HANDBOOK OF CHILDREN'S LITERACY

Handbook of Children's Literacy

Edited by

Terezinha Nunes

Peter Bryant

KLUWER ACADEMIC PUBLISHERS
DORDRECHT / BOSTON / NEW YORK / LONDON

Library of Congress Cataloging-in-Publication Data is available.

ISBN 1-4020-1620-4

Published by Kluwer Academic Publishers
PO Box 17, 3300 AA Dordrecht, The Netherlands

Sold and distributed in North, Central and South America
By Kluwer Academic Publishers,
101 Philip Drive, Norwell, MA 02061, U.S.A.

In all other countries, sold and distributed
By Kluwer Academic Publishers, Distribution Centre,
PO Box 322, 3300 AH Dordrecht, The Netherlands

Printed on acid-free paper

Printed and bound in Great Britain by Antony Rowe Limited.

Table of Contents

Introduction to the Handbook

TEREZINHA NUNES & PETER BRYANT

Handbooks offer invaluable contributions to novices as well as to experts in a domain. A review of research is always handy to the expert and is a way into expertise for a novice. Handbooks may have a more specific focus: handbooks and useful collections have been compiled on word spelling, dyslexia, or reading acquisition in bilingual contexts. We felt that it was time to edit a handbook that allowed the multifaceted nature of children's literacy to come to the foreground. By including such different sections as non-normative literacy learning and looking across languages, basic processes in word reading and text comprehension, and by looking at language instruction across time, we wish to make it salient that children's literacy is a phenomenon that must be investigated from a variety of perspectives, with diverse methods and in order to answer different questions. No single method, no isolated theory, no unique educational input can be expected to explain children's literacy. The variety and creativity of methods for investigating children's reading and writing increased considerably in the second half of the last century. This variety is represented in the Handbook, where readers will come across experiments using a diversity of measures, predictive studies, qualitative analyses of children's performance, intervention studies, and investigations of the social and historical contexts for the teaching of literacy. The editors who contributed to the organisation of the Handbook ensured that their sections offer this refreshing breadth of coverage of methods so that no generalisations about the elephant are made from exploring only its tail.

Theoretical accounts of children's literacy have also become increasingly more sophisticated in the last few decades. A major shift in the thinking about what is involved in literacy was accomplished when teachers, clinicians and researchers ceased to view reading and writing as simple perceptual and motor skills reinforced through repetition. When literacy became conceptualised as a linguistic and representational ability, new insights into its nature, development and the reasons for children's difficulty in literacy acquisition became possible. Literacy is now thought of as a generative ability: once we learn to read and spell, our reading and spelling are not restricted to the identification and production of the specific words we learned, we can read and spell words that we never saw before in print. We can even read and spell words that we never heard before. The processes of literacy acquisition must be conceived in a way that is in keeping with the generative and representational nature of literacy. Thus new theorising about literacy acquisition has explored from a progressively more varied range of perspectives the connections between oral and written language. These varied perspectives are represented in different chapters in the Handbook, and include phonological, morphological, grammatical and pragmatic aspects of language. Children's reading and spelling problems, the different authors show, can come from any of these aspects, which may be more important at one level of analysis than at others. Phonological and morphological analyses are emphasised in English more when the word level is concerned whereas the grammatical and pragmatic level (including inference making and genre issues) are discussed more often at the sentence and text level of analysis.

The Handbook will bring the readers further than these cognitive issues would on their own. Learners have motivations and individual characteristics – they come from different social backgrounds and might have different levels of exposure to print; they may have different views of themselves as learners and different levels of motivation; in today's multicultural world, they might be learning to read their mother tongue or a language which is not that of their own community; they might be bilingual in two oral languages or bilingual in an oral and a signed language; they might be blind and use a sensory input different from the visual letter we are used to. How do all these variations influence children's literacy? Will research develop methods that lead to the understanding of all of these variations just as possibilities created from similar processes or do these variations result in different processes?

The authors of the different sections contribute in their own ways to this discussion. No-one is a novice to the theme they are writing and because of their expertise they can identify issues of great significance to the particular angle from which they are considering children's literacy. We invite our reader to take the risk of looking at literacy from this multiplicity of angles. The result can be the discovery of new and unsuspected angles from which to understand the phenomenon of children's literacy.

A. Literacy: Basic Processes In Development

Introduction

PETER BRYANT & TEREZINHA NUNES

The time that it takes children to learn to read varies greatly between different orthographies, as the chapter by Sprenger-Charolles clearly shows, and so do the difficulties that they encounter in learning about their own orthography. Nevertheless most people, who have the chance to learn to read, do in the end read well enough, even though a large number experience some significant difficulties on the way. Most of them eventually become reasonably efficient spellers too, even though they go on make spelling mistakes (at any rate if they are English speakers) for the rest of their lives. So, the majority of humans plainly does have intellectual resources that are needed for reading and writing, but it does not always find these resources easy to marshal.

What are these resources? Do any of them have to be acquired? Do different orthographies make quite different demands on the intellect? Do people differ significantly from each other in the strength and accessibility of these resources? If they do, are these differences an important factor in determining children's success in learning to read and write? These are the main questions that the different chapters in this section on Basic Processes set out to answer.

In their quest for these answers, most of the chapters in this section concentrate on the beginnings of reading, and there are good reasons for their doing so. One powerful reason is the possibility that some of the basic processes in reading are not natural processes – not the product of an innate system or of children's informal experiences in the environment. Some basic processes may have to be acquired. They may simply not be part of our intellectual apparatus before we begin to learn to read and we may only acquire them as a result of being taught reading and spelling.

We certainly need to know which basic processes in reading are a natural part of a young child's cognitive apparatus, and which they have to acquire, perhaps with great difficulty. One possible candidate for a basic process which comes to children only through the experiences that they have when learning to read is the process of detecting, analysing and manipulating phonemes. The case for this claim has often been stated and many of the arguments for it are re-stated in this section's chapters. First of all there is a strong and totally uncontroversial relationship between children's performance in phoneme judgement tasks and the progress that they make in learning to read: the more sensitive and skilled children are in these phoneme tasks, the better readers and spellers they tend to

3

T. Nunes, P. Bryant (eds.), Handbook of Children's Literacy, 3–10.
© *2004 Kluwer Academic Publishers. Printed in Great Britain.*

be. Given that individual alphabetic letters, by and large, represent individual phonemes, this connection between children's success with phonemes and with reading in many different alphabetic orthographies is not really surprising. The surprise, if there is one, is how difficult it is for young children, and especially for children who have not yet learned to read, to isolate and distinguish phonemes. They are plainly at sea with various tests of "phoneme awareness" and it even takes them a long time to work out the relationship between alphabetic letters and phonemes.

The data on young children's difficulties with various oral tasks in which they have to detect and sometimes to manipulate phonemes are well known and have often been reviewed (Goswami & Bryant, 1990; Adams, 1990). These difficulties are also to be found in older children and in adults who, for one reason or another, have not learned to read and write an alphabetic script (Mann, 1986; Morais, Cary, Alegria & Bertelson, 1979; Morais, Bertelson, Cary & Alegria, 1986; Read, Zhang, Nie & Ding, 1986). This line of research suggests that children only become aware of phonemes as a result of learning to read an alphabet, which is an argument that gains some impressive support from studies of the development of pre-school children's ideas about the way that the alphabet works.

There is a lucid description of this kind of work, which began with the spectacular studies of Emilia Ferreiro and her colleagues (Ferrero & Teberosky, 1983; Ferreiro, 1999) on pre-school children's ideas about what alphabetic letters represent, in the chapter in this section by Liliana Tolchinsky. Tolchinsky, like Ferreiro, takes a constructivist approach to the question, and like Ferreiro, she argues that in their first attempts to link letters with phonological units pre-school children actually get the unit wrong. She claims on the basis of children's reactions to questions about what individual letters signify that children entertain the idea that letters represent syllables rather than phonemes. This is certainly a plausible hypothesis, and, to return to the theme of the results of oral tests of phonological awareness for a moment, the idea is certainly supported by research which shows that children can isolate and detect syllables in these oral tasks long before they can do the same with phonemes.

The relative ease of syllables and the relative difficulty of phonemes in phonological awareness tasks are not in themselves surprising. Syllables are, as Sprenger-Charolles points out in her chapter in this section, explicit phonological units, whereas phonemes are constructs which differ from language to language. Nevertheless some controversy surrounds the hypothesis that children's first idea of the alphabetic letter is that it represents a syllable. In Tolchinsky's chapter you will find a clear account of this difference of opinion. She writes about the disagreement between her own point of view and that of psychologists who adopted the "invented spelling" approach to young children's spelling. These psychologists have argued for the most part that children have no particular problem in working out that letters represent phonemes.

"Invented spelling" is the name given to a series of studies which began with the highly original work of Charles Read and which have continued with the notable research of Rebecca Treiman (see her chapter in this section) and her colleagues. This research has shown that when children begin to write their spelling is often strikingly unconventional, but that nevertheless it often contains a reasonable phonemic transcription of the sounds of the words that the children are trying to represent in their writings. The child who pinned the written injunction "B Kwyit: this is wr mi dadday wrx" on his father's study door was incorrect in his spelling of the word "quiet" and yet did manage to represent the phonemes in that complex word quite respectably. This example, which comes from the collection of young children's spellings assembled by Charles Read, also illustrates another theme of research on invented spelling which is that beginning spellers often confuse letter names with letter sounds. At first sight the rendering of "be" as "b" seems no more than a vowel omission and therefore a mistake at the phoneme level. But the letter name for "b" contains two phonemes and sounds exactly the same as the word "be". Read's idea was that children sometimes use the letter sound and sometimes the letter name when they try to represent the sounds of words, and that they only systematically depart from letter-phoneme correspondences when they use the letter names, for these often involve more than one phoneme.

Treiman does not deal with the Ferreiro's and Tolchinsky's syllabic hypothesis in her chapter in this section, but she does set out some of her evidence for the idea that children try systematically to use letters to represent phonemes even in their very early writings. She looks at children' omissions of vowels and argues that there are often good phonemic reasons for these omissions. For example, she shows that children are more likely to leave the vowel letter out in "girl" (see also the spelling of "works" as "wrx" above) than in "kept". Her argument about this difference is that young children try to represent each phoneme with a letter. However in the case of "girl" they are dealing with a syllabic "r" which in phonological terms is actually part of the vowel sound. "Girl" contrasts with words like "kept" where the consonant that follows the vowel is much more clearly separate from it.

The invented spelling work offers other evidence for its thesis that, in spelling at least, even very young children recognise the relationship between letter sounds and individual letters from the start. The most striking phenomenon is of young children representing sounds in their spelling which are certainly part of the word which they are trying to write, but of which adults are normally quite unaware. Two examples of these arresting phonetic transcriptions, both taken from Charles Read's opus, are "jragn" for "dragon" and "chrak" for "truck". The children seem to be the aware that the sounds that we produce as the first consonants of words beginning with "dr" and with "tr" are actually quite close to "j" and to "ch". Similarly the spelling of "water" as "wodr" by young American children looks like another example of the same phenomenon. In spoken American English, the typical pronunciation of a "t", when it is immediately preceded and followed by vowel sounds, is as /d/ (this transformation is known as the "intervocalic tap"), and American children often spell it as "d" too. (If this claim is right, then English children who do not usually adopt this pronunciation and are more likely to represent the intermediate "t" with a glottal stop, should be unlikely to make this particular mistake: we know of no evidence on this point.)

This difference in views is an interesting and important one, but there has been no systematic attempt to explain or resolve it. Tolchinsky's chapter provides an excellent basis for starting to look for such a solution. For one thing, it is clear from the evidence that Tolchinsky describes that on the whole the children who took part in Ferreiro and Teberosky's studies and in Tolchinsky's too tended to be younger and from lower socio-economic levels than those who contributed to the work on invented spelling. Ferreiro and Teberosky studied pre-school children in deprived areas. Read's corpus came mainly from children in an Ivy League campus university, and Treiman gathered hers from a suburban school in a prosperous United States city.

Other phonological units besides the syllable and the phoneme have played their part in psychological theories about learning to read and spell. We have to consider the possibility that intra-syllabic units (phonological units that are smaller than a syllable, but larger than a phoneme), like onset and rime, play a part too in the development of reading. Saada's chapter shows that, as with syllable tasks, pre-school children do quite well in oral phonological awareness tasks that require them to make judgements about onsets and rimes, though they do so with varying degrees of success. Her apt quotation from the conclusions drawn by Treiman and Zukowski (1996) makes the point well: "Sensitivity to syllable, onsets and rimes can develop without knowledge of a writing system. In contrast, phonemic sensitivity may result at least in part from experiences connected with the learning of an alphabetic writing system" (p 211).

The fact that very young children do reasonably well in onset and rime tasks and that there is considerable variability among them in their success in these tasks has given us an important research tool. It allows us to plot the relationship between how well children do in such tasks before they begin to learn to read and the progress that they make later on in reading and in reading-related tasks. This in turn makes it possible for us to see whether children's explicit awareness of phonological units in general rather than their specific ability to learn about phonemes is an important factor in determining how well they do in learning to read. As the chapter by Sprenger-Charolles demonstrates, there is plenty of evidence that pre-school children's performance in onset and rime tasks predicts children's eventual progress in reading pretty well. It also predicts how well they do later on in phoneme tasks.

Sprenger-Charolles also shows us that there are differences between different orthographies in the importance of children being sensitive to these intrasyllabic units and particularly to rime. There is now a great accumulation of evidence that the rime is much more important in learning to read in English, and perhaps in German, than it is in languages like Spanish, Greek and Italian. It is important to know this, but, as Sprenger-Charolles shows us, it is not so surprising. In English the relation between individual letters and phonemes is highly variable, particularly when it comes to vowel sounds: in English also the correspondence between letter sequences and rimes is very much more predictable and regular than letter-phoneme relations are. In contrast in the Spanish, Greek and Italian orthographies, the rime itself is often just a vowel sound and the representation of phonemes in writing is as consistent and predictable as the relation between letters and rimes. Thus attention to rimes can in principle help English children, much more than Spanish, Greek or Italian children, to put some order into letter-sound relationships, and the evidence that English children take advantage of this valuable aid is now quite considerable.

Nevertheless the precise role of the easier units of onset and rime in English-speaking children's reading is now a controversial issue. Several psychologists argue that phonemes are the crucial unit in English, as much as in other orthographies, and that English-speaking children's pre-school experiences with rime play little part, or no part at all, in helping them to learn to read. This is partly an empirical disagreement and partly a theoretical one. Some studies have not reproduced the predictive relation between pre-school children's abilities to discriminate rime and their reading later on, though others continue to do so. The unsettled theoretical question is whether children's pre-school phonological experiences have any bearing whatsoever on their learning to read later on. This is a serious issue since it has significant implications for pre-school education. Should we in the nursery make sure that children are given enhanced phonological experiences with phonological units that they can handle, in the hope that this will make them better readers later on? Or should we simply say that pre-school phonology has next to nothing to do with the activities that children must pursue when they learn to read and pay no attention at all to phonology in the nursery? We need to know.

To return to phonemes, all the evidence, as we have seen, suggests that children have a great deal of learning to do in order to isolate these small units and to work out the relationship between them and the alphabetic letters that signify them. Nevertheless, we learn from the chapter by Sprenger-Charolles that there are striking cross-linguistic differences in the speed and the nature of this learning. These differences provide us with valuable insights into the way that children do learn to handle phonemes and letters.

The overall regularity of grapheme-phoneme and phoneme-grapheme corre-spondences, of course, differs greatly between different orthographies. English comes off the worst in these comparisons. At the level of correspondences between single letters and phonemes it is a highly inconsistent orthography. This is an important point, but one that should be treated with caution. Sprenger-Charrolles herself distinguishes grapheme-phoneme correspondences (GPC) and phoneme-grapheme correspondence (PGC) and also between the regularity of the relationship between phonemes and letters and between other units, like rime, and letter sequences. We have to pay great attention to these more detailed distinctions in cross-linguistic comparisons between different orthographies.

There are other reasons for being cautious about the claim that English is a capricious orthography. As Treiman points out in her chapter in this section, we can see from the justly famous work of Venezky that there are regularities in English letter-sound relationships at other levels: these include various, often complex, conditional rules, such as the effect of adding a final "e" on a syllable or the effect of ending a syllable with a consonant doublet. In a different way the chapter in this section by Bryant and Nunes is also at pains to point out regularities in letter-sound relationships at the level of morphology. English must undoubtedly be treated as a morpho-phonic script.

These caveats are important but Sprenger-Charolles still makes a convincing claim that the variations between orthographies in the regularity of letter-sound relationships do have an effect on the speed with which children learn about these relationships. There is consistent evidence that children who have to learn an orthography which is characterised by consistent and regular letter-phoneme relationships are also able to read pseudo-words at an earlier age than children whose orthography is less predictable. The result is a fascinating one, since it suggests a powerful relationship between the trustworthiness of letter-phoneme correspondences and readiness of young children to use these relationships.

The point that morphology, as well as phonology, plays an important part in learning to read is the subject of the chapter in this section by Bryant and Nunes. In many orthographies regularities at the morphological level go beyond the phonological regularities in the script. The spelling of the English regular past tense affix is a good example. In different regular past verbs this allomorph is pronounced as /t/, /d/ or/zd/, but it is always spelled as "ed". This spelling is not an accurate phonetic transcription of any of these three endings, and so the connection is a morphemic one: the same morpheme is spelled in the same way despite differences in its sound.

There are morphemic connections with spelling which cannot be reduced to phonology in many other scripts as well. Greek is a highly predictable orthography from the point of view of GPC, but not so predictable in terms of PGC. The spelling of Greek vowel sounds is quite difficult because there are many more ways of spelling vowels than there are vowels in Greek. Although there seems to be no particular rule to help people to choose the correct spelling in the stems of Greek words, there are definite regularities in the spelling of inflections in this language. The same inflection is always spelled in the same way, and so children are greatly helped by learning about these morphemic connections.

It takes several years, as Bryant and Nunes' chapter shows, for children to learn about these connections between affix morphemes and spelling, but Treiman's chapter in this section makes the point that other morphemic regularities might be easier for children to grasp. She reports some of her own research which shows that beginning spellers in America are less likely to mis-spell the middle consonant as "d" in "biting" than in "water" even though the typical American pronunciation of this consonant is /d/ in both words. Treiman argues that children recognise that the stem of the two-morpheme word "biting" is "bite" and they tend as a result to preserve the "t" spelling when an affix is added. Thus there may be differences in the ease with which children connect spelling patterns to stem and affix morphemes, though why this should be so is not clear at the moment.

So far in our account of the chapters in this section we have concentrated on the mechanisms that are necessary for learning to read. To be relevant to our basic question, which is about learning to read, these must be mechanisms for learning, and yet remarkably little is written about the learning process in modern studies by psychologists on children's reading. The group of psychologists who have had the most to say about learning in this area are those who work with connectionist models. These models, which are the subject matter of the chapter by Brown and Chater, are based on the proposition that learning is the result of an accumulation of associative links in networks that lead to new and adaptive behaviours. The models assume that these networks allow people to detect and learn about statistical regularities, and when such models are applied to reading much of the interest is in the way people build up connections between sounds and orthographic sequences on the basis of the frequency the associations between them.

Most attempts to use connectionist models to account for reading have been applied to expert, adult reading, but the case that Brown and Chater make in their chapter is that such models can also be used in a fruitful way to account for the development of reading in childhood. Using the connectionist approach as a framework, Brown and Chater consider various possible explanations for developmental differences and in particular for the differences between the strategies adopted by beginning readers and by older, more expert children. In accounting for younger children's reading, Brown and Chater distinguish hypotheses in which the basic difference is that the input for these children is different in some way from an alternative hypothesis that they are much less able than older children to detect and therefore learn about statistical regularities. The advantage of considering these different possibilities is that they can be tested rigorously using connectionist methods. This approach is still in its infancy, but it is clearly a promising and potentially valuable one.

Brown and Chater's chapter sticks closely to the idea that learners use the strategies that are optimal for the particular situation that they are in. The final chapter in this section by Pretzlik and Chan pursues the idea that the effort that individual children put into learning to read varies greatly, and that much of this variation is determined by social and emotional factors. The authors of this chapter take up the idea that the main cause of this difference between children is that their own view of their reading abilities vary, and that those who see themselves as good readers are more likely to devote much of their time to reading than others who do not have such good self-perceptions. The claim is interesting and also disturbing, partly because it is clear from some of the evidence described by Pretzlik and Chan that children's assessments of their own reading abilities are not always accurate. So children, who are actually good at reading but perceives themselves as poor readers, could actually fall behind because of their own misperceptions.

The effects of self-perception on individual children's progress in reading could plainly be the reason for what is known as the Matthew effect, which is that good readers get relatively better and poor readers relatively worse over time. In fact the data on self perception not only produce an explanation for the Matthew effect, but also suggest a more sophisticated version of it – that the increasing separation of good and poor readers is due not to their initial successes and failures but to their own perceptions of whether they have done well or badly. This is a complicated claim, but complexities pile up on complexities when one turns to the reasons for children's self-perceptions. Pretzlik and Chan cite recent research that that shows quite clearly that teachers and peers have a considerable influence on individual children's views of their own progress in reading and spelling. This chapter makes a convincing case for considering the social and emotional contexts of children learning to read.

Taken together the chapters in this section provide a stimulating and comprehensive account of research on the basic processes that are involved in learning to read. The chapters review the main hypotheses and the research paradigms, and the picture that they present is of a research effort which is making good progress and is producing results and theoretical conclusions of great value and interest.

REFERENCES

Adams, M.J. (1990) Beginning to read. Boston: MIT Press.

Ferreiro, E. and Teberosky, A. (1983) *Literacy before schooling*. Exeter, New Hampshire: Heinemann Educational Books.

Ferreiro, E. (1999) Oral and Written Words. Are they the same unit? In T. Nunes (Ed.). *Learning to read: an integrated view from research and practice* (pp. 65-76). Dordrecht, The Netherlands: Kluwer.

Goswami, U. & Bryant, P. (1990). *Phonological skills and learning to read*. London: Erlbaum.

Mann, V.A. (1986) Phonological awareness: the role of reading experience. *Cognition, 24*, 65-92.

Morais, J., Bertelson, P., Cary, L. & Alegria, J. (1986) Literacy training and speech segmentation. *Cognition, 24*, 45-64.

Morais, J., Cary, L., Alegria, J. & Bertelson, P. (1979) Does awareness of speech as a sequence of phones arise spontaneously? *Cognition, 7*, 323-331.

Read, C., Zhang, Y., Nie, H. and Ding, B. (1986) The ability to manipulate speech sounds depends on knowing alphabetic spelling. *Cognition, 24*, 31-44.

Treiman, R., & Zukowski, A. (1996). Children's sensitivity to syllables, onsets, rimes and phonemes. *Journal of Experimental Child Psychology, 61*, 193-215.

A1. Childhood Conceptions of Literacy

LILIANA TOLCHINSKY

ABSTRACT

This chapter presents a developmental perspective on literacy that explores children's evolving knowledge even prior to being formally taught to read and write. It starts by comparing four different approaches within this perspective: (1) the earliest Vygotskian, (2) the constructivist, (3) the socio-cultural and (4) the "invented spelling" approach. It then advances to describing the methods used to gather toddlers and preschoolers ideas of literacy and presents the main conclusions on children's ideas about the practices of reading and writing, texts and discursive genres, the formal features of written marks and written strings and the representational meaning of writing. Finally, it concludes with two of the contributions of developmental approaches to literacy, which consist in turning literacy into a domain of knowledge that deserves to be studied developmentally and bringing back literacy activities to preschool education.

INTRODUCTION

Reading and writing are social practices in which a notational system is used for composing messages. These practices occur in multiple occasions and for many purposes. Therefore, the process of becoming literate includes both mastering the notational system and the ability to form and to interpret the messages. It also implies the acquisition of a full repertoire of linguistic forms and text like activities such as quoting, describing or exposing as well as the development of certain attitude toward the literal or inferential quality and the truth value of verbal expressions. Traditionally, this multifaceted process has been conceived as highly dependent on formal teaching. An alternative approach is to look at literacy from a developmental perspective and to explore children's evolving knowledge even prior to being formally taught to read and write. Research that follows this approach demonstrates that, in the process of becoming literate, children construct original and precocious ideas about the practices of reading and writing and about the formal features of writing systems and the resulting texts. These ideas are the building blocks for further learning.

T. Nunes, P. Bryant (eds.), Handbook of Children's Literacy, 11–29.
© 2004 *Kluwer Academic Publishers. Printed in Great Britain.*

Developmental approaches to literacy

The developmental approach to literacy originated during the late thirties with the work of Vygotsky and Luria (1926) whose aim was to explore "the pre-history of written language". They were among the first psychologists to consider writing as an object of psychological interest. They argued that the aim of scientific psychology was to study "higher order psychological functions", "uniquely human functions", and since writing was uniquely human, it should be a concern of scientific psychology. For them, reading and writing, are not mere instruments or motor skills) but rather produce profound attitudinal and ideological changes that go much further than cognitive and psychological changes (Vygotsky, 1978).

This strand of research was revived almost 60 years later in the groundbreaking work of Ferreiro, whose goal was to trace the "psychogenesis of writing from a constructivist point of view". Her work was followed by a remarkable amount of studies in different languages, scripts and cultural contexts (Ferreiro & Teberosky, 1979, in Spanish, Levin & Tolchinsky Landsmann, 1985,1987, in Hebrew; Pontecorvo & Zuchermamaglio, 1990, in Italian; Besse, 1996, in French; Chan & Nunes, 1999, in Chinese). The psychogenetic approach is based on Piagetian constructivism rather than on Vygotskian thinking. I strongly support this view and have worked with the belief that even when children have to incorporate knowledge of a conventional kind derived from their membership in a social community (e.g., through language), they must make that knowledge their own and re-construct it in his their terms. We also believe that no knowledge begins from zero but rather that all knowledge has a developmental story. It follows from this view that one should study the process of becoming literate from the earliest possible moment.

The third perspective was a parallel developmental one but within a more ethnographic socio-cultural approach. This was the work of Clay (1975), and Teale and Sulzby (1986), in what the latter termed "emergent literacy". They stress that children's interest in the written word does not emerge "naturally", and they looked for the circumstances that might trigger, propitiate, enhance or provoke reading and writing practices at home or in school settings. Their studies and many other related ones have demonstrated the extent to which family literacy practices can be of fundamental importance when it comes to succeeding at school (e.g., Heath, 1982; Scollon & Scollon, 1981, McLane & McNamee; 1990).

A fourth strand of thought among developmentalists concerned with literacy is the one known as "invented spelling". This began with the revolutionary work of Charles Read (1971) who was among the first to view spelling as a linguistic process in which children attempt to map the sound structure of words. He based his conclusions on the results of a study of children who began to write when they were between about 2.5 and 4 years old – that is, before they were able to read. Read was also among the first to discover the important role of letter names in identifying phonemes and the importance of a child's own name in this discovery.

The most interesting situations concerning spelling occur when children attempt to write phonemes that do not appear in the name of any letter. In such cases children resort to an adult search for models or invent their own spelling.

Studies based on those four approaches explored the way in which young children read and write before they start school and are taught to spell conventionally. However, the reasons for taking a developmental perspective, as well as the interpretations given to the findings, differed greatly between the approaches. Vygotsky and Luria's main aim was to determine the influence of social change on individual Psychology. They focused more on the instrumental use of written language than on the processes through which an object of knowledge is constructed. In spite of their concern with the early development of writing, they failed to appreciate any features in child's product that did not serve an obvious instrumental purpose.

In contrast to the Vygotskian aims, the main goal of the constructivist program has been to illustrate the interaction between an active learning individual and the specific features of an object of knowledge, i.e., writing. One of the main contributions made by this approach to literacy is the recognition of the formal work involved in early writing. Researchers working in this line discovered that there are important developmental processes that occur before and during children's discovery of the communicative function of writing and the relationship between letters and sounds.

In this respect the constructivist approach differs not only from that of Vygotsky and Luria but also from the "invented spelling" line of work. The crucial difference is that the latter concentrates on the relationship between the letters that children use and the composition of the words that they are attempting to write. Earlier attempts to write are considered "pre-communicative" by people working on invented spelling and therefore there is no search for any developmental regularity during that stage.

Finally, studies in emergent literacy are more closely attuned to Vygotskian aims than to the psychogenetic constructivist program, even though they sometimes neglect the cognitive work that children are performing when trying to make sense of a notational system.

In spite of these differences these lines of work marked a turning point in the research on writing. They led eventually to an epistemological redrawing of the boundaries of the traditional domains of development and they had a strong impact on the school approach to literacy.

On the reasons why children have precocious ideas about literacy

Why should children know something about reading and writing before being formally taught to read and write? One reason is that they are active and constructive learners. If children have been shown to have such wonderful ideas on, for example, where dreams come from, or how we know that two collections have a similar quantity of elements or what makes the crucial difference between dolls and human babies, why should they remain indifferent to the presence of labels, road signs, advertisement, books, calendars, hallmarks or the many uses of reading and writing in our community? Cultural information permeates our daily life even before birth and therefore there is no reason why children should behave as active learners only of objects, people or animals and not of social practices with notational systems. When I speak of children as *active* and *constructive* learners, I mean learners who are personally involved in using their own previously acquired knowledge in constant interaction with the information provided by the environment. Their previous knowledge transforms the impact of this information. With this assertion I am not denying the crucial role of teaching in developing literacy. I am just disputing the assumption that children merely absorb what they are taught, and I am arguing that childhood conceptions of literacy are the basis on which further instruction must build.

HOW CHILDREN'S IDEAS ABOUT LITERACY ARE GATHERED

Researchers interested in unveiling the pre-history of written language use a diversity of approaches, both naturalistic and experimental. Infants are observed while reading storybooks with their mothers both at home and at research laboratories. Toddlers and preschoolers are observed at home while they are engaged in self-initiated reading and writing activities or in activities suggested by their parents or other adults. Children are also observed in situations designed by the researcher. For example, they are asked to read a favourite storybook that has been read to them repeatedly; to write and reread a story of their own composition and to dictate to a friend or to the experimenter a story that they know.

In more controlled situations children are asked to sort cards displaying different combinations of letters, letters mixed with figures or with drawings to find out their criteria for making sense of notations. They may be required to match a card to a picture and then to say what they think is written on the card. Afterwards, the card may be removed and put under another picture to see whether the children's interpretation of the card is stable or changes with the picture. They may also be asked to write words or sentences that were selected by the experimenter with some defined criteria. For example, in order to discover whether children will use the same letters to write the same syllable or the same words, researchers ask them to write words that contain the same syllable in different words (like *table* and *cable*) or different sentences that contain the same words *(a girl is dancing* and *a girl is dancing and singing)*.

Although Luria used controlled tasks in his seminal study, "emergent literacy" researchers tend to prefer observational naturalistic studies whereas researchers involved in the constructivist approaches to literacy tend to prefer more controlled tasks applied in the contexts of clinical interviews. In addition "emergent literacy" researchers are more inclined to analyse socio-verbal interactions around literacy events, whereas within the constructivist approach a very careful analysis of children's productions and justifications is usually performed. The tasks used within the constructivist paradigm may seem to go beyond the children's level of expertise, but these tasks are given under the assumption that, when solving them, children will put into play ideas that they have actively constructed about the social practices in literacy, the regularities of texts and discourse, and the representational meaning of writing. Some of these ideas will now be reviewed.

On reading and writing

Children are able to recognize reading practices from a very early age. Even infants are intelligent participants in book-reading activities. While it is true that initially they use books for sucking, eating or squeezing, this reaction to books is relatively short lived. From 8 to 18 months of age children progress from attempts to eat the page to being able to participate fully in verbal dialogue while looking at the books. Children grasp the physical acts involved in reading, which are gazing, pointing, monitoring and they also become familiar with the typical language associated with books (Bus, van Ijzendorm, & Pellegrini 1995; Snow & Ninio, 1986).

At the age of two, children believe that they must look at the pictures in order to discover the story, but within a few months they start to make distinctions between text and pictures (Ferreiro, 1986). They give each a different name and state that it is the text and not the pictures that are read "because there are letters". Thus children realize that books are a particular kind of object – different from food, toys, pets or people- an object you look at and say something in a loud voice. They also realize that different information is extracted from pictures than from the accompanying letters.

Book reading is, however, a cultural practice that is not democratically distributed. It greatly depends on the accessibility in the community, to reading materials and on the availability of adults in charge of the children. This practice is also very much influenced by the affective dimensions of mother-child interaction and parental expectations (Bus & van Ijzendorm, 1988). It is not surprising then that bed-time stories and storybook reading have been found to have a determinant role in becoming literate, particularly on the way that children grasp the link between reading and writing.

Three-year-olds raised in deprived communities do have an internal representation of writing: for them writing means the production of marks on paper. However reading has no definite meaning for these children and is often confused with writing (Ferreiro, 1986). For example, children who had just jotted down some marks on a sheet of paper and were asked to read them back responded that they have already done so. Other children claimed that pencils were needed for reading. These results indicate that the nature of writing is understood at an earlier age because it leaves visible traces; it changes the object visibly, while reading does not. To grasp the nature of reading children must comprehend that marks have meaning, that they stand for something beyond themselves, and that by looking at them we can grasp what they say. Participation in the social uses of written language seems crucial for this realization. As we shall see, however, there is a constant interaction between knowledge that children obtain from engagement in functional activities and knowledge about the formal features of notations. By participating in book-reading children might very well learn about the features of letters, figures and their combinations.

On texts and discursive genres

In the Western tradition, texts become objects; they are artefacts that convey information through linguistic forms and graphic conventions. Besides the discursive forms in these texts, the spatial layout, and the links between pictures and writing also provide useful information. Texts are physical objects supporting discourse and although discursive forms can free themselves from a particular physical support part of their meaning is affected.

Preschoolers have a notion of the type of discourse to be expected from certain physical supports. If 4- to 5-year-olds are read a recipe from a storybook or a typical fairy-tale from a newspaper, they may react with surprise and deny that this sort of text is written there. Preschoolers are also able to distinguish between different types of texts. Hebrew speaking five year olds were asked (1) to write a fairy tale *Ami ve'tami (Hansel and Gretel)* and (2) to describe what the chocolate house in the tale looks like. Their knowledge of phonographic conventions of written Hebrew was very poor; most of them could draw Hebrew letters but they did not always know their phonic value. Nevertheless, their written outputs for the narrative and for the descriptions were organised very differently. The narrative was written in long lines of one letter after the other with hardly any internal spacing between them, except for the name of the protagonists, which sometimes appeared with blanks on both sides. The description, in contrast, looked similar to a list of isolated words (Sandbank, 2002). When asked to read what they had written they interpreted the long lines as full utterances, parts of the tale. When interpreting the description, however, they named the different elements in the house saying that there were "chocolates, candies and cookies". A similar graphic differentiation was found in comparisons between the way preschoolers write shopping lists and the way they write news, advertisements and poetry (Pontecorvo and Zucchermaglio, 1989; Tolchinsky Landsmann, 1992). Long before children gain a full command of the phonographic conventions of the written system, the graphic layout of their writing mimics the features of these different genres.

Toddlers and preschoolers also have a notion of discourse in terms of a unit that can be transported, transmitted and separated from a wider discourse. This metalinguistic knowledge is demonstrated, for example, by children's ability to quote. The idea that underlies quotation is that a linguistic entity is singled out and reproduced. Only an utterance that is recognised as such can be quoted. Children quote from 3 year of age, particularly in their retelling of narratives. They are able to reproduce pieces of talk performed by the different characters in a rather exact way. Slightly older children are also able to shift pronouns and verb tenses when they move from the story line to a quotation by a character. For example, they can say when telling the Hansel and Gretel story: *"and then she came I am ready to eat you"*. However, quotation is performed without any framing. The quoted part of discourse is marked by a shift in the pronoun and in the verb-tense but there is no mention of the interlocutor or the speech act *("and then the witch came and said: I am ready to eat you")* for introducing the quote. This change occurs in children's quotation behaviour usually after age 7 or 8 years. From this age children start to use speech verbs (say, tell) and to mention the interlocutor explicitly. The development in children's quotations suggests that they approach the learning process with the capacity to distinguish between two levels in the same passage: the matrix and the quotation. But, the lexical means to frame the different levels, qualifying one level as a-saying-by-someone, may be an outcome of increasing experience with texts. Note that if this were not the case, four-year-olds would never be able to understand the instruction: Would you like to write here "a child is playing with a ball?", because this requires a distinction between the matrix (Would you like to write here...) and the precise expression to be written ("a child is playing with a ball"). In writing we use quotation marks to differentiate between levels, but in speaking the distinction is based on a metalinguistic capability.

Another related ability that indicates very young children's metalinguistic knowledge-in-action is their capability to distinguish between what was said and what can be inferred (Pontecorvo and Orsolini, 1990). This is particularly clear in the context of commenting on or of retelling a narrative, or in the way that children dictate a story to an adult who is serving as a scribe. In these situations children have shown their ability to distinguish between what was said and what was invented or added. As in the case of quotation familiarity with text-like discourses enable children to use a more complex repertoire of indices (tense forms, person marks, connective) to separate the actual message from the truth-value.

On written marks and written strings

Letters have names and distinguishable shapes. They represent sounds and belong to a closed inventory. Sometimes the name coincides with their sound, sometimes not. The name of letter A is /ey/ although its sound differs when it appears at the beginning of the following two words: "America" and "aims". Sometimes "letter" applies to a family of graphic variations (e.g., letter b, means Capital B, italic B, script b-), each of which is an allograph of the letter b. However, in certain contexts and I are not interchangeable. The decoding of *iris* -the flower- and *Iris* -the name- is identical but, if you write the name in lower case it will be considered a spelling mistake because, according to spelling conventions, proper names must be written with capitals. In proofreading one must relate to i, I and Ii as different letters. Moreover, letters belong to an inventory that has an internal order – the alphabetic order, which is unrelated to their sound-meaning but is a strong cultural ritual and functions as an organizing principle. Letters are also distinguishable shapes.

Long before learning to read and write in a conventional way children know most of these "facts" about letters. They are able to recite the alphabet, they know their names and sometimes their sounds, and they are able of recognize them by their shape. This is not too surprising because this is the sort of information that most adults provide when they are preparing children for reading. It is surprising, however, that many preschoolers know some facts about combinations of letters that are almost certainly not taught explicitly. Long before knowing how to read conventionally they distinguish between possible and impossible combinations of letters in their language. Indeed, when letters are used for writing not every combination is acceptable or meaningful. Some strings of letters are acceptable but have no meaning (for example, "dag" and "doog"); others are neither acceptable nor meaningful (for example, "dgd", "ddd", "aaa" and "aei"), while only some are both acceptable and meaningful (for example, "dog" and "dig"). Every word in a language consists of a legal combination but the opposite is not so; not every legal combination is a word. Besides the constraint on combination, there are two other formal constraints on strings: number and internal variety.

One of the most surprising findings in the study of early literacy is that children recognise these constraints before learning to read. When asked to sort cards into those that are readable and those that are not, they are guided by two criteria: minimal number and sufficient variety of letters (Ferreiro & Teberosky, 1979). The mere presence of letters is not enough for something to be readable; if there are very few letters, the letter string is judged as "unreadable". Similarly if the same letter is repeated many times, the string is also judged as "unreadable". So, cards with individual letters (T) are not good for reading in the children's judgement, but equally too many letters can also lead to doubt. For these children, the ideal number of letters for something to be judged as readable is three or four. Cards containing this number of letters were chosen without any hesitation as being suitable for reading. It is not enough, however, to have the correct number of letters. There is also a concomitant need for a limited variety. When children compared MMMMMM, AAAAAA and MANTECA, they were left in little doubt as to the fact that only the last sequence was good for reading (Ferreiro & Teberosky, 1979; Tolchinsky, 2003).

The constraints of quantity and variety are task-sensitive but follow a clear rationale: they are stronger when asked to judge for readability rather than for "writability". When the instruction is changed and children are asked to say which cards "have writing on them" (Lavine, 1977), repetition of the same letter is better accepted than when they are asked to look for those that are good for reading. We suppose that the reason for that lies in the instruction (to say which cards "have writing on them"). Indeed, variety is a criterion for judging whether something can be read though not whether it can be written.

Sensitivity to formal constraints was found not only for the number of letters and their internal variety, but also for the combination of letters. Preschoolers, who are not yet looking for letter-sound correspondences, were able to distinguish between sequences of letters that are possible combinations in their language and those that are not. The most readily accepted combinations were those that occur with greatest frequency in their language. At the age of 5 children rejected strings containing repeated vowels or repeated consonants demonstrating their understanding that a word must integrate both types of letter (Pick, Unze & Bronwell, 1978). Even before the discovery of the alphabetic principle, children do pay attention to the word-components. In order to decide which combinations are "well written", they look both at the letters that are integrated within the string and at the general configuration of the string. Another aspect of children's conceptions is that they also have a clear development in their ways of writing and in their view of the representational meaning of writing before attaining conventional spelling.

On writing

Writing is indeed an ambiguous term. It refers at least to the process of producing material traces on any surface and to the products. An interesting finding about early literacy is that children precociously conceive of writing as a particular activity, which is different from drawing and from "making numbers". To prove this assertion, researchers must, first of all, convince children that they should try writing because three or four year olds look rather bewildered when asked to write a word or a sentence as they clearly believe that they not supposed to know how to write. This refusal, however, is already a sign of knowledge; it reflects a child's conviction that writing, as opposed to drawing, requires special marks that must be known (Brenneman, Massey, Machado and Gelman, 1996).

We have found very few children, even those in the youngest age group, who produce writing and drawings that cannot be distinguished. Just as their writing lacks the graphic features of writing, so their drawing lacks the figurative features of a "realistic" representation. We know, however, that even when their writing and drawing are indistinguishable, three or four distinctive motor plans can be clearly identified (Karmiloff Smith, 1992; Breneman et at., 1996). Drawing and writing stimulate the performance of different actions. Thus, when drawing children make wide continuous circular movements whereas when writing they lift their pencils off the page and interrupt their movements much more frequently. While they are engrossed in the process of production, it seems to be writing, but, once finished, when it is separate from the "writer", it does not look like writing.

Independently of language, socio-economic status, or micro cultural milieu (Gibson & Levin, 1975; Bissex, 1980; Clay, 1982; Harste, Burke & Woodward, 1984) three to four year olds produce writing patterns distinguishable from their drawings. But, even when the writing-products become distinguishable from the drawing-products it will take some time until the different writing-products a child produces are distinguishable from each other. Once 3- to 4-years-olds are persuaded to try, they usually do very similar "scrawls" for writing isolated words or very long sentences.

Figure 1. Example of undifferentiated writing by a 4:8 year old Spanish girl who was asked to write two words and a short sentence.

Looking at what a child has produced, it is impossible to recognize which scrawl represents the word and which the sentence. For that reason *this first phase* in writing development is usually called *undifferentiated* (Luria, 1929; Ferreiro, 1988). Figure 1 presents an example *of undifferentiated* writing by a 4:8 year-old Spanish speaking girl who was asked to write two words and a short sentence. The products displayed the features of form common to writing in almost any language – linearity, presence of distinguishable units, regularity of blanks and directionality – but they do not reflect either the sound pattern or the meaning of the words or the sentence that they are supposed to represent. Moreover, young children behave often as though the position of the writing or the writer himself, rather than any particular feature of the written display, will determine its meaning. Three- to four-year-olds were shown pictures under which was a written caption (for example, a picture of a tree under which was written the word TREE) and they agreed in that the written word was TREE. However, when this written word was moved to another picture, the reading of the word also changed (Bialystock, 1992; Ferreiro, 1982). Thus the same written word could come to mean "boat", if it was placed under the drawing of a boat.

During *the second phase* of writing development two processes indicate developmental changes in the representational status of writing: children's written products now conform to the constraints of number and variety of marks that children have posited for legibility, and children begin to introduce graphic hints to differentiate among their own productions that, sometimes, reflect the changes in the words that they are attempting to represent.

In this second phase of writing development, children explore the regularities of the notation system. How many signs should a string contain to be acceptable? How different should they be? In order to have a set of interpretable marks, children obey the condition of minimum number of written marks (around three) and minimal variety (avoiding having identical mark one after the other). The two constraints of number and variety also regulate children's writing and seem to hold true across languages and scripts. So Catalan, French, Italian, Mexican, Argentinean, and Israeli preschoolers were found to apply similar constraints to their written products. The letters used may differ. Indeed, very early children incorporate the letter of the writing systems in their community but the written outputs reflect the two formal constraints. Figure 2 shows an example of "formally constrained" writing by a five year old Spanish boy who was asked to write the ingredients of a recipe.

Figure 2. Example of "formally constrained" writing by a five-year old Spanish-speaking boy who was asked to write the ingredients of a recipe

He had to write *aceite* (oil), *maiz* (corn) and *harina* (flour). For this he used the letters of his name (Andres) and letter-like forms or maybe an "ay".

Another shared feature in development concerns the source of the conventional letters children used during this phase of development. At times they may use the letters from a particular word that they have learned (cat, house, etc.), but most frequently, as seen in Figure 2, the child's own name is the source and point of identification for the letters. This behaviour, which has been reported time and again in many different languages, may also indicate that children come to identify one or more written words as prototype of written texts, that is texts that are meaningful and well written. The child's underlying reasoning seems to be that since these particular letters form part of a meaningful text they can be trusted to produce other texts.

The rules, which the children impose on number and variety, are not mere inventions. They reflect the actual distribution of word length and intra-word variation found in real texts. English orthography also contains examples of this constraint. The reason for repeating letters in "egg' is to fulfil the preference for nouns, verbs and adjectives to be at least three letters long (Aronoff, 1994). In Spanish no written word contains the same letter repeated more than twice in consecutive position while in Hebrew very few words contain the same letter repeated three times in consecutive position. But this use of formal constraints also reflects an active selection because although it is true that there are very few single-letter words, they are the most frequently used in any text.

Beyond the formal constraints on their writing, children often use modes of differentiation that suggest a sensitivity to meaning. Luria observed that, at a given point, children began to introduce graphic differences into their writing as some "scrawls" took on a longer or more rounded appearance. This occurred when the sentences referred to objects that differed in shape and size. Ferreiro (1985) reported similar findings. Children suggested, for example, that "bear" should be written with more letters than "duck", since a bear is bigger than a duck. Their writing did not reflect differences in shape or colour but *only* differences in number and size. This is not an iconic representation because children are looking for correspondences between an intrinsic graphic resource of writing – number of marks – and a quantifiable feature of the referent.

We have detected similar phenomena (Levin & Tolchinsky Landsmann, 1990, Levin & Korat, 1992) with Hebrew speaking children and Chan and Nunes (1998) have found that five-year-old Chinese-speaking children would retain a figurative correspondence between what they wrote and the object being referred to even when producing accurate Chinese symbols. For example, in writing the word "elephant', they would overemphasize a long stroke to represent the trunk of an elephant.

Pontecorvo & Zucchermaglio (1988) asked Italian children to write diminutives, which in Italian sound longer than the base word, and plurals, which are constructed by suffixation. In the first case there is a contradiction between the referred object and the sounding of the word whereas in the second case there is not. Most children in this phase of development chose content, decreasing the number of marks despite the words sounding longer and repeating marks to represent the plurals. I have found a similar phenomenon of reflection of similarities and differences in meaning onto similarities and differences in writing (Tolchinsky Landsmann. 1991). I believe that this is the point at which children start to look at writing as a communicative tool. That is, they start to look for ways of introducing elements into their writing to show (to themselves or to others) the differences that they have heard.

The third phase in the development of writing is characterized by children's attempts at letter to sound correspondences. We have seen that from very early on children explore the features of writing and some of them help them to organize their written materials. But, these self-imposed limitations on number and variety imply that children, time and again, use the same forms in different combinations rather than creating new forms. This facilitates the attribution of meaning to individual letters. Once writing is formally constrained, it can be operated on, first, in order to create graphic differences, and subsequently to work out the value of the elements in relation to the spoken utterance that the children are trying to represent. This is the main task performed during the third phase of writing development. In the two preceding phases of development their writing showed that they are aware of the fact that writing is *somehow* related to language. Many 3- to 4-year-olds when required to read what they have written, repeat verbatim the word they were asked to write. They, thereby, indicate that they believe that what they say is somehow related to what is written. Children's initial attempt at mapping letters onto parts-of -utterance appear when they read back what they have just finished writing. At this phase they are not systematic at it. They follow the written marks, while segmenting the words into parts (for example, saying *choco-late*), syllables or a mixture of both. The need to accommodate the reading to the written form leads to different ways of breaking up the word. Sometimes a child elongates the sound of a part; sometimes he cuts it short. The process of systematic correspondence is facilitated when this uttering is produced in front of a written string of few and distinct marks. The features of the written string pave the way to looking for a more articulated meaning to the graphic elements. With time (and probably more experience with print and /or writing activities segmentation systematically becomes syllabic. Children look for a term-to-term correspondence between number of syllables and written marks. Once they start working out the idea that writing is a representation of sounds, syllables become the first systematic unit of correspondence. Evidence for the syllabic hypothesis is provided by case analyses and in-depth longitudinal studies of Argentine and Mexican children carried out by Ferreiro and her collaborators (Ferreiro & Teberosky, 1979). Initial corroboration of the syllabic hypothesis was also provided by my own studies and those undertaken by Levin and Korat (1987) with Israeli children and by a further study comparing Spanish-speaking and Hebrew-speaking children.

It is not surprising that the syllable is the initial unit of correspondence. It is well established, since the earliest studies reported by Rosner & Simon, that children tend to segment words into syllables before they segment into phonemes. I should perhaps clarify that I am speaking about intentional segmentation. Infants are capable of categorical perception of sounds almost from birth (De Casper & Fifer, 1980; Eimas, Siqueland, Juscyk & Vigorito, 1971), but the intentional breaking down of a word into parts "smaller" than syllables rarely occurs before the age of 5.

Syllables are natural units of segmentation; they have phonic substrata, whereas phonemes are linguistic constructs. Therefore, it is understandable that when children start segmenting words to map on to letters, they do so in terms of syllables. Initially the main preoccupation within this age group is the correspondence between the *number* of syllables and the *number* of letters. When children are concerned mainly with quantitative correspondence, any letter will apparently do. At this point, a child's specific knowledge about letter-names and their respective sound values plays an important role.

Two processes are active in this undertaking; on the one hand, there is the analysis of the word; and on the other, a child's knowledge of the conventional sound value of the letters. It may be the case that some syllables – usually the initial one – receive conventional letters, while for the others letters are assigned arbitrarily. It may also occur that some children can identify one or more letters by their sound-value and use them, in a non-systematic way, when they recognize the presence of that sound in a word. We may, therefore, find some words that have not yet been analysed and are written with a quite arbitrary choice of letters; some that have been partially analysed and as the child knew some letters these have been used; and some for which, by chance, the child knew all the letters. These various possibilities are typical of any process of transitional knowledge. Eventually the two processes converge, and then the written product will include a letter with its conventional sound- value for each syllable. Figure 3 shows an example of syllabic mapping by a Spanish-speaking girl who was asked to write the same recipe as in Figure 2.

Figure 3: Example of syllabic mapping by a Spanish-speaking girl who was asked to write the same recipe as in figure 2.

For *aceite* (oil) – at the top – she used A for the first syllable (#a). E for the second (#cei#) and T for the third (#te#). For *maiz* (corn) – in the middle – she used A for the first syllable (#ma#) and S (#is#) for the second and for *harina* (flour) – at the bottom – she uses A for the first (#a), I (#ri#) for the second and A (#na) for the third.

The syllabic hypothesis has not gone unchallenged. It has been called into question mainly by studies carried out in English. There is no mention of a "syllabic period" in Bissex's (1980) case analysis of the literacy development of her English- speaking son, Paul -although some of the examples she provides might be interpreted in terms of syllabic mapping. Although several authors, as well as many parents and teachers, have noted that preschoolers and first graders "miss" letters (writing VKT for vacation), this is not usually interpreted as syllabic mapping. The usual interpretation is simply that children omit letters (Shimron, 1993). Kamii (1993) suggested that in English there must be a sort of consonantal stage rather than a syllabic one. The strongest attack against the "syllabic hypothesis" was made by Treiman and her associates. Treiman, Tincoff & Daylene Richmond-Welty (1996) suggested, in line with Ehri (1993), that "children begin to create links between printed words and spoken words from a very early age by finding links between letters in printed words and the names of the letters in the spoken words" (p. 512), which North American children learn very early in the context of preschool or family activities.

There is no doubt that children's knowledge of letter-names does play an important role in the acquisition of writing. However, knowledge about letter-names is only one of the factors that influences the development of writing, and it does not operate in the same way in every language and script. One possibility is that the syllabic hypothesis is language-specific: a hypothesis that would hold true for syllable-timed languages such as Spanish, Italian and Chinese but not for English. In general, segmentation strategies are influenced by the phonological structure of the language. Many more cross-linguistic studies are needed before we can reach a definitive answer.

Children exposed to alphabetic systems, systems in which individual letters roughly represent phonemes, will eventually discover the alphabetical principle: that phonemes can be represented by letters so that whenever a particular phoneme occurs in a word, and in whatever position, it can be represented by the same letter. As with most developmental acquisitions, the transition to alphabetic writing is gradual and related to children' s reading and writing experience. There is no sudden shift from a developmental period in which words are regulated by syllabic correspondences to a period in which words are regulated by alphabetic correspondences. Intermediate phases can be identified in which children produce syllabic-alphabetic mapping. Some syllables are exhaustively represented, while others are not. For example, the word *gato* (cat), written GAO, where the first syllable is exhaustively represented (#*ga*# written GA) while the second #*to*# is not.

Situations also arise in which information stemming from different sources creates conflict and children regress to more primitive ways of writing and equally privileged situations in which children arrive at more advanced solutions which cannot be generalized.

The transition is also word-sensitive. Children learn to write certain words alphabetically before others. This may depend on the structure of the word, on the extent to which the word-components present any difficulty of pronunciation, on the way that word-components are represented orthographically and, on children's previous knowledge of the letters that are used to represent the word. If the word forms part of a child's familiar vocabulary of written words, he or she will probably write it alphabetically earlier and more frequently than one, which is completely unknown.

It is in this transition to the alphabetic principle that the specific characteristics of the phonological and morphological structures of a language, and the way in which these characteristics are reflected in the script, play a crucial and distinctive role. It is an exciting experience to see how children attempting to assemble a word try to cope with different sources of information. At times it is a painstaking process during which they seek to conciliate on-line information from different sources with previously stored representations. Children are not only worried by letter-to-sound mapping which sometimes leads to unwanted products. They may also be worried about the outward shape of the letters, which do not always come out as planned, and about what they have already written on the piece of paper, which sometimes acts as an aid but at other times gives rise to conflicts that are not easy to overcome. Eventually these different sources of information become integrated and children learn to write conventionally. Indeed, the alphabetic phase does not indicate the end of writing development, only the very beginning. Children have still a long way ahead to master the multiple faces of literacy

THE CONTRIBUTION OF RESEARCH ON DEVELOPMENTAL LITERACY

I have examined some childhood conceptions on literacy through a discussion of studies in which children were asked to write and read in their own way. These have served to identify the different aspects involved in a child's construction of knowledge about the practices, the notational system, the types of discourse and the resulting texts. Obviously, these are just a minute part of the many other situations that could have been used, and the many that have indeed been used, to observe the development of literacy. The underlying hypothesis is that there is a construction process to which we can gain access by having children interpreting and producing writing. The basic rational underlying this approach is that literacy practices are both the source and the outcome of knowledge. At any level children approach the notational environment and the writing activities with some ideas but, at the same time they observe regularities, they map talk onto the observed graphic shapes and they make inferences about functions and functioning. Children are constantly using socially transmitted knowledge to build further knowledge. This is evident in the formal constraints that they put on readability, in their search for syllabic correspondences and their gradual recognition of the alphabetic principle.

One crucial attainment of this perspective is that literacy can now be seen as a domain of knowledge in a similar sense to physical knowledge or mathematical knowledge. It is a domain that deserves to be studied developmentally. Another attainment is that literacy didactic activities can be part of preschool education. Currently, a large number of schools all over the world take a child's out-of-school knowledge as the starting point for instructional processes. At a very early age child's knowledge about writing is taken into account and expanded upon. Spontaneous writing and multiple types of texts are integrated in daily school activities. From writing their own name and the names of the rest of the children, to writing prescriptions when playing doctors, letters to the major, poetry, songs, newspaper stories. Whatever the project to be developed, kindergartens, preschools or first grades include reading and writing activities without any limit concerning the letters or the text to be used. The criterion for inclusion is the interest of the theme or project and the need to write not the particular difficulty of a sound combination.

Further research should be extended to evaluate the extent to which early literacy is related to literate growth beyond the early years of schooling as well as the extent to which early literacy educational programs contribute to children development as creative, critical and participant members of their community.

REFERENCES

Aronoff, M. (1994). Spelling as Culture. In W. C. Watt (Ed.), *Writing Systems and Cognition* (pp. 67- 87). Dordrecht: Kluwer.

Besse, J. M (1996). An approach to writing in kindergarten. In C. Pontecorvo, M. Orsolini, B. Burge & L. Resnick (Eds.), *Children's early text construction* (pp. 17-144). Mahwah, NJ Lawrence Erlbaum.

Bialystok, E. (1992). Symbolic representation of letters and *numbers. Cognitive Development, 7,* 301-316.

Bissex, G. (1980). *GNYS AT WRK. A child learns to write and read.* Cambridge, MA: Harvard University Press.

Brenneman, K., Massey, C., Machado, S. & Gelman, R. (1996). Notating knowledge about words and objects: preschoolers' plans differ for "writing" and drawing. *Cognitive Development, 11,* 397-419.

Bus, A.G & van Ijzendorm, M. H. (1988). Mother-child interactions, attachment, and emergent literacy: A cross sectional study. *Child Development, 59,* 1262-1273.

Bus, A.G, van Ijzendoml, M. H., & Pellegrini, A.D. (1995). Joint book reading makes for success in learning to read. A metaanalysis on intergenerational analysis of literacy. *Review of Educational Research, 65,* 1-21.

Clay, M. (1972). Reading: the patterning of complex behavior. London: Heineman.

Clay, M. (1982). *What Did I Write? Beginning Writing Behaviour.* London: Heinemann Educational Books.

Chan, L. & Nunes, T. (1998). Children's understanding of the formal and functional characteristics of written Chinese. *Applied Psycholinguistics, 12,* 115-131 ,

Ehri, L.C. (1993). English orthography and phonological knowledge. In Scholes (Ed.), *Literacy and language analysis* (pp. 21-43). Hillsdale, NJ: Erlbaurn.

Eimas, F.R., Siqueland, E.R., Juscyk, P., & Vigorito, J. (1971). Speech perception in infants. *Science, 171,* 303-306.

Ferreiro, E. (1986). The interplay between information and assimilation in beginning literacy. In W. Teale & E. Sulzby (Eds.), *Emergent Literacy: Writing and Reading* (pp. 15- 49). Norwood, NJ: Ablex.

Ferreiro, E. (1988). L'écriture avant la lettre. In H. Sinclair (Ed.), *La production de notations chez le jeune enfant: langage, nombre, rythmes et melodies* (pp. 17-70). [The production of notations in young children: language, number, rythms, and melodies]. Paris: Press Universitaire de France.

Ferreiro, E., & Teberosky, A. (1979). *Los sistemas de escritura en el desarrollo del niño*. Mexico: Siglo XXI. [published in English under the title *Literacy before schooling*).

Harste, J. C., Woodward, v. A., & Burke, C. L. (1984). *Language stories and literacy lessons*. Porthmouth, NH: Heinemann Educational Books.

Heath, So B. (1983). *Ways with words*. Cambridge: Cambridge University Press

Kamii, C., Long, R., Manning, G. & Manning, M. (1993). Les conceptualisations du systeme alphabetique chez les jeunes enfants anglophones. *Etudes de Linguistique Appliquee, 91*, 34-47.

Karmiloff-Smith, A. (1992). *Beyond Modularity: A Developmental Perspective on Cognitive Science*. Cambridge, MA: MIT Press/Bradford Books.

Lavine, L. 1977. Differentiation of Letter-like Forms in Pre-reading Children. *Developmental Psychology, 23*, 89-94.

Levin, I. & Korat, 0. (1993). Sensitivity to phonological. morphological and semantic cues in early reading and writing in Hebrew. *Merrill-Palmer Quarterly, 39*, 233-251.

Levin, I., & Tolchinsky Landsmann, 1990. Becoming literate: Referential and Phonetic Strategies in Early Reading and Writing. *European Journal of Behavioural Development, 12*, 369-384.

Luria, A. R. 1929/1978. The Development of Writing in the Child. In M. Cole (Ed.), *The Selected Writings of A. R. Luria*. (pp. 145-194). New York: M.E Sharpe Inc.

McLane, J. B. & McNamee, G. D. 1990. *Early Literacy*. Cambridge, MA: Harvard University Press.

Pick, A., Unze, M. G., Brownell, C. A. , Drodzal, J. G., and Hopman, M. (1978). Young Children's Knowledge of Word Structure. *Child Development, 49*, 669-680.

Pontecorvo, C. & Zuchermaglio, C. (1988). Modes of differentiation in children's writing construction. *European Journal of Psvchology of Education, 1*, 371- 385.

Pontecorvo, C. & Zucherrnamaglio, C. (1990). Learning text composition in early literacy. In H. Mandl, E. De Corte, S.N Bennett & H.F. Friedrich. (Eds.), *Learning and instruction. European Research in International Context. V 01*. 22, Oxford: Pergamon Press.

Pontecorvo, C. & Zucchennaglio, C. (1989). From Oral to written text: How to analyze children dictating stories. *Journal of Reading Behavior, 2*, 109-125.

Read, Ch. (1971). Pre-school children's knowledge of English phonology. *Harvard Educational Review, 4*, 1-34.

Sandbank, A. (2002). The Interplay Between the Conventions of the Writing System and the Written Language in Writing Texts. In L. Tolchinsky *Developmental aspects in learning to write* (p 55-76) Dordrecht: Kluwer

Scollon, R. & Scollon, S. B. K. (1981). *Narrative. Literacy and Face in Interethnic Communication*. Norwood, NJ: Ablex.

Shimron, J. (1993). The Role of Vowels in Reading: A Review of Studies of English and Hebrew. *Psychological Bulletin, 114*, 52-67.

Snow, C., & Ninio, A. (1986). The contracts of literacy: What children learn from learning to read books. In W. Teale, & E. Sulzby (Eds.), *Emergent literacy: Writing and reading* (pp. 116-138) Norwood, NJ: Ablex.

Teale, R. & Sulzby, E. (1986). *Emergent Literacy: reading and writing*. Norwood, NJ: Ablex.

Tolchinsky Landsmann, L. & Levin, I. (1985). Writing in preschoolers: An age related analysis. *Applied Psycholinguistics, 6*, 319 -339.

Tolchinsky Landsmann, L. & Levin, I. (1987). Writing in four- to six-year-olds: representation of semantic and phonetic similarities and differences. *Journal of Child Language. 14*, 127-144.

Tolchinsky Landsmann, L. (1988). Form and meaning in the development of written representation. *European Journal of Educational Psychology, 3*, 385-398.

Tolchinsky, L. (1999). *The cradle of culture and what children know about writing and numbers before being taught*. Makwah: Lawrence Erlbaum Associates.

Tolchinsky-Landsmann, L. (1991). The Conceptualization of Writing in the Confluence of Interactive Models of Development. In Tolchinsky-Landsmann (Ed.). *Culture, Schooling and Psychological Development* (pp. 87-111). Norwood, J: Ablex.

Vygotsky, L. (1978). *Mind in Society*. Cambridge, MA: Harvard University Press.

FURTHER READINGS

Adams, M. J. (1991). *Beginning to read: Thinking and learning about print*. Cambridge, MA: MIT Press.

Barton, D. (1994). *Literacy: An introduction to the ecology of written language*. Oxford: Basil Blackwell.

Bialystok, E. (1992). Symbolic representation of letters and numbers. *Cognitive Development, 7*, 301-316.

Bissex, G. (1980). *GNYS AT WRK. A child learns to write and read*. Cambridge, MA: Harvard University Press.

Brennemann, K., Massey, C., Machado, S., & Gelman, R. (1996). Notating knowledge about words and objects: Pre-schoolers' plans differ for "writing" and "drawing." *Cognitive Development, 11*, 397-419.

Karanth, P., & Suchitra, M. G. (1993). Literacy acquisition and grammaticality judgments. In R. Scholes (Ed.), *Literacy and language analysis* (pp. 143-156). Hillsdale, NJ: Lawrence Erlbaum Associates.

Pontecorvo, C. & Rossi, F. (2001) Absence, negation, impossibility and falsity in children's first writing. In L. Tolchinsky (Ed.), *Developmental aspects in learning to write* (pp. 13-32). Dordrecht: Kluwer Academic

Ravid, D. and Tolchinsky, L. (2002). Developing linguistic literacy: A comprehensive model. *Journal of Child Language, 29*, 417-447.

Read, C. (1986). *Children's creative spelling*. London: Routledge and Kegan Paul.

A2. Phonology and Spelling

REBECCA TREIMAN[1]

ABSTRACT

It has often been suggested that the English spelling system is so capricious that children must rely largely on rote memory to learn how to spell in English. However, Venezky's (1970) demonstration that the English spelling system is more orderly than was thought before encouraged researchers to examine how children go beyond rote memorization in learning to spell. In a series of publications beginning in 1971, Read demonstrated that young children's spellings are often systematic attempts to translate genuine phonological distinctions, even though these spellings may be mistaken from the point of view of the conventional script. For example, the fact that children sometimes spell the opening sound of *truck* as *ch* reflects a real phonological difference between words whose spellings begin with "tr" and those whose spellings begin with "t" followed by a vowel. More recent research (e.g., Treiman, 1993) has amply confirmed that many of children's beginning spellings are guided by their understanding of phonology. For example, most Americans do not pronounce a separate vowel sound in words like *girl*, and young American children often misplace the letter for the vowel sound in such words or leave it out altogether, as in the errors GRIL and GRL. In British English, in contrast, words such as "girl" and "better" are pronounced without an "r" sound. Young British children are much more likely than their American counterparts to leave out the *r* when writing these words. English has morphological as well as phonological regularities, and some of these also influence the spellings of quite young children. For example, when the "t" sound is preceded and followed by a vowel in American speech, its pronunciation approaches that of a "d." This is reflected in the writing of beginning American spellers who are quite likely, for example, to write *water* as WODR. Such errors are more likely to occur in one-morpheme words, like *water*, than in two-morpheme words, like *biting*, where the first morpheme, in this case *bite*, ends in a "t" sound. Children's willingness to maintain the *t* spelling in these latter words supports the

---

[1] Preparation of this chapter was supported by grants from the National Science Foundation (SBR-9807736, BCS-0130763). and the March of Dimes Birth Defects Foundation (12-FY00-51). Thanks to Lia Sotak for comments on a draft of the chapter.

31

T. Nunes, P. Bryant (eds.), Handbook of Children's Literacy, 31–42.

conclusion that from the start their spellings reflect their understanding of linguistic patterns – phonological and morphological – and not just rote learning.

INTRODUCTION

The goal of this chapter is to review the research on the role of phonology in children's spelling. I will focus on how children learn to spell in English, particularly on the early stages of spelling development. The theme of the chapter is that learning to spell is a linguistically guided process, not simply a process of rote memorization. We must look closely at the structure of the language and at children's knowledge of that structure if we wish to understand the spelling errors that children make. One aspect of the structure of language – its phonological or sound structure – plays an especially important role in children's early spelling. Its role will be the focus of this chapter.

SPELLING AS ROTE VISUAL MEMORIZATION

Traditionally, it was thought that learning to spell in English is a process of rote memorization. So capricious is the English writing system, so illogical are spellings such as *could* and *island*, that learners have no choice but to laboriously memorize words' spellings. On this view, learning to spell requires much diligence and attentiveness but little linguistic skill or creativity. Children memorize words for their weekly spelling tests in much the same way that they memorize other dull (to them) facts, such as that Sacramento is the capital of California.

If learning the spelling of a word involves storing an arbitrary string of letters in memory, then the same principles that govern other forms of serial learning should apply to spelling. For example, the position of an item in the to-be-memorized string should have the same impact on spelling as on other memorization tasks. Spellers should show a serial position effect such that they perform relatively well on the initial and final letters of a word and poorly on the middle letters. Indeed, a serial position curve of this kind often appears in spelling (Jensen, 1962; Kooi, Schutz, & Baker, 1965). Such findings could be taken to suggest that misspellings such as LRN for *learn*, in which children omit letters from the middle of a word, are similar to errors in which people omit items from the middles of other to-be-memorized sequences. (Throughout this chapter, children's misspellings of words will be indicated in upper-case letters.) Misspellings such as GRIL for *girl*, in which children reverse two letters, are thought to be similar to reversal errors in other memorization tasks, as when people interchange two digits of a memorized telephone number.

This view of spelling as rote visual memorization has implications for the classification of children's spelling errors. On this view, misspellings should be seen in relation to the letters of a word's conventional spelling. Errors should be classified as omissions, reversals, or substitutions of particular letters in the to-be-memorized form.

SPELLING AS A PHONOLOGICALLY GUIDED PROCESS

The work of Richard Venezky (Venezky, 1970) set the stage for a change in thinking about spelling and spelling acquisition. Venezky's analyses of the spelling-sound relationships in some 20,000 English words showed that the writing system of this language is more predictable than often believed. To be sure, the English writing system is not characterized by the simple one-to-one relationships between *graphemes* (letters or letter groups) and *phonemes* (units of sound) that prevail in certain other alphabetic writing systems, such as Finnish. In English, a single grapheme often corresponds to more than one phoneme, as when *c* stands for "k" in *cake* but "s" in *city*. (Units of sound will be indicated in quotation marks throughout the chapter.) Also, a single phoneme often has more than one potential spelling, as when the "long a" sound is written as *ay* in *bay* and *mayor* but as *ai* in *bait* and *aid*. What is often overlooked is that these variations are typically not random. As Venezky pointed out, one can often predict which pattern will occur based on the position of the letter or phoneme in the word and the word's morphological structure (i.e., the smaller meaningful units or *morphemes* that it contains). For example, the *ay* spelling of "long a" usually occurs at the end of a morpheme, as in *bay*, or before a vowel, as in *mayor*. The *ai* spelling generally appears in other positions, as in *bait* and *aid*. As another example, a medial "short e" sound in a monosyllabic word is generally spelled as *e*, as in *bed*. However, the "short e" sound of *health* is spelled as *ea* rather than as *e*, corresponding to the fact that the word is related to *heal*. Not all English spellings are predictable, of course. The *s* in *island* and the *ai* in *plaid* seem to be genuine exceptions. Still, the English writing system is more principled than often believed (see Kessler & Treiman, 2001, 2003).

Venezky's work focused primarily on spelling-to-sound translation rather than on sound-to-spelling translation. The work thus has more direct implications for theories of word pronunciation and its development than for theories of spelling. However, Venezky's discussion of the linguistic patterns in the English writing system encouraged researchers to examine how spellers learn and use the patterns. The work set the stage for viewing spelling errors not only in relation to the conventional spelling of a word but also in relation to the word's linguistic structure.

Charles Read (1971, 1975a, 1975b, 1986) was one of the first investigators to study the development of spelling in English as a linguistic process rather than a process of rote visual memorization. Read's conclusions were based, in part, on a detailed study of young children who began to spell before they had received much formal instruction in spelling or reading. Preschoolers such as these may compose messages such as WAN YOU GAD I CHANS SEND IS OL I LADR. AD DOW GT ANE CHRIBLS, messages that contain many unusual spellings and that may be difficult for adults to read. This one says: When you get a chance send us all a letter. And don't get any troubles (Read, 1975b). Read examined the commonalities among different children's spellings and the ways in which the children represented various linguistic features. To bolster his conclusions, he also carried out experimental studies with young children. This combination of naturalistic and experimental research proved fruitful, with the naturalistic data pointing to certain phenomena that were then examined in greater detail in the experiments.

Read concluded that learning to spell is a linguistic process, more akin to learning to talk than to memorizing arbitrary sequences such as telephone numbers. When children acquire their spoken language, they learn about the patterns in the system and apply their generalizations to new instances, sometimes with surprising results. For example, a preschooler might say "I holded the baby" rather than "I held the baby." "Holded" is an error when judged against the conventional system, but it reveals an appreciation of how the English past tense is typically formed. Similarly, the preschool orthographer cited above wrote CHRIBLS instead of *troubles*. This is an error when judged against the conventional writing system, but it reveals the child's belief that the first part of *troubles* sounds like the first part of *chubby*. The sounds are indeed similar: The articulation of "t" becomes close to that of "ch" when "t" precedes "r." A similar phenomenon occurs for "d," which is pronounced similarly to "j" when it comes before "r."

The child who wrote CHRIBLS for *troubles* is not unique. Other precocious spellers studied by Read produced similar renditions of "t" before "r." Moreover, children sometimes misspelled "d" before "r" as *j* or *g*, as in JRAGIN for *dragon*. Such misspellings reflect the way in which children classify the sounds of their language, one aspect of their linguistic knowledge. Supporting this interpretation, experimental work reported by Read (1975a) showed that some young children do not consider the first sound of *truck* to be the same as the first sounds of *turkey* and *tie*, as adults do and as the conventional English writing system assumes. Instead, these children consider the first sound of *truck* to match the first sounds of *church* and *chicken*. The children's invented spellings testify to their own understanding of English phonology.

Are only gifted preschoolers able to invent spellings that reflect their conceptions of words' phonological forms? To determine whether more typical children do the same, I examined the writings produced by middle-class first graders who attended a state-supported school in the Midwestern United States (Treiman, 1993). These first graders were not precocious or advanced. What distinguished them from many other children was that their teacher was a strong believer in the *whole-language* approach to reading and writing instruction. Advocates of this view (e.g., Goodman, 1986) believe that children will pick up what they need to know about the relations between spellings and sounds from the reading and writing that they do. It is felt that children should not work with isolated words or isolated sounds but that they should read meaningful and interesting texts. Independent writing is thought to be important, especially writing that grows out of the children's own experiences. In line with the whole-language philosophy, the teacher in the first-grade classroom that I studied expected her students to write daily. She encouraged them to spell words on their own, and she did not tell the children how to spell words even if they asked. Invented spelling is a teaching tool in other classrooms as well, although this teacher's refusal to provide the correct spelling of a word even when a child requests it is rather unusual. The school district did mandate that the children memorize a list of six spelling words each week, beginning in the second half of the first-grade year. The teacher complied with this requirement.

The first graders in my 1993 study made many of the same kinds of spelling errors discovered by Read (1971, 1975a, 1975b, 1986). For example, the first graders produced spellings such as CHRAP for *trap* and JEAD for *drowned*. Thus, it is not just precocious children who begin to write at an early age who show a sensitivity to the phonological structure of language in their spelling. My findings further revealed that the spelling errors discovered by Read were just the tip of the iceberg. A number of other intriguing errors that were motivated by phonology emerged in the first graders' classroom spellings. My co-workers and I have carried out a number of experiments to examine these phenomena in more detail (Bernstein & Treiman, 2001; Cassar & Treiman, 1997; Reece & Treiman, 2001; Treiman, 1985a; Treiman, 1985b; Treiman, 1991; Treiman, 1994; Treiman, Berch, Tincoff, & Weatherston, 1993a; Treiman, Berch, & Weatherston, 1993b; Treiman, Broderick, Tincoff, & Rodriguez, 1998; Treiman & Cassar, 1996; Treiman, Cassar, & Zukowski, 1994; Treiman, Goswami, Tincoff, & Leevers, 1997; Treiman & Tincoff, 1997; Treiman, Zukowski, & Richmond-Welty, 1995). These studies, like my naturalistic study of first graders, were carried out with children from the Midwestern United States. Together, the naturalistic and experimental work provides a picture of how early spelling is guided by phonology and other types of linguistic knowledge, what kinds of errors occur among beginning spellers, and why children make these errors.

Consider the words *girl* and *her*. The first graders in my naturalistic study often omitted the vowels when they spelled such words, producing errors such as GRL and HR (Treiman, 1993). Studies in which children were asked to spell dictated real and made-up words revealed the same phenomenon among other groups of kindergarten and first-grade children from the United States (Reece & Treiman, 2001; Treiman et al., 1993a; Treiman et al., 1997). The results of these studies show that children are much more likely to omit the vowels of words such as *girl* and *her* than the vowels of words such as *kept* and *him*. Such differences emerge even when the two types of words are comparable in length (e.g., *girl* and *kept* are both four letters), consonant-vowel spelling pattern (e.g., *her* and *him* both contain a consonant letter followed by a vowel and another consonant), and frequency of occurrence in the English language. It is difficult to explain the difference in vowel omission rates if we view spelling as purely a matter of rote memorization of letter sequences. On that view, one might expect a fair number of vowel omissions in both *girl* and *kept* because the vowel letter is the third letter of a four-letter sequence in both cases. However, it would be difficult to explain why vowel omissions are more common with *girl* than *kept*. The difference in the rate of vowel omissions becomes easier to understand if we view spelling as guided by phonology. In American English, the phonological form of *girl* contains a *syllabic* "r" (i.e., an "r" that takes the place of the vowel at the centre of the syllable); it does not contain a separate vowel phoneme preceding an "r." Because the spoken form of the word does not include a separate vowel, it makes sense that children would often fail to include a vowel letter in their spellings. Children who have begun to grasp the alphabetic principle expect it to be implemented in a simple fashion such that each phoneme in a spoken word is translated with a single letter. *Girl* – with its initial "g", medial syllabic "r," and final "l" – is most naturally spelled as GRL. In contrast, *kept* has a true vowel phoneme in its pronunciation. Children therefore usually include a vowel letter when spelling this word. As these examples show, we can begin to understand why children make the spelling mistakes they do if we consider the phonological structures of words.

In *girl* and *her*, the syllabic "r" is stressed. Syllabic "r" also occurs in unstressed form in American English. For example, *doctor* and *tiger* end with an unstressed syllabic "r." Children from the United States often fail to include a vowel letter in such cases. For example, they may produce errors such as DOCTR for *doctor* and TIGR for *tiger*, omitting the vowel that should appear in the second syllable of the word. We may compare children's omissions of the second vowel in words such as *doctor* and *tiger*, on the one hand, and words such as *basket* and *salad*, on the other. The two types of words are similar in frequency, length, and consonant-vowel spelling pattern. However, *doctor* and *tiger* do not contain a separate vowel in the second syllable, whereas *basket* and *salad* do. Correspondingly, children are much more likely to include a vowel letter when spelling the second syllables of *basket* and *salad* than the second syllables of *doctor* and *tiger*. This result points, again, to an effect of phonology on spelling. It further implies that labelling an error as an omission of a letter from the word's conventional spelling may not shed much light on the basis for the error. One must consider the word's phonological form – in this case, whether it contains a syllabic "r" – as well as its standard spelling.

As children gain experience with the English writing system, they observe that the conventional printed forms of *her*, *girl*, and *learn* contain vowel letters. These are letters that the children did not anticipate based on their phonological representations of the words. In some cases, children are also explicitly taught that all words should be spelled with at least one vowel. As a result of such teaching (if provided) and their exposure to conventional print, children begin to include vowel letters in their spellings of words like *her*, *girl*, and *learn*. Children sometimes make an interesting kind of spelling error during this learning process: They use a vowel letter, but they put it in the wrong place. For example, children may spell *girl* as GRIL or *teacher* as TETRE (Reece & Treiman, 2001; Treiman, 1993; Treiman et al., 1993a; Treiman et al., 1997). Looked at superficially, these errors involve the reversal of two letters from the conventional spelling of the word – *i* and *r* in the case of *girl*, and *e* and *r* in the case of *teacher*. However, errors such as GRIL for *girl* and TETRE for *teacher* are more common than errors such as KPET for *kept* and BASKTE for *basket*. If the misordering of letters from the memorized spelling of the word were all that was involved, one would not expect to find such a difference. The different error patterns for the two types of words reflect differences in the words' phonological structures. Because there is no separate vowel phoneme preceding the syllabic "r" in the spoken form of *girl*, the word's phonological form provides no guidance on where any vowel letter should go. Given this lack of phonological underpinning, children sometimes put the vowel letter in the wrong place. *Kept*, in contrast, has a vowel phoneme after the "k" and before the final cluster in its spoken form. Children who treat spelling as a map of phonological structure thus know that they should place the vowel letter between the letters corresponding to the initial and final consonants. We gain a deeper understanding of children's spelling errors by acknowledging the importance of phonology in the spelling process than by classifying errors into such superficial categories as omissions and reversals.

Further evidence of the role of phonology in spelling comes from comparisons between children who speak different dialects of the same language. If phonology contributes importantly to spelling, then phonological differences among dialects may show themselves in spelling. To determine whether this is so, my colleagues and I (Treiman et al., 1997) compared the spellings of children who spoke two dialects of English – American English, as spoken by children from the Midwestern United States, and Southern British English. As discussed above, young children from the Midwestern United States are more likely to misspell *girl* as GRL than as GIL or GUL. Young children from Southern Britain, we found, show the opposite pattern. They often include a vowel letter but omit the *r*, as in GUL. Differences are also found on words like *doctor*. For American children, omissions in the second syllable tend to involve the vowel. For British children, it tends to be the *r* that is omitted. If spelling were only a matter of rote visual memorization, then we would expect to see similar errors by children from the United States and children from Britain. After all, the two groups of children encounter virtually the same conventional spellings (with a few differences such as *color/colour* and *recognize/recognise*). The finding that American and British children make different types of spelling errors on certain words supports the idea that spelling is guided by phonology. The key phonological difference in this case is that Southern British English is a *non-rhotic* dialect. Speakers of this dialect do not include an "r" when saying a word such as *girl*. When they pronounce *doctor* in isolation (and it appears to be the way in which words are pronounced in isolation that is critical for spelling), they also omit the "r." It is thus not surprising that young British children often produce spelling errors such as GUL and DOCTE. Most varieties of American English, including the Midwestern dialects that my colleagues and I have studied, are *rhotic*. This means that an "r" is present in words such as *girl* and *doctor*. American children typically include an *r* when spelling such words.

Intriguingly, dialect-related differences in spelling are not confined to words that are pronounced differently in American English and British English. Differences are found, too, on certain words that are pronounced alike in the two dialects. Consider the word *pizza*. In both American and British English, this word ends with a short unstressed vowel, called a *schwa*, when it is pronounced in isolation. However, the British children in our study (Treiman et al., 1997) frequently spelled such words with a final *r*, as in PISER. The American children rarely made such errors. What is the reason for this difference? For British children, the spoken form of *pizza* ends with the same unstressed schwa as the spoken forms of *doctor*, *tiger*, *after*, and so on. British children learn that schwa is often spelled not with a single-letter grapheme but with a *digraph*, or two-letter spelling. The digraph consists of a vowel letter, most often *e*, followed by *r*. British children generalize this pattern to the final vowel of words like *pizza*, producing errors such as PISER. These errors show that children pick up the relationships between phonology and spelling and generalize these patterns to new instances. They sometimes create spellings based on words' phonological forms rather than reproducing spellings from memory.

Another example of a dialect-related generalization error is BARTH for *bath*. My colleagues and I (Treiman et al., 1997) observed errors of this kind among the British children that we studied. Other examples are PARS and PRS for *pass*. In Southern British speech, *bath* has the same "ah" vowel sound as *card*. Children sometimes use the *ar* spelling (or just the *r*) that they have seen in *card* when attempting to spell words like *bath*. That is, they generalize the *ar* spelling that they have associated with the "ah" vowel of *card* to the "ah" vowel of *bath*. Note that *bath* does not contain an "r" sound in its pronunciation in non-rhotic dialects. Errors like BARTH for *bath* reflect a generalization process rather than an attempt to represent an "r" phoneme that is heard in the word itself.

In our cross-dialect study (Treiman et al., 1997), dialect-related generalization errors in spelling did not necessarily become less common as spelling ability increased. For example, British children with spelling ages of about 8 and 9 years old according to a standardized test actually made more errors like PISER for *pizza* than British children with spelling ages of about 6 and 7. Misspellings such as BARTH for *bath* were also found among the more advanced spellers. A certain amount of experience with the conventional writing system is necessary to learn that the schwa vowel may be spelled with the digraph *er* and that "ah" may be spelled as *ar*. These patterns are fairly complex in that a single phoneme is represented with a two-letter grapheme rather than a single letter. Once children have learned these digraph spellings, they sometimes extend them to cases in which they do not apply, much as a child learning to talk sometimes extends the regular past tense marker to irregular verbs.

With enough experience, children learn the conventional spellings of common words such as *pizza* and *bath*. However, Treiman and Barry (2000) found that even adults sometimes produce dialect-related errors when attempting to spell less common words. Consider the following misspellings from British university students: SCUBER for *scuba*, KARKI for *khaki*, and CARSKET for *casket*. These misspellings are similar to the PISER and BARTH errors that are found among British children. American college students rarely make these particular types of spelling errors, although they sometimes misspell the words in other ways. These results suggest that phonology continues to be involved in spelling even into adulthood. This conclusion fits with other work that has found phonological effects in adult spellers (e.g., Kreiner, 1992; Kreiner & Gough, 1990); it does not support the view that skilled spellers generally bypass phonology (e.g., Burt & Fury, 2000).

In English, it is not enough to learn which grapheme or graphemes may be used to symbolize each phoneme. When a phoneme may be represented with more than one grapheme – as most English phonemes can – children must also learn when each spelling is appropriate. As Venezky (1970) pointed out, one can often predict which of several possible graphemes will be found in a particular word based on various linguistic factors. One example, mentioned earlier, is that the "long a" sound is generally spelled as *ay* at the end of a morpheme or before a vowel, as in *bay* and *mayor*. In other positions, the *ai* spelling is more likely (e.g., *aid*, *bait*). The alternation between *ay* and *ai* is one instance of a general pattern that applies to digraphs. Digraphs ending with *y* and *w* typically occur at the ends of morphemes and before vowels, whereas those ending with *i* and *u* are more often found in other positions. This pattern does have some exceptions. For example, *growl* has *ow* before a consonant in the middle of a morpheme, where *u* would normally be expected. Still, the pattern holds true in many cases. Another example of a context-conditioned spelling alternation involves "k." The *ck* spelling of "k" occurs in the middles and at the ends of words but not at the beginnings, where *c* or *k* is more common. This pattern has no exceptions, in that no English words begin with *ck*.

Evidence from Treiman (1993) suggests that children begin to learn about the effects of positional context on spelling as early as first grade. For example, the first graders in that study were more likely to produce spellings such as SEILF and PLEW, which follow the alternation pattern described above, than spellings such as AI and EWT, which do not follow this pattern (by having a digraph ending in *i* at the end of a word or a digraph ending in *w* before a consonant). Also, the first graders did not often produce spellings such as CKES, with *ck* at the beginning of a word.

Further evidence of children's sensitivity to the effects of position on spelling comes from experimental work. In one study, Treiman (1993) asked kindergartners, first graders, second graders, and college students to look at pairs of nonwords and decide which item in each pair looked more like a real word should look. Sample pairs are *nuck-ckun* and *moil-moyl*, where the first member of each pair follows one of the patterns described above and the second member of the pair does not. Even the kindergartners, who were tested near the end of the school year and who were reading at a beginning first grade level, were slightly but significantly above the level expected by random guessing (56% correct, where 50% is expected by chance). By second grade, correct responses occurred 83% of the time, and by adulthood, 95%. These results, together with those of Cassar and Treiman (1997), suggest that even young children have some inkling that spelling patterns vary in a systematic way with word position. This knowledge expands and deepens as children encounter a variety of words and make generalizations from them.

It is not just a phoneme's position in a word that can affect its spelling. Even when position is held constant, the identity of the surrounding units may influence a phoneme's spelling. Kessler and Treiman (2001) documented this phenomenon. As one example, the "short e" sound is sometimes spelled as *ea* before "d," as in *bread* and *head*. It is rarely so spelled before "p". Adults appear to use the surrounding consonants as a cue to the spelling of a vowel. For example, having learned that the "e" sound of *friend* is spelled as *ie*, they are more willing to generalize this spelling to "chend," in which the "nd" after the vowel is maintained, than to "cheth," in which different consonants surround the vowel (Treiman & Zukowski, 1988; see also Treiman, Kessler, & Bick, 2002). It is not clear when and how children begin to use phonemic context as a cue to spelling. The results of Goswami (1988) suggest that units consisting of a vowel and final consonant play a special role from early on in the development of spelling. In that study, children who were given a "clue word" such as *beak* were able to use the clue to help them spell related words; the benefit was significantly greater for words that shared the vowel and final consonant of the clue word (e.g., *peak*) than for words that shared the initial consonant and vowel (e.g., *bean*). However, the findings of Nation and Hulme (1996) suggest that young children show no particular priority for vowel + final consonant units. In their research, children did not make significantly more analogies when a vowel + final consonant unit was shared than when some other unit was shared. Bernstein and Treiman (2001) found similar results. Further research is needed to study how children use context in choosing among alternative spellings for phonemes and when the ability to use different types of context emerges.

The research reviewed so far shows that spelling is guided to a large extent by phonology. One important aspect of learning to spell is learning how the phonological structure of language is symbolized in print. When children's conceptions of phonological structure do not match those embodied in the conventional writing system, or when the links between phonology and spelling are complex, spelling errors may occur. Importantly, the errors are usually not random or haphazard. The misspellings reflect children's belief that the visual forms of words map the phonological structure of the language.

BEYOND PHONOLOGY

Learning to spell in English involves learning about the way in which the phonological form of the language is symbolized in print. However, this is not all that it involves. English spelling also reflects other aspects of linguistic structure, including the morphological structure of the language. Children must learn about this aspect of the system as well. As one example of how this takes place, consider the American English pronunciation of medial "t." This sound is typically pronounced with a quick tap of the tongue against the upper part of the mouth, called a *flap*, when it occurs before an unstressed vowel. Flaps are voiced (i.e., the vocal cords vibrate during their articulation), and in this way are similar to "d." American children often spell a word like "water" as WODR, representing the flapped "t" with *d* (Read, 1975a; Treiman, 1993; Treiman et al., 1994). This error makes sense given the pronunciation of the word. With "biting," children can avoid making an error on the flap if they consider the word's morphological structure. "Biting" is composed of the stem "bite" (which ends with a "t" that is not flapped when the stem is pronounced by itself) and the inflectional ending

"ing." If children maintain the spelling of the stem when spelling the inflected word, they can avoid errors like BIDING for "biting." Studies have shown that children begin to be able to do this from an early age (Treiman et al., 1994; see also Treiman & Cassar, 1996). Further discussion of the role of morphology in spelling may be found in the chapter by Bryant and Nunes (this volume).

CONCLUSIONS

We have seen, in this chapter, that learning to spell in English is to a large extent a linguistic process. Memorization plays some role, for example in learning about the *s* of *island*, but there is much more to spelling than rote memory. From an early age, children treat spellings as maps of linguistic structure. They create spellings that reflect their knowledge of linguistic form. This chapter has focused on one particular aspect of linguistic form – phonology. Children's conceptions of phonology do not always match those that are assumed by the conventional English writing system. For example, children may classify the first sound of "troubles" as a member of the "ch" category rather than as a member of the "t" category. In addition, children take time to master the more complex mappings between phonology and spelling, as when a single phoneme is represented with two letters. By considering these and other factors, we can begin to understand the logic behind children's misspellings. Even when children's spellings are incorrect, as they often are, the spellings may reveal a good deal of linguistic knowledge.

REFERENCES

Bernstein, S., & Treiman, R. (2001). Learning a novel grapheme: Effects of positional and phonemic context on children's spelling. *Journal of Experimental Child Psychology, 79,* 56-77.

Burt, J. S., & Fury, M. B. (2000). Spelling in adults: The role of reading skills and experience. *Reading and Writing: An Interdisciplinary Journal, 13,* 1-30.

Cassar, M., & Treiman, R. (1997). The beginnings of orthographic knowledge: Children's knowledge of double letters in words. *Journal of Educational Psychology, 89,* 631-644.

Goodman, K. S. (1986). *What's whole in whole language.* Portsmouth, NH: Heinemann.

Goswami, U. (1988). Children's use of analogy in learning to spell. *British Journal of Developmental Psychology. 6,* 21-33.

Jensen, A. R. (1962). Spelling errors and the serial-position effect. *Journal of Educational Psychology, 53,* 105-109.

Kessler, B., & Treiman, R. (2001). Relationships between sounds and letters in English monosyllables. *Journal of Memory and Language, 44,* 592-617.

Kessler, B., & Treiman, R. (2003). Is English spelling chaotic? Misconceptions concerning its irregularity. *Reading Psychology, 24,* 291-313.

Kooi, B. Y., Schutz, R. E., & Baker, R. L. (1965). Spelling errors and the serial-position effect. *Journal of Educational Psychology, 56,* 334-336.

Kreiner, D. S. (1992). Reaction time measures of spelling: Testing a two-strategy model of skilled spelling. *Journal of Experimental Psychology: Learning, Memory, and Cognition, 18,* 765-776.

Kreiner, D. S., & Gough, P. B. (1990). Two ideas about spelling: Rules and word-specific memory. *Journal of Memory and Language, 29,* 103-118.

Nation, K., & Hulme, C. (1996). The automatic activation of sound-letter knowledge: An alternative interpretation of analogy and priming effects in early spelling development. *Journal of Experimental Child Psychology, 63,* 416-435.

Read, C. (1971). Pre-school children's knowledge of English phonology. *Harvard Educational Review, 41,* 1-34.

Read, C. (1975a). *Children's categorization of speech sounds in English (NCTE Research Report No. 17).* Urbana, IL: National Council of Teachers of English.

Read, C. (1975b). Lessons to be learned from the preschool orthographer. In E. H. Lenneberg & E. Lenneberg (Eds.), *Foundations of language development* (Vol. 2, pp. 329-346). New York: Academic Press.

Read, C. (1986). *Children's creative spelling.* London: Routledge & Kegan Paul.

Reece, C., & Treiman, R. (2001). Children's spelling of syllabic /r/ and of letter-name vowels: Broadening the study of spelling development. *Applied Psycholinguistics, 22,* 139-165.

Treiman, R. (1985a). Phonemic awareness and spelling: Children's judgments do not always agree with adults'. *Journal of Experimental Child Psychology, 39,* 182-201.

Treiman, R. (1985b). Spelling of stop consonants after /s/ by children and adults. *Applied Psycholinguistics, 6,* 261-282.

Treiman, R. (1991). Children's spelling errors on syllable-initial consonant clusters. *Journal of Educational Psychology, 83,* 346-360.

Treiman, R. (1993). *Beginning to spell: A study of first-grade children.* New York: Oxford University Press.

Treiman, R. (1994). Use of consonant letter names in beginning spelling. *Developmental Psychology, 30,* 567-580.

Treiman, R., & Barry, C. (2000). Dialect and authography: Some differences between American and British spellers. *Journal of Experimental Psychology: Learning, Memory, and Cognition, 26,* 1423-1430.

Treiman, R., Berch, D., Tincoff, R., & Weatherston, S. (1993a). Phonology and spelling: The case of syllabic consonants. *Journal of Experimental Child Psychology, 56,* 267-290.

Treiman, R, Berch, D., & Weatherston, S. (1993b). Children's use of phoneme-grapheme correspondences in spelling: Roles of position and stress. *Journal of Educational Psychology, 85,* 1-12.

Treiman, R., Broderick, V., Tincoff, R., & Rodriguez, K. (1998). Children's phonological awareness: Confusions between phonemes that differ only in voicing. *Journal of Experimental Child Psychology, 68,* 3-21.

Treiman, R., & Cassar, M. (1996). Effects of morphology on children's spelling of final consonant clusters. *Journal of Experimental Child Psychology, 63,* 141-170.

Treiman, R., Cassar, M., & Zukowski, A. (1994). What types of linguistic information do children use in spelling? The case of flaps. *Child Development, 65,* 1318-1337.

Treiman, R., Goswami, U., Tincoff, R., & Leevers, H. (1997). Effects of dialect on American and British children's spelling. *Child Development, 68,* 211-227.

Treiman, R., Kessler, B., & Bick, S. (2002). Context sensitivity in the spelling of English vowels. *Journal of Memory and Language, 47,* 448-468.

Treiman, R., & Tincoff, R. (1997). The fragility of the alphabetic principle: Children's knowledge of letter names can cause them to spell syllabically rather than alphabetically. *Journal of Experimental Child Psychology, 64,* 425-451.

Treiman, R., & Zukowski, A. (1988). Units in reading and spelling. *Journal of Memory and Language, 27,* 466-477.

Treiman, R., Zukowski, A., & Richmond-Welty, E. D. (1995). What happened to the "n" of sink? Children's spellings of final consonant clusters. *Cognition, 55,* 1-38.

Venezky, R. L. (1970). *The structure of English orthography.* The Hague: Mouton.

SUGGESTED FURTHER READINGS

Brown, G. D. A. and N. C. Ellis (1994). *Handbook of spelling: Theory, process and Intervention.* Chichester, England: Wiley.

Treiman, R. (1993). *Beginning to spell: A study of first-grade children.* New York: Oxford University Press.

A3. Linguistic Processes in Reading and Spelling: The Case of Alphabetic Writing Systems: English, French, German and Spanish

LILIANE SPRENGER-CHAROLLES[1]

ABSTRACT

The aim of this chapter is to provide a survey of the development of word reading and spelling in alphabetic writing systems. We assume that the processes that beginning readers rely on partially depend on the specific characteristics of each language, and not only on general principles common to all languages. In particular the weight of the indirect phonological route depends on the degree to which the different writing systems represent the spoken language which they encode. To illustrate this claim, we will review studies carried out with English-, French-, German- and Spanish-speaking children. After a presentation of the main specific linguistic characteristics of these four languages, we shall review the psycholinguistic literature. Our main arguments will be that (1) at the beginning of reading acquisition, the orthographic lexicon is not yet operating, therefore, children rely on their speech knowledge to establish relations between spoken and written language; (2) these relations are easier to establish when "spelling-to-sound" correspondences are transparent; (3) the units of "spelling-to-sound" correspondences depend on the linguistic peculiarities of each specific language; (4) the constitution of the orthographic lexicon is a consequence of the consolidation of the associations between "spelling-to-sound" correspondences.

INTRODUCTION

Young children might be able to understand a text that is read to them and yet still be unable to understand the same text when they have to read it by themselves. If this happens, their reading difficulties cannot be explained by a failure in comprehension – the goal of reading – but are due to an inability to master some

---

[1] Acknowledgement: I would like to thank Willy Serniclaes, Danielle Béchennec, Jesus Alegria and Sylvia Defior for their very helpful comments. The help of Sally Gerome in proof reading this chapter is gratefully acknowledged.

43

underlying mechanisms specific to reading. There is now overwhelming evidence that these mechanisms that are located at the word level are fairly automatic in skilled readers. This is crucial because of the limited capacity of the reader's information processing. The more attentional cognitive resources the reader uses for word identification (i.e. the more s/he tries to guess words out of context), the less cognitive resources remain available for understanding the text. An important question therefore is how a child acquires automaticity in word reading.

Most reading models assume two different mechanisms (or routes) for word access: a direct orthographic route and an indirect phonological route. The first involves direct connections between a written word and its occurrence in the orthographic lexicon of the subject. This route is generally used to read high frequency words, whether they are regular or irregular. The indirect route involves "spelling-to-sound" correspondences. This route works fine for regular words, like "table" in English or in French, but not for words like "have" in English or "femme" in French that transgress frequent "spelling-to-sound" correspondences.

The aim of the present chapter is to provide a survey of the development of word reading and spelling in alphabetic writing systems. We assume that the processes that beginning readers rely on partially depend on the specific characteristics of each language, and not only on general principles common to all languages. In particular the weight of the indirect phonological route depends on the degree to which the different writing systems represent the spoken language which they encode. To illustrate this claim, we will review studies carried out with English-, French-, German- and Spanish-speaking children (referred to from here on as English, French, German and Spanish children). After a presentation of the main specific linguistic characteristics of these four languages, we shall review the psycholinguistic literature. Our main arguments will be that:

- at the beginning of reading acquisition, the orthographic lexicon is not yet operating; therefore, children rely on their speech knowledge to establish relations between spoken and written language;
- these relations are easier to establish when "spelling-to-sound" correspondences are transparent;
- the units of "spelling-to-sound" correspondences depend on the linguistic peculiarities of each specific language;
- the constitution of the orthographic lexicon is a consequence of the consolidation of the associations between "spelling-to-sound" correspondences.

PHONOLOGICAL AND ORTHOGRAPHICAL SPECIFICITIES OF ENGLISH, FRENCH, GERMAN AND SPANISH

The letters of the alphabet are not connected with sounds but with phonemes. A phoneme is a family of sounds whose function is to signal a difference in meaning in a language. The fact that "bat" and "pat" differ in meaning demonstrates that /p/ and /b/ are English phonemes even if the sounds of [p] in "paper", "spoon" and "top" differ from one another. In Spanish, the fact that "pero" (but) and "perro" (a dog) differ in meaning indicates that two different phonemes for *R* exist. This is not the case in French where the differences between the two *R*s may be only a dialectal difference, and not a phonemic difference related to a difference in meaning.

Each letter of the alphabet was designed in principle to represent one specific phoneme. A major problem emerges when there are more phonemes than letters to represent them. For example, whereas the alphabet has five letters for vowels, as in oral Spanish, more than 14 simple vowels are found in English, French and German (Delattre, 1965). To spell English, French and German vowels, it is thus necessary to use either diacritic markers (i.e. the umlaut in German which differentiates *u* /u/ and *ü* /y/), or more than one letter (i.e. *ou* for /u/ in French as opposed to *u* /y/). As a consequence, the graphic unit that corresponds to the phoneme is not the letter but the grapheme. A grapheme may be simple (a one-letter grapheme, without diacritic markers) or complex (a letter with a diacritic marker or a digraph composed of more than one letter).

The vocalic system of English, French, German and Spanish

Most of the differences between the phonological and the graphemic structure of the English, French, German and Spanish languages are related to their vocalic system that may include monothongs and diphthongs, nasal vowels and a neutral vowel (Delattre, 1965; see also for English, Taylor & Serniclaes, 1998 and for German, Taylor & Serniclaes, 1999).

Length differences, which are similar to differences between open and closed vowels, allow the 14 main monothongs to be grouped into pairs (/i/I/, /y/Y/, /u/U/, /e/ɛ/, /ø/œ/, /o/ɔ/, /a/ɑ/). German has all seven pairs of monothongs. In English, there is no /y/Y/, but there are /i/I/, /ʊ/u/, /e/, /ʌ/ɜ/, /ɒ/ɔ/ and /æ/ɑ/. In French, there is only one /i/, one /y/, one /u/, and the problem of whether the other series (/e/ø/o/a/ vs /ɛ/œ/ɔ/ɑ/) represent 4 or 8 phonemes is unsolved. In Spanish, there are only five monothongs (/i/, /u/, /e/, /o/ and /a/). There are also 3-4 nasal vowels in French, nasality being not a distinctive feature in the three other languages. A neutral vowel /ə/, that is a sort of home base to which the tongue returns frequently in the course of speech, is found in German and French, but to a smaller extent than in English where almost all vowels can become a schwa in an unstressed syllable.

In Spanish, the five letters of the alphabet *i*, *u*, *e*, *o* and *a*, represent the five monothongs. In German, the umlaut differentiates /y/Y/ from /u/U/, /o/ɔ/ from /ø/œ/, and /a/ from /ɛ/, i.e. *ü* versus *u*, *o* versus *ö* and *a* versus *ä*, but there are also alternative spellings, i.e. *eu* for /ø/ (*adieu* /adjø/), *e* for /ɛ/ (*Antenne* /anɛtən/) and *y* for /y/ (*physic* /fysi:k/). Vocalic lengthening is mainly achieved by doubling the vowel (B*oo*t, *Aa*l), by adding a silent *h* after the vowel (B*oh*ne) or by adding the vowel *e*, after *i* (*Biene*). In addition, the presence of a double consonant indicates that the preceding vowel is short (*offen*). This system, which has few exceptions, is simpler for reading than for spelling because long vowels can be spelled in more than one way.

One of the main characteristics of the spelling of French vowels is the high number of digraphs (*ou* for /u/ as opposed to *u* for /y/, *eu* for /ø/œ/, and *a*, *i*, *o*, *u* + *n* or *m* for nasal vowels), but diacritic markers can also be used (for example, *é* and *è* for /e/ɛ/). Some of the digraphs have no simpler orthographic equivalents (*ou*, and the four nasal vowels), others have simpler allographs (*au*, *eau*, also spelled *o*), and alternative spellings are also found (i.e. *an* /ã/ also spelled *am*, *en* or *em*...; *in* /ɛ̃/ also spelled *im*, *en*, *ein*, *ain*...). But with the main exceptions of *e*, which can be /e/, /ɛ̃/, /ə/, or even /a/, and of *en*, which can be / ã / or /ɛ̃/, French graphemes representing vowels mainly refer to the same phonemes (Catach, 1986; Véronis, 1986). Therefore, in French, grapheme-phoneme correspondences for vowels are highly predictable, whereas phoneme-grapheme correspondences are not so easy to manipulate because it is often necessary to choose between alternative spellings for a particular vocalic phoneme (see also Peereman & Content, 1998).

It is not possible to explain the spelling of English monothongs without taking into account the following consonants, the number of syllables of the word and the word stress (Deschamps, 1994). First, for short vowels in monosyllabic words, grapheme-phoneme correspondences exhibit few exceptions. The grapheme *i* mainly corresponds to the phoneme /i/ as in *pit*, the grapheme *e* to /e/ as in *bed*, the grapheme *a* to /æ/ as in *bag*, the grapheme *o* to /ɒ/ as in *pot*; however, the grapheme *u* either corresponds to /ʊ/ as in *put* (/pʊt/) or to / ʌ / as in *but* (/bʌt/). Nevertheless, in order to read short vowels correctly, it is necessary to know also that they cannot be found at the end of a word, and that they are always followed by a non-silent consonant. The presence of a postvocalic *r* modifies the preceding vowel (*e*, *i*, *u*, *ea*, *o* become /ɜ:/ in *firm*, *hurt*, *pearl* or *world*). Second, the spelling of long vowels is very complicated. For example, eleven graphemes may correspond to the phoneme /i:/ (i.e. *e*, *i*, *ee*, *ea*, *ae*, *ei*, *ie*, *ey*, *ay*, *eo* and *oe* as in *theme*, *machine*, *see*, *sea*, *caesarean*, *conceive*, *niece*, *key*, *quay*, *people* and *subpoena*). Finally, English is clearly distinguished from the three other languages by the presence of the schwa /ə/. This neutral vowel is found in German and French, but is almost always written *e*. In English the majority of unstressed vowels turn out to be a schwa. According to Delattre (1965), over 50% of the vowels in connected speech can be neutralized in English. Therefore, when reading English words, you can be right half of the time if you use a schwa instead of the specific vocalic graphemes! Yet, to spell the same words correctly, it is necessary to memorize the specific vocalic grapheme, which corresponds to the neutral vowel.

Diphthongs are not found in French, but English, German and Spanish share three main diphthongs, /ai/, /au/ and /oi/; /ei/ is specific to Spanish (Delattre, 1965). To spell German and Spanish diphthongs, the letters that correspond to their sub-phonemes are used: *ai*, *au*, *oi* and *ei*. The Spanish spelling of these diphthongs has few exceptions, except for *i* that can be spelled *y* at the end of a word (*bailar*/*fray*, *boina*/*doy*, *beige*/*ley*). In German, alternative spellings can be found for /ai/ (spelled *ai* in *Laib* but *ei* in *Ameise*) and /oi/ (spelled *äu* or *eu* as in *äu*geln and h*eu*te). The spelling of English diphthongs is highly unpredictable. They can be represented by a single letter grapheme or by a digraph. For example, *i*, *y*, *ir*, *igh(t)* but also *uy* and *aiX* correspond to /ai/ in f*i*ne, tr*y*, f*i*re, l*igh*t, b*uy* and *ai*sle. In addition, all English vowels are more or less diphthonguised, i.e. articulated in a constant movement. Thus, the quality of the starting vowel progressively changes from the beginning to the end. This phenomenon is not easy to represent graphically. According to Delattre's analysis (1965), the closest transcription of the English *do*, *know* and *bee* turns out to be [dddəUUUuuuuw], [nnnɔɔɔɔoow] and [bbbIIiiij]. As compared to Spanish, German and French, in English, grapheme-phoneme as well as phoneme-grapheme correspondences for vowels are thus clearly more difficult to master.

The consonantal system of English, French, German and Spanish

Twenty letters of the alphabet can be used to spell the consonants. This number is similar to the number of consonantal phonemes in English (22 + 2 semi-consonants), French (17 + 3 semi-consonants), German (21 + 1 semi-consonant) and Spanish (17 + 2 semi-consonants). To explain the consonantal system of these four languages, we can divide the consonants into 3 main categories, stop, fricative and resonant (Delattre, 1965).

For stop consonants, the four languages share six oral non-affricates (/p/b/, /t/ d/, /k/g/) and three nasals (/m/n/ plus the palatal /ɲ/ in French and Spanish or the palato-velar /ŋ/ in English and German). Affricate stops can be found in English (/tʃ/dʒ/), in German (/pf/ts/) and in Spanish (/tʃ/). These four languages only share two fricatives /f/ and /s/. The fricatives /v/z/ and /ʃ/ʒ/ are present in English, French and German, but not in Spanish. Other fricatives are only found in one or two languages, two dentals in English and Spanish (/θ/ð/), one palatal in German (/ç/), one pharyngeal in German and Spanish (/χ/), one glottal in English and German (/h/), and the three Spanish fricatives (/β/ð/γ/) that correspond to the voiced stops /b/d/g/ (b/d/g/ occur word-initially, while /β/ð/γ/ occur intervocalically). The resonant *L* and *R* are found in the four languages, but they are not pronounced in the same manner. In addition, in Spanish, two *R*s can be found, one short with one flap and one long with multiple flaps, plus two *L*s, a latero-dental /l/ and a latero-palatal /λ/. The system has to be completed by three semi-consonants, /j/ which can be found in the four languages, /w/ which is not present in German, and the French /ɥ/ (Delattre, 1965).

The Table in the Appendix summarizes the spellings of the consonants and semi-consonants in the four target languages. Some of the consonantal phonemes are represented mainly by the same grapheme whereas for others alternative spellings can be found. Some of the grapheme-phoneme ambiguities are observed in all four languages; for example, the graphemes *g*, *c*, *s* and *t* usually correspond to different phonemes. Other ambiguities are present only in one language; for example, in German, a change between the voice-voiceless consonants /b/p/, /d/t/, /g/k/, /v/f/, /z/s/ at the end of the words (or of the morphemes) is observed. In addition, the letter *x* is not used to represent the pharyngeal /χ/ in Spanish and German, where *x* is almost always pronounced [ks]. In French and in English, *x* keeps the Spanish and the German pronunciation [ks] in *sexy*, but is also read [gz] in *exact*, [z] in *xenophobia* (in English) and *deuxième* (in French), and [s] in *soixante* in French.

Another reading problem, specific to French and English, is that some written consonants are silent. In English, at the beginning of a word, *kn* become /n/ as in *know*; *ps* becomes /s/ as in *psychology*; *wr* become /r/ as in *write*. The grapheme *gh* is silent before *t* as in *fight*, and at the end of a word as in *high* (except after *ou*), *t* and *k* disappear between *f* or *s* and *n* or *l* as in *soften*, *castle* and *muscle*. In addition, *L* and *R* are not clearly articulated in postvocalic position as in *help*, this phenomenon being stronger for *R* which only lengthens the preceding monothong as in *barn*, *bird*, *board*, etc. When the preceding vowel is a diphthong, a weak *R* appears as in *bare* or *bear* /beəʳ/ (Delattre, 1965). In French, the silent consonants are mainly at the end of the words but are often pronounced with the following word when it begins by a vowel. For example, *petit lit* is pronounced /pətili/ while *petit ami* is pronounced /pətitami/, not /pətit/ami/ nor /pətiami/. In general, the problem of the French final silent consonant is due to the fact that the morphological markers for the plural, as well as most of the verbal flexions, either are not pronounced or modify the pronunciation of "*e*" when they follow this grapheme (i.e., *leS pouleS mangeNT*/le pulə mãʒə /; *mangeR* /mãʒe/).

Another difficulty of the spelling of English and French consonants is related to the fact that they can be geminated without clear phonological properties, except in two cases. First, in French and in English *ss* always corresponds to /s/, never to /z/. Second, in French, the presence of a double consonant modifies the pronunciation of the vowel *e* which corresponds to /e/ɛ/ as in *nette* and not to /ə/ as in *petit*. Therefore, gemination mostly penalizes word spelling.

Compared to Spanish, grapheme-phoneme and phoneme-grapheme correspondences for consonants in English, and to a lesser extent in French and in German, appear to be less consistent. English grapheme-phoneme correspondences for vowels are nevertheless deeper than those for consonants and clearly deeper than the Spanish, the German and the French systems for vowels. This is shown indirectly in the appendix in which there seems to be less correspondence between pronunciation and spelling in English than in Spanish, German and French.

Other differences between English, French, German and Spanish

In English, German and Spanish, words have some degree of phonetic independence as each full word has its own stress. In English, however, the place of word stress is highly variable (Delattre, 1965), thus penalizing the reading of vowels that have to become a schwa in an unstressed position. The variability of stress location is smaller in German (Delattre, 1965). Spanish shows a definite tendency for fixed stress position on the penultimate syllable, except for bi-syllabic words (Delattre, 1965). In French, children cannot make stress errors in word reading as there is mainly a word-group stress. In addition, there is a preponderance of open syllables in French and in Spanish, whereas in English and in German, the majority of syllables have a closed structure (Delattre, 1965). Therefore in French and in Spanish – not in English and in German – the rime unit mostly corresponds to a vowel. As a consequence, a model of reading that attaches importance to the role of the rime units in the beginning of reading acquisition (see Goswami and Bryant, 1990) may be more suitable for English and German than for French and Spanish.

From linguistic description to statistical analyses

These descriptive data are partially congruent with the statistical analyses of Ziegler, Jacobs and Stone (1996; see also Ziegler, 1999 and Ziegler, Stone & Jacob, 1997). The authors have compared the degree of bi-directional consistency of orthography-to-phonology in monosyllabic words in English, French and German, not in Spanish. Inconsistency was defined at the orthographic and phonological rime levels. In regard to orthography-to-phonology (O-P) rime consistency, a word was considered inconsistent when its orthographic rime can be read in more than one way. In regard to phonology-to-orthography (P-O) rime consistency, a word was considered inconsistent when its phonological rime can be written in more than one way. The degree of O-P inconsistency is higher in English (12.9%) than in German and French (5.8 and 4.9%). The degree of rime inconsistency is higher for P-O than for O-P in all three languages, and much higher for P-O in French (50.3%) than in English (28%) or in German (25.9%). The differences between English and the two other languages are less than those expected according to our linguistic description based on grapheme-phoneme and phoneme-grapheme correspondences (GPC and PGC, see also Table in the Appendix) and to the fact that the 40 English phonemes can be spelled by 1120 graphemes (Coulmas, 1996) whereas the 35 French phonemes can be spelled by 130 graphemes (Catach, 1986), the 40 German phonemes by 85 graphemes (Valtin, 1989) and the 29-32 Spanish phonemes by 45 graphemes. The differences between observed rime level and expected phoneme level based results may be due to a strong decrease in inconsistencies when taking into account rimes in monosyllabic words, particularly for English vowels.

De facto, at the grapheme-phoneme level, the vowel consistency ratio for GPC appears very low in English and very high in French (48% vs. 94%, Peereman & Content, 1998) whereas for PGC it is similar in both languages (67% in English and 68% in French). However, only monosyllabic words were included in the

Ziegler et al.'s and Peereman et al.'s databases and, at least in French, monosyllabic words represent only a small percentage (6.70%, that is 2396 of the 36,000 words in the Micro Robert, 1986, according to Content, Mousty & Radeau, 1990); this restriction could bias the results.

From linguistic description to psycholinguistic processing

In the history of civilizations, as well as in the acquisition of language, written language takes a second place to spoken language. Human brains are first mapped out by spoken language processing. This can explain why phonological processing may be the core of reading acquisition. To corroborate this hypothesis via research on reading acquisition in Spanish, German, French and English, the most impressive argument is that even in English and in French, the efficiency of early reliance on phonological processing predicts later reading achievement. Nevertheless, due to the opacity of English orthography, reading acquisition may be more difficult in English than in the three other languages, especially Spanish and German. Moreover, the units of phonological processing may be based on the linguistic peculiarities of each specific language; for example, we can expect more errors with vowels than with consonants in English. We will try to answer these questions by examining the current literature on reading and spelling acquisition in English, French, German and Spanish.

Before we begin, we would like to recall that one of the problems of "phonocentrism" based on grapheme-phoneme correspondences is that phonemes are not easily perceptible in the spoken language because of coarticulation. For example, the spoken word *car* is pronounced in a single articulatory gesture. In alphabetic written systems each grapheme that corresponds to a phoneme is represented separately (c + a + r). Therefore, the child has to understand that the spoken word /kar/ is composed of three units in order to be able to match the graphemic form of this word with its phonemic equivalent. Phonemic awareness is thus linked to reading abilities. This important question is out of the scope of the present chapter (see Defior, this volume).

PHONOLOGICAL PROCESSING IN READING/SPELLING IN SPANISH, GERMAN, FRENCH AND ENGLISH

Reliance on phonological processing is assessed here by four main indicators; first by performance on pseudowords that cannot be processed via the orthographic route; second by the regularity effect, which is the difference between the processing of regular and strongly inconsistent grapheme-phoneme correspondences (e.g. *tAble* in French or English compared to *fEmme* in French or to *hAve* in English); third the production of regularizations with words involving inconsistent grapheme-phoneme correspondences (e.g., the word *Nation* read /nati-on/ in German, /nati-õ/ in French and /neiti-on/ in English or the word *abogado* read with the phonemes /b/, /g/, /d/ in Spanish (see Appendix); fourth by a strong correlation between pseudoword and word processing. Reliance on the orthographic route is shown by the fact that frequently seen items are better processed, i.e. high frequency words better than low frequency words and real words better than pseudowords.

Spanish, German, and French children

The regularity effect is difficult to use in Spanish because correspondences between graphemes and phonemes are rarely inconsistent (see above). Therefore, in order to assess if children rely on the phonological route, researchers generally take into account either pseudoword performance or the difference between the processing of a pseudoword and a real word. In spite of certain discrepancies in the studies, it seems that even very young Spanish children rely on efficient phonological skills. For example, 5 year-olds were able to read and spell more than 90% of bi-syllabic pseudowords including or not inconsistent graphemes such as *c* and *g* (Cuetos, 1989). Very high scores on pseudoword reading were also found in poor and good readers of the second grade (Valle-Arroyo, 1989). The pseudowords scores reported in other studies of Spanish children were slightly lower (Defior, Justicia & Martos, 1996; Sebastian-Gallès & Parreño-Vacchiano, 1995). However, Cuetos used only short pseudowords whereas Defior et al. relied on short and long pseudowords and Sebastian-Gallès & Parreño-Vacchiano on long pseudowords with inconsistent graphemes such as *c* and *g*. These differences in test items may explain Cuetos' higher scores. Concerning reliance on orthographic skills, when performance on pseudowords was compared to that of words, a lexicality effect emerged, even in young Spanish readers (Defior et al., 1996; Valle-Arroyo, 1989). Inconsistent findings emerged for the frequency effect. No effect was observed in the Valle-Arroyo study, whatever the grade level (2nd, 4th or 6th), whereas, surprisingly, Defior et al. found such an effect for the younger children (1st to 3rd Grade), but not for the older children (4th to 6th Grade). The difference in results for the frequency effect may be accounted for by pseudowords and words being presented on the same list in the Valle-Arroyo study, but not in the Defior et al. study. When subjects have to read words mixed with pseudowords, phonological processing is strengthened, and thus the frequency effect could disappear.

Beginning German readers – like Spanish children – seem to be able to make an early and efficient use of phonological processing (Wimmer and Hummer, 1990). After 8 months of reading instruction, 7.5 year-old first graders were asked to read and spell pseudowords and words, mostly one or two-syllable items with consistent grapheme-phoneme correspondences. The test items were presented on the same list, except for a spelling test. High scores were reported for pseudoword and word reading (68% and 87%), and for pseudoword spelling (70%), the lowest scores being observed in a word spelling task (59%). In another study, 8;5 to 10;5 year-old German dyslexics and non-disabled readers were asked to read words and pseudowords presented on different lists (Wimmer, 1993). Even the younger impaired readers reached a high level in the reading tasks and the performance of the non-disabled readers was very accurate. These results show that even first graders rely on well developed phonological processing. The fact that a lexicality effect emerged in the Wimmer and Hummer (1990) study also indicates that first graders are able to use their orthographical knowledge. However, high correlations were observed between pseudoword and word reading or spelling in the Wimmer and Hummer (1990) study as well as between pseudowords and high frequency words in the Wimmer (1993) study. This suggests that German children mostly rely on phonological processing to process words, even high-frequency words.

In a French longitudinal study, 6;6 to 7 year olds were asked twice (in the middle and at the end of the first grade) to read and spell high or medium frequency regular and inconsistent words, and pseudowords matched in orthographical difficulties to the regular words (Sprenger-Charolles, Siegel and Bonnet, 1998b). The inconsistent words contained either a low frequency grapheme or a silent grapheme in a non-terminal position (for example, femme [fam], woman; sept [sɛt], seven). Two levels of grapheme-phoneme consistency had been defined for the regular words and the pseudowords. At the first level, the items included only simple graphemes, each corresponding to one phoneme; the second-level items included context-independent digraphs. Only two digraphs have been used (*ou* /u/ and *ch* /ʃ/) because they have no simpler equivalents; therefore, the children were not expected to encounter more difficulties in spelling than in reading which would have been the case if we had used a frequent digraph such as *au* which has a simple and more frequent allograph "o".

Words and pseudowords were separately presented. In the middle of the first grade, high frequency words were not processed any better than medium frequency words and regular words not any better than pseudowords, neither in reading nor in spelling. At the end of the first grade, a frequency effect emerged in reading and in spelling and a lexicality effect was found, but only in reading (correct responses were 88% vs 80%, for regular word vs pseudoword reading; 78% vs 76%, for regular word vs pseudoword spelling). However, children processed regular words better than inconsistent words, whatever the test session (40% vs 7% in the first reading session and 87% vs 38% in the second; for spelling, 37% vs 5% and 73% vs 13%). The difference between regular and inconsistent words even increased between sessions as did the mean percentage of regularization errors. As in the Wimmer and Hummer study (1990), strong correlations between regular words and pseudowords were observed both in reading and in spelling. These results indicate that French children mostly rely on phonological processing in the beginning of reading and spelling acquisition and that the weight of this processing even increases with time. They also indicate that the orthographic lexicon is progressively set-up in reading and – though to a lesser extent – in spelling.

In comparisons of pseudoword reading and spelling with items of approximately the same degree of orthographical difficulty in Spanish (Cuetos, 1989), German (Wimmer and Hummer, 1990), and in French (Sprenger-Charolles et al., 1998b), 5 year-old Spanish children appear to reach a higher level than 7 year-old French children and than slightly older German children. The fact that a similar level of accuracy was observed for French and German children may not be due only to the use of highly regular grapheme-phoneme correspondences in the Sprenger-Charolles et al. (1998b) study, as suggested by another French study (see the results of regular words including digraphs either with allographs or with several possible pronunciations depending on the orthographic context, study 1, in Sprenger-Charolles & Casalis, 1995). The reading scores observed at the end of the first grade in that study were similar to those of the Sprenger-Charolles et al. study (1998b). Nevertheless, in the Sprenger-Charolles and Casalis study, the presence of digraphs strongly penalized word spelling.

Graphemic complexity mostly affecting word spelling in French was reported in the Leybaert and Content study (1995). The results of Alegria and Mousty (1994) also showed that French second graders (7;7) perfectly spelled context-independent graphemes – including bigraphs – whereas their scores for context-dependent graphemes were low. In addition, for inconsistent graphemes such as *s*, *ss* or *c* (for /s/) strong differences emerged between the dominant spelling (*s*) and the non-dominant spellings (*c* or *ss*), even when the non-dominant spelling was the most common grapheme in a specific context (e.g., *ss* in intervocalic position). It was only by grade 5 that the correct spelling of the different French contextual graphemes appeared to be mastered. These results were replicated in another study (Alegria and Mousty, 1996) that also indicated that word frequency had no impact on the performance of the younger children (beginning of 2nd grade). Thus, French children appear to begin to spell using a simplified set of phoneme-grapheme correspondences with no lexical involvement.

The weight of phonological processing in Spanish, German and even in French, may be a result of the use of phonic methods. The aim of the Leybaert and Content study (1995) was to assess this hypothesis. They looked at the development of reading and spelling skills in children instructed either by a phonic method (PH), or by a whole-word method (WW). The phonological skills of the WW second graders were weaker than those of PH group. Nevertheless, the former compared to the latter showed no indication of a greater reliance on word specific knowledge. Paradoxically, some elements even suggested that word specific knowledge could be less developed in the WW group. For example, WW second graders obtained lower scores than their PH age mates for the reading and spelling of irregular words. According to the authors, these results suggest that the acquisition of phonological skills constitutes a necessary step in the construction of the orthographic lexicon.

The role of phonological processing in the development of reading and spelling will be examined later. Before, we will give an overview of what happens with English children, who, compared to Spanish-, German- and, even, to French children learn to read in a language with a deeper orthography.

English versus French, German and Spanish children

The acquisition of phonological processing in English seems to be slow and difficult. Mean accuracy for pseudoword reading at the end of grade 1 typically ranges from 20% to 60% (Jorm, Share, MacLean & Matthew, 1984; Juel, Griffith & Gough, 1986; Siegel & Ryan, 1988; Vandervelden & Siegel, 1995). For example, Siegel and Ryan (1988) found that normal readers reached an almost perfect level in pseudoword reading only by the age of 9 years. It appears difficult to compare these results to those obtained with Spanish, German and French children because of the strong specificity of the English orthography. Consequently, we only examine comparative studies in which items were matched across languages to take into account comparable difficulties in spelling and pronunciation relationships.

In a cross-linguistic study, Bruck, Genesee and Caravolas (1997) followed English and French children (5;9 to 7 year-olds). Phonological awareness was assessed in the middle of kindergarten and word versus pseudoword reading at the end of grade 1. High frequency regular monosyllabic words sharing spelling patterns commonly taught to grade 1 children were selected. Pseudowords were constructed by changing the first letter of words. The French and English items were equated in number of letters and in grapheme-phoneme correspondences. Although the French children had fewer preliteracy opportunities and no reading instruction in kindergarten, at the end of grade 1 they obtained higher scores than their English peers on pseudoword and word reading (63 vs 36% and 76 vs 52%). In addition, the predictors of reading achievement were not the same in the two groups. The most significant predictor was onset-rime awareness for the English children and syllable segmentation for the French children. The phonological awareness results are congruent with the specificities of English and French languages (see here above) and the reading results may be explained by learning to read being easier in a more consistent orthography.

The reading skills of English and German children were assessed by Wimmer and Goswami (1994). Seven-, eight- and nine-year-olds were instructed to read number-words which are similar in the two languages (e.g. *three-drei*). Pseudo-words were derived from number-words by exchanging the consonantal onsets, including thus phonological units that were typical for each orthography. To make sure there were no differences in naming or articulatory speed, the children were asked to name the numerals corresponding to the number-words as quickly as possible. No differences between English and German children emerged for the numeral and the number-word conditions. However, the pseudoword reading scores of 7- and 8 year-old English children were lower than those of 7-year old German children (70% vs 90%). In addition, high correlations between pseudoword and word reading times were observed in the youngest German group, but not in the youngest English group. These results suggest that German children, but not English children, rely on the same phonological processing to read pseudowords and words, and that the phonological skills of the German children are more efficient than those of the English children.

These results were reproduced in the Frith, Wimmer and Landerl study (1998). In a first experiment with 7-, 8- and 9-year-olds, English and German words which were similar in spelling, pronunciation, meaning and familiarity were used (e.g. *Summer/Sommer*). Pseudowords were derived from the words by exchanging the onset (*Rummer/Rommer*). English children performed less well on words (80 vs 95%). Although in scoring the reading of the English pseudowords the criteria were lenient, the difference was much greater for pseudowords (59 vs 88%), especially for the younger children (7-year-olds, 45 vs 85%). In a second experiment, the effects of frequency and lexicality were manipulated. For high frequency words, 8-year-old English and German children obtained similar results but English children lagged behind their German peers both with low frequency words and with pseudowords.

The same children were asked to read trisyllabic pseudowords with simple open syllables and without consonant clusters (e.g. *tarulo, surimo*). Accuracy and reaction times were computed. The scores of the 8-year-old English children still were lower than those of their German peers, for accuracy (70% vs 99%) and for time latencies (4.3 sec per stimulus [$SD = 2.1$] vs 1.9 [$SD = 0.9$]).

In a parallel study French children were required to read similar trisyllabic pseudowords (i.e. *tibulo, butiro*) presented in a list including more complex and phonologically similar bisyllabic pseudowords (i.e. *tribul, tirbul; blutir, bultir*); thus, the French task favored errors. In spite of this, the French 8-year-old average readers obtained high scores for the reading of the trisyllabic pseudo-words (84% for accuracy and 1.4 sec per stimulus [$SD = 0.3$] for time latencies (see Sprenger-Charolles & Siegel, 1997 and the results of the 8-year-old average readers in Sprenger-Charolles, Colé, Lacert & Serniclaes, 2000).[1] The Frith et al. and the Sprenger-Charolles studies did not handle time latencies in the same way. In the former study, children were instructed to press the mouse button as soon as they felt able to read the word aloud; reading latencies were measured from onset of stimulus presentation. The French measure was more direct; the responses were recorded by the integrated speech sampler of a computer; correct responses time latencies were computed via the analysis of the speech signal. However, this methodological difference cannot account for the large differences observed between French and English children for reaction times. In this very simple reading task, English 8-year-olds clearly showed a lesser mastery of phonological processing than their German and French counterparts.

In another comparative study, 7-, 8 and 9-year-old English, Spanish and French children were required to read monosyllabic and bisyllabic words and pseudowords which were orthographically and phonologically analog or non-analog (*cake* or *ticket* vs *dake* or *bicket* vs *foaj, verrpil*, Goswami, Gombert &

---

[2] These results were published together with those of another list of pseudowords in Sprenger-Charolles et al. (2000).

Barrera, 1998). The principal aim of this study was to assess the degree of reliance on analogical processing in reading in the three languages. For each age level, the three groups were matched as closely as possible for reading age and for their knowledge of the real words from which the pseudowords were derived. Spanish children relied on efficient phonological processing based on grapheme-phoneme correspondences as suggested by their high scores for pseudoword reading (89%), the incidence of the stimuli length on their performance and the non-significant effect of analogy. An accuracy difference between the French and the English children (72% vs 52%) suggested the phonological skills of the former to be more efficient than those of the latter. In both groups, an effect of analogy was found, indicating that these children relied on reading units larger than grapheme-phoneme correspondences. However, for French children at least, the effect of analogy may be explained by confusing factors, such as the presence of very rare French bigraphs in the non-analog items (i.e., *nm, nl, ts, ae* or *oa* in the median position, see Content & Radeau, 1988). It is worth noting that in other studies no clear evidence that beginning readers relied on an analogical mechanism based on rime was found (see for reading and spelling in French, Sprenger-Charolles et al., 1998b; for reading in English, Bruck & Treiman, 1992; Frith et al., 1998).

Another issue is that in English in word and in pseudoword reading and spelling, errors involve vowels more often than consonants (Bryson & Werker, 1989; Fischer, Liberman & Shankweiler, 1977; Fowler, Liberman & Shankweiler, 1977; Fowler, Shankweiler & Liberman, 1979; Frith et al., 1998; Siegel & Faux, 1989). This difference was not found in German (Frith et al., 1998; Wimmer, 1993) or in French (Sprenger-Charolles & Siegel, 1997). These results are congruent with the predictions following from the linguistic description (see above).

To summarize, studies with young Spanish, German, and French children indicated strong and early reliance on phonological processing, both in reading and in spelling. Indicators of reliance on orthographic processing were also found in reading. Nevertheless, beginning readers and spellers mostly relied on phonological processing as suggested by the very high correlations observed between pseudoword and word processing. These studies also clearly showed dramatic differences in reading and spelling levels to the detriment of English children compared to Spanish, to German and to French children. These results might have been due to differences in orthographic consistency, but also to differences in instructional approach, the two factors being interrelated. Consistent orthography lends itself to systematic teaching by a phonic method, whereas inconsistent orthography demands more complex methods. However, French children taught by a phonic method reach a higher level of phonological and, surprisingly, of orthographic skills, than children taught by a whole-word method (Leybaert and Content, 1995) and a systematic phonic approach also seems to help English children (see for a review Snowling, 1996).

Nevertheless, the strongest influence seems to be that of the language to which the children are exposed. Learning to read in a consistent orthography leads to the use of phonological processing whereas learning to read in an inconsistent orthography leads to a lesser reliance on this processing, and, perhaps, to the use of non-phonological compensatory strategies. As noticed by Frith et al. (1998), English children, compared to German children, showed a significantly stronger tendency to make errors in which the target item (word or pseudoword) was replaced by another word and to be more sensitive to word frequency. These results suggest that English children might use top-down lexical representations to supplement error-prone bottom-up processes.

DEVELOPMENTAL TRAJECTORY

In the studies reviewed so far, Spanish, German and French – but not English children – were observed to rely strongly on phonological processing from the early stages of reading and spelling acquisition. This raises the question of the role of phonological processing in the developmental trajectory. Some researchers postulate that the orthographic lexicon is set-up gradually through the phonological route (see Ehri, 1998; Perfetti, 1992; Share, 1995). To corroborate this hypothesis, the most impressive argument is that even in English and French, the efficiency of early reliance on phonological processing predicts later reading achievement.

Substantial correlations have been found between pseudoword reading and exception word reading in English (e.g., Baron, 1979; Freebody & Byrne, 1988; Gough & Walsh, 1991; Stanovich & West, 1989). In addition, in the early stage of reading acquisition in English, phonological errors such as regularization were common for good readers and rare for poor readers (Siegel & Kerr, 1996). Longitudinal studies also suggested that good "decoders" learn to read more quickly than children with poor phonological skills. For example, in a longitudinal study, Jorm, Share, MacLean and Matthews (1984) followed two groups of kindergartners, "good decoders" and "non-decoders". The results indicated that the early good decoders improved in reading more than the "non-decoders". At the end of the second grade, they were nine months ahead in a word reading test. Another example is provided by the Byrne, Freebody and Gates (1992) study. The authors examined the evolution of two groups of second grade poor readers, one with adequate phonological skills and below average word specific knowledge (the "phoenicians"), and the other with average sight word recognition ability but poor phonological skills (the "chinese"). The results showed that the scores obtained by Phoenician readers improved between sessions – even for irregular words – while a deterioration in word reading skills was observed for the "Chinese" readers.

Similar tendencies were observed with French children. For example, second graders with a low level of phonological reading skills were also found to have a poor level of orthographic skills whereas children with efficient phonological skills had well developed orthographic skills (Leybaert & Content, 1995). In two short-term longitudinal studies of French children, early reliance on the phonological procedure was also found to be predictive of later efficiency of the orthographic procedure. In the first study (Sprenger-Charolles et al., 1998b) early phonological skills evaluated in the middle of the first grade by pseudoword processing were found to be predictive of performance on irregular words at the end of the same grade, whereas the reverse was not observed, in reading or in spelling. The other study (Sprenger-Charolles et al., 1998a) compared children with high and low levels of expertise in orthographic skills, as assessed by an orthographic choice task at the end of second grade. The second grade "experts" were the children who, in first grade, had been found to rely more strongly on phonological processing in reading aloud, in spelling and in silent reading. The acquisition of phonological skills seems thus to constitute a necessary step in the construction of the orthographic lexicon.

TENTATIVE EXPLANATION

Phonological processing thus seems to be the core of reading acquisition. This might be explained by the fact that reliance on phonological processing permits pseudowords as well as known and unknown regular words to be read. Through the use of phonological processing, and through the comparison of words phonologically decoded and those that are part of their oral vocabulary, children can learn to associate graphemes with phonemes and/or other types of orthographic units with phonological units (onset-rime, syllable).

It is important to note that even highly inconsistent words contain some regular grapheme-phoneme correspondences and that some inconsistencies are only a question of grapheme frequency. For example, the use of grapheme-phoneme correspondences in English leads to the pronunciation of the high frequency word *have* as /heiv/. Knowing that /heiv/ does not exist, but that the word /hæv/ does, children can infer that "a" must be read as /æ/ and not /ei/ in this word. Children may learn most of the relationships between orthography and phonology through this procedure. Because of grapheme-phoneme and of word frequencies, strong associations between orthographic and phonological units enable children to gradually construct their orthographic lexicon which permits the use of the direct route. Nevertheless, even when the direct route is functional, children may still have recourse to phonological processing and this processing becomes more and more efficient as a result of the consolidation of the associations between sublexical orthographic and phonological units.

In this framework, the level of grapheme-phoneme consistency is the major factor that determines the ease or difficulty of learning to read (see also the connectionist model of Plaut, McClelland, Seidenberg, & Patterson, 1996). Because of the consistency of grapheme-phoneme correspondences, this learning scheme works better in shallow orthographies than in deeper ones, i.e. in Spanish, German and French compared to English, or in Spanish compared to French.

Orthographic consistency could even have a long-lasting influence as suggested by the study of Paulesu, Demonet, Fazio, McCrory, Chanoine, Brunswick, Cappa, Cossu, Habib, Frith and Frith (2001) in which Italian, French and English adult average and dyslexic readers were compared.

In addition, the associations between graphemic and phonological units could depend on the specificities of each language. For example, the studies we reviewed suggested that the process of building associations for vowels in English is difficult. Therefore, in English, vowels may be associated with consonants only in a second phonological cycle (see Berent & Perfetti, 1995) whereas in German and French, consonants and vowels might blend together on-line. In English, vowels could also be processed with the following consonants because their pronunciation is often more consistent when taking into account the word rime, i.e. the vowel + the consonantal coda (see Goswami and Bryant, 1990).

In this framework, the fact that spelling scores are lower than reading scores may be due to the asymmetry between grapheme-phoneme and phoneme-grapheme correspondences. Whereas, for example, in German and in French, grapheme-phoneme correspondences are quite predictable, phoneme-grapheme correspondences are not so easy to manipulate because it is often necessary to choose between alternative spellings for a particular phoneme (see Table in the Appendix). In addition, knowledge of a spoken word may facilitate the reading of this word, but not the choice of its correct spelling. For example, in French, knowledge of the oral form /tablo/ does not facilitate the spelling of this word because the phoneme /o/ may be spelled *o* as in *numéro*, *au* as in *noyau* or *eau* as in *chateau*. This might explain why children begin to spell using a simplified set of phoneme-grapheme correspondences with no lexical involvement (Alegria & Mousty, 1994, 1996).

However, to be able to map graphemes with phonemes correctly, or phonemes with graphemes, children have to rely on well-specified phonological representations. If the child's phonological representations are not well specified, then the connections between graphemes and phonemes will be difficult to establish. This will be the case for dyslexic children who, according to current literature, have been shown to have deficient phonological representations (see Adlard & Hazan, 1998; Godfrey, Syrdal-Lasky, Millay & Knox, 1981; Manis, McBride-Chang, Seidenberg, Keating, Doi, Munson & Petersen, 1997; Mody, Studdert-Kennedy & Brady, 1997; Serniclaes, Sprenger-Charolles, Carré & Demonet, 2001; Werker & Tees, 1987). As a consequence, not only their phonological reading skills, but also their orthographic skills, will probably be impaired.

REFERENCES

Adlard, A., & Hazan,V. (1998). Speech perception in children with specific reading difficulties (Dyslexia). *The Quarterly Journal of Experimental Psychology, 51A*, 153-177.
Alegria, J., & Mousty, P. (1994). On the development of lexical and non-lexical procedures of French-

speaking normal and disabled children. In G.D.A. Brown, & N.C. Ellis (eds.). *Handbook of spelling: Theory, process and intervention* (pp. 213-226). New York, Wiley and Sons.

Alegria, J., & Mousty, P. (1996). The development of spelling procedures in French-speaking, normal and reading disabled children: Effects of frequency and of lexicality. *Journal of Experimental Child Psychology, 63*, 312-338.

Baron J. (1979). Orthographic and word-specific mechanisms in children's reading of words. *Child Development, 50*, 60-72.

Berent, I., & Perfetti, C.A. (1995). A Rose is a REEZ: The two cycles model of phonology assembly in reading English. *Psychological Review, 102*, 146-184.

Bruck, M., Genesee, F., & Caravolas, M. (1997). A cross linguistic study of early literacy acquisition. In B. Blachman (Ed.), *Foundations of reading acquisition and dyslexia: Implications for early intervention* (pp. 145-162). Mahwah (NJ), Lawrence Erlbaum.

Bruck, M., & Treiman, R. (1992). Learning to pronounce words: The limitation of analogies. *Reading Research Quarterly, 27*, 375-388.

Bryson, S.E., & Werker, J.F. (1989). Toward understanding the problem in severely disabled readers. Part I: Vowel errors. *Applied Psycholinguistics, 10*, 1-12.

Byrne, B., Freebody , P., & Gates, A. (1992). Longitudinal data on the relations of word-reading strategies to comprehension, reading time and phonemic awareness. *Reading Research Quarterly, 27*, 141-151.

Catach, N. (1978). *L'orthographe*. Paris: Presses Universitaires de France.

Catach, N. (1980). L'orthographe français: Traité théorique et pratique. Paris: Nathan.

Content, A., & Radeau, M. (1988). Données statistiques sur la structure orthographique du Français. *Cahiers de Psychologie Cognitive/European Bulletin of Cognitive Psychology.Special issue*, 1-87.

Content, A., Mousty, Ph., & Radeau, M. (1990). Brulex: une base de données lexicales informatisée pour le Français écrit et parlé. *Année Psychologique, 90*, 551-66.

Coulmas, F. (1996). *The Blackwell Encyclopedia of Writing Systems*. Oxford, UK : Blackwell.

Cuetos, F. (1989). Lectura y escritura de palabras a traves de la ruta phonologica. *Infancia y Aprendizaje, 45*, 71-84.

Defior, S., Justicia, F., & Martos, F. (1996). The influence of lexical and sublexical variables in normal and poor Spanish readers. *Reading and Writing: An Interdisciplinary Journal, 8*, 487-497.

Delattre, P. (1966). Studies in French and comparative phonetics. The Hague: Mouton.

Deschamps, A. (1994). De l'écrit à l'oral et de l'oral à l'écrit: Phonétique et orthographe de l'anglais. Paris: Ophrys.

Ehri, L.C. (1998). Grapheme-Phoneme knowledge is essential for learning to read words in English. In J.L.Metsala & L.Ehri (Eds.), *Word recognition in beginning literacy* (pp. 3-40). Mahwah (NJ): Erlbaum.

Fischer, F.W., Liberman, I.Y., & Shankweiler, D. (1977). Reading reversals and developmental dyslexia: A further study. *Cortex, 14*, 496-510.

Fowler, C.A., Liberman, I.Y., & Shankweiler, D.(1977). On interpreting the error pattern of beginning readers. *Language and Speech, 20*, 162-173.

Fowler, C.A., Shankweiler, D., & Liberman, I.Y. (1979). Apprehending spelling patterns for vowels: A longitudinal study. *Language and Speech, 22*, 243-252.

Freebody, P., & Byrne, B. (1988). Word-reading strategies in elementary school children: Relations to comprehension, reading time, and phonemic awareness. *Reading Research Quarterly, 23*, 441-453.

Frith, U., Wimmer, H., & Landerl, K. (1998). Differences in phonological recoding in German- and Spanish-speaking children. *Scientific Study of Reading, 2*, 31-54.

Godfrey, J.J., Syrdal-Lasky, A.K., Millay K.K., & Knox, C.M. (1981). Performance of dyslexic children on speech perception tests. *Journal of Experimental Child Psychology, 32*, 401-424.

Goswami, U. C. & Bryant, P. (1990). *Phonological skills and learning to read*. Hove (East Sussex): Lawrence Erlbaum Associates LTD.

Goswami, U., Gombert, J.E., & Fraca de Barrera, L. (1998). Children's orthographic representations and linguistic transparency: nonsense word reading in English, French and Spanish. *Applied Psycholinguistics, 19*, 19-52.

Gough, P. B., & Walsh, M.A. (1991). Chinese, Phoenicians, and the orthographic cipher of English. In S.A. Brady & D. P. Shankweiler (eds.). *Phonological processes in literacy: A tribute to Isabelle Y. Liberman* (pp. 199-209). Hillsdale (NJ): Erlbaum.

Jorm, A.F., Share, D.L., MacLean, R., & Matthews, R.G. (1984). Phonological recoding skill and learning to read: A longitudinal study. *Applied Psycholinguistics, 5*, 201-207.

Juel, C., Griffith, P. L., & Gough, P. B. (1986). Acquisition of literacy: A longitudinal study of children in first and second grade. *Journal of Educational Psychology, 78*, 243-255.

Leybaert, J., & Content, A. (1995). Reading and spelling acquisition in two different teaching methods: A test of the independence hypothesis. *Reading and Writing: An Interdisciplinary Journal, 7*, 65-88.

Manis, F.R., McBride-Chang, C., Seidenberg, M.S., Keating, P., Doi, L.M., Munson, B., & Petersen, A. (1997). Are speech perception deficits associated with developmental dyslexia ? *Journal of Child Experimental Psychology, 66*, 211-235.

Mody, M., Studdert-Kennedy, M., & Brady, S. (1997). Speech perception deficits in poor readers: Auditory processing or phonological coding? *Journal of Experimental Child Psychology, 64*, 199-231.

Paulesu, E., Demonet, J.-F., Fazio, F., McCrory, E., Chanoine, V., Brunswick, N., Cappa, S.F., Cossu, G., Habib, M., Frith, C.D., & Frith, U. (2001). Dyslexia, Cultural diversity and *Biological unity. Science, 291*, 2165-2167.

Peereman, R., & Content, A. (1998). Quantitative analysis of orthography to phonology mapping in English and French (on-line). ttp://homepages.vub.ac.be/~acontent/OPMapping.html.

Perfetti, C. (1992). The representation problem in reading acquisition. In P. Gough, L. Ehri & R. Treiman (Eds). *Reading Acquisition* (pp. 107-143). Hillsdale (NJ): Erlbaum.

Plaut, D. C., McClelland, J. L., Seidenberg, M. S., & Patterson, K. E. (1996). Understanding normal and impaired word reading: Computational principles in quasi-regular domain. *Psychological Review, 103*, 56-115.

Robert, P. (1986). Micro-Robert. Dictionnaire du français primordial, nouvelle édition revue et mise à jour. Paris: Dictionnaires le Robert.

Sebastian-Gallés, N., & Parraño-Vacchiano, A. (1995). The development of analogical reading in Spanish. *Reading and Writing: An Interdisciplinary Journal, 7*, 23-38.

Share, D.L. (1995). Phonological recoding and self-teaching: Sine qua non of reading acquisition. *Cognition, 55*, 151-218.

Siegel, L.S., & Faux, D. (1989). Acquisition of certain grapheme-phoneme correspondences in normally achieving disabled readers. *Reading and Writing: An Interdisciplinary Journal, 1*, 37-52.

Siegel, L.S., & Kerr, A. (1996). *An analysis of the reading errors of good and poor beginning readers.* Society for the Scientific Study of Reading. New-York, April 1996.

Siegel, L. S., & Ryan, E. B. (1988). Development of grammatical sensitivity, phonological, and short–term memory in normally achieving and learning disabled children. *Developmental Psychology, 24*, 28–37.

Serniclaes, W., Sprenger-Charolles, L., Carré, R., & Démonet, J.F. (2001). Perceptual categorization of speech sounds in dyslexics. *Journal of Speech and Hearing Research, 44*, 384-399.

Snowling, M. (1996). Contempory approaches to the teaching of reading. *Journal of Child Psychology and Psychiatry, 37*, 139-148.

Sprenger-Charolles, L., & Casalis, S. (1995). Reading and spelling acquisition in French first graders: Longitudinal evidence. *Reading and Writing: An Interdisciplinary Journal, 7*, 1-25.

Sprenger-Charolles, L., & Siegel, L.S. (1997). A longitudinal study of the effects of syllabic structure on the development of reading and spelling skills in French. *Applied Psycholinguistics, 18*, 485-505.

Sprenger-Charolles, L., Siegel, L.S., & Béchennec, D. (1998a). Phonological Mediation and Orthographic Factors in Silent Reading in French. *Scientific Study of Reading, 2*, 3-2.

Sprenger-Charolles, L., Siegel, L.S., & Bonnet, P. (1998b). Reading and spelling acquisition in French: The role of phonological mediation and orthographic factors. *Journal of Experimental Child Psychology, 68*, 134-165.

Sprenger-Charolles, L., Colé, P., Lacert, P., & Serniclaes, W. (2000). On Subtypes of Developmental Dyslexia: Evidence from Processing Time and Accuracy Scores. *Canadian Journal of Experimental Psychology (Special Issue on Early Literacy and Early Numeracy), 54*, 87-103.

Stanovich, K. E., & West, R. F. (1989). Exposure to print and orthographic processing. *Reading Research Quarterly, 24*, 402-433.

Taylor, J., & Serniclaes, W. (1998). Phonetics and Phonology. In René Dirven & Marjolijn Verspoor, (eds.). *Cognitive Exploration of Language and Linguistics* (pp. 107-135). London: Benjamins.

Taylor, J., & Serniclaes, W. (1999). Sprachliche Laute: Phonetik und Phonologie. In Ralf Pörings & U. Schmitz (Eds.), *Sprache und Sprachwissenshaft. Eine kognitiv orientierte Einführung* (pp. 107-134). Tübigen: Gunter Narr.

Valle Arroyo, F. (1989). Reading errors in Spanish. In P.G. Aaron & R.M. Joshi (eds.). *Reading and writing disorders in different orthographic systems* (pp. 163-175). Dordrecht: Kluwer Academic Press.

Valtin, R. (1989). Dyslexia in the German language. In P.G. Aaron & R. Malatesha Joshi (Eds.), *Reading and writing disorders in different orthographic systems* (pp. 119-135). Dordrecht: Kluwer Academic Press.

Veronis, J. (1986). Etude quantitative sur le système graphique et phono-graphique du français. *European Bulletin of Cognitive Psychology, 6*, 501-553.

Werker, J.F., & Tees, R.C. (1987). Speech perception in severely disabled and average reading children. *Canadian Journal of Psychology, 41*, 48-61.

Wimmer, H. (1993). Characteristics of developmental dyslexia in a regular writing system. *Applied Psycholinguistics, 14*, 1-33.

Wimmer, H., & Goswami, U. (1994). The influence of orthographic consistency on reading development: Word recognition in English and German children. *Cognition, 51*, 91-103.

Wimmer, H. & Hummer, P. (1990). How German speaking first graders read and spell: Doubts on the importance of the logographic stage. *Applied Psycholinguistics, 11*, 349-368.

Ziegler, J. (1999). La perception des mots, une voie à double sens? *Annales de la fondation Fyssen, 13*, 81-88.

Ziegler, J., Jacobs, A., & Stone, G. (1996). Statistical analysis of the bidirectional inconsistency of spelling and sound in French. *Behavior, Method, Research, Instruments and Computer, 28*, 504-515.

Ziegler, J., Stone, G., & Jacobs, A. (1997). What's the pronunciation for –OUGH and the spelling for / u/ ? Database for computing feedforward and feedback inconsistency in English. *Behavior, Method, Research, Instruments and Computer, 29*, 600-618.

SUGGESTIONS FOR FURTHER READING

Coulmas, F. (2003). *Writing systems. An introduction to their linguistic analysis.* Cambridge: Cambridge University Press (Cambridge textbooks in linguistics)

This new textbook provides an accessible introduction to the major writing systems of the world.

APPENDIX: PHONEME-GRAPHEME CORRESPONDENCES IN SPANISH, GERMAN, FRENCH AND ENGLISH

		STOP		
	Spanish	**German**	**French**	**English**
/p/	P posta /'posta/	P-PP-B^{inc} Poste /pɔst/ Pappe /'papə/ ab /ap/	P-PP poste /pɔst/ approche /aprɔʃ/	P-PP post /pəʊst/ approach /ə'prəʊtʃ/
/b/	B^{inc}-V^{inc} baca /'baka/ vaca /'baka/	B^{inc}-BB bei /bai/ Ebbe /'ɛ:bə/	B-BB table /tablə/ abbé /abe/	B-BB table /'teɪbl/ ebb /eb/
/t/	T tentar /ten'tar/	T^{inc}-TT-D^{inc}-TH alt /alt/ Bett /bɛt/ Hand /hant/ Theater /te'ɑ:tər/	T^{inc}-TT-TH halte /altə/ cette /cɛt/ théâtre /teɑtrə/	T^{inc}-TT halt /hɒlt/ sitting /'sɪtɪŋ/
/d/	D^{inc} dado /'daðo/	D^{inc}-DD adoptieren /adop'ti:rən/ addieren /a'di:rən/	D-DD-DH^e adopter /adɔpte/ addition /adisjɔ̃/ adhérer /adere/	D-DD adopt /ə'dɒpt/ addition /ə'dɪʃən/ adhere /əd'hɪə ^{r}/
/k/	C^{nc}-K-QU clima /'klima/ kilo /'kilo/ que /ke/	C^{inc}-K-KK-CK CH^e-G^{inc} Klima /'kli:ma/ Akkord /a'kort/ Clou /klu/ Rock /rɔk/ Quatsch /kvatʃ/ Chronik /'kro:nik/ Tag /tɑ:k/	C^{inc}-CC-Q(U) K-CK-CH^e climat /klima/ accord /akɔr/ kilo /kilo/ ticket /tikɛ/ quand /kɑ̃/, coq /kɔk/ quadruple /kwadryplə/ chronique /krɔnik/	C^{inc}-CC-K-CK QU^{inc}-Q-CH climate /'klaɪmət/ accord /ə'kɔ:d/ kilo /'ki:ləʊ/ ticket /'tɪkɪt/ quay /ki:/ quick /kwɪk/ school /sku:l/
/g/	G^{inc}-G(U)^{inc} garaje /ga'raχe/ guerra /'gerra/ guardia /'gwarðja/	G^{inc}-GG Garage /ga'rɑ:ʒə/ Aggression /agrɛ-/	G^{inc}-GG-G(U)^{inc}-C^e garage /garaʒ/ aggraver /agrave/ guerre /gɛr/ aiguille /egɥij/ second /səgɔ̃/	G^{inc}-GG-G(U)^{inc}-GH^{inc} garage /gæ'rɑ:ʒ/ /-rɪdʒ/ aggravate /'ægrəveɪt/ guard /gɑ:d/ language /'læŋgwɪdʒ/ ghost /gəʊst/
/m/	M flamear /flame'ar/	M-MM Blume /'blu:mə/ Flamme /'flamə/	M^{inc}-MM ami /ami/ flamme /flam/ (Nasal vowels: bombe /bɔ̃b/)	M-MM flame /fleɪm/ flammable /'flæməblə/
/n/	N naciòn /na'θjon/	N-NN Nation /natsi'o:n/ dann /dan/	N^{inc}-NN nation /nasjɔ̃/ bonne /bɔn/ (Nasal vowels: bon /bɔ̃/)	N-NN nation /'neɪʃən/ granny /'grænɪ/
/ɲ/	ñ niño /'niɲo/		GN gagner /gaɲe/	
/ŋ/	NG parking /parkiŋ/	NG-N(K) Angst /aŋst/ Onkel /'oŋkəl/	NG parking /parkiŋ/	NG-N(K) parking /'pɑ:kɪŋ/ think /θɪŋk/

/pf/	**PF** Pferd /pfe:rt/			
/ts/	**Z^{inc}-C^{inc}-TZ-T^{inc}** zentral /tsɛn'trɑ:l/ circa /'tsirka/ Putz /puts/ Nation /natsi'o:n/			
/tʃ/	**CH** chàchara /'tʃatʃara/			**CH^{inc}-TCH** such /sʌtʃ/; scotch /skɒtʃ/
/dʒ/				**J-G^{inc}-DJ-DG** job /dʒɒb/ agenda /ə'dʒendə/ adjust /ə'dʒʌst/ bridge /brɪdʒ/

FRICATIVE

	Spanish	**German**	**French**	**English**
/ß/^{cp}	**B^{inc}-V^{inc}** baba /'baßa/ uva /'ußa/			
/f/	**F** foto /'foto/	**F-FF-V^{inc}-PH** Feld /fɛlt/ Giraffe /gi'rafə/ Photo /'fo:to/ Vater /'fɑ:tər/	**F-FF-PH** fable /fabl(ə)/ affirme /afirm(ə)/ photo /foto/	**F-FF-GH^{inc}-PH** fable /'feɪbl/ affirm /ə'fɜ:m/ photo /'fəutəu/ laugh /lɑ:f/
/v/		**W-V^{inc}** Vase /'vɑ:zə/ Wagen /'vɑ:gən/	**V-W** vase /vɑz(ə)/ wagon /vagɔ̃/	**V-W^{inc}** vase /vɑ:z/ or /veɪz/ wagon /'væɡən/
/θ/	**Z-C^{inc}** nariz /na'riθ/ cerca /'θerka/			**TH^{inc}** theater /'θɪətə^r/
/ð/^{cp}	**D^{inc}-DH^e** dado /'daðo/; adherir /aðe'rir/			**TH^{inc}** this /ðɪs/
/s/	**S** salchicha /sal'tʃitʃa/	**S^{inc}-SS-ß** als /als/ Kissen /'kisən/ Soße/'zo:sə/	**S^{inc}-C^{inc}/Ç-SS** **T^{inc}-X^e-SC** saucisse /sosis/ tasse /tas/ centre /sɑ̃trə/ ça /sa/ nation /nasjɔ̃/ six /sis/ science /sjɑ̃s/	**S^{inc}-C^{inc}-SS-SC** sausage /'sɒsɪdʒ/ assess /ə'ses/ cease /si:s/ science /saɪəns/
/z/		**S^{inc}-(T)Z** Rose /'ro:zə/ setzen /'zɛtsən/	**S^{inc}-Z-X^{inc}** rose /roz/ zéro /zero/ deuxième /døzjɛm/	**S^{inc}-Z** rose /rəuz/ zero /'zɪərəu/
/ʃ/		**SCH-S^{inc}-CH^{inc}** Charge /'ʃarʒə/ Tasche /'taʃə/ Straße /'ʃtrɑ:sə/	**CH-SCH** charge /ʃarʒə/ schema /ʃema/	**SH-CH^{inc}-SCH-T^{inc}** machine /mə'ʃi:n/ schedule /'ʃedju:l/ share /ʃeə^r/ nation /'neɪʃən/
/ʒ/		**G^{inc}-J^{inc}** Garage /ga'rɑ:ʒə/ Journalis- /ʒurnal---/	**G^{inc}-J** garage /garaʒ/ jeudi /ʒødi/	**G^{inc}-S^{inc}** garage /gæ'rɑ:ʒ/ /-rɪdʒ/ measure /'meʒə^r/

| /ç/ | | CH^{inc} G^{inc}
trächtig /'trɛçtiç/ | | |

| /ɣ/^{cp} | G^{inc}
abogado /aßo'ɣaðo/ | | | |

| /χ/ | J-G^{inc}
jarabe /χa'raße/
gente /'χente/ | CH^{inc}
Nacht /naχt/ | | |

| /h/ | | H
Höhe /'hø:ə/ | | H
hair /heə^r/ |

RESONANT

	Spanish	German	French	English
/r/	R^{in} curioso /ku'rjoso/	R-RR kurios /kuri'o:s/ irregulär /iregu'lɛ:r/	R-RR curieux /kyrjø/ irrégulier /iregylje/	R^{inc}-RR curious /'kjʊərɪəs/ irregular /ɪ'regjʊlə^r/
/rr/	RR-R^{inc} perro /'perro/ raro /'rraro/			
/l/	L color /ko'lor/	L-LL Kolorit /kɔlɔ'ri:t/ mille /'milə/	L-LL^{inc} couleur /kulœr/ ville /vil/	L-LL color /'kʌlə^r/ billow /'bɪləʊ/
/ʎ/	LL millón /mi'ʎon/			

SEMI-CONSONANT

	Spanish	German	French	English
/j/	I^{inc}-Y viaje /'bjaχe/ ya /ja/	J^{inc}-L^e Billard /'biljart/ ja /ja:/	I^{inc}-(I)LL^{inc}-Y^{inc} ciel /sjɛl/ paye /pɛj/ fille /fij/	Y^{inc}-I^{inc} ... million /'mɪljən/ yes /jes/ new /nju:/
/ɥ/			U^{inc} (+I) tuile /tɥil/	
/w/	U^{inc} sueño /'sweɲo/		OI-OU loi /lwa/ oui /wi/	W^{inc} walk /wɔ:k/

inc: inconsistent graphemes (more than one pronunciation)
e: examples of exceptional grapheme-phoneme correspondences
cp: contextual phoneme (/ß/,/ɣ/,/ð/ in Spanish)

A4. Connectionist Models of Children's Reading

GORDON D. A. BROWN & NICK CHATER

ABSTRACT

This chapter focuses on connectionist models of reading development, and outlines several different ways in which connectionist modelling both has been, and could be, used to advance the theoretical understanding of reading development.

Several different developmental possibilities are distinguished in the context of a discussion of connectionist models. In connectionist terms literacy development could in principle be constrained by various distinct factors, including at least (a) the small or unrepresentative nature of the fragment of the spelling-to-sound mapping system early learners are exposed to; (b) the length of time a learning mechanism requires to develop a good model of the statistical structure of the language; (c) the slow development of the representations that allow the relevant generalisations to be learned, and (d) more general limitations in the representational capacity of the learning system throughout development. Computational modelling allows a clear and explicit distinction between, and exploration of, each of these factors.

In reality, of course, it is likely that limitations on literacy development are a composite of these and other factors, and that the factors interact with one another to define a rather complex developmental trajectory. But this is precisely the point at which connectionist modelling may make a useful contribution, because the examination of artificial learning systems may allow us to tease apart the contributions of the different elements in a way that will never be possible by empirical investigation alone.

INTRODUCTION

This chapter focuses on connectionist models of reading development, and outlines several different ways in which connectionist modelling both has been, and could be, used to advance the theoretical understanding of reading development.

At the heart of connectionist models and their application to psychological theorising is the *learning* ability of such models, i.e., their ability to learn associations between patterns (such as the written forms of words and their pronunciations) after exposure to those associations. Connectionist models thus

T. Nunes, P. Bryant (eds.), Handbook of Children's Literacy, 67–89.

provide a possible approach to modelling reading development according to which developmental progression can be viewed simply in terms of increasing amounts of learning. We argue that such an approach is inadequate. In order to study the time-course of development in more detail, or to understand individual differences in reading learning, it is necessary to examine a range of additional possible constraints on the developmental process. A theme of the present chapter is the distinction between *single-factor* and *multi-factor* connectionist models of reading development. Various connectionist models focus on the effects of a single source of developmental constraint (such as the number of connections and units available to a model, or the quality of its phonological representations). We adopt a statistical approach to connectionism (see e.g. Chater, 1995; McClelland, 1998), according to which connectionist learning is a kind of statistical inference and the end-point of learning in a connectionist reading network is a probabilistic model of the mapping between spelling and sound and connectionist learning is a type of statistical inference. This statistical approach leads us to the idea that there are several different possible sources of developmental constraint in connectionist models, and to the suggestion that a complete connectionist model of reading development will need to incorporate the interactive effects of several different developmental limitations.

Connectionist models are at the forefront of theorising about the processes that underlie skilled adult reading, and much empirical effort continues to be directed at evaluating recent connectionist models of reading and their competitors (for recent examples, see Coltheart et al., 2001; Cortese, 1998; Perry & Ziegler, 2002; Rastle & Coltheart, 1999, 2000; Van Orden, Pennington, & Stone, 2001; Weekes, 1997; Zorzi, 2000). However until recently work on reading *development* has received somewhat less direct attention by connectionist modellers, despite a number of interpretations of reading development within a connectionist (e.g. Ans, Carbonnel, & Valdois, 1998; Berninger et al., 2000; Brown, 1997; Harm & Seidenberg, 1999; Hulme et al., 1991, 1995; Manis et al., 1996; Plaut, McClelland, Seidenberg, & Patterson, 1996; Seidenberg & McClelland, 1989; Thomas & Karmiloff-Smith, in press; Zorzi, Houghton, & Butterworth, 1998a) or more general (Van Orden, Pennington, & Stone, 1990) framework. As Thomas and Karmiloff-Smith note, specifically developmental approaches may be needed within connectionism, in contrast to the accounts of acquired language disorders that initially received more attention.

Despite this, we argue here that the understanding gained from connectionist models of reading is of considerable relevance to some of the most hotly debated current issues in the experimental reading development literature. For example, connectionist modelling has helped psychologists to gain a clearer understanding of the importance of phonological representations in early reading. We also identify ways in which connectionist models could in future research be used to inform debate on questions concerning the levels of spelling-to-sound analysis that should be taught to children (e.g. low-level correspondences between graphemes and phonemes vs. a focus on higher-level sublexical units such as onsets and rimes). Connectionist models could also be used to investigate the relative contributions, and interactive effects, of learners' individual differences and their instructional experience, and so allow derivation of testable hypotheses in a neglected area of empirical research.

In the first part of this chapter we describe the basic features of connectionist models of reading. We then briefly relate connectionist models to statistical approaches and the "rational analysis" approach to human cognition. In the final part of the chapter we discuss ways in which literacy developmental may be and has been approached using connectionist networks. Several different approaches are possible, although they are not usually distinguished clearly in the literature. We also provide specific examples of some ways in which connectionist models of reading have enhanced our understanding of normal reading development and of children's reading problems.

CONNECTIONISM: BASIC PRINCIPLES

Many excellent introductions to connectionism and its psychological applications are available (e.g. Bechtel & Abrahamsen, 1991; Elman et al., 1996; Levine, 1991; McLeod, Plunkett, & Rolls, 1998; Quinlan, 1991), and we do not attempt to provide a comprehensive overview here. However the basic features can be summarised briefly. This section can be omitted by readers familiar with basic knowledge of connectionist principles.

Connectionist accounts of behaviour are often seen as providing an alternative or a supplement to traditional cognitive-level accounts of psychological phenomena. Symbolic accounts focus on the use of *rules* and *strategies*. Reading provides a paradigmatic example of a case where rules (such as grapheme-phoneme correspondence rules) could be used to derive outputs for regular items (i.e. words with regular pronunciations, in the case of reading) while a separate list of "exceptions" is maintained for cases where the rules will not produce the right outcome. Connectionist models in contrast emphasise the *association* between input and output pairs, without making reference to explicit rules, and are able to learn quasi-regular mappings (such as that between spelling and sound) without recourse to separate lists of rules and exceptions. For example, Rumelhart and McClelland's (1986) model of the acquisition of the past-tense forms in English employed a simple pattern associator that learned associations between verb-stems and past-tense verbs without making reference to explicit rules. This early model was claimed to provide a demonstration of how rule-like behaviour could be generated through learning regularities of the environment, even though no explicit rules were incorporated into the system, and more recent work has developed and refined the claim (see Elman et al., 1996, for a review). Questions concerning the general adequacy of such models in accounting for the relevant phenomena, and questions concerning the proper interpretation of the models demonstrations, have been among the most widely-debated questions within cognitive science over the past decade (e.g. Chater & Oaksford, 1990; Fodor & Pylyshyn, 1988; Marcus, 1995; Pinker & Prince, 1988).

Thus much of the interest in connectionist models of reading and verb tense learning has been due to the claims that such models may provide a radical alternative to symbolic cognitive accounts of the same phenomena. We emphasise here, however, that the question of whether connectionist models have aided understanding of the relevant psychological processes such as reading development can be evaluated separately from these wider issues. Whatever one's views on the adequacy of connectionist models as accounts of cognition in general, it is beyond doubt that the attempts to build implemented models of reading have led to an enhanced understanding of the kinds of psychological mechanisms that must be involved. It is the latter claim that we illustrate here: connectionist model-building can shed light on psychological processing whether or not connectionist models can or will supplant or supplement alternative, symbolic, rule-based models.

What are the relevant features of connectionist models? Connectionist networks consist of many individual (subsymbolic) computing units which are heavily interconnected. These approximations to "brain-like" architectures have been shown in many models to give rise to many behavioural qualities that typify human cognition, including learning capacity, graceful degradation of performance under less than optimal conditions, use of a single mechanism to process regular and exceptional instances of a phenomenon, and flexible access to memory content (see, e.g., Rumelhart & McClelland, 1986; McLeod et al., 1998).

How do these connectionist systems work? We can illustrate with a very simple fictional model of reading – a model that can read only two or three words (this connectionist network is very much simpler than any that has been seriously proposed as a model of human reading, but can serve as an illustration for some basic points).

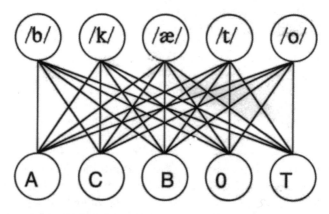

Figure 1. An unrealistic connectionist network for spelling-to-sound translation.

All the circles in the diagram, in both the top row and the bottom row, are units or nodes in the small network. These are often thought of as simplified artificial neurons. The circles in the bottom row represent units that can be activated by the letters in a printed word. Each unit has associated with it an "activation value", often between 0 and 1, or a binary value of 0 or 1 (the latter corresponding simply to "ON" or "OFF"). So if the printed word CAT was presented to the network, for example, the nodes standing for "C", " A ", and "T" would be "ON" and all the other letter units would be "OFF". We have indicated this by shading the relevant units on the diagram. Thus the bottom row of units, which would often be called the "input units", or the "input layer" can be used to represent several different words. Thus the word BAT would be represented by switching on just the first, third, and fifth units.

Each circle in the top layer (of "output units") represents a single phoneme node. Thus a pattern of activation of the output units can represent a possible pronunciation of a word (e.g. the nodes that would correspond to the pronunciation /kæt/).

Units in a connectionist networks are typically interconnected both within and between layers, with connections of variable strengths. The number of layers may vary, with spelling-to-sound correspondences explicitly represented at several levels (e.g. Brown, 1987; Norris, 1994) or with input and output layers directly connected (e.g. Zorzi, Houghton, & Butterworth, 1998b). These connections allow the activity value of one unit to influence, and be influenced by, the activity value of other units. In the figure we have only drawn connections between the input (orthographic) units and the output (phonological) units. Every input unit is connected to every output unit. In typical connectionist models of reading the input to a network is specified as a pattern of activity over the orthographic units (e.g. the pattern corresponding to the written word CAT). An output is then calculated on the basis of the input activation ad the connection strengths. In the simplified model in the Figure, we could assume that each output units that is connected by a solid line (connection strength of 1) to an input unit that is activated (ON) will itself become activated. When CAT is presented, therefore, the correct pronunciation /kæt/ will become represented as a pattern of activation over the output units. The network can then be said to have produced the correct pronunciation of the written word CAT.

Thus the toy model in the Figure illustrates how the written or spoken forms of words can be represented as patterns of activity over a connectionist model's units, and how a pattern of activity over one population of units can give rise to a pattern of activity over a different population of units depending on the connection strengths between different units. The model employs a simple form of *distributed representations* – note that each unit participates in the encoding of many different words, and each word is represented as a pattern of activity distributed over many different units. There is no one-to-one mapping between words and units. Some more realistic connectionist models of reading have much more distributed representations, in that there are no single units corresponding to letters and phonemes in the language, but instead letters and phonemes are themselves represented as a pattern of activity distributed over many units.

The model in the figure also illustrates many of the problems that have to be overcome in a plausible connectionist model of reading; one of the most important distinguishing characteristics of different models concerns their solutions to these problems. First, the model depicted would only work accurately for a language in which there is a simple and reliable correspondence between letters and phonemes. However many more realistic models are able to produce the correct pronunciations of irregular words (such as HAVE or PINT) mainly by virtue of two mechanisms that we did not include in our simple model. First of all, weights are graded, not all-or-none. Thus a given set of letter units, or combinations of letter units, may be strongly connected to the units that represent the most frequent pronunciation of that letter or set of letters, and less strongly connected to possible but less common pronunciations. Secondly, and importantly, many connectionist models of reading include a separate population of units, called *hidden units*. Hidden units are located between input units and output units; typically every input unit is connected to every hidden unit, and every hidden unit is connected to every output units, but input units and output units are not directly connected. The inclusion of hidden units allows a network to form internal representations of clusters of inputs, and this can allow a network with hidden units to solve problems that can't be solved by a network without hidden units (see Bechtel & Abrahamsen, 1991; Quinlan, 1991, for an introduction).

A second immediately apparent limitation of the network in Figure 1 is that there is no *ordering mechanism*. It is straightforward to activate the units corresponding to the letters in a word (e.g. the B, A, and T in BAT), but this fails to specify the order of the letters and therefore would assign the same representation to TAB as to BAT. This is clearly unsatisfactory. Real connectionist models of reading have adopted a variety of more or less adequate solutions to this problem. To simplify the explanation, we describe the case of orthographic representations, although similar considerations apply to both the phonological and orthographic representations. One solution to the ordering problem involves dedicating a unit to the representation of every *ordered triple* of letters or phonemes contained in the word. For example, the orthographic form of a word such as HAVE contains the four triples _HA + HAV + AVE + VE_ (where "–" represents a word boundary). One input unit could be dedicated to each of the triples that would be necessary to represent all words in English. A variant of this general scheme was used in the connectionist model of reading developed by Seidenberg and McClelland (1989). The simple system involving a one-to-one correspondence between each unit and a specified triple is not feasible in a large-scale model, because too many units would be required (except for very small vocabularies). The actual implementation therefore uses distributed representations, in which each unit participates in the encoding of many different triples. Each triple is then represented as a pattern of activity over many different units. Triples of phonetic features, rather than triples of phonemes themselves, were used in the Seidenberg and McClelland (1989) model's phonological (output) representations.

Alternative schemes for representing the order of letters and phonemes in a word have been used in different models (e.g. Bullinaria, 1995, 1997; Plaut et al., 1996; Sejnowski & Rosenberg, 1987; Seidenberg & McClelland, 1989). We address these in more detail below, as one of the main conclusions from research has been that the precise nature of the representations that are employed is responsible for quite detailed aspects of the behaviour of a given model. Indeed, the development of plausible mechanisms for representing the order of letters and phonemes within words remains a central task for connectionism. However, as we show below, despite considerable ongoing research aimed at identifying limitations of current connectionist models of reading (see e.g. Coltheart et al., 1993; 2001; Cortese, 1998; Perry & Ziegler, 2002; Rastle & Coltheart, 1998, 2000) current connectionist models of skilled adult single word reading can account for a range of effects of such as word frequency, spelling-to-sound regularity, and their interactions (e.g. Seidenberg & McClelland, 1989; Plaut et al., 1996).

Learning in connectionist models

When considering the *development* of reading in a connectionist model, a question of central interest is whether and how a connectionist network can learn a set of connection strengths between its units such that the network is able to produce the correct pronunciation of all or most of the words it has been presented with. Indeed, the ability of networks to learn an appropriate set of connection strengths has been central to the interest in such models within psychology over the past 15 years. Learning in the models may be achieved by the gradual adjustment of connection strengths, in proportion to the discrepancy between an actual pattern of activity and the desired (target) pattern. Connection strengths are usually set to small random values initially, with the result that at first there is no systematic relation between the pattern of activation presented to the network's input units (i.e., the spelling of a word) and the resulting pattern of activation on the network's output units (i.e., the network's estimate of the pronunciation of that word). However a suitable learning algorithm can make gradual changes in the strengths of the links so that a given input gradually comes to activate the appropriate output. Returning to our simple example network, suppose for example that when the B letter input unit is switched on, there is a strong connection between it and the /k/ output phoneme unit, but only a weak link to the /b/ output phoneme unit. The learning algorithm will slightly reduce the strength of connection to the /k/ output unit, and slightly increase the strength of connection to the /b/ output unit. This has the consequence that the next time the B letter input unit is switched on, the output produced by the network in response to this unit will be a little more accurate.

The study of learning mechanisms within connectionist networks is a large research area in itself, and the learning algorithms are more complex when networks include hidden units (which are crucial to enable successful performance on many realistic tasks). Nevertheless successful learning is often possible (Rumelhart, Hinton, & Williams, 1986), with the result that the patterns of activity across one layer of the network (e.g. the input units) can become associated with specific patterns of activity across a different layer (e.g., the output units). The network gradually comes to represent the statistical properties of the associations between input and output patterns. This can give rise to rule-like behaviour, without explicit rules being built into the network. In all cases, the basic mechanism is one of gradual changes in the connection strengths between different units of the network, such that there are gradual improvements in the accuracy with which the desired, or "target", output pattern becomes represented over the network's output units in response to the presentation of a given pattern over the input units.

Because connectionist networks often learn the statistical regularities of a system (such as the orthographic-to-phonological mapping system) only gradually, they can be used to model the gradual emergence of the knowledge of such a system (see Elman et al., 1996, for a review of connectionism and developmental issues). This means that they have the potential to provide *developmental* accounts of performance in domains such as reading (Ans, Carbonnel, & Valdois, 1998; Berninger et al., 2000; Brown, 1997; Harm & Seidenberg, 1999; Hulme et al., 1991; Manis et al., 1996; Seidenberg & McClelland, 1989; Thomas & Karmiloff-Smith, in press; Van Orden, Pennington, & Stone, 1990; Zorzi, Houghton, & Butterworth, 1998a), with developmental progression being seen at least partly as the result of increasing amounts of learning. However the most successful applications of connectionist models to reading have been in accounting for empirical data that reflect skilled adult readers' sensitivity to the statistical structure of the language, such as word frequency effects, various measures of the regularity of the spelling-to-sound mapping system, and the interactions between frequency and regularity effects (Plaut et al., 1996).

CONNECTIONISM, READING AND STATISTICS

Before examining specific examples of the gains in understanding that have been achieved by studying connectionist models of reading development, it is helpful to take a step back and consider *why* connectionist models may be successful (to the extent that they are) in modelling skilled adult reading. One possible reason for the success of connectionist models of reading in mirroring the performance of skilled readers may be that both the connectionist models and human readers are both learning to converge on statistically optimal solutions to the problem of predicting phonology from orthography. To the extent that readers and connectionist networks are faced with the same learning problem, and to the extent that both skilled adult readers and fully-learned connectionist networks embody statistically optimal solutions to this learning problem, it should not surprise us that they behave in similar ways.

But is this a plausible account? It is now widely believed that much of human perceptual and cognitive behaviour can be understood as an optimal reflection of the statistical structure of the environment – that is, the decisions and solutions that are adopted by the human processing system are the best that can be achieved given the probabilistic structure of the input. The "rational analysis' of cognitive processes (Anderson, 1990; see also Shepard, 1987) seeks to explain cognitive performance by reference to the structure of the environmental problems that the cognitive system is adapted to perform. This approach seeks to answer the question of why the cognitive system performs as it does. The central idea is that, in the context of a specific task, human cognitive mechanisms are optimally adapted to the statistical nature of the environment in which they operate. Anderson applied this approach successfully to the analysis of human memory and categorisation (see e.g. Anderson & Milson, 1989; Anderson & Schooler, 1991) and rational analysis is now a significant theme in cognitive psychology (see e.g. Chater & Oaksford, 1999, and the many models in the Oaksford & Chater, 1998, collection).

Following this tradition, we have argued elsewhere that the behaviour of the adult human single-word reading system can be understood as behaviour that is optimal given the statistical structure of the mapping between orthography and phonology (Brown, 1995; Brown, 1998). We dubbed this the ROAR model (for Rational Optimal Adaptive Reading). The ROAR model assumes that single word reading can be viewed as a statistical process, requiring computations of the most probable pronunciation of a given orthographic string (given the known statistical properties of the spelling-to-sound mapping system). According to what we termed the Optimal Reading Hypothesis, skilled adults read with maximum efficiency, given the statistical structure of the mapping from orthography to phonology in English. If this is so, we would expect their reading speed for individual words to reflect the spelling-to-sound consistency of items in such a way as to respect the consistency ratio just described. Brown (1995) reviewed evidence consistent with this claim, and took this to be consistent with the suggestion that readers are behaving in a statistically optimal way given the structure of the English spelling-to-sound mapping system (see also Jared, McRae and Seidenberg, 1990; and, especially, Treiman, Mullennix, Bijeljac-Babic, & Richmond-Welty, 1995).

Thus skilled adult readers can be viewed as having internalised, and being adaptively responsive to, the statistical structure of the relevant problem domain (in this case, the mapping between orthography and phonology). Note that this approach is very different from formal modelling of the *mechanisms* hypothesised to underlie reading, for it assumes that it is possible to specify the optimal strategy of reading independently of the actual mechanism assumed to implement the processing. In the specific case of reading, for example, the aim is not to characterise the mechanisms that underpin reading by building an appropriate model, but to understand why it is that we read in the way that we do (as opposed to having evolved or acquired some other mechanism that works in a different way). In other words, the approach enables a shift from the question *what kind of mechanism underpins reading* to the rather deeper question *why do we have the reading mechanism that we do*? Almost all research in the psychology of reading and reading development has been aimed at answering the former question, but a complete understanding of reading development will require the latter question to be addressed.

Although the "rational analysis" approach can lead to implementation-independent characterisations of optimal behaviour, it may be that connectionist architectures provide particularly suitable mechanisms for modelling the internalisation of statistical models of the environment (the spelling-to-sound mapping system, in the case of reading). It has been shown that, under some circumstances, connectionist networks can be seen as learning machines that discover a statistically optimal solution to the associative mapping problems they are faced with (for reviews, see Chater, 1995; McClelland, 1998). According to this view, connectionist learning mechanisms lead to the development of a statistical model of the relevant aspect of the world. One possible explanation for the success of connectionist models of reading is, therefore, that both skilled adult readers, and connectionist networks, are attempting to perform optimally in the face of the statistical structure of the problem facing them. The implications of this kind of approach for reading *development* are less clear, however, and it is these that we explore here.

RATIONAL ANALYSIS, CONNECTIONISM, AND DEVELOPMENT

The rational analysis approach has received less attention from developmentalists, perhaps because the notions of development and learning are concerned with trajectories towards a (possibly optimal) end state, but such questions are quite separate from those concerned with the optimality or otherwise of different developmental trajectories towards that end point. The nature of the task facing children may be very different from that facing skilled adults, and so the type of behaviour that would qualify as "optimal" may, correspondingly, be very different. It is to this issue that we now turn.

As we have indicated, one way of looking at connectionist learning algorithms is as a kind of statistical modelling (see Chater, 1995) – as in a statistical technique like multiple non-linear regression, the network must, after it has learned, be able to apply different weightings to different inputs and input combinations in order to calculate the correct output from those inputs. A large literature has shown that connectionist networks can, under some circumstances, learn to make (locally) optimal statistical inferences (see McClelland, 1998, for a review and the suggestion that connectionist networks also provide a method for exploring deviations from optimality). This would be consistent with the idea that the performance of fully-learned connectionist models mirrors the performance of skilled human readers just to the extent that both have acquired good models of the statistical structure of spelling-sound correspondences. If this general account is correct, it can help us to understand why connectionist models may provide a good account of skilled adult reading. But is there equally good reason to believe that connectionism will provide equally good models of the process of *learning* to read? We can distinguish different ways in which connectionism may be relevant to the development of a task such as reading.

SOURCES OF DEVELOPMENTAL IMPROVEMENT

Considerations from the rational analysis approach suggest several different ways in which the performance of a system for learning to read might be developmentally limited, and suggest possible reasons for the different decoding strategies that may be used by children. An advantage of connectionist modelling of reading development, we will suggest, is that the respective contributions of the different possible sources of developmental limitations can potentially be disentangled.

We distinguish various possibilities below. To summarise: For the learning system to respond optimally to the problems facing it, several different conditions must be met. First, the sample of language (the reading vocabulary) to which the learning system is exposed must reflect the statistical characteristics of the full system (because the learner can't derive an optimal solution to a problem it is not exposed to). Second, the learner must be able to represent the input appropriately, or the input to the internal learning system will again not adequately reflect the structure of the problem domain. Third, the learner must have sufficient exposure to the problem to enable learning. Finally, there must be sufficient internal representational capacity for the problem solution to be stored. There is ample psychological evidence that all of these factors influence the speed and efficiency of literacy acquisition, but not all have received equal attention in the connectionist modelling literature. Furthermore, it seems likely that more than one of these factors is likely to impact upon development in a significant way. We suggest that the construction of explicit connectionist models provides an ideal opportunity for studying the interactive effects, and relative importance, of these various factors influencing reading. We now consider each of these possibilities in turn.

Impoverished input

Connectionist models can be used to examine the behaviour (e.g. the generalisation performance) of networks trained on a small fragment of the spelling-to-sound mapping system (e.g. Zorzi et al., 1998a). Two related questions arise. First, we can ask whether children's reading can be understood as optimal in the light of the fragment of language to which they have been exposed. Second, we can ask about the generalisation performance that could be achieved by a given learning system on the basis of the fragment they have experienced.

One theoretical possibility is that children are behaving optimally in the light of the learning experience they have had. Consider for example the case of a child who has been exposed to a reading vocabulary of just 200 words. The reading strategies adopted by the child might be highly optimal given the statistical structure of the spelling-to-sound correspondences in those 200 words. Of course, such an extreme view is untenable in the light of the difficulty that children have in the early stages of literacy acquisition. However, the suggestion is nonetheless useful to consider, because it raises the possibility that reading strategies that appear maladaptive from the perspective given by skilled adult reading may be much more suited to the smaller fragment of the language to which children have been exposed. Furthermore, such considerations could have important practical implications. For example, different units of spelling-to-sound correspondence might be optimal for children than for adults, simply because the children's reading vocabularies are much smaller. In particular, the rime-based units of spelling-to-sound correspondence that appear to offer the greatest amount of predictability in the mapping between spelling to sound when a large sample of vocabulary is analysed (Treiman et al., 1995) might not be the optimal units for children to use in the light of their different, and smaller, vocabularies. In a smaller vocabulary, there will be many different rimes, and relatively few words sharing any particular rime. Therefore rime-based representations might provide a much less productive basis for generalisation over a small vocabulary than over a larger vocabulary. If so, it would be risky to assume that, because the irregularity of the language as a whole is reduced when rime-level correspondences are used, rime-based spelling-to-sound correspondences are the best to use in the early instruction of children.

There is little direct evidence that optimal strategies differ as a function of reading vocabulary size, because little empirical attention has been given to the statistical characteristics of children's early reading vocabularies (although, as reviewed elsewhere in this volume, there is ample evidence that children' s reading strategy changes developmentally). However this is exactly the kind of issue that connectionist learning models, and statistical models more generally, can help address. If the solutions that connectionist networks find to the problem of developing a statistical mapping of the relationship between spelling and sound differ as a function of reading vocabulary size, this could point to reasons for the different reading strategies adopted by younger children. This would represent an important departure from the more traditional intuition that early readers have simply not yet developed the "best" reading strategies, towards a position according to which early readers have discovered the best solution to different problem from that facing skilled adult readers. Little work along these lines has yet been undertaken within a connectionist tradition.

An alternative issue concerns fragment-based generalisation performance. Relatively few studies have looked at the generalisation performance of networks trained on small vocabularies. However, as Share (1995) noted, the "self-teaching" of reading may be an important factor in literacy development, in contrast to "direct teaching" of the entire language. Zorzi et al. (1998a), using a two-layer network to examine acquisition of spelling-to-sound relations, found that exposure to a small number of words did permit their network to generalise to novel items. Stronger "lexical analogy" effects were shown by the network when the training vocabulary was small (86 words), reflecting the particular items in the training set, even though the model did not incorporate explicit lexical representations.

An obvious direction for future work would involve examination of the type of limited vocabulary that, when learned, promotes the best generalisation. In addition, future studies may examine whether different composition of vocabularies would lead to optimal generalisation when the learning system has impaired phonological representations (see below). Berninger et al. (2000) have already argued for a close connection between connectionist modelling and instructional practice. They suggest that models should be "instructionally explicit" as well as "computationally explicit", and use insights from connectionist models to structure feedback in actual instruction. Consistent with the expectations from connectionist models, they find that direct linkages between orthography and phonology promoted the best generalisation, while onset and rime-based training appeared less effective.

Distorted input

A related view to the "impoverished input" position above is that the reading vocabulary experienced by children is not only much smaller than that available to adult readers, but also systematically "distorted" in that the statistical properties of the spelling-sound mapping of the child' 's reading vocabulary are qualitatively different from the statistical properties of the complete language. In modelling skilled adult reading with a connectionist model, Plaut et al. (1996) found that representing the frequency distribution of words in the training set accurately was important if the right combination of observed nonword reading, frequency effects, and regularity effects were to be shown by the trained model. Thus the precise statistical structure of the input is important in determining the mature behaviour of the learning system.

This kind of consideration could provide a further reason why the optimal strategy for children might be different from the optimal strategy for skilled adult reasons. This would be consistent with the possibility that the use of different strategies by children than adults might reflect the different database available to children, rather than the inability of children to represent the regularities within the database they know about. A contrasting possibility is that an input that is appropriately and systematically distorted during the early stages of learning may make it easier for a network to learn a complex input-output mapping system if this enables the network to find an approximate solution quickly without being led into spurious and inescapable local minima due to a multitude of irregularities (Elman, 1993). Again, it would be nonsensical to suggest that the whole of children's reading strategies are determined solely by the structure of the input they have been exposed to, and that there are no other developmental constraints. Yet the suggestion that *some* of the different reading strategies exhibited by children are due to the statistical structure of the input they receive is much more plausible, as can be illustrated by example. It is well established in other domains (such as verb-tense learning) that the behaviour of a network can change when the composition of its input changes (e.g. Plunkett & Marchman, 1991, 1993; Rumelhart & McClelland, 1986). Another example concerns the need to co-represent regular and irregular items. In studying the acquisition of language systems, particularly the system responsible for the formation of past tense verb forms in English, Plunkett and Marchman (1991) have delineated some important constraints on the conditions under which exceptions and regularities/sub-regularities can become represented within the same system. Such considerations are critical in literacy acquisition. As just one example, it appears that very irregular items (such as HAVE; cf. CAVE, RAVE, SAVE etc.) can only become stably represented by the learning system if they are sufficiently high in frequency. If the (token) frequency of exceptional items is too low, then it is difficult or impossible for the correct output to become associated with them, for the tendency to regularise those items due to the high frequency of regular items becomes too strong. Therefore it appears to be no accident that in language systems such as the English spelling-to-sound system the irregular items tend to be high in token frequency. This appears to be a computational consequence of the need to represent exceptions and regularities in the same system. This has important pedagogical implications. It suggests, for example, that it might be a mistake to minimise use of irregular items in the early stages of learning to read, for the irregular items will be difficult or impossible to represent if they are too low in token frequency. There is a dearth of empirical evidence on this question, although our own initial studies have found little evidence that current reading materials or learning experiences are structured appropriately in this regard.

Insufficient learning

A very different view, and one implicitly (if perhaps inappropriately: Share, 1985) adopted by most current connectionist models of reading, is that limiting factors in the early stages of reading are best characterised in terms of an inadequate internalisation of the statistical structure of the spelling-to-sound system to be learned chiefly because of insufficient exposure (not enough trials of learning). On this position, then, children are exposed to the same "problem" as are skilled adult readers, but have not yet developed an optimal solution to the problem just because they have not had enough trials of learning.

Several connectionist models of adult reading implicitly take this position because they present the full to-be-learned vocabulary, in all its richness, to a model right from the very earliest stages of learning. There is no increase in the size of the reading vocabulary to which the model is exposed as learning in the model progress; development is simply seen as correlated with "amount of learning" rather than with any concomitant change in the nature of the mapping to be learned (although see the Zorzi et al., 1998a, study cited above for an exception).

Nevertheless, a number of connectionist models have found parallels between the changing performance of networks over training and the developmental stages seen in children's literacy development (see e.g. Plaut et al., 1996; Seidenberg & McClelland, 1989). For example, the initial Seidenberg and McClelland (1989) model observed greater effects of spelling-sound regularity early in development, as do children. Zorzi et al. (1998a), using their two-layer network described above, found that increasing amounts of training on a large vocabulary captured a number of developmental phenomena and extracted similar statistical regularities to those discovered by children. Although no training was given on isolated letter-sound mappings, good nonword generalisation was evident fairly early in training. Spelling and sound onsets and rimes became aligned, and the influence of the final consonants (in the monosyllabic words on which the network was trained) on vowel pronunciation increased with training, consistent with the idea that through experience children develop sensitivity to rime-level correspondences (e.g. Treiman et al., 1995).

Ans et al. (1998) examined reading development in a network that included both a "global" word-level procedure and a segment-level procedure. They found similarities between children's reading behaviour and the performance of the network early in training, with greater effects of spelling-sound regularity early in training and also behaviour consistent with a shift from alphabetic to more global orthographic processing. Both strategies could be used by the network at all stages, but the mixture changed with reading experience.

Bullinaria (1997) examined development in reading and other areas, with a particular focus on the "alignment problem" (essentially, the problem of knowing which substrings of letters correspond to which substrings of phonemes). He found that, with development, the networks learned to solve the alignment problem by effectively choosing their own training set and thereby solving the alignment problem. A network can learn to choose a good set of targets / alignments by choosing the alignment-target that first best with its existing knowledge.

Note that connectionism can potentially provides some insight into why it is that an extensive amount of learning may be advantageous or necessary, by making clear the conditions under which learning will lead to effective generalisation. Good generalisation and maintenance are produced when learning is gradual and incremental (the underlying system only changes by a small amount in response to each presented exemplar) and when *interleaved learning* is employed. This means that different examples are not presented all at once, in blocks, but rather are "interleaved" (so that, for example, irregular examples would be interspersed amongst regular exemplars). McClelland, McNaughton and O'Reilly (1995) provide an extensive discussion of the respective advantages and disadvantages of different types of learning in connectionist-like architectures, and suggest the need for separate "episodic" and "semantic" memory systems that involve different learning methods (fast, one-shot learning vs. slower, gradient-descent interleaved learning) and consequently have complementary pattern of strengths and weaknesses (see also French & Chater, 2002).

We emphasise, however, that simple developmental accounts of reading within a connectionist account are unlikely to capture the relevant patterns of psychological performance unless they go beyond the idea that early development can be captured in a model simply in terms of an insufficient number of trials of learning, to take account also of the different nature of the input to developing systems.

Inadequate representations

Another possible source of developmental constraint, and one that would be consistent with much psychological evidence, is that the reading learning system has an impaired ability to *represent* the relevant structure in the world (here, the orthographic and phonological structure of words), and that it is this provides the main source of developmental limitation. Thus even if the learning reader is faced with a statistically representative sample of the problem domain, and has ample exposure to the input-output pairings that must be learned, no method of learning will permit discovery of the best problem solution if the internal cognitive system cannot represent the input and output patterns in such a way as to permit the required generalisations to be represented. A long tradition of psychological research on reading development, much of which is reviewed in the present volume, has focused on the role of children's phonological representations in developing reading, and suggested that the lack of good phonemic representations may underpin the poor literacy performance of children. In computational terms, this is an example of the "inadequate representations" view, and a range of connectionist work that is consistent with the suggestion that representational inadequacy may indeed give rise to the specific pattern of difficulty seen in children with literacy problems, as we now illustrate briefly.

It is well established that there is a clear link between children's awareness of the sound structure of the language and the speed and ease with which they acquire literacy (e.g. Bradley & Bryant, 1983; Goswami & Bryant, 1990; Wagner & Torgesen, 1987; see also several chapters in the present volume). This led to the "phonological deficit" model of reading disability (e.g. Stanovich & Siegel,

1994), according to which a core deficit in phonological skills leads to developmental delay in reading. However the nature of the causal relationships between the specificity of phonological relationships and the reading learning process have not always been made explicit. Furthermore, purely verbal formulations of the phonological deficit account of reading disability led to predictions that have not been confirmed (Brown, 1997; Metsala, Stanovich, & Brown, 1998). Connectionist models have added to our understanding in both these cases.

Following the influential connectionist reading model of Seidenberg and McClelland (1989), subsequent research has demonstrated that the nature of the representations available to a connectionist model of reading is an important determinant of its performance. The Seidenberg and McClelland model was criticised for its inability to assign psychologically realistic pronunciations to many nonwords (Besner, Twilley, McCann & Seergobin, 1990). Further research revealed that this limitation arose partly because the model used triple-based representations of the type described above, in which triples of letters such as HAV or VE_ or phonetic features were used to represent the orthographic and phonological forms of words respectively. (In fact, the representations were distributed over input and output units in a rather more complex way than that described here; a full description can be found in Seidenberg & McClelland, 1989, but is not essential for present purposes.)

As Plaut et al. (1996) make clear, the adoption of representations such as this can lead to difficulty in acquiring relatively low-level spelling-to-sound correspondence, such as those between individual graphemes and phonemes, due to what they term the *dispersion problem*. This arises when the same letter-to-sound correspondence must be learned in several different contexts, as such dispersion effectively dilutes the amount of training received by the network on a given correspondence. In a triple-based representation, letters and phonemes are assigned a different representation according to where in a triple they occur. Thus the letter R at the beginning of a triple has, as far as the model is concerned, nothing in common with an R occurring at the end of a triple. The fact that these are the same letter is not represented, and so they will effectively be treated as different letters by the model. This impairs the ability of the model to learn generalisations between graphemes and phonemes. Improved nonword performance can be obtained if more fine-grained input and output representations are used. These allow the network more easily to capture generalisations at the level of graphemes and phonemes (e.g. Brown, 1997; Bullinaria, 1995; Harm, 1998; Harm & Seidenberg, 1999; Norris, 1994; Plaut et al., 1996). Therefore a model that is provided with explicit representations at many different levels will perform well (Norris, 1994; see also Phillips et al., 1993).

Furthermore, it has been argued that some paradoxical deficits associated with developmental dyslexia may be explained in terms of the specificity of the representations given to the model (Brown, 1997; Harm & Seidenberg, 1999; Manis et al., 1996; Metsala & Brown, 1998; Plaut et al., 1996). For example,

Brown (1997) directly compared the performance of a network with "good" phonological representations (similar to those used by Plaut et al., 1996) to the performance of a network with "impaired" phonological representations (similar to those used by Seidenberg & McClelland, 1989). For some comparisons the networks were given different amounts of training so that they were matched on word reading accuracy (analogous to the "reading age match" design used with children). The "impaired" network was worse at nonword reading but, more interestingly, showed normal-sized effects of spelling-sound regularity, consistent with the data (Metsala et al., 1998).

The influential Harm and Seidenberg (1999) model considers phonological dyslexia in terms of decay in or damage to the weights in a phonological attractor network, and was used to demonstrate that a network will learn more easily if it is provided with prestructured phonological output representations (see also Hulme, Snowling & Quinlan, 1991; Hulme et al., 1995). More specifically, Harm and Seidenberg demonstrated the importance of pretraining (or parallel training) of phonological representations. The trained phonological system allows encoding of dependencies across output phoneme slots in a more sophisticated way than was possible with earlier networks. The "clean up units" allow a precise output to be produced even if the output system is given less explicit input. When a network is pretrained on phonological word forms, or has the ability to learn the phonological information at the same time as learning to read, it learns to generalise better (as evidenced by nonword reading) than does a network that does not have the ability to represent phonological knowledge in the same way. One important conclusion is that the difference between impaired and unimpaired networks is primarily seen on nonword rather than word reading. Importantly for the understanding of normal and impaired reading development in children, simulations showed an interaction between instruction and phonological representation, such that explicit instruction is particularly important when phonological representations are impaired.

Other approaches have also been adopted. Ans et al. (1998) characterised developmental phonological dyslexia in terms of impaired acquisition of segment-level traces. Zorzi et al. (1998a) compared the behaviour of their two-layer network, in which orthographic and phonological representations made direct contact with each other, to the behaviour of a modified network in which orthography-phonology connections could only be made indirectly (via a layer of hidden units). When the network was trained on a small vocabulary of items, generalisation performance was much less good in the models with only indirect orthography-phonology connections, essentially because the model learned to adopt a lexical strategy. Thus factors other than the specificity of phonological representations are important for achieving good generalisation after training on a small vocabulary.

Impaired general internal representational capacity

The final view that we list here places the main source of developmental improvement in yet another place – increasing general representational capacity of networks with development (a "maturation" factor: see Elman et al., 1996). It could be that much of the developmental increase in ability that is seen in normal literacy development is not primarily due to the nature of the input that learners experience, to the way that input is represented, or to inadequate opportunity for learning, but instead due to the insufficient capacity of the developing system to represent the problem solutions. In connectionist networks this can be represented by a developmental increase in the number of units of connections available to represent mappings (e.g. Seidenberg & McClelland, 1989). Few reading development models have varied the capacity of networks dynamically during learning, but several have examined the effects of restricting computational resources throughout learning. For example, several different studies have modelled forms of developmental dyslexia by varying the number of hidden units available to a connectionist learning system (e.g. Brown, 1997; Bullinaria, 1997; Plaut et al., 1996; Seidenberg & McClelland, 1989; see also Thomas & Karmiloff-Smith, in press). Brown argued that, when a network comparison analogous to a reading age match is carried out, seemingly paradoxical effects of impaired nonword reading combined with preserved effects of spelling-to-sound regularity can be observed.

As with the other possible constraints on development we have outlined above, it is unclear how maturational factors such as numbers of hidden units or connections might interact with other developmental factors. As Plaut et al. (1996) note, the task facing hidden units is harder if imperfect phonological output information is available, because a more accurate pattern of activation must be passed to the output layer if no clean-up mechanism is available.

We also note that there can be advantages for learning of starting with a large amount of computational capacity then gradually reducing it via network pruning (e.g. Mozer & Smolensky, 1989). The benefit of such an approach appears to be that it sometimes enables the network to find an approximately correct solution to a difficult problem without being overly "distracted" early on in learning by the fine-grain detail of the irregularities in the training set.

SUMMARY AND CONCLUSIONS

We have distinguished several different developmental possibilities. Literacy development could reflect children's exposure to an increasingly large or representative fragment of the spelling-to-sound mapping system that they must learn. Alternatively, literacy development could be limited primarily by the fact that it takes a long time to develop a good model of the statistical structure of the domain; because the representations that allow the relevant generalisations to be

86 *Gordon D. A. Brown & Nick Chater*

learned develop only gradually, or because of developmental improvement in the representational capacity of the learning system early in development.

In reality, of course, it is likely that limitations on literacy development are a composite of these processes, and that the processes interact with one another to define a rather complex developmental trajectory. But this is precisely this point at which connectionist modelling may make a useful contribution, because the examination of artificial learning systems may allow us to tease apart the contributions of the different elements in a way that will never be possible by empirical investigation. For example, we can exert complete control over the nature of the input (orthographic) and output (phonological) representations that a connectionist network has available to it, and we can also have complete control over the reading vocabulary that it must learn. We can therefore conduct investigations to examine the speed of learning of a given vocabulary, and the resulting generalisation to unfamiliar items, as a function of the particular input and output representations that a model is provided with. Such analyses may permit the development of specific hypotheses concerning the best way of structuring the early instructional experiences of children in such a way as to permit maximum generalisation, and may allow the modelling of multi-factor rather than single-factor explanations of reading development within connectionist models.

REFERENCES

Anderson, J. R. (1990). *The adaptive character of thought*. Hillsdale, NJ: Erlbaum.
Anderson, J. R., & Milson, R. (1989). Human memory: An adaptive perspective. *Psychological Review, 96*, 703- 719.
Anderson, J . R., & Schooler, L. J. (1991). Reflections of the environment in memory. *Psychological Science. 2.* 396-408.
Ans, B., Carbonnel, S., & Valdois, S. (1998). A connectionist multiple-trace memory model for polysyllabic word reading. *Psychological Review, 105*, 678-723.
Bechtel, W. & Abrahamsen, A. A. (1991). *Connectionism and the Mind: An Introduction to Parallel Processing in Networks*. Cambridge MA: MIT Press/Bradford Books.
Berninger, V. W., Abbott, R. D., Brooksher, R., Lemos, Z., Ogier, S., Zook, D., & Mostafapour, E. (2000). A connectionist approach to making the predictability of English orthography explicit to at-risk beginning readers: Evidence for alternative, effective strategies. *Developmental Neuropsychology, 17*, 241-271.
Besner, D., Twilley, L., McCann, R. S. & Seergobin, K. (1990). On the association between connectionism and data: Are a few words necessary? *Psychological Review, 97*, 432-446.
Bradley, L., & Bryant, P. E. (1983). Categorising sounds and learning to read -causal connection. *Nature, 301*, 419-421.
Brown, G. D. A. (1995). A rational analysis of reading: Spelling-to-sound translation is optimal.
Brown, G. D. A. (1987) Resolving inconsistency: A computational model of word naming. *Journal of Memory and Language, 23*, 1-23.
Brown, G. D. A. (1997). Connectionism, phonology, reading, and regularity in developmental dyslexia. *Brain and Language, 59*, 207-235.
Brown, G. D. A. (1998). The endpoint of reading instruction: The ROAR model. In J. L. Metsala & L. C. Ehri (Eds.), *Word recognition in beginning literacy*. Mahwah, NJ: LEA (pp. 121-138).
Bullinaria, J. A. (1995). Neural network models of reading: Solving the alignment problem without

Wickelfeatures. In J. P. Levy, D. Bairaktaris, J. A. Bullinaria, & D. Cairns (Eds.), *Connectionist models of memory and language*. London: UCL Press. (pp. 161-178).

Bullinaria, J. A. (1997). Modeling reading, spelling, and past tense learning with artificial neural networks. *Brain and Language. 59*. 236-266.

Chater, N. (1995). Neural networks: the new statistical models of mind. In J. P. Levy, D. Bairaktaris, J. A. Bullinaria, & D. Cairns (Eds.), *Connectionist models of memory and language*. London: UCL Press. (pp. 207-227).

Chater, N., & Oaksford, M. (1990). Autonomy, implementation and cognitive architecture: A reply to Fodor and Pylyshyn. *Cognition, 34*, 93-107.

Chater, N., & Oaksford, M. (1999). Ten years of the rational analysis of cognition. *Trends in Cognitive Science. 3*. 56-65.

Coltheart, M., Curtis, Atkins, P., & Haller, M. (1993). Models of reading aloud: Dual-route and parallel-distributed-processing accounts. *Psychological Review, 100*, 589-608.

Coltheart, M., Rastle, K., Perry, C., Langdon, R., & Ziegler, J. (2001). DRC: A dual route cascaded model of visual word recognition and reading aloud. *Psychological Review, 108*, 204-256.

Cortese, M. J. (1998). Revisiting serial position effects in reading. *Journal of Memory and Language, 39*, 652-665.

Elman, J. L., Bates, E. A., Johnson, M. H., Karmiloff-Smith, A., Parisi, D., & Plunkett, K. (1996). *Rethinking innateness: A connectionist perspective on development*. Cambridge, MA: MIT Press.

Elman, J. L. (1993). Learning and development in neural networks: The importance of starting small. *Cognition, 48*, 71- 79.

Fodor, J., & Pylyshyn, Z. (1988). Connectionism and cognitive architecture: A critical analysis. *Cognition, 28*, 3-71.

French, R. M., & Chater, N. (2002). Using noise to compute error surfaces in connectionist networks: A novel means of reducing catastrophic forgetting. *Neural Computation, 14*, 1755-1769.

Goswami, U., & Bryant, P. E. (1990). *Phonological skills and learning to read*. Hove: Lawrence Erlbaum Associates Ltd.

Harm, M. W. (1998). *Division of labor in a computational model of visual word recognition*. Unpublished PhD dissertation, University of Southern California, August 1998.

Harm, M. W., & Seidenberg, M. S. (1999). Phonology, reading acquisition, and dyslexia: Insights from connectionist models. *Psychological Review, 106*, 491-528.

Hulme, C., Quinlan, P., Bolt, G., & Snolwing, M. J. (1995). Building phonological knowledge into a connectionist model of the development of word naming. *Language and Cognitive Processes, 10*, 387-391.

Hulme, C., Snowling, M., & Quinlan, P. (1991). Connectionism and learning to read: Steps towards a psychologically plausible model. *Reading and Writing, 3*, 59-168.

Jared, D., McRae, K. & Seidenberg, M. S. (1990). The basis of consistency effects in word naming. *Journal of Memory and Language, 29*, 687- 715.

Levine, D. S. (1991). Introduction to neural and cognitive modeling. Hillsdale, NJ: LEA.

Manis, F., Seidenberg, M., Doi, L., McBride-Chang, C., & Peterson, A. (1996). On the basis of two subtypes of developmental dyslexia. *Cognition, 58*, 157-195.

Marcus, G. F. (1995). The acquisition of the English past tense in children and multilayered connectionist networks. *Cognition.,56*, 271-179.

McClelland, J. L. (1998). Connectionist models and Bayesian inference. In M. Oaksford & N. Chater (Eds.), *Rational models of cognition*. Oxford: OUP. (pp. 21-53).

McClelland, J. L., McNaughton, B. L., & O'Reilly, R. C. (1995). Why there are complementary learning systems in the hippocampus and neocortex: Insights from the successes and failures of connectionist models of learning and memory *Psychological Review, 102*, 419-457.

McLeod, P., Plunkett, K., & Rolls, E. T. (1998). Introduction to connectionist modelling of cognitive processes. Oxford: OUP.

Metsala, J. L., & Brown, G. D.A. (1998). Normal and dyslexic reading development: The role of formal models. In R. M. Joshi & C. Hulme (Eds.), *Reading and Spelling: Development and disorders*. Mahwah, NJ: LEA. (pp. 235-262).

Metsala, J. L., Stanovich, K. E., & Brown, G. D.A. (1998). Regularity effects and the phonological deficit model of reading disabilities: A meta-analytic review. *Journal of Educational Psychology, 90,* 279-293.

Mozer, M. C., & Smolensky, P. (1989). Using relevance to reduce network size automatically. *Connection Science, 1,* 3-16.

Norris, D. (1994). A quantitative model of reading aloud. Journal of Experimental Psychology: Human Perception and Performance, 20, 1212-1232.

Oaksford, M., & Chater, N. (1998). (Eds.) *Rational models of cognition.* Oxford: OUP.

Perry, C., & Ziegler, J. C. (2002). Cross-language computational investigation of the length effect in reading aloud. *Journal of Experimental Psychology: Human Perception and Performance, 28,* 990-1001.

Phillips, W. A., Hay, I. M., & Smith, L. S. (1993). Lexicality and pronunciation in a simulated neural net. *British Journal of Mathematical and Statistical Psychology, 46,* 193-205.

Pinker, S. & Prince, A. (1988). On language and connectionism: Analysis of a parallel distributed processing model of language acquisition. *Cognition, 28,* 73-193.

Plaut, D. C., McClelland, J. L., Seidenberg, M. S. & Patterson, K. E. (1996). Understanding normal and impaired word reading: Computational principles in quasi-regular domains. *Psychological Review, 103,* 56-105.

Plunkett, K., & Marchman, V. (1991). U-shaped learning and frequency effects in a multi-layered perception: Implications for child language acquisition. *Cognition, 38,* 43-102.

Plunkett, K., & Marchman, V. (1993). From rote learning to system building: Acquiring verb morphology in children and connectionist nets. *Cognition. 48.* 21-69.

Quinlan, P. (1991). *Connectionism and Psychology.* London: Harvester.

Rastle, K., & Coltheart, M. (1998). Whammies and double whammies: The effect of length on nonword reading. *Psychonomic Bulletin & Review, 5,* 277-282.

Rastle, K., & Coltheart, M. (1999). Serial and strategic effects in reading aloud. *Journal of Experimental Psychology: Human Perception and Performance, 25,* 482-503

Rastle, K., & Coltheart, M. (2000). Serial processing in reading aloud: Reply to Zorzi (2000). *Journal of Experimental Psychology: Human Perception and Performance, 26,* 1232-1235.Rumelhart, D. E., Hinton, G. E. & Williams, R. J. (1986). Learning internal presentations by error propagation. In D. E. Rumelhart and J. L. McClelland (Eds.), *Parallel Distributed Processing: Explorations in the microstructure of cognition (Vol.1).* Cambridge, MA: Bradford Books/ MIT Press.

Rumelhart, D. E. & McClelland, J. L. (1986). On Learning the Past Tenses of English Verbs. In I. L. McClelland & D. E. Rumelhart (Eds.), *Parallel Distributed Processing: Explorations in the microstructure of cognition (Vol. 2).* Cambridge, MA: MIT Press/Bradford Books.

Seidenberg, M. S. & McClelland, J. L. (1989). A distributed, developmental model of word recognition and naming. *Psychological Review, 96,* 523-568.

Sejnowski, T. J. & Rosenberg, C. R. (1987). Parallel Networks that learn to pronounce English Text. *Complex Systems, 1,* 145-168.

Share, D. L. (1995). Phonological recoding and self-teaching: Sine qua non of reading acquition. *Cognition, 55,* 151-218.

Shepard, R. N. (1987). Towards a universal law of generalization for psychological science. *Science, 237,*1317-1323.

Stanovich, K.B., & Siegel, L. S. (1994). Phenotypic performance profile of children with reading disabilities: A regression-based test of the phonological-core variable-difference model. *Journal of Educational Psychology, 86,* 24-53.

Thomas, M., & Karmiloff-Smith, A. (in press). Are developmental disorders like cases of adult brain damage? Implications from connectionist modelling. *Behavioural and Brain Sciences.*

Treiman, R., Mullennix, J., Bijeljac-Babic, R., & Richmond-Welty, E. D. (1995). The special role of rimes in the description, use, and acquisition of English orthography. *Journal of Experimental Psychology: General, 124,* 107-136.

Van Orden, G. C., Pennington, B. F., & Stone, G. O. (1990). Word identification in reading and the promise of subsymbolic psycholinguistics. *Psychological Review, 97,* 488-522.

Van Orden, G. C., Pennington, B. F., & Stone, G. O. (2001). What do double dissociations prove? *Cognitive Science, 25,* 111-172.

Wagner, R. K., & Torgesen, J. K. (1987). The nature of phonological processing and its causal role in the acquisition of reading skills. *Psychological Bulletin, 101,* 192-212.

Weekes, B. S. (1997). Differential effects of number of letters on word and nonword naming latency *.Quarterly Journal Of Experimental Psychology, 50,* 439-456.

Zorzi, M. (2000). Serial processing in reading aloud: No challenge for a parallel model. *Journal of Experimental Psychology: Human Perception and Performance, 26,* 847-856.

Zorzi, M., Houghton, G., & Butterworth, B. (1998a). The development of spelling-sound relationships in a model of phonological reading. *Language and Cognitive Processes, 13,* 337-371.

Zorzi, M., Houghton, G., & Butterworth, B. (1998b). Two routes or one in reading aloud? *Journal of Experimental Psychology: Human Perception and Performance, 24,* 1131-1161.

SUGGESTED FURTHER READINGS

Elman, J. L., Bates, E. A., Johnson, M. H., Karmiloff-Smith, A., Parisi, D., & Plunkett, K. (1996). *Rethinking innateness: A connectionist perspective on development.* Cambridge, MA: MIT Press.

Harm, M. W., & Seidenberg, M. S. (1999). Phonology, reading acquisition, and dyslexia: Insights from connectionist models. *Psychological Review, 106,* 491-528.

Thomas, M., & Karmiloff-Smith, A. (in press). Are developmental disorders like cases of adult brain damage? Implications from connectionist modelling. *Behavioural and Brain Sciences.*

ACKNOWLEDGEMENTS

The research described here was partially supported by a grant from the Leverhulme Trust (U.K.). We thank Jonathan Solity for many helpful discussions. Correspondence concerning this article should be addressed to Gordon D.A. Brown, Department of Psychology, University of Warwick, Coventry, CV4 7AL, U.K. Email: G.D.A.Brown @warwick.ac.uk.

A5. Morphology and Spelling

PETER BRYANT & TEREZINHA NUNES[1]

ABSTRACT

Phonemes as well as morphemes are represented in many written languages, including English, Greek, French and Portuguese. Morphology is such an important feature of written English that it has been defined by some linguists as a morpho-phonemic script. In this chapter it is suggested that there are at least four types of situation where knowledge of morphemes is necessary for word spelling and reading: (1) when there is more than one way to represent a sequence of sounds, spelling is often determined by morphology (e.g., the end sounds of "emotion" and "magician" are the same but spelling differs for morphological reasons); (2) there may be phonological changes in the base form when an affix is added to it but the spelling of the base form is often preserved, maintaining the meaning connection between the two forms clear (e.g., the final consonant sound in "magic" changes when the suffix "ian" is added but the spelling is preserved); (3) the fixed spelling of an affix – such as the "ed" for past regular verbs – may actually flout letter sound correspondences (e.g., "list" and "kissed" have the same rime but "list" is spelled phonetically whereas "kissed" represents the past tense in a way that flouts letter-sound correspondences); and (4) sometimes a decision about where to parse words in reading is crucial for word identification and is based on the morphemes it contains (e.g., in the words "unimportat" and "uniform" the sequence "uni" is parsed differently because "un" and "uni" are the prefixes in these words, respectively).

Research showing how children learn about morphological representation is relatively recent but much has already been accomplished in this domain. The chapter presents evidence that systematic representation of morphemes in spelling is a relatively late acquisition in comparison with the systematic representation of phonemes. Evidence is also available to suggest that children's awareness of grammar and morphology is a predictor of their later ability to represent morphemes systematically and it is thus a possible cause of progress in this aspect of literacy. Finally, intervention studies show that improving children's awareness

[1] Preparation of this chapter was supported by grants from the ESRC and MRC. The authors are thankful to these institutions for their support.

T. Nunes, P. Bryant (eds.), Handbook of Children's Literacy, 91–118.
© 2004 *Kluwer Academic Publishers. Printed in Great Britain.*

of morphology has a positive effect on their reading in general and their spelling of words where morphology is represented.

INTRODUCTION: WHAT HAVE MORPHEMES TO DO WITH READING AND SPELLING

A large proportion of the words in the English language, and an even larger proportion in many other languages, contain more than one morpheme, and this has dramatic and important consequences both for reading and for spelling these languages. A morpheme is a unit of meaning. "Lock" is a one-morpheme English word – either a noun or a verb – and "unlock" is a two-morpheme word, for the "un" at the beginning reverses the meaning of the verb. "Unlocked" is a three-morpheme word because the added /t/ sound at the end, which is spelled as "ed", is another unit of meaning. It makes the verb "unlock" into a past verb or a past participle.

In principle there may be no need for readers or spellers to know anything at all about the morphemic structure of such words. It is just possible that children could learn the specific spellings of all three of the individual words in this set of words ("lock", "unlock", "unlocked") without ever paying any attention to the morphemic relationships between them. It is most unlikely, however, that children do ignore the structure of the words that they are learning to read and spell in this way, and the most pressing reason for suggesting that they might learn to take morphemic relations into account is that it is a great help to do so. Attention to the morphemic structure of words can make the job of learning to read and write a great deal easier.

The importance of parsing morphemes

Knowledge about morphemes removes many of the ambiguities that would otherwise perplex beginning readers and spellers. Consider, for example, the different pronunciations of the letter sequence "sh" in the two words "rushing" and "mishap", both of which are two-morpheme words. The "sh" sequence usually acts as a digraph which represents a single phoneme, /ʃ/. This is how things are in the first of the two words, "rushing". Here the "sh" sequence falls entirely within the first morpheme and represents the last phoneme in that morpheme. Thus the "sh" sequence is treated as a unit, as is normally the case. In the second word, "mishap, the two letters lie on different sides of the morpheme boundary, and no longer act as a unit, since each letter represents a different sound: "s" represents the final phoneme in the first morpheme and "h" the opening sound of the second morpheme. The morpheme boundary is the reason why the letter sequence represents one grapheme in "rushing" and two graphemes in "mishap".

The nature of the morphemes also has an effect: different morphemes, which share common spelling patterns, are sometimes pronounced in different ways. An example is the "un" opening sequence which is pronounced in one way in, for example, in the word "untied" and in quite another way in "united". It will surely help a child to realise that words like "unit" "unite" "unity" and "united" share a common stem and therefore a common pronunciation, in which the "un" sequence represents a different sound than it does in words like "untied" and "unlocked" where "un" represents a whole morpheme.

Constancy in spelling the same morpheme even though the sound varies

So the same spelling pattern is pronounced in different ways in different morphemes, and – the other side of this coin – the same morpheme is often spelled in the same way, despite variations in the way that it is pronounced in different words. Let us take as our first example the past-tense inflectional morpheme in English regular past verbs. In speech the past tense inflection comes in three different sounds, as we can see from the words "filled" "kissed" and "waited". The last sounds of these three past verbs are /d/, /t/ and /ɪd/ respectively, and yet they are all spelled in the same way. The "ed" ending is therefore a spelling sequence that represents a particular morpheme and not a particular sound.

The plural inflectional morpheme is another example of constancy in spelling at the level of the morpheme rather than of the sound of an inflectional ending. The spelling for regular plural endings is invariably "s", if the inflection is one phoneme, and "es" if there are two phonemes to this plural ending, as in "fishes". However, the sound of the one-phoneme ending is not always /s/, as in "cats": in words like "buns" and in "trees" the sound of the final plural inflection /z/, and yet it is always spelled with an "s". So here too there is a simple morphological rule, which is to spell all one-morpheme plural inflections as "s", whether their sound is "s" or "z". It is fine to spell "freeze" with a "z" but quite wrong to write the word "trees" with this ending.

Morphemic spelling constancy also plays a part in the spelling of stem morphemes. In English and in several other languages the stem of a derived word is often spelled in the same way as the word from which it was derived even when it is pronounced differently. "Heal" and "health" and "muscle" and "muscular" are two well-known examples (Marsh, Friedman, Welch & Desberg, 1980: Marsh, Friedman, Desberg & Saterdahl, 1981: Marsh & Desberg, 1983). These "derivational constancies", as they are called (Templeton & Bear, 1992) serve a useful educational and cultural purpose. They are a clear reminder that certain words share a common stem and therefore a common meaning, even though these stems are pronounced in different ways.

The same sound spelled in different ways when it represents a morpheme and when it does not

The basic difference between "freeze" and "trees" that we have already mentioned is that the first of these words is a one-morpheme word while the second contains two morphemes. The spelling for the ending of the one-morpheme word is phonetic (it conforms to grapheme-phoneme rules): in contrast the spelling of the last phoneme of the two-morpheme word is determined by a morphemic spelling rule. This contrast between one- and two-morpheme English words is exactly the same in the case of the regular past tense endings that we have already mentioned. "List" and "kissed" share a common rime ending and so do "hand" and "banned". The last phonemes of "list" and of "hand" are spelled phonetically, according to grapheme-phoneme correspondence rules. However exactly the same last phonemes are spelled as "ed" in "kissed" and "banned" because the sound represents the past tense morpheme in both of these words.

The spelling of words that end in /ks/ is a striking example of a simple, and completely consistent, morphological English spelling rule that is based on the difference between one- and two-morpheme words. In singular nouns, which in English have no inflection, the /ks/ ending is always spelled as "x" or "xe" ("fox", "tax" "axe"). In English plural nouns, however, the spelling for this same end sound is always "cks" or "ks"/"k(e)s"("socks", "books" "lakes") because of the hard-and-fast rule that the plural inflection in regular plural nouns must be spelled as "s" to denote that it is a suffix added to the stem.

The rule that this ending is spelled as "x" in one-morpheme words, but as "cks" or "ks" in two-morpheme words, also applies to present verbs in English. We finish "I fix" with an "x", because "fix" is a one-morpheme verb, but we put an added "s" on the verbs "He picks/looks/bakes" because these are all two-morpheme verbs where the final /s/ sound is the third person singular inflection and the written final "s" represents the existence of that added morpheme.

Thus the spelling of morphemes often provides more information than speech itself. An extreme example of the helpfulness of morphologically based spelling is in the way that the plural ending is spelled in French. In French the plural ending on nouns, adjectives and verbs is silent, but it appears in writing. We do not hear the "s" on the end of the noun and the adjective in the phrase "les maisons blanches", or the "nt" at the end of "ils regardent", but we spell these endings when we write such words in French. Thus French writing explicitly signifies the plural ending, while speech does not.

The same sound can be spelled in one way when it represents one morpheme and in another way when it represents a different morpheme

Perhaps because English is a relatively uninflected language, which therefore contains many one-morpheme words, the most remarkable instances of morphological spelling tend to be those of the kind that we have just considered, where particular sounds are spelled phonetically in a one-morpheme words but in a different way in a two-morpheme words. In more inflected languages, such as modern Greek and Portuguese, it is easier to find instances where different inflectional morphemes or derivational morphemes share the same sound as each other but are spelled in different ways. Thus the contrasts in these languages tend to be between different two-morpheme words rather than between one- and two-morpheme words.

There are, for example, several different ways of spelling the long /i/ vowel sound in Greek (Aidinis, 1998: Bryant, Nunes and Aidinis, 1999). When this sound is at the end of a word it can signify a masculine plural (-οι), a feminine singular (-η), a neuter singular nominal or adjectival inflection (-ι) or a third person singular verb ending (-ει). Note that these four suffixes sound exactly the same as each other, but are spelled in four entirely different ways, each of which is a legitimate spelling for that sound. The clue to choosing the right spelling for each inflection is therefore entirely morphological. Figure 1 gives a verse from a reading book in Greek in which all the lines end with a word with this ending, and it shows the different spellings for this sound.

Such contrasts between two-morpheme words with morphemes that sound the same but are spelled differently, for morphological reasons, are very common in Portuguese too. For example, the words "princesa" and "pobreza" share the same sounding two-syllable ending, which contains the /z/ sound but is spelled differently in the two-words, because the "esa" ending indicates a female title and the "eza" ending signifies an abstract noun.

The same kind of contrast exists in English too. One rather striking example is the contrast between regular plural endings and possessive endings. Both these endings sound the same but they are spelled differently because of the use of the apostrophe to represent possession. The phrases "The boy's drink" and "The boys drink" sound the same in spoken language but have entirely different meanings, and this difference is represented in writing by the presence in one phrase, and the absence in the other, of an apostrophe.

Another example is the group of words that end in the syllable /ən/ as in the two words "institution" and "magician". These final syllables are pronounced in the exactly same way as each other, and they are both derivational morphemes, but they are spelled differently. The rule is that when the morpheme transforms the word into an abstract noun, it is spelled as "ion" ("confession, protection"): when it transforms the word into a person who is an agent, the same sound is spelled as "ian" ("logician", "optician"). Of course, sometimes morphemes, which have different meanings but which sound the same, are also spelled in the same way as each other. The comparative ending ("bigg-er") and the agentive ending ("hunt-er") is a case in point. It is an interesting question whether children become more aware of morphemic differences when these co-incide with spelling differences ("ion/ian") than when they do not ("er").

Ξύπνα, ξύπνησε, παιδί.
Κικιρίκου, οἱ πετεινοί.
Φύγε, νύχτα σκοτεινή,
τὸ πουλάκι κελαηδεῖ.
Ξύπνα, ἐφάνηκε ἡ αὐγή.
Πάει πιὰ ἡ νύχτα αὐτή.
Ἦρθε ἡ χαρὰ στὴ γῆ.

Figure 1. A page from a Greek reading book which gives a simple poem in which the words at the end of each line all end in the same sound as each other. The sound is /ɪ/ and the figure illustrates that it is spelled in several different ways. Each different way represents a different suffix morpheme.

Conclusions about the need to know about morphemes in order to learn to read and to spell

Our argument so far is that some knowledge of morphemes and of their connection with spelling patterns could, in principle, be a powerful aid to a child learning to read and write. This knowledge could reduce much of the ambiguity in reading and spelling. Children who use it should have no difficulty in understanding why they should write "list" and not "lissed", or "optician" and not "opticion". They should also be able to break up difficult words that they are trying to read into meaningful and readable segments.

However, the fact that morphological knowledge could help them does not mean that children do automatically take advantage of this knowledge when they learn to read and to spell. There is an alternative possibility, which is that children learn to recognise and to spell the sort of words that we have been discussing in a rote manner. There are even instances, as we shall see later, where children might follow some lower-level orthographic rule which leads them to appear to respect morphological spelling rules even though the rules that they are following are not morphological ones. One must not assume, a priori and without any evidence, that children's morphological knowledge plays an important part in learning to read and to spell. One needs empirical evidence to make this kind of a statement.

At least four kinds of evidence are needed here:

- First we have to look for signs of learning that is distinctively morphological. We have argued for a distinction between learning about grapheme-phoneme correspondences and learning morphologically based spelling rules. If the distinction is a valid one, it is likely that these two kinds of learning do not take place at exactly the same time in children's development. In that case, it should be possible to tease them apart by studying the developmental course of learning to read and spell.

- Secondly, we need evidence about how children learn morphologically-based spelling rules. In this chapter we will show that, as children progress from using just phonological rules to using both phonological and morphological rules, much of their new learning is their own construction.

- Thirdly, we must show that this new learning really does involve genuine morphological rules and cannot be reduced to specific word-bases associations. The acid test here is to investigate their knowledge of these morphologically based spelling rules with the help of pseudo-words whose grammatical function is clear from the context that these pseudo-words are in. If children put an "ed" ending on a pseudo-word which from the context is obviously a past verb, but not on a pseudo-word which ends with the same sound sequence but clearly has the status of a noun, they must be using a genuine rule, and not relying on specific spelling knowledge.

- Fourthly, we should look for connections between children's knowledge of the morphemic structure of words in the spoken language and the progress that they make in reading and spelling.

The process of learning about morphologically based spelling rules must depend on some understanding of the morphemic structure of words in the spoken language. It follows that the greater awareness and knowledge that a child has about morphemes in the spoken language, the faster and more effective this child's learning about spelling rules based on morphemes is likely to be.

In the rest of this chapter we shall try to satisfy all four requirements.

The first requirement – grapheme-phoneme correspondence first and morphologically-based rules later

Children's learning about morphological spelling rules is distinctive and different from phonological learning in two ways. The time-scale is different. Children learn about morphological spelling rules at a different time and a different rate than they learn about grapheme-phoneme correspondences.

The best evidence for this gap between learning to write alphabetically and learning to write conventional, morphologically determined, spellings is the widely-accepted phenomenon of invented spelling (Read, 1986). In the first stages of writing, children depend heavily on grapheme-phoneme correspondences, or at any rate on their own version of these correspondences, and they usually ignore conventional spellings for affix morphemes. The past tense ending, for example, is quite consistently ignored in children's early writing, as Figure 2, which is a story written by a 7-year old girl, attests. The work of Read (1986) and of Treiman (1993) and of several others has shown quite unambiguously that children make no attempt at first to adopt the conventional "ed" past tense ending, but simply write the ending phonetically.

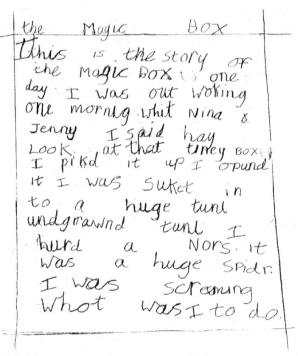

Figure 2: The opening page of a story written by a 7 year-old girl which illustrates the predominance of phonetic spellings for past verb endings at this age. Note the spellings for "picked" "opened" and "sucked".

Children's initial avoidance of morphemic distinctions in spelling suggests that they first go through a phase during which they conquer the alphabetic principle, and only later turn to morphology as well. However, both Read and Treiman suggest that there is at least one exception to this general pattern. This concerns the rule that the plural suffix in nouns is spelled as "s" even though the sound of the suffix is often /z/ (e.g. "birds", "smiles", "fishes"). The reason for thinking that children understand this rule is that they apparently obey it: for the most part they use the letter "s", and hardly ever the letter "z", to write the plural ending even when its sound is /z/. However, they might disdain the letter "z" merely because it is an infrequent letter anyway. (Shakespeare went as far as calling "z" the "unnecessary letter".) We could only be sure that children understand the rule that "s" is the right way to spell the plural ending if they spell the /z/ ending in other, non-plural, words, like "jazz" or "choose" (many /z/ ending non-plural words end in "se") differently from plural words.

Kemp (2000: see also Kemp and Bryant (2003)) has pointed out, however, that a child who puts "s" at the end of "buns" but "z" at the end of "jazz" may not be doing so for morphological reasons. Children, she argued, could learn this distinction on the basis of frequency of certain letter patterns. Kemp's point was that in virtually all non-plural English mono-syllabic words ending in /z/, this final end sound is immediately preceded by a vowel ("jazz" "craze"). In contrast, the sound preceding the /z/ ending in most plural mono-syllabic nouns is a consonant ("buns"). Thus children could learn, on the basis of frequency alone, that "z"s do not follow a consonant – that there are no sequences like "mz" "nz" or "lz", and that the /z/ sound should be represented as "s" immediately after these letters.

To obey these particular frequency-based associations in this way would lead to fairly good but not to completely correct spelling of the /z/ ending. Anyone who obeys these associations would spell the plural endings for nouns whose stems ends in a consonant ("buns") correctly. This person would also do well with /z/ ending words, whose penultimate sound is a short vowel, since there are no English nouns whose stem ends in a short vowel. Every /z/ ending mono-syllabic word in English whose penultimate phoneme is a short vowel is a non-plural word ("buzz" "fizz") and should not be spelled with an "s" at the end.

However, one category of /z/ ending words would not be spelled well by someone obeying a frequency-based rule. Words whose /z/ ending follows a long vowel can either be plural nouns or non-plural words. There are plenty of plural nouns ("pleas" "fees" "pies") and non-plural words ("please" "seize") in this category, and therefore there is no consistent way of telling, on the basis of frequency alone, whether these words should end in "s" or in some other spelling ("se", "ze").

Thus anyone who obeys frequency-based associations, rather than morphological rules about the /z/ ending, will spell the plural /z/ sounding endings of nouns whose stem ends in a consonant correctly, and also the endings of non-plural mono-syllabic /z/ ending words, whose penultimate sound is a short vowel.

However, they will, make many errors with /z/ ending words whose penultimate sound is a long vowel ("craze", "ways").

Kemp found exactly this pattern (many more errors with plural and non-plural words whose penultimate sound was a long vowel than with the other two categories) in tasks involving real words and pseudo-words with school children of 5-9 years. She even found the same pattern, though in not so strong a form, when she gave the same pseudo-word task to adults. Even adults, to some extent at least, followed frequency-based associations in preference to a morphologically-based rule. An interesting aspect of Kemp's results was that adults who had been to university did better on this task than those who had not. Going to university, it seems, does wonders for one's knowledge of morphologically based spelling rules.

Kemp's interesting work is a useful warning against concluding too rapidly that children are following a morphological spelling rule when there are other possible explanations for the spelling patterns that they are using. It also demonstrates how elusive these rules seem to be – not only to children but to some adults as well. Certainly much other work shows that children's learning of the conventional spellings for inflectional morphemes takes a great deal of time. The rule about the /ks/ ending that we mentioned above is a clear instance. We have shown (Bryant 2002) that children of 5-9 years often fail to assign "x" endings to one-morpheme and "s" endings to two-morpheme words that have this final sound. They get better at doing so as they grow older, but even at the age of 9 years their spelling of this final sound is by no means perfect, and they are particularly weak in pseudo-word tasks which are the definitive test of their knowledge of the morphological spelling rule.

Our own work (Nunes, Bryant & Bindman, 1997) also confirms that English-speaking children are very slow indeed to adopt the past tense "ed" ending. We conducted a longitudinal study of 363 children whose ages in the study ranged from 6 through to 11 years, and in the course of this study we gave the children spelling tasks involving the words presented in Table 1. These were ("ed" ending) regular past verbs and also non-verbs with similar sounding endings and irregular past verbs which also ended with the same sounds but whose endings were spelled phonetically. Our results with the younger children confirmed that a sizeable number of them simply ignored the "ed" ending with regular verbs and wrote these endings phonetically. The developmental improvement in the use of this difficult ending was quite marked. However it was not comprehensive. Many of the oldest children did not put this ending on all the regular verbs, even though these were all frequent and well-known words.

Children are also in striking difficulty with the apostrophe (Bryant, Devine, Ledward & Nunes, 1997). Younger children (9-10 year olds) tend to leave it out altogether in genitive (possessive) words: older children (11 and 15 year olds) put it in more often, but almost as often in the wrong words (plural nominatives) as in the right ones. We shall return to this pattern of children's spelling getting worse with some words at the same time as it gets better with others later in this chapter.

**Table 1. The words that the children had to spell
in the Nunes et al. (1997) longitudinal study**

	/d/ ending	/t/ ending
Regular past verbs		
	called	dressed
	covered	kissed
	filled	laughed
	killed	learned
	opened	stopped
Irregular past verbs		
	found	felt
	heard	left
	held	lost
	sold	sent
	told	slept
Non-verbs		
	bird	belt
	cold	except
	field	next
	gold	paint
	ground	soft

There is hardly any dispute about children's slowness in learning correct conventional spellings for words whose spelling depends on their morphemic structure. Nor is there much disagreement that children do eventually find out about these spellings. But it is hard to find a consensus about how they learn about these spellings. This is a subject that researchers have entirely neglected until quite recently.

The second requirement: how children learn the new morphological spelling rules

Learning to spell better – learning to spell worse

It is tempting to argue that children learn any topic that they encounter at school just by being taught it and for no other reason. But this is not a good answer to the question of how children learn about morphological spellings, and it is certainly not a complete answer. It is incomplete because there are spelling rules which are not taught at school but which children nevertheless learn about. We shall deal with one of these, which concerns the difference between English regular and irregular verbs, later on in this chapter.

Another reason for not using teaching as a catch-all explanation of their learning about morphological spelling rules is the shape of the learning. If children were simply learning a rule by being told about it, one would expect them to go directly from a state of not knowing the rule to knowing it. This, as we shall now see, is not the case.

In all the cases that we have been discussing children have to learn to represent the same sound with different spellings in different words. Typically they start by using one spelling for this and avoiding others. So, as we have seen, they initially spell /d/ and /t/ endings as "d" and "t" which means that they are right in the case of non-verbs like "list" and of irregular verbs like "slept" but wrong with regular past verbs like "kissed" and "clapped". At this stage they clearly lack the morphological rule that past verbs end in "ed".

If it were a matter simply of learning the rule by being told it, we would expect that children would change rather suddenly from spelling words like "kissed" as "kist" to spelling them correctly, and that at the same time they would continue to spell the endings of non-verbs and of irregular past verbs correctly. But this is not what happens. Our longitudinal study (Nunes et al., 1997) showed that many children take an intermediate step. They begin by avoiding the "ed" spelling entirely. Then they go on to use this spelling for some words ending in /d/ and /t/, but they use it with the wrong types of words as well as with the right ones. In this intermediate stage they put "ed"s on the ends of some regular verbs but also on the ends of some non-verbs and irregular past verbs.

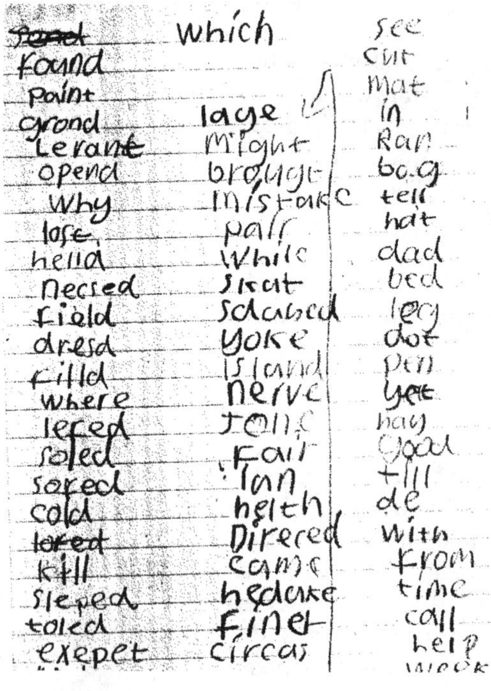

Figure 3. Examples of misplacements of the "-ed" ending in the spelling of a 7½-year-old English schoolboy.

Figure 3 gives an example of a 7 year old boy's spelling of the words in Table 1 together with some other words. The pattern of this boy's spelling is quite typical.. He managed not use the "ed" spelling when it was needed, writing "filled" as "filld" and "dressed" as "dressd". However he did apply the "ed" ending all over the place, and often in entirely the wrong places. His spelling of "slept" as "sleped" and of "sold" as "soled" may not seem so surprising, since these are past verbs, even though they are not regular ones. "Necsed", "sofed" and "direced" are much more striking since these are non-verbs. Thus the boy's misspellings demonstrate that he is probably not using any morphological criteria, when he decides how to spell /d/ and /t/ endings even though he has adopted the "ed" spelling which is the correct conventional spelling for an inflectional morpheme.

These misuses of the "ed" ending in irregular past verbs and in non-verbs were extremely common. By the end of our study 71% of the children had made this mistake with irregular past verbs and 56% with non-verbs. Our longitudinal data also confirmed that this kind of mistake was the main feature of a genuinely intermediate phase of a three-phase development. First the children did not use the "ed" spelling: then (the intermediate phase) they used it altogether too generously with non-verbs as well as with past verbs, and finally they used it with past verbs only and eventually just with regular past verbs.

The developmental picture is much the same with English children's spelling of the /ks/ ending (Bryant, 2002). We used the technique of giving children written sentences with a missing word, and then dictating the whole sentence including the missing word, which the child then had to write in. The words they had to write – the missing words – had /ks/ endings, but some were one-morpheme (e.g. "fox", "mix") and others two-morpheme (e.g. "socks", "picks") nouns and verbs.

We also worked with pseudo-words. We dictated sentences like "Bob crecks the windows every morning". The children had to write the /ks/ ending pseudo-word, and the surrounding sentence provided the context which made it clear whether this pseudo-word represented a one-morpheme or a two-morpheme word.

The pseudo-word task produced clear and surprising results. Six-year-old children hardly ever used the "x" ending, and so they spelled the endings of the two-morpheme more successfully than the endings of the one-morpheme pseudo-words. Between the ages of 6 and 8 years their use of "x" increased, but it increased as much with the inappropriate two-morpheme pseudo-words as with the appropriate one-morpheme ones. Thus, here is another example of children getting worse with some words while they get better with others. We must add that 9-year old children did genuinely improve. They used the "x" spelling more with the appropriate words and less with inappropriate words that the younger children.

The appearance of new mistakes with /ks/ words between the ages of 6 and 8 years is yet another example of children of a striking, and quite general, developmental sequence in spelling. When children begin to use apostrophes, when they start to give /d/ and /t/ ending words the "ed" ending and when they first use both the "x" and the "s" ending for /ks/ ending words, their spelling gets better and iut gets worse at the same time. They go through a phase of spelling some words worse than they did before, at the same time as they are spelling others better than they did before.

This strange and interesting intermediate spelling phase is not at all a purely Anglophone phenomenon. Here are some examples from other languages, starting with the effect of different stress patterns in Portuguese. In most Portuguese words the stress is on the penultimate syllable, but there are exceptions. One concerns the very frequent final /u:/ sound. Most words that end in /u:/ do follow the typical pattern of having the stress on the penultimate syllable. In all these words the final /u:/ sound is spelled as "o" (e.g. "gato" meaning "cat"). Young Portuguese-speaking children initially find this spelling ("o" for /u:/) rather difficult because it violates the grapheme-phoneme correspondence of "u" for /u:/ that they learned when they learned about the alphabet. They often make the mistake of writing "gato", for example, as "gatu".

There are, however, Portuguese /u/ ending words which have a different, and unusual, stress pattern. In these words the stress is on the last syllable – on the /u:/ in fact- and this affects the spelling of that sound. In all these words the final /u:/ is spelled as "u". "Bambu" is one example and "caju" another.

Nunes, Roazzi and Buarque (2003) were the first to show that beginning spellers usually write /u:/ sounds as "u" and thus misspell words like "carro" as, for example, "carru". They found too that, as children grow older, they spell /u:/ endings as "o" more often than before, which means that they get better at spelling words like "carro". But they also reported the more surprising result they actually become less successful than they were before with words like "bambu" because they now begin to give these the "o" ending as well: they misspell "bambu" for example as "bambo".

Later still they manage to distinguish these two kinds of word quite well, and this suggests that they eventually do learn the stress-related rule. This final step is also surprising in a way, because the children in this study had not been taught this complex rule. Their learning of the rule was probably implicit.

We find a rather similar sequence in French children. Michel Fayol and his colleagues (Totereau, Thenevin and Fayol, 1997: Fayol, Thenevin, Jarousse, & Totereau, 1999) looked at their spelling the plural morphemes which, as we have remarked, are mostly silent in French. These ingenious researchers found that beginning spellers usually omit these plural inflections when writing plural words. Later on they begin to include the "s" plural inflection for nouns and adjectives. However, they also tend to put this ending at the ends of verbs ("Les garcons manges") as well. When they are older they do begin to adopt the "nt" plural ending, but at first they sometimes make the opposite mistake: they sometimes put this on plural nouns and adjectives as well ("Les femment mangent"). Eventually they learn that the plural inflection is spelled as "s" in nouns and adjectives and as "nt" in verbs. This study gives us yet another example of children adopting a new spelling pattern without being clear about the rule for using it, and of spelling some words worse at the same time as spelling others better than before during an intermediate phase. The child who puts "nt" at the end of the noun "femme", having previously used the correct "s" ending for this word, does not at first know the rule for the new spelling that he or she has just begun to use. It seems that, here as in the other examples, the child must have the experience of using the new spelling, wrongly as well as rightly, before understanding its purpose.

Greek children follow this sequence too. Greek has an extremely regular orthography: one can tell exactly how any Greek word is pronounced from its spelling. However, as we have seen, several sounds in Greek are spelled in more than one way. We have already considered the example of the long /ɪ/ vowel sound, which can be spelled as η, ι, ει, and οι. There are other instances. The /o/ sound is spelled either as "o" or "ɪ" and the /ey/ sound either as "ε" or as "αι". So the Greek child has to choose, and in many instances morphology can help him or her make the choice. Whenever these sounds represent the whole or a part of an inflectional morpheme at the end of a word, there is no ambiguity at all in their spelling. Each inflectional morpheme has its own fixed spelling.

Two studies have shown that Greek children tend at first to adopt one spelling only where there alternative spellings for the same sound and to apply this preferred spelling quite generally. Aidinis, 1998 (see also Bryant, Nunes and Aidinis, 1999) has shown this in a cross-sectional study and Chliounaki (unpublished: but see Chliounaki and Bryant (2002)) in a longitudinal one. Beginning spellers use "o" rather than "ɪ","ε" rather than "αι" and either "η" or "ι" rather than "ει" and "οι". (Note their preference for single letters over digraphs.)

Chliounaki's longitudinal study has already established a developmental pattern with which we are becoming quite familiar. Her data cover the spelling of 6-year old children in their first year at school. In the first of two sessions during that year, Chliounaki found that many of them used one spelling only for sounds like /i/ for which there are alternative spellings. We shall take as an example words ending in /o/. Some words ending in this sound are neuter singular nouns, and their final sound is spelled as "o". Others are first person singular verbs, in which case the final /o/ is spelled as "ω". Many children in the sample wrote both kinds of words with an "o"ending and thus were right in the case of singular neuter nouns but wrong with first person singular verbs. Six months later on Chliounaki also found that a high proportion of these children began to use the "ω" as well as the "o" at the ends of such words. However, most of these children sometimes applied the new "ω" spelling not only to first person verbs, which is correct, but also on occasion to neuter nouns as well, which is quite wrong. They spelled the noun endings worse than before at the same time as they spelled the verb endings better.

So when children adopt new morphologically –based spellings they do not always use these new spellings correctly. They do not progress seamlessly from not using a spelling sequence to using it in the correct place. They seem to need an intermediate phase in which they sort out for themselves the underlying rules for the new spellings.

Sorting the rule out: Is construction the answer?

Some time during this striking intermediate phase, in which children start to spell worse than before, as well as better than before, they must learn the correct underlying principles for conventional morphological spellings. The clue to the nature of this learning must lie in the fact that children adopt the new spelling patterns before they understand the rules for these new spellings. It looks as though they have to try these patterns out first in order to understand them properly.

Our own hypothesis is that children have to construct these spelling rules for themselves. We argue that they need to experiment with the new spellings themselves before they can understand the rules behind them properly. That indeed is the whole point of the intermediate phase. It is a time for experimenting.

We are not claiming that children have to work things out entirely on their own, without any help from their teachers or parents or friends. These people are an essential part of the experiment. If children are experimenting effectively, they have to pay attention to the outcome of their experiments, and an important part of that outcome should take the form of comments and corrections from teachers and others. So other people should play a vital part in the process of construction, but the centre of it is still the child actively trying out new ways of writing and studying the results of their actions.

The idea of construction in children's learning is of course a Piagetian one (e.g. Piaget & Inhelder, 1974). One of Piaget's main claims was that children have their own ideas about the rules that govern the world that they live in, and they do everything that they can to understand this world within this theoretical framework. However, when they realise that their theory has stopped coming up with coherent explanations for their experiences or solutions to new problems that they encounter, they eventually start to create a new and more sophisticated theory than the one that they have held to up till now.

Thus Piaget's theory was that children start with an inadequate rule and apply it as widely and as often as they can. However, eventually and inevitably, they discover that the simple rule does not cover everything that happens to them. Their first response to these encounters with exceptions to their present rule is to stick to the same kind of rule but adjust and extend it to take account of the exceptions. These adjustments then lead them into new experiences, which eventually lead them to abandon the first and inadequate kind of rule and to construct a radically new and more sophisticated one. So there are three steps from one rule to a radically new one. First the child notices exceptions to the rule that he or she has been following. Then the child tinkers with this rule in order to try to cope with the exceptions. This tinkering leads to new experiences which then give the child the information that s/he needs to form a completely new kind of rule on a radically different level.

It is not hard to apply this theoretical analysis to developmental sequences that we have found in children's spelling. First children concentrate entirely on alphabetic rules that are based on grapheme-phoneme correspondences. Next they find that there are other ways of spelling the sounds than are to be found in a simple alphabetic code. The children realise that "ed", for example, is a legitimate, though slightly odd way of writing /d/ and /t/ endings, and now they alternate between the straightforward alphabetic spelling and the new "ed" spelling. At this stage (the intermediate phase in the sequence) they are still using a phonologically-based rule, that particular sounds are spelled with particular letters, but they incorporate the idea of alternative spellings for the same sound. As a result they will now have experiences and feedback from writing the new "ed" sequence themselves. In the end these new experiences eventually and rather slowly lead the children to take the third step of learning the morphological basis for deciding whether or not "ed" is the right ending for the word in question. This is an entirely new kind of rule, and a much more sophisticated one.

Thus, in our analysis, as in Piaget's theories about children's construction of logic, children's attempts to shore up the old rule, almost perversely, provide them with the experiences that they need in order to learn the new rule. The child who in the intermediate phase, spells the final /t/ sometimes as "t" and sometimes as "ed" without any good way of choosing between these two spellings will *as a result of doing so* learn a new rule for using both of these spellings.

The third requirement: Testing with pseudo-words to see if children learn genuine morphological rules

Children must have some knowledge of the morphological structure of familiar words in order to be able to make the jump from a phonologically based approach to a morpho-phonemic set of rules. They cannot hope to understand when to use "ed" and "cks" endings and when not to, unless they can tell whether the words that they are dealing with are one- (*mist, fox*) or two- (*kissed, socks*) morpheme words. So much is obvious. But we still need to know whether a lack of morphological knowledge is a constraint in learning about morphologically-based spelling rules. Are children at first held back from learning these rules by an inadequate knowledge of the morphemic structure of the words in their vocabulary?

If we believed much of what is written about young children's morphological knowledge, the answer that we would have to give to this question would be a resounding "No". The prevailing opinion (e.g. Pinker, 1994) is that children have a good working knowledge of morphological structure at an early age and long before they learn about the conventional spellings for morphemes that we have been discussing. This widespread optimism can be traced back to the well-known experiment by Berko (1958) with pseudo-words. Berko's method was to inject a pseudo-word into a meaningful context that made the grammatical status of the word very clear. The children, whose ages ranged from 4- to 11-years, would then be asked to complete a sentence using the new word in a context that required a morphological transformation. Berko's most famous example is the single-to-plural "wug" transformation. The experimenter, using pictures, said to the child "Here is a wug. Now there is another one. Now there are two??", and asked the child to complete the sentence. The transformations that the children had to make were all from one- to two-morpheme words. They had to add a morpheme.

The children's performance in this task is usually described as entirely successful, but this is not right. They did indeed do well with the "wug" example. The pre-school (4- and 5-year-old) children turned in a score of 76% correct, while the older children were right 97% of the time. But they were much less successful with other pseudo-words. For example, only 14% of the pre-school (4- and 5-year-old) children managed a singular-to-plural "niz-nizzes" transformation successfully, and even the older children, with a score of 33% correct, were in difficulty with that example.

Much the same kind of extreme variation was found with present-to-past verb transformations. The children did well when the transformation was from the present "bing" to the past "'binged" (60% and 85% correct in the two age groups respectively), but remarkably badly with a "mott-motted" (32% and 33% correct) transformation. What is the reason for these variations?

One possible explanation turns on the fact that the difficult transformations in Berko's study were those in which last phoneme in the one-morpheme pseudo-word was also the characteristic sound (or one of the characteristic sounds) of the morpheme which they were being asked to add to that word. The ending of "niz" is the same as the ending of "knees". The last phoneme of "mott" is the same as the last phoneme of "kissed". Perhaps children are aware that plurals can end in the sound /z/ and past verbs in /t/, but do not understand that these are affixes added to a stem. So when they are asked to say "niz" in the plural, and "mott" in the past they register that these already have a plural or past ending and decide to add nothing to them. This hypothesis is different from Berko's, who argued that the reason for "niz" and "mott" being difficult was that the right suffixes for them, /ɪz/ and /ɪd/ are relatively infrequent, but it is at least as plausible. Whatever the explanation for the children's difficulties, these difficulties undoubtedly exist, and so the idea that morphological knowledge, or lack of it, might be a constraint in learning about morphologically-based spellings is a plausible one.

The question about the constraint is this: is children's success in learning about morphologically based *spelling* rules determined in any way by the extent of their knowledge of the morphological structure of words in their *spoken* vocabulary? Before even trying to answer this question, we have to defend and justify an assumption that is part of it. This assumption is that children do definitely learn morphological spelling rules, rather than just learning the spelling of two or three morpheme words by rote. This assumption is, of course, also part of the hypothesis that we have been developing through this chapter. But how can we so sure that it is a justifiable one?

The data that support this assumption most strongly come from written versions of the Berko task. We ourselves (Bryant, Nunes & Snaith, 2000) have found that 8 and 9 year old children are more likely to spell the ending a pseudo-word like "chaild" with an "ed" if it is embedded in a context that gives it the status of a past verb ("Yesterday we all chaild at home") than if the context clearly makes it a non-verb ("In France most people keep at least one chaild in each bedroom").

As we mentioned earlier in this chapter, we also have similar results with the spelling of the /ks/ ending (Bryant, 2002). Initially this morphological spelling rule causes children a lot of difficulty but eventually they realise, to some extent at least and even with pseudo-words, that they should spell the /ks/ ending in one morpheme words as "x" or "xe" and in two-morpheme words as "cks" or "kes".

Children's success in using the conventional spellings for morphemes with pseudo-words in these studies is strong evidence that they understand and use morphologically based spelling rules, at least to some extent. It should be noted that their performance in such tasks is far from perfect, and, in case you want to shrug of their successes as obvious, remember the negative results that we reported earlier over the morphological rule for spelling /z/ ending words. Most children, and many adults, blithely ignored the simple morphological rule for this ending and rely on frequency-based associations instead.

These pseudo-word tasks are an absolutely essential tool for anyone who wants to discover whether children really do understand morphological spelling rules and are not relying on rote learning. There is no other way to establish whether or not they are using these rules. Yet the method has not been used much. The pseudo-word spelling studies that we have reported have been entirely with inflectional morphemes, and not with all of them, and we know of no such studies with derivational morphemes.

Using pseudo-words to discover implicit learning

The learning that we have been discussing could be either explicit or implicit,. The distinction between implicit and explicit learning is widespread, and there is plenty of good evidence for the importance of both kinds. The distinction is important because it is relevant to teaching. Is it better to give children explicit instruction about morphological spelling rules, or should we make sure that they are given the right kind of practice to build up a sufficient stock of implicit knowledge about these rules?

Little is known either about the degree of explicit knowledge that children have of this type, or of any type, of spelling rule, and we do not have much information either about the explicit instruction that children are given about morphemes and spelling. In the current British national curriculum for reading and spelling ("The Literacy Hour") there are arrangements for the specific teaching about some morphological spelling rules, like the spelling of the past tense ending, but we cannot tell yet whether this translates into children becoming explicitly aware of these rules and consciously using them in reading and writing.

We do, however, know of one instance of a morphologically-based rule which is not taught explicitly because teachers themselves have no explicit knowledge of the rule, but which children do manage to learn, at least to some extent. This rule –quite a simple one – also concerns the English past tense ending.

Some past verbs end in the sound /d/ or /t/, and yet seem to break the "ed" rule, because these /d/ and /t/ endings are spelled phonetically. These are past verbs like "slept", "felt", "went", "heard" and "found". Typically these apparent exceptions are high frequency and therefore quite important words. Children are usually taught that they are exceptions to the general "ed" rule, which is true at a surface level, but does not describe the underlying rule.

At a deeper level, there is a conditional spelling rule that accounts both for the past verbs whose endings are spelled as "ed" and for past verbs whose endings are spelled phonetically. This rule is about the relation between the sounds of the stems of the verb the present and past tenses. In some cases these present and past tense stems sound exactly the same, as do the stems in "kiss/kissed", "kill/killed" "clap/clapped" and "pur/purred". In other cases the sounds of the two stems are different, usually because of a vowel change from the present to the past tense stem: some examples are "hear/heard", "sleep/slept", "feel/felt", "find/found". In the first group of verbs (same sounding stem in present and past) all the past verb endings are spelled as "ed". However, in the second group (different sounding stems in present and past) the endings are spelled as "d" or "t".

This is the actual rule. Verbs with the same sounding stem in present and past have "ed" endings in the past. Verbs with a different sounding stem in present and past do not have the "ed" ending and their endings are spelled according to traditional grapheme-phoneme correspondence principles. We know of only one exception to this rule. The single, rather irritating, exception is "pay/paid". Thus the endings of all past verbs with stems that sound different to the present stem are spelled phonetically. The endings of all but one of the past verbs whose stem sounds the same as in the present tense are spelled as "ed".

This is a clear, simple and apparently teachable rule, but it is hardly known and it is not taught in English schools. We interviewed 21 primary school teachers about past tense endings and all of them answered that most past verbs that end in /d/ or /t/ are spelled as "ed", but that there are some exceptions to this rule. Thus their answers were at a surface level, and none of these teachers showed any knowledge of the deeper rule that we have just described. Our attempts to elicit some explicit knowledge of this rule from some of their pupils were also fruitless. We are certain, therefore, that neither children, nor teachers, have any explicit knowledge of the deeper rule, despite its economy and its simplicity.

What about the possibility of some implicit knowledge of this untaught rule?

We (Bryant, Nunes and Snaith, 2000) looked for this type of knowledge in a series of experiments, with 8- and 9-year-old children, in which we used pseudo-verbs. In these experiments we always followed the same method, which was to dictate a passage that contained the same pseudo-verb in the present tense or as an infinitive, and in the past tense. These passages made it clear whether the stem of this entirely new verb sounded the same or different in the infinitive or in the present tense and in the past. In half the passages the stem sounded the same in present and past: "Harry is a chailer. At the moment he is chailing the teacher's book. He /chaild/ another one this morning". In the other half it sounded different: "Harry is a cheller. At the moment he is chelling the teacher's book. He /chaild/ another one this morning. If children follow the stem-based rule, they should spell the missing word as "chailed" in the first and as "chaild" in the second passage.

Each child had before her a written transcript of this passage, except that one word was missing (signified by a gap in the written passage). The missing word, which the child had a to write in, was always the past pseudo-verb. We dictated the whole passage including the past pseudo-verb, and the child's task was to put this missing verb in the gap provided as soon as he or she heard the word.

We wanted to know whether the children would assign the "ed" ending more to pseudo-verbs with the same-sounding stems in present and past than to pseudo-verbs with different sounding stems in present and past. Would they also spell the endings of different-sound past pseudo-verbs phonetically more often than the endings of same-sound past pseudo-verbs?

The answers to both these questions were positive. In three different experiments we found that 8- and 9-year old children do treat the two-kinds of pseudo-verbs differently. In all three experiments there was a consistent and significant difference between the two conditions, in the number both of "ed" endings (more in same- than in the different-sound past pseudo-verbs) and also of phonetically spelled endings (more in different- than in the same-sound past pseudo-verbs).

This result is striking and surprising. Children learn, though never perfectly, a rule which they cannot articulate, of which they almost certainly have no conscious awareness at all, and which they are never taught at school or anywhere else. This rule, though simple, is more sophisticated than a straightforward phonological spelling rule or a straightforward morphological one. It is a conditional rule that relies on a combination and a co-ordination of morphological and phonological knowledge. Yet the children managed to learn something about it on their own without any help from other people.

We also have a constructivist explanation for children's ability to learn about this rule for themselves. The children may be constructing the untaught rule for themselves, and the constructive process might be much the same as when they originally learned to use "ed". It may be that the active experience of using the "ed" ending both with same- ("clapped") and with different-sound past verbs ("sleped") gives children the information that they need to learn the conditional rule about the different between same- and different-sound stems.

One question raised by these results is about the possible effects of explicit instruction of this teachable, rule. It is possible that children can only learn it on their own and would not be helped by explicit instruction. On the other hand, explicit instruction may help them to a complete grasp of a rule that otherwise they would grasp only incompletely. The question has strong educational implications. We need to know how explicit the teacher ought to be about these morphological rules.

The fourth requirement – Morphological knowledge should be related to morphological spelling

There is a serious gap in current research on morphological knowledge and morphological spelling rules. If, as we have argued, pseudo-word spelling tasks are the acid test of children's knowledge of morphological spelling rules, then these tasks must be the outcome measure in any attempt to answer the question with which we started this section. Our initial question was whether the extent of children's general morphological knowledge constrains and determines their success in learning morphological spelling rules. To find an answer, we must surely relate measures of their knowledge of the morphological structure of spoken words to their success in a pseudo-word spelling task which tests their knowledge of morphologically-bases spelling rules. Yet, as far as we know, only one such study has ever been done.

This does not mean that the question itself has been neglected. On the contrary some of the best minds in reading research have given it the closest attention. But the outcome measures in these studies have for the most part been inadequate. From this point of view the relevant studies fall into two groups, those in which the outcome measure is some general measure of reading or spelling, and those where the outcome measure is more specifically related to the understanding of morphologically-based spelling rules. This second category is obviously the better of the two, since the question to be answered is about understanding and use of morphological rules in spelling. Studies that actually measure this understanding are closer to answering the question than studies that do not.

Here are some examples of the first category. Fowler and Liberman (1995) report a study in which they compared children of two age levels in their standards of reading and in their relative success in two morphological awareness tasks. These were production tasks, in which the child had to produce a derived word on the basis of a one-morpheme cue e.g. the experimenter said "Four: The horse came in ————" and the child had to supply the missing, derived, word. In one task the phonological relation between the cue and the derived word was transparent (e.g. four: fourth) while in the other it was not transparent. In the second condition the stem was pronounced differently in the one-morpheme cue and in the derived word (e.g. five: fifth).

Fowler and Liberman reported that this complex condition was a good predictor of reading levels, but they concluded that the reason for this connection was probably more to do with the children's phonological skills than with their morphological knowledge. They argued that it takes more phonological acuity to understand that "fifth" is related to "five" than that "fourth" is related to "four", because there is a greater phonological distance between the first than to the second of these pairs. This is pure conjecture, of course, and it is quite easy to come up with the obvious counter-argument that it must take a particularly strong sense of morphemes to get over the phonological disparity between "five" and "fifth" and see that they are morphologically related.

Nevertheless Fowler and Liberman's doubts about the importance of morphological awareness were bolstered by another comparison that they made. This took the form of a reading level match, which is a powerful comparison that the Haskins group have used all too rarely. They compared younger children whose reading was above average for their age with older children whose reading was average or worse than that. The reading level of the two groups was, as a consequence, the same, and Fowler and Liberman's argument was that if the greater difficulties of the older group were due in any way to a lack of morphological awareness, they should actually score worse in the morphological production tasks than the younger children who were clearly having no great difficulty in learning to read.

They found no such result. The younger and older groups' morphological scores were much the same, and Fowler and Liberman argued that children's morphological awareness may be determined, at least partly, by their reading experiences, rather than the other way round. This last idea is an important and a plausible one, and it deserves to be pursued. However there are serious reasons for caution about this particular study.

We have already touched on the trouble, which is that the outcome measure is too broad. Standardised tests of reading are not precise enough instruments to measure the effect of morphological knowledge on the correct use of morphological spelling rules. One needs specific outcome measures that test children's use of these spelling rules precisely. More general measures do not work because there are so many other influences on children's reading than their awareness of morphemes, as the many varied chapters in this Handbook attest.

Much the same point can be made about an otherwise interesting and sophisticated study by Carlisle (1995). She conducted a longitudinal study with Production and Judgment tests of morphological awareness. Her study also included tests of phonological awareness and of the children's reading comprehensions. She reported quite strong relations between all these variables in the first and second grade. Although Carlisle argued that children's general morphological knowledge does play a part, she ends up agreeing with Fowler and Liberman that it is hard to disentangle this form of awareness from phonological awareness. This caveat may, however, be quite unnecessary. Again the general nature of the reading measure makes it impossible to tease out any specific contribution of children's morphological knowledge. Again we need specific outcome measures as well as specific predictors.

Studies with specific outcome measures do exist. In a well known experiment Rubin (1988) administered tests not only of morphological awareness tasks (the Berry-Talbot test which uses Berko-type procedures and also Carlisle's own more explicit test of morphological judgements), but also children's of ability to adopt conventional spellings for suffixes in inflected and derived words. She found a strong relation between the morphological awareness scores and the children's knowledge of morphological spelling rules. This is a fine and important result, but there are two reasons for being cautious about it. One is that Rubin's test of children's morphological spellings, sensitive and ingenious as it was, nevertheless only contained real words. As we have seen, one has to have pseudo-words as well to avoid the possibility of specific rote learning and to establish that a rule has definitely been learned.

The other reason for caution is that in Rubin's study there was no measure of the other form of awareness waiting in the wings – phonological awareness. The claims made by Fowler and Liberman and by Carlisle make it essential for anyone trying to make a specific connection between morphological knowledge and morphological spelling to establish that this connection is not some by-product of the children's phonological skills.

This second problem, at any rate, was avoided in another study in which the outcome measure was a specific test of the use of morphological spelling rules. This was a longitudinal study by Bryant, Nunes and Bindman (2000) in which the outcome measure was a highly specific test of children's learning about one particular morphological spelling rule, the use of the apostrophe in spelling the possessive. Apostrophes cause English-speaking children a great deal of difficulty, and it is perfectly obvious that many adults never manage to learn the apparently simple rule for inserting apostrophes in possessive words. Yet there is little research on this stubborn difficulty. (We know of only one other study (Bryant, Devine, Ledward & Nunes, 1997) on the topic, besides the one that we are describing here.)

The Bryant, Nunes and Bindman study covered a period of 19 months. In the opening session and in another session 11 months later we gave children, who at the outset were aged 6, 7 and 8 years, a Word Analogy test in which we presented, for example, first the present and then the past tense of a verb, and then presented another word and asked the children to make the same transformation (the actual procedure was slightly more complex than this since it involved a puppet making the first of the two transformations). In the second of these two sessions we tested the children's phonological skills. We gave them a phoneme oddity task, in which the experimenter said three words at a time, two of which shared a common phoneme either at the beginning (log, *pet*, lid) or at the end (*film*, keeps, box) of the words, while another word (the odd word) did not contain this phoneme. The child's task was to tell us which was the odd word out.

In the third session, which came 8 months later, we gave children a test of their knowledge about the use of apostrophes to denote possession. In this test we provided the children with written sentences, which were incomplete in that one word was missing. That word, as the context made clear, was either singular possessive (genitive) word or a nominative or accusative plural word. Thus all these missing words ended in "s". Then we dictated the whole sentence, including the missing word. Some examples of these various sentences are "The *dog's* tail is wagging." "The *dogs* are barking." "Is this the *boy's* football." "Look at the *boys* playing football." In all these examples the missing word is the italicised one. The child's task was to write in that word, and the question was whether he or she would leave out the apostrophe in the plural, nominative or accusative words and put it in the possessive words.

The children, whose ages now were 8, 9 or 10 years, did not do well in this apostrophe task, but their scores varied a lot, and the most interesting result for us was the extent to which the morphological (Word Analogy) and the phonological (Phoneme Oddity) tasks, given in the earlier sessions, predicted their success with the apostrophes. The clear answer was that the morphological scores predicted the children's performance in the apostrophe task. In a hierarchical multiple regression, in which the outcome measure was the children's performance in the apostrophe task, we entered age, IQ and the children's overall reading levels first, and thus controlled for the effects of differences in these powerful variables. Nonetheless, the morphological scores in the initial and the following session both accounted for a significant portion of the variance in the apostrophe task. In contrast the phonological scores were nowhere near being successful predictors of the children's scores in the apostrophe task, even though these same phonological scores predicted their reading levels very well indeed, as they usually do.

This result is the strongest evidence that there is for an independent and specific contribution of morphological knowledge to children's learning of morphologically based spelling rules. However, it concerns one spelling contrast only – the contrast between regular plural endings and possessive endings. It is a start, but we badly need much the same kind of study with other morphological rules such as regular past tense inflectional endings and the contrast between the – ian and the –ion derivational endings.

SUMMARY

We began this chapter by showing that there are many morphologically-based spelling rules in English and in other European orthographies, and that these are rules of great importance. Then we set out four requirements for establishing that children learn some, at least, of these rules. These were that:

We should show that children learn phonologically-based and morphologically based spelling rules at different times

We should be able to chart the course and the nature of their learning of morphologically-based rules

We should be able to show, with the use of pseudo-words, that the children are learning genuine rules and not specific word associations

We should demonstrate strong and specific connection between children's morphological knowledge and their success in learning morphologically-based spelling rules.

The evidence that we have presented goes a long way to fulfil all four of these criteria. Children do learn the morphological rules some time after conquering the basis grapheme-phoneme associations, and so morphological learning definitely follows phonological learning in the acquisition of spelling rules.

There are too some interesting data on the way that children learn the morphological rules: the patterns of generalisation and overgeneralisation of the new spelling patterns are evidence that the learning of morphological spelling rules takes a distinctive course.

It is also clear, from research with pseudo-words that in some cases at least children are learning genuine, abstract, rules. That appears to be the case with the "-ed" past tense inflection and with the contrast between one and two morpheme words ending in /cs/. However, there is a serious need to extend this use of pseudo-word tests to other morphological spelling rules as well. As Kemp's (2000: see also Kemp and Bryant, 2003) work clearly shows, we cannot assume genuine rule learning in every case. Her experiments demonstrated that even the simple spelling rule for plural endings, that "s" is the always correct spelling for regular plural endings whether the sound of the ending is /s/ or /z/, seems to escape many adults and most young children.

Finally, there is some evidence – but again not enough yet – of a strong and specific connection between children's explicit awareness of morphological structure and their success in learning morphologically based spelling rules. The connection between morphological knowledge and learning how to spell morphemes seems plausible and almost tautological, and yet it had proved terribly difficult to provide hard and convincing evidence that the connection exists. One study does show that it plays an important part in learning a particular morphological rule – the contrast between plural and possessive endings – but that is just a start. We badly need similar work with other morphological spelling rules.

What else needs to be done? In our view, the last of the four questions raises the most pressing problems, because of its clear educational implications. If learning how to spell morphemes depends on children's understanding that words can be broken up into morphemes, surely we should teach them about morphological structure as well as about spelling patterns. So researchers must do more well-designed longitudinal studies which measure, in a controlled and convincing manner, the connections between how much children know about particular morphemes and how well they learn the spelling rules for these morphemes.

If, as we predict, studies of this sort do show a strong connection between these two variables, their direct implication will be that we should be teaching children about morphemes. This conclusion immediately suggests another type of study – the intervention study. If teaching is needed, how do we do it? And if we do succeed in teaching children about morphemic stricture, will this in turn affect their spelling. So far, psychologists have stayed clear of intervention studies as far as morphemes are concerned. In our view, this kind of research, when it happens, will establish once and for all how important it is for children to be aware of the morphological structure of the words that they speak and to be able think about this structure when they when they are learning how to spell these words correctly.

REFERENCES

Aidinis, A. (1998) Phonemes, morphemes and literacy: evidence from Greek. Unpublished Phd. thesis. Institute of Education, University of London.

Berko, J. (1958) The child's learning of English morphology. *Word, 14*, 150-177.

Bryant, P., (2002) Children's thoughts about reading and spelling. *The Scientific Study of Reading, 6*, 199-216.

Bryant, P., Devine, M., Ledward, A. & Nunes, T. (1997) Spelling with apostrophes and understanding possession. *British Journal of Educational Psychology, 67*, 93-112.

Bryant, P., Nunes, T. & Aidinis, A. (1999) Different morphemes, same spelling problems: cross-linguistic developmental studies. In M. Harris & G. Hatano (Eds.) *Learning to read and write: a cross-linguistic perspective* (pp. 112-133). Cambridge: Cambridge University Press.

Bryant, P., Nunes, T. & Bindman, M. (2000) The relations between children's linguistic awareness and spelling: the case of the apostrophe. *Reading and Writing, 12*, 253-276.

Bryant, P., Nunes, T. & Snaith, R. (2000) Children learn an untaught rule of spelling. *Nature, 403*, 157-158.

Carlisle, J. F. (1988). Knowledge of derivational morphology and spelling ability in fourth, sixth and eighth graders. *Applied Psycholinguistics, 9*, 247-266.

Chliounaki, K. and Bryant, P. (2002) Construction and learning to spell. *Cognitive Development, 17*, 1489-1499.

Fayol, M., Thenevin, M.-G., Jarousse, J.-P. & Totereau, C. (1999) From Learning to Teaching to Learn French written morphology. In T. Nunes (Ed.) *Learning to Read: an integrated view from research and practice* (pp. 43-64). Dordrecht, The Netherlands: Kluwer.

Fowler, A. E. and Liberman, I. Y. (1995) The role of phonology and orthography in morphological awareness. In L.B. Feldman (Ed.), *Morphological aspects of language processing.* (pp. 157-188). Hillsdale, NJ: Lawrence Earlbaum.

Kemp, N. (2000) The representation of morphology in children's spelling. Unpublished thesis. Oxford: Oxford University.

Kemp, N. & Bryant, P. (2003) Do bees buzz? Rule-based and frequency-based knowledge in learning to spell the plural-s. *Child Development, 74*, 63–74.

Marsh, G. & Desberg, P. (1983) The development of strategies in the acquisition of symbolic skills. In D. R. Rogers and J. A. Sloboda (Eds.), *The Acquisition of Symbolic Skills* (pp. 149-154). New York: Plenum Press.

Marsh, G., Friedman, M. P., Desberg, P. and Saterdahl, K. (1981) Comparison of reading and spelling strategies in normal and reading disabled children. In M. Friedman, J. P. Das & N. O'Connor (Eds.), *Intelligence and Learning* (pp. 363-367). New York: Plenum Press.

Marsh, G., Friedman, M. P., Welch, V. & Desberg, P. (1980) The development of strategies in spelling. In U. Frith (Ed.), *Cognitive Processes in Spelling*. London: Academic Press.

Nunes, T., Bryant, P. & Bindman, M. (1997) Morphological spelling strategies: developmental stages and processes. *Developmental Psychology, 33,* 637-649.

Nunes, T., Roazzi, A. & Buarque, L. L. (2003) Learning to mark stress in written Portuguese. *Faits de Langue*, in press.

Piaget, J. & Inhelder, B. (1974) *The child's construction of quantities*. London: Routledge & Kegan Paul.

Pinker , S. (1994) *The Language Instinct*. London: Penguin Books.

Read, C. (1986) *Children's Creative Spelling*. London: Routledge & Kegan Paul.

Rubin, H. (1988) Morphological knowledge and early writing ability. *Language and Speech, 31*, 337-355.

Templeton, S. & Bear, D. R. (Eds.) (1992) *Development of orthographic knowledge and the foundations of literacy*. Hillsdale, NJ: Lawrence Erlbaum.

Totereau, C., Thenevin, M.-G. & Fayol, M. (1997) The development of the understanding of number morphology in written French. In C. A. Perfeti, L. Rieben & M. Fayol (Eds.), *Learning to spell: Research, Theory and Practice across Languages* (pp. 97-114). Mahwah, NJ: Lawrence Erlbaum Ass.

Treiman, R. (1993). *Beginning to spell*. New York: Oxford University Press.

SUGGESTED FURTHER READINGS

Harris, M. & Hatano, G. (1999), *Learning to read and write. A cross-linguistic perspective*. Cambridge: Cambridge University Press.

Nunes, T., Bryant, P. & Bindman, M. (1997) Morphological spelling strategies: developmental stages and processes. *Developmental Psychology, 33,* 637-649.

Nunes, T., Bryant, P. & Olsson, J. M. (2003) Learning morphological and phonological spelling rules: An intervention study. *The Scientific Study of Reading, 7*, 289-307.

Perfeti, C. A., Rieben, L. & Fayol, M. (1997), *Learning to spell: Research, Theory and Practice across Languages*. Mahwah, NJ: Lawrence Erlbaum Ass.

Templeton, S. & Bear, D. R. (Eds.) (1992), *Development of orthographic knowledge and the foundations of literacy*. Hillsdale, NJ: Lawrence Erlbaum.

A6. Children's Self-Perception as Readers

URSULA PRETZLIK & LILY CHAN

ABSTRACT

Reading self-perception refers to a set of beliefs, observations and attitudes that children have about themselves as learners especially related to reading and reading related activities. Reading is central to children's academic progress; they read in and out of school – all over the world – and depending on their specific needs they "choose" their tools from range of scripts and languages.

A positive attitude by parents, teachers and the children themselves towards academic work and scholastic achievement supports the learning process. Quite possibly subtle "messages" conveyed by teachers in form of verbal, written and behavioural feedback to pupils about their ability and academic performance influence not only the view pupils have of themselves, but also the view they have of their classmates' expectations within the classroom. When pupils are aware of what is expected from them, their performance is likely to be in accordance with those expectations. It therefore follows that teachers' expectations of their pupils – high or low – influences a pupil's academic performance.

At long last a child's self-perception as reader is receiving attention. Bear in mind that reading self-perception does not relate directly to objective measures of academic performance or to the perceptions of significant others such as peers and teachers. These measures are designed to explore the view the child holds about his or her performance. They are not designed to predicting actual academic performance, that is not their intended propose. Research into this area began in the 1990s when four measures designed to assess children's perception about their reading ability became available.

Self-perception – a psychological construct – refers to the core of a person's self-awareness. The construct enables children to describe themselves, to appraise what they are like and to put importance onto these evaluations. In our chapter we attempt to give an account of how children feel about themselves and their learning and their reading in particular. First we introduce the theoretical background that relates to a person's self-concept; once we have established this basic ideas we consider research methods and research designs, which are used to measure a child's self-concept in general and reading self-perception in particular. Finally we propose to you as practitioners and researchers that children's reading

T. Nunes, P. Bryant (eds.), Handbook of Children's Literacy, 119–146.
© 2004 *Kluwer Academic Publishers. Printed in Great Britain.*

self-perception should be considered within the context of the child's social situation – especially the teacher and the classmates.

INTRODUCTION

The self is fundamental to all social concepts. Self-perception, a psychological construct, refers to the core of an individual's self-awareness. It enables individuals to describe themselves, to evaluate the different features of this description and to apportion importance to those features. Self-perception also facilitates an appreciation as to how the features combine to produce what they recognise as themselves. The self is a strong motivating force behind human behaviour and its development starts at an early age.

Children do not react automatically to everyday experiences. They tend to interpret consciously what is happening around them. They consider events unfolding and take notice of the behaviour of others, which in turn affects them. Their response to these experiences depends partly on their evaluation and partly on the manifestation of other people's evaluations of them – a framework characteristic of the theory introduced by Cooley (1902) and Mead (1934).

When children enter school, they already bring with them a bias towards achievement or failures resulting from home experience, including parental influence and interest. Their self-perception dictates the expectations they have for themselves and therefore affects their management and performance in the school environment. School children notice and sense not only how their teacher interacts with them, but also how the same teacher interacts with the other children in the classroom. Nash (1976), Crocker and Cheeseman (1988), Pitkänen and Nunes (2000), and Nunes and Pretzlik (2000) have shown that young children have the ability to assess accurately a teacher's perception of them and their classmates.

The symbolic interactionist theorists (e.g. Cooley, 1902; Mead, 1934; Harter, 1996) put forward the notion that children first observe the way in which significant others react to them and then respond to that reaction. Here "significant others" are defined as those people who are sufficiently important to children for the children to regard signals given by them as a measure or comparison of their own abilities. Significant others intensify or reduce children's feelings of security and insecurity, and contribute to increases and decreases in their feelings of helplessness. As a result it can be said that significant others are capable of promoting or diminishing a child's sense of worth (Burns, 1982; Babad, Bernieri & Rosenthal, 1991; Saracho, 1991; Harter, 1998).

Close family members are the first significant others in a child's life. However, from the time children enter school, teachers and peers also have influence on how children see themselves. Teachers' assessments of their pupils are communicated through verbal and non-verbal behaviour. Pupils interpret this behaviour and the interpretations they make contribute to the development of a concept of self as a learner within the school and more specifically within the environment of the classroom.

For children to be able to distinguish between their own and others' abilities first requires an understanding of how abilities are structured – for example, whether teachers and parents differentiate between academic domains, between children's performance in sport, maths and literacy or if they hold broader, more universal views of children's competence. The notion of a universal self-concept, put forward in the 1960s (e.g. Coopersmith, 1967; Rosenberg, 1965), has been revised and extended through a multidimensional, hierarchical model first proposed by Shavelson, Hubner and Stanton (1976). This hierarchical model, as well as the revised version by Marsh and Shavelson (1985), was developed within the context of children's education and it can therefore be assumed that this model includes and is related to an academic self-concept, on that divides itself into a variety of related domains.

The self is not a simple unitary concept, but a complex system made up of different constructs or domains each of which deserves to be investigated in its own right. In this chapter the focus tends to lean towards one aspect of children's academic self and their self-perception as readers.

In the following section the theoretical background related to children's self-concept is going to be introduced first. The theoretical background is followed by a discussion on how children's self-concept can be measured. Then some approaches, which permit to measure children's self-perception of their reading ability, are presented. Finally, we propose that the academic self-concept – reading in particular – should to be looked at in light of a child's social situation, including their teacher and peers.

THEORETICAL BACKGROUND OF CHILDREN'S SELF-CONCEPT

William James, who lived in the United States, began to write down his ideas about the self in the 1890s. Generally recognised as the first psychologist to develop a theory of self-concept, James proposed that the self is essentially private and sometimes well concealed. The self-concept, according to James, is formed by individuals through their perception and their subsequent internalisation of the views and behaviours others have of them. He set a precedent and anticipated many of the subsequent developments in self-concept theory.

James (1892; also in Allport, 1985) identified two distinct but intimately intertwined aspects of self. He makes a basic distinction between the "I" and the "Me": the I as the self-as-knower – and the me as the self-as-known. That is to say the I is the object of a person's perception when that person reflects on him or herself. Although James regarded the global self to be the I – and the empirical self to be the Me – the Me is defined as the sum total of everything a person calls his or her own. The I-self is the active observer, whereas the Me-self is the observed – the result of self-observations through others' eyes.

James classified three components in descending order of importance; in his theory they make up a major part of the Me-self. The material self incorporates the bodily self and all a person can call "mine". The bodily self is the innermost part of the material self. James states that a certain amount of bodily egotistical behaviour is needed to form the base for "other selves", from which the hierarchical scale of constructs is derived. The social self reflects the recognition received from others. Given the potential for variation in the characteristics that others might recognise, James notes that a person has as many social selves as there are individuals who recognise this person and who carry images of him or her in their minds. His concept of the social self anticipated the importance of the evaluations by specific and generalised others that was to become an important focus of symbolic interactionists such as Cooley (1902) and Mead (1934). The spiritual self was regarded by James as the most enduring aspect of the self and includes an individual's thoughts, dispositions and moral judgements. From a historical perspective, James' theory formed the foundation for future theories, especially those theories of the self, based on the premise of the individual evaluating him or herself within a hierarchical (vertical) and multidimensional (horizontal) model.

A positive self-concept is known to be an advantageous quality in many areas of life, including in young people's educational processes. To study the structure of a self-concept and in particulare pupils' self-concept as learners a number of researchers used Susan Harter's model (1985; e.g. Entwisle, Alexander, Pallas & Cadigan, 1987), while others have applied Marsh and Shavelson's model (1985; e.g. Byrne, 1996; Skaalvik & Hagtvet, 1990; Marsh, Craven & Debus, 1991; Blatchford, 1997). It is generally assumed that academic achievements and the perception of self within an academic context are related. Of the issues addressed by researchers concerning self-concept and academic achievement, the one that has been the most complex has been the question of whether academic self-concept influences academic achievement, or whether instead, academic achievement influences academic self-concept.

Byrne (1984) reported that for every study that argues in favour of the impact of academic self-concept on academic achievement, there is a comparable one that claims the opposite to be true. Of 23 studies reviewed, 11 argued for a causal flow from self-concept to academic achievement, 11 for an academic achievement to self-concept flow, and only one study was unable to determine a direction at all. For a review of the literature on the link between academic achievement and self-concept, the reader is advised to refer to Hattie (1992) and Byrne (1996).

According to Harter (1986), Marsh and Shavelson (1985) and others, self-concept is a multidimensional construct. For example, distinctions have been made by Harter between global characteristics of a child "I am happy the way I am', social characteristics "I have as many friends as I want', school performance "I can do my school work quickly' and reading performance "I am good at reading long words". The Marsh and Shavelson model consist of domains, which divide and multiply as children learn, develop and get older (e.g. Byrne &

Shavelson, 1986; Marsh, 1986). Moving from the top to the bottom of this hierarchical image, the structure becomes increasingly differentiated. More specifically, global self-concept that sits on the top divides into two main dimensions – the academic self-concept and the non-academic self-concept. These two dimensions then sub-divide once more – the academic dimension into subject areas such as mathematics and English, and the non-academic dimension into areas such as the social, the emotional and the physical self. In sum, this model can be thought of as pyramid-shaped, organised with perceptions of a general self-concept at the top, inferences about sub-areas such as academia, social relationships and sports somewhere in the middle and a variety of behaviours related to more specific situations at its base. For example, children's perceptions of their ability to read may affect their self-perceptions of overall levels of academic competence and these in turn will modify their perceptions of global self-concept (see Byrne, 1996 for a detailed description and diagrams).

Despite the rich and dynamic beginning of the theory of self-concept first provided by James (1892; 1899) research and measurement advances have progressed slowly. Unfortunately James did not evaluate his elegant supposition and more specifically neither did he evaluate the distinction and interdependence he reported between the Me-self and the I-self. Yet, subsequent researchers have turned their attention to assessing the self as an object of perceived knowledge and judgement and more recently the I-self has been considered with a focused on children's development of the self (see Hattie, 1992; Bracken, 1996; Ferrari & Sternberg, 1998; Harter 1999). In this chapter we write with children in mind.

METHODOLOGICAL ISSUES RELATED TO ASSESSING SELF-PERCEPTION IN CHILDREN

Studies that attempt to measure either self-perception in general (global, which is unidimensional) or children's self-perception in particular (academic, which itself is multidimensional, e.g. maths, art, reading), from the start run into a number of methodological difficulties. One such difficulty is to locate and choose a valid and reliable measuring tool – a safe way of assessing self-perception. Many researchers have developed their own instruments, many of which were poorly checked for reliability and validity. In the past these instruments have often been crudely described and were difficult to locate. Contemporary self-concept research reflects progress in two areas: (a) newly developed self-concept instruments designed to measure multiple facets of the construct and (b) more substantive self-concept research designed to take these multiple facets into account (Byrne, 1996).

The two main methods used to measure self-perception in children are self-report and observation. Self-report involves responding to statements or items related to the way an individual thinks of him or herself or the way a significant other – for example the class teacher or a peer – perceives one of the pupils. Of the many possible self-report methods rating scales, checklists, Q sort, open-ended interviews, ranking others and self-ranking should be considered when designing a project linked to children's self-perception. Observational methods can be carried out by a one or more than one observers. Behaviours are often recorded using simple pencil and paper methods. The results of these real life observations can be supported through audio recordings, which are transcribed. Observations can also be recorded on video and analysed at a later stage. Data can be obtained in a structured way by use of a checklist or rating scale covering valid verbal interaction and behaviour categories.

MEASURES: CHILDREN'S SELF-CONCEPT

Children's self-esteem is often measured through rating scales. They are constructed to enable the child to respond to a set of specific, predetermined questions or statements (e.g. Wylie, 1974; Harter, 1985; Piers, 1984; Battle, 1992; Bracken, 1992; Coopersmith 1984; Brown & Alexander, 1991; Marsh, 1990).

Harter's (1982) original measure The Perceived Competence Scale for Children questionnaire and the Revised Version (Harter, 1985) were developed to elicit children's domain specific judgements of their own competence, as well as a global perception of their worth or esteem as a person. When this measure was first developed through interviews and observations with a large cross section of children and young people, separate sub-scales emerged. The Perceived Competence Scale for Children questionnaire taps competence domains such as Physical Appearance through statement such as "Some children wish something about their face or hair looked different." BUT "Other children like their face and hair the way they are." Behavioural Conduct "Some children do things they know they shouldn't do." BUT "Other children hardly ever do things they know they shouldn't." Scholastic Competence "Some children are pretty slow at finishing their work." BUT "Other children can do their work quickly." Social Acceptance "Some children are always doing things with a lot of children." BUT "Other children usually do things by themselves." Athletic Competence "Some children feel that they are better than others their age at sport." BUT "Other children don't feel that they can play as well." plus Global Self-worth "Some children are very happy being the way they are." BUT "Other children wish they were different".

This measure is designed for children between the ages of eight and 18. According to Harter, by the age of eight children not only make discrete judgements about their competence in different domains, but they have already constructed a view of their general self-worth as a person – over and above the specific competence judgement. Three age appropriate scales have derived from the original scale and are widely used. They are: (1) the Pictorial Scale of Perceived Competence and Social Acceptance for Younger Children for children from four to seven years (Harter & Pike, 1984), (2) the Self-Perception Profile for Children rating scale for school age children from seven to 13 years (Harter,

1985), and (3) for the Self-Perception Profile for Adolescence rating scale for young people from 13 to 18 years (Harter, 1988).

For school age children, the Self-Perception Profile for Children rating scale has shown to be a valid and reliable self-report instrument suitable for use with children of "reading" age. Children's perception of self-esteem is looked at both directly through Global Self-worth and indirectly through domain specific judgements. Each sub-scale is made up of six statements where the children indicate what sort of a person they perceive themselves to be. The part statement on the left of the scale, for instance, says "Some children often forget what they learn' and the part statement on the right "Other children remember things easily". After the children indicate the answer most appropriate for them, they are asked whether this is "Really true for me' or "Sort of true for me". The range of scores for each statement is 1 to 4 and the possible range for each sub-scale is 6 to 24. This question format not only provides a 4 point ordinal data record of a child's perception of competence and self-worth, but also efficiently reduces a child's tendency to give socially desirable responses.

In general, results from rating scales provide valuable information and are relatively objective. Furthermore, their data are suited to quantitative analysis and results can be compared within and between individuals. Nonetheless, two drawbacks should be born in mind when considering this method. Firstly, the completion of a rating scale requires a certain degree of verbal competence for children to understand the questions put to them and for them to be able to verbalise their answers related to these questions. Secondly, because of the confined structure of a questionnaire and its demand on cognitive maturity, detailed descriptive information is invariably lost along the way.

In the next section we will describe some contemporary academic self-concept measures (e.g. Marsh, 1990a; 1990b; Pitkänen & Nunes, 2000; Chapman & Tunmer, 1993; Henk & Melnick, 1995; Gambrell, Palmer, Codling & Mazzoni, 1996). They have been designed to reflect children's self-perception independently from their academic achievement. Academic self-concept itself does not relate directly to objective measures of academic performance or to the perceptions a child's academic achievement of significant others, peers and teachers for example. These measures are designed to explore what children think their academic performance is like and what they feel about their academic performance. The academic self-concept measures are not designed to predict children's actual academic performance – that is not their intended purpose.

MEASURES: CHILDREN'S SELF-PERCEPTION AS READERS

Learning to read is a key activity and is central to children's academic progress. All over the world children read and write at home and in school – they use a variety of scripts and languages according to their geographical and social position.

Teachers have long recognised that motivation is crucial to young children learning to read (Dweck & Leggett, 1988). A positive attitude by parents, teachers and the children themselves towards reading supports the learning process. Initial reading difficulties can lead to poor academic performance, which in turn will result in negative self-perceptions and negative learning attitudes (Stanovich, 1986).

As a number of complex and interacting variables are likely to be involved, children's self-perception as readers is difficult to measure. These variables include the child's temperament, cognitive ability, and social and educational experiences. Due to the difficulties involved in following children's development and in order to incorporate the challenge to understand some of these changes, qualitative research methods such as ethnography, case studies, interviews and observations, should be considered by researchers in addition to quantitative methods which include rating scales and structured observations.

If, for example, a researcher wants to find out how two poor readers in a primary school are supported by the teacher and their peers and how they perceive themselves as readers, they could use a range of qualitative methods. The researcher might observe the whole class and the two poor readers in particular. They could undertake one-to-one interviews with the poor readers, their peers and the teacher. The findings might then show that the two poor readers described having good peer support in the classroom and felt they had learned basic reading skills. When comparing their self-perception as readers to that of their classmates no significant difference might be found. If this were the case, then this would be a positive result in its own right. The danger, however, would be to misinterpret this result by generalising the finding based on just two pupils and so to conclude that poor readers don't have lower self-esteem than good readers.

Reading self-perception refers to a set of beliefs, perceptions and attitudes that children have about themselves as learners in reading and reading related activities (Wilson, Chapman & Tunmer, 1995). Despite increasing recognition of the significance of young children's self-perception as readers, there was in the past a virtual absence of research on its development during the onset of the acquisition process. Two main reasons contribute to this lack of empirical evidence; one stems from conflicting ideas about the structure and timing of the emergence of young children's academically related self-perception, and the other from a lack of measures of self-perception suitable for young readers.

However, children's reading self-perception is currently receiving attention. Research into this area began in the 1990s when four instruments designed to measure reading self-concept became available. They are the Reading Self-Concept Scale (Chapman & Tunmer, 1993; Wilson et al., 1995), the Reader Self-Perception Scale (Henk & Melnick, 1995), the Motivation to Read Profile (Gambrell et al., 1996) and Children's Self-Perception as Readers (Pitkänen & Nunes, 2000). In the following section, these four instruments will be discussed and some of their characteristics highlighted.

THE READING SELF-CONCEPT SCALE

In 1993 Chapman and Tunmer published the Reading Self-Concept Scale. It measures children's ability to describe themselves as readers and is relevant for beginning readers to children with three to four years reading experience. The items are designed to assess a range of reading-related self-perceptions. Ten questions make up the practice section and another thirty the three sub-components – Competence in Reading, Difficulties in Reading and Attitudes toward Reading. The sub-components in turn form the main section of the scale.

The children begin by answering the practice section, which helps them become used to the interviewer and to the format of the scale. Practice items include "Do you like climbing trees?", "Is painting pictures hard for you?" or "Can other kids swim better than you?". Next come ten statements to assess Competence in Reading, i.e. "Can you work out what a story means?", "Are you good at fixing up mistakes in reading?" and "Can you work out hard words in a story even if there are no pictures?". Ten questions assess Difficulty with Reading i.e. "Is reading in the class hard for you?", "Do you make lots of mistakes in reading?" or "Is it hard for you to understand stories you have to read in class?". And finally another ten questions assess Attitudes Towards Reading i.e. "Do you feel good when you do reading work?", "Do you like reading in class?" or "Do you like reading at home?".

The negative questions are carefully worded, for example "Do you find it hard to understand the stories you have to read in class?" rather than "I can't understand the stories I have to read in class". The three sub-components are made up of 30 questions and these are presented to the child in a mix order design. A scoring key helps the researcher keep count.

The Reading Self-Concept Scale is administered during one-to-one interviews where each of the statements is read aloud to the child. The interview tends to last about 25 minutes. A 5-point Likert-type scale is used to record the answers. The scores are from no, never (1); no, not usually (2); child understands sentence but is not sure (3); yes, usually (4); to yes, always (5). The authors reported solid internal reliability for their scale ($\alpha = .85$ at 5 years; $\alpha = .84$ at 6 years and $\alpha = .85$ at 7 years).

Using this measure, Chapman and Tunmer (1993) explored the theoretical consistency of the three sub-components mentioned above. These components originate from the reading area of academic self-concept based on Marsh and Shavelson's model (1985), namely, children's perceptions of Competence in Reading, their perceptions of Difficulty with Reading, and Attitudes Towards Reading. Perceptions of Competence refer to beliefs regarding their own ability and strengths such as "Are you good at remembering words?" Perceptions of Difficulty refer to beliefs that reading activities are hard and problematic, for example "Do you need extra help in reading?" Attitudes to reading are defined in terms of affinity and feelings "Do you like reading in class?" Chapman and Tunmer report that a clear distinction between perceptions of competence and perceptions of difficulty should be made. The distinction is important because young children often hold positive self-perceptions of ability, while perceiving that they have reading difficulties. A low rating on self-concept items in perceptions of competence does not necessarily reflect the kind of reading difficulties children face at home and in the classroom. Such difficulties may lead some of them to have negative reading self-perceptions.

Clarity of items is a fundamental contributor to the validity of a scale. Thus it is necessary to consider whether some children may understand the language used in the scale, but still have difficulties with the content; for examples "Are you good at remembering words?", "Can you work out hard words by yourself when you read?" may pose problems for young children who are still developing insight into what reading involves.

A difficulty Chapman and Tunmer fail to consider is that "...children's self evaluations are mainly a reflection of other people's evaluation" (Cooley, 1902). The 30 statements which make up the Reader Self-Perception Scale are based entirely on children's observation of their own performances, and do not include any kind of social feedback regarding their reading. On entrance to school, teachers as well as other pupils, become important influences on how children view themselves as learners (Rosenthal & Jacobson, 1968). It is, therefore, crucial that a rating scale includes children's assessment of their own ability as well as their views about others' perception of their own reading ability. Results of the Reading Self-Concept Scale would be enhanced if additional measures were introduced to take into account academic performance, the perception of the academic performance by the pupils, as well as what the pupils believe the teacher thinks of their reading, writing and comprehension ability.

THE READING SELF-PERCEPTION SCALE

Henk and Melnick (1995) developed the Reader Self-Perception Scale to assess how children of primary school age feel about themselves as readers. Test results can be used for whole groups or individual assessments, as well as intervention studies. The scale is based on the theoretical framework of Bandura's self-efficacy (1977; 1982). Here, self-efficacy is defined as "a person's judgements of her or his ability to perform an activity, and the effect this performance has on the on-going and future conduct of the activity" (Henk & Melnick, 1995; p. 471). Perceptions of self-efficacy are assumed to influence children's over all academic achievement, and reading in particular. Children, who perceive themselves as good readers, tend to choose to read, whereas children, who perceive themselves as poor readers, tend to avoid reading. Similarly children, who perceive themselves as good readers, are inclined to put more effort into a reading task and enjoy doing so whereas children with a lower perception of their reading ability generally put less effort into a reading task (Bandura & Schunk, 1981; Dweck, 1999). It can therefore be said that the effect of performance in the first place influences performance at a later stage. Good readers become better readers and poor readers lag behind.

The Reading Self-Perception Scale is a reliable and valid measure designed for children in the 4, 5 and 6th grade of primary school. It can be administered in small groups and completed within approximately 20 minutes. Thirty-two items assess self-perceptions represented by four sub-scales. The sub-scales are (1) Progress, made up of 9 items, is defined as how a pupil's perception of present reading performance compares with their performance in the past. For example "When I read I need less help then I used to" and "I am getting better at reading". (2) Observational Comparison, made up of 6 items, deals with how children perceive their reading performance compared with the performance of their classmates. For example "I seem to know more words than other kids when I read" and "I read better than other kids in my class". (3) Social Feedback, made up of 9 items, includes direct or indirect input about reading ability from teachers, classmates, and family members "Other kids think I am a good reader" and "People in my family think I read pretty well". Finally (4) Physiological State, made up of 8 items, refers to internal feelings that children experience while reading. Examples are "I feel good inside when I read" and " I feel comfortable when I read". Internal reliabilities for the four scales have been reported as good, ranging from (α =. 81 to α =. 84).

Using this scale and similar to Chapman and Tunmer's own scale, children are asked to indicate how strongly they agree or disagree with each item on a 5-point Likert-type scale. The items in Observational Comparison and Physiological States are similar to the section of Perception of Competence in reading and Attitudes to reading in the Chapman and Tunmer scale. However, the notion that literacy learning is socially situated and influenced by significant others is incorporated into Henk and Melnick's Reader Self-Perception Scale. They assume that while establishing reader self-perceptions, individual children take into account social feedback from others such as teachers, peers and parents. In this rating scale, there is a strong component of how children perceive other people's opinions of them as readers "My teacher thinks I am a good reader" or "My classmates like to listen to me read". Recent studies have shown that children's self-perception of ability relative to others has important implications in the build up of their own perceptions (Blumenfeld, Pintrich, Meece & Wessels, 1982; Pitkänen & Nunes, 2000; Nunes & Pretzlik, 2000; Tsolaidou & Pretzlik, 2000).

The Motivation to Read Profile

Reading motivation is defined "by an individual's self-concept and the values the individual places on reading" (Gambrell et al., 1996; p. 519). The Motivation to Read Profile designed by Gambrell et al. consists of two related instruments and a combination of methods: the Reading Survey and the Conversational Interview.

The Motivation to Read Profile assesses children's perception of self as readers and the value they attach to it.

The scale is applicable for children from grade 2 to grade 6, and can be administered either individually or in small groups taking about 20 minutes. The authors report good validity and high inter-rater reliability of the scale ($\alpha = .75$ for self-concept and $\alpha = .82$ for value; pre-and post-test reliability $\alpha = .68$ for self-concept and $\alpha = .70$ for value).

The first part of the measure consists of 22 statements. There are two sample items (1) I am in second, third, fourth, fifth or sixth grade (2) I am – a boy/a girl". Ten statements define children's Self-concept as a Reader, "I read – not as well as my friends; about the same as my friends; a little better than my friends or a lot better than my friends". Another ten statements define their Value of Reading, i.e. "I think reading is – a boring way to spend time; an OK way to spend time; an interesting way to spend time or a great way to spend time". All of the statements are responded to on a 4-point scale. The statements are answered on an even number scale designed to avoid neural, central responses. In this case the children have to make a clear decision when answering each item. In order to avoid response bias in the form of "yes" or "no" throughout, some items are graded from most to least positive and others from least to most positive.

The purpose of the interview is to supplement quantitative data provided by the questionnaire with qualitative data. The first part of the assessment – the ratings scale – is extended by a conversational one-to-one interview. For the second part of the assessment the teacher or researcher takes about 20 minutes to talk to the children about their motivations to read. Where possible the interview should be taped and transcribed. The interview schedule consists of 14 predetermined, open-ended questions, which in turn are divided into three sections. They are (1) Narrative reading, i.e. "Tell me about the most interesting story or book that you have read this week (or last week). Take a few minutes to think about it. (Waiting time) Now, tell me about the book or story." (2) Informational reading, i.e. "Think about something important you learned recently, not from your teacher and not from television, but from a book or some other reading material. What did you read about? (Waiting time) Tell me about what you learned." and (3) General reading, i.e. "Tell me about your favourite author. Again, take a few minutes to think about it (Waiting time)". Children's responses can be probed. Questions such as "What else can you tell me?" or "Is there anything else?" are used during the interview. Throughout the interview the children are encouraged to give free responses, which relate directly to them and their experiences.

The Motivation to Read Profile (Gambrell et al., 1996) is somewhat similar to the Reading Self-Concept Scale (Henk & Melnick, 1995). Both measures include statements with reference to children's own observations of reading ability and motivation to read. They also give children a chance to refer to significant others' observations of reading ability and motivation and thereby touch on symbolic interactionist theories of self put forward by Cooley (1902) and others. Children observe the way in which others – family members or the teacher – react to them as readers and report on the observations.

READING ABILITY: SELF-PERCEPTION AND PERCEPTION BY OTHERS

A further line of theoretical research suggests that academic self-concept is affected by a frame of reference effect where academic self-concept involves a self-assessment of relative and not absolute competence (Marsh, 1990a; 1990b; Bouffard & Vezeau, 1998). Common sense would dictate that children base their views of themselves as learners on the "reality" of their ability – that is to say on their actual school performance. However, this is not necessarily so. Hattie (1992) reported results from 128 studies where academic self-concept and academic achievement were compared. From 1,136 correlations 944 were found to be positive, 22 zero and 170 negative. The relationship between self-concept and performance was shown to be weak – the average correlation was $r = .21$.

Self-perception in the context of school is not only about actual ability – it also depends how teachers and peers regard their pupil (Stipek & Lupita, 1984; Scott, Murray, Mertens & Dustin, 1996; Nunes & Pretzlik, 2000). The ability of children to accurately rank their academic ability depends on their ability to see their position from a viewpoint of outside observers (Nicholls, 1978).

In the 1970s Nash set out to discover whether seven and eight year old children could assess themselves relative to their peers in reading ability – in terms of who is better or worse than themselves at reading – and produce a rank order of perceived ability. It was found that children are well aware of their position in class. Not only were they aware of their position, but also they were found to do so according to their self-perception (Nash, 1976). Children who were seen to be "good" at schoolwork put themselves forward as "clever" and vice versa.

In their study Crocker and Cheeseman (1988) replaced the methodology of using self-report questionnaires and one-to-one interviews with naturalistic observations in the classroom and rankings about class work by pupils and teachers. Each child was given the names of all the children in the classroom on separate pieces of paper. They were then asked to sort these names into two piles – those who the child thought were better then he or she at school work and those who the child thought were not as good as he or she at school work. These relative self-rankings were converted to a percentage score of children perceived to be "better than me" for each class. To gain data on teacher estimates of children's academic ability, they were asked to rank all the children in the class for "good at school work". This was done with regard to the teacher's daily experience and without reference to standardised test results. Next, correlations between pupil-teacher ranking were carried out to explore the agreement between teachers' academic criteria and their pupils understanding of it.

Crocker and Cheeseman's methodology was extended in studies conducted by Pitkänen and Nunes (2000) and Tsolaidou and Pretzlik (2000). Pupils' self-perception of their reading and maths ability was obtained during two one-to-one interviews. They were asked to sort the photographs of the other children in the classroom first for reading and one week later for maths. On each occasion each child was asked to sort the photographs into three piles "he/she is better than me", "as good as me" or "not as good as me". The children also completed standardised IQ, reading and spelling as well as maths tests to provide results of their actual academic performance. Teachers' perception of their pupils' general ability for learning, for reading and for maths was ranked on three occasions, one week apart. Results from the teacher rankings and their pupils' actual academic performance, and pupil ranking and their actual academic performance were compared. Regression analyses were then applied to the data from pupils' self-perception related to their performance and the teachers' perceptions of academic performance were compared. It was found that the children's perception of themselves was not significantly related to their academic performance. However, their self-perception as learners was significantly related to the perception of their academic performance reported by the teacher and that of the peers.

RESEARCH DESIGNS

A research design in the area of self-perception, as in other areas of enquiry, depends first and foremost on the research question. Frequently developmental and educational research includes a question about how certain aspects about behaviours, feelings or abilities change over time. There are three main research designs for this kind of question: cross-sectional, longitudinal and cross-lag.

Cross-sectional design

A cross-sectional design involves selecting children from different age groups so that results from observations, questionnaires or interviews can be compared across and within the groups. This design has the advantage of being relatively easy to set up – children are assessed at one point in time. It also makes such studies quick to carry out and is relatively cheap and efficient. Participants are unlikely to drop out and if they do then same-age children can replace them.

Results from data, where children of differing ages are compared, give a snapshot of their self-perception at a given point in time, but are unable to explain what developmental history the perception of self might have followed. The data are ineffective in providing a description of how children came to acquire their self-perception.

Day to day occurrences influence children's self-perceptions; Collison (1974) for example found that the self-concept of young children could be altered by a single incident. In his study 8-year-old children were given the first half of the Piers-Harris Self-Concept Scale (Piers & Harris, 1964) followed by a maths test.

Half of the group was told that they had performed badly on the test and the other half was told that they had performed well. The group then completed the second half of the self-concept scale. It was found that the children, who had received negative feedback after completing the first half of the test, scored considerably lower in their self-concept scores on the second part of the scale than children who had received positive feedback halfway through the experiment. This result suggests that events immediately prior to a self-esteem or self-concept interview may influence results. This difficulty can be overcome by adopting a longitudinal approach, where children are assessed more than once, and will contribute to the validity for measuring children's self-concept.

Longitudinal design

An alternative to the cross-sectional design is a longitudinal design. Using this method a group of children are studied repeatedly at different points in time. The time intervals may be relatively short (days or weeks) or long (months or years). The two main strengths of this design are that major patterns of development can be identified, as well as individual differences, and that such studies provide the researcher with data that will show relationships between earlier and later behaviours, feelings and abilities.

The process of change is seen more clearly when a longitudinal design is employed. When a group of children's perception of self is tracked, data can explain whether differences in one of the domains or dimensions of self at Time 1 really are related to differences in the domains or dimensions of self at Time 2 or Time 3. Detailed patterns of change can be detected this way. Finding such patterns depends on three basic elements: the methodology used (e.g. observations, questionnaires, interviews), how frequently the testing takes place, and how the data are analysed.

Despite producing conceptual advantages, longitudinal designs are used less frequently than cross-sectional designs. This is often due to practical disadvantages. Longitudinal studies take a long time to complete, which in turn leads to a long wait for meaningful results to emerge. Longitudinal research is more expensive than cross sectional research, and is more likely to be affected by participant and researcher attrition. Loss of participants during a long-term investigation may lead to a biased group.

Cross-lagged design

This research design has cross-sectional and longitudinal components, in which groups of participants born in different years are followed over time. The two designs are combined to overcome some of the limitations of cross-sectional and longitudinal research. This combination leads to a cross-lagged design where two or more variables at two or more points in time are under investigation. Among the design advantages is that it permits researchers to find out whether cohort effects are operating by comparing children of the same age born in different years. It is also possible to make cross-sectional and longitudinal comparisons using the data from the same children.

SOME FACTORS AFFECTING SELF-PERCEPTION

Academic performance

A strong link between a domain judged important by children and their self-esteem in that domain suggests that the match between children's aspirations and performance is a major factor in determining how they feel about themselves (Harter, 1988). Children may not think Athletic Competence to be important yet value their Scholastic Competence highly. As reading forms a core part of children's academic progress, the appraisal of children's academic abilities has serious consequences for their overall development in the educational context. One of the elements, which relate to children's reading self-concept, is the accuracy of their assessment of their reading ability. Recognising a notable relationship between their perceived ability and their actual ability leads children to examine the cause of their success and failure in a logical, mature manner, and recognising the cause of their success or failure will enable them to act accordingly.

Dweck (1999) suggests that the hallmark of successful pupils is their love to learn. She and her colleagues found that successful pupils tend to seek challenges, value their own efforts, and persist with the task in hand when faced with difficulties. Those pupils, who perceive reading as valuable and important and who enjoy it, will read in a more structured and active way than those pupils who take little pleasure and interest in it. In other words learning is to some extent reliant on self-motivation and high motivation to read is directly related to a positive self-concept as a reader (Dweck & Elliott, 1983).

DEVELOPMENTAL LEVEL

As discussed earlier, the sense of self is not simply instinctive, but is developed through a process of personal and interpersonal experiences. It is changeable and incorporates a potential for growth and development. Pre-school age children's self-concepts are diffuse and loosely organised. Young children do not differentiate between externalised behaviour and underlying ability. They tend to see themselves in terms of the way they look, what they do, what they are called, and what toys or books they posses. The self becomes more definite when children are able to describe themselves in relation to others and when they consider others describing them.

The purpose of a study by Jambunathan and Norris, 2000 was to examine the relation between language competence and self-competence among 3 and 4 year old children. Thirty-nine children with no known language problems completed the Pictorial Scale of Perceived Competence and Social Acceptance for Young Children (Harter & Pike, 1984) and the Preschool Language Assessment Instrument (Blank, Rose & Berlin, 1978). Results found in this study show that the perception of self-competence among young children is related to their language competence. While the self-concept becomes established in the early years of childhood, it nevertheless remains flexible during the primary school years (Schunk, 1990).

It appears that during the period of the home-to-school transition, children's academic self-concept begins to emerge. Entwisle et al., (1987) investigated a large racially diverse sample (673 children aged 5 years), taking into account how the children forged their academic self, and especially the extent to which evaluation of significant others versus self-perception was influenced. Through interviews with parents, beginning pupils and their teacher during the first school year it was found that at the end of the first year at school pupils' evaluation of their own academic ability was a the main contributor to their self-perception as learners. It was not – as has been found with older pupils – the view significant others such as parents, teachers and peer had of them (e.g. Nunes & Pretzlik, 2000).

Current thinking about the self-concept supports the notion that the academic self is made up of a multitude of factors; for example, maths, physics, art, sport and reading. However, where young children are concerned the findings are less clear. While some research has found that young children have relatively undifferentiated self-concepts (for a review see Bracken, 1996) other research shows (Marsh et al., 1991) academic self-concept dimensions, such as reading and maths, to be differentiated even among young children (5- to 7-year-old children). Nevertheless, there is some agreement among researchers that differentiation between various self-concept domains increases with age. As children get older they are better able to express themselves and describe what they like, what they are good at and how they feel about their performance.

Harter (1982) reports that from about 8 years of age children develop domain-specific evaluations of their competence and adequacy in addition to an increased global concept of their worth as individuals. It needs to be born in mind that self-report measures – dependent on children's verbal abilities – are generally used to assess developmental trends. Children are asked to report the way they perceive themselves. Discrepancies in results may be due to a variety of factors, including the information that is available to the child at the time of interview and the child's cognitive maturity to process the information presented. Markus (1977) suggests that a child's attempt to organise, summarise or explain behaviour will result in the formation of cognitive structures. These structures are often referred to as self-schemata. Self-schemata are cognitive generalisations made by the individual about the self. These generalisations are derived from past experience and help to organise and guide the processing of self-related information contained in the individual's social experience (Markus, 1980).

The relationship between the concept of causal ordering of self-concept and academic ability vary with age, as well as definitions of self-concept and the kind of measure of academic performance used.

THE DEVELOPMENT OF A READING SELF-CONCEPT

Taking the hierarchical model (Marsh & Shavelson, 1985) as the theoretical framework the next level will now be considered – the move from children's academic self-concept to their self-perception as readers.

Numerous studies have shown that self-concept strongly influences achievement (e.g. Marsh, 1986; 1990; Song & Hattie, 1984) – the better pupils feel about themselves the better their school performance. Other studies support the theory that achievement strongly influences self-esteem – the better the school performance the better pupils feel about themselves (e.g. Newman, 1984; Skaalvik & Hagvet, 1990). These opposing views led Chapman and Tunmer (1997) to look at two relationships. (1) Whether an association exists between initial reading self-concept (at the beginning of formal education) and later reading achievement and (2) whether an association exists between pre-reading skills at entry of formal schooling and later reading self-concept. The design was longitudinal lasting for 30 months and included 152 children of these 112 completed all tasks. At the beginning of the study the children were 5 years old and were starting formal schooling.

At Time 1 the pre-reading scales included a phoneme deletion task, a sound-matching task, a letter identification task, and an oral vocabulary scale – the Peabody Picture Vocabulary Test (Dunn & Dunn, 1981). The children completed the scales within the first four weeks of the first year in school. Reading self-concept was assessed by means of the Reading Self-concept Scale (Chapman & Tunmer, 1995), and was first completed after the children had been in school for six weeks. At Time 2 during the second year in school, the children completed the Burt Word Reading Test (Gilmore, Croft & Reid, 1981) a contextual priming task, and the Reading Self-concept Scale. Finally, at Time 3 – twelve months later – during the children's third year in school, the Burt Word Reading Test, a revised version of the comprehension sub-test of the Neale Analysis of Reading Ability (Neal, 1988) and the Reading Self-concept Scale were administered.

It was found that reading self-concept is moderately stable during the first three years of schooling. The Reading Self-Concept Scale correlation for Time 1 with Time 2 is $r = .39$. There is some indication that reading self-concept becomes more stable between the second and third grade ($r = .49$), but there is no significant relationship between pre-school reading skills and beginning reading self-concept. The results of correlations between the reading factors and reading self-concept show a steady increase over time ($r = .11$, $r = .21$, and $r = .35$). These results suggest that associations between self-perception and ability begin to form during the second and third grade. An interactive relationship between children's reading performance and reading self-concept then starts to emerge. However, Chapman and Tunmer (1997) concluded that young children do not develop their reading self-concept solely as a result of their actual reading attainment. More work is needed to explore other factors, which contribute to children's perception as to what kind of readers that they think themselves to be.

These findings indicate that children begin school unaware of how they feel about themselves as readers. Chapman and Tunmer put forward the idea that young children's development of a reading self-concept is in a state of flux, and that changes take place in response to formal reading instructions in the class room and to the relationship between reading performance and reading related tasks.

This may be so but – as has already been suggested in this chapter – significant others including teachers and peers contribute notably to the emergence of children's self-perception as learners and this includes their self-perception as readers. A study by Nunes & Pretzlik (2000) asked if pupils' self-perception as readers might be influenced by their performance and also by their teacher's and their peers' judgement of them. Fifty-nine children aged 10 to 11 and two teachers took part. These pupils completed the Schonell Spelling Test and Reading Test (Schonell & Goodacre, 1974) and reported on their self-perception as readers. The teachers ranked them in order of their perception of pupils reading ability. It was found that teachers are accurate in their judgements of pupils' academic performance – a significant relationship was found between children's ability and teacher judgement ($r = .69$). However, when applying a regression analysis much more variance in children's self-perception as readers was explained by social factors than by academic performance (50% after controlling for IQ; 16% after controlling for performance in reading). Teacher and peer judgements of academic ability were shown to be in close agreement. Their judgement made a significant contribution to explaining pupils' self-perception as learners in general and as readers in particular after partialling out the effect of actual performance. It can therefore be concluded that teacher and peer judgements reinforce each other and are not independent of each other.

Beginning readers, who experience early success, will engage in the process of reading with pleasure and enjoyment. Beginning readers, who experience initial difficulty on the other hand, may initiate a chain of escalating negative "Matthew effects" (Stanovich, 1986). That is to say, children, who experience initial difficulties, interact less with print, obtain less pleasure from reading, and are less motivated to engage in reading-related activities, read less and therefore practice less. A negative Matthew effect will lead young readers to slower progress than those children who experience initial success and therefore may initiate a feeling of low self-esteem and difficulties in other areas. There is some suggestion that reading programmes with emphasis on developing poor readers' reading skills can reverse the flow of negative Matthew effects (e.g. Reading Recovery Programme; Clay, 1987). Stanovich (1986) argues that the most effective way to recover from negative Matthew effects is instruction. By providing intensive reading support for children, who experience difficulties, the extra practise and positive learning periods should lead to increased confidence and skills levels, and improved reading self-concept. Those pupils, who perceive themselves as being good, competent students, generally experience positive changes in achievement in the relevant academic domain (Anderman, et al., 2001). The pupils are able to maintain a positive self-image; and this positivity then translates into constructive attitudes and beliefs about the academic domain.

Wilson Chapman and Tunmer (1995) tested the hypothesis that reading intervention programmes improve reading skills and lead to improvements on the Reading Self-Concept Scale of poor beginning readers. Twenty-six 6-year-old children, who were amongst the bottom 20% in the Diagnostic Survey (Clay, 1985), completed the Reading Self-concept Scale (Chapman & Tunmer, 1995) before and after undergoing the Reading Recovery Programme (Clay, 1987). Daily a trained teacher provided individual reading instruction. Upon completion of the 20-week Reading Recovery programme, the children showed significant improvement in their book level reading scores. However, their reading self-concept had not improved. Wilson et al., (1995) suggest that one possible explanation for the lack of improvement in reading self-concept may be the lack of specific support or instruction by this intervention programme to alter the children's negative belief systems. Children's attitudes about themselves as learners and as readers and their negative perception of competence in reading are likely to be associated with early reading failure. Furthermore, the social environment of the school had not been taken into account – including how teachers and other pupils viewed this "lowest achievers in reading" group and how these significant others might have inspired and motivated the children as readers.

The child in the social environment of the school

The role of feedback from significant others is one of the main pathways through which children learn about themselves. This explanation forms part of social learning theory (Bandura, 1977); it is suggested that rewards in the form of positive social feedback are more important in learning than actual performance had been considered in the past. However, the theory was never strongly supported by research findings. Social comparison theory (Festinger, 1954), on the other hand, argues that people use significant others in their environment as frames of reference in forming self-assessment. The social comparison theory is somewhat similar to the notion of symbolic interactionists (e.g. Cooley, 1902; Mead, 1934) where "the looking-glass" hypothesis is emphasised.

Theorists of the symbolic interactionist movement, which followed on from James' work, provide a further perspective on the relationship between the individual and society and vice versa. In contrast to James, the symbolic interactionists put stress on how an individual's social interactions with others profoundly shape the self. The self is considered to be primarily a social construction developed through linguistic exchanges with others (Harter, 1999). Feedback from significant others – parents, siblings in the home setting, peers and teachers in the school environment – is an essential part of a child's everyday life. Parents and siblings become less significant at school age, but the role of teachers and other pupils takes on special significance especially during middle childhood.

For Cooley significant others constitute a social mirror into which the individual looks to discover opinions and perceptions about the self. Here the mirror reflects perceived evaluations of others. Cooley suggests that what develops into the self is what individuals imagine others are thinking of their appearance, actions, abilities and so on. According to this theory the internalisation of others' opinions about the self is one of the critical elements in a child's thinking process and prepares the way for a developmental perspective on how the attitudes of others are incorporated into the self. To summarise, from early childhood concepts of self develop from observing how significant others respond: "In the presence of one whom we feel to be of importance, there is a tendency to enter into and adopt by sympathy his judgement of ourselves" (Cooley, 1902; p. 175).

Mead elaborates the themes identified by Cooley with a greater insistence on the role of social interaction, particularly the use of language. For him, *"We appear as selves in our conduct insofar as we ourselves take the attitude that others take toward us. We take the role of what may be called the "generalised" other. And in doing so we appear as a social object, as selves' do* (Mead, 1925; p. 270). The concept of the generalised other, according to Mead, implies that the child is reacting to more than one set of specific others, with whom he or she is interacting, i.e. the home environment. The child comes to adopt the perspective of a more generalised group of significant others who share a particular societal perspective on the self, i.e. the school environment.

In sum the social interactionist school of thought emphasises the importance of the opinions of others in shaping the self-concept – through social interaction. Children not only take into account feedback from specific significant others, but also from the process as a whole, through which more generalised attitudes toward the self are adopted. This then leads to contemporary findings where although cognitive levels, existing academic self-concept and school grades are important in indicating a pupil's performance. Research has shown that there are two other influences to be considered – comparisons with "significant others" in the same subject group and "significant others" in a different subject group (Marsh, 1993; Marsh, 1986; Marsh & Craven, 1991).

According to Marsh, pupils use an internal/external reference model, which describes how academic self-perceptions are formed. For instance, a positive verbal self-perception is more likely when pupils measure their verbal performance in relation to their peers (external comparison). When, on the other hand, their verbal performance is better than their mathematical performance it is described as an internal comparison. Empirical findings show that verbal and maths self-perceptions are not related to each other, although verbal and maths performance was related. Pupils' verbal self-perception is also related to verbal performance and maths self-perception is related to maths performance. Marsh states that these findings indicate that pupils are aware of their own abilities in different academic areas and that, at the same time, academic self-perceptions are influenced by processes other than academic performance, that is to say, they way they are perceived by their peers.

In a study by Cole (1991) 360 pupils aged 10 years from 18 classrooms reported in the autumn and in the spring on how much they liked their classmates and whether their classmates liked them. It was found that pupil's acceptance by their peers in the autumn was a predictor of their self-report scores on the Social Acceptance sub-scale of the SPPC (Harter, 1982) in the spring. This result shows that these pupils' acceptance by their peers influenced changes in their self-perceptions of social acceptance – children who were reported to be accepted by their peers developed a more positive view of themselves and vice versa. The school environment provides children with abundant dimensions for shaping and reshaping the "sense of self" – in social and in academic terms.

Because pupils spend a considerable amount of their time within the school environment, teachers and pupils act as important significant others in the formation of their academic and social self-conception. The development of an academic self is elicited through experiences at school – such as regular objective and subjective evaluation of academic performance and regular social interactions with peers and teachers. Pupils are given opportunities to develop differentiated components – they understand that behaviour is not always in accordance with their potential. According to Schunk (1990), children evaluate their classroom performance against an absolute and a normative criterion.

Absolute criterions are fixed and relate to their actual performance, whereas normative criterions are based on and related to the performance of others, namely their peers.

THE POWER OF TEACHERS

Quite possibly teachers' subtle "messages" in the form of feedback to children about their ability and academic performance influence not only their view of themselves, but also their classmates' expectations of their academic performance within the group. If pupils are aware of what is expected, their performance is likely to be in accordance with those expectations (Connell & Ilardi, 1987; Eshel & Kurman, 1991; Jackson & Bracken, 1998). It therefore follows that the expectation teachers holds of their pupils will influence pupils' academic performance and behaviour with others.

Research published in *Pygmalion in the Classroom* (Rosenthal & Jacobson, 1968) indicates that expectations held by teachers correspond to pupils' performance. According to Rosenthal and Jacobson's study the teachers' expectations have a direct influence on individual pupil's school performance. That is to say if a teacher thinks highly of a pupil's performance that pupil's school performance will improve and vice versa. Pupils behave according to their teacher's perception of them as pupils and as a consequence the teacher's "prophecy" is "self-fulfilled" (Rogers, 1991). Because pupils' self-concept as learners has also been shown to play a vital part in their performance at school (Pitkänen & Nunes, 2000), it is important that they develop and maintain a positive view of their competencies. As was theorised by Cooley and others, children's self-concept develops mainly through interactions with significant others.

Following the Pygmalion in the Classroom study (Rosenthal & Jacobson, 1968) where it was shown for the first time that teachers were able to influence pupils in a powerful way, the expectancy phenomenon was explored further. Palardy (1969) identified two groups of teachers; one group believed that boys learn to read at the same rate as girls and the other group that boys are slower than girls in learning to read. The children were pre-tested as they entered school for the first time, and results revealed no difference in verbal ability between the girls and the boys. Yet, at the end of the school year post-test results showed that the boys, who were taught by a teacher believing girls to have a higher verbal ability, scored significantly lower in their reading tests than the girls. At the same time results from the group of children whose teacher thought boys and girls to be equally good at learning to read at the beginning of the school year had similar reading ability scores at the end of the year. These findings strongly suggest that reading scores can be affected by teacher expectations.

Teachers' awareness of their pupils' quality and quantity of verbal and non-verbal communication, influences children's self-concept as learners. As discussed earlier, self-concept is associated directly with academic performance. Brophy (1979) shows that for a child to obtain a favourable self-concept, she needs to be not only successful, but also to perceive herself as successful, and that this may depend on the child's interpretation of the messages put out by the teacher. In the 1960s Jackson and Strattner (1964) and Brookover, Thomas and Patterson (1964) found that children's perceptions of their academic performance do directly effect their subsequent schoolwork. Children, who see themselves as poor pupils, may attribute errors and failures to a lack of ability. In the eye of the children such feelings confirm that their negative self-concept is correct and so a vicious circle begins. Skaalvik and Hagvet (1990) – similar to Stanovich (1988) – report that young children (8 to 10 years) with positive self-perceptions of their academic ability approach new school tasks with confidence. The success with completing those tasks will, in turn, boost their confidence in their ability as learners whereas pupils with negative self-perceptions of their academic ability will tend to approach new tasks more hesitantly.

When Pitkänen and Nunes (2000) investigated the extent to which 6-year-olds can estimate their academic performance in maths and reading relative to their teacher's perception of them, they found that children's self-ranking of performance in reading and maths strongly agreed with their teacher' ranking. However, when the actual performance was measured through standardised tests, only moderate agreement was found between the children's self-perception and their actual performance. This result shows that the children's self-perception as learners is related more strongly to their teacher's view of them rather than to their actual academic achievements.

When controlling for actual performance in IQ, maths and verbal ability, teachers' perceptions of their pupils' standard of reading ability was indeed shown to influence the pupils' self-perception of ability (Pitkänen & Nunes, 2000). It therefore follows that skilled readers are viewed as "good" pupils whereas less skilled readers – despite their competence in other academic domains – are regarded as "poor" pupils. Teachers favourable perception of competent readers makes such children think of themselves as competent across domains and vice versa. This finding supports the Shavelson, Hubner and Stanton, (1976) and Marsh and Shavelson (1985) models, which refer to self-concept as a multi-dimensional and hierarchical construct where academic domains are independent from each other. Pitkänen and Nunes conclude that classroom teachers in their "position of power" are able to influence the way children perceive themselves as learners. Teachers' expectations of their pupils may lead to causal effects.

The influence of the teacher in the classroom is considerable. Pupils learn quite quickly the various academic criteria used by teachers to judge academic output. Self, peer, and teacher perceptions of intelligence and verbal and maths ability were found to be in significant agreement with each other. The way pupils perceive themselves as learners are influenced not only by their performance but also through social influences in the classroom (Crocker & Cheesman, 1988; Nunes & Pretzlik, 2000). This aspect and those aspects mentioned earlier in this chapter contributes to a child's self-perception as a reader and ought taken into consideration when future research is being planned.

REFERENCES

Allport, G. (ed.) (1985). *William James Psychology the Briefer Course.* Indiana: University of Notre Dame Press.

Anderman, E., Eccles, J., Yoon, K., Roeser, R., Wiegfield, A. & Blumenfeld, P. (2001). Learning to value mathematics and reading: Relations to mastery and performance oriented instructional practices. *Contemporary Educational Psychology, 25,* 76-95.

Babad, E., Bernieri, F. & Rosenthal, R. (1991), Students as judges of teachers' verbal and non-verbal behaviour. *American Educational Research Journal, 28,* 211-234.

Bandura, A. (1977). Self-efficacy: Toward a unifying theory of behavioural change. *Psychological Review, 84,* 191-215.

Bandura, A. (1977). *Social learning theory.* Englewood Cliffs, NJ: Prentice-Hall.

Bandura, A. (1982). Self-efficacy mechanism and human agency. *American Psychologist, 37,* 122-147.

Bandura, A., & Schunk, D. (1981). Cultivating competence, self-efficacy, and intrinsic interest through proximal self-motivation. *Journal of Personality and Social Psychology, 41,* 586-598.

Battle, J. (1992). Culture-Free Self-Esteem Inventories. Austin TX: Pro-Ed.

Blank, M., Rose, S. A. & Berlin, L. J. (1978). Preschool Language Assessment Instrument: The Language of Learning in Practice. New York: The Psychological Corporation.

Blatchford, P. (1997). Students' Self Assessment of Academic Attainment: accuracy and stability from 7 to 16 years and influence of domain and social comparison group, *Educational Psychology, 17*, 345-359.

Blumenfeld, P. C., Pintrich, P. R., Meece, J. & Wessels, K. (1982). The formation and role of self-perceptions of ability in elementary classrooms, *The Elementary School Journal, 82(5)*, 401-420.

Bouffard, T., & Vezeau, C. (1998). The Developing Self-System and Self-Regulation of Primary School Children. In M. Ferrari, and Sternberg, R.J. (eds.), *Self-Awareness: Its Nature and Development* 246-272. New York: The Guilford Press.

Bracken, B. (1992). Multidimensional Self Concept Scale. Austin, TX: Pro-Ed.

Bracken, B. (1996). Handbook of Self-Concept, Developmental, Social and Clinical Considerations. Chichester: John Wiley & Sons.

Brookover, W., Thomas, S. & Patterson, A. (1964). Self-concept of ability and school achievement. *Sociology of Education, 37*, 271-278.

Brophy, B. (1979), "Teacher Behaviour and its Effects". *Journal of Educational Psychology, 71*, 733-750.

Brown, L., & Alexander, J. (1991). Self-Esteem Index. Austin TX: Pro-Ed.

Burns, R. B. (1982). *Self-Concept Development and Education*. London: Holt, Rinehart and Winston.

Byrne, B. M. (1984). The General/Academic Self-concept. Nomological Network: A review of construct validity research. Review of Educational Psychology, 54(3), 427-456.

Byrne, B. M., (1996). Academic Self-Concept: Its Structure, Measurement, and Relation to Academic Achievement. In B. Bracken (ed). Handbook of Self-Concept, Developmental, Social and Clinical Considerations. Chichester: John Wiley & Sons.

Byrne, B. M., & Shavelson, R. J. (1986). Adolescent self-concept: Testing the assumption of equivalent structure across gender. *American Educational Research Journal, 24*, 365-385.

Chapman, J. & Tunmer, W. (1993). Reading Self-Concept Scale. Palmerston North, New Zealand: Educational Research and Development Centre, Massey University.

Chapman, J. & Tunmer, W. (1995). Development of young children's reading self-concepts: an examination of emerging sub-components and their relationship with reading achievement. *Journal of Educational Psychology, 87*, 154-167.

Chapman, J. & Tunmer, W. (1997). A longitudinal study of beginning reading achievement and reading self-concept. *British Journal of Educational Psychology, 67*, 279-291.

Clay, M. (1985). *The early detection of reading difficulties*. Auckland, New Zealand: Heinemann.

Clay, M. (1987). Implementing Reading Recovery: Systematic adaptations to an educational innovation. *New Zealand Journal of Educational Studies, 22*, 35-58.

Cole, D. (1991). Change in self-perceived competence as a function of peer and teacher evaluation. *Developmental Psychology, 27*, 682-688.

Connell, J. P. & Ilardi, B. C. (1987). Self-system concomitants of discrepancies between children's and teachers' evaluations of academic competence. *Child Development, 58*, 1297-1307.

Cooley, C. (1902). *Human nature and the social order*. New York: Scriber's.

Coopersmith, S. (1967). *The antecedents of self-esteem*. San Francisco. CA: Freeman.

Coopersmith, S. (1984). Coopersmith Self-Esteem Inventory. Paolo Alto, CA: Consulting Psychologist Press.

Crocker, T. & Cheeseman, R. (1988). The ability of young children to rank themselves for academic ability, *Educational Studies, 14(1)*, 105-110.

Dunn, L. M. & Dunn, L. (1981). Peabody Picture Vocabulary Test. Circle Pines, MN: American Guidance Service.

Dweck, C. S. (1999). *Self-Theories: Their Role in Motivation, Personality, and Development*. Sussex: Psychology Press.

Dweck, C. S. & Elliott, E. (1983). Achievement motivation. In P. H. Mussen (ed.), *Handbook of child psychology* 643-692. New York: Wiley.

Dweck, C. S. & Leggett, L. (1988). A Social-Cognitive Approach to Motivation and Personality. *Psychological Review, 95*, 256-273.

144   *Ursula Pretzlik & Lily Chan*

Entwisle, D. R., Alexander, K.L., Pallas, A.M., & Cadigan,D. (1987). The Emergent Academic Self-Image of First Graders: Its Responce to Social Structure. *Child Development, 58,* 1190-1206.

Eshel, Y., & Kurman, J. (1991), "Academic Self-Concept, Accuracy of Perceived Ability and Academic Attainment". *British Journal of Educational Psychology, 61,* 187-196.

Ferrari M., & Sternberg, R.J. (1998). *Self-awareness: Its Nature and Development.* New York:The Guilford Press.

Festinger. (1954). A theory of social comparison processes. *Human Relations, 7,* 117-140.

Gambrell, L. B., Palmer, B.M., Codling, R.M., & Mazzoni, S.A. (1996). Assessing motivation to read. *The Reading Teacher, 49,* 518-533.

Gilmore, A., Croft, C. & Reid, N. (1981). *Burt Word Reading Test: New Zealand Revision.* Wellington, NZ: New Zealand Council for Educational Research.

Harter, S. (1982). The Perceived Competence Scale for Children. *Child Development, 53,* 87-97.

Harter, S. (1985). *The Self-Perception Profile for Children.* Denver, CO: University of Denver.

Harter, S. (1986). Cognitive-developmental processes in the integration of concepts about emotions and self. *Social Cognition,* 4(2), 119-151.

Harter, S. (1988). *The Self-Perception Profile for Adolescents.* University of Denver, Denver, CO.

Harter, S. (1996). Historical Roots of Contemporary Issues Involving Self-Concept. In B. Bracken (ed). Handbook of Self-Concept, Developmental, Social and Clinical Considerations. Chichester: John Wiley & Sons.

Harter, S. (1998). The Development of Self-Representations. In W. E. Damon, N. (ed.), *Social, Educational and Personality Development* (5th ed.) 3, 553-617. New York: John Wiley.

Harter, S. (1999). *The Construction of the Self.* New York: The Guilford Press.

Harter, S., & Monsour, A. (1992). Developmental Analysis of Conflict Caused by Opposing Attributes in the Adolescent Self-Portrait. *Developmental Psychology, 28,* 251-260.

Harter, S., & Pike, R. (1984). The Pictorial Scale of Perceived Competence and Social Acceptance for Young Children. *Child Development, 55,* 1969-1982.

Hattie, J. (1992). *Self-Concept.* New Jersey: Lawrence Erlbaum Associates.

Henk, W., & Melnick, S. (1995), "The Reader Self-Perception Scale (RSPS): A new tool for measuring how children feel about themselves as readers". *The Reading Teacher, 48,* 470-482.

Jackson & Strattner (1964). Meaningful learning and retention: noncognitive variables, *Review of Educational Research Association,* 513-523.

Jackson, L., & Bracken, B. (1998), "Relationship Between Students' Social Status and Global and Domain-Specific Self-Concepts". *Journal of School Psychology, 36,* 233-246.

Jambunathan, S. & Norris, J. (2000). Perception of self-competence in relation to language competence among preschoolers. *Child Study Journal, 30(2),* 91-101.

James, W. (1892). Psychology: The briefer course. New York: Henry Holt.

James, W. (1899). Talks to Teachers on Psychology and to Students on Some of Life's Ideals. New York: Dover.

Markus, H. (1977). Self-schemata and processing information and the self. *Journal of Personality and Social Psychology, 35,* 63-78.

Markus, H. W. (1980). The self in thought and memory. In D. Wegner and R. Vallacher (eds.), *The self in social psychology.* New York: Oxford University Press.

Marsh, H. W. (1986). Verbal and Math Self-Concepts: An Internal/External Frame of Reference Model. *Americal Educational Research Journal, 23,* 129-149.

Marsh, H. W. (1990a), "Influences of Internal and External Frames of Reference on the Formation of Math and English Self-Concepts". *Journal of Educational Psychology, 82,* 107-116.

Marsh, H. W. (1990b), "The Structure of Academic Self-Concept: The Marsh/Shavelson Model". *Journal of Educational Psychology, 82,* 623-636.

Marsh, H. W., (1993). The multidimensional structure of academic self-concept: Invariance over gender and age. *American Educational Research Journal, 30,* 841-860.

Marsh, H. W. & Craven, R.G. (1991). Self-Other Agreement on Multiple Dimensions of Preadolescent Self-Concept: Inferences by Teachers, Mothers, and Fathers. *Journal of Educational Psychology, 83,* 393-404.

Marsh, H. W., Craven, R.G., & Debus, R. (1991). Self-Concepts of Young Children 5 to 8 Years of Age: Measurement and Multidimensional Structure. *Journal of Educational Psychology, 83,* 377-392.

Marsh, H. W., & Shavelson, R. J. (1985). Self-concept: Its multifaceted, hierarchical structure. *Educational Psychologist, 20,* 107-125.

Mead, G. (1925). The genesis of the self and social control. *International Journal of Ethics, 35,* 251-273.

Mead, M. (1934). *Mind, self, and society.* Chicago: University of Chicago Press.

Nash, R. (1976). *Teachers expectations and pupil learning.* London: Routledge.

Neale, M. D. (1988). Neal Analysis of Reading Ability – Revised. Hawthron, Australian Council of Education.

Newman, R. S. (1984). Children's achievement and self-evaluations in mathematics: A longitudinal study. *Journal of Educational Psychology, 76,* 857-873.

Nicholls, J. (1978). The Development of the Concept of Effort and Ability, Perception of Academic Attainment and the Understanding that Difficult Tasks Require more Ability. *Child Development, 49,* 800-814.

Nunes, T., & Pretzlik, U. (2000). Is intelligence really all verbal and reading ability? *XVIth Biennial Meeting of ISSBD.* Beijing, China.

Palardy, J. (1969). What teachers believe – what children achieve. *Elementary School Journal, 69,* 371-374.

Piers, E. V. (1984). *Revised manual for the Pier-Harris Children's Self-Concept Scale.* Los Angeles: Western Psychology Services.

Piers, E. V. & Harris, E. (1964). Age and other correlates of self-concept in children. *Journal of Educational Psychology, 55,* 91-95.

Pitkänen, J., & Nunes, T. (2000). Teachers' representations of intelligence and their consequences for pupils. *XVIth Biennial Meeting of ISSBD.* Beijing, China.

Rogers, C. (1991). Early admission: early labelling. In P. Light, R. Carr and M. Woodhead (eds.), *Growing Up in a Changing Society,* 163-178. London: Routledge.

Rosenberg, M. (1965). *Society and adolescent self-image.* Princeton, NJ: Princeton University Press.

Rosenthal, R. & Jacobson, L. (1968). *Pygmalion in the Classroom.* New York: Holt, Rinehart and Winston, Inc.

Saracho, O. N. (1991). Teacher expectations of students' performance: a review of the research. *Early Child Development and Care, 76,* 21-41.

Schonell, F. (1955), *Schonell Reading and Spelling Tests.* Edinburgh: Oliver and Boyd.

Schonell & Goodacre (1974). Graded Word Reading Test. The Psychology and Teaching of Reading, 5th edition of Edinburgh: Oliver and Boyd.

Schunk, D. (1990). Goal setting and self-efficacy during self-regulated learning. *Educational Psychologist, 25,* 71-86.

Scott, C. G., Murray, G.C., Mertens, C., & Dustin, R.E. (1996). Student Self-Esteem and the School System: Perceptions and Implications. *Journal of Educational Research, 89,* 286-293.

Shavelson, R.J., Hubner, J.J., & Stanton, G.C. (1976). Self-concept: Validation of Construct Interpretations. *Review of Educational Research,* 46(3), 407-441.

Skaalvik, E. M., and Hagtvet, K.A. (1990). Academic Achievement and Self-Concept: An Analysis of Causal Predominance in a Developmental Perspective. *Journal of Personality and Social Psychology, 58,* 292-307.

Song, I. S., & Hattie, J. (1984). Home environment, self-concept, and academic achievement: A causal modelling approach. *Journal of Educational Psychology, 76,* 1269-1281.

Stanovich, K. E. (1986), "Matthew effects in reading: Some consequences of individual differences in the acquisition of literacy". *Reading Research Quarterly, 21,* 360-407.

Stanovich, K. E. (1988). Explaining the differences between dyslexic and the garden-variety poor readers: The phonological-core variable-different model. *Journal of Learning Disabilities, 21,* 590-612.

Stipek, D. J., and Lupita, T.M. (1984). Children's Judgements of their own and their Peers' Academic Competence. *Journal of Educational Psychology, 76,* 75-84.

Tsolaidou, K., & Pretzlik, U. (2000). Do Teachers perceive or create pupils' individual differences? *British Psychological Society Developmental Annual Conference* Bristol UK.

Wilson, M. G., Chapman, J.W., and Tunmer, W.E. (1995). Early Reading Difficulties and Reading Self-Concept. *Journal of Cognitive Education, 4,* 33-45.
Wylie, R. C. (1974). The self-concept (Vol. 1, rev. ed.) Lincoln: University of Nebraska Press.

SUGGESTED FURTHER READINGS

Burns, R. B. (1981), The self-concept in theory, measurement, development and behaviour. New York: Longman Group Limited.
Dweck, C. S. (1999). *Self-Theories: Their Role in Motivation, Personality, and Development.* Sussex: Psychology Press.
Harter, S. (1996). Historical Roots of Contemporary Issues Involving Self-Concept. In B. Bracken (ed). Handbook of Self-Concept, Developmental, Social and Clinical Considerations. Chichester: John Wiley & Sons.
Stanovich, K. E. (1986), "Matthew effects in reading: Some consequences of individual differences in the acquisition of literacy". *Reading Research Quarterly, 21,* 360-407.

B. Reading and Writing Texts: An Overview

Introduction

ALISON F. GARTON & CHRIS PRATT

The ability to read and write involves a complex set of skills that develop during childhood. To be effective, reading and writing both require the maintenance of a topic over several sentences and arguably develop as an extension of the ability to hold a conversation with another person. However, there are some unique characteristics of text production and understanding that warrant special attention. The Chapters in this Section of the Handbook each address the topic in a different way and highlight the diversity of research and the range of sub-topics that constitute story-telling and understanding texts.

The terms text, story, discourse and narrative are often used interchangeably, although each has a technically different meaning and some authors make important distinctions. While story and narrative may be used as synonyms for "tale", text and discourse refer more to the medium, in the former case extended passages, most commonly found in books and the latter, discourse, refers generally to discussion or dialogue (the spoken word). The capacity to produce and understand narrative texts and discourse requires the acquisition of linguistic devices that permit cohesion, such as words, pronouns, anaphoric reference, connections such as "and" and "because" and grammatical constructions such as the active and passive voices. Cohesion itself is an important research topic and has been distinguished by Karmiloff-Smith and colleagues from coherence (Karmiloff-Smith, Johnson, Grant, Karmiloff, Bartrip & Cuckle, 1993) where the latter refers to rules that operate to organise the content of a story. This distinction is discussed at greater length in the Chapter by Garton and Pratt. In addition, children have to learn how language forms and functions inter-relate. Functions necessary for extended discourse or text include creating a timeline (past, present, future), connecting clauses temporally or causally, and ensuring that the text is divided appropriately to reflect the organisation of actions and events.

Story telling and understanding cohesive extended discourse or narrative are rich areas for research. Topics studied include looking at how children develop these capabilities, how adults understand and create texts, including the use of writing technologies, as well as research that looks at the interrelationship between reading, writing, thought and culture. Much research has focused on the social aspects of learning to read and write (Garton & Pratt, 1998) as well as on specific components such as describing and defining what constitute skills of

T. Nunes, P. Bryant (eds.), Handbook of Children's Literacy, 149–153.
© 2004 *Kluwer Academic Publishers. Printed in Great Britain.*

understanding (see Chapters by Oakhill & Cain, and Fayol). Olson (1994) reminds us that, in the tradition of McLuhan (1962), literacy is an instrument of cultural and scientific development, and that writing in whatever form or in whatever medium enables us to view our world and our culture. Writing too can be regarded as responsible for the development of thought although Olson believes this position may have been overstated.

The relationship between reading, writing and literacy is important when we are considering texts and discourse in the broadest sense, to include all forms of extended talking and writing, production and comprehension. In terms of writing, this must embrace such technologies as word processors and their effect on the writing process as well as on the outcome or product and on the human mind and scientific, artistic and cultural thinking.

Genres are types of texts and can be used to reveal the importance of being able to read, write and understand material that is linked thematically, structurally and causally. Genre is the term used to describe different forms of story and includes such narratives as scripts, fiction and personal experiences (Pan & Snow, 1999). These genres require different content, language forms and organisational structures, reflecting their different functions. Scripts represent recurrent actions and events, such as what happens when catching a train or at a football match. They represent typical scenarios, actions and events, and children can begin to produce naïve scripts from an early age. These become increasingly generalised but contain more detail in terms of particular events and timing. Personal experiences are told about specific events that happened in one's past; they thus use the pronoun *I* and the past tense. When young children talk about personal experiences, they often do not contextualise their story. For example, they may talk about a particular event that occurred whilst on holiday without stating that that was when the event took place. With increasing age however, the personal experience stories become more varied and occasionally elaborated and embellished.

Fictional stories include a start (an identifiable event), a problem requiring resolution, and the resolution. Often these are stylised in the form of "Once upon a time...", based on other stories, or on personal experience such as "When we were walking down the street...". Typically, the past tense is used, and again, the stories become more complex as children's language develops, their imagination increases and they can deal with more abstract content.

Different story types require different forms and functions of language. Reading and writing texts require different skills but a broad definition of literacy to include reading and writing takes into account these different competencies (Garton & Pratt, 1998). In addition, different forms of literacy require different competencies, for example reading and understanding the form guide for a horse race requires a different set of literacy skills than those required for reading Homer's *The Odyssey*. Children have to learn the conventions associated with different genres as well as acquiring the component skills necessary for skilled reading and writing. Much research has focused on one activity or the other and as noted earlier, there are key differences between reading and writing and these are described in the Chapter by Fayol. These differences relate both to the cognitive activities required in text production and text comprehension, themselves related to the way the texts are organised and processed.

Fayol distinguishes between the conceptual dimension of narratives, that is the representation of events and actions, and the rhetorical dimension, that is the textual or linguistic structure of narratives. In acquiring or learning how to produce or understand narratives, children have to impose organisation or sequences on texts before they can understand or produce them. The imposition of structure on texts requires several component skills, including knowledge, memory and language. Children who show poor comprehension skills often have difficulties with some of these component skills, as discussed in detail by Oakhill and Cain in their Chapter. Studies on the development of children's comprehension skills recognise that a range of inter-related abilities including knowledge of syntax and semantics as well as cognitive skills such as making inferences and remembering text is required for accurate understanding of texts. However, while there are identifiable factors, it is not clear whether these skills are as a consequence of learning to comprehend texts or do themselves lead directly to improved reading comprehension.

The question of causality is also discussed in the Chapter by Salomon, Kozminsky and Asaf who examine the relationship between the "technological environment" (namely word processing tools) and the production of texts (or writing). They distinguish between the "effect of" the technology versus the "effect with" technology use. The former refers to long-lasting writing-related changes in cognition, strategies and abilities as a consequence of using the technology while the latter refers to changes in cognition or performance while using a word processor and its particular features. In both cases, use of the technology is prompting change in the writing process, but these changes may lead to more enduring changes in the way texts are produced or understood. Salomon and colleagues discuss this issue at length and highlight the mixed state of the research, the results and the implications. The interesting lesson from the review of research indicates that technology *per se* does not influence children's writing. What is important however is the learning environment created as a function of using the technology. Collaborative learning environments that support and stimulate writing activities enable children to monitor their writing, to reflect on the process and the product and to become aware of the activity.

Collaboration is also identified as an important component in children's early book reading. Garton and Pratt use the scaffolding metaphor to describe how joint book-reading between very young children and their mothers introduces children to books and serves as a basis for later reading. Early book-reading has been linked with later successful reading and literacy skills, including comprehension skills. Precursors to the skills associated with reading comprehension can be fostered in the supportive parent-child relationship; again however the direction of causality is not clear and research needs to be conducted to answer questions of linkages.

In their Chapter, Tunmer and Chapman examine three different views regarding the use of context in learning to read. According to the first view reading increasingly relies on redundancies of language to make predictions about the text that has yet to be read. The second view suggests that reading can develop efficiently only if the child avoids using context to identify words. They argue that recent evidence would challenge both of these views and supports the third view that context can be used effectively if it is in conjunction with word decoding skills based on letter-sound or grapheme-phoneme correspondences to assist beginning readers read unfamiliar words. Context on its own is not sufficient to determine what is an unfamiliar word and at times word decoding skills are also not sufficient without context. However if context is used in conjunction with developing grapheme-phoneme correspondence knowledge it can assist the child by constraining the possibilities for an unknown word. Thus the child progresses by using both context and word identification skills and again it should be noted that self-regulation and monitoring of reading skills are essential for children to make progress in learning to read.

The Chapters in this Section of the Handbook thus explore to varying extents how texts are produced and understood. It is clear that skilled readers can be identified as having certain characteristics and certain skills, but whether these are a cause or a consequence of reading still has not been determined. A recurrent theme in the Chapters is that a supportive instructional environment that encourages awareness and appreciation of the written word assists in children becoming skilled at understanding and producing the written word.

Finally, why is the study of text understanding and production so important? It has been argued by key theorists such as Bruner (1990) that through the construction and understanding of stories, humans deal with and understand their experiences, their thoughts and their minds. As Olson (1994) notes, literacy, the reading and writing of texts, is a social phenomenon and involves the participation in a "textual community" of readers or writers who share a common way of way of reading and interpreting. In other words, to be literate requires participation in a socio-cultural community and to read and understand texts, stories, discourse and narratives that are relevant and important to that community and to contribute to that community through talk and writing.

The construction of meaning is fundamental to human psychology. Bruner (1990) makes the distinction between the paradigmatic and the narrative forms of thought, the former being the relation between human experience and its meaning and the latter referring to stories or narratives, the vehicle by which meaning is communicated. This view highlights the fundamental importance of finding meaning in experiences as a way of understanding human culture and development. This has been further extended to the application of narrative approaches to personal and management needs. Story telling and listening thus encapsulate things such as narrative therapy, personal development, and management development. The need to talk about and listen to the lived experiences of the self and others has become a tenet of modern living in the 21st Century, and is based on the capacity to talk, read and write extended discourse and text. It is also based on the philosophical and theoretical position that the construction of meaning through narratives underpins the development of the human mind.

Furthermore, stories reflect cultural differences and different value systems. During development, children's early socialisation experiences embrace cultural values and beliefs and find expression in oral and written stories. Stories told to children also have a range of other functions including those of entertainment, of affirmation of good and condemnation of bad, of rewarding good behaviour and punishing transgressions, and so on; again with cultural differences. Narratives or texts are thus researched for examining cultural and social differences between children, differences that are observed in different linguistic and cognitive skills. For adults, society is organised through texts and scripts and it is sometimes the hallmark of an advanced society to have laws, bureaucracies, education systems and religion based on beliefs and mores that have been written down. A certain literacy, or common way of reading, writing and interpreting texts, is necessary for these beliefs to be shared. In addition, science and the arts (particularly literature and poetry) require a shared participation in particular forms of literacy. These varied skills in adults and how they develop in children are precisely those described by the authors of the Chapters in the Handbook.

REFERENCES

Bruner, J.S. (1990). *Acts of meaning*. Cambridge, MA: Harvard University Press.
Garton, A.F. & Pratt, C. (1998). *Learning to be literate: The development of spoken and written language* (2nd Edition). Oxford: Blackwell.
Karmiloff-Smith, A., Johnson, H., Grant, J., Jones, M-C., Karmiloff, Y-N., Bartrip, J., & Cuckle, P. (1993). From sentential to discourse functions: Detection and explanation of speech repairs by children and adults. *Discourse Processes, 16*, 565-589.
McLuhan, M. (1962). *The Gutenberg galaxy*. Toronto: Toronto University Press.
Olson, D.R. (1994). *The world on paper*. Cambridge: Cambridge University Press.
Pan, B.A., & Snow, C.E. (1999). The development of conversational and discourse skills. In M. Barrett (Ed.) *The development of language* (pp. 229 – 249). Hove: Psychology Press Ltd.

B1. The Development of Comprehension Skills

J. V. OAKHILL & K. CAIN

ABSTRACT

This chapter provides an overview of the research into the development of children's reading comprehension skills. A number of aspects of comprehension skill that might limit the development of effective and efficient comprehension are considered. These areas range from efficiency of decoding and meaning access at the level of single words, through syntactic development, to inference making and integration of the ideas in the text as a whole. Areas that may affect comprehension development, such as amount of reading experience and motivation to read, are also discussed briefly. The chapter ends with a discussion of causal issues in the development of comprehension skill.

INTRODUCTION: WHAT DOES IT MEAN TO COMPREHEND?

There is relatively little research on the development of children's reading comprehension, and no developmental model of reading comprehension. In this chapter, we discuss some of the important component skills for comprehension and how they develop (but not necessarily in the context of reading). We also discuss studies that have attempted to map both the development of these skills and their relation to the development of reading comprehension.

This chapter is not the place to go into current theories of (adult) text comprehension (for summaries of recent research on this topic, see Gernsbacher, 1994), but we should consider the main aspects of comprehension – what it means to comprehend. We can view the process of understanding a text as one that results in a representation of the state of affairs the text describes: A representation that is often referred to as a *Mental Model* (e.g. Johnson-Laird, 1983) or a *Situation Model* (Kintsch, 1998). Our view is that efficient text understanding leads to an integrated and coherent representation of the content of a text. In order to derive such a representation, the reader will need to engage in a number of processes. We outline these processes here, but do not mean to imply that the order in which we list them in any way corresponds to the order in which a reader applies them. It is likely, rather, that in efficient text comprehension, some or all of these types of processing are going on in parallel.

155

T. Nunes, P. Bryant (eds.), Handbook of Children's Literacy, 155–180.
© *2004 Kluwer Academic Publishers. Printed in Great Britain.*

First, the reader will need to derive and integrate the meanings of the individual words, sentences and paragraphs. The derivation of meaning obviously cannot take place in isolation, because the individual words and sentences need to be interpreted with respect to the text as a whole. Second, he or she will need to derive the key ideas or themes of the text. In understanding a story, for instance, the main characters and their motives, and the plot of the story, need to be determined. Third, readers need to make inferences to fill in information that is left implicit in the text. This point is well illustrated by the following very short text from Charniak (1972) which, despite its length, requires a number of inferences if it is to be fully understood:

Jane was invited to Jack's birthday party. She wondered if he would like a kite. She went to her room and shook her piggy bank. It made no sound.

To understand this text in any meaningful way, we need to make inferences based on our knowledge of the conventions surrounding birthday parties and money: the requirement to take a present, saving money and the need for money to buy presents. Someone who did not understand birthday parties, piggy banks or money would find even this simple story impossible to understand. There are other inferences to be made as well: Jane is not simply *wondering* if Jack would like a kite, she is planning to buy him one (for his birthday present). Similarly, the implication of the *lack of sound* in the last sentence is far from explicit, but we understand that there are going to be some implications for Jane's plans, and might even begin to predict what might happen next in the story (if it were longer).

THE DEVELOPMENT OF COMPREHENSION

It might seem reasonable to assume that, once children have learned to decode reasonably efficiently, comprehension will follow automatically. After all, the children are already proficient at understanding the spoken language and, in general, reading and listening comprehension are highly correlated, particularly when decoding differences are small. For college students, correlations of between .82 and .92 have been found (Gernsbacher, Varner and Faust, 1990; Palmer, MacLeod and Davidson, 1985).

Garton and Pratt (1998, p. 248) suggest, however, that children's listening comprehension may not be as good as it seems from their everyday interactions. The situation in which language is spoken provides many cues, as well as those provided by tone of voice, facial expression and intonation pattern of the utterance. In addition, adults often modify their speech and/or provide additional information when talking to children. Such factors may give the impression that a child's understanding is better than it really is.

There are, however, also reasons why beginning readers might have problems that are specific to reading. One is that written language makes use of syntactic constructions and vocabulary that may not be familiar to children from their everyday spoken interactions. Children have to learn the "language of books". Garton and Pratt also suggest that written language demands the integration of information across extended tracts of discourse in a manner that spoken language usually does not (of course, in a spoken interaction, the listener can also stop and ask the speaker for clarification if a referent is not clear. The text cannot be interrogated).

In this chapter, we consider studies that have used a variety of measures to assess the development of comprehension, including the ability to answer questions about a text, and various types of memory for aspects of a text. Free recall is often used (with some justification) as an index of a reader or listener's understanding of a text. In general, recall and comprehension are highly correlated. As Bower (1978) puts it: "Superior memory seems to be an incidental by-product of fully understanding a text" (p. 212).

Speed and efficiency of single-word decoding and semantic access

The reason why slow and laboured (even though accurate) word decoding may affect the development of comprehension is fairly obvious. If a reader is struggling through a text, and finding word decoding slow and effortful, then their short-term memory will be taxed, and there will be little processing resources left for comprehension. Children who are beginning to read may have particular problems – their difficulties with word recognition may leave little cognitive capacity for comprehension processes. Furthermore, as Smith (1975) points out, the rapid loss of information from short-term memory makes it difficult for slow readers to hold information from earlier in a sentence to integrate it with what comes later (by the time they have struggled to the end of a sentence, they have forgotten how it began!).

Naturally, decoding skills improve with age and practice, so a related assumption would be that, as children's reading develops, they need to devote less time to word decoding and have more time free for comprehension. There is empirical support for this pattern of development – Curtis (1980) showed that, by the later primary school grades, comprehension skills replace decoding skills as the most important predictors of reading skill. Similarly, Saarnio, Oka and Paris (1990) showed that the reading comprehension of younger (grade 3) children is primarily determined by decoding skills, but by grade 5, the ability to use context to derive meaning plays a more important role in the prediction of comprehension skill.

There is, however, also evidence that children do not make good progress in comprehension (even listening comprehension) if their decoding is delayed. In a longitudinal study, in which she monitored the progress of children in grades 1-4, Juel (1988) found that, although good and poor readers started out with rather similar, and age-appropriate, listening comprehension, the poor readers made no progress in listening comprehension between grades 2 and 4. The good readers, however, continued to made steady progress. Juel suggests that this lack of progress may be related to the fact that poor readers are not able to read as much (either in school or at home) as good readers. Thus, they probably do not develop relevant knowledge and experience of texts and how they are structured, and without this practice in reading for comprehension, their listening comprehension also tends to suffer.

There is no evidence to suggest that the relation between speed of decoding and comprehension skill is causal. If it were, then one would expect that training in rapid decoding would have a direct effect on comprehension skill. However, experiments designed to test this hypothesis have been singularly unsuccessful in showing such a training effect. For instance, Fleischer, Jenkins & Pany (1979) trained a group of poor readers to recognise words as rapidly as the good readers. They then gave them test passages containing the trained words. Although speed of word decoding was improved by the training, comprehension was not. Such findings suggest that automaticity of decoding has only an indirect influence on comprehension skill – perhaps allowing it to develop rather than influencing it directly. It may also, of course, be the case that, at least after the initial stages of reading acquisition, good comprehenders simply read more, and their decoding skills increase because of the amount of practice they have in reading, rather than vice-versa.

It is difficult to obtain reliable measures of speed and automaticity of lexical and semantic access in young children. However, Gitomer, Pellegrino and Bisanz (1983) devised a method of measuring semantic processing speed that takes into account the differing amount of time it takes children of different ages to make responses in experiments. They found that both speed of access, and the ability to make use of information about the semantic category of a word, increase between 8 and 10 years. In a similar experiment, Chabot, Petros and McCord (1983) also showed an increase in semantic processing speed with age and reading ability. Such results suggest that young children's comprehension may be limited at least to some extent by the speed with which they are able to access the meanings of individual words.

Vocabulary development

Vocabulary knowledge is one of the best predictors of reading comprehension (Carroll, 1993; Davis, 1944, 1968; Thorndike, 1973). Thorndike found correlations of between .66 and .75 between reading comprehension and vocabulary knowledge.

There are major problems in estimating the size of a child's vocabulary at different ages (see Beck and McKeown, 1991), so we will not consider that aspect of vocabulary development in any detail. In any case, as Beck and McKeown point out, the process of becoming aware of new words is not the same as "knowing" those words. It may take some time before new words are sufficiently securely and richly represented to affect a child's comprehension. It has long been thought that a major source of new vocabulary is reading (Huey, 1908; Thorndike, 1917), presumably through a process of inferring new meanings from context. However, Werner and Kaplan's (1952) results suggest that context may not be all that helpful. They explored children's developing ability to use context to assign meanings to unknown (nonsense) words. They gave children, aged 9 to 13, a set of 6 sentences all containing the unknown word. They found that performance improved with age, and that a particular problem for the younger children was that they were not able to come up with a single meaning that would fit all six sentence contexts. However, this task was difficult in that it required the reader, in one sitting, to constantly refine the meaning of the nonsense word as more information became available, a task that requires the consideration and integration of the hypothesised meanings from all six sentences. So, although derivation of word meanings from context can occur, particularly in older children, the available evidence suggests that context has only rather weak effects on vocabulary development (for a brief review, see Beck and McKeown, 1991). Moreover, research on the process of acquiring meaning from context suggests that learning a word is not simply a matter of extracting the meaning from the context. Rather, it is likely to be a gradual process of learning the meaning in small increments. Beck and McKeown suggest either that oral contexts may play a larger and continuing role during the school years than was previously thought, or that children's vocabulary size has been hugely overestimated.

Mezynski (1983) reviewed eight vocabulary training studies that found differential effects of training on comprehension. She concluded that the successful transfer effects found by Beck, Perfetti and McKeown (1982) may have been, at least in part, an artefact of the particular training tasks. In their programme, they not only manipulated how frequently the trained words were seen, but also encouraged elaborative semantic processing of language by comparing target words with their synonyms. This focus on synonyms, and the importance that Beck et al. placed on background context, may have taught children to think about the reading process more generally, rather than simply encouraging them to learn the specific items trained. Mezynski argues that this training may have promoted a more active and, therefore, more appropriate, reading style, which resulted in comprehension improvements.

Whatever the precise details of how vocabulary is learned, the fact is that reading comprehension and vocabulary are highly related. An obvious and tempting interpretation of the high correlations is that having a good vocabulary *causes* the development of reading comprehension. If too many words are unknown, then they will disrupt reading for meaning. However, as is the case with single-word decoding, training studies have not provided evidence for this direct causal relation (e.g. Jenkins, Pany and Schreck, 1978; Tuinman and Brady, 1974). So, as with word recognition, knowing the meanings of the words in a text may be necessary, but not sufficient, for good comprehension. Indeed, a study by Eldredge, Quinn and Butterfield (1990) showed that reading comprehension is a stronger cause of general vocabulary growth than vice-versa in the 2nd grade.

They used a cross-lagged panel design, and then employed path analysis to verify the relationships implied by the cross-lagged analysis. The cross-lagged correlations showed that reading comprehension measured at the beginning of the school year accounted for 47% of variability in vocabulary achievement measured at the end of the school year, whereas vocabulary achievement measured at beginning of the school year accounted for only 34% of variability in reading comprehension achievement at end of the school year. The authors then used LISREL to test between five different theoretical models, and found that the best-fitting model was one in which early comprehension skill predicted growth in vocabulary knowledge, but not vice-versa. This model produced, for example, a superior fit to one in which the relation between growth in vocabulary knowledge and in comprehension was fully reciprocal. So, although some reciprocity cannot be entirely ruled out by these data, the findings clearly suggest that early reading comprehension is a stronger cause of general vocabulary growth than vice-versa. One possible interpretation of this finding is that extensive reading (a possible result of better comprehension) may be instrumental in vocabulary acquisition, a position supported by later studies of the relation between exposure to print and vocabulary growth (Echols, West, Stanovich and Zehr, 1996). These findings (that exposure to print improves vocabulary) can be taken to contradict other research findings (discussed earlier) which suggested that children of this age are not good at deriving word meanings from context. However, there may be a crucial difference between trying to get children to infer word meanings from context, and the more natural acquisition of word meanings that occurs during reading. The studies by Stanovich on exposure to print suggest that the occurrence of a word in numerous different contexts may provide the reader with an opportunity to come up with hypotheses, and to gradually refine their understanding of the meaning of that word.

A causal link between vocabulary and reading comprehension is also implied by models of reading that emphasise the importance of fluency and automaticity of access to word meanings (e.g. Laberge and Samuels, 1974; Perfetti and Lesgold, 1977), as mentioned in the previous section. However, the evidence for such a relation is equivocal. Some training studies have succeeded in improving vocabulary knowledge (e.g. Beck, Perfetti and McKeown, 1982; Jenkins, Pany and Schreck, 1978; Tuinman and Brady, 1974), but not all of them have shown corresponding increases in comprehension skill. However, this failure could be because the training was not sufficiently extensive. Indeed, Beck et al. argued that for vocabulary instruction to have effects on reading comprehension, it is necessary to increase not just the number of words learned, but also the fluency with which the meanings of new words can be accessed. Thus, there is some evidence that both the number of words known by an individual, and the ease with which word meanings can be accessed, influences text comprehension.

Of course, reading comprehension and vocabulary may be related indirectly by a third factor. A likely candidate for such a mediator is verbal IQ (see Anderson and Freebody, 1981). It may be that the more intelligent individuals have a greater ability to learn from context, and that this ability also enables them to develop an extensive vocabulary (for further discussion, see also Daneman, 1988).

Syntactic development

It used to be thought that children's syntactic development was more-or-less complete at about 5 years, but more recent work shows that their syntax continues to develop – albeit in more subtle ways – long after this age (summaries of these later developments can be found in Oakhill and Garnham, 1988, Chapter 3 and, more recently, in Garton and Pratt, 1998, Chapter 5). Not only is children's command of syntax in their oral language still developing when they begin to learn to read but, as pointed out earlier, written language is not "speech written down" and in order to become proficient readers, children have to learn how to interpret the unfamiliar syntactic forms that are particular to written language (e.g. Reid, 1970, 1983).

We need to distinguish between syntactic knowledge and syntactic awareness. Syntactic knowledge is required to extract meaning from different syntactic constructions, e.g. the sort of knowledge that is needed to appreciate the meaning of active vs. passive constructions. Such knowledge may be implicit. By contrast, syntactic (or grammatical) awareness is regarded as explicit knowledge, involving deliberate and controlled reflection on language. Syntactic awareness is not necessarily required to extract meaning but would, for example, be used in decisions about grammatical well-formedness.

Clearly, (implicit) knowledge about syntactic forms is necessary to comprehend particular grammatical constructions and, thus, might be expected to be related to comprehension level. Syntactic awareness has been proposed to influence reading ability in two different ways. Tunmer and Bowey (1984) suggested that such skills may help children to detect and correct reading errors and, thus, enhance comprehension monitoring (the topic of comprehension monitoring will be considered in a separate section, later). Second, Tunmer and Hoover (1992) have proposed that syntactic awareness may aid word recognition if children are able to use the constraints of sentence structure to supplement their rudimentary decoding ability.

Using an oral cloze task, Willows and Ryan (1986) found that syntactic awareness was related to both reading comprehension and decoding in 6-8 year olds even after vocabulary ability and non-verbal IQ had been taken into account. However, semantic knowledge may have influenced performance on this task, because the correct filler must be selected on the basis of both the word's meaning (semantics) and its grammatical function. In another study with 6 year olds, Bowey and Patel (1988) used a sentence correction task, performance on which is not necessarily reliant on semantic knowledge. Performance on this measure did not account for significant variance in either reading comprehension or word reading accuracy after individual differences in vocabulary had been taken into account. Thus, there is little support for a direct relation between explicit measures of syntactic awareness and reading comprehension. Recent work of our own indicates that there might be developmental differences in the influence of syntactic knowledge on comprehension. In our longitudinal study, we found that syntactic ability (TROG: Bishop 1982) did not predict comprehension skill (or word reading accuracy) in 7-8 year olds after vocabulary and IQ had been taken into account, but that it explained significant variance in reading comprehension (but not reading accuracy) in the same sample of children one year later (Oakhill, Cain and Bryant, in press).

Evidence from Tunmer and colleagues suggests that there might be a reciprocal relation between reading ability and syntactic awareness. Using a reading-level match design, Tunmer, Nesdale and Wright (1987) found that younger good readers were better than older poor readers on two measures of syntactic awareness, an oral cloze task and a sentence correction task. Thus, poor readers may be developmentally delayed in syntactic awareness. In a subsequent study, Tunmer (1989) assessed children's syntactic awareness at the end of the first year of school and then a year later. Performance on these measures predicted both word decoding and listening comprehension, and these two skills in turn predicted reading comprehension. However, a recent study by Blackmore and Pratt (1997) failed to find a direct relation between pre-school grammatical awareness and later reading comprehension. Thus, the precise relation between reading comprehension and syntactic knowledge and awareness is not clear.

One explanation for a relation between syntactic abilities and reading comprehension more generally, is that two are related by phonological processing ability. This hypothesis has been extensively explored by Shankweiler and colleagues (see Shankweiler, 1989, for a review) in relation to syntactic knowledge. According to their account, comprehension difficulties arise when children are unable to set up or sustain a phonological representation of the incoming verbal information. As a result, they experience difficulties in retaining and processing this information in verbal working memory and, thus, have problems parsing syntactically complex constructions (see e.g. Smith, Macaruso, Shankweiler, and Crain, 1989). The relation between phonological processing and syntactic awareness was addressed in a study of 8-year-olds conducted by Gottardo, Stanovich and Siegel (1996). In support of the phonological limitation hypothesis, they found that syntactic awareness did not account for significant variance in either word reading or reading comprehension after performance on measures of working memory and phonological awareness had been controlled for. However, the length of the sentences used in their grammatical awareness task may have placed heavy demands on working memory, thereby affecting the pattern of the results (Blackmore and Pratt, 1997). In addition, we have found evidence that children can have comprehension problems in the absence of phonological difficulties (Cain, Oakhill and Bryant, 2000). So, even if the adequacy of a child's phonological representation does constrain their syntactic skills, it certainly cannot be regarded as the basis of all comprehension difficulties.

Understanding text structure

Once the sentences in a text have been understood, they must be integrated to provide an interpretation of the text as a whole. This integration will depend on many skills and abilities, but an important one is the ability to appreciate which are the main ideas in a text (what it is about) and to understand how it is structured.

Identification of main ideas

Johnston and Afflerbach (1985) considered that the ability to identify the main ideas in a text was the "essence of reading comprehension". Young readers have difficulties in recognising the central theme or main ideas from a passage of prose, and even 12-13 year-olds sometimes have difficulties in discriminating between relevant and irrelevant information in a text (Brown and Day, 1983).

Various studies have shown that children's ability to state the main topic of a text increases markedly from 2nd to 6th grade. For instance, Yussen (1982) showed that younger children (he tested children from grades 2,5 & 8) were poor at selecting the main idea of a story sequence (though even 2nd grader children can, to some extent, abstract the main ideas, Danner, 1976). In Yussen's study, the older children were also better at putting sequences of pictures into order to form a story, though somewhat surprisingly, these two abilities were not related.

As children develop, they not only get better at selecting the main point in a story, they also change their minds about what sort of information is most important. Stein and Glenn (1979) classified stories into "story grammar" categories and they found that 1st graders usually picked the *consequences of actions* as most important, whereas 5th graders picked the *goals* of the main characters. These results suggest that 1st grade children have consistent ideas about what is important in a story, but that their ideas differ from those of older children.

Sensitivity to hierarchical structure

Many recent theories of text comprehension have drawn attention to the fact that information in a text is hierarchically structured. This structure arises because a well-written text is focused round one or more main ideas, with subsidiary ideas and trivial details subordinated to the main ones. The proper understanding of a text depends on the reader's sensitivity to the relative importance of the ideas in it (see, e.g., Meyer, 1977).

However, Brown and Smiley (1977) showed that children find it difficult to judge the relative importance of ideas in a text, and that such competence develops rather late. They tested 8-, 10-, 12- and 18-year-olds' ability to classify the ideas in folk tales into one of four importance categories. The young adults showed highly concordant ratings, whereas the 8-year-olds were almost completely unable to do the task, and even 12-year-olds were only reliably able to distinguish between the highest and lowest levels of importance. Interestingly, however, the information that the subjects recalled from the stories was dependent on level of importance, such that even the youngest subjects recalled more important than unimportant ideas. Brown and Smiley suggest that this discrepancy between children's explicit awareness of importance levels and the effect that importance has on text recall may be related to differences in *metacognitive* skills at different ages. Younger children have less insight into their own understanding, a topic which we discuss in more detail below. In summary, hierarchical structure is a common feature of texts, and sensitivity to that structure is necessary for comprehension. Younger children find it difficult to make explicit judgements about what is important in a story. However, Brown and Smiley's work suggests that young children do pay more attention to the important ideas in a text, even though they cannot say what those ideas are.

Understanding the logical structure of the text

Another important element in comprehension is understanding how the ideas in a text are related. One way to assess children's understanding of narrative structure is to get them to tell stories themselves. Children's narratives become more coherent with age (see Baker and Stein, 1981, for a review of children's developing sensitivity to logical structure and knowledge of what makes a good story). Children also expect certain types of information to occur in stories. When crucial types of information are missing, they often add them in when retelling a story, so that the retold story conforms to the story as they expected it to be. Similarly, if a story is told with the events out of order, children often restore it to a more normal order when they retell it. For instance, Stein (1979) distorted written stories by moving specific statements from their original positions. She tested 2nd and 6th graders, and found that, although the older children recalled more in general, the qualitative patterns of recall were similar in the two age groups: the distorted stories were recalled less well than the original ones, and became more difficult to recall the further the statements were moved from their original positions. However, there were developmental differences, in that the older children were more likely to move the statements back to their original position when they recalled the stories, or at least repeated the statement in that position. Stein interpreted these findings as evidence for children's growing knowledge of story grammars, but they could equally well be considered as a reflection of children's growing knowledge about the world and about typical sequences of events in it (see below).

Trabasso and Stein (1997) explored differences in telling of picture stories in pre-schoolers and 2nd graders. Some of the pre-schoolers (age 4-5 years), tended to name, identify and describe the pictures. However, the majority of even the younger children, and almost all of the 2nd graders used knowledge of goal plans and psychological and physical causality to produce a causally and/or episodically well-formed story from the picture sequence (see also Trabasso and Nickels, 1992).

In summary, it is certainly likely that children's knowledge about typical story sequences will develop with age and experience, and that such development will aid their text comprehension. It is also likely that, as children acquire knowledge, and use goal plans to interpret everyday events, they will become more adept at constructing coherent, integrated representations of such events (whether they be actual or fictional).

Learning to make inferences

In order to understand a text, it is necessary to establish the connections between the ideas in it. However, writers leave many things implicit, and inferences are crucial to this process of connecting up ideas, since they enable the reader to fill in "missing information" in a text. Inferences may be of two main types: coherence and elaborative. Coherence inferences are necessary, in that they require that information explicitly provided in the text is integrated to establish cohesion between different sentences. Such inferences may require that information from general knowledge is incorporated with information in the text itself, to make links and to fill in missing details. Elaborative inferences are, as the name suggests, inferences that elaborate on and embellish information in the text, but which are not strictly necessary to understanding. Broadly, developmental studies of inference skills show that young children are able to make the same inferences as older ones, but are less likely to do so spontaneously (they may only do so when prompted or questioned, e.g. Casteel and Simpson, 1991; Omanson, Warren and Trabasso, 1978; Paris and Lindauer, 1976; Paris and Upton, 1976). We first discuss the development of inference making in general, and then focus on two aspects in particular: the use of prior knowledge in inferential processing, and the relation between inferential processing and text memory.

Paris, in particular, has carried out numerous studies of children's developing ability to make inferences. Many of his studies were based on the ideas of Bransford and his co-workers (e.g. Bransford, Barclay and Franks, 1972), who stressed that comprehension is a constructive and integrative process. For example, Paris and Carter (1973) argued that, if children construct a meaning-based representation of a text, then they should "recognise" sentences that are consistent with the meaning of the text, but which did not actually occur in them. The children in their study were read short passages, such as the following:

The bird is inside the cage.
The cage is under the table.
The bird is yellow.

The children then had to say whether or not they had heard a series of sentences from the stories, some of which had actually been presented, and some of which were consistent with the meaning of the text (true inferences, e.g. The bird is under the table). Children aged 7 and 10 consistently accepted true inferences as sentences they had already heard, but rejected new sentences that were not consistent with the meaning (e.g. The bird is on top of the table). Indeed, the probability of children identifying items from the stories and true inferences as old information did not differ significantly. These findings suggest that children of both ages integrated the information from different sentences and stored abstract, meaning-based representations, rather than specific words or sentences. The younger children made more errors overall, but the pattern of errors was similar for both age groups. Further studies, however, suggested that there were problems with this original study. In particular the sentences could be discriminated based on differences in wording as well as differences in meaning (further details can be found in Oakhill and Garnham, 1988, Chapter 5).

As an alternative to the false recognition paradigm, Paris and Lindauer (1976) developed a cued recall procedure, which eliminates some of these problems. This procedure, in which words are used to prompt the recall of previously-presented sentences, provides a cleaner measure of inferential processing in children. Paris and Lindauer tested 1st, 3rd and 5th graders, to see whether they routinely inferred highly-probable instruments that were not specifically mentioned (e.g. a knife for cutting steak). There were two versions of each sentence, one in which the instrument was explicitly mentioned (i.e. the information in parentheses was included) and one in which it was not: The workman dug a hole in the ground (with a shovel).

After listening to the sentences, the names of instruments (implied or explicit) were given as cues, and the child had to try to recall the relevant sentence. The findings were that 5th graders recalled almost as many sentences when the cues were implicit as when they were explicit. The implicit/explicit difference was much larger for the 3rd graders, and larger still for the 1st graders. The finding that there was almost no difference between explicit and implicit cues for the oldest children implies that they were able to make the inferences that enabled them to use the implicit cues to retrieval. However, even the 6 year-olds could choose the appropriate instrument for the implicit sentences in a subsequent test. So, it seems that even 1st grade children can make such inferences when the situation demands them, but they do not often *spontaneously* infer the instruments, either when they hear the sentences, or when they are given the cue words to prompt recall.

In a further experiment, Paris and Lindauer asked 1st grade children to act out the sentences as they were presented. In this condition, they found no difference between explicit and implicit mentions of the instrument. Presumably the requirement to act out the sentences forced the children to make appropriate inferences. Related work by Paris, Lindauer and Cox (1977) also showed that strategies that encourage children to elaborate on a text (in this case, making up a story about it) increased inferential processing in 6-year-olds, again suggesting the idea that younger children are able to make the same inferences as older ones, but are less likely to do so spontaneously.

Following the pioneering work of Paris and his co-workers in this area, a number of other researchers showed that both coherence and elaborative inferences (see above) increase with age (Ackerman, 1986, 1988), though Ackerman (1988) and Ackerman and McGraw (1991) report results which led them to suggest that younger children may be making *different* inferences, but not necessarily *fewer* inferences than older children and adults. Ackerman (1986) discusses some of the potential reasons for age-related differences in inference making. He suggests that younger children's greater tendency for non-integrative processing directly affects their ability to establish referential cohesion, but only indirectly affects causal elaboration. Thus, even if young children were encouraged to engage in more integrative processing, their difficulties with elaborative inferencing may remain. Their difficulties may be in part related to their inability to see the need for an elaborative inference. Ackerman (1988) has attempted to look in more detail at the *reasons* why younger children make fewer inferences. He concludes that even 1st graders are very well able to make at least some kinds of inference in some situations. However, young children are more dependent than older children and adults on contextual support (i.e. clues) to the inference. Developmental differences in inference making have often been attributed to differences in integration of information with age. However, Ackerman's study demonstrated that even young children are able to integrate information, at least to make the "reason inferences" which he studied. Ackerman suggests that inference failures cannot be attributed wholly to inference ability or integration or processing problems, but probably also have to do with the ways in which concept knowledge and concept prominence are organised in the listener's story representation.

Some recent work of our own (Cain and Oakhill, 1999), suggests that the ability to make at least some types of inferences is not something that simply comes with reading experience. That study showed that poor comprehenders performed worse on an inference task than did younger average readers who had the same absolute level of comprehension skill. Such a design enables the influence of comprehension skill and inference skill to be disentangled. The difference in inference skills between younger normal readers and older poor comprehenders could not have resulted from the younger children's superior comprehension (because they were at the same level of comprehension skill as older poor comprehenders). Thus, a causal link from inference making to comprehension skill is a possibility.

Inferences and prior knowledge

Another way of thinking about inference is that at least some forms of inference making require the incorporation of prior knowledge, memories and personal experiences into the mental representation of a text. For example, in order to infer that a shovel was used to dig a hole, the reader has to use the knowledge that holes in the ground are typically dug with shovels, and thus go beyond the information that is explicitly stated in the text about digging holes. There are numerous demonstrations that prior knowledge and individual expertise influence comprehension in skilled readers (e.g. Pichert and Anderson, 1977; Spilich, Vesonder, Chiesi and Voss, 1979). Thus, many inferences rely on knowledge of the world, and such knowledge is obviously developing in young children. So, there may be many texts that young children find difficult to understand because they have not got the relevant background information, and so cannot make the relevant inferences. Not surprisingly, there is a good deal of evidence that prior knowledge influences both comprehension and memory for text in children (see, e.g. Brown, Smiley, Day, Townsend and Lawton, 1977; Owings, Petersen, Bransford, Morris, and Stein, 1980). It can not only alter the amount that is recalled, but can also influence children's perceptions of what is important, and can affect the types of intrusions that occur in text recall.

While it is known that there are age-related differences in both inference skills and in general knowledge, there is very little work on how the availability of knowledge is related to the development of inference making skill. A recent study by Barnes, Dennis and Haefele-Kalvaitis (1996) addressed this issue, and showed that the ability to make inferences develops with age, independently of the influence of knowledge. Barnes et al. trained children (aged between 6 and 15 years) on a novel knowledge base. Once the children had learned the knowledge base to criterion, they read a multi-episode story and were asked questions about it that required inferences that drew on that knowledge base. The results showed that ensuring that the knowledge was equally available to all children did not attenuate age-related differences in inference making.

More generally, the increase in text recall with age is also thought to be attributable to concomitant increases in general knowledge. It is well known that text recall increases with age (e.g. Brown and Smiley, 1977; Mandler and Johnson, 1977). A problem with such studies is that they use exactly the same (typically very simple) passages for the different age groups. Thus, the older subjects would be expected to have less new information to learn compared with the younger ones. In a study in which an attempt to equate passage difficulty to grade level was made, Drum (1985) found no overall increase in the proportion of text ideas recalled as a function of age in immediate recall (she tested grades 5, 8 and 11, and college-level readers). However, contrary to the results for immediate recall, the older subjects recalled more information from the passages when recall was tested after a delay of a week. A likely explanation of these results is that, even though immediate verbatim recall did not increase with age, the older subjects produced text representations that were better integrated with prior knowledge, and which were, therefore, more stable over time.

Inference and memory for text

It is reasonable to suppose that inference making and story memory might be interrelated because inference making is likely to lead to a better-integrated, more coherent text representation, which will be better remembered. Paris and Upton (1976) suggested that inference-making may help with the encoding of text into memory, and demonstrated that the making of inferences helps children to remember a story. In their experiment, children aged between 5 and 11 heard short stories, and were asked questions about each story immediately afterwards. Half of the questions required recall of verbatim information, and half required an inference. Paris and Upton found that ability on both types of question increased with age but, even when improvement in memory for the exact wording of the texts was taken into account, there was still an age-related increase in the ability to make inferences.

The relation between inference making and text recall has, however, been questioned by Omanson Warren and Trabasso (1978). They conducted an experiment in which they asked 8-year-olds to make inferences about the intentions and actions of the main protagonist in a story. There were three versions of the story. In one, the protagonist's motives were not mentioned; in the second they were socially desirable, and in the third, undesirable. In all three cases the children listened to the story, were tested on a variety of inferential questions, and were then asked to recall the story. The inclusion of information about motives resulted in more correct inferences, but did not improve recall in general. In a second experiment, children aged 5 and 8 were matched on their ability to remember information that was crucial to the inferences, but the 8-year-olds still made more inferences than the younger children. These findings suggest that the ability to make inferences increases with age, but independently of text memory.

Comprehension monitoring

Older successful readers reflect on what they have just read: whether it made sense, whether or not they enjoyed it, what they learnt, and what the main points were. Such reflection on one's own reading can, and should, also take place during the course of comprehension. *Comprehension monitoring* is the term usually applied to this process of assessing whether one's comprehension is progressing in a satisfactory manner, and might also include the ability to know how to remedy any comprehension problems, if they are detected. In such circumstances, skilled readers might re-read part of the text, ask for assistance, or use a dictionary. Here, however, we concentrate on the first aspect. Comprehension monitoring is one of the *metalinguistic* skills that children acquire as their linguistic skills develop: the ability to reflect on the use of language. A more general survey of recent research on the development of children's metalinguistic skills can be found in Garton and Pratt (1998, Chapter 7).

In general, younger children are less likely to realise that they do not understand, and do not know what to do about it if they do realise (see Baker and Brown, 1984; Markman, 1981 for reviews). They are, for example, unable to detect that crucial information is missing from a text. For instance, Markman (1977) assessed children's ability to detect inadequacies in instructions for how to play a game or perform a magic trick. In both cases, some crucial information was omitted. The younger children (1st graders) generally failed to realise that there was any problem with the instructions until they tried to carry them out. Older children (3rd graders) realised more rapidly that the instructions were incomplete.

In another study, Markman (1979) used texts that were logically inconsistent. Young children were poor at spotting even gross inconsistencies, such as those in the following passage:

Ants
Everywhere they go they put out a special chemical from their bodies. They cannot see this chemical, but it has a special odour. An ant must have a nose in order to smell this chemical odour. Another thing about ants is that they do not have a nose. Ants cannot smell this odour. Ants can always find their way home by smelling this odour to follow the trail.

Markman asked children from grades 3, 5 and 6 to make suggestions about the changes, if any, that would be needed to make such texts easier to understand. Surprisingly, a substantial proportion of the texts were judged to be fully comprehensible even by the oldest children, although there was some improvement with age. Such results suggest that younger children are not building such a well-integrated model of a text or set of instructions because, if they were, they would necessarily spot inconsistencies. Markman and Gorin (1981) showed that children's apparent inability to find problems could be explained, at least partially, by the standards that they use to evaluate their comprehension, and also by their unwillingness to criticise written material. They gave children (aged 8 and 10) different sorts of instructions before they read passages that contained both falsehoods and inconsistencies. Some children were told simply to look for problems, others were specifically told to look either for falsehoods, or for inconsistencies. In each case, they were given several examples. Both kinds of specific instructions increased the children's ability to identify the kind of problem mentioned, though there was greater improvement in the older children's performance.

Task effects in comprehension monitoring

Although there is a general tendency for comprehension monitoring to improve with age, the extent to which it is demonstrated can be affected quite dramatically by aspects of the task, and by instructions (see Baker, 1984a; Garner, 1987, chapter 5).

For example, children are more likely to report problems when they are forewarned of them (Markman, 1979), or if the task is given game-like qualities (the children are asked to pretend they are editors, or detectives, e.g. Garner, 1980; Grabe and Mann, 1984; de Sousa and Oakhill, 1996). They are also more likely to report failures when the criteria are more explicit, for instance when they are assessing whether or not instructions work (Markman, 1977), than when they have to select their own criteria, as is the case when they are looking for text inconsistencies.

An example of these task effects is that, whereas the 3rd graders in Markman's (1977) study often reported problems with instructions even before they attempted to carry them out, children of the same age and older in her later study completely missed blatant inconsistencies, such as those in the passage about ants, above. There is some evidence that even pre-school children show some competence in evaluating their comprehension if the conditions are right (see Baker, 1984b, Wimmer, 1979).

A further complication, pointed out by Baker (1984a), is that passages may be incomprehensible for different reasons. For instance, the "ants" passage above is *internally inconsistent* – there is a conflict between different pieces of information in the passage itself. Other passages may present conflicts with prior knowledge, which presents an *external* standard against which they can be evaluated. Finally, uncommon or nonsense words make passages difficult for a different reason – they are not in the child's vocabulary. The ability to monitor these different types of text problem do not necessarily develop in parallel. Garner (1981), for example, found that poorer readers are less likely to notice problems arising from internal inconsistencies than those arising from difficult vocabulary.

Baker (1984a) compared spontaneous and instructed use of the three criteria for detecting comprehension problems, outlined above: internal inconsistency, external inconsistency, and vocabulary. She tested 9- and 11-year-olds (and also compared good and poor readers at each age). Half of the children were instructed about the criteria they should apply, and the other half were simply told to look for problems. Consistent with previous research, the older and better readers identified more problems than the younger and poorer readers. Interestingly, when Baker looked at the number of times a criterion was used, she found that the 9-year-old children complied with the instructions just as often as the 11-year-olds. However, they were less likely to use the criteria correctly.

Why do children have problems with comprehension monitoring?

Baker's findings conflict with the view that younger children are less willing to criticise written material. Baker suggests, rather, that even when younger children know what problems they might encounter, they may still fail to identify problems because they do not always use the criteria consistently and effectively – perhaps because they cannot cope so efficiently with the competing demands on their cognitive resources.

Ruffman (1996) has suggested that some form of information processing limitation is important in explaining children's difficulties with comprehension monitoring. In a study that will be discussed in more detail below, Vosniadou, Pearson and Rogers (1988) showed that children's difficulties often arise because they fail to remember the logically inconsistent premises. Because information processing capabilities are known to develop with age (for a summary, see Oakhill, 1988), it is likely that children's capabilities in comprehension monitoring will show a concomitant increase. However, Ruffman also argues that the extent to which children are predisposed to derive a single conclusion from a text is at least as important as their information processing capabilities. Evidence from a variety of cognitive tasks indicates that children are much more likely to acknowledge that another person does not have complete knowledge, or has misunderstood, than they are to attribute lack of knowledge or misunderstanding to themselves. In other words, when children make mistakes, they are much more likely to do so because they attribute knowledge, rather than ignorance, to themselves.

One way to get round this problem of children being over-confident in their own knowledge, is to use non-verbal assessments of comprehension monitoring. For instance, Harris, Kruithof, Terwogt, and Visser (1981) measured 8- and 11-year-olds' reading times for a line of text that was not consistent with the title of the passage. They also asked the children to point out explicitly any problems with the texts they were reading. They found that, although the 11-year-olds were better at explicitly recognising which line was inconsistent, children of both ages spent more time reading the lines that were inconsistent with the titles. Harris et al. argued that the inconsistent lines generated some sort of signal even to the younger children that there was something wrong with the text, causing them to re-read the inconsistent line, or to look back to earlier text, but they were less likely to realise the implications of the signal than the older children. Subsequent work by Zabrucky and Ratner (1986) produced similar findings. They found that both 3rd and 6th graders spent more time reading inconsistent, than consistent, target sentences, but that the 3rd graders were less likely to report inconsistencies. Thus, larger discrepancies between the on-line and off-line measures of comprehension evaluation were found for the younger than for the older children.

These data also indicate that comprehension monitoring does not necessarily entail explicit awareness of the problem in the text. In the Harris et al. study, mentioned above, the children seemed to have some implicit sensitivity to the problems, even when they could not explicitly identify the problem.

How are comprehension and comprehension monitoring related?

It is not clear to what extent comprehension and comprehension monitoring are separate subskills or related aspects of the same process. For instance, Ellen Markman (1981, p. 75) suggests that information about comprehension is often a by-product of the attempt to understand. In some cases, active comprehension monitoring may not be necessary – the reader simply needs to engage in comprehension. Vosniadou, Pearson and Rogers (1988) also proposed that the ability to detect errors in a text is related to the ability to construct a good representation of the meaning of the passage. They asked 1st, 3rd and 5th graders (mean ages 6.5, 8.7 and 10.7 years) to detect familiar falsehoods and unfamiliar factual contradictions in narrative texts. The children were able to detect the familiar falsehoods better than the unfamiliar contradictions but, when familiarity was controlled, no differences were found. However, when the children's recall was compared to their comprehension monitoring, it was found that detection of inconsistencies was poorest for precisely those texts that were recalled least well. The authors conclude, therefore, that children are more likely to fail to detect inconsistencies because they do not represent the inconsistent pieces of information in memory in the first place, rather than because they are unable to compare the representations of the inconsistent parts of the text. They further suggest that younger children's difficulties in such tasks may be compounded by inadequate or incompatible prior knowledge.

In summary, children's ability to reflect on their own comprehension develops over the primary school years. Younger children's difficulties with comprehension monitoring may be partly due to their lack of awareness of appropriate standards for evaluating their comprehension. Older children, by contrast, use multiple-standards in a flexible manner, and are more likely to build a coherent text representation which, in turn, aids their comprehension monitoring. Markman (1981) suggests that, without the ability to reflect on one's own comprehension, comprehension itself will suffer. However, others have suggested that it is comprehension that is fundamental to monitoring. Whatever the case, there is no evidence for a *causal* link between metalinguistic awareness and comprehension skill. In fact, both Vygotsky (1962) and Donaldson (1978) have argued that it is the process of learning to read that is responsible for increasing the child's language awareness, rather than the other way round.

Reading experience

In this section, we discuss briefly what is known about the effects of reading experience out of school: both being read to, and voluntary reading. It is plausible that reading to children may have some indirect effects on the development of comprehension. For instance, adults reading to children may explain unknown vocabulary items to them, and children are exposed to the "language of books": the more complex syntactic structures and longer sentences that are common in books but not in spoken language. Reading to children might make them more interested in reading themselves, or more keen to learn to read (see Garton and Pratt, this volume), and increased motivation might, in itself, lead to advances in reading comprehension.

A common belief is that children should be encouraged to spend more time engaged in reading outside school because it is supposed that greater exposure to print will increase reading ability and reading-related skills. However, although children who read a lot tend to be good comprehenders (for a review see Guthrie and Greaney, 1991), the causal direction of this link is not clear: It may be that good comprehenders are children who enjoy reading and who, therefore, choose to read a lot, rather than the other way round (see, for example, the discussion of Juel's study, above).

Several studies have clarified the nature of this link between print exposure and comprehension. For instance, Anderson, Wilson and Fielding (1988) showed that text comprehension in 5th grade was predicted by amount of reading (based on diaries of amount of time spent reading outside of school), even when earlier (2nd grade) text comprehension was taken into account. Their finding that amount of reading predicted growth in comprehension between 2nd and 5th grade led them to conclude that amount of book reading has a causal role in reading comprehension skill. Similarly, Cipielewski and Stanovich (1992) found that amount of reading (measured by the Title Recognition Test) was highly predictive of reading comprehension in 5th grade, even after 3rd grade reading comprehension had been taken into account. Echols et al. (1996) showed that measures of exposure to print were highly predictive of reading comprehension one year later, even when an assessment of general verbal ability (PPVT) had been taken into account. Thus, there is still a relation between print exposure and reading comprehension, even when the tendency for those who are high-verbal to be more avid readers is taken into account. Even more surprising are the results of a study by Cunningham and Stanovich (1997) in which they investigated the predictors of growth in reading comprehension from 1st to 11th grade. They found that their measures of exposure to print were highly predictive of growth in comprehension skill. Conversely, 1st grade reading ability (whether measured by single-word or comprehension indices) was highly predictive of 11th grade exposure to print, even when 11th grade reading comprehension had been partialled out. These data suggest that reading comprehension and exposure to print are likely to act in reciprocal relation to each other, over long periods of time. Cunningham and Stanovich's data demonstrate that individual differences in exposure to print predict growth in reading comprehension throughout the elementary school grades. Furthermore, the rapid early acquisition of reading ability seems to help children develop the lifetime habit of reading, regardless of their eventual level of comprehension skill.

Not only has the time spent reading outside of school been related to growth in reading comprehension, but so has time spent reading in school. Most studies in this area also suffer from the problem that the data are correlational – time spent reading is related to comprehension skill, but it is not clear what is causing what. However, studies that have attempted to address the issue of causality provide some evidence that amount of time reading does cause an increase in comprehension ability. For instance, Taylor, Frye and Maruyama (1990) found that subsequent reading comprehension was improved in a group of students who were given additional time to read, and Morrow (1996, cited by Guthrie, Van Meter, Hancock, Alao, Anderson and McCann, 1998) has confirmed this finding in an experiment with children who were assigned additional reading time in their classrooms.

Purpose and motivation for reading

Of course, all these factors discussed above may depend crucially on the individual child's motivation and interest in what they are reading. In order to become proficient readers and good comprehenders, it is not enough to possess the cognitive skills necessary for reading: Children must also be motivated to engage in literacy activities. Wigfield and Guthrie (1997) showed that motivation to read predicts growth in reading and, as we discussed above, amount of reading has been shown to be causally linked to gains in comprehension. A direct relation between readers' intrinsic motivation and their text comprehension has also been shown (Guthrie, Van Meter, Hancock, Alao, Anderson and McCann, 1998). A further study by Guthrie, Wigfield, Metsala and Cox (1999) included all three variables together: text comprehension, amount of reading and motivation to read. They found that reading motivation was a direct predictor of reading amount, even when the contributions of previous achievement, passage comprehension, prior knowledge and reading efficacy were taken into account. These findings held for 3rd, 5th and 10th grade students. They also found that amount of reading predicted reading comprehension in all age groups, even when a number of variables that correlate with reading comprehension (previous achievement, prior knowledge, reading efficacy and reading motivation) were controlled. The view of those authors is that one of the main contributions of motivation to text comprehension is that motivation increases amount of reading, which in turn has an impact on reading comprehension.

SUMMARY AND CONCLUSIONS

In this chapter, we have considered a number of factors that may influence the development of children's reading comprehension, either independently or in combination. These factors include word decoding, vocabulary and syntactic skills, knowledge of text structure, inference making and comprehension monitoring, and factors extrinsic to the text such as amount of reading experience and motivation. Whereas clear correlational links have been shown between comprehension skill and other variables, most of the available data do not permit conclusions about the likely direction of the link between a particular skill or ability and reading development, so in most cases there is no direct evidence that the link is causal. In some instances, it is clear that the link is not directly causal –

in the case of word level skills, for instance. Although it is obvious that a certain level of competence in word reading will be essential for comprehension, beyond this level there is no evidence to suggest that efficient decoding, in itself, causes comprehension skill to develop. Many of the skills that we have discussed, such as appreciation of how texts are structured, are likely to be by-products of comprehension skill, rather than essential to its development. Indeed, it is likely that the pattern of causation is complex, and probably often involves reciprocity between a particular skill and comprehension development. This reciprocal relation may well be mediated, at least in part, by reading experience and motivation to read. For instance, it is clear from Juel's longitudinal study that the poor readers (who were unable or unmotivated to read either in or out of school) made very little progress in listening comprehension. It is also likely that the relative contribution of different skills to reading comprehension varies with stage of development. For instance, the relative contribution of word level and higher order skills probably depends on age and ability (see, e.g. the earlier discussion of Curtis's work). One clear conclusion from this survey is that studies of the longitudinal development and interrelations between children's comprehension skills and strategies are very much needed.

REFERENCES

Ackerman, B. P. (1986). Referential and causal coherence in the story comprehension of children and adults. *Journal of Experimental Child Psychology, 41*, 336-366.

Ackerman, B. P. (1988). Reason inferences in the story comprehension of children and adults. *Child Development, 59*, 1426-1442.

Ackerman, B. P. and McGraw, M. (1991). Constraints on the causal inferences of children and adults in comprehending stories. *Journal of Experimental Child Psychology, 51*, 364-394.

Anderson, R.C. & Freebody, P. (1981). Vocabulary Knowledge. In J.T. Guthrie (Ed.), *Comprehension and Teaching,* (pp. 77-117). Newark, Delaware: International Reading Association.

Anderson, R. C., Wilson, P. T. and Fielding, L. G. (1988). Growth in reading and how children spend their time outside of school. *Reading Research Quarterly, 23*, 285-303.

Baker, L. (1984a). Spontaneous versus instructed use of multiple standards for evaluating comprehension; effects of age, reading proficiency, and type of standard. *Journal of Experimental Child Psychology, 38*, 289-311

Baker, L. (1984b). Children's effective use of multiple standards for evaluating their comprehension. *Journal of Educational Psychology, 76*, 588-597

Baker, L. & Brown, A.I. (1984). Metacognitive skills and reading. In P.D. Pearson (Ed.). *Handbook of Reading Research, Vol. 1*, New York: Plenum Press, (pp. 353-394).

Barnes, M. A., Dennis, M. & Haefele-Kalvaitis, J. (1996). The effects of knowledge availability and knowledge accessibility on coherence and elaborative inferencing in children from six to fifteen years of age. *Journal of Experimental Child Psychology, 61*, 216-241.

Beck, I. C. & McKeown, G. (1991) Conditions of Vocabulary Acquisition. In R. Barr, M.L. Kamil, P. Mosenthal, and P. D. Peason (Eds.). *Handbook of Reading Research, Vol. 2*. (pp. 789-814). New York: Longman.

Beck, I. C., Perfetti, C.A. & McKeown, G. (1982). Effects of long-term vocabulary instruction on lexical access and reading comprehension. *Journal of Educational Psychology, 74*, 506-521.

Bishop, D. (1982). *Test for the Reception of Grammar.* Manchester, England: Chapel Press.

Bower, G. H. (1978). Experiments on story comprehension and recall. *Discourse Processes, 1,* 211-231.

Bowey, J. A., & Patel, R. K. (1988). Metalinguistic ability and early reading achievement. *Applied Psycholinguistics, 9,* 367-383.

Bransford, J. D., Barclay, J. R. & Franks, J. J. (1972). Contextual prerequisites for understanding: Some investigations of comprehension and recall. *Journal of Verbal Learning and Verbal Behavior, 11,* 717-726.

Brown, A. L. & Day, J. D. (1983). Macrorules for summarizing texts: The development of expertise. *Journal of Verbal Learning and Verbal Behavior, 22,* 1-14.

Brown, A. L. & Smiley, S. (1977). Rating the importance of structural units of prose passages: A problem of metacognitive development. *Child Development, 48,* 1-8.

Brown, A. L., Smiley, S. S., Day, J., Townsend, H. & Lawton, S. C. (1977). Intrusion of a thematic idea in children's recall of prose. *Child Development, 48,* 1454-1466.

Cain, K. & Oakhill, J. V. (1999). Inference making and its relation to comprehension failure. *Reading and Writing, 11,* 489-503.

Cain, K., Oakhill, J. V. & Bryant, P. E. (2000). Phonological skills and comprehension failure: A test of the phonological processing deficit hypothesis. *Reading and Writing, 13,* 31-56.

Carroll, J. B. (1993). Human Cognitive Abilities: A Survey of Factor-Analytic Studies. New York: Cambridge University Press.

Casteel, M.A. & Simpson, G. B. (1991). Textual coherence and the development of inferential generation skills, *Journal of Research in Reading, 14,* 116-129.

Chabot, R. J., Petros, T. V. & McCord, G. (1983). Developmental and reading ability differences in accessing information from semantic memory. *Journal of Experimental Child Psychology, 35,* 128-142.

Charniak, E. (1972). Towards a model of children's story comprehension. M.I.T. AI Laboratory Memorandum AI-TR, Number 266.

Cipielewski, J. & Stanovich, K. E. (1992). Predicting growth in reading ability from children's exposure to print. *Journal of Experimental Child Psychology, 54,* 74-89.

Cunningham, A. E. & Stanovich, K. E. (1997). Early reading acquisition and its relation to reading experience and ability 10 years later. *Developmental Psychology, 33,* 934-945.

Curtis, M.E. (1980). Development of components of reading skills. *Journal of Educational Psychology, 72,* 656-669.

Daneman, M. (1988). Word knowledge and reading skill. In. M. Daneman, G. MacKinnon & T.G. Waller (Eds.), *Reading Research: Advances in Theory and Practice, Vol. 6.* San Diego: Academic Press.

Danner, F. W. (1976). Children's understanding of intersentence organisation in the recall of short descriptive passages. *Journal of Educational Psychology, 68,* 174-183.

Davis, F. B. (1944). Fundamental factors in reading comprehension. *Psychometrika, 9,* 185-197.

Davis, F.B. (1968). Research in comprehension in reading. *Reading Research Quarterly, 3,* 499-545.

de Sousa, I. & Oakhill, J.V. (1996). Do levels of interest have an effect on children's comprehension monitoring importance? *British Journal of Educational Psychology, 66,* 471-482.

Donaldson, M. (1978). *Children's Minds.* Glasgow: Collins

Drum, P. A. (1985). Retention of text information by grade, ability and study. *Discourse Processes, 8,* 21-52.

Echols, L. D., West, R. F., Stanovich, K. E. & Zehr, K. S. (1996). Using children's literacy activities to predict growth in verbal cognitive skills: A longitudinal investigation. *Journal of Educational Psychology, 88,* 296-304.

Eldredge, J. L., Quinn, B. & Butterfield, D. D. (1990). Causal relationships between phonics, reading comprehension, and vocabulary achievement in the second grade. *Journal of Educational Research, 83,* 201-214.

Fleischer, L. S., Jenkins, J. R. & Pany, D. (1979). Effects on poor readers' comprehension of training in rapid decoding. *Reading Research Quarterly, 15,* 30-48.

Garner, R (1980). Monitoring of understanding: An investigation of good and poor readers' awareness of induced miscomprehension of text. *Journal of Reading Behavior, 12,* 55-64.

178   *J. V. Oakhill & K. Cain*

Garner, R. (1981). Monitoring of passage inconsistency among poor comprehenders: A preliminary test of the "piecemeal processing" explanation. *Journal of Educational Research, 74*, 159-162.

Garner, R. (1987). *Metacognition and Reading Comprehension*. Norwood, N.J.: Ablex.

Garton, A., & Pratt, C. (1998). Learning to be literate: The development of spoken and written language (2nd ed.). Oxford, England UK: Blackwell Publishers, Inc.

Gernsbacher, M. A., Varner, K. R. & Faust, M. E. (1990). Investigating differences in general comprehension skill. *Journal of Experimental Psychology: Learning, Memory and Cognition, 16*, 430-445.

Gernsbacher, M. A. (Ed.) (1994). *Handbook of psycholinguistics*. San Diego, CA, USA: Academic Press, Inc.

Gitomer, D. H., Pellegrino, J. W. & Bisanz, J. (1983). Developmental change and invariance in semantic processing. *Journal of Experimental Child Psychology, 35*, 56-80.

Grabe, M., & Mann, S. (1984). A technique for the assessment and training of comprehension monitoring skills. *Journal of Reading Behavior, 16*, 131-144.

Guthrie, J. T. & Greany, V. (1991). Literacy acts. In R. Barr, M. L. Kamil, P. Mosenthal, and P. D. Peason (Eds.). *Handbook of Reading Research, Vol. 2*. New York: Longman. (pp. 68-96).

Guthrie, J. T., Van Meter, P., Hancock, G. R., Alao, S., Anderson E. & McCann, A. (1998). Does concept-oriented reading instruction increase strategy use and conceptual learning from text? *Journal of Educational Psychology, 90*, 261-278.

Guthrie, J. T., Wigfield, A., Metsala, J. L. & Cox, K. E. (1999). Motivational and cognitive predictors of text comprehension and reading amount. *Scientific Studies of Reading, 3*, 231-256.

Harris, P. L., Kruithof, A., Terwogt, M. & Visser, T. (1981). Children's detection and awareness of textual anomaly. *Journal of Experimental Child Psychology, 31*, 212-230.

Huey, E. (1968) *The Psychology and Pedagogy of Reading*. Cambridge, Mass.: MIT Press (originally published 1908).

Jenkins, J. R., Pany, D. & Schreck, J. (1978). Vocabulary and reading comprehension: Instructional effects. *Technical Report No. 100*. Urbana-Champaign, IL: Center for the Study of Reading.

Johnston, P. & Afflerbach, P. (1985). The process of constructing main ideas from text. *Cognition and Instruction, 2*, 207-232.

Johnson-Laird, P. N. (1983). Mental Models: Towards a Cognitive Science of Language, Inference, and Consciousness. Cambridge: Cambridge University Press.

Juel, C. (1988). Learning to read and write: A longitudinal study of 54 children from first through fourth grades. *Journal of Educational Psychology, 80*, 437-447.

Kintsch W. (1998). *Comprehension: A Paradigm for Cognition*. Cambridge: Cambridge University Press.

Laberge, D. & Samuels, S. J. (1974). Toward a theory of automatic information processing in reading. *Cognitive Psychology, 6*, 293-323.

Mandler, J. M. & Johnson, N. S. (1977). Remembrance of things parsed: Story structure and recall. *Cognitive Psychology, 9*, 111-151.

Markman, E.M. (1977). Realizing that you don't understand: A preliminary investigation. *Child Development, 48*, 986-992.

Markman, E.M. (1979). Realizing that you don't understand: Elementary school children's awareness of inconsistencies. *Child Development, 50*, 643-655.

Markman, E.M. (1981). Comprehension Monitoring. In W.P. Dickson (Ed.) *Children's Oral Communication Skills* (pp. 61-84). London: Academic Press.

Markman, E. M. & Gorin, L. (1981). Children's ability to adjust their standards for evaluating comprehension. *Journal of Educational Psychology, 73*, 320-325.

Meyer, B. J. F. (1977). The structure of prose: effects on learning and memory and implications for education practice. In R. C. Anderson, R. Spiro & W. E. Montague (Eds.) *Schooling and the Acquisition of Knowledge* (pp. 179-200). Hillsdale, N.J.: Lawrence Erlbaum Associates.

Mezynski, K. (1983). Issues concerning the acquisition of knowledge: Effects of vocabulary training on reading comprehension. *Review of Educational Research, 53*, 253-279.

Oakhill, J. (1988). The development of children's reasoning ability: Information-processing approaches.

In K. Richardson & S. Sheldon (Eds.), *Cognitive development to adolescence: A reader* (pp. 169-188). Hove, England UK: Lawrence Erlbaum Associates, Inc.

Oakhill, J., & Garnham, A. (1988). *Becoming a skilled reader*. Oxford, England UK: Basil Blackwell, Inc.

Oakhill, J. V. Cain, K. & Bryant, P. E. (2003, in press). The dissociation of single-word reading and text comprehension: Evidence from component skills. *Language and Cognitive Processes*.

Omanson, R. C., Warren, W. M., & Trabasso, T. (1978). Goals, inferences, comprehension and recall of stories by children. *Discourse Processes, 1,* 337-354.

Owings, R. A., Petersen, G. A., Bransford, J. D., Morris, D. & Stein, B. S. (1980). Spontaneous monitoring and regulation of learning: A comparison of successful and less successful fifth graders. *Journal of Educational Psychology, 72,* 250-256.

Palmer, J., MacLeod, C. M., Hunt, E. & Davidson, J. E. (1985). Information processing correlates of reading. *Journal of Memory and Language, 24 (1),* 59-88.

Paris, S. G. & Carter, A. (1973). Semantic and constructive aspects of sentence memory in children. *Developmental Psychology, 9,* 109-113.

Paris, S. G. & Lindauer, B. K. (1976). The role of inference in children's comprehension and memory for sentences. *Cognitive Psychology, 8,* 217-227.

Paris, S. G., Lindauer, B. K. & Cox, G. L. (1977). The development of inferential comprehension. *Child Development, 48,* 1728-1733

Paris, S. G. & Upton, L. R. (1976). Children's memory for inferential relationships in prose. *Child Development, 47,* 660-668.

Perfetti, C. A. & Lesgold, A. M. (1977). Discourse comprehension and sources of individual differences. In M. A. Just & P. A. Carpenter (Eds.), *Cognitive processes in comprehension* (pp. 141-183). Hillsdale, N.J.: Lawrence Erlbaum Associates.

Pichert, J. W. & Anderson, R. C. (1977). Taking different perspectives on a story. *Journal of Educational Psychology, 69,* 309-315.

Reid, J. F. (1970). Sentence structure in reading primers. *Research in Education, 3,* 23-37.

Reid, J. F. (1983). Into print: Reading and language growth. In M. Donaldson, R. Grieve & C. Pratt (Eds.) *Early Childhood Development and Education* (pp. 151-165). Oxford: Basil Blackwell.

Ruffman, T. (1996). Reassessing children's comprehension-monitoring skills. In C. Cornoldi & J. V. Oakhill (Eds.) *Reading Comprehension Difficulties: Processes and Intervention* (pp. 33-67). Mahwah, N. J.: Lawrence Erlbaum Associates.

Saarnio, D. A., Oka, E.R. & Paris, S.G. (1990). Developmental predictors of children's reading comprehension. In T. H. Carr & B. A. Levy (Eds.) *Reading and its Development: Component Skills Approaches* (pp. 57-79). New York: Academic Press.

Shankweiler, D. (1989). How problems of comprehension are related to difficulties in word reading. In D. Shankweiler & I. Y. Liberman (Eds.) *Phonology and Reading Disability: Solving the Reading Puzzle* (pp. 35-68). Ann Arbor: University of Michigan Press.

Smith, S. T. Macaruso, P. Shankweiler, D. & Crain, S. (1989). Syntactic comprehension in young poor readers. *Applied Psycholinguistics, 10,* 420-454.

Smith, F. (1975). *Comprehension and Learning*. New York: Holt, Rinehart and Winston.

Spilich, G. S., Vesonder, G. T., Chiesi, H.L. & Voss, J.F. (1979). Text processing of domain-related information for individuals with high and low domain knowledge. *Journal of Verbal Learning and Verbal Behavior, 18,* 275-290.

Stein, N. L. (1979). How Children understand stories: A developmental analysis. In L.G. Katz (Ed.) *Current Topics in Early Childhood Education, Vol. 2.* (pp.261-290). Norwood, N.J.: Ablex.

Stein, N.L. & Glenn, C. G. (1979). An analysis of story comprehension in elementary school children. In R. O. Freedle (Ed.) *New Directions in Discourse Processing, Vol. 2.* (pp 53-120). Norwood, N.J.: Ablex.

Taylor, B. M., Frye, B. J. & Maruyama, G. (1990). Time spent reading and reading growth. *American Educational Research Journal, 27,* 351-362.

Thorndike, E. L. (1917). Reading as Reasoning: A Study of mistakes in paragraph reading. *Journal of Educational Psychology, 8,* 323-332.

Thorndike, R. L. (1973). Reading Comprehension Education in Fifteen Countries. New York: Wiley.

Trabasso, T. & Nickels, M. (1992). The development of goal plans of action in the narration of a picture story. *Discourse Processes, 15,* 249-275.

Trabasso, T. & Stein, N. (1997). Narrating, representing, and remembering event sequences. In P. W. van den Broek, P. J. Bauer & T. Bourg. *Developmental Spans in Event Comprehension and Representation.* Mahwah, N.J.: Lawrence Erlbaum Associates.

Tunmer, W. E. (1989). The role of language-related factors in reading disability. In D. Shankweiler & I. Y. Liberman (Eds.) *Phonology and Reading Disability: Solving the Reading Puzzle* (pp. 91-131). Ann Arbor: University of Michigan Press.

Tuinman, J. J. & Brady, M. E. (1974). How does vocabulary account for variance on reading comprehension tests? A preliminary instructional analysis. In P. Nacke (Ed.), *Twenty-third National Reading Conference Yearbook.* Clemson, SC: The National Reading Conference.

Tunmer, W. E., Nesdale, A. R., & Wright, A. D. (1987). Syntactic awareness and reading acquisition. *British Journal of Developmental Psychology, 5 (1),* 25-34.

Vosniadou, S., Pearson, P. D. & Rogers, T. (1988). What causes children's failures to detect inconsistencies in text? Representation versus comparison difficulties. *Journal of Educational Psychology, 80,* 27-39.

Vygotsky, L. S. (1962). *Thought and Language.* Cambridge, Mass.: MIT Press.

Werner, H., & Kaplan, E. (1950). Development of word meaning through verbal context: an experimental study. *Journal of Psychology, 29,* 251-257.

Wigfield, A., & Guthrie, J. T. (1997). Relations of children's motivation for reading to the amount and breadth or their reading. *Journal of Educational Psychology, 89 (3),* 420-432.

Willows, D. M. & Ryan, E. B. (1981). Differential utilisation of syntactic and semantic information by skilled and less skilled readers in the intermediate grades. *Journal of Educational Psychology, 73,* 607-715.

Wimmer, H. (1979). Processing of script deviations by young children. *Discourse Processes, 2,* 301-310

Yussen, S. R. (1982). Children's impressions of coherence in narratives. In Hutson, B.A. (Ed.) *Advances in Reading/Language Research,* Vol. 1. JAI Press Inc., (pp. 245-281).

Zabrucky, K. & Ratner, H. H. (1986). Children's comprehension monitoring and recall of inconsistent stories. *Child Development, 57,* 1401-1418.

SUGGESTED FURTHER READINGS

Cornoldi, C. and Oakhill, J.V.(Eds) (1996) Reading Comprehension Difficulties: Processes and Remediation. Mahwah, N.J.: Lawrence Erlbaum Inc.

Garton, A. and Pratt, C. (1998) Learning to be Literate: The Development of Spoken and Written Language. 2nd Edition. Oxford: Basil Blackwell. Especially chapters 5, 6, 7 and 9.

B2. Text and Cognition

MICHEL FAYOL

ABSTRACT

In this chapter, we summarize the observations concerning performance, knowledge and processes that have been described regarding the use of narratives by adults and their acquisition by children. In the first part we will consider the processes adults employ in comprehension and in production. We will thus be able to illustrate the principle dimensions involved in the treatment of narrative. These will then be discussed individually in the examination of work undertaken regarding their development in children from 4 or 5 to 12 years. In the second section, we will then report the facts acquired concerning the acquisition and learning of the organisation of events, the textual structure of narrative and, finally, the skills involved in textualisation.

INTRODUCTION
TEXT AND COGNITION: ON UNDERSTANDING AND PRODUCING NARRATIVES

The study of the comprehension and production of written texts and their development in respect of age and/or schooling level makes it necessary to distinguish between a number of dimensions concerning the relationships between text and cognition. This necessity is more apparent when one attempts a study of narrative. This textual type is in effect the only subject of this nature to have been the object of extensive research carried out both on adults and on children of different ages, in comprehension as well as production. Here, we shall limit ourselves to a summary of recorded observations concerning performance, knowledge and processes that have been described regarding the use of narratives by adults and their acquisition by children. In the first part we will consider the processes adults employ in comprehension and in production. We will thus be able to illustrate the principle dimensions involved in the treatment of narrative. These will then be discussed individually in the examination of work undertaken regarding their development in children from 4/5–12 years. In the second section, we will then report the facts acquired concerning the acquisition and learning of the

T. Nunes, P. Bryant (eds.), Handbook of Children's Literacy, 181–197.

organisation of events, the textual structure of narrative and, finally, the skills involved in textualisation.

ACTIVITIES INVOLVED IN COMPREHENSION AND PRODUCTION

Listening and reading comprehension

To understand a discourse or a text is to construct a mental model of the described situation (Bower & Morrow, 1990; see for overviews concerning text understanding, Britton & Graesser, 1996 and van Oostendorp & Goldman, 1999). This is a quasi-perceptual, analogue representation of the evoked entities which is less precise and less complete than in the case of perception (Johnson-Laird, 1983; Oakhill, Garnham & Vonk, 1989). This representation is elaborated on the basis of explicit textual information provided by words organised into sentences in accordance with the syntax specific to a given language. These sentences are themselves sequentially organised as text types which are more or less conventional and constraining (Fayol, 1991a). The words and their organisation induce the evocation of cognitive representations, the concepts and the relations between them. The processing performed in order to understand a text therefore interrelates both textual and cognitive dimensions, both the linguistic elements and the concepts and relations evoked by them. It demands that readers possess linguistic and conceptual knowledge and are able to mobilise both without being overwhelmed by the task.

The activity of comprehension is goal-directed. It is mobilised relative to a text and as a function of the reader's objective (e.g., amusement, search for information, to understand how to assemble a model or cook a recipe). It takes place in real time. As we know, listeners as well as readers have limited information processing capacities (Just & Carpenter, 1992; Kintsch & van Dijk, 1978). Depending on the characteristics of the text, their familiarity with the lexicon, the relative complexity of the sentences, their prior knowledge in the field discussed by the text and the objectives set for them or which they have set for themselves, they must therefore allocate their attention in the most suitable and effective way possible. Text processing is thus a highly constrained cognitive activity. The allocation of resources must allow for the elaboration of a mental model as close as possible to that which is required by the task. As far as the narrative is concerned, the construction of a causal chain linking the different actions to the individual's desired objectives probably provides a good approximation of what constitutes a relevant mental model, even though other aspects must be taken equally into consideration (Trabasso & Sperry, 1985).

To summarise, text comprehension primarily requires the capacity to process the linguistic aspects of text, words and sentences. It also requires a knowledge of the domain and textual type which makes it possible to draw inferences from concepts and connections which are explicitly marked in the text, and to fill in gaps in the narrative, which are always, in varying degrees, elliptical. Finally, it presupposes that people can monitor their own comprehension and consequently adapt the rhythm and objectives of their information acquisition. The mobilised operations must also, in their entirety, remain within the limits of the subject's processing capacities.

Narrative production

Understanding a narrative equates more or less to de-linearising pieces of information which are presented or processed in sequence, for the simple reason that listening and reading are sequential activities. This de-linearisation results in the creation of a representation which is simultaneously compatible with the text, the reader's prior knowledge of the field and the intention of the writer who has chosen to emphasise a particular character or action. In contrast to the process of comprehension, the producer of a text (e.g. a narrative) does not have to infer an intention or a content. He or she already possesses these elements, even if the relevant information for the narration is not all easily and quickly accessible. The narrator's task is therefore to focus on an event and to communicate the corresponding information by selecting the most appropriate items as a function of the pursued objective, the listeners and the conceptual and linguistic knowledge of the interlocutors.

If the author considers the chosen theme to be sufficiently interesting, he starts his narration. This requires the sequence of facts in the mental model to be easily accessible so that they can be converted into textual form if so required for the listeners or readers' understanding. As well as understanding, producing a text is a higly demanding activity which requires the efficient on-line coordination of both lower-level processes (e.g. lexical access, syntactic frame construction) and higher-level processes (e.g. elaborating ideas and conceptual relations) (for a review, see Torrance & Jeffery, 1999).

The canonical organisation of narratives plays a key role here. In effect, the narrative structure, which approximately follows the order of events (Denhière, 1984; Fayol 1985), constitutes, as it were, a plan for the retrieval of information from memory. It operates as a cue system for items grouped in categories. The activation of a higher-level category makes possible the retrieval of the elements contained within it and thus provides information about what needs to be formulated and, simultaneously, makes it possible to remember what has already been so. This results in the facilitation effects of the narrative structure on performances in comprehension, recall and story summarising tests (Kintsch, Mandel & Kozminsky, 1977; Stein & Nezworski, 1978).

Narration obliges the author to manage two complementary constraints inherent in the linearity of the text production. On the one hand, it is necessary to introduce new information, without which the narrative would have no interest.

On the other, he must ensure continuity between those elements previously introduced and those which emerge as the narrative unfolds. This assumes that the author possesses marker systems – punctuation, connectors, pronouns, articles – and that he employs them appropriately.

Overall, there are numerous studies which investigate and attempt to model adult performance in narrative comprehension and production. These studies can be subdivided on the basis of the levels which they address: with "high-level" corresponding to the construction of the mental model and an interpretation corresponding to the recipient and the quantity of prior knowledge (Fayol, 1997 a; Levy & Ransdell, 1996; Rijlaarsdam, van den Bergh & Couzjin, 1996) and "low-level" relating to the linguistic processing of words and sentences (Bock & Levelt, 1994; Levelt, 1989). The question of textual structures occupies an intermediate position between content-based and textualisation-based approaches (Fayol, 1991 a). However, in terms of the conceptions and methods involved it is closer to the linguistic perspective. We have decided to devote a sub-section to each of these dimensions in order, on the one hand, to provide a brief summary of the data observed in adult subjects and, on the other, to present the data and problems relating to acquisition and learning.

Three dimensions of narrative processing

The research cited above has made it possible to distinguish between a dimension which can be thought of as conceptual and which relates to the representation of the sequences of events and another more specifically linguistic dimension, while also indicating a distinction between a rhetorical dimension which relates to the structure of narrative texts and another which draws on the lexical-syntactical aspects arising from textualisation.

The conceptual dimension of narratives

The conceptual dimension concerns the mental representation of situations and events as well as their temporal or causal relations. It has given rise to numerous theoretical approaches, of which the most important of those concerned with narrative was developed by Schank and Abelson (1977). This theory postulates that actions are organised in terms of the goals pursued by actors who produce these actions in order to overcome the obstacles which oppose the attainment of these goals. It permits a formulation in terms of causal networks (Trabasso, Secco and Van den Broek, 1985). These networks appear as chains of events, linked together by temporal, causal or other connections. We use the term "framework" to designate these sequences of events (i.e. neither verbalised, nor drawn) which underlie narration.

The textual structure of narratives

The rhetorical dimension relates to the fact that the linguistic formalisation of narratives is not limited to a mere listing of characters, places, objects and events. Work in the 1970s clarified the effects of organisations which generally became known as "narrative superstructures". Numerous models were mapped out, but the similarities prevail greatly over the differences. Every narrative consists of a frame specifying places, moments and characters. The frame is introduced at the start of the narrative as a result of the practical constraints imposed by the need for effective communication. There next follows a trigger which introduces an obstacle which generally hinders the main character in the attainment of his or her objectives. The obstacle induces an emotional reaction together with the elaboration of a sub-goal, aiming to remove or bypass the obstacle. The main character makes one or more attempts, more or less successfully, until the final result is achieved (Mandler & Johnson, 1977; Stein & Glenn, 1979).

Textualisation

All narratives involve one or more characters who have to be introduced and then referred to as events progress. Languages use specific markers to perform different functions. For example, the first appearance of new characters or objects is preceded by an indefinite article (e.g. a man entered). Subsequent references use definitive determiners, articles (e.g. the man), pronouns (e.g. he) and demonstrative adjectives (e.g. this man). In general, the use of these markers, which is highly stereotyped, causes no problems in adults whether in narratives or in other types of text.

Another linguistic dimension relates to the marking of the continuity or discontinuity of events. Narratives describe the sequence of events in which connections can differ in their nature and degree from the simple parallel unfolding of two activities (e.g. the man was walking/a car was passing) to a close causal connection (e.g. the shot was fired/the man fell). Here, as well, markers exist which indicate the degree and nature of the connections: conjunctions (e.g. and, by, so) (Bestgen & Costermans, 1997; Noordman & Vonk, 1997; Townsend, 1997); punctuation marks (Fayol, 1997 b: Heurley, 1997); verbal forms (e.g. preterite; past progressive) which make it possible to distinguish between the foreground actions and the background facts and situations (e.g. the man was walking/a noise caught his attention) (Bonnotte & Fayol, 1998; Fayol, Hickmann, Bonnotte & Gombert, 1993).

ACQUISITION AND LEARNING OF THE COMPREHENSION AND PRODUCTION OF NARRATIVES

The development of causal chains

To understand or produce narratives, people need to possess knowledge of the way events unfold in reality. The modelling of this knowledge has led Schank & Abelson (1977) to propose the concepts of script and schema. A script corresponds to knowledge which relates to a recurring everyday situation which follows a stereotypical sequence. Scripts are acquired through the repetition of approximately identical situations associated with the same objectives. They are acquired very early; first as sequences of non-verbalised actions (e.g. bathing a doll) and then as verbally evokable structures (French & Nelson, 1985). Their two essential characteristics, the goal-directedness and the order of the sequence of events, appear very early. The sequence of actions, at first relatively free, becomes rigid, to the point that children either re-establish the canonical order when it is not respected or eliminate the deviant events (Bauer & Thal, 1990; Hudson & Nelson, 1983). It subsequently becomes more flexible again (Slackman, Hudson & Fivush, 1986). The events included in the script become more and more typical (Slackman & Nelson, 1984).

Scripted knowledge of ordered sequences of events, or "scenic" knowledge of spatial arrangements, is indispensable for the understanding and production of stories. It constitutes, in effect, knowledge which is shared by the interlocutors, and which permits efficient communication, emphasises the essential pieces of information while taking the familiar facts and situations as given. When an unexpected event intervenes or when an obstacle arises the sequence of events does not progress as usual and the situation becomes a potential narrative subject. This is something which has to be discovered by children and which will be more or less reinforced depending on their social environment and culture (Fayol, 1991 b). The unfamiliarity is perceived, and is seen as the impetus for the subsequent actions of the hero. The organisation of the actions can then be modelled by replicating the organisation of a causal chain as previously established.

To summarise, knowledge of frameworks and the regularities which characterise them allows the authors and recipients of narrative texts to construct mental models of situations, either from evocations or illustrations, or in order to produce texts by performing reconstructions on the basis of partial information brought together through the use of inferences.

The development of these chains of events, though emerging somewhat later, approximately replicates the development of scripts, for reasons which are easy to identify. They all rest on chronological-causal relations between facts associated with goals. The difference resides in the unexpected character of the former and the highly predictable and stereotypical nature of the latter. Thus, the evaluation of the unpredictability of an event supposes that the usual scenario is known, even if this is not sufficient in itself. Before children are 5 years old, their productions contain very few focused chronological-causal sequences. (Applebee, 1978; Pitcher and Prelinger 1963). The youngest (3 years) simply juxtapose sequences of facts without establishing interrelations which can be clearly identified by adults. It is the reactions and objectives of the characters that are missing. At 3 years, this absence may be a due to a misunderstanding of the subject matter. At 4 and above, this is no longer true. Questions asked to 4 and 5-year-olds reveal that they are aware of how events are linked and motivated (Trabasso & Nickels, 1992; Trabasso, Stein, Rodkin, Munger & Baughn, 1992). To summarise, there is a real development, but this seems to have more to do with the ability to mobilise knowledge, notably with regard to the elements involved in the sequencing of events, rather than new acquisitions (van den Broek, Lorch & Thurlow, 1996).

The facts reported above lead us to expect children of 6 years and above to achieve performances if not equal to then at least to close to those which characterise adults. Texts gathered from 6 to 8-year-olds are often of a level of organisation equivalent to that which Applebee (1978) attributes to children of 5 years. Furthermore, there is a clear development between the ages of 6 and 10 years, which goes from the juxtaposition of facts without a detectable relation between them to the integration of events in one or more chronological-causal chains, and which passes, at around 9 years, through a period during which narratives are based on an often dominant script, as well as on the narration of an unexpected event (Fayol, 1991 b). In other words, the ability to write coherent stories primarily develops at around 4 to 8 years and is increasingly refined between 8 and 10 years, with certain authors finding practically no change between 9 and 11 years (Fitzgerald, 1984). Nevertheless, there are major and persistent interpersonal differences (Peterson & McCabe, 1983). Arguments emerging from the study of comprehension suggest that at least some children between 6 and 8 years still have difficulty in integrating causal information in the course of reading narratives. It is the ability to organise narrative texts that seems to be lacking among those with a lower level of comprehension.

Oakhill and Yuill (1996, Yuill & Oakhill 1991; see alson Cain, 1996) have also shown that poor comprehenders have difficulty in making inferences and establishing connections between the ideas of a text. These difficulties are not limited to the processing of writing, but extend to comprehension in general. Three hypotheses have been proposed to account for the difficulties of poor comprehenders. The first considers that these subjects, whether children or adults, lack the necessary knowledge regarding the sequencing of actions. The second postulates that these subjects do not have sufficient contact with narrative productions in order to be able to determine what form they should take and how to treat them in terms of this organisation. The third suggests that the major difficulty for children with limited comprehension or poor narrative relates to their limited processing capacity (McCutchen, 1995). This hypothesis has received indirect confirmation. Oakhill & Yuill (1996) have reported that poor comprehenders have significantly less working memory capacity than subjects with a high level of comprehension. According to this conception, the increased difficulty experienced with regard to one of the components of a complex activity such as the comprehension or production of narratives is sufficient to reduce performance in this activity (Bourdin & Fayol, 1994, 1996).

In summary, the study of the development of comprehension and production of chronological-causal chains reveals two paradoxical facts. On the one hand, the acquisition and implementation of these chains appear at a very early age, since they are available from the age of 5 and even earlier (Sperry & Sperry, 1996). On the other hand, the study of reading comprehension and written composition reveals that the construction of mental models corresponding to these chains develops again between 6 and 10 years. All this suggests that the transition to the written mode, because of the specific communication situations which distinguish it from the spoken mode (Fayol, 1997 a), together with the new constraints imposed on processing, induces a reduction or stagnation of the ability to mobilise knowledge relating to the causal chains and the inferences they permit.

Narrative grammars and structures

Narrative grammars attempt to apply to the narrative the principles and conceptions which have been used with sentences. The aim is to define an exhaustive set of narrative categories, e.g. frame, trigger, reaction, endeavour, result, conclusion – and relations between these categories – to make possible, to be simultaneous with, to cause, to succeed – making it possible, on the basis of a finite number of rules, to produce and understand an infinite number of stories (and only stories) which have never been heard before (Mandler & Johnson, 1977; Thorndyke, 1977). Such grammars may be conceived of either as formal systems for the notation and elaboration of stories, or as simply translating the regularities of conventional narratives thus resulting in a narrative superstructure.

Numerous studies have shown that the *narrative superstructure* has an impact on the behaviour of adults and children (Mandler, 1987). Adults process the first and last sentences of a narrative episode more slowly when they are inserted in a narrative than when they are read in isolation (Haberlandt, Berian & Sandson, 1980). Moreover, any modification to the conventional order of narrative categories at the time of their presentation carries with it a supplementary processing cost, a cost which, for example, manifests itself in an increase in reading time (Mandler & Goodman, 1982). Equivalent results have been gathered with children of 7 to 10 years (Frochot, Zagar & Fayol, 1987).

Most studies have concentrated on production. The narratives containing all the constituents of the conventional order are better remembered than those which do not respect these constraints (Yussen, Stright, Glysh, Bonk, Lu & Al Sabaty, 1991). This effect has been observed in children of different cultures from

4-5 years of age. Nevertheless, younger subjects tend to recall certain narrative categories less well than adults: notably the reactions and goals (Mandler, Scribner, Cole & De Forest, 1980).

As research into the impact of causal chains has shown, the earliest narratives rarely respect the organisational framework – trigger/complication – endeavour/action(s) – resolution. It is not until children reach the age of 7 or 8 years that this superstructure becomes dominant. Notably, the positioning of the framework elements at the start of the narratives occurs only at a relatively late age (Fayol, 1991 b). This appearance of a formally identifiable framework is concurrent with the standardised use of the imperfect in French or the past progressive in English and pluperfect as well as expressions such as "the day before" (i.e. la veille in French) and "the next day" (i.e. le lendemain in French). These verbal forms and expressions form part of the narrative conventions, which vary from culture to culture. By contrast, younger children tend to produce a summary of the event as they would in everyday speech and then subsequently expand on this.

It appears extremely plausible that the acquisition of narrative schema is linked to the exposition of a corpus of written narratives. In effect, only these narratives exhibit the corresponding organisational regularities. Varnhagen, Morrison and Everall (1994) have shown that performance in recall and production depends on educational level, regardless of age. These findings suggest that the prolonged and repeated reading of and exposure to narrative texts help children acquire the characteristic regularities of the narrative superstructure. This hypothesis predicts that individuals who do not benefit from such exposure do not develop this schema. The data obtained by Cain (1996) confirm that subjects with a low level of comprehension are precisely those whose narrative productions diverge the most from the narrative superstructure and that these subjects have also had less contact than others with written narratives (see also Dickinson & Trabors, 1991).

The results of Varnhagen et al. reveal that the regularities of the narrative superstructure are acquired through a process of implicit learning. However, Fitzgerald and Spiegel (1983) have developed a training programme for the discovery and use of the *narrative superstructure* in writing. Children taught in this way have shown a significant improvement in production as well as in comprehension.

Overall, the facts concerning the acquisition and use of the narrative schema appear to be highly consistent. This schema facilitates the integration of information during comprehension and ensures the completeness and respect of the conventional character of written narratives during production. Its operation is not equivalent to that of the chronological-causal relations. It constitutes in effect a conventional rhetorical organisation which can only be acquired through exposition of a corpus of texts presenting the corresponding regularities. It is acquired at a very early age and depends strongly on direct contact with written narratives. However, explicit tuition-based learning proves effective both in production and comprehension, even at a relatively advanced age.

The processing of linguistic markers

The construction of a mental model of the described situation while reading or listening cannot be performed without taking account of the linguistic markers. These guide the activation of factual knowledge and procedures for processing. Additionally, the production of a narrative for a listener/reader requires certain lexical and syntactical choices to be made. The author, like the recipient, must make use of marker systems which are associated to facts or procedures in an approximately regular manner. Here we consider two of these sub-systems, one which assures the marking of interpropositional relations (connectors and punctuation); and one which permits the introduction and the referencing of referents (determiners and pronouns) (Fayol, 1997a, 1997b).

Linearisation in production introduces an initial problem: it is necessary to juxtapose information which may be more or less closely related. This requires the existence of a system of markers indicating the degree (punctuation) and the nature (connectors) of the relations between propositions or successive paragraphs (Fayol, 1997b). This system supplies the reader with indications as to the segmentation of information (i.e. separating facts from one another) and to their integration (i.e. elaborating a unified representation from the set of propositions). Both corpus studies and experimental research show that adults do indeed use the markers in a manner appropriate to their function.

Research concerning the acquisition/learning of these markers has demonstrated the need to consider connectors and punctuation separately. The former are acquired very early and in an order which can be found in all languages (Kail & Weissenborn, 1991). Furthermore, they are used in speech at an early age even when children are handling unfamiliar subject matter (French & Nelson, 1985; Hudson & Shapiro, 1991). We might therefore have expected them to emerge at the same time as children's initial written productions. Corpus analyses have shown that this is far from being the case and that it is often necessary to wait until 3rd grade (9 years) before they emerge (Fayol, 1991b). This "delay" is due to the fact that the texts produced by the youngest subjects have no thematic unity and that the event sequences that are recounted do not require the use of markers other than *and* or *then/after*. Once these sequences become chronological-causal in nature, productions include the relevant connectors and no development is observed. Studies of reading/comprehension have confirmed these results. It therefore appears that as far as the most elementary connectors are concerned, there is no development in processing between the ages of 5 and 10 (Fayol & Mouchon, 1997).

Things are very different when we consider punctuation. Since these markers are not acquired until children engage in written language, both their forms and their functioning are acquired in parallel. Although this discovery continues from the age of 6 to 12 years, it respects, from the outset, the regularities characteristic of adult production. The occurrence of a full stop, with or without a capital letter, delimits episodes or blocks of information which possess a thematic unity and this is confirmed by the associated pause lengths (Foulin, Chanquoy & Fayol, 1989).

The comma appears latter and is immediately applied to segmentations with a lesser level of importance. The other punctuation marks appear later (Ferreiro & Zucchermaglio, 1996). We have a less advanced understanding of how punctuation is processed during comprehension (Fayol, Gaonac'h & Mouchon, 1992). Our understanding of the acquisition of punctuation is more advanced in the field of production than in that of comprehension. However, the observed facts are consistent with those relating to the functioning of the connectors.

Linearisation gives rise to a second problem. While some information is juxtaposed even though the links between the items are weak or non-existent, other items of information are separated by one or more propositions even though conceptually closely related. To signal this continuity, languages possess units which make it possible to indicate references while providing more or less complete information concerning the referents (number, gender, case depending on the language). The functioning of these markers is now well understood in adult subjects. Their productive acquisition appears to take place in two phases. The first relates to situational speech. Here, children soon learn, with greater or lesser success, to associate determiners and pronouns with situations. The markers are used in a primarily deictic way. It is not until the age of 7-8 years that we observe an intratextual functioning of these markers which associates, for example, indefinite articles with new entities and definite articles with those that have already been evoked or which uses a proper noun followed by pronouns to refer to the main character in a narrative (De Weck, 1991; Hickmann, 2000; Hickmann, Kail & Roland, 1995; Karmiloff-Smith, 1979, 1981). This mode of intratextual operation appears relatively late and is correlated with the appearance or modification of the use of other markers such as verbal forms, and in particular the imperfect or preterite, or adverbial expressions such as *the day before/the day after* in the place of *yesterday/tomorrow*.

The processing of anaphoric references and determiners in comprehension has been studied in depth in adult subjects but less so in children. Nevertheless, the available data reveals that the comprehension of pronouns is problematic for them and especially so in the case of poor readers. However, experiments involving interpretational training have shown that these obstacles can be easily overcome (Oakhill & Yuill, 1996; Yuill & Oakhill, 1991). In the same way as for the *narrative superstructure*, these results suggest that the errors and difficulties of poor readers are due not to an inability but are more likely the result of inadequate contact with texts and/or the impossibility of performing in parallel the tasks of reading and integrating the referents into a representation. It is not learning but implementation that causes the problems.

TOWARDS AN INTEGRATIVE CONCEPTION

According to a cognitive perspective, the processing of a narrative, both in production and in comprehension, is a complex activity which simultaneously mobilises different representational levels and procedures. We have therefore been led to distinguish between a conceptual, chronological-causal type of representation which relates to goal-endeavour-result sequences, a rhetorical representation – the narrative schema – which refers to a conventional textual organisation and linguistic subsystems which can be used to mark specific items of information. These distinctions are based on empirical data which show that acquisition, difficulties and functioning vary as a function of these dimensions.

The acquisition of the chronological-causal dimensions of actions constitutes a prerequisite for the comprehension and production of narratives. In effect, subjects must possess mental categories which allow them to represent situations and draw inferences. This demands specific knowledge which is associated with concrete situations as well as inferential abilities which continue to develop between the ages of 6 and 15 years (Barnes, Dennis & Haefele-Kalvaitis, 1996). Most of this knowledge is probably acquired by means of action schemas during children's interaction with the physical and social environment.

The acquisition of the organisation of goals and actions, though universal and learned at an early age, is not in itself sufficient since the conventional forms of narratives go beyond these organisations even if they do take account of them. They add information, the aim of which is doubtlessly to provide sufficient data to permit the recipient to understand the narrative. While this pragmatic and textual dimension is just as fundamental as the preceding one, it cannot be acquired under the same conditions. As studies of difficulties and comparisons of populations and the effects of training have shown, it is both frequent and prolonged contact with written narratives and interaction with adults (and peers?) on the subject of these texts that encourage acquisition. The same reasoning applies to the more specifically linguistic aspects. The learning of the markers and their operation requires a corpus of examples and a set of activities involving the interpretation and production of linguistic markers.

Each of the dimensions we have considered may be affected by specific difficulties (Liles, Duffy, Merritt & Purcell, 1995). Each can also be the object of preventive or corrective action. Training in the establishment of inferences on the basis of goal-actions-results type relations have effectively improved the performances of poor comprehenders. The same is true of the explicit teaching of the narrative superstructure. In other words, while the dimensions we have discussed are usually acquired implicitly, it is possible to induce this learning by means of direct teaching coupled with exercises. These observations establish a continuity between acquisition and learning which deserves to be studied more widely and in greater depth.

The comparison of the performances of children of the same age asked to produce narratives on the basis of different media or in different situations or to understand certain narratives and produce others reveals two problems. The first relates to the effect of the pragmatic conditions on productions. This effect is both trivial and lacks an adequate theoretical basis. The work conducted by linguists interested in speech production has opened up avenues of investigation which have not been pursued even though it is they alone that can enable us to examine phenomena as problematic as the relative difficulty in the use of verbal forms (present vs. past) as a function of the situation of utterance. The second problem relates to the obvious gap in performance between judgements of narrative nature (is it a narrative?) and comprehension and production (Stein & Glenn, 1979; Stein & Nezworski, 1978). Children of 5 years of age who are presented with texts corresponding more or less to the conventional narrative organisation systematically choose the one which conforms most closely to the canonical organisation, just as adults do. However, the productions of children of the same age have usually not reached this level. This type of performance gap suggests that, in our reasoning, we need to distinguish between the availability of knowledge and its implementation and coordination. In a capacity-based view, the management of a complex task such as processing a narrative necessitates the coordinated mobilisation of different items of knowledge and procedures. This coordination itself could be costly and lead to performances which are inferior to those that might be expected on the basis of assessments of the subject's knowledge. This reduction in performance with reference to potential may vary as a function of level of development and interpersonal differences. This line of reasoning also leads us to evoke, on the one hand, the effect of activities in which certain components are rendered easier and, on the other, the impact of metacognitive guidance on performance enhancement (Ehrlich, 1999).

REFERENCES

Applebee, A.N. (1978). *The child's concept of story: Age two to seventeen*. Chicago: The University of Chicago Press.

Barnes, M.A;, Dennis, M. & Haefele-Kalvaitis, J. (1996). The effect of knowledge availability and knowledge accessibility on coherence and elaborative inferencing in children from six to fifteen years of age. *Journal of Experimental Child Psychology, 61*, 216-241.

Bauer, P.J. & Thal, D.J. (1990). Scripts or scraps: Reconsidering the development of sequential understanding. *Journal of Experimental Child Psychology, 50*, 287-304.

Bestgen, Y. & Costermans, J. (1997. Temporal markers of narrative structure: Studies in production. In J. Costermans and M. Fayol (Eds.), *Processing interclausal relationships* (pp. 201-218). Mahwah, N.J.: Lawrence Erlbaum associates Publishers.

Bock, K. & Levelt, W.J.M. (1994). Grammatical encoding. In M.A. Gernsbacher (Ed.), *Handbook of psycholinguistics* (pp. 945-984). New York: Academic Press.

Bonnotte, I. & Fayol, M. Cognitive representations of predicates and the use of past-tenses in French: A developmental approach. *First Language, 17*, 75-101.

Bourdin, B. & Fayol, M. Is written language production really more difficult than oral language production? *International Journal of Psychology*, 1994, *29*, 591-620.

Bourdin, B. & Fayol, M. Mode effects in a sentence production task. *CPC/Current Psychology of Cognition*, 1996,*15*, 245-264.

Bower, G. H. & Morrow, D.G. (1990). Mental models in narrative comprehension. *Science, 247*, 44-48.

Britton, B. K. & Graesser, A. C. (1996). *Models of understanding text*. Mahwah, N.J.: Lawrence Erlbaum associates Publishers.

Cain, K. (1996). Story knowledge and comprehension skill. In C. Cornoldi and J. Oakhill (Eds.), *Reading comprehension difficulties* (pp. 167-192). Mahwah, N.J.: Lawrence Erlbaum associates Publishers.

Denhière, G. (1984). *Il était une fois. Compréhension et souvenir de récits.* [Once upon a time. Comprehending and remembering stories]. Lille: Presses Universitaires de Lille.

De Weck, G. (1991). *La cohésion dans les narrations d'enfants.* [Cohesion in children's narratives]. Neuchâtel, Paris: Delachaux et Niestlé.

Dickinson, D. K. & Tabors, P. O. (1991). Early literacy: Linkages between home, school and literacy achievement at age five. *Journal of Research in Childhood Education, 6,* 30-44.

Ehrlich, M. F. (1999). Metacognitive monitoring of texte cohesion in children. In H. van Oostendorp et S.R. Goldman (Eds.), *The construction of mental representation during reading* (281-302). Mahwah, N.J.: Lawrence Erlbaum associates Publishers.

Fayol, M. (1985). *Le récit et sa construction.* [Narratives and its building up]. Neuchâtel, Paris: Delachaux et Niestlé.

Fayol, M. (1991 a). Text typologies: a cognitive approach. In G. Denhière and J.P. Rossi (Eds.), *Text and text processing.* Amsterdam: North Holland Publisher.

Fayol, M. (1991 b). Stories: A psycholinguistic and ontogenetic approach to the acquisition of narrative abilities. In G. Pieraut Le Bonniec and M. Dolitsky (Eds.), *From basic language to discourse basis processing* (pp; 229-243). Amsterdam: Benjamin.

Fayol, M. (1997 a). *Des idées au texte.* [From ideas to text composition]. Paris: Presses Universitaires de France.

Fayol, M. (1997 b). On acquiring and using punctuation: A study in written French. In J. Costermans and M. Fayol (Eds.), *Processing interclausal relationships processing* (pp. 193-204). Mahwah, N.J.: Lawrence Erlbaum associates Publishers.

Fayol, M., Gaonac'h, D. & Mouchon, S., (1992). L'utilisation des marques de surface lors de la lecture: L'exemple de la ponctuation. [Using surface markers in reading: The example of punctuation marks]. *Scientia Paedagogica Experimentalis, 29,* 83-98.

Fayol, M, Hickmann, M., Bonnotte, I. & Gombert, J.E. (1993). French verbal inflections and narrative context: A developmental perspective. *Journal of Psycholinguistic Research, 22,* 453 -478.

Fayol, M. & Mouchon, S. (1997). Production and comprehension of connectives in the written modality. A study of written french. In C. Pontecorvo (Ed.), *Writing development: An interdisciplinary view processing* (pp. 193-204). Amsterdam: John Benjamins.

Ferreiro, E. & Zucchermaglio, C. (1996). Children's use of punctuation marks: The case of quoted speech. In C. Pontecorvo, M. Orsolini, B.Burge, and L. Resnick (Eds.), *Children's early text construction processing* (pp. 177-206). Mahwah, N.J.: Lawrence Erlbaum associates Publishers.

Fitzgerald, J. (1984). the relationship between reading ability and expectations for story structures. *Discourse Processes, 7,* 21-41.

Fitzgerald, J. & Spiegel, D.L. (1983). Enhancing children's reading comprehension through instruction in narrative structure. *Journal of Reading Behavior, 15,* 1-17.

Foulin, J. N., Chanquoy, L. & Fayol, M. Approche en temps réel de la production des connecteurs et de la ponctuation ponctuation. [An on-line study of the production of connectives and punctuation marks]. *Langue Française,* 1989, n 81 p. 21-39.

French, L. A. & Nelson, K. (1985). *Children's acquisition of relational terms: Some ifs, ors, and buts.* New York: Springer Verlag.

Frochot, M., Zagar, D. & Fayol, M. (1987). Effets de l'organisation narrative sur la lecture de récits. [The impact of narrative organisation on reading stories]. *L'Année Psychologique, 87,* 237-252.

Haberlandt, K., Berian, C. & Sandson, J. (1980). The episode schema in story processing. *Journal of Verbal Learning and Verbal Behavior, 19,* 635-650.

Heurley, L. (1997). Processing units in written texts: Paragraphs or information blocks? In J. Costermans and M. Fayol (Eds.), *Processing interclausal relationships processing* (pp. 179-200). Mahwah, N.J.: Lawrence Erlbaum associates Publishers.

Hickmann, M. (1997). Information status and grounding in children's narratives: A crosslinguistic perspective. In J. Costermans and M. Fayol (Eds.), *Processing interclausal relationships processing* (pp. 221-244). Mahwah, N.J.: Lawrence Erlbaum associates Publishers.

Hickmann, M. (2000). Le développement de l'organisation discursive. [The development of discourse organisation]. In M. Kail and M. Fayol (Eds.), *L'acquisition du langage. Vol. 2. Le langage en développement. Au-delà de trois ans.* [Language acquisition. Vol. 2. The developing language. From 3 y-o onwards]. Paris: Presses Universitaires de France.

Hickmann, M., Kail, M. & Roland, F., (1995). Cohesive anaphoric relations in French children's narratives as a function of mutual knowledge. *First Language, 15,* 277-300.

Hudson, J. & Nelson, K. (1983). Effects of script structure in children's story recall. *Developmental Psychology, 19,* 625-635.

Hudson, J. & Shapiro, L. R. (1991). From knowing to telling: The development of children's script, stories, and personal narratives. In A. McCabe and C. Peterson (Eds.), *Developing narrative structure processing* (pp. 89-136). Hillsdale, N.J.: Lawrence Erlbaum Associates Publishers.

Johnson-Laird, P. N. (1983). *Mental models.* Cambridge, MA: Cambridge University Press.

Just, M. A. & Carpenter, P. A. (1992). A capacity theory of comprehension. *Psychological Review, 99,* 122-149.

Kail, M. & Weissenborn, J. (1991). Conjunctions: Developmental issues. In G. Pieraut Le Bonniec and M. Dolitsky (Eds.), *From basic language to discourse basis processing* (pp. 125-142). Amsterdam: Benjamin.

Karmiloff-Smith, A. (1979). *A functional approach to child language: A study of determiners and reference.* Cambridge, UK: Cambridge University Press.

Karmiloff-Smith, A. (1981). The grammatical marking of thematic structure in the development of language production. In W. Deutsch (Ed.), *The child's construction of language processing* (pp. 122-147). New York: Academic Press.

Kintsch, W. & van Dijk, T.A. (1978). Toward a model of text comprehension and text production. *Psychological Review, 85,* 363-394.

Kintsch, W. (1988). The use of knowledge in discourse processing: A construction-integration model. *Psychological Review, 95,* 163-182.

Kintsch, W. Mandel, T.S. & Kozminsky, E. (1977). Summarizing scrambled stories. *Memory and Cognition, 5,* 547-552.

Levelt, W. J. M. (1989). *Speaking: From intention to articulation.* Cambridge, MA: MIT press.

Levy, C. M. & Ransdell, S. E. (1996). *The science of writing.* Mahwah, NJ: Lawrence Erlbaum associates Publishers.

Liles, B. Z., Duffy, R. J., Merritt, D. D. & Purcell, S. L. (1995). Measurement of narrative discourse ability in children with language disorders. *Journal of Speech and Hearing Research, 38,* 415-425.

Mandler, J. (1978). A code in the node: The use of story schema in retrieval. *Discourse Processes, 1,* 14-35.

Mandler, J. (1987). On the psychological validity of story structure. *Discourse Processes, 10,* 1-29.

Mandler, J. & Jonhson, N. S. (1977). Remembrance of things parsed: Story structure and recall. *Cognitive Psychology, 9,* 111-151.

Mandler, J. & Goodman, M. S. (1982). On the psychological validity of story structure. *Journal of Verbal Learning and Verbal Behavior, 21,* 507-523.

Mandler, J., Scribner, S., Cole, M. & De Forest, M. (1980). Cross-cultural invariance in story recall. *Child Development, 51,* 19-26.

McCutchen, D. (1995). Cognitive processes in children's writing: developmental and individual differences. *Issues in Education, 1,* 123-160.

Mouchon, S., Fayol, M. & Gaonac'h, D. (1995). On-line processing of links between events in narratives. *Current Psychology of Cognition, 14,* 171-193.

Noordman, L. G. M. & Vonk, W. (1997). The different functions of a conjunction in constructing a representation of the discourse. In J. Costermans and M. Fayol (Eds.), *Processing interclausal relationships processing* (pp. 75-94). Mahwah, N.J.: Lawrence Erlbaum associates Publishers.

Oakhill, J., Garnham, A. & Vonk, W. (1989). The on-line construction of discourse models. *Language and Cognitive Processes, 4,* 263-286.

Oakhill, J. & Yuill, N. (1996). Higher order factors in comprehension disability: Processes and remediation. In C. Cornoldi and J. Oakhill (Eds.), *Reading comprehension difficulties processing.* (pp. 69-92). Mahwah, N.J.: Lawrence Erlbaum associates Publishers.

Peterson, C. & McCabe, A. (1983). *Developmental psycholinguistics: Three ways of looking at a child's narrative.* New York: Plenum.

Pitcher, E. G. & Prelinger, E. (1963). *Children tell stories: An analysis of fantasy.* New York: International Universities Press.

Poulsen, D., Kintsch, E., Kintsch, W. & Premack, D. (1979). Children's comprehension and memory for stories. *Journal of Experimental Child Psychology, 28,* 379-403.

Rijlaarsdam, G., van den Bergh, H. & Couzjin, M. (1996). *Theories, models, and methodology in writing research.* Amsterdam: Amsterdam University Press.

Schank, R. C. & Abelson, R. (1977). *Scripts, plans, goals, and understanding.* Hillsdale, N.J.: Lawrence Erlbaum associates Publishers.

Slackman, E. A., Hudson, J. A. & Fivush, R. (1986). Actions, actors, links, and goals: The structure of children's event representations. In K. Nelson (Ed.), *Event knowledge: Structure and function in development processing* (pp. 47-69). Hillsdale, NJ: Lawrence Erlbaum associates Publishers.

Slackman, E. A. & Nelson, K. (1984). Acquisition of an unfamiliar script in story form by young children. *Child Development, 55,* 529-540.

Stein, N. L. & Glenn, C. G. (1979). An analysis of story comprehension in elementary school children. In R. O. Freedle (Ed.), *New directions in discourse processing* (pp. 53-120). Norwood, NJ: Ablex.

Stein, N. L. & Nezworski, T. (1978). The effect of organisation and instructional set on story memory. *Discourse Processes, 1,* 177-193.

Sperry, L. L. & Sperry, D. E. (1996). Early development of narrative skills. *Cognitive Development, 11,* 443-465.

Thorndyke, P. W. (1977). Cognitive structures in comprehension and memory of narrative discourse. *Cognitive Psychology, 9,* 77-110.

Torrance, M. & Jeffery, G. (1999). *The cognitive demands of writing.* Amsterdam: Amsterdam University Press.

Townsend, D.J. (1997). Processing clauses and their relationships during comprehension. In J. Costermans and M. Fayol (Eds.), *Processing interclausal relationships* (pp. 265-282). Mahwah, N.J.: Lawrence Erlbaum associates Publishers.

Trabasso, T. & Nickels, M. (1992). The development of goal plans of actions in the narration of a picture story. *Discourse Processes, 15,* 249-275.

Trabasso, T. & Sperry, L. (1985). Causal thinking and the representation of narrative events. *Journal of Memory and Language, 24,* 612-630.

Trabasso, T., Secco, T. & van den Broek, P. (1985). Causal cohesion and story coherence. In H. Mandl, N. Stein and T. Trabasso (Eds.), *Learning and comprehension of text processing* (pp. 83-111). Hillsdale, NJ: Lawrence Erlbaum associates Publishers.

Trabasso, T., Stein, N. L., Rodkin, P. C., Munger, M. P., & Baughn, C.R. (1992). Knowledge of goals and plans in the on-line narration of events. *Cognitive Development, 7,* 133-170.

van den Broek, P. (1994). Comprehension and memory of narratives. In M. A. Gernsbacher (Ed.), *Handbook of psycholinguistics processing* (pp. 539-588). New York: Academic Press.

van den Broek, P. & Trabasso, T. (1986). Causal networks versus goal hierarchies in summarizing texts. *Discourse Processes, 9,* 1-15.

van den Broek, P., Lorch, E. P. & Thurlow, R. (1996). Children's and adults' memory for television stories: The role of causal factors, story grammar categories, and hierarchical level. *Child Development, 67,* 3010-3028.

van Oostendorp, H. & Goldman, S. R. (1999). *The construction of mental representations during reading.* Mahwah, N.J.: Lawrence Erlbaum.

Varnhagen, C. K., Morrison, F. J. & Everall, R (1994). Aging and schooling effects in story recall and story production. *Developmental Psychology, 30,* 969-979.

Yuill, N. & Oakhill, J. (1991). *Children's problems in text comprehension.* Cambridge, UK: Cambridge University Press.

Yussen, S. R., Stright, A. D., Glysch, R. L., Bonk, C. E., Lu, I. & Al-Sabaty, I. (1991). Learning and forgetting of narratives following good and poor text organisation. *Contemporary Educational Psychology, 16,* 346-374.

SUGGESTIONS FOR FURTHER READING

Britton, B.K. and Graesser, A.C. (1996). *Models of understanding text.* Mahwah, N.J.: Lawrence Erlbaum associates Publishers.

Cornoldi, C. and Oakhill, J. (Eds.), *Reading comprehension difficulties processing.* Mahwah, N.J.: Lawrence Erlbaum associates Publishers.

Costermans, J. & Fayol, M. (1997), *Processing interclausal relationships.* Mahwah, N.J.: Lawrence Erlbaum associates Publishers.

McCabe, A. & Peterson, C. (Eds.), *Developing narrative structure processing.* Hillsdale, N.J.: Lawrence Erlbaum Associates Publishers.

McCutchen, D. (1995). Cognitive processes in children's writing: developmental and individual differences. *Issues in Education, 1,* 123-160.

Torrance, M. & Jeffery, G. (1999). *The cognitive demands of writing.* Amsterdam: Amsterdam University Press.

B3. The Use of Context in Learning to Read

WILLIAM E. TUNMER & JAMES W. CHAPMAN

ABSTRACT

This chapter examines the theoretical arguments and empirical evidence in support of three views of the use of context in beginning reading. According to the first view the development of reading ability is largely a matter of learning to rely increasingly on the syntactic and semantic redundancies of language to generate hypotheses about the text yet to be encountered . In contrast, the second view holds that progress in reading can only occur if children avoid using context to identify words and instead concentrate on taking advantage of the systematic mappings between subcomponents of written and spoken words. The third view proposes that using the constraints of sentence context in conjunction with gradually improving word-level skills enables beginning readers to identify unfamiliar words and thus increase both their word-specific knowledge and knowledge of spelling-sound patterns. The available evidence tends to support the third view, although more research is needed to determine whether phonological factors and sensitivity to context contribute differentially to the use of context in reading as a function of age.

INTRODUCTION

There are at least three strategies that beginning readers can use to identify unfamiliar words in connected text. They can use their developing knowledge of mappings between subcomponents of written and spoken words to generate the word's pronunciation, they can analogise to known words that are stored in lexical memory, and, in combination with incomplete information from a partial decoding attempt, they can use the constraints of sentence context to narrow the possibilities of what the word might be. This chapter is concerned with two questions relating to the use of the latter strategy. First, how does the ability to use the constraints of sentence context contribute to the development of word identification skill in beginning readers? Second, what skills are necessary for the development of the ability to use context to identify unfamiliar words in text?

A preliminary distinction is crucial. Context certainly contributes to the *interpretation* of words identified in text, as demonstrated by the disambigua-

T. Nunes, P. Bryant (eds.), Handbook of Children's Literacy, 199–212.
© 2004 *Kluwer Academic Publishers. Printed in Great Britain.*

tion of words with multiple meanings (e.g., "His *sentence* was five years and three months' versus "His *sentence* was awkwardly constructed"). Context also influences text comprehension by facilitating the integration of new information into the reader's knowledge base. For example, the sentence "The cloth ripped but the haystack saved him" would be difficult to comprehend in isolation but is readily understood in the context of a passage about a man parachuting from an airplane (Bransford, 1979). There is no doubt, then, that context plays an important role in what the reader does with words after they have been recognized. However, we are concerned with what occurs prior to that point, with how the beginning reader uses context in the *identification* of words in text.

THEORETICAL BACKGROUND

There are two strongly opposing views on the use of context in beginning reading. The first derives largely from the work of Goodman (1967) and Smith (1971), according to whom skilled reading is primarily an activity of using the syntactic and semantic redundancies of language to generate hypotheses, or guesses, about the text yet to be encountered. Efficient readers are thought to pay little attention to the majority of words of text because language follows a predictable pattern. Only a minimal amount of word-level information is therefore needed to confirm language predictions. On the basis of these claims, Goodman and Smith argued that unlike fluent readers, poor and beginning readers are less able to make use of contextual redundancy in ongoing sentence processing. Reading instruction should therefore focus primarily on teaching beginning readers to use sentence context cues as the primary strategy for recognizing words in text. Children should be encouraged to monitor for meaningfulness and to make corrections only when necessary to make sense. When children encounter a difficult word they should be encouraged to guess what the word might be and receive praise if the response fits the context, even if the response is incorrect.

Children should also be taught to use mappings between letters and sounds (i.e., graphophonemic cues), but only very sparingly and mainly as backup support to confirm language predictions. Explicit and systematic instruction in letter-sound correspondences is discouraged for two reasons. First, concentrating too heavily on learning letter-sound correspondences may result in children losing the natural insight that print is meaningful. Second, English orthography contains so many irregularities that focusing too much attention on teaching letter-sound correspondences will not only waste valuable time but possibly even confuse children and impede progress. Rather, instruction in the use of spelling-sound relationships should almost always arise *incidentally* in the context of reading connected text, according to this view.

In opposition to the views of Goodman and Smith is the claim that language prediction skill is not important in either learning to read or skilled reading. The major assumption underlying the theoretical model of reading proposed by Goodman and Smith is that natural human language is very predictable and highly redundant. As stated by J. Smith and Elley (1994), two proponents of the Goodman and Smith view of reading, "Mature language users become very good at predicting the meaning of a speaker or an author and can often predict the exact word" (pp.77-78). Linguists, however, would strongly disagree. One of Noam Chomsky's (1965) greatest insights into the nature of human language was that virtually every sentence we produce or comprehend is novel, never having appeared before in the history of the universe. Because natural human languages are discrete combinatorial systems with the mathematical property of recursion, the number of sentences that a speaker can potentially understand or produce is without limit. Pinker (1994) describes this fundamental feature of human languages:

> If a speaker is interrupted at a random point in a sentence, there are on average about ten different words that could be inserted at that point to continue the sentence in a grammatical and meaningful way. (At some points in a sentence, only one word can be inserted, and at others, there is a choice from among thousands; ten is the average.) Let's assume that a person is capable of producing sentences up to twenty words long. Therefore the number of sentences that a speaker can deal with in principle is at least 10^{20} (a one with twenty zeroes after it, or a hundred million trillion). At a rate of five seconds a sentence, a person would need a childhood of about a hundred trillion years (with no time for eating or sleeping) to memorize them all. In fact, a twenty-word limitation is far too severe. (pp. 85-86)

Predictability is clearly not a feature of written or spoken language. Prior context provides little, of any, help in predicting each successive word in a sentence like the one just read.

Empirical support for this claim comes from Gough (1983) who found that under ideal conditions (where the material was familiar to the reader and there were no time constraints), the average predictability of content words (nouns, verbs, adjectives, etc.) is about 10%, compared to about 40% for function words (e.g., *on*, *to*, *the*), which are typically short, high-frequency words that the child can already recognize. Because the information conveyed by words varies inversely with their frequency, beginning readers who use sentence context as the primary strategy for reading text are faced with the following dilemma: While they are to depend on the meaning of the passage to infer the meanings of its less familiar words, the meaning of the passage depends disproportionately on the meanings of its *least* familiar and *least* predictable words. Consequently, unless children are reading very low-level texts with repeated sentence structures, a high degree of predictability, and a large amount of picture support, they will have at best a 1 in 10 chance of guessing the word.

Contrary to Goodman and Smith's claim that poor and beginning readers are less able to use sentence context to identify words as they read, research using discrete-trial reaction tasks (in which children are asked to name words preceded by either congruous, incongruous or neutral contexts) has shown that the effect of context on speed of ongoing word recognition during reading *decreases* with increasing age, grade level, reading ability, word familiarity and stimulus quality (see Stanovich, 1980, 1984, 1986, for reviews). Studies that have examined accuracy of recognizing words in isolation and in context report a similar pattern of results. Nicholson (1991), for example, found that context aids weaker, younger readers, but is not helpful for better, older readers. On the basis of such findings, Stanovich concluded that poor readers compensate for difficulties in word recognition by relying more on sentence context to facilitate ongoing word recognition. In contrast, good readers are less reliant on syntactic and semantic information because they are more proficient in using word-level information.

According to this view, then, less skilled readers should be discouraged from compensating for poor word recognition skill by relying on context. Instead, they should be encouraged to take advantage of the systematic mappings between subcomponents of written and spoken words. Sublexical analyses involving phonological information will then result in positive learning trials (i.e., correct word identifications), which in turn lead to the amalgamation of orthographic (i.e., the specific letter sequence) and phonological representations in lexical memory (Ehri, 1992). These amalgamated representations, or word-specific knowledge, provide the basis for rapid and efficient access to the mental lexicon, which in turn frees up cognitive resources for allocation to comprehension and text integration processes. Because lexical access that is inefficient and capacity draining will disrupt the temporary representation of text in working memory, children who are having trouble identifying the individual words of text quickly and accurately will encounter difficulty in comprehending what they are reading. In summary, the recommendations for reading instruction following from either of the two opposing views on the role of language prediction skill in beginning reading are counter-productive from the perspective of the other.

An alternative view to the two just described proposes that language prediction skill enables beginning readers to *combine* knowledge of the constraints of sentence context with incomplete graphophonemic information to identify unfamiliar words (including irregularly spelled ones) and thus increase both their word-specific knowledge and knowledge of grapheme-phoneme correspondences (Nation & Snowling, 1998; Tunmer & Hoover, 1992). The ability to use contextual information allows beginning readers to monitor accuracy in word identification by providing them with immediate feedback when their attempted responses to unfamiliar words in text fail to conform to the surrounding grammatical context. This occurs when a candidate word from the mental lexicon results in either a violation of a strict subcategorisation rule, which governs the syntactic structures into which a word can enter (e.g., "The boy *slept* the bed"), or a violation of a selectional restriction rule, which places constraints on how words of different form classes can be combined (e.g., "The cage *slept*.").

According to this view contextual information will only be useful if children are aware of the importance of the alphabetic code and have developed or been taught self-improving strategies for acquiring spelling-sound relations. The use of sentence context as backup support to confirm hypotheses about what unfamiliar words might be, based on incomplete spelling-sound knowledge, will help children to increase their word-specific knowledge from which additional spelling-sound correspondences can be induced. Children who have become active problem solvers with regard to graphic information will therefore use contextual cues to supplement word-level information rather than to substitute for it. Identifying unfamiliar words by using the constraints of sentence context in conjunction with gradually improving word-level skills will in turn enable beginning readers to accumulate even more spelling-sound knowledge, which, according to Ehri (1992), provides the basic mechanism for acquiring word-specific knowledge.

This view of the role of context in learning to read has important implications for beginning reading instruction. Instead of teaching children to use sentence context as the primary strategy for recognizing unfamiliar words in text (with letter-sound cues being used only very sparingly and mainly to confirm language predictions), beginning readers should be encouraged to look for familiar spelling patterns *first* and to use context to confirm hypotheses about what unfamiliar words might be, based on available word-level information. The major disadvantage of relying entirely on context to guess words is that not only will this strategy result in missed learning trials when context is insufficient to make a guess, but it will also result in *misleading* learning trials when a prediction is contextually appropriate but nevertheless incorrect. Deficient and misleading data will almost certainly impede progress. In response to the claim that English orthography is too irregular to be of much use, it can be argued that because no word in English is completely phonologically opaque, even irregularly spelled words (e.g., *stomach*, *castle*, *money*, *glove*) provide some accurate phonological cues to the word's identity. When beginning readers apply their developing knowledge of spelling-to-sound patterns to unfamiliar exception words, the result will often be close enough to the correct phonological form that sentence context cues can be used to arrive at a correct identification (e.g., "He couldn't find his *money*".).

REVIEW OF RESEARCH

A common objection to the conclusions of the preceding section is that many children learn to read quite satisfactorily through an instructional approach that places primary emphasis on the use of context to identify words in text. At this point we must avoid a common source of misunderstanding by recognizing that most children (probably 75%) will independently discover the enormous value of learning to read in an alphabetic orthography regardless of the method of instruction to which they are exposed. In support of this claim are results from a longitudinal study of beginning literacy development in New Zealand where children are encouraged to rely primarily on context to identify unfamiliar words in text (Tunmer, Chapman, Ryan & Prochnow, 1998). As part of this study children were asked the following question, once in Year 1 and again in Year 2: "When you are reading on your own and come across a word that you don't know, what do you do to try to figure out what the word is?" The children's responses were coded according to whether any reference was made to the use of word-level information, no reference was made to the use of word-level information, or no response was given. Examples of word-level responses included "sound it out," "hear all the letters," "think of the sounds," "listen to what the letters are," "look at the beginning, middle and end, then I try to work it out." Examples of text level responses included "guess," "think, guess what the word is," "read it all over again," "I miss it, carry on, then see what makes sense," "I leave it," "read on," "have a look at the picture," "put my finger on the book and try the other words and get a word that makes sense."

Results indicated that despite what they are normally encouraged to do, the majority of Year 1 and Year 2 children said that they used word-level information to identify unfamiliar words in text (52.1% and 66.2%, respectively). Although these results are important, the more interesting question is whether there is a relationship between what children say they do to identify unfamiliar words when they are in Year 1, and their reading achievement in Years 2 and 3. On all reading and reading-related measures there were highly significant differences between the groups that consistently favoured the children who reported using word-level information to identify unfamiliar words. Tunmer et al. also examined the relationship between Year 1 response category and placement in Reading Recovery, a nationally implemented remedial reading program. They found that children who were placed in Reading Recovery after a year of reading instruction were over 4½ times more likely to have indicated in their first year of schooling that they preferred using text level information when confronted with an unfamiliar word in text. In summary, the children in Year 1 who said they used word-level information to identify unfamiliar words consistently performed better on all reading and reading-related measures one and two years later and were much less likely to require Reading Recovery than children who preferred to use text level strategies such as contextual guessing.

To examine the relationship between the use of context and the development of word-specific knowledge Adams and Huggins (1985) asked good and poor readers in Grades 2 through 5 to read a frequency-graduated (from high to low) series of 50 irregularly spelled words, first in isolation, and then in underdetermining contexts (e.g., "The football hit him in the stomach," in which the target word was *stomach*). They found that accuracy of recognizing irregular words of "intermediate familiarity" (which varied with age and ability) improved markedly with context for every age and ability group, and concluded that "the facilitative potential of context is a function of the subjective familiarity of the word to be recognized" (p. 274).

From an analysis of the children's responses as they progressed through the list, Adams and Huggins identified three stages in the development of word-specific knowledge. Words at the beginning of the list were read quickly and accurately, even in the absence of context. This reflects the most advanced stage of development. The orthographic representations of these words have become fully consolidated in the mental lexicons of the readers. During the second or transitional stage of development, a point was reached in the list (which varied across children) at which the words were recognized with hesitation or not at all in isolation but were read correctly in context. It is at this stage that beginning readers are able to combine partial word-level information with sentence context cues to identify unfamiliar words. As the children progressed beyond this section of the list (which lasted for a span of 5 to 10 words) to the more difficult words of lower frequency, they began making more errors, until eventually most of their responses were incorrect with or without context. This reflects the first stage of development of word-specific knowledge. A defining characteristic of this stage was the strong tendency for children to pronounce words in accordance with canonical spelling-to-sound rules. As Adams and Huggins (1985) pointed out, "Although distinctly incorrect, such responses can also be seen as not-so-distant approximations to the correct words" (p. 276). This finding is consistent with Ehri's (1992) claim that spelling-sound knowledge is essential for acquiring word-specific knowledge.

Although the findings of the Adams and Huggins study suggest that language prediction skill may contribute to the development of word-specific knowledge, there remains the question of whether the ability to use the constraints of sentence context is a source of individual differences in learning to read. That is, are differences in language prediction skill related to differences in the rate at which children progress through the stages of sight word acquisition identified by Adams and Huggins? Suggestive evidence comes from studies reporting positive correlations between grammatical sensitivity and context-free word recognition ability and/or phonological recoding ability, which is the ability to translate letters and letter patterns into phonological forms (see Tunmer & Chapman, 1998, for a review). A commonly used measure of phonological recoding ability (or letter-sound knowledge) is the ability to pronounce correctly pseudowords such as *dut*, *sark*, *tain*, and *thrain*.

The grammatical sensitivity measure that most directly assesses language prediction skill is the oral cloze task, in which the child is asked to listen to incomplete sentences and to supply the missing word. Willows and Ryan (1986) found that performance on the oral cloze task was significantly related to reading achievement in a sample of first-, second-, and third-grade children even after the effects of age, general cognitive development, short-term memory, and vocabulary knowledge were statistically controlled. Tunmer, Nesdale and Wright (1987) used a reading-level match design in which good, younger readers were matched with poor, older readers on several measures of reading ability and on verbal intelligence. They found that the good readers scored significantly better than the poor readers on two measures of grammatical sensitivity, an oral cloze task and a word-order correction task. In support of the suggestion that language prediction skill may influence reading by helping children acquire phonological recoding skill, Stanovich, Cunningham and Feeman (1984) found that performance on an oral cloze task correlated more highly with phonological recoding than did their measure of phonological sensitivity. In fact, the oral cloze correlated more highly with phonological recoding than with any of the other variables included in the study (general intelligence, listening comprehension, word recognition speed, and reading comprehension).

Because of the correlational nature of these studies, it is possible that the strong relationships observed between grammatical sensitivity and reading simply reflect the indirect contribution of some third factor such as phonological sensitivity, which has been shown to be related to both grammatical sensitivity and reading ability. Grammatical sensitivity is thought to facilitate the development of word recognition skill by enabling beginning readers to use context to identify unfamiliar words, which in turn, increases their word-specific knowledge and knowledge of grapheme-phoneme correspondences. Grammatical sensitivity should therefore make a contribution to the development of word recognition ability that is distinct from that made by phonological sensitivity. In support of this claim, Tunmer (1989) found in a longitudinal study that grammatical sensitivity in first grade was significantly related to phonological recoding in second grade after the effects of verbal intelligence, general cognitive ability, and phonological sensitivity were partialed out.

Tunmer and Chapman (1998) carried out two experiments to explore further the hypothesis that the combination of partial decoding knowledge and contextual sensitivity is an important mechanism by which unfamiliar words in text can be identified. The purpose of the first experiment was to determine the *potential* contribution of letter-sound knowledge and sentence context to reading irregularly spelled words. Sixty-seven Year 2 and Year 3 children were given a mispronunciation correction task involving a hand-held puppet that said words the "wrong way". The child's task was to try to figure out what the puppet was trying to say. The mispronounced words presented to the children were all formed from the regularized pronunciations of irregularly spelled content words of varying print frequency. For example, the word *stomach* was pronounced as *stow-match*. The children were presented with a total of 80 regularized pronunciations and managed to figure out about a third of them. When these same mispronounced words were presented in context in another test session, the children's performance more than doubled. For example, when the puppet said, "The football hit him in the *stow-match*," most children immediately said the word was *stomach*.

It is important to note that the contexts used in the task were deliberately underdetermining ones, which research indicates is the more naturally occurring situation. As noted earlier, the average predictability of content words (i.e., nouns, verbs) in running text is less than 10% (Gough, 1983). When the 80 sentence contexts were presented as an oral cloze task to a separate sample of children, the average predictability of the target words was in fact below 10%. In summary, the results of the first study clearly indicated that the letter-sound information contained in irregularly spelled words is potentially very useful, especially when combined with sentence context cues.

The purpose of the second study was to determine the relative contributions of language prediction skill and letter-sound knowledge to the identification of unfamiliar words in underdetermining contexts. A sample of 289 Year 2 and Year 3 children were given several tests, including an oral cloze task as a measure of language prediction skill, a pseudoword decoding task as a measure of letter-sound knowledge, and a contextual facilitation task. In the latter task the children were asked to read aloud the same 80 irregularly spelled words that were used in the first experiment, first in isolation and then, in another test session, in underdetermining contexts that were read aloud by the experimenter.

The results of the contextual facilitation task indicated that, as expected, accuracy of recognizing words improved with context. Of greater interest was the finding that children with moderate or emerging knowledge of spelling-to-sound patterns showed the largest absolute gains when the words were presented in context. These were children whose percentile scores on the pseudoword decoding test ranged from 31 to 70. It appears that the ability of these children to take advantage of the available letter-sound information in exception words was not sufficiently advanced that they could identify many of the words in isolation. However, when the words were presented in underdetermining contexts, the performance of these children greatly improved. In contrast, the isolated word scores and contextual facilitation scores of the poor decoders were relatively low, suggesting that if beginning readers are unable to make use of the letter-sound information provided in exception words, context will be of little or no help. The absolute gains of the good decoders were also low, but this was because their ability to recognize words in isolation was so high, which limited the opportunity for improvement with context. When contextual facilitation was re-calculated as the ratio of contextual gain to potential improvement (as indicated by the number of words presented in isolation that were *not* correctly identified), the relationship between pseudoword decoding and relative contextual gain was a linearly increasing function. What these data clearly indicate is that although good decoders do not need to rely on context as often because of their superior ability to recognize words in isolation, when they do rely on context, they are much more likely to identify unfamiliar words than less skilled readers.

Following Rego and Bryant (1993), children's ability to read words in context that they could not read in isolation was also assessed by the number of words read correctly when the first 15 words missed in isolation were presented in context (the Rego and Bryant scoring procedure and the ratio of contextual gain to potential improvement yielded the same pattern of results). A scatterplot of the relation of letter-sound knowledge to reading unfamiliar words primed by context provided further support for the suggestion that only children who had begun to acquire knowledge of letter-sound correspondences were able to benefit from context. The scatterplot revealed that, although many children performed well on pseudoword decoding and poorly on contextual priming, no children performed poorly on pseudoword decoding and well on contextual priming. Letter-sound knowledge appears to be necessary for taking advantage of sentence context. Consistent with Ehri's (1992) claim that the development of word-specific knowledge depends centrally on phonological recoding ability, a similar pattern of results was observed in the scatterplot of the relation of letter-sound knowledge to identifying exception words in isolation. Out of 289 children, there was not a single child who was good at identifying exception words but poor at pseudoword decoding. Knowledge of spelling-to-sound patterns is essential for learning to identify words, including irregularly spelled ones.

Further statistical analyses of the data were carried out to determine the relative importance of letter-sound cues and sentence context cues to learning to read. The results indicated that letter-sound knowledge (as measured by pseudoword decoding) made a much greater contribution to the identification of unfamiliar exception words in context than did language prediction skill (as measured by performance on an oral cloze task). That is, even in the extreme case of learning to identify irregularly spelled words, knowledge of spelling-to-sound patterns is much more important than the ability to use the constraints of sentence context. This finding and the finding that letter-sound knowledge is necessary for taking advantage of the constraints of sentence context in identifying unfamiliar words, provides further support for the suggestion that beginning readers should use context to supplement word-level information rather than to substitute for it.

DISCUSSION

The latter findings would appear to conflict with those reported by Rego and Bryant (1993) who, in a longitudinal study, tested children at two points during their first year of schooling, when the mean ages of the children were 5 years, 6 months and 5 years, 11 months. Contextual facilitation in reading was assessed by the number of words that the children were able to read correctly when the first 10 words that they missed on a standardized test of context free word recognition were placed in sentence contexts read aloud by the experimenter. Rego and Bryant found that three measures of grammatical sensitivity (including an oral cloze task) taken in the first session each predicted priming by context in the second session after controlling for the effects of age, general intelligence, vocabulary knowledge and verbal memory. However, two measures of phonological sensitivity failed to make independent contributions to priming by context, although each predicted invented spelling ability in the second session.

A possible explanation of the failure to find a significant independent predictive relationship between phonological sensitivity and priming by context is that most of the children tested might not have reached the stage in the development of their word recognition skills during which they would have begun relying more heavily on phonological skills. In the second session the children performed at floor levels on a pseudoword decoding test (Rego, 1991), and in a standardized test of context free word recognition ability, 30 of the 54 children could not read a single word. The mean number of words read correctly was 0.35. Given these considerations and the fact that the children tested in the Tunmer and Chapman (1998) study were in their second or third year of schooling (with a mean age of 6 years, 11 months), it is possible that phonological skills contribute to the use of context in reading unfamiliar words at a somewhat later stage of reading development than that studied by Rego and Bryant.

In support of this suggestion are results from a longitudinal study reported by Tunmer and Chapman (1996) in which the literacy development of 152 children in 22 schools was tracked from school entry to the middle of Year 3. Multiple regression analyses were carried out with prereading measures at the beginning of Year 1 as predictor variables and priming by context at the end of Year 2 as the criterion variable. The extraneous variables, which were entered first, included age, listening vocabulary (as measured by the Peabody Picture Vocabulary Test), and verbal memory (as measured by a non-word repetition test). There were two measures of phonological sensitivity (sound matching and phoneme deletion) and two measures of grammatical sensitivity (word order correction and oral cloze). The measures of phonological and grammatical sensitivity each made an independent contribution to the variance in the priming by context measure after controlling for the effects of the extraneous variables. However, when the two phonological sensitivity measures were first entered into the regression equation along with the extraneous variables, only one of the grammatical sensitivity measures (word order correction) made an independent contribution to priming by context, accounting for only 1.6% of the variance. In contrast, when the two grammatical sensitivity measures were first entered along with the extraneous variables, each measure of phonological sensitivity made a strong, independent contribution to priming by context, with sound matching accounting for 5.4% of the variance and phoneme deletion accounting for 8.6% of the variance.

A similar pattern of results was obtained from multiple regression analyses in which the predictor variables were measures taken at the end of Year 1 and the criterion variable was again the priming by context measure taken at the end of Year 2. To control for autoregressive effects, performance on a standardized measure of context free word recognition ability at the end of Year 1 was also entered as an extraneous variable. The grammatical sensitivity measures were the same as those at the beginning of Year 1. However, phonological skill was assessed by two new measures, phoneme segmentation and pseudoword decoding. As before, the phonological and grammatical measures each made an independent contribution to priming by context when entered into the regression equation after the extraneous variables. The phonological measures also made strong, independent contributions to priming by context after the two grammatical sensitivity measures and extraneous variables had been entered into the regression equation. Phoneme segmentation accounted for 4.8% of the variance and pseudoword decoding accounted for 5.9% of the variance. In contrast, when a similar analysis was carried out for the grammatical sensitivity measures, only the oral cloze reached significance ($p < .05$), accounting for only 1.4% of the variance. In summary, the findings from the longitudinal study suggest that during the second year of formal literacy instruction, phonological skills make a much greater contribution to the ability to use context in reading than grammatical sensitivity.

Despite these results, however, contradictory findings have been reported for older children. In a study of Year 3 and Year 4 children (with an average age of 8 years, 10 months), Nation and Snowling (1998) found that word identification and comprehension skills were positively related to the use of context to facilitate word recognition (as measured by the ratio of contextual gain to the number of words presented in isolation that were not correctly identified). However, pseudoword decoding was not significantly related to contextual facilitation. Rather, listening comprehension and word-level semantic skills were the best predictors of contextual facilitation. Given that the variability for pseudoword decoding was reasonably high (i.e., the children were not performing at ceiling levels), this finding is somewhat puzzling. If partial decoding in combination with sensitivity to contextual constraints results in more words being read correctly in context than in isolation, then individual differences in letter-sound knowledge would be expected to be related to the quality of the partial decoding. It is possible that for older children the quality of their partial decodings is so advanced (e.g., *stow-match* for *stomach*) that only sensitivity to contextual constraints is important at this stage of development. As noted earlier, the opposite holds for poor decoders. That is, for beginning readers who are unable to make use of the letter-sound information available in unfamiliar words, context will be of little or no benefit to them (Tunmer & Chapman, 1998). Because the Rego and Bryant (1993) study focused on 5-year-olds, the Tunmer and Chapman (1998) study on 6-year-olds, and the Nation and Snowling (1998) study on 8-year-olds, a longitudinal study that spans across these ages is needed to determine whether phonological factors and sensitivity to contextual constraints contribute differentially to the use of context in reading as a function of age.

Another important issue raised by the Nation and Snowling (1998) study concerns the scoring procedure used to assess contextual facilitation. The pattern of results Nation and Snowling reported differed greatly according to whether contextual facilition was scored as the absolute difference between reading words in isolation and in context, or as the ratio of absolute contextual gain to potential improvement (as indicated by the number of words presented in isolation that were not correctly identified; see Tunmer & Chapman, 1998). As Nation and Snowling pointed out, because skilled readers make fewer errors when reading words in isolation, they have less opportunity to show improvement with context. The ratio measure is therefore a more appropriate measure of contextual facilitation than the absolute measure. Consistent with the findings of Tunmer and Chapman (1998), Nation and Snowling found that skilled readers were better able to make use of context than less-skilled readers when the ratio scoring procedure was used.

In an analysis of different scoring methods that used the data from the Tunmer and Chapman (1998) study, Allerup and Elbro (1998) argued against the use of the ratio scoring procedure to examine the question of whether better readers are "supported more by context than are poorer readers in the initial phases of reading development" (p. 411). However, Allerup and Elbro misunderstood what the ratio procedure was designed to measure. Both the ratio measure and the measure used by Rego and Bryant (1993) assessed children's ability to read words in context that they could not read in isolation; that is, their ability to *use* context if they needed to, not the overall extent to which they *relied* on context in reading text. Making this distinction is essential because it allows the following possibility, which is the major conclusion drawn from this review: skilled readers are better than less-skilled readers in using context to identify unfamiliar words in text because of their superior phonological recoding and/or grammatical sensitivity skills, but they rely less on context than less-skilled readers to read the words of text because of their superior context free word recognition skills.

REFERENCES

Adams, M.J., & Huggins, A. (1985). The growth of children's sight vocabulary: A quick test with educational and theoretical implications. *Reading Research Quarterly, 20*, 262-281.

Allerup, P., & Elbro, C. (1998). Comparing differences in accuracy across conditions or individuals: An argument for the use of log odds. *The Quarterly Journal of Experimental Psychology, 51A*, 409-424.

Bransford, J.D. (1979). *Human cognition: Learning, understanding, and remembering.* Belmont, CA: Wadsworth.

Chomsky, N. (1965). *Aspects of a theory of syntax.* Cambridge, MA: MIT Press.

Ehri, L.C. (1992). Reconceptualizing the development of sight word reading and its relationship to reading. In P. Gough, L. Ehri, & R. Treiman (Eds.), *Reading acquisition* (pp.107-143). Hillsdale, NJ: Lawrence Erlbaum Associates.

Goodman, K.S. (1967). Reading: A psycholinguistic guessing game. *Journal of the Reading specialist, 6*, 126-135.

Gough, P.B. (1983). Context, form and interaction. In K. Rayner (Ed.), *Eye movements in reading: Perceptual and language processes* (pp. 203-211). San Diego, CA: Academic Press.

Nation, K., & Snowling, M.J. (1998). Individual differences in contextual facilitation: Evidence from dyslexia and poor reading comprehension. *Child Development, 69*, 996-1011.

Nicholson, T. (1991). Do children read words better in context or in lists? A classic study revisited. *Journal of Educational Psychology, 83*, 444-450.

Pinker, S. (1994). *The language instinct: How the mind creates language.* New York: Harper Perennial.

Rego, L. (1991). *The role of early linguistic awareness in children's reading and spelling.* Unpublished doctoral dissertation, University of Oxford, England.

Rego, L., & Bryant, P. (1993). The connection between phonological, syntactic and semantic skills and children's reading and spelling. *European Journal of Psychology of Education, 8*, 235-246.

Smith, F. (1971). *Understanding reading: A psycholinguistic analysis of reading and learning to read.* New York: Holt, Rinehart & Winston.

Smith, J.W.A., & Elley, W.B. (1994). *Learning to read in New Zealand.* Auckland, New Zealand: Longman Paul.

Stanovich, K. (1980). Toward an interactive-compensatory model of individual differences in the development of reading fluency. *Reading Research Quarterly, 16,* 32-71.

Stanovich, K. (1984). The interactive-compensatory model of reading: A confluence of developmental, experimental and educational psychology. *Remedial and Special Education, 5,* 11-19.

Stanovich, K. (1986). Matthew effects in reading: Some consequences of individual differences in the acquisition of literacy. *Reading Research Quarterly, 21,* 360-406.

Stanovich, K., Cunningham, A.E., & Feeman, D.J. (1984). Intelligence, cognitive skills and early reading progress. *Reading Research Quarterly, 19,* 278-303.

Tunmer, W.E. (1989). The role of language-related factors in reading disability. In D. Shankweiler & I. Liberman (Eds.), *Phonology and reading disability: Solving the reading puzzle.* (pp. 91-131). Ann Arbor, MI: University of Michigan Press.

Tunmer, W.E., & Chapman, J.W. (1996, August). *Language prediction skill and beginning reading.* Paper presented at an Invited Symposium at the Twenty-Sixth International Congress of Psychology, Montreal, Canada.

Tunmer, W.E & Chapman J.W. (1998). Language prediction skill, phonological reading ability, and beginning reading. In C. Hulme & R.M. Joshi (Eds.), *Reading and spelling: Development and disorder* (pp. 33-67). Hillsdale, NJ: Lawrence Erlbaum Associates.

Tunmer, W.E., Chapman, J.W., Ryan, H., & Prochnow, J. (1998). The importance of providing beginning readers with explicit training in phonological processing skills. *Australian Journal of Learning Disabilities, 3,* 4-14.

Tunmer, W.E., & Hoover, W. (1992). Cognitive and linguistic factors in learning to read. In P. Gough, L. Ehri, & R. Treiman (Eds.), *Reading acquisition* (pp.175-214). Hillsdale, NJ: Lawrence Erlbaum Associates.

Tunmer, W.E., Nesdale, A.R., & Wright, A.D. (1987). Syntactic awareness and reading acquisition. *British Journal of Developmental Psychology, 5,* 25-34.

Willows, D.M., & Ryan, E.B. (1986). The development of grammatical sensitivity and its relationship to early reading achievement. *Reading Research Quarterly, 21,* 253-266.

SUGGESTED FURTHER READINGS

Nation, K., & Snowling, M.J. (1998). Individual differences in contextual facilitation: Evidence from dyslexia and poor reading comprehension. *Child Development, 69,* 996-1011.

Nicholson, T. (1991). Do children read words better in context or in lists? A classic study revisited. *Journal of Educational Psychology, 83,* 444-450.

Rego, L., & Bryant, P. (1993). The connection between phonological, syntactic and semantic skills and children's reading and spelling. *European Journal of Psychology of Education, 8,* 235-246.

Stanovich, K. (1984). The interactive-compensatory model of reading: A confluence of developmental, experimental and educational psychology. *Remedial and Special Education, 5,* 11-19.

Tunmer, W.E & Chapman J.W. (1998). Language prediction skill, phonological reading ability, and beginning reading. In C. Hulme & R.M. Joshi (Eds.), *Reading and spelling: Development and disorder* (pp. 33-67). Hillsdale, NJ: Lawrence Erlbaum Associates.

B4. Reading Stories

ALISON F. GARTON & CHRIS PRATT

ABSTRACT

This chapter focuses on how children learn about reading through reading stories and being read stories. Early book reading has been linked with benefits to literacy in early childhood. Both the skills required in learning to read and the process of reading are described. In particular, it is argued that the social context in which early literacy takes place is extremely important both in facilitating and constraining the rate and direction of reading development. Issues examined include early book reading, the transition from picture books to stories, the shift from listening to stories to understanding them, the specific components of understanding stories, enhancing the environment to encourage reading and finally, using the knowledge and skills learned through listening to construct stories. An integrative approach is taken, highlighting the close relationship between the written and oral aspects of literacy development.

INTRODUCTION

"Reading stories" is a suitably ambiguous phrase (and title for a book chapter) that can refer to the actual activity through which children acquire or develop the skill of reading as well as the processes by which extended text, narrative and discourse are discovered and mastered by children. That is, the term can refer to both the joint book reading activity between children and parents (the "what") as well as the means by which independent reading is attained (the "how"). The use of the phrase "reading stories" allows us to examine book reading as a developmental activity as well as how the activity assists in the process of reading development. Under this rubric, we will also consider the benefits for children of learning to read. Specific benefits include enhanced later language development, enhanced cognitive skills and the educational advantages that flow from reading. Other aspects that have been researched are the development of creativity, the enjoyment of books and reading as an activity *per se* and the development of warm and empathic relationships between the child and others when reading books.

In learning to read stories, there are at least two successive phases (Garton & Pratt, 1989, 1998). Current terminology has dubbed these phases "emergent literacy"

T. Nunes, P. Bryant (eds.), Handbook of Children's Literacy, 213–228.
© 2004 Kluwer Academic Publishers. Printed in Great Britain.

(Whitehurst & Lonigan, 1998 – a term they attribute to Clay, 1966, but which has also been used by others including Bus, 1994, Dickinson, 1995, and Hall, 1987) to characterise the development of literacy along a continuum. This development consists of the acquisition of the skills, knowledge and attitudes in learning to read and write and encourages the researcher to look for precursors to reading as well as continuities in the processes. A review by Whitehurst and Lonigan (1998) focuses on emergent literacy by firstly cataloguing the component skills and knowledge and then by focusing on the role of the environment in supporting or constraining the development of these skills and knowledge. This chapter will use the general emergent literacy characterisation in relation to the reading of stories by, with and to young children as they develop towards independent and confident readers. The two phases that we shall distinguish are early book reading and components of reading comprehension. This chapter will focus almost exclusively on the first phase in all its guises as the development of reading comprehension is covered in the chapter by Oakhill and Cain in this volume.

Our chapter will examine emergent literacy in the context of reading stories, and will do so within a developmental framework, looking at opportunities available for the encouragement of reading in young children and how this translates into skills, knowledge and attitudes. The main focus will be on young children up to about 5 or 6 years of age, once they are beginning school although some of the research on reading comprehension has been conducted with older children. We will draw on research that looks at continuities in the development of reading and examines the implications of activities related to reading for children's future reading skills, particularly in relation to stories.

Theoretical context

The theoretical framework adopted here and developed in Garton and Pratt (1989, 1998) is adapted from the theories proposed by Vygotsky and Bruner who emphasise the importance of social interaction for the development of knowledge, in particular, knowledge of symbolic systems such as spoken language, reading and writing. Vygotsky (1962) contended that social interaction created language and the integration of different tool and sign systems (for practical and symbolic purposes respectively) by the developing child were what gave raise to new and increasingly sophisticated behaviour. Use and integration can only take place through social interaction and are particularly facilitated by the "zone of proximal development" (Vygotsky, 1978) a theoretical notion that described the (child's) movement from potential to actual development capabilities in interaction with an adult or more capable peer. That is, Vygotsky emphasised the social and constructivist nature of the child's developing knowledge and skills, with the adult guiding and monitoring the child as he or she becomes aware of the significance of the tool or sign and integrated into a higher level of skill or behaviour. Collaborative social interaction is regarded as the key to development.

Bruner (1983) developed the notion of language as a mental tool that facilitates representation of the world. He drew on the notion that language and other symbolic systems) are best encouraged and hence develop in a functional way through social interaction. In his study of language development, he sought to demonstrate how children's communicative intentions were guided and enhanced through interaction with a parent so that the product was not only an awareness of the functions of language but also the use of language to communicate with others. One of the scenarios explored by Bruner was early shared book reading, which he examined specifically in relation to how its predictable and regular structure could, over time, give the child a framework within which to learn not just the words of language but its uses. The use of book reading as a social interaction context laid the basis for the subsequent studies into the relationship between such exposure to books and the language therein and subsequent language and reading abilities.

Early book reading

Research on book reading has obvious links with the study of the processes of reading. We have argued previously (Garton & Pratt, 1989, 1998) that the social opportunity between a parent and young children can assist both spoken language development in the early years and reading development in the preschool years. In support of this view, Bus (1994) reviewed the evidence for the important role of the parent in emergent literacy, or reading, in the context of the book reading paradigm. The research reviewed highlighted how important it was to have the child actively involved in the activity. Bruner's scaffolding analogy is a useful way of explaining how book reading uses a social relationship, in this case, the parent-child relationship, to facilitate later reading in the child. After reviewing a range of literature, Bus concluded that book reading as an activity lays the basis for reading, and furthermore, that adults are attuned to their children's emergent literacy skills and knowledge.

Earlier research, such as that of Wells (1985a, 1985b, 1985c) and Olson (1977, 1984) and also studies reported in Dickinson (1995), looked at the relationship between spoken language acquisition (via book reading) and later reading and literacy skills, in terms of the processes required for learning. This research assumes that there is a relationship between book reading and early vocabulary development (see deLoache & deMendoza, 1987, for evidence to support this claim), and that this early learning of the structural aspects of language extends to the facilitation of reading at a later age. In general, it is argued that while children are acquiring spoken language, the context provides cues for interpretation of, for example, the language input the child receives from the parent. In book reading, the context is used as a vehicle for the child learning such things as social routines and the use of labels to name things or to represent activities, together with other ways of representing information, such as numbers and pictures. The books involved are frequently those that have clear pictures of items assumed to be reasonably familiar to young children, and often arranged either alphabetically with words beginning with B on one page, for example, or in identifiable groupings, such as "Animals".

It is clear that both shared book reading and early exposure to print are elements in the home literacy environment which are linked both to early language abilities and to success in later reading. The evidence has been summarised elsewhere (Bus, van IJzendoorn & Pellegrini, 1995; Whitehurst & Lonigan, 1998). The research on the relationship of book reading to later reading abilities has examined both the component skills of literacy (including spoken language and vocabulary skills) as well as the importance of the social or interactional processes for later reading. This latter perspective also incorporates other aspects of the home literacy environment such as number of books in the home, use of public library facilities and exposure to print by other family members such as older brothers and sisters and the influence of these individually or collectively on the child's development of reading.

Bus, van IJzendoorn and Pellegrini (1995) conducted a meta-analysis of the outcomes for children of early book reading. They focused specifically on the frequency of parent-child book reading with preschool children and the resultant advantages recorded in language growth, emergent literacy and subsequent reading achievement. Bus et al. note the increasing reporting in the research literature of the use of early book reading in lower socio-economic families in order to enhance the literacy opportunities for such children and the assumed later educational benefits. Clearly, this type of intervention is important if there are measurable later benefits for the children.

In conducting their meta-analysis, Bus et al. selected studies which had measured the frequency of book reading between parents and their pre-school aged children. They argue that most research has collected information on the frequency of book reading and there is little variation in the frequency measures used. Furthermore, many of the qualitative differences between parents have been found not to relate to parental characteristics (as one might initially assume) but to the frequency of book reading. Although they acknowledge there may be individual differences in reading style between parents, any research examining such qualitative differences has been too diverse to be included in any meta-analysis. Bus et al. further note that socio-economic differences, themselves related to such things as access to and ownership of books, should be incorporated in any meta-analysis of the effects of early shared book reading.

Six hypotheses were tested by Bus at al. (1995). These related to predicted positive literacy outcomes including enhanced later language and reading skills. They also made some predictions about the magnitude of the hypothesised effects including taking into account socio-economic status, the extent to which the studies are controlled experiments rather than correlational studies, and the extent to which the strength of any association relates to the age at which the outcomes are measured. Drawing from some 40 studies with over 3000 children, Bus et al.

found an overall effect size (that is, the standardised difference between the groups or variables being considered) of $d=0.59$ for the association between book reading and subsequent language outcome measures, with a range of $d=0.00$ to $d=1.51$. This overall effect size corresponds to a mean correlation of $+0.28$. The effect sizes varied depending on the outcome measures, with the largest effect ($d=0.67$) for the association between early book reading and later language skills, and lower effect sizes for book reading and emergent literacy outcomes ($d=0.58$) and for book reading and reading achievement ($d=0.55$). Contrasts between low- and high socio-economic families did not yield the anticipated differences, nor did whether the studies were experimental or correlational/longitudinal. Effect sizes were greatest for the youngest children in the sample suggesting that age at the time of literacy outcome measurement can explain some of the variation in effect size.

The value of the meta-analysis by Bus and colleagues is that it starts to unravel some of the complexities of the relationship between early shared book reading and the claimed benefits. It uses the burgeoning literature in this area and carefully breaks down the relevant process variables as well as the outcomes. The analysis affirms the assumption that shared book reading promotes a literate attitude in children and confirms the value of intergenerational reading programs. That is, early parent-child shared reading has clear advantages for later language and reading.

From picture books to stories

A further consideration in early book reading is the nature of the books themselves. As noted earlier, many of the early books that parents and children read together are picture books where labelling of the familiar items depicted (such as animals or furniture) is the main activity, although some enterprising parents weave a story around these items and some books themselves include a broad integrative text. However, as we have drawn attention to previously (Garton & Pratt, 1989, 1998), in homes where books are read to children, there is frequently a shift when the child reaches about 2 years of age to the reading of stories from books. In such books the text is usually simple, with a single sentence on a page for example, and is clearly supported by the illustrations. As children get older, two developments can occur. The original simple story can be embellished either by the parent or by the use of a more complex variation of the already known story (for example, stories such as Snow White can be told simply or there can be further development of the characters or their surroundings, lending more texture to the tale). Or, the children can be read more complex stories in addition to those simple ones already in the repertoire. In either case, children are being exposed to more and more complex language, to less reliance on the illustrations and to extended text integrated over time and space. Using a situation that is familiar (book reading), parents can begin to introduce variety in text, to decrease the extent to which the context (the book) supports the text, and to extend the text to integrate further ideas over time. Many parents engage in such behaviour unwittingly, guided by their child's grasp of the existing stories and need for novel information.

Children are, through listening to stories being read, learning about how the language of texts is organised. Unlike language used in more general social conversations, written story language exists only in the context of reading a particular book and relies on that context for its interpretation. However, children probably do not realise that the written language requires the supportive context and to them, it may apparently exist independently of that context. However, it does not and can not exist as decontextualised language, spoken in conversation and children have to learn to appreciate this distinction. An adult and child reading a story with an extended theme can use the pictures to contextualise the written words, and can also elaborate on the illustrations through further conversation either with or without the contextual cues provided in the book. These elaborations help the child to make the distinction between spoken and written language and the contexts within which they are used and the contexts they can create.

Any contextualisation can vary, depending on the circumstances of the story telling. Garton and Pratt (1989, 1998) give the example of the availability of many children's stories on audio cassette (usually accompanied by the book). While children will sit and listen to such tapes with a parent present, they would be unlikely to be able to follow the accompanying text alone. They may give the appearance of doing so if the activity has been shared previously and become so routinised that the child knows when to turn the page. However some children will not sit and listen to a tape alone. It is clear, and the research reviewed by Bus et al. substantiates this, that what is important is the establishment and maintenance of a context shared by the parent and the child. In the case of listening to an audio tape, the child and parent together listen to the tape and follow the text as if the parent were doing the reading.

The above discussion has concentrated almost exclusively on situations where parents read from a book to their children. What happens in the case of narratives that parents "make up" and tell to their children without the support of pictures? There may be a shared context for the child to work out the story as these stories are often based on common experiences between the adult and the child and the child knows what is being talked about. Sometimes, the context is created by the parent telling the story, with the development of a world and characters shared by the child and the parent. For example, the author Roald Dahl's books were developed from stories he made up and related to his children. In some of these children's books, incredible worlds are described and improbable events occur – products of his imagination – but given life in the context of bed-time stories told to children. But as earlier, the essential component for the story telling is the joint adult-child participation.

From listening to comprehension

What happens when children listen to stories? How does listening to stories facilitate later language and reading skills? We hold a view that is not inconsistent with that of other researchers and invokes the notion of children internalising some abstract characteristics of language and its use in both the spoken and written forms. Alternatively, a modular view could be invoked, whereby by exposure to more and more complex stories, with more complex structures and greater use of decontextualised language requires the use of specific modules in the brain which come into play as and when the child is developmentally ready. We subscribe in this case to the previous view, if only because at this time, the evidence for it is more convincing.

In trying to work out the meaning in the language of a story, irrespective of the context or whether there is an explicit context, the language becomes the focus of the child's cognitive activity and attention. In so doing they begin to work out the relationship between any context and the language. This task is helped by the realisation that the language of stories is the same language as that used in social conversation wherein language creates the context. In book reading, the context supports the language although even when there are pictures, they tend to represent only a small part of the action, particularly as children move on from picture books *per se* to story books. Children become aware that the meaning of language is inherent in the structure of the language used in telling the story (or in the conversation), regardless of the contextualisation provided by the pictures or the shared knowledge. Children come to appreciate that language is a system of representation and can accordingly be used independently of the objects, people, events, actions and places it stands for. Furthermore, it can be used and interpreted in other and different contexts. That is to say, the reading of stories to children initially not only extends their experiences past the here and now (useful for the contextualisation and hence the understanding of language), but it allows them to detach language from the context and for language to become an object of awareness and knowledge.

Components of reading comprehension

Another aspect of reading stories is examination of the development or acquisition of the component skills and knowledge required by children when understanding the written word. Such knowledge and skills are essential for reading stories and deriving meaning from the written word. However, the comprehension of what is read does not follow on automatically from being able to read the words and previously we have distinguished three reasons for this (Garton & Pratt, 1989, 1998). Briefly, firstly, reading comprehension depends on listening comprehension skills and the latter may not be as well developed as we might infer from the children's behaviour in everyday interactions with their routinised and regular form and structure. Such consistency and predictability may aid children's comprehension and give the impression of greater ability than would be the case in less familiar and unstructured contexts. Studies such as those conducted by Markman (1979) and Tunmer, Nesdale and Pratt (1983) have examined the extent to which school-aged children are able to use cues to meaning provided in stories being read to them. Generally speaking, the greater the contextual material in the stories, the greater the ease with which children can understand, that is, extract the correct meaning from, the stories. Also, children improve in their listening comprehension with age and can extract the correct meaning from fewer contextual cues as they get older. Such experimental contexts however are not the same as a naturalistic story-telling context in the home for example, where other cues to meaning may be available for use by the children as well as the opportunity for further elaboration or discussion to assist children to understand.

Secondly, written language makes use of syntactic constructions that are infrequent in the spoken form of the language. This includes use of language in such contexts as instructions for an appliance or a board game, and in different written materials such as newspapers, street directories or timetables. Interestingly, such difficulties may be encountered when children begin to use basal readers at school as Reid (1983) has commented, after surveying such early reading books, that at that time many did contain structures not commonly or frequently found in spoken language. Children apparently therefore may have to deal with unfamiliar constructions when faced with learning to read.

Thirdly, comprehension of the written word often requires integrating complex information across extended discourse to a much greater extent than spoken language does. Research on listening comprehension invariably shows that children cannot keep track of information across sentences, either by failing to detect ambiguities in such extended text or by taking longer to read anomalous sentences than non-anomalous ones. It is also important to note that reading accuracy does not necessarily predict reading comprehension, as the two may be separate skills.

Encouraging children to read stories

There are two main ways in which children can be encouraged to read stories and to improve their story reading ability, firstly through the use of early intervention strategies that enhance emergent literacy skills and knowledge and secondly through strategies which develop and improve the comprehension skills of poor readers. A further but possibly unrelated strategy, because the facilitative effect on reading stories is not yet known, is through the encouragement of narrative skills in children. Peterson, Jesso and McCabe (1999) speculate that the encouragement of decontextualised language, prompted through the use of parental questions and careful listening, must affect the development of narrative skills. This must then not only assist language skills in general but it also increases awareness of such decontextualised uses of language which itself can have only a positive effect on reading.

Enhancing emergent literacy

The enhancement of emergent literacy not only has benefits for children's later reading ability, but it also allows researchers to test assumptions and hypotheses about the relationships between developmental signs and precursors of reading as well as about causal relationships amongst skill and knowledge components believed to be involved in reading and the reading process. Typically researchers or educators intervene with children who are "at risk" of not being exposed to early literacy environments or who have, for whatever reason, not developed one or more of the skills or knowledge claimed necessary for reading stories fluently and accurately.

Because of the reported success of early book reading on later reading, Dickinson (1995) and Whitehurst and Lonigan (1998) have drawn attention to the need for and the success of intervention programs. In particular, home and family intervention programs (sometimes referred to as intergenerational programs) have attracted attention because of the strength of their theoretical underpinnings as well as the practicality of their implementation. Four characteristics of book reading are noted as making it practical for use in intervention programs: It is a discrete activity that can easily be duplicated; it is a regular feature of home and school life; it is valued in literate cultures; and once established as a routine, can foster emotional closeness. Dickinson (1995) and Whitehurst and Lonigan (1998) review a range of intervention programs that have been used successfully in homes and schools to promote higher levels of literacy in the target populations. Both short- and long-term benefits must be evaluated and the facilitative effect on subsequent reading achievements assessed. There is however a firm commitment to such intervention programs and their value in enhancing literacy and educational opportunities for young children and their parents.

Whitehurst and Lonigan (1998) summarise a range of interventions that facilitate emergent literacy and speculate about a possible developmental model of emergent literacy, in the context of our current knowledge about how children learn to read which they argue is sparse. They conclude by suggesting some research initiatives and social policy directions both for interventions and for educational practice.

Interventions identified by Whitehurst and Lonigan (1998) as possibly enhancing emergent literacy include dialogic or shared reading, use of "little books", changes in the literacy environment, intergenerational family literacy, phonological sensitivity, and whole language instruction. These will be considered along two dimensions, namely indirect and direct. Indirect approaches use adults or the environment as vehicles to engage and encourage children in their reading. The relevant interventions are dialogic reading, use of "little books", intergenerational family literacy programs and changes in the classroom. Direct approaches, on the other hand, target the child and train or instruct children in one or more of the component skills required for reading. Indirect approaches tend to use a social framework to support the program, both practically and theoretically, as the interactional aspect is regarded as important to the success of the intervention. That is, the programs are derived from theories which emphasise the social interactional nature of reading development and the importance of interaction to children's development of reading. While indirect approaches are not anti-social nor asocial, the interactional aspect of the intervention or program is not essential to its success and the programs are derived typically from theory and research into cognitive development. An example of each type of intervention is given below.

Dialogic reading refers to shared reading in which the child learns to become the story teller (Whitehurst & Lonigan, 1998). Instead of the adult reading the story, he or she becomes an active listener, asking questions, prompting the child to give additional information and generally acting in a supportive way, rather like Bruner's "scaffold". Children's responses, as well as their attempts at reading, are encouraged through praise and repetition, and parents "up the ante" by encouragement of greater sophistication in the language used, in the responses elicited and in adherence to the printed word. It has been claimed that such shared reading involving parental support and encouragement of the reader role in the child has produced significant improvements in the language skills of children from middle and upper-income families (Whitehurst & Lonigan, 1998). Such marked changes are not noticed in children from lower-income families attending child care, although the effects are apparently maintained at least in the short term.

Direct interventions with children include those with origins in training in phonological sensitivity. With preschool children, programs that are designed to enhance phonological awareness typically demonstrate improvements in later reading (Bryant & Bradley, 1985; Lundberg, Frost & Petersen, 1988). Research conducted with school-aged children who are just beginning to learn to read (all reviewed in Byrne, 1998) has clearly shown the benefits of training children in phonological awareness, specifically through teaching them the alphabetic principle. Byrne and colleagues developed a program, *Sound Foundations* (Byrne & Fielding-Barnsley, 1991), which focuses on phoneme identity as a means of bringing to a child's awareness the relevance of the alphabetic principle. This principle offers a level of linguistic representation that, according to Byrne, enables the best hypothesis about language children can make. By realising that alphabets comprise phonemes, Byrne argues that children can begin to learn to read with a workable hypothesis instead of relying on more laborious ways of approaching reading such as remembering entire sequences of letters or words. This principle though does have to be taught explicitly (Byrne, 1996). Programs such as *Sound Foundations* that teach children directly about the linguistic representation lead to improved phonological awareness in children, which itself has been linked to positive effects on reading (e.g., Bryant, Bradley, MacLean & Crossland, 1989).

Developing the grammar of story telling

Children need to develop the capacity firstly to understand and then to create stories themselves. Stories, if they are well-formed, have an implicit structure, a grammar, which organises the sequence of events. Such a structure comprises a setting then an event (often unexpected) that initiates the subsequent action or response. This response may take several attempts (which allows for development of character or of optional actions), and is followed by consequences (successful or unsuccessful), with a final reaction or action to conclude the story. The episodic nature of stories and their predicability (at least in books or stories developed for young children) allow such a characterisation of the form of the story and also ensure that children can grasp the structure and reproduce it in their own attempts at writing stories later.

Olson and Gee (1988) briefly reviewed the research on children's development of story grammar. Using a structure similar to that described above, they surmise that children who have heard many stories told to them internalise the structure which then provides the mental scaffold, or schema, around which they organise the structure of stories of their own creation. Evidence for this conjecture is presented, both from the perspective of how children use such story schemas in understanding and remembering (by retelling) stories – they apparently do – and also from a developmental perspective. Olson and Gee provide evidence for three developmental trends: Children and adults recall the same story patterns; adults recall more detail but the story structure is the same; as a corollary, children produce increasingly complex stories with age with more logical and purposeful behaviour and greater internal story coherence; and thirdly older children can better recall information presented in a disorganised manner than younger children.

From this knowledge base, Olson and Gee outline some strategies that might be used to instruct children in story grammar. Noting the poorer comprehension skills of young children, they advocate the use of direct teaching methods such as s story map or discussing story grammar with children after reading them a story. Any of these direct methods capitalises on the knowledge children already have about a story structure, using a "bootstrapping" technique to assist children in their understanding of story structure. Such an explicit understanding has benefits for comprehension as well as for the writing of stories by the children themselves.

Work with slightly older children has focused on how they understand (and tell) stories which require the linking of ideas and concepts across extended time (for example, Karmiloff-Smith, 1986). It is assumed that stories allow the development of ideas, through sentences to narrative structures. Discourse cohesion, referring to the use of linguistic devices that bind together sentences thematically, is important not only as a development in children's capacity to understand and tell extended stories but it also offers an explanation of how this function of language is acquired and used. Early work by Karmiloff-Smith (1986) with children telling stories from a series of linked pictures, demonstrated that although 5-year-old children were able to describe each picture, they were not integrating the stories. That is, although their language use was reasonably sophisticated, they were not using devises such as pronouns to refer to already mentioned characters or words like "and" to link the pictures. The linguistic capacities to create a narrative structure for a cohesive story develop later (by around age 9 years). Subsequently, similar research by Spinillo and Pinto (1994) with 4- to 8-year-old children demonstrated that experimental variation (picture-prompt of stories versus free story production, for example) could elicit differing levels of narrative structure. The former experimental situation elicited more sophisticated narrative structure. Age and cultural differences in this ability were also noted with older, literate, children performing at a higher level than younger, preliterate ones, and 4-year-old Italian children performing at a higher level than their English counterparts, probably due to differences in the age at which children start attending pre-schools (the Italian children being in their second year and the English ones in their first). It is speculated that the schooling advantage is due to longer exposure of Italian children to interactions in the school setting which accounts for their higher ability to produce stories.

Parental differences in narrative elicitation have been linked to literacy acquisition as well as the transmission of social and cultural traditions and values. Peterson and McCabe (1992) examined how parents elicit stories, or narratives, from their children. Specifically they examined how differences in parental narrative styles influence the structure and form of the narratives created by children. They found a close correspondence between certain parental elicitation techniques (such as the use of questions) and children's narrative skill. For example, a mother who continually uses questions as a general means of obtaining information from her child was found not only to continue to use that technique when asked to elicit a story from her child but also that child's narrative language would be structured accordingly. This research demonstrated that from as young as 2 years of age, children's capacity to construct stories was linked to the form of the parental language used both generally and specifically in the experimental context.

Working with 3- to 9-year old children, Trabasso, Stein, Rodkin, Park Munger and Baughn (1992) investigated the elicitation of narratives by a sequences of pictures. In many ways this study extended the prior work of Karmiloff-Smith, using a different explanatory framework. In particular, Trabasso et al. wished to study how careful planning of the story by the children was reflected in greater cohesion in the subsequent narratives. Interestingly the younger children seemingly interpreted the task as describing one-by-one each picture in isolation. Older children demonstrated greater cohesion in their story-telling, taken as evidence for superordinate planning, linking the people and actions in the pictures. In a quite different approach, Hickmann and Schneider (1993) looked at the errors children made when telling stories and if and how they are able to recover story cohesion after making an error. Essentially, they were concerned with the development of self repairs, that is the awareness of errors and their correction, by children, using the narrative as a context. In terms of our interest here on the development of the grammar of story telling, this study showed that with increasing age (from age 5 years) children used the discourse context when correcting errors (in contexts where the correction was elicited) and demonstrated an increasing capacity to correct errors "on line", thus maintaining cohesion in the narrative.

A more recent investigation into children's and adults' awareness of discourse was conducted by Karmiloff-Smith, Johnson, Grant, Jones, Karmiloff, Bartrip and Cuckle (1993). They distinguished between cohesion, as described earlier, and discourse coherence which refers to the structure of a narrative via the specification of a rule system that organises or constrains the propositional content of a story. The authors examined the repairs made by 7- to 11-year-old children and adults in order to develop a theory about the constraints that operate in extended discourse. Karmiloff-Smith and colleagues used reaction time data as well as structured interviews to ascertain the detection of errors and repairs in discourse showing that detection, and awareness, improved with increasing age. As awareness was postulated to equate with knowledge, it was argued that detection of repairs together with qualitative confirmation of such detection showed that linguistic devices used in stories such as pronouns somehow act to constrain what can be detected. Furthermore, the effects are noted at different linguistic levels, namely, word, sentence or propositional level.

Karmiloff-Smith et al. in their examination of the knowledge children and adults had of the linguistic markers of discourse cohesion found that the discourse-level functions of nouns and pronouns were not available to metalinguistic awareness in the same way that the sentence-level functions of the same markers were. That is, the use of noun and pronoun (or the detection of repairs to their appropriate use) were more easily recognised at the intra- or inter-sentence level than at the extended discourse level. This difference in the detection of repair categories was mirrored in the children's and adults' capacity to provide explanations for the repairs because, it is speculated, when two different linguistic functions are encoded by the same markers simultaneously, they compete for on-line processing resources and only one is accessible to awareness. One function is at the discourse level – the coherence of the narrative – the other is at the level of linguistic structure, the discourse cohesion. These levels of encoding develop at different rates. Discourse-level encoding is relevant to on-line processing as decisions need to be made over a longer time span and hence may not be available for reflection. Discourse cohesion functions can be handled more immediately. This research is important because it permits the development of a model that proposes the acquisition of multiple levels of linguistic representations which ultimately permit the understanding and use of extended narratives by children and adults. It also demonstrates how narratives are constructed by children and the structural changes that may occur during their development.

CONCLUDING COMMENTS

The usefulness of reading stories to children is often judged in terms of the later social and educational benefits noticed particularly on starting school (Hewison & Tizard, 1980; Wells, 1985a, 1985c, 1987; Cunningham, Stanovich & West, 1994; Dickinson, 1995, Tough, 1977, 1983; and Bus, 1994). The social benefits include such things as enhanced spoken language including communication and conversational skills as well as cognitive benefits (Stanovich, 1986). It is generally claimed that educational benefits arise from the any one or all of the following, each of which has been alluded to or reviewed in this chapter: Children have greater familiarity with the language of books; they have developed the concept of a story; and perhaps most importantly, they know that meaning can be extracted from the printed page, they can understand and use discourse and narrative, and most importantly of all, children enjoy reading stories.

REFERENCES

Bruner, J. S. (1983). *Child's talk: Learning to use language*. Oxford: Oxford University Press.

Bryant, P. E., & Bradley, L. (1985). *Children's reading problems*. Oxford: Basil Blackwell.

Bryant, P. E., Bradley, L., MacLean, M., & Crossland, J. (1989). Nursery rhymes, phonological skills and reading. *Journal of Child Language, 16*, 407-428.

Bus, A. (1994). The role of social context in emergent literacy. In E. Assink (Ed.), *Literacy acquisition and social context* (pp. 9-24). London: Harvester Wheatsheaf.

Bus, A., van IJzendoorn, M., & Pellegrini, A. (1995). Joint book reading makes for success in learning to read: A meta-analysis on intergenerational transmission of literacy. *Review of Educational Research, 65*, 1-21.

Byrne, B. (1996). The learnability of the alphabetic principal: Children's initial hypotheses about how print represents spoken language. *Applied Psycholinguistics, 17*, 401-426.

Byrne, B. (1998). *The foundations of literacy*. Hove, Sussex: Psychology Press.

Byrne, B., & Fielding-Barnsley, R. (1991). *Sound foundations*. Sydney, Australia.

Clay, M. M. (1966). *Emergent reading behaviour*. Unpublished doctoral dissertation, University of Auckland.

Cunningham, A. E., Stanovich, K. E., & West, R. F. (1994). Literacy environment and the development of children's cognitive skills. In E. Assink (Ed.), *Literacy acquisition and social context* (pp. 70-90). London: Harvester Wheatsheaf.

DeLoache, J., & DeMendoza, O. (1987). Joint picturebook interactions of mothers and 1-year-old children. *British Journal of Developmental Psychology, 5*, 111-123.

Dickinson, D. K. (Ed.) (1995). Bridges to literacy: Children, families and schools. Oxford: Blackwell.

Francis, H. (1987). Cognitive implications of learning to read. *Interchange, 18*, 97-108.

Garton A. F., & Pratt, C. (1989). *Learning to be literate: The development of spoken and written language*. Oxford: Basil Blackwell.

Garton A. F., & Pratt, C. (1998). *Learning to be literate: The development of spoken and written language* (2nd ed). Oxford: Blackwell.

Hall, N. (1987). *The emergence of literacy*. Sevenoaks: Kent: Hodder & Stoughton.

Hewison, J., & Tizard, J. (1980). Parental involvement and reading attainment. *British Journal of Educational Psychology, 50*, 209-215.

Hickmann, M., & Schneider, P. (1993). Children's ability to restore the referential cohesion of stories. *First Language, 13*, 169-202.

Karmiloff-Smith, A. (1986). Some fundamental aspects of language development after age five. In P. Fletcher & M. Garman (Eds.), *Language acquisition* (2nd ed) (pp. 455-474). Cambridge: Cambridge University Press.

Karmiloff-Smith, A., Johnson, H., Grant, J., Jones, M-C., Karmiloff, Y-N., Bartrip, J., & Cuckle, P. (1993). From sentential to discourse functions: Detection and explanation of speech repairs by children and adults. *Discourse Processes, 16*, 565-589.

Lundberg, I., Frost, J., & Petersen, O. (1988). Effects of an extensive program for stimulating phonological awareness in preschool children. *Reading Research Quarterly, 23*, 263-284.

Markman, E. M. (1979). Realising you don't understand: Elementary children's awareness of inconsistencies. *Child Development, 50*, 643-655.

Olson, D. R. (1977). From utterance to text: The bias of language in speech and writing. *Harvard Educational Review, 47*, 257-281.

Olson, D. R. (1984). "See! Jumping!" Some oral antecedents of literacy. In H. Goelman, A. Oberg & F. Smith (Eds.), *Awakening to literacy* (pp. 185-192). Portsmouth, NH: Heinemann Educational Books.

Olson, M. W., & Gee, T.C. (1988). Understanding narratives: A review of story grammar research. *Childhood Education, 64*, 302-306.

Peterson, C., Jesso, B., & McCabe, A. (1999). Encouraging narratives in preschoolers: An intervention study. *Journal of Child Language, 26*, 49-67.

Peterson, C, & McCabe, A. (1992). Parental styles of narrative elicitation: Effects on children's narrative structure and content. *First Language, 12*, 299-321.

Reid, J. (1983). Into print: Reading and language growth. In M. Donaldson, R. Grieve & C. Pratt (Eds.), *Early childhood development and education* (pp. 151-165). Oxford: Basil Blackwell.

Spinillo, A.G., & Pinto, G. (1994). Children's narratives under different conditions: A comparative study. *British Journal of Developmental Psychology, 12*, 177-194.

Stanovich, K. (1986). Matthew effects in reading: Some consequences of individual differences in the acquisition of literacy. *Reading Research Quarterly, 21*, 360-407.

Tough, J. (1977). *The development of meaning*. London: George Allen and Unwin Ltd.

Tough, J. (1983). Children's use of language and learning to read. In R.P. Parker & F.A. Davis (Eds.), *Developing literacy* (pp. 55-67). Delaware: International Reading Association.

Trabasso, T., Stein, N.L., Rodkin, P.C., Park Munger, M., & Baughn, C.R. (1992). Knowledge of goals and plans in the on-line narration of events. *Cognitive Development, 7*, 133-170.

Tunmer, W. E., Nesdale, A. R., & Pratt, C. (1983). The development of young children's awareness of logical inconsistencies. *Journal of Experimental Child Psychology, 36*, 97-108.

Vygotsky, L. S. (1962). *Thought and language*. Cambridge, MA: MIT Press.

Vygotsky, L. S. (1978). *Mind in society: The development of higher psychological processes*. Cambridge, MA: Harvard University Press.

Wells, C. G. (1985a). *Language development in the pre-school years*. Cambridge: Cambridge University Press.

Wells, C. G. (1985b). *Language, learning and education*. NFER-Nelson.

Wells, C. G. (1985c). Preschool literacy related activities and later success in school. In D. R. Olson, N. Torrance & A. Hildyard (Eds.), *Literacy, language and learning: The nature and consequences of reading and writing* (pp. 229-255). Cambridge: Cambridge University Press.

Wells, C. G. (1987). *The meaning makers*. London: Hodder and Stoughton.

Whitehurst, G. J., & Lonigan, C. J. (1998). Child development and emergent literacy. *Child Development, 69*, 848-872.

SUGGESTIONS FOR FURTHER READING

Garton, A. F. and Pratt, C. (1998). *Learning to be literate: The development of spoken and written language* (Second edition). Oxford: Blackwell.

Olson, D. R. (1994). *The world on paper*. Cambridge: Cambridge University Press.

Olson, D. R. and Torrance, N. (Eds.) (1991). *Literacy and orality*. Cambridge: Cambridge University Press.

B5. Computers and Writing

GAVRIEL SALOMON, ELY KOZMINSKY & MERAV ASAF

ABSTRACT

The technological environment, in which writing takes place, affects both writing and cognition. However, this depends on the design of the technological tools that support writing and their use. The chapter reviews writing with technological tools, specifically writing with word processors and related tools. We argue that the reported mixed effects of using computer tools in students' writing, should be analyzed according to the long lasting "effect off" vs. the direct "effect with" technology usage paradigm, coupled with the types of students' literacy activities and the context of their learning environment. The direct "effect with" word processors tend towards more easy production but less planning and less meaningful revisions. Instructionally guiding tools, such as Computerized Supported Intentional Learning Environment (CSILE) and Writing Partner, that provide scaffolding and stimulate writing-related cognitions, improve self-regulation and metacognitive monitoring of the writing activities. Collaborative-based writing tools, synchronous and asynchronous, embedded in meaningful learning environments provide another dimension of knowledge construction. In these environments, writing becomes an important mediation channel together with additional supporting "mindtools", such as outliners. These mindtools can produce not just sequential essays but hypertexts that provide additional means of constructing and presenting knowledge.

INTRODUCTION

All forms of writing require some kind of material technology. First, writing requires what Bolter (1991) has defined as a "writing space", that is "the physical and visual field defined by a particular technology of writing" (p. 11). Second, writing requires implements that enable the process of writing – the wedges used to inscribe clay tablets by the Sumerians, the quill, the plume, the pen or the keyboard. And third, writing requires craftsmanship, a "teche" (Ellul, 1964) without which the technology-as-material and tools would be useless.

Importantly, technologies designed to extend human communication and knowledge construction capacities affect the role that craftsmanship has to play.

229

T. Nunes, P. Bryant (eds.), Handbook of Children's Literacy, 229–246.
© *2004 Kluwer Academic Publishers. Printed in Great Britain.*

As technologies change, nowadays entailing capacities that mimic, even exceed, human ones, so does the required craftsmanship. New technologies de-skill older craftsmanship replacing it with a new one. Copying by hand the Holy Scriptures must have required a very different craftsmanship than writing with a ball pen. And as professional writers often testify (Snyder, 1994), writing with a word processor is a profoundly different process requiring yet another kind of craftsmanship and possibly different ways of conceiving of writing and reading a text (Haas, 1996). Does this technology-determined change of craftsmanship leave any lasting cognitive footprints on a child's mind?

Writing not only serves to turn (preexisting) private thoughts into a permanent public record, thereby extending memory (Donald, 1991), but it also shapes the writer's thoughts and ideas: "Our graphic systems not only preserve information but also provide models, which allow us to see our language, our world, and our minds in a new way" (Olson, 1994, p. 258). But whereas this may be the general case, one would need to ask whether and how the technology of writing affects children's writing in any profound and unique way. Does the way writing is carried out – by chiseling signs into stone, by inscribing on wax, or by writing on paper – differentially determine the generation of ideas, the quality, structure or fluency of the written product? Does the technology of writing matter in terms of the immediate cognitions involved in writing? Moreover, does the shift from one to another technology of writing (particularly the shift to computer-based writing and communication) affect the writer's more lasting and transferable writing-related capabilities?

Such questions are not new. They have been raised in the past by scholars such as McLuhan (1972), and Ong (1982). Although writing is both a *cultural* practice as well as an *individual's* cognitive activity, the question of how writing with different technologies affects the mind has been addressed at mainly the cultural level. Thus, McLuhan (1972) argued that print has laid the foundations for the assembly line, for mass production, and for cause-and-effect thinking; Ong (1982) argued that "Without writing the literate mind would not and could not think the way it does...Writing has transformed human consciousness" (p. 78). Concerning writing in particular, Bangert-Drowns (1993) has postulated that "The computer as a tool, as a spread sheet, data base, networking link, graphic generator, calculator, and word processor is transforming the way the 'information age' society lives and works" (p. 70). Bolter (1991) speculated that print-based writing "expects the humanities, including metaphysics and ethics, to be relatively stable and hierarchically organized" (p. 234). Hypertext, he argued, has very different expectations. We will return to this argument later on.

While such large-scale effects may indeed take place on a cultural level, we are concerned here more with the minds of individual children. Olson (1977) tried to bridge the gap between the cultural and the individual level, pointing both to the differences between oral and literate cultures and between pre-literate and literate children. What about the role of technology, particularly as children become initiated into a technology-based culture of literacy? Would writing and communicating with computers affect their processes and products of writing, and their acquisition of writing-related capabilities any differently from the way print-based writing may have affected them? Haas (1996), based on a Vygotskian notion of socio-culture mediation, argued that technology does matter, significantly affecting individual's writing and cognitions. We do not espouse technological determinism; we are fully aware that the way one chooses to use technology plays no lesser a role than that played by the technology. Clearly, technology, the person using it and the culture within which it is been used play reciprocal roles in affecting each other. While being cognisant of this reciprocity, we nevertheless wish to deal here with the question of technology's effects on children's writing.

Different kinds of "effect", different usages of technology

Not all effects are born equal. Thus, we need to introduce a distinction between effects "with" a technology and effects "of" it (Salomon, Perkins, & Globerson, 1991). Effects "with" a technology pertain to changes in cognitions or performance, such as more intensive employment of metacognitions or a lengthier phase of essay planning, improved spelling, or more paragraph revisions. Such changes take place *while* a student is writing *with* a particular word processor, or with the help provided by in-process prompts (e.g., Reynolds & Bonk, 1996). However, effects of this kind, although often desirable, are not necessarily maintained over time and writing occasions when writing is done with another technology. These are effects that are contingent upon the presence of the technology that enables them and occur only during its use. On the other hand, effects "of" a technology pertain to more lasting and generalisable changes of writing-related cognitions, strategies, abilities and dispositions that are the *consequence* of writing with, say, a prompting word processor. These become manifest when writing takes place in the absence of the technology that brought about these changes.

We need to keep this distinction in mind when we ask how and under what conditions does this or that technology affect writing processes, products and capabilities. Effects with, say, a word processor on cognitions activated during essay planning are not necessarily the same as those more durable and generalisable essay planning dispositions and abilities developed as a consequence of using that tool. Indeed, being able to engage in more meaningful revision when probed by a program such as Reynolds and Bonk's (1996) Generative-Evaluative Computerized Prompting tool, does not mean that the students have become better at revising their essays or more disposed to engage in revision in the absence of that tool. Improved performance (effects with a tool) is not the same as improved ability or mastery (effects of a tool's usage).

But effects of what? Computers are neither a uniform technology nor are literacy-related activities with computers uniform. In fact, there is a continuum of tools and usages along which research and development attempts can be arranged. This continuum ranges from the simplistic to the more elaborate, and from the stripped down, non-instructional tool, to whole encompassing instructional settings (Bangert-Drowns & Kozma, 1989).

Specifically, on one side of the continuum we have the employment of word processors for essay writing, the effects of which were often studied in the early years of computer use. On the other side of the continuum we have the design of whole new learning environments, most often based on constructivist and social-cooperative principles (e.g., Lamon, *et al.*, 1996). In between the two poles we have semi-intelligent guidance and prompt-providing writing tools as well as guided idea organizers and outlining tools. These, usually stand-alone tools, are not necessarily part of a whole new kind of learning environment. However, unlike typical word processors they often entail a partner-like quality, guiding the writer to think about the essay's readers and provide prompts for revision (e.g., Bonk & Reynolds, 1992). In other cases, the prompts during planning, production, and revision serve as externalized metacognitive-like guides that are contingent upon the writer's inputs (Zellermayer, Salomon, Globerson, & Givon, 1991).

In light of the variety of tools and usages as illustrated above, it appears that the question of whether, how and to what extent does the computer technology for writing affect the processes, products and capabilities of writing in general or of planning in particular is unanswerable in its general form. Any generalisation pertaining to the influence of "The Computer" on children's planning and writing (as distinguished from the possible influence on a whole generation or culture) would be unwarranted. As is so often the conclusion arrived at in educational research and in particular in what concerns the effects of word processors on children's writing, the answer is "It all depends" (Cochran-Smith, 1991). And "it" depends on what particular tools and instructional arrangements are the source of the alleged effect, what is being affected, how it is affected, and what kinds of literacy activities the students become engaged in while working with the technology. In the next sections we briefly review the field according to the continuum of tools mentioned earlier.

Word processors

The common assumption pertaining to the use of word processors was that the opportunities afforded by the tool for planning, writing, but mainly essay revising, will change writing processes, products and abilities. One of the first fully developed studies was that of Diaute (1985) whose findings did not support the expectation that word processing will affect planning and writing in any meaningful way. The findings of other researchers, employing only word processors without particular instruction, were consistent with Diaute's (see review by Dahl & Farnan, 1996). For example, Haas (1989, 1996) carried out one of the few studies on the effects of word processors on essay planning and found that it resulted in less planning than writing by hand. She also found that planning pertained less to global and conceptual aspects of the essays and more to technical and sequential ones. Thus, her elementary school age writers tended not to have a sense of the whole text. It is possible that, given the known attraction of word processors, they "lure" the children to turn more quickly to the production of essays, while forgoing planning. Still, Bangert-Drowns (1993) report that the overall quality of the essays produced with word processors tends to be of somewhat higher quality. But the effects found are marginal. Were the evaluators of the essays impressed by the essays' length or by their clean and errorless drafts? Or is it possible that due to mechanical ease, planning becomes more distributed throughout the writing process when writing with word processors? Research so far does not provide clear answers to such questions.

Several researchers reported that word processors enable and promote collaborative writing, resulting in higher quality essays and in the writers' greater awareness of the writing process (Bruce, Michaels and Watson-Gegeo, 1985; Crook, 1994; Davies, 1989; Dickinson, 1986; Snyder, 1994). However, this slightly increased awareness does not seem to manifest itself in essay revision. Revision of essays written with word processors, unlike those written by hand, seem to be more distributed throughout the writing process (Owston, Murphy, & Wideman, 1992). However, again, when using word processors, students do not appear to have a 'sense of the whole text' (Haas, 1989, 1996), thus revising more mechanical elements (such as correcting errors up to the sentence level), than conducting global revisions (e.g., Bridwell-Bowels, Johnson, & Brehe, 1987). This can be due to the difficulty of reading on-line (e.g, Gould & Grischkowsky, 1984), the limited information viewed on the computer screen (Haas, 1996), or due to the lack of global planning.

In all, results of the research on writing with word processors yielded weak and often mixed results and has been critically summarized by Cochran-Smith (1991) and by Peacock and Beard (1997). The latter concluded as follows:

> [M]any of the supposed benefits of word processing have not been confirmed by research evidence. In addition, many devotees fall victim to simplistic technological determinism ... and enthusiastic qualitative accounts frequently ignore considerable teacher assistance when reporting improvements attributed to word processing (p. 289).

Instructionally-guiding tools

The theoretical rationale underlying the question of whether word processors affect children's writing is, as we have seen, pretty slim. Why, indeed, should word processing, in of itself, have any profound effects on writing, save a few shallow, mechanical effects? The empirical evidence tends to generally bear this out in its weak and mixed results. The picture changes when instruction is added to the computer-based activity. There are two kinds of instruction that should be mentioned here. One kind of instruction is independent of any computer affordance or activity but may be *accompanied* by the latter, as when students are didactically taught about different writing genres and are then sent to the word processor to write an essay in one of the genres (e.g. Nuvoli, 2000).

The second kind, and of much greater relevance here, consists of instruction, tutorship, or guidance which is built into a computer tool in a way that capitalizes on the computer's capabilities and affordances, on the one hand, and evokes, scaffolds, guides or overtly simulates writing-related cognitions, on the other. One such early tool was designed by Woodruff, Bereiter & Scardamalia (1981-1982) in which "14-years-old students composed for the first time opinion essays on a computer, using an interactive program that led them after each sentence through a branching sequence of questions designed to induce means-end planning of the next sentence" (described in Bereiter and Scardamalia, 1987, p. 138). Another tool of that kind was designed by Diaute (1985), incorporating such on-line prompts as "Can your reader see, hear or feel what you have described?". Most prompting programs that developed later on followed these early examples. They often provided prompts that addressed writers' planning, writing and revising metacognitions, expecting not only to attain effects *with* the programs during prompted writing, but also more lasting effects of it, as when students learn to prompt themselves on their own, thus acquiring an ability for self-prompting.

The strong emphasis on prompting and on modeling writing-related metacognitions is justified on the grounds that, as Bereiter and Scardamalia (1987) have pointed out, since the process of writing lacks the guidance, feedback and prompting of face to face conversation, it becomes an unsupported, unguided autonomous process. Older and better developed writers rely quite heavily on their self-regulatory capabilities, continuously conversing with themselves in lieu of the absent partner. However, younger writers experience great difficulty in self-regulating their planning and idea production since live conversation entailing continuous inputs does not require these (Bereiter & Scardamalia, 1987). That is, live conversation does not prepare the child for the kind of self-regulations that writing requires. Thus, prompting elementary school children's memories during writing ("What else do you know about this?"), or prompting them to provide explanations and elaborations appear to facilitate the number of discourse elements they use in their essays quite significantly. The provision of metacognitive-like prompts is supposed to serve in both a compensatory function of procedural facilitation for the not-yet developed self-regulation as well as a model for such to be emulated. Whereas the former would facilitate writing while the prompts are provided, the latter would become manifested in the form of improved self-regulation.

The designs and studies by Bonk and Reynolds (1992) and Reynolds and Bonk (1996) serve as good examples of this genre of computer-based writing tools. Bonk and Reynolds (1992) designed a word processor to provide upon request generative and evaluative prompts (e.g., "Ask yourself: What other ideas does this suggest?"; "Think about the problem or original topic. Is everything you've said needed or related to it?"). Participants, sixth, seventh and eighth grade students, were required to request the prompts a particular number of times during three writing sessions.

The findings of this study failed to support the researchers' expectations. Perhaps most importantly, the incident of meaningful changes in writing that coincided with the prompts constituted only 14% of all changes, suggesting that many of the prompts the students were exposed to were not acted upon. Overall, although the prompted students engaged in somewhat less surface revisions, they did not engage in any more meaningful revisions, relative to non-prompted students. This was particularly pronounced for the younger (sixth grade) students who seemed to benefit somewhat more from the generative rather than from the evaluative prompts. This led the researchers to consider the possibility that students of this younger age may not yet be capable of benefiting from externally-provided writing-specific prompts for they may not yet know how to act upon them. Revision, as also found out by others (e.g., Bereiter & Scardamalia, 1987) turns out to be particularly difficult for younger students.

A number of factors may account for these results. One such factor, also identified by Zellermayer *et al.*, (1991), may well be the difficulty or reluctance poor writers have in reading the sometimes lengthy prompts. Another, more profound factor concerns the absence of any relationship between the text being produced and the prompts accessed. The provided prompts are supposed to model metacognitive activity. But action-specific, real-life metacognitions, whether regulating writing or reading, planning or revising, are by their very nature highly contingent on the ongoing activity. One would hope that, capitalizing on the computer's affordances, its provided prompts would be textually and structurally contingent upon one's actual writing. They were not. Also, the effects studied in the prompting studies mentioned so far concerned effects *with* the technology, attained while prompting took place. Effects *of* prompting, manifested in more lasting, transferable improvements in specific writing-related self-regulation, were not seriously investigated in these studies. Does computer-generated, contingent prompting improve writing *ability* (not just performance) through an increased tendency to engage in self-regulation?

The study by Zellermayer, Salomon, Globerson, and Givon (1991) addressed the latter two issues – contingency of the prompts on the young writers' inputs, and their effects on the writers' tendency to become self-regulating in the absence of the prompting tool. That study, employing the computerized Writing Partner, was based on the assumption that a computer tool can function in a child's zone of proximal development (Vygotsky, 1978) by offering an explicit and dynamic model of regulation that can be "internalized" to serve in a cognitive function as self-regulation. This assumption was tested in an earlier study with a *Reading Partner*, that provided ongoing metacognitive guidance during text reading (Salomon, Globerson, & Guterman, 1989). Seventh graders reading eleven texts with the *Reading Partner* showed significantly better reading comprehension of unguided texts than their peers in the other two groups; they also showed significant improvements in essay writing quality a while later, suggesting that such a guiding tool can have generalisable effects in the form of a greater disposition to employ reading and writing-related metacognitions for self-regulation.

The *Writing Partner* tool employed by Zellemayer *et al.* (1991) in a subsequent study, was designed to facilitate writers' move from "knowledge telling" to "knowledge transforming" (Bereiter & Scardamalia, 1987). It strongly emphasized the guidance through the planning phase but also guided the writers through writing and revision of their essays. Middle school children were led to brainstorm their main ideas and assign these ideas to particular categories such as hero, triggering event, conflict, setting, timing, resolution, minor event, and the like. The writers associated their ideas with appropriate icons and keywords. Using this icon-based format of outline-planning, the students could then arrange the icons/ideas in a two dimensional space. All that pre-writing information was kept in the computer's memory. During writing itself, the computer could "identify" in a semi-intelligent fashion the keywords used in the planning phase and present the writers with content appropriate metacognitive-like questions: e.g., "Does John, your hero, have any feelings? Did you mention them?"; "If this is a conflict, have you got an idea how it will be resolved?", etc. Students could also request help when they felt difficulties during writing and be guided by the program to self-diagnose their difficulties (e.g., "If you are stuck, how would a movie continue the story?"; "Think of another opening such as ..."). Revision entailed similar choices and guides.

Findings were quite clear: Receiving unsolicited prompts lead to the writing of superior essays with the tool and later on also without it. The unsolicited guides benefited good and poor writers alike. Still, in line with other studies, revision processes were not affected by writing with the guidance of the tool as much as planning processes were.

It thus appears that a computerized tool – (a) that provides a developmentally appropriate model of writing-specific metacognitions; (b) which offers novel, useful, and learnable cognitive functions particularly geared to the planning phase of writing; and (c) whose guidance is contingent on writers' inputs, can be emulated and used both as an aid to performance and as a cultivator of more lasting and transferable capabilities (Salomon, 1988).

However, such computer-based procedural facilitation of writing is based on a relatively narrow, albeit traditional, conception of literacy as an isolated, decontextualized activity. As pointed out by Flower (1996), textual literacy as practiced in schools suffers from an exclusive focus on individual performance and from a preoccupation with the manipulation of context-free symbolic information. This agrees well with the claim that students often learn to write while word processing without having any words to process and without having a real audience to write to. The alternative view suggests seeing literacy as a "social practice of making texts, supported by explicit instruction in the problem-solving strategies a writer brings to the rhetorical situation" (Flower, 1996, p. 27). Emphasis thus shifts to what Flower calls "literate action", which – inspired by a more general conception of cognitions that are situated in the real world and embedded in particular contexts (e.g., Lave & Wenger, 1991) – translates into collaborative, contextualised writing.

The question thus arises as to whether team-based planning, whereby students engage in collaborative essay planning and writing that resembles literate action and facilitates socially distributed cognitions, improves planning quality and following that – writing. Employing the *Writing Partner*, Elliott and Salomon (1992, unpublished) carried out a study with Australian young female students, considered poor writers. The students planned essays collaboratively or individually and then wrote the essays either in teams or alone. The differences between the two modes of essay planning were striking: Team planning was significantly more elaborate, more thoughtful, took far more time than individual's planning, and had a clear and strong effect on the overall quality of the essays, whether written alone or in teams. Interestingly, although essays written in teams did not differ in their overall quality from those written alone, the students participating in team writing claimed that they preferred to write alone. Apparently, planning is an activity that affords team-work more than text production.

The design of whole new learning environments

The improvement in planning and in subsequent quality of collaborative writing suggests that it depends not only on the computerized tool as a stand-alone. The findings suggest that a deeper change may be required, one that is based on the conception of literacy (in fact, intellectual activity and learning in general) as a socially and culturally embedded activity. Such a conception of literacy has many implications. One important implication concerns the idea of writing for a real, personally and socially significant audience; a second implication is that writing is to be done in the service of one's engagement in an authentic problem or issue, rather than as a process designed to serve itself (e.g., Williams *et al*, 1998). Cohen and Riel (1989) have found that seventh graders' quality of essays written for distance peers was significantly better than the quality of essays written for their teacher. Similarly, Riel (1990) found that the performance of fourth graders on a standard test of basic skills improved significantly as a function of writing for a peer audience and particularly as a function of editing the essays of peers for a classroom newspaper.

Writing activities involving teams, peer audiences, and problem solving contexts cannot be carried out very well in traditional learning environments. Indeed, researchers and educational designers have in recent years felt a need for a new conceptualisation of the contexts of learning in general and writing in particular, and consequently for the redesign of appropriate learning environments. The impetus for such a move came from three closely related sources – the above mentioned criticism of the isolated writer engaged in near-sterile writing exercises, new conceptions of learning, and the availability of computer technology that could help in turning these conceptions into actual classroom practices.

There are two closely interrelated conceptions of learning that underlie and guide the design of novel learning environments. The first conception of learning regards learning as a constructive process, whereby learners do not absorb, acquire, or internalize knowledge but rather construct it in their own way: "Children don't *get* ideas, they *make* ideas" (Kafai & Resnick, 1996, p. 1). A number of implications follow from this basic tenet. One such implication is that learning and actual doing – in the form of problem solving, writing or designing a product – are closely interwoven (Perkins, 1992). Thus, for example, one learns to write by having a real problem to solve and write about. A second implication is that students' activities, the ones that are to lead to learning, need to be goal oriented. Thus writing, for example, is to be carried out within the context of problem solving and as part of that process rather than as an isolated, often content and context-independent activity. Writing becomes a tool in the service of problem solving and designing (Andrade & Perkins, 1998).

The second conception, closely related to the previous one, pertains to the issue of social learning. The origins of this conception go back to the Vygotskian theory that development entails inter-personal processes that can become intra-personal ones within a child's zone of proximal development. It is also based on more recent theoretical developments concerning the socially distributed nature of cognitions (e.g., Resnick, 1991; Cole & Engestrom, 1993), the relationships between individual and social learning (e.g., Salomon & Perkins, 1998), and findings showing the actual learning attainments of student teams (e.g., Slavin, 1994).

These conceptions, when put together, lead to the design of new team-based, exploration- and problem solving-oriented, information rich, and non-didactic learning environments. Student activities, writing in particular, become integrated into the exploratory, communicational, team-based activities, whereby writing is carried out for the purposes of problem solving and communication and for specific real-life audiences. One such environment is the Computer Supported Intentional Learning Environment (CSILE) of Bereiter and Scardamalia (see e.g., Scardamalia, Bereiter, & Lamon, 1994). CSILE is a computer-based environment designed to promote intentional learning of students by providing the guidance and technological means to facilitate knowledge construction. Students carry out in writing discussions about selected issues, problems and questions they themselves raise ("I wonder why an offspring will resemble one parent and not the other", a question raised by one participant during an ongoing exploratory exchange about heredity). The discussions are a-synchronic whereby a student may enter an idea, hypothesis, a possible explanation, question, insight, and the like, and will place it under one of these categories. Gradually, a communal database becomes created, shared by all, driven by students' curiosity and knowledge, and based on the information they gather from a variety of sources.

Since the discussions are a-synchronic, writing is one of the backbones of the process, being the main medium for students' exchanges of ideas, exploration, argumentation, and questioning. It is thus not surprising that students of varying ages in CSILE classes showed impressive effects *with* CSILE, particularly with respect to the quality of arguments raised, the extent to which counter examples were discussed, the number of causal explanations provided, the analogies and predictions offered, and the like (e.g. Hakkarainen, Lipponen, & Jaervelae, 2001). Most importantly, though, also clear and strong effects *of* CSILE were recorded in the area of reading, using standard tests, and in the area of writing. These effects are particularly important to note since no direct instruction in reading or writing was provided.

In another project CSILE was combined with two other projects: *Fostering Communities of Learners* (Brown & Campione, 1994) and *The Adventures of Jasper Woodbury* (Cognition and Technology Group at Vanderbilt, 1992) into one project – *Schools For Thought* (SFT) (Lamon, *et al.*, 1996). In that project students carried out research and discussions in teams on topics such as planning a trip to Mars. While dealing with such a problem, students had to pull in knowledge from a variety of disciplines and communicate through CSILE among themselves and with experts outside the classroom. Teams became experts in their respective sub-topics and then became reorganized in a jigsaw manner. Writing was one of the major media of communication, but to no lesser an extent also a tool with which each team could gradually construct its own products.

As is typical of this genre of novel, constructivist learning environments, writing was not a focus of instruction in SFT classes. Students' readings served their writing, and their writings served their needs to communicate to share knowledge, to try out new ideas, to critique, and to argue. But since good, clear, comprehensible written communication was very much the norm, it should come as no surprise that writing quality showed impressive improvements. Thus, for example, the reports written within the "Mission to Mars" and the "Endangered Species" projects by the sixth graders were "better than almost anything we have seen from sixth-grade classrooms ... Students wrote more, organised better, used better and more complex sentence structure, and improved in punctuation, capitalisation, and usage. Knowledge and their ability to express it were impressive" (Lamon, *et al.*, 1996, p. 262).

As for effects *of* the project, the writing ability of SFT and control group students was assessed based on essays students wrote. Students were asked to write an essay about "If you could change something about your world, what would you change? Why? How?". Analyses showed that SFT students scored significantly higher on overall quality than control students in the same schools – controlling for prior differences in students' language ability. SFT students also scored higher on eight of ten categories including structural aspects of introduction, transitions, and conclusion; content aspects of argument and coherence, and mechanical aspects of spelling and vocabulary. When divided into high, medium, and low scorers (based on the standard achievement test scores), SFT students outscored control students at each level (Secules, *et al.*, 1997).

However, not always do such improvements show up on standard achievement tests of language mechanics such as punctuation, grammar and vocabulary. This was also the results of some CSILE evaluations. There is a clear discrepancy between the researchers', parents' and teachers' observations, on the one hand, and the students' performance on standard achievement tests, on the other. One explanation is that the latter does not tap the kind of writing that is emphasized and practiced in the SFT classrooms. Writing in the SFT classrooms emphasizes research, collaborative planning and composition for real purposes, for real audiences and for idea-constructive and communicational purposes. Typical state-mandated standard achievement tests often do not focus on these. Quite clearly, an evaluation of the quality of writing in SFT classes, as in other novel technology-intensive constructivist learning environments, needs to take into consideration the new approaches to literacy that emphasize literate practices that are embedded in a mindful, purposeful and social context (Flower, 1996). New measures need to be devised to tap development of children's literacy along these lines.

Studies of the kind just described have one major drawback. In the novel constructivist learning environments, with their highly integrated social, curricular, instructional and technological components, it is impossible to determine the extent to which the technology, in and of itself, leads to any specific literacy improvements (Salomon, 1991). Thus, if one asks how much does computer technology really matter, meaning how strong are its "net" effects, other things held constant, it would be impossible to provide an answer. While it is true that the computer, when properly used, is essential in realizing the educational conceptions underlying the new class of learning environments, it is quite impossible to single out its unique effects. Paradoxically, to be truly effective, one needs to design novel learning environments that emphasize team-writing within a context of, and in the service of, meaningful problems to be solved. However, the very systemic approach to the orchestration of such learning environments makes it quite impossible to determine the exact contribution of technology to the improvement in writing or in learning. Authenticity overrides certitude; considerations of effective instruction take precedent over scientific-analytic rigor.

Lessons to be learned

The conclusion stated above still leaves open the question we have started out with: What non-trivial difference does technology make in the process of writing and in the process of acquiring writing-related skills? Many of the studies designed to answer this question, particularly the ones carried out with word processors, arrived at weak or mixed results. Other studies with stronger effects are the ones that "confounded" the technology with instruction or embedded it in a complexly integrated learning environment. In this light, one would be tempted to respond to our initial question by arguing that technology, in and of itself, does not really matter that much for children's writing; instruction does (Clark, 1983).

Let us carry out a hypothetical experiment by examining a more extreme case. We could ask whether such a conclusion would still hold when the technology shifts more dramatically from writings in the typical linear manner, having a beginning, a middle and end, to a vastly different kind of writing: hypertext. Hypertexts involve textual nodes and links among them, yielding a web, rather than a continuous text. Although each node may entail "regular" text, it is the absence of any predetermined organisation of the nodes that makes hypertexts so unique. Hypertext "texts" allow movement from one node to another in a great variety of directions in endless combinations, and without necessarily having any preset order. Movement within a network of such links, typical of multimedia programs, would fit well a constructivist conception of learning whereby students literally construct their own texts while exploring a topic (Cunningham, Duffy & Knuth, 1993).

What implications follow from here for writing in hypertext style? According to Bolter (1991), hypertext-like writing will lead to the abandonment of the ideal of uniform, high culture, with its standardisation and unification, leading to a (postmodern) network of diverse and non-hierarchical cultures. If all combinations of hypertext are legitimate so are all points of view, perspectives and interpretations. To this one could add that hypertext writing is not guided by a desire to attain logical coherence and continuity along a story line or an argument. Rather, hypertext is guided by a desire to link together in a more logical or more associative manner a loose collection of diverse textual items. Writers do not have to envision a single structure for their writing products nor a single kind of audience; different audiences could construct the text each for its own purpose and each in its own way.

Hypertexts are profoundly different from regular texts and this difference warrants the expectation that hypertext writing is likely to affect the process, the qualitative nature and the competencies of writing. Indeed, initial reports suggest that the way students go about writing hypertexts is very different from the way they usually write regular essays (Lehrer, Erickson, Love & Connell, 1994). It is because of this rather profound qualitative difference between the forms of writing distinguishing regular texts from hypertext, that in this case, unlike that of word processors, writing is likely to change significantly. Contrary to the hype associated with them, word processors did not call for a kind of writing that was qualitatively different from what writing by hand called for. The texts were still linear, they still had to have a beginning, middle and end, they still were supposed to have coherence and continuity, and they still had to be addressed to a particular audience. On the other hand, hypertext appears to change the very nature of the text to be produced and thus the very nature of the process of writing, and, of course, its outcomes. Whether it will affect writing *capabilities* remains to be seen.

There is a possible lesson here. A new technology may affect the processes, products and possibly also the capabilities of writing to the extent that what it affords, demands, evokes, guides, supplants or models is *profoundly* different (yet manageable) from its predecessor. Word processors do not meet this criterion. According to Jonassen (2000), word processors are merely *productivity tools* that cannot restructure and amplify the thinking of the writer compared with *mindtools* that can be used to represent knowledge. The computer tool *Inspiration* (www.inspiration.com), to use one example, has hypertext qualities and thus can be expected to exert strong effects on outlining and writing.

There is an instructional corollary to this lesson. The value of computer technology for the improvement of children's writing and for the cultivation of writing-related capabilities greatly depends on the extent to which its employment amplifies, activates, models, supplants or guides cognitive processes that are germane to the process of writing, on the one hand, and different from the ones affected by other technologies, on the other. The relative effectiveness of some of the guidance-providing tools described earlier results from the fact that the processes they modeled and offered for "internalisation" were both necessary for better writing to take place and – relative to practical alternatives – novel.

The examination of writing when embedded within novel learning environments leads to yet another lesson to be learned. Research on word processing approached the tools as a given, something akin to a natural phenomenon, the effects of which can be studied "as they are". The question asked was how does the use of word processors affect writing, without, in most cases, trying to deliberately design computers or their use to serve particular instructional purposes. In comparison, research on writing-related guidance did not treat the computer as a given; the strength of that research was in the way it treated computers as tools that can be designed for instruction. The same applies to instructionally-oriented outliners and idea organizers. The design of novel learning environments went even farther than that by designing whole classroom cultures in which computer-based writing through communication played an important role. There is thus a big difference between studying what computers *do* and what computers *can be made to do*. It is the difference between what Herbert Simon (1982) has defined as the study of the natural and the study of the artificial, respectively. The study of the artificial deals "not with the necessary but with the contingent – not with how things are but with how they might be" (Simon, 1982, p. xi). Thus, designs capitalize on computers' potential strengths, such as their built-in intelligence, their motivating power, or their language-parsing ability, to see how and to what extent they can be made to make a difference.

The study of computer writing and children can of course be fit into both the science of the natural and the science of the artificial. Studying computers and children's writing in the tradition of the former would contribute to a deeper understanding of how culture and technology relate to cognition and literacy; studying what computers can be made to do to children's literacy would contribute to the field of literacy education.

There is another possible lesson to be learned from the difference between the two approaches, a lesson bearing on the distinction we have made between effects *with* and *of* the computer. This lesson has wider implications for literacy education. We have seen that computers can be made to have reliable effects on writing during their use (effects "with"). But there is only very little evidence to show that their use, even with built-in guidance and even when embedded within novel learning environments, has lasting and generalisable effects on writing-related capabilities or dispositions. Only a few studies showed transfer effects on writing-related metacognitive mastery or on writing quality in the absence of the tool. One reason for this paucity is that many researchers have taken effects "with" as evidence for effects "of", thus, for example, regarding improved planning or writing quality while being guided by a semi-intelligent tool as if it shows improved planning ability.

But there may be another, far more profound reason that transcends research finesse. The reason is that short term interventions may lead mainly to performance effects "with" a computerized tool, effects that are contingent on the presence of the tool: More and better planning, more ideas, better essay organisation, more meaningful editing, and the like. For more lasting and generalisable effects "of" writing with a tool – better planning *ability*, a disposition to shift from "knowledge telling" to "knowledge transforming", and the like, one would need a far longer time span.

It appears that hardly any effects on writing-related capabilities and dispositions can be attained in a "shot in the arm" like instructional manner. Nevertheless, writing with computers is here to stay and evolve. Bolter's (1991) "writing space", which was limited to the permanent record left by the pen or typewriter, has acquired additional features, such as: an editable memory for ease of transforming the recorded ideas; variation of fonts and markings for communicating subtleties of tone and emphasis; hyperlinking for pointing to additional relations within and beyond the produced text; an easy accommodation of non-textual material, such as tables, graphs, pictures, and video and voice clips; and, integration of the main writing tool, the word processor, with presentation, transformation, organisation, and communication tools. While the new technologies are yet not matured, and many features may be superfluous or in need of further refinement, the little "teche" (Ellul, 1964) is already sharpening his or her craft.

REFERENCES

Andrade, H. L. G., & Perkins, D. N. (1998). Learnable intelligence and intelligent learning. In R. J. Sternberg & W.M. Williams (Eds.) *Intelligence, instruction and assessment: Theory in practice.* (pp. 67-94). Mahwan, NJ: Lawrence Erlbaum Associates.
Bangert-Drowns, R. L. (1993). The word processor and an instructional tool: A meta-analysis of word processing in writing instruction. *Review of Educational Research, 63,* 69-93.

Bangert-Drowns, R. L., & Kozma, R. B. (1989). Assessing the design of instructional software. *Journal of Research on Computing in Education, 21,* 241-262.

Bereiter, C., & Scardamalia, S. (1987). *The psychology of written composition.* Hillsdale, NJ: Lawrence.

Bolter, J. D. (1991). The shapes of WOE. *Writing on the Edge, 2,* 90-91.

Bonk, C. J., & Reynolds T. H. (1992). Early adolescent composing within a generative-evaluative computerized prompting framework. *Computers in Human Behavior, 8,* 39-62.

Bridwell-Bowels, L., Johnson, P., & Brehe, S. (1987) Composing and computers: Case studies of experienced writers. In A. Matsuhashi (ED.),*Writing in real time: Modeling production processes* (pp. 81-107). Norwood, NJ: Ablex.

Brown, A. L., & Campione, J. C. (1994). Guided discovery in a community of learners. In K. McGilly (Ed.), *Classroom lessons: Integrating cognitive theory and classroom practice* (pp. 229-270). Cambridge, MA: MIT Press/Bradford Books.

Bruce, B., Michaels, S., & Watson-Gegeo, K. (1985) How computers change the writing process. *Language arts, 62,* 143-149.

Clark, R. E (1983). Reconsidering research on learning from media. *Review of Educational Research, 53,* 445-459.

Cochran-Smith, M. (1991). Word processing and writing in elementary classrooms: A critical review of related literature. *Review of Educational Research, 61(1),* 107-155.

Cohen, M. and Riel, M. (1989).The effect of distant audiences on students' writing. *American Educational Research Journal, 26,* 143-59.

Cole, M., & Engestrom, Y. (1993). A cultural-historical approach to distributed cognition. In Salomon, G. (Ed.). *Distributed cognitions: Psychological and educational considerations* (pp. 1-46). Cambridge: Cambridge UP.

Crook, C. (1994). Computers and the collaborative experience of learning. London: Routhledge.

Cognition and Technology Group at Vanderbilt (1992). The Jasper Series as an example of anchored instruction: Theory, program description, and assessment data. *Educational Psychologist, 27(3),* 291-315

Cunningham, D.J., Duffy, T.M. & Knuth, R.A. (1993). The textbook of the future. In C. McKnight, A. Dillon, and J. Richardson, (Eds.), *Hypertext: A Psychological Perspective* (pp.19-49). London: Horwood Publishing.

Dahl, K. L., & Farnan, N. (1996). *Children's Writing: Perspectives from research.* Newark, DE: IRA.

Davies, G. (1989). Discovering a need to write: The role of the teacher as collaborator. In M. Styles (Ed.) *collaboration and writing.* Milton Keynes: Open UP.

Diaute, C. (1985). *Writing and computers.* Reading, Mass.: Addison-Wesley Publishing Company.

Dickson. D. K. (1986). Cooperation, collaboration and a computer: Integrating a computer into a first-grade writing program. *Research in the Teaching of English, 20,* 97-123.

Donald, M. (1991). *Origins of the human mind: three stages in the evolution of culture and cognition.* Cambridge, MA: Harvard U.P.

Elliott, A., & Salomon, G. (1992). *Effects of the writing partner on writing ability* (unpublished).

Ellul, J. (1967). *The technological society.* New York: Alfred A Knopf.

Flower, L. (1996). Collaborative planning and community literacy: A window to the logic of learners. In L. Schauble, & R. Glaser (Eds.), *Innovations in learning new environments for education,* (pp. 25-48). Mahwah, NJ: Lawrence Erlbaum Associates.

Gould, J. D., & Grischkowsy, N. (1984). Doing the same work with hard copy and with cathode-ray tube computer terminals. *Human Factors, 26,* 323-337.

Haas, C. (1989). 'Seeing it on the screen isn't really seeing it': Computer writers' reading problems. In G. E. Hawisher & C. L. Selfe (Eds.), *Critical perspectives on computers and composition instruction* (pp. 16-29). New York: Teachers College Press.

Haas, C. (1996). Writing technology: Studies on the materiality of literacy. Mahwah, NJ: Lawrence Erlbaum Associates.

Hakkarainen, K., Lipponen, L., & Jaervelae, S. (2001). Epistemology of inquiry and computer-supported collaborated learning. In T. Koschmann & H. Rogers (Eds.), *CSCL 2 carrying forward the conversation: Computers, cognition and work* (pp.129-156). Mahwah, NJ: Lawrence Erlbaum Associates.

Jonassen, D.H. (2000). Computers as mindtools for schools: Engaging critical thinking (2nd edition). Prentice-Hall.

Kafai, Y. B., & Resnick, M. (Eds.) (1996). *Constructionism in practice: Designing, thinking, and learning in a digital world.* Mahwah, NJ, USA: Lawrence Erlbaum Associates.

Lamon, M., Secules, T., Petrosino, A. J., & Hackett, R. (1996). Schools For Thought: Overview of the project and lessons learned from one of the sites. In L. Schauble and R. Glaser (Eds.), *Innovations in learning: New environments for education* (pp. 243-288). Mahwah, NJ: Lawrence Erlbaum Associates

Lave, J., & Wenger, E. (1991). *Situated learning: Legitimate peripheral participation.* Cambridge: Cambridge UP.

Lehrer, R., Ericson, J., Love, M., & Connell, T. (1994). Learning by designing hypermedia documents. *Computers in the Schools,* 10, 227-254.

McLuhan, M. (1972). *The Gutenberg galaxy: The making of typographic man.* Toronto, University of Toronto Press.

Nuvoli, G. (2000). Revisions of text with word processing. *Psychological Reports, 87,* 1139-1146.

Olson, D. R. (1977). From utterance to text: the bias of language in speech and writing. *Harvard Educational Review, 47,* 257-81.

Olson, D. R. (1994). *The world on paper.* Cambridge: Cambridge UP.

Ong, W.J. (1982). *Orality and Literacy.* London: Routledge.

Owston, R. D., Murphy, S., & Wideman, H. H. (1992). The effects of word processing on students' writing quality and revision strategies. *Research in the Teaching of English, 26,* 249-276.

Peacock, M. and Beard, R. (1997). "Almost an invincible repugnance"?: Word processors and pupil writers. Educational Review, 49, 283-94.

Perkins, D. N. (1992). Smart schools: From training memories to educating minds. New York: The Free Press.

Resnick, L. B. (1991). Shared cognition: Thinking as social practice. In L.B. Resnick, J.M. Levine, & S.D. Teasley (Eds.), *Perspectives on socially shared cognition,* (pp. 1-20). Washington, DC: American Psychological Association.

Reynolds, T. H. & Bonk, C. J. (1996). Facilitating college writers' revisions within a generative-evaluative computerized prompting framework. *Computers and Composition, 13,* 93-108.

Riel, M. (1990). Cooperative learning across classrooms in electronic learning circles. *Instructional Science, 19,* 445-66.

Salomon, G. (1988). AI in reverse: Computer tools that turn cognitive. *Journal of Educational Computing Research, 4,* 123-139.

Salomon, G. (1991). On the cognitive effects of technology. In L. T. Landsmann (Ed); *Culture, schooling, and psychological development. Human development, 4,* (pp. 185-204). Norwood, NJ: Ablex Publishing Corp.

Salomon, G., Globerson, T., & Guterman, E. (1989). The computer as a zone of proximal development: Internalizing reading-related metacognitions from a Reading Partner. *Journal of Educational Psychology, 81,* 620-627.

Salomon, G. & Perkins, D. N. (1998). Individual and social aspects of learning. *Review of Research in Education, 23,* 1-24.

Salomon, G., Perkins, D. N., & Globerson, T. (1991). Partners in cognition: Extending human intelligence with intelligent technologies. *Educational Researcher, 20,* 2-9.

Scardamalia, M., Bereiter, C., & Lamon, M. (1994). The CSILE project: Trying to bring the classroom into World 3. In K. McGilly (Ed.), *Classroom lessons: Integrating cognitive theory and classroom practice.* (pp. 201-228). Cambridge, MA: The MIT Press.

Secules, T., Cottom, C.D., Bray, M.H., Miller, L.D., & the Cognition and Technology Group at Vanderbilt (1997). Creating Schools for thought: Creating learning communities. *Educational Leadership* 54(6):56-60.

Simon, H. (1982). *The science of the artificial.* Cambridge, MA: MIT Press.

Slavin, R. (1994). *Cooperative learning: Theory, research, & practice* (2nd ed.) Boston: Allyn & Bacon.

Snyder, I. (1994). Writing with word processors: The computer's influence on the classroom context. *Curriculum Studies, 26,* 143-162.

Vygotsky, L. S. (1978). *Mind and society.* Cambridge, Mass: Harvard University Press.

Williams, S. M., Burgess, K. L., Bray, M. H., Bransford, J. D., and the Cognition and Technology Group at Vanderbilt (1998). Extending learning communities. In D. Chris (Ed.), *Learning and technology.* Alexandria, VA: ASCD.

Woodruff, E., Bereiter, C., & Scardamalia, M. (1981-1982). On the road to computer assisted compositions. *Journal of Educational Technology Systems, 10(2),* 133-148.

Zellermayer M., Salomon, G., Globerston, T. & Givon, H. (1991). Enhancing writing-related metacognitions through a computerize Writing-Partner. *American Educational Research Journal, 28,* 373-391.

REFERENCES FOR FURTHER READING

Bangert-Drowns, R. L. (1993). The word processor and an instructional tool: A meta-analysis of word processing in writing instruction. *Review of Educational Research, 63,* 69-93.

Cochran-Smith, M. (1991). Word processing and writing in elementary classrooms: A critical review of related literature. *Review of Educational Research, 61(1),* 107-155.

Haas, C. (1996). Writing technology: Studies on the materiality of literacy. Mahwah, NJ: Lawrence.

Jonassen, D.H. (2000). Computers as mindtools for schools: Engaging critical thinking (2nd edition). Prentice-Hall.

Salomon, G. & Perkins, D. N. (1998). Individual and social aspects of learning. *Review of Research in Education,* 23, 1-24.

C. Non-Normative Development in Children's Literacy

C1. Reading and Spelling Difficulties

CARSTEN ELBRO

Although this section is about problems with literacy, it presents, in condensed form, a long series of success stories. Perhaps most impressively, the advances in theory and practice presented in this section cover multiple aspects of literacy problems, e.g., definitions, occurrence, variability, causes, prediction and intervention, studied by means of many different scientific methods from psychology, linguistics, neurology, genetics, pedagogy and sociology. The advances have been accomplished through a high degree of collaboration across disciplines, and a common wish to understand and to help children with literacy difficulties, although much more money and glamour might have been gained from efforts to move market shares from one company to another.

There are many aspects of reading and spelling difficulties which are not covered, or not covered in any detail, by the section. One such aspect is the consequences of reading difficulties – for schooling, education, vocational training, social status, self concept as a learner etc. These consequences are strong and well documented (e.g., Ceci, 1986). The special teaching methods and their effects are not covered either. In the present volume, focus is on early intervention, an area where much progress has been made in the last decades. But this focus must not lead to the false impression that nothing can be done beyond the initial teaching of reading. Student-controlled corrective feedback during reading certainly is effective (e.g. Wise, Ring & Olson, 2000), even though many students with reading difficulties have difficulties turning knowledge of letter-sound-relationships into fluent word recognition (Olson, Wise, Johnson & Ring, 1997).

The section consists of two main parts. The first part is concerned with reading difficulties which have no obvious explanation. Problems with word recognition (decoding) are dealt with at the behavioural (including education), neurological, genetic and social levels. In addition, reading comprehension problems are covered. The second part is committed to reading in special populations. In two such populations, reading and spelling problems are very frequent, namely in children with specific language impairments, and in deaf children (and adults). In the third group, blind children and adults, reading is not such a problem.

T. Nunes, P. Bryant (eds.), Handbook of Children's Literacy, 249–256.
© 2004 *Kluwer Academic Publishers. Printed in Great Britain.*

DYSLEXIA: SPECIFIC PROBLEMS WITH THE ALPHABETIC SYSTEM OF WRITING

So what is dyslexia exactly? Although it is a simple question on the surface, it is as old as research into dyslexia itself. In her chapter on *The Concept of Dyslexia*, Casalis unfolds the history of the definitions of dyslexia and other difficulties with learning to read. She demonstrates how both classical and recent definitions share a core element of *surprise*. There are children for whom it is surprisingly difficult to learn to read. There are children who show a persistent discrepancy between apparent potential and achievement. Recent research on dyslexia has focussed on the nature of the reading problem rather than on the exclusionary criteria (what dyslexia is not). The search has been for specific problems in reading which are shared by many people with reading difficulties that are not explained by obvious causes. As pointed out by Casalis, an excellent candidate for such a core difficulty is specific problems in word identification – as opposed to, for example, specific problems with language comprehension in reading. More specifically, most difficulties with word decoding can be traced back to problems with letter-sound associations (see, for example, Lyon, 1995). Hence, dyslexia could be defined as *a problem with the acquisition of the basic alphabetic principle of the writing system*.

A problem with the acquisition of the alphabetic principle is probably the most basic difficulty that can arise with written language. After all, writing consists of letters which, in principle, represent systematic units of speech, phonemes. Problems with the basic alphabetic principle may have many causes, they may take various forms, and they may have consequences of varying degrees of severity. They might even exist in the context of other problems – such as low IQ, poor educational possibilities, attentional disorders etc.

Problems with the alphabetic principle of the writing system may take many shapes. Differences between alphabetic writing systems (orthographies) are one source of variation in dyslexia. Writing systems vary along several dimensions. One important dimension is grapheme-phoneme transparency. Some orthographies are much more regular than the English one; some even approach a simple phoneme alphabet, such as Finnish, Greenlandic, Spanish, and Turkish. In languages with such more simple letter-sound correspondences than in English, dyslexia appears to be more of a speed problem than an accuracy problem in word decoding (Landerl, Wimmer, & Frith, 1997; Wimmer, 1993). Only in the very first phase of learning to read in such languages may dyslexic children show a serious accuracy problem (Wimmer, 1996).

Like other people, no two dyslexics are completely alike. The variations in dyslexic reading and spelling behaviour have attracted considerable research interest mostly because of the possible differences in underlying causal mechanisms that they might reflect. Research has almost exclusively been concerned with variation in only one dimension: the degree to which phonological recoding (spelling words out) is involved. At one end of this continuum are the laborious letter-by-letter readers ("surface" type), and at the other end are the more frequent whole-word readers ("phonological" deficit type). Although it has not been established whether dyslexic reading behaviour is significantly more varied along this continuum than normal reading behaviour (e.g. Elbro, 1990; Stanovich, Siegel, Gottardo, Chiappe & Sidhu, 1997), much research effort has focussed on this variation. In their chapter on *Individual Differences in Dyslexia* Margaret Snowling and Yvonne Griffiths discusses variation in dyslexic reading behaviour from several perspectives: single case research, models of normal reading development, comparisons with acquired dyslexias, and computer-supported models of reading and spelling behaviour ("connectionist" models). Whilst the symptoms of dyslexia towards the "phonological" deficit end of the continuum are well in line with the phonological core account of dyslexia, the symptoms at the "surface" end of the continuum present a challenge to the common understanding of dyslexia. Snowling and Griffiths list a number of possible causes including, for example, limited print exposure and slow speed of access to phonological representations of whole words. External validation of the behavioural differences in dyslexia would seem to be called for. Both the biological and genetic levels of investigations might offer such validation.

THE BIOLOGY AND GENETICS OF DYSLEXIA

There is no doubt that the human brain is the *biological* site of dyslexia and most of the other reading difficulties. For generations brain research methods that were too crude to have much to offer in the way of understanding the nature of dyslexia. This has changed dramatically over the last two decades so that neurological research is now the most rapidly expanding field in dyslexia research. Hence, Nicky Brunswick's chapter on the neurological bases of dyslexia covers a wide field. A relatively small part of the field is concerned with the structure of the brain. Magnetic resonance imaging (MRI) can provide in vivo images of "slices" of the brain with a very fine spatial resolution indeed. Details as small as about a square millimetre can be discerned. Such images render the obvious question answerable: does a dyslexic brain look any different from a normal brain? The answer is: perhaps some small ones. There are a number of independent findings that suggest that language areas in the right temporal lobe may be more equal in size to the corresponding areas in the left temporal lobe in dyslexics than in normal readers. The dyslexic brain is more "balanced" than the normal brain, which in three out of four cases features an asymmetry (left larger than right). However, these images of the structure of the brain do not disclose anything about the function of the brain.

Functional imagery is arguably more informative about the brain bases of dyslexia. Brunswick's chapter gives an overview of the recent techniques and the findings. The advantages and shortcomings of each of the techniques are highlighted helping the reader to interpret the discrepancies between findings from different techniques: EEG, ERP, MEG, PET, fMRI. The findings are many, and there are many brain sites that may show different patterns of activity in dyslexic and normal readers – under various task requirements and in different orthographies (e.g. Paulesu *et al.*, 2000). It is truly breathtaking to view pictures of the brain while people are thinking – and exhibiting problems with reading. The techniques are certainly promising, but it seems fair to say that brain research in dyslexia is still in its infancy. The challenges are many and fundamental. The most serious challenge concerns the interpretation of individual differences in activity levels. Normally, a subtraction technique is employed whereby activity in a "rest" or "control" situation is subtracted from the activity on the experimental task. A relatively low on task activity is usually interpreted simply as "a failure to activate" certain areas of the brain. But one alternative explanation is that the low on task activity stems from a relatively high "rest" or "control" activity. When subtracted from a normal level of on task activity, the resulting task activity will appear relatively small. Another problem with interpretation stems from the fact that there may be at least two (and possibly more) causes behind a low activity in a particular area of the brain: a high degree of specialisation (automaticity) or a "failure to activate" the area. Hence, it is not self evident that high activity levels indicate better functioning. Finally, dyslexic individuals are usually compared with normal readers who find the tasks easier to solve. Hence, differences in activations patterns may also reflect (simple) differences associated with levels of task difficulty levels and not only deviant patterns of cognitive processing.

It is well known that dyslexia runs in families. It is also the case that there are about twice as many boys as girls who receive special education because of reading and writing difficulties. One major question is why this is so. Is it because of genetic inheritance, or is it social (environmental) influences: nature or nurture? Jim Stevenson tells the developing success story of behaviour-genetic research in reading and dyslexia in his chapter *Epidemiology: Genetic and Social Influences on Reading Ability*. The chapter has several important messages for teachers, researchers, and educational planners. One message is that the genetic influences on reading development are not a question of either or. They can be sensibly described in probabilistic terms: the risk of becoming dyslexic is partly genetically determined. Or they can be described in popular terms: differences in reading development are moderately influenced by genetic variation. The educational implication of this is the exact opposite of the commonly held view. The implication is that the more we wish to counteract the genetic influences on reading acquisition, the more we need to know about them. We can carry out a more specific intervention when we know exactly what we wish to intervene against. Another positive implication is that as the genetic influences are brought to light, the contours of the environmental influences also become sharper. One such environmental factor is associated with being a later born child (number 4 or later) in a large family.

Naturally, reading ability is not inherited directly. Programmes for the human cells' production of amino acids are. The causal chain which ultimately leads to differences in ease in learning to read is, so far, almost unknown. The exciting message from recent research is that we now hold both ends of the chain in our hands. There are certain "markers" on the chromosomes which correspond to the presence or absence of specific reading difficulties in individual members of families prone to dyslexia.

READING COMPREHENSION DIFFICULTIES

Dyslexia is a specific problem with the acquisition of word decoding abilities. Obviously, reading comprehension is affected when word decoding is a problem. But could it also be that comprehension problems exist even in the context of accurate and fluent decoding? This question has attracted an increasing amount of interest both in practice and in research. Demands on reading comprehension have increased radically over the last generation as higher education has become a must for an burgeoning part of the population. Increasing numbers of young adults have to acquire knowledge and basic job-related qualifications through reading. The growing demands for learning through text highlights comprehension problems which were not considered previously.

The chapter *Reading Comprehension Difficulties* by Kate Cain and Jane Oakhill offers a comprehensive overview of the research into the multifaceted nature of reading comprehension difficulties and their cognitive correlates. The authors focus mainly on difficulties above the word level, though they acknowledge the crucial importance of word decoding and vocabulary knowledge. They provide a detailed account of the various types (or symptoms) of poor comprehenders' failure to integrate current text with previously read text and with background knowledge. This account may provide teachers and educators with a rich source of inspiration for the development of new ways of teaching reading comprehension to those who need it the most. The account may also offer insights into problems with spoken language comprehension. However, the research in reading comprehension problems is much more sparse than the research into dyslexia and decoding problems, even though comprehension problems are notoriously more complex. Numerous areas deserve to be researched. To mention just two examples: first, very little is known about the *causal* relations between basic cognitive functions (e.g. working memory) and specific component processes in reading comprehension such as inference making or use of context to derive word meanings. Second, practically nothing is known about the specificity of reading comprehension difficulties: to what extent do they exist independently of problems with listening comprehension? Which kinds of text structures and features are specific to written language as opposed to spoken language, and how might they give rise to independent processing problems?

EARLY IDENTIFICATION AND INTERVENTION

In most cases, problems with literacy acquisition can be predicted well before anyone notices a problem. Numerous studies have shown that the strongest predictors are pre-literacy skills, most notably letter knowledge, phonological awareness, and various measures of naming abilities. Together these predictors account for reading outcomes in about 80% or more of preschool children. This knowledge means that resources may be more efficiently targeted to children who really need the extra attention and instruction. And it provides essential input for theoretical models of the cognitive and linguistic foundations of reading and its development

Two chapters by Carsten Elbro and Hollis Scarborough, *Early Identification* and *Early Intervention*, cover the recent advances in early prediction and early prevention of reading difficulties. In a sense, the second chapter disconfirms the first because it is indeed possible to prevent reading difficulties, i.e., to falsify the prediction. It is now very clear that preschool intervention can substantially reduce the incidence and severity of reading difficulties. This is the case for both unselected groups of children and for well known at-risk groups such as children with specific language impairments, children of dyslexic parents, and children from socio-economic deprived environments

However, these and other very positive findings should not be used to hide the problems and challenges in early prediction and intervention. So far, early identification has almost exclusively been attempted with respect to problems with decoding, typically occurring during the first two years of primary school. There is a dearth of studies of early predictors of other types of problems with literacy, most notably with specific reading comprehension problems. One reason is that comprehension problems cannot be identified as early as decoding problems, so prediction of comprehension problems is more time consuming and costly than prediction of decoding problems. Another reason is that other types of reading difficulties are yet ill defined. Perhaps longitudinal prediction studies that span a longer time can contribute to better definitions of reading difficulties that are not simple consequences of initial problems with word decoding. As for intervention studies, one of the major challenges is to make the concept of phoneme identity accessible to those many at-risk children who do not profit from current teaching practices. Perhaps other aspects of their linguistic abilities and awareness need to be engaged first. Also, prediction studies indicate that various naming abilities contribute independent variance to reading development. Yet, the possible causal relation between ease of lexical access and reading acquisition still has to be studied in experimental intervention studies.

LITERACY DIFFICULTIES IN SPECIAL POPULATIONS

Since reading is a linguistic activity, it ought not come as a surprise that *children with specific language impairments* (SLI) before school generally find it more difficult to learn to read than other children. Yet, it is still a tradition in many countries that speech therapy for SLI children is clearly distinguished from measures to support the reading development for these children. The lacuna between speech and reading support means that many SLI children suffer from reading difficulties in the first school years that could have been predicted and, to some extent, prevented – had the speech and reading services been better integrated. Julie Dockrell and Geoff Lindsay's chapter, *Specific Speech and Language Difficulties and Literacy*, thus has considerable implications for practice. The authors begin with an account of the notion of specific language impairments and then provide a detailed overview of the various types of language difficulties and their known consequences for reading. It should be noticed that not all types of language impairment are equally detrimental to reading. Also, some language abilities may subserve compensatory strategies. Such knowledge is of primary importance when remedial efforts are targeted, planned and carried out.

The theoretical implications of the documented links between well described language impairments and reading difficulties are vast but, unfortunately, almost unexplored. For example, how can it be that a substantial number of preschool children with phonological disorders do *not* acquire reading difficulties? Is it possible to classify phonological disorders into those that usually result in later reading difficulties, and those that do not. Could it be that only some phonological disorders reflect some, yet unknown, more fundamental disorder which is most likely to give problems with literacy acquisition?

Deaf children are not language disordered, yet the majority of them have severe problems learning to read,' generally much more severe problems than congenitally blind children have. Jesus Alegria explains in his chapter, *Deafness and Reading*, why this is so. Deaf children appear to have two types of problem: the first problem is that their first language is normally sign language, not spoken language. The second problem is that the elements of sign language do not correspond to the sound segments of spoken language. While the first problem gives rise to vocabulary and syntactic constraints on reading, the second problem is a severe obstacle in the acquisition of word decoding ability. It does not make sense for congenitally deaf children to try to spell out words in order to read them. So reading new words continues to be a problem for deaf children. Against this background, it is no surprise that the deaf children with the best oral language are generally among the better readers. What is a puzzle is how deaf children acquire phonological representations of words. Alegria's chapter gives a review of some of the well documented sources of this acquisition. The chapter also discusses a number of other intriguing questions about deafness and reading, for example, why it is that early proficiency with sign language and the presence of two (as opposed to one) deaf parents are positive correlates of reading development in deaf children.

Blind children commonly learn to read braille, the alphabetic system where letters are represented by patters of dots from a 6 dot matrix. Since most blind children speak normally and are likely to be even more aware of the sounds of

256 *Carsten Elbro*

language than seeing children, learning to read does not pose extraordinary difficulties to them. Hence, the section ends on a positive note with Susanna Millar's chapter about *Reading by Touch in Blind Children and Adults*. Naturally, visually dependent meanings of words may be less well represented in the vocabulary of a blind child, and comprehension may be affected correspondingly. But real problems with literacy acquisition have mostly the same reasons in blind as in hearing children. They are related to problems with identification of speech sounds. In addition, some blind children have problems with the tactile input, e.g., problems with keeping track of the words and lines.

Taken together, the chapters on reading in special populations underscore the importance of language skills for literacy. Reading requires not only the language comprehension abilities necessary for understanding spoken language, but also puts special emphasis on the access to the particular linguistic segments that are represented in writing. The primary units of the alphabetic code are the single sounds and the letters that represent them. When the child's access to the identity of these single sounds is impeded, then the child is at high risk for reading difficulties. Fortunately, there are many ways in which children can be helped to acquire such awareness of phoneme identity. And well-documented positive effects of intervention abound as never before.

REFERENCES

Ceci, S. J. (Ed.) (1986). Handbook of Cognitive, Social, and Neuropsychological Aspects of Learning Disabilities (especially Vol. 1 part IV, and Vol 2 part III). Hillsdale, NJ: Lawrence Erlbaum.

Elbro, C. (1990). *Differences in Dyslexia. A Study of Reading Strategies and Deficits in a Linguistic Perspective*. Copenhagen: Munksgaard.

Landerl, K., Wimmer, H., & Frith, U. (1997). The impact of orthographic consistency on dyslexia: A German-English comparison. *Cognition*, 63, 315-334.

Lyon, G. R. (1995). Toward a definition of dyslexia. *Annals of Dyslexia*, 45, 3-27.

Olson, R. K., Wise, B., Johnson, M., & Ring, J. (1997). The etiology and remediation of phonologically based word recognition and spelling disabilities: Are phonological deficits the "hole" story? In B. A. Blackman (Ed.) *Foundations of reading acquisition and dyslexia. Implications for early intervention*, (pp. 305-326). (Mahwah, NJ: Lawrence Erlbaum).

Paulesu, E., McCrory, E., Fazio, F., Manoncello, L., Brunswick, N., Cappa, S. F., Cotelli, M., Cossu, G., Corte, F., Lorusso, M., Pesenti, S., Gallagher, A., Perani, D., Price, C., Frith, D., & Frith, U. (2000). A cultural effect on brain function. *Nature neuroscience*, 3(1), 91-96.

Stanovich, K. E., Siegel, L. S., Gottardo, A., Chiappe, P., & Sidhu, R. (1997). Subtypes of developmental dyslexia: Differences in phonological and orthographic coding. In B. A. Blachman (Ed.), *Foundations of Reading Acquisition and Dyslexia* (pp. 115-141). Mahwah, NJ: Lawrence Erlbaum.

Wimmer, H. (1993). Characteristics of developmental dyslexia in a regular writing system. Applied *Psycholinguistics* 14, 1-33.

Wimmer, H. (1996). The early manifestation of developmental dyslexia: Evidence from German children. *Reading and Writing: An Interdisciplinary Journal*, 8, 171-188.

Wise, B. W., Ring, J., & Olson, R. K. (2000). Individual differences in gains from computer-assisted remedial reading. *Journal of Experimental Child Psychology*, 77(3), 197-235.

C2. The Concept of Dyslexia

SÉVERINE CASALIS

ABSTRACT

Developmental dyslexia is a term used to describe a particular disability or learning difficulty which appears in the process of learning to read. Developmental dyslexia is considered to differ from acquired dyslexia, a term used to refer to the loss of the ability to read after a brain accident. The concept of developmental dyslexia rests on the notion of a discrepancy between a level of performance expected on the basis of IQ and an observed achieved level. The classical definition is based upon criteria that exclude particular cases – it describes what is not dyslexia. The definition, and in particular the IQ discrepancy, has been the object of much criticism. As will be discussed, it has led to much confusion without really helping to promote an understanding as to what dyslexia actually involves. Research on reading difficulties has identified dyslexia as a specific reading-related problem as opposed to a general learning problem. Dyslexia is characterised by a failure in the word identification system, and does not imply – as opposed to other reading problems – a comprehension failure. Moreover, a number of studies have identified the major cause of word identification failure in dyslexia, word recognition depends on phonological abilities. Indeed, dyslexia is associated with poor segmental analysis – that is, poor performance in tasks that require segmenting words into its constituent sounds – and more generally with poor performance in tasks involving phonological processing.

INTRODUCTION

The term dyslexia refers to two distinct kinds of reading difficulty. Acquired dyslexia refers to the disturbance of reading ability in a person who has previously learned to read normally, but who lost this ability as a result of brain damage. Developmental dyslexia concerns difficulties associated with the process of learning to read. This chapter focuses on developmental dyslexia, specifically in the field of research related to cognitive psychology. The main questions about the concept of developmental dyslexia (hitherto termed simply dyslexia) concern the definition of the term and the specificity of the trouble. As will be seen, a definition of dyslexia is an area of dispute. The dispute lies in the existence and the identification of a group

257

T. Nunes, P. Bryant (eds.), Handbook of Children's Literacy, 257–273.

of children specifically retarded in reading, distinct from other learning disabilities. Indeed, there are many possible reasons why a child may have difficulty learning to read. The concept of dyslexia lies in the assumption that specific difficulties in learning to read are different in nature and in causal factors from other reading disabilities. Finally, the debate may concern all the domains in which a differentiation between subgroups, – based on necessarily arbitrary criteria- is considered as useful or not in regard to both comprehension of the problems and their remediation.

THE CLASSICAL DEFINITION OF DYSLEXIA.

The first article in medical literature on dyslexia was written by Morgan in 1896. The term used then was not "dyslexia" but "word blindness". This term had previously been applied to patients who lost their reading abilities due to cerebral disease. In addition to Dejerine's (1892) findings in an autopsy of a "pure word blindness" case – a disconnection of the right visual cortex from the left angular gyrus – Morgan attributed the cause of word blindness to defective development of the left angular gyrus. Sometime later, Hinshelwood (1917) noted a parallelism between acquired and developmental word blindness. The neuropathologist Orton indicated in an article published in 1925 that some cases of developmental word blindness had led him to analyse "reading disability [as] a graded series in severity, that is not generically graded to mental retardation". Orton (1937) described five syndromes of delay or disorder in language acquisition, a contribution to the provision of a unified view of the language system. In particular, Orton noticed the frequency of delay in the acquisition and use of spoken language and stuttering. Dyslexia was considered to be associated with a delayed development of the entire language system. As Richardson (1992) points out, a marked resurgence of interest in dyslexia was associated with the work of Geschwind (1962), who emphasised an anatomical basis for reading disorders. Since the seventies, the psychology of reading has greatly developed, and interest in dyslexia is considerable: numerous articles and books have been devoted to the subject. But, however far the knowledge of learning disabilities has increased, disagreement about the definition of dyslexia remains in the scientific community and the question as to who is dyslexic or not is still an object of debate (see for example Stanovich, 1996).

The classical definition of dyslexia doesn't tell us what dyslexia *is*, only what it *is not*. Thus, the World Federation of Neurology (1968) defined dyslexia as a "disorder manifested by difficulty in learning to read despite conventional instruction, adequate intelligence, and sociocultural opportunity. It is dependent upon fundamental cognitive abilities which are frequently of constitutional origin" (Critchley, 1970). In identifying dyslexic children, researchers and practitioners rule out children who have a sensory impairment (auditory deficit or non corrected visual defect), an emotional disturbance, or neurological damage. While there are many reasons why a child fails to read, dyslexia is defined as a failure in learning to read which cannot be explained by those reasons. In other words, dyslexia is seen as an "unexpected" impairment of reading acquisition, i.e. not connected with a visible cause. A current working definition has been proposed by the International Dyslexia Organisation (1994) and discussed by Lyon (1995): "Dyslexia is one of several distinct learning disabilities. It is a specific language-based disorder of constitutional origin characterised by difficulties in single word decoding, usually reflecting insufficient phonological processing. These difficulties in single word decoding are often unexpected in relation to age and other cognitive and academic abilities; they are not the result of generalised developmental disability or sensory impairment [...]". Likewise, the term "dyslexia" is often considered as being related to "specific reading disability (or retardation)" because the problem occurs without a general context of backwardness. However, many researchers prefer the term "specific reading disability" due to the fact that "dyslexia" has a controversial status. As will be seen later, specific reading retardation (in other words dyslexia) is distinguished from general retardation. The relevance of this distinction will be discussed later, but it is important to note that specific reading retardation is associated with normal or superior IQ, whereas general learning disabilities which include a reading disability are associated with a lower IQ.

Dyslexia is often seen as unexpected due to the fact that it cannot be attributed to obvious causes. One area of focus concerns IQ levels, and there is a definition of dyslexia which emphasizes an IQ/reading level association. In this case, dyslexia is defined by a discrepancy between the obtained and the expected reading ages. Indeed, as Rutter and Yule (1975) point out, a traditional way of measuring under-achievement involves the use of an achievement ratio which utilizes the ratio between the child's mental age and his achievement age. For example, a 10-year-old child with a mental age of 8 years is expected to have a reading-age of 8 years; inversely a 10-year-old child with a mental age of 12 years is expected to reach a reading level corresponding to 12 years. Knowing the correlation between age, IQ and reading, one can calculate an expected value in reading given the value of IQ for each age. It is thereby possible to examine whether a child's reading score is above or below the expected value, given his/her age and IQ. On this basis, children can be identified who have reading scores significantly lower than expected. Such children are identified as dyslexic.

The discrepancy between actual reading level and the expected reading level has been crucial to the concept of dyslexia, whatever was its operationalisation: a reading level gained by the dyslexic child 18 or 24 months below the predicted value based on both age and IQ for example. While this may be valuable only for young children, other criterion can be chosen – the cut-off in terms of standard deviation for example: performance is considered as abnormal if it falls 1.65 standard deviations below the mean. The "discrepancy" view is reinforced by the fact that, in some large studies, the distribution of reading scores showed a "hump" on the left side: more children failed to learn to read than the normal gaussian curve would have indicated (e.g. Yule, Rutter, Berger and Thomson,

1974). However, the "hump" is controversial and has failed to be systematically replicated. For example, instead of a "hump", Rodgers (1983), who studied 8000 children, found a "little button" in the left of the gaussian curve (see also, Share, McGee, McKenzie, Williams and Silva 1987, Shaywitz *et al.*, 1992). Beyond the question of the distribution shape of the frequency of scores, which may depend on technical factors (like items' difficulty level), the specificity of dyslexia among other reading disabilities was important in the validation of the concept.

The IQ-reading discrepancy concept has lead to confusion. It must be emphasised that although this definition is commonly used, it is not based on verifiable hypotheses. In particular, some authors have pointed out that if dyslexia as a syndrome exists, it must affect people with low income, or lower IQ, or anything else. It should be emphasised that the classical definition was often used by researchers whose aim was to conduct research under conditions as pure as possible. In these circumstances, the temporary elimination of factors which might increase variability may be necessary. This will result in the exclusion of many cases and so, while this may be acceptable in the research context, it must be acknowledged that caution in the selection of a population *does not* validate *de facto* such a definition by exclusion. Of course, the use of such an approach is even more critical in a practical educational context, because it eliminates subjects on arbitrary and unfounded criteria.

The major problem of the classical definition is the implicit assumption made about IQ (Stanovich, 1986, 1996, Siegel, 1988): to rule out poor readers because of low IQ suggests that low IQ explains poor reading performance. However no reading acquisition model assigns a central role to intelligence, while there are models which do emphasize the role of phonological ability (Share, 1995). Moreover, while reading achievement and IQ may be correlated after a few years (about 0.7), correlation is rather low in the first year (Stanovich *et al.*, 1984). Correlation becomes increasingly important, due to the fact that reading promotes the development of abilities and knowledge which are measured in IQ tests. As a result, a poor reader's IQ score may progressively decrease: because he/she doesn't read, he/she cannot develop the knowledge and ability required in the IQ tests as well as the same age peers who can read. The IQ decreases because he/she doesn't read, not the reverse. To explain a poor reading score by a low IQ may therefore be incorrect. Moreover, what can be said about a child who has simultaneously a high IQ (let's say 140) and an average reading score, corresponding to his chronological age? Is that child dyslexic? Inversely, how should children be considered who read above the predicted value given by their IQ? Some hyperlexic children have exceptionally good reading levels in spite of a low IQ. It seems that IQ may not predict reading. If, at least at the beginning, reading and IQ are poorly correlated, how can failure in reading be explained by a low IQ?

It appears that a satisfactory definition of dyslexia cannot be provided by the classical approach; more importantly, the concept of dyslexia remains unclear using such a definition. The current definition is more precise and certainly may help to clarify the debate. The question of characterisation of difficulties and underlying process may be deepened however. In this respect, two issues are important and concern the specificity and characteristics of dyslexia. First, to what extent do specific disabled readers (dyslexic) differ from general backward readers? Second, are their reading and associated underlying processes fundamentally different from those of other children? These questions are briefly discussed in the following sections.

STUDYING THE SPECIFICITY OF DYSLEXIA: THE WORD RECOGNITION FAILURE

In order to know whether there is something specific in dyslexia, it is necessary to understand whether dyslexic people are qualitatively different from normal readers and whether dyslexic children differ from retarded readers who fail to fit the criterion. Recent research on reading difficulties attempts to find characteristics shared by the majority of people whose reading difficulties are not explained by obvious causes. The first question may be analyzed in terms of the delay/deviance problem. Two possibilities appear: according to the delay hypothesis, disabled readers perform in a way similar to younger children of the same level. In the deviance hypothesis, the reading score is the same in the different groups of readers, but the performance is due to a different subprocess in the different groups. It means thus that the same level of performance was reached in a different manner, and suggests a deviance in the way the level of performance is achieved. What is a "reading level"? In order to assess reading level, two kinds of tests may be used: comprehension tests and decoding tests. Decoding tests assess the basic ability to read words. This ability involves a subcomponent and the functioning of the subcomponent can be studied when the decoding level is the same for different children. Comprehension reading tests involve both decoding – a specific reading activity- and comprehension – a nonspecific activity involved in reading and listening. A study matching groups on comprehension then investigates whether the relative contribution of the subskills determining comprehension ability is the same in the compared groups. Two cases are considered in respect of the different information drawn from these comparisons.

Listening comprehension and word recognition

The simplistic view of reading (Gough & Tunmer, 1986) states that the comprehension ability in reading is the product of two abilities: the decoding ability (word recognition) and listening comprehension ability.

Each of these factors is necessary, but not sufficient, for success in reading. Theoretically a poor level of reading comprehension may have two distinct causes: a poor decoding ability or a poor listening comprehension ability. Of course, a poor reading comprehension score may come from poor abilities in both domains. In order to understand what is specific in disabled readers (dyslexia), as opposed to other backward readers, the comparison involving both comprehension and word identification is particularly relevant. The question of specificity of dyslexia from the comprehension/decoding discrepancy point of view necessitates comparisons of three groups: dyslexics, normal young readers, and globally disabled readers. Studies have broken down this question into three distinct comparisons.

If dyslexic readers' comprehension of oral language is consistent with their normal-range intelligence and educational background, then their listening comprehension should be significantly higher than their word recognition. Bruck (1988) found that when dyslexic and normal readers were matched on reading comprehension, dyslexics performed significantly worse on word identification (see also Elbro, 1990). Conversely, Conners and Olson (1990) compared dyslexics (15.6 years old) and normal readers (10.4 years old) on word recognition scores. The dyslexics performed significantly better than the younger, normal readers on listening comprehension, even though their listening comprehension was low for their age. This latter result illustrates the long term effects that the practice of reading may have on general verbal abilities. The consequences of reading for verbal and cognitive abilities, called the Matthew effect, have been discussed in Stanovich (1986). As reading influences some linguistic and cognitive abilities, dyslexics may not develop those abilities as well as their chronological-age peers. In the Conners & Olson study, dyslexics showed better reading comprehension abilities than younger children of the same reading age even though the difference was slight. The superiority of the dyslexics in reading comprehension compared to reading-level matched children suggests that the different components involved in reading comprehension are differently represented in young normal and dyslexic readers. Thus, a specificity appears in such studies in so far as comprehension is higher in dyslexics than their own word recognition level.

Poor readers and the lag hypothesis

Is this discrepancy distinctive of dyslexics compared to other poor readers? How do other poor readers behave? Are their difficulties also specific or could they well be characterised as delayed readers? In order to examine variability in learning to read, Stanovich tested the lag hypothesis. Following this hypothesis, general poor readers are characterised by a general lag, affecting all reading components. To examine this hypothesis, Stanovich (1988) compared skilled third-grade children with less skilled fifth-grade children, both groups reaching the same level of reading comprehension. He compared their performance on thirteen measures related to reading (for example: vocabulary, rhyme production, pseudoword naming, etc.). Results indicated that both groups performed similarly on all but one measure (letter naming time). The extreme convergence of the profile of the two groups indicates that the poor readers group does not suffer from a specific impairment, but its acquisition is delayed: cognitively, they resemble younger children who are at the same stage of reading development. This result (see also Stanovich, Nathan & Zolman, 1988) strongly supports the developmental lag hypothesis of the reading problems of non-dyslexic children.

Dyslexic and other poor readers

Aaron (1987) compared the two groups of disabled readers. All the subjects of the study were college students who performed three or more years below expectation. Two groups were formed on the basis of subjects' IQ: subjects who had an overall score of 95 or above (that is, average or above average) were placed in the dyslexic group. Subjects who had a full scale IQ of 85 or below were placed in the non-specific reading disability group. Subjects whose IQ score fell between 85 and 95 were not included in the study. The authors hypothesised that if dyslexia is qualitatively different from other reading disabilities, differences would appear between the groups on different measures. Six differences appeared between the two groups matched on reading comprehension. First, the dyslexic group showed poor decoding skills, in comparison to the nonspecific reading disability group, whereas the listening comprehension scores differed between the two groups of disabled readers; the group identified as dyslexic did not differ from normal readers in comprehension scores. The performance of the group with nonspecific reading problems was below that of both dyslexic and of normal readers. Other differences were also found in the following domains: rate of reading when comprehension was required, on-line monitoring of comprehension, understanding of syntactically ambiguous sentences, and type of reading errors committed (Aaron, Kuchta, Grapenthin, 1988, Aaron, 1987, Aaron, 1995). More recently, Nation and Snowling (1998) have shown that the reading process differs also in the use of contextual information from the text. Generally poor readers showed more contextual facilitation than good readers, thus replicating the results of Perfetti & Hogaboam (1975). However, the two groups differed in the use of contextual information: children with poor reading comprehension skills failed to benefit from context, whereas dyslexics showed the greatest contextual facilitation. Thus, the process implied in reading comprehension distinguished specific poor readers from those who were poor readers and poor comprehenders.

Dyslexia as a comprehension vs word recognition discrepancy

On the basis of the reading comprehension score, it is thus possible to differentiate here two populations of disabled readers which show different patterns when compared with comprehension- matched normal readers. The globally retarded readers have reached the same level of reading comprehension with the same profile as normal readers: no significant differences were found between poor and young readers, except for a few measures strongly related to chronological age (as speed for example). Thus, poor readers are characterised by a general lag or delay in reading acquisition. Inversely, when comparing dyslexic children with comprehension matched children, some significant differences appear: in particular, the older dyslexic readers have poorer decoding skills. They have achieved the same reading comprehension level because they have better vocabulary, memory, or other cognitive skills than the younger readers of the same reading age. What is important is that they have reached the same level in a different way. Consequently, they cannot be considered as simply delayed. Their high cognitive skills allow them to compensate for their poor decoding skills.

These studies validate the notion that there are two possible sources of comprehension reading failure. One is constituted by comprehension problems, one by decoding problems. It doesn't imply that decoding problems are met only in children of normal or superior IQ. The IQ difference results from the fact that both groups are equated on comprehension and that comprehension is correlated with IQ. Decoding is independent of IQ. Consequently, children who display specific decoding disability should be found on all the IQ levels. However, following the simple view model, listening comprehension should be considered in parallel. This leads us to view that dyslexics are children who display a discrepancy between reading and listening comprehension or, in others words, who fail specifically in word identification.

UNDERLYING FACTORS IN DYSLEXIA

It is helpful to consider two main questions in order to understand the concept of dyslexia. First, is there a specificity of dyslexia in the word recognition subcomponent? Second, is the word recognition deficit explained by a cause or a body of causes common to a large majority, if not all, of dyslexic children? In other words, are we able to find causes of failure in word recognition that fit a large number of cases? Since both questions are more deeply discussed in the following chapters, we will only draw out the main trends in order to examine the concept of dyslexia.

Is there a specificity of dyslexia in the reading process?

The first question concerned word recognition components. Classically, two main procedures are considered (Coltheart, 1978). In the sublexical – also known as phonological – procedure, spelling-to-sound correspondences are involved. In the lexical – also termed orthographic – procedure, representations from the visual analysis are directly mapped onto orthographic representations that are stored in a mental lexicon. The question arises as to whether dyslexic children show a similar pattern of subcomponent involvement in word recognition, when compared to reading-level matched normal readers. Generally, studies showed a disadvantage for the phonological/sublexical procedure in dyslexic children: dyslexics were found to read significantly less pseudowords than control matches (Olson *et al.*, 1989, Rack, Snowling & Olson, 1992). The pseudoword deficit – assessed by an imprecise or slow pseudoword decoding – has been evidenced in several languages, even those that have a regular and transparent orthography (Wimmer, 1993). However, such a result was not found in all studies; Treiman and Hirsh-Pasek (1985), for example, found no difference between groups. Although these contradictory results may arise from technical reasons, they suggest two conclusions. First, *generally*, a pseudoword reading deficit, is associated with poor performance in tasks that require segmenting words into their constituent sounds and is characteristic of dyslexics. Second, there could be an important variability in the dyslexic population as well as in the nondyslexic population (Bryant & Impey, 1986). Indeed, a growing corpus of evidence indicates at present that word recognition patterns differ among dyslexic children (Broom and Doctor, 1994). Moreover, recent studies that examined large groups of dyslexics clearly indicate an important heterogeneity in reading process (Casalis, 1995, Castles and Coltheart, 1993, Manis, Seidenberg, Doi, McBride-Chang and Peterson, 1996, Seymour, 1986 Sprenger-Charolles, Colé, Serniclaes and Lacert, 2000). Consequently, it is not clear that dyslexics read on the basis of the same process and, hence, dyslexia may not be a unique syndrome. It should, however, be considered that, insofar as the studies did not integrate a developmental dimension, such a variability remains difficult to interpret. To what extent do differences represent different developmental stages? A recent study by Snowling, Goulandris and Defty (1996) showed that the nature of dyslexia changed over time, even if the phonological deficits were at the core of the reading impairment. At present, caution is shared among the scientific community, and, in the absence of evidence, heterogeneity is largely admitted, even if the phonological route deficit is recognised as the main trouble in dyslexia.

A cause of dyslexia: the phonological module

The second question concerns underlying factors. For nearly twenty years, a very large corpus of evidence has shown that dyslexics suffer from deficits in their phonological processing abilities. These well-established deficits concern various aspects of phonological processing. Dyslexic children are incapable of analysing speech into phonological segments (Bryant and Bradley, 1985, Lecocq, 1986). In those measures called "phonological awareness tasks", dyslexic children show poorer performance than younger normal readers, matched on reading level. This incapacity is localised in the phonological sphere: the dyslexics are incapable of removing a phoneme from a word but not a note from a musical sequence (Morais, Cluytens & Alegria, 1984). They also display poor phonological short-term memory abilities (Mann & Liberman, 1984, Brady, 1991) and slowness in naming (Denkla & Cutting, 1999, Wolf, 1999). It has been shown that deficits in phonological awareness are causally related to reading difficulties (Bryant & Bradley, 1983, Lundberg, Frost & Petersen, 1988). Those deficits may be caused by anomalies in speech perception and, more precisely, in phoneme categorisation (Werker & Tees, 1987, Manis, McBride-Chang *et al.* 1997). Moreover, some remedial studies have shown that phonetic discrimination training in reading disabled children may enhance their score in phonemic awareness tasks (Hurford, 1990). The phonological deficit has also been explained in terms of poor underlying phonological representations. According to Fowler (1991), differences in the representation of phonological segments of different lengths may determine linguistic and metalinguistic development. Segmental analysis depends on the nature of the segments i.e., syllables, phonemes, rhymes. Segmental analysis may be impaired by the lack of precision or completeness of representation of these segments. Swan and Goswami (1997a, 1997b) have tested this hypothesis and found that the variation in the precision of phonological representation may explain some differences in phonological awareness scores (see also Elbro, 1996, for a related view).

An aspect that might be particularly enlightening in understanding dyslexia is that phonological impairment does persist into adulthood, even if reading problems are overcome. For example, Elbro, Nielsen & Petersen (1994) found that adults diagnosed as dyslexic during childhood continue to confuse phonologically similar words. Gallagher, Laxon, Armstrong & Frith (1996) were interested in the phonological abilities of well-compensated dyslexic adults i.e., adults who have learned to read well but have had a diagnosis of dyslexia in childhood. Although their academic achievement was high, their performance in pseudoword reading was poor, and they were slow in a phoneme inversion task, digit and word naming speed. Thus, reading disability is associated with a specific process impairment which persists even though reading processes evolve. While this well-established pattern of results may validate the concept of dyslexia, it should be noted that other poor readers may also display some phonological deficits (Juel, 1988, Juel, Griffith & Gough, 1988, Jorm, Share, Matthews & Maclean, 1986). However, in contrast to other poor readers, dyslexic children manifest deficits only in the phonological sphere, whereas other poor readers exhibit deficits in a larger variety of domains (Ellis & Large, 1987). For the latter population, some of these deficits may be causally related to their comprehension reading disability. Inversely, the deficit in dyslexia is localised in the phonological core. Stanovich (1988) proposed a framework which accounts for variation in reading with the phonological-core variable-difference model. This model associates dyslexia with a specific phonological-core deficit, without considering the IQ discrepancy. It provides a clearer definition of dyslexia, based on phonological deficit and which clearly differentiates dyslexics from general poor readers. Actually, there is a large consensus among researchers to associate reading difficulties in dyslexia with poor phonological abilities.

Finally, a somewhat contradictory view emerges. On the one hand, particularly in group studies, dyslexia is associated with both poor segmental analysis abilities and poor performance on the sublexical component (as measured in pseudoword reading). On the other hand, heterogeneity is acknowledged, and while cases of dyslexia are presented without any associated deficit (Castles & Coltheart , 1996), some visual deficit has been reported in isolated cases (Romani, Ward and Olson 1999). Thus, while it is acknowledged that the phonological module is implicated in dyslexia, other underlying deficiencies are not eliminated, even though, at present, they are not defined and appear rather unclear. In other words, dyslexia is associated with a phonological deficit, but this criterion is not exclusive. Children who perform high on phonological tests, but who are very poor in word recognition, are considered as dyslexic.

BIOLOGICAL AND ENVIRONMENTAL FACTORS IN DYSLEXIA

Heritability

The constitutional origin of dyslexia has been emphasised in both classical and current definitions. In the neurological field, the dyslexics' brain has been shown to display some particularities in the cellular organisation (ectopies, microgenesis, etc.) and in a higher incidence of lateralisation of the *planum temporale* than in the normal population (Galaburda, 1989).

Also part of the constitutional origin in the concept, the question of heritability takes a part in the concept of dyslexia. Vogler, DeFries and Decker (1985) have documented the family nature of reading problems. They estimated that the chance of a dyslexic boy having a dyslexic father was 40%, and the chance of having a mother dyslexic is 35%, for a girl, the proportion is about 17-18%, without considering the sex of the parents. The proportion for a dyslexic boy is five to seven times higher than the probability of finding a dyslexic child who does not have a dyslexic parent, and, for a girl, ten to twenty times greater. However, the presence of family transmission is a necessary but not sufficient piece of evidence for genetic etiology. The obvious confound is the shared environment within families.

The influence of genetic factors while controlling for environmental factors is helpfully investigated in twin studies. The rationale of the twins studies is as follows: monozygotic (MZ) and dizygotic (DZ) twins share the same environment, but they differ in terms of genetic similarity: whereas monozygotic twins have identical genes, dizygotic share their genes to the same degree as siblings, that is 50%. This difference allows a distinction to be made between what is genetically transmitted and what is environmentally shared. If dyslexia has a genetic etiology, then MZ twins would be more likely than DZ twins to share a reading disability. DeFries, Fulker and LaBuda (1987) observed that there was more difference in reading performance between DZ twins than MZ twins. More recently, Olson (1994) found that for both phonological and orthographic coding, genetic factors appeared to be more influential than shared environment. Furthermore, phonological recoding and orthographic knowledge are found to be equally inheritable. Thus, it appears that reading disorders may be genetically transmitted to some degree. This does not mean that dyslexia is directly genetically transmitted nor that one can find a gene responsible for reading disability.

Social factors

When considering a whole group of poor readers, it is clear that they come more often than not from low Socio-Economic Status (SES). In practice, both the classical and current definitions rule out from the dyslexic population children from very low SES because it is recognised that their low social conditions may directly affect their academic achievement. However accepting that because dyslexic children could come from any social background does not mean that reading problems are independent from social background.

Raz and Bryant (1990) have found that SES differences directly affect both the components of reading, word identification and comprehension. They found that word identification depended on phonemic awareness for children from lower and higher SES. SES differences in phonemic awareness emerged only after children entered school and were exposed to some reading instruction. In a recent study, however, Bowey (1999) observed that phonological sensitivity differs between high and low SES children as early as the kindergarten stage. Such a difference was found in preschool children even when IQ performance and linguistic factors were taken into account.

Prognosis of poor reading abilities may depend on several factors, such as the severity of the deficit, presence of behavioral problems and social background (Waring, Prior, Sanson and Smart, 1996). Thus, social factors may both play a role in determining reading problems and in resolving them. However, the reciprocal relation is also true: future SES depends on reading level probably more than the reverse. Thus the question of remediation is crucial for dyslexics.

REMEDIATION

As indicated before, an important characteristic of dyslexia is the fact that reading problems continue to be evident in adulthood, even when differences in SES and IQ are taken into account (Pennington *et al.*, 1990). In fact, it appears that difficulty to remediate is a recurrent characteristic of dyslexia. In a study that aimed to remediate reading ability in poor readers in first grade, Vellutino, Scanlon *et al.* (1996) found that it was easy to obtain improvement in about two thirds of them whereas one third (dyslexic) were difficult to remediate. The groups differed on a range of abilities, which reinforces the idea that dyslexics present a specific profile. However, both persistence of reading difficulties and difficulty to remediate do not mean that remediation is impossible. Studies that emphasize specific training on phonological abilities (Hurford, 1990) have found some improvement in the domain. Otherwise, remediation that emphasizes the relation between graphemic and phonemic information is acknowledged as achieving better effects.

CONCLUSION

The concept of dyslexia is considered controversial. First of all, it is obvious that reading disabilities are along a continuum, and putting limits in order to define categories depends on arbitrary criteria. Why should one consider as dyslexic children whose reading level falls 24 months or 18 months below the expected level? Second, the term "dyslexia" may evoke both unity and biological origins. How can we ascertain that the reading difficulty of a child is biological in origin? Moreover, manifestations of dyslexia are far from homogeneous. However, it is undeniable that some children display profound difficulty in learning to read, without a context of general disabilities, emotional disturbance, brain damage or sensorial deficit. Moreover, the deficit of these children is located in the word identification domain. Whether the proportion of such children is above a predicted value or not is not important. Research has to explain why these children fail to read. The identification of such a population ("unexpected" failure in learning to read) has allowed one to specify components that might be involved in dyslexia and to develop research of causality in reading problems. Identification of so-called dyslexic children has led to highlight the role of phonological abilities as the underlying process in word recognition. The strict restriction of "dyslexic" to certain poor readers allows development of research and does not impede the extension of results to other populations, that may be more heterogeneous. Certainly, a major problem with the classical definition of dyslexia (the use of exclusion criteria and especially the IQ discrepancy) has led to much confusion – because IQ is not a good measure of potential for reading development and such a link lies on hypotheses yet to be tested. As indicated earlier on, a clearer concept of dyslexia emerges when the specific word recognition failure is considered as the basis of dyslexia. It may then be operationalised by a discrepancy between reading level and listening comprehension. It should be noticed that fundamentally the concept of dyslexia continues to rest on the discrepancy between an actual level of reading achievement and a predicted level of achievement.

Comparisons involving a comprehension level match design emphasize specificity of word identification failure in dyslexic children. The merit of these studies is to distinguish two kinds of poor readers: some have problems in word identification and some have problems in comprehension. The latter are improperly called poor readers. They would best be called poor comprehenders.

A difficulty in understanding the concept of dyslexia is linked to the fact that comprehension is correlated with IQ, while word identification is not. Thus, a study that matches both groups of poor readers on reading comprehension may select only the dyslexic that have skilled comprehension (that is often associated with a normal or superior IQ). But this doesn't mean that only normal or superior IQ children may encounter word identification failure. However, if this word identification failure arises in a child with a low IQ, comprehension may also be low. It appears that the concept of dyslexia becomes clearer if it is associated with a word identification deficit, independently of IQ. The principal cause lies in phonological deficits, even if, at the present time, it is not possible to ensure that it is a unique impairment in all cases of word identification failure. Data of reading processes show effectively a heterogeneity. This heterogeneity poses a problem firstly because it is difficult to interpret variation independently of a longitudinal context and, secondly because orthographic failure is not clearly associated with an underlying process deficit.

The fact that dyslexia may not constitute a unitary process and that difficulties are located along a continuum does not invalidate the concept of dyslexia. Certain children do encounter specific difficulties in establishing a functional word identification system. Their reading difficulties lie only in this failure. All their other difficulties are best interpreted as consequences of poor reading. This is not the case of other poor readers who may encounter a range of difficulties associated with reading and language. From this distinction, remediation may be oriented in two separate directions. For dyslexic children, word identification has been established as the cause of their reading difficulty. Thus they could benefit from the development of phonological awareness and specific training in this domain may be useful. For the other poor readers, comprehension must be enhanced by special training (for poor comprehenders) and if necessary (for children who display both deficits) in both word identification and comprehension.

REFERENCES

Aaron, P. (1987). Developmental dyslexia: is it different from other forms of reading disability? *Annals of Dyslexia*, 37, 109-125.

Aaron, P. G. (1995). Differential diagnosis of reading disabilities. *School Psychology Review*, 24,(3), 345-360.

Aaron, P. G., Kuchta, S. & Grapenthin, C. T. (1988). Is there a thing called dyslexia? *Annals of Dyslexia*, 38, 33-49.

Bowey, J. A. (1995). Socioeconomic status differences in preschool phonological sensitivity and first-grade reading achievement. *Journal of Educational Psychology*, 87, 476-487.

Bradley, L. & Bryant, P. (1983). Categorizing sounds and learning to read – a causal connection. *Nature*, 301, 419-421.

Brady, S. (1991). The role of working memory in reading disability. In S. Brady & D. Shankweiler (Eds): *Phonological Processes in Literacy: A tribute to Isabelle Liberman* (pp. 129-151). Hillsdale, N.J., Lawrence Erlbaum Associates.

Broom, Y. M. & Doctor, E.A. (1994). Developmental dyslexia: contrasting pattern of performance on a diagnostic psycholinguistic assessment. *South African Journal of Psychology*, 24, 219-227.

Bruck, M. (1988). The word recognition and spelling of dyslexic children. *Reading Research Quarterly*, 23, 51-69.

Bruck, M. (1992). Persistence of dyslexics' phonological awareness deficits. *Developmental Psychology*, 28, 874-886.

Bryant, P. & Bradley, L. (1985). *Children's reading difficulties*. Oxford: Blackwell.

Bryant, P. & Impey, L. (1986). The similarities between normal readers and developmental and acquired dyslexics. *Cognition*, 24, 121-137.

Casalis, S. (1995). Apprentissage de la lecture et dyslexies de l'enfant (Learning to read and developmental dyslexia). Lille: Presses Universitaires du Septentrion.

Castles, A. & Coltheart, M. (1993). Varieties of developmental dyslexia. *Cognition*, 47, 149-180.

Castles, A. & Coltheart, M. (1996). Cognitive correlates of developmental surface dyslexia: A single case study. *Cognitive Neuropsychology*, 13(1), 25-50.

Coltheart, M. (1978). Lexical access in simple reading tasks. In G. Underwood (Ed): *Strategies in information processing* (pp. 151-216). London: Academic Press.

Conners F. A. & Olson, R.K. (1990). Reading comprehension in dyslexic and normal readers: a component-skills analysis. In D. A. Balota, G. B. Flores d'Arcais, K. Rayner (Eds). *Comprehension processes in reading* (pp. 557-579). Hillsdale: Lawrence Erlbaum Associates.

Critchley, M. (1970). *The dyslexic child*. London: William Heineman Medical Books.

DeFries, J. C., Fulker, D. W. & LaBuda, M. C. (1987). Evidence for a genetic etiology in reading disability of twins. *Nature*, 329, 197-215.

Déjérine, J. (1892). Contribution à l'étude anatomo-pathologique et clinique des différentes variétés de cécité verbale (Contributions to the anatomo-pathological study of the different varieties of verbal deficiencies). *Memoriale Société biologique*, Fev, 27, 61.

Denckla, M. B. & Cutting, L. E. (1999). History and significance of Rapid Automatized Naming. *Annals of Dyslexia*, 49, 29-42.

Elbro, C. (1996). Early linguistic abilities and reading development: a review and a hypothesis. *Reading and Writing. An Interdisciplinary Journal*, 8, 453-485.

Elbro, C., Nielsen, I. & Petersen, D. (1994). Dyslexia in adults: evidence for deficits in non-word reading and in the phonological representation of lexical items. *Annals of Dyslexia*, 44, 205-226.

Elbro, C., Rasmussen, I. & Spelling, B. (1996). Teaching reading to disabled readers with language disorders: a controlled evaluation of synthetic speech feedback. *Scandinavian Journal of Psychology*, 37, 140-155.

Ellis, A. & Large, B. (1987). The development of reading: as you seek so shall you find. *British Journal of Psychology*, 78, 1-128.

Fowler, A. E. (1991). How early phonological development might set the stage for phoneme awareness. In S. Brady & D. Shankweiler (Eds). *Phonological process in literacy. A tribute to Isabelle Liberman* (pp. 97-118). Hillsdale, NJ: Erlbaum.

Gallagher, A. M., Laxon, V., Armstrong, E. & Frith, U. (1996). Phonological difficulties in high functioning dyslexics. *Reading and Writing. An Interdisciplinary Journal*, 8, 499-509.

Geschwind, N. (1962). The anatomy of acquired disorders of reading. In J. Money (Ed). *Reading disability, progress and research needs in dyslexia* (pp.115-159). Baltimore: The Johns Hopkins University Press.

Gough, P. B. & Tunmer, W. E. (1986). Decoding, reading and reading ability. *Remedial and Special Education*, 7, 6-10.

Hinshelwood, J. (1917). *Congenital word blindness*. London: H.K. Lewis.

Hurford, D. P. (1990). Training phonemic segmentation ability with a phonemic discrimination intervention in second- and third- grade children with reading disability. *Journal of Learning Disabilities*, 23, 564-569.

Jorm, A., Share, D., Matthews, R. & MacClean, R. (1986). Behaviour problems in specific reading retarded and general reading backward children: a longitudinal study. *Journal of Child Psychology and Psychiatry*, 27, 33-43.

Juel, C. (1988). Learning to read and write: a longitudinal study of 54 children from first through fourth grades. *Journal of Educational Psychology*, 80, 437-447.

Juel, C., Griffith, P. L. & Gough, P. B. (1986). Acquisition of literacy: a longitudinal study of children in first and second grade. *Journal of Educational Psychology*, 78, 243-255.

Lecocq, P. (1986). Sensibilité à la similarité phonétique chez les enfants dyslexiques et les bons lecteurs (Sensibility to phonetic similarity in dyslexic children and normal readers). *L'Année Psychologique*, 86, 201-221.

Lundberg, I., Frost, J. & Pertersen, O. (1988). Effects of an extensive program for stimulating phonological awareness in preschool children. *Reading Research Quarterly*, 23, 263-284.

Lyon, G. R. (1995). Toward a Definition of Dyslexia. *Annals of Dyslexia*, 45, 3-27.

Manis, F. R., McBride-Chang, C., Seidenberg, M., Keating, P., Doi, L.M., Munson, B. & Pertersen, A. (1997). Are speech perception deficits associated with developmental dyslexia? *Journal of Experimental Child Psychology*, 66, 211-235.

Manis, F. R., Seidenberg M., Doi, L. M., McBride-Chang, C. & Peterson, A. (1996). On the bases of two subtypes of developmental dyslexia. *Cognition*, 58, 157-195.

Mann V. A. & Liberman, I. Y. (1984). Phonological awareness and verbal short term memory. *Journal of Learning Disabilities*, 17, 592-599.

Morais, J., Cluytens, M. & Alegria, J. (1984). Segmentation abilities of dyslexia and normal readers. *Perceptual and Motor Skills*, 58, 221-222.

Morgan, W. P. (1896). Word blindness. *British Medical Journal*, Nov 7, 1378.

Nation, K. & Snowling, M. J. (1998). Individual differences in contextual facilitation: evidence from dyslexia and poor reading comprehension. *Child Development*, 69, 996-1011.

Olson, R., Foltz, G. & Wise, B. (1986). Reading instruction and remediation with the aid of computer speech. *Behavior Research Methods, Instruments and Computers*, 18(2), 93-99.

Olson, R. K. (1994). Language deficits in "specific" reading disability. In A. M. Gernsbacher (Ed). *Handbook of Psycholinguistics* (pp. 895-916). San Diego, CA: Academic Press.

Olson, R. K., Wise, B., Conners, F., Rack, J. & Fulker, D. (1989). Specific deficits in component reading and language skills: genetic and environmental influences. *Journal of Learning Disabilities*, 22, 339-348.

Orton, S. T. (1937). Reading, writing and speech problems in children. New York: Norton.

Pennington, B. F., Van Orden, G. C., Smith, S. D., Phyllis, A. G. & Haith, M. M. (1990). Phonological processing skills and deficits in adult dyslexics. *Child Development*, 61, 1753-1778.

Perfetti, C. & Hogoboam, T. (1975). Relationship between single word decoding and reading comprehension skill. *Journal of Educational Psychology*, 67, 461-467.

Rack, J. P., Snowling, M. J. & Olson, R. K. (1992). The nonword reading deficit in developmental dyslexia: a review. *Reading Research Quarterly*, 27, 29-53.

Raz, I. S. & Bryant, P. (1990). Social background, phonological awareness and children's reading. *British Journal of Developmental Psychology*, 8, 209-225.

Richardson, S. O. (1992). Historical perspectives on dyslexia. *Journal of Learning Disabilities*, 25, 40-47.

Rodgers, B. (1983). The identification and prevalence of specific reading retardation. *British Journal of Educational Psychology*, 53, 368-373.

Romani, C., Ward, J. & Olson, A. (1999). Developmental surface dysgraphia: what is the underlying cognitive impairment? *The Quarterly Journal of Experimental Psychology*, 52A, 97-128.

Rutter, M. & Yule, W. (1975). The concept of specific reading retardation. *Journal of Child Psychology and Psychiatry*, 16, 181-197.

Seymour, P. H., (1986). *Cognitive analysis of dyslexia*. London: Routledge and Kegan Paul.

Share, D. (1995). Phonological recoding and self-teaching: sine qua non of reading acquisition. *Cognition*, 55, 151-218.

Share, D. L., McGee, R., McKenzie, D., Williams, S. & Silva, P. A. (1987). Further evidence related to the distinction between specific reading retardation and general reading backwardness. *British Journal of Developmental Psychology*, 5, 35-44.

Shaywitz, S. E., Escobar, M. D., Shaywitz, B. A., Fletcher, J. M. & Maknuch, R. (1992). Evidence that dyslexia may represent the lower tail of a normal distribution of reading ability. *New England Journal of Medicine*, 326, 145-150.

Siegel, L. S. (1988). Evidence that IQ scores are irrelevant to the definition and analysis of reading disability. *Canadian Journal of Psychology*, 42, 468-478.

Snowling, M. J., Goulandris, N., Defty, N. (1996). A longitudinal study of reading development in dyslexic children. *Journal of Educational Psychology*, 88, 653-669.

Sprenger-Charolles, L., Colé P., Serniclaes, W. & Lacert, P. (2000). On subtypes of developmental dyslexia: evidence from processing time and accuracy scores. *Canadian Journal of Experimental Psychology*, 54, 88-104.

Stanovich, K. E. (1986). Matthews effect: some consequences of individual differences in the acquisition of literacy. *Reading Research Quarterly*, 21, 360-406.

Stanovich, K. E. (1988). Explaining the differences between the dyslexic and the garden-variety poor readers: The phonological-core variable difference model. *Journal of Learning Disabilities*, 22, 590-612.

Stanovich, K.E. (1996). Toward a more inclusive definition of dyslexia. *Dyslexia*, 2, 154-166.

Stanovich, K. E., Cunningham, A. E. & Feeman, D. J. (1984). Intelligence, cognitive skills, and early reading progress. *Reading Research Quarterly*, 19, 278-303.

Stanovich, K. E., Nathan, R. G. & Zolman, J. E. (1988). The developmental lag hypothesis in reading: longitudinal and matched-reading level comparisons. *Child Development*, 59, 71-86.

Stanovich, K. E., Nathan, R. G., & Vala-Rossi, M. (1986). Developmental changes in the cognitive correlates of reading ability and the developmental lag hypothesis. *Reading Research Quarterly*, 21, 199-202.

Swan, D. & Goswami, U. (1997). Phonological awareness deficits in developmental dyslexia and the phonological representations hypothesis. *Journal of Experimental Child Psychology*, 66, 18-41.

Swan, D. & Goswami, U. (1997). Picture naming deficits in developmental dyslexia : The phonological representations hypothesis. *Brain and Language*, 56, 334-353.

Treiman, R. & Hirsh-Pasek, K. (1985). Are there qualitative differences in reading behavior between dyslexics and normal readers? *Memory and Cognition*, 13, 357-364.

Vellutino, F. R., Scanlon, D. M., Sipay, E. R., Small, S. G., Pratt, A. & Denckla, M. B. (1996). Cognitive profiles of difficult-to-remediate and readily remediated poor readers: early intervention as a vehicle for distinguishing between cognitive and experiential deficits as basic causes of specific reading disability. *Journal of Educational Psychology*, 88, 601-638.

Vogler, G. P., DeFries, J. C. & Decker, S. N. (1985). Family history as an indicator of risk for reading disability. *Journal of Learning Disabilities*, 18, 419-412.

Waring, S., Prior, M., Sanson, A. & Smart, D (1996): Predictors of "recovery" from reading disability. *Australian Journal of Psychology*, 48, 3, 160-166.

Werker, J. F. & Tees, R. C. (1987). Speech perception in severely disabled and average reading children. *Canadian Journal of Psychology*, 41, 48-61.

Wimmer, H. (1993). Characteristics of developmental dyslexia in a regular writing system. *Applied Psycholinguistics*, 14, 1-33.

Wolf, M. (1999). What time may tell: towards a New Conceptualization of Developmental Dyslexia. *Annals of Dyslexia*, 49, 3-28.

Yule, W., Rutter, M., Berger, M & Thompson, J. (1974). Over- and under-achievement in reading: distribution in the general population. *British Journal of Psychology*, 44, 1-12.

SUGGESTED FURTHER READINGS

Hulme, C. & Snowling, M. J. (1997) (Eds), *Dyslexia, Biology and Cognition*. London: Whurr Publishers.

Lundberg, I., Tonnessen, F. E., & Austad, I. (1999). *Dyslexia: advances in theory and practice*. Dordrecht (The Netherlands): Kluwer Academic Publishers.

C3. Developmental Dyslexia: Evidence from Brain Research

NICKY BRUNSWICK

ABSTRACT

According to Beaumont (1982), "a psychology without any reference to physiology can hardly be complete. The operation of the brain is relevant to human conduct, and the understanding of how the brain relates to behaviour may make a significant contribution to understanding how... psychological factors operate in directing behaviour" (p. 4). This view of the importance of brain research to our understanding of cognitive and behavioural processes has gained ground in the past 20 years with the development of neuroimaging techniques (such as Positron Emission Tomography, Magnetoencephalography and functional Magnetic Resonance Imaging) and improvement in sophistication of other methods (such as Electroencephalography and Event-Related Potentials). These methods have been used extensively by cognitive neuroscientists to study the relationship between the brain's activity and processing of language in developmental dyslexics and control readers. This chapter reviews the major developments in cellular analysis, electrophysiology and neuroimaging as applied to developmental dyslexia and evaluates explanations for the neurophysiological and neuroanatomical differences between developmental dyslexics and unimpaired readers.

INTRODUCTION

Attempts to relate aspects of linguistic processing with underlying physiology have a long history in neuroscience and pre-date the identification of developmental dyslexia. The pioneering investigations of the mid-19th century were driven by neurologists studying individuals whose spoken language processing skills had been impaired or lost through brain injury (Broca, 1861; Wernicke, 1874). These early studies were among the first to illustrate the importance of the left hemisphere to the processing of language, specifically the production of speech.

Half a century later, investigators began to suggest that abnormalities in the left hemisphere may contribute to the language disorder, developmental dyslexia. In 1925, Orton suggested that delayed neurological development within the

T. Nunes, P. Bryant (eds.), Handbook of Children's Literacy, 275–291.
© 2004 Kluwer Academic Publishers. Printed in Great Britain.

language system of the brain was responsible for a failure of the left hemisphere to develop unilateral linguistic superiority over the right hemisphere. This inhibition of normal cerebral (i.e. left hemisphere) dominance for language was thought to be responsible for the difficulty that developmental dyslexics had in distinguishing mirror images of letters (i.e. b and d). Although subsequent research has shown Orton's theories to be incorrect, they were nonetheless important in suggesting that dyslexia was in some way associated with anomalous cerebral lateralisation.

The development of neuroimaging techniques has facilitated investigation of the relationship between psychology and physiology in normal, healthy adults and children. Recent studies have not only associated specific brain areas, notably within the temporo-parieto-occipital regions of the left hemisphere, in the production and comprehension of language, but have related specific areas of brain activation with specific aspects of language processing (Price, 1997). These studies are discussed in detail later. First, however, we will consider the evidence for and against structural abnormalities in developmental dyslexia.

Developmental dyslexia and brain structure

As the human brain matures, the size of the left temporo-parietal region increases and neurons in the right hemisphere diminish (Brown, Hulme, Hyland & Mitchell, 1994). This combination of development and attrition produces the leftward asymmetry in the posterior of the hemisphere (including the planum temporale) which is consistently seen at post-mortem, in brain scans, and which is present in foetuses, in children and in adults (Galaburda, Corsiglia, Rosen & Sherman, 1987; Morgan & Hynd, 1998). Some have suggested that this asymmetry represents the anatomical substrate for language in the left hemisphere (Galaburda et al, 1987). While the precise relationship between this asymmetry and competent language processing has yet to be determined, a great deal of evidence indicates that deviation from this "normal" asymmetry is associated with impaired language processing, such as poor reading comprehension or poor phonological processing skill (see review by Beaton, 1997).

It is unsurprising, then, that neuroanatomical evidence suggests that this pattern of asymmetry is not as common in developmental dyslexics as in unimpaired readers. Structural measures indicate that dyslexics are more likely to display either symmetry or reversed asymmetry in regions of the left hemisphere, including the planum temporale (Galaburda, Menard & Rosen, 1994) and in more posterior regions encompassing the temporal lobes and occipital and parieto-occipital regions (Hynd & Semrud-Clikeman, 1989; Tallal & Katz, 1989) (see Figure 1). More fine-grained anomalies have been observed by Rae and colleagues who noted reduced cell density in temporo-parietal cortices and cerebella of dyslexics relative to controls (Rae, Lee, Dixon, Blamire, Thompson, Styles, Talcott, Richardson & Stein, 1998).

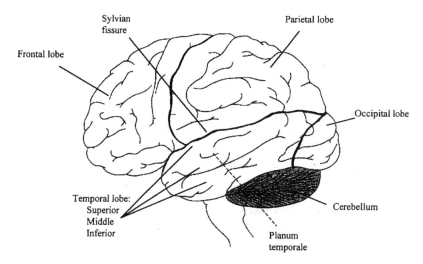

Figure 1. The left hemisphere of the human brain

Abnormal patterns of planum temporale a/symmetry have been linked with the language processing deficits which are characteristic of dyslexia (Rumsey, Nace, Donohue, Wise, Maisog & Andreason, 1997). Dyslexics with rightward asymmetry of the parieto-occipital region, for example, have demonstrated significantly poorer verbal skills than readers without this reversed asymmetry (Hier, LeMay, Rosenberger & Perlo, 1978). As language production is normally the responsibility of specific areas within the left hemisphere, this is not inconsistent with the hypothesis that left hemisphere impairment is associated with poor language. Developmental dyslexics with reversed asymmetry have also been found to show significant discrepancies between their verbal abilities and their non-verbal abilities (Rosenberger & Hier, 1980). Semrud-Clikeman et al have reported a link between various linguistic processing deficits (poor verbal comprehension, decoding and naming skills) and reversed or symmetrical plana, and suggest that the planum temporale may be a "general language processing centre" (Semrud-Clikeman, Hynd, Novey & Eliopulos, 1991, p. 238).

The dyslexics' problems may be the result of under-development of the left hemisphere. In these readers, for example, the left cerebral hemisphere is poorly developed and provides an inadequate substrate for development of competence in verbal skills (Bishop, 1990). The alternative possibility is that rather than representing under-development of the left hemisphere, physiological symmetries in dyslexic brains may be the result of an over-development of the right hemisphere (Kaufman & Galaburda, 1989). This symmetry/reversed asymmetry may be due to the unexpected failure of neuronal attrition in the right hemisphere, possibly as a result of the dyslexics' continued reliance on right hemisphere neurons to support the left hemisphere's impaired language processing functions (Hermann & Zeevi, 1991). Either of these possibilities would indicate that the development of functional lateralisation is necessary for the acquisition of reading and that the reading impairments in the majority of developmental dyslexics may be associated with the temporo-parietal cortices of the brain (Larsen, Hoien, Lundberg & Odegaard, 1990).

The mapping of morphological differences between dyslexic and non-dyslexic brains, particularly in regions which mediate aspects of language production and comprehension, is important for suggesting possible physiological loci for the cognitive impairments experienced by dyslexic readers. These structural measures alone are not sufficient, however, to provide a clear understanding of the precise role of physiological factors in linguistic processing. It is also necessary to demonstrate differences between dyslexic and non-dyslexic readers in the functioning of these brain regions during cognitive processing. The development of brain imaging techniques has provided the means with which we are able to investigate these cognitive processes at work in competent reading and at fault in dyslexia. In this way, neuroimaging provides an opportunity to extend our knowledge of dyslexia as gleaned from behavioural measures alone.

Developmental dyslexia and neuroimaging

Functional activation of the brain may be studied using a number of techniques including Electroencephalography (EEG), Event-Related Potentials (ERPs), Magnetoencephalography (MEG), Positron Emission Tomography (PET) and functional Magnetic Resonance Imaging (fMRI).

While these techniques index different mechanisms of brain functioning, and each has been used to investigate sensory and cognitive processes involved in developmental dyslexia, care must be taken in the selection of such neuroimaging techniques when studying language processing. Each technique has disadvantages as well as advantages. For example, the precise relationship between the measures of brain activation and brain function is not always clearly understood; the temporal resolution of the techniques (the length of time required to detect brain responses) varies greatly, and the degree of invasiveness of each technique makes some unsuitable, or even prohibited, with certain groups of individuals, such as children or women (see below).

Electroencephalography (EEG)

EEG provides a measure of the brain's electrical activity, recorded via electrodes placed normally on the scalp. The electrical activity of millions of post-synaptic dendrites of brain cells is amplified many times to produce the EEG signal which comprises four frequencies: delta, theta, alpha and beta. The alpha frequency predominates during rest and is replaced by other frequencies during the perception, or active processing, of a stimulus. The delay between signal production and detection is in the region of 1-10 milliseconds.

Researchers employing EEG have variously reported that – relative to controls – dyslexics display either attenuated or increased EEG activity depending on the testing condition, the EEG waveband and brain region being studied. During rest, for example, lower levels of alpha activity have been reported in the temporal and parieto-occipital brain regions of adult dyslexics than in controls with eyes closed (Ahn, Prichep, John, Baird, Trepetin & Kaye, 1980; Byring, 1986). No differences in any waveband are reported between dyslexic children and age-matched controls during rest with eyes open (Ortiz, Exposito, Miguel, Martin-Loeches & Rubia, 1992; Rippon & Brunswick, 1998; Rippon & Brunswick, 2000).

Further evidence of task-related EEG abnormalities has been found in the brains of developmental dyslexics during the performance of reading-related tasks. Landwehrmeyer, Gerling and Wallesch (1990), for example, observed that dyslexic participants (with moderate severity "dyslexia pure") showed reduced activity (cortical negativity) in the left hemisphere during reading, during visual (orthographic) error detection and during auditory-visual antonym selection. This is interpreted as reflecting a generalised left hemisphere cortical deficit in these dyslexics.

Dyslexia has also been associated with increased alpha activity in frontal regions during phonological processing (Rippon & Brunswick, 1998); with left frontal, mid-temporal and posterior fronto-central alpha increases during speech perception, reading and the processing of nonsense syllables (Duffy, Denckla, Bartels & Sandini, 1980); and with alpha increases in temporo-parietal regions during auditory phonemic discrimination (Ortiz et al, 1992). As task-related alpha suppression is associated with attention (Ray & Cole, 1985), these findings may indicate reduced "cortical readiness" in the dyslexics during language processing.

More recently, Rippon and Brunswick (2000) observed significant increases in frontal theta activity in dyslexic children during phonological processing but not during visual processing, while control readers showed a task-related decrease in theta amplitude. Evidence suggests that theta decreases with practice and with reduced attentional requirements associated with improvements in cognitive skill. Dyslexics also showed a marked parieto-occipital (right > left) asymmetry in beta amplitude – which indexes cognitive activity – in both tasks (visual and phonological); the controls again showed a consistent pattern of amplitude reduction. While this asymmetry in the dyslexics (also reported by Ortiz et al, 1992) seems to reflect the application of an appropriate strategy for the visual processing task in which they were successful, it suggests the application of an inappropriate strategy for the phonological processing task in which they were unsuccessful.

These findings offer evidence of a physiological basis for the behavioural deficits in developmental dyslexia although the precise relationship between EEG activity and brain function is unclear. It is possible that only the most severe disorganisation may be detected in the EEG under simple testing/rest conditions while more subtle changes in functional localisation between dyslexic and normal readers may only be apparent in the EEG signal during cognitive processing.

Event-Related Potentials (ERPs)

The ERP represents an averaged segment of EEG activity from which the background noise has been diminished through repeated stimulus presentation. The brain's response to a single stimulus would be imperceptible within the EEG, while the averaged response across many presentations is clear. Major ERPs typically recorded in language studies are the N100 (a negative peak occurring approximately 100 milliseconds post-stimulus onset), the N200 and P200 (negative and positive peaks occurring at 200 msecs), and the P300 (a positive peak at 300 msecs) (see Figure 2); the N400 (a negative peak at 400 msecs) is also receiving increasing attention.

Early ERP studies of dyslexia relied upon very simple paradigms to investigate sensory/attentional processes (indexed by the N100, N200 and P200). Researchers reported smaller amplitude ERPs recorded from the left parietal region of dyslexic readers than of controls in response to either passively-viewed flashes of light (N180: Preston, Guthrie & Childs, 1974; N200: Conners, 1971) or visually-presented words (N180: Preston et al, 1974; N200: Symann-Louett, Gascon, Matsumiya & Lombroso, 1977). Others found smaller differences in relative P200 amplitude to words and passively-viewed light flashes in left parietal regions of poor readers than of controls (Preston, Guthrie, Kirsch, Gertman & Childs, 1977).

More recent studies have used rather more relevant language processing tasks. Brunswick and Rippon (1994), for example, employed a dichotic listening task with 7-11 year old dyslexics and age-matched controls. Although these two groups did not differ in terms of behavioural performance on the task, the control readers produced significantly greater N100 amplitudes in the left temporal region than the dyslexics; the dyslexics displayed approximately symmetrical activity bilaterally. Similarly, Shucard, Cummins & McGee (1984), reported reversed ERP (N200, P200) asymmetries recorded from the temporo-parietal region in dyslexics

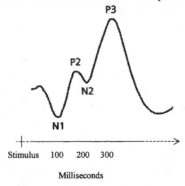

Figure 2. The major components of the ERP waveform

during language tasks, while Chayo-Dichy and Ostrosky-Sollis (1990) observed no inter-hemispheric differences in ERP activation during the processing of verbal and non-verbal stimuli. This symmetry/reversed asymmetry appears to be the result of lesser involvement of the dyslexics' left hemisphere rather than greater involvement of the right.

In addition to differences in the early waveforms, dyslexic and control readers are distinguishable in terms of later ERP waveforms (P300 and N400) which index cognitive processes. For example, smaller amplitude/longer latency P300s have been observed in dyslexic children than in controls (Holcomb, Ackerman & Dykman, 1986; Taylor & Keenan, 1990), and also in dyslexic men with a history of ADHD (Duncan, Rumsey, Wilkniss, Denckla, Hamburger & Odou-Potkin, 1994). In this latter study, no differences in P300 amplitude were found between dyslexics without ADHD and control readers, although differences were found in auditory P300 scalp distribution of dyslexics (with and without ADHD) and controls. Relative to the controls, the dyslexics showed a more asymmetric (right > left) P300 distribution at the frontal sites, while controls showed a more asymmetric (right > left) distribution at the parietal sites. Differences in P300 amplitude/latency have been interpreted as reflecting inefficient cognitive processing by the dyslexics and an ineffective allocation of attentional resources.

The N400 is a measure of semantic processing that has shown numerous, but seemingly inconsistent, differences between dyslexics and controls. Some researchers have observed an attenuated N400 in dyslexics (Stelmack & Miles, 1990; Johannes, Mangun, Kussmaul & Münte, 1995 – although this effect was observed in response to high frequency words only), while others have reported an enhanced N400 in dyslexic children (Neville, Coffey, Holcomb & Tallal, 1993). Taken together, these data may reflect the dyslexics' subtle difficulties with semantic memory and integration.

Although EEG and ERP measures are sensitive to temporal changes in mental activity, the techniques are hampered by poor spatial resolution (it is difficult to localise specific sources of brain activation with any great accuracy). Most of the activation recorded at the scalp is presumed to have originated from the neocortex in the region of the recording electrode, although signals originating at more distal cortical sites might often make a significant contribution to the activity observed at a given scalp recording site; this makes accurate functional localisation very difficult. These factors make the meaningful interpretation of EEG data difficult with respect to underlying functional neuro-anatomy beyond the level of the cortical lobes. The development of magnetoencephalography has addressed this problem.

Magnetoencephalography (MEG)

Magnetoencephalography is a functional imaging technique which allows the measurement of perceptual and cognitive functions relatively accurately in time and space. It does this by providing a sophisticated three-dimensional measure of the magnetic fields produced by neuronal activation. Although the ability to infer the 3-D distribution of electrical sources in the brain from scalp-recorded MEG has fundamental physical limits (the spatial resolution of this technique is typically 5mm), the temporal resolution of MEG is in the same millisecond range as EEG. This temporal resolution makes MEG a useful technique for measuring rapid changes in cortical activity associated with language processing.

One study of dyslexia using MEG found that while control readers show strong MEG activation of the left inferior temporo-occipital region within 200 milliseconds of silently reading real words and pseudowords, dyslexics fail to activate this region within this time window (Salmelin, Service, Kiesilä, Uutela & Salonen, 1996). Some of the dyslexics displayed a late response in the inferior temporo-occipital region (between 400-700 milliseconds post stimulus onset), albeit to a significantly lesser extent than the controls. Other dyslexics failed to show any such activation within the left temporal lobe. Conversely, the dyslexics showed activation in the left inferior frontal lobe (approximately corresponding to Broca's area) while the controls did not. The majority of the control readers produced greater activation in response to pseudowords than words (in the left middle temporal lobe and central sulcus), as did half of the dyslexics (in the temporo-parieto-occipital region). This pattern suggests that in dyslexics the modality-independent naming system, of which the temporal gyrus forms a part (see Price & Friston, 1997), is failing to activate, or at least activating significantly more slowly, than in the control readers.

A follow-up study by the same group investigated dyslexics' processing of words within sentences (Helenius, Salmelin, Service & Connolly, 1999). This study employed a semantic evaluation paradigm in which the last word of each sentence was either expected ("The piano was out of tune") or semantically anomalous ("The pizza was too hot to sing"). Contrary to the earlier results, this task elicited anatomically similar responses from good and dyslexic readers. In the majority of respondents from both groups a region of the left superior temporal cortex was activated; some respondents (controls and dyslexics) also produced activation within the left temporo-parietal and temporo-occipital regions and in inferior parietal cortex. The two groups differed significantly, however, in the time-course of their activations: the dyslexics' activations were delayed by approximately 100 milliseconds relative to those of the controls. The authors suggest from these findings that although the sentences provided contextual support for word identification, thus facilitating reading for the dyslexics and making the process more cortically-similar to that of the controls, the responses of the dyslexics were not normal. Their delayed activations may reflect a less precise synchronisation of neural populations with the result that more temporally extended activations lead to increasing shifts in latency in a system that depends on serial stages.

One possible confound in these studies, however, was that the design demanded silent reading with no overt response (except to occasional target words in the first study), thus there is no measure of accuracy. Although the behavioural tasks were simple, the findings may be confounded by performance differences in the dyslexics' and controls' reading of the stimuli, particularly the non-words. It may be that the dyslexics' failure to activate the temporal language areas within the given time window in the first study reflects a failure to decode the stimuli with sufficient accuracy to activate the semantic and naming areas of the brain. The provision of a context in the second study may have served to prime the recognition of the words, helping to compensate for some of the problems of early word recognition.

Whilst MEG represents a powerful tool for investigating the neural correlates of developmental dyslexia, the installation and running of equipment necessary for recording MEG is so expensive and unwieldy that few MEG centres exist at present. Even within these centres few studies have investigated dyslexia.

Positron Emission Tomography (PET)

Positron Emission Tomography is used to measure brain activation either by monitoring regional cerebral blood flow following the intravenous administration of radioactive water ($H_2^{15}O$) or by measuring metabolism of radioactive glucose. Neuronal activity in the brain increases both blood flow to active regions and metabolic activity in these regions. The radioactive elements within the water or glucose emit positrons which are detected in higher concentrations at neuronally-active regions of the brain than at inactive regions. While PET images have fairly good anatomical resolution (brain regions can be identified to within 2-6 mm), the technique is hampered by its poor temporal resolution: it takes 30-90 seconds to obtain a final image which represents an average response across many stimulus presentations. This poor temporal resolution makes PET unable to detect changes in the brain which may only last a fraction of a second. An additional problem is the highly invasive nature of the technique. The introduction of a radioactive tracer, usually intravenously, precludes the use of the technique with children (non-clinical individuals younger than 18 cannot be tested), with non-clinical pre-menopausal women, or with anyone who is needle-phobic.

Studies using PET suggest that developmental dyslexia may be the result of disconnection within the language regions of the brain. This hypothesis was first proposed by Paulesu and colleagues, based on the findings of a study in which they recorded brain activation in dyslexic and control readers during the performance of a visual rhyme judgement task and a short-term memory task (Paulesu, Frith, Snowling, Gallagher, Morton, Frackowiak & Frith, 1996). Although no behavioural differences emerged, the brain regions activated by the groups differed. During each task the control readers produced activation in Broca's area, Wernicke's area and the insula while the dyslexics showed more circumscribed activations in Broca's area and Wernicke's area but none in the insula. Whereas the dyslexics only engaged regions strictly necessary for

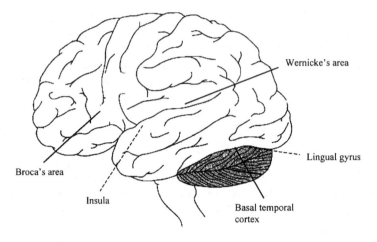

Figure 3. Language areas of the brain

performing the tasks, the competent readers engaged the entire language system in an automatic synchronised manner. This automaticity within the language system, which facilitates fluent mapping between the sight of a written word and the corresponding articulatory sequence of the spoken word, is thought to be mediated via the insula.

Further evidence of disconnection in dyslexic brains has been reported by Horwitz, Rumsey & Donohue (1998). They observed significant activation in the left angular gyrus and extrastriate visual areas in occipital and temporal cortex, including superior occipital/basal temporal gyri, parts of the lingual and fusiform gyri, part of Wernicke's area and Broca's area (see Figure 3), in control readers during the reading of pseudowords (e.g. "phalbap" and "chirl"). During the reading of low frequency irregular words (e.g. "choir" and "pharaoh") the control readers showed significant activation in the angular gyrus and the left lingual and fusiform gyri. The dyslexics, by contrast, failed to show activation in the angular gyrus and the inferior frontal region, the fusiform or lingual gyri, irrespective of the type of task. Thus, it would appear that the angular gyrus may be functionally disconnected from the left hemisphere language system in developmental dyslexics.

Rumsey et al (1997) had previously reported that relative to controls, dyslexics demonstrated reduced activation of mid to posterior temporo-parietal cortex, in particular the left superior and middle temporal gyri, left fusiform and right perirolandic region. Unfortunately, the behavioural performance of the two groups in this study was not matched and the dyslexics performed less accurately than the controls. It is possible that the activation differences may reflect the dyslexics' greater difficulty in performing the task. Furthermore, as the presentation of stimuli was self-paced, the dyslexics performed more slowly than the controls, seeing fewer stimuli; thus it is possible that the greater temporal lobe activations of the controls may reflect greater auditory stimulation received by these readers as they heard their own voices reading more of the words.

These issues were addressed by Brunswick and colleagues in a series of PET studies involving explicit and implicit reading of simple words and pseudowords (Brunswick, McCrory, Price, Frith & Frith, 1999) and word/pseudoword repetition (McCrory, Frith, Brunswick & Price, 2000). The selection of simple words and pseudowords ensured no behavioural differences between dyslexics and controls.

Across all three studies, regions of common activation were found in the two groups: in bilateral frontal, superior temporal and cerebellar/fusiform regions, left thalamus and right inferior parietal cortex, representing the classical language areas. Significant task-specific between-group differences were also observed.

Of particular interest in the explicit reading task (and in support of Salmelin et al's (1996) MEG finding) was reduced activation in the left basal temporal gyrus, the cerebellum and the medial lingual/occipital gyrus in dyslexics relative to controls, in conjunction with greater activation in Broca's area. It is hypothesised that the dyslexics' greater activation of this region – which is involved in articulatory coding (Démonet, Chollet, Ramsay, Cardebat, Nespoulous, Wise, Rascol & Frackowiak, 1992) – may reflect their greater effort in reading the stimuli. Alternatively, it is possible that this activity may be a by-product of weak connectivity between the anterior and posterior components of the language system (as reported by Paulesu et al, 1996). Thus, these findings support neuropsychological evidence that both dyslexics and non-dyslexics rely on a common distributed language system for word recognition but they activate anterior and posterior parts of this system differently, even when reading successfully.

In the implicit reading task, when dyslexics and controls made non-linguistic judgements about the physical form of word, pseudoword and false font stimuli, the dyslexics again demonstrated reduced levels of activation in inferior parietal cortex, in the left frontal operculum surrounding the most anterior part of the insula, and in middle temporal, inferior temporal and posterior basal temporal cortices.

One region was consistently under-activated in dyslexics relative to controls whether reading was explicit or implicit: the left middle/basal temporal region. This reduced activation in a region associated with phonological processing relates to the comprehensive phonological processing impairments displayed by dyslexics, and in particular to a selective impairment in lexical phonological retrieval. Differences in activity in this posterior basal temporal region are particularly interesting because it is activated in concert with the left frontal operculum/insula as part of the naming system which is critical either in the specification or retrieval of phonological information (Price & Friston, 1997). This component of the language system is likely to be the source of a primary impairment in developmental dyslexia. Evidence from tasks requiring phonological retrieval (e.g. Spoonerism tasks, rapid naming, phoneme fluency) support this suggestion that dyslexia involves a core deficit in accessing phonological codes.

In McCrory et al's (2000) repetition task, irrespective of word type, dyslexics showed less activation than controls in the right superior temporal cortex (notably, BA22), the right post-central gyrus and the left cerebellum. The previous two studies showed that dyslexics activate these regions normally when reading, suggesting that this observed neural manifestation of dyslexia is task-specific, i.e. functional and not structural. Other studies with normal readers have associated attending to the phonetic structure of speech with a decrease in right hemisphere activity (Zatorre, Meyer, Gjedde and Evans, 1996); therefore, it is suggested that in this dyslexic sample, lower right hemisphere activation may indicate less processing of non-phonetic aspects of speech, allowing greater salience to be accorded to phonological aspects of attended speech.

More recently, Paulesu, Démonet, Fazio, McCrory, Chanoine, Brunswick, Cappa, Cossu, Habib, Frith and Frith (2001) have used PET to demonstrate a "universal neurocognitive basis for dyslexia". These researchers reported reduced left hemisphere activity – particularly in the middle temporal gyrus, the inferior and superior temporal gyri and the middle occipital gyrus – in the brains of English, Italian and French dyslexics during reading.

Taken together these studies indicate that dyslexics share a common deficit in phonological processing; how this manifests in functional imaging investigations is context-specific and depends on the demands of the experimental task.

Functional Magnetic Resonance Imaging (fMRI)

Functional Magnetic Resonance Imaging is a technique which measures changes in oxygen levels in the blood vessels of the brain. Changing concentrations of oxygen in the haemoglobin around sites of brain activation alter the magnetic properties of the blood; these are detected by the fMRI scanner. This technique appears to offer the best combination of temporal resolution (changes in blood flow are detected within 1 second) and spatial resolution (brain regions can be identified to within 1-3 mm) currently available. However, attempts to measure functional activation within the language regions using fMRI are hampered by technical difficulties: the fMRI scanner is very noisy, so auditory language processing tasks can be difficult to run; individuals who are claustrophobic may experience severe discomfort whilst lying inside the scanner, and differences in the density of tissue (cerebral cortex, cerebro-spinal fluid, sinusoidal cavities and skull) around the inferior temporal regions produce difficulties in obtaining clear images.

fMRI has been used, however, to provide evidence in support of the phonological hypothesis of dyslexia. Shaywitz and colleagues, for example, presented dyslexic and control readers with a battery of reading tasks, the successful completion of which relied increasingly upon phonological processing (Shaywitz, Shaywitz, Pugh, Fulbright, Constable, Mencl, Shankweiler, Liberman, Skudlarski, Fletcher, Katz, Marchione, Lacadie, Gatenby & Gore, 1998). In addition to performing the behavioural tasks significantly more poorly than the controls, the dyslexics showed a significantly different pattern of brain activation, most notably in Wernicke's area, the angular gyrus and the striate cortex, in which the dyslexics showed relative underactivation, and in the inferior frontal gyrus, in which they showed overactivation. Further differences were found in left and right hemisphere activation in the angular gyrus and basal temporal cortex (BA37): in each case, activations in the controls were greater in the left hemisphere than in the right; in the dyslexics, activations were greater in the right hemisphere than in the left. These findings support evidence presented above (Salmelin et al, 1996; Brunswick et al, 1999), in relating anomalous functional activation in anterior and posterior language areas of dyslexics' brains to the phonological difficulties which "characterise" dyslexia (see also Georgiewa, Rzanny, Hopf, Knab, Glauche, Kaiser & Blanz, 1999).

As well as supporting the phonological hypothesis of dyslexia, fMRI studies of developmental dyslexia have provided evidence of impairments in low-level visual processing. One focus of these studies has been the functioning of the magnocellular (M) layers of the lateral geniculate nucleus (LGN) and their projections onto area V5 of the visual cortex (see Figure 4); this region is specialised for the processing of visual motion. Abnormalities in the structure or functioning of the M pathways would impair the efficiency of visual motion processing which would be reflected in anomalous activation of V5 (Eden, VanMeter, Rumsey, Maisog, Woods & Zeffiro, 1996).

Evidence from various sources has pointed to the existence of such abnormalities and to a selective processing deficit within the M systems of dyslexics. Anatomical post-mortem evidence, for example, has indicated the presence of anomalously small cells within the M layers of the LGN in dyslexic brains (Livingstone, Rosen, Drislane & Galaburda, 1991). Psychophysical evidence has revealed impaired

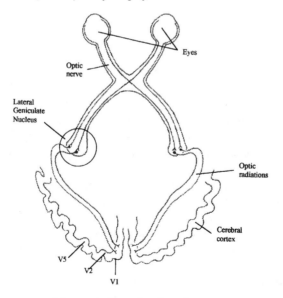

Figure 4. The visual pathway

performance of dyslexics on motion discrimination tasks (Felmingham & Jakobson, 1995), while PET data have provided evidence of a lack of functional connectivity within the dyslexic brain between the left angular gyrus and the temporo-occipital cortex including V5 (Horwitz et al, 1998). Such data have been interpreted within the framework of the M theory of dyslexia as reflecting general impairments in temporal processing in the visual and auditory modalities as well as, possibly, the vestibular and motor systems (Stein & Walsh, 1997).

Eden et al's seminal investigation of the functioning of V5 in dyslexics, using fMRI, found that while coherently-moving low contrast random dots failed to activate V5 in dyslexics, in control readers this brain region was activated bilaterally. No differences in activation were observed between the two groups in V1 (primary visual cortex) or V2 in response to stationary, high-contrast, patterns; regions V1 and V2 receive information about direction of movement from the M layers of the LGN and transfer this information to region V5. These findings suggest a neurophysiological basis for the subtle visuo-perceptual processing deficits previously reported in dyslexics. Disruption of the mechanism underlying the normal functioning of V5 has been implicated in the disturbance to motion detection and in the more general temporal processing impairments characteristic of dyslexia (Stein & Walsh, 1997).

In another series of studies, Demb and colleagues observed activation in V5 in the brains of dyslexics as well as controls in response to moving dots although the control readers produced higher levels of activation than the dyslexics in regions V5 and V1 (Demb, Boynton & Heeger, 1998). No significant group differences were observed in response to moving stimuli of high mean luminance. Given that the lower the luminance of a visual stimulus the greater the relative responsiveness of the M system, this offers support to the M pathway deficit hypothesis of dyslexia.

SUMMARY

The results from the neuroimaging studies of developmental dyslexia provide strong evidence of abnormalities (structural and functional), particularly within the left hemisphere and particularly within the temporal and temporo-parietal regions. All of the techniques have indicated reduced activity in the "traditional language areas" of the left hemisphere of dyslexics relative to controls; all have indicated reduced activity in the posterior basal temporal/temporo-parietal cortex of dyslexics; and all have indicated increased activity in left hemisphere frontal areas (e.g. Broca's area) in dyslexic brains.

These abnormalities emerge even when the two groups of readers are equated in terms of behavioural performance. If participants vary in their ability to perform a task, investigation of behavioural performance and brain activation yields information as to the use of possible compensatory strategies and the involvement of different brain regions to support these strategies. Future longitudinal brain imaging studies of dyslexics, from the time in childhood when their dyslexia is identified to when they become highly compensated adult dyslexic readers, would provide valuable information about the development and adoption of these compensatory strategies. Whatever the relationship between functional imaging measures of the brain and dyslexia, these measures represent objective clinical tools for investigating the development of dyslexia. With the exception of PET, all techniques may be used with children considered to be at risk of developing reading problems, even prior to the emergence of the symptomatic difficulties of developmental dyslexia, and they may be used to track the development of impairments.

To be truly effective in mapping local neuronal activity, an imaging technique needs both millimeter precision in localising regions of activated tissue and sub-second temporal precision for characterising changes in patterns of activation over time. As discussed above, however, current brain imaging techniques differ not only in what they measure (which aspect of neuronal activity is chosen as an index of functional activity), but also in the degree of accuracy with which they measure it (their anatomical and temporal resolution). Where apparently inconsistent results have been reported by research teams employing different techniques, these differences may be the direct result of inherent differences in the techniques in terms of what they measure. For example, Eden et al's reporting of abnormalities in the M pathway associated with dyslexia has been questioned by researchers using other neuroimaging techniques, such as MEG (Vanni, Uusitalo, Kiesilä & Han, 1997) or ERPs (Johannes, Kussmaul, Münte & Mangun, 1996). However, whereas Eden's fMRI detects changes in blood flow related to neuronal activity, providing an index of firing rate, Vanni et al's MEG records changes in neural synchrony, while Johannes et al's ERPs are averaged electrical voltage potentials recorded from the neocortex. Rather than telling different stories, these different data sets may in fact be pointing to different aspects of the same story and should be explored further.

In view of the pros and cons of each functional imaging technique, future attempts at localising regions of neural activation in dyslexics and normal readers should involve the possibility of combining techniques (see Mazziotta & Toga, 1996). The benefit of such integration is the optimal measuring of both temporal and spatial dynamics of sensory and cognitive processing. Future research will reveal the extent to which this integration may succeed in expanding our knowledge of the neural bases of normal language functioning and of developmental dyslexia.

REFERENCES

Ahn, H., Prichep, L., John, E. R., Baird, H., Trepetin, M. & Kaye, H. (1980). Developmental equations reflect brain dysfunctions. *Science*, 210, 1259-1262.

Beaton, A. A. (1997). The relation of planum temporale asymmetry and morphology of the corpus callosum to handedness, gender and dyslexia: a review of the evidence. *Brain and Language*, 60, 2, 255-322.

290   *Nicky Brunswick*

Beaumont, J. G. (1982). *Introduction to Neuropsychology*. Oxford: Blackwell Scientific Publications.

Bishop, D. V. M. (1990). *Handedness and Developmental Disorder*. Hove, UK: Lawrence Erlbaum Associates.

Broca, P.P. (1861) Remarques sur le siege de Ia faculté du langage articule, suivies d'une observation d'aphemie (New observation of aphemia produced by a lesion of the posterior half of the second and third frontal convolutions). *Bulletin de Ia Société Anatomique*, 36, 330- 357.

Brown, G. D. A., Hulme, C., Hyland, P. D. & Mitchell, I. J. (1994) Cell suicide in the developing nervous system: A functional neural network model. *Cognitive Brain Research*, 2, 1, 71-75.

Brunswick, N. & Rippon, G. (1994). Auditory event-related potentials, dichotic listening performance and handedness as indices of lateralisation in dyslexic and normal readers. *International Journal of Psychophysiology*, 18, 3, 265-275.

Brunswick, N., McCrory, E., Price, C. J., Frith, C.D. & Frith, U. (1999). Explicit and implicit processing of words and pseudowords by adult developmental dyslexics: a search for Wernicke's Wortschatz? *Brain*, 122, 1901-1917.

Byring, R. F. (1986). EEG correlation topography in poor spellers. *Electroencephalography and Clinical Neurophysiology*, 63, 1, 1-9.

Chayo-Dichy, R. & Ostrosky-Sollis, F. (1990). Neuroelectric correlates of dyslexia. *Revista Mexicana de Psicologia*, 7, 109-119.

Conners, C. K. (1971). Cortical visual evoked response in children with learning disorders. *Psychophysiology*, 7, 418-428.

Demb, J. B., Boynton, G. M. & Heeger, D. J. (1998). Functional magnetic resonance imaging of early visual pathways in dyslexia. *Journal of Neuroscience*, 18, 6939-6951.

Démonet, J.-F., Chollet, F., Ramsay, S., Cardebat, D., Nespoulous, J.-L., Wise, R., Rascol, A. & Frackowiak, R.S.J. (1992). The anatomy of phonological and semantic processing in normal subjects. *Brain*, 115, 1753-1768.

Duffy, F. H., Denckla, M. B., Bartels, P. H. & Sandini, G. (1980). Dyslexia: regional differences in brain electrical activity by topographic mapping. *Annals of Neurology*, 7, 412-420.

Duncan, C. C., Rumsey, J. M., Wilkniss, S. M., Denckla, M., Hamburger, S. D. & Odou-Potkin, M. (1994) Developmental dyslexia and attention dysfunction in adults: brain potential indices of information processing. *Psychophysiology*, 31, 386-401.

Eden, G. F., VanMeter, J. W., Rumsey, J. M., Maisog, J. M., Woods, R. P. & Zeffiro, T. A. (1996) Abnormal processing of visual motion in dyslexia revealed by functional brain imaging. *Nature*, 382, 66-69.

Felmingham, K. L. & Jakobson, L. 5. (1995). Visual and visuomotor performance in dyslexic children. *Experimental Brain Research*, 106, 467-474.

Galaburda, A. M., Corsiglia, J., Rosen, G. D. & Sherman, G. F. (1987). Planum temporale asymmetry: Reappraisal since Geschwind and Levitsky. *Neuropsychologia*, 25, 853-868.

Galaburda, A. M., Menard, M. T. & Rosen, G. D. (1994). Evidence for aberrant anatomy in developmental dyslexia. *Proceedings of the National Academy of Sciences of the United States of America*, 91, 8010-8013.

Georgiewa, P., Rzanny, R., Hopf, J.-M., Knab, R., Glauche, V., Kaiser, W.-A., & Blanz, B. (1999) fMRI during word processing in dyslexic and normal children. *NeuroReport*, 10, 3459-3465.

Helenius, P., Salmelin, R., Service, E. & Connolly, J. (1999). Semantic cortical activation in dyslexic readers. *Journal of Cognitive Neuroscience*, 11, 535-550.

Hermann, H. T. & Zeevi, Y. Y. (1991). Interhemispheric interactions and dyslexia. In J. F. Stein (Ed.), *Vision and visual dyslexia*, 271-279. London: Macmillan.

Hier, D. B., LeMay, M., Rosenberger, P. B. & Perlo, V. P. (1978). Developmental dyslexia. Evidence for a subgroup with a reversal of cerebral asymmetry. *Archives of Neurology*, 35, 90-92.

Holcomb, P. J., Ackerman, P. T. & Dykman, R. A. (1986) Auditory event-related potentials in attention and reading disabled boys. *International Journal of Psychophysiology*, 3, 263-273.

Horwitz, B., Rumsey, J. M. & Donohue, B. C. (1998) Functional connectivity of the angular gyrus in normal reading and dyslexia. *Proceedings of the National Academy of Sciences of the United States of America*, 95, 15, 8939-8944.

Hynd, G. W. & Semrud-Clikeman, M. (1989). Dyslexia and neurodevelopmental pathology: relationships to cognition, intelligence and reading skill acquisition. *Journal of Learning Disabilities*, 22, 4, 204-2 16.

Johannes, S., Kussmaul, C. L., Münte, T. F. & Mangun, G. R. (1996). Developmental dyslexia: passive visual stimulation provides no evidence for a magnocellular processing defect. *Neuropsychologia*, 34, 11, 1123-1127.

Johannes, S., Mangun, G. R., Kussmaul, C. L. & Münte, T. F. (1995) Brain potential in developmental dyslexia: differential effects of word frequency in human subjects. *Neuroscience Letters*, 195, 183-186.

Kaufmann, W. E. & Galaburda, A. M. (1989). Cerebrocortical microdysgenesis in neurologically normal subjects – a histopathologic study. *Neurology*, 39, 238-244.

Landwehrmeyer, B., Gerling, J., Wallesch, C. S. (1990). Patterns of task-related slow brain potentials in dyslexia. *Archives of Neurology*, 47, 791-797.

Larsen, J., Hoien, T., Lundberg, I. & Odegaard, H. (1990). MRI evaluation of the size and symmetry of the planum temporale in adolescents with developmental dyslexia. *Brain and Language*, 39, 289- 301.

Livingstone, M. S., Rosen, G. D., Drislane, F. W. & Galaburda, A. M. (1991). Physiological and anatomical evidence for a magnocellular deficit in developmental dyslexia. *Proceedings of the National Academy of Sciences of the United States of America*, 88, 18, 7943-7947.

Mazziotta, J. C. & Toga, A. W. (1996). Speculations about the future. In A. W. Toga & J. C. Mazziotta (Eds), *Brain Mapping: The Methods*, 445-457. London: Academic Press.

McCrory, E., Frith, U., Brunswick, N. & Price, C. (2000) Abnormal functional activation during a simple word repetition task: a PET study of adult dyslexics. *Journal of Cognitive Neuroscience*, 12, 5, 753-762

Morgan, A. E. & Hynd, G. W. (1998). Dyslexia, neurolinguistic ability, and anatomical variation of the planum temporale. *Neuropsychology Review*. 8, 2, 79-93.

Neville, H. J., Coffey, S. A., Holcomb, P. J. & Tallal, P. (1993) The neurobiology of sensory and language processing in language-impaired children. *Journal of Cognitive Neuroscience*, 5, 235-253.

Ortiz, T., Exposito, F. J., Miguel, F., Martin-Loeches, M. & Rubia, F. J. (1992). Brain mapping in dysphonemic dyslexia: in resting and phonemic discrimination conditions. *Brain and Language*, 42, 3, 270-285.

Orton, S. T. (1925). Word blindness in school children. *Archives of Neurology and Psychiatry*, 14, 581-615.

Paulesu, E., Démonet, J.-F., Fazio, F., McCrory, E., Chanoine, V., Brunswick, N., Cappa, S. F., Cossu, G., Habib, M., Frith, C. D. and Frith, U. (2001) Dyslexia: Cultural diversity and biological unity. *Science*, 291, 5511, 2165-2167.

Paulesu, E., Frith, U., Snowling, M., Gallagher, A., Morton, J., Frackowiak, R. S. J. & Frith, C. D. (1996). Is developmental dyslexia a disconnection syndrome? Evidence from PET scanning. *Brain*, 119, 143-157.

Preston, M. S., Guthrie, J. T. & Childs, B. (1974). Visual evoked responses in normal and disabled readers. *Psychophysiology*, 11, 452-457.

Preston, M. S., Guthrie, J. T., Kirsch, I., Gertman, D. & Childs, B. (1977). VERs in normal and disabled adult readers. *Psychophysiology*, 14, 8-14.

Price, C. J. (1997). Functional anatomy of reading. In R. S. J. Frackowiak, K. J. Friston, C. D. Frith, R. Dolan, & J. C. Mazziotta (Eds.), *Human Brain Function*, 301-328. London: Academic Press.

Price, C. J. & Friston, K. J. (1997). Cognitive conjunction: A new approach to brain activation experiments. *Neuroimage*, 5, 4, 261-270.

Rae, C., Lee, M. A., Dixon, R. M., Blamire, A. M., Thompson, C. H., Styles, P., Talcott, J., Richardson, A. J. & Stein, J. F. (1998). Metabolic abnormalities in developmental dyslexia detected by H-1 magnetic resonance spectroscopy. *Lancet*. 351, 1849-1852.

Ray, W. J. & Cole, H. (1985). EEG alpha activity reflects attentional demands and beta activity reflects emotional and cognitive processes. *Science*, 228, 750-752.

Rippon, G. & Brunswick, N. (1998). EEG correlates of phonological processing in dyslexic children. *Journal of Psychophysiology*, 12, 3, 261-274.

Rippon, G. & Brunswick, N. (2000). Trait and state EEG indices of information processing in developmental dyslexia. *International Journal of Psychophysiology*, 36, 3, 251-265.

Rosenberger, P. B. & Hier, D. B. (1980). Cerebral asymmetry and verbal intellectual deficits. *Annals of Neurology*. 8, 300-304.

Rumsey, J. M., Nace, K., Donohue, B., Wise, D., Maisog, J. M. & Andreason, P. (1997). A positron emission tomographic study of impaired word recognition and phonological processing in dyslexic men. *Archives of Neurology*, 54, 5, 562-573.

Salmelin, R., Service, E., Kiesilä, P., Uutela, K. & Salonen, 0. (1996). Impaired visual word processing in dyslexia revealed with magnetoencephalography. *Annals of Neurology*, 40, 2, 157-162.

Semrud-Clikeman, M., Hynd, G. W., Novey, E. S. & Eliopulos, D. (1991). Dyslexia and brain morphology: relationships between neuroanatomical variation and neurolinguistic tasks. *Learning and Individual Differences*, 3, 225-242.

Shaywitz, B., Shaywitz, S., Pugh, K., R., Fulbright, Constable, T., Mencl, E., Skudlarski, Liberman, A. R., Shankweiler, D., Katz, L., Fletcher, J., Lacadie, C., Marchione, K., Gatenby, C., & Gore, J. (1998) Functional disruption in the organization of the brain for reading in dyslexia. *Proceedings of the National Academy of Sciences of the United States of America*, 95, 2636-2641.

Shucard, D., Cummins, K. & McGee, M. (1984). Event-related brain potentials differentiate normal and disabled readers. *Brain and Language*, 21, 2, 318-334.

Stein, J. & Walsh, V. (1997). To see but not to read; the magnocellular theory of dyslexia. *Trends In Neurosciences*. 20, 4, 147-152.

Stelmack, R.M. & Miles, J. (1990) The effect of picture priming on event-related potentials of normal and disabled readers during a word recognition memory task. *Journal of Clinical and Experimental Neuropsychology*, 12, 887-903.

Symann-Louett, N., Gascon, G. G., Matsumiya, Y. & Lombroso, C. T. (1977). Waveform differences in visual evoked responses between normal and reading disabled children. *Neurology*, 27, 156-159.

Tallal, P. & Katz, W. (1989). Neuropsychological and neuroanatomical studies of developmental language/reading disorders: recent advances. In C. von Euler, I. Lundberg & G. Lennerstrand (Eds), *Brain and Reading*, 183-196. London: MacMillan.

Taylor, M. J. & Keenan, N. K. (1990). Event-related potentials to visual and language stimuli in normal and dyslexic children. *Psychophysiology*, 27, 318-327.

Vanni, S., Uusitalo, M. A., Kiesilä, P. & Hari, R. (1997). Visual motion activates V5 in dyslexics. *NeuroReport*, 8, 1939-1942.

Wernicke, C. (1874). *Der Aphasische Symptomenkomplex* (The aphasia symptom complex). Breslau, Poland: Cohen & Weigert.

Zatorre, R., Meyer, E., Gjedde, A. & Evans, A. (1996) PET studies of phonetic processing of speech: review, replication and re-analysis. *Cerebral Cortex*, 6, 21-30.

SUGGESTIONS FOR FURTHER READING

Beaton, A. A. (1997). The relation of planum temporale asymmetry and morphology of the corpus callosum to handedness, gender and dyslexia: a review of the evidence. *Brain and Language*, 60, 2, 255-322.

Brunswick, N., McCrory, E., Price, C. J., Frith, C.D. & Frith, U. (1999). Explicit and implicit processing of words and pseudowords by adult developmental dyslexics: a search for Wernicke's Wortschatz? *Brain*, 122, 1901-1917.

Habib, M. (2000) The neurological basis of developmental dyslexia – An overview and working hypothesis. Brain, 123, 2373-2399.

Paulesu, E., Frith, U., Snowling, M., Gallagher, A., Morton, J., Frackowiak, R. S. J. & Frith, C. D. (1996). Is developmental dyslexia a disconnection syndrome? Evidence from PET scanning. *Brain*, 119, 143-157.

C4. Epidemiology: Genetic and Social Influences on Reading Ability

JIM STEVENSON

ABSTRACT

The epidemiology of reading disability (RD) has been studied in a number of large scale surveys of the general population. The aim of such research is to identify correlates of RD which may indicate possible significant causal factors. One specific aspect of epidemiology is that which investigates the co-occurrence of RD in families. This approach can identify the extent to which RD is influenced by genetic and various types of environmental influences. The results suggest that RD without associated low ability is more often found in boys than girls. Many of the correlates of RD are also associated with low general ability. One of the specific social correlates of RD is being a later born child in a large family. Genetic differences between children make a substantial contribution to RD. Molecular genetic investigations are starting to identify particular sources of genetic variation that contribute to RD on chromosomes 6 and 15. It is argued that RD represents one of the major areas where complex cognitive skills can be analysed in terms of the genes contributing to functional variation. It will therefore play an important part in furthering our understanding of the relationships between genes and brain structure and function.

INTRODUCTION

Epidemiology is the study of the pattern of the occurrence of a condition within the general population. Its aim is to identify the prevalence of a condition and the significance of social and other factors that may be correlated with variation in prevalence. In the broadest sense it includes the study of genetic influences by examining the pattern with which a condition occurs within a family – genetic epidemiology. This chapter will examine what has been learnt about the social and genetic factors associated with reading disability (RD). This research lies at the heart of the nurture-nurture debate (Plomin, 1994) as it relates to RD. Just to what extent do genetic differences between children or experiential factors at home or at school account for the failure to develop adequate reading skills? These studies can

T. Nunes, P. Bryant (eds.), Handbook of Children's Literacy, 293–311.
© 2004 Kluwer Academic Publishers. Printed in Great Britain.

answer this question at the population level – in general what are the relative contributions to RD from these two sources. The chapter will cover some recent findings on the molecular genetic study of RD. This can start to answer the question at the level of the individual – how likely is that this child carrying these genes will develop RD. At present this risk cannot be determined at the individual level with any accuracy but progress is being made.

In the work to be summarised below the epidemiology of RD will be examined. RD is used in a non-specific sense to represent poor reading and/or poor spelling ability. In addition for some studies the differentiation needs to be made between RD that occurs in the context of general low ability and RD that represents a specific cognitive disability.

Epidemiology provides evidence on prevalence which is needed for planning the provision of services. It is essential to know how many children are affected and where they are found in terms of geographical or social variation. In addition epidemiology may be helpful in identifying appropriate methods for case identification in the population for example via screening procedures either for the condition itself or for a marker of the condition. The issues relating to screening for literacy difficulties have been well discussed by Singleton (1997).

Epidemiology also provides data for development of an understanding of the aetiology of a condition. Here consistent associations between social, developmental or biological features can be used to identify possible causes of RD. Being a non-experimental approach (i.e. based upon the observation of correlations within the population), the demonstration of causality from epidemiological evidence alone can never be certain. Without recourse to experimental manipulation, the findings from epidemiology are open to the problem of a correlated third factor producing the observed relationship between RD and another characteristic. In addition many of the associated factors with RD may be correlated amongst themselves. It can therefore be problematic to identify the effect on RD of any one particular influence.

One of the difficulties with the epidemiology of RD and with the estimation of prevalence rates is that there is a lack of consensus about how RD should be defined. Indeed the evidence is most convincing that RD is simply the extreme on a continuum of underlying relative ability and that there may be no distinct categorical judgement that can be made about whether RD is present or absence – it is a question of degree. This means that putting a cutting point on reading under-achievement, whether this judgement is made in relation to general ability or not, is possibly artificial. It was proposed by Rutter and Yule (1975) that an etiologically distinct group of specific reading retarded children could be identified at the bottom of the range of reading achievement in relation to IQ i.e. a "hump" in the distribution. This view has proved controversial despite subsequent supported evidence from other epidemiological studies (Stevenson, 1998). It is this issue that will be considered first in the critical review of the epidemiological literature. However first some of the terminology in genetic epidemiology needs to be defined.

THEORETICAL BACKGROUND

Genetic epidemiology analyses the pattern of occurrence of RD or the correlations between the reading score of relatives. It attempts to estimate the impact of the genetic and environmental similarities between relatives on their resemblance for reading. This quantitative genetic approach to the analysis of individual differences and development, assumes that there are a number of discrete influences producing resemblance within families and differences between families. As far as genetic influences are concerned the emphasis is placed upon additive genetic factors ie genes that have an independent and additive influence in variation in the phenotype (in this case reading ability). This is a simplification since it ignores interaction between pairs of genes (such as dominance effects) and interactions between different genes (epistasis effects). These non-additive genetic influences can be examined but require more complex designs and larger samples than have been available for RD to date (see Plomin *et al.* 1997 under further reading for a more extended discussion of these assumptions).

As far as environmental influences are concerned, these are divided into those that produce resemblance within families and those that produce differences. The shared environment are non-genetic influences that produce resemblence between brothers and sisters and also contribute to some of the differences seen between families. The non-shared environmental influences are ones that generate differences between brothers and sisters. One of the features of research applying behaviour genetic analysis to child development has been the recognition of the power of non-shared environmental influences on a range of cognitive and behavioural characteristics (again see Plomin *et al.*, 1997 for further details).

A theoretical model is constructed that predicts the degree of resemblence between relatives. For example genetically identical twins (monozygotic or MZ) will have a resemblence reflecting the size of genetic and shared environmental influences on RD. On the other hand the resemblence between non-identical twin pairs (dizygotic or DZ) will reflect again the shared environment but only half the impact of genetic variation (on average DZ twins and other siblings share half their genes). In adoptive families children's resemblence will reflect the influence of the shared environment alone since they do not have a biological parent in common.

These models, or predictions of the degree of similarity between relatives, are then compared with the correlations obtained between measures of reading or the presence of RD in different types of relative. Parameter estimates are obtained for the size of the effects of genetic, shared or non-shared environmental influences on reading. The size of the genetic effect is called "heritability" and is an estimate of the proportion of the variation in reading ability that is explained by genetic differences between individuals.

It is beyond the scope of this chapter to provide details of the methods used in quantitative genetic analysis. It is also not feasible to detail the variety of molecular genetic approaches that are being developed. A good review of these techniques and their application to developmental psychology is provided by Plomin & Rutter (1998).

CRITICAL REVIEW OF THE LITERATURE

Epidemiological studies of RD

A strong case against the hump notion of Rutter and Yule (1975) was provided from the data obtained by Shaywitz, Escobar, Shaywitz, Fletcher & Makuch (1992) on 414 children from the general population. They found no excess of individuals underachieving at reading in relation to attainment expect from their IQ. They conclude that RD is essentially on a continuum and that relative achievement conforms to a normal distribution. They went on to argue that in terms of the nature of the cognitive deficit underlying RD, that the discrepancy from IQ and the low achievement groups did not differ (Fletcher *et al.*, 1994). However the RD was identified, phonological processing deficits were present. These findings supported the phonological-core variable-difference mode proposed by Stanovich (Stanovich & Siegel, 1994).

The original Rutter and Yule (1975) definition of specific reading retardation identified a prevalence rate of approximately 5%. If the Shaywitz *et al.* (1992) argument is accepted then prevalence rates for RD are essentially arbitrary since relative ability is on a continuum and no specific degree of under-achievement has precedence.

The case for the distinction between specific reading retardation (SRR) and reading backwardness (RB) was partly based on the hump in the distribution of reading attainment relative to IQ. It was also based on differences in the characteristics associated with the two types of RD. These included a history of speech and language disability (more marked in RB), the type of behaviour disturbance shown (antisocial behaviour in SRR and a range of disturbance in RB). It was argued by Rutter and Yule (1975) that this was indirect evidence that the origins of RD in these two groups may be different. At that stage it was unknown whether the SRR and RB distinction also reflected a difference in the underlying nature of the reading deficit in terms of cognitive abilities. The case for such a qualitatively different cognitively based disability (dyslexia) required other evidence.

One attempt to derive an indirect estimate of the prevalence of dyslexia as differentiated sub-group of RD children was made by Miles (1991). Using data from a national cohort of children a prevalence estimate of between 2 and 4% was obtained. The differentiation that was made here was that the child had first to show reading underachievement (a difference between reading or spelling attainment and a measure of intelligence) and then those with additional "dyslexic signs" were identified.

One of the characteristics that Rutter and Yule claimed was distinctive about children with specific reading retardation was the more marked sex ratio in this group compared to those that showed general reading backwardness.

There could not be a more readily ascertained characteristic than gender but nevertheless there has been considerable controversy over the extent to which RD is associated with gender. It has been argued (Shaywitz, Shaywitz, Fletcher, & Escobar, 1990; Shaywitz, Towle, Lessne & Shaywitz, 1988) that the supposed excess of RD in males is a product of biases within schools that result in the more ready identification and referral for remediation of RD in a boy than in a girl.

However the excess of males with the form of RD not associated with low overall ability is a robust finding (Stevenson, 1992). The original Isle of Wight and Inner London studies (Rutter & Yule, 1975) were based on research ascertained samples an found an excess of males in the specific reading retarded group but not in the group with general reading backwardness. Later epidemiological studies have shown a similar specific excess of males. Lewis, Hitch & Walker (1994) found that with a definition of specific reading difficulties that identified 3.9% of the population the sex ratio was 3.2:1 males to females (an imbalance that was not found for arithmetic difficulties). For RD associated with low general ability the sex ratio was reduced to 1.3:1. These figures are based on a total population sample of 1206 British school children aged 9- to 10-years. In the USA too the excess of males (sex ratio 3.2) has been reported with a reduced ratio (1.3) for poor reading with generalised learning disabilities (Badian, 1999). The agreement between these two school based epidemiological studies is remarkable. Therefore not withstanding the evidence to be reviewed below that the nature of the underlying reading deficit is the same for children with specific reading retardation and reading backwardness, at least as far as one of the correlates is concerned there does seem to be an indication that boys are more vulnerable to development of specific reading retardation than RD in general. This suggests a etiologically heterogeneity for RD.

Nevertheless the demonstration of much more equal sex ratio in epidemiological rather than a service identified RD cases, is a good illustration of the distortion that can occur if the search for associations with RD is based on referred cases rather than systematic study if a whole population. The methodology and statistical issues in such two stage epidemiological surveys has been reviewed by Dunn *et al.* (1999).

A wide range of environmental influences on reading ability and general intelligence was investigated in a sample of 550 twin children age 13 years (Stevenson & Fredman, 1990). The aim of the study was to identify environmental correlates of individual differences in reading ability that were independent of those on general intellectual ability and to use multiple regression procedures so that the independent effect of the correlated environmental factors could be determined.

They found that a number of social factors were consistently associated with reading accuracy (Neale Analysis of Reading Ability) and on the Schonell single word reading and spelling test. In an initial univariate analysis these factors could be divided into those that are antecedents or plausible causes low reading age: gender (boys worse), parental occupation (social class), parental education, mother's mental health, father's reading habits and family size and those that could be either causes or consequences of the child's poor reading – mother's criticisms of the child and parental help with homework. Even though it is reasonable to assume that parental occupation, social class and metal health are antecedents of the child's reading ability, for the parents these factors may have in part been influenced by their own history of RD (Elbro, Nielsen & Petersen, 1994).

When Stevenson & Fredman used a multiple regression approach only social class, family size and mother's education remained significant predictors. Moreover when IQ was added to the regression equation only family size retained a significant association with variation in reading. This suggests that the majority of the family and social influences on reading are ones that enhance general ability too. Being a later born child in a large family is however a specific risk factor for poor reading attainment. These results were obtained on a British sample. A similar pattern has been obtained in studies from the USA of little residual impact of the home environment on school achievement once general ability was taken into account (Bradley & Caldwell, 1984).

An important feature of the data in the study by Stevenson & Fredman (1990) was that an earlier quantitative genetic analysis had been carried out on the reading scores. This showed that when the original reading and spelling measures were analysed that, in addition to genetic effects, the environmental influences were roughly equally divided between the shared and non-shared environment. When residuals were obtained after regression onto IQ, the predominant environmental effect was non-shared. It should be noted that twin data alone cannot differentiate between non-shared environmental influences and the effects of measurement error. A separate test-retest study had provided estimates of reliability that could be used to refine the estimates of the non-shared environment alone in this particular (Stevenson *et al.*, 1987). The important feature of these estimates of genetic and environmental influence is that they were obtained not by direct measurement of the environment but rather from a priori theoretical assumptions. They are however consistent with the Stevenson & Fredman (1990) results of measured environmental influences, where the shared environmental influences, reflecting factors such as the enriching qualities of the home, were ones that effected IQ as much as reading.

In the Stevenson & Fredman (1990) analysis there was some evidence that maternal depression was related to the child's cognitive development. In this analysis there was no evidence that this feature of the child's family background was specifically related to reading ability. A previous study of younger children did suggest that aspects of the mothers' mental state and early mother-child relationship was related to later reading ability (Richman, Stevenson & Graham, 1982). A similar finding has been reported by Estrada *et al.* (1987). The mechanisms whereby maternal depression can impact on the child, including the child's cognitive development, have been reviewed (Cummings & Davies, 1994: Kelly, Morisset, Barnard, Hammond & Booth, 1996).

There have been a number of large scale surveys that have establish the social and familial correlates of poor reading attainment. For example the epidemiological study on the Isle of Wight showed that parental attitudes to literacy as reflected in for example the number of books in the house correlates with reading ability of the children (Rutter, Tizard & Whitmore, 1970). More recently a series of studies by Adele and Allen Gottfried (e.g. Gottfried, Fleming & Gottfried, 1998) have identified the way such features of the home environment have an enduring impact on the children's intrinsic academic motivation. These effects are not simply explained by social class differences since structural equation modelling showed that the impact of the stimulating home remained when social class was introduced into the models. However in a review of such studies (Scarborough & Dobrich, 1994), there was a surprisingly modest impact of reading to children on later attainments.

The specific impact of social class on the core phonological skills of literacy have been difficult to determine. Phonological sensitivity has not been found to be related to social class in some studies (MacLean, Bryant & Bradley, 1987; Raz & Bryant, 1990)), whilst in others it has been (Bowey, 1995; Lonigan, Burgess, Anthony & Barker, 1998). Lonigan *et al.* (1998) discuss this inconsistency in the literature and the potential importance such an effect might have in explaining the origins of social class differences in literacy. It should be emphasised that social class itself (as determined by parental occupation) is only a marker for other more fundamental influences on reading development. The social class of the family is related to reading because it is associated with other more immediate influences on reading such the amount of reading with the child a parent undertakes, the extent to which the family uses language games with the child in the pre-school years or with some factor outside the family such the quality of schooling during the early years.

It is important to consider the impact of such broad social class influences on reading as part of a bi-directional process. The social class of family of origin may influence the child's literacy development and their level of literacy will contribute to their own later occupational status. There is evidence that children with poor reading attainment in middle childhood continue fail at school, leave school early and experience difficulties making transitions into working life (Maughan, Hagell, Rutter & Yule, 1994; Maughan, 1995). Indeed it has been suggested that the rate of RD in runaway or homeless street youths is as high as 52% (Barwick & Siegel, 1996).

One of the most consistent findings which was noticed from the first systematic studies of RD, is that it tends to reoccur in a families across and within generations (Hinshelwood, 1907). Genetic epidemiology attempts to identify whether the pattern of occurrence in families is due to genetic or environmental transmission and, if genetic, the type of genetic mechanisms that is responsible e.g. dominant recessive, sex-linked or autosomal. The quantitative analysis of family data and in particular of some especially informative families – those with twins or adopted children – can identify the extent to which RD is influenced by genetic or environmental differences between children i.e. heritability. The findings from the genetic epidemiology of RD will now be considered.

Quantitative genetic studies of RD

Once the familial nature of RD had been initially identified, it was some time before the clear evidence was obtained·that this arose from genetic factors rather than from social transmission within families. This came from twin studies that were published during the 1980's. The Colorado Twin Reading study (DeFries & Fulker, 1987; DeFries, Fulker & LaBuda, 1987) and the London Twin Reading study (Stevenson *et al.*, 1987) provided complimentary evidence about the role of genetic and environmental factors. The two twin studies were based on large representative samples but in the case of the Colorado study each twin pair had one member who was RD whilst in the London study the twins are representative of the full range of reading ability. Between them these studies provided evidence that genetic differences between children contributed about half the variance in reading ability. There have been subsequent twin studies that have replicated this finding (Reynolds *et al., 1996*).

Having established the role of genetic factors in RD, interest has moved to try to identify factors that might indicate those for whom genetic influences were more marked. For example Stevenson *et al.* (1987) suggested that there might be an age related decline in heritability for reading whilst that for spelling ability was maintained. This hypothesis was tested in the Colorado data by DeFries, Alarcon and Olson (1997). When the sample was divided into those above and those below the age of 11.5 years a different pattern of heritability was obtained. Reading had a higher heritability in the younger group compared to the older confirming the prediction made by Stevenson *et al.* (1987). By contrast the heritability of spelling was maintained across age and indeed there was some evidence that it increased as children got older.

Using data from the Colorado Adoption Project the sources of continuity and discontinuity in reading achievement have been examined. Wadsworth, Fulker & DeFries (1999) have shown that genetic factors are responsible for the stability of individual differences in reading scores. Importantly there was no evidence of novel genetic or shared environmental influences at the older age (12 years). Changes in ability between the ages of 7 and 12 years were associated with non-shared environmental influences (e.g. instructional methods, teachers, peers etc). To summarise these age related changes, it is apparent for reading but not for spelling that the significance of genetic factors declines with age. The nature of these genetic influences remains the same over time. The same shared environmental influences operate across the childhood years but only have a modest impact. Non-shared factors are present and play a particular role in producing changes in reading ability from age to age.

In addition to the moderation of heritability by age, the possibility of differences in the size of genetic effects for more and less able children has also been examined. Using data from the Colorado Twin study, twins were divided into those with a full scale IQ greater than 100 and those less than 100. Wadsworth, Olson, Pennington & DeFries (1998) found that there was a significant difference (p < .03) between the heritabilities for the higher IQ children (0.72) and those of below average intelligence (0.43). The conclusion therefore is that environmental factors play a greater role in reading difficulties experienced by lower IQ children.

Finally it would appear that sex may also be a moderator of genetic effects. Knopnik, Alarcon & DeFries (1998) found that the genetic correlation between the sexes was significantly less than one (0.59) which indicates that the genes that influence RD in males are not identical to those operating in females. This again emphasises the possible heterogeneity in the origins of RD.

These studies have been based upon a quantitative genetic analysis of RD. Interest is now centring on how to identify the particular genes that might be contributing to RD. However such molecular genetic studies need to be based on a more detailed understanding of the structure of genetic and environmental influences on reading and related abilities. For example the distinction has been made between two aspects of emergent literature skills. These are abilities such as phonological awareness and letter knowledge and in contrast to language and conceptual knowledge (Whitehurst & Lonigan, 1998). The influences on each of these aspects of emergent literacy skills are likely to be different and they will have a greater salience at different stages of literacy acquisition (Wagner *et al.*, 1997).

The Colorado and London studies examined the influence of genetic factors on different underlying cognitive processes in reading. It was found that phonological processing (ie. sub-lexical units) in reading were more strongly influenced by genetic factors than the ability to read based upon orthographic regularities (Olson *et al.*, 1989; Stevenson, 1991; Castles *et al.*, 1999).

A study attempting to identify the complex pattern of genetic influences on reading and related abilities was undertaken by Hohnen & Stevenson (1999). Using two samples of twins aged 6 and 7 years they were able to show that the genes influencing general intelligence and general language ability were also related to individual differences in the early stages of reading ability. They did not find any evidence of specific genetic associations between phonological ability and literacy. Instead these two aspects of cognitive development were associated via shared genetic influences on general language and via a specific shared environmental influence. It is interesting to note that the latter is consistent with previous studies which have shown that the experience of rhymes and a specific training in phonological awareness can enhance reading development (Bryant *et al.*, 1990).

The results of these quantitative genetic studies explain why the attempts to identify broad social influences on RD have failed to explain more that 20-30% of the variance e.g. Stevenson & Fredman (1990). These approaches measure RD in just one family member, usually a child of specific age, and then try to identify the factors that vary between families that account for variation in reading attainment. The quantitative genetic studies suggest that genetic factors play a significant part in RD and that many of the important experiences that influence RD are differences within families. These influences will not be identified by epidemiological studies of the kind usually carried out. The effects of the non-shared environment can only be detected in studies that incorporate measures on more than one child within a family. On the other hand the relatively minor impact of shared environmental influences on RD can be shown in studies of just one family member. This was demonstrated in a cross national study by Stevenson, Lee, Stigler & Lucker (1984). They found that at age 11 years few of the measures of family background or of parent child interaction differentiated between average and poor readers in samples from Japan, Taiwan and the United States.

Molecular genetic studies of RSD

Alongside the quantitative genetic studies mentioned above, molecular genetic techniques have been applied to RD. These represent one of the most extensive sets of replicated molecular genetic investigations of complex cognitive abilities. There were initial linkage studies suggesting that a gene on chromosome 15 might play a role in RD (Smith *et al.*, 1983). Subsequent analysis of this same set of families suggested an additional gene on chromosome 6 might play a role (Smith *et al.*, 1991). A study of linkage in small samples also suggested to linkage chromosome 1 (Rabin *et al.*, 1993).

The best evidence of linkage to date centres on chromosome 6. Using a sample of siblings and an independent sample of twins Cardon *et al.* (1994,1995) found linkage to markers on a region of chromosome 6(6p21.3). Subsequently Grigorenko *et al.* (1997) also found evidence of linkage for specific forms of RD in six extended multi-affected families to a similar region of chromosome 6. The Cardon *et al.* (1994,1995) study was based upon a composite measure of RD. A further analysis of the twins from that sample, but using three more specific phenotypes (ie. word recognition, phonological decoding and orthographic coding) found deficits in each facet of reading to be linked to the 6p21.3 region (Gayan *et al.*, 1995).

One essential requirement for linkage studies of these complex characteristics is to obtain replication in independent samples. Gayan *et al.* (1999) obtained a new sample of 126 sib-pairs and found evidence for linkage for orthographic, phonological and word recognition to markers D6S276 and D6S105. This overlaps with the region identified by Cardon *et al.* (1994,1995). A similarly wide range of RD related deficits were found to be linked to exactly the same markers in a UK based study by Fisher *et al.* (1999). The striking feature of this replication is that it has been found using different forms of linkage analysis, different measures of RD, different samples and by different research teams. It should however be noted that there has been a report of a non-replication of linkage to chromosome 6 by Field and Kaplan (1998). They used a measure of pseudoword reading similar to the pronounceable non-words adopted by Gayan *et al.* (1999). They suggest that the non-replication might be due either to sample differences or possibly from differences in linkage analysis approaches. Until the Field and Kaplan (1998) data are analysed using the QTL approach adopted by Cardon *et al.* (1994, 1995), Gayan *et al.* (1999) and Fisher *et al.* (1999) the significance of this non-replication is difficult to evaluate.

A different pattern of linkage results for RD has been reported by Grigorenko *et al.* (1997). They too found linkage to chromosome 6, but only for a phonological awareness phenotype and not for single-word reading. The initial reports from this study suggested that the region on chromosome 6 for which linkage was obtained was somewhat different from that identified by Cardon *et al.* (1994, 1995). It has been suggested subsequently that the position of some of the markers used are in fact in the same 6p21.3 region (Gayan *et al.*, 1999).

Grigorenko *et al.* (1997) found single-word reading to be linked to a marker on chromosome 15 (D15S143). Using spelling disability in seven multiply affected families, Schulte-Korne *et al.* (1997) found linkage to the same marker on chromosome 15 (marker D15S143). The significance of this region of chromosome 15 has been confirmed in a sample of over 100 parent/proband trios (Morris *et al.*, 2000). Using closely spaced markers a susceptibility gene for RD was located at chromosome 15q15.1. Grigorenko *et al.* (1998) also have reported findings on an enlarged sample of eight families and have found linkage to chromosome 1 (marker D1S199) for a phonological decoding phenotype. Previous reported linkage of RD to chromosome 1 had been made by Rabin *et al.* (1993).

There is strong evidence of linkage of RD to chromosome 18p11.2 (Fisher *et al.*, 2002). They were able to replicate this linkage in three independent sample of families. They conclude that a gene at this position is probably a general risk factor for dyslexia, influencing several reading-related processes.

As reviewed above, the quantitative genetic evidence suggests both shared and some independent genetic influences on difference features of RD. The molecular genetic studies seem to indicate that some of the shared genes may be situated on chromosome 6 and chromosome 18. Additional specific genes may also be on chromosome 6 or possibly located on chromosome 15 and 1.

The pattern of these results do not suggest a clear isolation of genetic influences on the two broad pathways in the two route model of reading (Coltheart *et al.*, 1993). A meta-analysis of the abilities of children with RD has shown that the predictions from the two route model are not supported at the phenotypic level (Metsala, Stanovich & Brown, 1998). The phonologically based deficit in pseudo-word reading was found but RD children also showed the same regularity effect as reading aged matched controls. The latter is the greater proficiency in reading regular compared to irregularly spelt words. Under the two route model this is thought to arise from the possibility of reading unfamiliar regular words via the sub-lexical route. The Metsala *et al.* (1998) result appears to be inconsistent with the two route model of reading. By contrast connectionist models of reading have produced just this pattern of deficit i.e. poor pseudoword reading and a "normal" regularity effect. Recently Coltheart *et al.* (2001) have suggested that a duel route cascade model of reading is superior to the parallel distributed model. These uncertainties over the nature of the psychological processes underlying the RD phenotype need to be resolved before the molecular genetic studies can begin to produce a coherent and consistent pattern of results on genetic effects on sub-types of RD. The complexity of this issue and the progress that has been made in integrating findings from neuropsychological and cognitive studies, brain imaging and genetics has been comprehensively reviewed by Grigorenko (2001). The results to date suggest that there is unlikely to be a simple relationship between specific genes identified and features of the underlying cognitive deficits.

READING AND BEHAVIOUR

One well replicated epidemiological finding is the co-occurrence of RD with behaviour problems in children. This is now better understood in the light of the genetics evidence reviewed above. In particular it has been repeatedly found that RD tends to co-occur with externalising behaviour problems such as hyperactivity or attention deficit hyperactivity disorder (ADHD) and conduct disorder. Stevenson (1996) reviewed the possible origins of comorbidities between these three conditions and concluded that both hyperactivity and RD arose from basic underlying but separate cognitive deficits. In contrast conduct disorder did not have a distinctive cognitive profile. The nature of the underlying cognitive deficit for RD was essentially that of a phonological processing difficulty. For hyperactivity the situation was less clear as to whether the underlying deficit was one of attentional control, executive function or behavioural inhibition.

One possible mechanisms producing comorbidity is that of shared genetic influences. An estimate the genetic correlation between RD and hyperactivity was made by Stevenson *et al.* (1993).They were able to show that the data from the Colorado and the London Twin Reading Studies produced values for the bivariate group heritability of 0.32 and 0.21 respectively. This is an indication of the extent to which genetic factors are shared. This finding has been replicated in a large study of twins from the Australian Twin Registry (Hay *et al.*, 1999). The are however suggestions from an American family study (Faraone *et al.*,1993) that these two conditions do not co-segregate (i.e. are not inherited together) and therefore that ADHD and RD are etiologically distinct. At present this incompatibility between the results of twin and family studies has yet to be resolved.

To date, there is no molecular genetic evidence that might help to decide this issue. It has been suggested that since the 6p21.3 locus is close the HLA region on chromosome 6, that genes effecting immune system dysfunction might play a role. In addition the evidence of a possible deficiency in C4B complement protein in children with ADHD has led Warren *et al.* (1995) to suggest that this gene situated in the HLA region is a good candidate for a shared genetic influence on ADHD and RD.

In addition to genetic influences, there were a number of more distal causes of conduct disorder, hyperactivity and RD which were themselves intercorrelated. These include factors most strongly related to conduct disorder such as family dysfunction (e.g. marital discord and inconsistent discipline), related to hyperactivity, such as disrupted parenting and related to reading disability, such as maternal depression. The origin of the correlation between these more distal causes possibly lay in social disadvantage (e.g. Biederman *et al.*,1995). There are therefore a number of environmental as well as genetic mechanisms which will be leading through to the association between ADHD and RD.

DISCUSSION

In contrast to the acquisition of spoken language, which has been subject to the biological processes of evolution, learning to use written language is has emerged through social conventions. It is this difference in naturalness that makes learning to read so much more difficult for children than learning to speak. For a clear and concise account of the consequences of that distinction see Liberman (1991). Some minimal level of instruction is essential for reading acquisition. However given that instruction is available, biological (genetic) differences between children play a major role in determining how readily reading will be acquired.

Studies of the pattern of cognitive and language skills of children with RD (Morris *et al.*, 1998) suggest that these genetic factors are likely to involve the functioning of phonological processing. The phonological dyslexic subtype was a identified by difficulties with reading non-words and real words across age. Surface dyslexia on the other hand seemed to represent an age limited delay in the acquisition of word recognition. The validity of these two subtype had been argued by Castles & Coltheart (1993), however the genetic evidence suggests that it is the phonological processing related disabilities that carry the most substantial genetic influence on RD.

The evidence of familiality has made it sensible to conduct longitudinal studies of children who are at risk for RD because of a family history. Such studies have been concerned not just the identify the emergent cognitive and language abilities of these children but also to identify environmental factors which may carry some of the familial risk (Lyytinen, 1997; Scarborough, 1991). For example, Scarborough has shown that such at risk children who later became RD had, in addition to weak early syntactic abilities, a less frequent exposure to print, especially solitary book activities. This may also feedback into the reading process so that more successful readers seek out more print exposure and thereby help to promote further their own development: the reverse holds for poor readers (Stanovich & West, 1989; Cunningham & Stanovich, 1997). This is the so-called Matthew effect in reading (Stanovich, 1986). These "environmental" influences may of course be mediating some of the genetic effects on RD but may nevertheless be open to intervention.

Indeed it should not be assumed that because a characteristic has a high heritability that it is not amenable to effective intervention. It was pointed out by Tizard (1975) that the high heritability of height was in no way inconsistent with the substantial increases in height in the general population in the UK during the first part of the twentieth century. This mean gain in height could not be due to changes in the genetic make-up of the population. It was a consequence of environmental changes such as nutrition and public health. This was produced even though 90% of the variation in height at any given time was due to genetic differences between individuals. This means that effective teaching is certainly possible for children with RD. The strong genetic basis of the condition does not preclude marked changes in reading ability in response to instruction.

Once the heritabilty of different forms of RD is known, it becomes possible to search for the genes responsible using molecular genetic techniques. RD is the complex psychological condition whose quantitative and molecular genetic basis is best understood. This coupled with the emerging literature on the structural and functional imaging of the brain during reading (Paulesu *et al.*, 1996) and for individuals with RD, provides the basis for a concerted investigation of the links between genes, gene products (proteins), gene expression in the brain and the related functional variations.

The complex mechanisms whereby genes influence development are becoming better understood and the differentiation of genes that regulate normal development from those that might be involved in quantitative trait differences is starting to be made (Tautz & Schmid, 1998). The range of single genes that have an impact on brain and behaviour is extensive and the interplay between them and their interactions with variation in environments is being explored (Wahlsten, 1999). The significance of advances in molecular genetics for developmental studies is becoming clear (Plomin & Rutter, 1998) and literacy development is likely to remain at the forefront of studies relating genes to complex cognitive skills.

The evidence from epidemiology that has investigated both social and genetic associates of RD suggests aetiological heterogeneity. Although the evidence is clearly supports a phonological processing core for RD regardless of the child's general intellectual level, this underlying disability can arise from a number of causes. The correlates of RD with and without low IQ are some what different (e.g. sex ratios) and the twin evidence suggests that environmental factors have a greater role to play in RD in children with lower IQ.

Heterogeneity is also found in the molecular genetic studies. The pattern of occurrence in families with multiple members effected by RD does not correspond with any simple single gene transmission. There will be a set of genes involved in such a complex cognitive skill and it is likely to be a large set. Any one of these genes will only contribute a small amount to the development of the RD phenotype. There is no such thing as "the RD gene" but by identifying those genes that do play a role, insight into genetic variation and brain function will start to emerge.

REFERENCES

Badian, N. A. (1999). Reading disability defined as a discrepancy between listening and reading comprehension: A longitudinal study of stability, gender differences, and prevalence. *Journal of Learning Disabilities, 32*,138-148.

Barwick, M. A., & Siegel, L. S. (1996). Learning-difficulties in adolescent clients of a shelter for runaway and homeless street youths. *Journal of Research on Adolescence, 6*, 649-670.

Biederman, J., Milberger, S., Faraone, S. V., Kiley, K., Mick, E., Albon, S., Warburton, R. & Reed, E. (1995). Family environment risk factors for ADHD – A test of Rutter's indicators of adversity. *Archives of General Psychiatry, 52*, 464-470.

Bowey, J. A. (1995). Socioeconomic status differences in pre-school phonological sensitivity and first grade reading achievement. *Journal of Educational Psychology, 87*, 476-487.

Bradley, R. H. & Caldwell, B. M. (1984). The relation of infants' home environment to achievement test score in first grade: A follow-up study. *Child Development, 55*, 803-809.

Bryant, P. E., MacLean, M., Bradley, L. L., & Crossland, J. (1990). Rhyme and alliteration, phoneme detection, and learning to read. *Developmental Psychology, 26*, 429-438.

Cardon, L. R., Smith, S. D., Fulker, D. W., Kimberling, W. J., Pennington, B. F., & DeFries, J. C. (1994). Quantitative trait locus for reading-disability on chromosome-6. *Science, 266*, 276-279.

Cardon, L. R., Smith, S. D., Fulker, D. W., Kimberling, W. J., Pennington, B. F., & DeFries, J. C. (1995). Quantitative trait locus for reading disability: *Science, 268*, 1553.

Castles, A. & Coltheart, M. (1993). Varieties of developmental dyslexia. *Cognition, 47*, 149-180.

Castles, A., Datta, H., Gayan, J., & Olson, R. K. (1999). Varieties of developmental reading disorder: genetic and environmental influences. *Journal of Experimental Child Psychology, 72*, 73-94.

Coltheart, M., Curtis, B., Atkins, P., & Haller, M. (1993). Models of reading aloud – dual-route and parallel-distributed-processing approaches. *Psychological Review, 100*, 589-608.

Coltheart, M., Rastle, K., Perry, C., Langdon, R., & Ziegler, J. (2001). DRC: A dual route cascaded model of visual word recognition and reading aloud. *Psychological Review, 108*, 204-256.

Cummings, E. M., & Davies, P. T. (1994). Maternal depression and child-development. *Journal of Child Psychology and Psychiatry, 35*, 73-112.

Cunningham, A. E., & Stanovich, K. E. (1997). Early reading acquisition and its relation to reading experience and ability 10 years later. *Developmental Psychology, 33*, 934-945.

DeFries, J. C., Alarcon, M., & Olson, R. K. (1997). Genetic aetiologies of reading and spelling deficits: Developmental differences. In C. Hulme & M. Snowling (Eds.), *Dyslexia: Biology, cognition and intervention* (pp. 20-37). London: Whurr.

DeFries, J. C., & Fulker, D. W. (1987). Multiple regression analysis of twin data: etiology of deviant scores versus individual differences. *Acta Geneticae Medicae Et Gemellologiae, 37*, 1-13.

DeFries, J. C., Fulker, D. W., & LaBuda, M. C. (1987). Evidence for a genetic aetiology in reading disability of twins. *Nature, 329*, 537-539.

Dunn, G., Pickles, A., Tansella, M., Vazquez Barquero, J. L. (1999). Two-phase epidemiological surveys in psychiatric research. *British Journal of Psychiatry, 174*, 95-100.

Elbro, C, Nielsen, I. & Petersen, D. K. (1994). Dyslexia in adults – evidence for deficits in non-word reading and in the phonological representation of lexical items. *Annals of Dyslexia, 44*,205-226.

Estrada, P., Arsenio, W. F., Hess, R. D. & Holloway, S. D. (1987). Affective quality of the mother-child relationship: Longitudinal consequences for children's school-relevant cognitive functioning. *Developmental Psychology, 23,* 210-215.

Faraone, S. V., Biederman, J., Lehman, B. K., Keenan, K., Norman, D., Seidman, L. J., Kolodny, R., Kraus, I., Perrin, J., & Chen, W. J. (1993). Evidence for the independent familial transmission of attention-deficit hyperactivity disorder and learning-disabilities -results from a family genetic-study. *American Journal of Psychiatry, 150,* 891-895.

Field, L. L., & Kaplan, B. J. (1998). Absence of linkage of phonological coding dyslexia to chromosome 6p23-p21.3 in a large family data set. *American Journal of Human Genetics, 63,* 1448-1456.

Fisher, S. E., Marlow, A. J., Lamb, J., Maestrini, E., Williams, D. F., Richardson, A. J., Weeks, D. E., Stein, J. F., & Monaco, A. P. (1999). A quantitative-trait locus on chromosome 6p influences different aspects of developmental dyslexia. *American Journal of Human Genetics, 64,* 146-156.

Fisher, S. E., Francks, C., Marlow, A. J., MacPhie, I. L., Newbury, D. F., Cardon, L. R., Ishikawa-Brush, Y., Richardson, A. J., Talcott, J. B., Gayan, J., Olson, R. K., Pennington, B. F., Smith, S. D., DeFrieS, J. C., Stein, J. F., & Monaco, A. P. (2002). Independent genome-wide scans identify a chromosome 18 quantitative-trait locus influencing dyslexia. *Nature Genetics, 30,* 86-91.

Fletcher, J. M., Shaywitz, S. E., Shankweiler, D. P., Katz, L., Liberman, I. Y., Stuebing, K. K., Francis, D. J., Fowler, A. E., & Shaywitz, B. A. (1994). Cognitive profiles of reading disability: Comparisons of discrepancy and low achievement definitions. *Journal of Educational Psychology, 86,* 6-23.

Gayan, J., Olson, R. K., Cardon, L. R., Smith, S. D., Fulker, D. W., Kimberling, W. J., Pennington, B. F., & DeFries, J. C. (1995). Quantitative trait locus for different measures of reading-disability. *Behavior Genetics, 25,* 266.

Gayan, J., Smith, S. D., Cherny, S. S., Cardon, L. R., Fulker, D. W., Brower, A. M., Olson, R. K., Pennington, B. F., & DeFries, J. C. (1999). Quantitative-trait locus for specific language and reading deficits on chromosome 6p. *American Journal of Human Genetics, 64,* 157-164.

Gottfried, A. E., Fleming, J. S., & Gottfried, A. W. (1998). Role of cognitively stimulating home environment in children's academic intrinsic motivation: a longitudinal study. *Child Development, 69,* 1448-1460.

Grigorenko, E. L., Wood, F. B., Meyer, M. S., Hart, L. A., Speed, W. C., Shuster, A., & Pauls, D. L. (1997). Susceptibility loci for distinct components of developmental dyslexia on chromosomes 6 and 15. *American Journal of Human Genetics, 60,* 27-39.

Grigorenko, E. L., Wood, F. B., Meyen, M. S., Pauls, J. E. D., Hart, L. A., & Pauls, D. L. (1998). Linkage studies suggest a possible locus for dyslexia near the rh region on chromosome. *Behavior Genetics, 28,* 470.

Grigorenko, E. L. (2001). Developmental dyslexia: An update on genes, brains, and environments. *Journal of Child Psychology and Psychiatry, 42,* 91-125.

Hay, D. A., McStephen, M., Levy, F. and Martin, N. (1999). Combining twin and co-twin designees to understand the development and differentiation of ADHD. Paper presented at the International Society for Research into Child and Adolescent Psychopathology Conference, Barcelona, 17-20 June 1999.

Hinshelwood, J. (1907). Four cases of congenital word-blindness occurring in the same family. *British Medical Journal, 1,* 608-609.

Hohnen, B., & Stevenson, J. (1999). The structure of genetic influences on general cognitive, language, phonological, and reading abilities. *Developmental Psychology, 35,* 590-603.

Kelly, J. F , Morisset, C. E., Barnard, K. E., Hammond, M. A., Booth, C. L. (1996). The influence of early mother-child interaction on pre-school cognitive/linguistic outcomes in a high-social-risk group. *Infant Mental Health Journal, 17,* 310-321.

Knopik, V. S., Alarcon, M., & Defries, J. C. (1998). Common and specific gender influences on individual differences in reading performance: a twin study. *Personality and Individual Differences, 25,* 269-277.

Lewis, C., Hitch, G. J., & Walker, P. (1994). The prevalence of specific arithmetic difficulties and specific reading difficulties in 9-year-old to 10-year-old boys and girls. *Journal of Child Psychology and Psychiatry, 35,* 283-292.

Liberman, A. M. (1991). Observations from the sidelines. *Reading and Writing, 3,* 429-433.

Lonigan, C. J., Burgess, S. R., Anthony, J. L., & Barker, T. A. (1998). Development of phonological sensitivity in 2- to 5-year old children. *Journal of Educational Psychology, 90,* 294-311.

Lyytinen, H. (1997). In search of precursors of dyslexia: A prospective study of children at risk for reading problems. In C. Hulme & M. Snowling (eds.), *Dyslexia: Biology, cognition and intervention* (pp108-130). London: Whurr Publishers.

MacLean, M., Bryant, P., & Bradley, L. (1987). Rhymes, nursery rhymes and reading in early childhood. *Merrill-Palmer Quarterly, 33,* 255-282.

Maughan, B. (1995). Annotation – long-term outcomes of developmental reading problems. *Journal of Child Psychology and Psychiatry, 36,* 357-371.

Maughan, B., Hagell, A., Rutter, M., & Yule, W. (1994). Poor readers in secondary-school. *Reading and Writing, 6,* 125-150.

Metsala, J.L., Stanovich, K.E. & Brown, G.D.A. (1998). Regularity effects and the phonological deficit model of reading disabilities: A meta-analytic review. *Journal of Educational Psychology, 90,* 279-293.

Miles, T. R. (1991). On determining the prevalence of dyslexia. In M. Snowling & M. Thompson (eds.), *Dyslexia: Integrating theory and practice* (pp. 144-153). London: Whurr Publishers.

Morris, D. W., Robinson, L., Turic, D., Duke, M., Webb, V., Milham, C., Hopkin, E., Pound, K., Fernando, S., Easton, M., Hamshere, M., Williams, N., McGuffin, P., Stevenson, J., Krawczak, M., Owen, M. J., O'Donovan, M. C., & Williams, J. (2000). Family-based association mapping provides evidence for a gene for reading disability on chromosome 15q. *Human Molecular Genetics, 9,* 843-848.

Morris, R. D., Stuebing, K. K., Fletcher, J. M., Shaywitz, S. E., Lyon, G. R., Shankweiler, D. P., Katz, L., Francis, D. J. & Shaywitz, B. A. (1998). Subtypes of reading disability: Variability around a phonological core. *Journal of Educational Psychology, 90,* 347-73.

Olson, R., Wise, B., Conners, F., Rack, J., & Fulker, D. W. (1989). Specific deficits in component reading and language skills: genetic and environmental influences. *Journal of Learning Disabilities, 22,* 339-348.

Paulesu, E., Frith, U., Snowling, M., Gallagher, A., Morton, J., Frackowiak, R. S. J., & Frith, C. D. (1996). Is developmental dyslexia a disconnection syndrome – evidence from pet scanning. *Brain, 119,* 143-157.

Plomin, R. (1994). Genetics and experience: The interplay between nature and nurture. Thousand Oaks, CA: Sage.

Plomin, R. & Rutter, M. (1998). Child development, molecular genetics and what to do with genes once they are found. *Child Development, 69,*1223-1242.

Rabin, M., Wen, X. L., Hepburn, M., Lubs, H. A., Feldman, E. & Duara, R.. (1993). Suggestive linkage of developmental dyslexia to chromosome 1p34-p36. *Lancet, 342,* 178.

Raz, I. S., & Bryant, P. (1990). Social background, phonological awareness and children's reading. *British Journal of Developmental Psychology, 8,* 209-225.

Reynolds, C. A., Hewitt, J. K., Erickson, M. T., Silberg, J. L., Rutter, M., Simonoff, E., Meyer, J., & Eaves, L. J. (1996). The genetics of children's oral reading performance. *Journal of Child Psychology and Psychiatry, 37,* 425-434.

Richman, N., Stevenson, J. & Graham, P. (1982). *Pre-school to school: A behavioural study.* London: Academic Press.

Rutter, M., Tizard, J. & Whitmore, K. (1970). *Education, health and behaviour.* London: Longmans.

Rutter, M. & Yule, W. (1975). The concept of specific reading retardation. *Journal of Child Psychology and Psychiatry,16,* 181-197.

Scarborough, H. (1991). Antecedents to reading disability: Pre-school language development and literacy experiences of children form dyslexic families. *Reading and Writing, 3,* 219-233.

Scarborough, H. & Dobrich, W. (1994). On the efficacy of reading to preschoolers. *Developmental Review, 14,*245-302.

Schulte-Korne, G., Grimm, T., Nothen, M. M., Muller Myhsok, B., Propping, P., & Remschmidt, H. (1997). Evidence for linkage of spelling disability to chromosome 15. *American Journal of Medical Genetics, 74,* 661.

Shaywitz, S. E., Escobar, M. D., Shaywitz, B. A., Fletcher, J. M., & Makuch, R. (1992). Evidence that Dyslexia may represent the lower tail of a normal distribution of reading ability. *New England Journal of Medicine, 326,* 145-150.

Shaywitz, S. E., Shaywitz, B. A., Fletcher, J. M., & Escobar, M. D. (1990). Prevalence of reading Disability in Boys and Girls. *Journal of the American Medical Association, 264,* 998-1002.

Shaywitz, S. E., Towle, V. A., Lessne, D. K., & Shaywitz, B. A. (1988). Prevalence of dyslexia in boys and girls in an epidemiological sample – contrasts between children identified by research criteria and by the school-system. *Annals of Neurology, 24,* 313-314.

Singleton, C. (1997). Screening early literary. In J.R. Beech & C. Singleton (eds.), *The psychological assessment of reading* (pp.67-101). London: Routledge.

Smith, S. D., Kimberling, W. J., Pennington, B. F., & Lubs, H. A. (1983). Specific reading disability: identification of an inherited form through linkage analysis. *Science, 219,* 1345-1347.

Smith, S. D., Kimberling, W. J. & Pennington, B. F. (1991). Screening for multiple genes influencing dyslexia. *Reading and Writing, 3,* 285-298.

Stanovich, K. E. (1986). Mathew effects in reading: Some consequences of individual differences in the acquisition of literacy. *Reading Research Quarterly, 21,* 360-407.

Stanovich, K. E., & Siegel, L. S. (1994). Phenotypic performance profile of children with reading disabilities: A regression-based test of the phonological-core variable-difference model. *Journal of Educational Psychology, 86,* 24-53.

Stanovich, K. E. & West, R. F. (1989). Exposure to print and orthographic processing. *Reading Research Quarterly, 24,* 402-433.

Stevenson, H. W., Lee, S., Stigler, J & Lucker, G. W. (1984). Family variables and reading: A study of mothers of poor and average readers in Japan, Taiwan and the United States. *Journal of Learning Disabilities, 17,* 150-156.

Stevenson, J. (1988). Which aspects of reading-ability show a hump in their distribution. *Applied Cognitive Psychology, 2,* 77-85.

Stevenson, J. (1991). Which aspects of processing text mediate genetic effects? *Reading and Writing: An Interdisciplinary Journal, 3,* 249-269.

Stevenson, J. (1992). Evidence for a genetic etiology in hyperactivity in children. *Behavior Genetics, 22,* 337-344.

Stevenson, J. (1992). Identifying sex-differences in reading-disability – lessons from a twin study. *Reading And Writing, 4,* 307-326.

Stevenson, J. (1996). The hyperactive child at school. In S. Sandberg (Ed.), *Hyperactivity disorders of childhood.* (pp. 382-432). Cambridge: Cambridge University Press.

Stevenson, J. & Fredman, G. (1990). The social environmental correlates of reading ability. *Journal of Child Psychology and Psychiatry, 31,* 681-694.

Stevenson, J., Graham, P., Fredman, G., & McLoughlin, V. (1987). A twin study of genetic influences on reading and spelling ability and disability. *Journal of Child Psychology and Psychiatry, 28,* 229-247.

Stevenson, J., Pennington, B. F., Gilger, J. W., DeFries, J. C., & Gillis, J. J. (1993). Hyperactivity and spelling disability – testing for shared genetic etiology. *Journal of Child Psychology and Psychiatry , 34,* 1137-1152.

Tautz, D. & Schmid, K. J. (1998). From genes to individuals: Developmental genes and the generation of the phenotype. *Philosophical Transactions of the Royal Society of London Series B, 353,*231-240.

Tizard, J. (1975). Race and IQ: the limits of probability. *New Behaviour, 1,* 6-9.

Wadsworth,S. J., Fulker, D. W. & DeFries, J. C. (1999). Stability of genetic and environmental influences on reading performance at 7 and 12 years of age in the Colorado Adoption Project. *International Journal of Behavioral Development, 23,* 319-332.

Wadsworth, S. J., Olson, R. K., Pennington, B. F., & Defries, J. C. (1998). Differential genetic etiology of reading disability as a function of IQ. *Behavior Genetics, 28,* 483-484.

Wagner, R. K., Torgesen, J. K., Rashotte, C. A., Hecht, S. A., Barker, T. A., Burgess, S. R., Donahue, J., & Garon, T. (1997). Changing relations between phonological processing abilities and word-level reading as children develop from beginning reading to skilled readers: A 5-year longitudinal study. *Developmental Psychology, 33,* 468-479.

Wahlsten, D. (1999). Single-brain influences on brain and behaviour. *Annual Review of Psychology, 50,* 599-624.

Warren, R. P., Odell, J. D., Warren, W. L., Burger, R. A., Maciulis, A., Daniels, W. W., & Torres, A. R. (1995). Reading-disability, attention-deficit hyperactivity disorder, and the immune-system. *Science, 268,* 786-787.

Whitehurst, G. J., & Lonigan, C. J. (1998). Child development and emergent literacy. *Child Development, 69,* 848-872.

SUGGESTED FURTHER READINGS

For an introduction to the theories, methods and findings in quantitative and molecular genetic analysis in behaviour genetics see:

Plomin, R., DeFries, J. C., Mcclearn, G. E., & McGuffin, P. (2000). *Behavioral genetics.* (Fourth ed.). New York: Worth.

For a clear and accessible account of the principles and methods in epidemiology see:

Sackett, D. L., Haynes, R. B., Tugwell, P. (1991). *Clinical epidemiology: a basic science for clinical medicine. Second edition.* Boston: Little, Brown & Co.

C5. Reading Comprehension Difficulties

KATE CAIN & JANE OAKHILL

ABSTRACT

In this chapter we consider the nature and the source of difficulties experienced by children with a specific type of comprehension deficit, children who have developed age-appropriate word reading skills but whose reading comprehension skills lag behind. As discussed elsewhere in this volume, text comprehension is a complex task that involves many different cognitive skills and processes. Consequently, there are many different aspects of the reading process where difficulties may arise, which may, in turn, contribute to these children's poor comprehension. In this chapter, we examine the evidence that impairments at the word-, sentence-, and discourse-level play a causal role in this population's comprehension difficulties. In addition, we consider whether deficits in cognitive abilities such as memory skills and general intelligence, and factors such as amount of exposure to print, contribute to poor comprehension.

INTRODUCTION

A child requires two skills to be a successful and independent reader: They must be able to decode[1] the individual words on the page and they must be able to comprehend the text. Word decoding and reading comprehension are highly related skills: correlations between these skills fall within the range of 0.3 to 0.77 (Juel, Griffith & Gough, 1986; Yuill & Oakhill, 1991). When decoding and reading comprehension difficulties are concomitant, problems with understanding can arise because laboured word decoding leaves the reader with insufficient processing capacity to compute the relations between successive words, phrases, and sentences to construct a coherent and meaningful representation of the text (e.g. Perfetti, 1985). However, accurate decoding skills do not ensure adequate reading comprehension. Approximately 10% of (British) school children have adequate

---

[1] In this context, we use the term decoding to refer to word recognition in general, which may be accomplished, for example, by recoding from graphemes to phonemes, by sight recognition, or by analogy (e.g. Ehri, 1999).

T. Nunes, P. Bryant (eds.), Handbook of Children's Literacy, 313–338.

decoding skills but poor reading comprehension (Stothard & Hulme, 1996; Yuill & Oakhill, 1991). Furthermore, these children demonstrate a general deficit in text comprehension, performing poorly on assessments of both reading and listening comprehension (Cain, Oakhill & Bryant, 2000a; Stothard & Hulme, 1992). Thus, decoding deficits are not an obvious source of their reading comprehension difficulties. This chapter is concerned with the nature and the source of the text comprehension difficulties (for both written and spoken text) experienced by this particular population, to whom we refer to as less skilled comprehenders.

Text comprehension is a complex task that involves many different cognitive skills and processes. Consequently, there are many different aspects of the reading process where difficulties may arise and which, in turn, affect text comprehension, e.g. word-level, sentence-level and discourse-level. In addition, cognitive abilities such as memory skills and general intelligence, and factors such as amount of exposure to print, may also affect comprehension. In this chapter we assess the evidence that deficits in each of these areas are a source of the problems that less skilled comprehenders have with text comprehension. In using this framework we are not suggesting that language processing takes place within a strictly modular system. We are simply using this categorisation to impose a workable structure on the chapter. Indeed, as will become clear during the course of our review, there is evidence that the processing of verbal information at three different language levels (word, sentence and discourse) can affect performance at another level in both a bottom-up and top-down manner. Another proposal that we explore is the distinction made by Perfetti, Marron and Foltz (1996) that comprehension may be affected by both knowledge and processing skills (e.g. vocabulary and inference making, respectively).

As mentioned above, weak decoding skills can adversely affect reading comprehension performance. Many studies investigating comprehension skills have either used an assessment of reading comprehension that confounds these two variables or have not controlled for individual differences in word reading skill (e.g., Forrest-Pressley & Waller, 1984; Jetton, Rupley & Willson, 1995; Kirby & Moore, 1987; Nation & Snowling, 1999; Paris & Jacobs, 1984; Smith, Macaruso, Shankweiler & Crain, 1989). Therefore, the extent to which such studies address comprehension difficulties rather than just general reading difficulties is unclear. For this reason, we concentrate on studies that have included measures of decoding skill and reading comprehension in this review. If measures of both these components are taken, the influence of decoding on comprehension level can be taken into account when analysing data or decoding skill can be held constant for the populations being studied. The latter procedure, matching groups for decoding skill, has been adopted by us and other researchers in much of the work that we discuss in this chapter (e.g. Yuill & Oakhill, 1991). Typical characteristics of groups from our research are shown in Table 1. As well as the issue of subject selection, there are a number of issues concerning the appropriate experimental design to test causal hypotheses, discussion of which is beyond the scope of this chapter. We refer the interested reader to Cain, Oakhill

Table 1 The mean scores (and standard deviations) of typical groups

	Less skilled comprehenders (N = 14)	Skilled comprehenders (N = 12)	Comprehension -age match (N = 12)
Chronological age	7,7 (4.44)	7,7 (4.04)	6,6 (3.88)
Sight vocabulary	37.21 (4.00)	37.42 (3.00)	32.92 (2.91)
Word reading accuracy in context	7,9 (5.17)	7,11 (5.73)	6,7 (4.98)
Reading comprehension	6,7 (3.87)	8,1 (5.14)	6,8 (3.11)

Note. Where appropriate, ages are given as years, months with standard deviations in months.

and Bryant (2000a) for further details on these issues in relation to reading comprehension.

The structure of the remainder of this chapter is as follows. In the following four sections we review the different potential sources of deficit, as outlined above. In the final discussion section, we relate these findings to a model of text representation and consider directions for future research.

WORD-LEVEL DEFICITS AS A SOURCE OF TEXT COMPREHENSION FAILURE

In this section we review work that investigates whether word-level difficulties are related to higher-level text comprehension deficits.

Speed and automaticity of decoding

Slow or inaccurate word reading may affect comprehension because it uses up limited processing capacity that is necessary for text comprehension processes such as integration (Perfetti, 1985). Identification of poor comprehenders who have accurate word recognition skills does not rule out the possibility that their word processing skills are slower and less efficient than those of good comprehenders. However, in several studies, assessments of word reading speed, automaticity of decoding and accuracy of nonword reading have revealed no differences between skilled and less skilled comprehenders (Oakhill, 1981; Stothard & Hulme, 1996).

Phonological skills

Phonological skills are strongly associated with word reading development (e.g. Bradley & Bryant, 1983; Wagner & Torgesen, 1987) and children with dyslexia commonly experience difficulties with the phonological representations of words (Hulme & Snowling, 1992). Phonological processing deficits have also been posited as an underlying cause of poor readers' comprehension difficulties in that they impair the reader's ability to retain verbal information in working memory and, thus, complete higher-level processing for meaning (see Shankweiler, 1989, for a review). Shankweiler and colleagues have repeatedly demonstrated differences between good and poor readers' ability to retain and process verbal information in a phonological form. However, this work did not take individual differences in word reading skill into account, so it does not demonstrate a direct relation between comprehension skill and phonological processing.

We know of only two studies that have investigated the relation between phonological processing skill and reading comprehension, whilst controlling for word reading ability (Cain, Oakhill & Bryant, 2000b; Stothard & Hulme, 1996). Both studies failed to find differences between skilled and less skilled comprehenders' performance on a range of tasks that involved the storage of phonological stimuli, and the isolation and manipulation of phonemes. Cain *et al.* did find a relation between comprehension skill and one phonological assessment, a version of Bradley and Bryant's (1983) odd-word-out task. The authors speculated that the poor comprehenders' difficulties with this task may reflect their weak working memory skills and subsequent work has confirmed that performance on this task is more dependent upon working memory than other phonological awareness tasks (Oakhill & Kyle, 2000). We discuss the relation between memory and comprehension skill in more detail later on.

Vocabulary and semantic knowledge

Word knowledge is highly correlated with reading comprehension ability in both children and adults (Carroll, 1993), but the relation between the two is not clear. Limited vocabulary knowledge does not always impair comprehension (Freebody & Anderson, 1983, but see Wittrock, Marks & Doctorow, 1975) and vocabulary knowledge *per se* does not appear to be sufficient to ensure adequate comprehension of larger units of text (e.g. Pany, Jenkins & Schreck, 1982). As already noted, several researchers have demonstrated that children can experience text comprehension difficulties even when vocabulary knowledge is controlled for (Ehrlich & Remond, 1997; Oakhill, Cain & Yuill, 1998; Stothard & Hulme, 1992).

Although simple vocabulary knowledge may not be a strong determinant of comprehension skill, individuals who possess a rich and interconnected knowledge base may comprehend text better than those whose representations are sparse. For example, Spilich, Vesonder, Chiesi and Voss (1979) demonstrated that prior knowledge about the topic of a text facilitates reading comprehension. Thus, if word meanings are poorly represented in semantic memory, less information will be accessed and perhaps fewer relations between concepts will be made than if a rich semantic representation for word meaning exists. A study by Nation and Snowling (1998a) found differences between good and poor comprehenders on a measure of semantic fluency: the Word Association subtest from the Clinical

Evaluation of Language Fundamentals-Revised (CELF-R, Semel, Wiig and Secord, 1987). In this test, children have to provide as many category members of a category name (e.g. animals) as possible. Nation and Snowling found that poor comprehenders produced fewer instances than did good comprehenders. In a further study, they compared the priming of words that were related by category but differed with respect to associative strength occurrence in both good and poor comprehenders (Nation & Snowling, 1999). For example, the word pairs "cat-dog" and "aeroplane-train" are both related by category, but the latter pair co-occurs in texts less frequently than "cat-dog" and, therefore, has a lower associative strength. Good comprehenders showed priming for both types of word pair, whereas poor comprehenders only showed priming for word pairs that had high associative strength as well as a category relation.

It is unclear whether Nation and Snowling's studies demonstrate semantic weaknesses in children with specific comprehension problems, because the good and poor comprehenders were not matched for word reading accuracy or for vocabulary skills. Thus, it is possible that the good comprehenders' superior performance on this task was due to their better word reading and/or vocabulary skills, rather than their superior discourse-level comprehension. Indeed, when skilled and less skilled comprehenders are matched for both word reading accuracy and sight vocabulary, we find that they produce comparable numbers of exemplars in the semantic fluency test (Cain, Oakhill & Lemmon, under review). Therefore, we suggest that limited semantic knowledge may be related to comprehension difficulties in certain populations of less skilled comprehenders but not others.

Whether or not these discrepant findings are due to population differences, it is important to establish the process by which the individual differences in the range and richness of semantic representations may arise in the first place. One plausible mechanism for vocabulary acquisition is to infer the meanings of unfamiliar vocabulary items from context (Daneman, 1988; Nagy, Herman & Anderson, 1985). Another source of variance (and one that may contribute to knowledge differences) is differential exposure to print (e.g. Stanovich, 1993). We shall consider these hypotheses in later sections.

Summary

There is a strong relation between general reading ability and decoding efficiency, phonological skills and vocabulary knowledge. However, children with text comprehension difficulties do not necessarily have deficient decoding skills: some poor comprehenders have fluent and accurate word reading skills. Furthermore, although a phonological processing deficit is a plausible source of the text comprehension difficulties experienced by poor word readers, there is no evidence for a direct relation between the tasks assumed to measure phonological processing and reading comprehension skill. There is some evidence that individual differences in semantic representation are related to comprehension performance, but not all studies have included vocabulary controls. To date the direction of the relation between these two skills has not been addressed: whether good semantic knowledge is a by-product of experience in reading and understanding text or whether it is (in part) contributing to success in text comprehension. However, there is evidence that individual differences in time spent reading account for differences in the growth of vocabulary knowledge (Echols, West, Stanovich & Zehr, 1996), so this is an important area for future investigations.

SENTENCE-LEVEL DEFICITS AS A SOURCE OF TEXT COMPREHENSION FAILURE

Once words have been recognised and their meanings retrieved, the meaning of the sentence must be established. Knowledge about syntactic constraints can aid this process because knowledge about the meanings and order of the noun and verb phrases may be insufficient to establish who did what to whom in sentences such as the following: "The mouse that scared the elephant was chased by the cat". It is perhaps not surprising then that measures of syntactic awareness correlate with measures of reading ability (e.g. Bowey, 1986a; Siegel & Ryan, 1989). First, we consider the relation between reading comprehension and sentence structure. In the second part of this section we consider the extent to which grammatical and semantic constraints may be related to text comprehension via their influence on word comprehension and word recognition.

Syntactic knowledge

There are two ways in which grammatical knowledge may directly facilitate comprehension. It facilitates the comprehension of sentences such as the example above where semantics might be misleading. It has also been suggested that grammatical knowledge may facilitate the detection and correction of reading errors, thereby enhancing comprehension monitoring (Bowey, 1986b; Tunmer & Bowey, 1984). Not all children with discourse-level comprehension problems demonstrate deficits in syntactic knowledge (Yuill & Oakhill, 1991). However, a study by Stothard and Hulme (1992), using the same measure as Yuill and Oakhill, revealed differences between skilled and less skilled comprehenders. It is important to assess memory skills when investigating sentence understanding. Some studies indicate that memory, rather than knowledge, limitations underlie poor sentence-level comprehension (e.g. Smith, Macaruso, Shankweiler & Crain, 1989), whereas others do not (Bentin, Deutsch & Liberman, 1990). We also need to consider the nature of the relation between syntactic skills and text comprehension: do good syntactic skills arise through good reading comprehension experience, or are they a pre-requisite for skilled comprehension? The precise relation between syntactic knowledge and comprehension is still open for investigation.

Use of sentence context

This section considers work exploring the relation between comprehension skill and the ability to use sentence context to aid both word comprehension and word reading.

The first piece of evidence that less skilled comprehenders make less use of sentence context when constructing meaning comes from an early study by Oakhill (1983). This study was designed to investigate a particular type of inference, an instantiation, where the reader infers a specific meaning of a common noun from the sentence context. For example inferring that "fish" is most likely a "shark" in the following sentence: "The fish frightened the swimmer". Less skilled comprehenders made fewer instantiations than did skilled comprehenders, suggesting that their local processing of text is less influenced by the semantic content of the sentence.

The context of a sentence may also enable the reader to select the appropriate meaning of an ambiguous word. Gernsbacher and Faust (1991) explored this process in college students, who were classified as either good or poor comprehenders. (The students' word reading skills were not reported, but presumably individual differences in word reading do not influence reading comprehension skill in a population of college students to the extent that they might do in a population of school children.) The students were presented with sentences that provided either a neutral or biasing context for the final word, which could take two meanings, e.g. "he picked up the spade" or "he dug with the spade". The task was to decide whether a target word, "garden", was related to the overall meaning of the sentence. Both good and poor comprehenders made use of the biasing context, which suggests that adults with comprehension difficulties are not deficient in their use of sentence context to guide meaning.

Tunmer and Bowey (1984) proposed that children might use the constraints of sentence structure to supplement basic letter-sound knowledge to facilitate word recognition. We know of only one study that has investigated whether sentence context facilitates poor comprehenders' ability to read words, rather than comprehend them (Nation & Snowling, 1998b). In this study, children heard a non-constraining sentence frame such as "I went shopping with my mum and my ____". They were then presented with one of two different word types on a computer screen. Some had an exceptional spelling-sound pattern, "aunt" for the example above. Other items were words with a regular pronunciation, such as "cash", that had a neighbour with an inconsistent pronunciation, for this example "wash". Accuracy and reading times were recorded. Good comprehenders benefited more than poor comprehenders from the context for both types of word. Because the sentences were constructed so that the final word was not predictable, it is likely that both syntactic and semantic knowledge contributed to performance in this task. Nation and Snowling conclude that impoverished contextual facilitation skills may adversely affect growth in word reading skill of poor comprehenders. Thus, they may develop into garden-variety poor readers, with weak decoding and comprehension skills, unable to use their comprehension skills to bootstrap their word reading development.

Summary

These studies suggest that at least some children with specific comprehension problems experience difficulties with sentence structure. Clearly, further studies are necessary to establish whether some poor comprehenders are delayed in their acquisition of particular syntactic structures, and the direction of any link between comprehension and syntactic knowledge.

Less skilled comprehenders are less likely to make use of sentence context to guide their comprehension of common nouns. But adults with weak comprehension skills are able to use a biasing sentence context to guide their interpretation of an ambiguous noun. Further work with children is necessary to determine when and how sentence context affects word comprehension, and the direction of the relation. Finally, there is some evidence that good comprehenders are less likely to use context to aid word recognition. However, it is not known whether this impairment is a source of higher-level comprehension difficulties or a by-product of them.

TEXT-LEVEL DEFICITS AS A SOURCE OF READING COMPREHENSION FAILURE

The higher-level text-processing skills that we consider are integration and inference making, anaphoric reference, use of discourse-level context, and story structure. We also examine metacognitive knowledge and processes. We have explored these skills in some detail, and find that it is at this level of processing (and knowledge) that differences between good and poor comprehenders are most reliably found. Furthermore, our investigations into some of these areas have begun to address the issue of causality using a comprehension-age match design and training studies. Thus, we are able to draw some conclusions about the most plausible direction of these relations.

Text integration and inference making

Inference making ability is a valuable component skill of reading comprehension. Not all details are explicitly mentioned by the author, so the reader must generate links between different parts of a text and use general knowledge to fill in missing detail, in order to construct an adequate and coherent representation of the text.

Early work by Oakhill revealed that less skilled comprehenders are poor at making inferences when reading or listening to text. Relative to skilled comprehenders, less skilled comprehenders generate fewer constructive inferences, i.e. inferences which require the reader to integrate information from two different sources (Oakhill, 1982), and they are poor at incorporating general knowledge with information in the text to generate simple inferences (Oakhill, 1984). Memory for the text itself did not appear to be the source of their difficulties in these studies.

In recent work we have investigated whether knowledge deficits are a possible source of the less skilled comprehenders' difficulties, given that this knowledge is crucial for the second type of inference described above (Cain, Oakhill, Barnes & Bryant, 2001). We used a procedure that was developed by Barnes and colleagues (e.g., Barnes & Dennis, 1998) that enabled strict control of individual differences in general knowledge. Children were taught a set of facts about an imaginary planet, called Gan. For example, "The flowers on Gan are hot like fire"; "The ponds on Gan are filled with orange juice". Once this knowledge base had been learned, children were read a multi-episode story and were then asked questions to assess their ability to generate inferences. In order to draw these inferences, children had to incorporate an item from the knowledge base with a premise in the text. Recall of the knowledge base was assessed once more at the end of the story and only responses to inference questions for which the knowledge base item was recalled were included in the final analysis. Even when knowledge was controlled for in this very strict way, less skilled comprehenders generated fewer inferences than did the skilled comprehenders.

Another study (Cain & Oakhill, 1999a) included a comprehension-age match group and, thus, sheds some light on the likely direction of the relation between comprehension skill and inference making. In this study, less skilled comprehenders were significantly poorer than skilled comprehenders at generating two types of inference: those that required them to integrate information between two sentences, and those for which they had to incorporate general knowledge with information provided in the text in order to establish adequate sense. The less skilled comprehenders were also significantly poorer than the comprehension-age match group on the first type of inference. We concluded, therefore, that deficient inference making skills were not the result of inferior reading comprehension skills in general, because the less skilled and comprehension-age match groups were matched on this measure. The less skilled comprehenders' difficulties could not be attributed to poor memory for the text, because recall of verbatim detail from the story was comparable for all groups. Again, there was no evidence that general knowledge was the source of difficulty: When an inference was not made, additional questions revealed that all children had the requisite knowledge to make these inferences. Instead, this result suggests that difficulty with the process of inference making contributes to poor reading comprehension.

Two training studies support this proposed direction of causality. In the first, Yuill and Joscelyne (1988) taught children to make inferences from key "clue" words in deliberately obscure texts. In one story, the text does not state explicitly that the main character was lying in the bath, but this setting can be inferred from words such as "soap", "towel", and "steamy". After training, the children were tested on similar types of story. The less skilled comprehenders benefited more from the training than the skilled group. In another study, Yuill and Oakhill (1988) trained children to make the same type of lexical inference and also to generate questions to test their understanding. The less skilled comprehenders who had received this training made substantial gains in comprehension on the Neale comprehension sub-test, relative to the skilled comprehenders.

Our work, thus far, has demonstrated that less skilled comprehenders have persistent problems with inference making in both reading and listening comprehension tasks. However, the source of the less skilled comprehenders' inference making difficulties is not clear. There is no evidence that memory for the text and/or general knowledge deficits are a fundamental source of difficulty, although they might well be in other populations. One type of knowledge deficit that has not yet been extensively studied is knowing how to make an inference. The training studies may have been successful because they taught the less skilled comprehenders this skill. Another factor to consider is working memory, the capacity to store and process information simultaneously. Performance on working memory tasks discriminates between good and poor comprehenders and we discuss this factor in the section on cognitive processes.

Anaphoric processing

An anaphor is a linguistic device that maintains referential continuity within a text. An anaphor can be a pronoun, such as "he", and takes its meaning from its antecedent in another (preceding) part of the text. "John" is the antecedent for the anaphoric pronoun "he" in the following: "John was very tired, so he went to bed". Anaphoric links can be made both within and between sentences. Anaphoric resolution is, thus, similar to inference making, in that the reader must make links between different parts of the text to maintain coherence.

Oakhill and Yuill compared skilled and less skilled comprehenders' ability to supply and resolve anaphors in three studies. In the first study (Yuill & Oakhill, 1991, expt. 4.4) children were presented with 2-clause sentences, such as "Peter lent his coat to Sue because she was cold". In this example, the antecedent (Sue) of the anaphor (she) is cued because there is only one female antecedent in the main clause. Less skilled comprehenders were worse at resolving the anaphors overall, whether or not a cue was present. A second experiment (Oakhill & Yuill, 1986) demonstrated that less skilled comprehenders were also poorer than skilled comprehenders at supplying the correct anaphor (either "he" or "she") in sentences such as the following "'Steven gave his umbrella to Penny in the park because ___ wanted to keep dry". A final experiment (Yuill & Oakhill, 1988) explored anaphoric reference more generally by using four types of cohesive ties: reference, ellipses, substitutions, and lexical ties. The text used was longer and more naturalistic than the short ones used in the above studies. Again, less skilled comprehenders were poorer at resolving these cohesive ties.

Ehrlich and colleagues have extended this line of research in their exploration of anaphoric processing in French children. Ehrlich and Remond (1997) demonstrated that 9-year-old less skilled comprehenders were generally impaired in resolving both pronoun and general noun anaphors, and had particular difficulty with object pronouns that had distant antecedents. In other studies, this group of researchers has explored the link between anaphoric processing and metacognitive skill (the latter is discussed in detail below).

Ehrlich (1996) compared 13- and 15-year-old skilled and less skilled comprehenders' ability to detect inconsistencies in expository texts. The inconsistencies occurred where nouns with contrasting meanings replaced noun phrase anaphors. Less skilled comprehenders detected fewer of these contradictions than did the skilled group. In a later experiment, Ehrlich, Remond and Tardieu (1999) found that 10-year-old less skilled comprehenders also detected fewer anaphoric inconsistencies.

These studies demonstrate that less skilled comprehenders of different ages have difficulties with anaphoric processing: they are poor at resolving anaphors, supplying appropriate anaphors, and detecting inconsistent anaphors. Clearly a difficulty in establishing anaphoric reference will affect the reader's ability to construct a coherent and integrated representation of the text. A deficit in using these devices may, therefore, lead to text comprehension problems. However, to our knowledge, no studies investigating the direction of the relation between these skills have been undertaken.

Use of context at the discourse-level

In this section we review work that has investigated whether poor comprehenders experience deficits in their ability to use the context of a story to establish meaning.

A recent study explored less skilled comprehenders' ability to use story context to derive the meanings of novel vocabulary items (Cain, Oakhill, & Elbro, in press). Good and poor comprehenders read short texts that contained an unknown (made-up) word, the meaning of which could be derived from information contained in one of the story sentences. This sentence occurred either immediately after the unknown word or later in the story after some additional filler sentences. In general, less skilled comprehenders were poorer at this task than the skilled comprehenders. However, they were particularly impaired on stories where the additional filler sentences separated the occurrence of the unknown word and the helpful sentence context, a condition where the working memory demands of the task were greatest. As mentioned in the section on semantic knowledge, skill in making discourse-level inferences may be an important determinant of vocabulary acquisition (e.g., Daneman, 1988; Jensen, 1980; Sternberg & Powell, 1983). Thus, a weakness in this higher-level ability may affect subsequent vocabulary growth, and lead to lower-level deficits in word level knowledge.

Sometimes a reader may come across a phrase in a text that cannot be interpreted by reference to a single sentence. Instead, he or she must use the overall theme of the text to make sense of it. We have investigated this skill by studying children's ability to determine the meanings of idioms (Cain & Oakhill, 1999b). Idioms are figurative expressions that are often categorised into two types: Transparent idioms, such as "to skate on thin ice", whose meaning can be deduced from the component words, and opaque idioms, such as "to kick the bucket", whose meaning has become obscure and must be learned. Children were presented with short stories that contained an idiom, some of which were novel. For both 8 year olds and 10 year olds we found that skilled comprehenders were more likely than less skilled comprehenders to produce interpretations that were either accurate interpretations of the idioms or a plausible figurative interpretation. The less skilled comprehenders' interpretations of these phrases were less likely to be based on the context of the story as a whole, and included literal interpretations of these phrases that were implausible within the context of the story.

Less skilled comprehenders experience particular difficulty with the use of story context to facilitate understanding of unknown words and phrases in text. This higher-level process may be an important mechanism for acquiring information from context in everyday reading and, thus, impairments in the use of context may affect vocabulary growth. We need to establish whether a deficit in the use of context leads to reading comprehension (and word level) problems or is a result of such difficulties.

Metacognition

In this section we discuss work which assesses the relation between metacognitive aspects of reading and comprehension ability. Metacognition has been defined as "*Knowledge about* and *regulation of* cognitive states and processes" (Kurtz, 1991, emphasis added). For example, knowledge about the goals of reading, and the ability to monitor and regulate one's reading to meet the demands of the current task. We shall adopt this distinction in our review.

Knowledge

It is not surprising that younger and poorer readers have limited knowledge about reading, and that they tend to focus on the word reading rather than the meaning construction aspects of the task (Myers & Paris, 1978; Paris & Jacobs, 1984). However, there is some evidence that poor comprehenders place a greater emphasis on word-level aspects of reading, compared to skilled comprehenders (Garner & Kraus, 1981-1982; Yuill & Oakhill, 1991). For example, Yuill and Oakhill (1991) found that less skilled comprehenders regard poor decoding skills as a particularly important indicator of reading difficulties. Skilled and less skilled comprehenders differ in their knowledge about both the aims of reading and also about how to repair comprehension failures (Cain, 1999). Furthermore, both English and Italian poor comprehenders demonstrate impaired knowledge about which reading strategies are appropriate for different reading situations, e.g. studying or reading for pleasure (Cain, 1999; Pazzaglia, Cornoldi, & de Beni, 1995). Although these studies demonstrate that metacognitive differences are related specifically to comprehension ability, it is not yet clear whether these knowledge differences arise through differential reading experience or whether they (in part) contribute to individual differences in comprehension skill.

Processes

An important comprehension skill is the reader's ability to regulate their reading to the demands of the current task. If an individual realises that their comprehension is inadequate, they can take appropriate steps to remedy the situation although, as noted above, less skilled comprehenders may not always possess the necessary metacognitive knowledge for such action.

A popular method used to assess skill in monitoring one's comprehension is an inconsistency detection task. In this task, children read short texts containing inconsistencies either between different parts of the text, i.e. conflicting information given in two sentences, or between information given in the text and external information, such as general knowledge. Oakhill, Hartt and Samols (1996) found that less skilled comprehenders were less accurate than skilled comprehenders in detecting nonsense words and anomalous phrases in short narratives. In a second experiment, the less skilled comprehenders were also poorer at detecting pairs of sentences that were contradictory. The difference was more pronounced when the contradictory sentences were separated by filler text, which the authors attribute to individual differences in working memory capacity. This study indicates a processing difficulty for less skilled comprehenders.

Ehrlich's studies on anaphoric processing (Ehrlich, 1996; Ehrlich, Remond, & Tardieu, 1999) suggest that skilled comprehenders may have lacked knowledge about how to repair comprehension failure. For example, the skilled compre-henders not only spent longer reading the inconsistent parts of the text, but they were more likely to look back to the preceding text when an inconsistency was encountered. Ehrlich, Remond and Tardieu (1999) found that the less skilled comprehenders' evaluations of their understanding indicated that they were aware to some extent of their difficulties with these texts. Other work (Cataldo & Oakhill, 2000) also indicates that strategy knowledge may play a role. In this study, Italian school children were required to look back through narrative texts to locate the answers for particular questions. The search strategies that they used were recorded. Less skilled comprehenders used less sophisticated strategies for locating information. For example, they would begin their search at the beginning of the narrative, rather than starting at the paragraph that contained the answer.

There is also a relation between reading comprehension skill and the ability to regulate reading style for different reading goals (Cain, 1999). This study included a comprehension-age match group in order to assess the most plausible direction of any relation between these two skills. Children read short stories under different instruction conditions, such as "skim read" or "read to study". Both the skilled comprehenders and the comprehension-age match group adapted their reading to the instructions, reading more quickly in the "skim read" condition than in the "study" condition. Furthermore, as predicted, their comprehension of the text was poorest in the "skim read" condition and best in the "study" condition. Neither reading speed nor comprehension of the stories was affected by instruction condition for the less skilled comprehenders. The differences found between the less skilled comprehenders and the comprehension-age match group indicate that the ability to set and reach suitable reading targets is not simply a by-product of reading comprehension level. We interpret these findings as evidence that the ability to adapt reading in different situations may be one source of the less skilled comprehenders' general text comprehension difficulties. We have administered tests of comprehension monitoring to the cohort participating in our longitudinal study (Oakhill, Cain & Bryant, in press). We find that a child's performance on this measure when aged 8 years predicts their general reading comprehension ability a year later. Thus, there is some evidence that this skill is necessary for growth and development of comprehension skills.

Less skilled comprehenders are poor at monitoring their understanding of both narrative and expository text. Their ability to search through text and to regulate their reading style is also poor. Furthermore, there is some indication that their knowledge about reading and repair strategies is inadequate. The extent to which knowledge and processing deficits interact warrants further investigation. However, there is some evidence that a weakness in the latter skill may contribute to comprehension difficulties.

Story structure knowledge

Knowledge about the organisation of texts increases throughout middle childhood, although the majority of studies have concentrated on narrative texts (e.g., Stein & Glenn, 1982). Children's recall of stories indicates that tacit knowledge of the structural importance of story units is related to general reading ability (Smiley, Oakley, Worthen, Campione & Brown, 1977). Perfetti (1994) proposes that a possible source of comprehension failure is inadequate knowledge about text structures, which may arise because of insufficient reading experience.

Several studies have found that less skilled comprehenders demonstrate poorer awareness of text structure than do skilled comprehenders. Yuill and Oakhill (1991) presented skilled and less skilled comprehenders with stories, either aurally or in picture form. The task was to select the main point of the story from a choice of four statements, the others being the main setting, the main event, and an incorrect main point. Less skilled comprehenders were poor at selecting the main point of the story in both presentation conditions. In another study, they investigated the connectives that children included in stories that they either retold (after the experimenter), or narrated from picture sequences. In the retelling task, less skilled comprehenders and skilled comprehenders produced comparable numbers of the connectives that appeared in the original version, but the skilled comprehenders were more likely to include additional connectives. When required to narrate the story told by a picture sequence, less skilled comprehenders produced fewer causal connectives and used referential ties ambiguously. Thus, less skilled comprehenders have difficulties with elements of cohesion that make a story well structured and integrated. Less skilled comprehenders also demonstrate weaknesses with other aspects of text structure. Using a production task, Cain and Oakhill (1996) assessed the structural quality of stores narrated from topic prompts, such as "Pirates", and also picture sequences. When given the topic prompt, less skilled comprehenders produced more poorly organised stories than both skilled comprehenders and a comprehension-age match group. However, their stories were better integrated when narrated from the picture sequence. A later study (Cain, in press) replicated this earlier finding and demonstrated that less skilled comprehenders can also benefit from a title that states the overall direction or point of the story, e.g. "How the pirates lost their treasure".

Several points arise from these studies. First, poorer performance by the less skilled comprehenders, relative to the comprehension-age match group, indicates that the ability to produce structured coherent stories does not simply arise from good reading comprehension experience. Rather, a deficit in this skill is more plausibly associated with the causes of poor comprehension. Second, less skilled comprehenders are able to tell coherent stories when given appropriate help. This finding is supported by a study that assessed skilled and less skilled comprehenders' understanding of abstract stories (Yuill & Joscelyne, 1988). When provided with a title that described the main point of the abstract story, less skilled comprehenders benefited more than did the skilled comprehenders.

Other work has demonstrated a relation between comprehension skill and children's knowledge about the information carried by particular features of text, namely story titles, beginnings and endings. Cain (1996) found that less skilled comprehenders were poor at explaining the types of information that are found in story titles. More than 80% of skilled comprehenders could give appropriate examples of the sort of information contained in a story title, such as "tells you what its about and who's in it", whereas less than one quarter of the less skilled comprehenders were able to do so. The latter group were more likely to respond that a title "tells you whether you like the story or not" and some stated that titles do not tell the reader anything at all! Less skilled comprehenders were also the least aware that the beginnings of stories might contain important information about settings and characters. This work indicates that they have less explicit awareness about these textual features, which can be useful aids for the reader, helping them to invoke relevant background information and schemas.

This work demonstrates that less skilled comprehenders have impaired sensitivity to the function of different parts of a story. In addition, they are poor at comprehending and producing stories unless given support in the form of integrated picture sequences and titles. There is some evidence to suggest that some aspects of story knowledge and the ability to structure stories are determinants of reading comprehension skill. As yet, we cannot state whether the differences found between skilled and less skilled comprehenders arose from processing or knowledge differences. The support provided by picture sequences and goal-directed titles may have freed up useful processing resources enabling the less skilled comprehenders to plan more integrated stories and/or to use a variety of connectives. On the other hand, less skilled comprehenders may have inadequate knowledge about the function of particular connectives, and also story structure and story schemas, knowledge which the helpful prompts may have provided. However, although less skilled comprehenders are poor at explaining the information contained in a variety of textual features, they clearly have some tacit awareness of such cues, benefiting from integrated and goal-directed titles in comprehension and production tasks.

Summary

Less skilled comprehenders experience difficulties with a wide-range of text-level comprehension skills: inference making, anaphoric processing, structuring stories, metacognitive knowledge and monitoring skills, use of context at the discourse-level. There is some evidence that deficits in first four areas might lead to general text-level comprehension difficulties. Such findings need to be followed up by training studies which, if successful, would provide ways to remediate some of the difficulties experience by less skilled comprehenders.

COGNITIVE PROCESSES

Memory skills

In order to understand prose, the reader must be able to hold information in memory whilst computing the relations between successive words and sentences in order to construct a coherent, integrated representation of the text.

Short-term memory

There is little evidence that the ability to store information in short-term memory is related to specific comprehension difficulties. Less skilled comprehenders' recall of strings of words or digits is comparable to that of their skilled peers (Oakhill, Yuill & Parkin, 1986; Stothard & Hulme, 1992). However, other research suggests that less skilled comprehenders' may have a very selective impairment in the passive storage of verbal information.

Nation, Adams, Bowyer-Crane, and Snowling (1999) found that good and poor comprehenders' recall of concrete nouns (e.g., tooth, fruit) was comparable, but that less skilled comprehenders were poorer when the items to be recalled were abstract (e.g., luck, pride). They conclude that the poor comprehenders' impairment is a reflection of underlying semantic weaknesses. Whereas the good comprehenders were aided by both phonological and semantic representations of the items to be recalled, the poor comprehenders had impoverished semantic knowledge and were thus at a disadvantage when they had to remember certain stimuli, such as abstract words. This restriction in short-term memory could affect later processing and, therefore, lead to text-level deficits. This hypothesis is certainly interesting, and warrants further exploration, but there is an alternative explanation of these findings that should first be ruled out. Nation *et al.* did not match their good and poor comprehenders for word knowledge (neither word reading accuracy nor vocabulary). Thus, the poor comprehenders that they studied may have had poorer phonological representations of the abstract words because they had weaker word recognition and vocabulary skills, which could have resulted in storage and recall difficulties.

Working memory

As mentioned previously, the reader (or listener) must generate links between different sentences and ideas in order to construct an integrated representation of a text. To achieve this objective, information must be held in memory whilst concurrently carrying out processing operations, i.e., storing the information from one sentence whilst reading the next one. This more active function of memory is known as working memory.

Daneman and Carpenter (1980, 1983) developed the Reading Span Test to measure working memory capacity. The task requires the individual to read and understand a series of sentences (the processing component) whilst concurrently remembering the final word from each sentence (the storage component). Performance on this task is significantly correlated to college students' comprehension skill. Yuill, Oakhill and Parkin (1989) demonstrated that less-skilled comprehenders are poorer on working memory tasks relative to skilled comprehenders (even tasks that require the processing of numbers and not sentences). They propose that this impairment in the ability to store and process information simultaneously may account for the less-skilled comprehenders' difficulties in resolving anomalies and generating inferences from text. Two recent studies have demonstrated that children's reading comprehension skill is specifically related to the processing and storage of verbal material: comprehension level was not related to performance on spatial working memory tasks (Nation *et al.*, 1999; Seigneuric, Ehrlich, Oakhill, & Yuill, 2000).

As mentioned above, Nation and colleagues propose that the memory limitations found in their population of poor comprehenders reflect underlying semantic weaknesses. Another possibility, originally proposed by Gernsbacher (e.g., Gernsbacher, Varner & Faust, 1990), is that limitations arise from difficulties in inhibiting irrelevant information. For example, Gernsbacher and colleagues found that adult poor comprehenders had trouble in rejecting the inappropriate meaning of an ambiguous word. Good comprehenders were quick to reject such meanings. Another group of researchers working with adult good and poor comprehenders have found that the poor comprehenders often erroneously recalled items from previous trials (de Beni, Palladino, Pazzaglia, & Cornoldi, 1998). The relation between inhibition and comprehension skill needs to be explored in relation to children's comprehension problems.

Although working memory limitations are related to comprehension impairments, it still not clear how the working memory difficulty arises, and which aspects of the task are affected. Furthermore, the work reported so far does not address the issue of whether working memory limitations are a cause or a consequence of reading comprehension difficulties. Studies that have included a comprehension-age match have not ruled out the possibility that working memory differences are the result of differential reading experience, rather than causally related to comprehension skill (Cain, 1994; Stothard & Hulme, 1992). Indeed, Tunmer (1989) has proposed that practice at representing and manipulating linguistic information may facilitate working memory ability.

Verbal ability

In adult populations, reading comprehension skill is related to verbal IQ (e.g. Sternberg & Powell, 1983). Stothard and Hulme (1996) found that children who were less skilled comprehenders obtained low verbal IQ scores relative to their performance IQ. They conclude that less skilled comprehenders have a specific deficit in their verbal skills. We gave the same assessments to similarly selected groups of skilled and less skilled comprehenders (Cain, Oakhill & Bryant, 1999). Like Stothard and Hulme's sample a significant difference between the groups was only evident on the verbal IQ measure. However, the less skilled comprehenders' mean pro-rated verbal IQ score was 97, which is within the "average" range. Other recent work indicates that deficits in verbal intelligence alone cannot completely explain variance in reading comprehension. Oakhill, Cain and Bryant (in press) found that particular comprehension skills such as inference making, comprehension monitoring, story structuring ability, and working memory capacity, predicted variance in reading comprehension skill, even after verbal intelligence scores and vocabulary had been accounted for.

A general assumption is that adequate levels of intelligence are necessary for good comprehension skills to develop. Alternatively, good comprehension may lead to better performance on measures of IQ. It is important to determine the direction of the relation between reading comprehension and verbal IQ, because it may affect our approach to remediation of comprehension difficulties. Indeed, there is some evidence for the second proposal: Stanovich (1993) has shown that reading experience can foster growth in general verbal ability. Perhaps greater experience in reading and understanding text develops vocabulary knowledge and skills such as inferencing and integration skills, which may facilitate performance on IQ tests. It is plausible, therefore, that a reciprocal relation exists: an individual requires a basic level of intelligence to be able to read and comprehend text, but experience and practice in comprehension skills may then lead to IQ gains.

Exposure to print

As stated in previous sections, inadequate knowledge about semantics, text structure, reading strategies etc. may arise because of insufficient reading experience. Differences in reading experience will also lead to differences in children's experience of processes important for comprehension, such as working memory, use of context, inference making etc. Several studies have found a relation between children's reading comprehension and the time they spend reading (Anderson, Wilson, & Fielding, 1988; Cipielewski & Stanovich, 1992; Taylor, Frye, & Maruyama, 1990). Cunningham and Stanovich (1997) have found that exposure to print accounted for unique variance in grade 11 reading comprehension even after earlier reading comprehension skill had been taken into account. Thus, experience with print can predict later comprehension skill, over and above initial comprehension level.

It is likely that mechanisms such as use of context, inference making skill, and comprehension monitoring, share variance with initial comprehension skill. Thus, the amount and type of practice a child gets may be important for growth in these areas, and also comprehension in general, in addition to skill proficiency at an early age. The amount of time engaged in reading will determine the amount of experience a child has with comprehension skills, which may help to strengthen these skills and make their use more automatic. Time spent reading will also affect the likelihood that the reader will come into contact with a range of vocabulary and text genres.

We have found that 7–8-year-old skilled and less skilled comprehenders matched for word reading accuracy do not differ on a measure of print exposure (Cain, Oakhill & Bryant, 2000a). That finding does not rule out the possibility that these groups may differ in their reading experience as they grow older. Presumably, children with poor comprehension skills derive less pleasure from reading, thus the extent to which they engage in reading as a pastime may reduce over the years, relative to that of peers with initially good comprehension skills.

Thus, we would predict that groups of skilled and less skilled comprehenders who were originally matched for word reading and vocabulary skills may differ on these measures later in time, with less skilled comprehenders becoming "garden-variety" poor readers (see also Nation and Snowling, 1998b). However, a more complicated pattern may emerge. Stanovich (1993) reports work with adults who exhibited a discrepancy between their print exposure and reading comprehension ability. He found that individuals with high levels of reading experience but relatively poor comprehension skills actually did better on a measure of receptive vocabulary than did good comprehenders who read little, and that the two groups were comparable on several other verbal cognitive measures. These data suggest that experience with print can, in part, compensate for modest comprehension skill.

However, once differences in word reading skill are apparent, differences in comprehension may be further increased. Better readers will engage with texts that have more difficult and less frequent vocabulary, more difficult syntactic constructions, and more complex text structures. For this reason, it is important to ensure in studies investigating causes of comprehension failure that skilled and less skilled comprehenders are initially matched for their contextual word reading abilities.

Summary

There is little evidence that populations with specific comprehension deficits experience difficulties with the simple storage of verbal information, but it is apparent that they have limitations in their ability to store and process simultaneously. The source of these difficulties, possibly semantic deficiencies or weak inhibition skills, remains to be established. Furthermore, the direction of the relation between working memory and reading comprehension is not yet clear. There are indications that another posited source of comprehension problems, general verbal ability, cannot fully account for comprehension skill deficits. In addition, evidence from adult populations indicates that this skill may interact reciprocally with reading comprehension over time. Differential exposure to print may provide differential opportunities to practice text comprehension skills and, thus, be an important factor in reading development.

CONCLUSIONS

This chapter was concerned with the nature and source of the difficulties experienced by children who have delayed reading comprehension in the presence of adequate word reading and vocabulary. These children experience deficits with many types of knowledge and processes that are important to reading. Their problems are most reliably found on tasks that assess text-level comprehension skills, such as inference making, anaphoric processing, comprehension monitoring, the use of discourse-level context, and knowledge and use of story structure. The results from both training studies and those adopting a comprehension-age match design indicate that deficits in both inference making ability and story production may be causally linked to text comprehension difficulties. Further work is necessary to establish the likely direction of the relation between other text-level skills and reading comprehension ability.

As well as the text-level difficulties experienced by less-skilled comprehenders, impairments in the use of sentence-level context and some syntactic structures have also been reported. Although some researchers report word-level semantic deficits, others do not, and it may be the case that these discrepancies reflect population differences, such that different populations of poor comprehender experience different fundamental weaknesses. Currently, the extent to which children with text-level reading comprehension difficulties also experience deficits at the word and/or sentence level is not known. Further work is necessary to establish whether and how such impairments may be related to text comprehension difficulties in general. In addition, we need to determine the direction of causality between such weaknesses and inadequate comprehension. For example, semantic deficits may lead to text level comprehension difficulties or, alternatively, inadequate text processing skills may impair the acquisition and richness of semantic representations.

The picture that emerges of less skilled comprehenders from the studies we have reviewed is of children who are able to integrate information locally in a text, but who are not able to produce a coherent Mental Model (see Johnson-Laird, 1983) of the text as a whole. Such problems are apparent in both their understanding and their production of stories – they do not seem to be able to plan a globally coherent story, but can produce locally coherent text. Thus, such children could be characterised as lacking a "drive for coherence" in both comprehension and production of text. It is not, at the moment, clear what underlies this inability to produce causally linked and well-integrated text models. It may be that less-skilled comprehenders know less about, or are less willing to use, strategies in comprehension. Or, it may be that the strategies that they try to use to build integrated models are less effective than those of skilled comprehenders, perhaps because of some fundamental differences in information-processing ability between the groups.

When investigating comprehension failure, we should also be aware of the limitations of experimental comparisons between skilled and less skilled comprehenders. As Cornoldi, de Beni, and Pazzaglia (1996) point out, such studies do not establish whether less skilled comprehenders *in general* present a particular deficit or whether *every* less skilled comprehender presents that deficit. They looked at the performance of 12 less-skilled comprehenders on a range of different comprehension-related tasks. Different children exhibited different profiles of skill strength and deficit. For example, one child demonstrated metacognitive deficits but no working memory deficits, whilst another demonstrated working memory deficits but no metacognitive deficits, although the majority were impaired on some of the assessments of these two skills. Given the number of cognitive skills associated with good reading comprehension, it would be surprising (and discouraging from a remediation point of view) if *all* the abilities associated with good reading comprehension were deficient in *all* less skilled comprehenders. Cornoldi *et al.*'s analysis suggests that the population of children with comprehension difficulties is far from homogenous. It may be that different types of poor comprehender exist: some may have a fundamental weakness in working memory that restricts their ability to make inferences, whilst others may have the necessary working memory capacity to perform such tasks, but lack the relevant metacognitive and strategic knowledge. Thus, different children may fail to construct coherent representations of text because of different underlying impairments.

As this review has demonstrated, we have now established many areas in which children with text-comprehension difficulties demonstrate weaknesses. Work investigating the causal relation between comprehension skill and these deficits is still in its infancy. However, given the range of knowledge and processing problems associated with poor comprehension, and the complex nature of the reading comprehension task itself, it is likely that different children will experience different patterns of deficit.

REFERENCES

Anderson, R. C., Wilson, P. T., and Fielding, L. G. (1988). Growth in reading and how children spend their time outside of school. *Reading Research Quarterly, 13*, 285-303.

Barnes, M. A. & Dennis, M. (1998). Discourse after early-onset hydrocephalus: Core deficits in children of average intelligence. *Brain and Language, 61*, 309-334.

Bentin, S., Deutsch, A., & Liberman I. Y. (1990). Syntactic competence and reading ability in children. *Journal of Experimental Child Psychology, 48*, 147-172.

Bowey, J. A. (1986a). Syntactic awareness and verbal performance from preschool to fifth grade. *Journal of Psycholinguistic Research, 15*, 285-306.

Bowey, J. A. (1986b). Syntactic awareness in relation to reading skill and ongoing comprehension monitoring. *Journal of Experimental Child Psychology, 41*, 282-299.

Bradley, L. & Bryant, P. E. (1983). Categorising sounds and learning to read: A causal connexion. *Nature, 301*, 419-421.

Cain, K. (1994). An investigation into comprehension difficulties in young children. Unpublished D.Phil. thesis. University of Sussex.

Cain, K. (1996). Story knowledge and comprehension skill. In C. Cornoldi & J. V. Oakhill (Eds.), *Reading Comprehension Difficulties: Processes and Remediation* (pp. 167-192). Mahwah, NJ: Lawrence Erlbaum Associates.

Cain, K. (1999). Ways of reading: How knowledge and use of strategies are related to reading comprehension. *British Journal of Developmental Psychology, 17*, 293-309.

Cain, K. (in press). Text comprehension and its relation to coherence and cohesion in children's fictional narratives. *British Journal of Developmental Psychology*.

Cain, K. & Oakhill, J. (1996). The nature of the relationship between comprehension skill and the ability to tell a story. *British Journal of Developmental Psychology, 14*, 187-201.

Cain, K. & Oakhill, J. V. (1999a). Inference making and its relation to comprehension failure. *Reading and Writing. An Interdisciplinary Journal, 11*, 489-503.

Cain, K. & Oakhill, J.(1999b). "Comprehension skill, context, and the interpretation of figurative language." Paper presented at the sixth annual meeting of the Society for the Scientific Study of Reading, Montreal, April 1999.

Cain, K., Oakhill, J. V., & Bryant, P. E. (1999). "Reading comprehension failure: Profiles of individuals from different populations. "Paper presented at the 1999 biennial meeting of the Society for Research into Child Development, Albuquerque, April 1999.

Cain, K., Oakhill, J. V., & Bryant, P. E. (2000a). Investigating the causes of reading comprehension failure: The comprehension-age match design. *Reading and Writing. An Interdisciplinary Journal, 12*, 31-40.

Cain, K., Oakhill, J. V., & Bryant, P. E. (2000b). Phonological skills and comprehension failure: A test of the phonological processing deficit hypothesis. *Reading and Writing. An Interdisciplinary Journal, 13*, 31-56.

Cain, K., Oakhill, J., & Elbro, C. (in press). The ability to learn new word meanings from context by school-age children with and without language comprehension difficulties. *Journal of Child Language*.

Cain, K., Oakhill, J. V., & Lemmon, K. (under review). Individual differences in the inference of word meanings from context: the influence of reading comprehension, vocabulary knowledge, and memory capacity.

Cain, K., Oakhill, J. V., Barnes, M. & Bryant, P. E. (2001). Comprehension skill, inference making ability and their relation to knowledge. *Memory and Cognition, 29*, 850-859.

Carroll, J. B. (1993). *Human Cognitive Abilities: A Survey of Factor-Analytic Studies*. New York: Cambridge University Press.

Cataldo, M. G., & Oakhill, J.V. (2000). Why are poor comprehenders inefficient searchers? An investigation into the effects of text representation and spatial memory on ability to locate information in a text. *Journal of Educational Psychology, 92*, 791-799.

Cipielewski, J., & Stanovich, K. E. (1992). Predicting growth in reading ability from children's exposure to print. *Journal of Experimental Child Psychology, 54*, 74-89.

Cornoldi, C., De Beni, R., & Pazzaglia, F. (1996). Profiles of reading comprehension difficulties: An analysis of single cases. In C. Cornoldi and J. Oakhill (Eds.), *Reading comprehension difficulties: Processes and interventions* (pp. 113-136). Mahwah, NJ: Lawrence Erlbaum Associates.

Cunningham, A. E., & Stanovich, K. E. (1997). Early reading acquisition and its relation to reading experience and ability 10 years later. *Developmental Psychology, 33*, 934-945.

Daneman, M. (1988). Word knowledge and reading skill. In M. Daneman, G., MacKinnon, & T. G. Waller (Eds.), *Reading research: Advances in theory and practice, vol. 6 (*pp. 145-175). San Diego, CA, US: Academic Press.

Daneman, M., & Carpenter, P. A. (1980). Individual differences in working memory and reading. *Journal of Verbal Learning and Verbal Behavior, 19*, 450-466.

Daneman, M., & Carpenter, P. A. (1983). Individual differences in integrating information between and within sentences. *Journal of Experimental Psychology: Learning, Memory and Cognition, 9*, 561-584.

De Beni, R., Palladino, P., Pazzaglia, F., & Cornoldi, C. (1998). Increases in intrusion errors and working memory deficit of poor comprehenders. *Quarterly Journal of Experimental Psychology: Human Experimental Psychology, 51A*, 305-320.

Echols, L. D., West, R. F., Stanovich, K. E., & Zehr, K. S. (1996). Using children's literacy activities to predict growth in verbal cognitive skills: A longitudinal investigation. *Journal of Educational Psychology, 88*, 296-304.

Ehri, L. C. (1999). Phases of development in learning to read words. In J. Oakhill & R. Beard (Eds.), *Reading Development and the Teaching of Reading (pp 79-108)*. Oxford, UK: Blackwell.

Ehrlich, M. F. (1996). Metacognitive monitoring in the processing of anaphoric devices in skilled and less skilled comprehenders. In C. Cornoldi & J. V. Oakhill (Eds.), *Reading Comprehension Difficulties: Processes and Remediation*. (pp. 221-249). Mahwah, NJ: Lawrence Erlbaum Associates.

Ehrlich, M. F., & Remond, M. (1997). Skilled and less skilled comprehenders: French children's processing of anaphoric devices in written texts. *British Journal of Developmental Psychology, 15,* 291-309.

Ehrlich, M. F., Remond M., & Tardieu, H. (1999). Processing of anaphoric devices in young skilled and less skilled comprehenders: Differences in metacognitive monitoring. *Reading and Writing. An Interdisciplinary Journal, 11,* 29-63.

Forrest-Pressley, D. L., & Waller, T. G. (1984). *Cognition, Metacognition, and Reading.* New York: Springer Verlag.

Freebody, P., & Anderson, R. C. (1983). Effects on text comprehension of differing proportions and locations of difficult vocabulary. *Journal of Reading Behavior, 15,* 19-39.

Garner, R., & Kraus, C. (1981-1982). Good and poor comprehender differences in knowing and regulating reading behaviors. *Educational Research Quarterly, 6,* 5-12.

Gernsbacher, M. A., & Faust, M. (1991). The mechanism of suppression: A component of general comprehension skill. *Journal of Experimental Psychology: Learning, Memory and Cognition, 17,* 245-262.

Gernsbacher, M. A., Varner, K. R., & Faust, M. (1990). Investigating differences in general comprehension skill. *Journal of Experimental Psychology: Learning, Memory and Cognition, 16,* 430-445.

Hulme, C. & Snowling, M. (1992). Deficits in output phonology: A cause of reading failure? *Cognitive Neuropsychology, 9,* 47-72.

Juel, C., Griffith, P. L., & Gough, P. B. 1986). Acquisition of literacy: A longitudinal study of children in first and second grade. *Journal of Educational Psychology, 78,* 243-255.

Jensen, A. (1980). *Bias in Mental Testing.* New York: Free Press.

Jetton, T. L., Rupley, W. H., & Willson, V. L. (1995). Comprehension of narrative and expository texts: The role of content, topic, discourse, and strategy knowledge. In Hinchman, K. A., Leu, D. J., & Kinzer, C. K. (Eds.) *Perspectives on literacy research and practice. Forty-fourth yearbook of the national reading conference* (pp. 197-204). Chicago: International Reading Conference.

Johnson-Laird, P. N. (1983). *Mental Models.* Cambridge: Cambridge University Press.

Kirby, J. R., & Moore, P. J. (1987). Metacognitive awareness about reading and its relation to reading ability. *Journal of Psychoeducational Learning, 2,* 119-137.

Kurtz, B. E. (1991). Cognitive and metacognitive aspects of text processing. In G. Denhiere and J.-P. Rossi (Eds.), *Text and Text Processing* (pp. 77-103). North Holland: Elsevier.

Myers, M., & Paris, S. G. (1978). Children's metacognitive knowledge about reading. *Journal of Educational Psychology, 70,* 680-690.

Nagy, W. E., Herman, P. A., & Anderson, R. C. (1985). Learning words from context, *Reading Research Quarterly, 20,* 233-253.

Nation, K. & Snowling, M. J. (1998a). Semantic processing and the development of word-recognition skills: evidence from children with reading comprehension difficulties. *Journal of Memory and Language, 39,* 85-101.

Nation, K. & Snowling, M. J. (1998b). Individual differences in contextual facilitation: evidence from dyslexia and poor reading comprehension. *Child Development, 69,* 996-1011.

Nation, K. & Snowling, M. J. (1999). Developmental differences in sensitivity to semantic relations among good and poor comprehenders: evidence from semantic priming. *Cognition, 70,* 81-83.

Nation, K., Adams, J. W., Bowyer-Crane, C. A., & Snowling, M. J. (1999). Working memory deficits in poor comprehenders reflect underlying language impairments. *Journal of Experimental Child Psychology, 73,* 139-158.

Oakhill, J. V. (1981). Children's Reading Comprehension. Unpublished D.Phil. Thesis. University of Sussex.

Oakhill, J. V. (1982). Constructive processes in skilled and less- skilled comprehenders' memory for sentences. *British Journal of Psychology, 73,* 13-20.

Oakhill, J. V. (1983). Instantiation in skilled and less-skilled comprehenders. *Quarterly Journal of Experimental Psychology, 35A,* 441-450.

Oakhill, J. V. (1984). Inferential and memory skills in children's comprehension of stories. *British Journal of Educational Psychology, 54,* 31-39.

Oakhill, J.V. & Kyle, F. (2000). The relation between phonological awareness and working memory. *Journal of Experimental Child Psychology, 75*, 152-164.

Oakhill, J. V., & Yuill, N. M. (1986). Pronoun resolution in skilled and less skilled comprehenders: Effects of memory load and inferential complexity. *Language and Speech, 29*, 25-37.

Oakhill, J. V., & Yuill, N. M. (1988). Understanding of anaphoric relations in skilled and less skilled comprehenders. *British Journal of Psychology, 79*, 173-186.

Oakhill, J.V, Cain, K. & Bryant, P. E. (in press). The dissociation of single-word reading and text comprehension: Evidence from component skills. *Language and Cognitive Processes*.

Oakhill, J. V., Cain, K. & Yuill, N. (1998). Individual differences in young children's comprehension skill: Toward an integrated model. In C. Hulme and R. M. Joshi (Eds.), *Reading and Spelling: Development and Disorders* (pp. 343-367). Mahwah, NJ: Lawrence Erlbaum Associates.

Oakhill, J.V. Hartt, J. & Samols, D. "Comprehension monitoring and working memory in good and poor comprehenders" Presented at the XIVth Biennial ISSBD Conference, Quebec City, August 12-16 1996.

Oakhill, J. V., Yuill, N. M., & Parkin, A. (1986). On the nature of the difference between skilled and less-skilled comprehenders. *Journal of Research in Reading, 9*, 80-91.

Pany, D., Jenkins, J. R., & Schreck, J. (1982). Vocabulary instruction: effects of word knowledge and reading comprehension. *Learning Disability Quarterly, 5*, 202-215.

Pazzaglia, F., Cornoldi, C., & de Beni, R. (1995). Knowledge about reading and self-evaluation in reading disabled children. *Advances in Learning and Behavioral Disabilities, 9*, 91-117.

Paris, S. G., & Jacobs, J. E. (1984). The benefits of informed instruction for children's reading awareness and comprehension skills. *Child Development, 55*, 2083-2093.

Paris, S. G., & Myers, M. (1981). Comprehension monitoring, memory and study strategies of good and poor readers. *Journal of Reading Behavior, 13*, 5-22.

Perfetti, C. A. (1985). *Reading Ability*. Oxford: Oxford University Press.

Perfetti, C. A. (1994). Psycholinguistics and reading ability. In M. A. Gernsbacher (Ed.), *Handbook of Psycholinguistics*, (pp. 849-894). San Diego: Academic Press.

Perfetti, C. A., Marron, M. A., & Foltz, P. W. (1996). Sources of comprehension failure: theoretical perspectives and case studies. In C. Cornoldi & J. V. Oakhill (Eds.), *Reading Comprehension Difficulties: Processes and Remediation* (pp. 137-165). Mahwah, NJ: Lawrence Erlbaum Associates.

Seigneuric, A., Ehrlich, M.-F., Oakhill, J.V. & Yuill, N.M. (2000). Working memory resources and children's reading comprehension. *Reading and Writing. An Interdisciplinary Journal, 13*, 81-103.

Semel, E., Wiig, E. H., & Secord., W. (1987). *Clinical Evaluation of Language Fundamentals - Revised*. San Diego, CA: The Psychological Corporation.

Shankweiler, D. (1989). How problems of comprehension are related to difficulties in decoding. In D. Shankweiler & I. Y. Liberman (Eds.), *Phonology and Reading Disability: Solving the Reading Puzzle*, (pp. 35-68). Ann Arbor: University of Michigan Press.

Siegel, L. S. & Ryan, E. B. (1989). Development of working memory in normally achieving and subtypes of learning disabled children. *Child Development, 60*, 973-80.

Smiley, S. S., Oakley, D. D., Worthen, D., Campione, J., & Brown, A. L. (1977). Recall of thematically relevant material by adolescent good and poor readers as a function of written versus oral presentation. *Journal of Educational Psychology, 69*, 381- 387.

Smith, S. T., Macaruso, P., Shankweiler, D., & Crain, S. (1989). Syntactic comprehension in young poor readers. *Applied Psycholinguistics, 10*, 429-454.

Spilich, G. J., Vesonder, G. T., Chiesi, H. L., & Voss J. F. (1979). Text processing of domain-related information for individuals with high and low domain knowledge. *Journal of Verbal learning and Verbal Behavior, 18*, 275-290.

Stanovich, K. E. (1993). Does reading make you smarter? Literacy and the development of verbal intelligence. In H. Reese (Ed.), *Advances in Child Development and Behavior, vol. 24*, (pp. 133-180). New York: Academic Press.

Stein, N. L., & Glenn, C. G. (1982). Children's concept of time: The development of a story schema. In W. J. Friedman (Ed.), *The Developmental Psychology of Time*, (pp. 255-282). New York: Academic Press.

Sternberg, R. J., & Powell, J. S. (1983). Comprehending verbal comprehension. *American Psychologist,* *38*, 878-893.

Stothard, S. E., & Hulme, C. (1992). Reading comprehension difficulties in children: The role of language comprehension and working memory skills. *Reading and Writing. An Interdisciplinary Journal, 4*, 245-256.

Stothard, S. E., & Hulme, C. (1996). A comparison of phonological skills in children with reading comprehension difficulties and children with word reading difficulties. *Journal of Child Psychology and Child Psychiatry, 36*, 399-408.

Taylor, B. M., Frye B. J., & Maruyama, G. M. (1990). Time spent reading and reading growth. *American Educational Research Journal. 27*, 351-362.

Tunmer, W. E. (1989). The role of language-related factors in reading disability. In D. Shankweiler, & I. Y. Liberman (Eds.), *Phonology and Reading Disability: Solving the Reading Puzzle*, (pp. 91-132). Ann Arbor: University of Michigan Press.

Tunmer, W. E., & Bowey, J. A. (1984). Metalinguistic awareness and reading acquisition. In W. E. Tunmer, C. Pratt, & M. L. Herriman (Eds.), *Metalinguistic Awareness in Children* (pp. 144-168). New York: Springer-Verlag.

Wagner, R., & Torgesen, J. K. (1987). The nature of phonological processing and its causal role in the acquisition of reading skills. *Psychological Bulletin, 101*, 192-212.

Wittrock, M. C., Marks, C., & Doctorow, M. (1975). Reading as a generative process. *Journal of Educational Psychology, 67*, 484-489.

Yuill, N., & Joscelyne, T. (1988). Effect of organisational cues and strategies on good and poor comprehenders' story understanding. *Journal of Educational Psychology, 80*, 152-158.

Yuill, N. & Oakhill, J. (1988). Understanding of anaphoric relations in skilled and less skilled comprehenders. *British Journal of Psychology, 79*, 173-186.

Yuill, N. & Oakhill, J. (1991). *Children's Problems in Text Comprehension: An Experimental Investigation.* Cambridge: Cambridge University Press.

Yuill, N. M., Oakhill, J. V., & Parkin, A. J. (1989). Working memory, comprehension skill and the resolution of text anomaly. *British Journal of Psychology, 80*, 351-361.

C6. Early Identification

CARSTEN ELBRO & HOLLIS S. SCARBOROUGH[1]

ABSTRACT

Most cases of reading difficulties can be predicted. This chapter provides a survey and a discussion of the research evidence. Across more than 60 samples, there is considerable agreement that the strongest preschool predictors are the children's budding orthographic abilities (e.g. letter knowledge), phoneme awareness, and measures of productive language (e.g. naming). This appears to hold for both unselected samples and for groups of children at risk for reading difficulties, e.g. children of dyslexic parents, and children with specific language impairments. With combined measures, prediction accuracy generally approaches 90% and without doubt is of practical importance. In comparison, non-verbal abilities and socioeconomic factors are much less predictive of individual reading development although socioeconomic factors exert a strong influence on school standards. The chapter also discusses a number of challenges to current prediction models. These include possible non-linearity between predictors and reading outcomes; e.g. the possibility that some predictors are particularly good indicators of problems with reading acquisition, but do not distinguish well between children who will become superior readers and others. It is also likely that prediction depends on the age of the child at which verbal abilities are measured, with basic productive and receptive measures being more predictive in younger children. We also discuss how and when reading outcomes are measured can influence prediction.

INTRODUCTION

It is expected that children will learn to read and write in school. Children differ considerably in how readily they do so, however. For those who progress most slowly in literacy acquisition, unfortunately, the consequences can be grave. Academically, these children are likely to struggle throughout their school years,

---

[1] Support for the preparation of this chapter was provided, in part, by NOS-S grant No. 124811/541 to the first author and Grant No. HD-01994 to Haskins Laboratories.

T. Nunes, P. Bryant (eds.), Handbook of Children's Literacy, 339–359.
© 2004 *Kluwer Academic Publishers. Printed in Great Britain.*

with poor reading and writing skills often hampering achievement in other areas also. Furthermore, these children's confidence in their abilities and their motivation to engage in reading and writing activities may be lowered, which can exacerbate the academic difficulties. Because the negative consequences of early reading failure may extend into many other aspects of a child's life, it is widely agreed that attempts should be made to identify children at risk for reading difficulties at a young age, and to intervene so as to minimize their difficulties in learning to read or even to prevent them entirely.

This chapter concerns the issue of early identification of children who are most likely to develop reading problems. From research on the prediction of early reading achievement from measures taken prior to schooling, much has been learned about the kinds of knowledge and skills that are lacking in at-risk children, and about the feasibility of using assessments of such abilities for the practical purpose of screening entering students.

Prediction research is also a source of clues regarding the cause(s) of early reading failure, and a strong theoretical understanding of how and why reading problems occur is essential for effective intervention. However, causal links can only be established through experimentation; i.e., by evaluating the success of attempts to help children develop abilities which are believed to be causally related to reading development. Therefore, research into the causes of reading difficulties and work on practical intervention are closely linked. Chapter C7 of this handbook deals with early intervention from this joint perspective.

It has been nearly a century since Henri Binet's initial efforts to predict which children will have the greatest difficulty in school by examining their skills and abilities. Numerous prediction studies have been conducted since, but we will focus primarily on work from the past few decades, during which attention has shifted from IQ to a host of other potential predictor variables. Most such longitudinal research has commenced at about kindergarten age, shortly before children receive formal school instruction in reading. In several recent studies, however, predictor measures have been taken at even younger ages, mainly during the preschool years but in some cases even in infancy.

EARLY LANGUAGE AND LITERACY SKILLS PREDICT FUTURE READING

Scarborough (1998a) presented a comprehensive review of the published prediction studies. This included a meta-analysis of those that followed children from school entry age (typically, 4.5 to 6 years) through one to three years of school, based on 61 samples of size 30 or greater. Table 1 lists the mean (and median) correlations between outset abilities and subsequent reading achievement.

Several important patterns are revealed by Table 1. These conclusions pertain also to several newer prediction studies that were not included in the meta-analysis (Badian, 2000; Catts, Fey, Zhang & Tomblin, 1999, 2001; Hindson, 2001;

Table 1 Average correlations between kindergarten predictor variables and later reading scores, based on a meta-analysis of findings from 61 research samples (from Scarborough, 2001).

Predictor Variable	# of Samples	Mean r	Median r
Measures Requiring the Processing of Print			
Rudimentary Reading: letter-sound knowledge or entire "readiness" battery	21	.57	.56
Letter identification: naming of upper- and lower-case letters.	24	.52	.52
Print concepts: familiarity with the mechanics and purposes of book reading	7	.46	.49
Measures of Oral Language Proficiency			
General Language Index: expressive and receptive skills	4	.46	.47
Phonological Awareness	27	.46	.42
Expressive ("Naming") Vocabulary	5	.45	.49
Sentence or Story Recall	11	.45	.49
Rapid Serial Naming Speed	14	.38	.40
Verbal IQ	12	.37	.38
Receptive Language (syntactic)	9	$\leqslant$.37	.40
Receptive Vocabulary	20	.33	.38
Expressive Language Skills	11	.32	.37
Verbal Memory (digit or word list recall)	18	.33	.33
Receptive Language (semantic)	11	.24	.25
Speech Production (pronunciation accuracy)	4	–	.25
Speech Perception (phoneme discrimination)	11	.22	.23
Measures of Nonverbal Abilities			
Visual Memory	8	.31	.28
Nonverbal IQ	8	.26	.25
Motor Skills	5	.25	.26
Visual Discrimination	5	.22	.20
Visual-Motor Integration	6	.16	.13

Lonigan, Burgess & Anthony, 2000; Muter & Snowling, 1998; Olofsson & Niedersøe, 1999;. Pisecco, Baker, Silva & Brooke, 2001).

First, it is very clear that nonverbal (visual, motor, and visuo-motor) skills account for very little variance in reading acquisition. Likewise, speech perception and speech production differences at this age are surprisingly uninformative about future reading achievement (but these may be more potent predictors from younger ages, as discussed below). These findings suggest that screening for these abilities would be ill-advised for detecting children at risk, and that preschool programs that aim to improve perceptual functioning and intersensory integration are unlikely to have any major positive impact on children's literacy development.

Second, among the verbal abilities that have been studied, expressive measures are somewhat more predictive than receptive measures, especially for vocabulary. This may reflect the fact that the reliability of expressive measures is inherently higher, since guessing can distort receptive scores. Or it may mean that the requirement to retrieve words and construct sentences on production tests affords greater sensitivity for distinguishing between at-risk and not-at-risk children.

Third, several domains of language abilities (phonology, morphology, vocabulary, syntax), and both "basic" and "metalinguistic" skills in these domains, appear to be predictive, not just one. In this regard, it should be noted that in addition to the language measures listed in the table, syntactic awareness has also been found to be a strong predictor of reading, although it has rarely been included in prediction studies (Bohannon, Warren-Leubecker, & Hepler, 1984; Muter & Snowling, 1998; Tunmer & Hoover, 1992).

Fourth, not surprisingly, measures of emerging *written* language skills are also among the best predictors of subsequent reading abilities. Knowing the names of letters, for instance, has consistently been the strongest single predictor variable, accounting for unique variance in achievement beyond that accounted for by oral language abilities. Likewise, measures of print concepts, including familiarity with the functions and basic conventions of the written word, have also been found to predict reading development.

The table does not reveal, however, the degree of association *between* measures, and the extent to which they overlap as predictors (i.e., account for the same portion of variance in reading). In the Copenhagen prediction study summarised below, less than half of 11 significant predictors of reading difficulties contributed unique information to the prediction (Petersen & Elbro, 1999). The overlap between predictors was thus considerable. Some practical and theoretical implications of this will be discussed below.

SOCIO-CULTURAL PREDICTORS OF READING ACHIEVEMENT

Socio-cultural factors appear to be less predictive of individual reading achievement than are the linguistic abilities of children. It has long been recognised that there is a very strong relationship between the average achievement level at a school and the average socio-economic (SES) stratum of families whose children attend that school. At the individual level, however, differences in the incomes, education levels, and occupations of children's parents are not well correlated (typically, less than .25) with future reading achievement. Hence, researchers have recently focussed less on demographic factors and more on aspects of a child's early environment that contribute to later academic differences, directly or indirectly by influencing preschool skill development.

Home experience factors have been studied intensively during the last decades. Somewhat contrary to common views, the relationships of home literacy practices and expectancies to literacy development are not especially strong. For instance, two recent meta-analyses of studies of the impact of parents' reading to their children each showed significant but modest average correlations of .28 (Bus, van IJzendoorn & Pellegrini, 1995; Scarborough & Dobrich, 1994). Similarly, in a nationally representative sample of 22,000 beginning kindergartners in the United States, a correlation of only .21 was obtained between the frequency of parent-child reading and letter knowledge (West, Denton & Germino-Hausken, 2000). Other indicators of home literacy, such as the amount of reading material in the home and the frequency of library visits, have also been found to correlate significantly, but not strongly, with children's reading development. These findings, and those from other recent studies (e.g., Frijters, Barron & Brunello, 2000), indicate that probably no more than 8% of the variance in early literacy skills is directly accounted for by differences in home literacy environments. For the purpose of identifying children at risk for reading difficulties, therefore, home experience differences are less informative than measures of children's early language and literacy skills.

Somewhat stronger predictive relations have been found for the reading *abilities* of parents, rather than their reading habits. As discussed below, specific reading difficulties (dyslexia) among the parents is a particularly strong risk factor for the children, at least in part because variation in reading ability has been shown to be genetically influenced (e.g., DeFries & Alarcon, 1996; Gilger, Borecki, Smith, DeFries & Pennington, 1996). Once parental reading ability is controlled in prediction analyses, the influences of socio-economic predictors are substantially reduced (Elbro *et al.*, 1998).

COMBINING PREDICTORS

As noted earlier, preschool language and literacy skills are not independent, but instead are intercorrelated to a considerable degree. This means that it is no trivial question whether the prediction of reading outcomes will increase when various predictors are combined. Scarborough (1998a) identified nine studies in which several preschool tests were combined to improve the prediction of reading outcomes in the first grades. On average 57% of the variance in reading was accounted for (R = .75) across the seven studies that reported results from multiple regression analyses. This figure is certainly higher than what is obtained with any single measure. So it seems clear that the prediction of reading outcomes may be strengthened by the inclusion of a number of preschool variables, each accounting for some unique as well as shared variance. Most studies have included measures of both letter knowledge and phonological awareness, but other predictors in their batteries have been dissimilar, and have not usually included the kinds of oral language measures (e.g., story recall and naming skills) that, individually, are best correlated with reading. Hence, it is possible that even stronger prediction results might be obtainable by using a few well-chosen measures.

Prediction studies have included up to 28 preschool predictor variables. Apart from the practical demands of using such an extensive battery, it also is a potential threat to the reliability of the combined measure of risk. Inclusion of

344   *Carsten Elbro & Hollis S. Scarborough*

more predictors in the preschool battery increases the error variance, or "noise". Not all this noise is detected in the traditional prediction studies because they are not really predictive, but rather retrospective. They predict in the rear mirror and ask the question: What characterised the children with reading delays when they were younger? In contrast, true prediction estimates require a predefined set of predictors with predefined weights used in a new group of children

It should not come as a surprise, therefore, that the predictive power seems to drop in replications within the same population but at a later age; compare, for instance, de Hirsch, Jansky, & Langford (1966) with Jansky, Hoffmann, Layton, & Sugar (1989) and Badian (1982) with Badian (1988). The predictive power also decreases from the initial study to a second study with new participants within the same age range; compare Silver & Hagin (1981) with Mantzicopoulos & Morrison (1994), and Hurford *et al.* (1993) with Hurford *et al.* (1994). Likewise, Petersen and Elbro (1999) reported a 10% drop (from 80 to 70%) in the correct classification rate when the original prediction model (Elbro *et al.*, 1998) was used with a new sample of children. While this drop may not be of substantial theoretical importance, it certainly is serious in practice. Practical aspects of the prediction of literacy delays in individual children are taken up in the following section.

PREDICTION OF INDIVIDUAL OUTCOMES

From a theoretical perspective it is important to be able to predict a significant amount of variance in literacy development. Significant predictors can be highly informative to theoretical models of the processes of literacy and its development. But accounting for variance in achievement is not the same as predicting the outcome for an individual child. Reading researchers are ordinarily satisfied if they can account for 25-60% of the variance in some measure of reading (corresponding to multiple correlation coefficients ranging from .50 to .75). However, this leaves a great deal of the variation among children unexplained, so that many errors of prediction will occur for individual children.

The percentage of individual outcomes (reading disabled or not) that have been correctly predicted from multiple risk measures has ranged from 89 to 92 across studies. Sensitivity (the proportion of children who developed reading disabilities who were correctly designated as at risk on the predictor battery) ranged from 56 to 93, and specificity (the proportion of normal achievers whose successful outcomes were correctly predicted) was between 80 and 95. Thus, while normal reading is predicted quite accurately, a rather high proportion of children who develop problems are not identified early on.

To illustrate, typical results from one study (Petersen & Elbro, 1999) are shown in Table 2. Prediction of the individual reading development of 150 children was based on six preschool measures: letter knowledge; three measures of phonological and morphological awareness; distinctiveness of pronunciation; and dyslexia in the

Table 2. Observed reading abilities at the beginning of second grade as a function of predicted reader group. Cut-off value $p = 0.50$. Overall prediction rate is 86% (from Petersen & Elbro, 1999)

Observed dyslexic	Predicted normal	Predicted accuracy	Prediction
Dyslexic	21	14	60%
Normal	7	108	94%

family). Children with severe problems with the acquisition of word decoding in grade 2 were classified as "dyslexic' following a cut off criterion corresponding to the 11th percentile in a group of children from families without reading problems. The reading outcome was predicted correctly for 129 (86%) of the children.

As is typical, the prediction was much less accurate for children who developed reading problems (60%) than for children with no problems (94%). To understand the lower sensitivity than specificity, however, one must understand that it is largely a function of the relative sizes of the observed groups. Current statistical techniques seek to maximise the *overall* prediction rate. To do so, a high prediction rate is essential in the largest subgroup of children, and accuracy is less important in the smaller group (i.e., children with literacy problems). This bias is also reflected in the "underprediction" of the children with literacy problems: only 28 children were predicted to be at risk whereas 35 children were considered to have problems.

It is easy to alter this bias, though this is rarely done. Table 3 is based on the same data and the same predictors as Table 2. The only difference is that the cutoff point has been changed so as to include more children in the at-risk group (now 34). This has lead to an increase in the sensitivity (from 60 to 68%) at the expense of a decrease in specificity (from 94 to 90%). Sensitivity may be further increased, but always at the expense of the specificity.

Table 3. Observed reading abilities at the beginning of second grade as a function of predicted reader group. Cut-off value $p = 0.60$. Overall prediction rate is 85%

Observed	Predicted dyslexic	Predicted normal	Prediction accuracy
Dyslexic	23	11	68%
Normal reader	12	104	90%

The balance between sensitivity and specificity of a prediction model is not primarily a research matter, but a practical and ethical matter. The more efficient, economical, and harmless the intended treatment for at-risk children, the more important it is to provide this treatment to all children who might possibly need such assistance; i.e. high *sensitivity* is desirable. Conversely, with only inefficient, expensive, and potentially harmful treatment available, great care should be taken *not* to offer this treatment to children who might not require it; i.e., high *specificity* is essential. Our point here is that for practical purposes, the prediction formula itself does not provide any well-founded criterion for differentiating between children at risk and those who are not. Such cut points must be selected based on the particular educational situation in which risk designations are being made.

EFFECTS OF LANGUAGE AND ORTHOGRAPHY

Most of the published prediction studies have been conducted in English. To our knowledge, no study has systematically examined the possible effects of language or orthography on prediction by using exactly the same predictors within comparable samples from populations that speak different languages or use different kinds of orthographies to represent language in print. Nevertheless, less strict comparisons can be made with some caution.

From the information available, there are no indications that the oral language itself matters. Prediction studies done in several languages (all represented with alphabetic orthography) have provided results which are not significantly discrepant from the pattern in table 1. The languages include Danish (Elbro, *et al.*, 1998; Frost, 2001), Dutch (Wesseling, 1999), Finnish (Lyytinen, Ahonen, & Räsänen, 1994), French (Sprenger-Charolles, Siegel, & Béchennec, 1998), German (Schneider & Näslund, 1993), Swedish (Lundberg, Olofsson & Wall, 1980). Even for Chinese, which has a non-alphabetic writing system, phonological awareness has been shown to predict progress in learning to read (Ho & Bryant, 1997); not surprisingly, however, visual abilities also appear to play a strong role in prediction of Chinese literacy, which is generally not the case for children learning to read alphabetic orthographies.

It should be noted, however, that the strength of phonological awareness as a predictor appeared to be weaker in the Austrian (German-speaking) sample studied by Wimmer, Mayringer & Landerl (2000). Their results suggest that a more "regular' (transparent) writing system, like that for German, may decrease the relative importance of phonological awareness as a predictor of reading achievement. That is, initial reading development in German was not much affected by whether a child entered school with normal or poor phonological awareness, but was instead predicted by naming and novel word learning abilities. However, poor phonological awareness did predict later acquisition of irregular spellings (such as of English loan-words). It may be, therefore, that it is easier to learn about the sound structure of spoken language when there is a simple relationship between printed and spoken words than when the relationship is less straightforward. On the other hand, Austrian schools invariably use a synthethic phonics approach, so instructional differences may also explain the observed differences from English findings.

PREDICTION IN AT-RISK POPULATIONS

At-risk populations are children who are known to have an increased risk of developing reading difficulties based on an aspect of their backgrounds, rather than based on skills assessed at the outset of schooling. Such populations include children diagnosed early with specific language impairments, children of dyslexic parents, and children from socioeconomically depressed neighborhoods who attend academically low-performing schools. It is important to identify such groups of children with a heightened risk for the same reasons as it important to be able to predict reading failure in general. But at-risk populations have also been studied because the relatively frequent occurrence of reading difficulties in such populations allows for studies of relatively small samples.

Educationally disadvantaged children

As noted earlier, children who enter a school (typically, one in a poor community) at which students have historically been low achievers are very likely to become poor readers relative to national norms. This prediction, however, holds for the entire group, and has little to do with individual differences in reading achievement relative to other children receiving the same educational opportunities. Because the main research emphasis has been on raising achievement of *all* students at such schools, few attempts have been made to predict individual outcomes. There are some indications, however, that the same entering skills that predict reading in the general population – letter knowledge, print concept knowledge, phonological awareness, and oral language abilities – contribute similarly to achievement differences in these at-risk children (Juel, Griffith & Gough, 1986; Snow, Barnes, Chandler, Goodman & Hemphill, 1991; Walker, Greendwood, Hart & Carta, 1994; Whitehurst & Lonigan, 2001).

Children with specific language impairments

Children who were diagnosed in the preschool years as having a specific language impairments (SLI) are a much-studied at-risk group. (See Dockrell & Lindsay, this volume). It is very well documented that many SLI children later have reading difficulties (in addition to continued language weaknesses) in their school years (e.g. Aram & Hall, 1989; Baker & Cantwell, 1987; Catts, 1991; 1993; Hauschild & Elbro, 1992; Nauclér & Magnusson, 1998; Rescorla, 1999; Stothard, Snowling, Bishop, Chipchase & Kaplan, 1998). Certainly, not every child with SLI becomes dyslexic, but milder reading problems occur quite often, particularly when early language impairments extend beyond expressive phonological (speech production) difficulties. Across several studies, strong predictors of future reading skills of children with SLI have included phonological awareness, naming vocabulary, speeded naming, and metasyntactic skills. These predictors are also among the strongest in unselected samples, suggesting that the predictors of poor reading development among SLI children may not differ much from those in unselected samples. However, performance IQ may have a stronger influence on reading development in SLI children, presumably because those with high IQ are better able to compensate for their language problems (Snowling *et al.*, 2000).

Children of dyslexic families

Reading abilities (and disabilities) tends to run in families. Hence, children of dyslexic parents are another group at a high risk for reading difficulties. When children have one or more dyslexic first-degree relatives (a dyslexic parent, sister or brother) their risk for dyslexia is increased by a factor of four or even more (Gilger, Pennington & DeFries, 1991). Scarborough (1998a) estimated, based on several studies, that approximately 40% of the offspring of dyslexic parents develop reading disabilities, but only about 10% or fewer of the offspring of unaffected parents do (a 6.0 odds increase of the risk). Very similarly, Borstrøm and Elbro (1997) reported that 40 percent of their (untrained) at-risk children became dyslexic as compared to only 8 percent of the comparison group (a risk increase of odds 7.7). It bears mentioning, however, that all such estimates vary depending on the criteria used to define reading disabilities in children and in adults.

In this group both genetic and social environmental factors may contribute to risk. There is considerable evidence for a genetic contribution to variation in reading abilities – or, more accurately, in a predisposition to be weaker or stronger in one or more skills that are important to reading (DeFries & Alarcon, 1996; Gilger, Borecki, Smith, DeFries & Pennington, 1996; Olson & Gayan, 2001). In addition, the reading habits and academic goals of parents who are poor readers may also contribute adversely to the literacy development of their children, although evidence in support of this notion is not strong (Scarborough, Dobrich & Hager, 1991).

In the 1980's, Scarborough (1989, 1990, 1991) followed groups of children of dylexic parents, and a comparison sample (of similar background and IQ) from unaffected families, from age 2.5 through 8 years; in addition, 66 of these 78 children were again studied at age 14 (Scarborough, 1998b). By the end of second grade, 22 of the 34 at-risk children, but only 2 of the 44 controls, were a year or more behind in reading, and this pattern of achievement differences related to familial risk persisted through eighth grade, and presumably beyond. (The unnaturally high proportion of at-risk cases in the sample resulted from intentional over-representation through recruitment and sample selection.)

Because the participants were volunteers, they can be assumed to be self-selected for factors that would tend to enhance positive outcomes, such as the willingness to participate in a long-term project and a desire to learn more about child development. Especially among families with dyslexia, participation might also have been motivated by concerns about their toddler's early development. Given the very similar estimates of familial risk rates (see above) and other findings in this sample compared to others, however, these possible selection biases appear not to have unduly affected the results.

By age 2½, differences were already evident between the at-risk children who later became dyslexic and the children who did not have reading difficulties. On average, the latter were similar in nonverbal abilities but stronger in receptive and especially expressive language proficiency in all domains, although not on all skills at all ages. At the outset, they produced longer and more syntactically complex utterances and made many fewer articulation errors in their speech. Morpho-syntactic and vocabulary skills differentiated the groups at ages 3 and 4 years, and at age 5 the largest differences were seen in expressive vocabulary, phonological awareness, and letter knowledge. It is reassuring that these are also among the most powerful predictors found in unselected samples of children of this age (Table 1). Especially from a theoretical perspective, it is interesting that the initial syntactic differences were found to account for some additional variance in reading outcomes even after readiness skills at age 5 were statistically controlled in a multiple regression. Finally, an unexpected finding was that although the amount of parent-preschooler shared reading (based on parent report) was only weakly related to reading development, the children who became poor readers were observed by their mothers to spend much less time at ages 3 to 4 engaged in solitary book activity, suggesting that early attitudes as well as developing skills may influence these children's early literacy experiences and eventual reading abilities.

In the past decade, Scarborough's findings have largely been confirmed and extended in several studies conducted in many countries, including England (Gallagher, Frith & Snowling, 2000), Finland (Lyytinen, Ahonen, & Räsänen, 1994), Norway (Hagtvet, 2000), USA (Pennington, Lefly & Boada,1999), Australia (Hindson, 2001; Byrne, Fielding-Barnsley, Hindson, Mackay, Newman & Shankweiler, 1998), and Denmark (Elbro *et al.*, 1998; Petersen & Elbro, 1999). Across different languages and alphabetic systems, in comparison to other preschoolers, those at risk due to familial dyslexia consistently exhibit a wide array of weaknesses in early language and emerging literacy abilities but not nonverbal skills, and these differences are reliably associated with reading abilities many years later. Quite remarkably, in the Finnish study, even infants' electrophysiological responses to speech versus nonspeech stimuli were consistent with these risk-based differences in verbal ability. Furthermore, another promising predictor variable – the distinctiveness of a child's phonological representations of words – was identified in the Danish sample. It is expected that much more information of both theoretical and practical value will soon become available from these studies, some of which are ongoing.

Comparison with unselected samples

The next question is whether the predictors in at-risk populations are the same as those in unselected populations. Several studies have followed unselected samples of children from preschool into primary school (e.g. Bryant, Maclean, Bradley & Crossland, 1990; Catts, Fey, Zhang & Tomblin, 1999; Shapiro *et al.*, 1990). The vast majority of these studies have found reliable associations between early language abilities and reading acquisition.

A more direct comparison between at-risk children (from dyslexic families) and not-at-risk children was made in the Copenhagen longitudinal study. In general, no significant interactions were found that involved predictors and at-risk status (Elbro *et al.*, 1998; Petersen & Elbro, 1999). Also, the strongest predictors in the at-risk group were much the same as those found in unselected samples: letter knowledge, phoneme awareness (e.g. syllable deletion), and phonetic distinctiveness of pronunciation (accurate naming).

A related question of both theoretical and practical importance is whether family at-risk status can fully be explained in terms of poor language skills of the sort that predict dyslexia. Have we managed to "unpack" the factors that are imbedded in the at-risk status that follows from having a dyslexic parent? Or does at-risk status still have some predictive value even when the known language predictors are accounted for? Results from the Copenhagen study indicate that at-risk status was indeed captured by the language predictors. At-risk status did not contribute to the prediction of dyslexia when differences in letter knowledge, phonological awareness and distinctiveness of pronunciation had been accounted for (Elbro *et al.*, 1998). However, recent analyses in a bigger group of children indicated that at-risk status still contributed some prediction after controlling for early language skills (Petersen & Elbro, 1999). A safe conclusion is that *if* at-risk status "contains" factors that are not covered by the already known early language skills, these unknown factors have only a modest influence.

ISSUES OF CAUSALITY

Although many preschool measures of language abilities have been found to be significant *predictors* of literacy delays, they may not be independent *causes* of literacy delays. So far, among the strong predictors, only phonological awareness and perhaps vocabulary abilities have been shown in experimental studies to be causally related to literacy problems (as reviewed in the next chapter of this volume). Other predictors have either failed to obtain a causal status in experimental studies or have not been subjected to experimental manipulation at all. For example, although rapid naming may be easy to measure and a relatively powerful predictor, naming speed is hard to improve in young children (de Jong & Frielink, 2000). And if it is hard to improve, there is little room for studies of possible effects on literacy acquisition. On the other hand, some prerequisites may be relatively easy to improve, but their effects on reading acquisition may either be modest (e.g. letter knowledge) or trivial from a theoretical perspective (e.g. rudimentary literacy skills). In addition there are several potential complications in establishing cause-and-effect relationships in reading development. Some of these will be considered in the remaining sections of this chapter.

Non-linear relationships between predictors and outcomes

Most prediction studies have employed linear regression techniques with continuously distributed variables. That is, they have sought to obtain best-fitting linear regression equations for predicting reading measures from predictors across a wide range of ability. However, not all variation in reading ability is equally important. Most would agree that it is essential to predict (to prevent) initial failure in learning to read, while it is less imperative to predict which children will become superior readers. Yet different sets of predictors, or different strengths of various predictors, may be relevant to identifying future reading at the low end than the high end of the continuum. In other words, the weaknesses of to-be-poor readers may not be the mirror image of the strengths of to-be-superior readers.

One kind of non-linear relationship of interest is illustrated in figure 1. Such a pattern is seen when development of a predictor skill is *necessary but not sufficient for successful* reading acquisition. The example in the graph shows such a

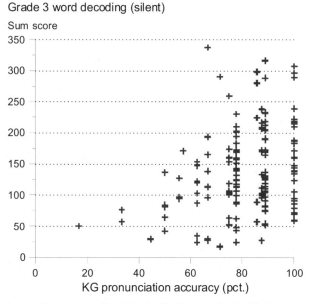

Figure 1. A non-linear relationship (a "half correlation") between pronunciation accuracy in early KG and word decoding in early Grade 3 (r = 0.32)

relationship between the quality of phonological representations in preschool children and the reading level of the same children at the beginning of grade 3 (Elbro, 1999, based on data from Petersen & Elbro, 1999). Although this pattern could result to some extent from a ceiling effect on the predictor, a similar pattern has been reported for early phonological awareness and later reading attainment (Gough, 1998).

This particular relationship is called a "half correlation" because the scores fall within a triangle (in the lower right corner of the diagram). There are no children with low scores on the prerequisite measure and high reading outcome, as indicated by the lack of data points in the top left portion of the graph. This indicates that a high score on the prerequisite measure is a necessary precondition for attaining a good reading ability in the first school years. However, there are children with high scores on the prerequisite measure who nonetheless have low reading scores. So it seems that a high score on the prerequisite measure is not sufficient for the development of a good reading ability.

Such a "half correlation" is not a trivial deviation from a linear relationship. A half correlation cannot exceed $r = 0.5$ (the correlation coefficient for the data presented in Figure 1 is 0.32). This might be one reason why "pronunciation accuracy' reportedly has a low predictive power (Table 1). Relationships of this sort may also easily be washed out by more straightforward effects of other early language skills in, for example, a multiple linear regression analysis. The correlation is quite weak in children with normal to high scores on the predictive measure; it is only the children with poor abilities on the predictive measure who really differ from the rest of the children in terms of their reading development. Since most prediction studies are mainly concerned with the prediction (and prevention) of reading difficulties, not with prediction of superior reading, it may be reasonable to avoid analyses that assume linearity, such as standard multiple linear regression. Instead regression techniques for prediction of group memberships (e.g. logistic regression) may often be more appropriate.

Discovering deviations from linearity is important for both theory and practice. It is essential that they be taken into account in models of the causal relationships between early language abilities and later reading development. Some early language abilities may be of critical importance without being sufficient – such as quality of phonological representations and access to phoneme size units of speech. Other language abilities may not be of equal critical importance for differentiating children at greatest risk from others, but instead have a strong impact on the ease of literacy acquisition throughout the whole range of reading abilities. Such other factors could be vocabulary size and speed of access to lexical items in the mental lexicon (illustrated in Figure 2). From a practical point of view, furthermore, relying on analyses of only linear relationships may yield a misleading picture of how to identify these children and what skills should be the focus of intervention.

Grade 3 word decoding (silent)

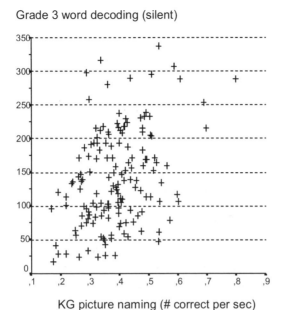

KG picture naming (# correct per sec)

Figure 2. A linear relationship between picture naming ability (number of correct per second) in early KG and word decoding in early Grade 3 (r = 0.38)

Prediction depends on when preschool skills are measured

In several longitudinal studies, reading outcomes have been predicted by different language abilities at different preschool ages, as reviewed by Scarborough (2001). For instance, in her longitudinal study, Scarborough (1990) found that from measures taken at age 2½ years, the complexity of spoken sentences and the accuracy of word pronunciations were the best indicators of whether a child would become a disabled reader. At ages 3 and 4, sentence processing and vocabulary (especially their production), but not speech, were the aspects of language that best predicted outcomes. From 5, the significant predictors were among those that are most consistently found in other prediction studies (cf. table 1); namely, phonological awareness (matching of rhymes and initial phonemes), expressive vocabulary, and letter knowledge.

There may be several reasons why later literacy delay is predicted by different language abilities at various points in age. Of course, it is difficult completely to rule out psychometric reasons, such as differences in sensitivity between various measures of early language abilities. Yet, one theoretical possibility with far reaching implications is that there may not be one linear causal chain that leads from one underlying cause through a number of other causes until it manifests itself in a reading delay. Rather, it may be that some underlying and persisting factor (possibly of genetic origin) may cause different problems at different stages of language development. An analogous relationship between cause and symptoms is seen for illnesses such as diabetes. Untreated, it may lead to a whole range of symptoms, any one of which may not necessarily be caused by preceding ones (Scarborough, 2001).

When a language impairment manifests itself in different forms over the preschool years, this may simply mean that it is easier to measure certain language deficits at some times (when the skill ordinarily undergoes rapid growth) than at others (when growth is slower). For example, impairments in syntactic skills may be most detectible from age 2 to 4 years, when syntactic development is particularly rapid by unimpaired preschoolers. Non-linear growth may also make language impaired children appear normal at times when other children reach a plateau, a hypothesised phenomenon that has been called "illusory recovery" (Scarborough & Dobrich, 1990). The recovery is only illusory because they will be left behind as soon as the other children enter a new developmental spurt.

The notion of illusory recovery may also help explain the void between preschool speech therapy and remedial teaching of reading in primary school. As reviewed earlier, a language impaired child who has successfully acquired age appropriate expressive phonology and syntax at the age of six may still be at risk of reading delays in school. The speech therapist may be satisfied with the progress of the child, but the recovery may be only illusory and the child may experience severe problems with learning to read and write.

Prediction depends on when and how reading abilities are assessed

Without question, reading is a multifaceted skill, and each component must develop through instruction and practice in order for the child to become a good reader. In predicting reading achievement, not enough attention has been paid to the question of which components of reading are predicted by particular early skills, and whether such relationships are the same at the earliest stages of reading as at later ones. In the first few grades, difficulty in word recognition and decoding is the greatest obstacle to progress for children who struggle, and hence the aspect of reading that is the focus of much instruction and assessment in the early school years. Most beginning students can readily handle language of the texts (which tend not to be very challenging in structure or content at this age), but may be unable to identify the printed words. Similarly, it is well known that decoding accuracy develops before decoding speed and fluent reading. Finally, once word recognition skills have been sufficiently developed, the main obstacle to progress is difficulty in comprehending complex texts.

Therefore, it is possible that somewhat different early abilities predict reading development at different skill levels, or more likely that the relative potency of predictors may shift depending on when outcomes are measured. For example, it may be that the initial phases of decoding development are predicted mainly by access to segmental phonology since such access is important in order to discover how spellings are related to speech sounds. Conversely, during a later phase the development of decoding speed may become more important – and differences in reading speed may be related to earlier measures of oral language fluency. And increasingly over time, broader cognitive and linguistic abilities needed for text comprehension may begin to contribute most heavily to prediction.

Fortunately, this issue has begun to be addressed in recent longitudinal research, in which a broader array of reading skills have been assessed and/or outcomes at older ages have been obtained. For example, measures of naming speed have been found to be more important predictors of third grade reading than of second grade reading (Elbro, 1997). It has also been shown that the association of letter knowledge in kindergarten to later reading scores remains strong throughout the elementary school years, whereas correlations between phonological awareness and reading achievement tend to be weaker for long-term rather than short-term prediction (Badian, 1995). Furthermore, the relative predictive strengths of phonological and sentence processing abilities have been shown to reverse when comprehension rather than word recognition skill is used as the outcome measure of reading in grade 2 and later (Catts *et al.*, 1999, 2001).

As more is learned about such changes in the relationship between early abilities and various later reading components over time, this should contribute to a clearer and more complete understanding of the bases for reading difficulties and to greater accuracy in identifying children at risk for reading failure. Even so, it must be remembered that prediction based on current knowledge is quite accurate, and that there is strong temporal stability of reading abilities from grade 1 onwards. This suggests that the overall picture is unlikely to be dramatically altered, but only modulated, by future findings.

Unexamined possibilities

It is very conceivable that there may be important characteristics of preschoolers that have been largely neglected in prediction research, but that may be able to provide important additional information about risk. For example, background knowledge of facts and concepts is acknowledged to facilitate reading comprehension, and lack of such knowledge has been shown to hinder comprehension not just of literature but also of texts assigned in other content areas (National Research Council, 1998). Acquired background knowledge is probably a distinct capability not tapped by vocabulary and IQ measures (with which it certainly overlaps), and thus may hold promise as predictor of reading achievement at older ages. In addition, children's motivation to read and their attitudes toward literacy may partly be reflected already in early language and literacy abilities, but may still be of value in its own right for identifying which young children are most likely to have difficulty learning to read (Scarborough & Dobrich, 1994).

CONCLUSIONS

Enormous strides have been made in research over several decades on the early prediction of subsequent reading difficulties, and high levels of accuracy in identifying children at risk for reading problems have been attained in several studies. Prediction models are now so powerful that they are indeed of practical relevance, for example when resources must be allotted to children with high risks of reading failure.

Nevertheless, we have also pointed to several unresolved issues and gaps in knowledge that remain to be addressed. The issues include some quite fundamental ones. For example, we know that letter knowledge, phoneme awareness and picture naming are powerful predictors for children learning to read in English, but it may be that phoneme awareness is a somewhat less strong predictor for children learning to read in a more regular orthography. After all, English is the exception, whereas regular orthographies are the more common. It may also be that the relative importance of various predictors depends on the level of reading proficiency we aim to predict. Perhaps phoneme awareness is more important to the initial phases in reading development than to later phases. Conversely, naming (lexical retrieval) may be of greater importance to the development of fluency and comprehension, which typically accelerate *after* the initial phases of development. And it may certainly be the case that some predictors are relevant for predicting problems in reading, but not for predicting superior reading – because they are not linearly related to the entire continuum of reading abilities but rather are a characteristic (or possible cause) of certain impending problems.

To be sure, we will probably never be able to predict or prevent *all* reading difficulties, but prediction is likely to improve to some degree as the research becomes more sophisticated in its skill assessments and data-analytic techniques. Our growing knowledge about early prediction not only has practical importance, but also contributes to the theoretical challenge of expanding and refining current hypotheses about the relationships between preschool language and literacy developments and later reading abilities. To that end, experimental intervention research is also critical, and that is the topic taken up in the next chapter.

REFERENCES

Aram, D. M., & Hall, N. E. (1989). Longitudinal follow-up of children with preschool communication disorders: treatment implications. *School Psychology Review, 18*, 487-501.

Badian, N. A. (1982). The prediction of good and poor reading before kindergarten entry: A 4-year follow-up. *Journal of Special Education, 16*, 309-318.

Badian, N. A. (1988). Predicting dyslexia in a preschool population. In R. L. Masland & M. W. Masland (Eds.), *Preschool Prevention of Reading Failure* (pp. 78-103). Parkton, Maryland: York Press.

Badian, N. A. (1995). Predicting reading ability over the long term: The changing roles of letter naming, phonological awareness, and orthographic knowledge. *Annals of Dyslexia, 45*, 79-96.

Badian, N. A. (Ed.). (2000). *Prediction and prevention of reading failure.* Timonium, MD: York Press.

Baker, L., & Cantwell, D. P. (1987). A prospective psychiatric follow-up of children with speech/ language disorders. *Journal of the American Academy of Child and Adolescent Psychiatry, 26,* 546-553.

Bohannon, J., Warren-Leubecker, A., & Hepler, N. (1984). Word awareness and early reading. *Child Development, 55,* 1541-1548.

Borstrøm, I., & Elbro, C. (1997). Prevention of dyslexia in kindergarten: Effects of phoneme awareness training with children of dyslexic parents. In C. Hulme & M. Snowling (Eds.), *Dyslexia: Biology, Cognition and Intervention* (pp. 235-253). London: Whurr.

Bryant, P. E., Bradley, L., MacLean, M., & Crossland, J. (1989). Nursery rhymes, phonological skills and reading. *Journal of Child Language, 16,* 407-428.

Bus, A. G., van IJzendoorn, M. H., & Pellegrini, A. D. (1995). Joint book reading makes for success in learning to read: A meta-analysis on intergenerational transmission of literacy. *Review of Educational Research, 65,* 1-21.

Byrne, B. Fielding-Barnsley, Rl, Hindson, B., Mackay, C., Newman, C., & Shankweiler, D. (1998, April). *Early intervention with children at risk for reading disability: A mid-term report.* Paper presented at the conference of the Society for the Scientific Study of Reading, San Diego, CA.

Catts, H. W. (1991). Early identification of dyslexia: Evidence from a follow-up study of speech-language impaired children. *Annals of Dyslexia, 41,* 163-177.

Catts, H. W. (1993). The relationship between speech-language impairments and reading disabilities. *Journal of Speech and Hearing Research, 36,* 948-958.

Catts, H., Fey, M., Zhang, X., & Tomblin, J. B. (1999). Language basis of reading and reading disabilities: Evidence from a longitudinal study. *Scientific Studies of Reading, 3,* 331-361.

Catts, H. W., Fey, M. E., Zhang, X., & Tomblin, J. B. (2001). Estimating the risk of future reading difficulties in kindergarten children: A research-based model and its clinical implementation. *Language, Speech, and Hearing Services in Schools, 32*(1), 38-50.

DeFries, J.C., & Alarcon, M. (1996). Genetics of specific reading disability. *Mental Retardation and Developmental Disabilities Research Reviews, 2,* 39-47.

de Hirsch, K., Jansky, J. J., & Langford, W. S. (1966). *Predicting reading failure. A preliminary study.* New York: Harper & Row.

de Jong, P. F., & Frielink, O. (2000). *Rapid Automatic Naming: Easy to measure, hard to improve.* Paper presented at the Annual Meeting of the Society of the Scientific Study of Reading, July 2000, Stockholm.

Elbro, C. (1997, April). *Different language abilities predict poor and good reading in the early grades.* Paper presented at the American Educational Research Association meeting in Chicago.

Elbro, C. (1999, April). The identification of individual eggs in an omelette: How low quality of phonological representations of lexical items predicts phonological processing difficulties with spoken and written language. In B. F. Pennington (Chair), Longitudinal studies of children at family risk for dyslexia: Results from four countries. Symposium conducted at the meeting of the Society for Research in Child Development, Albuquerque, NM.

Elbro, C., Borstrom, I., & Peterson, D. K. (1998). Predicting dyslexia from kindergarten. The importance of distinctness of phonological representations of lexical items. *Reading Research Quarterly, 33*(1), 36–60.

Frost, J. (2001). Differences in reading development among Danish beginning-readers with high versus low phonemic awareness on entering Grade one. *Reading and Writing. An Interdisciplinary Journal, 14,* 615-642.

Gallagher, A., Frith, U., & Snowling, M. (2000). Precursors of literacy delay among children at risk of dyslexia. *Journal of Child Psychology and Psychiatry, 41,* 203-213.

Gilger, J. W., Borecki, S. D., Smith, S. D., DeFries, J. C., & Pennington, B. F. (1996). The etiology of extreme scores for complex phenotypes: An illustration of using reading performance. In C. H. Chase, G. O. Rosen, & G. F. Sherman (Eds.), *Developmental dyslexia.* Baltimore: York Press.

Gilger, J. W., Pennington, B. F., & DeFries, J. C. (1991). Risk for reading disability as a function of parental history in three family studies. *Reading and Writing. An Interdisciplinary Journal, 3,* 205-217.

Gough, P. (1998, April). *Phonemic awareness as a predictor of reading achievement.* Paper presented to the conference of the Society for the Scientific Study of Reading, San Diego CA.

Hagtvet, B. (2000). Prevention and prediction of reading problems. In N. A. Badian (Ed.), *Prediction and prevention of reading failure* (pp. 105-131). Timonium, MD: York Press.

Hauschild, K. M., & Elbro, C. (1992). *Hvad blev der af dem? En efterundersøgelse af børn fra Taleinstituttet i København* ('What became of them? A follow-up study of children who were refered to the Copenhagen Speech Institute'). Copenhagen: Audiologopædisk Forening. Monografi nr. 15.

Hindson, B. (2001). The linguistic and cognitive characteristics of preschoolers at risk for developmental reading disability. University of New England, Australia. Doctoral dissertation.

Ho, C. S., & Bryant, P. (1997). Phonological skills are important in learning to read Chinese. *Developmental Psychology, 33,* 946-951.

Hurford, D. P., Darrow, L. J., Edwards, T. L., Howerton, C. J., Mote, C. R., Schauf, J. D., & Coffey, P. (1993). An examination of the development of phonemic processing abilities in children during their first-grade year. *Journal of Learning Disabilities, 26,* 167-177.

Hurford, D. P., Schauf, J. D., Bunce, L., Blaich, T., & Moore, K. (1994). Early identification of children at risk for learning disabilities. *Journal of Learning Disabilities, 27*(6), 371-382.

Jansky, J. J., Hoffmann, M. T., Layton, J., & Sugar, F. (1989). Prediction: A six-year follow-up. *Annals of Dyslexia, 39,* 227-246.

Juel, C., Griffith, P. L., & Gough, P B. (1986). Learning to read and write: A longitudinal study of children in first and second grade. *Journal of Educational Psychology, 78,* 243-255.

Lonigan, C. J., Burgess, S. B., & Anthony, J. L. (2000). Development of emergent literacy and early reading skills in preschool children: Evidence from a latent variable longitudinal study. *Developmental Psychology, 36,* 596-613.

Lundberg, I., Olofsson, & Wall, S. (1980). Reading and spelling skills in the first school years predicted from phonemic awareness skills in kindergarten. *Scandinavian Journal of Psychology, 21,* 159-173.

Lyytinen, H., Ahonen, T., & Räsänen, P. (1994). Dyslexia and dyscalculia in children – risks, early precursors, bottlenecks and cognitive mechanisms. *Acta Paedopsychiatrica, 56,* 179-192.

Mantzicopoulos, P. Y., & Morrison, D. (1994). Early prediction of reading achievement: Exploring the relationship of cognitive and noncognitive measures to inaccurate classifications of at-risk status. *RASE. Remedial and Special Education, 15,* 244-251.

Muter, V., & Snowling, M. (1998). Concurrent and longitudinal predictors of reading: The role of metalinguistic and short-term memory skills. *Reading Research Quarterly, 33,* 320-327.

National Research Council (1998). *Preventing reading difficulties in young children.* Washington, DC: National Academy Press.

Nauclér, K., & Magnusson, E. (1998). Reading and writing development: Report on an ongoing longitudinal study of language-disordered and normal groups from pre-school to adolescence. *Folia Phoniatrica et Logopaedica, 50,* 271-282.

Olofsson, A., & Niedersøe, J. (1999). Early language development and kindergarten phonological awareness as predictors of reading problems: From 3 to 11 years of age. *Journal of Learning Disabilities, 32,* 464-472.

Olson, R. K., & Gayan, J. (2001). Brains, genes, and environment in reading development. In S. B. Neuman & D. K. Dickinson (Eds.), *Handbook of early literacy research* (pp. 81-94). New York: Guilford Press.

Pennington, B. F., Lefly, D. L., & Boada, R. (1999, April). *Phonological development and reading outcomes in children at family risk for dyslexia.* In B. F. Pennington (Chair), Longitudinal studies of children at family risk for dyslexia: Results from four countries. Symposium conducted at the meeting of the Society for Research in Child Development, Albuquerque, NM.

Petersen, D. K., & Elbro, C. (1999). Pre-school prediction and prevention of dyslexia: A longitudinal study with children of dyslexic parents. In T. Nunes (Ed.), *Learning to read: An integrated view from research and practice* (pp. 133-154). Dordrecht: Kluwer.

Pisecco, S., Baker, D. B., Silva, P. A., & Brooke, M. (2001). Boys with reading disabilities and/or ADHD: Distinctions in early childhood. Journal of Learning Disabilities, 34, 98-106.

Rescorla, L. R. (1999), July). *Outcomes of late talkers: Academic and language skills at age 13.* Paper presented at the meeting of the International Association for the Study of Child Language, San Sebastian, Spain.

Scarborough, H. S. (1989). Prediction of reading disability from familial and individual differences. *Journal of Educational Psychology, 81,* 101-108.

Scarborough, H. S. (1990). Very early language deficits in dyslexic children. *Child Development, 61,* 1728-1743.

Scarborough, H. S. (1991). Antecedents to reading disability: Preschool language development and literacy experiences of children from dyslexic families. *Reading and Writing. An Interdisciplinary Journal, 3,* 219-233.

Scarborough, H. S. (1998a). Early identification of children at risk for reading disabilities. Phonological awareness and some other promising, predictors. In. In B. K. Shapiro & P. J. Accrado & A. J. Capute (Eds.), *Specific reading disability: A view of the spectrum* (pp. 75-119). New York: York Press.

Scarborough, H. S. (1998b). Predicting the future achievement of second graders with reading disabilities: Contributions of phonemic awareness, verbal memory, rapid naming, and IQ. *Annals of Dyslexia, 48,* 115-136.

Scarborough, H. S. (2001). Connecting early language and literacy to later reading (dis)abilities: Evidence, theory, and practice. In S. B. Neuman & D. K. Dickinson (Eds.), *Handbook of early literacy research* (pp. 97-110). New York: Guilford Press.

Scarborough, H. S., & Dobrich, W. (1990). Development of children with early language delays. *Journal of Speech and Hearing Research, 33,* 70-83.

Scarborough, H. S., & Dobrich, W. (1994). On the efficacy of reading to preschoolers. *Developmental Review, 14,* 245-302.

Scarborough, H. S., Dobrich, W., & Hager, M. (1991). Literacy experience and reading disability: Reading habits and abilities of parents and young children. *Journal of Learning Disabilities, 24,* 508-511.

Schneider, W., & Näslund, J. C. (1993). The impact of early metalinguistic competencies and memory capacity on reading and spelling in elementary school: Results of the Munic longitudinal study on the genesis of individual competencies (LOGIC). *European Journal of Psychology of Education, 8,* 273-287.

Shapiro, B. K., Palmer, F. B., Antell, S. E., Bilker, S.; et-al (1990). Detection of young children in need of reading help: Evaluation of specific reading disability formulas. *Clinical Pediatrics, 29,* 206-213.

Silver, A. A., & Hagin, R. A. (1981). *SEARCH manual.* New York: Wiley.

Snow, C. E., Barnes, W. S., Chandler, J., Goodman, J. R., & Hemphill, L. (1991). *Unfulfilled expectations: Home and school influences on literacy.* Cambridge, MA: Harvard University Press.

Sprenger-Charolles, L., Siegel, L. S., & Béchennec, D. (1998). Phonological mediation and semantic and orthographic factors in silent reading in French. *Scientific Studies of Reading, 2,* 3-30.

Stothard, S. E., Snowling, M. J., Bishop, D. V. M., Chipchase, B. B., & Kaplan, C. A. (1998). Language-impaired preschoolers: A follow-up into adolescence. *Journal of Speech, Language and Hearing Research, 41,* 407-418.

Torgesen, J. K., Wagner, R. K., & Rashotte, C. A. (1999). Prevention and remediation of severe reading disabilities: Keeping the end in mind. *Scientific Studies of Reading, 1,* 217-234.

Tunmer, W. E., & Hoover, W. A. (1992). Cognitive and linguistic factors in learning to read. In P. B. Gough, L .C. Ehri, & R. Treiman (Eds.), *Reading acquisition* (pp. 175-214). Hillsdale, NJ: Erlbaum.

Walker, D., Greenwood, C., Hart, B., & Carta, J. (1994). Prediction of school outcomes based on early language production and socioeconomic factors. *Child Development, 65,* 606-621.

Wesseling, R. (1999). Quality of phonological representations: Etiology and remediation of dyslexia. Amsterdam: Free University. Doctoral dissertation.

West, J., Denton, K., & Germino-Hausken, E. (2000). America's kindergartners: Findings from the early childhood longitudinal study, kindergarten class of 1998-99, Fall 1998. Washington, DC: National Center for Education Statistics.

Whitehurst, G. J., & Lonigan, C. (2001). Emergent literacy: Development from prereaders to readers. In S. Neuman & D. Dickinson (Eds.), *Handbook of early literacy research* (pp. 11-29). New York: Guilford.

C7. Early Intervention

CARSTEN ELBRO & HOLLIS S. SCARBOROUGH[1]

ABSTRACT

Many cases of reading difficulties can be prevented. There is no longer good reasons to "wait and see" and expect that a child "grows out" of his or her difficulties. It is now clear that preschool activities that direct the child's attention directly towards the sound (phoneme) structure of the spoken language are beneficial for the child's reading development. Such awareness paves the way for the child's understanding of the nature of the alphabetic principle of writing. Adding letter knowledge to phoneme awareness takes the child a step further towards literacy. Several studies are reviewed that indicate such early intervention has positive effects both in undivided classrooms and in small, targeted groups. Further, it is also beneficial both for unselected groups of children and for groups of at-risk children such as children with language impairments, children from dyslexic families, children from socioeconomically disadvantaged families, or children who have poorly developed phoneme awareness and letter knowledge for a variety of reasons. In addition, early book-reading interventions have been found to promote vocabulary knowledge and semantics – both in unselected groups and in children with poor vocabularies. The chapter concludes with calls for further research into "treatment resisters", i.e., children who do not benefit even from the best of our efforts at early intervention, and for research in early intervention to promote language comprehension skills that are essential for reading.

INTRODUCTION

Intervention means to step in and take some action intended to divert the child from his or her present course onto a better one. With respect to reading, the goal of intervention is to do something extraordinary that helps the child avoid reading

---

[1] Support for the preparation of this chapter was provided, in part, by NOS-S grant No. 124811/541 to the first author and by Grant No. HD-01994 to Haskins Laboratories. We wish to thank Jane Oakhill for her many astute comments.

T. Nunes, P. Bryant (eds.), Handbook of Children's Literacy, 361–381.

difficulties that would otherwise lie ahead. Intervention may take many different forms, from play-like language activities in preschool classes to intensive supplemental tutoring for beginning readers who are falling behind.

Intervention can be undertaken at various points during the course of reading development: *before* formal reading instruction begins (in kindergarten or earlier); *during* the early phases of reading instruction (usually in first and second grade); and *beyond* the primary grades. Intervention before formal instruction aims to strengthen the language and emergent literacy abilities that contribute to success in learning to read; hence intervention at the earliest point has the goal of *preventing* reading difficulties. Intervention during the primary grades typically targets not just the prerequisite abilities but also the early reading skills being taught; the goal is for initial difficulties to be overcome so that future achievement will not be jeopardised. Later interventions necessarily are aimed at remediating existing weaknesses in reading, often with a focus on teaching compensatory strategies in addition to strengthening fundamental skills.

This chapter will focus on early intervention[2] (i.e., with kindergartners and younger preschoolers) and on its important relationships to the prediction research that we have already reviewed in Chapter C6. Early prevention programs can be fruitfully informed by early prediction studies in several ways. First, the prediction results provide guidance as to what early skills should be the focus of intervention. Strengthening the known predictor skills is most likely to serve the goal of preventing difficulty in learning to read when instruction begins. Conversely, it is unlikely that children would benefit significantly from instruction in skills or abilities that are not predictive of reading development. Second, although early intervention could in principle be carried out with all children, this is not always desirable, feasible, or cost effective. Instead, therefore, it is often appropriate and economical to target prevention programs toward those children who are more in need of support than others. To that end, the results of prediction studies can help us decide how to identify children who are at greatest risk for reading failure. In addition, studies of early intervention reflect back on early prediction, contributing to a stronger theoretical understanding of the course of literacy development from the preschool to the school years. When strengthening an early skill is shown to be effective in raising future achievement (and reducing the incidence of later reading problems), this provides evidence that the skill in question does indeed bear a causal relation to reading acquisition, and is not just a correlate or marker of risk. Without such evidence, accurate and complete theoretical models cannot be established.

The practical motivations for early intervention to prevent subsequent reading difficulties are widely accepted.

---

[2] The focus on early intervention does *not* imply that intervention at a later point is useless. There is evidence that intervention during the primary grades can be highly effective, and perhaps as effective as preschool intervention (see National Reading Panel, 2000, chapter 2-1).

First, from an institutional perspective, it can potentially be of great value. Especially in the United States, it is widely felt that many children who now receive special educational services would not have needed such costly remedial intervention if their reading difficulties had been addressed at much younger ages (National Research Council, 1998). There is great hope that investing in early prevention efforts will insure that nearly all children learn to read successfully in the primary grades, freeing up resources to provide intensified later intervention for the few children who most need it.

Second, from the child's perspective, the benefits of successful early intervention are potentially far-reaching. As noted earlier, the consequences of low achievement in the primary school grades are dire, affecting not just academic progress in other subjects but also social and emotional adjustment. Early intervention has the immense human advantage that it may minimise the period during which the child encounters any difficulties, thereby forestalling the snowballing negative sequelae ("Matthew effects") that may be even more debilitating than the reading problem itself.

Knowledge derived from research on successful (and unsuccessful) interventions is as indispensable from a theoretical viewpoint as from a practical viewpoint. Well-conducted intervention studies are a critical source of evidence about the causes of reading difficulties. Conversely, even the most well-established precursors in longitudinal prediction studies may be only *indirectly* related to subsequent reading failure, or may even be merely markers of risk for reading difficulties but be otherwise irrelevant to reading acquisition. The correlational prediction studies reviewed in the preceding chapter of this volume can tell us only that certain reliable indicators of risk can be observed before a child exhibits difficulties in learning to read. Intervention studies, on the other hand, are experimental by nature, and can thus confirm or disconfirm whether progress in learning to read is indeed affected by helping children improve abilities that are hypothesised to be of critical importance for reading. Reading-specific, positive effects of intervention are unlikely to occur unless the trained abilities are causally related to reading. The relationship might not be a direct one, but a causal relationship must exist.

TARGETED VERSUS UNIVERSAL EARLY INTERVENTION

One approach to early intervention is to provide all kindergarteners with a high quality educational program that promotes the development of critical reading-related skills that have been identified in research. Typically, this is accomplished *not* through formal reading instruction, but through developmentally appropriate classroom activities and games. Even though it is well established that there are wide differences among kindergarteners in their abilities and knowledge when they enter school, it is also likely that much of this variability reflects the early educational histories of the children rather than intrinsic differences among them in the capacity to learn. Hence, it is argued, exposing all children to a solid kindergarten curriculum and excellent teaching will overcome initial differences, in particular by bringing the skill levels of the least-prepared students up to the levels of better-prepared students by the time formal instruction commences.

This approach, which has been taken in several intervention studies to date, has some clear advantages. When entire classrooms are studied, with students randomly assigned to classrooms and with the intervention program implemented in some classrooms but not others (ideally, on the basis of random assignment), comparisons between treatment and non-treatment groups can readily be carried out. Large numbers of participants can be studied, allowing for detailed analyses of subgroups. Children at risk need not be identified or treated any differently from their classmates, and if the intervention is successful, they (and their peers) may never become aware of their initial weaknesses and the risk associated with them. Thus far, however, this approach has more often been taken in Grade 1 than in kindergarten (e.g., Foorman, Francis, Fletcher, Schatschneider & Mehta, 1998; Lie, 1991; Scanlon & Vellutino, 1996), so how far earlier intervention might go toward preventing reading difficulties is difficult to judge from the few studies with kindergartners, discussed below. Also, it is widely believed that most children (perhaps 75-90%) will successfully learn to read regardless of the type of instruction they receive. If so, comparing treatment and control groups (especially alternative-treatment controls) from unselected samples is likely to yield rather weak effects overall, even if there are substantial benefits for the small minority of at-risk children (whose outcomes are of greatest interest).

An alternative approach is to provide early intervention to targeted groups that have been identified as most likely to encounter difficulties in learning to read. These groups include economically disadvantaged children, preschoolers with a history of speech-language impairments, offspring of parents with reading disabilities, and kindergartners who do poorly when their skills are measured prior to the start of formal reading instruction. Note that these at-risk groups are not mutually exclusive, but may overlap considerably. That is, a child may be from a family of poor readers *and* may attend a low-performing neighborhood school *and* may have a preschool language impairment *and* may exhibit weaknesses in reading-related skills at the time of school entry. Despite this, targeted interventions have typically recruited at-risk children on the basis of a single risk factor, so we will discuss such interventions separately in what follows.

One advantage of targeted interventions is that they are potentially applicable at younger ages, before children enter kindergarten. Also, available resources are not devoted mainly to treating children who are not at risk, and thus whose futures would probably not be altered much by participation. On the other hand, participation in targeted interventions is more likely to be voluntary, so research samples may not be population-representative, raising questions about the generalisability of the findings. Furthermore, there are ethical questions raised by designs in which at-risk children are randomly assigned to a control group rather than to one receiving the preferred treatment. Also, when young children are identified as at risk, such labelling raises concerns about possible negative consequences (stigmatisation, setting a self-fulfilling prophecy in motion, and so forth), although evidence is sorely lacking with regard to this important question. Nevertheless, because the reading difficulties of targeted populations are of such particular concern, there has been a considerable amount of intervention research with at-risk samples.

In what follows, we will first describe the methods and results of intervention programs that have been used with unselected samples. We will then turn to the findings for studies of particular targeted groups.

EARLY INTERVENTION WITH UNSELECTED GROUPS

Several intervention studies have been conducted in randomly assigned samples of kindergarten children. Guided by theory and the results of prediction research, these programs have mainly sought to strengthen one or more of a small set of reading-related skills and abilities: letter knowledge and rudimentary reading skills; phonological awareness; oral language skills (especially vocabulary); and familiarity with books and reading.

Letter knowledge and rudimentary reading skills

Knowing the letters of the alphabet, understanding the alphabetic principle (that letters represent the speech sounds of oral language in a systematic way), learning basic sound-spelling correspondences, and recognizing some basic "sight words" (like *the, you, is*, etc.) are the literacy skills that have traditionally been introduced in the beginning phases of reading instruction. When the prevention of reading difficulties is addressed through kindergarten interventions with entire classes, therefore, the issue is usually not *whether* to introduce children to such matters but *when* and *how* to do so in the most effective and developmentally appropriate ways. On the one hand, some have favoured providing stimulating and print-rich settings and activities in which children can discover rudimentary literacy skills for themselves, through experiences driven by curiosity, a supportive environment, and teachers who are alert to opportunities to bring these aspects of reading and writing to the children's attention when the occasion arises. In brief, this approach involves indirect, implicit, and embedded instruction. On the other hand, other educators advocate that kindergarten activities instead be designed to teach these fundamental skills in a direct, explicit, and systematic way. That is, games, songs, read-alouds, and so forth are designed to be used in a particular sequence, with learning based not just on experience but also on direct and explicit teaching of the subject matter. This does not mean, however, that there is any less emphasis on avoiding formal lessons in favour of engaging and brief play-like activities as the context for such instruction at young ages.

Although this debate continues, with strongly held views on both sides, the evidence to date favours the use of a more direct, explicit, and systematically sequenced introduction to letter knowledge and foundational reading skills. This conclusion was reached in a comprehensive evaluation of instructional methods by an expert panel in the United States (National Reading Panel, 2000), based on their review of published reports on the teaching of basic alphabetic skills in kindergarten and the primary grades. While it is probably true that some children will progress satisfactorily regardless of the approach taken, less positive outcomes for the class as a whole are obtained from indirect and child-initiated instruction. That is, particularly for the students who were less skilled at the outset, more explicit assistance is needed in mastering the rudiments of reading. Simply starting earlier does not foster successful reading acquisition by these students, but only makes their weaknesses visible at an earlier time than otherwise.

Importantly, instruction in letter knowledge *alone* does not seem to pave the way towards reading development (refs. in Adams, 1990). The negative outcomes of training studies suggest that knowing letters is like knowing the parts of a bicycle without being able to ride it. Knowing letters is probably necessary but not sufficient, and thus has to be combined with other information about the nature of the alphabetic writing system. A key link in helping children to grasp the alphabetic principle, and thereby to gain familiarity with spelling-sound correspondences, is phonological awareness, another reading-related skill that can successfully be introduced at the kindergarten level or somewhat earlier.

Phonological awareness and phonemic awareness

Phonological awareness is, most fundamentally, an appreciation of the fact that spoken words consist of phonological elements such as syllables and various smaller units. The smallest of these, called *phonemes*, are what graphemes (letters and letter combinations) usually represent when the word is written down. Clearly, understanding this "alphabetic principle" depends on the child's having noticed the existence of speech sounds, and especially of individual phonemes. Otherwise, how could the child understand what is meant when a teacher says, for example, "The letter B stands for the first sound in *boy*."? For this reason, phonological awareness is among the best predictors of future reading achievement. Many programs have been developed to train phonological awareness in young children, and there is abundant evidence that many game-like activities can readily direct children's attention to the phonological structure of words, not just in kindergarten but even in four-year-olds (e.g., Byrne & Fielding-Barnsley, 1990; Solity, 1996; Treiman & Baron, 1983). The use of phonological awareness training programs in kindergarten and preschool classrooms has grown dramatically over the past decade.

The results of experimental training studies have consistently indicated that structured language activities that help young children focus on sound segments within words are indeed beneficial for their later reading development. This conclusion was recently confirmed by a meta-analyses conducted by the National Reading Panel (2000). (See also Ehri *et al.*, 2001) Moreover, there is evidence that the benefits of such early training can persist for many years (Byrne, Fielding-Barnsley & Ashley, 2000).

To illustrate, consider the well-known Bornholm study (Lundberg, Frost & Petersen, 1988; Lundberg, 1994). In it, all kindergarten teachers on the Danish island of Bornholm were invited to participate in a study of phonological awareness training with their students, and nearly all consented to participate (N = 235). Kindergartners from another area of Denmark, who were from comparable socioeconomic backgrounds, served as a comparison group (N = 155). The language activities designed to enhance phonological awareness took place for about 15 minutes every day over an 8 month period. These activities proceeded from general listening tasks to language tasks involving gradually smaller units, from whole words, to syllables and rhymes, to single phonemes. The children's gains in phoneme awareness were impressive, averaging one standard deviation across types of phonological manipulation tasks (segmentation, synthesis, rhyming). These gains were very specific to phonological awareness, with no advantage for the experimental children in terms of letter knowledge, vocabulary, or math abilities in the kindergarten year. Nevertheless, when followed up in first grade, the trained group earned higher scores than the controls on tests of spelling and, marginally, word reading. Most impressive, however, was that the benefit of early phonological awareness training strengthened over time, such that by the end of the second grade, the experimental children significantly outperformed the control children in both reading and spelling.

The experimental materials and teaching methods from the Bornholm study have been translated into other languages and very similar results have been reported from German (Schneider, Küspert, Roth, Visé, & Marx, 1997), Spanish (Cary & Verhaeghe, 1994), and American English (Brennan & Ireson, 1997); see also Adams, Foorman, Lundberg, & Beeler (1998). It is interesting to note, furthermore, that in one of the German studies reported by Schneider and colleagues, some teachers did not complete the final part of the program, which focussed on isolating single phonemic segments. The children in those classes did significantly worse than the other participants on subsequent tests of both phoneme awareness and reading and writing. This result underscores the importance of the awareness of *single phonemes* as a stepping stone to initial reading development. Note that the term *phonemic* awareness is used to denote this particular aspect of phonological awareness, the attainment of which is more likely to require explicit instruction or literacy (Bowey, 2000; Bowey & Francis, 1991; Stanovich, 1992).

From a theoretical perspective, another noteworthy aspect of the Bornholm project (and several others) is that instruction in letters was not provided in conjunction with the oral phonological training. This is important because the positive effects of the program on later reading achievement suggest that phonemic awareness is indeed causally related to learning to read. The nature of this relationship is apparently not unidirectional, however, since the reverse has also been demonstrated, namely that learning to read causes gains in phonemic awareness (Ehri & Wilce, 1980; Perfetti, Beck, Bell & Hughes, 1987) In novice readers (but perhaps not at later periods of reading acquisition), phoneme awareness may serve a *catalytic* function, in the sense that it helps set the stage for understanding the function of letters and for making the connections between graphemes and phonemes (Frost, 2001).

From a practical perspective, however, teaching phoneme awareness *with* letter manipulation provides considerably more benefit for learning to read and spell than does phonological awareness training *without* letters (National Reading Panel, 2000, chapter 2-1). Across more than 80 independent samples, the average effect size when letters were taught was almost twice as large as when phonological awareness was trained in isolation. In sum, the research strongly indicates that kindergarteners are helped most when phonological awareness and letter knowledge, and the relation between them, are the focus of classroom activities.

Oral vocabulary and knowledge about literacy

Whereas phonological awareness, letter knowledge, and rudimentary reading skills probably contribute most heavily to the acquisition of "bottom up" (word recognition and decoding) skills, other strong predictors of future reading are more likely to be precursors of "top down" comprehension of text. Of these, the most attention has been paid to vocabulary acquisition, but oral comprehension abilities and familiarity with "concepts of print" have also been examined. In early interventions to foster the development of these skills, kindergartners or younger preschoolers (individually or in groups) have received increased or enhanced exposure to joint book-reading experiences with an adult, relative to a control group. Although merely increasing the amount of book-reading has produced semantic gains (e.g., Feitelson, Kita & Goldstein, 1986; Robbins & Ehri, 1994; Senechal & Cornell, 1993), even larger effects have been obtained when the manner, rather than just the amount, of this activity is altered, for instance by providing the meanings of unfamiliar words in the story (e.g., Elley, 1989), or by having the children answer questions about such words (e.g., Senechal, 1997). It has also been reported that gains in semantic skills and print concepts vary depending on the style adopted by the adult reader, and that different reading styles may be more effective at different points in literacy development (e.g., Reese & Cox, 1999; Teale & Martinez, 1996).

The most comprehensive and widely used intervention of this sort is "dialogic reading," a program developed by Whitehurst and his colleagues. In many studies, parents or teachers of children in the treatment group have been trained to (a) evoke greater verbal participation from the child by asking questions that require more than a yes-no answer; (b) provide feedback on the child's language productions, such as by extending or recasting them; and (c) challenge the child by encouraging dialogue about aspects of the storybook that are not already familiar territory. Adults in the control groups have read equally often to the children, but in their customary ways. After relatively brief (one month) interventions, group differences in expressive vocabulary were observed in two early studies with unselected samples (Whitehurst, Falco, Lonigan, Fischel, DeBaryshe, Valdez-Menchaca & Caulfield, 1988; Arnold, Lonigan, Whitehurst, & Epstein, 1994). As will be described below, dialogic reading interventions have also been successfully conducted with a variety of targeted at-risk populations.

EARLY INTERVENTION FOR KINDERGARTNERS WITH WEAK READING-RELATED SKILLS

From the prediction research reviewed in the previous chapter, it is clear that children who begin school with weaknesses in oral language and emergent literacy skills (revealed by screening assessments) are at risk for future reading difficulties. Targeting those children for special training during the kindergarten year has been shown to be effective in raising their skills levels in several areas, and follow-up assessments of later reading achievement have shown that the benefits of intervention can be long-lasting.

Phonological awareness, letter knowledge, and rudimentary reading skills

In the Bornholm study described earlier, separate analyses were conducted for 50 children (25 from the experimental group and 25 controls) whose phonological awareness scores were lowest at the outset (Lundberg, 1994). In the control group, as one would expect, the low-scorers exhibited significantly slower progress in reading than the other controls, confirming that the initial weakness in this skill was indeed an indicator of risk. In the experimental groups, however, the children who were originally the poorest in phoneme awareness, but who received training in phonological awareness, were able to read as well as the normal children in the control group when they reached grade 3. The early intervention thus appears to have prevented many of the reading problems that might otherwise have occurred.

Because a lack of letter knowledge is also a risk factor, it is common for initial weaknesses in both phonological awareness and alphabetic skills to be addressed in training (e.g., Schneider *et al.*, 1999; Torgesen, Wagner & Rashotte, 1997) When phonological awareness training alone has been contrasted with training that also familiarised children with letters, the combination has usually produced more robust benefits for reading acquisition (Ehri *et al.*, in press; National Reading Panel, 2000).

Positive short-term and/or long-term benefits of early phonological awareness training (with or without letters) have also been reported from numerous other intervention studies with at-risk children learning to read other languages and orthographies, including German (Schneider *et al.*, 1999), Hebrew (Bentin & Leshem, 1993), Spanish (Defior & Tudela, 1994), and English (e.g., Bradley & Bryant, 1983; Byrne, Fielding-Barnsley, & Ashley, 2000; Fox & Routh, 1976, 1984; O'Connor, Jenkins & Slocum, 1995). These and other studies further suggest that phoneme segmentation is a key to other types of phoneme manipulation, and that there is little advantage to using a wide variety of phonological tasks work over just one or two (Ehri *et al.*, in press; National Reading Panel, 2000).

Vocabulary and oral language

Effects of book-reading interventions to promote language abilities have been examined not just in unselected groups (as described above) but also in samples of children who earned low scores on pretests of vocabulary knowledge. In a study of such 3- to 5-year-olds in daycare setting, Hargrave and Senechal (2000) compared groups that received the dialogic reading program (Whitehurst *et al.*, 1988; described earlier) on a regular basis for a month versus an equivalent number of more conventional shared reading experiences with the same books. Although both groups acquired some new words that had been introduced in the books, only the dialogic reading group also showed gains on a post-test of expressive vocabulary. Robbins and Ehri (1994) compared vocabulary growth resulting from bookreading exposure for children who obtained low versus high scores on a vocabulary pretest, and found that greater gains were made by the children with larger initial vocabularies. Hence, although shared bookreading does appear to foster vocabulary growth in children who need it, they may benefit less than other children from this intervention, presumably due to the same limitations that hindered prior vocabulary acquisition. More intensive and/or frequent intervention may therefore be necessary to overcome initial weaknesses in these children's knowledge of words and their meanings.

EARLY INTERVENTION FOR CHILDREN FROM DYSLEXIC FAMILIES

As described earlier, if one or more members of a child's immediate family have a history of reading disability (dyslexia), this family background places the child at high risk for having difficulty in learning to read. Although children from dyslexic families would thus be an obvious target group for early intervention, this has rarely been undertaken. In part, this may be because the logistics of such programs are complicated. These children do not attend special preschools or clinics, making recruitment of large samples difficult. Also, denying intervention to a control group that is similarly at risk poses ethical questions. To our knowledge, only three intervention studies with this population have been conducted, two in Australia (Byrne *et al.*, 1997; Byrne, in press; Hindson, 2001) and the other in Copenhagen (Borstrøm & Elbro, 1997; Petersen, 2000).

The first Australian intervention concerned 54 children aged 4 in the kindergarten grade. All of the children had a first degree relative (parent or older sibling) with dyslexia as confirmed by a history of reading difficulties and poor reading performance at the time of the study. The at-risk children were taught in small groups (with one to six children) for one 40-minute session per week over a period of 16 to 20 weeks. The aim of the teaching was to make the children aware of the principle of phoneme identity, i.e., that words can share the same sounds. Teaching and subsequent testing focussed on initial and final consonants. Based on results from the first 40 of the children who completed the program it seemed clear that phoneme identity was much harder to detect for the at-risk children than for a not-at-risk group studied earlier (Byrne & Fielding-Barnsley, 1990). In the at-risk group 32% of the children did not progress at all in phoneme awareness during training, and a further 20% of the children showed only marginal progress. These figures may be compared to 5% and 2%, respectively, in the not-at-risk group. Hence, it appears that a relatively high proportion of at-risk children are resistant to early intervention which works well in other populations. This result suggests that at-risk status indeed is associated with the ability to acquire phoneme awareness. However, the long term outcome for reading is yet to be reported.

The second Australian intervention features a dedicated control group but is still in progress. However, a preliminary report (Byrne, in press; Hindson, 2001) suggest that the at-risk children do benefit from the intervention in terms of initial progress with reading. They were achieving grade-appropriate scores in reading once they reached school.

The Copenhagen study targeted somewhat older children from dyslexic families. In Denmark children start in the kindergarten grade the year they become 6; formal instruction in reading commences one year later in grade 1. In this study, 88 children of dyslexic parents were followed from the beginning of kindergarten until the beginning of the third grade. (A follow up assessment at grade 7 is in progress.) During the kindergarten year, a random sample of 36 of these children (from 27 different classrooms) were involved in an extensive and intensive program aimed to improve their attention to initial sounds in words. The program, which lasted about half an hour every day for 14 weeks, replaced some of the normal kindergarten activities. The program was multi-modal in the sense that it comprised activities involving attention to articulation, speech sounds, and letter forms; no reading was involved, however. The progress of this treatment group was compared to that of 52 at-risk untrained controls (from 44 classes) and with that of 48 untrained not-at-risk children. At the beginning of the second grade, the reading development of children in the three groups was assessed with a variety of reading tests. Some results are summarised in Table 1.

Table 1. Number of children in each of three groups identified in the beginning of second grade as either normal or possibly dyslexic (i.e., with low scores in phonological decoding, below 10th%ile in the normal control group).

Reading status at the beginning of grade 2	At-risk children		Normal
	Exp.	Contr. 1	Contr. 2
Possibly dyslexic	6	21	4
Possibly normal	30	31	44

In the table, the Grade 2 reading status classifications are based on composite scores on two tests of phonological decoding, namely pseudoword reading and pseudo-homophone detection (i.e., deciding which of two printed pseudowords would, if they were read aloud, sound like a real word).

The cut-off point for reading difficulties was set at 8 percent (4/48) in the not-at-risk group which corresponds to a conservative estimate of the proportion of children who are likely to receive some kind of special assistance at school. Using the same cut-off point, 40% of the untrained at-risk children displayed difficulties, as expected given their family backgrounds. A significantly smaller proportion, only 17% (6/36), of the trained at-risk children showed similar signs of difficulties, indicating that training in phonological awareness and letter knowledge was effective in facilitating subsequent reading acquisition by these children. Significant positive effects were also found a year later at the beginning of the third grade (Petersen, 2000).

Unfortunately, in neither study were the at-risk children entirely "inoculated" against reading difficulties as a result of participating in a preschool program aimed at strengthening phoneme awareness and letter knowledge. There was still an elevated incidence of reading disabilities in trained at-risk groups (compared to not-at-risk controls) in both the Copenhagen and Australian samples. In the latter, the best predictor of how individual children would fare over subsequent years was the ease with which the preschool intervention lessons were mastered, rather than the skill level attained by the end of the program. In the Copenhagen study, the best predictor of a child's response to the training program was the quality of phonological representations of whole words. Some children had poor pronunciations of long, but familiar words, such as *chocolate, library*, and *elephant*, and these children generally profited less from the training program and had poorer reading development than other at-risk children (Elbro, 1998; Elbro, Borstrøm, & Petersen, 1998; Petersen, 2000).

EARLY INTERVENTION FOR CHILDREN WITH PRESCHOOL LANGUAGE IMPAIRMENTS

Preschoolers are said to have specific language impairments (SLI) when their oral language development is significantly delayed in the absence of any hearing deficit, general developmental disability, or other condition in which language delay occurs as a secondary symptom. Children diagnosed with SLI are at considerable risk for future reading difficulties as well as for persisting or recurring oral language weaknesses that undoubtedly exacerbate their difficulties with written language (e.g. Aram & Hall, 1989; Catts; 1993; Hauschild & Elbro, 1992; Nauclér & Magnusson, 1998; Rescorla, 2000, 2002; Stothard, Snowling, Bishop, Chipchase & Kaplan, 1998). Because their language problems are identified during the preschool period, it is common for them to receive therapy from a speech-language pathologist prior to (and often during) the early school years. The effectiveness of such intervention has been evaluated in many research studies, but only recently has attention turned to the question of whether benefits might be seen for literacy development as well as for oral language proficiency.

Oral language skills

The methods of speech-language interventions are varied, and necessarily depend on the nature and scope of the child's language impairment. That is, preschool intervention is not the same for all children with SLI, but is individually tailored to strengthen receptive and/or expressive proficiency in one or more aspect of language (vocabulary, syntax, morphology, pragmatics) and/or speech. There is ample evidence that a variety of conventional therapies can be effective in helping children overcome their oral language impairments by the time they enter kindergarten (Fey, 1990; Friedman & Friedman, 1980), although their recovery may sometimes be "illusory" (Scarborough & Dobrich, 1986), as discussed in the preceding chapter. With regard to whether such intervention also reduces these children's risk for future reading difficulties, however, the evidence to date is not very promising. For example, the amount of therapy that a child has received has been unrelated to future reading achievement in correlational studies (Aram & Nation, 1980; Bishop & Adams, 1990; Bishop & Edmundson, 1987; Stark, Bernstein, Condino, Bender, Tallal & Catts, 1984), and the prevalence of reading disabilities in the primary school grades does not appear to be reduced for children who receive therapy, even if their language abilities improve dramatically (Fey, Catts & Larrivee, 1995; Huntley, Holt, Butterfield & Latham, 1988; Yancey, 1988). However, there has not been enough investigation of this issue to warrant a firm conclusion. It could turn out that the improvement of oral language capabilities is a necessary but not sufficient condition for successful reading acquisition by these children, and that their development of other necessary skills (such as phonological awareness) has been impeded by the preschool language impairment and thus also needs intervention prior to schooling.

Phonological awareness

Because children with SLI have difficulties with basic language abilities, one might fear that metalinguistic activities would be well beyond their capabilities. Fortunately, this is not always so. A number of studies have documented that some language impaired children *can* learn to manipulate speech sounds – and that such activities do appear to be beneficial for their subsequent reading development (Korkman & Peltomaa, 1993; Warrick, Rubin, & Rowe Walsh, 1993). Even children whose language impairments are associated with more general developmental delays have been reported to benefit from phonological awareness activities in kindergarten (O'Connor, Notari-Syverson, & Vadasy, 1998; O'Connor, Notari-Syverson, & Vadasy, 1996). The extent to which language impaired children's risk for reading difficulties is reduced, however, has not yet been firmly established.

EARLY INTERVENTION FOR SOCIOECONOMICALLY DISADVANTAGED CHILDREN

The risk for reading difficulty is very high for children who live in poor neighborhoods and attend schools with high rates of below-grade reading, and numerous factors – many extrinsic to the child – undoubtedly contribute to this (Vernon-Feagans, Hammer, Miccio & Manlove, 2001). When they enter school, these children often exhibit weaknesses that are similar to those seen in other at-risk groups; namely, in letter knowledge; phonological awareness; vocabulary; print concepts knowledge; and so forth. Consequently, the same sorts of interventions to strengthen these skills have been provided to disadvantaged children as to other children at risk for reading difficulties.

Phonological awareness, letter knowledge, and rudimentary reading skills

Children from low-income families have been observed to know fewer letters and be less aware of the phonological structure of spoken words than children from more affluent backgrounds (e.g., Bowey, 1995; Brady, Fowler, Stone, & Winbury, 1994; Duncan & Seymour, 2000; Raz & Bryant, 1990; West, Denton & Germino-Hausken, 2000). Training in phonological awareness and letter knowledge has been shown to be effective in several studies with this population, and subsequent gains in reading achievement (relative to untrained students) have been demonstrated (Blachman, Ball, Black, & Tangel, 1994; Brady, Fowler, Stone & Winbury, 1994; Gross & Garnett, 1994; Tangel & Blachman, 1992).

Vocabulary, language comprehension, and print concepts

More so, perhaps, than in other at-risk groups, oral language abilities and familiarity with print concepts are often rather weak in children from disadvantaged communities (e.g., Dickinson & Snow, 1987; Hart & Risley, 1995; Snow, Barnes, Chandler, Goodman & Hemphill, 1991). This problem has most often been addressed through interventions that provide kindergartners (or younger preschoolers) with frequent adult-child book-reading. This is sometimes delivered via print-rich kindergartens with frequent read-alouds (e.g., Karweit, 1989; Mason, Kerr, Sinha & McCormick, 1990) or through family literacy programs to involve parents also (Wasik, Dobbins & Herrmann, 2001). Unfortunately, children's reading achievement outcomes have not always been obtained when these programs have been implemented or evaluated, so evidence for their efficacy is sparse and sometimes ambiguous. Recent evidence also suggests that the amount of verbal stimulation, through peer conversations and teacher-child exchanges, is remarkably low in many child care centres and preschools serving disadvantaged children, suggesting that many opportunities (besides book reading) for promoting language growth are missed in their early years (Dickinson & Sprague, 2001). Based on these observations, a program has recently been developed to educate preschool teachers and child care providers about ways to promote language and literacy development, but no evidence is yet available regarding its effects on future reading achievement.

One important finding that has emerged from book-reading intervention studies is that the nature of the adult-child interaction, and not just the regular occurrence of book reading, contributes to the child's language and literacy development. Several studies have examined the relative effectiveness of various ways of sharing books with disadvantaged children. Their findings converge on the conclusion that a critical element of such intervention is that enriching verbal interactions, involving much participation by the children, take place during book reading (e.g., Karweit, 1989; Dickinson & Sprague, 2001). As described earlier, such interactions are a major component of Whitehurst's dialogic reading program, which has repeatedly been shown to produce reliable gains in vocabulary and emergent literacy skills of economically disadvantaged children (Valdez-Menchaca & Whitehurst, 1992; Whitehurst, Epstein, Angell, Payne, Crone, & Fischel, 1994). These findings indicate that the major benefits of dialogic reading apparent occur at young ages (ages 4 and 5), when a strong relationship between vocabulary gains and emergent print skills is seen. When follow-up reading assessments at grades 1 and 2 were conducted for a large recent sample of low-income children, however, the further development of vocabulary was influence solely by early vocabulary differences, and further progress in reading (word recognition and decoding) depended only on early phonological awareness and alphabetic knowledge (Whitehurst, Zevenbergen, Crone, Schultz, Velting, & Fischel, 1999). These findings underscore the need for early interventions that strengthen a wide range of reading-related abilities, including letter knowledge, phonological awareness, and oral language (Whitehurst & Lonigan, 2001).

Broad-based cognitively enriching interventions

To a greater extent than children at risk for other reasons, children of poverty are likely to achieve poorly not just in reading but in other academic subjects also. Consequently, intervention efforts targeted to this population are not always specifically designed to prevent reading difficulties alone, and thus often involve training in a broader range of cognitive (and non-cognitive) abilities. In the United States, there have been numerous early intervention projects for disadvantaged children, many of which have examined cognitive and academic outcomes throughout childhood, adolescence, and even early adulthood (e.g., Berrueta-Clement, Schweinhart, Barnett, Epstein & Weikart, 1984; Campbell, Pungello, Miller-Johnson, Burchinal & Ramey, 2001; Gray, Ramsey & Klaus, 1982).

The characteristics of these programs have differed considerably in terms of the nature and duration of the preschool intervention. Barnett (2001) recently reviewed reading achievement outcomes for 37 studies that followed the children's development through grade 3 or later. He concluded that although many studies have failed to demonstrate long-term benefits of early childhood intervention, this is likely to be the result of methodological flaws. The best-designed studies have produced substantial and persisting gains in reading achievement (and other areas) and reductions in rates of grade retention and special education placement. Most of these successful programs have begun in infancy and continued until kindergarten, and have provided highly intensive, full-day, year-round, child care at centres (rather than the home). Although less costly in the short run, one-year kindergarten interventions have unfortunately been far less effective in preventing reading difficulties in this population.

CONCLUSION

Many experienced kindergarten teachers might argue that the present chapter has few implications for early reading instruction that are not already a part of their everyday practice. It is certainly possible to find teaching materials several generations old that recommend activities for novice readers that direct their attention to the sounds of speech, help them to discover the alphabetic principle and make connections between speech sounds and letters, build their vocabularies through rich verbal interactions, and increase their familiarity with the conventions, mechanisms, purposes, and rewards of reading. The first author's basic reader, first published in 1927 (Eskildsen, 1959, 29th printing), is just one example. Even so, the recent scientific literature has some very important messages for practitioners as well as researchers.

To begin with, there is no doubt that research has greatly expanded our knowledge and understanding of reading and its acquisition. Many long-held beliefs have been shown to be entirely erroneous; e.g., that children who have difficulty learning to read are lazy or unintelligent; that 4- and 5-year-olds are maturationally unable to benefit from activities that promote learning about the rudiments of reading; that boys are much more likely than girls to develop reading disabilities; and so forth. Results from correlational and especially intervention studies have narrowed down the list of likely causes of most reading problems to a very few, ruling out many candidates that predominated in theories of reading disabilities for much of the past century (e.g., visual deficits, emotional problems, intersensory integration, etc.). Contemporary explanations for reading failure, although admittedly not complete, are supported by replicated empirical findings rather than anecdotal evidence or just beliefs.

From a practical standpoint, this greater understanding has been an invaluable guide to designing, implementing, and evaluating early prevention programs that are demonstrably effective in regular kindergarten instruction and in interventions targeted for children who are identified as at risk for reading difficulties. The dozens of studies that we have reviewed, most conducted in the past 20 years, attest to the impressive advances that have been made in this area. This rapidly accumulating knowledge base about what works (and what doesn't) for promoting successful reading acquisition will, it is hoped, have several benefits for educators.

For instance, a widely held and reasonable assumption is that teachers will be most effective when they recognize and understand their students' cognitive and linguistic accomplishments that precede, influence, and result from learning to read. With such understanding, teachers need not rely exclusively on a set of teaching techniques that was taught to them in the past, but can interpret children's comments and errors in optimal ways, and can be more flexible in adopting instructional goals, materials, and activities that are most appropriate to the current skill levels of the students. The knowledge gained from research should also, we hope, make education more resistant to the tides of fads and fashion, because making informed choices about educational policy and practice should be easier when some options are supported by strong empirical evidence and others are not.

Despite the advances that have been made toward preventing reading difficulties, there remains much to be learned through further intervention research. One critical need is the development of more powerful methods for strengthening the comprehension component of reading, which is too often neglected until the later elementary school years. Fortunately, the past few years have seen an upsurge in interest in this issue, particularly with regard to promoting rapid increases in vocabulary skills. Also, although contemporary programs for training novice readers in phonological awareness and letter knowledge are quite effective, nevertheless a nontrivial proportion of at-risk youngsters fail to respond well to these interventions. The obstacle(s) for these so-called "treatment resistors" are not well understood at present, although research efforts are underway to address this great concern. Finally, another positive trend in intervention research, and one that we heartily endorse, is an increased collaboration between educational researchers and experienced, innovative practitioners. Researchers and teachers have much to learn from each other, as both groups are increasingly coming to appreciate.

REFERENCES

Adams, M. J., Foorman, B. R., Lundberg, I., & Beeler, T. (1998). *Phonemic awareness in young children: A classroom curriculum*. Baltimore, MD: Paul Brookes.

Aram, D. , & Nation, J. (1980). Preschool language disorders and subsequent language and academic difficulties. *Journal of Communication Disorders, 13*, 159-179.

Arnold, D. H., Lonigan, C. J., Whitehurst, G. J., & Epstein, J. N. (1994). Accelerating language development through picture-book reading: Replication and extension to a videotape training format. *Journal of Educational Psychology, 86*, 235-243.

Barnett, W. S. (2001). Preschool education for economically disadvantaged children: Effects on reading achievement and related outcomes. In S. Neuman & D. Dickinson (Eds.), *Handbook of early literacy research* (pp. 421-443). New York: Guilford.

Bentin, S., & Leshem, H. (1993). On the interaction between phonological awareness and reading acquisition: It's a two-way street. *Annals of Dyslexia, 43*, 125-148.

Berrueta-Clement, J. R., Schweinhart, L .J., Barnett, W. S., Epstein, A. S. & Weikart, D. P. (1984). *Changed lives: The effects of the Perry High/Scope Educational Research Foundation (No. 8)*. Ypsilanti, MI: High/Scope Press.

Bishop, D. V. M., & Edmunsdon, A. (1987). Specific language impairment as a maturational lag: Evidence from longitudinal data on language and motor development. *Developmental Medicine and Child Neurology, 29*, 442-459.

Bishop, D. V. M., & Adams, C. (1990). A prospective study of the relationship between specific language impairment, phonological disorders and reading retardation. *Journal of Child Psychology and Psychiatry, 31*, 1027-1050.

Borstrøm, I., & Elbro, C. (1997). Prevention of dyslexia in kindergarten: Effects of phoneme awareness training with children of dyslexic parents. In C. Hulme & M. Snowling (Eds.), *Dyslexia: Biology, Cognition and Intervention* (pp. 235-253). London: Whurr.

Bowey, J. A. (2000).A case for early onset-rime sensitivity training in at-risk preschool and kindergarten children. In N. A. Badian (Ed.), *Prediction and prevention of reading failure* (pp. 217-245). Timonium, MD: York Press.

Bowey, J. A., & Francis, J. (1991). Phonoological analysis as a function of age and exposure to reading instruction. *Applied Psycholinguistics, 12*, 91-121.

Brady, S. A., Fowler, A. E., Stone, B., & Winbury, N. (1994). Training phonological awareness: A study with inner-city kindergarten children. *Annals of Dyslexia, 44*, 27-59.

Brennan, F., & Ireson, J. (1997). Training phonological awareness: A study to evaluate the effects of a program of metalinguistic games in kindergarten. *Reading and Writing. An Interdisciplinary Journal, 9*, 241-263.

Byrne, B., Fielding-Barnsley, R., & Ashley, L. (2000). Effects of preschool phoneme identity training after six years: Outcome level distinguished from rate of response. *Journal of Educational Psychology, 92*, 659-667.

Byrne, B. & Fielding-Barnsley, R. (1990). Acquiring the alphabetic principle: A case for teaching recognition of phoneme identity. *Journal of Educational Psychology, 82*, 805-812.

Byrne, B. Fielding-Barnsley, R., Hindson, B., Mackay, C., Newman, C., & Shankweiler, D. (1998,

April). *Early intervention with children at risk for reading disability: A mid-term report.* Paper presented at the conference of the Society for the Scientific Study of Reading, San Diego, CA.

Campbell, F. A., Pungello, E. P., Miller-Johnson, S., Burchinal, M., & Ramey, C. T. (2001). The development of cognitive and academic abilities: Growth curves from an early childhood educational experiment. *Developmental Psychology, 37*, 231-242.

Dickinson, D. K., & Snow, C. E. (1987). Interrelationship among prereading and oral language skills in kindergartners from two social classes. *Early Childhood Research Quarterly, 2*, 1-25.

Cary, L., & Verhaeghe, A. (1994). Promoting phonemic analysis ability among kindergartners. *Reading and Writing. An Interdisciplinary Journal, 6*, 251-278.

de Jong, P. F., & Frielink, O. (2000). *Rapid Automatic Naming: Easy to measure, hard to improve.* Paper presented at the Annual Meeting of the Society of the Scientific Study of Reading, July 2000, Stockholm.

Dickinson, D. K., & Sprague, K. E. (2001). The nature and impact of early childhood care environments on the language and early literacy development of children from low-income families. In S. Neuman & D. Dickinson (Eds.), *Handbook of early literacy research* (pp. 263-280). New York: Guilford.

Duncan, L. G., & Seymour, P. H. K. (2000). Socio-economic differences in foundation-level literacy. *British Journal of Psychology, 91*, 145-166.

Ehri, L. C., Nunes, S., Willows, D., Schuster, B., Yaghoub-Zadeh, Z., & Shanahan, T. (2001). Phonemic awareness instruction helps children learn to read: Evidence from the National Reading Panel's meta-analysis. *Reading Research Quarterly, 36*, 250-287.

Elbro, C., Borstrøm, I., & Petersen, D. K. (1998). Predicting dyslexia from kindergarten. The importance of distinctness of phonological representations of lexical items. *Reading Research Quarterly, 33*, 36-60.

Elbro, C. (1998). When reading is "readn" or somthn. Distinctness of phonological representations of lexical items in normal and disabled readers. *Scandinavian Journal of Psychology, 39*, 149-153.

Elley, W. B. (1989). Vocabulary acquisition from listening to stories. *Reading Research Quarterly, 24*, 174-187.

Eskildsen, C. (1959, 29th printing, org. 1927). *Ole Bole ABC.* København: Gjellerups Forlag.

Feitelson, D., Kita, B., & Goldstein, Z. (1986). Effects of reading stories to first graders on their comprehension and use of language. *Research on the Teaching of English, 20*, 339-356.

Fey, M. E. (1990). Understanding and narrowing the gap between treatment research and clinical practice with language-impaired children. Future of Science and Services Seminar (1990, Rockville, MD). *ASHA Report Series, American Speech Language Hearing Association, 20*, 31-40.

Fey, M. E., Catts, H. W., & Larrivee, L. S. (1995). Preparing preschoolers for the academic and social challenges of school. In M. E. Fey, J. Windsor, & S. F. Warren (Eds.), *Language intervention: Preschool through the elementary years. Communication and Language Intervention Series, Vol. 5*, pp. 3-37.

Foorman, B. R., Francis, D. J., Fletcher, J. M., Schatschneider, C., & Mehta, P. (1998). The role of instruction in learning to read: Preventing reading failure in at-risk children. *Journal of Educational Psychology, 90*, 37-55.

Fox, B., & Routh, D. K. (1984). Phonemic analysis and synthesis as word attack skills: Revisited. *Journal of Educational Psychology, 76*, 1059-1064.

Fox, B., & Routh, D. K. (1976). Phonemic analysis and synthesis as word-attack skills. *Journal of Educational Psychology, 68*, 70-74.

Friedman, P., & Friedman, K. A. (1980). Accounting for individual differences when comparing the effectiveness of remedial langue teaching methods. *Applied Psycholinguistics, 1*, 151-170.

Frost, J. (2001). Differences in reading development among Danish beginning-readers with high versus low phonemic awareness on entering grade one. *Reading and Writing. An Interdisciplinary Journal, 14*, 615-642.

Gray, S. W., Ramsey, B. K., & Klaus, R. A. (1982). *From 3 to 20: The Early Training Project.* Baltimore: University Park Press.

Hargrave, A. C., & Senechal, M. (2000). A book reading intervention with preschool children who have limited vocabularies: The benefits of regular reading and dialogic reading. *Early Childhood Research Quarterly, 15,* 75-90.

Hart, B. & Risley, T. (1995). *Meaningful differences.* Baltimore: Paul H. Brookes.

Hindson, B. (2001). Linguistic and cognitive characteristics of preschoolers at risk for developmental reading disability. Doctoral dissertation, University of New England (Australia).

Huntley, R. M., Holt, K. S., Butterfield, A., & Latham, C. (1988). A follow-up study of a language intervention programme. *British Journal of Disorders of Communication, 23,* 127-140.

Korkman, M., & Peltomaa, A. K. (1993). Preventive treatment of dyslexia by a preschool training program for children with language impairments. *Journal of Clinical Child Psychology, 22,* 277-287.

Lie, A. (1991). Effects of a training program for stimulating skills in word analysis in first-grade children. *Reading Research Quarterly, 26,* 234-250.

Lundberg, I. (1994). Reading difficulties can be predicted and prevented: A Scandinavian perspective on phonological awareness and reading. In C. Hulme & M. Snowling (Eds.), *Reading Development and Dyslexia* (pp. 180-199). London: Whurr Publishers.

National Reading Panel. (2000). Teaching children to read: An evidence-based assessment of the scientific research literature on reading and its implications for reading instruction. Washington, DC: The National Institute of Child Health and Human Development (http://www.nichd.nih. gov/ publications/nrp/smallbook.htm).

National Research Council (1998). Preventing reading difficulties in young children. Washington, DC: National Academy Press.

O'Connor, R. E., Notari-Syverson, A., & Vadasy, P. F. (1996). Ladders to literacy: The effects of teacher-led phonological activities for kindergarten children with and without disabilities. *Exceptional Children, 63,* 117-130.

O'Connor, R. E., Jenkins, J. R., & Slocum, T. A. (1995). Transfer among phonological tasks in kindergarten: Essential instructional content. *Journal of Educational Psychology, 87,* 202-217.

O'Connor, R. E., Notari-Syverson, A., & Vadasy, P. (1998). First-grade effects of teacher-led phonological activities in kindergarten for children with mild disabilities: A follow-up study. *Learning Disabilities Research and Practice, 13*(1), 43-52.

Petersen, D. K. (2000). What do you get if you add mmm/ to ice? Training phoneme awareness in kindergarten. An intervention study with children of dyslexic parents. In N. A. Badian (Ed.), *Preschool prediction and prevention of reading failure* (pp. 247-273). Baltimore, ML: York Press.

Raz, I. S., & Bryant, P. (1990). Social background, phonological awareness and children's reading. *British Journal of Developmental Psychology, 8,* 209-225.

Rescorla, L. (2000). Do late-talking toddlers turn out to have language and reading outcomes a decade later? *Annals of Dyslexia, 50,* 87-102.

Rescorla, L. (2002). Language and reading outcomes to age 9 in late-talking toddlers. *Journal of Speech Language and Hearing Research, 45,* 350-371.

Robbins, C. & Ehri, L. C. (1994). Reading storybooks to kindergartners helps them learn new vocabulary words. Journal of Educational Psychology, 86, 54-64.

Scanlon, D. M., & Vellutino, F. R. (1996). Prerequisite skills, early instruction, and success in first-grade reading: Selected results from a longitudinal study. *Mental Retardation and Developmental Research Reviews, 2,* 54-63.

Scarborough, H. S., & Dobrich, W. (1994). On the efficacy of reading to preschoolers. *Developmental Review, 14,* 245-302.

Schneider, W., Küspert, P., Roth, E., Visé, M., & Marx, H. (1997). Short- and long-term effects of training phonological awareness in kindergarten: Evidence from two German studies. *Journal of Experimental Child Psychology, 66,* 311-340.

Schneider, W., Ennemoser, M., Roth, E., & Kuespert, P. (1999). Kindergarten prevention of dyslexia: Does training in phonological awareness work for everybody? *Journal of Learning Disabilities, 32,* 429-436.

Senechal, M., & Cornell, E. H. (1993). Vocabulary acquisition through shared reading experiences. *Reading Research Quarterly, 28,* 360-374.

Senechal, M. (1997). The differential effect of storybook reading on preschoolers' acquisition of expressive and receptive vocabulary. *Journal of Child Language, 24*, 123-138.

Snow, C. E., Barnes, W. S., Chandler, J., Goodman, J. R., & Hemphill, L. (1991). *Unfulfilled expectations: Home and school influences on literacy.* Cambridge, MA: Harvard University Press.

Stanovich, K. E. (1992). Speculation on the causes and consequences of individual differences in early reading acquisition. In P. Gough, L. Ehri, & R. Treiman (Eds.), *Reading acquisition.* Hillsdale, NJ: Erlbaum.

Stark, R., Bernstein, L., Condino, R., Bender, M., Tallal, P., & Catts, H. (1984). Four year follow-up study of language-impaired children. *Annals of Dyslexia, 34*, 49-68.

Teale, W. H., & Martinez, M. G. (1996). Reading aloud to young children: Teachers' reading styles and kindergartners' text comprehension. In C. Pontecorveo, M. Orsolini, B. Burge, & L. B. Resnick (Eds.), *Children's early text construction* (pp. 321-344). Mahwah NJ: Erlbaum.

Torgesen, J. K., Wagner, R. K., & Rashotte, C. A. (1997). Prevention and remediation of severe reading disabilities: Keeping the end in mind. *Scientific Studies of Reading, 1*, 217-234.

Valdez-Menchaca, M. C., & Whitehurst, G. J. (1992). Accelerating language development through picture book reading: A systematic extension to Mexican day-care. Developmental Psychology, 28, 1106-1114.

Warrick, N., Rubin, H., & Rowe Walsh, S. (1993). Phoneme awareness in language-delayed children: Comparative studies and intervention. *Annals of Dyslexia, 43*, 153-173.

West, J. Denton, K., & Germino-Hausken, E. (2000). America's kindergartners: Findings from the Early Childhood Longitudinal Study, kindergarten class of 1998-99, Fall 1998. Washington, DC: National Center for Educational Statistics.

Whitehurst, G. J., Falco, F. L., Lonigan, C., Fischel, J. E., DeBaryshe, B. D., Valdez-Menchaca, M. C., & Caulfield, M. (1988). Accelerating language development through picture pbook reading. Developmental Psychology, 24, 552-558.

Whitehurst, G. J., & Lonigan, C. (2001). Emergent Literacy: Development from Prereaders to Readers. In S. Neuman & D. Dickinson (Eds.), *Handbook of early literacy research* (pp. 11-29). New York: Guilford.

Whitehurst, G. J., Arnold, D. S., Epstein, J. N., Angell, A. L., Smith, M., & Fischel, J. E. (1994). A picture book reading intervention in day-care and home for children from low-income families. *Developmental Psychology, 30*, 679-689.

Whitehurst, G. J., Epstein, J. N., Angell, A. L., Payne, A. ., Crone, D. A., & Fischel, J. E. (1994). Outcomes of an emergent literacy intervention in Head Start. *Journal of Educational Psychology, 86*, 542-555.

Yancey, P. S. (1988). Speech- and language-impaired three and four year olds: A five year follow-up study. In R. L. Masland & M. W. Masland (Eds.), *Preschool prevention of reading failure* (pp.52-77). Parkton, MD: York Press.

C8. Individual Differences in Dyslexia

MARGARET J. SNOWLING & YVONNE M. GRIFFITHS[1]

ABSTRACT

With the phonological deficit hypothesis of dyslexia as a back-drop, this review discusses the issue of how individual differences in its behavioural manifestation should be conceptualised. It begins by reviewing ways of classifying children with dyslexia from a clinical perspective and proceeds to describe the cognitive neuropsychological approach to classification that has focused on the reading and spelling profiles of such children. It argues that children's reading difficulties should be couched within the framework of typical reading development and that sub-typing systems that have not acknowledged developmental data have limitations. An interactive model of learning to read is used to propose that individual differences in dyslexia depend upon the severity of the phonological processing difficulties experienced by an individual child, the proficiency of other cognitive skills and the environment in which they learn.

INTRODUCTION

Although the first case of unexpected reading difficulty in childhood was described over a century ago (Morgan, 1896), the definition of dyslexia continues to be debated (Lyon, 1995; Stanovich, 1994; Tonnessen, 1997). Dyslexia is commonly defined as a specific difficulty in learning to read, despite normal IQ and adequate educational opportunity. It is a disorder of development that primarily affects the acquisition of literacy and the most widely accepted view is that it lies on the continuum of language disorder. Thus, dyslexia is characterised by verbal processing deficits (Vellutino, 1979) and a specific theory that will be considered here views impairments in phonological processing to be at its core (Brady &

---

[1] This chapter was prepared with support from Wellcome Trust grant 040195/Z/93/A to Margaret Snowling and a Dyslexia Institute/University of York studentship to Yvonne Griffiths.

T. Nunes, P. Bryant (eds.), Handbook of Children's Literacy, 383–402.
© *2004 Kluwer Academic Publishers. Printed in Great Britain.*

Shankweiler, 1991; Morton & Frith, 1995; Snowling, 1995; Stanovich & Siegel, 1994; see Brady, 1997, for a review).

The phonological deficit theory of dyslexia is compelling. First, it is well grounded in theory. The strong developmental association between phonological skills and learning to read forms a back-drop to much dyslexia research (Goswami & Bryant, 1990; Share, 1995). The theory also makes sense of the different manifestations of dyslexia across the age-span from pre-school (Scarborough, 1990) to adulthood (Pennington, van Orden, Smith, Green & Haith, 1990; Paulesu, Snowling, Gallagher, Morton, Frackowiak, & Frith 1996). Second, phonological sensitivity shares heritable variance with reading skills (Olson, Wise, Conners, Rack & Fulker, 1989) and importantly, there is substantial evidence that interventions that enhance phonological skills facilitate reading development in dyslexia (Snowling, 1996).

The traditional view concerning the mechanisms that account for the relationship between phonology and learning to read is that children who do well on tests of phonological awareness are quick to understand how phonemes and graphemes relate in the orthography, and to use this knowledge of letter-to-sound rules as a self-teaching device (Share, 1995). Hence, successful reading depends upon learning explicitly how to assign sounds to letters sequentially, and to blend them to synthesise a pronunciation. However, an alternative view (Ehri, 1992; Rack *et al.*, 1992; Laing & Hulme, 1999) argues instead for a direct mapping mechanism according to which children at the very earliest stages of learning to read are able to set up direct mappings between orthography and phonology. According to this view, children learn to read by directly mapping sequences of letters to their pronunciations and not by relying on decoding rules (Marsh. Friedman, Welch & Desberg, 1981).

From the cognitive perspective, the phonological deficit theory proposes that delayed phonological development in dyslexia affects the development of phonological representations that are the foundation for orthographic development (Snowling & Hulme, 1994; Metsala, 1997). In turn, awareness of the phonological components of spoken words is not available at a time when this is critical for the acquisition of reading and spelling skills (Elbro, Borstrom & Petersen, 1998; Fowler, 1991). Typical consequences are a slow rate of literacy development, poor generalisation of word reading skills to nonword reading and poor spelling development (Snowling, 2000 for a review).

A significant problem for the phonological deficit hypothesis, however, is the existence of cases of developmental dyslexia that do not appear to have phonological processing impairments. This chapter will consider the extent to which a unitary theory of dyslexia can explain the variation seen among dyslexic children. We begin by examining the different ways in which dyslexic children have been classified into sub-types, and then go on to describe an alternative approach that investigates how cognitive skills can explain the variety of reading behaviours seen in dyslexia (Griffiths & Snowling, 2002). We argue that the existence of children with quite different reading profiles is consistent with a view that there is continuous variation in underlying cognitive and linguistic skills in dyslexia, in interaction with reading experience. We end by proposing a version of the phonological deficit theory that can account for individual differences in children's reading difficulties.

THE CLASSIFICATION OF DYSLEXIC CHILDREN

The attempt to classify dyslexic children into different sub-types has a long tradition. Influenced by the medical model, some of the earliest forms of classification grouped dyslexic children according to their neuropsychological symptoms. Kinsbourne and Warrington (1963) used patterns of sub-scores on the Wechsler Intelligence Scales as a means of classification. Children with a Performance IQ at least 20 points lower than their Verbal IQ scores who had associated problems with finger differentiation and right-left orientation were described as having developmental *Gerstmann syndrome*. Children with the opposite pattern, higher Performance than Verbal IQ, were described as having *language-retardation*. However, as Kinsbourne & Warrington (1963) noted, these categories fail to account for many poor readers.

Mattis, French and Rapin (1975) also used a neuropsychological approach to classify a group of dyslexic children with 90% success. The largest subgroup, 48% of the sample, had problems with speech articulation, graphemic motor skills and poor sound blending and were described as having "articulatory and grapho-motor dysco-ordination' difficulties. Twenty-eight percent who had difficulties with naming and labelling were considered to have a 'language disorder' and the smallest subgroup (14%) had 'visuo-spatial difficulties', predominantly problems with visual discrimination, and visual memory. Using similar methodology, Denckla (1977) identified five sub-groups of dyslexia, the majority having some form of language deficit. One subgroup had globally poor language abilities, another poor articulation and grapho-motor skills and a third with an 'anomic' repetition 'disorder' encompassing deficits in naming (with a tendency to make semantic errors), poor digit span and sentence repetition. There was also a subgroup with verbal learning and memory deficits and one described as having a 'dysphonemic sequencing disorder', with deficits in digit span, sentence repetition, and naming (all characterised by phonemic substitutions or reversals), with additional syntactic difficulties.

An alternative and more objective approach to the classification of children with dyslexia involves the use of multivariate techniques to examine statistical relationships among different neuropsychological deficits (Fletcher, Morris, Lyon, Stuebing, Shaywitz, Shankweiler, Katz and Shaywitz, 1997). In one such study, Doehring and Hoshko (1977) used factor analysis to delineate three subgroups of dyslexia on the basis of reading-related skills. The first group had severe oral reading difficulties but performed well on visual and auditory matching tasks. A second group demonstrated slow auditory-visual letter association skills and a third group with slow auditory-visual association of words and syllables had difficulties with phonic analysis, blending and sequencing. However, like the clinical approaches, this technique does not always reveal distinct and homogenous subtypes. Petrauskas and Rourke (1979) reported that between 20-50% of children in their sample could not be readily sub-typed using factor analytic techniques and Naidoo (1972) used cluster analyses to discern four subgroups of dyslexic readers, but found considerable overlap between the groups. A further problem is that clusters can reflect random departures from normality and may be spurious (Satz and Morris 1981).

Thus, early attempts to delineate subtypes of dyslexia had numerous limitations. Indeed it is worth noting that the sub-types that emerged were inevitably a function of the tasks used to test the dyslexic readers. These, in turn, reflected the disciplinary background or clinical experience of the researcher. Moreover, the factorial structure revealed was not always easy to characterise. From a theoretical perspective, a particular shortcoming was the failure to specify the nature of the reading disorder that the children manifested. Hence, it was never clear whether the deficits associated with particular sub-types were a necessary or sufficient explanation for the late emergence of reading in individual cases (Marshall 1984).

READING AND SPELLING PROFILES IN DYSLEXIA

The importance of differentiating dyslexic children according to the kinds of problems they have with reading and writing has long been recognised by those concerned with remediation (Mykelbust and Johnson 1962; Johnson and Mykelbust 1967). An influential approach to sub-typing that started from the reading and spelling errors made by dyslexic children was that of Boder (1971,1973). Boder's technique was simple. She began by presenting children with words to read aloud and noted those that were read automatically. She assumed that these words were already part of the child's sight vocabulary. When a word was not read immediately, she allowed 15 seconds for the child to attempt to decode it using phonic skills. She then gave a spelling test comprising words they had read correctly (known words) and words they had been unable to decode (unknown words).

Over sixty percent of the sample was described as *dysphonetic dyslexics*. They had a limited sight vocabulary and showed difficulties with word attack skills including phonic analysis and synthesis. They were said to spell "by eye' alone and were unable to spell words unless they were in their sight vocabulary. A second, smaller group (10%) of the children had difficulties in building up a sight vocabulary. This *dyseidetic* group read laboriously "by ear', being unable to memorise the visual shapes of words so to read them as a whole, and all of their misspellings were phonetic. Boder also identified a third group comprising 22% of her sample that showed errors typical of both the dysphonetic and dyseidetic groups. These children were the most severely handicapped since they could not draw upon either visual or phonic skills.

Boder's approach was well motivated and offered clinicians the opportunity to devise remedial programmes to suit the individual needs of dyslexic children, although it was not rigorous methodologically. A more formal approach to the classification of dyslexic children in terms of their reading and, to a lesser extent spelling performance, took its lead from the discipline of cognitive neuropsychology (Shallice, 1988) to become a dominant approach in the UK and Europe during the 1980s. It is to this approach that we now turn.

Analogies between acquired and developmental reading disorders.

Cognitive neuropsychologists who study the reading skills of neurological patients have described a variety of ways in which the adult reading system can fractionate following brain damage (see Ellis, 1994 for a review). Two contrasting patterns of breakdown involve the selective impairment of either the phonological pathway that is specialised for the reading of novel words, or the lexical or semantic pathway (Coltheart, 1978; Plaut, McClelland, Seidenberg & Patterson, 1996) that is involved in the reading of exception words. Patients with phonological dyslexia have impairments of the phonological reading system. They typically show poor reading of nonwords in the context of good reading of familiar words, and they make predominantly dysphonetic spelling errors. Patients with surface dyslexia can no longer recognise many words that were once familiar by sight (Patterson, Marshall & Coltheart, 1985). However, they retain the ability to sound out words to a degree, using the alphabetic properties of English. As a consequence of this strategy, they are prone to make regularisation errors on irregular words in English, such as *yacht*, or *colonel*, by treating them as one would a nonword. They also tend to spell phonetically.

The first case of phonological dyslexia in childhood was described by Temple and Marshall (1983). The case study was about a 17 year old girl, HM, who was reading around the 10 year level. HM produced all the characteristic symptoms of an acquired phonological dyslexic; she had difficulties reading novel words as well as long regular words and her reading errors included visual paralexias, e.g. press read as "pass" and derivational errors, e.g. imagine read as "image". Despite her decoding difficulties, HM was reported to read exception words well. In fact, she did not make many regularisation errors and did not show the usual advantage of regular over irregular words. When she mis-read words, her attempts tended to include components of other words, suggesting she was trying to use visual analogies.

Within the same framework, Coltheart, Masterson, Byng, Prior, & Riddoch (1983) described the case of CD, a 15 year-old dyslexic, with a reading-age of around 11 years. CD showed the pattern of deficit characteristic of acquired surface dyslexia. Consistent with this description, she read regular words better than irregular words, many of her reading errors were regularisations, e.g. quay →[kwɛɪ] ; come → [kəʊm]. However, in one respect CD was not typical of surface dyslexia; although she was observed to read phonologically, her 'sub-lexical' reading skills were not proficient and her reading of nonwords was not as good as might be expected. More intact nonword reading has been reported in subsequent cases of developmental surface dyslexia, both in children (MI; Castles & Coltheart, 1996) and in adults (JAS; Goulandris & Snowling, 1991; Allan; Hanley, Hastie & Kay, 1992).

Thus, the cognitive neuropsychology offered a principled approach to the classification of dyslexia, by reference to a model of reading development. However, it was not without its critics (Snowling, 1983; Wilding, 1989). An important issue, as with all single case research, was the representativeness of the cases that were described. Seymour (1986), following a case-series of such children, concluded that the dyslexic population is heterogeneous but without distinct sub-types. Furthermore, as Bryant and Impey (1986) showed, there is also variation in the reading skills of normal readers. This normal variation clearly needs to be taken account of before concluding that a particular set of reading behaviours is the hallmark of a specific sub-type of dyslexia.

More generally, a problem for the cognitive-neuropsychological approach was that it was not couched in developmental terms. As Frith (1985) pointed out, it is possible to conceptualise dyslexia in its classic form as a failure to proceed to the alphabetic phase of development, when children first begin to use phonological skills for reading. The profile of phonological dyslexia exemplifies this phase of development well (Seymour & Elder, 1986). However following developmental arrest at this stage, literacy acquisition can often proceed, so that the profile of surface dyslexia might emerge as a consequence of reading delay with failure to progress further. What is important then is to try to explain the reading behaviour of dyslexic children in terms of their underlying cognitive skills and to highlight in particular, deficiencies in the processes considered to be pre-requisites for satisfactory literacy acquisition.

A DEVELOPMENTAL PERSPECTIVE ON DYSLEXIA

Snowling, Stackhouse and Rack (1986) used Frith's (1985) model of literacy acquisition as a framework for examining the association between the cognitive deficits of seven dyslexic readers and the patterns of reading difficulty observed. By dividing the cases according to reading level, they also made a preliminary assessment of how reading experience might be related to changes in reading and spelling profile – in some cases as a response to teaching.

The study involved three dyslexic children reading at the 7-year-level and four older dyslexics who had attained a reading age of at least 10 years; all had poor nonword reading skills and were classified as showing developmental phonological dyslexia. The study also included two groups of normally developing readers, reading at the 7- and the 10- year levels for the purpose of developmental comparison.

Consistent with Frith's hypothesis, the dyslexic children, particularly those of low reading age, appeared to be arrested in the logographic phase of development. Thus, their reading was inherently inaccurate with a preponderance of visual errors and there was a notable absence of the regularisation errors seen frequently among controls. In all cases but one, nonword reading skills were impaired relative to reading-age matched controls; the exception was a boy who had received extensive tutoring and a second boy had difficulties with two- but not one-syllable nonwords. In similar vein, the spelling skills of the dyslexics were poorer overall than the controls and they showed a marked tendency to make dysphonetic spelling errors, e.g., FISH as fine, BUMP as bunt, GEOGRAPHY as gorphy.

Whilst there was some variation between cases, all displayed the phonological deficits that have been shown to characterise dyslexia, including problems of phonological awareness, verbal memory and nonword repetition. It seemed reasonable to conclude that deficiencies in the phonological processes that are required for successful literacy development had caused a difficulty in acquiring alphabetic skills (cf. Campbell and Butterworth, 1985). However, in some cases, progress to the alphabetic phase had been possible, especially where the child had benefited from remediation.

One of the children studied by Snowling *et al.* (1986), JM, was followed longitudinally to assess the effects his phonological difficulties would have on learning to read in the long term. When first seen, JM was 8 years old and, although a boy of superior intelligence, he had only just begun to read and spell. At this stage in his development, he was what could be described as a 'logographic' reader – he could read words but not new or unfamiliar words and his spelling was dysphonetic e.g. he spelled CAP as gad, POLISH as bols and REFRESHMENT as refent. JM made roughly half the average rate of progress in his literacy development over the next four years, and his reading profile did not change (Snowling and Hulme, 1989); he still had significant difficulty in nonword reading and his spelling remained dysphonetic.

JM was next tested when he was 13 years old (Hulme and Snowling, 1992). One of the main aims of this study was to pinpoint the locus of his phonological processing deficit by administering tests that placed differential emphasis on phonological input and phonological output processing. A test of complex nonword discrimination revealed that JM's auditory processing of speech input was intact. He also had no difficulty discriminating words from confusable nonwords when compared with RA-controls in a lexical decision task. In contrast, JM had great difficulty when required to repeat the complex nonwords he had discriminated – in fact, his performance fell outside of the range of normal controls when asked to repeat the stimuli. Taken together, these data provided powerful evidence for a differential deficit in JM affecting output phonology.

The finding of selective deficits at the level of output phonology in JM suggested that output phonological representations play an important role in learning to read. Hence, Hulme and Snowling (1992) proposed that children use output phonology when mapping the letters in printed words onto the sound structure of spoken words. The development of such mappings is critical to progress through the alphabetic phase of development. JM lacked stable output representations and it seemed therefore that the development of his sight vocabulary had been delayed. Furthermore, he had been unable to abstract and use letter-sound rules to facilitate his reading because of his output difficulties.

The conclusion that JM's orthographic development was constrained by his phonological difficulties seems, on the face of it, clear-cut. To place his reading difficulties in context, it is interesting to note that Vellutino and Scanlon (1991) reported a retrospective analysis of several hundred impaired readers showing that as many as 83% were deficient in mapping alphabetic symbols to sound. So, the theory that phonological deficits affect transition to the alphabetic phase of literacy development has considerable currency. It is plausible that a proportion of those who gain alphabetic skill do so in response to remediation. But, are there additional or different deficits associated with developmental surface dyslexia that impede progress?

One of the first hypotheses to be forwarded about the cause of the surface dyslexic profile in childhood was that a perceptual deficit affected the acquisition of visual word forms, at least in a minority of cases of 'dyseidetic' dyslexia (Boder, 1973). More recently, Goulandris and Snowling (1991) reported the case of JAS, a dyslexic undergraduate who resembled a surface dyslexic in her performance. JAS performed competently on phonological tasks but her visual memory for both letters and for abstract shapes was severely impaired. Thus, it was plausible that her poor visual memory had compromised the development of orthographic skills perhaps, by limiting her ability to remember the graphemic sequences that represent the varying spelling patterns of English (see Romani, Ward and Olson (1999) for a modification of this view)

However, the finding that surface dyslexia is associated with visual memory deficits has not been replicated consistently (Castles and Coltheart, 1996; Hanley *et al.*, 1992; Seymour and Evans, 1993). As we have seen, this might be because, in some cases the profile of surface dyslexia comes about as the consequence of remediated phonological problems, while other times it reflects a more specific cognitive deficit implicating visual processing.

The regression approach to sub-typing

A different approach to the classification of children into sub-types in relation to patterns of reading performance in the normal population was described by Castles and Coltheart (1993) who studied a sample of 53 dyslexic children. Fundamental to this approach is the use of regression to identify dyslexic children whose reading of either nonwords or exception words falls outside of the expected range for their age. Castles and Coltheart initially focused on individuals for whom a single 'component' reading skill was outside the normal range. On this criterion, 8 (15%) of their sample could be classified as having a specific deficit in nonword reading (phonological dyslexia) and 10 (19%) as having a specific deficit in exception word reading (surface dyslexia). Using a less stringent method, Castles and Coltheart went on to identify the proportion of individuals who were outside the normal range for both component skills, but more so for one than the other. Using this criterion, they were able to classify 55% of their sample as phonological, and 30% as surface developmental dyslexics.

The method chosen by Castles and Coltheart to identify sub-types of dyslexia made reference to a normative sample of children of the same age as the children with dyslexia. These children, by definition, read at a higher level than the dyslexics. If relative efficiency of different reading strategies is bound to the overall level that the reader has attained, then extrapolation from the reading patterns of children at one level to another is an inappropriate way of defining abnormal patterns of reading (Snowling, Bryant & Hulme, 1996; Stanovich, Siegel & Gottardo, 1997).

Following Castles and Coltheart's (1993) procedure, but using a more rigorous reading-age matched design, Manis, Seidenberg, Doi, McBride-Chang and Peterson (1996) identified relatively few children who demonstrated dissociations between nonword and exception word reading, once reading age was taken into account. Specifically, they classified 12/51 phonological and 1/51 surface dyslexics in this way. The remaining 75% of the sample showed a normal (though delayed) pattern of reading performance. A similarly low incidence of sub-types was also reported by Stanovich *et al.*, (1997) with 74% of children showing component reading skills within the normal range.

An important feature of the Manis *et al.*, (1996) and Stanovich *et al.*, (1997) studies is that these investigators went on to compare the children conforming to the description of phonological dyslexia with those considered to show the surface profile on tests of phonological and orthographic processing skill. The phonological task used by Manis *et al.* (1996) required the child to listen to a nonword and say what came immediately before or after a target phoneme, e.g., which sound comes before the [t] sound in /skwupt/? The orthographic choice task required the child to decide which of two visually presented letter strings was a correctly spelled word, e.g., streat/street. Stanovich *et al.* (1997) used the Rosner auditory analysis test (Rosner & Simon, 1971) as their phonological measure; this task required the child to delete either a syllable or phoneme from a spoken word and say what was left. Their orthographic measure was a 'word-likeness choice' task which required the child to decide which nonword letter string was more 'word-like' than the other, e.g., filf-filk. In both studies, when compared with younger reading age-matched controls, children identified as showing a phonological dyslexic profile showed poor phonological awareness skills. In contrast, the performance of children with a surface dyslexic profile was indistinguishable from that of normal reading-age controls, even on tasks measuring orthographic skill.

The most straightforward interpretation of these results is that surface dyslexia is characterised by a delayed pattern of reading development, whilst developmental phonological dyslexia represents a developmental reading disorder. A similar conclusion was reached by Snowling, Goulandris and Defty (1996) who carried out a detailed case study of two children conforming to each profile. It is important to note, however, that this conclusion does not address the important question of what accounts for by far the largest majority of dyslexic children: those who cannot be classified into a distinct sub-type. A comprehensive theory of dyslexia must account not only for the cognitive deficits that underlie the disorder but also for variation in its behavioural manifestations (Morton & Frith, 1995).

Predictors of nonword and exception word reading skill among dyslexic readers

In a recent study of our own involving a sample of 58 dyslexic readers, we took a slightly different approach to the investigation of individual differences (Griffiths 1999). Our starting point was the knowledge that phonological awareness is an excellent predictor of individual differences in normal reading development, and that dyslexic children showing different reading profiles have been found to differ in phonological skills. In addition, we noted that it is not unusual in development for children to compensate for basic deficits by drawing on compensatory resources; in dyslexia, children differ not only in the severity of their phonological deficit but also in the proficiency of skills, such as visual memory or semantic processing (Snowling, Goulandris & Stackhouse, 1994).

From previous studies, we expected that it would be possible to identify relatively few sub-types using the regression methodology. We therefore decided to use a multivariate approach to determine the concurrent predictors of individual differences in component reading skills among dyslexic children. We assessed each child's ability to read nonwords and exception words before proceeding to investigate their performance on tests of phonological awareness (phoneme deletion and rhyme production), phonological processing (nonword repetition, verbal short-term memory and speech rate), visual memory for abstract shapes and vocabulary knowledge. In addition, we included two tests tapping speed of information processing, in line with current ideas that some dyslexic children suffer a double deficit affecting phonological awareness and processing rate (Bowers & Wolf, 1993).

There were substantial correlations between measures of phoneme awareness and both nonword reading and exception word reading among our dyslexics and their younger reading-age matched controls. As a group, however, the dyslexic readers were no worse at exception word reading than the controls, and regression analyses did not identify predictors of exception word reading once overall reading attainment (or exposure to print) was taken into account. In contrast, there were several important predictors of nonword reading. In both normal reader and dyslexic samples, phonemic awareness accounted for independent variance in nonword reading after age and reading skill were taken into account. More importantly, further analyses focusing on the dyslexic readers alone, revealed three predictors of the ability to read novel words. First, as predicted, phonological processing was a strong predictor of nonword reading, accounting for 8% of unique variance in this skill. Second, both visual memory and speed of processing accounted for independent variance in nonword reading. Interestingly, the contribution of phonological awareness was not significant when variations in phonological processing had been controlled.

The results of this study are broadly in line with the conclusions of Manis, Stanovich and their colleagues (op cit). In our study, we were able to classify 16 (27%) children as having a phonological dyslexic profile and only one (2%) as surface dyslexic. However, to the extent that such children can be considered extremes on a distribution of nonword reading skill, individual differences on this continuum were predicted by phonological processing skills; in general terms, children with more of a surface dyslexic-like profile have relatively good phonological ability while those with a phonological dyslexic profile have more severe phonological deficits (Griffiths & Snowling 2002). There are additional predictors too. The ability to remember sequences of visual items is associated with better nonword reading skills. In addition, speed of processing influences reading profile in that children with a slow speed of processing tend to be better non-word readers. Furthermore, we found that the tendency to regularize exception words among dyslexics was associated with good nonword reading.

It is perhaps important to stress that the kind of analysis outlined here is quite compatible with the fact that, clinically, quite marked differences in reading profile can be observed. Indeed, as we show below, it is possible to select from most samples of dyslexic children, a number who show rather clear-cut patterns of deficit. NW and CHD were two such children whom we first assessed when they were 10 years 8 months old (Griffiths, 1999). Both were well behind in their reading development (each had a reading age of 8 years 9 months) and their spelling was more impaired. The performance of these children on tests of nonword and exception word reading and on related processing tasks is summarised in Table 1.

NW shows many of the features of surface dyslexia. His nonword reading was relatively good considering his overall level of reading ability, while his exception word reading was more impaired. Indeed 67% of his reading errors were regularisations, e.g., he read SWORD as [swɔːd], and NINTH as [nɪnθ] and his spelling errors were primarily phonetic, e.g, he spelled INSTRUMENT → 'instroment', QUALITY → 'qualety', DESCRIBE → 'discribe'. By contrast, CHD showed many of the features of phonological dyslexia. Although his exception word reading was at the same level as that of NW, he could read only 31% of the nonword set given to both boys. He made relatively fewer regularisation errors (50%) and a higher proportion of lexicalisations and nonword substitutions indicating a failure to apply phonological strategies, e.g., he read WOUNDED as [ʊ], and REACT as [riːtʃ], ACHE [æ]-[tʃ] and AISLE

**Table 1. Performance of two dyslexic children, NW and CHD,
on tests of reading and reading-related skills**

	NW	CHD
Word reading (WORD)	34 (raw score)	34 (raw score)
Nonword reading	63%	31%
Exception word reading	36%	36%
Regularisation errors	67%	50%
Phoneme deletion	63%	46%
Nonword repetition	82%	63%
Verbal Memory span	3.5	3.3
Speech rate	2.6 words/sec	1.8 words/sec
Visual Memory span	2.5	3.5
Speed of Processing	4th (percentile)	66th (percentile)

as [ɪlz]. CHD's spelling was characterised by a large proportion of dysphonetic spelling errors, e.g, he spelled DESCRIBE → discrap, QUALITY → quaty, ELECTRIC → eletric, PARAGRAPH → powergrapth, and ELEPHANT → elephat. Although he was able to reconstruct the number of syllables in the word, he would often reduce consonant clusters to single letters, and errors on single phonemes would often be substitutions for phonemes which may only differ by a single phonetic feature (e.g. substituting a [b] for a [p] sound).

The pattern of reading profile demonstrated by NW and CHD was, in each case, associated with a distinctive pattern of behaviour on the other cognitive tasks they were given. NW's phonological awareness skills were quite good for his level of reading ability. On a test of phoneme deletion which required NW to take-away a specified sound from a spoken nonword, and say what remained, (e.g. [baɪs] without the [b] would give ['ice'], he managed to get 63% correct, whereas CHD scored only 46%. Likewise, NW's phonological processing skills, as measured by nonword repetition, verbal memory and speech rate were better than those of CHD.

One of CHD's strengths was his speed of information processing, as assessed by the coding and symbol search sub-tests from the WISC III, and his visual memory span for a set of abstract shapes was average for his age. On these tasks, NW displayed weaknesses. It is perhaps also worth noting that CHD scored higher on a test of print exposure than NW.

The cases of NW and CHD illustrate how two dyslexic readers, of similar age and overall ability, and reading at the same level may show markedly different profiles. However, the balance of their strengths and weaknesses is such that their behaviour is predictable in a principled way from a model of reading behaviour in which individual differences in reading strategy are the consequence of developmental interactions between phonological processing skills, visual and speed of processing resources

Taken together, the findings of our study are consistent with a modified version of the phonological deficit hypothesis. Dyslexic children do have phonological deficits. However, unsurprisingly, the severity of their phonological impairment is variable. Some dyslexic children show phonological impairments when compared with younger reading-age matched controls, others only in relation to age-matched peers. Nonetheless, it is reasonable to suppose that the phonological deficit is implicated in reading failure in both cases. Furthermore, the impact of the deficit can be moderated by other cognitive skills. We have argued elsewhere that some dyslexic children rely heavily on sentence context to get around their problems at the level of word decoding (Nation & Snowling, 1998). We suggest here that a child's visual memory capacity can also afford a compensatory resource for learning (cf. Hulme & Snowling, 1992). Our results also imply that a child with slow speed of processing has better chance of developing phonological reading strategies than one with fast processing speed, although this does not guarantee they will be able to learn to read the exception words of English (cf. Bowers, 1995).

TOWARDS AN UNDERSTANDING OF INDIVIDUAL DIFFERENCES IN READING DISABILITY

The hypothesis that we have forwarded concerning the role of cognitive skills in the development of dyslexic children's nonword reading skills takes for-granted that reading development is an interactive process. It seems to us that the conclusion that poor phonological skills are at the basis of reading impairment in dyslexia is inescapable (Stanovich & Siegel, 1994). However two independent factors, visual memory and speed of processing represent secondary 'risk' or 'protective' factors when identified in association with a phonological deficit (Vellutino, Scanlon, & Tanzman 1991). How can the interaction of these factors be conceptualised in relation to what is known about the process of learning to read?

For a theoretical explanation of phonological and surface dyslexia, Manis *et al.* (1996) turned to the connectionist model of reading of Seidenberg and McClelland (1989). In this model, reading was conceptualised as the transfer of patterns of activation between sets of orthographic input and phonological output units, via a set of hidden units. The network was gradually trained to learn the associations between orthographic and phonological strings by a process of feedback using a learning algorithm known as back propagation. The associations were coded by means of weights on the connections that change as a function of learning. An important feature of this model and others like it is that, as the model learns, the knowledge that it embodies generalises (Van Orden, Pennington & Stone, 1990). Thus, such models read words that they have not been trained on with reasonable success, and show higher performance on regular words with consistent spelling-sound mappings than on inconsistent or exception words. Connectionist models, such as this, provide a useful framework for the analysis of developmental disorders because these can be traced to limitations either in the representations involved in the learning process or to the processing resources available.

From the perspective of Seidenberg and McClelland's (1989) model, Manis *et al.* (1996) proposed that phonological dyslexia could arise as a consequence of deficits at the level of phonological representations (Brown, 1997; Fowler, 1991; Snowling & Hulme, 1994; Swan & Goswami, 1997). In contrast, surface dyslexia might be due to a computational resource limitation causing slowness in learning. Alternatively, it could arise in the same way as phonological dyslexia, but where the child had received extensive training in phonics. They left open the possibility that a visual deficit, affecting orthographic representations, could bring about this profile.

The data from our recent study can be similarly interpreted within the connectionist framework. To do this we must first describe a recent modification of the Seidenberg and McClelland (1989) model implemented by Harm and Seidenberg (1998). In this model the phonological network was pre-trained before learning trials began, in an analogous way to that in which a child's phonological development proceeds prior to the start of learning to read. Within this model, Harm and Seidenberg simulated acquired phonological dyslexia by reducing the network's capacity to represent phonological information. One way of doing this involved imposing a degree of weight decay within the phonological network. Speculatively, we suggest that our measure of phonological processing can be conceived of as an index of weight decay; dyslexic children with poorer phonological processing skills suffer greater weight decay. A more severe impairment of phonological representation was created by also severing connections within the phonological layer. In an analogous manner, the dyslexic children in our study with poorer phonological awareness, who by default also had poorer phonological processing, had more severe impairments of nonword reading.

In the study we have just described, a second constraint on the operation of the phonological pathway was signalled by poor visual memory. Harm and Seidenberg 's simulations show that the more severe the phonological deficit, the more the network has to draw upon general processing resources. Visual memory might be thought of here as part of a more general processing resource. Within this view, differences in general processing capacity can moderate the extent to which poor phonology disrupts the ability to read nonwords.

Current connectionist models are silent as to the role of speed of processing in the determination of patterns of reading behaviour. Our suggestion is that children who demonstrate slow speed of processing have difficulty setting up connections between orthography and phonology because activations across orthographic and phonological units are mis-timed. Similar proposals linking slow speed of processing with difficulties in establishing memory representations for printed words have been made recently by Wimmer, Mayringer and Landerl (1998) on the basis of findings from German speaking dyslexic children who do not show deficits in phonological awareness, and Bowers and Wolf (1993). In short, a mis-timing of sources of activation may have its principle effect on the acquisition of orthographic knowledge, leaving slow and laborious decoding possible.

The phonological representations view articulated here has close similarities with the 'phonological core-variable difference model' of Stanovich and his colleagues (Stanovich & Siegel, 1994). According to Stanovich and Siegel (1994), poor phonology is related to poor reading performance, irrespective of IQ; poor readers differ from normal readers in skills close to the phonological core of the deficit (e.g. phonological awareness), and discrepancy-defined poor readers differ from generally poor readers in skills further from the core (e.g., listening comprehension and working memory). The phonological-core variable deficit model is silent about individual differences in dyslexia. By contrast, the phonological representations hypothesis implies that phonological deficits can interact with underlying cognitive strengths and weaknesses to determine individual differences in reading behaviour. In our view, a child's reading deficit is predicted by the 'severity' of their phonological deficit in interaction with their profile of strengths and weaknesses.

CONCLUSIONS

In this chapter we have reviewed a range of different approaches to the classification of children with dyslexia. There have been a number of recurring themes. Despite their appeal to the clinician who sees a wide range of different phenomena in the behavioural symptoms of dyslexia, none of the approaches have been successful in assigning all dyslexic children to a sub-type. In every taxonomy to date, a significant number of children have been left unclassified and the theoretically motivated distinction between developmental phonological and developmental surface dyslexia also fail to capture the range of variation observed.

A second theme is that the largest sub-type of dyslexia is associated with language processing impairments. Arguably, the theme is replicated in the larger numbers of children showing phonological than surface dyslexia. A recent subtyping study using cluster analysis, reported by Fletcher *et al.* (1997), came to similar conclusions. Nine sub-types of reading disability were identified following the assessment of 232 children of mixed abilities on a large battery of cognitive measures. Five of these sub-types were described as 'specific', predominantly consisting of dyslexic children. Four of these five specific subtypes included children displaying impairments on a phonological awareness measure, with variations in accompanying impairments in rapid automatised naming and verbal short-term memory. The fifth specific subtype included children who were not impaired in phonological awareness but on measures which involved rapid and/or sequential processing (the 'rate deficit' group). The other clusters comprised the normal ability children, a global language impaired subgroup, and the majority of the below average ability subgroups.

It might be argued that the attempt to relate differences in literacy profile with associated cognitive skills is essentially correlational and therefore not without its shortcomings. However, as Bishop (1998) has pointed out, since dissociations in development are rare, developmental associations are important because they can highlight the dependence of changes in one cognitive system on the acquisition of skills in related domains. With respect to dyslexia, it seems likely that the failure to learn to read (and spell) along normal lines is a direct consequence of phonological deficits. However, in determining individual differences in reading skill, these differences interact with other factors, such as the semantic and visual skills that children bring to bear by way of compensation, and the ways in which they are taught (Vellutino *et al.*, 1991).

An important methodological consideration often neglected by researchers exploring the nature of individual differences in developmental dyslexia is the problem of external validation of variation in dyslexia. Stanovich *et al.* (1997) explored the stability and reliability of the phonological and surface dyslexic subtypes identified in their sample using a CA- matched group of normal readers. Additional measures of nonword and word reading included in the battery allowed the authors to examine what proportion of dyslexic children could be classified as either phonological or surface dyslexia when a CA-match design was employed but using alternative measures for classification of the sample. One reanalysis employed nonword reading as the measure of sublexical skills and word reading as the measure of lexical reading skills, and the other used spelling performance as the indicator of lexical skills. No child who fulfilled the criteria for surface dyslexia using the original method of classification was also reliably classified across both these additional methods. In contrast, six children originally classified as phonological dyslexics were consistently classified when these alternative measures were employed. Hence, the phonological subtype would appear to be a more reliable and distinct subtype than the surface dyslexic profile.

A recent behaviour genetic analysis of the heritability of word recognition skills in twins selected from the extremes of a distribution representing relative strength in phonological and orthographic processing is consistent with this view (Castles, Datta, Gayan & Olson, 1999. In this study, the contribution of environmental variance to the word recognition skills of children with a "surface-dyslexic" profile was greater than to those with a "phonological dyslexic" profile, and they also had poorer scores on a test of print exposure. In contrast, almost two thirds of the variance in word recognition scores for the phonological-dyslexic subgroup was due to genetic factors pointing to a possibly inherited deficit in spoken language skills.

In a related study, Olson, Datta, Gayan and DeFries (1999), investigated the heritability of word recognition in children who varied in speed of processing. The slowest third of the group who were significantly poorer on orthographic tasks, showed a relatively low heritability for word recognition deficits, but a high shared-environment influence. The opposite pattern was seen for the high speed group. These findings complement the results we have reported which suggest speed of information processing speed may be an important cognitive skill which may 'modify' the effects of variations in a phonological deficit on an individual's behavioural profile of reading development. Studies of the heritability of different forms of dyslexia are at a relatively early stage though Grigorenko *et al.* (1997) have reported evidence consistent with the idea that different genetic substrates underlying different 'types' of dyslexia. Further empirical research is required before a full understanding is possible of how the problems of different dyslexic children can be traced to the neurobiological substrate.

REFERENCES

Bishop, D. V. M. (1998). Cognitive neuropsychology and developmental disorders: Uncomfortable bedfellows. *Quarterly Journal of Experimental Psychology, Section A-Human Experimental Psychology, 50*, 899-923.

Boder, E. (1971). Developmental dyslexia: prevailing diagnostic concepts. In H. R. Myklebust (Ed.), *Progress in learning disabilities and a new diagnostic approach*, (pp. 293-321). New York: Grune & Stratton.

Boder, E. (1973). Developmental dyslexia: A diagnostic approach based on three atypical reading-spelling patterns. *Developmental Medicine and Child Neurology, 15*, 663-687.

Bowers, P. G. (1995). Tracing symbol naming speed's unique contributions to reading disabilities over time. *Reading and Writing: An Interdisciplinary Journal, 7*, 189-216.

Bowers, P. G., & Wolf, M. (1993). Theoretical links among naming speed, precising timing mechanisms and orthographic skill in dyslexia. *Reading and Writing: An Interdisciplinary Journal, 5*, 69-85.

Brady, S., & Shankweiler, D. (Eds.). (1991). *Phonological Processes in Literacy*. Hillsdale, NJ: Erlbaum.

Brady, S. A. (1997). Ability to encode phonological representations: an underlying difficulty for poor readers. In B. Blachman (Ed.), *Foundations of Reading Acquisition and Dyslexia: Implications for Early Intervention, (pp 21-48)*. Mahwah, New Jersey: Lawrence Erlbaum Associates.

Brown, G. D. A. (1997). Connectionism, phonology, reading, and regularity in developmental dyslexia. *Brain and Language, 59*, 207-235.

Bryant, P. E., & Impey, L. (1986). The similarities between normal readers and developmental and acquired dyslexic children. *Cognition, 24*, 121-137.

Campbell, R., & Butterworth, B. (1985). Phonological dyslexia and dysgraphia in a highly literate subject: a developmental case with associated deficits of phonemic processing and awareness. *Quarterly Journal of Experimental Psychology, 37A*, 435-475.

Castles, A., & Coltheart, M. (1993). Varieties of developmental dyslexia. *Cognition, 47*, 149-180.

Castles, A., & Coltheart, M. (1996). Cognitive correlates of developmental surface dyslexia: a single case study. *Cognitive Neuropsychology, 13*, 25-50.

Castles, A., Datta, H., Gayan, J., & Olson, R. K. (1999). Varieties of reading disorder: genetic and environmental influences. *Journal of Experimental Child Psychology, 72*, 73-94.

Coltheart, M. (1978). Lexical access in simple reading tasks. In G. Underwood (Ed.), *Strategies of information processing*, (pp. 151-216). London: Academic Press.

Coltheart, M., Masterson, J., Byng, S., Prior, M., & Riddoch, J. (1983). Surface dyslexia. *Quarterly Journal of Experimental Psychology, 35*, 469-495.

Denckla, M. (1977). Minimal brain dysfunction and dyslexia: Beyond diagnosis by exclusion. In M. E. Blaw, I. Rapin, & M. Kinsbourne (Eds.), *Topics in Child Neurology*, New York: Spectrum Publication.

Doehring, D. G., & Hoshko, I. M. (1977). Classification of reading problems by the Q technique of factor analysis. *Cortex, 13*, 281-294.

Ehri, L. C. (1992). Reconceptualising the development of sight word reading and its relationship to recoding. In P. B. Gough, L. C. Ehri, & R. Treiman (Eds.), *Reading Acquisition* (pp. 107-143). Hillsdale, NJ: Erlbaum & Associates.

Elbro, C., Borstrom, I., & Petersen, D. K. (1998). Predicting dyslexia from kindergarten: The importance of distinctness of phonological representations of lexical items. *Reading Research Quarterly, 33*, 36-60.

Ellis, A. W. (1994). *Reading, Writing and Dyslexia. A Cognitive Analysis.* (2nd ed.). Hove, UK: Lawrence Erlbaum Associates.

Fletcher, J. M., Morris, R., Lyon, G. R., Stuebing, K. K., Shaywitz, S. E., Shankweiler, D. P., Katz, L., & Shaywitz, B. A. (1997). Subtypes of dyslexia: An old problem revisited. In B. Blachman (Ed.), *Foundations of Reading Acquisition and Dyslexia* (pp. 95-114). Mahwah, New Jersey: Lawrence Erlbaum Associates.

Fowler, A. (1991). How early phonological development might set the stage for phoneme awareness. In S. A. Brady & D. P. Shankweiler (Eds.), *Phonological processes in literacy: A tribute to Isabelle Liberman* (pp. 97-117). New Jersey: Erlbaum.

Frith, U. (1985). Beneath the surface of developmental dyslexia. In K. Patterson, M. Coltheart, & J. Marshall (Eds.), *Surface Dyslexia: Neuropsychological and cognitive studies of phonological reading* (pp. 301-330). London: Erlbaum.

Goswami, U., & Bryant, P. E. (1990). *Phonological skills and learning to read.* London: Erlbaum.

Goulandris, N., & Snowling, M. J. (1991). Visual memory deficits: A plausible cause of developmental dyslexia? Evidence from a single case study. *Cognitive Neuropsychology, 8*, 127-154.

Griffiths, Y.M. (1999). Individual differences in developmental dyslexia. Unpublished DPhil thesis, University of York.

Griffiths, Y.M. & Snowling, M.J. (2002). Predictors of exception word and nonword reading in dyslexic children: the severity hypothesis. *Journal of Educational Psychology, 94*, 34-43.

Grigorenko, E.L., Wood, F.B., Meyer, M.S., Hart, L.A., Speed, W.C., Shuster, B.S. & Pauls, D.L. (1997). Susceptibility loci for distinct components of developmental dyslexia on chromosome 6 and 15. *American Journal of Human Genetics, 60*, 27-39.

Hanley, J. R., Hastie, K., & Kay, J. (1992). Developmental surface dyslexia and dysgraphia: an orthographic processing impairment. *Quarterly Journal of Experimental Psychology, 44A*, 285-320.

Harm, M. W., & Seidenberg, M. S. (1998). Phonology, reading acquisition and dyslexia: Insights from connectionist models. *Psychological Review, 106*, 491-528.

Hulme, C., & Snowling, M. (1992). Phonological deficits in dyslexia: a reappraisal of the verbal deficit hypothesis. In N. Singh & I. Beale (Eds.), *Current perspectives in learning disabilities,* (pp. 270-331). New York: Springer-Verlag.

Johnson, D. J., & Mykelbust, H. R. (1967). *Learning Disabilities: Educational Principles and Practice.* New York: Grune and Stratton.

Kinsbourne, M., & Warrington, E. K. (1963a). Developmental factors in reading and writing backwardness. *British Journal of Psychology, 54*, 145-156.

Laing, E., & Hulme, C. (1999). Phonological and semantic processes influence beginning readers' ability to learn to read words. *Journal of Experimental Child Psychology, 73*, 183-207.

Lyon, G, R. (1995). Toward a definition of dyslexia. *Annals of Dyslexia, 45*, 3-27.

Manis, F. R., Seidenberg, M. S., Doi, L. M., McBride-Chang, C., & Petersen, A. (1996). On the bases of two subtypes of developmental dyslexia. *Cognition, 58*, 157-195.

Marsh, G., Friedman, M., Welch, V., & Desberg, P. (1981). A cognitive development theory of reading acquisition. . In G. Mackinnon & T. G. Waller (Eds.), Reading Research: Advances in Theory and Practice (Vol. 3, pp. 199-221). New York: Academic Press.

Marshall, J. C. (1984). Toward a rational taxonomy of the developmental dyslexias. In R. N. Malatesha & H. A. Whitaker (Eds.), *Dyslexia: A global issue.* (pp. 211-232). The Hague: Martinus Nijhoof.

Mattis, S., French, J. M., & Rapin, I. (1975). Dyslexia in children and young adults: three independent neuropsychological syndromes. *Developmental Medical Child Neurology, 17*, 150-163.

Metsala, J. L. (1997). Spoken word recognition in reading disabled children. *Journal of Educational Psychology, 89*, 159-169.

Morgan, W. P. (1896). A case of congenital word blindness. *British Medical Journal, 2*, 1378.

Morton, J., & Frith, U. (1995). Causal modelling: a structural approach to developmental psychopathology. In D. Cicchetti & D. J. Cohen (Eds.), *Manual of developmental psychopathology,* (pp 357-390). New York: Wiley.

Mykelbust, H. R., & Johnson, D. J. (1962). *Dyslexia in Children. Exceptional Children, 29*, 14-25.

Naidoo, S. (1972). *Specific Dyslexia*. London: Pitman Publishing.

Nation, K., & Snowling, M. J. (1998). Semantic processing and the development of word recognition skills: evidence from children with reading comprehension difficulties. *Journal of Memory and Language, 39*, 85-101.

Olson, R. K., Datta, H., Gayan, J., & DeFries, J. C. (1999). A behavioral-genetic analysis of reading disabilities and component processes. In R. Klein & P. McMullen (Eds.), *Converging methods for understanding reading and dyslexia* (pp133-152). Cambridge, MA: MIT Press.

Olson, R. K., Wise, B. W., Connors, F., Rack, J., & Fulker, D. (1989). Specific deficits in component reading and language skills: genetic and environmental influences. *Journal of Learning Disabilities, 22*, 339-349.

Patterson, K., Marshall, J. C., & Coltheart, M. (Eds.). (1985). *Surface dyslexia: Neuropsychological and cognitive studies of phonological reading*. Hove, UK: Lawrence Erlbaum Associates.

Paulesu, E., Frith, U., Snowling, M., Gallagher, A., Morton, J., Frackowiak, F. S. J., & Frith, C. D. (1996). Is developmental dyslexia a disconnection syndrome? Evidence from PET scanning. *Brain, 119*, 143-157.

Pennington, B. F., Orden, G. C. V., Smith, S. D., Green, P. A., & Haith, M. M. (1990). Phonological processing skills and deficits in adult dyslexics. *Child Development, 61*, 1753-1778.

Petrauskas, R. J., & Rourke, B. P. (1979). Identification of subtype of retarded readers: A neuropsychological, multivariate approach. *Journal of Clinical Neuropsychology, 1*, 17-37.

Plaut, D. C., McClelland, J. L., Seidenberg, M. S., & Patterson, K. (1996). Understanding normal and impaired word reading: Computational principles in quasi-regular domains. *Psychological Review, 103*, 56-115.

Romani, C., Ward, J., & Olson, A. (1999). Developmental Surface Dysgraphia: What is the underlying cognitive impairment? *Quarterly Journal of Experimental PsychologyA, 52*, 97-128.

Rosner, J., & Simon, D. (1971). The auditory analysis test: An initial report. *Journal of Learning Disabilities, 4*, 40-48.

Satz, P., & Morris, R. (1981). Learning disability subtypes: A review. In F. J. Pirozzdo & M. C. Wittrock (Eds.), *Neuropsychological and cognitive processes in reading* (pp. 109-141). New York: Academic Press.

Scarborough, H. S. (1990). Very early language deficits in dyslexic children. *Child Development, 61*, 1728-1743.

Seidenberg, M. S., & McClelland, J. (1989). A distributed, developmental model of word recognition. *Psychological Review, 96*, 523-568.

Seymour, P. H. K. (1986). *A cognitive analysis of dyslexia*. London: Routledge and Kegan Paul.

Seymour, P. H. K., & Elder, L. (1986). Beginning reading without phonology. *Cognitive Neuropsychology, 1*, 43-82.

Seymour, P. H. K., & Evans, H. M. (1993). The visual (orthographic) processor and dyslexia. In D.M. Willows, R.S. Kruk, & E. Corcos (Eds.), *Visual processes in reading and reading disabilities* (pp. 317-346). Hillsdale, NJ: Erlbaum.

Shallice, T. (1988). *From neuropsychology to mental structure*. Cambridge: Cambridge University Press.

Share, D. L. (1995). Phonological recoding and self-teaching: sine qua non of reading acquisition. *Cognition, 55*, 151-218.

Snowling, M. (1980). The development of grapheme-phoneme correspondence in normal and dyslexic readers. *Journal of Experimental Child Psychology, 29*, 294-305.

Snowling, M. J. (1983). The comparison of acquired and developmental disorders of reading. *Cognition, 14*, 105-118.

Snowling, M. J. (1996). Annotation: Contemporary approaches to the teaching of reading. *Journal of Child Psychology and Psychiatry, 37*, 139-148.

Snowling, M. J. (2000). *Dyslexia*. Second Edition. Oxford: Blackwell Publishers.

Snowling, M. J., Bryant, P. E., & Hulme, C. (1996). Theoretical and methodological pitfalls in making comparisons between developmental and acquired dyslexia: Some comments on A. Castles and M Coltheart (1993). *Reading and Writing: An Interdisciplinary Journal, 8*, 443-451.

Snowling, M. J., Goulandris, N., & Defty, N. (1996). A longitudinal study of reading development in dyslexic children. *Journal of Educational Psychology, 88*, 653-669.

Snowling, M. J., Goulandris, N., & Stackhouse, J. (1994). Phonological constraints on learning to read: Evidence from single-case studies of reading difficulty. In C. Hulme & M. J. Snowling (Eds.), *Reading development and dyslexia* (pp. 86-104). London: Whurr Publishers.

Snowling, M. J., & Hulme, C. (1989). A longitudinal case study of developmental phonological dyslexia. *Cognitive Neuropsychology, 6*, 379-403.

Snowling, M. J., & Hulme, C. (1994). The development of phonological skills. *Philosophical transactions of the Royal Society B, 346*, 21-28.

Snowling, M. J., Stackhouse, J., & Rack, J. (1986). Phonological dyslexia and dysgraphia: a developmental analysis. *Cognitive Neuropsychology, 3*, 309-339.

Stanovich, K., Seigel, L. S., & Gottardo, A. (1997). Progress in the search for dyslexia subtypes. In C. Hulme & M. Snowling (Eds.), *Dyslexia: Biology, Cognition and Intervention*, (pp 108-130). London: Whurr.

Stanovich, K. E. (1994). Does dyslexia exist? *Journal of Child Psychology and Psychiatry, 35*, 579-595.

Stanovich, K. E., & Siegel, L. S. (1994). The phenotypic performance profile of reading-disabled children: a regression-based test of the phonological-core variable-difference model. *Journal of Educational Psychology, 86*, 24-53.

Swan, D., & Goswami, U. (1997). Phonological awareness deficits in developmental dyslexia and the phonological representations hypothesis. *Journal of Experimental Child Psychology, 60*, 334-353.

Temple, C., & Marshall, J. (1983). A case study of developmental phonological dyslexia. *British Journal of Psychology, 74*, 517-533.

Tonnessen, F. E. (1997). How can we best define 'Dyslexia'? *Dyslexia, 3*, 78-92.

Van-Orden, G., Pennington, B., & Stone, G. (1990). Word identification and the promise of sub-symbolic psycholinguistics. *Psychological Review, 97*, 488-522.

Vellutino, F. R. (1979). *Dyslexia: Research and Theory*. Cambridge, MA: MIT Press.

Vellutino, F. R., & Scanlon, D. M. (1991). The pre-eminence of phonologically based skills in learning to read. In S. Brady & D. Shanweiler (Eds.), *Phonological processes in literacy: A tribute to Isabelle Liberman*, (pp 237-257). Hillsdale, NJ: Lawrence Erlbaum.

Wilding, J. (1989). Developmental dyslexics do not fit in boxes: Evidence from six new cases studies. *European Journal of Cognitive Psychology, 1*, 105-127.

Wimmer, H., Mayringer, H., & Landerl, K. (1998). Poor reading: A deficit in skill-automatisation or a phonological deficit? *Scientific Studies of Reading, 2*, 321-340.

C9. Specific Speech and Language Difficulties and Literacy

JULIE E. DOCKRELL & GEOFF LINDSAY

ABSTRACT

This chapter explores the relationships between oral language skills and literacy in children with specific speech and language difficulties. We consider the heterogeneous nature of the population of children with language difficulties and provide evidence to support the view that children with specific language problems experience a variety of problems with the language system. The extent and nature of any associated literacy problems will be related to the particular domain of language processing that is compromised. The ways in which language difficulties may serve as barriers to literacy development are considered. It is argued that semantics, syntax, metalinguistic abilities and attention must be considered in addition to phonological factors if we are to develop and an accurate picture of the links between language and literacy. A dynamic model with the relative importance of different factors at different developmental stages needs to be considered.

INTRODUCTION

Language and literacy

Children with specific speech and language difficulties experience problems with the acquisition and processing of oral language skills. The problems are characterised by a protracted rate of language development as well as particular difficulties with subcomponents of the language system (see Bishop, 1997 or Leonard, 1998 for reviews). Reading is grounded in oral language skills and it is therefore not surprising that children who experience difficulties with oral language frequently experience difficulties with literacy. By corollary many poor readers also experience difficulties with oral language. Recently Catts, Fey and Tomblin (1997) estimated that as many as 50 per cent of poor readers have language deficits that go beyond phonological processing. These problems include difficulties with expressive and receptive vocabulary and syntax or wider problems with comprehension of text and making inferences. The link between oral language and literacy raises a number of important questions about the

T. Nunes, P. Bryant (eds.), Handbook of Children's Literacy, 403–435.
© *2004 Kluwer Academic Publishers. Printed in Great Britain.*

relationship between language and literacy and the possible linguistic precursors of literacy problems.

This link between language and literacy has led some researchers to argue that there may be a continuum between developmental language disorders and reading problems and that these problems may share the same underlying processing deficits. Reading, writing, talking and understanding share many similar processes but there are also important differences between them. Moreover, children can experience a variety of difficulties within the language system and/or different kinds of reading problems. Establishing the nature of the links between the different sets of problems is of key practical and theoretical importance.

In this chapter we will argue that children who experience specific speech and language difficulties are not a homogeneous group. Not only do the children experience a range of problems with the language system they frequently have additional problems. The diversity of the group should lead us to question univariate predictions of development and ask the more precise question 'Which kinds of language difficulties lead to particular patterns of reading difficulty'? There are presently partial answers to this question but there are many gaps in our current understanding of the processes. The first half of the chapter considers criteria for the identification of specific language difficulties and the various ways that the difficulties are manifested. In the second section we consider the links that exist between specific speech and language difficulties and literacy.

We have chosen to use the term 'specific speech and language difficulty' to denote the children who have primary difficulties with the language system. The children form a mixed group in terms of language problems (Fletcher, 1991; Conti-Ramsden *et al.*, 1997; Conti-Ramsden and Botting, 1999). Terminology varies across the literature. Some researchers have opted to use the term 'language learning disability' as a term to encompass both language and literacy difficulties. Since the overlap between difficulties with language and literacy is still a matter of debate the criteria for this needs careful consideration. Other researchers have chosen not to distinguish between specific and non-specific language problems – "We make no distinction between children with specific and nonspecific language impairments. Both groups of children have language learning deficits, and it is these impairments, not non-verbal cognitive deficits, that should be directly related to reading development" (Catts and Kamhi, 1999:66). In the present chapter to clarify the basis of claims made in research papers we either define the sample used or opt for the terminology used by the researchers. The concept of discrepancy between verbal and non-verbal skills is discussed in more detail in the section that follows.

CHILDREN WITH SPECIFIC SPEECH AND LANGUAGE DIFFICULTIES

Language delays and disorders are associated with a broad range of developmental problems including hearing loss (both conductive and sensorineural), developmental delay, pervasive developmental disability and Down syndrome, with as many as 13% of all children experiencing some form of language difficulty (Beitchman, Nair, Clegg and Patel, 1986). A specific difficulty with the language system is generally considered to be a developmental language disorder that occurs in the absence of general learning difficulties, hearing loss, motor disorders, socio-emotional dysfunction or frank neurological deficit.

The children and their difficulties have been described in a variety of ways. The confusion that exists is reflected in the variety of terms that have been used to describe the children. These include terms such as *Developmental aphasia, Specific language impairment*, and *Developmental disorders of language*. This list is not all inclusive and specific terms are also used to describe particular types of problems. These include *grammatical specific language impairment* or *word-finding difficulties*.

Tomblin, Records and Zhang (1996) determined the prevalence rate of specific speech and language difficulties to be 7.4% among five-year-olds.[1] A higher ratio of boys to girls is affected (Johnston, Stark, Mellits and Tallal, 1981). Recent research with twins and adoption studies has highlighted the key role of genetic factors in children's early language delays (Bishop, North and Donlan, 1995; Felsenfeld and Plomin, 1997; Lewis and Thompson, 1992; Tomblin and Buckwalter, 1998). Research with twins indicates that in 2-year-olds with very low vocabulary scores the environment accounted for only 18% of the variance in contrast to the 69% of the variance accounted for in the typically developing group (Dale *et al.*, 1998). These results support the view that for the children with low vocabularies there is a high genetic component. While these results indicate that there was less scope for variation in the low vocabulary group salient environmental differences could make a difference. The critical role of non-word repetition as a genetic marker of language impairment has also been highlighted (Bishop *et al.*, 1999). Although considerable debate exists about the ways in which non-word repetition can account for the variety of deficits presented by these children, poor non-word repetition should, perhaps, be considered to be one risk among many potential language related risk factors.

Identifying a specific speech and language difficulty

The identification of language difficulties, per se, is problematic. Conventional classification systems include categories related to specific language problems. The International Classification of Diseases (ICD-10, WHO, 1992) describes the category of 'specific developmental disorders of speech and language' while the

---

[1] In Tomblin's study children had normal non-verbal IQs, and scored at least 1.25SDs below the mean on two or more of five composite language measures.

Diagnostic and Statistical Manual IV (American Psychiatric Association, 1994) uses the term 'developmental language disorder'. The criteria to make this specific diagnosis centre on three issues:

I.   Performance on a language test below the child's chronological age
II. A discrepancy between the child's language skills and their non-verbal abilities
III. Language disabilities that cannot be attributed to any other cause

Performance on language tests

The first criterion captures the essential notion that the child's language must be delayed from the norm or presents a different pattern from the norm. At one level this should be obvious. However, this norm itself is not easy to characterize. There is considerable diversity in the rate at which children acquire language, especially in the pre-school period (Bates, Dale and Thal, 1995) and the use of differing selection criteria can result in the identification of different numbers of children, and of children manifesting differing types of problems (Dockrell, 2001). Leonard (1998) argues that "Even if fully half of all late-talking two-year-olds have significant language problems when they reach school age, the fact that the remaining half do not indicates that a diagnosis of SLI before age three is currently not feasible" (p. 183).

Performance on non-verbal tasks

Having established a delay, this on its own is not sufficient to decide that a child has a *specific* problem with language. It is also necessary to consider the child's developmental profile more generally. The second point narrows the potential group of children by requiring that a discrepancy exists between the child's language skills and their non-verbal ability. Traditionally specific speech and language difficulties have been defined by contrasting an average or above-average non-verbal cognitive ability with oral language skills that are significantly lower. The discrepancy criterion is based on the assumption that since verbal skills are compromised non-verbal ability is a more appropriate (reliable and valid) measure of intellectual functioning.

The notion of a *significant discrepancy* is problematic. Firstly, it is important to decide how much of a difference is significant. Aram and his colleagues (Aram, Morris and Hall, 1992) have shown that variations in the discrepancy criteria that are used can make a 25% difference in the number of children identified as language 'disordered'. Even with the least restrictive criteria they found that 40% of a sample of children who were defined by clinicians as language disordered would not have been identified as having a language disorder using discrepancy criteria alone. It is also important to realize that on their own discrepancies often fail to account for the diversity of children's performance in different language and cognitive tasks. This may be particularly problematic when a child is experiencing an additional learning difficulty. There is the added complication that for some children with SSLD their performance on non-verbal tasks appears to 'drop off' as they get older (Conti-Ramsden, Botting, Simkin and Knox, 2001). Consequently, while the use of discrepancies may be a helpful framework for structuring our understanding of children's development, the complexity of the identification process creates doubts about the reliability and validity of the procedure. Children may be having major and specific language problems and yet be missed with these identification processes. Nonetheless while the relationship is not straightforward the majority of researchers and practitioners use some form of discrepancy between language abilities and non-verbal abilities to identify *specific* problems with the language system.

Lack of alternative explanation for the problem

Perhaps the most commonly used core criterion to identify children with a specific speech and language difficulty is that their language problems *cannot* be explained in terms of other cognitive, neurological or perceptual deficits. The previous section has highlighted some of the difficulties in ruling out wider cognitive problems (as measured by IQ). Yet it does not necessarily follow that children who are experiencing other sensory problems or neurological difficulties may not also have specific language problems. Certainly practitioners report the co-occurrence of other difficulties with 'specific speech and language difficulties' (Dockrell and Lindsay, 2000). Moreover, it is likely that whether or not the language problem is viewed as specific will depend on the age and context of the identification. Thus, for example a child identified at 8 with a specific reading difficulty who has significant and marked language problems may not be conceptualised as having a specific speech and language difficulty. Equally a four-year-old with chronic otitis media and additional language problems would be excluded from the current identification procedures. Research studies vary in the extent to which they adhere to exclusionary criteria.

Samples of children with specific speech and language difficulties will vary and it is likely that samples drawn from different groups, such as community, language unit or clinical sample, will differ. To try and alleviate these problems a number of different identification criteria have been suggested.

Frameworks for identification

One of the most common frameworks used to identify children for research purposes is that of Stark and Tallal (1981). In this case a series of both inclusionary and exclusionary criteria are used. Specifically the following test results must be obtained: Performance IQ of at least 85 and at least one of the following:

1. Receptive language score at least 6 months below mental age (MA)
2. A combined language score of at least 12 months below the lower of MA or chronological (CA)
3. An expressive language score which is at least 12 months below the lower of the MA or CA.

The language delay score raises critical issues for age-related identification. A six month delay at three-years of age would be a major cause for concern. In contrast a six-month delay at 12 is more likely to reflect normal variation. In both cases the sensitivity of the measures is paramount. The tight use of the IQ criterion and the language discrepancy scores raises major practical problems. There is marked variation in the IQ cut-off points used by different researchers (Plante, 1998). Moreover there are significant differences across non-verbal tests for performance levels (Swisher, Plante and Lowell, 1994). In the Swisher *et al.* (1994) study the mean IQ varied by as much as 10 points over three different measures. These identification problems are particularly acute given that, for a variety of reasons, the non-verbal IQ scores of children with SLI are commonly lower than those of normally developing children (Conti-Ramsden, Hutcheson and Grove, 1995).

The variety in the children's level of non-verbal functioning reflects practitioners' views of the diverse nature of the population (Dockrell, George, Lindsay and Roux, 1997). The IQ criterion becomes important if there is evidence of an impact on the child's functioning. This is currently an issue of debate (see Leonard, 1998:184-185). Catts and Kamhi (1999) argue there is little evidence to support a differentiation based on non-verbal functioning and Fey, Long and Cleave, (1994) report that gains in grammatical skill were not markedly different between children with IQs above or below 85. In contrast there is suggestive evidence from some longitudinal studies (Bird, Bishop and Freeman, 1995; Stothard *et al.*, 1998) that non-verbal ability may play a role in prognosis. However, it is currently unclear to what extent more severe language problems may lead to subsequent reduced non-verbal scores. The exclusion of children with scores within the range typically educated in mainstream school may run the risk of excluding children who would benefit from a more detailed analysis of their language needs and may result in their difficulties being subsumed under other categories of learning difficulty.

The problems that exist with measures of non-verbal ability are of equal relevance to language measures. There is general agreement that a representative set of language tests is needed to identify children with specific speech and language difficulties and that a single measure is never sufficient. Rather a profile of the child's language skills needs to be obtained. Yet not all language tests are sensitive to language problems to the same degree. When Plante and Vance (1994) examined 21 tests that purported to identify language difficulties in pre-school children (aged three to four) their findings were disconcerting. They assessed 20 children with SLI (specific language impairment) and 20 normally developing children, both groups of children had non-verbal abilities within the average range. The original diagnosis of SLI was made by clinics and schools referring the children to the study on the basis of performance on standardised tests and clinical judgement of impaired language. Only 38 per cent of the tests met half the necessary criteria for test use and of the four acceptable tests administered to the children only one test (SPELT-II) discriminated in an acceptable way between the language impaired and non-language impaired children. Moreover, giving the children more language tests did not improve the identification rate. Identification criteria need to be specified and justified and will need to be supported by detailed analyses of the types of language problems experienced by the children.

Summary

There are currently a number of difficulties surrounding the identification of children with SSLD. In the early years this involves an appropriate cut-off point between typical and atypical development. As children get older a particular issue arises about whether the children's language skills are commensurate with their general abilities or whether language is a specific difficulty in and off itself. Nonetheless there is no doubt about the existence of a group of children whose language and communication skills do not follow the typical developmental trajectory. A major concern is specifying what problems exist within the language system and what factors are responsible for the variation in developmental patterns.

THE LANGUAGE SYSTEM – WHAT GOES WRONG?

Profiling children's problems

Language difficulties are commonly divided into two basic categories – expressive language disorder and mixed receptive and expressive problems (DSM-IV, 1994). DSM IV also allows phonological disorder, stuttering disorder and language disorder not otherwise specified. A simple two-level system has a number of limitations as Bishop (1997:35) points out. Moreover, for many children their pattern of language difficulty changes over time (Conti-Ramsden and Botting, 1999). Even when obvious problems resolve difficulties may be evident in formal assessments (Bishop, North and Donlan, 1996).

An important step in developing our understanding of difficulties with the language system has come from accounts that specify the subcomponents that are important for effective language use. These subcomponents include grammar, vocabulary, phonology and pragmatics. Each of the subcomponents of the language system can be studied and assessed independently. However, this does not mean that the components work independently. They interact in the overall process of comprehending and producing language. Analysis of children's language has shown that children can have difficulties with each of the subcomponents of the language system. Table 1 presents a summary of the six key areas that have been the focus of investigation. In this table the nature of the problems identified are briefly described and the implications and key issues mentioned. In section 6 the barriers that these specific difficulties pose for subsequent literacy development will be considered.

Given the variety of ways in which the language system can be impaired and the general dissatisfaction with the definition and identification of the children there has been a move towards distinguishing subtypes of language impairment. These subtypes involve various combinations of the processes outlined in Table 1. Establishing an empirically based classification system would be an important step towards classifying the disorder and would provide a means of testing the relationship between various patterns of speech and language problems and the child's literacy competencies. One of the most commonly cited approaches to subtypes is that proposed by Rapin and Allen (1987). The six groups are presented in Table 2.

A critical issue in the use of classification systems is the basis for their construction. A variety of different methods have been used. Rapin and Allen (1987) used clinical assessment to classify the children but standardised assessments (Aram and Nation, 1975; Beitchman et al., 1989; Bishop and Edmundson, 1987) and linguistic measures (Fletcher, 1991) have also been used. Each system for classification has resulted in different subgroupings. For example, Fletcher (1991) identified four subgroups of children with specific language impairment: one group with rate and fluency problems but who were generally error-free, a second with phonological/grammatical problems who were dysfluent, a third where semantic referencing problems were implicated, and a fourth group who were relatively fluent but with linguistic structure building problems. In contrast Aram and Nation (1975) formed six groups and Beitchman et al. (1989) using a community sample identified 4 groups of children based on a number of standardised language measures: one with normal language, a second described as having poor comprehension, a third with poor articulation, and a fourth who were low overall and had associated motor problems. Conti-Ramsden, Crutchley and Botting (1997) have derived a series of clusters based on psychometric test performance but complemented by the clinical judgment of experienced teachers and speech and language therapists. They found a reasonable similarity with the Rapin and Allen (1987) classification system but there were key differences between them. The age of the Conti-Ramsden et al. (1997) sample is also important. These children were seven years of age and all spending 50% or more of their school time in language units and were therefore experiencing pronounced problems. Our own analyses (Dockrell and Lindsay, 2002) of seven-year children identified through professionals in local education authorities provided a three factor solution of the analysis of the children's language scores; a factor that could broadly be defined as lexical/syntactic, a factor that was phonological and a

Table 1 – Problems with Subcomponents of the Language System

Problem identified	Production	Comprehension	Nature of the problem	Implications	Key issues	Indicative Studies
Auditory processing	✓ (possibly)	✓	Impairments in the ability to perceive rapidly presented verbal material of brief duration (possibly also non-verbal material)	Even children who pass hearing tests may have subtle auditory problems that have consequent effects for processing oral language	Can these difficulties account for all language problems? Are the problems in discrimination or discrimination in particular contexts or the forming of phonological representations?	Tallal, Stark and Mellits (1985) Leonard, McGregor and Allen (1992) Sussman (1993) Tallal et al. (1996)
Phonological problems	✓	✓ (some sounds)	Problems have been noted in perceiving phoneme constancy across different word contexts, in encoding phonological information and in phonological awareness.	Impoverished input to the grammatical system. Difficulties in establishing phonological representations of new words.	Is the immature phonological processing secondary to or independent from auditory discrimination?	Dollaghan (1987) Kahmi, Lee and Nelson (1985) Magnusson and Nauclear(1993) Bird and Bishop (1992)
Vocabulary	✓	✓	Delays in use of first words and subsequent reduced vocabulary rates. Associated problems with word-finding. Currently evidence to suggest that the acquisition of verbs may be differentially impaired.	Implications for age of first word combinations and later vocabulary acquisition in school-based contexts. May have implications for the nature and extent of the children's wider verbal knowledge base	The link between slower rates of acquisition/ smaller vocabularies is presently unclear. Need to specify the relationship between lexical and semantic acquisition. Can children's vocabularies be accounted for by reduced efficiency of working memory?	Rice, Buhr and Oetting, (1992) Oetting, Rice and Swank, (1995) Gathercole and Baddeley (1990) Dockrell, Messer, George and Wilson (1998)

Problem identified	Production	Comprehension	Nature of the problem	Implications	Key issues	Indicative Studies
Syntax	✓	✓	Problems manifested in a number of ways – simplifications of speech output, omissions of function words and shorter utterances. Morphologically complex words can be particularly problematic	Difficulties with comprehension will affect critical aspects of verbal interactions. Failure to understand oral grammatical forms has implications for understanding of written text. Difficulties in producing correct forms fluently will impact on interactions and may have direct implications for written language production.	The extent to which the difficulties are best explained as a maturational failure of innate syntactic abilities or reduced information processing resources	Leonard, (1989) Fletcher and Ingham, (1996) Van der Lely and Stollwerck (1997) Bishop (1994)
Pragmatics		✓	Problems in understanding and using language in social situations.	Difficulties in understanding connected discourse and drawing inferences.	Necessity to disentangle lack of relevant knowledge to draw inferences or failure(s) with social cognition.	Nippold and Fey (1983) Bishop and Adams (1989)

Table 2 – Subgroups of children with specific speech and language difficulties

Subtype	Problems
Verbal auditory agnosia	severe difficulties in comprehension, production is also poor
Verbal dyspraxia	have normal comprehension but poor expressive skills related to articulation
Phonological programming syndrome	oral-motor capacities are normal but there are deficits in the production of speech sounds
Phonological-syntactic difficulties	production and comprehension are impaired
Lexical-syntactic deficit	characterised by word finding difficulties, problems in producing connected speech
Semantic-pragmatic difficulties	ability to produce and understand meaningfully utterances is impaired despite normal grammatical skills

final factor that included memory related language tasks (sentence length and alliteration).

There are a number of issues to consider with all these attempts to classify the children's language performance. The results will depend on the measures used (which psychometric tests), the age at which the children are assessed (with more fine-grained results arising with older children where there is scope for differentiation), the level at which the language system is evaluated, the educational context in which the child is placed, and the flexibility in the way the classification system is used.

If it were established that particular classification systems were predictive of patterns of improvement, indicative of appropriate intervention or indicated differential effects on later educational attainment this would indeed provide strong evidence for their validity. However, at present these issues have yet to be comprehensively addressed. Nonetheless unless we work within well-defined frameworks it will not be possible to address these issues. For example, there is strong evidence that children who have both receptive and expressive difficulties fair worse than those with expressive difficulties alone. Moreover, it is likely that the cooccurence of other difficulties such as attention problems, difficulties in the planning and execution of motor programs and behaviour problems will increase the complexity of the process (Beitchman *et al.*, 1986; Benasich, Curtiss and Tallal, 1993). As Bishop states "Once we understand what it is about language that can give children particular difficulty, we can devise better ways of indexing underlying problems, and it is these indices … that have the best chance of providing us with meaningful classifactory framework" (1997:37).

Delayed or disordered language?

On the whole classification systems are relatively neutral on whether the children's language performance should be conceived as a "delay" or 'disorder'. This may well reflect the descriptive nature of classification systems. Yet attempts to *explain* the children's patterns of language difficulties have frequently centered on the question of delay or deviant acquisition patterns. Stark, Mellits and Tallal (1983) and Bishop and Rosenbloom (1987) draw a logical distinction between language delay and language disorder. In the latter case children's language acquisition is thought to follow a *different* pattern from the norm with, for example, a child experiencing difficulties with a particular syntactic structure or producing speech in a dysfluent fashion. A delay suggests that the child is acquiring language in a normal fashion but at a slower pace than their age-matched peers. Thus, a quantitative gap exists between the child's skills as compared to children of a similar age. In contrast deviant or disordered language implies a qualitatively different pattern of development, one that differs in the way in which language processing occurs and/ or the order in which the language is acquired. The evidence is mixed.

A number of studies have reported less frequent use of morphemes compared to matched samples (Clahsen, 1989) and asynchronies between lexical items and syntactic structures (Chiat and Hirson, 1987), both of which suggest deviance. In contrast other studies have produced evidence to support a delay explanation (Johnston and Kamhi, 1984). In general, studies that have supported a delay notion have focused on single components of the language system whereas those which highlight different patterns of development have examined relationships between various grammatical components. In an attempt to further address patterns of acquisition across components Curtiss, Katz and Tallal (1992) studied 28 language-impaired children and 32 matched controls over a period of five years. The acquisition patterns of the language impaired children were similar to those of their language matched peers, implying that the language impaired children were constructing grammars based on the same rules and principles. Nonetheless as the authors state their data only represent a sample of possible comparisons that could be made and their results do not rule out difference in the acquisition of certain forms.

Leonard (1998) has argued that the delay-deviance dichotomy does not adequately capture the variety of ways in which children with specific speech and language difficulties can differ from the norm. He identified five possible patterns of development: a delay where the child may experience both a late emergence of language and slower than average developmental path; a plateau where the child reaches a particular level of competence but proceeds no further; a profile difference where a different relationship from the norm exists between the subcomponents of the language system; abnormal frequency error where the child exhibits a type of error that can be seen in the language of a normally developing child but never in the same degree; a qualitative difference whereby the child produces unusual forms that are never seen in typical development.

Leonard's differentiated description helps us to focus on the possible differing patterns of development and forces the refinement of theoretical explanations of the problems. In what ways can we explain these differing patterns of development?

Explanations of the children's language impairments

Descriptions of the types of language problems experienced by the children do not provide the basis for guiding intervention nor do they provide a satisfactory basis for considering the links between language and literacy. In contrast adequate explanations should guide language interventions and provide links with the child's functioning more generally, including literacy. Explanations of language problems are generally offered in one of two ways: explanations that are language specific and often focus on the subcomponent under investigation and explanations that are at a more general level and reflect the wider cognitive system. A number of explanations focus on the children's grammatical performance. For example it has been argued that children lack the knowledge that morphological marking is obligatory (Rice and Wexler, 1996) or have an inability to learn inflectional rules (Gopnik, 1997). Indeed it has been speculated that children do not possess the basic competence for linguistic generalisation and need to learn on an item by item basis. The general consensus is that it is the degree of children's use of inflexions, not their absence that is the key. When children use inflexions they are usually appropriate (Leonard, 1998).

Others have explained the children's language problems as a result of speech processing limitations. It is argued that speech processing problems result in degraded phonological representations that influence the semantic and syntactic processes engaged in by the children. Phonology has been advanced as the link between speech perception difficulties and language problems (Joanisse and Seidenberg, 1998). Tallal (1990) has also identified impairments in perceiving rapid stimuli in the visual and tactile modalities in these children suggesting that the deficit is not specific to speech.

In contrast to explanations based within the language system it has been argued that the children might have difficulty with language because they may have access to fewer cognitive resources. There are cases where children with specific speech and language difficulties demonstrate partial mastery of a grammatical structure but that level of mastery varies across situations. Such a result is not consistent with a specific linguistic deficit. Rather it indicates that the ability is not well established and performance is influenced by the demands of the task. Further there is evidence that poor or reduced ability to store information in working memory could be a contributory cause to language difficulties. Gathercole and Baddeley (1990) found that children with language difficulties performed less well than typically developing children on a task that required immediate recall of non-words. The fact that the children with language difficulties were poorer than the younger language age matched controls is of particular significance. They concluded that the children with language difficulties could retain less material in their immediate memory. Thus, working memory can constrain the development of speech production which depends heavily on phonological storage capacity.

A defining characteristic of children with specific speech and language difficulties is that their non-verbal skills are at least within the average range. Arguments about discrepancies and primary problems are based on the understanding that the children experience no specific cognitive difficulties. Yet there is research that suggests that children can have subtle but significant cognitive problems across visual, auditory and tactile stimuli (Johnston, 1991; Stone and Connel, 1993).

In many respects the range of explanations offered to account for specific speech and language difficulties mirrors the different types of problems experienced by the children. Competing explanations exist not only to explain the "language" problem but also to explain problems within the subcomponents of the language system.

A major problem with current explanations is the ability to account for differences over time. For example a group of children originally studied by Tallal, Stark, Kallman and Mellits (1981) were followed up by Bernstein and Stark (1985). One of the previously observed deficits (discriminating tone pairs at short stimulus intervals) was no longer evident although the majority of children still met the criteria for SLI. Bishop has argued that such data "raises the possibility that a slow maturing auditory perceptual system might leave a legacy of language impairment, even after ceiling levels of auditory discrimination have been reached" (1997:229).

Summary

Children with specific speech and language difficulties experience a variety of problems with the language system, including problems with syntax, phonology and semantics. There are also cases where difficulties extend beyond these areas to include pragmatics, problem solving and inferencing. The extent and nature of any subsequent literacy problem is likely to be related to the particular domain of language processing that is compromised, with the likelihood of reading difficulties increasing with the number of language domains where problems are evident.

IMPLICATIONS FOR STUDIES OF LANGUAGE AND LITERACY

The extent and nature of the difficulties experienced by this group of children would suggest that they were highly susceptible to failure in language based tasks such as reading (both word recognition and comprehension), spelling and the content of written language. This brief review of the area raises four key issues that will complicate investigations of the link between specific speech and language difficulties and literacy. Firstly, the heterogeneous nature of the children's language problems suggests that investigations of language related tasks will need to take account of the variety of language difficulties. Children with comprehension problems, for example, may present different patterns of difficulty with reading than children who have only phonological problems. Of course, if they do not this has implications for our understanding of specific speech and language difficulties. Secondly, it is important to measure the children's level of non-verbal functioning and be explicit about the measures used. Thirdly, it is important to consider a range of reading skills in the same way that we consider a child's language profile, to consider the specific difficulties experienced with reading including accuracy of regular, irregular and pseudoword reading. Finally, since language profiles change with age it will be important to consider both the language ages and chronological ages of the children studied. This is particularly important since different measures of reading achievement at different times may be dependent on somewhat different language abilities, separately or in combination. For example, Sawyer (1992) investigated the relationship between language measures and reading for two cohorts of children entering kindergarten and then followed the children up over a 4-year period. She argues that for the younger children global language measures were related to measures of early reading achievement. These measures included letter and number naming. In contrast by first grade an additional effect of word and phoneme segmentation was evident on performance. By grade 2 comprehension also influenced word recognition and in grade 3, the final point of testing, word recognition and comprehension were essentially independent. Sawyer's results support the view that the impact of language processes on literacy may change over time and the choice of language and literacy measures will be critical in revealing differences.

Carrying out research with special populations brings certain constraints and the studies reported below have not met all of these criteria. However by considering all the studies it is possible to construct an emerging picture of the links between specific speech and language difficulties and literacy.

LANGUAGE AND LITERACY

Both retrospective research using clinical records and surveys of academic performance have highlighted the link between specific speech and language difficulties and reading disabilities. The data from Silva's study (Silva *et al.*, 1987) of 937 New Zealand children demonstrated that at nine and 11 years the reading scores of the children with language disorders were increasing at a significantly slower rate than those for the remainder of the sample. Children with receptive and expressive difficulties were more at risk for reading problems than those with either receptive or expressive problems alone. There is some suggestion that age-appropriate IQs can serve as a moderating variable, so where IQs are within the average range the problems are less severe (Richman, Stevenson and Graham, 1982; Silva, McGhee and Williams, 1985). More recently a number of concurrent and prospective studies have begun to address more detailed aspects of the link between language and literacy.

McArthur *et al.* (2000) found that 55% of a sample of children with specific reading difficulties met the criteria of specific language impairment while 51% of a sample with specific language impairment met the criteria of specific reading difficulties. The former were in reading classes and public schools while the latter were attending Language Development Centres. This study not only provides further evidence of the overlap between language and reading difficulties, it also poses important methodological questions of researchers who are examining one group or the other, rather than the nature of their relationship. For example, they question the concept of "specific" in each group and whether standard criteria of specific reading disability should be modified to include the absence of language impairment, given that while there is a relationship, reading difficulties are not inevitable among children with specific language impairment.

Concurrent studies of language and reading

In a concurrent study of 252 7-year-olds in English language units Botting Crutchley and Conti-Ramsden (1998) identified a high proportion of children with reading problems (defined as scores below the 28th centile). Severity varied within their subgroups, but those who were clustered as having semantic pragmatic problems had much better reading skills (with a mean score at the 66th centile) than the others. It is important to note that these reading measures only concerned decoding (British Abilities Scale Word Reading) and it is possible that these children with good decoding skills (pragmatics group) would be experiencing difficulties with comprehension.

Our work with a sample of 69 8-years olds in mainstream schools, units and special schools found a high rate of literacy difficulties (Dockrell and Lindsay, 1998). On the Macmillan Individual Reading Analysis (MIRA), both for accuracy and comprehension, and on Spelling and Early Number Scales (both from the British Ability Scales II [BAS-II]) the children in our sample consistently recorded mean scores below their chronological age level. Thirteen children failed to score at all and a total of 38% failed to score at an age equivalent of five years for reading. The regression analyses indicated that the phonological language measure was a significant correlate of all the education attainments measured. The general language measure was an important correlate of reading comprehension and early number skills whereas the language memory measure, predicted children's performance on early number skills and a language/education measure the Junior Rating Scale (Abraham and Lindsay, 1990). These results support the critical role for language in school attainments of 8-year-old children and further highlight the importance of identifying both the particular deficiencies in language and the tasks that the child is required to complete. Not all children scored outwith the norm for decoding and comprehension. However, clarifying this variation in the literacy skills of language impaired children has important implications for intervention. Evidence from longitudinal studies goes some way to addressing this issue.

Prospective studies of language and reading

Scarborough and Dobrich (1990) followed up four children with early language delay who showed severe and broad impairments in syntactic, phonological and lexical production. Three of these four children experienced delays in literacy despite normal or near-normal language proficiency at the age of 5. However, it was not possible from the children's preschool language skills to predict the differential success of the single child. Their data are important firstly because they demonstrate that even when children's language improves sufficiently to fall within the normal range, and despite the range of language measures, it was not possible to predict the reason only one child was successful and the others were not. One of the major limitations of the study is the size of the sample. A sample size of 4 is insufficient from which to predict differential success more generally.

Beitchman *et al.* (1996) report the results of a much larger study and in this case, since it was a community sample, there are comparative data with children who were not experiencing difficulties at five years of age. Their results demonstrate a link between the categories of language difficulties they identified when the children were 5 (see discussion in section 3.1) and the nature of their language problems and educational attainments at 12:5. The children in the high overall and the poor articulation group were functioning within the norm for both reading and spelling at 12:5. In contrast both the poor comprehension and the low overall groups scored lower, with the children in the low overall group fairing worse. However, even the low overall group had a mean standard score within the average range (86). No analyses of profiles of reading are available and the failure to document the nature of the children's language problems is a major limitation in drawing implications from this study.

It can be argued that because of the measures used by Beitchman *et al.* (1996) they fail to capture patterns of performance for children with specific speech and language problems. In contrast Stothard, Snowling, Bishop, Chipchase and Kaplan (1998) followed up 71 adolescents identified with speech and language impairment at age 4. When these children were initially followed up at age 5:6 the language problems of a significant proportion had resolved (Bishop and Edmundson, 1987). Non-verbal IQ was an important prognostic factor. There was a good outcome on language measures for 44% of the children with specific language impairment (normal non-verbal ability) but only for 11% of the general delay group. Further testing of this sample at 8:6 found that those with a good outcome performed normally on reading and spelling tasks (Bishop and Adams, 1990). At 15-16 the resolved SLI group showed few differences with their matched peers. They obtained slightly lower scores on tests of expressive and receptive vocabulary, picture naming and reception of grammar but they did show significant deficits on tasks tapping verbal short-term memory and phonological skills. Moreover they obtained significantly lower reading scores than their matched peers despite their similar language scores (mean composite standard score on the reading measure was 94). The persistent SLI group obtained significantly lower scores on all oral language measures in comparison with their matched controls and were experiencing significant problems with reading (mean composite standard score on the reading measure of 69). This long-term detrimental effect of persistent oral language impairments on reading and spelling has been noted in other well-designed studies (Goulandris, Snowling and Walker, 2000).

In an attempt to pinpoint causal factors more precisely a number of studies have narrowed the focus of the specific population that was investigated. In this vein Rhea Paul and her colleagues in Oregon investigated the implications of specific expressive delays. Paul (1996) reported that over 70% of children with a history of language delay had moved into the normal range of expressive language by kindergarten and even those who had not were able to function at the low end of the range on school achievement. Over 80% of children with a history of expressive delay had moved into the normal range of expressive language and school achievement by second grade and even those who continued to have immature expressive language did not differ significantly from peers with normal language histories in either reading comprehension or reading recognition. Of course it remains to be seen whether these children will have problems in adolescence as the Stothard *et al.* (1998) sample did, although a group of adolescents with resolved language difficulties did not have significant problems in the Goulandris *et al.* (2000) study.

The results from Bird, Bishop and Freeman (1995) from a study of 31 children with expressive phonological impairments present a rather different picture. The majority (24/31) of the children had significant literacy problems when followed up at 7:6 irrespective of whether the children also had broader language difficulties. The two measures that revealed significant differences between the children with good and poor literacy outcome were non-verbal scores on two WISC subscales and initial expressive phonology. That is those who did well, had milder phonological problems and were above average on non-verbal abilities.

The role of the speech processing system in reading attainment is complex. Stackhouse (2000) has argued that a developmentally intact speech processing system is *necessary* to develop language normally and is the foundation for written language development. Yet her own data make it clear that there is no simple relationship. The critical factor appears to be whether phonological representations are intact. Speech problems alone are less likely to lead to later literacy problems as both Paul (1996) and Stackhouse's (2000) data would suggest.

Examinations of children's performance on specific linguistic measures provide further evidence of the need to profile the children's language skills. Magnusson and Naucler (1990) found that measures of syntactic production and language comprehension administered to children with speech and language impairments before they entered school were related to reading achievement in grade1, but the best predictors were not standardised tests but measures of metalinguistic ability specifically phonological awareness. In a comparison of the phonological, lexical and syntactic skills of a sample of reading impaired and language impaired children Kamhi and Catts (1986) found considerable similarities in the difficulties that they experienced. The language impaired children performed worse than the reading impaired children on only three measures, all involving word and sentence repetition. Thus, their results suggest that children's mastery or lack of mastery of specific syntactic structures and word meanings will be reflected in their understanding of what they read or in the lexicon and grammar of written language.

Catts and Kamhi (1999) summarize preliminary results of a study of 225 language impaired children (half with average or above non-verbal IQs and half with moderately low non-verbal IQs). By the time the children had reached second grade approximately 52% of the total sample of children with language impairment performed one or more standard deviations below the mean on a composite measure of reading comprehension whereas 44% scored one or more standard deviations below the mean on a composite measure of word recognition. Both the severity of language difficulties and the degree of non-verbal deficit accounted for independent amounts of the variance.

The results of these studies raise a number of important questions (see also chapters by Elbro and Scarborough). Firstly there is strong evidence of the link between speech and language difficulties and early literacy skills, yet a significant proportion (precise figures depend on the study) of children at this point are still functioning within the norm. Secondly, there is supportive evidence from a number of the studies that average non-verbal intelligence may act as a moderator variable. Yet the interpretation of this result is complicated. Firstly, it may be that for children with milder problems their average non-verbal abilities can go some way to compensate for their language problems. Children with poor non-verbal skills and other language deficits may not be able to implement non alphabetic strategies. Alternatively it may be that in those studies where non-verbal IQ acts as a moderator variable the tests did not tap the non-verbal deficits that are characteristic of children with language problems (Johnston, 1994; Kamhi, 1981). Further, the age of the children is important. For example, pre-school children with specific speech and language difficulties may not show evidence of impaired non-verbal functioning because of the particular processes tested and developmental opportunity, while older children may produce evidence of impaired non-verbal functioning either because the demands of the tests have changed or because their limited language has impacted on their ability and experiences in other domains. Finally the Kamhi and Catts (1986) comparison between children with specific speech and language difficulties and specific literacy difficulties raises the issue of whether these populations should be viewed as the same, overlapping or separate?

Converging evidence

An alternative approach to those studies that identify children with language problems are studies that consider reading disabilities and associated language problems. Of course demonstrating that children with reading difficulties have language difficulties is not sufficient since it does not demonstrate that the language problems are causally related to reading problems. The language difficulties may be the consequence of the reading problem. Children who read less have less access to vocabulary, syntactic constructions and complex text. Studies that examine children who are at risk of reading problems provide more powerful evidence. Menyuk *et al.* (1991) in a study of children at risk of reading disabilities found that the best predictors of reading achievement were metalinguistic measures including phonological awareness although other measures of language proficiency were significantly associated with reading scores. Such results concur with the Magnusson and Naucler (1990) results cited above.

Scarborough (1990) in a seminal study of early dyslexics examined the role of language processing deficits in the etiology of reading difficulties. In this study syntactic differences among 2-year-olds corresponded most closely with the children's eventual outcomes but phonological production was also substantially impaired in the children who were later identified as poor readers.

Snyder and Downey (1991) evaluated the relationship between a broad range of language measures and the reading skills of 93 reading disabled and 93 typically developing children between the ages of 8 and 14. Their results serve to highlight the importance of a) considering developmental changes in language and literacy and b) elucidating how different kinds of oral language skills relate to reading performance at different points in time. Both the younger and older groups were deficient in word-decoding and there was little evidence to suggest that the older group had improved markedly. These difficulties had persisted over time although the children had received phonics based support. The children's comprehension performance also demonstrates links with oral language skills but the pattern of results is important. Both for the younger and older groups the predictors of reading success differed between the typically developing group and the reading disabled group. For example, for the younger reading disabled children both naming time and naming accuracy accounted for variance in reading comprehension whereas for the typically developing group differences in comprehension were primarily accounted for by a sentence completion measure. For the older reading disabled group the oral language skills that contributed were discourse processing scores, suggesting that these older children were compensating for their poor decoding skills by making greater use of top-down processes.

Individual differences in linguistic comprehension appear to be one of the best predictors of discourse-level contextual facilitation (Rego and Bryant, 1993). Further Nation and Snowling (1998b) have argued that it is comprehension rather than word-level semantic skills that are critical. They suggest that this is because listening skills/comprehension captures variance in syntactic as well as semantic skills. A clear prediction from these data is that children who have difficulties with oral language comprehension will have added difficulties with reading since they will not have recourse to a range of higher order inferencing skills which would potentially assist them when decoding becomes difficult. Moreover, such difficulties may not be evident in the initial stages of reading. This conclusion is substantiated by a study of 56 children with speech language impairments by Catts (1993). He found that the difficulties of the subjects with speech and language difficulties were observed in measures of word recognition in first and second grade and a measure of comprehension in second grade. Standardised measures of semantic-syntactic abilities accounted for differences in reading comprehension above that accounted for by phonology and rapid naming. As was the case with the assessment of language, a critical issue is when and how reading is measured and whether metalinguistic skills are tapped.

Gallagher, Frith and Snowling (2000) provide important supportive evidence about the key role of language in later literacy skills. These authors traced the early language skills in a group of children who were at genetic risk of dyslexia from the age of 3. Their literacy skills were measured at 6 where two groups were identified – literacy normal and literacy delayed. The children who were delayed in their literacy skills at 6 showed deficits in the majority of language domains assessed at 3 including vocabulary, expressive language, rhyme knowledge, digit span, letter knowledge and non-word repetition. The two groups did not differ on measures of non-verbal ability or speech motor articulation. Their results indicate that at age 6 the children's earlier speech and language measures and letter knowledge contributed independent sources of variance to literacy skill. The authors argue that children at risk of literacy delay experience specific difficulties in learning letter names and sounds.

Studies that compare these two populations and explore the language skills of children at risk of reading confirm the link between oracy and literacy. Further, they raise issues about the timing of measures of literacy and oracy with respect to the child's age. A general trend from the data is the importance of comprehension and the enduring impact of phonological problems. Although the children as a group are at risk there is much variability within the population (Bishop and Adams, 1990). Two major gaps in our understanding are evident. Firstly, without detailed analyses of the children's performance on particular reading tasks and evidence of how common these problems are across the different subgroups of language impaired children we are in a poor position to identify causal variables and thereby predict developmental outcomes. Secondly, unless we consider the wider implications of specific speech and language difficulties we may be failing to identify important variables which impact on performance and abilities to access the curriculum.

THE WAYS IN WHICH SPECIFIC SPEECH AND LANGUAGE DIFFICULTIES IMPOSE BARRIERS TO BECOMING LITERATE

Early experiences

As we have seen, children with specific speech and language difficulties have a range of other problems in addition to language. In this section we outline the ways in which these problems may affect their later experiences with reading. For example, young children's communicative environment and exposure to books and reading may affect early language skills and future reading. Children with language difficulties may be missing out on a range of literacy experiences. Much emphasis is placed nowadays on early book reading. Mogford-Bevan and Summersall (1997) have shown that there are difficulties in book reading for parents of children (2:6– 3:9) with language comprehension delays. Picture book reading occurs significantly less often in these dyads. This is despite adequate opportunities. Parents found the experiences unrewarding and there was a gradient of success in picture book reading depending on the severity of the language problem. Bornstein, Haynes and Painter (1998) have further demonstrated a role both for child-based and mother-based factors in the development of early vocabulary. If mothers of children with specific language difficulties are facing particular problems this will have detrimental effects on their children's preschool experiences. A range of early intervention projects aim to address this issue (Johansson, 1994; Manolson, 1983). Data from Gillam and Johnston (1985) indicates that other areas of preliteracy may be vulnerable in children with specific language problems. The preschool children in their study had difficulties with aspects of print awareness suggesting that even before reading these children were at a disadvantage.

Behavioural and emotional problems

The increased incidence of both behavioural and emotional disorders among children with language delay (Baker and Cantwell, 1987; Beitchman *et al.*, 1996; Silva *et al.*, 1987) raises further problems. Research suggests that children who are identified with attention deficit hyperactivity disorder (ADHD) are distinct from those with reading problems (Shaywitz, Fletcher and Shaywitz, 1994). Nonetheless increased rates of attention problems will reduce the children's opportunities to benefit from the implicit and explicit support to develop literacy skills. Recent work by Adams *et al.* (1999) has highlighted the importance of assessing both cognition and behaviour when planning the management of children with reading difficulties. Their study demonstrated a particularly high association between reading difficulties and children reported as hyperactive. Four per cent of the variance in concurrent reading attainment was accounted for by the teachers' ratings of behaviour even after the effects of IQ were controlled. In our own study (Lindsay and Dockrell, 2000) parents' ratings of their children's behaviour problems was predicted by both their language comprehension and their reading comprehension.

A recent study by Tomblin, Zhang, Buckwalter and Catts (2000) provides further evidence for the cooccurence of reading and behavioural difficulties among children with specific language impairment. They found that 52% of the language impaired group in second grade had a reading disability and 28,9% had behavioral disorder, in both cases the rates were significantly higher than average controls. They also examined the three-way interaction and found that the risk for behavioural difficulties in children with specific language impairment appeared to be related to their reading status; that is, children with specific language impairment have greater risks of behavioural difficulties owing to their associated reading difficulties. This study, therefore, suggests that reading and behavioural difficulties are not only independently related to language impairment, but that there is an interaction, with reading acting as a mediating factor, at least at second grade. Such results add weight to the contention that access to the curriculum will be impaired both independently by the language, reading and behavioural difficulties, but also that there are important associations which are additive in their impact. On the other hand, children who develop reading competence despite language difficulties are less likely to have behaviour difficulties.

Vocabulary and naming

The reduced receptive and expressive vocabulary of many of these children will restrict the range of materials that will be accessible. When children learn to read new words they typically already know something about the meaning of these words. This assumption may be misguided when working with children with specific speech and language difficulties. Limited vocabulary may serve to restrict the range of guesses that a child can make about a word that is difficult to decode. This has the potential of leading to further reductions in vocabulary since reading is an important way of increasing both vocabulary and general knowledge.

Word-finding difficulties are associated with reading problems linked to retrieval. Children with reading difficulties have been found to be slower on rapid naming tasks (Denckla and Rudel, 1976; Wolf, 1991). Our investigations of children with word-finding difficulties (Dockrell, Messer and George, 2001) indicate that these children can be on average a ¼ second slower in naming objects that they correctly identify in comprehension tasks than both chronological and naming age controls. Thus, if speed of naming is, as has been argued, related to reading independently of phonological awareness (Catts, 1993) then there is a strong likelihood that these children will experience difficulties in reading. However, a direct test of the relationship between word-finding and literacy did not result in a clear and inevitable link. Murphy, Messer and Dockrell (submitted) demonstrated that over 60% of the children with objectively identified word finding problems did not have difficulties with decoding and those that did have problems were more likely to have associated problems with comprehension as well. One of the limitations imposed by poor comprehension skills is the ability to use context to aid decoding and thus subsequent comprehension (Nation and Snowling, 1998a).

Phonology

Phonology is the major route for word-decoding and if there is impaired phonological processing this puts children at risk for literacy problems. A constant theme throughout the longitudinal and cross-sectional studies has been the powerful role of phonological difficulties in restricting the children's reading progress. Large differences have been found between good and poor readers in phonological memory and this mirrors the large differences that are commonly reported between the phonological memory skills of language impaired and typically developing children (Gathercole and Baddeley, 1990; Montgomery, 1995). A number of studies have examined language impaired children's ability to process phonological information. In the cross-sectional study reported in section 5 above (Dockrell and Lindsay, 1998; 2002) we found that over 50% of the sample of 69 children scored below the 15th centile on all phonological measures assessed by a phonological assessment battery (PHAB). Kamhi, Lee and Nelson (1985) found that language impaired children were poorer at dividing words into syllables, Dollaghan (1987) found that Language impaired children had more difficulty than age controls encoding phonological information of new words. Moreover, some authors have attributed the delays in naming of these children to retrieving phonological information from long-term storage (Leonard *et al.*, 1983). One of the most detailed studies of the language and reading skill of children with specific language difficulties has been carried out by Joffe (1997). Her results indicate that children with specific language impairments have great difficulty in the manipulation of phonological segments and are impaired compared with CA matches and LA matches. The children were also poorer than LA matches at reading nonwords, suggesting that their limited knowledge of the sound system restricts their use of grapheme, phoneme correspondence rules. A critical distinction needs to be made between poor phonological skills and poor phonological awareness as predictors of literacy outcomes. There is now consistent evidence that speech articulation problems on their own do not lead to literacy problems.

Syntax

Children's ability to produce and understand grammatical utterances has played a central role in our understanding of the oral language difficulties of children with specific speech and language difficulties. Why might such skills impact on reading? Two possible analyses must be considered. Firstly, the children's oral language measures might be related to their reading achievements: alternatively it may be the children's syntactic awareness which is the critical link. Some children with grammatical problems have significant difficulties in comprehension when grammar is used to signal contrasts in meaning. Given that written language is frequently low in redundancy such tasks might well place added demands on the children's processing of the language. Scarborough's data (1990; 1991) discussed earlier support the view that children who develop reading difficulties can have lower syntactic abilities than children who become normal readers later. In Scarborough's work, early syntactic abilities accounted for some unique variance in later reading scores. In contrast measures of oral grammatical competence (Test of the Reception of Grammar and Test for Examining Expressive Morphology) used by Joffe (1997) did not predict the reading or spelling of the children with specific language impairments. The age and criteria for selecting participants in these two contrasting studies are worthy of note and may suggest avenues for future research. Scarborough's sample were identified at 2:6 as being at risk of reading deficit because of their family history and were followed until the age of 8. In contrast Joffe's sample were identified at a mean age of 7:2 and were children with specific language impairments. These children were followed for a further 21 months. Assessments of younger children are likely to rely on syntactic measures and there may well be greater levels of differentiation at this point. Nonetheless Joffe's (1997) results question acceptance of simple causal connection between grammatical competence and literacy difficulties.

Evidence with normally developing children has demonstrated a strong causal connection between semantic and syntactic awareness and reading and spelling development (Rego and Bryant, 1993; Tumner, 1990). As mentioned previously metalinguistic skills feature as an important variable for the reading ability of children with specific speech and language difficulties. Joffe's data support this view. She demonstrated that syntactic awareness measures accounted for a significant amount of the variance in the reading and spelling of single words, and non-words, as well as prose reading and reading comprehension in her sample of language impaired children. These measures did not do so consistently across all her tests and times of measurement.

Comprehension and communication

Children with specific speech and language difficulties often have problems with comprehension and inferencing (see Bishop, 1997 for a review). Phonological difficulties have been considered the core of reading difficulties for some time now. However, there is an increasing indication that language comprehension skills are also important. Typically the strong contribution of verbal IQ (which includes language comprehension skills) has been controlled for statistically in reading studies but if we are to understand the causes of reading failure generally we need to look more broadly. It is argued that children who have comprehension difficulties have fewer resources for deciphering unfamiliar words and making inferences from texts (Nation and Snowling, 1998a; 1998b). Even when comprehension appears to be within the normal range on standardised tests difficulties with inferencing can remain. There is some suggestion that problems in story comprehension cannot simply be attributed to difficulties in understanding grammatical structure (Bishop and Adams, 1992). Interestingly the children in this study seem to be poor at story comprehension even when the stories were presented pictorially. These difficulties have particular ramifications for the comprehension of written texts. When children experience difficulties with reading comprehension these difficulties are not restricted to reading alone (Oakhill, 1982; 1983; Hulme and Snowling, 1992). Rather the reading comprehension problems are in line with other comprehension skills suggesting that the children are experiencing a global deficit in language.

Children with specific speech and language difficulties also experience communication breakdowns where problems occur in formulation and result in dysfluency (McLachlan and Chapman, 1988). Thus, there is a need to reduce linguistic demands for these children to support more fluent and increased coherence in narratives. A failure to understand and be understood could adversely affect teacher-student communication and thereby reduce the effectiveness of instruction.

Summary

In this section we have considered a range of different ways in which the language problems experienced by children with specific speech and language difficulties will impact on their ability to develop fluent literacy skills. Semantics, syntactics, metalinguistic ability, and attention must all be considered as elements of the reading process with phonological factors if we are to develop an accurate picture of the link between language and literacy. A critical issue is the time and type of assessment of language and reading measures. Yet if we are to target intervention appropriately the causal links must be established.

CONCLUSIONS

Literacy and language skills are related to a large degree, but we have argued in this chapter that teasing out the relationship between specific language difficulties and literacy skills is not straightforward. Language comprises a number of subskills which are interactively related with respect to children's development, probably in a hierarchical and time-ordered progression. However, children's language difficulties may be characterised by a number of different profiles, including various specific and also more general difficulties. This is also the case with literacy. For example, there is firm evidence for the importance of phonological skills in the development of literacy, and for children with difficulties in development in this domain having literacy problems. However, there is increasing evidence for the importance of difficulties at the word and higher levels. An important area for future investigations is to examine the role of different language abilities in explaining individual differences in word recognition and comprehension in children with speech and language difficulties: studies need to go further than descriptions.

Language problems are closely associated with literacy difficulties, but the interaction is complex. In some cases the language-based difficulties appear to be causally related to later problems, and this will be the major direction of causal relationship. This argument is a variant of Frith's (1997) model that has language system abnormality as an element at the biological level of a three stage causal modelling of dyslexia. However, our position is that the impact of language difficulties is broader than on phonological abilities, important though these are. There is also evidence for a two-way interaction, for example with impaired literacy leading to reduced opportunities to develop language. Furthermore, it is likely that there is also an interaction with development in that different aspects of language will be of importance for literacy at different stages. This is not to argue an absolute and clear- cut stage model, but rather a more dynamic model with relative importance of different factors. For example, while accuracy of letter or word recognition is a pre-requisite for the development of increased fluency and generalisation (e.g. recognition in different contexts), a broader experience may aid development of accuracy and fluency. Furthermore, the child's other strengths (e.g. non-verbal ability) or associated difficulties (e.g. distractibility, impaired self esteem) are important mediating factors. There is, therefore, no a priori reason to assume that all children's difficulties will be the same.

The implications of this analysis include the importance of pre-school intervention to aid children with developmental language difficulties, but the necessity to acknowledge a range of intervention foci depending on the nature of the child's difficulties. Secondly, children's language abilities and their early and emergent literacy skills should be investigated at school entry, and appropriate modifications to the early years curriculum and its delivery should be effected. In England it has been compulsory since September 1998 for all maintained schools to implement a baseline assessment scheme accredited by the Qualifications and Curriculum Authority (QCA). This is potentially an important opportunity to identify language difficulties not recognised pre-school, and early identification was one of the underlying purposes for the scheme. However, the current system is seriously deficient in the lack of requirement for evidence of the technical quality of the schemes used (Lindsay and Desforges, 1998). Nevertheless, the schemes will provide an opportunity to sensitise teachers to the issues, and require a limited assessment of every child: the danger, of course, is that poor schemes will produce unacceptable hit rates, with high numbers of false negatives.

The challenge for the future is to continue to identify the relationships between specific speech and language difficulties and problems with literacy, but at a more analytical level. This research agenda must be complemented by interventions which are derived from the evidence of causal associations, and by evaluations of identification and assessment procedures, and the intervention programmes which are based thereon. In this approach it is important to recognise the need to intervene at the level of both language and literacy, but with specific interventions, which may vary at different stages of the child's development. There are, therefore, implications for multi-professional collaboration in assessment, planning and implementing programmes by teachers, speech and language therapists, and of course parents.

REFERENCES

Abraham, J. E. and Lindsay, G. A. (1990). *Junior Rating Scale*. Windsor: NFER-Nelson.

Adams, J. W., Snowling, M. J., Hennessy, S. M. and Kind, P. (1999). Problems of behaviour, reading and arithmetic: Assessments of comorbidity using the Strengths and Difficulties Questionnaire. *British Journal of Educational Psychology, 69*, 571-585.

Aram, D., Morris, R. and Hall, N. (1992). The Validity of Discrepancy Criteria for Identifying Children with Developmental Language Disorders. *Journal of Learning Disabilities, 25*, 549-554.

Aram, D. and Nation, J. E. (1975). Patterns of language and behaviour in children with developmental language disorders. *Journal of Speech and Hearing Research, 18*, 229-241

Baker, L. and Cantwell, D. P. (1987). A prospective psychiatric follow-up of children with speech/language disorders. *Journal of the American Academy of Adolescent Psychiatry, 26*, 546-553.

Bates, E., Dale, P. and Thal, D. (1995). Individual differences and their implications for theories of language development. In P. Fletcher and B. MacWhinney (Eds), *Handbook of child language* (pp.96-151). Oxford: Basil Blackwell.

Beitchman, J., Hood, J. Rochon, J. Peterson, M., Mantini, T. Majumdar, S. (1989). Empirical classification of speech/language impairment in children. I Identification of speech and language categories. *Journal of the American Academy of Child and Adolescent Psychiatry, 28*, 112-117.

Beitchman, J., Nair, R., Clegg, M. and Patel, P. G. (1986). Prevalence of speech and language disorders in 5-year-old kindergarten children in the Ottawa-Careton region. *Journal of Speech and Hearing Disorders, 51*, 98-110.

Beitchman, J., Wilson, B., Brownlie, E. B., Walters, H. and Lancee, W. (1996). Long-term consistency in speech/language profiles: Developmental and academic outcomes. *Journal American Academy of Child and Adolescent Psychiatry, 35*, 804-814.

Benasich, A. A., Curtiss, S. and Tallal, P. (1993). Language, learning, and behavioural disturbances in childhood: a longitudinal perspective. *Journal of the American Academy of Child and Adolescent Psychiatry, 32*, 585-594.

Bernstein, L. E. and Stark, R. E. (1985). Speech-Perception Development In Language-Impaired Children – A 4-Year Follow-Up-Study. *Journal of Speech and Hearing Disorders, 50*, 21-30.

Bird, J. and Bishop, D. V. M (1992). Perception and awareness of phonemes on phonologically impaired children. *European Journal of Disorders of Communication, 27*, 289-311.

Bird, J., Bishop, D. V. M. and Freeman, N. (1995). Phonological awareness and literacy development in children with expressive phonological impairments. *Journal of Speech and Hearing Research, 38,* 446-462.

Bishop, D. V. M. (1989). *Test of Reception of Grammar*, 2nd Edition. (University of Manchester, The Author, Age & Cognitive Performance Research Centre).

Bishop, D. V. M. (1994). Grammatical errors in specific language impairment: competence or performance limitation? *Applied Psycholinguistics, 15,* 507-549.

Bishop, D. V. M. (1997). Uncommon Understanding: Development and Disorders of Language Comprehension in Children. Hove, East Sussex: Psychology Press.

Bishop, D. V. M. and Adams, C. (1989). Conversational characteristics of children with semantic-pragmatic disorder: II What features lead to a judgement of inappropriacy? *British Journal of Disorders of Communication, 24,* 241-263.

Bishop, D. V. M. and Adams, C. (1990). A prospective study of the relationship between specific language impairment, phonological disorders and reading Retardation. *Journal of Child Psychology and Psychiatry, 31,* 1027-1050.

Bishop, D. V. M. and Adams, C. (1992). Comprehension problems in children with specific language impairment: literal and inferential meaning. *Journal of Speech and Hearing Research, 35,* 119-129.

Bishop, D. V. M. and Edmundson, A. (1987). Language-impaired four-year-olds: distinguishing transient from persistent impairment. *Journal of Speech and Hearing Disorders, 52,* 156-173.

Bishop, D. V. M. and Rosenbloom, L. (1987). Classification of childhood language disorders. In W. Yule, M. Rutter (Eds) *Language Development and Disorders. Clinics in Developmental Medicine* (double issue), nos. 101-2. London: MacKeith Press.

Bishop, D. V. M., North, T., Donlan, C. (1996). Nonword repetition as a behavioural marker for inherited language impairment: Evidence from a twin study. *Journal of Child Psychology and Psychiatry, 37,* 391-403.

Bishop, D. V. M., Bishop, S. J., Bright, P., James, C., Delaney, T. and Tallal, P. (1999). Different origin of auditory and phonological processing problems in children with language impairment: evidence from a twin study. *Journal of Speech, Language, and Hearing Research, 42,* 155-168.

Bornstein, M. H., Haynes, M. O. and Painter, K. M. (1998). Sources of child vocabulary competence: a multivariate model. *Journal of Child Language, 25,* 367-393.

Botting, N., Crutchley, A. and Conti-Ramsden, G. (1998). Educational transitions of seven-year-old children with specific language impairment in language units: a longitudinal study. *International Journal of Language and Communication Disorders, 33,* 177-197.

Catts, H. W. (1993). The relationship between speech-language impairments and reading disabilities. *Journal of Speech and Hearing Research, 36,* 948-958.

Catts, H. and Kamhi, A. (1999). *Language and Reading Disabilities.* Boston: Allyn and Bacon.

Catts, H. W., Fey, M. and Tomblin, B. (1997). Language basis of reading disabilities. Paper presented at the society for the Scientific Study of Reading. Chicago, IL. (cited in Catts, H. and Kamhi, A., 1999) *Language and Reading Disabilities.* Boston: Allyn and Bacon.

Chiat, S. and Hirson, A. (1987). From conceptual intention to utterance: A study of impaired output in a child with developmental dysphasia. *British Journal of Disorders of Communication, 22,* 37-64.

Clahsen, H. (1989). The grammatical characterization of developmental dysphasia. *Linguistics, 27,* 897-920.

Conti-Ramsden, G. and Botting, N. (1999). Classification of children with specific language impairment: Longitudinal considerations. *Journal of Speech, Language and Hearing Research, 42,* 1195 -1204.

Conti-Ramsden, G., Botting, N., Simkin, Z. and Knox, E. (2001). Follow-up of children attending infant language units: Outcomes at 11 years of age. *International Journal of Language and Communication Disorders, 36,* 207-219.

Conti-Ramsden, G., Crutchley, A. C. and Botting, N. (1997). The extent to which psychometric tests differentiate subgroups of children with Specific Language Impairment. *Journal of Speech, Language and Hearing Research, 40,* 765-777.

Conti-Ramsden, G., Hutcheson, G. D. and Grove, J. (1995). Contingency and Breakdown: Children with Specific Language Impairment and their conversations with mothers and fathers. *Journal of Speech and Hearing Research, 38*, 1290-1302.

Curtiss, S., Katz, W. and Tallal, P. (1992). Delay versus deviance in the language acquisition of language-impaired children. *Journal of Speech and Hearing Research, 35*, 373-83.

Dale, P., Simonoff, E., Bishop, D. V. M., Eley, T., Oliver, B. Price, T., Purcell, Stevenson, J. and Plomin, R. (1998). Genetic influence on language delay in two-year-old children. *Nature Neuroscience, 1*, 324-328.

Denckla, M. B. and Rudel, R. G. (1976). Rapid automatized naming (RAN): Dyslexic differentiated from other learning disabilities. *Neuropsychologia, 14*, 471-479.

Dockrell, J. E. (2001). Assessing language skills in preschool children. *Child Psychology and Psychiatry Review, 6*, 74-85.

Dockrell, J. E. and Lindsay, G. (1998). The ways in which children's speech and language difficulties impact on access to the curriculum. *Child Language Teaching and Therapy, 14*, 117-133.

Dockrell, J. E. and Lindsay, G. (2000). Meeting the needs of children with specific speech and language difficulties. *European Journal of Special Needs Education, 15*, 24-41.

Dockrell, J. E. and Lindsay, G. (2002) The Impact of Specific Language Difficulties on Learning and Literacy. In Centre for Educational Research (Ed). Learning and Instruction: Recent research approaches. Athens: KEE.

Dockrell, J. E., Messer, D. and George, R. (2001). Patterns of naming objects and patterns in children with word finding difficulties. *Language and Cognitive Processes, 16*, 261-286.

Dockrell, J. E., George, R., Lindsay, G. and Roux, J. (1997). Professionals understanding of specific language impairments – Implications for assessment and identification. *Educational Psychology in Practice, 13*, 27-35.

Dockrell, J. E., Messer, D., George, R. and Wilson, G. (1998). Children with word-finding diffculties - prevalance, presentation and naming problems. *International Journal of Language and Communication Disorders, 33*, 445-454.

Dollaghan, C. (1987). Fast mapping of normal and language-impaired children. *Journal of speech and hearing disorders, 52*, 218-222.

Elliott, C. D., Smith, P. & Mcculloch, K. (1997). *The British Ability Scales II.* (Windsor, NFER-Nelson).

Felsenfeld, S. and Plomin, R. (1997). Epidemiological and offspring analyses of developmental speech disorders using data from the Colorado adoption project. *Journal of Speech Language and Hearing Research, 40*, 778-791.

Fey, M., Long, S. and Cleave, P. (1994). Reconsideration of IQ criteria in the definition of specific language impairment. In R. Watkins and M. Rice (Eds) *Specific Language Impairment in children.* (pp.161-178) Baltimore: Paul Brookes.

Fletcher, P. (1991). Subgroups in school-age language-impaired children. In P. Fletcher and D. Hall (Eds) *Specific Speech and Language Disorders in Children* (pp.152-165) London: Whurr.

Fletcher, P. and Ingham, R. (1995). Grammatical impairment. In P. Fletcher and B. MacWhinney (Eds) *The handbook of child language* (pp.603-622) Cambridge, MA: Blackwell.

Fredrickson, N., Frith, U. and Reason, R. (1997). Phonological Assessment Battery (PHAB). Windsor, NFER Nelson.

Frith, U. (1997). Brain, mind and behaviour in dyslexia. In C. Hulme and M. Snowling (Eds) *Dyslexia: Biology, Cognition and Intervention* (pp.1-19). London: Whurr.

Gallagher, A., Frith, U. and Snowling, M. (2000). Precursors of literacy delay among children at genetic risk of dyslexia. *Journal of Child Psychology and Psychiatry, 41*, 203-213.

Gathercole, S. E. and Baddeley, A. D. (1990). Phonological memory deficits in language-disordered children: Is there a causal connection? *Journal of Memory and Language, 29*, 336-360.

Gillam, R. B. and Johnston, J. R. (1985). Development Of Print Awareness In Language-Disordered Preschoolers. *Journal of Speech and Hearing Research, 28*, 521-526.

Gopnik, M. (1997). Language deficits and genetic factors. *Trends in Cognitive Sciences, 1*, 5-9.

Goulandris, N., Snowling, M. J. and Walker, I. (2000). Is dyslexia a form of specific language impairment? A comparison of dyslexic and language-impaired children as adolescents. *Annals of Dyslexia, 50*, 103-120.

Hulme, C. and Snowling M. (1992). Deficits in Output Phonology - An Explanation of Reading Failure. *Cognitive Neuropsychology, 9(1)*, 47-72.

Joanisse, M. and Seidenberg, M. (1998). Specific language impairment: a deficit in grammar of processing. *Trends in Cognitive Sciences, 2*, 240-247.

Joffe, V. L. (1997). The relationship between linguistic awareness and reading and spelling development in children with specific language impairment. D.Phil. Thesis, Oxford University.

Johansson, I. (1994). Language Development in Children with Special Needs – Performative Communication, translated by E. Thomas. London: Jessica Kingsley.

Johnston, J. R. (1991). Questions about cognition in children with specific language impairment. In J. F. Miller (ed.) *Research on Child Language Disorders: A Decade of Progress*. Austin, Tx: Pro-Ed.

Johnston, J. (1994). Cognitive abilities of children with language impairment. In R. Watkins and M. Rice (Eds) *Specific language impairment in children* (pp. 107-121). Baltimore: Brookes.

Johnston, J. and Kamhi, A. (1984). Syntactic and semantic aspects of the utterances of language-impaired children: The same can be less. *Merrill-Palmer Quarterly, 30*, 65-85.

Johnston, R. B., Stark, R., Mellits, D. and Tallal, P. (1981). Neurological status of language-impaired and normal children. *Annals of Neurology, 10*, 159-163.

Kamhi, A. G. (1981). Non-Linguistic Symbolic and Conceptual Abilities of Language-Impaired and Normally Developing-Children. *Journal of Speech and Hearing Research, 24*, 446-453.

Kamhi, A. G. (1986). Toward and understanding of developmental language and reading disorders. *Journal of Speech and Hearing Disorders, 51*, 337-347.

Kamhi, A. G. and Catts, H. W. (1986). Toward an Understanding of Developmental Language and Reading Disorders *Journal of Speech and Hearing Disorders, 51*, 337-347.

Kamhi, A., Lee, R. and Nelson, L. (1985). Word, syllable and sound awareness in language-disordered children. *Journal of Speech and Hearing Disorders, 50*, 207-213.

Leonard, L. (1997). *Children with specific language impairments*. Cambridge, MA: MIT Press.

Leonard, L., McGregor, K. and Allen, G. (1992). Grammatical morphology and speech perception in children with specific language impairment. *Journal of Speech and Hearing Research, 35*, 1076-1085.

Leonard, L., Nippold, M., Kail. R. and Hale, C. (1983). Picture naming in language-impaired children. *Journal of Speech and Hearing Research, 26*, 609-616.

Lewis, B. A. and Thompson, L. A. (1992). A study of developmental speech and language disorders in twins. *Journal of Speech and Hearing Research, 35*, 1086-1094.

Lindsay, G. and Desforges, M. (1998). *Baseline Assessment: Practice, Problems and Possibilities*. London: David Fulton.

Lindsay, G. and Dockrell, J. E. (2000). The behaviour and self-esteem of children with specific speech and language difficulties. *British Journal of Educational Psychology, 70*, 583-601.

MacLachlan, B. and Chapman, R. (1988). Communication breakdowns in normal and language-learning disabled children's conversation and narration. *Journal of Speech and Hearing Disorders, 53*, 2-7.

Magnusson, E. and Naucler, K. (1990). Reading and spelling in language disordered children – linguistic and metalinguistic prerequisites report of a longitudinal study. *Clinical Linguistics and Phonetics, 4*, 49-61.

Magnusson, E. and Naucler, K. (1993). The development of linguistic awareness in language-disordered children. *First Language, 13*, 93-111.

Manolson, A. (1983). *It takes two to talk*. Toronto: Hanen Early Language Resource Centre.

McArthur, G. M., Hogben, J. H., Edwards, V. T., Heath, S. M. and Mengler, E. D. (2000). On the 'specifics' of Specific Reading Disability and Specific Language Impairment. *Journal of Child Psychiatry and Psychology, 41*, 869-874.

Menyuk, P., Chesick, M., Liebergott, J., Korngold, B., D'Agostino, R. and Belanger, A. (1991). Predicting reading problems in at-risk children. *Journal of Speech and Hearing Research, 34*, 893-903.

Mogford-Bevan, K. P. and Summersall, J. (1997). Emerging literacy in children with delayed speech and language. *Child Language Teaching and Therapy, 13*, 143-159.

Montgomery, J. (1995). Sentence comprehension in children with specific language impairment: the role of phonological working memory. *Journal of Speech and Hearing Research, 38*, 187-199.

Murphy, N., Messer, D. and Dockrell, J. (submitted) The relationship between naming and literacy in children with word-finding difficulties.

Nation, K. and Snowling, M. (1998a). Individual differences in contextual facilitation: evidence from dyslexia and poor reading comprehension. *Child Development, 69*, 996-1011.

Nation, K. and Snowling, M. (1998b). Semantic processing and the development of word recognition skills: Evidence from children with reading comprehension difficulties. *Journal of Memory and Language, 39*, 85-101.

Nippold, M. and Fey, S. (1983). Metaphoric understanding in preadolescents having a history of language acquisition difficulties. *Language, Speech and Hearing Services in Schools, 14*, 171-180.

Oakhill, J. (1982). Constructive Processes In Skilled and Less Skilled Comprehenders Memory for Sentences. *British Journal of Psychology, 73*, 13-20.

Oakhill, J. (1983). Instantiation In Skilled And Less Skilled Comprehenders. *Bulletin of the British Psychological Society, 36*, A21-A21.

Oetting, J., Rice, M. and Swank, L. (1995). Quick incidental learning (QUIL) of words by school-age children with and without a language impairment. *Journal of Speech and Hearing Research, 38*, 434-445.

Paul, R. (1996). Clinical implications of the natural history of slow expressive language development. *American Journal of Speech and Language Pathology, 5*, 5-21.

Plante, E. (1998). Criteria for SLI: The Stark and Tallal Legacy and Beyond. *Journal of Speech, Language and Hearing Research, 41*, 951-957.

Plante, E. and Vance, R. (1994). Selection of preschool language tests: A data-based approach. *Language Speech and Hearing Services, 25*, 15-24.

Rapin, I. and Allen, D. (1987). Developmental dysphasia and autism in pre-school children: Characteristics and subtypes. Proceedings of the first international symposium on specific speech and language difficulties. London: Association for All Speech Impaired Children.

Rego, L. L. and Bryant, P. E. (1993). The connection between phonological, syntactic and semantic skills and children's reading and spelling. *European Journal of Psychology of Education, 8*, 235-246.

Rice, M. L., Buhr, J. and Oetting, J. (1992). Specific-language-impaired children's quick incidental learning of words: The effect of a pause. *Journal of Speech and Hearing Research, 35*, 1040-1048.

Rice, M. L. and Wexler, K. (1996). A phenotype of specific language impairment: extended optional infinitives. In M. L. Rice (Ed.) *Towards a Genetics of Language* (pp.215-237). Mahwah, NJ: Lawrence Erlbaum.

Richman, N., Stevenson, J. and Graham, P. J. (1982). *Preschool to School: A Behavioural Study*. London: Academic Press.

Sawyer, D. J. (1992). Language abilities, reading acquisition, and developmental dyslexia: a discussion of hypothetical and observed relationships. *Journal of Learning Disabilities, 25*, 82-95.

Scarborough, H. S. (1990). Very early language deficits in dyslexic children. *Child Development, 61*, 1728-1743.

Scarborough, H. S. (1991). Early syntactic development of dyslexic children. *Annals of Dyslexia, 41*, 207-220.

Scarborough, H. S. and Dobrich, W. (1990). Development of children with early language delay. *Journal of Speech and Hearing Research, 33*, 70-83.

Shaywitz, S. E., Fletcher, J. M. and Shaywitz, B. A. (1994). Issues in the definition and classification of attention deficit disorder. *Topics in Language Disorders, 14*, 1-25.

Silva, P. A., Williams, S. M. and McGee, R. (1985). A longitudinal study of children with developmental language delay at age three: Later intelligence, reading and behaviour problems. *Developmental Medicine and Child Neurology, 29*, 630-640.

Silva, P. A., Williams, S. M. and McGee, R. (1987). A longitudinal study of children with developmental language delay at age three: Later intelligence, reading and behaviour problems. *Developmental Medicine and Child Neurology, 29*, 630-640.

Snowling, M.J. (1996). Contemporary Approaches to the teaching of reading. *Journal of Child Psychology and Psychiatry, 37*, 139-148.

Snyder, L. S. and Downey, D. M. (1991). The language reading relationship in normal and reading disabled children. *Journal of Speech and Hearing Research, 34*, 129-140.

Stackhouse, J. (2000). Barriers to Literacy Development in Children with Speech and Language Difficulties. In D. Bishop and L. Leonard (Eds) *Speech and Language Impairments in Children: Causes, Characteristics, Intervention and Outcome.* Hove: Psychology Press.

Stark, R. and Tallal, P. (1981). Selection of children with specific language deficits. *Journal of Speech and Hearing Disorders, 46,* 114-122.

Stark, R. E., Mellits, E. D. and Tallal, P. (1983). *Behavioural attributes of speech and language disorders.* New York: Academic Press.

Stone, C. A. and Connell, P. J. (1993). Induction of a visual symbolic rule in children with specific language impairment. *Journal of Speech and Hearing Research, 36,* 599-608.

Stothard, S. E., Snowling, M., Bishop, D. V., Chipchase, B. B. and Kaplan, C. A. (1998). Language-impaired preschoolers: a follow-up into adolescence. *Journal of Speech Language and Hearing, 41,* 407-418.

Sussman, J. (1993). Perception of formant cues to place of articulation in children with language impairments. *Journal of Speech and Hearing Research, 36,* 1286-1299.

Swisher, L., Plante, E. and Lowell, S. (1994). Nonlinguistic deficits of language-impaired children complicate the interpretation of their nonverbal IQ scores. *Language, Speech, and Hearing Services in the Schools, 25,* 235-240.

Tallal, P. (1990). Fine-grained discrimination deficits in language-learning impaired children are specific neither to the auditory modality nor to speech perception. *Journal of Speech and Hearing Research, 33,* 616-617.

Tallal, P., Stark, R. and Mellits, D. (1985). Identification of language impaired children on the basis of rapid perception and production skills. *Brain and Language, 25,* 314-322.

Tallal, P., Stark, R., Kallman, C. and Mellits, D. (1981). A reexamination of some nonverbal perceptual abilities of language-impaired and normal children as a function of age and sensory modality. *Journal of Speech and Hearing Research, 24,* 351-357.

Tallal, P., Miller, S. L., Bedi, G., Byma, G., Wang, X., Nagarajan, S. S., Schreiner, C., Jenkins, W. M. and Merzenich, M. M. (1996). Language Comprehension in Language-Learning Impaired Children Improved with Acoustically Modified Speech, *Science, 271,* 81-84.

Tomblin, J. B. and Buckwalter, P. R. (1998). Heritability and poor language achievement among twins. *Journal of Speech Language and Hearing Research, 41,* 188-199.

Tomblin, J. B., Records, N. L. and Zhang, X. Y. (1996). A system for the diagnosis of specific language impairment in kindergarten children. *Journal of Speech and Hearing Research, 39,* 1284-1294

Tomblin, J. B., Zhang, X., Buckwalter, P. and Catts, H. (2000). The association of reading disability, behavioral disorders and Language Impairment among second grade children. *Journal of Child Psychology and Psychiatry, 41,* 473-482.

Tumner, W. E. (1990). The role of language prediction skills in beginning reading. *New Zealand Journal of Educational Studies, 25,* 95-114.

van der Lely, H. and Stollwerck, L. (1997). Binding theory and specific language impairment in children. *Cognition, 62,* 245-290.

Vincent D. and de la Mare M. (1990). *Macmillan Individual Reading Analysis* (MIRA). London: Macmillan.

Werner, E. O. and Kresheck, J. D. (1983). SPELT-II The Structured Photographic Expressive Language Test II.

Wolf, M. (1991). The word retrieval deficit hypothesis and developmental dyslexia. *Learning and Individual Differences, 3,* 205-223.

(1994). Diagnostic and Statistical Manual of Mental Disorders, Fourth Edition (DSM-IV). American Psychiatric Press, Inc. (APPI).

Suggested further readings

Please see Table 1.

C10. Reading by Touch in Blind Children and Adults

SUSANNA MILLAR

ABSTRACT

Scripts for the blind use touch as a substitute for vision. A number of different systems have been proposed at various times. But braille is undoubtedly the script most commonly used by blind people throughout the world. It is taught to visually handicapped children in India, in Japan, in Russia, in all the countries of continental Europe, as well as in the English speaking world. Most studies of reading by blind children and adults have been on braille. Braille is, consequently, the main focus in this chapter. Two other systems, "Moon" (simplified capital letters), and the "optacon" (vibrotactile stimulation of the fingertip) are discussed briefly. But braille (characters based on a six point matrix) is of special interest for understanding how touch functions. This chapter considers how the perceptual and orthographic basis of a tactual reading system relates to the language which it is intended to convey, and how it is acquired.

INTRODUCTION

Scripts for the blind use touch as a substitute for vision. A number of different systems have been proposed at various times. But braille is undoubtedly the script most commonly used by blind people throughout the world. It is taught to visually handicapped children in India, in Japan, in Russia, in all the countries of continental Europe, as well as in the English speaking world. Most studies of reading by blind children and adults have been on braille. Braille is, consequently, the main focus in this chapter. Two other systems, 'Moon' (simplified capital letters), and the "optacon' (vibrotactile stimulation of the fingertip) are discussed briefly. But braille (characters based on a six point matrix) is of special interest for understanding how touch functions, and how the perceptual and orthographic basis of a tactual reading system relates to the language which it is intended to convey.

The prevalence of braille as the main tactual reading system is instructive. The script is very often criticised as too difficult to recognise and too complicated to learn. But, unlike most other systems, it was invented by a blind person and later

T. Nunes, P. Bryant (eds.), Handbook of Children's Literacy, 437–457.

teacher of the blind, Louis Braille, because he was dissatisfied with the embossed print letter shapes that he had been forced to learn as a child in nineteenth century France. His script uses dot patterns instead of shapes.

Reasons for the preference are only now beginning to be understood, as touch is becoming of interest in its own right. For a long time, the fact that physical shapes can be recognised by touch, as well as by vision, seemed sufficient for the tacit belief that what suits vision must suit touch.

The use of tactual shapes for reading is surprisingly recent. Interest in the education of blind people can be traced to the eighteenth century "enlightenment" in France, and particularly to the writings of the philosopher and encyclopaedist, Diderot (1751). Valentin Haüy (1745–1822), a professor at the Bureau Academique d'Ecriture in Paris, explicitly cited Diderot to support his assumption that the blind would be able to read by touch. Haüy produced a system of embossed print letters which he introduced to blind people in the institute for the handicapped in Paris. It seems likely that this was the reading system that Louis Braille so disliked when he was sent to the Institut Nationale des Jeunes Aveugles in Paris at the age of ten, in 1819.

Louis Braille's own system evidently owed something to a tactual punctiform code that had been invented for use by the army. The inventor demonstrated the code at the school that Louis Braille attended when he was fourteen (Lorimer, 1997). Braille developed a much simpler matrix of 6 dots, and assigned alpha-numerical values to the patterns derived from that matrix. The same braille patterns, with relevant prefixes, are used also for numerical and musical notations. These are not discussed in the present chapter.

The complex history of how the current Braille system came to be accepted in competition with raised Roman letters and other sign systems, has been ably described by Lorimer (1997). The history and eventual assignment of Braille patterns to different languages and in different orthographies deserves far more attention by linguists than it has received so far (Daniels, 1996). But such questions are beyond the present brief.

The basic six dot braille system was adopted in the English-speaking world in the 1930s. The quest for improvements and further unification of the braille system is by no means at an end. For English-speaking braille users there is now an accredited authority which debates and decides on ongoing changes to braille rules. One very recent change is the introduction of capital letter signs that were previously used only in some English speaking countries. That rule did not yet figure in the braille learned by the children and adults who were subjects in braille studies reported in this chapter.

Writing was invented to convey language through means other than hearing. The question is thus how reading by touch takes place, and how it is acquired. It is not primarily about the characteristics of people who use it. Blind children do not form some special deviant group. It could even be said that reading by touch was originally invented almost as much for use by armies for secret communication in the dark (see earlier, & Geldard, 1974), as for people who cannot see enough to read print. The enquiry centers on the information that is available in touch without sight, and on the role of tactual information in conveying verbal messages.

What is usually called "touch" actually names combinations of inputs from touch, movement and (limb and body) postures. Movement has long been considered important for tactual perception. The fact that the combination of inputs from the three sources varies with the size, depth and physical composition of perceptual objects, has received much less attention. Nevertheless, the reference information that the combined conditions afford for shape coding has important bearings on findings with tactual symbol systems for reading.

The chapter is divided into sections which examine these. The braille system is described next, followed by findings on the perception of braille patterns as symbols for single letter and word names and sounds. The section examines what tactual features are picked up early in learning and with reading experience. The fourth section considers the progressive spatial organisation of finger movements and posture cues, and the adaptation of scanning movements to the verbal and spatial aspects of reading continuous texts for comprehension. Section five looks at findings on abbreviated (contracted) forms in spelling, writing and reading. The final sections discuss developmental aspects of blindness, methods of teaching, and briefly describe other tactual reading systems.

SOME FEATURES OF ENGLISH BRAILLE AND TACTUAL PERCEPTION.

English braille has some unique features that repay detailed analysis. The language that it represents is, of course, the same oral language as for print. But the characters differ radically from print in physical composition. The orthography of the braille system is also based, to a significant extent, on the same imperfectly alphabetic spelling as English print. However, braille also contains logographs, – characters that stand for whole words – as well as many other contracted and abbreviated forms.

The physical composition of braille is determined by the small, (6.2 mm) matrix of six (2 × 3) raised dots from which all characters derive (Figure 1). The patterns are thus not only very small, they also lack the distinctive features of most print letters, because the presence or absence of any dot in the matrix denotes a different character. Both characteristics are relevant to the recognition of braille letters, considered in the next section.

The braille alphabet has an eminently logical structure, as might be expected from a grandson of eighteenth century French Enlightenment. The number of dots assigned to the 26 letters of the alphabet increase in alphabetical order from one to six. The top four positions of the braille matrix or "cell' are used for the first ten letters of the alphabet. They extend to the lower two positions for the remaining sixteen letters, in a left to right order, though some of the more frequent letters (r) "win out', in consisting of fewer dots, over letters (q) that occur less frequently (Figure 1).

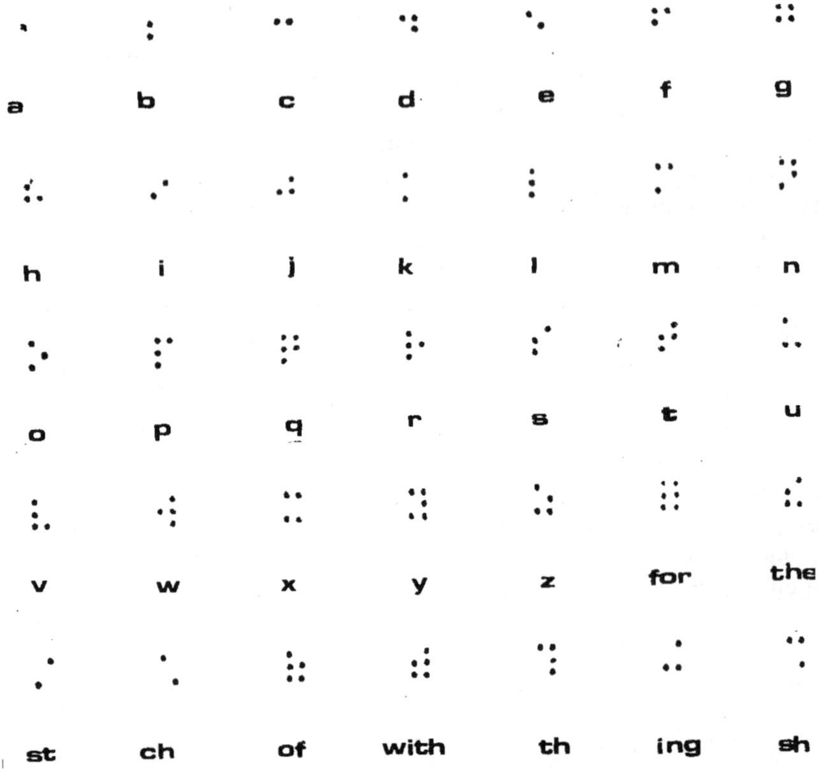

Figure 1. The braille alphabet and some single character contractions.

English braille comes in two main forms. Grade I uses orthographically "regular" (phonologically transparent) words in which, as in most French words, each character stands for the name and sound of a letter. The child first learns to associate the heard sound of a letter with the felt character that represents the sound. In principle, words can then be recognised ("sounded out") by integrating the sounds of sequentially felt letters and groups of letters (phonological method). Grade I used to be taught first, often in alphabetical order, though simple contractions are now often introduced quite early.

Grade II braille is based on English print spelling, but also contains a large number of different types of contractions. The simplest, and probably most useful, are the letter patterns themselves. Each letter of the alphabet, with the curious exception of the character for "o", also represents a word when the pattern stands alone, flanked by gaps on either side, as words are. On its own, the letter "p" reads "people" and "g" stands for "go". Other logographs, derived from further permutations of the six dot matrix, also represent frequently used words and syllables. Some examples are shown in Figure 1. Another class of contractions for useful words, syllables and endings is composed of single characters which have one to three preposed dots. Single character contractions, with and without the pre-posed dots, have to be used in words that contain the relevant letter sequence. Dots confined to the lower four positions of the cell are used for punctuation marks, some double consonants and pre-fixes.

Three factors in tactual perception need to be stressed in connection with the composition of braille patterns as language symbols. They are easily overlooked, because it is often forgotten that the combinations of inputs from touch, movement and posture cues in "touch" vary with the size and composition of perceptual objects. The point is that the small size and lack of distinctive features of braille afford few reference cues for the spatial aspects of reading. Secondly, though movement is known to be important, it is not always appreciated that in tactual reading, the intake of information occurs during finger movements (Bürklen, 1917/32; Davidson *et al.* 1980; Foulke, 1982; Kusajima, 1974). In visual reading, by contrast, information is taken in during fixation times, not during the saccadic (jump) eye-movements from one fixation point to the next. The third factor concerns the progressive organisation of hand and finger movements, relative to each other and to the script. It is especially relevant to the differentiation of verbal and spatial coding in the acquisition of braille.

TACTUAL AND VERBAL ASPECTS OF RECOGNISING SINGLE LETTERS AND WORDS

Touch is often tacitly regarded merely as a poor cousin of vision. Braille patterns look like quite simple global shapes (Figure 1). The most common early assumption was that Braille patterns are also initially perceived as global ("wholes" or "Gestalten") figures by touch (Bürklen, 1917/1932). An extensive and influential investigation of braille reading (Nolan & Kederis, 1969) found no evidence that words are recognised as global shapes, but attributed recognition errors to confusing the global outline shapes of different letters. The "global shape" view is also assumed in describing touch as similar to "blurred vision" (Apkarian-Stielau & Loomis, 1975). Visual errors were increased, to a level comparable to errors in touch, by reducing the visibility of print letters. However, the finding is not sufficient evidence that tactile patterns are initially perceived as global outline shapes (see also, Loomis, 1993).

The most influential view, nevertheless, has been that braille depends on letter-by-letter reading, and is difficult and slow, because poor tactual acuity makes letter shapes difficult to recognise. There are readers who read braille one letter at a time (see later). But it is not an adequate description of how braille reading takes place, or is acquired.

The evidence suggests that the salient features in initial (untutored) tactual perception of braille patterns are dot-gap density or "texture" cues, rather than global outline shapes. The most pervasive errors are missed dots (Nolan &

Kederis, 1969). Patterns with fewer dots are easier than similar shapes with more dots, partly because they are taught first, but also because figures with more dots differ less from each other in texture cues. It is not a question of counting the dots (e.g. Newman, Craig & Hall, 1987).

Braille patterns are certainly recognised less easily by touch than by vision (Millar, 1977a, 1997a; Newman, Sawyer, Hall & Hill, 1990). But the difficulty occurs in recognising, drawing, and naming the patterns early in learning, not in discriminating them (Millar 1977a, 1978a, 1985). Even naïve subjects, who have never encountered braille patterns before, can easily discriminate the patterns from each other (Katz, 1925; Millar, 1977a). The task difference is difficult to explain on the "global shape" view. If the initial tactile perception of a shape is based on its global outline, why should it be easy to discriminate between two shapes, but very difficult to recognise a single pattern (e.g. as new/old) or to draw the outline shape, even if not expertly? The task difference suggests rather that the features which are sufficient for discrimination (e.g. texture) are not identical with the features (e.g. outline shape) needed for recognition (the evidence is discussed later). Limited tactual acuity could not explain the task difference either. The small size of the braille matrix is a factor, especially in conjunction with the paucity of salient features in braille patterns. But the pad of the forefinger (mainly used for scanning) is one of the most sensitive areas of skin. Judged by 2-point thresholds (minimum distance to feel two points as separate), it is normally sufficient for the braille cell, though the threshold is somewhat higher in old age and severe diabetes (Bernbaum et at., 1989; Harley et at., 1985; Stevens, 1992; Stevens et.al., 1996). However, perception of braille patterns depends, in any case, on active movements, and not on the passive stimulation used in 2-point threshold measures.

The small memory span for tactual features (Millar, 1975) provides an important clue. Purely tactual features can be remembered in the short-term (Millar, 1975; Watkins & Watkins, 1977). However, recall spans seem to be limited to about three items (Millar, 1975, 1978b). Once characters can be named quickly, blind children have no problem in remembering much longer series of letters by name sounds (Millar, 1975), as would be expected for phonologically recoded items (e.g Baddeley, 1990; Conrad 1964, 1971). The very small recall spans for tactual features, prior to verbal recoding, suggest that the tactual features are not initially felt in economically organised form (e.g. Miller, 1956), such as simple global shapes. Louis Braille (see earlier) seems to have had the right hunch about punctiform inputs for reading by touch (Loomis, 1981; Millar, 1985a).

Direct evidence that dot-gap density cues are easier to recognise tactually than global shapes comes from studies which used a variety of different methods to test for aspects of global shape perception (Millar, 1975, 1977a, b, 1978a,b, 1985a). The studies have been reviewed before (Millar, 1981, 1994; 1997a). Briefly, the results show that matching braille patterns on dot density cues is significantly easier and more powerful than matching, a) in terms of continuous outline-shapes of the patterns, or (b) by the spatial location of dots, or (c) by matching on vertical symmetry versus asymmetry (a highly salient difference in vision) in slightly extended dot patterns. Also (d) matching braille letters was significantly worse when the formats differed slightly in dot-gap formats, even though the letters were identical in shape as well as in name, and (e) beginners needed training to recognise the same letters in somewhat enlarged format (Millar, l977a, b, 1978 a, 1985). Better readers did not require special familiarisation to generalise to larger shapes, but they also took longer over the enlarged (i.e. apparently easier) than over familiar formats.

Such findings are sometimes misunderstood as if it were asserted that touch "cannot" detect outlines, symmetry, spatial locations, nor generalise to identical shapes that differ in size. That is not, of course, the implication. Global shapes can certainly be perceived by touch. The point is that the implications of shape detection for teaching methods are not always immediately obvious.

The shape of words is a good example. Braille readers can detect the shape of braille words when asked to do so, and good readers are better at it (Millar, 1984 a). But good as well as slow readers preferred to match words by sound or meaning rather than by shape, and were also significantly better at detecting the sounds and the meanings of words than their shape (Millar, 1984 a). Dot numerosity, indicating word length, was picked up quite easily even by slow readers, by contrast. It is sometimes used as an additional cue to word length by fluent readers when confronted with perceptually degraded scripts (Millar 1997a).

The finding that word-shape is a very poor cue to the sound or meaning of words has some bearing on how the "word superiority" effect operates in braille. The effect, showing that words are recognised faster than their constituent letters, has been demonstrated for Braille (Krueger, 1982; Pring 1982). But it cannot easily be attributed to fast detection of the global shape of the words (Millar, 1984a). The effect is even less compatible with the assumption of letter-by-letter reading (Nolan & Kederis, 1969). The word superiority effect could not occur in braille at all, if it depended upon detecting each letter shape, recoding it by sound, and then integrating the sounds to recognise the word. Slow readers are certainly also slow at recognising letters, and reading speeds can be improved by training in character recognition (see Foulke, 1982). Moreover, beginning braille readers depend significantly more on phonological coding of letters and words in prose reading than proficient braillists (Millar, 1988a; 1990, 1997a). But such findings do not imply that fluent reading simply depends on faster pick-up and recoding of letter shapes.

Touch seems to be specialised more for texture, so that dot-density cues are more immediately obvious. Relatively poor coding of global shape, compared to vision, is entirely intelligible by the paucity of reference cues that the small size and lack of distinctive features of braille patterns affords in tactual conditions. Spatial tasks, including shape perception, depend on reference organisation. At least three sources of reference are redundantly available in normal visual conditions: (i) Current external (environmental) cues relative to which distinctive features can be specified; (ii) Specification of features relative to body-centred reference frames (e.g. the body midline, limb postures); and (iii) The relation of distinctive features to each other within patterns which determine their relative location and directions. All three sources of reference, and the informational redundancy that their coincidence provides, are severely reduced for braille patterns in touch. Without vision, current external reference cues are diminished or excluded. Active search for external anchor cues depends on prior information and/or experience in systematic scanning (Berla & Butterfield, 1977; Davidson *et al.*, 1972). Braille patterns are too small to relate any constituent feature accurately to body-centred cues (Millar, 1978a). The lack of distinctive features in the patterns makes it also difficult to determine the location of dots within patterns by reference to each other. It is not necessary to assume that people are normally aware of any of these sources of reference information, nor of their lack. But differences in reference information explain the findings on the tactual features that underlie braille reading at different levels of proficiency.

Evidence that initial detection of dot-gap density "textures" is easier than perceiving global shape is thus largely explained by the paucity of reference cues that the patterns afford in tactual conditions. The explanation also suggests how, in principle, spatial (shape) coding can be improved. Thus, it is possible to instruct even very young children to use different forms of reference information (Millar, 1985b). We have also shown that shape symmetry does not facilitate perception of small raised line configurations that were explored with one finger. But symmetry facilitated perception when self-referent cues were made salient, by initially aligning the two forefingers above the display, in line with the body midline, so that the forefingers scanned the display in parallel in the direction of the body midline (Ballesteros, Millar & Reales, 1998; Millar, 1978a; Millar, Ballesteros & Reales, 1994). Single Braille dot patterns are too small for simultaneous scanning by the two forefingers. The reference anchors needed for systematic scanning depend on the progressive organisation finger positions and directional movements (see later).

Evidence on fluent prose reading is discussed in the next section. But it is relevant to point out here that fluent readers, unlike beginners, adapt the mode of scanning to the reading task. Prose reading elicits smooth lateral scanning of temporally extended dot-gap (shear) patterns (Grunwald, 1966; Millar, 1987a). By contrast, letter detection in the same scripts elicits systematic (up/down/across) scanning of separate shapes. Young beginners shows neither pattern consistently (Millar, 1987a). By contrast, newly blind adults who have learned braille attempt to scan letter shapes systematically in all reading tasks (Millar, 1997a, 1997b). For adults beginners, there is a perceptual advantage of first learning enlarged (spaced) single characters (e.g. Newman *et al.*, 1984; Tobin *et al.*, 1986). Apart from the motivational advantage of greater perceptual ease, the spatial directions of the longer scanning movements that enlarged braille cells elicit can be monitored more easily.

The practical implications for teaching young children depend on the aims of reading. The finding that dot-gap density cues are relatively easy and salient in initial tactual discrimination, and have some affinity with the lateral (shear) patterns that underlie lateral scanning in later fluent prose reading, suggests that lateral scanning needs to be encouraged early, quite as much as perceiving patterns as global shapes, which is often the aim in early teaching. At the same time, the young child also has to learn to recognise single characters. These are not alternatives. Both forms of scanning have to be acquired.

THE ORGANISATION OF SCANNING MOVEMENTS AND SEMANTIC INFORMATION IN READING

Any one who has watched the hand movements of really proficient braille readers is struck by the smooth, light, even scanning movements of the hands over the text, and the smooth transitions by which the two hands seem to take over from each other in moving from one line to the next. Lines drawn by pencils attached to the reading fingers (Bürklen, 1917/1932), kymograph records (Kusajima, 1970, 1974), transcriptions of trajectories filmed from above (Eatman, 1942, quoted by Foulke, 1982), or from a horizontal position (Bertelson & Mousty, 1985) show apparently simultaneous trajectories by the two forefingers over different portions of text.

Grunewald's (1966) suggestion that the smooth lateral hand movements of fluent readers depend on scanning dynamically extended temporal patterns is supported by evidence (Millar, 1987a, 1997a). It has also sometimes been suggested that in fast reading the two hands actually read different portions of text simultaneously (Bertelson & Mousty, 1985; Bürklen, 1917/1932). An alternative suggestion (Kusajima, 1970) was that reading is fast because the two hands perform different functions. Another possibility was that the right hand scans ahead for gist, while the left checks individual words or features.

The views have very different practical implications. But more fine-grained data were needed for adequate tests. Video recording from below transparent surfaces, with simultaneous (1/100 sec) timing and voice output provided these (Millar, 1988 a). The exact time and precise (mm) location of braille dots on the centre of the fingerpads of the forefingers, during normal prose reading, could thus be viewed on the monitor and ascertained in frame-by-frame replay.

The Grunwald (1966) hypothesis, that temporally extended patterns are felt, involves shear patterns produced on the fingerpad by moving the finger laterally over the dot-gap patterns of cells. The findings (for details, see Millar, 1987a, 1997a) showed severe loss of comprehension in prose reading by fluent braillists in conditions that interfered with lateral (across the finger) shear patterns, compared to altered movements which preserved the lateral dot-gap relation of the moving finger to the orientation of the text. By contrast, letter search was not affected. Fluent readers explored letter shapes with systematic movements in both vertical and horizontal directions. Beginning and slow readers, by contrast, used the same unsystematic scanning movements with much regression in all conditions. They were able to understand some of the gist of the stories in text reading to about the same extent.

Three findings are worth noting: (i) There is a change, with proficiency, in the tactual information that is being picked up, which is not merely a question of better discrimination; (ii) Tasks seem to have an increasingly "top-down" effect in differentiating forms of scanning for different features; and (iii) Extended temporal (dot-gap density) shear patterns seem to underlie fluent reading for comprehension, while movements indicating shape coding are used for detecting single characters.

The overlap in time of hand movements by fluent readers on successive lines of text, as seen from above or sideways (see earlier), can be shown to result from separable spatial and verbal functions (Millar 1987b; 1997a), in line with suggestions by Kusajima (1970, 1974). The notion (Bertelson & Mousty, 1985; Bürklen, 1917/32) that two different portions of braille text can be read simultaneously is more improbable, in any case, if reading means taking in verbal information. Clearly, touching is not, as such, evidence for reading. In testing the two hypotheses, the minimum criterion for simultaneous reading (taking in verbal information) versus touching for some other purpose (e.g. checking a feature or location) was that the two forefingers should simultaneously touch one new (not previously scanned) letter (Millar, 1987a).

The evidence supports the notion that the two hands perform different functions in parallel (Millar, 1987a; Davidson *et al.*, 1992). Results from prose reading by fluent readers (Millar, 1987b), and further findings from readers with high (e.g. 188 wpm) reading rates (Millar, 1997a) showed that the two hands perform different functions simultaneously. Analyses were based on (1/100 sec) timing of the position of (blackened) Braille dots on the fingerpads (seen from below) in frame-by-frame analyses. Types and directions of finger movements on and above lines of text, and during transitions from one line to the next were also analysed. No simultaneous reading (touching two new letters) was found for transitions between lines of text for the fastest readers. Typically, these readers start to scan a new line of text with the left forefinger some hundredth of seconds after the right hand has moved from the last letter of the previous line, and is either touching the blank beyond it or is in transit (often above the text) to join the left hand. By the time the right hand joins the left, the left hand has read nearly to the middle of that line. The right forefinger then takes over, and reads on to the end of that line, as the left forefinger begins to move down to find the beginning of the subsequent line. Both hands thus read alternately, and both alternately perform spatial tasks alternately, moving to join the next line and locating the start or ends of lines. Consistent findings, which indicate that two-handed reading by fluent braillists is based on separable functions, since the forefingers touch the same cells for different portions of time, have been reported by Davidson *et al.* (1992).

The separation and alternation of spatial and verbal function of the hands shown by fluent readers is rarely found in poor readers. Beginning readers tend to "scrub' over the same letters and show many regressions (e.g. Bürklen, 1917/32; Kusajima, 1970; Merry, 1942, cited by Foulke, 1982; Millar, 1997a). They are not merely slow. Beginners typically fail to keep to the line of text, veering downwards, and fail to use the two hands in conjunction to keep the place. Interestingly enough, simultaneous touching (or overlap in time) of letters occurs quite frequently during regressions by slow readers. But these are typically over characters that have been touched many times before, and indicate checking procedures rather than "reading' in the sense of taking in verbal information from two locations in parallel. An entirely consistent finding is that reading with the two forefingers in adjacent positions is actually more frequent in slow than fast reading (e.g. Bertelson & Mousty, 1985; Buerklen, 1917/32; Kusajima, 1970/74; Millar 1997a).

Laterality studies on Braille have variously reported superior performance with the left hand, with the right hand, and no significant superiority for either hand on its own (e.g. Bradshaw *et al.*, 1982; Fertsch, 1947, Hermelin & O'Connor, 1971; Millar, 1977a, 1984b; Mutaguchi & Nakata, 1997; Newman, Brugler & Craig, 1988; Rudel, Denckla & Spalten, 1974; Sampaio & Philips, 1995; Semenza *et al.*, 1996; Wilkinson & Carr, 1987). Materials and reading tasks vary between studies from single letter discrimination, accuracy in letter naming, to prose reading speeds, and subjects range from just having learned a few letters, to a life-time of braille use. Such factors, as well as early teaching methods are, no doubt, involved. But they do not relate systematically enough to the contradictory findings to warrant direct theoretical inferences about hemisphere functions, nor prescriptions about which hand to use for Braille (for discussion, see Millar, 1994). There is no unequivocal evidence at present that either the right hand, or the left hand is better for braille learning, or leads to superior braille skills later.

There is, however, general agreement that reading with both hands tends to be better (see Foulke, 1982 for discussion). Blind children establish their own reading styles quite early on, including the hand they prefer for braille (not to be confused with handedness) when the task demands single hand reading. Individuals also differ considerably in the manner in which the two hands are deployed, including the amount of text read by the left and right hand by fluent readers (Millar, 1997a).

The progressive spatial organisation of hand movements to each other, and the progressive differentiation of spatial and verbal functions for the two hands, plays an important part in learning. Experienced braille teachers encourage beginners to adopt upright body postures. These facilitate the systematic use of the hands relative to the body and to the spatial layout of texts. In fluent reading, scanning relates to external cues in the text. Competent braillists scan the layout of text prior to reading. Assigning the spatial and verbal aspects of reading alternatively to the two hands seems to be associated mainly with fluent reading by people who have learned Braille early, possibly because more of the subsidiary skills have become "automatic" with extended experience.

The fact that Braille reading correlates with comprehension and memory, and is affected by priming, lexical ambiguity, syntactic and semantic difficulties in texts (e.g. Daneman & Carpenter, 1988; Hamann, 1996; Millar, l988b; 1990; Mousty & Bertelson, 1985, 1992; Nolan & Kederis, 1969) is hardly surprising. Lexically difficult (low frequency) words initiate regressions. There is evidence that regressive movements in reading revert to text locations that provide perceptual and orthographic aid to construing the meaning of the difficult word (Millar, 1988b, 1997a).

Braille readers use the semantic context when the perceptual input is poor (Millar, 1988b, 1990, 1997a). Semantic heuristics do not seem to be specific to young children, or to lack of proficiency, as such (Millar, 1988b; 1997a; Mousty & Bertelson, 1985), as is sometimes assumed in visual reading. Perceptually degraded (faint) words, that occur in semantically related versus unrelated contexts, show similar effects for experienced and beginning readers. Experienced braillists are simply better at recognising degraded braille, as well as at finding related terms to disambiguate the perceptual input (Millar, l988b; 1997a). Intelligent young readers often use gist to repair spatial errors (e.g. missing the first word on a line). The opposite also occurs.

Phonological strategies are also used as important aids when texts are difficult. Fluent readers can read easy texts silently without loss of comprehension or speed while mouthing an irrelevant syllable, which prevents covert articulation (rehearsal). But their comprehension is severely impaired with difficult texts in these conditions (Millar, 1990).

WRITING, READING SPEED, CONTRACTIONS AND SPELLING

There are still some blind readers who were taught to write by using a stylus and indented metal guide to prick out braille dots from the reverse side of the page. An early directive indicates how the "mirror-image reversal" writing was supposed to be taught (McFerrin, 1930). The author specifically warns against teaching beginners to write letters backwards by left-right reversals. He advises instead that braille dot numbers (conventionally, *1,2,3* for the vertically consecutive dots in the left column, and *4,5,6* for the right column of dots in the 2 × 3 cell) should be used to avoid confusions.

Typing machines that produce raised dots mechanically are relatively recent. The "Perkins" machine, still used currently for writing by young blind children, has a horizontal keyboard to produce the vertically oriented braille cell. The three horizontal keys on the left produce vertical dots 1, 2, 3, and are pressed, respectively, by the forefinger, middle and ring finger of the left hand. The three horizontal keys on the right produce dots 4, 5, and 6, and are pressed by the forefinger, middle and ring finger of the right hand. The vertical orientation of the Braille cell (two aligned columns of 3 dots) on the page in reading thus has to be matched to a horizontal layout of two adjacent rows of keys (left: 1, 2, 3; right: 4, 5 6) on the keyboard. Beginning readers often use the number by which the position of a dot in the cell is known, and the corresponding number of the key on the keyboard, quite overtly for both reading and writing. Some teachers deprecate the use of dot numbers for braille letters in reading. However, using dot numbers that designate both the positions of dots in the upright letter pattern, and the position of appropriate keys on the horizontal keyboard, is relatively easy. The alternative is to mentally rotate the spatial position of the two vertical columns in the braille pattern in reading by 90° in clockwise (for the left) and counterclockwise (for the right) directions to match the spatial positions on the keyboard. Such mental spatial rotation is known to be difficult even in sighted conditions. For some retarded readers writing with the "Perkins" is much easier than reading. It seems likely that this is due to the redundancy of associating letter sounds with dot numbers that also mark the relevant finger-key combinations (Millar, 1983; 1997a). Any deliberate use of such strategies seems to drop out with proficiency, in any case. Fluent readers describe the numbering strategy as "babyish" and say that they do not need it. Contracted characters for words and syllables are produced in the same fashion as letters. Once learned, they reduce the time it takes to write words.

The main reason for contractions is to speed prose reading. Tactual reading is certainly slower, on average, than visual reading. The usual estimate (250–300 words/minute) for visual reading is more often cited than documented for representative samples of the general sighted population. The low rate for braille (70–100 words/minute) that is usually quoted was found for blind adolescents (e.g. Nolan & Kederis, 1969). A somewhat higher average (104 wpm) has been estimated for adults (Foulke, 1964). Reading speeds also depend on texts and tests. High frequency word speeds (Tooze, 1962) can differ from speeds on braille versions of print comprehension tests, though there are some worrying downward trends between results for blind adolescent compared to the sighted (Greeney, Hill, & Tobin, 1998). On the other hand fluent (pre-University) students achieved reading rates of about 150 and 188 words/minute with quite difficult texts (Millar, 1997 a). Grunwald (1966) reported reading rates of 200 words/minute. At the same time, very slow reading (e.g. 30 words/minute) by highly educated former print readers can yield excellent understanding of difficult texts with many contracted forms. Reading by these subjects did indeed show letter-by-letter shape scanning (Millar, 1997a, b).

Contractions do, of course, complicate the learning process. The beginner has to learn, not only new characters, but also the rules which determine when abbreviations are to be used. The advantage in speed is also lost with contractions that occur infrequently (Lorimer *et al.*, 1982). Nevertheless, frequently occurring contractions can make reading much faster (e.g. Foulke, 1982), and are identified quite quickly (Nolan & Kederis, 1969). Slow readings of words in which contractions occur are often due to the low frequency of the words, rather than to the contractions as such (Nolan & Kederis, 1969). Findings both with Norwegian and English show that competent braillists read words faster in contracted than in uncontracted form (Bruteig, 1987; Millar, 1997a).

Contractions can present problems for spelling print, which blind children learn for general educational, and practical purposes, such as using computer keyboards for touch typing. Long-term familiarity with the sound-spelling-graphemic associations in scripts is probably the single most important factor in fast braille.

Evidence for long-term effects of different orthographic experience was found by comparing people, who had learned braille after reading print for nearly forty years, with fluent braillists with equal years of reading experience. The sentences contained words in which a logographic contraction (e.g. the character for "one" or "of") was either compatible with sound-spelling associations in print (e.g. "mONEy" and "prOFile"), or disrupted it (e.g. "atONE" and "proOF"). Former print readers took significantly longer to read words in which the contraction disrupted the sound-spelling association of print than words in which the same contraction was compatible with print sound-spelling associations. Fluent braillist did not differ in reading speeds for such words (Millar, 1995, 1997a). Immediately prior tactual presentation of the target words reduced the difference by former print readers. Prior auditory (cross-modal) presentation did not, though it speeded reading.

The findings have practical application for teaching adults to read Braille. Theoretically, they imply that associations between physical (tactual/auditory) features of the input and sound- spelling habits are (automatically) activated in fast reading (Millar, 1997 a).

BLINDNESS AND LEARNING TO READ

The old assumption that blind children use sounds without meaning ("verbalisms") is not tenable. Meaning is not derived only, or even mainly, from sight. Blind children's vocabulary (e.g. Tobin, 1972, 1992; Williams, 1956) does not need to lag behind the sighted, though many events do require more explanation than blind children often receive, and deficits have been reported (Elstner, 1983). However, evidence that even beginners use the semantic context to repair perceptual or spatial errors (see earlier), suggests that comprehension as such is not a major problem for normal blind children. But braille needs more cognitive skill than visual reading (Nolan & Kederis, 1969).

The phonological skills needed for learning to read print (e.g. Bryant & Bradley, 1985), are shown also by normal blind children. If anything, blind children attend more to speech sounds, and play with them (Elstner, 1983). A negative finding with nonsense (pseudo) homophones, suggesting that blind children do not use phonological coding strategies (Pring, 1985), was not replicated with braille words (Millar, 1984a). The degree of phonological coding varies with reading proficiency and the difficulty of texts (Millar, 1990, 1997), as in does in print reading (e.g. Hardyk and Petrinovitch, 1970). But several further studies also show that beginning braille readers rely heavily on sounds. Sentences and texts with homophone words that differ in feel, spelling (contracted vs uncontracted forms) and meaning are wrongly accepted because they sound the same. (Millar, 1988 b, 1995). Beginners can barely detect letters and words, let alone understand the text, if they have to articulate a meaningless syllable while reading silently, showing that they are using speech-based strategies (Millar, 1990, 1995, 1997a). As mentioned earlier, once naming is established, they also rely on fast phonological recoding in short-term memory for braille characters (Millar, 1975).

Sounds that the sighted can lip-read as well as hear may need additional attention by the blind to restore the advantage that redundant cues provide. More blind than sighted children also seem to have some hearing loss, and need speech therapy. The earlier survival of pre-term babies has increased the number of blind children with multiple handicaps and severe learning difficulties (see Fielder, Best and Bax, 1993).

Reading retardation in braille, as measured by word (Tooze, 1962) and prose reading (Lorimer, 1977) tests, by blind children of more or less average intelligence, is characterised by combined deficits in phonological and tactual scanning skills. Scanning movements bear a strong relationship to reading ability (Mommers, 1976). Joint place-keeping and systematic exploration movements by the two hands is unusually poor in these children (Davidson, Wiles-Kettelman, Haber & Appelle, 1980; Millar, 1997a; Mommers, 1976). A longitudinal study of congenitally totally blind retarded readers is reported in Millar (1997a).

Most attempts to improve Braille learning have concentrated on recognition of single characters, often by attempts to enlarge the cell either by spacing or by adding dots (e.g. Foulke, 1973, 1982; Foulke & Warm, 1967; Hall & Newman, 1987; Newman, 1985, 1987). Newly blind adults learn larger characters more easily (Tobin, 1988, Tobin *et al.* 1986), possibly because prior visual knowledge (Heller, 1993; Newman *et al.*, 1984, 1985, 1988, 1990) elicits systematic exploration of expected spatial features. Larger movements can be related more easily to reference anchors (see section 3). The Tobin (1988) reading scheme for adults starts with enlarged forms and then reduces them to the normal braille cell size. The scheme has the advantage that self-instruction is augmented by auditory feedback at all stages of learning, and introduces contractions quite early.

Teachers are divided on whether or not young beginners should first learn enlarged forms, and then change over to the normal format. Experimental findings with very young beginners are often based on practice with a very small subset of letters. There is no adequate empirical evidence on the long-term effects on later fluency of starting either with enlarged letters and changing to the normal format later, or of starting with the normal format, which then receives longer practice. What the findings, taken together, do show (section 3,4,5 & 6) is that fluent readers use lateral scanning for prose reading and quite different movements to detect single letters.

The most successful method with young blind children, in my experience, combined apparently different approaches to reinforce each other (Morgan, Lingard *et al.*, 1988). The sound for the letter, that is also the beginning sound of the contracted word that the letter represents (e.g. "g" for "go") can be used to reinforce each other. Young blind children respond well to redundancy (overlap) of texture and shape cues (Millar, 1986). It is not easy to introduce redundancy into braille without distorting the (cell) matrix. But the method used highly discriminable letters in small, regular (phonologically transparent) words. The conjunction enabled practice in blending and segmenting sounds, as well as in scanning single and combined letter patterns. Together with the same letters as logographs (single letter contractions for words), these words quickly form meaningful little sentences, enabling lateral scanning. The scheme was also made fun by attaching tiny toys, relevant to the key word.

Methods that combine attention to single sounds, in combination and segmented, together with the difference in scanning single characters and lateral scanning in conjunction with meaning and some fun, are likely to produce some of the redundancy that young beginners need. The main advantage for young beginners is the length of time, practice and training that can be devoted to Braille. The need for training and practice for adult learners is not sufficiently recognised (Pester, 1993).

ALTERNATIVE READING SYSTEMS:

"Moon" (invented in the mid-nineteenth century by the person it is named after) is recommended for severely learning disabled blind children who are not expected to be able to learn braille. The characters are embossed simplified (less cluttered) print capitals (Figure 2). The shapes are somewhat (7 × 7 mm) larger than the braille cell, and have some of the distinctive features of print which makes them much easier to feel as distinctive shapes (see section 3). Newly blind adults also sometimes learn Moon before going on to braille. The system is not primarily intended for fast prose reading, though it could, in principle, be used by people who find Braille too difficult. A "Moon writer" (Tobin, 1984) has been developed recently, and is available from the Royal National Institute for the Blind.

The "optacon" translates visual print into vibrotactile stimulation. The pad of the forefinger rests on a rectangular array of "benders". The right hand scans visual print text with an electronic device which translates print letters into patterns of vibrotactile stimulation. The reader needs to know print. Discriminability of vibrotactile stimuli has been studied extensively (for review, see Sherrick, 1990; Sherrick & Craig, 1982). The device has been quite successful, though it now seems to be in decline in favour of computer-aided devices.

There is a good deal of ongoing research which attempts make it possible for blind people use computers, mostly by using auditory inputs and/or feedback. Machines that produce braille automatically and translate between braille and print are also being produced (for information, see Gill & Peuleve, 1993). The limiting factor is cost. But even with the aid of computers, braille is still the main road to literacy for the blind at present.

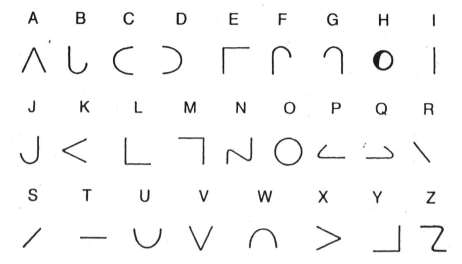

Figure 2. The Moon Alphabet

SUMMARY AND CONCLUSIONS

Tactual reading has often been viewed as a letter-by-letter process, based on the global shape of letters, which becomes faster with experience. Language skills are grafted onto this. The evidence reviewed here on braille is more consistent with a model in which language skills interact with the progressive spatial organisation of tactual scanning movements.

The specific "touch" combination of inputs from touch, movement and reference cues, that the size and composition of braille patterns afford, is less well adapted to (but does not exclude) global shape perception than to the perception of dot-gap density or "texture" cues, and to lateral time-extended dot-gap density patterns. The possibility of fast lateral scanning may explain why the system is still used in preference to more obviously shape-based tactual systems.

The acquisition of braille, suggested by the findings, can be summarised as follows:

(i) Young beginners rely on fast phonological recoding of tactually easy, but initially poorly organised dot-gap texture cues, picked up with relatively unsystematic scanning movements (sections 2, 3, 6);

(ii) Increased fluency depends on four main skills that interleave with language skills and demands (a) Progressive spatial anchoring of hand movements for place-keeping and place-finding, to scan dot-gap density patterns system-atically in association with the sounds of single characters, and to develop smooth lateral scanning of temporally extended patterns in association with the sounds and meanings of words and sentences (sections 3 & 4); (b) Adapting scanning movements to different verbal tasks by using smooth lateral scanning of laterally extended dot-gap density patterns for text comprehension, and specific local exploration for letter recognition (section 4 & 6); (c) assigning spatial and verbal functions alternately to both hands, to produce simultaneous processing from different (spatial and verbal) domains (section 4); and (d) Progressively closer ("automatic") links for the graphemic-orthographic- phonological associations of the script through experience and familiarity.

REFERENCES

Apkarian-Stielau, P. & Loomis, J.M. (1975). A comparison of tactile and blurred visual form perception. *Perception & Psychophysics, 18*, 362 -368.

Ballesteros, S., Millar, S. & Reales, M. (1998). Symmetry in haptic and in visual perception. *Perception & Psychophysics, 60*, 389-404.

Baddeley, A. D. (1990). *Human Memory: Theory and Practice*. Hillsdale: Lawrence Erlbaum Associates.

Bernbaum, M., Albert, S. G.,& McGarry, J. D. (1989). Diabetic neuropathy and braille ability. *Archives of Neurology, 46*, 1179-1181.

Bertelson, P., Mousty, P, & D'Alimonte, G. (1985). A study of braille reading: Patterns of hand activity in one-handed and two-handed reading. *The Quarterly Journal of Experimental Psychology, 37A*, 235-256.

Bradshaw, J. L., Nettleton, N.C. & Spehr, K. (1982). Braille reading and left and right hemispace. *Neuropsychologia, 20*, 493 – 500.

Bryant, P. E. & Bradley, L. (1985). *Children's Reading Problems*. Oxford: Basil Blackwell.

Bruteig, J. M. (1987). The reading rates for contracted and uncontracted braille of blind Norwegian adults. *Journal of Visual Impairment and Blindness, 81*, 19 -23.

Bürklen, K. (1917; translated by F. K. Merry, 1932). *Touch Reading by the Blind*. New York: American Foundation for the Blind.

Conrad, R. (1964). Acoustic confusions in immediate memory. *British Journal of Psychology, 55* 75 – 84.

Conrad, R. (1971). The chronology of the development of covert speech in children. *Developmental Psychology, 5*, 398 – 405.

Daneman, M. (1988). How reading braille is both like and unlike reading print. *Memory & Cognition, 16*, 497 – 504

Daniels, P. T. (1996). Shorthand. In P. T. Daniels & W. Bright (Eds.), *The World's Writing Systems*, Oxford: Oxford University Press.

Davidson, P. W. (1972). The role of exploratory activity in haptic perception: Some issues, data and hypotheses. *Research Bulletin, American Foundation for the Blind, 24*, 21-28.

Davidson, P. W., Appelle, St., Haber, R. N. (1992). Haptic scanning of braille cells by low- and high-proficiency blind readers. *Research in Developmental Disabilities, 13*, 99 – 111.

Davidson, P. W., Valenti, D., Reuter, S., Wiles-Ketteman, M., Haber, R. N. & Appelle, 5. (1980). Relationship between hand movements, reading competence and passage difficulty. *Neuropsychologia, 18*, 629-635.

Elstner, W. (1983). Abnormalities in the verbal communication of visually-impaired children. In A. E. Mills (Ed.), *Language Acquisition in the Blind Child: Normal and Deficient* (p.p. 18-41). London: Croom Helm.

Fertsch, P. (1947). Hand dominance in reading braille. *American Journal of Psychology, 60*, 335-349.

Fielder, A. R., Best, A. B., Bax, M. C. O. (Eds, 1993). *The Management of Visual Impairment in Childhood*. London: MacKeith Press.

Geldard, F. A. (Ed., 1974). *Cutaneous Communication Systems and Devices*. Austin, Texas: Psychonomic Society.

Gill, J. M. & Peuleve, C. A. (1993). Research Information Handbook of Assistive Technology for Visually Disabled Persons. London: The Tiresias Consortium.

Geeney, J. Tobin, M.J. & Hill, E. W. (1998). *Neale Analysis of Reading Ability: University of Birmingham Version*. London: Royal national Institute for the Blind.

Grunwald, A. P. (1966). A braille reading machine. *Science, 154*, 144-146.

Hamann, S. B. (1996). Implicit memory in the tactile modality: Evidence from braille stem completion in the blind. *Psychological Science, 7*, 284-288.

Hardyk, C. D. & Petrinovitch, L. R. (1970). Subvocal speech and comprehension level as a function of the difficulty level of the reading material. *Journal of Verbal Learning and Verbal Behavior, 9*, 12-17.

Harley, R. T., Randall, K., Pichert, J. W. & Morrison, M. (1985). Braille instruction for blind diabetic adults with decreased tactile sensitivity. *Journal of Visual Impairment and Blindness, 79*, 12-17.

Hartley, J., Tobin, M. J. Trueman, M. (1987). The effects of providing headings in braille text. *Journal of Visual Impairment and Blindness, 81*, 213 -214.

Hatta, T. & Moriya, K. (1988). Developmental changes of hemispheric collaboration for tactile sequential information. *International Journal of Behavioral Development, 11*, 451 -465.

Hermelin, B. & O'Connor, N. (1971). Functional asymmetry in the reading of braille. *Neuropsychologia, 9*, 431 435.

Heller, M. A. (1987). The effect of orientation on visual and tactual braille recognition. *Perception, 16*, 2911–298.

Heller, M. A. (1993). Influence of visual guidance on braille recognition: Low lighting also helps touch. *Perception & Psychophysics, 54*, 675 -681.

Heller, M. A. Rogers, G. J. & Perry, C. L. (1990). Tactile pattern recognition with the optacon: Superior performance with active touch and the left hand. *Neuropsychologia, 28*, (9), 1003-1006.

Katz, D. (1925). Der Aufbau der Tastwelt (The construction of the tactual world). Leipzig: Barth.

Krueger, L. (1982). A word-superiority effect with print and braille characters. *Perception & Psychophysics, 31*, 345-352.

Kusajima, T. (1970). Experimentelle Untersuchungen zum Augenlesen und Tastlesen (Experimental studies of visual and tactual reading). Neuburgweier: G. Schindele Verlag.

Kusajima, T. (1974). Visual Reading and Braille Reading: An Experimental Investigation of the Physiology and Psychology of Tactual Reading. New York: American Foundation for the Blind.

Loomis, J. (1993).Counterexample to the hypothesis of functional similarity between tactual and visual pattern perception. *Perception & Psychophysics, 54*, 179-184.

Lorimer, J., Tobin, M. J., Gill, J. & Douce, J. (1982). *A Study of Braille Contractions*. London: Royal National Institute for the Blind.

Lorimer, P. (1997). A critical evaluation of the historical development of the tactile modes of reading and an analysis and evaluation of researches carried out in endeavours to make the Braille code easier to read and to write. Birmingham: Ph.D. Thesis, Birmingham University.

Millar, S. (1975). Effects of tactual and phonological similarity on the recall of braille letters by blind children. *British Journal of Psychology, 66*, 193-201.

Millar, S. (1977a) Early stages of tactual matching. *Perception, 6*, 333 – 343.

Millar, S. (1977 b) Tactual and name matching by blind children. *British Journal of Psychology, 68*, 377- 387.

Millar, S. (1978 a) Aspects of information from touch and movement. In G. Gordon (Ed.), *Active Touch* (pp 215-227). London: Pergamon Press.

Millar, S. (1978 b) Short-term serial tactual recall: Effects of grouping tactually probed recall of braille letters and nonsense shapes by blind children. *British Journal of Psychology, 69*, 17 – 24.

Millar, S. (1981 b) Crossmodal and intersensory perception and the blind. In R.D. Walk & H-L. Pick, Jr. (Eds.), *Intersensory Perception and Sensory Integration*. (p.p. 281-314). New York: Plenum Press.

Millar, S. (1983). Language and active touch: Some aspects of reading and writing by blind children. In A. E. Mills (Ed), *Language Acquisition in the Blind Child: Normal and Deficient. (p.p. 167-186)*. London: Croom Helm.

Millar, S. (1984 a) Strategy choices by young Braille *readers. Perception, 13,* 567-579.

Millar, S. (1984 b) Is there a "best hand" for Braille? *Cortex, 13,* 567-579

Millar, S. (1985 a). The perception of complex patterns by touch. *Perception, 14,* 293-303.

Millar, S. (1985 b). Movement cues and body orientation in recall of locations by blind and sighted children. *Quarterly Journal of Experimental Psychology, 37A,* 293-279.

Millar, S. (1986) Aspects of size, shape and texture in touch: Redundancy and interference in children's discrimination of raised dot patterns. *Journal of Child Psychology and Psychiatry, 27,* 367-381.

Millar, S. (1987 a) The perceptual "window" in two-handed Braille: Do the left and right hands process text simultaneously? *Cortex, 23,* 111 – 222.

Millar, S. (1987 b) Perceptual and task factors in fluent Braille. *Perception, 16,* 52 1-536.

Millar, S. (1988 a) An apparatus for recording hand movements. *British Journal of Visual Impairment and Blindness, VI,* 87-90.

Millar, S. (1988 b) Prose reading by touch: The role of stimulus quality, orthography and context. *British Journal of Psychology, 72,* 87-103.

Millar, S. (1990). Articulatory coding in prose reading: Evidence from braille on changes with skill. *British Journal of Psychology, 81,* 205-219.

Millar, S. (1994). Understanding and Representing Space: Theory and Evidence from Studies with Blind and Sighted Children. Oxford: Clarendon Press.

Millar, S. (1995) Sound, Sense, Syllables and Word length in Prose Reading by Touch. Paper presented at the Scientific Meeting of the Experimental Psychology Society, Birmingham: July 12.

Millar, S. (1997 a). *Reading by Touch.* London: Routledge

Millar, S. (1997 b). Theory, experiment and practical application in research on visual handicap. *European Journal of Psychology of Education:* Special Edition *12,* 415-430.

Millar, S. Ballesteros & J. M. Reales (1994). Influence of symmetry in haptic and visual perception. Paper presented at the 35th Annual Meeting of the Pychonomics Society, St. Louis, Mo. November 11-13.

Miller, G. (1956). The magical number seven, plus or minus two: Some limits on our capacity for processing information. *Psychological Review, 63,* 81-97.

Mommers, M. J. (1976). Braille reading: Factors affecting achievement of Dutch elementary school children. *New Outlook for the Blind, 70,* 332-340.

Morgan, M. & Lingard M. (1988). *Braille for Infants: A Pre-school and Infant Level Reading Scheme.* London: Royal National Institute for the Blind.

Mousty, P. & Bertelson, P. (1985). A study of braille reading: I. Reading speed as a function of hand usage and context. *Quarterly Journal of Experimental Psychology, 31,* 217-233.

Mutaguchi, T. & Nakata, H. (1997). Development of braille reading rate in children who are congenitally blind. *Japanese Journal of Special Education, 35,* 11-18.

Newman, S. E., Brugler, T. S. & Craig, R. A. (1988). Immediate memory for haptically examined braille symbols by blind and sighted adults. *International Journal of Rehabilitation Research, 11,* 389-391.

Newman, S. E., Hall, A. D., Foster, J. D. & Gupta V, (1984). Learning as a function of haptic discriminability among items. *American Journal of Psychology, 97,* 359-372.

Newman, S. E., Kindsvater, M. B. & Hall, A. D. (1985). Braille learning: Effects of symbol size. *Bulletin of the Psychonomic Society, 23,* 189-190.

Newman, S. E., Sawyer, W. L., Hall, A.D & Hill, L. G. J. (1990). One modality is sometimes better than two. *Bulletin of the Psychonomic Society, 23,* 17-18.

Nolan, C. Y. & Kederis, C. J. (1969). *Perceptual Factors in Braille Recognition.* (AFB Research Series No.20). New York: American Foundation for the Blind.

Pester, E. (1993). Instruction for individuals who are blind adventitiously: Scheduling, expectations and reading interests. *Review: American Printing House for the Blind.* Louisville: Ky., *25,* 83-87.

Pring, L. (1985). Processes involved in braille reading. *Journal of Visual Impairment and Blindness, 79,* 252-255.

Rudel. R. G., Denckla, M. B. & Spalten, E. (1974). The functional asymmetry of braille letter learning in normal sighted children. *Neurology, 24,* 733-738.

Sampaio, E. & Philip, J. (1995). Influence of age of onset of blindness on braille reading performance with left and right hands. *Perceptual & Motor Skills, 81,* 131-141.

Semenza, C., Zoppello, M., Ogidiuli, 0. & Borgo, F. (1996). Dichaptic scanning of braille letters by skilled blind readers: Lateralization effects. *Perceptual & Motor Skills, 82,* 1071-1074.

Sherrick, C. E. (1991). Vibrotactile pattern perception: Some findings and applications. In M.A.Heller & W.Schiff (Eds), *The Psychology of Touch* (p.p. 189-217). Hillsdale, N.J.: Lawrence Erlbaum.

Sherrick, C. E. & Craig, J. C. (1982). The psychology of touch. In W.Schiff & E. Foulke (Eds), *Tactual Perception: A Sourcebook*. (pp. 55-81). New York: American Foundation for the Blind.

Stevens, J. C. (1992). Aging and spatial acuity of touch. *Journal of Gerontology, 41,* 35-40.

Stevens, J. C., Foulke, E., Patterson, M. Q. W. (1996). Tactile acuity, aging, and Braille reading in long-term blindness: *Journal of Experimental Psychology: Applied, 2,* 91-106.

Tobin, M. J. (1972). *The Vocabulary of the Young Blind Schoolchild:*. Birmingham: College of Teachers of the Blind.

Tobin, M. J. (1984). A Moon Writer. *The New Beacon, LXVIII,* 173-176.

Tobin, M. J. (1988). Beginning Braille. *The New Beacon, LXXII,* 81-82.

Tobin, M. J. (1992). The language of blind children. Communication, words and meanings. *Language & Education, 6,* 177-182.

Tobin, M. J. Burton, P, Davies, B. T. & Guggenheim, J. (1986). An experimental investigation of the effects of cell size and spacing in braille: with some possible implications for the newly-blind adult learner. *The New Beacon, LXX,* 829, 133 – 135.

Tooze, F. H. G. (1962). *The Tooze Braille Speed Test*. Bristol: The College of Teachers of the Blind.

Watkins, M. J. & Watkins, O. C. (1974). A tactile suffix effect. *Memory & Cognition, 2,* 176 180.

Warm, J, & Foulke, E. (1968). Effects of orientation and redundancy on the tactual perception of forms. *Perceptual & Motor Skills, 27,* 83-89.

Wilkinson, J. M., & Carr, T. H. (1987). Strategic hand use preferences and hemispheric specialisation in tactual reading: Impact of the demands of tactual coding. *Brain & Language, 32,* 97-123.

SUGGESTED FURTHER READINGS

Millar, S. (1997). *Reading by Touch*. London: Routledge (now Taylor & Francis).

Millar, S. (1994). Understanding and Representing Space: Theory and Evidence from Studies with Blind and Sighted Children. Oxford: Clarendon Press.

C11. Deafness and Reading

JÉSUS ALEGRIA

ABSTRACT

This chapter analyses the reading and spelling skills of deaf persons. It is first noted that reading achievement is usually weak in this population. The data and theory about reading acquisition and reading troubles in the case of hearings suggest two main causes to explain this situation. The first is not specifically related to reading understanding. It is the well-documented inability of deaf children at the linguistic (lexical-semantic and morphosyntactic) level and their weakness in general world knowledge. It is argued that these problems can at least partially be compensated by using Sign Language. Empirical evidence indicates that children exposed to signs, and specially deaf children with deaf parents, tend to have better results in reading comprehension than those exposed to classical oral methods. It is suggested that the positive role of Sign Language on reading comprehension results from its contribution to the development of general world knowledge and some aspects of vocabulary shared by oral and sign languages.

The second cause is reading specific. Current models of reading attribute an essential role to phonology at two distinct levels of written information processing: pre- and post-lexical codes. The former codes intervene in written word identification while the latter are activated after word identification and participate in written sentence understanding. The relevance of pre-lexical phonological coding in the deaf depends on the existence of a phonological lexicon accessible through phonological codes. This is obvious in hearings children but not in the case of the deaf. It is argued however that lip-reading and Cued-Speech do create phonological representations of words that can be accessed through phonological coding. This is specially true of children exposed to Cued-Speech at their homes from an early age. These children develop phonological representation of speech similar to those of the hearing and their mechanisms of written word identification and spelling are also similar.

Post-lexical phonological codes participate in reading comprehension as a memory device. It has been demonstrated that numerous deaf children, specially those exposed precociously and early to Cued-Speech, do use phonological codes is different tasks including working memory and reading comprehension. The data reviewed here demonstrate that reading achievement scores are strongly related with phonological coding in working memory probably because these code

T. Nunes, P. Bryant (eds.), Handbook of Children's Literacy, 459–489.

are the most efficient for written sentences processing. It is concluded that high levels of reading comprehension (a level compatible with high school studies) cannot be reached on the bases of exclusive Sign Language ability. Oral language phonology seems to be a necessary condition for reaching high literacy levels.

INTRODUCTION

The situation

It is well established that deaf persons generally present important reading and spelling difficulties. Twenty years ago in a carefully conducted study Conrad (1979) examined the reading level reached by nearly all of the students leaving special school for hearing impaired children in England and Wales from 1974 to 1976. He used the Wide-span Reading Test (Brimer, 1972) that consists in a series of pairs of sentences, one has a missing word that has to be found in the other sentence. The median reading age for the entire population was 9;0 (years;months). In the subgroup presenting hearing losses greater than 86 dB, about 50% of the students were totally illiterates (reading age 7;0 years which is the zero level of the test). Finally, if it is admitted that a functional level of literacy is not reached before a reading age of 11–12 years, less than 15% percent of this population reached this level.

Conrad underlines the remarkable coincidence of his results with those obtained by DiFrancesca for 17,000 hearing impaired children in the USA. The reading age of the 15- to 16-year-old groups in this study was 9;2. Similarly, Trybus and Krashmer (1977) examined a sample of about 1,000 hearing impaired persons of 20 and older. They found the median reading achievement to be equivalent to about grade four; only 10% of the oldest group have reached the eighth-grade level in reading. It is sometimes assumed that reading ability improves after leaving school. Hammermeister (1971) examined reading abilities of a group of adults up to thirteen years beyond school-leaving age and found that reading comprehension did not improve, despite an increase in vocabulary.

Studies conducted in the eighties and nineties basically confirm those just mentioned. Allen (1986) has examined the group of deaf students involved in the norming of the Stanford Achievement Test (SAT). He found that the reading level increases from 8 to 15 years at a rate of about five times slower than in hearing children. As a result, the difference between deaf and hearing children tends to increase as a function of time (Harris, 1994). Furthermore, no improvements were observed between 15 and 18 (the last age considered in the study). A plateau at a reading level at about third grade seems to be reached (see also Paul & Jackson, 1994). Different criteria of functional reading have been proposed. All are more or less arbitrary. If the reading achievement level of fourth or fifth grade were to be adopted as a criterion for functional literacy, as it is usually done for hearing populations, then more than 30% of the school leavers would be deemed illiterate (see Furth, 1966; Lichtenstein, 1998; Marschark & Harris, 1996; for additional evidence and discussion).

In spite of this rather dramatic situation concerning average reading ability in deaf students, there are considerable individual differences, and some deaf students achieve a much higher competence in reading than others. It is thus important to examine these individual differences because they may suggest potential causes of reading disability. One obvious factor is the hearing loss itself. In order to understand the meaning of the factors that determine reading ability, we shall briefly presents a theoretical framework of reading mechanisms and reading acquisition.

A general theoretical framework for reading acquisition and reading disability

Although the reading levels of deaf people have been extensively studied their reading processes have received little attention. In order examine this issue it is necessary to specify a general theoretical context in which empirical data could be understood. Most of the chapters of this volume concern this notion, so that it is sufficient here to concentrate on the aspects of current cognitive theories that concern directly deaf reading.

Reading theories assume that this ability involves *specific abilities*, the most important of which is written word identification mechanisms, and *non specific abilities*, such as those involved in spoken language understanding – that is, parsing sentences and integrating the results into the readers' knowledge base. It has been argued that these two abilities exhaust all of the variance in reading comprehension (Gough, Hoover & Peterson, 1996; Gough & Tunmer, 1986; Hoover & Gough; 1090). Gough *et al.* have called this notion "the simple view of reading", which supposes that reading and understanding a text is the product of word decoding and speech understanding. The failure in one or in the other inevitably provokes reading problems.

The distinction between specific and non specific reading abilities has found empirical support by the presence of cases demonstrating a double dissociation. Some hearing children with normally developed written word decoding skills may have poor reading comprehension. They also present difficulties at spoken language comprehension (Healy, 1983; Stothard & Hulme, 1992; Oakhill & Juill, 1996). In contrast, dyslexic children present specific troubles at word decoding level without problems at the linguistic or general ability level.

In the context of deafness it is worth emphasising that each one of these abilities, specific as well as non-specific, involves phonological coding. This unique term indicates two sorts of codes differing by their nature and function. In word processing, phonological coding is a pre-lexical activity (i.e., it occurs before word recognition) and plays a major role in the process of word identification. In sentence processing, however, the phonological codes involved are post-lexical. In sentence processing, phonological codes are activated after the identification of individual words and have a mnemonic function – that is, they are involved in remembering the initial portions of a sentence in order to make sense of the whole sentence.

Written word processing exploits the regularities in letter-sound correspondences, i.e. in the mapping between spoken words and their alphabetic representation. This mapping plays a determinant role in reading acquisition because it provides readers with a tool for recognising words they knows from spoken language but which they have never seen before. For beginning readers this represents most of the word they encounter in print. It is widely recognised that learners must proceed to an explicit analysis on speech at phonological level in order establish the relationships between oral and written language so that they can exploit the alphabetic code (Bertelson, 1886; Bradley & Bryant, 1983; Byrne, 1992; Ehri, Morais, Alegria & Content, 1987; see also relevant chapters in this volume). Reading backwardness has been interpreted as a failure in the establishment of this mapping. In accordance with this notion, dyslexics are reported as presenting troubles at phonological analysis (Bruck, 1992; Frith, 1997; Gallagher, Laxon, Armstrong & Frith, 1996; Morais & Mousty, 1992; Rack, Snowling & Olson1992; Casalis, this volume).

Besides word decoding skills, reading comprehension requires the ability to bring to bear on the reading processes knowledge of the language that the reader has gained from experience with spoken language (sign language for deaf children who know it). This activity involves memory and it is a well documented fact that post-lexical phonological codes are strongly involved in working memory (WM) (Baddeley, 1986; Baddeley & Hitch, 1974; see Brady, 1991; for the relationships between Working memory and reading difficulties).

As reading skill advances a decrease in the correlation between word decoding and reading comprehension may be expected and an increase in the correlation between listening and reading comprehension (Hoover & Gough, 1990). This is because as word processing abilities develop and become automatic, individual differences at this level tend to disappear. Children who remain poor word decoders, and obviously dyslexic children, may compensate using higher-level linguistic abilities (Stanovich, 1980). Several studies have shown that poor readers rely more on contextual constraints in word decoding than good readers (Perfetti, Goldman & Hogaboam, 1979; Perfetti, & Hogaboam, 1975; Stanovich & West, 1979; 1983).

A final point that is worth considering concerns interactions between specific and non-specific determinant of reading ability. Reading acquisition in hearing children begins by the time they possess linguistic knowledge: lexical, syntactic, and pragmatic, acquired through their social interactions. The first steps in reading acquisitions capitalise on this knowledge. As reading ability increases, language ability also increases as a results of the reading activity itself (Nunes, Bryant, & Bindman, in press). Complex syntactic structures as well as some sophisticated aspects of vocabulary are usually not present in spoken language and can only be acquired through printed material. It has been shown that dyslexic adults matched in reading level with children of third and fourth grade know more words than their younger pairs. This difference disappears at fifth grade, suggesting that from this level onwards vocabulary increases more from reading than from spoken interactions (Greenberg, Ehri & Perin, 1997). This data exemplifies the notion that the relationship between reading and language is one of reciprocal causation (Stanovich, 1986).

Examining reading abilities in deaf children: which are the (good) questions

The data and theorising about reading mechanisms, reading acquisition and the associated difficulties in normally hearing summarised earlier on cannot be ignored when considering reading in deaf persons. My view is that the notions discussed so far allow for an understanding of the exact nature of the problem and consequently for considering adequate solutions and reasonable aims.

Two notions seem particularly important to underline. The first concerns the idea that phonology plays an essential role in reading and that two different kinds of phonology must be considered, one that is involved at word decoding and the other that is involved at higher levels of reading comprehension. The hearing literature shows that individual differences at phonological level are extremely important determinants of reading skills, may be the most important. So it is necessary to examine the phonological skills of the deaf, both pre- and post lexical; their existence, origin, and function will be examined in detail later in this chapter.

The second notion derived from the hearing literature that is important in the context of reading acquisition by deaf people concerns the reciprocal relation between higher level linguistic knowledge and reading. A closely related notion concerns the existence and the origin of this linguistic knowledge. The exposure to spoken language guarantees for hearing children a sufficient linguistic base to start learning to read. This is frequently not the case for deaf children. Reading is often supposed to be a source – often the most important – of language acquisition.

The great debate about oral versus sign language education might be examined in this context. Pure oral methods start from the obvious fact that speech is not acquired naturally by deaf children, as it is in the case of hearing children. Deaf children must be carefully taught through residual hearing, lip-reading which gives visual cues about phonology, and tactile kinaesthetic feedback from articulation. Despite important efforts the results are often unsatisfactory. This has induced some educational settings to introduce methods aimed at improving speech perception by enhancing visual phonological information. The most widely spread and successful is Cued-Speech, which will be discussed in some detail in a later section in this chapter.

Sign languages, in contrast, are rich systems of manual communication acquired by children exposed to them in infancy in much the same manner that hearing children acquire spoken language. This explains their considerable attraction. Sign languages have a lexicon of signs, morphemic devices for building complex words out of simple ones, and grammatical rules for combining words into sentences (Klima & Bellugi 79; Siple, 1978). The basic question to consider is how print, which represents spoken language, can be articulated with linguistic knowledge developed through sign language. An obvious obstacle is the absence of a shared pre-lexical as well as post-lexical phonology between these two systems. As far as the option for sign language means renouncing to develop phonological skills, the success of this educational route in promoting reading acquisition depends on several factors. First, the possibility of creating word identification skills without the help of pre-lexical phonology, that is to say without exploiting the alphabetic code. The limits of such a project are not known and must be empirically established. Second, the possibility of using linguistic and general knowledge developed through sign language to understand written spoken language. This is necessarily incomplete because oral syntax and sign syntax are radically different. The question is how much oral syntax may be acquired using written language as the unique input.

The difficulties of this educational route in promoting reading skills, among some other reasons, has brought educators to consider a mixed system called "Total Communication" or "Bilingual Programs. Children are exposed to a communication system combining signs borrowed from sign language and spoken language, from which the system morphology and syntactical structure are taken. Words and morphemes are also represented using finger spelling, where each letter of the alphabet is represented by one gesture. These systems are called Signed English. Signed French, or more generally, Signed Spoken Language (SSL). These systems are easier to acquire than pure oral language due to the use of signs. They are closer to spoken language, from which they have the borrowed the syntactic structure, but they do not give information about the sub-lexical phonological structure of lexical items.

DETERMINANTS OF READING ABILITY IN DEAF PERSONS

The picture outlined in the review of reading achievement by deaf students was rather pessimistic. There are, however, considerable individual differences that are worth examining because they suggest potential causes of reading disability.

Individual differences in language knowledge.

Individual differences in reading comprehension in poor deaf readers are not the result of specific reading problems. These difficulties largely reflect global deficits in linguistic knowledge, which is certainly the main determinant of the reading difficulties of deaf learners. Before considering individual differences of reading ability itself it is important to examine the differences at linguistic level and their possible origin.

Vocabulary

Lexical acquisition by deaf children in classical oral educational settings is generally extremely slow (Mohay, 1984; Golding-Meadow, 1985). The lexical explosion observed in hearing children revealing an autonomous increase of vocabulary is absent in the deaf (Gregory & Mogford, 1981). As a result, at the onset of primary school orally educated deaf children posses a vocabulary of about 200 words, which is clearly insufficient to start learning to read (Meadow; 1980).

Numerous studies involving deaf children after several years of schooling demonstrate that they remain delayed. A survey using the Peabody Vocabulary Test with 15 year-old deaf students showed that they possess vocabulary levels as low as hearing pre-schoolers (Ives, 1974; Hine & MacDonald, 1974). Similar results have been repeatedly obtained in other studies (King & Quigley, 1985; Marschak, 1995; Miklebust, 1960; Quigley, 1984).

Linguistic development in a sign language context do not differ in any essential manner from oral language Prinz & Prinz, 1979; for recent contributions see the books edited by Emmorey & Lane, 2000, and Chamberlain, Morford & Mayberry, 2000). Similarly educational programs including signs (SSL) tend to produce better results at lexical development than pure oral methods. Schlesinger and Meadow (1972), for example, have follow a deaf child exposed to signed English at his home between 1;3 and 3;4. A lexical explosion was observed and at the end of this period the vocabulary has reached 604 items which is far greater than the values obtained with classical oral methods.

Morphology and syntax

In a detailed series of studies, Quigley and his associates have found that deaf children have severe problems with syntax (Quigley, Smith & Wilbur, 1974 Quigley *et al.* 1976; 1977). They have examined the syntactic abilities of deaf students from 10 to 19 year. The results show that the average 18-year-old deaf has a syntactic ability of about those of an 8-year-old hearing child with some interesting differences among English structures: question formation, complementation, and pronominalisation are the poorest while the simplest negation and conjunction structures the best (see also Brown, 1984; Cooper, 1967; Odom, Blanton *et al.* 1967; and Dubuisson & Vincent-Durroux, 1991, in French, Volterra & Bates, 1989, in Italian).

Bilingual methods including signs in the education of deaf children have weaker effects on syntax than they have on vocabulary. Dood, McIntosh, and Woodhouse (1998) in a longitudinal study with children exposed to a Total Communication program have found that morphology and syntax were the most impaired linguistic abilities. The mean length utterance (abbreviated as MLU) age reached 3;4, which was more than 6 years below the children's current chronological age. The delay in sentence comprehension was somewhat inferior: 3;9. Examination of the children's strategy to understand English indicated a strong tendency to impose a subject-verb-object structure to all of sentence forms and to disregard grammatical devices (plural-singular markers and prepositions). The notion that vocabulary usually reaches higher level than syntax has also been documented by Harrris (1994). In her study, deaf and hearing children matched for single word reading level presented important differences in text comprehension, with the deaf being poorer than the hearing (Bishop, 1983; Schick, 1992).

Vocabulary and syntax data clearly show that most deaf children have important difficulties when they were pre-schoolers and that their progress with age remains weak because of the reciprocal relations between language knowledge and reading ability (the Mathew effect, see Hurry, this volume). Initial poor linguistic abilities in deaf children may produce poor reading performance and, as a consequence, this reading difficulty deprives them from an important source of linguistic knowledge. Waters and Doehring (1990) have separately evaluated several linguistic abilities – including vocabulary and syntax – of a group of deaf young people from 7 to 20 years and their reading achievement. Strong correlation between these two measures were observed at each age and at each reading level. More important, the authors pointed out that scatter plot showed that the subjects who have better reading skills tend to have better spoken-language skills, whereas but the reverse was not true. This suggest that reading problems stem for global linguistic deficits. Marschak and Harris (1996) have proposed that before starting reading instruction linguistic knowledge must have reached a critical mass. Reading itself will then play its role in the acquisition of vocabulary and syntax.

Individual differences in reading comprehension.

In the Conrad (1979) study, three factors strongly correlated with reading level were carefully analysed: hearing loss, intelligence (non-verbal intelligence evaluated with the Raven's Matrices), and the use of "internal speech" in working memory (WM), which was evaluated comparing the immediate recall for series of rhyming words (do, who, few, etc.) with series of non rhyming words (home, lane, bean, etc.). The rationale was that speech recording as a tool for maintaining information in WM would reduce performance for rhyming compared with non-rhyming items (this difference will be called the rhyming effect).

Hearing loss and non-verbal intelligence played independent roles. When considering the former factor, children with a hearing loss up to 85 dB were better readers than those with a greater loss (median reading ages 10;0 and 7;6, respectively). The comparison of reading scores of children above and below the median in the intelligence test showed a difference of about two years in favour of the former group at each hearing loss level.

Internal speech evaluated with the rhyming effect was strongly correlated with hearing loss, memory span and with reading ability. Young people who used speech codes scored 1;6 to 2;9 years ahead in reading even after controlling for hearing loss and non verbal intelligence. Conrad concluded that "the degree of deafness in itself is not a major factor in reading comprehension" but "whether or not the child has acquired the use of internal speech" (p 157). This is an important notion from both theoretical and practical reasons because internal speech, at least at first sight, cab be expected to be under the control of educational factors.

Wandel (1989; in LaSasso, 1998a, b) used Conrad's (1979) methods and materials with 90 deaf students from 7 to 16 years exposed to different communication systems: Oral, Total Communication and Cued-Speech. The results showed that Oral and Cued-Speech children were more prone to use speech in working memory than those in a Total Communication background.

More recently, Lichtenstein (1998) examined the relationships between reading processes and speech coding in WM with deaf students (mean age 20;10). He adopted Conrad's technique as well as a detailed questionnaire in which the subjects were requested to report their own introspection about coding in WM and in reading: speech, sign, finger spelling, and visuo-orthographic codes. Reading ability was correlated with memory span and with both speech coding scores (rhyming effect) and reported speech coding. Together these measures accounted for 40% of students spelling scores and 30% of reading comprehension. This confirmation of Conrad's work is important because the present population was educated in a variety of ways, including sign language (44.5% of the subjects used sign language as their ordinary manner to communicate). It is worth mentioning that even the students with no oral education showed the increase in reading skills as a function of speech coding.

An additional factor that has been recurrently reported as related to reading ability concerns the exposure to sign language. This is often indirectly established showing that deaf children with deaf parents are usually better readers than children with hearing parents. In Conrad's study (1979), the deaf children of deaf parents read at about two grades above a carefully constructed control group of deaf children with hearing parents (see also Jensema & Tribus 1978; Marscharh, 1993; Meadow, 1968; Prince & Strong, 1997; Schlesinger & Meadow, 1972; Stukless, 1966; Vernon & Koh; 1970).

Such findings have led some authors to propose that early exposure to sign language plays a positive role in reading comprehension because it gives the child a first language (sign language) which facilitates the processing of some aspect of a second (oral) language. It must be recognised, however, that deaf and hearing parents of deaf children differ not only in their competence in signing but also, for example, in social and cultural issues which determine academic and personal expectations concerning their sons (Marschark, 1993). This notion is certainly important but it cannot explain all of the effects of belonging to a family of deaf. Strong and Prinz (1997) compared the reading ability of groups of deaf children from deaf and from hearing mothers and found the classic difference. The authors evaluated independently the child's ability in sign language and established three groups, low, medium, and high ability. When this factor was controlled difference between groups disappear with one exception: in the low group the difference in English literacy as a function of the hearing status of the parents remained.

Several authors have challenged the notion that sign language *per se* facilitates the acquisition of high levels of literacy in a second language. It is worth noticing that sign language and spoken language differ radically at the level of morphology and syntax. Marschak and Harris (1996) state quite reasonably that sign language (American or British in their discussion but the notion can be generalised to other sign languages) will facilitate reading of English or Chinese in the same manner. This implies that the facilitation takes place at a rather abstract level which is by no means equivalent to the level at which spoken languages and their printed form are related, that is to say the phonological level (LaSasso, 1998a, b). It seems obvious that the knowledge of structural aspects of spoken language must help written language acquisition. Jensema and Trybus (1978) have reported data that can be understood in this perspective. They have compared deaf children from families with one and with two parents being deaf. In the former case speech was the primary form of communication while in the later it was sign. In both cases, however, the children were presented with sign language. The reading level reached by the children with only one parent deaf was superior to the level reached by the other group.

Some aspects of the Lichtenstein (1998) study are worth mentioning in the present discussion. Besides searching for the presence of speech coding in working memory, this author also examined for codes based on sign, as well as on finger spelling and visuo-orthographic patterns. The technique was similar to the one used to detect speech coding. In order to determine sign coding the author compared recall for lists of items presenting similarity in sign structure, "queremic" similarity, with the recall of a control list which did not presented such similarity. Some previous studies had demonstrated that deaf signers do code using sign representations (Bellugi, Klima & Siple, 1975; Klima & Bellugi, 1979). In the present experiment however queremic similarity effects were absent and individual evaluations of this effect were not correlated with subjective reports of using sign to memorise and to read. Besides no correlation was observed between the use of sign language to communicate and the use of speech coding in reading and in working memory. Lichtenstein points out that students who virtually never use speech to communicate reported using speech codes for processing written English. It is suggested that sign coding is not a useful coding device in memory and reading. As a matter of fact, queremic distinctiveness of the items in the control list did not aid memory. These observations confirm Hanson's (1982) findings that second generation deaf children with American Sign Language (ASL) as first language do use speech coding in memory tasks involving both signs and words and that speech coding was correlated with memory span.

To conclude it seems that the positive effects of sign language knowledge on reading cannot be attributed to any aid at the level of coding. Speech codes seem to be the most efficient tool to code spoken language in memory and in reading.

The data reviewed so far allow for a weak conclusion that any successful system to convey information may help future reading acquisition. The efficiency of this help may obviously depend on the connection between the knowledge it conveys, the knowledge represented in written language and the codes involved in reading. Written material simultaneously represents several levels of knowledge:

- general world knowledge which is non specifically linguistic;
- specific linguistic knowledge encoded at the level of vocabulary, morphology and syntax;
- and specific knowledge of the language at phonological level.

The positive effects of sign language on reading comprehension can probably be explained by its contribution to the development of general world knowledge as well as some aspects of the vocabulary, which it shares with spoken language. Morphology and syntax of sign language, however, differ in important aspects from spoken language (see Burman & Pretzlik, this volume) so that it cannot help reading comprehension at this level. Some authors have speculated that early sign language acquisition might help the acquisition of a second (oral) language and through this participate in reading comprehension. Compelling data are not available on this matter (see LaSasso, 1998b; for a critical examination of this hypothesis).

The exposure to Total Communication systems incorporating signs into spoken language syntactic structures have been reported as being as efficient as sign language at reading acquisition level (Marschark & Harris, 1996). These systems, unlike pure sign language, represent the morphological and syntactic structure of spoken language, so that they can in principle be a better support for the acquisition of the corresponding written language. This has important con-sequences for deaf early education because sign languages are only available to deaf parents while signed versions of spoken languages are more easily accessible to hearing parents. Similar considerations have been applied to hearing teachers of the deaf (Woodward & Allen, 1987). It is clear that it is easier for them to develop a real competence in signing a spoken language than in sign language.

Finally post-lexical speech (phonological) codes seem to be specially well adapted to process written information. The data discussed in this section suggest that this is because they are optimal for fulfilling memory needs in reading. This may explain the recurrent correlation observed between spoken ability and both memory span and reading ability.

An important point for further discussion concerns the relationships between the spoken language ability and speech intelligibility. Possessing useful phonological representations of language does not necessarily imply speech ability, as shown by the results reported by Bishop and Robson (1989), who demonstrated that congenitally speechless individuals present the rhyming effects in memory tasks.

PHONOLOGY AND READING IN DEAF PERSONS

The notion of phonology is typically attached to auditory information. If this were true, profoundly deaf persons would not have phonological codes. We shall argue that phonology is an abstract notion that includes sensory information other than auditory. Lip-reading, for example, gives the deaf child information about the sequence of units that forms words. Dodd, McIntosh, and Woodhouse (1998) state that "phonology is the linguistic system of contrasts that governs how speech sounds may be combined to convey meaning". If the term "speech sounds" was replaced by "abstract speech units", then the notion of phonology as a system of contrasts might be detached from the notion of auditory input. The function of those units is to create minimal contrastive sequences that permit to differentiate pairs of items like /pin/-/bin/ and /pin/-/tin/. It is clear that lip-reading gives information that does not allow for the discrimination of the former pair but allows for the discrimination of the latter. Dodd has convincingly argued that lip-reading and obviously residual hearing provide deaf pre-schoolers useful phonological information that may be revealed in different tasks involving speech processing and representation. In this section we shall first review evidence demonstrating that at least some deaf persons do possess phonological representations, then the visual origin of those representations will be discussed.

Phonological representations in deaf children: convergent evidence from different paradigms

A great number of cognitive activities involve phonological coding. The main reason is that phonological codes are a central device in WM, which has ubiquitous functions in human cognition. The experiments on WM in deaf students reviewed earlier on demonstrated that phonological coding was positively correlated with memory span, reading comprehension, and speech intelligibility, suggesting that phonological codes are optimal for written language understanding.

The role of WM in written language understanding has been examined in a more direct manner using the "tongue-twisting" paradigm. Bell, France, and Perfetti (1991) submitted hearing college students to a semantic acceptability task of written sentences which contained several words beginning either with stop consonants: /t d/, or fricatives: /s z/. In addition the subject have to retain series of digits presenting either the same (stops) or different consonants (fricatives) than the sentences. The results show specific interference effects indicating that working memory is the locus of written sentence processing and that processing activates phonological codes. This has been confirmed with less skilled readers from second to fourth grades (McCutchen & Crain-Thoreson, 1994). Hanson, Goodell, and Perfetti (1991) have demonstrated a tongue-twister effect with deaf college students whose first language was ASL. They concluded from these results that, despite ASL, phonological coding was in principle available for these students and that they did use phonological codes during silent reading, suggesting that phonological codes are the most adapted to written language processing. This conclusion is consistent with results presented earlier on in this chapter.

Another important source of evidence concerning the use of phonological coding by the deaf is word spelling. A possible procedure to spell a word consists in activating its phonological code and translating it into the sequence of letters according with systematic rules. Similar results may by obtained using whole orthographic representations without any participation of phonological codes and translation rules. Some results have suggested that deaf spellers may rely exclusively on orthographic representations (Dodd, 1980). It seems clear, however, from other studies that deaf students do use phonology to spell (see Campbell, 1994; for a review). Hanson, Shankweiler, and Fischer (1983), and Burden and Campbell (1994) in English, Leybaert and Alegria (1995) and Leybaert (2000) in French, have shown that words that have a consistent spelling (the sequence of letters may be derived from their surface phonology using rules), were better spelled than words presenting inconsistencies. Besides, an important proportion of misspellings were homophones of the target word. These effects were correlated with speech intelligibility as was the case for phonological coding in WM.

Convergent data have been collected using the rhyme decision paradigm (for ex. saying whether the names of two pictures rhyme or not) Campbell & Wright (1988) have shown that deaf youngsters tend to rely on spelling. They consider that words rhyme only if they have identical orthographic endings. However this is not necessarily the case as shown by the fact that phonological codes based on lip-reading have been demonstrated (Dodd & Hermelin, 1977; Charlier & Leybaert, 2000). Interestingly these representations are under specified because lip-reading do not transmit some phonetics contrasts. As a results misspelling ("sponch" for *sponge* and "oufert" pour *ouvert* in English and French respectively; Leybaert, 1998) as well as rhyming decision errors reflect this fact revealing identical mechanisms operating on the same codes. Charlier & Leybaert (2000) however have examined the performance of children exposed to CS before the age of 3 on a rhyming decision task. The results showed that sensitivity to the rhyme develops before the acquisition if written language and that lip-reading errors were absent suggesting that the phonological representations underlying the responses were completely specified (see further data and discussion later in the chapter).

The Stroop colour-word interference paradigm has been used with deaf children because it reveals automatic word identification and the consecutive activation of the corresponding phonological code (Leybaert, Alegria & Fonck, 1983; Leybaert & Alegria, 1993). This paradigm consists in presenting colour names written in colour to the participants, whose task it is to name the colour used in the presentation rather than read the colour word. The interference effect is shown in the response latencies, which are considerably larger if the word presented is a colour name, which interferes with naming the colour in which it was written, than if the word is not a colour name. The Stroop interference is considerably greater in a colour naming than in a manual response task, where the participants would press a key with a dot of matching the colour of the letters used to present the word. (Pritchatt, 1968). It has been hypothesised that in the naming condition the word and the colour inputs automatically evoke their corresponding phonological codes. The greatest part of the interference comes from the competition between these two phonological output codes. In the manual response condition, however, the interference is weaker because the phonological code evoked by the identification of the written word does not interfere (or not so much) with the colour-naming task (Lupker & Katz, 1981). In a series of experiment (Leybaert, Alegria & Fonck, 1983; Leybaert & Alegria 1993) compared the manual with the naming Stroop interferences in two groups of orally trained deaf subjects, one having good and the other poor speech-intelligibility, and in a group of hearing controls. In the manual response condition the interference was significant and basically identical in the three groups. A significant and rather substantial increase of interference was observed in the naming task only in the hearing and in the good speech-intelligibility deaf groups. These results indicate that written word as well as colour identification automatically evoke the corresponding phonological output code in the deaf who have developed intelligible speech.

To summarise, the experimental evidence examined so far clearly demonstrates that at least some profoundly deaf children do possess phonological codes and that this is not an exceptional situation. Individual differences at speech intelligibility were correlated with phonological coding. It is interesting to note that in some cases – rhyming effects in WM and in the Stroop task – the activation of phonological codes had detrimental effects on performance (in the Stroop case the subjects were totally aware of the negative effects of their tendency to pronounce the word's name). The fact that phonological codes participate in these conditions suggests that their activation is not under the subject's control as it might be he case in spelling and in rhyming decision tasks.

The theoretical framework outlined in this chapter made a clear distinction between pre- and post-lexical phonological codes. The codes at play in all of these experiments are post-lexical, that is to say they are evoked after the activation of lexical item. It makes sense that those codes were related with speech production.

Lip-reading and speech perception in deaf and hearing persons

The basic input for deaf people that might help the elaboration of phonological representations is Lip-Reading (LR). Numerous arguments demonstrate that this is the case. Each time explicit speech production, oral as well as written, is examined in deaf students the specificity observed is easily explained in terms of LR. Dodd (1976) has shown that more that 60% of the oral production errors in orally educated deaf results from the ambiguities of LR: stopping ("tip" for "ship"), suppression of final syllables ("ma" for "mat"), suppression of weak syllables ("nana" for "banana") etc. Spelling errors are of the same kind (Leybaert & Alegria, 1995, Leybaert, 1998).

The role assigned to lip-reading until the mid 70s was real but theoretically modest. It was recognised that lip-reading improves speech understanding in poor hearing conditions (Binnie, Montgomery & Jackson, 1974; Erber, 1969, 1974; Sumby & Pollack, 1954). LR information was supposed to be optional, that is to say that it can be exploited if the subject feels that it could be useful, and ignored otherwise. Data collected during the last 20 years, however, have shown that when the listener sees the speaker's face, he cannot ignore the LR information. The visual information accompanying speech production inevitably integrates into an audio-visual compound which is identified as a speech-sound that can differ from the auditory signal. McGurk and McDonald (1976) showed that seeing a face pronouncing the syllable /ga/ together with a simultaneous auditory /ba/ produces an intermediate percept /da/. If auditory and visual stimuli are inverted, that is, when the visual stimulus presents a bilabial feature, /ba/ or /pa/, this feature is inevitably included in the subject's perception, which sounds /bga/ or /bda/. These results have been confirmed and their consequences for speech processing theories have been discussed amply (Burnham, 1998; Green, 1998; Liberman & Mattinbly, 1985; Massaro 1987; Summerfield, 1987, 1989; see Campbell, Dodd & Burnham, 1998; for an excellent collection of papers concerning this notion). The main point of these theories is that speech processing must be considered as an auditory visual phenomenon.

Studies concerning the McGurk effect from a developmental point of view have shown that it is present in 4-6 year-olds (McGurk & McDonald, 1976; Massaro, 1987) but also in infants. Using the paradigm of preference, Dodd (1977) has shown that 10- to 16-week-old infants devote more attention to speech when sound and lip movements were synchronised than when they were out-of-synchrony. Kuhl and Meltzoff (1982) and McKain, Studdert-Kennedy, Spieker, and Stern (1983) have demonstrated that 4- to 6-month-old infants presented with two faces prefer to look at the face executing the articulatory gesture corresponding to the stimulus simultaneously presented through audition. Finally using the habituation paradigm Burnham and Dodd (1996) have shown that the 4- to 6-month-old infants are susceptible to the McGurk effect.

In the context of the present discussion concerning phonological access to linguistic representations in the deaf, it could be extremely important to determine how LR information has acquired its phonological value. It may be hypothesised that it is the case because hearing individuals are exposed to massive and highly correlated audio-visual speech. The data concerning audio-visual speech perception in infants casts some doubt on this notion. A pre-wired speech processor to deal with phonological information including LR is available in infancy. It is conceivable then that the exposure to LR alone, as is the case of infants born profoundly deaf, could activate the speech processor. The notion that LR is integrated into the speech perception device leads to the conclusion that there must be sufficiently abstract speech representations, common to both the auditory and the visual speech signals (see Summerfield, 1987, 1991).

Cued-Speech: a manual aid to lip-reading

Lip-reading alone is insufficient to deliver much useful speech because of its intrinsic ambiguity. To take an example from the earliest referential items, French words like "papa" /papa/ and "maman" /mamã/ are identical at LR. This situation has frequently brought speech therapists and teachers of the deaf to add systematic signals, usually visual but sometimes tactile to LR, in order to reduce the ambiguity of LR.

Cued Speech (CS) has been developed to help deaf children to understand speech by eliminating LR ambiguity (Cornett, 1967; see LaSasso, 1989b; for a recent description of the English version; Alegria, Charlier & Mattys, 1999; for the French version, and Torres & Ruiz, 1996 for the Spanish).

Language acquisition and speech processing

Data concerning language development in deaf children exposed to CS at their homes before the age of 2 years (Home-CS children) have shown that these children develop a vocabulary similar to their hearing pairs (Cornett, 1973; Nash, 1973; Périer, 1988). Similarly, morphosyntactic data collected with deaf children do not differ from normal hearing children. Moseley, Williams-Scott and Anthony (1991) have examined the MLU and the 14 first English morphemes (Brown, 1973) of a deaf child of 3;10 year. The results were within the hearing norms (see also Kilpila, 1985, and Metzger, 1994, in LaSasso 1998).

In a French study (Alegria, Hage & Périer, 1991) have examined the capacity of a group of Home-CS children to deal with French grammatical gender. The phonological marks concerning the grammatical gender are noun endings which sound masculine or feminine. The child task consists in to associate this endings with the determinants which are also marked for gender (i.e. *la* fourch*ette* (the fork) typically feminine, *le* cam*ion* (the lorry) typically masculine). It is difficult to deal with this task for two main reasons. First word endings are not systematically related to gender (some endings are unmarked, i.e. *la loi* (the law) – *le roi* (the king)). The second reasons concerns specially deaf children. It results from the fact that both word-endings and determinants are difficult to perceive in LR. So that CS was expected to transmit this specially tenuous phonological information more precisely than classical oral methods. Two groups of children were considered, a Home-CS and a group precociously and intensively trained by oral methods. The children in both groups were matched for vocabulary knowledge and lip-reading ability. The groups differed in the attribution of grammatical gender to unfamiliar words indicating that the Home-CS group have succeed at elaborating a superior ability to derive grammatical gender from phonology cues.

Speech perception in deaf children of school age using Cs has been examined in some experimental studies (Nicholls & Ling, 1982; Charlier, Hage, Alegria & Périer, 1990; Alegria, Charlier & Mattys, 1999). Groups of deaf children knowing CS were submitted to a sentence comprehension task, word identification, and/or pseudo words processing, presented with LR alone or LR accompanied with CS. Without exception CS significantly and substantially improved speech performance compared with LR alone. In the Alegria *et al.* (1999) experiment a Home-CS group and a School-CS group were compared. The former group included children who had started using CS with their parents at home as the ordinary way to communicate before the age of 2. The school group had begun later (usually at 6) and used CS exclusively at school. The results showed that the gain induced by CS relative to the LR condition was significantly greater in the Home-CS group than in the School-CS group (despite the fact that the former group was younger than the latter). The difference favouring the home-CS group was especially important in pseudo-word processing. The differences between these two groups remained when the duration of the exposure to CS was statistically controlled. This indicates that pure, non-lexical phonological processing depended more strongly on precautions of exposure to CS than to the duration of the exposure *per se.*

It may be hypothesised from these data that exposure to CS allows the children to elaborate speech representations which are completely specified. Evidence in favour of this notion has been obtained using the rhyming decision task and examining spelling production errors of deaf children precociously exposed to CS. In the experiment by Charlier and Leybaert (1998) previously commented, half of the non-rhyming pairs were similar at lip-reading level (for example the pair: *train- pied*, the items' endings do not rhyme but are identical for lip-reading). Performance in the Home-CS and School-CS groups in the non-rhyming condition reached 90% and 68% correct. The results indicate that the Home-CS group possess phonological representations of words presenting contrasts which are not transmitted by LR.

In a spelling task using high-frequency and low-frequency words, Leybaert (1999) examined in a quite precise manner the errors of Home-CS and School-CS youngsters and a group of hearing controls. The frequency of phonetically acceptable spellings in the Home-CS group was indistinguishable from the scores of the hearing controls and greater than those of the School-Cs group. It is worth mentioning that the three groups were matched for global spelling level and that hearing and Home-Cs groups were younger than the School-CS group (8;9, 8;10 and 11;1 respectively). It is concluded that the development of completely specified phonological representations of speech underlying spelling depends on the phonetic accuracy of the input to which the children are exposed in pre-school years, including auditory and visual input.

READING MECHANISMS IN THE DEAF

The problem under consideration in this section concerns the mechanisms used by deaf people to understand written information. A theory derived from hearing subjects' data, summarised in the first section of this chapter, indicates that two main problems must be examined: word identification on the one hand and sentence parsing and other higher level processes of meaning extraction from texts on the other hand.

Word identification processes

Despite non trivial differences between models of written word identification, all of them include a phonological assembling device which elaborates sublexical phonological strings from orthographic information, and a corpus of global orthographic representations of words which permits their identification. The main question concerns the existence of a sublexical device in deaf readers. The function of such a device is twofold: it allows for the identification of words which do not have an orthographic entry, and it contributes to the elaboration of these orthographic entries (Ehri, 1991; Gough & Juel, 1991; Perfetti, 1991; Share 1999). The relevance of the phonological assembler depends on the existence of a functional phonological access to the lexicon. It is obvious that elaborating phonology from print is useless without a phonological access to lexical knowledge. The data reviewed in the previous section show that at least deaf children whose lip-reading abilities have been successfully exploited do have access to phonological codes. Phonological access, however, might be absent in deaf signers. It must be recognise that this is not necessarily the case because deaf signers are exposed to lip-reading and because finger-spelling, which is integrated in sign language, might play a role at this level. The question must be examined on empirical grounds.

The paradigms of lexical decision and of naming, combining factors like word frequency and lexicality with item length and spelling-to-sound regularity, have been used to determine the contribution of phonological assembling and orthographic access procedures to word identification in several studies.

Using the naming paradigm a group of 19 orally educated deaf youngsters aged from 14 to 20 years was tested (see Alegria & Leybaert, 1991; Leybaert, 1993; for a more extended report of these data). Naming latencies and naming errors were recorded. Three aspects of the results demonstrate the participation of phonological assembling. The first was their basically correct pronunciation of pseudowords. The performance for pseudowords derived from words by changing one letter (e.g. tur from dur (hard)) was poorer than the performance for the corresponding words. This effect of lexicality was not due to the articulatory familiarity of the words as shown by the fact that pseudohomophones (pseudowords pronounced like real words) showed a reliable effect of lexicality, which was significantly smaller than the one obtained with the non-homophonic pseudowords.

A second source of evidence of phonological assembling activity with words was obtained by combining frequency and length. The effect of frequency was obtained with latency as well as with accuracy scores. As expected, the effects of length were weaker for the frequent than for the infrequent words indicating that phonological assembling was mainly used to identify unfrequented words for which a lexical orthographic access was not available.

Thirdly, series of irregular words were considered. The application of an assembling procedure in this case produces regularisations (for example, reading / fem/ instead of /fam/ for *femme* (woman)) that can interfere with the post-lexical correct pronunciation directly found in the lexical address. Special precautions were to be taken because sometimes deaf children produced the regularised response not only when presented with the written version of some words, but also in picture manning or when spontaneously pronouncing them. This is because the internal phonology associated with lexical items comes sometimes from the orthographic version of the word (see previous discussion on the rhyme decision task in Campbell & Write, 1988, and Charlier & Leybaert, 1998). To eliminate this artefact the subjects were asked to name a drawing of each of the irregular words used in the experiment. Only those words correctly pronounced in this case were considered. The naming results showed a reliable effect of regularity, which was greater with infrequent than with frequent words.

Using the lexical decision paradigm Burden and Campbell (1994) examined a group of deaf school leavers of 14;6 years with a reading age of 9;6. The results revealed significant effects of regularity for infrequent words at both response latencies and response accuracy, similar to the results for a control group of hearing children paired with them for reading comprehension.

Transler, Leybaert & Gombert (1999) have explored assembling abilities in deaf students asking them to choose among two items the one which is "more similar" compared with a model item. The notion of similarity was not explained to the subject. It was expected that his choices may reveal something about the units on which comparison were done. The results strongly depended on the speech intelligibility of the children. The high intelligibility group as well as the hearing control gave phonologically motivated choices. They choose homophones instead of orthographically similar items and showed sensitivity to the syllabic structure of the items (with the CVC-CV model: *paulni, paulto* (CVC-CV) will be preferred to *paulot* (CV-CVC)).

These data lead to the conclusion that written word identification in orally educated deaf children is not restricted to orthographic recognition but that they possess and use a phonological assembler. It seems likely that an important proportion of deaf persons possesses lexical entries that are accessible via a phonological path.

Important differences between deaf students as a function of educational factors are likely to be observed. Hickson, Woodyant, Cue & Dodd (in press) have done a longitudinal study with 8 children educated in a total communication setting. For 5 out of the 8, sign was the dominant modality for communication while the others mainly used speech. The errors observed in a naming task showed a dichotomy between these groups. The errors produced by the children who signed were consisted mainly in either reading refusals or substitutions based on salient parts of the word (*under* for *undid*, *stand* for *stamps*). Refusals revealed that children did not use decoding procedures for the words that were not immediately recognised through a stored orthographic code. In contrast, errors of children who used speech showed a high proportion of mispronunciations (*brife* for *brief*) indicating that they did use a phonological decoding strategy.

The case of word identification in deaf signers presents considerable interest from a theoretical as well as a practical standpoint. It would seem less likely that these persons use phonological codes in word identification. Some authors, however, have evoked the possibility that children who communicate by sign may use fingerspelling to elaborate a link between written words and the internal sign representations, so that, unknown printed words might be coded in a familiar finger-spelled version in a way similar to phonological assembling, and succeed at word identification. Hirsh-Pasek and Treiman (1982) have shown that deaf children improve word identification only when they were encouraged to fingerspell written words that are in their finger-spelling vocabulary. However, Treiman and Hirsh-Pasek (1983) in an experiment with successful readers whose first language was sign language and who have poor oral skills failed to find evidence of fingerspelling recoding in a correct/incorrect sentence decision task (see also Lichtenstein, 1998). In the critical condition sentences presented numerous repetitions of finger-spelling handshapes aimed at disturbing sentence processing if fingerspelling codes were used. It must be said that this paradigm clearly concerns post-lexical codes though the results do not imply that fingerspell codes are not used in word identification (but see Mayberry & Waters, 1987).

Some authors, however, using also the lexical decision and the naming paradigms have failed to find any evidence of phonological assembling activity in word identification. Waters and Doehring (1990) submitted a group of orally educated deaf students aged from 7 to 20 years to several lexical decision tasks. In one task spelling to sound regularity of the items was manipulated. The second task used the technique elaborated by Meyer, Schvaneveldt and Rudy (1974) in which pairs of items are shown and the subject has to decide whether both are words or not. The items may be phonologically and/or orthographically similar (i.e. *hold-bold*, *light-bite*, *cough-tough*, *chair-white*). The results show an important effect of age, the younger subjects being slower than the older, but phonological coding effects were absent at all ages.

Similarly Beech and Harris (1991) submitted a group of deaf students of 9;6 years with a reading age of 7;6 years to a lexical decision task. They found that children correctly rejected pseudohomophones and accepted irregularly spelled words far better than hearing controls, suggesting that their decision did not rely on phonological assembling procedures. Some aspects of the results were somehow surprising. A post-hoc comparison between a group of fluent signers with no spoken language skills and another group presenting the opposite pattern failed to show any difference at phonological decoding level. The author concluded that deaf students rely exclusively on a sight vocabulary to identify written words even though they possess good oral abilities. In a recent longitudinal study these authors have examined the progress at word reading in deaf students during the first two years of school (Harris & Beech, 1995). The results showed a significant and strong correlation (r = .71) between word reading and phonological skills evaluated with an "oddity test", in which the subject has to indicate which drawing among three or four has a name which does not rhyme with the others (Bradley & Bryant, 1983). The authors recognise that this correlation is a bit surprising taking into account the absence of evidence of phonological coding in word identification. It might be supposed that the children possessed phonological representations of words and were able to analyse them into constituents, as shown by their ability to answer to the oddity question, but they did not use those units in word reading.

A similar conclusion can be drawn from an additional experiment reported by Waters and Doehring (1990) with a group of 15 orally trained deaf youngsters from 15- to 22-years old and presenting an important reading ability span (from 4th to 12th grade). They were presented with the lexical decision tasks previously discussed and, as was the case in the main experiment, their results showed an absence of spelling-to-sound regularity effects. These subjects were also presented with a series of tasks involving an explicit spelling-to-sound procedure (for example, to point to a picture among four which corresponded to a printed pseudohomophone). The results showed that the better readers were faster and committed fewer errors than the poorer readers in these tasks. The conclusion is that good deaf readers are able to abstract phonological information when this is necessary but that they do not use this ability spontaneously in reading words. The authors speculate that this may result from their limited oral vocabulary, which makes phonological access less useful for them than it is for hearing readers. These data, together with those from the Beech and Harris (1991) study, point towards an interesting dissociation between pre- and post-lexical phonological coding.

Recent work concerning word identification mechanisms in hearing people has introduced a distinction between automatic and strategic phonological coding (see Berent & Perfetti, 1995 for a discussion). For example, the regularity effects in classical naming and in lexical decision tasks obtained with deaf or hearing children may result from the use graphophonemic regularities as a consciously controlled strategic. It would be interesting to demonstrate that phonological codes are indeed automatically generated during word identification. In the hearing literature strong evidence has been reported for phonological activity during the first 100 ms of word identification. One of the methods of documenting this phenomenon consists in using the paradigm known as priming. In a priming reading study, participants are exposed to a word – the prime – for a very short duration and then to a second word – the target word – that is assumed to be either related or not to the prime. A priming effect is obtained when recognition of the target word is facilitated after the prime in comparison to recognition when the prime was not presented. If a mask – that is, another stimulus – is presented between the prime and the target word, the facilitation effect tends to disappear. Priming has been used in the assessment of phonological effects by presenting successively the prime and the target separated by a mask (e.g. series of XXXX), aimed at interrupting the processing of the prime. The prime is of short duration (e.g. 50 ms). A response (naming or lexical decision) to the target word has to be performed. The relationships between prime and target are manipulated as well as the time interval between them (Stimulus Onset Asynchrony, SOA). When the prime is a homophone of a word semantically related to the target word (in French *ocean* may be primed by *maire* (major) which is homophonous of *mer* (sea) and also by the pseudohomophone *merre*); facilitation is observed relative to the case where no relationship exists between prime and target. The SOA values of less than 100 ms have been shown to produce facilitation (Van Orden, 1987; Ferrand & Grainger, 1992; Terrand, Granger & Segui, 1992). Some of the experiments examined so far using classical naming and lexical decision tasks suggest that deaf children use assembling procedures from phonological codes. It would be interesting to determine the exact status, strategic or automatic, of these codes. To the best of my knowledge there is only one published experiment using this method with deaf subjects. Paire-Ficoud and Bédoid (1996) used an SOA of 100 ms, with prime and mask of 50 ms each. The semantic priming effect mediated by phonological similarity was absent in the deaf group. The authors manipulated the factor "visibility" of the prime word in terms of LR. This factor appeared to be significant, suggesting that LR codes are rapidly and automatically activated following the presentation of a printed word. This has important consequences concerning the access to the lexicon. It is obvious that more experimental work concerning these issues is necessary especially in the context of educational options for deaf children.

Higher level linguistic resources and word identification

Reading comprehension depends on two basic devices, firstly low level specific word identification abilities and secondly, high level general linguistic and non-linguistic knowledge. Empirical data discussed in the first section of this chapter showed that poor word decoding abilities can be – and generally are – compensated for by the use of higher level knowledge. Poor hearing decoders strongly rely on linguistic constraints to identify written words (Perfetti *et al.*, 1979; Stanowitch & West, 1979, 1983). Since written word processing depends on phonological abilities it was expected that deaf readers must also rely heavily on higher level resources to understand texts.

This prediction has been directly examined in an experiment considering the role of context in word identification in deaf as well as hearing people (Fischler, 1985). A group of 40 undergraduate deaf students from Gallaudet College and 40 hearing college students as controls was presented with a lexical decision task. An introductory sentence was presented followed by the target item, which could be either the most likely completion, an unlikely but congruous completion, or an incongruous one. Both groups showed the expected word predictability effect: decision times were faster to likely than to unlikely words and incongruous words were the slowest. The effect of predictability was greater in deaf than in hearing students. Besides, the subjects, deaf as well as hearing, who were slower to recognise words in isolation were more disrupted by incongruous than acceptable words. Subjects who are somewhat slower appear to rely more on contextual information as predicted by the compensatory model of reading comprehension (Stanowich & West, 1981; 1983, and Perfetti *et al.*, 1979).

The literature shows that the level of reading comprehension reached by hearing children with poor written word processing ability remains poor despite contextual help. Compensation seems to be only partial, so that word identification ability determines the upper limit of reading comprehension. This has important consequences for deaf readers who are poorer at word decoding that their hearing peers. In the experiment by Fischler (1985) mean decision times for words in neutral contexts were considerably slower in deaf than in hearing students (753 and 571 ms respectively).

The notion that deaf students do exploit contextual information to identify written words has several important consequences. The first one concerns the availability of higher order knowledge to compensate for poor word identification abilities. In the case of hearing children this knowledge develops through ordinary interactions with their social partners. This is often not the case in deaf children due to their limited linguistic and social experiences. Obviously sign language is a good candidate to help deaf children create a corpus of linguistic and world knowledge which might support reading comprehension. The positive effects that sign language produces in reading comprehension reported by some authors can reasonably be attributed to the semantic features of signed languages, which share basic semantic features with spoken language.

These positive effects of sign language are inevitably limited to the aspects of language shared by both systems, that is to say semantics. Sign language morphology and syntax are radically different from spoken language. As a consequence sign language cannot help the reader as those levels.

Moreover phonological coding which cannot develop on pure sign language basis plays an important role in syntactic analysis. The ability to attend to sequential relations among words and to relate function words with other lexical items in the sentence heavily depends on the availability of an efficient memory device. Data reviewed in detail in the second section of this chapter showed a strong relationship between speech coding in working memory, memory span and reading ability (Conrad, 1979). Lichtenstein (1998) has added to Conrad's analysis the notion that sign coding cannot replace efficiently speech coding as a device to maintain English linguistic information in memory. This was true even in sign educated students. The author mentions that students who virtually never use speech to communicate reported using speech for processing written English. This clearly suggests that, even in a sign language educational option, an important dosage of spoken language must be included if relatively high levels of reading comprehension are to be expected.

CONCLUSION

It is impossible to conclude a chapter about reading comprehension and deafness without taking part in the debate on oral versus sign language education of deaf children. If reading were absent from the debate, I do think that the situation would be totally different. Sign language is a language and as such it allows the deaf person to have exchanges as rich and creative as it is the case in all human communities. This notion is widely admitted now and does not need to be defended. The problem arises when reading is included in the educational project. A sufficiently high level of reading ability seems to be out of reach if education is exclusively based on sign language. The reason is that print represents spoken language and print processing uses spoken language devices which are absent in sign language. Spoken and sign language are intrinsically different in all of the formal aspects of language, that is phonology and syntax. As a consequence transfer from one to another is not immediate. Some educators defend the pure sign language option stating that it is possible to use linguistic and general knowledge developed through sign language to understand written spoken language. The data and theory examined in this chapter do not confirm this hypothesis and compelling evidence in its favour has not been provided by the defenders of this option. Showing that sign educated deaf children have often better reading skills than orally educated students does not demonstrates that the former have reached sufficiently high reading levels – such as a level compatible with high school studies.

It must be admitted that some reading ability can be reached on pure sign bases. The possibility to elaborate a relatively wide orthographic lexicon without phonological support, that is to say without exploiting the alphabetic code, has been evoked by the defenders of pure sign education. This notion explicitly rejects, or at least reduces at a minimum, the participation of syntax in printed language understanding. The limits of such a project are not known and must be empirically established.

It has been demonstrated already that lip-reading combined with Cued Speech allows for the development of completely specified phonological representations of speech which efficiently support reading acquisition and print processing. To conclude it seems fair to recognise to each educational option its merits. A pragmatic solution which considers bilingual education adapted to each particular case seems necessary. The parents' status, deaf or hearing, is an important factor to take into consideration. For deaf parents it is absurd to renounce to sign language to communicate with their deaf child. Oral education is however indispensable if a high level of reading is expected. For hearing parents an oral option based on Cued Speech can be easily adopted. Early exposure to this method produces remarkable results in reading and spelling. The use of sign language in this case is not indispensable as far as reading is involved but can be motivated on different grounds.

REFERENCES

Alegria, J., Charlier, B. & Mattys, S. (1999). Phonological processing of lipread and Cued-Speech information in the deaf. *European Journal of Cognitive Psychology, 11*, 451-472.

Alegria, J., & Leybaert, J. (1991). Mécanismes d'identification des mots chez le sourd (Mechanisms of word identification in the deaf). In R. Kolinski & J. Morais (Eds), *La reconnaissance des mots dans les différentes modalités sensorielles (Word recognition in different sensory modalities)* (pp. 277-304). Paris: Presses Universitaires de France.

Allen, T. E. (1986). Patterns of academic achievement among hearing impaired students: 1974 and 1973. In A.N.Schildroth and M. A. Karchmer (Eds), *Deaf children in America*. San Diego, CA : College-Hill Press.

Bishop, D. V. M. & Robson, J. (1989). Unimpaired short-term memory and rhyme judgements in congenitally speechless individuals: implication for the notion of articulatory coding. *Quarterly Journal of Experimental Psychology, 41A*, 123-140.

Baddeley, A. (1976). *The psychology of memory*. New York : Basic Books.

Baddeley, A. D. (1986). *Working memory*. Oxford: Clarendon Press.

Baddeley, A. & Hitch, G. S. (1974). Working memory. In G. H. Bower (Ed.), *The psychology of learning and motivation* (vol. 8). New York: Academic Press.

Beech, J. R. & Harris, M. (1991). The prelingually deaf young reader : a case of reliance on direct lexical access ? *Journal of Research in Reading, 20*, 105-121.

Bell, L. C. & Perfetti, C. A. (1994). Reading skill: some adult comparisons. *Journal of Educational Psychology, 86*, 244-255.

Bellugi, U., Klima, E. & Siple, P. (1974/75). Remembering in signs. *Cognition, 3*, 93-125.

Berent, I. & Perfetti, C. A. (1995). A Rose is a REEZ: the two cycles model of phonological assembly in reading English. *Psychological Review, 102*, 146-184.

Bertelson, P. (1986). The onset of literacy: liminal remarks. *Cognition, 24*, 1-30.

Binnie, C. A., Montgomery, A.A. & Jackson, P. L. (1974). Auditory and visual contributions to the perception of consonants. *Journal of Speech and Hearing Research, 17*, 619-630.

Bishop, D. (1983). Comprehension of spoken, written and signed sentences in childhood language disorders. *Journal of Child Psychology and Psychiatry, 23*, 1-20.

Bishop, D. V. M. & Robson, J. (1989). Unimpaired short-term memory and rhyme judgements in congenitally speechless individuals: implication for the notion of articulatory coding. *Quarterly Journal of Experimental Psychology, 41A*, 123-140.

Bradley, L. & Bryant, P. (1983). Categorising sounds and learning to read : A causal connexion. *Nature, 301*, 419-421.

Brady, S.A. (1991). The role of working memory in reading disability. In S.A. Brady & D.P. Shankweiler

(Eds), Phonological processes in literacy: A tribute to Isabelle Liberman (pp. 129-152). Hillsdale, N.J.: Lawrence Erlbaum.

Brimer, A. (1972). *Wide-span Reading Test*. London: Nelson.

Brown, R. (1973). *A first language: The early stages*. Cambridge, MA: Harvard University Press.

Brown, J. B. (1984). Examination of grammatical morphemes in the language of hard-of-hearing children. *Volta Review, 86*, 229-238.

Bruck, M. (1992). Persistence of dyslexics' phonological awareness deficits. *Developmental Psychology, 28*, 874-886.

Burnham, D. (1998). Language specificity in the development of auditory-visual speech perception. In R. Campbell, B. Dodd & D. Burnham. *Hearing by Eye II. Advances in the psychology of speechreading and auditory-visual speech* (pp. 27-60). Sussex (U.K.): Psychology Press.

Burden, V. & R. Campbell (1994). The development of word coding skills in the born deaf: An experimental study of deaf school leavers. *British Journal of Psychology, 72*, 371-376.

Burnham, D. & Dodd, B. (1996). Auditory-visual speech perception as a direct process : The McGurk effect in infants and across languages. In D. Stork & M. Hennecke (Eds), *Speechreading by humans and machines*. Berlin: Springer-Verlag.

Byrne, B. (1991). Experimental analysis of child's discovery of the alphabetic principle. In L. Rieben & Ch. Perfetti (Eds), *Learning to read: basic research and its implications* (pp. 75-84). Hillsdale, N.J.: Lawrence Erlbaum Ass.

Campbell, R. (1991). Speech in the head? Rhyme skill, reading, and immediate memory in the deaf. In D. Reisberg (Ed.), *Auditory Imagery*. Hillsdale, N.J.: Lawrence Erlbaum Ass.

Campbell, R., Dodd, B., & Burnham, P. (1998). *Hearing by Eye, vol. 2*. London: Psychology Press.

Campbell, R. & Wright, H. (1988). Deafness, spelling and rhyme: how spelling supports written word and picture rhyming skills in deaf subjects. *The Quarterly Journal of Experimental Psychology, 40A*, 771-788.

Chamberlain, C., Morford, J. P. & Mayberry, R. I. (2000). *Language acquisition by eye*. London: Lawrence Erlbaum Ass.

Charlier, B. L., Hage, C., Alegria, J. & Périer, O. (1990). Evaluation d'une pratique prolongée du LPC sur la compréhension de la parole par l'enfant atteint de déficience auditive (Evaluation of the effect of prolonged practice of cued speech on the level of language comprehension acquired by deaf children). *Glossa, 22*, 28-39.

Charlier, B. L. & Leybaert, J. (2000). The rhyming skills of deaf children educated with phonetically augmented speech reading. *The Quarterly Journal of Experimental Psychology, 53A(2)*, 349-375.

Conrad, R. (1979). *The deaf school child*. London: Harper and Row.

Cooper, R. L. (1967). The ability of deaf and hearing children to apply morphological rules. *Journal of Speech and Hearing Research, 10*, 77-86.

Cornett, O. (1967). Cued speech. *American Annals of the Deaf, 112*, 3-13.

Cornett, O. (1973). Comments on the Nash case study. *Sign Language Studies, 3*, 93-98.

Di Francesca, S. (1971). Academic achievement results of a national resting program for hearing impaired students. New York: Academic Press.

Dodd, B. (1976). The phonological system of deaf children. *Journal of Speech and Hearing Disorders, 41*, 185-198.

Dodd, B. (1977). The role of vision in the perception of speech. *Perception, 6*, 31-40.

Dodd, B. (1979). Lip reading in infants: Attention to speech presented in- and out-of-synchrony. *Cognitive Psychology, 11*, 478-484.

Dodd, B. (1980). The spelling abilities of profoundly deaf children. In U. Frith (Ed.), *Cognitive processes in spelling*. London: Academic Press.

Dodd, B., & Hermelin, B. (1977). Phonological coding by the prelinguistically deaf. *Perception and Psychophysics, 21*, 413-417.

Dodd, B., McIntosh, B. & Woodhouse, (1998). Early lipreading ability and speech and language development of hearing-impaired pre-schoolers. In R. Campbell, B. Dodd, & D. Burnham (Eds), *Hearing by eye II* (pp. 229-242). London: Psychology Press.

Dubuisson, C. & Vincent-Durroux, L. (1991). L'enseignement de la langue maternelle aux déficients auditifs (The teaching of mother tongue to the hearing impaired). *Glossa*, 27, 32-37.

Ehri, L. (1991). Learning to read and spell words. In: L. Rieben & Ch. Perfetti (Eds), *Learning to read : basic research and its implications* (pp. 33-46). Hillsdale, N.J.: Lawrence Erlbaum Ass.

Emmorey, K. & Lane, H. (2000). *The signs of language revisited*. London : Lawrence Erlbaum Ass.

Erber, N. P. (1969). Interaction of audition and vision in the recognition of oral speech stimuli. *Journal of Speech and Hearing Research, 12*, 423-424.

Erber, N. P. (1974). Visual perception of speech by deaf children. Recent developments and continuing needs. *Journal of Speech and Hearing Research, 39*, 178-185.

Ferrand, R. & Grainger, J. (1992). Phonology and orthography in visual word recognition : evidence from marked non-woprd priming. The Quarterly *Journal of Experimental Psychology, 45*, 353-372.

Fischler, I. (1985). Word recognition use of context, and reading skill among deaf college students. *Reading Research Quarterly, 20*, 203-218.

Furth, H. (1996). Thinking without language : Psychological implications of deafness. New York : Free Press.

Goldin-Meadow, S. (1985). Language development under atypical learning conditions: Replication and implications of a study of deaf children of hearing parents. In K. E. Nelson (Ed.) *Children's language, Vol. 5*. Hillsdale, N.J., Lawrence Erlbaum Ass.

Gough, P. B. & Juel, C. (1991). The first stages of word recognition. In L. Rieben & Ch. Perfetti (Eds), *Learning to read: basic research and its implications* (pp. 47-56). Hillsdale, N.J.: Lawrence Erlbaum Ass.

Gough, P. B. & Tummer, W.E. (1986). Decoding, reading, and reading disability. *Remedial and Special Education, 7*, 6-10.

Green, K. P. (1998). The use of auditory and visual information during phonetic processing: implications for theories of speech perception. In R. Campbell, B. Dodd and D. Burham (Eds), – *Hearing by Eye, vol 2.* (pp. 3-26). London: Psychology Press.

Greenberg, D., Ehri, L. C. & Perin, D. (1997). Are word-reading processes the same or different in adult literacy students and third-fifth graders matched for reading level ? *Journal of Educational Psychology, 89*, 262-275.

Gregory, S. & K. Mogford (1981). Early language development in deaf children. In B. Woll, J. Kyle & M. Deuchar (Eds), *Perspectives on British Sign Language and deafness*. London: Croom Helm.

Hage, C. & Alegria, J. (in preparation). The development of grammatical gender morphophonology in deaf children exposed to Cued-Speech.

Hage, C., Alegria, J. & Périer, O. (1991). Cued speech and language adquisition: the case of grammatical gender morpho-phonology. In D. S. Martin (Ed.), *Advances in cognition, education, and deafness*. Washington, D.C.: Gallaudet University Press.

Hammermeister, F. K. (1971). Reading achievement in deaf adults. *Journal of Reading Specialist, 116*, 25-28.

Hanson, V. L. (1982). Short-term recall by deaf signers of American Sign Language: Implications of encoding strategy for order recall. *Journal of Experimental Psychology: Learning, Memory and Cognition, 8*, 572-583.

Hanson, V. L., Goodell, E. W. & Perfetti, C.A. (1991). Tongue-Twister effects in the silent reading of hearing and deaf college students. *Journal of Memory and Language, 30*, 319-331.

Hanson, V. L., Shankweiler, D. & Fisher, F. W. (1983). Determinants of spelling ability in deaf and hearing adults: access to linguistic structure. *Cognition, 14*, 323-344.

Harris, M. (1994). Reading comprehension difficulties in deaf children. Paper presented at the *Workshop on Comprehension Disabilities*. Centro Diagnostico Italiano. Milan, Italy.

Harris, M. & J. Beech (1994). Reading development in prelingually deaf children. In K. Nelson and Z. Reger (Eds), *Children's Language*. Hillsdale, N.J.: Lawrence Erlbaum Ass.

Healy, J. (1982). The enigma of hyperlexia. *Reading Research Quarterly, 17*, 319-338.

Hickson, L., Woodyant, G., Cue, C. & Dodd, B. (in press). A longitudinal study of the linguistic abilities of children with severe and profound hearing impairment.

Hine, W. D. & P. J. MacDonald (1976). The screening survey of hearing-impaired children in the Midlands and North of England. Language results, University of Manchester, Department of Audiology and Education of the Deaf.

Hirsh-Pasek, K. & Treiman, R. (1982). Recoding in silent reading. Can deaf child transform into a more manageable form ? *Volta Review, 84*, 71-82.

Hoover, W. A. & Gough, P.B. (1990). The simple wiew of reading. *Reading and Writing, 2*, 127-160.

Ives, L. A. (1974). A screening survey of 2060 hearing-impaired children in the Midlands and North of England. Language results. *Supplement to the British Deaf News.*

Jensema, C. J. & Tribus, R. J. (1978). Communicating patterns and educational achievement of hearing in paired children. Washington, D.C.: Gallaudet. College of Demographic Studies.

Kipila, B. (1985). Analysis of an oral language sample from a prelingually deaf child's Cued Speech: A case study. *Cued Speech Annual, 1*, 46-59.

King, C. M. & Quigley, S.P. (1985). *Reading and deafness.* San Diego, C.A.: College Hill Press.

Klima, E. & U. Bellugi (1979). *The signs of language.* Cambridge, Mass.: Harvard University Press.

Kuhl, P. K. & A. N. Meltzoff (1984). The intermodal representation of speech in infancy. *Infant behavior and development, 7*, 361-81.

LaSasso, C. & Metzger, M. (1998). An alternate route for preparing deaf children for conveying traditionally spoken languages. *Journal of Deaf Studies and Deaf Education, 3*, 265-289.

Leybaert, J. (1993). Reading ability in the deaf: the roles of phonological codes. In M. Marschark & D. Clark (Eds.), *Psychological Perspectives on Deafness*, (pp. 269-309). New York: Lawrence Erlbaum Ass.

Leybaert, J. (1998). Phonological representations in deaf children: the importance of early linguistic experience. *Scandinavian Journal of Psychology, 39*, 169-173.

Leybaert, J. (2000). Phonology acquired through the eyes and spelling in deaf children. *Journal of Experimental Child Psychology, 75*, 291-318.

Leybaert, J. & Alegria, J. (1993). Is word processing involuntary in deaf children? British *Journal of Developmental Psychology, 11*, 1-29.

Leybaert, J. & Alegria, J. (1995). Spelling development in hearing and deaf children: evidence for the use of morpho-phonological regularities in French. *Reading and Writing, 7*, 89-109.

Leybaert, J., Alegria, J. & Fonck, E. (1983). Automaticity in word recognition and word naming by the deaf. *Cahiers de Psychologie Cognitive, 3*, 255-272.

Liberman, A. M. & Mattingly, I. G. (1985). The motor theory of speech perception revised. *Cognition, 21*, 1-36.

Lichtenstein, E. H. (1998). The relationship between reading processes and English skills of deaf college students. *Journal of Deaf Studies and Deaf Education, 1*, 234-248.

Lupker, S. J. & Katz, A. N. (1981). Input, decision and response factors in picture-word interference. *Journal of Experimental Psychology: Human Learning and Memory, 7*, 269-282.

Marschak, M. (1993). *Psychological development of deaf children.* New York: Oxford Univ. Press.

Marschak, M. & Harris, M. (1996). Success and failure in learning to read: a special case (?) of deaf children. In J. Oakhill & C. Cornoldi (Eds), *Children reading comprehension disabilities*, Hillsdale, N.J.: Lawrence Erlbaum Ass.

Massaro, D. W. (1987). Speech Perception by ear & eye. In B. Dodd & R. Campbell (Eds), *Hearing by eye: the psychology of lip-reading.* London: Lawrence Erlbaum Ass.

Mayberry, R. & Waters, G.S. (1987). Deaf children recognition of written words: Is fingerspelling the basis. Paper presented *in the Society for Research in Child Development.* Baltimode, MD.

McGurk, H. & McDonald, J. (1976). Hearing lips and seeing voices. *Nature, 264*, 746-748.

McKain, K., Studdert-Kennedy, M., Spieker, S., & Stern, D. (1983). Infant intermodal speech perception is a left-hemisphere function. *Science, 219*, 1347-1348.

Meadow, K. P. (1968). Early manual communication in relation to the deaf child's intellectual, social and communicative functioning. *American Annals of the Deaf, 113*, 29-41.

Metzger, M. (1994). First language acquisition in deaf children of hearing parents: Cued English input. Georgetown University.

Meyer, D. E., Schvaneveldt, R.& Rudy, M.G. (1974). Functions of graphemic and phonemic codes in word recognition. *Memory and Cognition, 2*, 309-321.

Myklebust, H. R. (1960). *The psychology of deafness.* New York : Grune & Stratton.

Mohay, H. (1984). A preliminary description of the communication systems evolved by two deaf children in the absence of a sign language model. *Sign Language Studies, 34,* 73-90.

Morais, J., Alegria, J. & Content, A. (1987). The relationships between segmental analysis and alphabetic literacy: An interactive view. *Cahiers de Psychologie Cognitive, 7,* 415-438.

Morais, J. & Mousty, P. (1992). The causes of phonemic awareness. In: J. Alegria, D. Holender, J. Morais, & M. Radeau (Eds), *Analytic approaches to human cognition* (pp. 193-212). Amsterdam: North-Holland,.

Moseley, M., Williams-Scott, B. & Anthony, C. (1991). Language expressed through Cued-Speech: A preschool case study. Paper presented at *the American Speech and Hearing Association*, Atlanta, G.A. Nov. 1991.

Nash, J. E. Cues or signs: a case study in language acquisition. *Sign Language Studies, 3,* 79-91.

Nicholls, G. H. & Ling, D. (1982). Cued speech and the reception of spoken language. *Journal of Speech and Hearing Research, 25,* 262-269.

Odom, P. B., Blanton, R. L. & Nunnally, J. C. (1967). Some "cloze" technique studies of language capability in the deaf. J*ournal of Speech and Hearing Research, 10,* 816-827.

Paire-Ficoud, L. & Bédoid, N. (1996). Code phonologique précoce et lisibilité labiale des mots chez le lecteur entendant et le lecteur sourd profond pré-lingual (Phonological coding and lip readability of words in hearing and profoundly deaf children). *Revue de Neuropsychologie, 6,* 239-250.

Paul, P. & Jackson, D. W. (1994). Towards a psychology of deafness:Theoretical and empirical perspectives. Boston: Allyn & Bacon.

Perfetti, C. A. (1991). Representations and awareness in the acquisition of reading competence. In: L. Rieben & Ch. Perfetti (Eds), *Learning to read: basic research and its implications* (pp. 33-46). Hillsdale, N.J.: Lawrence Erlbaum Ass.

Perfetti, C. A., Goldman, S. R. & Hogaboam, T. W. (1979). Reading skills and the identification of words in discourse context. *Memory and Cognition, 7,* 273-282.

Perfetti, C. A. & Hogaboam, T. W. (1978). Reading skill and the role of verbal experience in decoding. *Journal of Educational Psychology, 70,* 717-729.

Périer, O. (1987). L'enfant à audition déficiente: Aspects médicaux, éducatifs, sociologiques et psychologiques (The hearing impaired child: Medical, educational, sociological and psychological aspects) *Acta Oto-rhino-laryngologica belgica, 41, 129-420.*

Prince, P. & Strong, (1995). The interrelationship among cognition, Sign Language and literacy. Paper presented at the *18th International Congress on Education of the Deaf.* Tel Aviv, Israël, July 18-20, 1995.

Prinz, P. M. & E. A. Prinz (1979). Simultaneous acquisition of ASL and spoken English in a hearing child of a deaf mother and a hearing father. Phase 1: Early lexical development. *Sign Language Studies, 25,* 283-296.

Pritchatt, D. (1968). An investigation into some of the underlying associative verbal processes of the Stroop colour effect. *The Quarterly Journal of Experimental Psychology, 20,* 351-359.

Quigley, S. P., Wilbur, R., Power, D., Montanelli, D. & Steinkamp, M. (1977). *The language structure of deaf children.* University of Illinois. Institute for Child Behavior and Development.

Quigley, S. P. & Paul, P. V. (1984). *Language and Deafness.* San Diego: College-Hill Press.

Quigley, S. P., Smith, M. & Wilbur, R. (1974). Comprehension of relativized sentences by deaf students. *Journal of Speech and Hearing Research, 17,* 325-341.

Rack, J. P., Snowling, M.J. & Olson, R. K. (1992). The nonword reading deficit in developmental dyslexia : a review. *Reading Research Quarterly, 57,* 42-71.

Schlesinger, H. & Meadow, K. P. (1972). *Sound and sign. Childhood deafness and mental health.* Berkeley, CA : University of California Press.

Share, D. L. (1995). Phonological recoding and self-teaching : *sine qua non* of reading acquisition. *Cognition, 55,* 151-218.

Share, D. L. (1999). Phonological recoding and orthographic learning : a direct test of the self-teaching hypothesis. *Journal of Experimental Child Psychology, 72*, 95-129.

Siple, P. (1978). Linguistic and psychological properties of American Sign Language signs and printed English words by congenitally deaf signers. In P. Siple (Ed.), *Understanding language through sign language research*. New York: Academic Press.

Stanovich, K. E. (1980). Interactive-compensatory model of reading. *Reading Research Quarterly, 16*, 32-71.

Stanovich, K. E. (1986). Matthew effects in reading: Some consequences of individual differences in the acquisition of literacy. *Reading Research Quarterly, 21*, 360-406.

Stanovich, K. E. & West, R. F. (1979). The effects of orthographic structure on the word search performance of good and poor readers. *Journal of Experimental Child Psychology, 28*, 258-267.

Stanovich, K. E. & West, R. F. (1981). The effect of sentence context on on-going word recognition: Tests of a two-process theory. *Journal of Experimental Psychology: Human Perception and Performance, 7*, 658-672.

Stanovich, K. E. & West, R. F. (1983). On priming by a sentence context. *Journal of Experimental Psychology : General, 112*, 1-36.

Stothard, S. & Hulme, C. (1996). A comparison of reading comprehension and decoding difficulties in children. In C. Cornoldi & J. Oakhill (Eds), *Reading comprehension difficulties: Processes and intervention* (pp. 93-112). Hillsdale, N.J. : Lawrence Erlbaum Ass.

Strong, M. & Prinz, P.M. (1997). A study of the relationship between ASL and English literacy. *Journal of Deaf Studies and Deaf Education*.

Stukless, E. R. & Birch, J. W. (1966). The influence of early manual communication on the linguistic development of deaf children. *American Annals of the Deaf, 111*, 452-460.

Sumby, W. & Pollack, I. (1954). Visual contributions to speech visibility in noise. *Journal of the Acoustic Society of America, 26*, 212-215.

Summerfield, Q. (1987). Some preliminaries to a comprehensive account of audio-visual speech perception. In B. Dodd & R. Campbell (Eds.), *Hearing by eye: the psychology of lip-reading* (pp. 3-52). London: Lawrence Erlbaum Ass.

Summerfield, Q. (1991). Visual perception of phonetic gestures. In: I. G. Mattingly & M. Studdert-Kennedy (Eds). *Modularity and the motor theory of speech perception*. Hillsdale, New Jersey: Lawrence Erlbaum Ass.

Torres, S. & Ruiz, M. J. (1996). La palabra complementada: introduccion a la intervencion cognitiva en logopedia (Supporting language: introduction to the cognitive intervention in speech therary). Madrid : CEPE.

Transler, C., Leybaert, J. & Gombert, J. E. (1999). Do deaf children uses phonological syllables as reading units? *Journal of Deaf Reading and Deaf Education, 4*, 124-143.

Treiman, R. & Hirsh-Pasek, K. (1983). Silent reading: Insights from second-generation deaf readers. *Cognitive Psychology*, 39-65.

Trybus, R. J. & Karchmer, M. A. (1977). School achievement scores of hearing impaired children: National data on achievement status and growth patterns. *American Annals of the Deaf*, Directory of Programs and Services, *122*, 62-69, 569-574.

Van Orden, G. D. (1987). A ROWS is a ROSE : spelling, sound and reading. *Memory and Cognition, 15*, 181-198.

Vernon, M. & Koh, S. D. (1970). Early manual communication and deaf children's achievement. *American Annals of the Deaf, 116*.

Volterra, V. & Bates, E. (1989). Selective Impairment of italian grammatical morphology in the congenitally deaf: a case study. *Cognitive Neuropsychology*, 6, 273-308.

Wandel, J. E. (1989). Use of Internal Speech in reading by Hearing and Hearing Impaired Students in Oral, Total Communication and Cued-Speech programs. Unpublished manuscript, Columbia University, New York.

Waters, G. & Doehring, D. G. (1990). The nature and role of phonological information in reading acquisition: insights from congenitally deaf children who communicate orally. In T. Carr & B. A.

Levy (Eds.), *Reading and its development: Component skills approaches*. San Diego: Academic Press, pp. 323-373.
Woodward, J. & Allen, T. E. (1987). Classroom use of ASL by teachers. *Sign Language Studies, 54*, 1-10.

SUGGESTED FURTHER READING

Some important contributions to the question of reading and deafness have been published after this chapter was written. I would like to mention the issue of the *Journal of Deaf Studies and Deaf Education*, Volumes 5 and 6, published in 1999 and 2000 respectively, both devoted to this matter; and a series of papers concerning reading acquisition based on American Sign Language appeared in *Language Acquisition by Eye*, in C. Chamberlain, J. P. Morford, and R. I. Mayberry (Eds.) LEA, London, 2000. The studies concerning cochlear implants have not been considered in this chapter because they are not directly related to reading. It is obvious however that this technique has major effects on phonological processing. Consequently it will influence reading acquisition and print processing in the same extent as other devices aimed at facilitating phonological processing.

D. Literacy Concepts and Instruction

Introduction: Teaching Literacy: What Practices, When and Why?

ANNE-MARIE CHARTIER

In western societies nowadays everyone is supposed to be able to read. Therefore many of the characteristic features of reading are so familiar and seem so natural that they have become invisible. Almost all the researchers who have been working on reading and on the way children learn to read (or not) live in countries which mass-produce books and newspapers and where one resorts to writing and reading in nearly every social activity; all children in these countries go to school for more and less prolonged periods in their lives and the teaching profession is nurtured on long pedagogical traditions (textbooks, regular progression, exercises and debates on methods). These characteristics make up a spontaneous reference framework for researchers: all of them acknowledge that a child should normally be able to read at the age of about seven or eight; that "normal" reading is visual and silent – one reads on one's own, at one's own pace; that reading consists in processing the information contained in a text from a language point of view (writing codes) and knowledge (written contents); and that the reading medium informs readers at once about the content and form of a text (whether he opens a dictionary, a novel, a newspaper or a letter). Thus research on reading (carried out in laboratory experiments, data from school curricula, national or international assessment tests, surveys on populations of good or bad adult or child readers) confirms the features which characterises reading as it is commonly practised in societies offering regular schooling at the end of the 20th century.

Two facts have driven researchers to inquire into this pattern and become aware of its presuppositions: the discovery of a significantly high degree of illiteracy in developed societies on the one hand, and the observation of precocious learning on the other. The behaviour and knowledge of those who are not complete non-readers, nor experts at reading, have compelled one to define more precisely what "being able to read" means. Indeed an illiterate adult – or a child who cannot yet read – are nevertheless capable of mastering a whole range of information on writing and reading. The boundary between readers and non-readers is therefore not as distinct as their designations indicate; moreover it shifts positions according to countries, times and social groups. A person who would have been labelled literate by people around them at a given time and place would be considered illiterate in another. Reading is not only a cognitive skill; it is also a

T. Nunes, P. Bryant (eds.), Handbook of Children's Literacy, 493–497.
© *2004 Kluwer Academic Publishers. Printed in Great Britain.*

social practice whose historical cultural and linguistic dimensions have to be clarified.

A third fact has recently contributed to this awareness: new writing technologies and the use of computers. Reading on a screen implies a whole change in habits linked to printing. Computers introduce new relationships between reading and writing enabling readers to interfere on the text in the course of reading. The interface man-machine is changing the criteria of reading skills that had been elaborated by disconnecting reading and writing at a time when manuscript production was a gesture clearly separated from the delivery of a printed book. Therefore individuals presently considered readers according to the previous criteria could soon be considered illiterate if they are unable to manipulate new writing technologies.

The chapters that compose the present section are an attempt to shed light on these different aspects. According to David Olson, to grasp "the cognitive consequences of literacy" one must accept that writing is a symbolic language at odds, rather than in continuity, with oral language, contrary to what usual approaches indicate. In fact, oral comprehension and written comprehension can be treated as two forms of linguistic information processing for which one is required to master both linguistic codes and knowledge of contents; the major difference is that writing is a delayed instrument of communication, which disconnects the time of production and that of delivery, whereas oral interlocution allows permanent interactions between speaker and interlocutor. To Olson, this is not the prevailing characteristic: writing is actually a specific instrument of communication, but it is also a language representation system. Therefore, it is impossible to learn to read without learning to portray elements that oral language does not make it necessary to elucidate: phonemes, words, sentences. Because of their linguistic discoveries, readers organise the logic of their thought, the forms of their reasoning and the way they consider links between words and objects differently from illiterates. Reading leads them to adopt a metalinguistic position, for writing is a very incomplete retranscription of words, since the writer is not there to underscore and explain what he wants to say – unlike the speaker. Any reading therefore demands an interpretation taking the specificity of writing signs into account.

The specific characteristics of written language account for the variety of the social usages deriving from it. These have varied in the course of history, as we learn from the history of reading which allows us to understand by comparison how present reading can be defined in its particular features. This argument is in keeping with Roger Chartier's (1993) analysis, that considers the major transformations of reading. Western tradition has often seen in printing a revolutionary discovery, which has allowed a massive spread of writing. Recent findings have shown that it is not the technical invention in itself that produced the transformations of modern times after Gutenberg, for other civilisations have known printing without experiencing the same results.

Social and political specific contexts are necessary for reading to spread outside literate circles. However, writing which separates words with spaces, after replacing continuous writing commonly used in antiquity, made visual reading possible through the direct recognition of words without saying them aloud. This transformation took place in the Middle Ages and altered intellectual habits at a time when oral collective reading and silent individual reading coexisted in the social environment. Reading on a screen nowadays implies another change by transforming the links between reading and writing and suppressing the material differences between the media (newspapers, books, magazines). And yet, these differences are those which readers rely on to distinguish different texts from the point of view of the form and content in the structured world of printing.

The history of reading is not the history of teaching how to read. Traditionally this history is often limited to that of pedagogical methods, which have improved in the course of centuries thanks to the progress of knowledge (on language and learning) and transmission techniques (teaching materials, textbooks). This linear cumulative vision overlooks the fact that each era has had a reading pedagogy adapted to its own cultural aims. Indeed, according to Anne-Marie Chartier, religious conflicts urged Churches to launch a first literacy campaign of the common people in 16th century Europe. Contents and teaching methods were radically different depending on whether one aimed at giving the children of the elite a literate Christian culture (Latin classics) or teaching ordinary children to read (and not to write) so as to make them learn catechism, read their prayers and attend a service. When education imposed itself as a political and no longer a religious necessity, the methods invented by private tutors to teach the elite could not be adopted for collective teaching to diffuse secular knowledge. New writing technologies that children could easily master were necessary to make it possible to teach both reading and writing to whole groups of pupils. It was the dawn of the era of compulsory schooling. Reading was the starting point of learning, and no longer its goal. From the end of the 19th century debates on methods (synthetical or analytical methods, methods aiming at helping decipher or recognise words directly) concerned not only private education but also compulsory schools.

All teachers at the beginning of the 20th century thought that in countries offering regular schooling, literacy would soon become widespread. Academic failure and persistent illiteracy among adults despite schooling sowed doubt over these expectations and triggered off many attempts to find causes. Those attempts which concern the acquisition of school reading are far more numerous that those regarding adults. The chapter by Daniel Wagner provides a systematic comparison of the knowledge relating to the literacy of both adults and children, which usually represent distinct areas of research. It considers the facts based on cultural environment, cognitive tests and the language under consideration. This research has important political consequences: it can direct decisions concerning the language used to learn to read given that it is still spontaneously thought better to learn in one's mother tongue. What is to be done when one deals with a language which is not written during the learning phase?

This research also concerns teaching methods depending on whether they are given in proper schools or in a less formal way particularly during literacy campaigns aimed at illiterate adults. On which conditions are literacy courses effective? How can illiterate adults or poor readers despite years and years spent at school be taught to read again? To Wagner the ability to read has to be handled like an evolving reality, dependent on life-space as well as on life-span.

What is known of the young children's first steps in learning? The article by Madelon Saada-Robert traces the research done into "Early Emergent Literacy". First acquisitions are not only the result of formal teaching. What part do written habits of a family play in the children's first experiences, particularly what is read to them (albums, picture books, tales etc.)? Are precocious skills in oral language a factor likely to make the teaching of reading precocious? The article summarises numerous studies which have allowed to better group together the stages which children go through in order to master the codes of an alphabetical language: time of logographic processing of writing, gradual awareness of the sound value of words, morphological and orthographical aspects of the writing of words. However, whereas research, in the main, deals with the teaching of writing and of reading in a separate way, later studies have sought to underscore the possible interactions between both processes with particular interest in how revealing the "invented writing" produced by young children can be, not only the elaboration of writing codes but also, the effect on their skills, that is to say reading.

Research into reading has had significant effects on teaching methods. Indeed, the processes used by skilled readers have directed the learning processes proposed to beginners. As shown in the article by Jane Hurry, since the seventies, the opposition between phonic methods centred on the acquisitions of codes and global methods centred on text comprehension has turned to the advantage to phonic methods. All researchers today agree that it is essential to master graphophonemic relations to learn how to read. This is essential, but not enough. Indeed, a teaching method is not only a sequence of taught contents. It also includes learning methods and teaching styles. What information can be gathered from comparative research into different teaching methods? Whether it is teaching contents or teaching ways, results are not necessarily the same. Moreover certain teaching contents (e.g., lexical enrichment) have no visible effect in the short term but can prove effective in the medium term. Far from imposing a unique teaching curriculum, comparative research into reading methods is a way to inquire rigorously into the relationships between teaching and learning to read, didactic theory and pedagogical practice.

Thus specific features of written culture (Olson), teaching methods (Chartier, Hurry), elements to be taken into consideration in precocious learning and learning failures (Wagner; Saada-Robert) present reading ability as a skill whose components cannot in principle be defined once and for all; they vary according to cultural aims, social constraints and academic environment. New research alone can enable us to assess the effects and the limitations of the changes brought about by new information and communication technologies whose socio-cultural cognitive and pedagogical consequences cannot yet be observed with enough objectivity.

REFERENCES

Chartier, R. (1993) Lecteurs dans la longue durée: du *codex* à l'écran. In R. Chartier (Ed.), *Histoires de la lecture: un bilan des recherches* (pp. 271-283.) (Stories about reading: a review of research). Paris: Imec Éditions; Éditions de la Maison des Sciences de l'Homme.

D1 Literacy in Time and Space: Issues, Concepts and Definitions

DANIEL A. WAGNER[1]

ABSTRACT

Literacy is a term which continually evolves in meaning. Over the past several decades, researchers in industrialised countries have invested tremendous effort in attempting to better understand how children learn to read and write. In other (mainly developing) countries, literacy often is taken to mean the reading and writing skills adults needed in order to partake in social practices or in economic development. These two separate literatures – children's literacy and adult's literacy – have only rarely come into contact. "Life-span" literacy, then, refers to an approach which may be applied to literacy development across an individual's lifetime, from childhood to adulthood. "Life-space" literacy refers to the important social and cultural factors which influence individual literacy learning and literacy practice within and across contexts. This paper reviews the concepts of life span and life-space, and highlights some areas of useful intersection for future research and policy development. The basic argument is that the worlds of literacy, among child and adult learners, and across diverse parts of the globe, can be utilised synergistically to promote a more literate world.

INTRODUCTION

Literacy is a word that has meant different things to different people over hundreds (even thousands) of years. Comprehensive reviews of literacy's many definitions are too numerous to even list, especially when taking into account cultural and linguistic variations of the term and its meanings. In this short paper, the focus will be on two important dimensions (or rather parameters) of literacy that are at the

---

[1] Parts of this paper are derived from Wagner (1992). *Literacy: Developing the future*, Unesco Yearbook of Education, Paris: Unesco; and Wagner (1994). Life-span and life-space literacy: National and international perspectives. In D. Keller-Cohen (Ed.). *Literacy: Interdisciplinary conversations.* Cresskill, NJ: Hampton Press.

T. Nunes, P. Bryant (eds.), Handbook of Children's Literacy, 499–510.

same time both obvious and complex – namely, how literacy varies over time (ontogeny) and space (context).

Two stories help to illustrate the present thesis. The first takes place in Morocco, where an elderly woman sets the scene.

Oum Fatima has labored virtually every day of her 55 or so years of age, and with four children and a chronically ill husband unable to help financially, she could only hope to do housecleaning in the wealthier homes of the labyrinthian *medina* (or old city) of Marrakech.

Beyond regular washer-woman duties, it was normal for Oum Fatima to handle a gamut of contacts between the "outside world" and the home and children for which she worked so hard. Such activities varied enormously. On some days, the mailman would arrive with letters; Oum Fatima would deliver each to the addressee, knowing simply by the type of handwriting or script used – Arabic or French – who should receive which letter.

Once a month, the "electric man" would arrive to collect money for the month's charges; Oum Fatima handled this affair with just a question or two, drawing money from an earthenware jar in which she stashed odd coins and bills in anticipation of his visits. At the *souk* (market), Oum Fatima's skill in mental arithmetic and bargaining was legendary, Not only could she switch effortlessly between the several parallel currencies in use – dirhams, francs and rials (a base-five system) – but her ability to negotiate the lowest possible price made her a well-known figure in her *derb* (quarter). To those of her social class, as well as to those "higher up", Oum Fatima was a woman worthy of great respect.

The second relates to young American boy, who was five and growing up in a middle class well-educated family, when this observation was noted. Each night his mother and father would take turns reading to him, as they had done nearly every night since he was about two years old. Over the years, this boy became very involved in the stories told and stories recited. He knew what was on every page, though he still only knew the letters of the alphabet, and could not recognize more than few isolated words. With more time, practice and nurturance, his parents had every expectation that he would become a part of literate American society.

What is the relationship between these two disparate stories across time and space? There are two relevant linkages. First, each actor – Oum Fatima and the boy – are "normal" for their context. Each functions well, and neither is stigmatised for being "behind" or "underdeveloped," though neither would be considered to be extraordinarily intelligent by the terms of IQ or "intelligence" that are still widely applied in the U.S. and Europe. Second, both are *active* learners, and are motivated to seek new information with all the skills they possess. Are these individuals "deficient" in "basic skills?" Probably the answer is "yes," by current Western normative definitions of literacy. Could each of them learn more of such skills? Yes, of course. But, unfortunately, it will not be easy. Oum Fatima has her busy life to lead, and so does this 5-year-old boy. Fortunately for the boy, however, his parents will likely provide him with a rich literate environment that it will be impossible for him to escape from the world of books and print.

Thus, in their own milieu, both Oum Fatima and the boy are contributors to their contexts, and should not be stigmatised as "deficient." But how do we create contexts for individuals to wish to read, even though they may function reasonably well in the lives they currently lead? This fundamental problem – essentially one of culture – is basic to literacy work today. The boy will, in great likelihood, become literate if things continue as they are. Oum Fatima will continue to be a smart lady with print and numbers, but still unable to read or write with competence, and unlikely to ever change.

In sum, literacy is practiced in ways that can and should be understood across the life span and across life-spaces, whether in America or in Africa. It is becoming increasingly clear that in a number of fundamental ways, a more literate society cannot be created in America or elsewhere without a more comprehensive conceptual framework – one that explicitly attempts to link children's acquisition of literacy with that of adult's, and one that assumes that there is no single normative theory to literacy development. Thus, while the present volume focuses on children's literacy, this paper will use research on both child and adult literacy in order to draw certain ontological distinctions.

CONCEPTUALISING LIFE-SPAN AND LIFE-SPACE LITERACY

While a comprehensive review and synthesis is not possible in this short paper, new conceptual linkages in literacy can be made, both for theory and practice. Literacy in children and adults is a useful domain to construct a new life span and life-space conceptualisation. The study of literacy acquisition appears to be heavily influenced by research undertaken in the industrialised world. Much of this research might be better termed the acquisition of reading and writing skills, with an emphasis on the relationship between cognitive skills and reading skills, such as decoding and comprehension. Most of this work has been carried out with school-aged children, rather than with adolescents or adults; and surprisingly little research on literacy acquisition has been undertaken in the Third World and on non-Western languages (but see Wagner, Venezky & Street, 1999, for a broad based counterexample). Despite these gaps in the research literature, it is possible to put forward a number of conclusions about how literacy is acquired across different societies. The present conceptual framework for life span and life-space literacy utilizes three dimensions for the collection and interpretation of findings: environmental-cultural, linguistic, and cognitive-psychometric.

The environmental-cultural dimension

Children. In industrialised countries, it is usually assumed that most children grow up in "literate households," that is with both parents educated and able to read and write proficiently. While specialists in industrialised countries are now much more likely to discuss the diversity of their respective societies (also useful as explanations for the diversity of literacy achievement in the entire population), the so-called " average child" typically starts to come into contact with written language about the age of three or four years, beginning with what has been termed the preliterate skills of scribbling and storybook "reading." (Ferreiro & Teberosky, 1982; Sulzby & Teale, 1991; Vygotsky, 1978). Subsequently, children are socialised for literacy through many years of attendance in school, reinforced by parents who read and wish their children to read.

Naturally, this normative, schematic, and idyllic picture of literacy learning in industrialised countries leaves out many children in today's world, both in those (industrialised) countries and in the developing world. With respect to illiteracy or low literacy in former colonies, specialists have stressed the importance of class structure and ethnicity/race as explications of differential motivation and socialisation of young literacy learners. Some specialists claim that many minority and marginalised children in industrialised countries (constituting what is sometimes called the "Fourth World") are simply unmotivated to learn to read and write in the cultural structure of the school (Bourdieu, 1977; Ogbu, 1999, Vermes & Kastenbaum, 1992). This approach to understanding social and cultural differences in literacy and school achievement has received increased attention in that it avoids blaming children for specific cognitive deficits, while focusing attention more on changes in the social and political structure of schooling.

Such an approach to children's literacy achievement in developing countries seems to have received only modest attention from specialists in developing countries, most of who appear to see the problem of illiteracy in broader social and economic terms. Rather than focus on those who "fail" in the school system (which is usually the emphasis of Western social scientists), these researchers are mainly concerned with how to provide more literacy to the entire population. Thus, the developing country context is seen as one in which there is simply too little literacy in the environment (e.g., books, newspapers etc.), too few literate parents to teach and add value (or "cultural capital", after Bourdieu, 1977) to literacy in the home, and too few children who attend sufficient numbers of years of schooling to become literate.

Overall when consideration is given to children in low-literate settings (whether in the Third World or urban ghettos of the Western countries), the environmental-cultural dimension of literacy learning provides a ready explanation for the lack of literacy acquisition among children and youth. As societies become more literate (measured in terms such as greater numbers of educated and literate parents), the environmental-cultural dimension of literacy development can be expected to play a more nuanced and selective role in what statisticians term the explanation of variance.

Adults. Compared to the considerable progress made in understanding the acquisition of literacy in children, far less is known about literacy acquisition in adults, though the research base has grown substantially over the past decade (see the research-policy review by Wagner & Venezky, 1999).

In contrast to the study of children, adults who do not learn to read and write in industrialised countries are often considered to be "failures," since they should have learned to read and write in school. Children, while eventually stigmatised in school for failing to read adequately by the end of primary school, are nevertheless given time to develop skills "naturally," through home and school learning. By contrast adult illiterates or low-literates are assumed, in most industrialised countries, to already have failed. This distinction is exceedingly important, and is one of the key issues in adult literacy work today. Especially in industrialised countries, where the population density of literacy and literacy requirements are relatively high, the illiterate and low- literate individual may become demoralised by the stigmatisation of illiteracy. Thus, the motivation to achieve and to become literate is a critical element in the success of most contemporary adult literacy programs in industrialised countries.

The situation may be more mixed in poor developing countries. With a population density of literate individuals so much lower and a less substantial need for literacy in everyday life, the stigmatisation factor may be considerably diminished, as in the story of Oum Fatima described earlier. Nonetheless, even though literacy in many Third World countries is still a domain reserved primarily for the educated classes, the uneducated and illiterate may, for a variety of socio-historical reasons, perceive themselves to be stigmatised and unable to break the cycle of poverty and illiteracy. Thus, motivation for learning can be just as great a problem for adult literacy programming in developing countries as it is in industrialised ones.

Cultural and environmental explanations for adult illiteracy and low-literacy in industrialised and developing countries are quite similar, and reside principally in the individual's lack of school-based learning (through non-attendance or premature dropout). As in the case with children, the low incidence of schooling, as well as lack of participation in adult literacy programs and campaigns, may be seen as a sociological and cultural phenomenon. Adults, certainly more than young Children, are prone to making decisions independently across most societies. This means that the dual coercive and supportive influences of parents and teachers have considerably less influence on the adult learner than on the child learner. As a result, motivational forces may not only be reduced, but also the incentives for participation in literacy programs may be largely or entirely absent for adults in developing countries.

While statistics on adult literacy programs are far from adequate, statistics on participation can be quite revealing (and disappointing) for providers of literacy services. In industrialised countries it is now widely acknowledged that low literacy: levels in the working population in industrialised nations is considerably below previous estimates, and hovers at about 25% of the adult population (OECD, 1995). In addition, the available evidence suggests that more than half the new adult literacy students in America drop out before having completed four weeks of their program (Wagner & Venezky, 1999). Similarly, it has been reported that low participation rates are an important factor in the inability of many developing countries with significant adult literacy program investments to make significant progress toward improved adult literacy rates (Wagner, 1995).

The linguistic dimension

Children. More than two decades ago, Downing (1974) published *Comparative Reading,* which surveyed the acquisition of reading skills across different languages and different orthographies. Based on his work and others, we know that mastery of the spoken language is a typical prerequisite for fluent reading comprehension in a given language.

Until fairly recently, it has been taken as " axiomatic" (cf. Unesco, 1953) that learning to read in one's "mother-tongue" or first language is *always* the best educational policy for literacy provision, whether for children or adults. Based on several well-known research studies undertaken in the 1960's, it has been generally assumed that children and youth who had to learn to read in a second language were at a disadvantage relative to others who learned in their mother tongue. While this generalisation probably holds true in many of the world's multilingual societies, more recent research has shown that there may be important exceptions (Dutcher, 1982; Engle, 1975; Wagner, et al., 1989).

We also know that languages that have a relatively close correspondence between spelling and sounds (such as Spanish) tend to make literacy learning easier than in languages where there exist many exceptions to "sounding out" rules (such as in the English language). Yet, it has also been shown, contrary to earlier anecdotal information, that reading problems (and disabilities) exist in all known written languages, even those in which there is no spelling-sound correspondence, such as in Chinese (Stevenson, et al., 1982).

Overall, it can be concluded that while important differences exist amongst languages (written and spoken), the normal healthy child, with the proper environmental supports (including direct and indirect instruction), ought to be able to learn to read and write successfully by the age 5-7 years. That there remain large individual differences in literacy achievement is usually thought to be explicable by addressing individual level approaches to literacy learning.

Adults. It has been often assumed by national and international development agencies that the language learning characteristics of children are roughly the same for adults. Indeed, there are extremely few references to the child-adult distinction in the international policy arena (see, however, Chall, 1999). Generally speaking, international and national policy makers inmost countries appear to assume that, like children, it is preferable to teach adults in their mother tongue rather than in a second language. The only caveat is that a few governments, putting learning efficiency aside, may prefer a second (usually metropolitan or European) language for the larger purposes of economic development. In the developing world, especially, there have been many about-faces on language of teaching policies, such that a clear record of language policy for adult learning is virtually non-existent. The scientific research literature is similarly absent on the topic of first and second language and literacy learning in adults.

In second language learning (oral and aural skills), the available literature seems to be varied in its conclusions. Contrary to popular belief, some specialists believe that adults are faster at second language learning than are children, particularly with respect to syntactic and lexical development; by contrast, children may out-distance adults in learning proper pronunciation of a second language, since their muscular habits are less ingrained (McLaughlin, 1985). Thus, it is doubtful that adults should be considered "like children" in the domain of second language learning, as they possess many more lexical items in their native language than children, and have cognitive and metalinguistic skills that are may make second language learning far easier than it is for children.

Thus, the picture of second language and literacy learning is more uncertain with adults. Even if literacy learning in the mother tongue is necessarily easier than in a second tongue (and this has yet to be substantiated), it does not follow that adult literacy should always be taught in the mother tongue. For example, the presumed cognitive advantage of learning a first literacy in one's mother tongue may be small relative to the motivational aspects of learning to read in the second language/literacy. In the few studies which have looked at the preferred language of literacy in adult literacy programs, policy makers have often been surprised to find that individuals often prefer the metropolitan language of literacy to the relatively ineffective (for economic purposes) mother tongue local language, whether in the U.S. or developing countries (Wagner, 1995).

In sum, linguistic factors in adult literacy acquisition are just beginning to be empirically understood. However, in most countries around the world, the issue of "which language of literacy" is often bound up in a host of political issues. Oftentimes it is difficult to obtain objective information on adult preferences, as political figures and lobbyists tend to take opposing positions on the issue of language learning.

The cognitive-psychometric dimension

Children. Perhaps the greatest quantity of research on literacy has been undertaken within the traditions of psychological testing, developed at the beginning of the twentieth century in Western countries. Because studies using psychometric tests (usually on samples of Western middle-class school children) demonstrated that reading ability was statistically correlated with cognitive skills such as perceptual discrimination, eye movements and aural (auditory) discrimination, it was concluded that these skills (the ones that correlate most highly with reading skill) are the basis for effective reading (cf. Barr et al., 1991). This finding, which has been replicated many times, has had major ramifications for literacy instruction the world over.

First it was concluded that such basic cognitive skills (termed "pre-reading" skills) necessitate direct instruction (of these same skills) in the school curriculum. As a result the past several decades have seen a tremendous growth in the use of basal textbooks which stress the learning of cognitive skills and an instructional approach favoring the decomposition of the reading task into simple skill (or subskill) components. One main example is the emphasis on "sounding out" of simple words or word-like strings (morphemes).

Second, it was suggested that children who were "slow learners" of literacy (sometimes termed "dyslexics") were thought to lack certain cognitive skills, therefore requiring remedial instruction on the skills themselves (rather than more practice on reading itself). This approach to seeing literacy acquisition as a consequence of the basic cognitive skills or subskills that underlie reading led to a long term tendency of reading and literacy specialists to emphasize the individual learner as the "cause" of his or her reading deficiencies (e.g. Vellutino & Denckla 1991).

Third, the cognitive approach has led to a number of important theories of reading and literacy acquisition. One of the most prominent has been termed the "stage theory" of reading (Chall, 1983). In this theory, it was proposed that all children (and, implicitly, adults as well) would normally learn to: (1) decode the alphabet; (2) learn to read written language; and then (3) read to learn from the written language. Accordingly, these are stages that all readers must go through to become proficient in any written language. While this theory has been hotly debated in the United States, it has yet to be tested widely in other societies.

Finally, since most of the research upon which these conclusions are drawn have been based on Western middle-class children, cultural and linguistic factors have tended to be minimised. It was only with the advent of ethnographic studies (e.g., Street, 1996) that the cognitive-psychometric perspective came under especially critical review, particularly with respect to the large-scale literacy problems in developing countries and amongst minority populations in industrialised countries.

Adults. While there exists a vast literature on the cognitive and psychometric properties of literacy acquisition in children, the opposite is largely true in studies of adult literacy acquisition. Work is only just beginning on establishing testing equivalencies amongst the varied standardised tests currently used to measure adult literacy learning in Western countries. Since almost no direct assessment of adult skills (i.e., out of school literacy and basic skills) has taken place in developing countries, there is little basis upon which to form solid conclusions for other parts of the world.

As with language learning, it has usually been assumed (due to lack of relevant data) that adults learn literacy like children do, perhaps faster or perhaps slower, depending on the commentator and on the limited research cited. However, it is often taken for granted that adults can learn to read in "crash" courses in a matter of weeks or months in literacy campaigns, even though it is usually assumed to take years in children (Amove & Graff, 1987). Whether such adult literacy learning is retained for functional use is seldom explored, and this area of research has just begun to receive serious attention (Wagner, 1998).

In summary, when data from research studies are brought together, it may be seen that considerable progress has been made in understanding the life span acquisition of literacy in children and adults, particularly in industrialised societies. Far less is known about literacy acquisition in a truly global *or life-space* perspective, and in multilingual societies. Since the bulk of non-literate people live in these areas of the world, there is much more that needs to be known if we are to improve literacy provision in the coming decades.

We can also see that there are certain similarities between children's literacy learning and adult learning, such as in the early emphasis on alphabet learning and decoding. But important differences are also apparent. Perhaps most important is the observation that learning to read may have enormously different personal significance to adults than to children, who tend to be socialised and instructed by parents and teachers (and even obliged) into literacy. Motivation will depend greatly on differing perceptions of literacy learning, and these may vary enormously by context and across individuals. Similarly, there are numerous studies of second language literacy learning in children, but relatively few with adults. A comprehensive life span approach will require a filling in of the "empty cells" across the life cycle. In sum, despite some important preliminary conclusions that carry across life spans and life-spaces, much work remains to be done to construct a comprehensive and intersecting research base in this field.

POLICY IMPLICATIONS OF A LIFE-SPAN AND LIFE-SPACE APPROACH

In the view presented above, literacy may be understood as a cluster of skills and practices which begins with early oral language skills in all children, and develops into literacy skills acquired and retained in varying degrees across the lifetime of the individual. Individuals who never come into contact with written materials will not learn to read, many who live in contact with the literate world may only learn a few of the practices and skills defined as literacy in the contemporary world, while others who are socialised in highly literate environments will, almost without exception, become literate themselves.

If present trends continue, particularly with the universalisation of primary schooling, the world of illiteracy will diminish sharply over the next century. Indeed, the number of "naive" illiterates – those with no knowledge that literacy exists and with no knowledge of the uses of literacy by others – is dwindling today; relatively few persons in industrialised fall into that category today. Nonetheless, demographics suggest that the absolute numbers of individuals with low literacy skills (e.g., with only a few years of primary schooling) continues to *increase* in many parts of the world, while in OECD countries, these trends are particularly sensitive to race, ethnicity and social class (OECD /Statistics Canada (1995).

Connect child and adult literacy theory with action

Both child and adult literacy programs need to benefit not only in terms of new knowledge, but also in the contexts in which literacy learning occurs. One relatively new area of work is "family literacy" where both children and adults learning to read together; for a review, see Gadsden (1999). Literacy researchers are still divided into roughly two camps -those who study children in schools, and those interest in adult and non-formal education. This gap must be bridged in the coming years or important opportunities for synergies between parental literacy and children's literacy will be lost.

Build on cultural strengths

Although obvious in everyday life, building on cultural strengths is a concept often ignored in educational programming for children and adults, Schools in many parts of the world often ignore the culture of minority groups and indigenous cultures in the formal educational system. Adult education programs also often fail to motivate learners when they utilize national (and even European languages) for instruction; literacy training ought to be built on the languages which people have the most motivation to learn. Furthermore, literacy programs can be built into family and social services, such as early childhood education programs, as well as in cooperation with agencies for health and workplace training. Clearly, to be effective, literacy and basic skills programs need to be much better linked with people's lives, home lives and life-spaces.

Literacy "campaigns" are not very effective

Talk of eradicating literacy, via national and international campaigns, sometimes creates the illusion that literacy learning can be achieved quickly, ubiquitously and inexpensively, and that such learning is virtually permanent. This perspective, from the available research, has been demonstrated to be erroneous on all counts. We have not yet integrated what we know and what we still need to know about the trajectory of life-span literacy skills. Some skills may increase, others may wane, all as a function of the practice and practices engaged in by individuals in a diverse and variegated set of life-spaces.

CONCLUSIONS

With the advent of new literacy initiatives for children and for adults in many countries worldwide, there is an increasing need to provide conceptual clarity to those who work in the field, as well as for those who are the recipients of educational programs. An appropriate conceptual framework for literacy across the life-span and across life-spaces is a useful, indeed necessary, way to think about literacy development in children and adults. The compartmentalised approaches of the past seem only to divide a field that is in greater need of coherence if we are to achieve a literate world in the future.

REFERENCES

Arnove, R. F. & Graft, H. J. (Eds.). (1987). *National literacy campaigns.* New York: Plenum.

Barr, R., Kamil, M. L., Mosenthal, R. B., & Pearson, P. D. (1991). (Eds.), *Handbook of reading research. Vol II.* New York: Longman.

Bourdieu, P. (1977). *Outline of a theory of Practice.* Cambridge: Cambridge University Press.

Chall, J. S. (1983). *Stages of reading development.* New York: McGraw-Hill.

Chall, J. S. (1999). Developing Literacy ... in children and adults. In D. A. Wagner (Ed.), *The future of literacy in a changing world, 73-94.* . Second edition, Revised and updated. Cresskill, NJ: Hampton Press.

Dutcher, N. (1982). *The use of first and second languages in primary education: Selected case studies.* World Bank Staff Working Paper No.504. Washington, DC: World Bank.

Engle, P. L. (1975). Language medium in early school years for minority language groups. *Review of Educational Research, 45,* 283-325.

Ferreiro, E. & Teberosky, A. (1982). *Literacy before schooling.* Exeter, NH: Heineman Educational Books.

Gadsden, V. L. (1999). Family literacy practice and programs. In D. A., Wagner, R. L. Venezky, & B. V. Street (Eds.). *Literacy: An International Handbook.* Boulder, CO: Westview Press.

Kirsch, J. S., Jungeblut, A., Jenkins, L., & Kolstad, A. (1993). *Adult literacy in America: A first look at the results of the National Adult Literacy Survey.* Washington, DC: National Center for Educational Statistics, U.S. Department of Education.

McLaughlin, B. (1985). *Second language learning in childhood.* (2nd Ed.). Hillsdale, NJ: Erlbaum.

OECD/Statistics Canada (1995). *Literacy, economy and society.* Paris: OECD.

Ogbu, J. U. (1999). Learning achievement in minority groups. Paper presented at the Annual Meetings of the American Educational Research Association.

Stevenson, H. W., Stigler, J. W., Lucker, G. W., Lee, S., Hsu, C. C., & Kitamura, S. (1982). Reading disabilities: The case of Chinese, Japanese, and English. *Child Development, 33,* 1164-1181.

Street, B. V. (1996). *Cross-cultural approaches to literacy.* Cambridge: Cambridge University Press.

Sulzby, E. & Teale, w. (1991). Emergent literacy. In R. Barr, M. L. Kamil, R. B. Mosenthal, & P. D. Pearson (Eds.), *Handbook of reading research. Vol II,* 727-758. New York: Longman.

UNESCO. (1953). The use of vernacular languages in education. *Monograph on fundamental education.* No.8. Paris: UNESCO.

Vellutino, F. R. & Denckla, M. B. (1991). Cognitive and neuropsychological foundations of word identification in poor and normally developing readers. In R. Barr, M. L. Kamil, R. B. Mosenthal, & P. D. Pearson (Eds.), *Handbook of reading research. Vol II, 571-608.,* New York: Longman.

Vermes, G. & Kastenbaum, M. (March 1992). Socio-linguistic minorities and scholastic difficulties in France. In D. A. Wagner & I. Puchner (Eds.). *World literacy in the year 2000: Research and policy dimensions 163-173.* Philadelphia: Annals of the American Academy of Political and Social Science.

Vygotsky, L. (1978). *Mind in society.* Cambridge, MA: Harvard University Press.

Wagner, D. A. (1995). Literacy and development: Rationales, myths, innovations, and future directions. *International Journal of Educational Development, 15,* 341-362.

Wagner, D. A. (1998). Literacy retention: Comparisons across age, time and culture. In H. Wellman & S. G. Paris (Eds.), *Global prospects for education: Development culture and schooling* (pp. 229-251). Washington, D.C.: American Psychological Association.

Wagner, D. A., Spratt, J. E. & Ezzaki, A. (1989). Does learning to read in a second language always put the child at a disadvantage?: Some counter-evidence from Morocco, *Applied Psycholinguistics, 10*, 31-48:

Wagner, D. A. & Venezky, R. L. (1999). Adult literacy: The next generation. *Educational Researcher, 28*, 21-29.

Wagner, D. A., Venezky, R. L., & Street, B. V. (Eds.) (1999). *Literacy: An International Handbook*. Boulder, CO: Westview Press.

D2 Teaching Reading: A Historical Approach

ANNE-MARIE CHARTIER

ABSTRACT

The historian endeavours to understand reading as it was taught in past times without comparing it with the present. He/she attempts to find out what written social practices were the point of reference for teachers, pupils and their parents and what were the means available to make this teaching possible. Besides, it is the opinions of the time and not contemporary standards that were the criteria according to which this teaching was said to be effective and why it was effective. Thus, between the 16th and 19th centuries, there were different teaching methods depending on whether they were aimed at restricted reading (religious texts of different forms of worships) or generalised reading (unknown religious or secular texts); depending on whether reading was taught from texts in Latin (catholic prayers) or in the vernacular (protestant prayers, secular texts); depending on whether teaching was carried out on an individual basis (tutors of the elite, teachers of rural schools) or in groups (simultaneous teaching requiring an clear cut curriculum, standardised books and trained teachers); depending on whether reading came before writing, or on the contrary the three R's (reading, writing and reckoning – or arithmetic) could be taught simultaneously, with the emergence of slates and pen nibs at the expense of goose quills. At the end of the 19th century, contemporary debates about analytical or synthetic, phonic or visual methods appeared.

At a time when everyone goes to school, it is necessary to understand why some pupils do not achieve well, and how it is possible to remedy the situation, particularly in a society where writing skills are gradually becoming as important as reading skills in the definition of illiteracy.

INTRODUCTION

In considering the meaning of the word "reading", we can say that we never stop becoming literate since we will always come across texts beyond our understanding. However, "reading" can be considered as a skill most children manage to master in a few years or in a few months. In this article, we will deal with the second meaning of the word "reading". Thus limited to the basic skill, reading is often considered

511

T. Nunes, P. Bryant (eds.), Handbook of Children's Literacy, 511–538.

as a skill more or less easy to acquire, depending on the difficulty of the spelling rules of each language (thus, Spanish is easier than English; Gray, 1956; Sprenger-Charolles, 2003). Studying teaching methods from a historical point of view can help to determine how teaching procedures have become more efficient with increasingly rigorous linguistic approaches, and with an improved understanding of the psychological processes implied in learning. Furthermore, teaching methods depend on what reading actually involved at the time considered. Reading practices and standard textbooks used by literate people need to be taken into account, and in this case reading basics involve literacy and culture. These methods cannot be historically compared as if their aim had always been to develop the same proficiency through various techniques of deciphering and interpretation (Hébrard, 1998). By studying the history of teaching reading, it should be possible to find out why age-old habits, like spelling a word syllable by syllable before reading it or teaching children in Latin, which nowadays seem to HINDER [prevent] rather than help learning were considered appropriate by generations of teachers before finally being subjected to criticism and abandoned. I will study teaching methods in this respect, and have selected a few examples taken from the sixteenth to the nineteenth century in order to show how cultural changes in reading conceptions and practices since the Renaissance have impacted on the way school-children have become acquainted with written culture.

INDIVIDUAL METHODS OF TEACHING READING IN LATIN

The ends and means of teaching reading

By the end of the Middle Ages, there were two ways of approaching written texts. The first one was the scholarly and intellectual approach corresponding to the traditional instruction of scholars in medieval universities. They learned the basics of Latin letters, syllables and whole words while at the same time becoming familiar with this new language by singing liturgical texts in chorus at church. By using plainchant, they had to articulate and pronounce syllabically, even though they did not understand what they were singing at first. Then grammar was introduced: scholars had to memorize a book of grammatical rules written in Latin, sometimes in verse so as to make it easier for oral memorizing, for example Donatus and his followers[1] (for further reading on the history of grammar, see Auroux, 1994, and Colombat, 1999.). Thus, students learned a language and its grammar at the same time while practising Latin orally with their masters and their

---

[1] Aelius Donatus wrote the *Ars minor* (by questions and answers) and *Ars Major* around 350-360. Reading is treated in the first part (letters, syllables, words, i.e. the basics) as an oral process. Alexandre de Villedieu's *Doctrinale*, circ. 1200, in verse. Despautère's *Commentarii Grammatici*, 1537.

fellows. Italian as well as French humanists severely criticised such teaching methods and rejected Medieval Latin as corrupt, even if it was easy to speak, to read and to understand (Grendler, 1984; Grafton, 1997). They advocated the reading of ancient writers, like Cicero, Virgil, Terence and Caesar, and they imitated these texts to create a vernacular literature, in a time when spoken language had no legitimacy or explicit rules of spelling and pronunciation. In fact, there was much debate among scholars about how to spell words (Blanche-Beneviste & Chervel, 1969; Baddeley, 1993), and spelling depended on writers or copyists, and after Gutenberg on printers. The argument in favour of learning Latin was its prestige as a sacred language and its position as the language of universal culture, as well as the simplicity of its spelling.

However, there were people not learned in Latin and yet who needed to write. The education of merchants developed very early in Italy, as well as in other urban areas of Northern or Western Europe. In Italy, in the sixteenth century, the masters of "abbaco schools" opened private or communal classes to teach commercial reckoning and calligraphy (Petrucci, 1983; Grendler, 1984; Black, 1987; Hébrard, 1995, Ruggero, 1999). After studying the basics of Latin, children started writing and reckoning (or "rithmetic) in the language of the day. Whereas scholars were required to write in Latin and read the chefs-d'oeuvre of past writers, merchants wanted to read and reckon in languages used in commercial exchanges. At the time, most people were unable to read and did not feel the need to. If necessary, they could appeal to a clerk for help – *literatus* and *clericus* were synonymous.

The gap between the great number of *illiterati* and the small number of *literati* was bridged by the Religious Reformation, whose policy was to teach everybody to read. As Luther wrote (see Gilmont, 1997),[2] nothing should prevent believers from having direct access to the Scriptures, whatever their sex or age, "whether it be a poor maid or a nine year old child". Laymen should be able to read in order to be able to see the fundamental truths of faith by themselves. The Protestant countries were foremost in translating the Scriptures into common language and developing universal literacy projects. The Catholic Church followed in their footsteps. The Council of Trent[3] (Julia, 1997) maintained that ordinary people should be instructed from childhood. Everyone should be able to read and memorize their catechism, so as not to make mistakes in dogma. That is why the Roman Church encouraged bishops and priests to develop instruction. In this context of schism in the Roman Church, religious persecution, wars and theological conflicts -hence the importance of words used in prayers and catechisms, the religious elite realised it was essential to develop universal literacy;

---

[2] In fact, Luther did not encourage people or children to read alone. Martin Luther, *M.L.O.*, IX, ed. Labor et Fides, Genève, p. 111.

[3] The Council (1545-63) condemned protestant heresies and affirmed the major points of truth in catholic faith.

most families had no such awareness. The two medieval traditions, the scholarly one and the practical one, which had both been elaborated by "professionals", provided the basic means for teaching adults and children for non-professional purposes. This development can be studied through three different types of document: the primers used to teach reading, the treatises describing teaching methods, and various accounts like students' or teachers' memories, scenes of classwork represented in images or literature and contracts between families and teachers, etc.

Teaching tools for beginners

The early tools used to teach reading have almost all disappeared. They were fragile and had no commercial value. Three prime tools could be found throughout Europe, or nearly: horn-books (in Italy carta or tavola, in France, charte, carte, palette or tablette, in England horn-book or battledore), ABC's (salterio, *Instructions chrétiennes*, primer, *Crisscross*) and readers (prayer books, books of Hours, *Civilités*). A late English engraving dating from 1622 shows how a horn-book was used in tutoring. The scene takes place in a study where we can see a table with an inkstand, a quill, an open book and a whip. A young child is holding the handle of a wooden board in his left hand, while in his right hand he is holding a pin which he is using to point out the letters he is naming or maybe his tutor is naming. The tutor is sitting in an armchair and he is looking over the shoulders of the child standing between his knees. The horn book already existed in the Middle Ages. From the sixteenth century onwards, the alphabet was no longer written (and later printed) in columns but in two lines. The first always began with a cross and consisted of the alphabet in small letters, and the second line, in capital letters. Children had to make the sign of the Cross before reading letters as well as prayers. Hence the name of Santa Croce, Croix-de-par-Dieu or Criscross (Christ's cross) given to ABCs in Italy, France or England. The Gothic fonts were gradually replaced by new Roman or Italic ones. The list of vowels came below the alphabet, sometimes but not always followed by the list of consonants and a few examples of syllables set in columns for instance A, E, I, O, U associated with B, C, and D. Finally, there was a prayer formula (the sign of the Cross and a psalm verse) and/ or a "longer text", like the Pater Noster in Latin or in the vernacular according to the country and the cult.

The second book was the ABC, a cheap booklet consisting of a few pages only and sometimes illustrated with wood engravings. Whereas the horn-book often belonged to the family, the ABC was the first and usually the only schoolbook. It was called a Psalter, more often than ABC or primer, because of the texts it contained. Unlike the Psalter printed for religious use, the school primer included an alphabet and a table of syllables. The same elements as in the horn-book could be found and they were arranged in a similar fashion – the Cross, the alphabet in upper-case and lower-case letters and a list of syllables which presented the "consonant-vowel" and "vowel-consonant" combinations. Primers usually gave only two-letter syllables, but in more elaborate primers – which were later copied in popular versions – three or even four letter syllables could be found. Then, there were the prayers, the Lord's Prayer and the Creed in Latin or the vernacular, the Ten Commandments, and the Ave Maria in Catholic countries. Other prayers included the Confiteor, the seven psalms of Penance, and various religious hymns, depending on different cults.

The third book introduced the pupils to longer texts. The opposition between primers and readers, still in use today, shows the gap between the two stages. The selected texts were not written especially for children. They were shortened versions of well-known texts. In Italy, the first reader imposed by tradition was the Donatello, a shortened Latin grammar. The other texts were used in the various religious services: Veni creator and the Vespers of the Virgin, translations of the Gospels and Psalms. There were lists of the truths that should be remembered. A new literary genre appeared during the Renaissance, which was called *Civilités*.[4] These books dealt with savoir-vivre and good manners. Short versions were made for children. They were often printed in "civilité types", imitating cursive writing, which helped children become acquainted with reading manuscripts. They were the only books dealing with secular subjects.

Individual teaching

Italian children started with the tavola, then they went on with the *salterio* and finished with the *Donatello* (Ruggero, 1999). French children started with the palette, then went on with the *Croix de par Dieu* and the *Civilités*, English children with the horn-book, the primer and finally the reader (Smith, 1974). Whether at school or at home, the time spent with each book was not fixed in advance, since individual teaching prevailed. It is not difficult to teach students in groups who can already read and write, by giving them lessons or exercises they can do silently together while the teacher is speaking, commenting or asking questions. For a long time however, it was considered impossible to teach illiterate people in groups. Reading lessons were always one to one. The teacher asked the child to come with his book and checked that he had memorised the preceding lesson – for instance, would ask the child to name the letters or the syllables he was supposed to know – then he taught him a new lesson, naming new letters or new syllables, and asked to repeat them several times before sending him back to his seat to practise by himself or with a fellow pupil. Another child would then be called. It must not be forgotten that children did not attend school regularly, that they arrived at irregular hours,

---

[4] Erasmus wrote in 1530 *De Civilitate morum puerum*, translated or imitated in many vernacular versions, which had a great success in schools from the seventeenth to the nineteenth century.

did not have the same ABCs and the lists of syllables, the characters and the lay out of pages differed from one book to another. Teaching a whole class would have required regular attendance and standard books. The amount of time granted to each pupil could not be long. Those, who could afford it, usually resorted to private tuition or tutorship. However, individual teaching enabled students to progress at their own pace, which, in some cases, meant fast.

Teaching basics

School books seemed to impose the same definite progression: when they were able to name letters and syllables, children read their first texts. The reading process implied spelling the letters in order to pronounce the syllable ([pe]-[a], [pa]) and then the word (Pa-ter, Pater). In fact, the children/students connected the signs identified in the page with the text known by heart (Pater Noster, qui es.). In short, in order to learn to read, spelling and reciting should be done at the same time. It is only in the second stage that the teacher asked for fluent reading, linking words or sequences of words. Here is an example of a teaching practice described in "the school ordinance" in Lutheran Saxony, in 1580: "When you are certain they have mastered the alphabet, teach them the syllables, using the Lord's prayer as your text. All this time pay close attention to their pronunciation, and do not allow the boys to slur or drawl their vowels and consonants in the manner of their natural speech, but make them separate and distinguish the sounds clearly from one another, as is done in Latin diction". It shall be remembered that in that Lutheran country prayers were still in Latin at that time: "What's the first letter in *pater*? It is a *p*. Show me the *p* in the alphabet. What comes after the *p*? an *a*. Show me the *a*. And so on".

Reading the sounds clearly separated and distinguished one from the other was considered as the model for good oral reading. It would not be considered today as fluent reading. In fact, the "stumbling reading" of beginners sounded not unlike the collective reading or saying of prayers at church – "as is done in Latin diction" (Strauss, 1981). Reading corresponded to this collective practice and, just as they used the notes to sing, even though they could not read them well, in the same way they used the texts to "read/say" the prayers slowly together at church. The fact that they uttered them with faith was in itself valuable and the pastor's role was to explain and develop the meaning, Sunday after Sunday. It was obvious that a child or an illiterate adult did not really understand what he/she was saying/reading. Reading did not mean "getting information", it meant praying – that is to say proving one's faith in God and remembering the text which expressed it. Written texts made it possible to say and repeat over and over again, without making errors, the words people had to meditate on when their true meaning was not directly given.

During this first learning period, pupils memorised and repeatedly revised a small number of written texts. Then they could start reading texts they did not know by heart, but which had already been heard in church, or which had been read at school by more advanced students (prayers, *Civilités*, etc.). The texts belonging to their catechism were always learnt and said aloud, before they were read. The pupil learnt to spell letters first, then pronounce the syllables, and transform the syllables into a whole word, the words into a sentence and finally the sentences into a whole text. This stage was like decoding a text orally while the teacher checked the accuracy of the reading. The exercise was supposed to enable pupils to read aloud new texts, as long as they were printed in familiar characters. Actually, very few people in European countries considered the acquisition of such a skill a social priority. In most cases, teachers had achieved their aims when their pupils knew exactly what was needed to take part in the religious life of the community. Yet, this modest initiation was often sufficient to enable young readers to read far more than the usual requisites. These bright students were considered naturally gifted and often they became churchmen or scholars.

The social efficiency of learning reading

The teaching methods set up by the Churches aimed at "restricted literacy" (Goody, 1977; 1987), a practice of reading without writing, and collective reading aloud, restricted and intensive reading (Wittman, 1997) – only a few texts were worth reading and were read again and again. Reading without writing: writing was unnecessary for the majority of people, since writing was necessary mainly for arthmetic and for commercial accounts or studying Latin classics, which involved other social and cultural worlds. Collective reading aloud – the "devotio moderna" was emerging and implied individual forms of spiritual life, like silent reading and re-reading or recollections of texts; but normally a text had to be read in a group. In this social ritual, the group and an external authority could guarantee its meaning. Whoever read by themselves might become heretical or misguided. As opposed to the indefinite variants of oral tradition, reading aloud ensured accuracy of written texts, while maintaining convivial forms of ritual and emotional experiences and did not exclude those who were not learned in religious or secular written culture – particularly from the reading of widely circulated printed books, such as chapbooks, almanacs, political pamphlets, tales of chivalry, romances and lives of saints. The aim of "restricted literacy" was made possible by teaching pupils to read in two different ways. They had to know basics – letters, syllables – in order to be able to reconstruct the words and they had to become gradually acquainted with written culture: first, they learnt by heart the texts to be read, while at the same time they experienced their meaning and value in the life of their community – teachers took children to attend church services- eventually, they were confronted with the texts themselves and started deciphering them.

LEARNING TO READ ONE'S OWN LANGUAGE (1600'S–1800'S)

Teachers of the ABCs: three contrasted Protestant examples

As the teaching of laymen to read aimed only at limited practice, there was no need for an elaborate methodology. Those pupils, who had difficulties mastering the alphabet with its numerous typographic variants, and who failed to memorize and combine syllables, were nevertheless able to use a text as a useful prompt, having heard it repeated in chorus by people around them. Was it really necessary to set up schools all over the country for such a result? The policies of European countries – as far as literacy was concerned – depended more on political than on pedagogical choices.

In the various German Lutheran states, churches relied on public authorities, under the supervision of pastors for the instruction of children, parents being considered incapable of such responsibility. In return, masters taught pupils to honour and obey their Prince. Compulsory regulations issued by public authorities encouraged regular and relatively early schooling. German teachers, as we have seen in Saxony in the preceding example, rapidly became "professionals". In the seventeenth century, after the Thirty Years' War, when the Duke of Sax-Gotha reformed schools, the *Schul-Methodus* published by the Duke recommended that each pupil should be given a reading book including a syllabary, the Gospel, a songbook and a book of arithmetic. The hymns of the Songbook – in German at that time – were sung in chorus, which perpetuated the slow syllabic reading to fit the music that the children discovered in church on Sundays. In 1698, the Duke created the first *seminarium scolasticum* to train masters. Such institutions developed throughout the eighteenth century under the influence of the Pietists. Then, prospective teachers learnt how to teach religion – Luther's small catechism, the reading of the Bible, the explanation of canticles and Sunday sermons – and also "the best ways to teach children to read".[5] As a result there were places where ancient and new treatises on reading were read carefully and repeatedly, like the century-old method of Ickelsamer[6] of analysing

---

[5] Curriculum for the Realeschule of Berlin (founded in 1748 by a pietist theologian, Hecker). In 1753, the King of Prussia made it the Royal Training School for Brandebourg.

[6] Valentin Ickelsamer (1501-1542), friend of Luther, published *A correct and quick Way to Learn Reading*, and *A German Grammar from which Every Man Can Teach Himself to Read*. In 1527, he wrote a primer *The shortest Way To Reading*. He proposed to teach the phonic power of letters from sounds to letters of words, and not the reverse, as usually: "Take the name Hans: you have four sound changes in this word, which are represented by four letters. First, you hear a strong exhaling noise, as when someone heaves a deep sigh. This is the H, which you breathe into the vowel A. Following this, there is a sound through the nose and finally you hear a sibilant like the hissing of a snake" (Gerald Strauss, op.cit., p. 97). A picture associated with each letter helped children to memorize the sound (a dog over the growl R, a cow over the moo-sound M, and so on) or the initial letter (*Mönch* for M (Monk), *Esel* for E (ass), *Ring* for R).

sounds, which had had little or no impact when it was released – it was beyond the usual abilities of teachers. The method had been circulated by the editor Peter Jordan, without training colleges, teachers learnt from colleagues or from books. This was what happened in England at that time.

In England, after 1534, when the Act of Supremacy declared Henry VIII the Supreme Head of the Church in England, primers were all written in English, and the first primer authorised by the King and the Church was published in 1540.[7] It included the Lord's Prayer, the Creed, the Articles of Faith, the Ten Commandments, preceded by an alphabet. These standard books it was hoped would make up for the shortage of competent teachers due to low wages and the increasing number of elementary schools. Several pedagogical treatises aimed at helping the people who wanted to teach. In 1570, John Hart published *A method or comfortable beginning for all unlearned whereby they may be taught to read English*, in which he explained how his book could enable anyone to teach without it becoming a full time occupation: "Some one such in a house as now can read our present manner, may be able to teach it to all the rest of the house, even the whiles their hands may be otherwise well occupied in working for their living, or otherwise being idle or sitting by the fire, without any further let or cost" (see Cressy, 1980). Edmund Coote, whose famous treatise *The English school-master* was reprinted 48 times between 1596 and 1696, thought that teaching children was an appropriate additional job for craftsmen: "Tailors, weavers, shopkeepers, seamsters... may sit at thy shop board, at thy looms, or at thy needle, and never hinder thy work to hear the scholars, after thou hast once made this little book familiar unto thee". While tutors and scholars were seeking solutions to the difficulties of written English[8] with its irregular spelling so confusing for beginners, others taught children without a didactic approach, the practice being "limited to the hearing of memorised lessons and the most elementary work with the alphabet and primer" (Cressy, 1988, p. 39). Meanwhile, printed texts were gradually improving with new editorial techniques. The primers were printed in big fonts, and used one syllable words (so there would be no problem for children to stress the word) and rhyming sentences to help being memorised. For instance, the *New England Primer* associated each letter with a picture and a distich (C: The Cat doth play/ And after slay; D: The Dog can bite/ A Thief at Night). That is why, when the demand for literacy did not correspond to a personal request from families, but was a response to the injunction of the Church supported by political authorities, the pedagogical

---

[7] The archbishop of Canterbury, Cranmer, who wrote the *Book of Common Prayer* thought that the Church of England would be unified by this official reference to a single book, founding a single and common interpretation. According to Olson (1994), that is a feature of Protestant reading, founded on literal meaning of texts, as in modern scientific discourse which followed.

[8] "Moreover, in the seventeenth and eighteenth centuries, great changes took place in vowel sounds, but at that time printing had so nearly fixed the spellings that changes were difficult. Today, we spell about as they did in the time of James I (1603-25) and pronounce as well as we can" (Mathews, 1966).

curriculum was limited and the result depended less on the professionalism of teachers than on the pupils' personal involvement and their good relationship with the teacher.

Mass education could be envisaged without schools. In some countries such as Sweden and Finland – the Church authorities, which were also Lutheran, relied on families to teach their children to read and learn their catechism (Johansson, 1981). For enforcement, the Church Law of 1686 obliged clergymen to check the proficiency of adults and children in an annual and solemn examination. Those who failed were not allowed to take part in the sacraments, i.e. the official ceremonies of civil as well as religious life. This system still prevailed when John Patterson, a Scottish Evangelist, became aware of it a century later: "The parents were the teachers of their children, till they reached the age of fourteen or thereabouts, when they attended the pastor or his assistant, to be prepared for confirmation and being admitted to the Lord's Supper. And as no person can be confirmed till he can read and repeat his catechism, or until confirmed, can give his oath in a court of justice, or get married, a great disgrace is attached to not being able to read; indeed, one who can not read is nobody in the eye of the law". "Reading and repeating the Catechism", the two tests of the examination revealed the concept of written culture at that time. As far as the aims were concerned, informal but intensive guidance provided by a relative rather than a professional could achieve satisfactory results. Private tuition, elsewhere reserved to the upper-class, had become the standard in Sweden.

Learning to read in a Catholic country: giving up Latin in France

In Catholic countries, ecclesiastical tradition as well as humanistic experiments argued in favour of Latin. The use of oral Latin prevailed because the spelling of words was regular. It was easier to memorize the correspondences between letters and sounds and to articulate syllables in Latin than in any vernacular language. The language spoken by princes was seldom spoken by children because of the number of dialects whose spelling had not been determined and whose pronunciation differed according to the area. In short, with Latin, children could discover the "principle" of the correspondences with an alphabet which was virtually phonetic. Thanks to this training, they would be able to read their mother tongue with some extra but rather limited practice. In 1654, this prevailing position was adopted by Jacques de Batencour, a Parisian priest, in his treatise *L'École paroissiale*. "As reading in French is much more difficult than reading in Latin, children should be able to read fluently in Latin first, Latin being the starting point for reading in French as it contains the same characters and syllables". He rejected learning from prayers because they were too well known: "To start with, ask the child to read a passage he does not know by heart, like the seven Psalms, and the Pater, Ave, Credo, Benedicite, or *Repons de la Messe*, because when you ask them to read what they already know by heart, they do not learn how to read at all" (de

Batencour, 1654). If this method is compared to the former ones, two changes can be detected. On the one hand, reading was no longer recognizing a text already known, but saying aloud an unknown text, which meant that a deciphering technique was essential. Therefore syllables had to be memorised, learnt by rote ("par routine") and also by rules ("par connaissance et jugement"). Everybody could realize that spelling does not enable you to infer their pronunciation, but is a great help to memorize them. On the other hand, a recurrent problem was solved by typography. Printers inserted hyphens or blanks between syllables in order to help the pupil, when the simple Consonant-Vowel (do-mi-ne) could not be applied (cle-mens). Yet, reading was probably easier for pupils if they articulated familiar words of their own language, instead of Latin words they did not understand. This argument, which had first been developed by Reformers, had become the argument of many French teachers, and first of all, tutors or masters in private boarding schools.

The tutors, whose pupils spoke French and not a dialect, rapidly chose to treat Latin as a second written language (Compère & Chervel, 1997; Waquet, 1998). When a pupil read aloud a text in French, he/she could hear words known and so came to the meaning of the text. As Thomas Guyot wrote, "it is a great mistake to start to teach children to read in Latin, as is usually done. French people already know French of which they know an infinite number of words; why do we not teach them first to read in French, as this method would be much quicker and less difficult?". Between the two aims, reading texts containing "an infinite number of words" and reading familiar prayers, there is a difference of nature and not of degree: from the start, tutors aimed at achieving an ability to permit the reading of any text and not just a limited corpus. As a consequence, the method of teaching had to follow rules. This is clear with the Jansenist teachers of Port-Royal (Delforge, 1985), who, for example, invented a new spelling technique to make the phonic power of consonants sound clearer. The usual names of letters (Bé, Cé, Dé, Effe) were replaced by a syllable, which showed the consonant power much better (Be, Ke, De, Fe).[9] By choosing to teach to read in French, a teacher became aware of the idiosyncrasies of this language, which could not be easily written with a Latin alphabet inherited from tradition. The typographical distinction between I and J, and between U and V made it possible to add two consonants which were not found in Latin. But the problem of the vowels, much more numerous in French than in Latin, raised a number of problems (Auroux & Calvet, 1973).[10] The grammarians debated spelling reforms, the uses of the accents,

---

[9] This spelling had been rediscovered by Py-Poulain Delaunay (*Méthode du sieur Py-Poulain de Launay ou l'art d'apprendre à lire en français et en latin*, 1719), approved by the Encyclopedists and it was in use in many schools in the nineteenth century.

[10] At that time, grammarians did not agree on what is called a sound in French. According to the *Grammaire* of Port-Royal, there were 10 vowels and 19 consonants, according to the grammarian Duclos, 17 vowels and 22 consonants. It is only at the beginning of the eighteenth century that we have a complete description of the sounds of French.

and the various ways of encoding the same sound. The master, who wanted to break with tradition and make new didactic choices had to study the language closely. So as to set up his own method, he had to determine the power of letters, how to separate syllables and whether the spelling was appropriate. Giving new names to letters was not merely technically convenient, but changed the representation of the relationship between oral and written languages.

In fact, popular literacy made steps forward thanks to new institutions. The last new teaching method developed in France by the Counter Reformation was devised by J. B. de La Salle. As he considered poor people not to be really concerned about their salvation "having no religion themselves", he tried to make schools of catechism attractive to urban populations. There were no tuition fees and pupils were taught the three R's in French, as was in the tradition for merchants. Thus he attracted the clientele of writing teachers and teachers of arithmetic, whose corporations took him to Court, because they had a well established monopoly on such teaching. He rallied not only poor people (as other charitable orders did), but also the popular urban elite – craftsmen and merchants. J. B. de La Salle broke away from individual teaching, caused of a lack of discipline and background noise in classrooms, thanks to "the simultaneous system" described in his famous treatise, *Conduite des Écoles chrétiennes* (1706). As a result, a greater number of children could work quietly together and were kept busy, even when their master was not teaching them. Such a method needed standard school books (written and published by the Brothers), organised classes of the same level, and strict discipline for the pupils as well as for the masters. Before writing and arithmetic, "there will be nine different types of lessons in Christian Schools: 1st, the chart of alphabet, 2nd, the chart of syllables, 3rd the syllabary, 4th primer, 5th the second book which those who can spell perfectly well will start reading [in syllables], 6th the third book which will teach children to read with pauses, 7th the Psalter, 8th the *Civilité*, 9th handwritten letters". All these devices were traditional, but there were a greater number of stages: the ABC chart (learnt in two months) and the syllable chart (in one month) had become large boards, in front of which several pupils used to stand together. The syllabary included the first prayers. The readers (between 3 and 6 months for each book) were the same for all, so that the children could read together. The best pupil in each group corrected his classmates and made them repeat the lesson while the master was teaching another group. Pupils went on to the next stage according to progress made. A Brother Inspector came once a month to examine them and decide whether they could go on, according to their achievements, which enabled him to control the masters at the same time. It was only at the end of this course that pupils learnt to read aloud texts in Latin, so that they could become altar boys. In fact, Latin as a language was no longer included in the curriculum and that broke with a long clerical tradition. The Brothers who were not priests were not allowed to study Latin, so that they could not be tempted to teach their most advanced students who would then want to join a grammar school.

The Christian Brothers' Schools became models of self-sufficient primary schools, separated from grammar schools, reserved for ordinary children and aiming at religious and secular teaching of the 3 R's in French. Prospective teachers were recruited among former pupils, who were thus socially promoted. This order of primary teachers, who were not learned in Latin or knowledge reserved for churchmen, had only to show (and not justify) good methods of reading, writing, counting and praying. Therefore the level of this training was below the level of German teachers, who studied in seminars with Pietist pastors. But thanks to the Rule, communal life and printing works, their efficiency was rapidly acknowledged, so that their methods were adopted by other charitable orders or lay masters. The division of the learning process into tiny and well-ordered steps had often been regarded as a consequence of a "Cartesian" conception of language learning – starting with the elements and gradually incorporating the whole. This concept must also be considered as a pragmatic decision to organize classwork efficiently, restrict teachers' initiatives and encourage pupils to stay longer at school. Whereas private tutors aimed at making children learn faster, J.B. de La Salle did the reverse. Parents often removed their children from school as soon as they could read, the learning process had to take longer so that religious knowledge and Christian habits were deeply implanted. For this founder, the main part of teaching took place orally – when every day the whole group said prayers, sang canticles, went to mass, recited their catechism and got ready for the sacraments. Teaching the 3 R's was the only means towards a Catholic education.

Experiments in theory and practice

There were three important changes in teaching reading between the sixteenth and eighteenth centuries. First, a linguistic change: as Latin, the universal written language was abandoned in favour of national languages, the old grammar – the science of Latin language – had to be revised and explicit representations of these spoken languages had to be constructed – vernacular grammars. Yet, teachers could not wait for rules to be laid down about pronunciation which kept changing, shifting regional accents and the unified spelling of words or the graphic material (22 letters only in the Latin alphabet). That is why the ABCs of petty schools reflected the traditional usages with the Latin pattern of spelling letters and then syllables, in its nearly unchanged vernacular version, while grammarian tutors invented innovative and efficient teaching devices in order to rationalise spelling, but these could be used only within the pupil-tutor relationship.

The second change was the use of spoken languages. It extended the aims of learning and brought about new standards. Formerly, chorus reading of liturgical and catechetic texts was considered sufficient. It was no longer the case when printed books multiplied. In towns earlier than in the country, in northern earlier than in southern Europe, teachers sought to introduce people to religious texts – spiritually necessary – as well as to secular texts – socially useful. Literacy was no longer restricted to reading prayers. Pupils had to read books and even manuscripts, and they also had to write and to reckon. The new treatises on education meant for the teachers of elementary schools reflected this evolution. As a result, learning to read became a greater challenge. The lists of syllables were longer and more complex since the various combinations of a language had to be mastered before reading whole words could be achieved. Because of this linguistic "abstraction", reading became hard for beginners and many children failed. This is the reason why old methods were more and more criticised while the private tutors' new methods were praised. They devised games to make it easier for children to memorize, like dice or cards making up syllables, and they used images. Others rejected the constraints of letter-spelling, in favour of the direct reading of the syllable[11] or even the whole word,[12] so that the pupils could read short texts right away. Others taught reading and writing at the same time – children wrote with chalk on slates – as they had noticed that "learning one helped for the other". Finally, a new trend of thinkers –including Rousseau – considered it worthless and harmful to teach children to read at too early an age. A child should be instructed by experience and speech and when he/she felt the need to read, would learn fast, whatever the method. Still what had become normal or usual for the instruction of elite – learning to read and write in one's own language in order to be able to read new texts – was still out of reach in ordinary schools.

The third change concerned methods of teaching. Teaching reading to a group of children was invented in France by the end of the seventeenth century (the simultaneous system of Christian Brothers' Schools) and in England by the end of the eighteenth century (the monitorial or mutual system).[13] Politicians were struck by these experiments more than by theoretical inventions – as they paved the way to universal literacy. They affected school equipment, with the need for standard teaching material, blackboards, tables and benches to separate children according to their levels. The job of teaching changed too. It had become a full time job for "professionals". They had to follow an explicit method, with clear criteria to assess

---

[11]For instance, *Le Quadrille des enfants*, de l'Abbé Berthaud, 1783.

[12]Gedike in Deutchland, Nicolas Adam and Sicard in France, for instance.

[13]John Lancaster opened a school for poor children in 1798 and the Lancasterian Society was created in 1808 to expand his work. In 1797, Andrew Bell, a clergyman of the Church of England, described a monitorial experiment in Madras in his book *An Experiment in Education*, and the Church of England in 1811 set up its National Society and opened schools for poor children according to the rules of the monitorial (or mutual) system. The two systems seemed simple, inexpensive and sufficient to provide reading, writing, arithmetic and basics of moral or religious instruction. The master gave tuition out of hours to monitors (about 10 or 11 years old); during the class, each monitor drilled a group of ten pupils, so it was possible to teach 150 or more children in the same class-room, under the supervision of only one master. Harold Silver, *The Concept of Popular Education; a study of ideas and social movements in the early nineteenth century*, London, 1965.

the progress of their pupils. Special, theoretical and practical training was needed for this job.

No institution, however, managed to integrate the three innovations in schooling systems so that they could be generalised. Linguistic experiments dealing with didactics in teaching reading remained the privilege of the pupils taught by tutors and or in boarding schools – collective teaching was set up within the traditional highly sequenced organisation of learning. Most children continued to learn to spell letters and to syllabify before reading a whole word, and they had to be able to read before being taught to write and count- if sufficient time remained.

LEARNING TO READ AND WRITE AT THE SAME TIME IN THE NINETEENTH CENTURY

The primers at the beginning of the 1800's: moral and patriotic books in the USA

In 1790, the *American Spelling Book* was published in Boston. A few years later, Noah Webster's book replaced the *New England Primer* published by John Gaine in London in 1683, which had become "the chief book of the time". The book was printed in small format and in close characters. It included an alphabet, long lists of syllables (197 combinations) and words, followed with texts as in former ABC's, illustrated with blurred small engravings. And yet it revealed a new approach to reading and new goals. That book definitely opened a new editorial era, that of mass production. The distribution of the *Blue Back Speller*, as it was named, brought him enough money to allow Webster to work on his dictionary. More than 10 million copies were distributed throughout the USA within thirty years (Russel & Fea, 1967). After 1840, steam printing presses made it possible to print in greater number and by the end of the century the number of copies approached a hundred million. A second characteristic is that religious contents had almost disappeared (2 pages out of 158) and been replaced by patriotic and moral catechism. The primer was one of three different stages, the second one being *The little Reader's Assistant* – stories from American history beginning with Columbus, a short grammar and a "Federal catechism being a short and easy explanation of the Constitution of the United States". The third stage, an *American Selection of Lessons in Reading and Speaking* was also meant for college students. It included speeches made by American political orators ("the writings which marked the revolution, which are perhaps not inferior to Cicero and Demosthenes") and lessons in national history and geography. This was the first example of a complete progression, which provided young Americans with all the texts that had to be known by the citizens of a free nation. In fact, even if they referred to knowledge for adults (ethics, politics or sciences), all the texts were especially written for children.

The third characteristic concerns the approach to teaching reading. Most of the book, 78 pages out of 158, is made up of lists of words, 80 to 180 on each page, each one appearing only once, "arranged in order by their number of syllables, and further into lists according to the similarity of phonetic elements" (Smith, 1974). Using written language as a basis, Webster wanted to normalize American pronunciation, fix the spelling and unify the country by its language as well as by its institutions. For the author of the dictionary, knowing words enable a person to transmit knowledge and verbalize their experience of the world. In this way, Webster belongs to the great tradition, from Comenius to Pestalozzi which considered that in order to teach children scientific or secular subjects – geography, botany or history – things had to be named before being dealt with. Webster's glossary offered knowledge to be acquired or to be shared. As he feared the harmful consequences of oral memory which he considered mechanical, he chose prose rather than verse to understand or to study.

"Reading is talking from a book"

Theoretical debates about the place of the word in the process of learning to read were at the centre of the debates in the nineteenth century: is the word the starting or the finishing unit? Sometimes the word is considered as a "whole", built from relationships between elements (letters and sounds, or syllables), sometimes the whole word has to be analysed in elements. For Webster, there were two stages, from syllables to words, and from words to sentences and he focused on the second stage. The child had first to imitate the master, a model of good pronunciation. In fact, if the pupil said the word properly, it was the step towards reading the sentence fluently. In 1829 J. Leavitt (*Easy Lessons in Reading*) wrote: "Children will never be allowed to pronounce a sentence or even a word, in that dull, monotonous humdrum style, which so often disgraces our common schools. It is a very useful practice for the teacher to read over a sentence, before the scholar, giving it proper pauses, inflection and emphasis, and then to require the scholar to repeat it, until he can pronounce it with propriety". The model of religious reading had been replaced by the model of oratorical reading, just as politicians, lawyers or scientists delivered their "lectures". The rules to achieve good reading required that words should be pronounced clearly, slowly, with pauses and the same intonation as the master's. The author added: "Try to understand every word as you go along", and "try to read as if you were telling a story to your mother, or talking with some of your playmates. *Reading is talking from a book*". Oral reading aimed at communicating with someone else as people did in the upper class – other children had to be taught to do that in school. The slow syllable reading, which was adapted to collective religious reading was then considered defective, that of a beginner or an illiterate adult. Then again, the ways to circulate this new model were not the same in tutorship or school teaching.

When mothers became teachers: the first literature for children

By the 1800's, women started to have access to written culture (Flint, 1993; Lyons, 1997). Reading scenes more and more often present women either reading by themselves or aloud to their children and relatives. Private tutors gave way to mothers, who had become readers, and were thus naturally promoted tutors of their children. When they addressed parents as well as schoolmasters, the authors of readers actually wrote for them. Women were ready to share the new approach to reading, secular as well as educational, moralizing as well as sentimental, offered by the handbooks available.

Mothers were advised to teach their children twice a day, for a short period of about a quarter of an hour in a cheerful atmosphere. Instead of punishing the child for his/her mistakes, progress should be rewarded and children should be encouraged to be curious about print. Whatever the method, they had to learn the names of letters first, then the syllables which could be uttered directly, without letters being spelt aloud. There was something new: what the child had learnt from his handbook could immediately be reused in other illustrated albums – often arranged around the alphabet (Le Men, 1984). Children with their mothers looked at the pictures, and, under the drawing of a dog or a drum or a farmer, they looked for the name of the animal, the object or the job represented. They came across letters and syllables already known and went on to the following pages. Finally, the mother read aloud the text about the dog, the drum or the farmer. So whereas the primer imposed a definite progression, the new picture books designed for children introduced a non-linear progression.

In this way, children could start reading when they were 3 or 4. The early introduction of their children to reading took place among other literacy practices a mother had in her charge: reading for relatives, keeping up to date the correspondence between the members of the family, and the family accounts. At a time when many adults, who did not go to school, learnt to read late in their lives (Castillo Gomez, 2002), all the new handbooks associated such learning with a young child's life and placed the appropriate age to learn before the age of reason. Rather than teaching rules, teachers were required appeal to intuition and memory through repetition and games. Social conceptions of education – how to speak to young children and what about – suddenly appeared in methods and images representing family relationships, domestic events, everyday habits and "good behaviour", which writers wished to inculcate. Reading books full of good and well-educated children, even though still immature, had become selective and distorting mirrors of society, while civic, scientific and moral readings were postponed.

Reading and writing at the same time: technical and pedagogical experiments

Making up texts for children had another consequence, which was directly related to teaching procedures: how could the progression be adapted to such young minds? Mothers combined the desire for reading aroused by everyday life with games and affective constraint. It was an efficient approach because the mother remembered what had been acquired and was being acquired, which enabled the tutor to move at the child's own pace until fluent reading was achieved. Yet, such guidance was not possible for large groups, which were necessarily restricted to the ABC's stage. A radical pedagogical change took place in teaching reading practices in the 1830s in England, and about ten years later in France. Learning the 3 R's at once became possible. The traditional pattern of the 3 R's which developed in the eighteenth century defined a course divided into three successive stages – reading, then writing, and then arithmetic (reckoning). The division into three different learning skills was particularly obvious as pupils had to pay more if they wanted to be taught to write and even more if they wanted to learn arithmetic. In addition to the economic obstacle, there was a material obstacle – as learning to write with a quill-pen could not be taught to a large group of pupils. The nib of the quill had to be constantly sharpened because it wore out fast and then spluttered and damaged the paper. Such practice could be carried out with a tutor or a master looking after only a few children – for instance in the Christian Brothers Schools, but definitely not with a whole class. This is the reason why teaching writing at an early age took place only in tutorship, and, even in this privileged relationship, reading always came before writing. Teachers had to wait until a child had acquired good penmanship and the ability to write freehand ("à main levée").

Teaching children to write at an early age required a political decision – equal tuition fees for reading and writing – and new technical devices. In Germany, the systematic use of slates to write words as the lesson was going on was very well described by Horace Mann, who visited Prussia in 1843, and found there that Ickelsamer's method was improved with the use of writing. In front of sixty pupils, he witnessed the teacher drawing a house on the blackboard and writing the word HAUS (twice: in script and "in the German letter"). The teacher ran over the forms of the letters with a rod, and the children did the same movements with their fingers in the air. Then, they copied the word on their slates. After that, the teacher drilled them in the sounds. The names of the letters were not given, only the H sound, the AU sound, and then the teacher showed how he combined the two sounds in a block. S was sounded, first alone, and then with the others, and then, the entire word was spoken. The teacher demonstrated how to draw a house, and the lesson (one hour) finished with a discussion on houses, personal anecdotes or remarks (Mann, 1884). Thanks to the slates, teachers could not only teach new words, but they could check that words already studied had been memorised. Dictations became pupils' daily routine. The use of slates rapidly spread to England and the USA where pupils used them throughout their school years. This new teaching device made it possible for very young children to go to school: they sat on benches with their slates on their knees and drew vertical lines or circles, i.e. lines of "i" and "o", while the master was teaching the older children. Letters were no longer shapes to be looked at and sounds to be listened to, but had become movements. The monitorial system of Lancaster had adopted the Indian technique of drawing letters with the finger in sand boxes. It could thus carry out the teaching of reading and writing at the same time.

The invention of metal pen nibs was a significant step. Simultaneously the price of paper went down. School furniture changed also – since all pupils had to write, they needed tables to put their papers on, note-books, pens and inkstands. Pupils' copy-books reflected the pedagogical changes, year after year. Writing exercises could be found in the lowest grades with vertical lines or circles, then they had to copy lines of letters of different sizes, then words and short sentences. Reading acquisitions were taken up again or even prepared in writing exercises. Whereas the main activity in class used to be the lesson -listening, learning, reciting-, by the 1840's a new pedagogical practice developed and this spread in the second half of the century, joining the lesson (reading/saying) and the exercises (reading/writing). Whatever the changes that took place later as far as content, method and goals were concerned, this is still the basis of to-day's teaching practice. From then on, teachers in elementary country schools, which prevailed in France and Southern Europe, could have several groups of different levels working at the same time, some of them with the teacher, others were busy, writing alone. The system "one grade-one master" prevailing in urban areas and particularly in Germany, England and the USA led printers to work out progressive handbooks adapted to different levels, to define annual contents and to provide a new reader for each year. Monitors, who were necessary to observe the progress of their fellow pupils through their response to oral questions, gradually disappeared since the exercises done by the pupils on their own were themselves a record of progress. "New" teachers had to mark copybooks, a new task, indeed.

New handbooks to teach reading

When considering the new generation of books following those changes it can be seen why the *Blue Back Speller*, in spite of its modern contents and aims, belongs to the old schooling system. Former primers include four "logical" parts – letters, syllables, words and sentences or texts – on the pattern of linguistic books, setting out, chapter after chapter, the different units of language. On the other hand, by the second half of the nineteenth century, primers set up a progression inside each page and throughout the book. In standard primers, four elements can be found within each page: at the top there is a picture surrounded by graphic material which differs according to the method – letters, syllables and words or a word, a syllable and a letter, or only a whole word. Then, there is a list of syllables and/or words (in which you drill the new elements combined with others learnt before) drilled, short sentences (which enable pupils to revise known words or to introduce new words "in a context"), and a sentence in cursive writing to be copied into the copybook. An age-old order disappeared – the alphabetical order was replaced by a new sequential arrangement, based on a progression involving many criteria of short/long vowels, "easy"/"difficult" consonants, sounds encoded by one or several letters.

On every page of the new standard, instructions printed in small characters are given to the teacher or the parents about what they should tell the children to do, how they should proceed, what should be memorised and the mistakes to avoid. The primer develops its didactic in the foreword and throughout the lessons, which proves that families and teachers were not yet familiar with such a method. For instance, the new lesson refers to what has already been studied, repetition is now the rule so that new words appearing on each page are gradually less numerous.[14] Review lessons appear at regular intervals, so that children can sum up what has been studied before: within the lesson, the same syllables are presented out of order to avoid mechanical reading, encouraged by systematic charts. The same words can be found several times, used in very similar yet different sentences (Is it an ox? It is an ox. It is my ox. *McGuffey's Primer* Lesson I[15]).

Another recurring feature is the introduction of engravings at the top of every page: the letter, the sound, or the syllable introduced are associated with a key-word whose image enables the child to conceptualize and recall it straightaway – a picture of an ox grazing in a field for the word "ox," of a pipe for the letter and the sound [p] (Cuissart, 1865), or of "cheval" (horse) for the syllable /al/ (Berthon, 1887). In the initial lessons, words are carefully selected so as to combine three features difficult to find together: they should represent easily identifiable objects, belong to every day vocabulary and have regular spelling. Thus, to start with, each letter can be given one "power" (value). In English, monosyllabic words are by far the most numerous. Because of the stresses and the rhythm, it is difficult or impossible to recognize a long word, when its syllables are pronounced one after the other. In French, the sound introduced can be represented by a letter in the middle of the word (U in "lune") but eventually, initial position (U in "usine") or final position (U in "menu") prevails. The typical sentences produced by these strong lexical constraints follow this pattern. "Can a pup run? Yes, a pup can run. All the pups can run. But a pup can not run as fast as a dog" (*McGuffey's primer*, lesson 64). The texts a child reads transmit no essential values; they deal only with what the children already know and are not meant to teach anything else other than how to encode and decode written language.

---

[14]These repetitions would seem quite limited to modern educators. Nila Banton Smith quotes studies on the average number of occurrences of words in primers between 1913 and 1929: words occurring only once or twice represented 43% of the material in 1913, and only 18% in 1929, whereas words occurring more than 11 times were 26% in 1913 and 33% in 1929. Between 1922 and 1931, the number of words fell from more than 400 to less than 300 (average for 7 American primers). Previously (in the *Blue Back Primer*, for instance) repetitions were prohibited.

[15]*McGuffey's primer*, 1836. The first lesson combines monosyllabic words of only two letters. McGuffey 's primer gradually superseded Webster's. Between 1836 and 1920, 132 million copies of the McGuffey's readers (one book for each level) were bought (Mathews, 1966, p. 102).

Finally the letters in the book are more and more often written in cursive and printing letters, to drill the children in the two representations of the written word. In the ABC's of animals, the word "ass", or "lion" is written below the picture which is surrounded by four letters (cursive capital and small letters on the right hand side, the printed characters on the left). Among books entitled "teaching and writing handbook", common in France at the end of the century, each line in printed letters is repeated in cursive letters. Others are less ambitious and only give the cursive version of the key-letter and a few syllables including it – it can be seen how the letters are linked together – and the final sentence which will be copied on the slates or in the copybook. The teaching of capital letters is postponed.

The fact that children have reached the end of the first stage of learning to read is symbolically marked at the end of the primer by a longer text and concludes with the learning of the ABC and the introduction of the following stage, which is more like "real" reading. For instance, the book of Cuissard develops *in fine* a philosophy of reading which clearly shows how learning to read and instruction are two different stages: "Now, you can read and you will soon be able to read lovely stories in books by yourselves. All human knowledge can be found in books. So, when you can read, you can become a scholar. You have to understand what you can read very well. To be able to understand what you read, you must not read too fast. This primer has taught you to learn one difficult problem at a time and constantly review what you have learnt. Keep this good habit. It is easy to overcome difficulties if you tackle them one after the other, and as long you do not forget what you have learnt, you will always progress fast enough".

Theoretical models in competition about how to read words: syllabic method, phonic method, whole-word method.

Throughout the nineteenth century, philosophers debated the learning processes. The rationalist approach advocated learning systematically from the parts to the whole, from the simple to the complex. The empiricist approach advocated learning analytically, from the perceptions provided by our senses to the various elements which make them up. The simple being abstracted from the whole is hard to find out by experience. This debate went on against a background of discussions about teaching reading. It focused on the status of the word and whether it should be considered as the starting or as the finishing unit. For those who supported spelling methods, the word was the whole which had to be apprehended from the perception of the letters. On the other hand, for those who supported the word-method, children should first understand the word as a whole and then proceed to the observation of its elements. Other educators considered the word as an element in larger units, i.e. the sentence and the text – knowing the vocabulary was essential – and children could proceed from the word to the sentence or from the sentence considered as the meaningful unit to the words (sentence method).

By the end of the century, the debates between authors of reading methods had made clearer the first conflict between supporters and detractors of spelling methods. In fact, between 1850 and 1900, spelling aloud the letters of each syllable had gradually become useless from a practical more than from a theoretical point of view, and writing exercises came into general use. Whatever the spelling method used – whether children spelled the names of letters as in the old method or the sounds of the letters as in the modern method, whether they read syllables (syllabic method) or whole words first (whole-word method) – it had no impact on the practice of copying. While he/she writes "ox" or "boy" ten times or more, the child learns to "spell" or mentally pictures the letters one after the other, combines them together and reads the word again directly. Writing makes it possible to link together slowly, but for ever, the "phonological awareness" with the "orthographic awareness", as cognitive psychologists would say to-day. Educators realised that, contrary to what could have been imagined, good reading did not necessarily ensure this link.

The first evaluations on this particular point took place at the end of the century. In 1880, in the USA, Walton picked out 108 different spellings of the word *whose*, 58 for *which*, and 208 for *scholar* in pupils' papers. The French Inspecteur Général Beuvain made the same observation in France in 1873. 77% of the children spelled the word *tuyaux* correctly but the remaining 23% produced 138 different spellings. Confronted with this orthographic inventiveness, Walton remained optimistic and concluded that "the word method of teaching beginners to read, with the constant exercise in writing, is the best means of making good spellers". This relationship between writing and learning to read had been empirically noted, but had no effect on the theoretical conceptions of reading still regarded as a basic skill unrelated to writing.

Nevertheless, spelling aloud letters was carried on in a ritual way, many teachers could not imagine a reading lesson without the smooth running song of the spelling,[16] and it was an easy way to correct dictations, – teachers asked children to spell aloud words they had written, but, in this case, the aim was to check the orthography without syllabification. It was no longer used to teach reading and the new generations of teachers who had studied in the 1900's did not use it any more. Still, repeatedly copying words or common expressions, fixes the written forms of words, which have already been studied or not yet studied. For instance, in an American primer dating from the 1880's, which used the whole-word method, at the bottom of the reading page, can be seen the sentence to be copied / written in cursive writing "I see a sled" – the drawing represents children playing with a sled in the snow. A note in small characters explains that "The teacher may direct the children to write the idiom "I see" four times more,

---

[16]Joseph Mayer Rice (*The Public-School System of the United States*, New-York, 1893) was so fascinated by the "concert recitations" he listened to in Cincinnati that he wrote them down on scores. Mathews (1966) published some examples (p. 112-114).

substituting for "sled", the words they have already learned to write "cat", "rat", "hat", "bed".[17] The pedagogical debates which started by the end of the century and went on into the twentieth century can not be understood without taking this new fact into account: teaching writing at an early age definitely affects reading skills and accelerates the direct reading of words and texts.

Primers taught regular words first and then irregular words, the skills achieved in the first steps help to progress to the following ones. The difficulties of written English led some linguists to argue for reforms in order to simplify spelling.[18] They supported the use in schools of the phonetic alphabets developed in the 1870s for scientific use to encode dialects or unwritten languages (Harrison, 1964). The Leigh's System (1873) the Shearer's Speller (1894, and the Scientific Alphabet (1902) had a limited impact in schools but interested specialists greatly before World War I in the USA and in England. These inventions were discontinued, however they were taken up again after World War II, when simplified spelling failed to be used generally,[19] but became a device to help beginners using ITA (Initial Teaching Alphabet).

A second way of teaching prevailed first in the USA, then in England, based on the whole-word method – a method which does not require an explicit analysis of sounds. With the irregular spelling of English, the systematic learning of correspondences between graphemes and phonemes proved to be impossible and discouraging and more children were likely to fail than to succeed. Experiments have shown that a child memorizes whole words very fast so that they can be used from the start of reading. Some forerunners in this trend have often been quoted, namely the German Gedicke (1753-1804), the French Jacotot (1790-1840), the American Pierce who wrote in 1844: "When they are perfectly familiar with the first words chosen, and the sentence which they compose, select other words, and form other sentences; and so on indefinitely" (Pierce, "On Reading", *American Institute of Instruction,* XIV, (1844) in Mathews, 1966, p 87). He assumed that in the stock of well-known words, children will gradually discover recurring elements which will enable them, by analogy, to read new words without help. That is why the whole-word method is also called look-and-say. It omits the code and focuses on units beyond words, i.e. on the understanding of texts. It was supported by all those, who were appalled by the linguistic and intellectual paucity of primers. Drilling exercises were devoid of content, and focusing on the code postponed an acquaintance with "real texts". Educators

---

[17]Swinton's *Primer and first Reader*, (circa 1880), quoted by Nila Banton Smith, *op. cit.* p. 151.

[18]The S.S.B. (Simplified Spelling Board) was founded in 1906 in the USA, and the S.S.S. ("Simplifyd Speling Sosyeti") in 1908 in London, and some primers were printed in "simplifyed speling".

[19]"A Spelling Reform bill was introduced in the House of Commons early in 1949. It failed of passage, but, in 1953, a bill was enacted which authorised a properly selected association or institution to institute researches with a view to reading and, if possible, eliminating the widespread inability of the children of Great Britain to read their own language". Mathews, 1966 p. 176. About the failure of spelling reforms in France, Blanche-Benveniste and Chervel, 1969, pp. 85-112.

thought children should be confronted as early as possible with literary texts, adapted to their ages – tales and stories for example. This can be found in many primers between 1890 and 1910. One preface can be read: "It is not believed desirable that children in these early grades have even a complete system of phonics. It is the aim to give in this manual only such work as experience has shown necessary to train children into independent power over words in their vocabulary" (Free & Treadwell, 1910). George Farnham considered that "the sentence is the unit of expression", thus founding the "sentence method or story method" (Farnham, 1895) from a theoretical point of view. This is how the story of the Little Red Hen (Judson & Bender, 1899) soon came to be translated across Europe and published in schoolbooks for beginners.

The primers' obsession with phonology was also questioned by the first scientific research on adult reading processes. Javal's experiments on eye-movements (1879) had shown that when somebody reads, his eyes do not sweep smoothly along the lines, but advance by jumps; during each brief pause, more or fewer words are taken in. Then, psychological and physiological investigations shifted the emphasis from oral reading to silent reading. Several reports defined expert reading as the individual, silent and quick processing of information. "For this reason, such factors as intonation, expression, pauses, and the like, are relatively insignificant". If reading is an ideo-visual process, is it really necessary to spend such time training children to read aloud? The fluent reader is someone who can "see" directly the meaning of the word in the written form, without any oral medium. It is the way spontaneously chosen by the supporters of the whole word method, which can be called look-and-mean rather than look-and-say. They were comforted in their choices by the very fast progress of children when they began to read short texts.

In 1908, when he examined the various methods in competition in schools, Huey (1908) foresaw that the ABC method, still in use in some classes, would soon be shelved and outdated. He talked about the technical progress of the phonic method but concluded that in the near future the look-and-say method would be increasingly implemented. The twentieth century opened up with an optimistic discourse: schooling had become universal and the combination of school policies, pedagogical experiments and scientific discoveries had virtually eliminated illiteracy. They would certainly overcome reading disabilities and, in the short run, children would be able to read texts without suffering the pangs of decoding first.

CONCLUSION: ILLITERACY ENDURES DESPITE COMPULSORY SCHOOLING

In concluding this historical survey, I will try to point out the changes which took place in this century. At the beginning of the 1900's, everybody was convinced that illiteracy could be eliminated. Anyone would soon be able to improve his or her knowledge at school and beyond school thanks to reading on their own. Yet, the problem of failure to learn reading appeared, almost as if it was a consequence of compulsory schooling. Indeed, if everybody goes to school, then the question must be asked why some children remain unable to read. Is it due to the child, the school or society? Throughout the century scientists developed a variety of answers. First, it was considered as a mental problem. In France, at the request of the education authorities, Binet 1904 set up a test to identify the children who needed remedial teaching. In this test, which looked like a school examination, he linked language, intelligence and development. There were three degrees of mental deficiency (severe, moderate, or slight): the child who cannot learn to speak, the child who will never learn to read, the child who can be re-educated and the normal child. Between these stages/degrees, there is a continuum, as far as the problem of language (oral and written) is concerned. The ability to learn to read is a feature of human intelligence just as speech. Fast learning is a sign of advanced, and therefore superior intelligence. If the standard of human intelligence is measured by exercises which imply formal and written language (Olson, 1994) must it be concluded that in today's world, more and more invaded by writing, illiterate people are doomed to become "abnormal"?

With such an approach, teachers could not be blamed for the failure of their pupils, since the reasons for the failure lie in the child himself. Other discoveries were needed to question the methods of teaching reading in schools. During World War I, many American soldiers were unable to execute written orders because they could not understand them. For the first time, there was a debate on the illiteracy concerning adults who had been to school. Educators were worried and the studies they published in specialised reviews gave arguments to the supporters of the whole-word methods considering them to be better for understanding texts. Similar events were recorded in Great Britain during World War II. According to the British Service, 25% to 30% of the soldiers were "functional illiterate", although by Binet's standards, they were "normal". From the 1950's, as more children stayed longer at school, comprehensive schools developed and teachers were for the first time confronted with pupils "unable to read", according to the standards of grammar schools. Educators tried to find new reasons , un-related to mental disabilities (Chartier, A-M, 1993) for this deficiency in literacy. They emphasised the importance of psychological problems such as dyslexia, and psycho-affective blocks, or social causes like the impact of television, cultural deprivation (poor social backgrounds) and linguistic patterns even pedagogical problems, unskilled teachers with a lack of appropriate training, and, last but not least, archaic or non relevant methods. Western Europe affected by the economic crisis of the 1970's realised that adult illiteracy was not only an American problem.

Throughout the twentieth century, the reading issue was at the centre of teaching crises. The debates began whenever it became obvious that the aims which had been assigned to and gradually achieved by schools were no longer adapted to what was actually required – for example reading and applying instructions at work, in the army, in the office or in the factory (finding useful information in documents, and writing administrative papers or commercial forms). New aims were added to old ones, reading novels for culture for example, or scientific handbooks for instruction. Schools had to train all children in all the different uses of reading, social or scholarly, utilitarian or cultural, recreational or educational. Therefore children had to be able to read on their own without help and quickly. Of course achieving aspirations in a short time is not feasible and it is no wonder that more pupils failed. Thus, people realised that literacy was not the universal tool that nineteenth century educators had imagined. Then they were convinced that, once someone had been taught the ABC, he/she would be able to read any text. Therefore all the difficulties observed on a large scale called into question prevalent teaching methods. In the USA and England, the whole-word method was put under the microscope and after violent debates the phonic method was reintroduced.[20] In France, the syllabic method focusing on the phonic code, was considered responsible for failures in secondary schools, and new didactics turned to whole-word methods, when English-speaking countries were given up.

Since the Renaissance, written culture has undergone a large number of radical changes in Western countries, and teachers have often been confronted with pupils resistant to literacy. This was not a problem as long as reading was only a means and not an end. During the Renaissance, reading aimed to improve knowledge of religious truths though everyone knew that you could be saved even if you were not learned and damned even if you were a scholar. The Revolution dreamt of enlightened citizens – that is to say, literate – but citizenship was considered as a right, even though it took some time to extend this right which was first reserved for a privileged few – the wealthy, the male, the white and the literate. At the end of the twentieth century, people needed to be able to read and write, in order to live a normal life in a world where writing is critical, despite the television and the telephone. Being literate is useful not only from a practical point of view, but even more so from a symbolical point of view. It is a sign of belonging to a common culture, as if, in our scholarly society, written language has acquired the status of a natural language, to understand and express, i.e. to read and write. One can imagine that the challenge of the twenty-first century will be concerned less with reading than writing, which may prove to be the significant cultural change under way at the end of the twentieth century. Debates about teaching methods are already moving from the pair "decoding-understanding" to the pair "encoding-producing a text". This will be enough to nurture new pedagogical experiments, indefinite research projects and interesting debates and clashes in conferences and playgrounds.

---

[20]A public debate began when Rudolf Flech published *Why Johnny Can't Read, and What You can Do about it*, (1955). Jeanne Chall (1967) gave a synthetic review of the different theoretical points of view, the practices in class-rooms and the assessments of different methods on children's skills.

REFERENCES

Auroux, S. & Calvet, L. (1994) De la phonétique à l'apprentissage de la lecture: la théorie des sons du langage au XVIIIe siècle (From phonetics to learning to read: phonological theory in the XVIIth century). *La Linguistique, 9,* 71-88

Auroux, S. (1994) *Histoire des idées linguistiques* (History of linguistic ideas). Liège: Mardaga

Baddeley, S. (1993). *L'orthographe française au temps de la Réforme* (French orthography during the Reform) Genève: Droz.

Berthon, J. (1887) *Méthode simultanée de lecture et d'écriture* (Simultaneous method for reading and writing) Paris: Librairie Godechaux.

Black, R. (1987) Humanism and education in Renaissance Arezzo. *I Tatti Studies, Essays in the Renaissance, 2,* 171-237 (The Harvard University Center for Italian Renaissance Studies, Florence).

Blanche-Benveniste, C. & Chervel, A. (1969) *L'orthographe* (Orthography). Paris: Maspéro.

Cavallo, G., Chartier, R. (eds), 1997, *L'histoire de la lecture dans le monde occidental,* Paris, Seuil, (Rome 1995), translation 1999, *A History of Reading in the West.* Cambridge: Polity Press.

Chall, J. (1967)*The Great Debate.* New York: McGraw Hill.

Chartier, A-M. (1993) La lecture scolaire entre sociologie et pédagogie (School reading between sociology and pedagogy). In M. Poulain (Ed.), *Lire France aujourd'hui* (pp. 89-135), Paris: Promodis.

Colombat, B. (1999) *La grammaire en France de la Renaissance à l'âge classique* (Grammar in the classic age of renaissance in France). Grenoble: ELLUG.

Compère, M. M. & Chervel, A. (1997), Les Humanités Classiques (Classic Humanities) *Histoire de l'Éducation,* 74, the whole volume, pp. 5-38, 187-203.

Cressy, D. (1980), *Literacy and the social order, Reading and Writing in Tudor and Stuart England.* Cambridge: Cambridge University Press.

Cuissart, E. (cir. 1865). *Enseignement pratique et simultané de la lecture, de l'écriture, de l'orthographe et du dessin* (The practical and simultaneous teaching of reading, writing, orthography and drawing). Paris, Picard et Kaan.

de Batencour, J. (1654), *L'école paroissiale* (Parish schools). Paris: Pierre Targa

Delaunay, P. (1719) *Méthode du sieur Py-Poulain de Launay ou l'art d'apprendre à lire en français et en latin* (Mr. Py=Poulain de Launay's method or the art of teaching reading in French and Latin). Paris:Nicolas Le Clerc

Delforge, F. (1985) *Les petites écoles de Port-Royal, 1637-1660* (Small schools in Port-Royal). Paris: Cerf.

Despautère (1537) *Commentarii Grammatici* (Comments on grammar). Paris: R. Estienne

Farnham, G. (1895). *The Sentence Method of Reading.* Syracuse: C.W. Bardeen.

Flint, K. (1993). *The Woman Reader, 1837-1914.* Oxford: Oxford University Press.

Flech, R. (1955). *Why Johnny Can't Read, and What You can Do about it.* New York: Harper and Brothers.

Free, M. & Treadwell, H. (1910). *Reading Literature-Series.* Peterson and Co.

Gilmont, J-F. (1997). Réformes protestantes et lecture (Protestant reform and reading). In G. Cavallo & R. Chartier (Eds.), *op. cit.* (pp. 249-278).

Goody, J. (1977). *The Domestication of the Savage Mind.* Cambridge: Cambridge University Press.

Goody, J. (1987) *The Interface between the Oral and the Written.* Cambridge: Cambridge University Press.

Grafton, A. (1997). Le Lecteur Humaniste (The humanist reader). In G. Cavallo & R. Chartier (Eds.), *Histoire de la lecture dans le monde occidental* (pp. 209-248). Paris: Seuil.

Gray, W. S. (1956). *L'enseignement de la lecture et de l'écriture* (The teaching of reading and writing). Genève: UNESCO.

Grendler, P. (1984) *Schooling Renaissance Italy, Literacy and Learning 1300-1600,* London-Baltimore: John Hopkins University Press.

Harrison, M. (1964). *The Story of the Initial Teaching Alphabet,* New-York, Toronto, London.

Hébrard J., (1998) Les savoirs élémentaires à l'époque moderne (elementary knowledge in modern times). *Histoire de l'Éducation,* 38, 7-58.

Hébrard, J. (1995) Des écritures exemplaires: l'art du maître écrivain en France entre XVIe et XVIIIe siècle (Models of writing: the scribe's art in France between the XVI and the XVII centuries). *Mélanges de l'école Française de Rome, Italie et Méditerranée, 107*, 473-523.

Houston, R. A. (1988) Literacy in Modern Europe. Culture and Education 1500-1800. London: Longman.

Huey, E. B. (1908) *The Psychology and Pedagogy of Reading.* New York: The Macmillan Co.

Johansson, E. (1981) The History of Literacy in Sweden. In H. J. Graff (Ed.). *Literacy and social development in the West: a reader* (pp. 151-182). Cambridge: Cambridge University Press.

Judson, H. P. & Bender, I. (1899) *Graded Literature Readers,* First Book, New-York: Merill and Co

Julia, D. (1997) Lecture et Contre-Réforme. In G. Cavallo & R. Chartier (Eds.), *op.cit.* (pp. 279-314).

Le Men, S. (1984). *Les abécédaires français illustrés du XIXe siècle* (The French illustrated primers of the XIXth centruty). Paris: Promodis.

Lyons, M. (1997) Les Nouveaux Lecteurs au XIXe siècle. Femmes, enfants, ouvriers (The new readers of the XIXth century. Women, children and workers). In G. Cavallo & R. Chartier (Eds) *op.cit.* (pp. 365-400).

Mann, H. (1844). *Common School Journal, VI,* 117-118.

Mathews, M. (1966) *Teaching to read, Historically Considered.* Chicago: University of Chicago Press.

Olson, D. (1994) *The World on Paper: The conceptual and cognitive implications of writing and reading.* Cambridge: Cambridge University Press.

Petrucci, A. (1983). Il libro manuscrito (The handwritten book). *Litteratura italiana. Produzione e consumo, 2,* 499-524. Torino: Enaudi.

Pierce, (1844) *On Reading.* American Institute of Instruction, XIV.

Rice, J. M. (1893) *The Public-School System of the United States.* New-York: missing publisher (suppress this quotation)

Russel, D. H. & Fea, H. R. (1967). Research on Teaching Reading. In N.L. Gage (Ed.). *Handbook of research on teaching.* Chicago: Rand McNally & Company (first published in 1963).

Silver, H. (1965) *The Concept of Popular Education; a study of ideas and social movements in the early nineteenth century,* London.

Sprenger Charolles, L. (2003) Linguistic processes in reading and spelling. The case of alphabetic written systems (in this book)

Smith, N. B. (1974) *American Reading Instruction.* Newark, Delaware: Silver Burdett and Company (first ed. 1934)

Strauss, G. (1981) Techniques of Indoctrination: the German Reformation. In H. J. Graff (Ed.) *Literacy and social development in the West: a Reader* (pp. 101-125), Cambridge: Cambridge University Press.

Waquet, F. (1998) *Le latin ou l'empire d'un signe. XVIe-XXe siècle* (Latin or the empire of a symbol). Paris: Albin Michel.

Wittman, R. (1997). Une révolution de la lecture à la fin du XVIIIe siècle? (A revolution in reading at the end of the XVIIIth century ?). In G. Cavallo & R. Chartier (Eds.), *Histoire de la lecture dans le monde occidental* (pp 331-364). Paris: Seuil.

SUGGESTED FURTHER READINGS

Cavallo, G. & Chartier. R. (1997). *Histoire de la lecture dans le monde occidental.* Paris: Seuil.

Goody, J. (1987) *The Interface between the Oral and the Written.* Cambridge: Cambridge University Press.

Olson, D. (1994) *The World on Paper: The conceptual and cognitive implications of writing and reading.* Cambridge: Cambridge University Press.

D3 The Cognitive Consequences of Literacy

DAVID R. OLSON

ABSTRACT

The cognitive consequences of literacy derive not only from the well known properties of writing, its fixity and its permanence, but more fundamentally from the metalinguistic or metarepresentational properties it inherits from direct and indirect quotation. Literacy sponsors attention to the linguistic form of an utterance – its phonology, its lexicon, its sentences and above all its sentence meaning – the meaning conveyed when expressions are "mentioned" rather than "used." A variety of cross-cultural and developmental evidence is used to assess this view and to show why schooling is such an important part of literacy.

INTRODUCTION

It is frequently noted that we, humans, are the kind of species that we are because we are a language-using species and that we have the kind of "civilised" culture that we do, at least in part, because we are a writing-using culture. Yet this obviousness creates a problem for the social sciences in that while it is clear that the availability of a language enhances communication greatly it is not at all clear if or how being either a speaker or a writer reorganizes cognition in any decisive way. Indeed, on one well known account (Fodor, 1975) speech has little impact on cognition as it is merely the expression of the known; similarly, on another well-known account (Scribner & Cole, 1981, p. 5), literacy has "little detectable impact on cognition", on "how we classify, reason, [or] remember". Much of the basis for claims and denials about the cognitive consequences of either speech or writing depends upon how one defines oral competence, literacy and schooling. If defined narrowly as bare speaking or bare reading ability, the consequences are comparably limited. If defined as the competence developed through years of training whether in becoming an oral rhetorician or in developing the competence to exploit the literate resources of an advanced bureaucratic society, the consequences are undoubtedly of major significance.

In this paper, I shall consider literacy broadly as including not only the ability to make and recognize marks but to exploit the texts and artifacts created around and by means of these marks. Generally, these include not just marks for sounds,

T. Nunes, P. Bryant (eds.), Handbook of Children's Literacy, 539–555.
© 2004 *Kluwer Academic Publishers. Printed in Great Britain.*

for words, for sentences, but also marks for number, algebra, graphs, charts and extended monological, essayist discourse which make possible a literate, or document culture. Although all cultures make some use of written marks, not all cultures have invented notational systems for representing spoken utterances nor such secondary notation systems as graphs, algebra, maps, written contracts, let alone written literature, science and philosophy. Yet, an understanding of the cognitive implications of literacy will, ultimately, have to account for the impact of this full range of notational, representational devices and accumulated artifacts. Defined broadly like this it is difficult to imagine anyone seriously denying the conceptual implications of writing. As Derrida (1976, pp. 30-31) has noted: "this factum of phonetic writing is massive: it commands our entire culture and our entire science". Yet while we have been much concerned with advancing and spreading literacy we have only recently begun to attempt to understand its social and cognitive implications.

To understand the cognitive consequences of literacy it may be necessary to distinguish the communicative functions of speech and writing from their representational or cognitive functions. If writing is seen exclusively in communicative terms, it will be seen as primarily expressing the known in a new medium. Even then the implications of writing for the accumulation and sharing of textual information across space and through time is momentus (Eisenstein, 1979).

Yet viewed only as a communication device, the impact of writing on cognition may be underestimated. If we think of writing not only as a means of communication but as a medium of representation, its implications for thinking become more accessible. Writing, on this view, is not only for communication but in addition a structure or system for representing ideas and meanings and, above all else, as a means for representing language. The implications for the further advance of thinking and the growth of knowledge derive from those representational and metarepresentational possibilities. All literate persons explore these representational possibilities but major contributions to these representational systems, as for example, in the invention of an alphabet, of numerals or of algebra, go down as major cultural and historical achievements.

Understanding the cognitive consequences of literacy is analogous to understanding the cognitive consequences of learning a language. There is a rich literature (Nelson, 1996) showing that children bring to the language learning task a highly structured cognitive system which allows them to perceive and act in a complex and comprehensible manner. Yet in learning a language, the child is not only learning a means of communicating the known. Rather that prior sensory-motor knowledge has to be reorganised to fit the lexical and grammatical features of the language. They have, for example, to reorganize their perceptual knowledge of, say, their *black cat,* into the grammatical structure "The cat is black". That is, language gives that knowledge a propositional form required for the formation and formulation of articulate knowledge. Secondly, the meta-representation of such propositions provides the basis for such conscious, intentional states as believing and intending and ultimately, for understanding other minds (Astington, Harris & Olson, 1988; Pemer, 1991; Wellman, 1990). Thus, learning a language is not only learning to communicate but also learning how to sort experience into socially agreed upon systems of knowledge. Admittedly, the language as structure has evolved to be easily learnable, that is, easily mapped on to the pre-linguistic experiences and intuitions of the learner. Yet, one can grant that without giving up the important notion that experience takes on its subject-predicate and hierarchical categorical form, at least in part, in the process of learning a language.

The relation between writing, literacy and cognition may be analyzed in similar terms. As mentioned, writing is a means of communication which extends the reach of utterances across space and through time (Innis, 1950; McLuhan, 1962; Eisenstein, 1979; Donald, 1991). Because it is fixed and relatively permanent, writing provides opportunities for accumulation and reorganisation of information that go far beyond the limitations of speech and human memory and gives writing a significant role in social and historical development. To understand a complex modern society requires that we see it as "textually mediated" (Smith, 1990). But, to return to our theme, writing is not only a communicational device, it is a mode of representation as well. Harris (1989, p. 99) states precisely this view: "The essential innovation which writing brings is not a new mode of exchanging and storing information but a new mentality". The work of such writers as Goody (1968, 1987), Ong (1982), Donald (1991), Smith (1990), Olson and Torrance (1996) have begun to spell out just what is involved in that new mentality. Others, Street (1984), Prinsloo and Breier (1996) and Doronilla (1996) have pointed out that these functions do not develop in a social vacuum. Writing maps on to, and, in ways not yet well articulated, transforms such large-scale social activities as law and government as well as the small-scale social activities involved in planning, record keeping, and networking for particular, local purposes. Both institutions and cultural practices change with the adoption of writing and documentation (Stock, 1983; Clanchy, 1993; Olson, 1994), and, by hypothesis, the cognitive practices of participants change accordingly. Just why writing matters, however, remains underspecified.

The link between culture and mind suggests that there is an identity between the structures that have been found to have an impact on cognition and those that are found to have an impact on the culture. Writing, in the sense of providing one with a stylus and a writing surface has little impact on cognition in the absence of appropriate knowledge how to make the best use of the technology. For example, children given a pencil and paper and asked to use notes to help them remember the locations and identities of playing cards often make notes which interfere with memory rather than aid it. Asked to make a note that would aid memory, one subject wrote; "Be sure to remember where the cards are" without noting where, in fact, they were! What matters is that they know and apply a notational system suitable to the task at hand, such as notating locations in terms of rows and columns (Escritt, 1998).

Similarly, knowing how to write numbers may have little effect on cognition unless one knows how to do computations with them. Computation with numerals, for example, in the form of long division, is the product of a long evolutionary history, the result of which has to be taught to children. Only then can written numbers affect cognition and then only if the learner recognizes that such computation is useful for some task at hand. This cultural invention, computations with numerals, and mathematical cognition are, thereby, closely interrelated. Similarly, a writing surface is important for remembering a list only if one knows how to write distinctive signs for each item to be remembered. Thus literacy is not merely access to the "tool" of writing but rather the competence with culturally-evolved notational schemes which may be used for particular cognitive functions. This partial identity between culture and cognition leads some writers to describe these cognitive functions in social terms as "cultural practices" (Wertsch, 1998). Yet it is important to recognize that cultures don't do anything; it is individuals, equipped with certain knowledge and available tools who do things, and the job of the psychologist is to understand just how that ability to do comes about.

Literacy has an impact on cognition, then, primarily through the evolution over time of notational forms the most important of which is writing, and the mastery of those notational forms by individuals. Sometimes, the form is invented in service of an existing function as in double-entry book keeping, at other times, it is the invention of a literate form which awaits a possible use, as in the case of pure mathematics and imaginative literature. We may now be in a position to understand Scribner and Cole's (1981) finding that knowing how to write had little cognitive impact on the Vai, a small traditional society in Liberia. As they noted, the script was a syllabary which segmented neither phonemes, words or sentences and the writing was used only for a limited set of functions such as letter writing. Such writing, they observed, was of little significance conceptually whereas schooling, learning to read and write a national language, had a marked effect. The contrast, however, is not between literacy and schooling but rather between two kinds or forms of literacy one of which could be acquired informally in a relatively brief period, while the other was sufficiently elaborated that its mastery required some years of schooling. Only the latter, for example, would include learning how to use a dictionary, derive synonyms and antonyms, or re-read, criticize and revise texts. Creating a dictionary is made possible by the metalinguistic knowledge of *words* which in turn appears to depend upon the availability of a word-based script. The Vai, of course, had neither lexicographers nor dictionaries. To put it simply, writing has an impact on cognition through culture, a culture of writing. Individual learners gain conceptual advantage through learning to deal with those literate resources. Thus culture and cognition are closely linked and a literate culture is critical to the development of a "literate mentality". On the other hand, it would be wrong to think that these domains of knowledge are just independent specialisations; rather, as I shall argue, they have a common base in the metalinguistic knowledge sponsored, to a large extent, by writing.

What are the properties of a literate culture which give rise to those aspects of cognition that we may describe as "literate"? Taken broadly, they include all those literate, documentary practices that are central to a modem bureaucratic society– law, economics, literature and the sciences. But fundamental to all of them is the availability of a permanent, repeatable notational system, a writing system or script capable of representing the surface structure of speech. This is the traditional meaning of writing although some writers have argued for the importance of broadening the definition to include all documentary practices (Boone & Mignolo, 1994; Harris, 1995).

WRITING AND THE CONCEPTION OF LANGUAGE: THE PSYCHOLOGY OF LEARNING TO READ AND WRITE

Writing systems of the world differ importantly in how they relate to spoken language. Lographic scripts, syllabaries and alphabets each have their own distinctive properties which readers must come to terms with in order to learn to read and write. Yet common to all writing systems is the fact that they represent language and not ideas or the world directly. In regard to alphabets, one of the major discoveries in the past 30 years is that in learning to read, children are learning something they did not already know *about the properties of their own speech*. This fact was long overlooked as children are normally speakers of the language they are learning to read. Hence, it was long assumed that what was required in learning to read was how to identify the visible marks as expressions of that oral knowledge, whether of sounds, words or sentences that they already possessed. The discovery, credit for which is usually given to the Alvin and Isabel Liberman, (Shankweiler & Liberman, 1972) is that, in fact, pre-readers lack the appropriate knowledge of the phonological segments represented by the letters of the alphabet. Consequently, learning to read is importantly a new form of "oral" competence, learning to analyze speech into the acoustic constituents to be represented by visible marks. While some writers took this new "meta" knowledge to be the natural outcome of advancing cognitive development (Hakes, 1980), a series of studies of adults in non-literate cultures showed that such knowledge never developed in the absence of exposure to the alphabetic script. Morais, Alegria and Content (1987) as well as Bertelson and de Gelder (1994) found that non-literate adults, unfamiliar with the conventions of alphabetic writing, were unable to segment oral speech into literacy-relevant constituents. It was concluded that that ability was a consequence of learning to read. It is worth mentioning that that analysis may be learned through oral means in anticipation of learning to read (Goswami & Bryant, 1990) but the critical fact is that to learn to read is in part learning to "hear" speech in a new way. As Adams, Treiman and Pressley (1998) point out "Literacy development at every level pivots on the ability to treat language itself as not merely an instrument, but an object of thought, analysis, and reflection." (p. 277)

An important question remains, however, as to whether this new knowledge is simply implicit knowledge of phonology made explicit (Adams, Treiman, & Pressley, 1998) or whether it is a matter of construing the perceptible properties of speech in terms of a set of rather abstract categories, that is, a model, provided by the script itself, a view suggested by Ferreiro and Teberosky (1982/1979), Olson (1994), and Blanche-Benveniste (1994, p. 70) who put it this way: "Literacy gives access to a representation of one's language largely different from the representation induced only by oral practice". This latter view is supported by the fact that the alphabet is not exactly an explicit phonology but rather a set of marks representing classes of discriminable sounds. As Grendler (1989, p. 194) pointed out "16th C humanist grammarians had no concept of phoneme other than that of letter". They thought that letters were the underlying constituents of speech whereas they are representations of classes of sounds (and sometimes of morphemes) selected in the interest of reading efficiency (Smith, 1994).

The impact of writing on one's conception of language is not exhausted by phonological segmentation. Concepts of words, sentences and texts appear to be equally dependent upon certain types of scripts. Although all cultures have a concept of a *tongue,* not all have a concept of *language* or of the phonological, lexical and grammatical properties of that language. Many of the world's non-literate cultures lack a concept of *word* in the sense of lexical item (Goody, 1968; Finnegan, 1977; Scribner and Cole, 1981). Indeed, the discovery that all the utterances in the world could be reduced to an itemisable set of lexical items, i.e., words, must have been as momentus to the first lexicographers as the fact that all the meaning bearing sounds of a language could be represented by a small set of marks, was to the first alphabet-makers. In fact, it is only modern phonological theories which have demonstrated that the sounds of a language are both more diverse and more highly integrated than those classes of sound represented by the letters of the alphabet suggest.

Pre-readers conceptions of words have been studied by a number of developmentalists. Piaget (1926; see also Sinclair, 1978) noted that young children conflated the properties of words with the properties of the objects they denoted, a phenomenon he described as *nominal realism* but he failed to note that the distinction may be a product of literacy. It was the students of children's literacy (Reid, 1966; Downing, 1987; Francis, 1975) who first noted that when asked what a word was, young children claimed that a word was something that was written. Children seemed not to realize that a word was equally something spoken! Ferreiro and Teberosky (1982/1979) were the first to note that when children begin to write, it is not at all obvious to them that the entities to be written are words, or indeed, that an utterance is composed of words. When children began to write, it seemed not to occur to them that the written marks corresponded to properties of the linguistic expression rather than to the object or meaning conveyed. Thus in writing a word like "boat", they assumed that the parts of the written sign must correspond to particular parts of the boat. Homer and Olson (1999) have shown that exposed to a piece of text which reads, for example,

"Three little pigs" and then told that it says "Three little pigs", pre-reading children often assume that each of the pieces of print corresponds to one of the pigs. Hence, when one word is covered up, they claimed that the expression now says "Two little pigs". Conversely, when asked to write "No little pigs" they claimed that it cannot be written because there are no pigs! Such evidence strongly suggests that children readily think of the meaning conveyed, that is, the world represented by the expression, rather than about the linguistic form of the expression itself. Again, it is reasonable to infer that learning to read and write a word-based script is instrumental in creating the consciousness of the primary linguistic elements, words. Olson and Homer argued that analyzing an utterance into distinctive lexical items is prerequisite to learning how to analyze words into phonological constituents represented by letters. Further, once words are distinguished, they may become objects of thought to be compared, organised into dictionaries and analyzed philosophically. Much of the western intellectual tradition is based on such metalinguistic reflection.

Harris (1986), too, has suggested that consciousness of words may be instrumental in clarifying the distinction between things, names and words. Further, he suggested that, historically, the failure to clearly distinguish things from names produces a form of emblematic symbolism which may extend to various gods and spirits and "is often bound up in various ways with word magic and practices of name-giving. It reflects, fundamentally. a mentality for which reality is still not clearly divisible into language and non-language, any more than it is divisible into the physical and the metaphysical, or into the moral and the practical" (1986, p. 13 1-2). Thus, a culture of writing may have been an important factor in "disenchanting" nature.

A similar argument may be made for the analytical notion of sentence. In written English, sentences are notationally indicated by capital letter and a full stop. Oral utterances are rarely identical to grammatical sentences. Learning to read and write is not only learning something about these conventions; it is a matter of coming to analyze one's own speech into units expressible by the grammatical form of the sentence. Reorganizing oral "idea units" (Chafe, 1985) into acceptable sentences is the task of literacy. And thinking about those sentences apart from the contextualised meanings they ordinarily convey is at the basis of literate thought.

How writing restructures thought

The conceptual implications of literacy arise, then, from turning language from something which is used into something which is mentioned; it is an exercise in metarepresentation. But it is not only the linguistic forms– sounds, words, sentences– which are metarepresented but also the types of meanings these forms express– word meaning and sentence meaning, in particular. The meanings of words find their way into dictionaries; sentence meanings, sometimes called decontextualised meanings (Donaldson, 1978) become the new tools of literate thought.

If writing is seen as merely an alternative to speaking and listening, the cognitive implications of writing will be missed. The significance of writing as an intellectual tool derives from the basic fact about writing; writing turns language into an object of thought. These objects include not only surface properties of speech, as mentioned, but forms of meanings as well. Writing is in principle metarepresentational; it represents not ideas but language. We have already seen that the very act of learning to read and write an alphabetic, word-based script brings with it a new awareness of some aspects of language. It remains to be shown how metarepresenting language contributes to a new, literate mode of thought.

Harris's (1989) conjecture is as follows: "The restructuring of thought which writing introduces depends on prizing open a conceptual gap between sentence and utterance" (1989, p. 104). Grice (1989) had earlier made an analytic distinction between sentence meaning and speaker meaning, the former the concern of linguists, the latter of everyone else. Harris's contribution was to suggest that writing brought that distinction into awareness. He continues: "Writing is crucial here because [scientific] inquiry presupposes the validity of unsponsored language. Utterances are automatically sponsored by those who utter them, even if they merely repeat what has been said before. Sentences, by contrast, have no sponsors: they are autoglottic abstractions".

Utterances are, of course, human actions. We do things with words as Austin (1962) pointed out. In saying something we are giving our warrant to the truth of what we express. Sentences, on the other hand, are linguistic abstractions in two ways. First, it is not clear that speakers even utter proper sentences; utterances are composed of "idea units" expressed by a burst of six or seven morphemes with one intonational contour (Chafe, 1985). The idea that a sentence expresses a complete thought is the view of the grammar teacher not a conversationalist. Second, sentences are abstractions in that they are "authorless", divorced from the immediacy of the current speaker. This is best seen in the case of direct and indirect quotation which we shall discuss presently. The hypothesis, here, is that writing is instrumental in bringing into consciousness both what a sentence may mean and what a speaker means by it. For Harris, writing exploits the gap between the two. This view is quite similar to my own view that writing, in the Western cultural tradition, exploits the space opened up between what is said and what is meant by it.

In a series of papers (Olson, 1977; 1994) my colleagues and I have shown that the say-mean distinction is one that children come to make systematically only in the early school years. In one study (Robinson. Goelman & Olson, 1983) we asked pre-school children to play a communication game in which a speaker, separated by a screen from a listener, attempts to describe an object in an array in such a way that the listener can pick up the identical object from a complementary display. These objects, however, differed in ways that required some adjectival modification such as the *big* red flower or the white dog *with spots* as the display also contained a small red flower and an unspotted dog. As speakers, pre-school children frequently omitted the necessary adjectives and the listener, therefore, selected an incorrect object. Prior to the age of 6 the majority of children agreed, inappropriately, that the fault lay with the listener for choosing the wrong object! By age 6 they tended to blame the speaker for his inadequate message. A second fact is more apposite. Children who blamed the listener, the younger children, also claimed that the speaker had said "the *big* red flower when the speaker had in fact only said "the red flower" but had meant "the big red flower". From such studies we inferred that pre-school children conflated what was said with what was meant, that is, they maintained no independent representation of the linguistic form of what was said. Later studies added details to this picture. Bonitatibus and Flavell (1985), Beal and Flavell (1984) found that children were more likely to fail to notice the ambiguity of an utterance if they had independent access to the intention it expressed. Lee, Torrance and Olson (2001) have shown that in the context of nursery rhymes children are particularly attentive to the wording (what was said) whereas in communicative contexts they are more attentive to the intended meaning (what was meant). What they lack is the ability to systematically distinguish between the two and to work out their relations, e.g., I said ... but I meant....", that is to "prize" open the gap between sentence and utterance.

But is this awareness of the distinction between *what is said* and *what is meant* simply a developmental achievement or is it a specialised competence attributable to literacy? Age does seem to be a necessary condition but is it a sufficient one? If this difficulty is to be traced to literacy rather than simply to the immaturity of children, it is necessary to show that even adult non-literates may have difficulty with these distinctions. Feldman (1991) has shown that oral cultures exploit a variety of ways of *saying* and *meaning* ranging from formal to extremely metaphorical. Further, Lucy (1993) has shown that reflexive uses of language are a universal property of language. Yet it remains unclear whether concepts such as *word, sentence* and *sentence meaning,* independent of their meanings in context, are clearly distinguished in non-literate cultures. Thus, although language functions may be more or less universal, literacy may be important to the kinds of detached sentence-meanings that make up the backbone of modern science and philosophy.

Some recent anthropological evidence (Urban, 1994) suggests that literacy may contribute to systematically distinguishing the sentence from the utterance, that is, the linguistic expression from its interpretation. Although direct quotation is part of the language, it is not always recognised as such. When asked "How do you say [in your mother tongue] 'Do you want to eat'", a non-literate adult informant may reply "No, I don't want to eat". That is, rather than treating the embedded expression "Do you want to eat" as a direct quotation, that is, as a verbal form, the informant interpreted it as an ordinary question, namely, whether he was hungry – which he denied. Pre-school children routinely make this confusion

(Olson & Hildyard, 1981). Literacy, it may be argued, is instrumental in refining and honoring that distinction. Indeed, the distinction between mention and use provides a way of understanding the special nature of literate thought.

Literate thought

There is a long and controversial literature on literacy and thinking (for a review see Cole and Scribner, 1974; Olson, 1994). Although anthropologists such as Levy-Bruhl (1926) collected numerous examples of what he called "participatory thought", that is, thinking which did not run strictly in accordance with normative principles of logic, Vygotsky and Luria (Luria, 1976) were among the first to report an experimental study of the reasoning processes of illiterate adults. Subjects were a group of adult peasants in a remote rural part of Central Asia tested in the 1920s prior to collectivisation and mass education. A typical protocol was as follows:

The following syllogism is presented: **In the far north, where there is snow, all bears are white. Novaya Zemlya is in the Far North and there is always snow there. What color are the bears there?**

"There are different sorts of bears."

Failure to infer from syllogism.
The syllogism is repeated.

"I don't know; I've seen a black bear, I've never seen any others... Each locality has its own animals: if it's white, they will be white; if it's yellow, they will be yellow."

Appeals only to personal, graphic experience.
But what kinds of bears are there in Novaya Zemlya?

"We always speak only of what we see; we don't talk about what we haven't seen".

The same.
But what do my words imply? The syllogism is repeated.

"Well, it's like this; our TSAR isn't like yours, and yours isn't like ours. Your words can be answered only by someone who was there, and if a person wasn't there he can't say anything on the basis of your words." (pp. 108-109)

While these observations are both amusing and replicable, their interpretation remains a matter of controversy. Cole and Scribner (1974) claimed that Luria was incorrect in interpreting this as an indication of a limitation in logical abilities. The ability to infer from premises appears to be universal as Cole and Scribner demonstrated by changing the format from counterfactuals to hypotheticals. that is, to reasoning from pretended premises. That is, while non-literate adults may fail to draw the correct inference from a statement which they have reason to doubt, such as those used by Luria, this is not a failure of logic as they succeed in drawing the correct inferences in a purely pretended or hypothetical situation. Both involved logical inference and hence it was concluded that literacy is not necessary for logical reasoning.

However, Cole and Scribner's conclusion is also subject to criticism. Admittedly, their evidence clearly indicates that illiterate subjects make inferences much like anyone else. Furthermore, a careful reading of the subject's response indicates the correct drawing of an inference from a hypothetical premise: "If they are brown, they will be brown". Indeed, few theorists have been so bold as to deny logical reasoning abilities to any human being. A more defensible claim is that the non-literate subjects refused or were unable to treat the given premises as grounds for the inference, that is, to reason syllogistically. There is no indication that subjects, without tutoring, could do that. Interestingly, some recent developmental research by Apperly and Robinson (1998) has shown that whereas even 4 year olds can reason from future hypotheticals, it is only some two years later, perhaps under the influence of schooling, that they can solve counterfactual problems of the sort studied by Vygotsky and Luria. Only the latter have been associated with literacy.

Frawley (1998) has interpreted the Luria reports as a problem in adopting an appropriate frame, whether colloquial, which Luria's subjects preferred, or schooled, which they could do only in some circumstances. Both accounts leave unanswered just what is involved in adopting the so-called "schooled" frame. In Olson (1994) I argued that Luria's subjects failed to treat the set problem as a fixed "text", treating it rather as an utterance which the subject tended to reject rather than as a given explicit text or document from which a logical inference could be drawn. As the transcript indicated, the subject said "I can tell nothing from your words". Harris (1995) as mentioned, would characterize such texts as "unsponsored" language, a characterisation that comes close to my notion of "autonomous text" (Olson, 1977). Yet, the concept of a "text" in this context remains somewhat vague and undefined.

What all of these accounts acknowledge is the special, indeed peculiar, nature of the problems Luria set for his subjects. This peculiarity is dubbed "schooled" by some of the above mentioned writers but what. one may ask, makes them schooled, as they were given out of school to subjects who never did attend school? The set problems are indeed school-like "texts" which call for a distinctive mode of interpretation. But how are we to characterize that mode?

DIRECT QUOTATION AS A MODEL FOR WRITTEN TEXT

One hypothesis which goes some distance in explaining both the special nature of the problem and the particular competence involved in solving it, is that such tasks depend upon grasping the grammatical and logical properties of direct quotation. Direct quotation is the prototypical case of mentioning an expression rather than using it. Stated another way, direct quotation involves metarepresentation, the ability to use language to refer to language (Lucy, 1993). In the simplest case, if John says "David said "I'm hungry"", the pronoun *I* loses its normal tie to the speaker, John, and becomes attached to the subject of the main clause, *David*. The pronoun has lost its normal reference in the context of direct quotation.

True, all languages have such reflexive capabilities but it is writing, it may be argued, which massively exploits that property. If this is true, it is no longer appropriate to think of speech as simply an alternative to writing. Rather, writing is to be seen as having, not the properties of speech generally, but the properties of direct and indirect quotation.

If we recall the problem in Luria's report, we may recognize it as having the properties of quoted rather than direct speech. Such expressions are *mentioned* rather than *used:* again, they report assertions rather than make them. What Luria's subjects are expected to do, I suggest, is treat the set problem as if it were quoted rather than direct speech and interpret it and respond to it accordingly. That, I would suggest, is the ability which tends to be underdeveloped in non-literate subjects and massively exploited by literate ones in that literacy is through and through a metalinguistic phenomenon. That suggestion would not only explain Vygotsky and Luria's findings, it would fit well with the observations by Urban (1994) suggesting the fragility of direct quotation in the translation efforts of non-literate adults and the findings on pre-literate children's lack of competence with direct quotation (Hickman, 1985). Third, it would explain the difficulties our children had when asked to write "Three cats" or "No cats". They attempted to represent the cats or their absence rather than the words mentioned in the quoted expression. That is, what they failed to recognize was the quotation marks implicit in the request. The suggestion, then, is that understanding a text is primarily a matter of understanding the peculiar nature of quoted as opposed to direct speech.

Quoted speech has the linguistic property of opacity, that is, the expression is taken as having a meaning but that meaning is immune from some contextual, deictic information. Technically, directly and indirectly quoted expressions are opaque in that they exclude the possibility of substituting terms by other terms even if those terms refer to the same object or event. In the case of direct quotation, if John says "I'm hungry," it cannot be reported directly as John said "I want something to eat" even if both refer to the same desired event. Young children fail to make such a distinction (Hedelin & Hjlmquist, 1988).

Indirect quotation, expressed by means of verbs of saying and verbs of thinking similarly display these properties of logical opacity. Children's under-standing of logical opacity may be studied via tasks having the following form. Subjects are told that a character, John, thinks that particular yellow ball is in a closet. What John does not know is that the yellow ball is soft. The subjects are then asked two questions: "Is the soft ball in the closet?" to which the correct answer is "Yes", and "Does John think that the soft ball is in the closet?" to which the correct answer is "No". Children in Western cultures solve such tasks at about age 6 at about the time they learn to read and write (Kamawar & Olson, 2001).

But those are just the properties that written texts exploit. They allow paraphrase and interpretation but they restrict, at the price of misrepresentation, direct quotation to the actual words employed and inference to the properties stated. Although the theory that writing is metarepresentational is by now quite widely accepted (Adams, Treiman & Pressley, 1998) the more specific hypothesis, that writing inherits the special properties of direct quotation and indirect quotation is new and only now coming in for empirical test. Apperly and Robinson (1998) and Kamawar and Olson (2001) have recently found that children's competence in drawing valid inferences from direct and indirect quotation, the problem of opacity, is solved only in the early school years and that it is highly related to children's understanding of the say-mean, that is, the sentence-utterance distinction, the task we have traditionally used to assess literate competence (see also Anderson, 1997 for similar findings).

While the appropriate studies have not yet been carried out cross-culturally, there is reason to believe that both pre-literate children and non-literate adults have some difficulty in managing the appropriate interpretation of direct quotation. The findings reported by Luria as well as those of Urban can be interpreted in this light. In both cases, subjects must make a "use-mention" or a sentence-utterance distinction and in both cases subjects find the distinction somewhat difficult if not impossible in other than simple contexts.

If these relations hold up to scrutiny, we may have achieved a general theory of the special nature of written texts and the special nature of the reasoning recruited in dealing with them. The theory has the advantage that it does not either assimilate written texts to oral speech nor does it describe them as totally distinctive. Rather, the claim is that writing picks up and elaborates one of the natural and universal functions of speech, the reflexive ability that makes direct quotation possible. But while that reflexive property remains limited in scope and application in speech, it becomes the central property of written texts.

It should be noted that written texts were not always seen as intrinsically opaque; recognizing that opacity depends in part upon the assumptions about reading. Morrison (1990, p. 68) noted that "[Twelfth-century] readers would peruse texts with a kind of redactive criticism, editing them and seeking epiphanies between the lines". That is, they apparently took themselves to be addressed by the text, largely overlooking the metarepresentational nature of the text. Both texts and their readings have to be shaped up to support and sustain their opacity; indeed schooling appears to be required. Olson and Astington (1990) showed that advanced levels of writing competence involves the mastery of a complex set of metalinguistic and cognitive concepts for specifying just how the writer intended the text to be interpreted, including such concepts as imply, assume, conclude, infer and the like and that higher levels of reading competence involved learning how to "take," that is, to interpret such texts. The mastery of the culture of writing, they argued, provides a learner with these new reflexive concepts in addition to the more limited concepts of word and sentence acquired in the early stages of learning to read.

In our modern way of writing in such institutional contexts as the school, a text is to be seen not a direct utterance but a direct quotation. That is to say, the formation of a written expression depends primarily upon sentence and textual meaning rather than on shared intentions as is the case with ordinary discourse. In the creation of the kinds of texts we accept as normative in our modern literate and bureaucratic society, one initially chooses a sentence to express a belief or intention or meaning. The reader (and the writer is just the first reader) then has available only the sentence in its context to use as a basis for constructing a meaning in a way exactly analogous to hearing a direct quotation. The meaning constructed on the basis of the sentence may be discrepant from the meaning actually intended. One of the two will have to be rejected. This requires that another sentence be generated to more precisely express a more justifiable meaning. And so on. The product is a set of sentences, a text, which when interpreted with the rules for direct quotation, convey the desired intended meaning. The detection of the gap between sentence meaning and utterance meaning, then, invites attempts at revision and formal correctness. Writing seems to be instrumental in both creating and bridging that gap.

Once one is conscious of the gap between the written form and the intended meaning it putatively expresses, it is possible to increase the mapping between the two, to allow for shaping and editing a text to make it say, so far as possible, neither more nor less that what is meant. This is at the base of written law, public documents and ultimately the standard manuals of all the sciences. And while such writing has some conceptual advantages, it also creates certain blind spots, namely, the assumption that textual or sentence meaning is the ultimate or true meaning rather than what it is in fact, namely, an expression of the beliefs and intentions of a writer. That mistaken assumption yields an extreme fundamentalism and literalism which may restrict as much as aid further thought. Yet when exploited as a specialised form of discourse, in its appropriate institutional context, it is an important factor in the creation of "objective" knowledge.

Writing systems are culturally evolved notational systems which provide categories in terms of which we come to think about our speech. I am fond of paraphrasing Whorf's famous dictum that "we dissect nature along lines laid down by our language". That paraphrase would say, rather, that "we introspect our language along lines laid down by our scripts". Seeing language in that new, metarepresentational way is what allows the distinctive mode of thought we identify with literacy.

REFERENCES

Adams, M. J.. Freiman, R. & Pressley, M. (1998). Reading, writing and literacy. In Damon, W (Ed.), *Handbook of Child Psychology*. Vol. 4, I. E. Seigel & K. A. Renninger (IA.), *Child psychology in practice,* 5th edition (pp. 275-355). New York: John Wiley & Sons.

Anderson, W. (1997). An investigation of the relationship between literacy, verbal ability and metarepresentational ability in normal young readers. Ph.D. dissertation. Department of Psychology, Fordham University, New York.

Astington, J. W., Harris, P. L., & Olson. D. R. (Eds.). (1988). *Developing theories of mind.* Cambridge: Cambridge University Press.

Apperly, I. A. & Robinson, E. J. (1998). Children's mental representation of referential relations. *Cognition, 67,* 287-309.

Austin, J. L. (1962). *How to do things with words.* Cambridge, MA: Harvard University Press.

Beal, C. R. & Flavell, J. H. (1984). Development of the ability to distinguish communicative intention and literal message meaning. *Child Development, 55,* 920-928.

Bertelson, P., & de Gelder, B. (1994). The cognitive psychology of literacy: Some basic findings. In L. Verhoeven (Ed.), *Functional literacy: Theoretical issues and educational implications* (pp. 151-162). Amsterdam: Benjamins.

Blanche-Benveniste, C. (1994). The construct of oral and written language. In L. Verhoeven (Ed.), *Functional literacy: Theoretical issues and educational implications* (pp. 151-162) Amsterdam: Benjamins.

Bonitatibus, G J. & Flavell, J. H. (1985). Effect of presenting a message in written form on young children's ability to evaluate its communication adequacy. *Developmental Psychology, 21, 455-461.*

Boone, E. & Mignolo, W. D. (Eds.). (1994). *Writing without words: Alternative literacies in Mesoamerica and the Andes.* Durham. NC: Duke University Press.

Chafe, W. (1985). Linguistic differences produced by differences between speaking and writing. In *D.* R. Olson, N. Torrance. & A. Hildyard (Eds.), *Literacy, language, and learning: The nature and consequences of reading and writing* (pp. 105-123). Cambridge: Cambridge University Press.

Clanchy, M. T. (1979). *From memory to written record: England, 1066-1307.* London: Edwin Arnold. (Second edition: Blackwell. 1993).

Cole, M. & Scribner. S. (1974). *Culture and thought: A psychological introduction.* New York: John Wiley & Sons. Inc.

Derrida, J. (1976). *Of grammatology* (G.Spivak. trans.). Baltimore, MD: Johns Hopkins University Press.

Doronilla, M. C. (1996). *Landscapes of literacy.* UNESCO.

Donald, M. (1991). *Origins of the modern mind: Three stages in the evolution of culture and cognition.* Cambridge, MA: Harvard University Press.

Donaldson, M (1978). *Children's minds.* Glasgow: Fontana/Collins.

Downing, J. (1987). Comparative perspectives on world literacy. In D. Wagner (Ed.), *The future of literacy in a changing world* (pp. 25-47). Oxford: Pergamon Press.

Eisenstein, E (1979). *The printing press as an agent of change.* Cambridge: Cambridge University Press.

Escritt, M. (1998). The influence of symbolic notation on memory in adults and children. Ph. D. Dissertation, Psychology Department, Queen's University.

Feldman, C. F. (1991). Oral metalanguage. In D. R. Olson & N. Torrance (Eds.), *Literacy and orality* pp. 47-65). Cambridge: Cambridge University Press.

Ferreiro, E. & Teberosky, A. (1982). *Literacy before schooling* (Los sistemas de escritura en el desarrollo del nino). Exeter, NH: Heinemann (English translation). Mexico DF: Siglo Veintiuno Editors. (Original work published in 1979).

Finnegan, R. (1977). *Oral poetry: Its nature, significance, and social context.* Cambridge: Cambridge University Press.

Fodor, J. A. (1975). *The language of thought.* New York: Crowell.

Francis, H. (1975). *Language in childhood: Form and function in language learning.* London: Paul Elek.

Frawley, W. (1997). *Vygotsky and cognitive science: Language and the unification of the social and computational mind.* Cambridge, MA: Harvard University Press.

Grendler, P. F (1989). *Schooling in Renaissance Italy: Literacy and learning 1300-1600.* Baltimore. MD: Johns Hopkins University Press.

Goody, J. (Ed.) (1968). *Literacy in traditional societies.* Cambridge: Cambridge University Press.

Goody, J. (1987). *The interface between the oral and the written.* Cambridge: Cambridge University Press.

Goswami, U. and Bryant, P. (1990). *Phonological skills and learning to read.* Hillsdale, NJ: Erlbaum.

Grice, P. (1989) *Studies in the way of words.* Cambridge, MA: Harvard University Press.

Hakes, D. T. (1980). *The development of metalinguistic abilities in children.* Berlin: Springer-Verlag.

Harris, R. (1986). *The origins of writing.* London: Duckworth.

Harris, R. (1995). *Signs of writing.* London: Routledge.

Harris, W. V. (1989). *Ancient literacy.* Cambridge: Cambridge University Press.

Hedelin, L. & Hjelmquist, E. (1988). Preschool children's mastery of the form/content distinction in spoken language. In K. Ekberg & P. E. Mjaavatn (Eds.), *Growing into the modern world* (pp. 639-645). Trondheim: The University of Trondheim, Norwegian Center for Child Research.

Hickman, M. (1985). Metapragmatics in child language. In E. Mertz & R. Parmentier (Eds.), *Semiotic mediation: Sociocultural and psychological perspectives (pp. 177-201).* New York: Academic Press.

Homer, B. & Olson, D. R. (1999). The role of literacy in children's concept of word. *Written Language and Literacy, 2, 113-137.*

Innis, H. (1950) *Empire and communications.* Oxford: Oxford University Press.

Kamawar, D. & Olson, D. R. (1999). Children's representational theory of language: The problem of opaque contexts. *Cognitive Development. 14, 531-548.*

Lee, E., Torrance. N., & Olson, D. R. (2001). Young Children and the Say/Mean Distinction: Verbatim and Paraphrase Recognition in Narrative and Nursery Rhyme Contexts. *J. Child Language,* 28, 531-543.

Levy-Bruhl, L. (1926). *How natives think.* London: George Allen & Unwin. (Original work published in 1910)

Lucy, J. A. (Ed.). (1993). *Reflexive language: Reported speech and metapragmatics.* Cambridge Cambridge University Press.

Luria, A. (1976). *Cognitive development: Its cultural and social foundations.* Cambridge: Cambridge University Press.

McLuhan, M. (1962). *The Gutenberg galaxy.* Toronto: University of Toronto Press.

Morais, J., Alegria, J., & Content, A. (1997). The relationships between segmental analysis and alphabetic literacy: An interactive view. *Cahiers de Psychologie Cognitive,7, 415-438.*

Nelson, K. (1996). *Language in cognitive development: emergence of the mediated mind.* New York. NY: Cambridge University Press.

Olson, D. R (1977). From utterance to text: The bias of language in speech and writing. *Harvard Educational Review, 47, 257-281.*

Olson, D. R & Astington, J. W. (1990). Talking about text: How literacy contributes to thought. *Journal of Pragmatics, 14, 557-573.*

Olson, D. R.& Hildyard, A. (1981). Assent and compliance in children's language. In W. P Dickson (Ed.), *Children's oral communication skills (pp. 313-335).* New York, NY: Academic Press.

Olson, D. R. (1994). *The world on paper: The conceptual and cognitive implications of writing and reading.* Cambridge: Cambridge University Press.

Olson, D. R. & Torrance, N. (Eds.) (1996). *Modes of thought: Explorations in culture and cognition.* New York: Cambridge University Press.

Ong, W. (1982) *Orality and Literacy: The technologizing of the word.* London: Methuen.

Perner, J. (1991). *Understanding the representational mind.* Cambridge, MA: Bradford Books/MIT press.

Piaget, J. (1929) *The child's conception of the world.* London: Kegan Paul. (Originally published in French in 1926).

Prinsloo, M. & Breier, M. (1996). *The social uses of literacy.* Amsterdam: John Benjamins.

Reid, J. F. (1966). Learning to think about reading. *Educational Research, 9, 56-62.*

Robinson, E. Goelman, H., & Olson, D. R. (1983). Children's understanding of the relationship between expressions (what was said) and intentions (what was meant). *British Journal of Developmental Psychology, 1, 75-86.*

Scribner, S. & Cole, M. (1981). *The Psychology of literacy.* Cambridge: Cambridge University Press.

Shankweiler, D. & Liberman, I. (1972). Misreading: A search for causes. In J. Kavanaugh & I. Mattingly

(Eds.), *Language by ear and language by eye: The relationships between speech and reading* (pp. 293-317). Cambridge, MA: MIT Press.

Sinclair, H. *(1978)*. Conceptualization and awareness in Piaget's theory and its relevance to the child's conception of language. In A. Sinclair, J. Jarvella, & W. Levelt (Eds.), *The child's conception of language* (pp. 191-200). Berlin: Springer-Verlag.

Smith, D. (1990). *Texts, facts, and femininity*. New York: Routledge.

Smith, F. (1994) *Understanding reading* (Fifth edition). Hillsdale, NJ: Erlbaum.

Stock, B. (1983). *The implications of literacy*. Princeton, NJ: Princeton University Press.

Street, B. (1984). *Literacy in theory and practice*. Cambridge: Cambridge University Press.

Urban, G. (1994). Externalization, replication and power. In M. Silverstein & G. Urban (Eds.), *Natural histories of discourse*. Chicago: University of Chicago Press.

Wellman, H. (1990). *The child's theory of mind*. Cambridge, MA: Bradford Books/MIT Press.

Wertsch, J (1998). *Mind as action*. New York: Oxford University Press.

SUGGESTED FURTHER READINGS

Olson, D. R. & Torrance, N. (Eds.) (1996). *Modes of thought: Explorations in culture and cognition*. New York: Cambridge University Press.

Verhoeven. L. (1994), Functional literacy: Theoretical issues and educational implications. Amsterdam: Benjamins.

D4 Comparative Studies of Instructional Methods

JANE HURRY

ABSTRACT

There are two central dimensions involved in the teaching of reading in the classroom: what should be taught (the curriculum) and how it should be taught (pedagogy). Decisions about what to teach are informed by theories of reading development. Comparison of different method of teaching reading overwhelmingly supports the important role of explicit phonics instruction in learning to read. Other important aspects of curriculum content have been less systematically researched, in part because of the difficulty of applying the privileged quantitative method to certain constructs. Pedagogy is informed by theories about learning. First, children must first spend enough time learning, not just being present but being engaged. This is made more challenging in the context of the classroom where typically children spend about two thirds of their time working alone or in independent groups and some techniques of keeping children "on task" are explored. Explicit instruction is consistently associated with better learning. It has been argued that the form that this instruction takes, the extent to which it employs a didactic method or one involving modelling, for example, should vary according to the complexity of the subject matter. However, generally, children learn what they are taught, but they learn it better if it is contextualised for them and if they are helped to grasp the principles behind the rules.

INTRODUCTION

The term "instructional method" is deceptively simple. This can be illustrated by considering a highly visible controversy around instructional methods between "phonics" and "whole language". The opposing methods represented are a skills based approach, involving explicit coverage of phonics and an inductive model of teaching where children are exposed to meaningful texts, and text construction on the assumption that they will work out the rules for themselves, as we do with spoken language.

The most immediately apparent difference between the two methods is in the content of what is taught, the curriculum. This is underpinned by their models of the reading process. In the skills based approach children are taught about the

T. Nunes, P. Bryant (eds.), Handbook of Children's Literacy, 557–574.

letters of the alphabet, about phonemic awareness, blending sounds, etc. In the whole language method children read books where meaning and purpose are emphasised.

Alongside the difference in the curriculum, differing assumptions are being made about the nature of the learning process. Those who teach phonics consider that children can learn and benefit from adult taught rules. Those who promote the whole language experience argue that the teacher's role is to expose children to a good learning environment. They consider that the abstract learning of de-contextualised skills is of very limited value as they are difficult for children to apply in the practical settings of their own work. These two models of learning map onto the classic dichotomy of adult-led versus child-centred teaching.

However, there is no necessary connection between what should be taught and how it should be taught. An earlier and equally fiercely contested argument raged around phonics versus "look and say" methods of instruction, nicknamed "the Great Debate" after Chall's book "Learning to Read: the great debate" (1967). In the 1960s the "look and say", or whole word method was ascendant in British and American primary schools. The "look and say" method shares certain things in common with the whole language approach. In particular both emphasise the importance of dealing with meaningful chunks of information and both marginalise the role of teaching decoding at the level of the phoneme. But the "look and say" method is more likely to employ teacher instruction of the core words used in a carefully designed series of books and rote learning of those words. The whole language approach is likely to eschew such direct methods, opting for a more implicit and inductive teaching style. It is also possible to apply different teaching styles, assuming different models of learning, in approaching phonics.

The term "instructional method" includes at least two distinct elements, curriculum and teaching style, with other important undercurrents such as motivation and assessment not drawn out here.

THE CURRICULUM

Choices about what to teach are essentially guided by the model of reading development adopted. To return to the example of the place of phonics in the curriculum, the importance of including material on letter sound has been extensively debated and researched. Underpinning this debate has been a dispute concerning the nature of the reading process. Whole language theorists such as Goodman (1986) and Smith (1979) proposed that laboured phonic decoding was the hallmark of the poor reader and that good readers concentrated on meaning and context. Phonic decoding was seen as a last resort in the reading process; it was cumbersome and distracted the reader from the essential task of understanding the meaning of a passage. For Goodman and Smith, the mature reading process consisted of making minimal use of the writing on the page and maximal use of knowledge of the world and the active problem solving strategies of predicting and inferring. The opposing view is that the critical insight in early reading is precisely the connection between letters and sounds that Goodman and Smith regard as marginal (eg. Stanovich,1986; Goswami and Bryant, 1990; Frith, 1985). The key to becoming a good reader is understanding and mastering the alphabetic code.

It is now clear that Goodman and Smith were wrong in thinking that skilled readers pay so little attention to the details of print. Research on the reading process in the 80s produced clear evidence that skilled readers attend closely to letters and words and in fact that it is the less skilled readers who rely more heavily on contextual clues to support their reading (Perfetti, 1985; Stanovich, 1986; Adams, 1990). It is no longer viable to argue that letter sound relationships are not important to reading. The debate has been transformed into an issue of how children learn such relationships.

Consistent with the research into the reading process, studies comparing curricula with and without explicit phonics tuition have found in favour of explicit phonics. Although some 30 plus years old, the Cooperative Research Studies in First Grade Reading Instruction (First Grade Reading Studies: Bond and Dykstra, 1967; Bond and Dykstra, 1997) deserve mention because they represent the most consistent broad based comparison of reading instruction available. Fifteen studies comparing six types of instructional method were analysed in an attempt to answer the question "which of the many approaches to initial reading instruction produces superior reading and spelling?" The six methods of instruction, which represented the most prominent methods at the time, were labelled Initial Teaching Alphabet (ITA), Basal (the use of a reading scheme, such as Ginn, with a controlled vocabulary of high frequency words to foster whole word recognition, a version of "look and say"), Basal plus Phonics, Language Experience (or Whole Language), Linguistic (the introduction of a controlled vocabulary of phonically regular words from which children can discover for themselves the relationships between letters and sounds) and Phonic/Linguistic. Of these, Basal was by far the most commonly used, with a contemporary survey finding that in more than 95% of schools, teachers relied heavily on a basal reading programme. Accordingly Basal programmes were compared with each of the other methods on a wide range of reading assessments. The Basal programmes were found to be of approximately equal effectiveness to ITA, Language Experience and Linguistic methods. It was found to be significantly less effective than Basal plus Phonics and Phonic/Linguistic. The results of this study have been used, quite rightly, as evidence of the importance of explicit phonics instruction. The first conclusion drawn by Bond and Dykstra on the basis of their results was that "word study skills must be emphasised and taught systematically". However, it is also worth reflecting on their second conclusion, that "combinations of programs.... often are superior to single approaches". Where curricula included phonics children's reading often benefited. However, phonics instruction never stood alone, it was always in addition to other elements of a reading curriculum.

At the same time that Bond and Dykstra were managing this large-scale comparative research, Chall (1967, 1997) was reviewing previous investigations on the same theme of early reading instruction. She found nine studies comparing look and say with a phonic method – all but one carried out before 1930. Although the children taught using the look and say method had an early advantage in some of the tests, by Grade 2 the phonics children were out-performing them. The comparison between look and say and phonics is truly a comparison of curricula, underpinned by different models of reading development. Those, who promoted the look and say method, believed that early phonics instruction was a mistake, that whole word recognition must come first. Chall's review is consistent with the later research on the reading process, confirming the importance of de-coding. She also analysed 25 studies comparing systematic and intrinsic phonics for beginning readers. These comparisons were really concerned with how to teach phonics rather than whether to teach phonics. She found that the explicit and systematic approaches were superior to the intrinsic ones. Consistent with findings emerging from the First Grade Reading studies, Chall concluded that the research from 1912 to 1965 showed that instructional methods with a code-emphasis produced better readers than methods with a meaning-emphasis.

Further confirmation of the superiority of methods including explicit phonics came from an analysis of 97 method comparison studies carried out between 1965 and 1978 (Pflaum, Walberg, Karegianes and Rasher, 1980). Pflaum and her colleagues found that in 73 of these studies, which included 30 different teaching methods, the experimental group significantly outperformed the controls. They concluded that "specifically designed instruction generally tends to produce more learning than less systematic instruction, assuming that control treatments may be less well thought out or operationalised compared with experimental treatments". They carried out a meta-analysis on the 30 studies, where means and standard deviations were reported and found that methods which included explicit, systematic phonics produced significantly larger gains than the others. This finding added further support to the proposition that explicit phonics instruction promotes reading progress. It should be said, however, that comparative studies of language experience methods were much fewer in number (only four such studies were listed) than those concerning phonics, and that none of the language experience studies could be included in the meta-analysis. The dearth of research on language experience or whole language approaches is a point to which I will return.

More recently, in the 1990s, the same picture emerges. Two classroom comparisons have found that early phonemic training, given by teachers as part of their normal programme, accelerates children's reading and spelling in comparison to controls. In a study by Blachman and colleagues, children were given phonological awareness training in groups of four or five, within the classroom and by a member of the teaching team (Blachman, Ball, Black, and Tangel, 1994). The 84 children made significantly more progress in reading and spelling than the no-intervention control group of 75. Morag Stuart (1999) compared classrooms using an off the peg phonics package (Jolly Phonics) with classrooms using "Big Books" to teach word level work (a fairly standard teaching practice in English schools and one recommended by the National Literacy Strategy). With the "Big Books" teachers, the researcher discussed the different ways in which big books could be used to foster word level work and ways of introducing letter names and letter sounds. These teachers were particularly asked to spend time on word level work. In other words they were advised to explicitly teach phonics in a way consistent with modern whole language classrooms. The researcher discussed the contents of the programme with the teachers using the commercial phonics package and gave them a training video. This study is interesting because both experimental and control group received explicit phonics instruction, but in the experimental classrooms phonics was foregrounded and the coverage was systematic. The children (five year olds) taught Jolly Phonics were significantly ahead of the control group in reading and spelling both immediately after the 12 week intervention and one year later.

Two comparative studies looking at children with reading difficulties found that adding explicit phonics tuition to a more broadly based reading programme significantly improved the effectiveness of the programme (Iversen and Tunmer, 1993; Hatcher, Hulme and Ellis, 1994). In the case of the Iversen and Tunmer study children receiving Reading Recovery made faster progress if given additional systematic phonics tuition. In the Hatcher et al study children receiving reading plus phonology tuition made greater reading progress than those receiving either reading or phonology alone. Similarly, a curriculum (direct code) which included work on concepts about print, the use of big books, writing and language games, and independent reading plus explicit phonics tuition, was more effective at improving the reading skills of at risk first and second graders than either embedded phonics instruction or whole language teaching (Foorman, Francis, Fletcher, Schatschneider and Mehta, 1998).

Despite the fact that many of the studies described above failed to use random assignment, and despite the fact that the phonics element varied from study to study, from sheer weight of numbers, the evidence for the value of explicit phonics instruction is quite overwhelming. It should clearly be part of every classroom reading programme, though until very recently there has been some resistance to a systematic coverage. However, another point needs to be made, and it is a very important one. Beyond their agreement about the importance of phonics within the reading curriculum, these studies clearly recognised the fact that such programmes had a code-emphasis but included other elements and that these elements were likely to be important. In the case of the study by Hatcher and his colleagues, these other elements were essential for significant reading progress (Hatcher et al, 1994). The same point has been made in different guises in recent writing on the subject of reading instruction (e.g. Adams, 1990; Freppon and Dahl, 1998). Stanovich and Stanovich remark that "there is no one who asserts that reading is merely a matter of decoding and word recognition" (1995).

They argue that word recognition is a necessary but not sufficient condition for good reading comprehension. This is entirely predictable from what we know about reading development.

- Children have to learn that print carries a message, and the rules of how it does so, often referred to as the concepts of print.
- Comprehension is aided by familiarity with the language of books (e.g. Donaldson, 1993).
- We know that fluent readers read without sounding words out letter by letter. Although they register individual letters (very rapidly) they look for letter chunks which they have learnt. They have progressed to what Frith described as the orthographic stage of reading development (Frith, 1985, see also Adams, 1990; Juel, 1991; Ehri, 1995). Such fluency is only achieved by lots of reading (e.g. Smith, 1978; Cunningham and Stanovich, 1991; Stanovich, 1986; Anderson, Wilson and Fielding, 1988).
- We know that reading comprehension relies on vocabulary and world knowledge as well as decoding (e.g. Stanovich, 1986; Stahl and Fairbanks, 1986).

There are other skills or strategies important to the reading process, but listing just a few will suffice to demonstrate that nobody argues that phonics instruction is all that should be included in the reading curriculum. Teachers are well aware of this as we can judge by their practice. For example, in an inspection of English primary schools carried out in 1991 in response to one of those intermittent political panics over reading standards, it was found that the vast majority of schools, children learnt about books and about phonics (HMI, 1990).

Unfortunately, systematic research into these other elements of the reading curriculum is sparse in comparison to the extensive work on phonic methods. For example, Chall remarked in 1967 that of the 38 studies on whole language that she unearthed, only two were comparative. In 1990s the picture had changed very little. There is still a dearth of quantitative research on whole language approaches (Klesuis, Griffith and Zielonka, 1991; Stall, McKenna & Pagnucco, 1994; Hempenstall, 1997). Proponents of whole language methods of teaching reading regard it as a philosophy rather than a "series of prescribed activities" (Goodman, 1992). In an attempt to capture a satisfactory definition of the "whole language" approach to the teaching of reading Bergeron (1990) reviewed all the journal articles published between 1979 and 1989. She concluded that whole language was a "unique enigma" for which no agreed definition existed. Moorman, Blanton and McLaughlin (1994) place its roots in the progressive movement of the 1920s and 30s, and particularly in the work of John Dewey. They comment that three central themes of this movement are frequently represented in the whole language literature:

1. Children are respected and placed at the centre of the learning experience.
2. Teachers interact with and guide their pupils, but do not dictate or direct outcomes.

3. Learning is seen as an intrinsically social event where children will do best where they see themselves as in a community of readers.

Whole language is seen by its adherents as a set of beliefs, a perspective rather than a practice (Altwerger, Edelsky and Flores, 1987). Not surprisingly this makes research difficult to operationalise.

Stahl and Miller (1989) found 51 studies comparing whole language or language experience approaches with basal reader approaches (which included the relevant First Grade Reading Studies (Bond and Dykstra, 1967). Overall they did not find much between the two approaches, neither of which emphasised explicit phonics. Whole language approaches tended to produce better results in kindergarten than in first grade. Stahl and Miller commented that whole language mirrored the social interactions found in literacy rich homes and that the approach may therefore be useful for introducing the basic concepts of print. However, their finding that whole language /language experience approaches were less effective for disadvantaged children suggests that the emphasis on social interaction failed to make up for limited early experience with books at home. In an update in 1994, Stahl and his colleagues (Stahl et al, 1994) commented on the relatively few studies comparing whole language with traditional approaches to reading carried out in the five years since their first meta-analysis. They found this surprising in light of the popularity of whole language approaches in the USA at this time, but it is consistent with the argument outlined above.

Whole language approaches do not lend themselves to comparative studies, both because of a lack of clearly identified reading outcomes and because of a philosophical unease with empirical research expressed by several of the leading whole language proponents. The lack of a clear definition of what constitutes whole language might be expected to produce an unusually large variance between programmes (as was indeed observed by Bond and Dykstra (1967)) relative to all the other teaching approaches examined. Where such variety is subsumed under one heading this undermines the value of meta-analyses. Stahl and his colleagues (1994) conclude that although it is teacher's beliefs which define them as using a whole language approach, it is their actions which are more relevant to children's achievement. Teachers with the same general beliefs act in rather different ways. Stahl et al also remarked that of the 45 comparative studies they looked at, only 20 (44%) measured reading achievement (Stahl et al, 1994). Twenty-two of the 45 studies (49%) used affective measures, such as attitude towards reading, orientation towards reading or self-esteem, a fact which again is consistent with the goals of the whole language approach. However, the studies surveyed failed to demonstrate that whole language encouraged more positive attitudes to reading than more traditional approaches. Because of the considerable variation between programmes classified as whole language, no detailed conclusions about the precise value of particular aspects of the curriculum can be drawn from this research.

Nonetheless, there are some studies which illustrate more precisely the value of teaching children things other than phonics. Central to all literature based programs is the importance of having students spend considerable amounts of time engaged with books, reading and being read to, responding to quality children's literature (Baumann and Levy, 1997). It has been claimed that from being read to, children learn about the concepts of print, they learn more about the world, they begin to understand the language of books, their vocabulary is increased and they develop a desire to read (Butler, 1979; Harris and Sipay, 1975; Holdaway, 1979). Studies of pre-school children have consistently shown that being read to regularly is associated with language development and predicts good reading progress (Chomsky, 1979; Clark, 1976; Durkin, 1966; Teale, 1978; Wells, 1986). The reading of "big books" or other shared reading in the first year or two of school has also been found to significantly improve children's reading and listening skills (Cohen, 1968; Elley, 1980, Elley and Mangubhai, 1983; Feitelson, Kita and Goldstein, 1986; Ricketts, 1982). Although there are no shortage of interpretations as to what aspect of the experience is helpful to children there is little in the way of evidence. Elley (1989) investigated the relationship between story reading and vocabulary development. He found that reading a story to seven year olds on three occasions over one week produced significant gains in vocabulary introduced by the book, compared to a control group.

Stahl and Fairbanks (1986) did a meta-analysis of the effects of vocabulary instruction. They selected 52 studies which met certain standards, including the use of a control group. They found that vocabulary instruction often had a significant effect on children's reading comprehension. The average effect size on comprehension of passages containing taught words was .97 – a large effect. The effect on more general reading comprehension as assessed by standardised tests was smaller – .30 – but still significant in many cases. These studies demonstrate empirically that improving vocabulary leads to improvements in reading comprehension. In other words the development of vocabulary is part of the reading process. However, by and large children learn new vocabulary not through direct instruction from their teachers but through their own reading (Adams, 1990; Nagy and Anderson, 1984). Teachers spend little time on direct vocabulary instruction (Durkin, 1979), but school age children learn a staggering 3,000 words or more per year (Adams, 1990). Nagy and Anderson (1984) found that the average fifth grader is likely to encounter between 16,000 and 24,000 unknown words per year in the course of reading. Which of these words are learnt is a function of how often they are encountered (repeated reading of text has been found to produce marked improvements in word recognition, fluency and comprehension: Herman, 1985; Sindlar, Monda and O'Shea, 1990; Taylor, Wade and Yekovich, 1985) and whether or not the child is trying to make sense of the text. So we come back to the importance of reading for meaning as we start to identify its significance within the process of children's reading development.

The emphasis in this section has been on what to include in children's reading curriculum, although perforce some aspects of how best to promote learning have also emerged. In the next section I will explicitly focus on the "how".

TEACHING STYLES

Although psychologists have produced theories of learning, there is no well-developed theory of instruction. However, certain important elements have been identified. Carroll (1963) drew attention to the importance of learning time, which has clear relevance for the classroom. He stated that mastery in a formal teaching context is a function of the ratio of the amount of time students actually spend on learning tasks (academic learning time) to the total amount of time they need. The time spent on learning is defined by the amount of time allowed for learning (the opportunity to learn) and the extent to which the student willingly and actively engages in the learning (perseverance). The amount of time needed to master a particular learning task is a function of the nature of the task, the student's ability and the quality of the teaching.

Not surprisingly, associations have consistently been found between student progress and both the amount of time allocated by the teacher to the curriculum area and the proportion of that time that students spent in active learning (Creemers, 1994, especially a study by Marzano et al, 1987 on effective reading instruction). Teacher management is an active device for creating time for learning and for ensuring that students actually spend their time on task (eg. The Leverhulme Primary Project, Wragg, 1993).

An example of this can be seen in a focused literacy programme (Literacy Intervention from Teachers – LIFT) which was influential in the development of the National Literacy Strategy (Hurry, Sylva and Riley, 1999). This programme offered a fairly structured classroom organisation linked to a whole language approach, an interesting marriage which exemplifies the interdependence of curriculum and teaching style. Particular features of the programme are: a literacy hour, during which every child is engaged in a literacy activity; the use of certain forms of direct instruction, for example the use of Big Books in a whole class teaching session, guided reading in ability groups using finely graded texts, and independent group activities structured to engage children in reading alone or to each other. Six LIFT Reception Year classes (4 and 5 year olds) were compared with six control classrooms offering a range of standard approaches to teaching literacy. Children were observed in order to describe the nature of the child's literacy experience in experimental and control classrooms and their reading progress was measured over the course of their first two years in school. Teachers in the LIFT classroom spent significantly more time on managing children and the children spent significantly more time reading and writing than children in the control classrooms (Sylva, Hurry, Mirelman, Burrell and Riley, 1999). Interestingly, it was the extra time LIFT children spent reading alone or to each other rather than to the teacher that was responsible for their additional academic learning time, a plausible result of additional teacher management. Children in LIFT classrooms made significantly greater progress in reading than the control children (Hurry, Sylva and Riley, 1999). Thus strong teacher management was seen to be associated both with an increase in the amount of curriculum time spent on (on task) reading and with additional reading progress.

Other ways to increase academic learning time have been explored. Children who do not read well or dislike reading, may fail to be actively engaged in reading activities. Since most reading takes place when children are working on their own or in groups and working independently from the teacher (eg. Galton, Hargreaves, Comber, Wall and Pell, 1999; Sylva, et al, 1999), teachers may find it difficult to ensure that poor readers get the practice they need. In order to maximise active learning time (perseverance), Mathes and her colleagues introduced a paired reading scheme in six First Grade classrooms (First-Grade PALS) (Mathes, Howard, Allen & Fuchs, 1998). More able readers were paired with less able readers and took on the role of "Coach". First-Grade PALS is composed of two set routines: Sounds and Words, a code-based activity following principles of the model of Direct Instruction (Carnine, Silbert & Kameenui, 1997), and Partner Read-Aloud, where children read and re-read a book together and re-tell the story to each other. The children worked in pairs for 35 minutes per day for 16 weeks. At the end of this time the children's reading progress was compared to that made by similar children in six similar control classrooms. The children in both types of classroom, First-Grade PALS and control, had spent around 11 hours per week on literacy activities, which included the paired reading in the experimental classrooms. The less able readers in the First-Grade PALS classrooms made significantly greater gains in reading, measured on a range of tests, than their peers in the control group. Paired reading had some significant effects on the reading of children of average ability but none for the more able group. This is as might be expected since the least able readers were always being "coached" by the more able readers and were therefore spending time on activities appropriate to their reading level. The children involved in paired reading did not spend more time on literacy activities than the control children, but presumably were more actively involved. Notice too that the correct match of pupil to task was important, illustrating the key role of assessment, which is a significant undercurrent in many comparative studies of instruction but is rarely explicitly discussed.

We might say that academic learning time is a necessary condition for learning to occur, but it is clearly not sufficient. It has been demonstrated that what is taught during that time is important. How it is taught is also significant.

As the evidence regarding the importance of phonics in beginning reading unfolded, the debate about whether or not to teach phonics essentially transformed into a question of how to teach phonics, some taking the position that such skills are best taught explicitly, others that it is better to let children induce them from meaningful reading. In a series of experiments Byrne showed how difficult it is to induce the alphabetic principle, both for children and adults (Byrne, 1998). For example, in one experiment university students learned four new symbols for the letters b, p, z, and s. These symbols were special in that they related to properties of speech. In speech, /b/ and /z/ are voiced, that is our vocal chords engage when we say them. The /p/ and /s/ are unvoiced. Similarly, /b/ and /p/ are bilabials, they are created in a particular place in the vocal cavity. The /z/ and /s/ are alveolars. The important point is that we can notice these features as we say the different letter sounds and the students were taught symbols which encoded these accessible features, but the connection was not made explicit. They were then asked to make decoding decisions about other letters, where the same phonetic features were represented using the same symbols. For example, students were asked if a symbol, which had been used to represent /b/ and /z/ – the voiced sounds – represented /v/ (a voiced sound) or /f/ (which is unvoiced). They performed at chance levels on the transfer task. They had not induced the symbol/phonic link. Byrne remarked that phonemes lack the visibility of larger units such as words and syllables. This makes the reliance on induction as a learning process for phonemes laborious and haphazard. Many children will probably get there in the end through induction, but it is not reliable. In fact, as we have seen, whole language and basal teaching methods, which rely on induction of grapheme/phoneme links, tend to be most successful in the first year or two of reading instruction. Curricula, which include explicit phonics, outstrip these inductive teaching methods after the first two years in school. If induction worked, but was slower than direct instruction, the opposite time trends would be expected. The results of comparative studies support Byrne's finding that induction of grapheme/phoneme links is surprisingly tricky, at least for some children. The alternative to induction is direct instruction of skills.

Children tend to learn what they are taught. Barr (1974) randomly allocated 32 beginning readers to "look and say" or "phonic" reading instruction. Before they were given their allotted instruction some children were predominantly sight-word readers, whilst others preferred a phonic approach. After eight months Barr found that most children had adopted the reading strategy that they were taught, irrespective of their previous approach. Similarly, Sowden and Stevenson (1994) compared two groups of children in their first year of school, one group being taught using a "look and say" approach, one using a mixture of "look and say" and phonics. The children were tested after six months in school. Children from the "look and say" classroom used whole word reading strategies almost exclusively, whereas children from the mixed method classroom used both whole word and phonological strategies – specifically the phonemic strategies which they had been taught.

Another example of the effects of direct instruction can be seen in the study by Elley (1989), already mentioned. Elley found that children learnt vocabulary from being read to by their teacher. He also found that how the story was read was important. Children were divided into three groups, A (experimental, n = 72), B (experimental, n = 55), and C (the control group, n = 51). The children in the experimental groups were read to both *with teacher explanation* (using various methods) and *without teacher explanation*. A cross-over design was used so that both Group A and Group B children heard stories under the two experimental conditions. Both story reading techniques produced vocabulary gains compared to the control group, who did not hear these stories. However, when the teacher explained new words in the context of the story, the gains were around three times greater than when the story was read without explanation.

There are also problems associated with direct instruction, which link to theories of learning. They hinge around the issue as to what extent children can be taught and to what extent children learn from their own actions and experience. As we saw above, they can be taught vocabulary through some form of direct instruction. However, their major route to expanding their vocabularies is through their own experience of reading. Byrne's remark, that links between sounds and phonemes are less easily induced than links between words or syllables and letter clusters is important here (Byrne, 1998). Some things are more accessible to induction than others. Teaching children about things that they can learn themselves is not a good idea. For one thing, the curriculum is too crowded to teach unnecessary skills. An example of this can be seen in the evaluation of a classroom programme designed by Byrne and Fielding-Barnsley (1991). In this evaluation, 64 children were taught about six key phonemes over 12 sessions. A well-matched control group of 62 children were taught about semantic classification over the same number of sessions. At the end of the 12 sessions the phonic group were significantly better at identifying the taught phonemes than the control group, but they also performed significantly better on six untrained phonemes. It would seem in this case that once children had been introduced to the principle of phoneme/grapheme links, they could generalise their learning to novel situations – that is they could induce links that they had not been directly taught. The underlying importance of this is not merely that curriculum time is saved, but also that children achieve a degree of independence in understanding a metalevel rule, which allows them to generalise to situations they will encounter on their own.

There has been a great deal written about the fact that teaching children rules does not guarantee that they can apply them. First, the teaching must be pitched to the right level. Secondly, children must understand how the abstraction of rules works in practice. For this reason "skill and drill" has been criticised as being too divorced from children's experience. Various ways of avoiding this problem have been explored. For example, Cunningham compared three different methods of teaching kindergarten and first grade children to read – two involving explicit phonics and one focusing on understanding stories (Cunningham, 1990). In the "skill and drill" phonics approach, children were taught phonemic awareness, phonemic segmentation and blending. Teaching methods were fun and interactive, but no link was made with children's own reading activities outside the lesson. In the "metalevel" approach, children were encouraged to talk about the links they could make between the lesson and their own reading. For example, they might be asked to try strategies such as "cutting up" words into their smallest pieces, thinking about what the words sounded like and then thinking about other words that sounded the same. Or, in the context of reading, they might be asked to decide if /b/a/t// fitted into a story about a baseball player. The value and utility of the skill for future reading was explicitly emphasised, modelled and contextualised. Both of the explicit phonics methods produced significant improvement in the children's reading, compared to the non-phonic method, and was consistent with the other evidence reviewed here. Both phonic methods were equally effective in improving children's phonemic awareness. However, for the first grade children, the "metalevel" approach was significantly more effective than the "skill and drill" method in improving their reading. Phonics skills learnt through the metalevel approach generalised better to a more global measure of reading. Byrne (1998) made a similar observation, "the more directly targeted the instruction (the more contextualised), the more thorough the acquisition" (p. 20).

It has been argued that different types of learning require different forms of instruction. Specifically, it has been remarked that what are described as "lower order" skills, involving predictable algorithms and facts, can be directly taught using "a highly ordered and consistent approach". "Higher order" skills – metacognitive skills – such as orientation, planning, testing, problem solving, evaluation and reflection, it is argued, require different instructional strategies (Creemers, 1994; Palinscar and Brown, 1989; Snow, Burns and Griffin, 1998; Rosenshine, Meister and Chapman, 1996). I think that this dichotomy between lower order and higher order skills is potentially misleading. However, let us examine the work on proposed instructional strategies for teaching higher order skills. There is quite an extensive literature on reading comprehension which is relevant here. Reading comprehension is a complex business. Rosenshine and his colleagues write that such a task "cannot be broken down into a fixed sequence of sub-tasks or steps that consistently and unfailingly lead to the desired end result" (1996). This makes direct instruction difficult and Durkin (1979) observed that out of 4,469 minutes of Grade 4 reading instruction, only 20 minutes were spent in comprehension instruction by the teacher. Teaching children cognitive strategies is an instructional response that has been explored as a way of helping teachers approach these more complex aspects of reading. Children are shown how to generate questions about texts and how to apply this questioning to what they read in order to support their comprehension. Although this does not lead directly in a step-by-step manner to comprehension, it is argued that the process allows children to develop internal procedures to understand text. Instructional techniques include teacher presentation, teacher modelling, teacher guidance of student practice and what is specifically referred to as reciprocal teaching.

A seminal study on reciprocal teaching was carried out by Palinscar and Brown (1984) with 12 year olds. The children had severe reading comprehension problems, but could decode at an age appropriate level. Although the children had received extra help with their reading, it had been aimed mainly at their decoding skills, which were no longer a problem. Palinscar and Brown developed a reciprocal teaching technique to foster children's comprehension and comprehension monitoring in an explicit way. Child and tutor took turns at reading a segment of text and then discussing various aspects of the text – paraphrasing main ideas, questioning any ambiguities, predicting the possible questions that might be asked about the segment, and hypothesizing about the content of the remaining passage segments. At the end of the training sessions the children's comprehension monitoring had improved substantially and so had their reading comprehension. Compared to their classmates, who had not been tutored, they had made substantially more progress in reading comprehension. The tutored group moved from the 7th to the 40th percentile compared with all the other seventh graders in the school.

Rosenshine, Meister and Chapman (1996) reviewed 26 comparative studies of direct instruction of comprehension strategies, all including equivalent experimental and control groups. In 17 of the studies, children were taught specific cognitive strategies of question generation. For example, they were given single word prompts for starting questions, such as *who, what, where, when, why* and *how*, or question stems, such as *"how are ... and ... alike?"* and *"what is the main idea of ..."*. Another technique involved teaching students to identify the main idea of a paragraph and then using this to generate questions. These 17 studies were described by Rosenshine and his colleagues as employing "traditional skill-based instruction". The other 9 studies involved reciprocal teaching (eg. Palinscar and Brown, 1984). Overall, instructing students in an explicit way about comprehension strategies was effective. When standardised tests were used, a median effect size of 0.36 was observed. When experimenter-developed comprehension tests were used, the median effect size was 0.86. These are medium to large effects.

These comparative studies demonstrate that teacher led or explicit instruction is effective for "higher order" skills. It is claimed that the method of explicit instruction differs somewhat from that considered appropriate for "lower order" skills, that it involves a heuristic, traditionally linked with informal inquiry-centered and discovery oriented teaching. Teaching "lower order" skills is seen as requiring didactic, formal, controlled instruction. However, the study by Cunningham (1990) illustrates that even the teaching of phonological skills, which might be described as "lower order", benefits from contextualisation and a certain amount of "metalevel" teaching. Byrne's (1998) work gives much the same message and there are copious references that catalogue the dangers of teaching children rules alone. Indeed, it has been argued that the hallmark of those, who find learning difficult, is their inability to either generate metacognitions or to apply them (Brown and Ferrara, 1985). It would seem that children learn what they are taught, but that they always learn it better if it is contextualised for them and if they are helped to grasp the principles behind the rules.

The definition of what constitutes direct instruction is vague. Broadly speaking it refers to academically focused, teacher-led, classrooms with specific, analytic goals. This teaching style appears to be an effective one. It seems that it can be applied to different kinds of learning. However, it does not capture everything of importance that happens in the classroom. For example, we have already identified the necessity of children reading to themselves. The average teacher spends the majority of her time interacting with pupils. In the ORACLE study, in

1976 teachers spent around 80% of their time relating directly to pupils. Thirty years later, in 1996, teachers spent 90% of their time working directly with their pupils (Galton, Hargreaves, Comber, Wall and Pell, 1999). Pupils however have a very different experience. In the same ORACLE classrooms in 1976 children were only interacting with the teacher for 15% of the time. Although this doubled to 30% in 1996, the majority of the time children still worked on their own (see also Tizard et al, 1988; Plewis and Veltman, 1997). Comparative studies in the area of reading, which address the learning taking place when children work alone or in small groups not lead by the teacher, are sparse. If children are spending 70% of their time in class away from their teachers, this element of their educational experience must not be neglected. Pupil motivation is likely to be particularly important in independent learning.

CONCLUSIONS

Comparative studies of methods of instruction have demonstrated that both what is taught and how it is taught are important. I have suggested that decisions about what to teach rely on theories of reading and that decisions about how to teach draw on theories of learning. However, it would seem that our understanding of the nature of the reading development process is particularly important. We use this knowledge in devising curricula, but we must also understand the elements involved in the process of reading in order to employ the direct teaching programmes that have proven powerful.

I have not attempted to cover all of the comparative studies of methods of reading instruction. This would be a monumental task. Rather, studies have been used to demonstrate a line of argument. I have also not focused on the methodological strengths and weaknesses of the studies reviewed, though I have excluded studies that were seriously flawed. All of the comparative studies have included controls, but random assignment to experimental or control group is the exception rather than the rule.

What has emerged is that research has demonstrated the importance of certain elements of instruction being included in the curriculum and the power of certain teaching styles. However, there is a danger here. Certain aspects of the reading process are more easily defined and researched than others. In particular there has been a huge amount of research on the role of phonics in children's reading. This work is of great value, but it has been observed that for many years teachers seemed to resist its message, to teach phonics explicitly. Direct or explicit instruction is an extremely effective method of teaching children, but comparative studies have tended to neglect other crucial areas of reading instruction – how we encourage children to read on their own, how we ensure that they attend to what they are reading and that they are attending to the right things in the right way. This leaves teachers to rely on what they can glean from their colleagues and their own experience in deciding what to undertake every day in their classrooms. It may lead teachers to conclude that research evidence is of limited value, failing to address central areas of their concern. If we are interested in the lessons of comparative studies being applied, we may have to expand our repertoire of research methods to address more of the research questions, which emerge from the experience of teaching 30 children at once.

REFERENCES

Adams, M. (1990). Beginning to Read: Learning and Thinking about Print. Cambridge, MA: the MIT Press.

Altwerger, B., Edelsky, C. &, Flores, B. (1987). Whole language: What's new. *The Reading Teacher, 41,* 144-154.

Anderson, R. C., Wilson, P. T., & Fielding, L. G. (1988). Growth in reading and how children spend their time outside of school. *Reading Research Quarterly, 23,* 285-303.

Barr, R. (1974). The effect of instruction on pupil reading strategies. *Reading Research Quarterley, 10,* 555-582.

Baumann, J. F. & Levy, G (1997). Delicate balances: Striving for curricular and instructional equilibrium in a second-grade, literature/strategy-based classroom. *Reading Research Quarterly, 32,* 244-275.

Bergeron, B. (1990). What does the term whole language mean? Constructing a definition from the literature. *Journal of Reading Behaviour, 22,* 301-330.

Blachman, B. A., Ball, E. W., Black, R. S. & Tangel, D. M. (1994). Kindergarten teachers develop phoneme awareness in low-income, inner-city classrooms. *Reading and Writing, 6,* 1-18.

Bond, G. L. & Dykstra, R. (1967). The co-operative research program in first-grade reading instruction. *Reading Research Quarterly, 2,* 5-142.

Bond, G. L. & Dykstra, R. (1997). The co-operative research program in first-grade reading instruction. *Reading Research Quarterly, 32,* 348-427.

Brown, A. L. & Ferrara, R. A. (1985). Diagnosing zones of proximal development, in J. V. Wertsch (Ed.), *Culture, Communication and Cognition: Vygotskian Perspectives* (pp. 273-305). Cambridge: Cambridge University Press.

Butler, D. (1979). *Cushla and her books.* London: Hodder & Stoughton.

Byrne, B. (1998). *The Foundation of Literacy.* East Sussex, UK: Psychology Press.

Byrne, B. & Fielding-Barnsley, R. (1991). *Sound foundations.* Sydney: Peter Leyden Educational Publishers.

Carnine, D., Silbert, E., & Kameenui, E.J. (1997). *Direct instruction reading.* Columbus, OH: Merrill.

Carroll, J. B. (1963). A model of school learning. *Teachers College Record, 64,* 723-733.

Chall, J. (1967) *Learning to Read: The Great Debate.* New York: McGraw Hill.

Chall, J. (1997) *Learning to Read: The Great Debate* (3rd edn). Orlando: Harcourt Brace.

Chomsky, C. (1979). Language and reading. In R. E. Shafer (Ed.), *Applied linguistics and reading* (pp. 112-128). Newark, Del: International Reading Association

Clarke, A. M. (1976). *Early Experience: myth and evidence.* London: Open Books.

Cohen, D. (1968). The effect of literature on vocabulary and reading achievement. *Elementary English, 45,* 209-217.

Creemers, B. P. (1994). *The Effective Classroom.* London: Cassell.

Cunnigham, A. E. (1990). Explicit versus implicit Instruction in Phonemic Awareness. *Journal of Experimental Child Psychology, 50,* 429-444.

Cunningham, A. E. & Stanovich, K. (1991). Tracking the unique effects of print exposure in children: Associations with vocabulary, general knowledge and spelling. *Journal of Educational Psychology, 83,* 264-274.

Donaldson, M. (1993). Sense and Sensibility: some thoughts on the teaching of literacy. In R. Beard (Ed.) *Teaching Literacy Balancing Perspectives* (pp. 36-60). Mawah, NJ: Lawrence Erlbaum.

Durkin, D. (1979). What classroom observations reveal about reading comprehension. *Reading Research Quarterly, 14,* 518-544.

Ehri, L. C. (1995). Phases of development in reading words. *Journal of Research in Reading, 18,* 116-125.

Elley, W. B. (1980). *Lessons learned about LARIC.* Christchurch, New Zealand: University of Canterbury.

Elley, W. B. (1980). Vocabulary acquisition from listening to stories. *Reading Research Quarterly, 26,* 174-187.

Elley, W. B. & Mangubhai, E. (1983). The impact of reading on second language learning. *Reading Research Quarterly, 19,* 53-67.

Feitelson, D., Kita, B., & Goldstein, Z. (1986). Effects of reading series-stories to first graders on their comprehension and use of language. Haifa, Israel: University of Haifa.

Foorman, B. R., Francis, D. J., Fletcher, J. M., Schatschneider, C., & Mehta, P. (1998). The role of instruction in learning to read: preventing reading failure in at-risk children. *Journal of Educational Psychology, 90,* 37-55.

Freppon, P. A. & Dahl, K. L. (1998). Balanced instruction: Insights and considerations. *Reading Research Quarterly, 33,* 240-251.

Frith, U. (1985). The usefulness of the concept of unexpected reading failure. Comments on reading retardation revisited. *British Journal of Developmental Psychology 3,* 15-17.

Galton, M., Hargreaves, L., Comber, C., Wall, D., & Pell, A. (1999). *Inside the Primary Classroom – 20 Years On.* London: Routledge.

Goodman, K. (1986). *What's whole in whole language?* Portsmouth, New Hampshire: Heinemann.

Goodman, K. (1986). Why whole language is today's agenda in education. *Language Arts, 69,* 354-363.

Goswami, U. & Bryant, P. (1990). *Phonological Skills and Learning to Read.* London: Lawrence Erlbaum.

HMI. (1990). *The Teaching and Learning of Reading in Primary Schools.* London: Department of Education and Science.

Harris, A. & Sipay, E. (1975). *How to increase reading ability (6th edn).* New York: McKay.

Hatcher, P. H., Hulme, C. & Ellis, A. W. (1994). Ameliorating early reading failure by integrating the teaching of reading and phonological skills: the phonological linkage hypothesis. *Child Development, 65,* 41-57.

Hempenstall, K. (1997). The Whole Language – Phonics Controversy: an historical perspective. *Educational Psychology, 17,* 399-418.

Heman, P. A. (1985). The effects of repeated readings on reading rate, speech pauses, and word recognition accuracy. *Reading Research Quarterly, 20,* 553-565.

Holdaway, D. (1979). *The Foundations of Literacy.* Sydney: Ashton Scholastic.

Hurry, J., Sylva, K. & Riley, J. (1999). Evaluation of a focused literacy teaching programme in reception and Year 1 classes: Children outcomes. *British Educational Research Journal, 25,* 637-649.

Iverson, A. & Tunmer, W. (1993). Phonological processing skills and the reading recovery programme. *Journal of Educational Psychology, 85,* 112-126.

Juel, C. (1991). Beginning Reading. In R. Barr, M. Kamil, P. Mosenthal & P.D. Pearson. (Eds) *Handbook of Reading Research Vol. II.* (pp. 759-788). New York: Longmans.

Klesius, J. P., Griffith, P. L., & Zielonka, P. (1991). A whole language and traditional instruction comparison: Overall effectiveness and development of the alphabetic principle. *Reading Research and Instruction, 30,* 47-61.

Marzano, R., Hagerty, P., Valencia, S. & DiStefano, P. (1987). *Reading Diagnosis and Instruction: Theory into Practice.* Engelwood-Cliffs, NJ: Prentice-Hall.

Mathes, P., Howard, J., Allen, S. & Fuchs, D. (1998). Peer-assisted learning strategies for first-grade readers: Responding to the needs of diverse learners. *Reading Research Quarterly, 33,* 62-94.

Nagy, W. & Anderson, R. (1984). How many words are there in printed school English? *Reading Research Quarterly, 19,* 304-330.

Palinscar, A. & Brown, A. (1984). Reciprocal teaching of comprehension-fostering and comprehension-monitoring activities. *Cognition and Instruction, 1,* 117-75.

Perfetti, C. A. (1985). *Reading Ability*. New York: Oxford University Press.

Pflaum, S. W., Walberg, H. J., Karegianes, M. L., & Rasher, S. P. (1980) Reading instruction: A quantitative analysis. *Educational Researcher, 9,* 12-18.

Plewis, I. & Veltman, M. (1995). Where does all the time go? Changes in pupils' experiences in year 2 classrooms. In M. Hughes (Ed), *Teaching and Learning in Changing Times* (pp. 1-16). Oxford: Blackwell.

Ricketts, J. (1982). The effects of listening to stories on comprehension and reading achievement. *Directions, 8,* 29-36 (University of the South Pacific, Fiji).

Rosenshine, B. (1979). Content, Time and Direct Instruction. In P. Peterson & H. Walberg (Eds), *Research on Teaching: Concepts, Findings and Implications* (pp. 28-56). Berkley: McCutchan Publishing Corporation.

Rosenshine, B., Meister, C., & Chapman, S. (1996). Teaching Students to Generate Questions: A Review of the Intervention Studies. *Review of Educational Research, 66,* 181-221.

Sindelar, P. T., Monda, L. E., & O'Shea, L. J., (1990). Effects of repeated readings on instructional and mastery level readers. *Journal of Educational Research, 83,* 220-226.

Smith, F. (1978). *Understanding reading (2nd edn.)* New York: Holt, Rinehart & Winston.

Snow, C. E., Burns, M. S. & Griffin, P. (1998). *Preventing Reading Difficulties in Young Children.* Washington: National Academy Press.

Sowden, P. T. & Stevenson, J. (1994). Beginning reading strategies in children experiencing contrasting teaching methods. *Reading and Writing, 6,* 109-123.

Stahl, S. A. & Fairbanks, M. M. (1986). The Effects of Vocabulary Instruction: A Model-Based Meta-Analysis, *Review of Educational Research, 56,* 72-110.

Stahl, S. A., McKenna, M. C., & Pagnucco, J. R. (1994). The Effects of Whole-Language Instruction: An Update and a Reappraisal. *Educational Psychologist, 29,* 175-185.

Stahl, S. A. & Miller, P. D. (1989). Whole Language and Language Experience Approaches for Beginning Reading: A Quantitative research Synthesis. *Review of Educational Research, 59,* 87-116.

Stanovich, K. E. (1986). Cognitive processes and the reading problems of learning disabled children: evaluating the assumption of specificity. In J. Torgesen & B. Wong (Eds.), *Psychological and educational perspectives on learning disabilities* (pp. 87-131). New York: Academic Press.

Stanovich, K. E. & Stanovich, P. J. (1995). How research might inform the debate about early reading acquisition. *Journal of Research in Reading, 18,* 87-105.

Stuart, M. (1999). Getting Ready for Reading: early phoneme awareness and phonics teaching improves reading and spelling in inner-city second language learners. *British Journal of Educational Research, 69,* 587-605.

Sylva, K., Hurry, J., Mirelman, H., Burrell, A., & Riley, J. (1999). Evaluation of a focused literacy teaching programme in reception and Year 1 classes: Classroom observations. *British Educational Research Journal, 25,* 617-635.

Teale, W. (1978). Positive environments for learning to read: What studies of early readers tell us. *Language Arts, 55,* 922-932.

Tizard, B., Blatchford, P., Burke, J., Farquhar, C., & Plewis, I. (1988). *Young Children at School in the Inner City.* Hove and London: Lawrence Erlbaum.

Wells, G. (1986). The meaning makers: Children learning language and using language to learn. London: Hodder and Stoughton.

SUGGESTED FURTHER READINGS

Adams, M. (1990). Beginning to Read: Learning and Thinking about Print. Cambridge, MA: the MIT Press.

Creemers, B. P. (1994). *The Effective Classroom.* London: Cassell.

D5 Early Emergent Literacy

MADELON SAADA-ROBERT

ABSTRACT

This chapter, organised in five sections, begins with a discussion of the general factors that influence the development of early literacy in young children, and ends with studies on some of the more specific components of emergent literacy.[1] The first section presents research on home environment and the role of parents in early literacy. These studies deal with socio-economic and cultural predictors, parental involvement in shared reading, and the relations between oral precocity and later written language. The second section investigates the more micro-social dimensions of early literacy, such as the quality of shared reading and the influence of the genre of books on literacy development. The third section presents research on preschool literacy development, including comparisons between contrasting instructional environments, teacher's perceptions of literacy, the emotional – relational dimensions of early literacy, and the socio-cultural approach to the analysis of preschool literacy. The fourth section points out some of the linguistic components involved in emergent reading and writing, such as children's understanding of the representational nature of literacy, text comprehension, word identification, alphabet knowledge, phonological and morphological awareness.[2] Finally, our own research paradigm will be briefly presented.

INTRODUCTION

This chapter is about the development and learning of early literacy in children, which for the most part takes place before school formal instruction. However, in a constructivist developmental perspective, there is no basis for treating the periods before and after school entry as two separate worlds. Children do not leave the outside learning environment when they enter the classroom. Literacy development

---

[1] I am particularly thankful to Marc Chapelle, José Favrel and George Hoefflin for the fruitful discussions concerning some arguments of this chapter, and to Emiel Reith for its final English version.

[2] Only some of the recent studies mentioned in this chapter are taken as prototypical, among all those who are actually dealing with the same topics.

T. Nunes, P. Bryant (eds.), Handbook of Children's Literacy, 575–598.

begins before formal schooling (Ferreiro & Teberosky, 1982), indeed "shortly after birth" (Lancy, 1994), and is influenced by the quantity and quality of literacy-related experiences in the home environment. An extensive body of research (reviewed in this chapter), which has been conducted mainly in homes, indicates that strong relations exist between meaningful storybook interactions and early literacy development. Entry to school, while remaining a transition into institutionalised instruction including a specific cultural initiation rite, should enable children to establish links between the different worlds – before and after school entry, outside and inside school – so that they progress towards socially integrated knowledge.

Literacy refers to the processes involved in the comprehension (reading) and production (writing) of texts (Pellegrini & Lee Galda, 1994). Two models attempt to explain literacy development: one posits "separate" pathways for reading and writing, the other stresses "interactive" processes (see below). In both cases, emergent literacy provides the developmental roots.

From a general point of view, both early and emergent literacy involve children learning in home or in homecare contexts, preschool or kindergarten environments, i.e. in any social context that enables them to develop literacy before they start formal school instruction in reading, writing and spelling. The term "emergent literacy" appeared in the early 1980s and was intended to reinforce a new conception of literacy as a process of becoming literate in the home, the community, day-care contexts, Head Start programs or kindergarten settings. The child is seen as the "constructor of his or her own literacy" (Sulzby & Teale, 1991). Under close examination, however, the concepts of emergent reading, emergent writing, and invented spelling, involve different theoretical frameworks, associated with different methodological designs and phenomena. Whereas emergent reading refers unambiguously to any sort of pre-reading practice, emergent writing and invented spelling involve two distinctions that should be noted: writing versus spelling, and emerging versus invented. Spelling, as one component of writing (Treiman & Cassar, 1996), concerns the scriptural ability to write words conventionally, according to its orthographic norm. Besides spelling, writing involves also textual-pragmatic components organised by high-order processes.

The 20-year history of invented spelling definitions refers mainly to spelling in untutored environments, and to children's own experimentation with meaning-form links, as well as spoken-written language links. Most researchers define invented spelling as children's ability to "sound units in words and associate letters with those units in a systematic though non-conventional way before being taught to spell or read" (Richgels, 1995, p. 99). We propose to call this the restrictive definition, i.e. based on two criteria: no formal instruction and explicit sound-letter correspondence. More recently, researchers working within a developmental approach have define invented spelling more broadly as the ability to socially produce functional semiological traces that are not yet letters, as well as the matching of sounds and letters (Jaffré, 1992; Jaffré, Bousquet &

Massonet, 1998). In short, the fact that children spell creatively in their family environment, in an experimental training setting or in the teaching/learning environment, shows that invented spelling is a social internalised ability, not a "natural" ability that emerges spontaneously in a pure individual development. Therefore, in our own studies involving on-line observation of children's strategies in the classroom (see below), we adopt a broad non-restrictive definition of invented spelling, which includes the developmental dimension and does not exclude the formal instructional context, enlarging it to all interactive and shared learning environments.

RESEARCH ON HOME ENVIRONMENT AND PARENT'S ROLE IN EARLY LITERACY

The main early predictors of later literacy development that have been studied recently are the socio-economic and cultural status of families, parental involvement and the quality of mother-child relationships, and finally oral language precocity. The role of these variables is usually studied using correlational or regression analyses.[3]

Socioeconomic-cultural status and the experiences of literacy

Teale's reference-work in this domain (Teale, 1986) discusses the influence of home background on young children's literacy development. He observed that all children, even those in the least literate families, have numerous experiences with written language, since literacy is used consistently to mediate daily living routine (making lists, paying bills, reading instruction, etc.). However, children who are read to – in more literate homes – show more advanced development in emergent literacy. By the time when children enter kindergarten at age 5 or 6 years, middle- and upper-middle-class children (defined by mother's educational levels, parental occupation, or income) exhibit more successful metalinguistic competencies than children who come from less advantaged environments. A higher degree of metalinguistic awareness is correlated with pre-reading print awareness and is predictive of a greater degree of achievement in reading and spelling (also in Bryant, MacLean, Bradley & Crossland, 1990; Dickinson & Snow, 1987; Warren-Leubecker & Carter, 1988).

In an attempt to define these relationships more precisely, Chaney (1994) focused on the relationships between social class, family literacy experiences,

---

[3] Without giving in details the results of significance analyses used in the studies, we shall mention as "significant" the differences tested at p < .05, and "very significant" the differences tested at p < .01.

language development, metalinguistic awareness and children's emergent literacy (mainly print awareness). His study involved 43 normally developing 3-year-old children enrolled in day-care centres, with parents differing on family incomes and years of mother-education. The children were tested with four language development tasks, 12 metalinguistic tasks and two tests of literacy knowledge. Their family literacy experiences were investigated through parents' interviews. The results showed that all children of the sample were involved in some literacy activities at home. In contrast to Teale's results – which were that lower income families read or write only when obliged by social necessity and never for pleasure (Teale, 1986) – Chaney found that 78% of the families in both lower and middle income groups read daily newspapers or books. Moreover, children's books were present in all families. All but one of the children in the entire sample were regularly read to by their parents, siblings, or grandparents.

According to the multiple regression analysis, family literacy experiences were a good predictor of language development and alphabetic concepts but not of metalinguistic and print awareness, nor of book concepts. Income was found not to be a predictor of language development, metalinguistic awareness, print awareness, alphabet concepts, or of book concepts. Language development was a good predictor of metalinguistic awareness, alphabetic and book concepts. The author concluded that social class is not a significant factor in determining metalinguistic tasks success. Once language development is controlled for, socio-economic factors play a minor role in predicting overall metalinguistic awareness. However, print awareness does appear to be related to social class variables. In the poorer and less-well educated families, the amount of literacy experiences varies considerably, and the alphabetic school-like play is less frequent. Even if the ability to recognize environmental print (signs and labels) develops in all young children, this does not necessarily lead to more advanced literacy skills such as print production (Dickinson & Snow, 1987).

Some recent studies involving detailed qualitative analyses of home literacy experiences and shared reading activities underline the influence of social class and the type and quality of parental involvement on later literacy development. For example, Purcell-Gates (1996) carried out a complete week of naturalistic observation in each of 20 low socio-economic status families. He analysed the discourse complexity occurring in the families and the 4-6 years old children's emergent literacy, their concepts of print, and their written and alphabetic principle knowledge. The type and the frequency of literacy events – in daily living routines, entertainment, school-related activities, work, religion, and in interpersonal communication at storybook time – varied a great deal, confirming Teale's (1986) findings. Children's understanding of the intentional nature of print was related both to the frequency of literacy events in the home, and to their personal involvement in these events. Children knew more about the alphabetic principle and the specific form of written language in homes where family members read and wrote for entertainment and leisure at more complex levels of discourse. In addition, parents' intentional involvement in their children's literacy learning increased once the children began formal literacy instruction in school. Parental involvement in children's literacy activities was also investigated by McCleaf Nespeca (1995) using standardised open-ended interviews with 9 low-income mothers. The existence of large differences in the amount and type of parental involvement in low-income families was confirmed; although all mothers considered reading aloud as very important, none remembered being read to as a child. Moreover, stressful conditions and unsafe areas of living are linked with less oral discourse and little effort to encourage children in writing or drawing, except for academic skills such as "drills" on the letters of the alphabet. In these families, shared reading consists mainly in questioning the child on factual cues, in the way that mothers think teachers do, and in pointing at words while reading. No oral discourse is engaged. In contrast to lower class families, middle-class parents engage children in more open-ended discussions about why events occur, and help children make links between every day experiences and the world of books.

Taylor (1995) carried out a study in 12 families which included a 6-year-old child attending 1st grade and which were identified as recurrent users of shared reading activities. These families were situated either in urban or in non-urban environments. Naturalistic data collected through home visits, structured interviews and family journals, provided the basis for a qualitative analysis of shared literacy activities – parental modelling through reading and writing, shared reading for pleasure, practical daily shared reading and writing – and oral language during recreation and work, mealtime, shared activities and bedtime. With respect to shared literacy activities, no significant difference was found between urban and non-urban families, but the amount of oral language activities and the types of shared reading varied according to the mother's educational level.

In short, socio-economic and cultural status have a low impact on daily literacy experiences in families. Nevertheless, differences appear at the micro-level of analysis: there is a great amount of variability in low-income and low-education families' experiences of literacy, and the amount and type of involvement in shared literacy is more closely linked to the families' conceptions of the formal teaching that their children will encounter later on.

In any case, home-shared literacy activities do have a significant incidence on oral language development and on early metalinguistic awareness. These findings help the discussion about ways in which school and home learning could build upon each other in producing early literacy development (Dickinson & Beals, 1994). Home-school relations should be reinforced by means of a "culture" of literacy, that is a complex of beliefs, knowledge and routines that ensure the foundation of children's development (Lancy, 1994). Parent programs, especially, with low socio-economic status families, usually attempt to establish this sort of relation (see below).

Do early talkers become early readers?

Because early exposure to storybook reading appears to be a main factor favouring later literacy development, oral language precocity has also gained the attention of authors. For instance, Crain-Thorenson and Dale (1992) designed a longitudinal study focusing on the role of verbal precocity in literacy development. Twenty-five children selected for verbal precocity at 20 months of age were tested at 24 months, 2½ years, and 4½ years, for language abilities (such as comprehension, word recognition, phoneme deletion), knowledge of print conventions and invented spelling. Children's verbal precocity, for which scores remained high, was found to have little effect on early reading, phonological awareness, concepts of print and invented spelling at age 4½. Instead, the frequency of story reading in the home and the child's engagement in story-reading episode appeared as significant predictors of language abilities at age 2½ and 4½ and of knowledge of print conventions at 4½ years. The authors emphasised the large variance in "effective" story-reading style among parents – in questioning, reading straight through, stopping when questioned. Furthermore, exposure to instruction in letter names and sounds was found to be a significant predictor of print knowledge, invented spelling and phonological awareness at age 4½ years.

Supporting emergent literacy through home environment

These results have lead to greater attention to home literacy experiences. At risk families are recommended to enter national programs that aim to help parents to create a supportive literacy environment in their home. A recent study (Saracho, 1997) analyses the qualitative changes in parental conceptions and activities related to literacy as a result of following such a program. Fifteen families, whose children attended kindergarten in a working-class community, participated in the workshop program. The workshop included the participation of the children's teachers and took place every two weeks over a 5-months period. Discussions were held regarding questions such as how to read books with children, how to engage children in discussions while reading books, how to record the books that are read, how to encourage children to read more books. In addition to comprehensive observations during the workshops, in-depth interviews with parents and teachers were conducted, and samples of the children's stories recorded. As the workshop progressed, it appeared that parents implemented what they learnt about literacy activities in school at home, i.e. by re-reading stories read by teachers, reading books provided by the school, developing language experiences through themes discussed in school, encouraging literacy activities that integrate reading in specific content (e.g., building of a book shelve together), assisting children in drawing pictures to represent letter names and sounds learned in school. Parents developed a wide variety of literacy activities using non-literacy resources (non-print materials linked to a story), literacy resources (newspapers, labels, alphabet noodles), library resources, and human resources. Finally, parents developed a positive conception of literacy and accepted new roles to assist in their children's development of literacy. Other studies have also pointed out the benefit of stimulating home literacy environments (Edwards, Fear and Harris, 1994; Svensson, 1994).

MICRO-SOCIAL DIMENSIONS OF EARLY LITERACY

Rather than merely determining the main factors that predict later literacy development, some authors focus on the micro-social dimensions of early literacy, such as the strategies of shared reading, children's involvement and "reading" strategies, as well as the influence of the genre of books that are chosen for shared reading.

Shared reading activities and children's involvement

Most studies on the role of interactive reading in emergent literacy focus primarily on the effects of a predetermined parent reading styles. Another paradigm consists of examining naturally occurring reading styles and assessing their success in eliciting children's involvement. Bus and van Ijzendoorn (1995) analysed both the characteristics of interactive mother-child reading, using Sulzby's scale of emergent reading (Sulzby, 1985), and the influence of more or less "secure dyads" in relation to mother-child attachment. The authors emphasised that "the learning process in the domain of literacy seems firmly embedded in the emotional context (...). Literacy is not the outcome of an environment enriched with written material but it strongly depends on parental ability to involve young children in literacy experiences" (Bus & van Ijzendoorn, 1995, p 1009). On the basis of a questionnaire, 350 mothers of 3-year-olds were matched into three groups: infrequently reading dyads (once or twice a week) and low socio-economic status (SES), frequently reading dyads (at least once a day) and low SES, frequently reading dyads and high SES. Children's individual behaviour was scored on a rating scale for attachment security, and the mother-child dyads were observed during shared reading, with respect to the degree of verbal elaboration.

There were four main results: 1) Differences according to low and high SES were found only with respect to the number of elaborations, not to their degree. 2) The mother-child attachment security was related to the frequency of reading: less secure dyads read less frequently, and children rated as insecure were less inclined to explore unknown aspects of their environment. 3) In the frequently reading group, interactive reading shaped by parents showed less elaboration revolving around books' pictures and text, which suggests that digressive tactics and supporting help in understanding were more characteristic among the infrequently reading group. 4) A developmental model of interactive reading is proposed (corresponding to Sulzby, 1985 independent reading scale), in which interactive reading follows a four-step strategy: commenting on the pictures; extended discussions primarily about pictures accompanying the reading; some discussion primarily about the story plot accompanying the reading; and finally reading the text while focusing the child's attention on the print. In line with Elster's findings (1994), this study showed a variety of different strategies in most dyads during interactive reading though certain strategies were dominant: some mothers mainly discussed the pictures while others mainly discussed the complex inferences necessary for story understanding.

Other studies have explored the nature of mother-child conversations during book reading, as related to contextualised past events, and its influence on later literacy. Reese (1995) analysed the conversations of 24 white middle-class mothers with their children at 40, 46, 58 months of age. They used a regression analysis to predict the children's emergent literacy at 70 months of age. Emergent literacy was assessed by five tasks: Peabody Picture Vocabulary Test, concept of print, decoding, story production and story comprehension. Over the 18-months observation period, mothers increased their use of contextualising utterances, especially in talking about past events, and this was a very strong predictor of 70-months children's print concepts, vocabulary and story comprehension skills, and a stronger predictor of these variables than of book reading per se. In contrast to many models of adult-child scaffolding these results do not support the notion that a decrease in contextualising utterances is a positive predictor of children's later literacy level. An increasing, not decreasing, level of contextualised comments positively predicted literacy. The authors concluded that there is a need for a new model of scaffolding in mother-child conversation during shared reading.

Does the genre of books influence written language?

In the hypotheses about emergent literacy, which is defined as a process of becoming literate (Sulzby & Teale, 1991), children are conceived as active creators. Literacy development is seen as the result of their search for new information in all types of resources – specific information about the alphabet, information about animals, plants, environment, and planned activities. Both non-fiction and fiction books, as well as multicultural books, are appropriate for leading the way to literacy. Some recent studies shed light on this issue (Reese & Harris, 1997; Scarborough & Dobrich, 1994; Zecker, 1996).

In reviewing thirty-one studies on reading aloud to children in home, Scarborough and Dobrich (1994) noticed that all of them refer to fictional storybooks, and a few of them mention technique books that help parents and children to build things together. Expository or informational books, such as alphabet and counting books, biography, technology, the arts, sports, history, are not used until elementary school. According to these authors, it is only recently that research begins to focus on the inherent value of non-fiction books, and on their role in developing a sense of inquiry and involvement in the world. Non-fiction books serve to inform, instruct, satisfy curiosity, answer questions, and afford broader knowledge. They offer clear distinctions between facts, theories and opinions. Non-fiction books are sources for learning, offering opportunities to search for information and to organize the search in other ways than reading from the first to the last page.

With respect to the writing aspect of literacy, Zecker (1996) found that narrative does not seem to be children's preferred choice of genre. In his study, 20 kindergartners and 20 first graders composed texts of three types – stories, personal letters, shopping lists – three times during the school year, and also re-read their productions. It was found that in young children, lists, not narratives, are the best-known genre. This study confirms Sulzby's categories of writing strategies (Sulzby, Barnhart & Hieshima, 1989): drawing, scribbling/letter-like forms, letter strings, copying, invented spelling, invented spelling/conventional mix, conventional writing. Zecker suggested adding the category of list-like writing. The results concerning children's re-reading of their compositions confirmed Sulzby's categories of emergent reading, i.e. describing pictures followed by paying attention to print, and finally conventional reading, with a list-like reading category added. A categorisation of genre concerning emergent literacy was described: narrative, all about expository, mixed text, one word/sentence. This study supported the hypothesis of the development of children's emergent literacy through text-specific characteristics.

In short, various micro-social dimensions, as in particular children's involvement in interactive reading, which is influenced by the frequency and verbal elaboration of shared reading in context of secure attachment, as the contextualisation of reading by discussing related events, and as the genre of books, appear to play an essential role in literacy learning and development.

PRESCHOOL LITERACY AND INSTRUCTION

Whereas research on home literacy considers both external predictors and micro processes involved in shared reading, research on preschool literacy presents a much greater homogeneity. In fact, the concept of emergent literacy is largely used in preschool context as an alternative to the classical "reading readiness skills" model of learning. Before focusing on the specific linguistic components in early literacy, we present some studies on literacy instruction in the kindergarten, on teacher's perceptions of literacy, and on the emotional-relational dimension of literacy acquisition. The sociocultural approach to preschool literacy will also be discussed.

Instructional environments and fostering emergent literacy

Two distinct types of instructional environments for fostering literacy in kindergarten are compared in most studies: the reading readiness skills program, and the emergent literacy environment. Corcoran Nielsen and Monson (1996) analyse their effects on literacy achievement in 83 children using a pre- and post-test design. Children in the emergent literacy environment, though considerably younger than those in the reading readiness skills program, make significantly greater gains in their concept of print, story retelling, writing, word reading, alphabet and sound/letter relationship. Enriched literacy environments for kindergarten children at any age, and particularly for children who are seen as "at risk" because of their young age at the time of their entry to kindergarten, are supported by the results of this study. These results confirm an earlier study by Whitehurst, Epstein, Angell, Payne, Crone and Fischel (1994) who analysed the effect of these two instructional environments on literacy knowledge of 167 4-year-olds attending Head Start program. According to the authors, the effect of the emergent literacy environment is highly significant for writing and print concepts, and for oral language in children who participated in shared reading at home as well as in the classroom. However, only one linguistic awareness subtest, which was identifying the first letter and sound of words, showed significant effects. The authors concluded that children from low-income families need frequent one-on-one language interactions with an adult to enhance their language skills. Head Start programs would be more effective in introducing even a few emergent literacy activities, if these effects were reinforced by shared reading practices in the family.

Putnam (1994) compared three early literacy programs commonly used in inner-city kindergartens: emergent literacy with whole language approach, writing to read with computer program, and reading readiness program. On the basis of on-line observations made in classroom, Putnam stated that in the reading readiness program, time devoted to direct instruction largely displaced reading aloud time, and that the reverse occurred in the emergent literacy approach. Children were also more conceptually engaged in their learning in this latter approach. McMahon, Richmond and Reeves-Kaselkis (1998) confirmed this result. They observed the degree of involvement in literacy activities in 192 children from 12 kindergartens. Children in emergent literacy classes showed a significantly higher involvement in using books and other reading materials, and in writing activity and interacting with contextual print. In contrast, children in the reading readiness classes showed a significantly higher involvement in the use of print related props – alphabetical order, letter-sound identification, and other reading sub skills. These authors argued that a complete retreat from all forms of skill instruction is not warranted, because many children may not conquer the alphabetic principle by sheer immersion in print alone or by listening to others read. More studies are needed to compare the effects of learning environments that promote reading readiness skills alone, or a combination of reading readiness skills and emergent literacy.

Teacher's perceptions of literacy

There is a difference between teachers' literacy conceptions of reading readiness skills practices and emergent literacy, with respect to the use of time, the content focus, and the types of interventions i.e. one-to-one, small groups, or one-to-all (Corcoran Nielsen & Monson, 1996). Emergent literacy kindergartens focus more time on coaching children, taking dictation, reading aloud, while reading readiness skills kindergartens spend most of the time on giving instruction and monitoring behaviour in paperwork activities. Emergent literacy kindergarten focus writing and reading aloud as the essential content, while reading readiness skills kindergarten focus procedural specific activities as the main content. McMahon et al. (1998) also state the differences between the two conceptions. The reading readiness skills conception involves no learning before age 5-6 years; the basic component of literacy acquisition is essentially concerned by visual-perceptual cues related to unit sounds; prerequisite skills are required and literacy instruction should be direct, systematic, sequential and should not follow an emotional value process. In contrast, the teachers' conceptions of emergent literacy assume that literacy development begins early in life, possibly at birth, through exposure to printed language; that reading and writing develop interrelatedly rather than sequentially; that children construct their own knowledge through active engagement; that language is learned through use and communicative purpose rather than through exercises, and that learning is a risky process involving errors and conflicts, proceeding from the known to the unknown. The teachers' conceptions of literacy seem to have high influence on literacy learning, particularly on the number and quality of children's voluntary involvement, which appear to be significantly higher in the emergent literacy classes.

Emergent literacy learning and dyadic interaction

Emergent literacy learning also needs to be studied in its emotional-relational dimension: for example, how do dyads composed of friends and non-friends support conflict and resolution in sharing book stories? In their one-year study, Pellegrini, Galda, Flor, Bartini and Charak (1997) used a path analysis measuring the effects of three levels of the dyad functioning: a) inhibition, b) conflict and resolution, c) emotional language and literate language. They found that the amount of conflicts during shared-reading was equal in both friend and non-friend dyads, but that the conflicts were better, and more rapidly, resolved in friend dyads. In addition, friend dyads generated more verbal interactions and more emotional/literate language than non-friend dyads.

The sociocultural perspective on emergent literacy analysis

Between a mainly cognitive approach and social-relational emphases in the study of literacy development, some research focuses on the semiotic dimension of emergent literacy, analysing the role of signs in mediated learning. Kantor, Miller and Fernie (1992), for example, explored the transactional aspect of print with the hypothesis that the meaning of signs was elaborated culturally by individuals in groups. An ethnographic research paradigm was used with 3 to 5-year-old kindergarten children attending a program based on constructivist-interactionist theories, in which the children were encouraged to create, solve problems, question, hypothesize, play, explain, etc. The curriculum was negotiated jointly by teachers and children. Teacher's literacy interventions were mostly concerned with informal writing activities based on spontaneous needs and interests expressed in school events and games, such as dictating pretend recipes to the teacher, playing writing, posting rules for cleanup, etc. Video recording and field notes of 2 hours each day, during one month in autumn, in winter, in spring, and interviews with children and parents, allowed the authors to describe means for developing literacy in kindergarten. These semiotic means involved activities such as planned literacy (e.g. journal writing, recipes, cards), arts and construction (e.g. writing a label, constructing with Lego, using media words and letters, etc.), lists and notes (e.g. writing a turn list, a note to remind) and activities with names (e.g. writing, dictating and reading names). Teacher-child interactions were added semiotic means to guide and validate the child's acquisition of literacy.

LINGUISTIC COMPONENTS OF EMERGING LITERACY LEARNING

Recent studies focus on the different linguistic components, such as the representational nature of literacy, the textual components, and the specific components that concern word units, morphemes, syllables, onset-rimes, and letters, involved at early stages in emerging literacy learning.

Children's understanding of the representational nature of literacy

The symbolic process involved in emergent literacy starts in the very early childhood period. This process involves an increasing complexification of various symbolisation abilities that develop through interaction with a variety of symbol systems. Children's understanding of the representational nature of symbols evolves by both internalising and purposely activating symbols. Pellegrini (1993) studied the effect of children's symbolic play on their literacy development. His findings indicated a strong relation between symbolic play and writing but not between symbolic play and reading. He concluded that reading and writing follow separate pathways of development, starting off as different things: reading – a second-order symbol system – finds its roots in oral language and peer conflicts, while writing – a first-order symbol system – is rooted in the interrelated symbolic process of peer play. Analysing both reading and writing related to prior symbols use, McMullen and Anderson Darling (1996), explore the ways in which 36 children aged 3-years became able to understand and to use external physical symbols in order to solve problems such as retrieving hidden objects on the basis of symbolic cues. Analysis of the retrieval strategies showed a transitional strategy between a mere trial and error, and a symbolic solving problem strategy, namely a perservative error strategy. This suggests that the transition to symbolic understanding is less abrupt than previously believed. Symbolic problem solving is considered as a central process in emergent literacy development, and, since it is not a "natural" part of development, teachers can play an important role in helping children to develop this process.

Recent studies (Bialystok, 1995; Jaffré, 1992; Pontecorvo Orsolini, Burge, & Resnick, 1996) also point out that, long before they can read and write conventionally, children show awareness of the semiotic property of written language, when they "read aloud" in a reader-like way, segmenting talk, accentuating written quoted speech, etc., or when they intend to "write" messages, and trace them in a pictographic manner including semantic units. More than a mere transcriptional process linking sounds and letters, literacy is now viewed mainly as a complex conceptual process of using signs to represent speech.

Relations between textual and other early literacy components

Text comprehension in 4-year-old low-income children was analysed by Dickinson and Smith (1994) in a context of interactive emergent reading with teachers. Three patterns of interactive reading characterised the teachers' dominant interventions: the co-constructive pattern (extended all-about conversations), the didactic-interactional pattern (children respond to questions), and the performance-oriented pattern (reading of introduced texts without discussion, followed by selective discussion about analytical organisation of text and vocabulary properties). The effects of these interactive reading patterns on children's vocabulary and comprehension were analysed using regression analysis. Gains in vocabulary and story comprehension were greater in the performance-oriented classrooms than in the didactic-interactional and the co-constructive classrooms. This suggests that the emergent reading environment per se does not ensure progress in literacy learning, as could be concluded by the studies comparing different kinds of literacy environments (see above). Another textual component to be considered concerns discourse cohesion, as part of comprehension that enables us to interrelate words in sentences and sentences in text, according to the type of text and audience. Discourse cohesion also ensures the progressive sequences of the textual organisation. Cox, Fang and White (1997) analysed how children of 4 and 5 years of age used cohesion in the two registers of oral language and literacy. A multivariate analysis showed no significant difference in the use of cohesiveness in the oral register but, in the written-literate register, a very significant difference appeared: children using non-narrative picture-based strategies of emergent reading, and oral-like strategies, do not use cohesiveness in story telling or dictation. In contrast, print-based strategies had a high effect on cohesiveness. These findings support the view that literacy development involves the apprehension both of specific, low-level, aspectual components and of general, high-level, textual components.

Relations between linguistic components in emergent reading

Whereas other chapters in this volume focus on one or the other components and processes involved in literacy, this section of the chapter presents only studies that contribute to the debate about the roots and development of early literacy. As for the roots, recent research on emergent reading raises new questions about the frontier between internal linguistic components and components that are not considered to be linguistic: for example, are picture-based strategies of book "reading", or even print-based strategies without autonomous deciphering, part of reading development? Where is the linguistic frontier between the information drawn from picture and from print? On the writing/spelling side of the question, should pictorial traces, semiologically intended, be considered as part of spelling development or not? These studies also allow us to question the nature of changes in the development of reading and writing/spelling: is development characterised by a progressive change of stages, a progressive change of strategy-dominance, or a progressive change within parallel strategies?

As was noted above, emergent reading abilities rely importantly on children's story comprehension acquired through interactive reading. Other studies demonstrate that children progressively understand print signs in texts from prior understanding of pictorial symbols, even though the qualitative step from symbolic to conventional sign representations is important. Elster (1994) analysed emergent reading strategies of 50 children, aged 4-5 years, in a school context. In this study, adults read books to children frequently over a week period, and each child was then asked to "read" his or her favourite book to the adult (a book chosen among those that were read by the adult). Two reading sequences were videotaped during one school year. In line with Sulzby's reference categories (Sulzby, 1985), three types of reading strategies were observed: picture-governed non-narrative talk (i.e. labelling objects and actions), picture-governed narrative talk (i.e. dialogue with the adult, narrative monologue, written-similar and written verbatim), and print-governed talk (i.e. aspectual and print narration). Whereas the youngest children used mostly non-narrative talk, the eldest ones produced mostly print-governed talk. But the main result of this study, which contrasted with Sulzby's results, was that all the children used different types of strategies at the same time during the year, and the strategy that they used depended on several factors such as the books' familiarity, the genre of text, the text sequence (beginning or end of the story), as well as the congruence of pictures and text. Microanalysis of emergent reading sequences showed that children generally began to "read" using the simplest strategies, and then switched to using more complex ones as the story progressed. In younger children the simplest non-narrative strategies were dominant while older children predominantly used print-governed strategies. Thus this study questioned the adequacy of the linear stage model of literacy development, as well as the dominance-progression model, and the model of parallel evolution of basic components (see below).

As for children's attention to print and their progressive awareness of internal units of text and words, storybooks should not be the only genre used in emergent literacy learning (Murray, Stahl and Ivery, 1996). These authors analysed the effects of three types of books used in three groups of kindergarten children: conventional alphabet books (capital letter and example words with corresponding pictures), letter-names books (pictures without words) and story-books. Measures of print concept, letter knowledge and phoneme awareness showed that there were no significant differences between the three groups on print concept and letter knowledge, but that the alphabet book group performed better than the other two groups in phoneme awareness. Thus, alphabet books provided children with the opportunity to link phoneme awareness with alphabet knowledge, because of phonemic information of the first letter's name such as B for bear, for beach, for bus, etc.

Phonological awareness, alphabetic knowledge and morphological awareness are the main components that have been analysed recently in relation to early reading. Whereas previous studies show that pre-school rhyme ability (the earlier phonological segmentation) is a major factor in later reading success, Johnston, Anderson and Holligan, (1996) claimed that both rhyme skills and alphabet knowledge in 4-year-old children are highly correlated with word reading and phonemic awareness. Analysing phonological awareness more closely, Treiman and Zukowski (1996) proposed a distinction between linguistic levels and the size of the segmentation. Five experiments present pairs of words and nonwords sharing some part of the word (for example pact–peel). Children aged 5 and 6 years are to recognize if the two words share something or not. The results suggest that phonological awareness is not a single homogenous ability. One source of heterogeneity is related to the linguistic level of the units involved: awareness of syllable develops earlier than awareness of intrasyllabic units (onset and rime), which in turn develop earlier than single phoneme awareness. Another source of heterogeneity seems to be the size of the linguistic unit, independently from the linguistic level; but the size criteria is not considered to be a determining factor in phonological recognition. Furthermore, all three levels of phonological awareness – syllable, onset-rime and phoneme levels – cannot be considered as prerequisites for learning to read: "Sensitivity to syllable, onsets and rimes can develop without knowledge of a writing system. In contrast, phonemic sensitivity may result at least in part from experiences connected with the learning of an alphabetic writing system" (Treiman & Zukowski, 1996, p 211).

Alphabetic instruction appears to play an important role in developing phonemic awareness (Seymour & Evans, 1994). These authors examined whether phonological development proceeds along a single path or a two-way path that includes lexical (words and morphemes) and non-lexical (sound-letter correspondence) components. The hypothesis that phonological awareness develops down hierarchical levels, from larger to smaller units, i.e. syllables to phonemes, was tested by measures of the contribution of alphabetic instruction, in a study of 80 children in nursery and elementary school. The results of three experiments indicated that access to phonemic segmentation depended on alphabetic instruction and may precede onset/rime and syllable segmentation. A dual foundation developmental model, involving logographic (direct recognition of whole words) as well as alphabetic and phonologic components as developmental roots of the orthographic final stage of reading was supported.

In addition to phonological awareness, a growing body of evidence suggests a high contribution of morphological awareness in emergent reading processes (Casalis & Louis-Alexandre, 2000). In this study, 50 French-speaking kindergartners were followed up to 2nd grade, and were assessed by phonological tasks, implicit and explicit morphological tasks (e.g. sentence completion versus segmentation and synthesis of words), and inflectional morphology tasks (e.g. feminine morphemes and verb tense, in words and pseudo-words). The results of this longitudinal study provided evidence for a link between early morphological awareness and learning to read. They also support the possibility of a causal connection, given that morphological scores in kindergarten predict reading ability in second grade. In the same vein, Elbro and Arnbak (1996) have shown that some dyslexic children benefited from morphological training for improving reading, and that this effect was specific and independent of phonological awareness.

Relations between linguistic components in emergent writing and spelling

Recent studies on emergent writing and invented spelling have investigated the following matters: writing as notational sign-based system, invented spelling as a developmental process, the role of logography, of letter name use, of phonology and morphology in writing/spelling early development. Unschooled children already have implicit knowledge of the differences involved in notational systems, such as drawing and writing (Brenneman, Massey, Machado & Gelman, 1996). Children who were asked to "draw a picture" and to "write the name of objects" depicted in drawings, drew mainly with continuous lines placed randomly on the page, but they "wrote" with discrete marks, mostly arranged in a linear fashion, from left to right on the page. This indicates, according to the authors, that children have early domain-specific knowledge about words and objects, even if they might still consider train to be a very long word, and butterfly a very short one. Marti (1997), in his study of early notational capacities in 4-year-old children, compared writing, numerical and pictorial notations, with respect to two criteria: a) the material and formal constraints of these different notational systems, and b) their semiotic properties as referring to reality. He found that, even though some differences appeared between the three notational systems, children developed notational capacities very early. Moreover, children's "notational theories" appear before they are able to read any notational sign.

Jaffré and David (1998) analysed invented spelling in French kindergarten workshops. They argued that both semiographic and phonographic components appear in early invented spelling, and they proposed a four-stage developmental model of invented spelling (Jaffré, 1995). Following the production of pictorial traces intended to represent words, a first logographic visual-based phase appears. Next there is an alphabetic phase with attempts at partial phonographic correspondence: this is followed by a second logographic phase that integrates morphological and phonographical knowledge, and later by the final ortho-graphic phase. Early on in this development, children conceptualise literacy according to two main principles (Ferreiro, Pontecorvo & Zucchermaglio, 1996): words have at least three letters (minimum quantity principle) and include different letters, without doubles (internal variety principle). In the process of conceptualising by re-inventing writing and spelling, the use of various genres of written texts, such as informative, expository texts (Boscolo, 1996; Teberosky, 1996), as well as imitative or narrative texts, with their communicative pragmatic own properties (aim, audience, etc.) should enable children to develop the specific components of literacy involved in the textual dimension of writing.

Other studies have described steps in spelling development within different languages (Levin, Share & Shatil 1996): a) production of scribbles, wavy lines, pseudo-letters or mock letters; b) making strings of random letters primarily taken from the child's name; and c) letter-sound correspondences, viewed as strictly invented spelling. Gombert and Fayol (1992), with French-speaking 3 to 6 years old children, insist on the fact that children never produce pictorial symbols (drawing) when they are writing. As for letter names, which, in contrast to punctuation marks, are conceptualised very early as part of the writing system (Ferreiro & Zucchermaglio, 1996), it is now widely stated that children first connect print and speech by noticing links between letters in printed words (B of beech), and letter names in the corresponding spoken words. For example, B in beech is identified earlier than B in bone (Treiman, 1994). In spelling, the strategy of using letter names (for example, "bee" written as B, or "are" written as R, "you" written as U, etc.) is often considered to constitute a typical stage in development. The findings of four experiments (Treiman & Zukowski, 1996) indicate that this claim is overstated. Letter-name effects depend on particular letters: the letter-name R is most likely to be used in spelling than the vowel-nasal names M and N. But the effects also depend on the chain of vowel and consonant: CC or CCV are more likely to be spelt with letter-names than other chains.

Another important component of literacy acquisition, analysed only recently, concerns the morphology or meaning-related form of words. This component develops essentially through writing/spelling activities in early elementary school curricula (Treiman & Cassar; 1996). The authors argue, like others (Nunes, Bryant & Bindman, 1997), that the phonological aspect is not the only descriptor of spelling acquisition, and that morphology, thought to be a late acquisition, is actually an early dimension of spelling, developing in parallel to phonology. These studies confirm that morphological marks are constitutive of invented spelling, and that they develop through several phases during the beginning of elementary school.

The even earlier development of morphology analysed in other studies (see above) could play a crucial role in the passage from phonographic to conventional orthographic spelling. Kamberelis and Perry (1994), who conducted a microgenetic study of invented spelling, describe how children come to grips with orthographic conventions. They assess the role of some of the processes involved in this passage, such as the connection between reading and spelling, which fosters the conceptualisation of words and metalinguistic explanations. More recently, Sulzby (1996) has discussed how interactive reading leads to the awareness of conventional orthography, especially through print-based reading strategies in which children are encouraged to take into account the specific dimensions of text, namely logographically familiar known words, letter-sound correspondence and comprehension.

Relations between reading and writing/spelling in early literacy

In contrast to Pellegrini and Galda (1994) who argue for two separate developmental pathways for reading and writing, according to the Vygotzkian model of two symbol systems – first-order symbolisation (symbolic play and writing) and second-order symbolisation (reading at once embedded with words) – others plead for an interactive model of development. Most of the studies presented in Perfetti, Rieben and Fayol (1997) support the interrelation of processes involved in learning to read, to write and to spell. Three interactive models have been proposed. A linear stage model (Frith, 1985) posits a first logographic stage that relies on reading, a second alphabetic stage related mainly to spelling, and a final orthographic stage requiring reading. A second model describes changes as a dominance of strategies (logographic, alphabetic, orthographic), which all appear in reading and spelling at the beginning of acquisition, rather than in successive, discrete stages (Elster, 1994; Rieben & Saada-Robert, 1997). A third model states that both logographic and alphabetic strategies develop in parallel, forming the dual foundation for later orthographic and morphographic strategies (Seymour, 1997). As for the processes involved in reading and spelling, they can be viewed as relying on a single representational system including phonological and visual processes and giving rise to the orthographic component of literacy (Perfetti, 1997).

Other processes are involved in both reading and spelling, such as memory, decoding, inventing and analogy processes (Ehri, 1997).

These studies provide strong arguments in favour of the conception of broad didactic situations including reading and writing (Chartier, Clesse, & Hébrard, 1998; Saada-Robert, Claret-Girard, Veuthey & Rieben, 1997; Perregaux, 1998 in multicultural contexts). In addition, the inter- and intra-individual differences underlined in several studies (Richgels, 1995; Rieben & Saada-Robert, 1991, 1997) are pointed out as a main characteristic of learning in preschool contexts.

The role of spelling in fostering reading abilities has only recently been analysed, although the contrary is commonly claimed. Richgels (1995) aimed to extend the restrictive "not being taught to read and spell" definition of literacy, to the classroom instructional design. He compares two groups of non word-reading kindergarten children aged 5 and 6 years, who were trained on phonetically simplified word-reading (for example PNO for piano): one group of 16 good inventive spellers, and one group of 16 poor inventive spellers. He found that good inventive spellers performed significantly better than poor inventive spellers at reading both easy words and difficult words. He suggests that "phoneme awareness, invented spelling and word reading comprise only a single, albeit a very significant, piece of the larger picture of children's developing literacy knowledge and competence", involving "meaning making, forms, meaning-form links and functions of written language" (Richgels, 1995, p. 107). In his conclusions about the didactical implications of research on literacy development, the author emphasised the need to involve all the above-mentioned dimensions in teaching approaches, including explicit work on specific components such as phoneme-grapheme correspondence. In the same way, Byrne (1998) argues for explicit instruction on the alphabetic component.

The relationship between the development of reading and spelling, phonological awareness and verbal working memory was examined further by Rohl and Pratt (1995) in a study with 76 pre-readers (mean age 5;8 years at the beginning of testing), who were followed over 2 years. The results of multiple regression analyses supported the theoretical position that both phonological awareness and verbal working memory contribute to the early stages of literacy acquisition. The study of Näslund and Schneider (1996) present a less optimistic view of the role of phonological awareness in later literacy development. They found that in 134 German kindergarten children (mean age 4;1 years), phonological awareness tasks varied highly in their prediction of later literacy performance (reading and spelling). This study also indicates that letter knowledge is less predictive than phonological awareness. Furthermore, phonological strategies seem to be acquired in spelling before they are acquired in reading (Huxford et al., 1992).

Returning to the issue of emergent literacy roots, a current debate questions the role of logography, as part of literacy development. According to Sprenger-Charolles (Sprenger-Charolles & Bonnet, 1995; Sprenger-Charolles, Béchennec, & Lacert, 1998), who conducted a longitudinal study with French kindergartners up to 1st grade, literacy develops mainly from phonological roots, without logography: "we did not find any traces of a first logographic stage" (Sprenger-Charolles et al., 1998, p. 62, translated from French). In other hypotheses logography is considered to be a foundation of literacy (Jaffré, 1995; Seymour, 1997). Our own current research aims to shed light on the role of logography in emergent literacy development.

A RESEARCH PARADIGM FOR THE STUDY OF SITUATED EMERGENT LITERACY

Most studies on emergent literacy use either experimental or ethnomethodological approaches. A new paradigm would consist in combining experimental, ethnological and psychogenetic[4] methods within an ecological context (Rieben & Saada-Robert, 1991, 1997). Our own "situated research" aims at studying the development and learning of emergent reading and writing in the ecological classroom context, and involves three dimensions: a) the elaboration of didactic problem-solving situations based on the linguistic components of emergent literacy; b) analyses of children's scores on psycholinguistic tasks, and analyses of children's strategies – based on microgenetic observations – in emergent reading and writing, reinforced by their metagraphic explanations; c) analysis of teachers' interventions observed during the on-line sequences of emergent reading and writing. The one-year longitudinal study involves French kindergartners (mean age 4; 1 years at the beginning of the study) engaged in didactic sequences of emergent reading and writing.

The main theoretical question deals with the root-status of logography in emergent literacy development, namely how children conceptualise the difference between the semio-pictorial dimension of literacy and the semio-graphical one, i.e. how pictures and text make sense for them. According to the first results of an exploratory study (Saada-Robert & Favrel, 2001; Saada-Robert & Hoefflin, 2000), complementarity between pictorial and print meanings seems most probable. Furthermore, picture-oriented strategies in emergent reading, and semiographic strategies combined with logographic strategies in emergent writing, could well constitute interactive roots of literacy development. This study should contribute new information to the debate about the model of a linear stage development (Frith, 1985), or the model of a parallel development of basic components (Seymour, 1997). Although our exploratory research does not yet allow any definite conclusion, both our previous studies (Rieben & Saada, 1997) and others (Elster, 1994) seem to point to an evolution comprising phases of dominant strategies, with emergent reading and writing evolving together from the very beginning of literacy development.

---

[4] The psychogenetic method consists in analysing longitudinal data within a comprehensive conceptual framework focused on the child's progressive constructs.

Further questioning for research on early literacy development should tackle more precisely situated learning microenvironments. Emergent literacy learning should be studied within the frame of problems such as the relations between picture and print in the early conceptualisation of literacy; the psycholinguistic status of logography; and finally, the processes that allow progression from phonographic to conventional orthography.

REFERENCES

Bialystok, E. (1995). Making concepts of print symbolic: Understanding how writing represents language. *First Language, 15*, 317-338.

Boscolo, P.(1996). The use of information in expository text writing. In C. Pontecorvo, M. Orsolini, B. Birge, & L. B. Resnick (Eds.), *Children's early text construction* (pp. 209-227). Hillsdale N.J: Lawrence Erlbaum.

Brenneman, K., Massey, C., Machado, S. F., & Gelman, R. (1996). Young children's plans differ for writing and drawing. *Cognitive Development, 11*, 397-419.

Bryant, P., Maclean, M., & Bradley, L. (1990). *Rhyme, language and children's reading. Applied Psycholinguistics, 11*, 237-252.

Bus, A.G., & van Ijzendoorn, M. H. (1995). Mothers reading to their 3-year-olds: The role of mother-child attachment security in becoming literate. *Reading Research Quarterly, 30*, 998-1015

Byrne, B. (1998). *The foundation of literacy*. Hove, UK: Psychology Press.

Casalis, S., & Louis-Alexandre, M. F. (2000). Morphological analysis, phonological analysis and learning to read French: A longitudinal study. *Reading and Writing. An Interdisciplinary Journal, 12*, 303-335.

Chaney, C. (1994). Language development, metalinguistic awareness, and emergent literacy skills of 3-year-old children in relation to social class. *Applied Psycholinguistics 15*, 371-394.

Chartier, A. M., Clesse, C., & Hébrard, J. (1998). *Lire, écrire: Produire des textes*. (Reading, writing: Text producing). Paris: Hatier Pédagogie.

Corcoran Nielsen, D., & Monson, D. L. (1996). Effects of literacy environment on literacy development of kindergarten children. *The Journal of Educational Research, 89*, 5, 259-271.

Cox, B. E., Fang, Z., & White O. B. (1997). Preschoolers' developing ownership of the literate register. *Reading Research Quarterly, 32*, 34-53.

Crain-Thoreson, C., & Dale, P.S. (1992). Do early talkers become early readers? Linguistic precocity, preschool language and emergent literacy. *Development Literacy, 28*, 421-429.

Dickinson, D. F. & Snow, C. E. (1987). Interrelationships among prereading and oral language skills in kindergartners from two social classes. *Early Childhood Research Quarterly, 2*, 1-25.

Dickinson, D. K. & Beals, D. E. (1994). Not by print alone: Oral language supports for early literacy development. In D. F. Lancy (Ed.). *Children's emergent literacy* (pp. 29-40). Wesport, Conn: Praeger.

Dickinson, D. K., & Smith, M. W. (1994). Long-term effects of preschool teachers' book readings on low-income children's vocabulary and story comprehension. *Reading Research Quarterly, 29*, 105-122.

Edwards, P. A., Fear, K. L., & Harris, D. L. (1994). Designing a collaborative model of family involvement in literacy: Researchers, teachers, and parents work together. In D. F. Lancy (Ed.). *Children's emergent literacy* (pp. 325-340). Wesport, Conn: Praeger.

Ehri, L. C. (1997). Learning to read and learning to spell are one and the same, almost. In C. A. Perfetti, L. Rieben, & M. Fayol (Eds.). *Learning to spell* (pp. 237-269). Mahwah, NJ: Erlbaum.

Elbro, C. & Arnbak, E. (1996). The role of morpheme recognition and morphological awareness in dyslexia. *Annals of Dyslexia, 46*, 209-240.

Elster, C. (1994). Patterns within preschooler's emergent readings. *Reading Research Quarterly, 29*, 403-418.

Fereiro, E., & Teberoski, A. (1982). *Literacy before schooling.* New York: Heinemann.

Ferreiro, E., & Zucchermaglio, C. (1996). Children's use of punctuation marks: The case of quoted speech. In C. Pontecorvo, M. Orsolini, B. Birge, & L.B. Resnick (Eds.). *Children's early text construction* (pp. 177-205). Hillsdale N.J: Lawrence Erlbaum.

Ferreiro, E., Pontecorvo, C., & Zucchermaglio, C. (1996). PIZZA or PIZA? How children interpret the doubling of letters in writing. In C. Pontecorvo, M. Orsolini, B. Birge, & L. B. Resnick (Eds.). *Children's early text construction* (pp. 145-163). Hillsdale N.J: Lawrence Erlbaum.

Frith, U. (1985). Beneath the surface of developmental dyslexia. In K. Patterson, J. Marshall & M. Coltheart (Eds.), *Surface dyslexia* (pp. 301-330). London: Erlbaum.

Gombert, J. E., & Fayol, M. (1992). Writing in preliterate children. *Learning and Instruction, 2*, 23-41.

Huxford, L., Terrel, C., & Bradley, L. (1992). "Invented" spelling and learning to read. In C. M. Sterling & C. Robson (Eds.). *Psychology, spelling and education* (pp. 159-167). Bristol: Multilingual Matters.

Jaffré, J-P. (1992). Le traitement élémentaire de l'orthographe: Les procédures graphiques (The elementary processing of spelling: Graphic procedures). *Langue Française, 95*, 25-48.

Jaffré, J-P. (1995) L'Acquisition de l'Orthographe (Spelling acquisition). In D. Ducard, R. Honvault & J-P. Jaffré (Eds). *L'orthographe en trois dimensions* (pp. 219). Paris: Nathan.

Jaffré, J-P., & David, J. (1998). Premières expériences en littératie (First experiences in literacy). *Psychologie et Education, 33*, 47-61.

Jaffré. J-P., Bousquet, S., & Massonnet, J. (1999). Retour sur les orthographes inventées (Back up on invented spelling). *Les dossiers des Sciences de l'Education, 1*, 39-52

Johnston, R. S., Anderson, M., & Holligan, C. (1996). Knowledge of the alphabet and explicit awareness of phonemes in pre-readers: The nature of the relationship. *Reading and Writing: An Interdisciplinary Journal, 8*, 217-234.

Kantor, R., Miller, S. M., & Fernie, D. E. (1992). Diverse paths to literacy in a preschool classroom: A sociocultural perspective. *Reading Research Quarterly, 27*, 185-201.

Kamberelis, & Perry (1994). A microgenetic study of cognitive reorganization during the transition to conventional literacy. In D. F. Lancy (Ed.). *Children's emergent literacy: From research to practice (pp. 93-123).* Westport, Conn: Praeger.

Lancy, D. F. (1994). *Children's emergent literacy: From research to practice.* Westport, Conn: Praeger.

Levin, I., Share, D. L., & Shatil, E. (1996). A qualitative-quantitative study of preschool writing: It development and contribution to school literacy. In M. Levy & S. Randell (Eds.). *The science of writing, theories, methods, individual differences and applications* (pp. 271-293). Hillsdale, NJ: Erlbaum.

Marti, E. (1997). Les débuts de la capacité notationnelle: Implications didactiques The beginning of notation: Didactic implications). Skhole. *Cahiers de la Recherche et du Developpement, 7*, 218-237.

McCleaf Nespeca, S. (1995). Parental involvement in emergent literacy skills of urban Head Start children. *Early Child Development and Care, 111*, 153-180.

McMahon, R., Richmond M. G., & Reeves-Kaselskis, C. (1998). Relationship between kindergarten teacher's perceptions of literacy acquisition and children's literacy involvement and classroom materials. *The Journal of Educational Research, 91*, 173-181.

McMullen, M. B., & Anderson Darling, C. (1996). Symbolic problem solving: An important piece of the emergent literacy puzzle. *Early Child Development and Care, 121*, 25-35.

Murray, B. A., Stahl, S.A., & Ivey, M. G. (1996). Developing phoneme awareness through alphabet books. *Reading and Writing: An Interdisciplinary Journal, 8*, 307-322.

Näslund, J. C., & Schneider, W. (1996). Kindergarten letter knowledge, phonological skills and memory processes: relative effects on early literacy. *Journal of Experimental Child Psychology, 62*, 30-59.

Nunes, T., Bryant, P., & Bindman, M. (1997). Spelling and grammar. In C. A. Perfetti, L. Rieben, & M. Fayol (Eds.). *Learning to spell* (pp. 151-170). Mahwah, NJ: Erlbaum.

Pellegrini, A. D. (1993). Ten years after: A reexamination of symbolic play and literacy research. *Reading Research Quarterly, 28*, 163-175.

Pellegrini, A. D., & Lee Galda (1994). Early literacy from a developmental perspective. In D. F. Lancy (Ed.). *Children's emergent literacy* (pp. 21-27). Wesport, Conn: Praeger.

Pellegrini, A. D., Galda L., Flor, D., Bartini, M., & Charak, D. (1997). Close relationships, individual differences and early literacy learning. *Journal of Experimental Child Psychology, 67*, 409-422.

Perfetti, C. A. (1997). The psycholinguistics of spelling and reading. In C. A. Perfetti, L. Rieben, & M. Fayol (Eds.), *Learning to spell* (pp. 21-38). Mahwah, NJ: Erlbaum.

Perfetti, C. A., Rieben, L., & Fayol, M. (1997). *Learning to spell*. Mahwah, NJ: Erlbaum.

Perregaux, C. (1998). Avec les approches d'éveil au langage, l'interculturel est au centre de l'apprentissage scolaire (With the language awareness approach, interculturalism is the centre of learning). *Bulletin suisse de linguistique appliquée, 67*, 101-110.

Pontecorvo, C., Orsolini, M., Birge, B., & Resnick L. B. (1996). *Children's early text construction*. Hillsdale NJ: Lawrence Erlbaum.

Purcell-Gates, V. (1996). Stories, coupons and the TV Guide: Relationships between home literacy experiences and emergent literacy knowledge. *Reading Research Quarterly, 31*, 406-428.

Putnam, L. (1994). Three different early literacy programs and their effects on inner-city kindrgartners' emerging sense of story. In D. F. Lancy (Ed.). *Children's emergent literacy* (pp. 285-308). Wesport, Conn: Praeger.

Reese, D. A., & Harris, V.J. (1997). "Look at this nest!" The beauty and power of using informational books with young children. *Early Child Development and Care, 127/128*, 217-231.

Reese, E. (1995). Predicting children's literacy from mother-child conversations. *Cognitive Development, 10*, 381-405.

Richgels, D. J. (1995). Invented spelling ability and printed word learning in kindergarten. *Reading Research Quarterly, 30*, 96-109

Rieben, L., & Saada-Robert, M. (1991).Developmental patterns and individual differences in the word-search strategies of beginning readers. *Learning and Instruction, 1*, 67-87.

Rieben, L., & Saada-Robert, M. (1997). Relations between word-search strategies and word-copying strategies in children aged 5 to 6 years old. In C. A. Perfetti, L. Rieben, & M. Fayol (Eds.), *Learning to spell* (pp. 295-318). Mahwah, NJ: Erlbaum.

Rohl, M., & Pratt C. (1995). Phonological awareness, verbal working memory and the acquisition of literacy. *Reading and Writing: An Interdisciplinary Journal, 7*, 327-360.

Saada-Robert, M., & Hoefflin, G. (2000). Image et texte: conceptions d'enfants de quatre ans en situation scolaire (Picture and text: children's conceptions at 4-years-old). *Archives de Psychologie, 68*, 83-99.

Saada-Robert, M., & Favrel, J. (2001). Lecture/écriture émergente en situation scolaire: Etude exploratoire de la logographie (Emergent reading/writing in school; Exploratory study of logography). *Proceedings of the 8th Conference of the International Association for the Study of Child Language* (pp. 232-249). Cascadilla Press

Saada-Robert, M., Claret Girard, V., Veuthey, C. & Rieben, L. (1997). Situations didactiques complexes pour entrer dans l'écrit (*Didactic settings for the entry into literacy*). Université de Genève, FPSE-Maison des Petits, Document interne n 9.

Saracho, O.N. (1997). Using home environment to support emergent literacy. *Early Child Development and Care, 127/128*, 201-216.

Scarborough, H.S., & Dobrich, W. (1994). On the efficacy of reading to preschoolers. *Developmental Review, 14*, 245-302.

Seymour, P. H. K. (1997). Foundations of orthographic development. In C.A. Perfetti, L. Rieben, & M. Fayol (Eds.), *Learning to spell* (pp. 319-337). Mahwah, NJ: Erlbaum.

Seymour, P. H. K., & Evans, H.M. (1994). Levels of phonological awareness and learning to read. *Reading and Writing: An Interdisciplinary Journal, 6*, 221-250.

Sprenger-Charolles, L., & Bonnet, P. (1995). New doubts on the importance of the logographic stage. *Cahiers de Psychologie Cognitive / Current Psychology of Cognition, 15*, 173-208.

Sprenger-Charolles, L., Béchennec, D., & Lacert, P. (1998). Place et rôle de la médiation phonologique dans l'acquisition de la lecture/écriture en français. *Revue Française de Pédagogie, 122*, 51-67.

Sulzby, E. (1985). Children's emergent reading of favorite storybooks: A developmental study. *Reading Research Quarterly, 20*, 458-481.

Sulzby, E. (1996). Roles of oral and written language as children approach conventional literacy. In C. Pontecorvo, M. Orsolini, B. Birge, & L.B. Resnick (Eds.), Children's early text construction (pp. 25-46). Hillsdale NJ: Lawrence Erlbaum.

Sulzby, E., Barnhart, J., & Hieshima, J. (1989). Forms of writing and rereading from writing: A preliminary report. In J. Mason (Ed.), *Reading/writing connections* (pp. 31-63). Needham Heights, MA: Allyn and Bacon.

Sulzby, E. & Teale W. H. (1991). Emergent literacy. In R. Barr, M. L. Kamil, P. Mosenthal, & P. D. Pearson (Eds.), *Handbook of Reading Research* (vol. 1, pp. 727-757). New York: Longman.

Svensson, A. K. (1994). Helping parents help their children: Early language stimulation in the child's home. In D. F. Lancy (Ed.). *Children's Emergent Literacy* (pp. 79-92). Wesport, Conn: Praeger.

Taylor, R. L. (1995). Functional use of reading and shared literacy activities in Icelandic homes: A monograph in family literacy. *Reading Research Quarterly, 30,* 194-219.

Teale, W. H. (1986). Home background and young children's literacy development. In W. H. Teale & E. Sulzby (Eds.), *Emergent literacy: Writing and Reading* (pp.173-205). Norwood, NJ: Ablex.

Teberosky, A. (1996). Informative texts of young schoolchildren. In C. Pontecorvo, M. Orsolini, B. Birge, & L. B. Resnick (Eds.), *Children's early text construction* (pp. 259-276). Hillsdale NJ: Lawrence Erlbaum.

Treiman, R. (1994). Use of consonant letter names in beginning spelling. *Developmental Psychology, 30,* 567-580.

Treiman, R., & Zukowski, A. (1996). Children's sensitivity to syllables, onsets, rimes and phonemes. *Journal of Experimental Child Psychology, 61,* 193-215.

Treiman, R., Tincoff, R., & Richmond-Welty, E. D. (1996). Letter names help children to connect print and speech. *Developmental Psychology, 32,* 505-514.

Treimann, R., & Cassar, M. (1996). Effects of morphology on children's spelling of final consonant clusters. *Journal of Experimental Child Psychology, 63,* 141-170.

Warren-Leubecker, A., & Carter, B. W. (1988). Reading and growth in metalinguistic awareness: Relations to socioeconomic status and reading readiness skills. *Child Development, 59,* 728-742.

Whitehurst, G. J., Epstein, J. N., Angell, A. L., Payne, A.C., Crone, D. A., & Fischel, J. E. (1994). Outcomes of an emergent literacy intervention in Head Start. *Journal of Educational Psychology, 86,* 542-555.

Zecker, L. B. (1996). Early development in written language: Children's emergent knowledge of genre-specific characteristics. *Reading and Writing: An Interdisciplinary Journal, 8,* 2-25.

D6 The Linguistic Consequences of Literacy

JOSÉ MORAIS & RÉGINE KOLINSKY

ABSTRACT

After a brief discussion of the concept of literacy and of the theories explaining metalinguistic development and its relations with language development, the empirical evidence on possible specific influences of literacy on both metalinguistic and linguistic abilities is examined. For each of these abilities, the lexical, morphological, syntactic, semantic and phonological components of language are separately dealt with. Although there are reasons to expect that literacy influences metalinguistic abilities in all these domains, unambiguous effects have only been obtained for metaphonological abilities, and particularly for the awareness of phonemes. Striking effects of literacy on some aspects, but not on others, of phonological processing involved in listening to speech are also observed. Those aspects that are permeable to the influence of literacy seem to correspond to late processing and to recognition strategies. Finally, it is emphasised that the main shortcoming of the literature concerned with literacy influences on both language and cognition is the lack, in most of the studies, of appropriate controls that would allow one to distinguish between literacy and other variables, in particular schooling.

INTRODUCTION

The influence of literacy on the development of language abilities has not been the object of systematic research. Although there are practical reasons for this relative neglect, among which the difficulty of finding and examining illiterate people in those countries where psychological science is more advanced, the most critical reasons are probably to be found at the theoretical and conceptual levels. For an influential line of thought, language is an "instinct" (cf. Pinker, 1994): it depends on genetic factors and develops unintentionally under the influence of exposure to linguistic communication in the first years of life. Under this view, literacy can be a derivation but certainly not an instrument of change of the fundamental language mechanisms. On the opposite theoretical pole, language, taken as verbal thought rather than as a capacity distinct from thought, is, no less than literacy, a historical cultural product (cf. Tulviste, 1991; Vygotsky, 1978). Given that this approach puts

T. Nunes, P. Bryant (eds.), Handbook of Children's Literacy, 599–622.
© *2004 Kluwer Academic Publishers. Printed in Great Britain.*

emphasis on the broader concept of culture, no much room is allotted to the specific effects of literacy. Besides, a methodological difficulty has been preventing developmental researchers from teasing apart the roles of chronological age, schooling and literacy (these two associated with socio-economic status) in the development of language-based abilities. Indeed, literacy usually starts around the age at which children begin to attend primary school, and the subsequent changes in those three variables are so strongly correlated, all positively, that disentangling them would require the experimenters to find very special situations. For all these reasons, handbooks of child psychology seldom present a chapter specifically devoted to the influence of literacy on either thought or language development.

The very concept of literacy requires some comment, since it is not attributed the same meaning by the different scholars. For a number of them, mainly cognitive psychologists (especially the ones who subscribe a modular view of mind), literacy is the ability to read and write. For others, mainly the "social-construction" – oriented psychologists, literacy is the whole corpus of knowledge and strategies that is acquired through the constant exercise of those abilities. The present authors adopt the first meaning for at least two reasons. First, it does not seem to be theoretically relevant to distinguish, within the individual's knowledge data basis, the part acquired through reading and writing from the part acquired through other forms of information processing. Second, contrary to general knowledge, the ability to read and write can be both defined operationally and estimated quantitatively.

Literacy is not an all-or-none quality. Yet, experimental work on literacy effects usually compares illiterate and literate people, i.e. adults who never learned to read and write and adults who are skilled readers and spellers, respectively. In some studies, however, intermediate levels of literacy are also contemplated: for example, adults who learned to read and write in childhood but who never attained good mastery of these abilities and who, for lack of practice, have become very poor readers and spellers. A related concept that is frequently encountered in the literature devoted to practical issues is "functional literacy". UNESCO (1970) defined it as a reading level equivalent to the American school system grade level of 5 (chronological age: around 10 years). But, for many theoretical issues, functional illiterates cannot be taken as illiterates. Although unable to read a large number of texts that are important in everyday life, the knowledge that "functional illiterates" once acquired of the written code allowed them to access consciously aspects of their language system of which fully illiterate people never become aware.

The scientific literature does, in general, distinguish illiterates from functional illiterates. However, there is a less overt conceptual confounding, which concerns both the illiterate adult and the preliterate child, and which can lead to erroneous interpretation of their behaviour. Both of them live in a literate community; therefore, the ways they understand and produce language, or even reflect about language, possibly undergo an indirect literacy influence. Thus, the behaviour of the illiterate is not necessarily the exact portrait of the illiterate mind.

In spite of this difficulty in assessing the influence of literacy on language and, more generally, on cognitive development, the research on this topic may contribute to answer a fundamental question about the modifiability of our mind. Language is a product of our biological evolution; literacy does not result from a biological necessity, but, since it capitalises on language, it is a "biologically secondary ability" (cf. Geary, 1995), that is, an ability which develops and improves with a specific form of practice. How much and what aspects of our language ability result from learning rather than from biology? And how much and what aspects of our learning-dependent language ability can be established at any time in life?

Theoretical background

Studies on the influence of literacy on language development increased in number, if not emerged, after it has been recognised that "knowing language" and "knowing about language" are distinct abilities with different age of onset and different temporal course. Knowing language refers to the ability that is supposed to exist implicitly or tacitly in the language user, and which supports basic speech comprehension and production skills. Without it there would be no language at all. Knowing about language refers to the ability to consciously reflect on language. In this case the term knowledge is not entirely appropriate: since it may include wrong statements, one would better call it "beliefs about language". We shall refer hereafter to these two types of abilities as linguistic and metalinguistic abilities, respectively.

Some psycholinguists proposed that metalinguistic abilities are the distinctive characteristic of a late phase of language development (e.g., Karmiloff-Smith, 1979). The function of these abilities would be to allow a reorganisation of linguistic categories consistent with a more abstract and more controlled level of processing. However, today it is widely accepted that the ability to read and write plays a critical role in the emergence and development of at least some metalinguistic abilities. Literate communication involves a special effort to control and improve comprehensibility. The written message, because it is permanent, remains accessible for re-evaluation and formal analysis (e.g., Donaldson, 1976). More specifically, acquiring reading and writing may be hard or may even not be possible if the learner does not become aware of some aspects of the speech structure (e.g., Rozin, Poritsky & Sotsky, 1971; Savin, 1972). These ideas, formulated in the early seventies, are at the origin of a huge amount of empirical and theoretical work on the relations between literacy and metalinguistic abilities. More recently, it was suggested that literacy may affect the very processes involved in understanding speech (e.g., Morais & Kolinsky, 1995).

The distinction between linguistic and metalinguistic abilities is actually a distinction between levels of representation and processing: unconscious or unintentional, the former; conscious or intentional, the latter. To a large extent, but perhaps not entirely so, the linguistic abilities are biologically primary and the metalinguistic ones biologically secondary. The notion that linguistic and metalinguistic abilities correspond to different types of knowledge has been sometimes overlooked, even in the relatively recent literature. For instance, since even babies demonstrate consonant discrimination abilities, the fact that illiterate adults are unable to delete intentionally the initial phoneme of a short utterance (Morais, Cary, Alegria & Bertelson, 1979) was judged by some authors as puzzling (see Morais, 1991 a, for anecdotal data on this assimilation of levels of representation). More recently, Coppens, Parente and Lecours (1998) still found necessary to refer to the fact that illiterate adults are able to discriminate minimal pairs (cf. Adrian, Alegria & Morais, 1995; Scliar-Cabral, Morais, Nepomuceno & Kolinsky, 1997) but unable to manipulate phonemes intentionally as an "apparent contradiction", and explained that "This apparent contradiction disappears if one considers that phonological decoding is a perceptual process whereas metalinguistic skills are a postperceptual skill (Kolinsky et al., 1987) (p.185)".

In the review of the literature that is presented below, the reader will find first a description of the evidence that suggests an influence of literacy on the metalinguistic abilities, and in a second section on the linguistic abilities. It is within each of these sections that most of the main components of language, the lexical, the morphological, the syntactic, the semantic and the phonological systems will be considered. Finally, the effects of literacy on brain organisation will be briefly evoked.

As the reader will notice, interpretation of a particular task as involving critically either linguistic or metalinguistic processes is not always easy. When our own interpretation diverges from that of the authors mentioned, this will be acknowledged. Whatever the right interpretation, this suggests that more theoretical work is needed to better specify the present concepts.

CRITICAL REVIEW OF THE LITERATURE

The influence of literacy on the development of metalinguistic abilities

There is a debate on the temporal course of metalinguistic development. According to the "interaction hypothesis" (Clark, 1978; Marshall & Morton, 1978), children begin to develop metalinguistic abilities during language acquisition, and as a support to it, around or even before 2 years of age. Self-corrections are considered to be an example of such metalinguistic behaviour. According to the "autonomy hypothesis" (e.g. Hakes, 1980), metalinguistic abilities develop much later, from ages 5 to 8. Establishing a bridge between the two hypotheses, Gombert (1992) proposed to distinguish true metalinguistic knowledge, which would not arise until children are 5- or 6-year old, from "epilinguistic" knowledge, i.e. knowledge about language that can be used in a non-intentional way. To what extent metalinguistic knowledge can evolve from epilinguistic knowledge is unclear. Although some authors (e.g. Lundberg, 1978) have suggested that the late emergence of metalinguistic abilities is related to cognitive development, in particular to the "decentration" process, the current prevailing view is that the passage to the intentional, systematic and abstract metalinguistic representations was made necessary by a particular learning process, namely literacy acquisition.

Lexical metalinguistic abilities

Children might become aware of words as separate entities within sentences or clauses only after they had learned to represent each word as a group of characters separated by an empty space from the other words or groups of characters. Cary (1988; see also Morais, 1987) asked illiterate adults to repeat short sentences presented to them orally and to introduce pauses between words. Most of the time, the participants segmented the sentences into main syntactic constituents. For instance, the sentence "O carro está parado a porta" yielded the segmentation "0 carro/está parado/a porta" (The car/stands/in front of the door) in the majority of the participants. One might say that this segmentation simply resulted from misunderstanding of the term "word". However, in a further experiment, a fresh group of participants was presented with the same sentences, but only after having received a series of six examples for which the correct response had been provided. These examples had no effect on the score. The only difference was a somewhat greater tendency to segment into syllabic units (10 percent and 2 percent of the responses in the situation with and without examples, respectively). Thus, the main syntactic constituents provided the most apparent units with meaning, and, if discouraged from making this kind of segmentation, illiterates sometimes shifted to segmentation into the most apparent phonological units, i.e. the syllables. One of the effects of literacy on language analysis would be to disclose the word unit.

However, this issue should be re-examined. As a matter of fact, more recently, Karmiloff-Smith, Grant, Sims, Jones & Cuckle (1996), testing 4- and 5-year olds, found that these children were able to isolate the "last word" or the last bit" in a sentence that was spoken to them and interrupted at some point. The authors claimed, on the basis of these results, that metalinguistic awareness could be a component of language acquisition, not a mere product of literacy. However, one should remark that the 4-year-old children who were successful in this test were judged by their teachers as being ready for reading instruction. It is well known that the children considered to be ready for reading tend to be those who are acquainted with written texts and to whom stories are read at home, very often with a combination of pointing and emphasis possibly calling their attention on individual words. Thus, the successful prereaders of Karmiloff-Smith et al.'s study could be influenced in their analysis of spoken language by their indirect experience of literacy.

The lexicon includes synonyms, i.e. different word forms for the same or similar meanings. To examine knowledge of synonyms, Doherty and Perner (1998) used a task in which the child is shown a picture, for example of a rabbit, and asked to name it – let us suppose he/she called it as rabbit – then a hand puppet names the same item in one of three ways: again as "rabbit", using a synonym ("bunny") or using a wrong name ("elephant"). The child is informed that the puppet's task was to name the item correctly but using a different name than the one he/she had proposed before, and he/she is asked to say whether the puppet succeeded. The results showed that most of the 4 year-old children tested are successful in this task. Knowledge of synonyms would thus precede literacy onset.

Doherty and Perner (1998) interpreted these results as indicating the presence of metalinguistic awareness, since the children's behaviour was not spontaneous but produced intentionally. According to them, the competence required by their task is metalinguistic because it requires to understand "language as a formal system carrying meaning" (p. 302). To be metalinguistic, a particular behaviour should "require attention to both formal and semantic aspects of language" (p. 302). But, then, the whole set of abilities requiring one to make abstraction of meaning and attend to or manipulate phonological attributes would not be considered as metalinguistic. In our opinion, Doherty and Perner's notion of metalinguistic abilities is too restrictive. Besides, we are reluctant to accept their task as truly metalinguistic. The fact that the children know more than one word referring to the same meaning and can use one or the other when asked to do so does not imply that they understand language as a formal system. In a similar vein, from the fact that a child knows that different cats are all cats it does not follow that he realises that an animal has to possess a specific set of properties and not to possess others, whatever they actually are, in order to be a cat. Children are not theoreticians of semantic concepts, even if they use these concepts in communication or formal experimental settings.

Morphological and syntactic metalinguistic abilities

As regards metalinguistic abilities related to morphology, one must take into account that in some languages, for instance French, the spelling of words may include silent letters which convey morphological information: the final "-nt" in verbal forms or "-s" in nouns, to indicate the plural, or a final consonant in the masculine form of the noun (as in "petit", "sot") which is pronounced in the feminine form ("petite", "sotte"). One may thus hypothesise that experience of the written word forms contributes to the development of morphological awareness. The fact that it is only by the third grade that the French-speaking child begins to exploit these morphological cues (Mousty & Alegria, 1996) suggests that he needs a relatively large experience of spelling before he becomes aware of these morphological relations. However, the hypothesis of a metamorphological development independent of literacy cannot be excluded.

Studies on syntactic awareness suggest that, while some forms are present before learning to read (for example, the ability to judge ungrammatical sentences as odd or silly emerges around the age of 4 years, cf. de Villiers & de Villiers, 1972, and Smith & Tager-Flusberg, 1982), others could emerge or develop as a function of either literacy or schooling. One study carried out in India (Karanth, Kudva & Vijayan, 1995), in which the authors evaluated both the comprehension of syntactic structure and judgements of grammaticality in unschooled children, aged 6 to 11 years, indicates that these two abilities still develop with age or, more exactly, with exposure to language. A schooling effect was also observed when these children were compared to schooled children of the same age, but the schooling variable was probably confounded with socio-economic status. The same caveat must be given as regards the interpretation of the results obtained by the same group (Karanth, Ahuja, Nagaraj, Pandit & Shivashankar, 1991, cited by Karanth, 1998) in a comparison of literate and illiterate adults on the same kind of tests. Although the authors suggest that literacy per se is a variable affecting grammaticality judgements, one would certainly be more prone to accept this claim if control people of the same socio-economic background but alphabetised at adult age ("ex-illiterates") had been tested too and had obtained better scores than the illiterates. A strict interpretation of the findings of this group is difficult because the authors do not feel the necessity of distinguishing literacy and schooling, and do not control for socio-economic status. As a matter of fact, they take the superior performance of the school-going children over the unschooled ones as "suggesting that these skills are enhanced by the acquisition of literacy" (Karanth, 1998, p. 151).

A relationship between measures of grammatical skills and judgements, on the one hand, and reading performance, on the other hand, was found in several studies that examined children. However, as pointed out by Bryant (1995), who provided a critical review of the literature, and contrary to the case of metaphonological abilities (see A.4. below) for those skills there is no unambiguous evidence on the direction of causality.

Semantic metalinguistic abilities

The classical studies by Luria (1976) on illiterate unschooled populations in Central Asia suggest that these individuals do not make classifications based on semantic categories or attributes but, instead, on associative or functional properties. However, this behaviour can be attributed to either illiteracy or lack of schooling, or both. Experiments comparing illiterate to ex-illiterate people, i.e. people who learned to read and write outside the school setting, on how aware they are of the structure of their semantic system remain to be done.

One study examined to what extent judgements of typicality, a variable relevant to the internal organisation of categories in the semantic system, vary as a function of reading level. Bjorklund and Bernholtz (1986) asked 13 year-old good and poor readers to make typicality judgements on items from 12 categories (tools, birds, clothing, etc.). While the ratings of the good readers were relatively similar to those of adults, those of the poor readers were similar to the ratings of a much younger group of normal readers from the third grade. This was observed for all the categories. Thus, conscious knowledge of item typicality seems to be influenced by literacy level. Nevertheless, in that study the impact of literacy may presumably be attributed to differences between groups in terms of reading experience and thus to acquisition of information through reading activities.

Phonological metalinguistic abilities

The alphabet is a code that represents language roughly at the level of units called phonemes. In order to be able to read and write alphabetic material, it is highly advantageous, if not necessary, to acquire conscious knowledge both of the alphabetic principle, i.e. that letters stand for phonemes, and of the particular alphabetic code, i.e. which letters stand for which phonemes. It has indeed been shown that learning to read and write in the alphabetic system promotes the acquisition of conscious representations of phonemes as well as the development of the ability to analyse spoken language into phonemes. These latter capacities are usually called phonemic awareness and conscious or intentional phonemic segmentation ability, respectively.

Children studies have generally shown a dramatic increase of performance on tasks supposed to reflect phonemic awareness, from kindergarten to first-grade. In one of those studies (Zhurova, 1973), children were shown dolls with coloured jackets and were told, for instance, that "the boy with the green jacket is Gan, the boy with the white jacket is Whan", etc. Then, they were tested for the retention of names and questioned about dolls with other (pink, etc.) coloured jackets. The rule for new jackets was used successfully by 12%, 39% and 100% of the children in the 4 to 5, 5 to 6 (kindergarteners), and 6 to 7 (first-graders) years age groups, respectively. In another famous study (Liberman, Shankweiler, Fischer & Carter, 1974), children were asked to play a game in which segments (either syllables or phonemes) of a word spoken by the experimenter had to be indicated by the number of taps. The authors found that none of nursery school children (mean age: 4.10) could segment by phoneme (i.e. reach a criterion of 6 consecutive errorless trials) while 46% could segment by syllable. The percentage of children who were able to segment by phoneme increased up to 17% in kindergarteners (5.10 years), and especially in first-graders (6.11 years), who reached 70%.

As Shankweiler and Liberman (1976) pointed out, the dramatic progress in intentional phonemic segmentation between ages 5 and 6 "might result from the reading instruction that typically begins between ages five and six. Alternatively it might be a manifestation of cognitive growth not specifically dependent on training". Some children studies yielded results that support the instructional hypothesis. In Denmark, where children begin literacy instruction one year later than in other industrialised countries, the improvement in intentional phonemic segmentation also tends to occur one year later (Skjelfjord, 1976). Testing children differing by some months of age at the beginning of the school year compared with testing at the same age but at two different periods in the school year showed that amount of instruction, rather than chronological age, is relevant (Alegria & Morais, 1979). Finally, type of instruction provokes very important differences, with the phonic method leading to much faster acquisition of phonemic awareness than the whole-word method (Alegria, Pignot & Morais, 1982).

Clear-cut evidence could be obtained by comparing illiterate adults, who had never been in school and never learned to read or write, and ex-illiterate adults, i.e. people of comparable age and background who had attended literacy classes as adults. That study, already briefly mentioned, was run in Portugal by Morais et al. (1979). The task was either to add a prespecified consonant at the beginning of a spoken utterance or to delete the initial consonant. The illiterates performed as poorly as first-grade Belgian beginning readers (less than 20% correct responses), whereas ex-illiterates reached the level of second-graders (more than 70% correct) (children data from Morais, Cluytens & Alegria, 1984). Morais, Bertelson, Cary and Alegria (1986) replicated these results and showed moreover that illiterates' inability to analyse language is not general, since most of them performed well in a task involving the deletion of the initial syllable. Conscious access to syllables does not depend crucially on alphabetic literacy, although this form of literacy probably provides useful cues for conscious syllabification. What alphabetic literacy specifically promotes is awareness of phonemes.

Contrary to the basic linguistic abilities, which can only develop in childhood, the awareness of phonemes may be elicited by learning to read at adulthood. A phoneme deletion training experiment yielded a significant improvement in the performance of illiterate participants (Morais, Content, Bertelson, Cary & Kolinsky, 1988). But one might consider this result as trivial. The very existence of ex-illiterates, or, in other words, the fact that even middle-aged illiterates can learn to read and write, and the high level of performance they reach in phoneme manipulation tasks constitute together a clear demonstration that there is no critical period for the acquisition of phoneme awareness.

The literature on metaphonological abilities has often confounded the notions of phonemic awareness and phonological awareness. In order to make clear what are the specific contributions of alphabetic literacy to those abilities, it is necessary to first unpack the notion of phonological awareness.

Phonological awareness is required when, for instance, one has to decide which of two evoked names is longer, or whether or not two nonsense utterances are identical. These tasks imply intentional judgements on phonology rather than the mere activation of phonological representations. In the same vein, most people are aware of some phonological properties when they appreciate or use rhyme and other phonological similarities in poetry, slogans, and puns. Phonological awareness is thus the capacity to represent phonological properties consciously.

As such it is a general, not very useful, concept, unless one specifies the phonological properties which an individual is aware of.

In particular, one should distinguish between analytic and holistic forms of phonological awareness. The latter do not imply segmentation and may be present before the onset of alphabetic literacy.

Some of these holistic forms of phonological awareness are certainly necessary to language development, like for example the self-corrections exhibited by children in the course of language acquisition. They provide a testimony of awareness of incorrect pronunciation: the child most probably realises the difference between incorrect and correct pronunciations.

Another illustration of a holistic phonological awareness is given by the task consisting in comparing the phonological length of a pair of evoked object names. This task yielded high scores in some of the illiterate adults tested by Kolinsky, Cary and Morais (1987). Participants were silently presented with a pair of standardised drawings. On neutral trials, drawings represented objects of the same physical size, which names varied however in phonological length. Sixty percent of illiterates obtained scores of at least 75% correct responses. The incongruent trials, where the longer word denotes the smallest object, were intended to indicate whether phonological awareness in illiterate people can resist semantic interference. Among the subjects who might be credited with this capacity, 83% obtained lower scores in the incongruent than in the neutral trials, though always above chance level. It thus seems that most of the subjects, rather than simply falling in the semantic trap, experienced an attentional conflict between semantics and phonology.

Holistic phonological awareness may also afford the possibility to accomplish some speech sound classification or detection tasks. Cary (1988) tested illiterate adults in the classification of triads of CV or VC spoken syllables. When two of the items not only shared a vowel, but were also perceptually close to each other (like in the triad /pe, be, si/), they were classified together most of the time. The proportion of correct classifications largely fell, however, when vowel sharing conflicted with the perceptual similarity of another pair, like in the triad /se, be, pi/, in which /be/ and /pi/ are globally more similar to each other than /se/ and /be/. The large difference in performance observed between the two situations suggests that illiterates may use some form of holistic phonological awareness to appreciate phonological similarity.

Most of the phoneme detection situations have yielded low scores in illiterates (e.g., Morais et al., 1986). However, unpublished data obtained by Fiadeiro, Cary and Morais suggest that illiterates may perform quite well when placed in very easy detection conditions, namely when a phoneme target which remains constant through the testing has to be found among very short stimuli. Most probably, illiterates were not using phonemic representations in this situation. The detection of /p/ in /pi/ or /pa/ but not in /vi/ or /va/ may actually result from a phonological similarity judgement between the pronounced target /pə/ and each of these stimuli.

The abilities of rhyme appreciation and production have been largely examined in the effort to distinguish between phonological and phonemic awareness. Like most preliterate children (see, e.g., Maclean, Bryant & Bradley, 1987), most illiterates are able to appreciate rhyme, and some are even able to produce it spontaneously. Morais et al. (1986) used a rhyme detection task in which subjects listened to 5 objects names while being presented with drawings. The first, target name, rhymed with one of the other names. Forty-eight percent of the illiterates obtained at least 75% correct choices of the rhyming name. In Bertelson, De Gelder, Tfouni and Morais (1989), Brazilian illiterates were presented with examples of word pairs that either rhymed or not. Then, they had to judge whether or not new pairs rhymed, erroneous responses being corrected. Seventy five percent of the illiterates reached the criterion of 6 consecutive correct responses. Illiterates can thus appreciate rhyme. Since illiterates usually fail subsyllabic segmentation tests (Morais et al., 1979; 1986; Bertelson et al., 1989), it seems that rhyme can be appreciated on the basis of holistic phonological awareness. In the same vein, note that Chinese emigrants in the Netherlands, who performed much better in phoneme tasks if they did become acquainted with the alphabetic system than if they did not, obtained similar levels of performance on a rhyme task (de Gelder, Vroomen & Bertelson, 1993).

The idea that rhyming ability does not necessary imply phonemic awareness is clearly supported by the observations made on illiterate poets (Cary, Morais & Bertelson, 1989; Morais, 1991 b). Despite their capacity to produce rhyme in their poems, illiterate poets are unable to perform tasks that, like consonant deletion or reversal, require phonemic awareness. The study of these people may be very helpful to determine those metaphonological abilities that do not strictly depend on alphabetic literacy. Illiterate poets are not only superior to non-poets in rhyme production; they also show higher rhyming discrimination than the best illiterate non-poets, as it was the case in a classification task requiring to distinguish rhyme from assonance (e.g., /bulə, **gumə, lumə**/).

Illiterate poets were also superior in a classification task requiring conscious knowledge of alliteration (initial consonant sharing). However, like for rhyme, responses apparently based on alliteration may not result from a subsyllabic or even phonemic analysis, but from a very fine attentional capacity to phonological similarities or discrepancies between utterances. As mentioned before, illiterates' phonological sensitivity is powerful enough to allow them to discriminate words that differ in one single phoneme (Adrian et al., 1995; Scliar-Cabral, Morais, Nepomuceno & Kolinsky, 1997). However, in order to make intentional judgements about phonology, some voluntary form of attention to speech sounds is necessary. Most of the illiterates possess this capacity to some extent, as shown by their rhyming and classification performances. Their attentional capacity suffers, however, from severe limitations. As already mentioned, they become unable to attend to vowel sharing when a conflicting, perceptually closer pair, is also available (Cary, 1988; see also Scliar-Cabral et al., 1997). Moreover, as observed by Cary and Morais (unpublished data reported by Morais, 1991 a), illiterates are quite unable to appreciate similarity based on consonant sharing, even when no other conflicting response is available, as in the triad /**lar, lɛv**, fɔʃ/. By contrast, illiterate poets, who scored highly in those tests, have developed some of these capacities.

Illiterate poets also suffer, however, from some limitations in phonological awareness. For instance, like non-poets, they are unable to classify together two items sharing the final consonant, like in /sɔl, **mal**, lidə/. In a similar vein, FJC, the most studied illiterate poet (Cary & Morais, unpublished data; see Morais, 1994), did not perform above chance level in three out of four classification tests in which phonemic identity conflicted with greater similarity of another pair. He only succeeded in vocalic classification of CV triads. This cannot be attributed to a general enhanced attention to vowels, given that FJC failed vocalic classification of VC triads. Selective attention to vowels was thus only displayed in a rhyming context. This is puzzling, since it appears to support a tautology: rhyming ability is due to rhyming ability! One possible interpretation of illiterate poets' rhyming and classification abilities is that confrontation with rhyming patterns of a popular poetry has led them to elaborate a rhyming lexicon (and/or suffixes and respective derivational rules) which helps them to increase, at the same time, the discriminability power of their phonological awareness. So, while their phonological awareness remains rather holistic, searching in their rhyming lexicon for convenient analogies allows them to put /si/ and /pi/ together from among /**si, pi**, be/, and helps them to distinguish true rhyme from assonance or alliteration.

In any case, the whole pattern of illiterate poets' results shows that the kind of phonological awareness that can be reached in the absence of alphabetic learning presents important limitations. Phonological awareness in non-alphabetic people is holistic, probably syllabic, and does not include selective attention to constituent phonemes. Even if one could distinguish a priori this capacity of phonemic selective attention from the capacity to represent phonemes in isolation and manipulate them intentionally, the empirical evidence suggests that the main *tour de force* is the acquisition of phonemic attention. Once this is acquired, under the influence of alphabetic literacy, the elaboration of conscious representations of phonemes may follow rather easily.

The influence of literacy on the development of linguistic abilities

Lexical abilities

Lexical knowledge increases hugely during the first years of schooling, mostly as a consequence of literacy ability. It seems that conversation with adults and TV watching contribute much less to this increase than reading activities. According to Nagy, Anderson and Herman (1987), the reading activities would account for about half of the 3,000 new words that a schoolchild of normal reading ability acquires each year. Outside school, good readers spend much more time reading than poor readers (fifth-graders at the percentile 90 would read 200 more text than their mates at the percentile 10, cf. Anderson, Wilson & Fielding, 1988) and therefore their knowledge of the lexicon is in all likelihood much greater.

In picture naming, illiterate (unschooled) participants have consistently been found to be inferior to literate (schooled) ones (Lecours et al., 1987, Rosselli, Ardila & Rosas, 1990; Reis, Guerreiro & Castro-Caldas, 1994). Tests of word and pseudo-word repetition have also usually yielded a much lower performance in illiterate participants than in literate ones (Reis & Castro-Caldas, 1995; Castro-Caldas, Petersson, Reis, Stone-Elander & Ingvar, 1998; Morais & Mousty, 1992). However, for both sets of studies, the conclusion that literacy is specifically responsible for the observed group differences is once again unwarranted. For example, it is worth noting that in the Castro-Caldas et al.'s (1998) study, the literates and illiterates had been matched by pairs, each participant of a pair one being the sister of the other participant. But the illiterate sister had not attended school at all, while the literate sister had achieved normal schooling in childhood. Therefore, the sisters differed from each other not only in literacy but also in schooling and, possibly, in acquired socio-economic status.

The idea that the observed group differences may be attributed to schooling and socio-economic factors rather than to literacy per se was supported for word and pseudo-word repetition. As a matter of fact, an ex-illiterate group was also tested in the experiment, run in collaboration with L. Cary and R. Campbell, that was reported by Morais and Mousty (1992). The results did not show any difference in either word or pseudo-word repetition between the illiterates and the ex-illiterates.

Morphological and syntactic abilities

Possibly relevant information is already described in the "Metalinguistic" section. A precise distinction between metalinguistic and linguistic knowledge is hard making for these components.

In Rosselli et al.'s (1990) study, the illiterates obtained lower performance compared to literates in understanding verbal commands, particularly for long and syntactically complex sentences, as well as in dealing with spatial relationships expressed verbally. But it should be recalled that literacy in this study was once again confounded with schooling.

Semantic abilities

It seems that, in free recall tasks, illiterates can use category organisation of the items when the categories are explicitly indicated to them or simply suggested by having them sort the items into piles (Cole, Gay, Glick & Sharp, 1971; Scribner, 1974). This would not be possible if the illiterates had no pre-existent semantic organisation.

Studies on the development of memory have shown that the tendency to spontaneously group items, for instance in recall, on the basis of semantic categories increases with schooling (e.g., Kail & Nippold, 1984). However, as for metalinguistic judgements on semantic properties, there is, as far as we know, almost no work attempting to highlight the specific role of literacy in this kind of developmental effect.

Phonological abilities

The recognition of spoken language includes the unconscious, mandatory and automatic operation of perceptual mechanisms that are biologically determined. The development of these mechanisms presumably requires critical experiences that take place in the usual conditions of early childhood. But recognition includes also processes which, while possibly being unconscious, mandatory and automatic, are acquired under the influence of explicit instruction and training. For instance, recognition of written words in the alphabetic system by beginning readers is based, at least partially, on a phonological assembling mechanism that is usually acquired through both alphabetic explicit instruction and progressive phonemic awareness. Phonological assembling is at the beginning an effortful, conscious activity, but later on it becomes unconscious: readers are not aware of using it in pseudo-word reading. There is thus no reason to discard a priori the idea that phonemic awareness may be at the origin of processes that intervene in the recognition of spoken words, or at least that it may influence the operation of some recognition processes. These processes may then become automatised, effortless, and unconscious.

The number of experimental studies of spoken word recognition in young preliterate children has greatly increased in the last years. The processes used by preliterates seem to be somewhat less directional and less oriented to the extraction of segmental information than the processes used by older, literate people. For example, adults generally display a higher rate of mispronunciation detection of the initial syllable than of the following ones. This effect is not observed in children (Cole & Perfetti, 1980). In a similar vein, in adults more than in children, words where some phonemes have been degraded or suppressed are judged less identifiable when those phonemes are initial than when they are not (Walley, 1988).

Studdert-Kennedy (1987) sustains that the rapid lexical growing that occurs around three years of age is contemporaneous with a passage from relatively holistic lexical representations to representations structured in terms of phonemes. This may be necessary, given the rapid increase of the proportion of words with many neighbours (Charles-Luce & Luce, 1990). The acquisition of alphabetic literacy may accelerate this developmental course, since literacy contributes to expanding the lexicon and therefore puts an additional pressure on the need for phonemically structured representations. A related question is whether alphabetic literacy can have similar effects on the processes of spoken word recognition, i.e., whether alphabetic people use more phonemically-based processes than non-alphabetic people. However, given the importance in speech recognition of mechanisms that are constrained both by universal properties of the speech production device and by very early linguistic experience, a large part of processing should be unaffected by alphabetic literacy. This part should, in principle, be the most peripheral and include at least the extraction of phonetic information from the speech input.

Below, we present some empirical evidence of both alphabetic literacy-independent and -dependent processes.

LITERACY-INDEPENDENT PROCESSES: AUTOMATIC EXTRACTION OF PHONETIC AND PHONOLOGICAL INFORMATION

Four types of phenomena have been investigated in illiterate Portuguese adults and compared to controls.

Categorical perception

Identification responses to sets of stimuli spanning the acoustic continuum that links two opposite values of a phonetic feature do not change in a smooth but rather abrupt manner (Liberman, Cooper, Shankweiler & Studdert-Kennedy, 1967). Castro and Morais (unpublished data; see Morais & Mousty, 1992) ran an experiment of word identification in which words differed in voicing (/balʌ/-/palʌ/ and /kɔlʌ/-/gɔlʌ/). Identification responses showed the usual curves of categorical perception, and there was no difference on the average between literates and illiterates.

McGurk effect

The visual information about the movements of the speaker's mouth can affect the perception of auditory information: adult (literate) listeners presented with a slightly ambiguous acoustic /ba/ and looking at a face that articulates /da/ silently may have the impression of hearing /da/ or even /bda/ (McGurk & McDonald, 1976). Morais, De Gelder and Verhaeghe (unpublished data; cf. Morais & Mousty, 1992) presented the auditory continuum /ba-da/ either in isolation, or simultaneously with the speaker's face on a video screen. In this last case, the two types of sensory information were either congruent or incongruent. In the pure auditory situation, there was no difference between literates and illiterates as far as the slope of the identification curve is concerned. This result converges with the previous one to indicate that phonetic categorisation, in terms of either place of articulation or voicing, is literacy-independent. In the auditory-visual situation, the literates' results confirmed once again the optical influence. Moreover, the shift in the identification curve was roughly the same in illiterates as in literates. The fact that there is no influence of literacy on the McGurk effect is consistent with the claim that the auditory-visual integration of phonetic information is carried out by a modular, biologically-wired device (Liberman & Mattingly, 1985).

Feature blending

The extraction of phonetic features may be inferred from the occurrence of some perceptual errors. For instance, when people receive the dichotic pair /ba-ta/ and erroneously recognise /pa-da/ above chance, one may interpret this error as the combination of the place of articulation value of the stimulus delivered to one ear with the voicing value of the stimulus delivered to the other ear (Day, 1968; Cutting, 1976). Morais, Castro, Scliar-Cabral, Kolinsky and Content (1987) examined this effect using dichotic presentations of CVCV Portuguese words in which the initial C was always a stop. In one third of the trials the initial consonants of the dichotic pair differed in both place of articulation and voicing. The task was to recognise the word presented in one, previously specified, ear. A significant proportion of phonetic feature blending was observed, which did not differ significantly between literates, semiliterates (with normal but short schooling in childhood) and illiterates. Thus, alphabetic literacy has no effect at the level where phonetic feature blending take place.

Migration errors

Following the logic of feature blending, we took advantage of the dichotic listening technique to elicit word illusions which should result from the erroneous combination of either phonetic features or larger parts of information, like phonemes or syllables (see Kolinsky, 1992; Kolinsky, Morais and Cluytens, 1995; Kolinsky & Morais, 1996). If such speech attributes can be wrongly combined, they must have been separately registered as independent units at some processing stage. In our situation, since the participant is asked either to detect a word target previously specified or to identify the presented stimulus, his/her attention is not called upon any word constituent. This experimental situation can thus be used for testing of illiterate as well as literate people.

Recent (unpublished) data that we have obtained on Portuguese-speaking literates (either European or Brazilian) indicate that the initial consonant of CVCV utterances is the attribute that "migrates" the most, compared to migrations of syllable and either voicing or place of articulation of the initial consonant (Kolinsky & Morais, 1992). Subsequent testing of illiterates, again from both Portugal and Brazil, yielded the same pattern of results (Kolinsky, Paiva, Cluytens & Morais, unpublished). This means that, at least for Portuguese, consonants have psychological reality at the perceptual level of processing, and that the role of consonants in speech perception can be demonstrated in a population that is unable to represent them consciously. The very same population which allowed us to show that conscious representations of phonemes are prompted by the learning of alphabetic literacy provides also a clear suggestion that unconscious perceptual representations of phonemes can develop prior to the onset of literacy. The same conclusion may be drawn from studies on young preliterate Portuguese children (Castro, Vicente, Morais, Kolinsky & Cluytens, 1995).

Alphabetic literacy effects

Alphabetic literacy affected other levels of processing in the task used by Morais et al. (1987).

Segmental versus global errors

Since all the phonemes of the dichotic words used in a trial were different, with the exception of the last vowel, it was possible to calculate the proportion of errors on one segment only, for instance on the initial consonant (segmental errors), and the proportion of errors on at least both segments of a syllable (global errors). The results showed that the proportion of segmental errors was higher in literates than in illiterates, whereas the proportion of global errors showed the opposite trend. This effect remained significant even when subgroups of same overall performance were compared. It was also observed in a further experiment (Castro & Morais, unpublished data) which used single-word but noisy presentations. This effect may reflect the availability in literates, who are aware of phonemes, of an attentional mechanism focusing on the phonemic structure of speech.

Models of spoken language processing generally admit that listeners may focus their attention on the level of information that is more appropriate to the task. The Morais et al.'s (1987) results suggest a more specific claim, namely that listeners can focus their attention on phonemic constituents even when they have to recognise whole words. This hypothetical attentional mechanism might be automatic or, instead, strategic and optional. In order to gather evidence on this issue, Castro and Morais (unpublished data; cf. Morais, Castro & Kolinsky, 1991) have compared two groups of literates tested in the noisy situation. The control group was simply required to recognise stimuli. Subjects of the experimental group were, in addition, informed about word structure and invited to pay attention to individual phonemes as a mean of improving performance. Despite the fact that the two groups obtained the same mean performance, segmental errors were proportionally more frequent in the experimental group. Thus, attention on the phonemic constituents of words is not automatic but, instead, constitutes a strategy.

Phonological fusions

Phonemic attention in spoken word recognition is presumably a consequence of phonemic awareness. The alphabetic literacy effect which we will now describe would stem, rather, from orthographic knowledge. Orthographic influences on metaphonology have been observed on rhyme judgements (Seidenberg & Tanenhaus, 1979) and phonemic detection (Taft & Hambly, 1985). In the present case, it takes place during lexical recognition and affects the occurrence of errors called phonological fusion. These errors are observed in dichotic listening when, for example, the stimuli "banket" and "lanket" yield the perception of "blanket"; they are barely affected by acoustic variables but largely by linguistic factors like the lexical status of illusory outputs (Cutting, 1975). Castro and Morais (unpublished data; see Morais et al., 1991) replicated this phenomenon with literate and illiterate Portuguese, using both pairs of words whose fusion would be consistent with orthography (e.g., "cara-lara" yielding the word "clara") and pairs whose fusion would not be consistent with orthography (e.g., "liz-fiz" yielding the word "feliz", which is written with "e" but is pronounced /fliʃ/). In the consistent case, the illusion was observed as frequently in literates as in illiterates. In the inconsistent case, while illiterates displayed the same illusory rate as in the consistent case, literates' orthographic knowledge inhibits the occurrence of phonological fusion, which they experienced at a much lower rate. This suggests that upper levels of processing in lexical access are permeable to orthographic representations.

To sum up, it appears that alphabetic literacy does not affect phonetic processing, but may have an effect on phonemic processing, either by contributing to a phonemic attentional strategy, or by allowing orthographic knowledge to influence the integration of phonemic sequences.

Literacy effects on brain organisation

Quite understandably, the knowledge of written words has to be represented in the brain. It was found, indeed, that an internal region of the left hemisphere is selectively activated by the presentation of sequences of letters that obey the phonotactic rules of the language, but not by the presentation of random sequences of letters (Petersen, Fox, Snyder & Raichle, 1990).

Several authors considered the hypothesis that illiterates display less left-hemisphere specialisation for language than literates. In spite of some discrepant results, it seems clear today that this hypothesis is wrong. The number of cases with aphasic symptoms due to left hemisphere lesions is similar in literate and illiterate subjects (Damasio, Castro-Caldas, Grosso & Ferro, 1976). Moreover, in the dichotic listening situation, when one calculates an index of laterality that takes differences in overall performance into account, the right-ear superiority for verbal material is similar in literates and illiterates (Castro & Morais, 1987).

More recently, the impressive PET-scan study carried out by Castro-Caldas et al. (1998) showed that, while there is no brain activation difference between literates and illiterates during word repetition, illiterates do not activate the same neural structures as literates during pseudo-word repetition. One can speculate that, when the phonological sequences cannot be found in the lexicon, the literates use for the perception of these sequences a phonological mechanism that capitalises in some way on the knowledge of the grapho-phonological correspondences. However, given that ex-illiterates are not better than illiterates on pseudo-word repetition (cf. Morais & Mousty, 1992), it seems that only a great experience with, and mastery of, the grapho-phonological correspondences, typical of schooled people, can support the development of such a mechanism.

DISCUSSION

The critical review of the literature presented above might leave the reader with the feeling that not much is known about the presence or absence of literacy effects on the development of linguistic and metalinguistic abilities. That feeling is justified as far as the lexical, morphological, syntactic and semantic components of language are considered. The situation is different as regards the phonological and metaphonological abilities. We believe that this situation is not mainly due to a greater traceability of the latter component. It is probably due, instead, to the fact that work on phonological and particularly phoneme awareness is part of a very important and highly productive field of research concerned with reading and writing acquisition and with the difficulties encountered by children in this acquisition.

Literacy is only one of the ways by which learning affects language development. Another, strongly related factor, is schooling. Most of the time, both factors are indistinguishable. But one has to admit that schooling incorporates many other experiences besides literacy. Moreover, it is possible to find unschooled literate people. Given the obligation for children of attending school in most countries, these people are actually ex-illiterates. Ex-illiterates provide us with a way of assessing the specific effects of literacy on cognitive and language development, thus controlling for schooling and, with some additional caution, for socio-economic status. A further possibility is to compare literate people with the same degree of schooling but who learned to read and write in different literacy systems. Unfortunately, not many studies have incorporated any of these two kinds of comparisons. We have seen that our group mainly used the

618   *José Morais & Régine Kolinsky*

comparison between illiterates and ex-illiterates. As regards the second approach, it has also been seldom used: Read, Zhang, Nie and Ding's (1986) study and de Gelder et al.'s (1993) study, both comparing alphabetised to non-alphabetised but literate Chinese readers, are exceptions among a few others. Thus most of the evidence available is inconclusive. A further methodological difficulty arises, as we have seen and will illustrate again in this section, from indirect literacy effects.

Whatever the difficulties, we should persist studying literacy effects. Literacy represents, for language, the greatest accomplishment of what can be called its secondary or derived abilities. While other primary biological abilities also gave rise to complex secondary functional systems with representational productivity (as it is the case for the musical and mathematical languages), literacy is probably the most widely used and the more important of these systems in our every-day life. For these reasons, it is certainly warranted to study literacy indeed, but also to attempt to specify how language is modified by literacy. To examine literacy effects should not lead to pay less attention to schooling effects, since both contribute to the formation, on the ground of our biopsychological capacities, of the so-called educated mind. The point is that the effects of each of these two variables should be disentangled from the other. The main recommendation that emerges from the state of the art in the literacy/schooling domain is that future research should cease to confound them. We disagree with Coppens et al.'s (1998) belief that "literacy is virtually impossible to separate from schooling" (p. 184), and above we adduced reasons to remain optimistic. The analytic challenge is the proper of all science.

Before concluding, we feel the necessity of alerting those who, from the academic world, have little if any acquaintance with the illiterates to the risk of an underestimation of the cognitive and linguistic functioning of these people. It happened several times that, presenting our findings on the illiterates' inability in the phoneme awareness tasks, we were gently reminded that perhaps our subjects had some general cognitive debility. Since our questioners were scientists, we eventually concluded that they were rightly asking for relevant data and therefore we included various IQ tests in the following studies. According to their performance on these tests, the illiterates were indeed cognitively deficient, but so were the ex-illiterates, too. We have now an answer. We could not demonstrate that illiterates are intelligent, but their putative low intelligence could not explain anyway their lack of phoneme awareness. Nor can the putative low intelligence of ex-illiterates explain why they were able to learn to read and write late in their life, as well as to develop phoneme awareness.

Kleiman (1998) quotes the following editorial from an important Brazilian newspaper: "The illiterate understands poorly what he hears and answers in a very imperfect way to the messages so received. The illiterate needs even more applied attention to what he sees". To counter this kind of portrait of the illiterate, Kleiman reports on work from her group analysing the oral discourse and more particularly the dictation of a letter by an illiterate syndicate leader to his secretary. Everything, the structure of the argument, the grammar and the lexis of this letter he could not write himself were "practically faultless" (p. 213). This is not only a clear example of indirect literacy influence. It is also a demonstration of intelligence and learning capacity.

REFERENCES

Adrian, J. A., Alegria, J., & Morais, J. (1995). Metaphonological abilities of Spanish illiterate adults. *International Journal of Psychology, 30*, 329-353.

Alegria, J., & Morais, J. (1979). Le développement de l'habileté d'analyse phonétique consciente de Ia parole et l'apprentissage de Ia lecture. (The development of the ability of conscious phonetic analysis of speech, and learning to read.) *Archives de Psychologie, 183*, 251-270.

Alegria, J., Pignot, E., & Morais, J. (1982). Phonetic analysis of speech and memory codes in beginning readers. *Memory and Cognition, 10*, 451-456.

Anderson, R. C., Wilson, P. T., & Fielding, L. G. (1988). Growth in reading and how children spend their time outside school. *Reading Research Quarterly, 23*, 285-303.

Bertelson, P., de Gelder, B., Tfouni, L. V., & Morais, J. (1989). Metaphonological abilities of adult illiterates: New evidence of heterogeneity. *European Journal of Cognitive Psychology, 1*, 239-250.

Bjorklund, D. F., & Bernholtz, J. E. (1986). The role of knowledge base in the memory performance of good and poor readers. *Journal of Experimental Child Psychology, 41*, 367-393.

Bryant, P. (1995). Phonological and grammatical skills in learning to read. In B. de Gelder & J. Morais (Eds.), *Speech and Reading. A Comparative Approach* (pp. 249-264). London: Erlbaum, Taylor & Francis.

Cary, L. (1988). A análise explícita das unidades da fala nos adultos não alfabetizados. (The explicit analysis of the speech units in non-alphabetised adults.) Unpublished Doctoral dissertation, University of Lisbon.

Castro, S. L., & Morais, J. (1987). Ear differences in illiterates. *Neuropsychologia, 25*, 409-417.

Castro, S.- L., Vicente, S., Morais, J., Kolinsky, R., & Cluytens, M. (1995). Segmental representation of Portuguese in 5- and 6- year olds: Evidence from dichotic listening. In I. Hub Faria & J. Freitas (Eds.) *Studies on the acquisition of Portuguese. Proceedings of the First Lisbon Meeting on Child Language* (pp. 1-16). Lisbon: Colibri.

Castro-Caldas, A., Petersson, K. M., Reis, A., Stone-Elander, S., & Ingvar, M. (1998). The illiterate brain. Learning to read and write during childhood influences the functional organization of the adult brain. *Brain, 121*, 1053-1063.

Charles-Luce, J., & Luce, P. A. (1990). Similarity neighbourhoods of words in young children's lexicons. *Journal of Child Language, 17*, 205-215.

Clark, E. V. (1978). Awareness of language: Some evidence from what children say and do. In A. Sinclair, R. J. Jarvella & W. J.M. Levelt (Eds.), *The child's conception of language* (pp. 17-44). Berlin: Springer-Verlag.

Cole, M., Gay, J., Glick, J. A., & Sharp, D. W. (1971). *The cultural context of learning and thinking*. New York: Basic Books.

Cole, R. A., & Perfetti, C. A. (1980). Listening for mispronunciations in a children's story: The use of context by children and adults. *Journal of Verbal learning and Verbal Behavior, 19*, 297-315.

Coppens, P., Parente, M. A. M. P., & Lecours, A. R. (1998). Aphasia in illiterate individuals. In P. Coppens, Y. Lebrun & A. Basso (Eds.), *Aphasia in atypical populations* (pp. 175-202). Mahwah, NJ: Lawrence Erlbaum.

Cutting, J. E. (1975). Aspects of phonological fusion. Journal of Experimental Psychology: Human Perception and Performance, 1, 105-120.

Cutting, J. E. (1976). Auditory and linguistic processes in speech perception: Inferences from six fusions in dichotic listening. *Psychological Review, 83*, 114-140.

Damasio, A. R., Castro-Caldas, A., Grosso, J. T., & Ferro, J. M. (1976). Brain specialisation for language does not depend on literacy. *Archives of Neurology, 33*, 300-301.

Day, R. S. (1968). Fusion in dichótic listening. *Dissertation Abstracts International, 29*, 2649B (University Microfilms No. 69-211).

de Gelder, B., Vroomen, J., & Bertelson, P. (1993). The effects of alphabetic-reading competence on language representation in bilingual Chinese subjects. *Psychological Research, 55*, 315-321.

de Villiers, P. A., & de Villiers, J. G. (1972). Early judgements of semantic and syntactic acceptability by children. *Journal of Psycholinguistic Research, 1*, 229-310.

Doherty, M., & Perner, J. (1998). Metalinguistic awareness and theory of mind: Just two words for the same thing? *Cognitive Development, 13*, 279- 305.

Donaldson, M. (1976). Development of conceptualization. In V. Hamilton & M. D. Vernon (Eds.), *The development of cognitive processes* (pp. 277-303). London: Academic Press.

Geary, D. C. (1995). Reflections of evolution and culture in children's cognition: Implications for mathematical development and instruction. *American Psychologist, 50*, 24-37.

Gombert, J. E. (1992). *Metalinguistic development*. London: HarvesterWheatsheaf.

Hakes, D. T. (1980). The development of metalinguistic abilities in children. New York: Springer-Verlag.

KaiI, R., & Nippold, M. A. (1984). Unconstrained retrieval from semantic memory. *Child Development, 55*, 944-951.

Karanth, P. (1998). Literacy and language processes — Orthographical and structural effects. In M. K. de Oliveira & J. Vaalsiner (Eds.), *Literacy in Human Development* (pp. 145-160). Stamford, Conn.: Ablex.

Karanth, P., Kudva, A., & Vijayan, A. (1995). Literacy and linguistic awareness. In B. de Gelder & J. Morais (Eds.), *Speech and Reading. A Comparative Approach* (pp.303-316). London: Erlbaum, Taylor & Francis.

Karmiloff-Smith, A. (1979). Language development after 5 years. In P. Fletcher & M. Garman (Eds.), *Language acquisition* (pp. 307-323). Cambridge: Cambridge University Press.

Karmiloff-Smith, A., Grant, J., Sims, K., Jones, M. C., & Cuckle, P. (1996). Rethinking metalinguistic awareness: representing and accessing knowledge about what counts as a word. *Cognition, 58*, 197-219.

Kleiman, A. B. (1998). Schooling, literacy, and social change: Elements for a critical approach to the study of literacy. In M. K. de Oliveira & J. Vaalsiner (Eds.), *Literacy in Human Development* (pp. 183-225). Stanford, Conn.: Ablex.

Kolinsky, R. (1992). Conjunctions errors as a tool for the study of perceptual processes. In: J. Alegria, D. Holender, J. Junça de Morais & M. Radeau (Eds.), *Analytic approaches to Human Cognition* (pp. 133-149). Amsterdam: North-Holland.

Kolinsky, R., & Morais, J. (1996). Migrations in speech recognition, *Language and Cognitive Processes* (special issue, A Guide to Spoken Word Recognition Paradigms), *11*, 611-619.

Kolinsky, R., Cary, L., & Morais, J. (1987). Awareness of words as phonological entities: The role of literacy. *Applied Psycholinguistics, 8*, 223-232.

Kolinsky, R., Morais, J., & Cluytens, M. (1995). Intermediate representations in spoken word recognition: Evidence from word illusions. *Journal of Memory and Language, 34*, 19-40.

Lecours, A. R., Mehler, J., Parente, M . A., Caldeira, A., Cary, L., Castro, M. J.,

Dehaut, F., Delgado, R., Gurd, J., Karmann, D. F., Jakubovitz, R., Osorio, Z., Cabral, L. S., & Junqueira, A. M. S. (1987). Illiteracy and brain damage: 1. Aphasia testing in culturally contrasted populations (control subjects). *Neuropsychologia, 25*, 231-245.

Liberman, A. M., Cooper, F. S., Shankweiler, D., & Studdert-Kennedy, M. (1967). Perception of the speech code. *Psychological Review, 74*, 431-461.

Liberman, A. M., & Mattingly, I. G. (1985). The motor theory of speech perception revised. *Cognition, 21*, 1-36.

Liberman, l. Y., Shankweiler, D., Fisher, M. F., & Carter, B. (1974). Explicit syllable and phoneme segmentation in the young child. *Journal of Experimental Child Psychology, 18*, 201-212.

Lundberg, I. (1978). Aspects of linguistic awareness related to reading. In A. Sinclair, R. J. Jarvella & W. J. M. Levelt (Eds.), *The child's conception of language* (pp. 83-96). Berlin: Springer-Verlag.

Luria, A. R. (1976). *Cognitive Development. Its Cultural and Social Foundations*. Cambridge, MA: Harvard University Press.

Maclean, M., Bryant, P., & Bradley, L. (1987). Rhymes, nursery rhymes, and reading in early childhood. *Merrill-Palmer Quarterly, 33*, 255-281.

Marshall, J. C., & Morton, J. (1978). On the mechanisms of EMMA. In A. Sinclair, R. J. Jarvella & W. J. M. Levelt (Eds.), *The child's conception of language* (pp. 225-239). Berlin: Springer-Verlag.

McGurk, H., & McDonald, J. (1976). Hearing lips and seeing voices. *Nature, 264*, 746-748.

Morais, J . (1987). Segmental analysis of speech and its relation to reading ability. *Annals of Dyslexia, XXXVII*, 126-141.

Morais, J. (1991 a). Phonological awareness: A bridge between language and literacy. In D. J. Sawyer & B. J. Fox (Eds.), *Phonological awareness in reading. The evolution of current perspectives* (pp.31-71*)*. New York: Springer.

Morais, J. (1991 b). Constraints on the development of phonemic awareness. In S. A. Brady & D. P. Shankweiler (Eds.), *Phonological Processes in Literacy. A Tribute to Isabelle Y. Liberman* (pp. 5-27). Hillsdale, NJ: Lawrence Erlbaum.

Morais, J. (1994). *L'Art de Lire. (The Art of Reading.)* Paris: Editions Odile Jacob.

Morais, J., Bertelson, P., Cary, L., & Alegria, J. (1986). Literacy training and speech segmentation. *Cognition, 24*, 45-64.

Morais, J., Cary, L., Alegria, J., & Bertelson, P. (1979). Does awareness of speech as a sequence of phones arise spontaneously? *Cognition, 7*, 323-331.

Morais, J., Castro, S. L., & Kolinsky, R. (1991). La reconnaissance des mots chez les illettrés. (Word recognition in illiterates.) In R. Kolinsky, J. Morais & J. Segui (Eds.), *La reconnaissance des mots dans les différentes modalités sensorielles: Etudes de psycholinguistique cognitive (Word recognition in the different sensory modalities: Studies in cognitive psycholinguistics.)* (pp. 59-80). Paris: Presses Universitaires de France.

Morais, J., Castro, S. L., Scliar-Cabral, L., Kolinsky, R., & Content, A. (1987). The effects of literacy on the recognition of dichotic words. *Quarterly Journal of Experimental Psychology, 39A*, 451-465.

Morais, J., Cluytens, M., & Alegria, J. (1984). Segmentation abilities of dyslexics and normal readers. *Perceptual and Motor Skills, 58*, 221-222.

Morais, J., Content, A., Bertelson, P., Cary, L., & Kolinsky, R. (1988). Is there a critical period for the acquisition of segmental analysis? *Cognitive Neuropsychology, 5*, 347-352.

Morais, J., & Kolinsky, R. (1995). The consequences of phonemic awareness. In B. de Gelder & J. Morais (Eds.), *Speech and Reading. A Comparative Approach* (pp.317-337). London: Erlbaum, Taylor & Francis.

Morais, J., & Mousty, P. (1992). The causes of phonemic awareness. In J. Alegria, D. Holender, J. Junça de Morais & M. Radeau (Eds.), *Analytic Approaches to Human Cognition* (pp. 193-211). Amsterdam: Elsevier.

Mousty, P., & Alegria, J. (1999). L'acquisition de l'orthographe: Données comparatives entre enfants normo-lecteurs et dyslexiques. (The acquisition of spelling: Comparative data of normal readers and dyslexic children.) *Revue Française de Psychologie, 126*, 7-21.

Nagy, W. E., Anderson, R. C., & Herman, P. A. (1987). Learning word meanings from context during normal reading. *American Education Research Journal, 24*, 237-270.

Pinker, S. (1994). *The language instinct.* New York: Morrow.

Read, C., Zhang, Y., Nie, H., & Ding, B. (1986). The ability to manipulate speech sounds depends on knowing alphabetic writing. *Cognition, 24*, 31-44.

Reis, A., & Castro-Caldas, A. (1997). Illiteracy: A bias for cognitive development. *Journal of the International Neuropsychological Society, 3*, 444-450.

Reis, A., Guerreiro, M., & Castro-Caldas, A. (1994). Influence of educational level of non-brain damaged subjects on visual naming capacities. *Journal of Clinical and Experimental Neuropsychology, 16*, 939-942.

Rosselli, M., Ardila, A., & Rosas, P. (1990). Neuropsychological assessment in illiterates: Language and praxic abilities. *Brain and Cognition, 12*, 281-296.

Rozin, P., Poritsky, S., & Sotsky, R. (1971). American children with reading problems can easily learn to read English represented by Chinese characters. *Science, 171*, 1264-1267.

Savin, H. B. (1972). What the child knows about speech when he starts to learn to read. In J. F. Kavanagh & I. G. Matting It (Eds.), *Language by ear and by eye* (pp.319-326). Cambridge, MA: MIT Press.

Scliar-Cabral, L., Morais, J., Nepomuceno, L., & Kolinsky, R. (1997). The awareness of phonemes: So close-so far away. *International Journal of Psycholinguistics, 13*, 211-240.

Scribner, S. (1974). Developmental aspects of categorized recall in a West African society. *Cognitive Psychology, 6*, 475-494.

Seidenberg, M. S., & Tanenhaus, M. K. (1979). Orthographic effects on rhyme monitoring. *Journal of Experimental Psychology: Human Learning and Memory, 5*, 546-554.

Shankweiler, D., & Liberman, I. Y. (1976). Exploring the relations between reading and speech. In R. M. Knights & D. J. Bakker (Eds.), *Neuropsychology of learning disorders: Theoretical approaches* (pp. 42-83). Baltimore: University Park Press.

Skjelfjord, V. J. (1976). Teaching children to segment spoken words as an aid in learning to read. *Journal of Learning Disabilities, 9*, 297-306.

Smith, C. L., & Tager-Flusberg, H. (1982). Metalinguistic awareness and language development. *Journal of Experimental Child Psychology, 34*, 449-468.

Studdert-Kennedy, M. (1987). The phoneme as a perceptuomotor structure. *Haskins Laboratories: Status Report on Speech Research*, SR-91, 45-57.

Taft, M., & Hambly, G. (1985). The influence of orthography on phonological representations in the lexicon. *Journal of Memory and Language, 24*, 320-335.

Tulviste, P. (1991). Cultural-historical development of verbal thinking: A psychological study. Commack, NY: Nova.

UNESCO (1970). Functional literacy: Why and how. Paris: UNESCO.

Vygotsky, L. S. (1978). *Mind in Society*. Cambridge, MA: Harvard University Press.

Walley, A. C. (1988). Spoken word recognition by young children and adults. *Cognitive Development, 3*, 137-165.

Zhurova, L. Y. (1973). The development of analysis of words into their sounds by preschool children. In C. A. Ferguson & D. I. Slobin (Eds.), *Studies of child language development* (pp. 141-154). New York: Holt, Rinehart & Winston.

FURTHER READINGS

Egan, K. (1997). *The Educated Mind.* Chicago: Chicago University Press.

Olson, D. R. (1994). *The World on Paper.* Cambridge, UK: Cambridge University Press.

Scribner, S., & Cole, M. (1981). *The Psychology of Literacy.* Cambridge, MA: Harvard University Press.

De Gelder, B., & Morais, J. (Eds.) (1995). *Speech and Reading. A Comparative Approach.* London: Erlbaum, Taylor & Francis.

De Oliveira, M. K., & Valsiner, J. (Eds.) (1998). *Literacy in Human Development.* Stamford, Conn.: Ablex.

E. Looking Across Languages

Introduction

TEREZINHA NUNES

This introduction to the section Looking across Languages seeks to identify different reasons for looking across languages to understand literacy development. Each chapter focuses on a different reason; they are discussed in turn.

The first reason to look across languages relates to how successful one can be in understanding a phenomenon if it cannot be compared to other contrasting cases. It is now widely recognised both in the study of cognitive development in general and also in the study of language development in particular that general theories cannot be developed without comparisons across cultures and across languages. Theories that aim at describing and explaining the processes involved in literacy acquisition in a general way must be tested across languages. Looking across languages can sharpen our awareness of classes of phenomena that we might not have considered if we only looked at our own language, just as looking across cultures allows us to treat what seems "natural" to us in our own environment as a product of culture.

In the study of literacy development, there is a need to consider both the nature of the oral language and the nature of the script. As Defior points out in the first chapter in this section, languages vary in the complexity of their oral structure. English, for example, has many more vowels than Spanish for a variety of reasons. One reason is that English includes a distinction between vowels articulated in the back or the front of the mouth: compare the pronunciation of "bad" and "bed" or "live" and "leave" to sense this distinction. Spanish and Portuguese, in contrast, do not include a distinction between front and back vowels. This difference between the oral languages requires of English speaking children a sensitivity to differences in vowel sounds which is not required of Spanish or Portuguese speaking children, whose languages include fewer distinctive features and thus fewer different vowels.

In spite of this difference between the number of vowels in oral English and Spanish, the number of letters used to represent vowel sounds in the two languages is the same. The consequence of trying to use a small number of vowels to represent a large number of vocalic sounds is that grapheme-phoneme correspondence rules in English must be more complicated and have to involve what is termed "hierarchical rules". The vowel sounds in words like "hat", "hate" and "dark" is quite different; this difference is marked by the letter E in the split diagraph A-E in "hate" and the letter R in "dark". Children learning to read

T. Nunes, P. Bryant (eds.), Handbook of Children's Literacy, 625–629.

English at first will use simply the letter A to represent all these three sounds, and only later will later master the complexity of these hierarchical rules. Languages that require fewer hierarchical rules in orthography are often termed *transparent*. Written Spanish is a much more transparent language than English.

A second reason to look across languages in the study of literacy acquisition is that there are differences between the way oral languages are represented in the writing systems they are associated with. Both English and Spanish are represented through an alphabet – i.e., both use letters to represent phonemes, which are the smallest units of sound. However, even here there are differences across languages. English represents sounds but also morphology: two words with the same stem are as a rule spelled in the same way even if the stem sound changes when a derivational suffix is added. For example, the word pairs "magic" and "magician" and "heal" and "health" have different sounding stems due to the addition of a derivational suffix but the stems are still spelled in the same way. The representation of morphology in spelling creates a new level of difficulty for some alphabetic languages, such as English, French and Greek. Examples from these languages were discussed in the first section of this handbook; the reader is referred to the chapters by Bryant et. al. and Fayol et al.

The acquisition of literacy in non-alphabetic languages is much less understood so far because less research is available. However, looking at these languages is important to help us understand the acquisition processes in reading acquisition more clearly by contrast or by analogy to observations in alphabetic languages. As discussed by Defior, non-alphabetic scripts include syllabaries, where each letter represents one syllable, and scripts such as Chinese, termed logographic, where each character represents morphemes and phonology simultaneously through different elements within the character. It is beyond the scope of this handbook to discuss how children learn to read and write in Chinese; the interested reader is referred to other works for an insight into this fascinating process (e.g., Chan & Nunes, 1998; Ho & Bryant, 1997; Huang & Hanley, 1995; Huang & Hanley, 1997; Shu & Anderson, 1997; 1999). However, research into how children learn to read and write in Chinese has helped researchers assess hypotheses that were proposed about learning to read in alphabetic languages. For example, it had been assumed for many years that Chinese children learn each character globally and by rote, without an understanding of how the writing system works and without the possibility of applying this knowledge to new words. This hypothesis was extended to suggest that different children learning to read English might adopt different styles, some being more analytical and taking advantage of the phonological representation in alphabetic scripts, whereas others would learn in a non-analytical way, similarly to Chinese children's learning processes. However, research on how Chinese children learn to read has shown that Chinese children don't learn in this global, non-analytical fashion. Like the learners of alphabetic languages, they have to learn to analyse the characters they are exposed to, apprehend their rules even if implicitly, and use these rules to pronounce and interpret novel characters, not encountered before. Furthermore,

Chinese children's progress in learning to read is predicted by their level of awareness of the sounds in their language, just like English children's progress is. The idea that English children could learn using a "Chinese style" becomes less credible when one considers that the Chinese children themselves do not learn their script in this global and rote manner.

The chapter by Nunes and Hatano pursues further issues about the connection between oral and written languages and differences across scripts. In contrast to Defior, who focused on phonological awareness and its relation to reading and spelling, Nunes and Hatano focus on morphological awareness. Defior points out that children must have phonological skills in order to learn oral language but that these skills remain largely implicit. When learning a written language, awareness of sounds becomes important because it is these sounds that are represented by letter. Nunes and Hatano extend the argument to the idea of morphological skills: much research has shown that we need to attribute morphological knowledge to children in order to understand how they acquire vocabulary in oral language. But, like phonological skills, this morphological knowledge seems to remain implicit. When children learn a script that represents morphology, their interaction with this new form of their own language becomes a factor in the development of morphological awareness.

Nunes and Hatano argue for yet another reason to look across languages: they suggest that it is possible for children to use their more abstract knowledge of the first written language they acquire to master a second written language. They support their view both with theoretical arguments and empirical findings. The theoretical argument is related to the idea that all children acquiring an oral language develop some form, even if implicit, of morphological knowledge. If this is the case, why should the connection between morphological awareness and literacy learning be a relation that is language specific? The empirical support comes from two types of study. The first shows that developmental processes in the acquisition of representations of morphology in writing is very similar in languages as different as English, French, Greek and Japanese. In all these languages, children seem to apprehend rules of representation, which they at first generalise to phonologically similar contexts until they realise the morphological nature of the rule. The second source of evidence comes from studies with bilingual children. These studies show that children do use what they learned in one language in the mastery of a second one.

The chapter that follows, by Sigel, explores different aspects of the transfer across languages. Sigel considers the transfer of diverse cognitive skills by looking at a diversity of situations where children are learning two languages. Although she recognises the significance of the context in which the languages are learned, she stresses that looking across different contexts in literacy learning is necessary if one wishes to generalise results regarding transfer across literacies. If children show transfer of knowledge across written languages irrespective of the contexts in which the languages are learned, it will be possible to conclude that transfer of knowledge across literacies is a general phenomenon, and is not restricted to situations where the languages are learned in a similar context.

This section closes with four case studies, where the context of language learning is brought to the foreground. Children may grow up in bilingual environments for such different reasons that it is important for researchers to learn to understand what these differences mean.

Bindman considers the case where a second language is learned for religious purposes and contrasts this situation with the learning of the same language as a second language but with a more general aim of becoming able to communicate orally, read and write. She locates this example within the classification system that has been developed to characterise literacy learning in a second language, providing insight into the consequences of the different modes of biliterate development in today's world. Her study is of great value because the children have the same first language and are learning the same second language: only the aims and mode of acquisition vary. Keeping the language constant while varying the context of acquisition can provide insight into the role of context in influencing transfer across languages.

Kumar also describes a situation where the second language and literacy under acquisition is kept constant but the differences between the learning situations are much larger. He stresses the meaning and consequences of the different contexts in which English literacy is learned in India and draws valuable lessons for a social analysis of biliterate development.

Pellicer draws our attention to a third case: that of bilingual children who only learn literacy in one of their languages. In the Mexican scene, it is not unusual for children who speak indigenous languages at home to learn Spanish literacy at school, without a comparable exposure to literacy in their own mother tongue. Pellicer's study shows the transfer of yet another concept across literacies, the concept of word, which studies of non-literate groups have shown to be a difficult one to attain (see Scribner & Cole, 1981, and Ferreiro, 1999, for example). Pellicer's work can make us aware of the fact that words are not phonological units in the stream of speech, but rather their identity as such involves a host of linguistic considerations. The children's success in transferring this concept is a testimony to the deep awareness of linguistic structures that they develop in contact with literacy in a second language.

The final case, analysed by Burman and Pretzlik, offers a brief look into the acquisition of English literacy by deaf children whose first language is a sign language. This very special case was included in the section Looking across Languages both as a way to offer another contrasting case but also as a stimulus for further research about deaf children's literacy. Unfortunately, as Burman and Pretzlik point out, theoretical insights into how deaf children who are users of a signed language can best be taught to read English are so far scarce. Efforts to develop the children's oral language seem to have attracted the attention of professionals who work with them whereas researchers seem to have concentrated on a single route to literacy, that which is based on phonological awareness. They suggest an alternative way, which seems well worth exploring further but stress that much more research is still needed before a clear path can be discerned.

These four cases studies are presented in chapters that differ in structure and focus from the preceding chapters in the Handbook. Their concern is with specific groups and their particular strengths and difficulties. As in all case studies, there are certainly more general lessons to be learned. It is important that the readers use these case studies as examples of how the specificity of biliteracy can raise issues not explored before in other contexts but can also provide more general lessons, which we can use in other situations. I found the reading of these case studies fascinating and hope the readers will feel the same way.

REFERENCES

Chan, L. & Nunes, T. (1998). Children's understanding of formal and functional constraints in written Chinese. *Applied Psycholinguistics, 19*, 115-131.

Ferreiro, E. (1999). Oral and written words. Are they the same units? *Learning to Read: An Integrated View from Research and Practice* (65-76). T. Nunes. Dordrecht, Kluwer.

Ho, C. S.-H., & Bryant, P. E. (1997). Learning to read Chinese beyond the logographic phase. *Reading Research Quarterly, 32(3)*, 276-289. Holm, A., & Dodd, B. (1996). The effect of first written language on the acquisition of English literacy. *Cognition, 59*, 119-147

Huang, H. S., & Hanley, J. R. (1995). Phonological awareness and visual skills in learning to read Chinese and English. *Cognition, 54*, 73-98.

Huang, H. S., & Hanley, R. (1997). A longitudinal study of phonological awareness, visual skills, and Chinese reading acquisition among first-graders in Taiwan. *International Journal of Behavioral Development, 20(2)*, 249-268.

Scribner, S. and M. Cole (1981). *The Psychology of Literacy*. Cambridge (MA), Harvard University Press.

Shu, H. & Anderson, R. C. (1997). Role of radical awareness in the character and word acquisition of Chinese children. *Reading Research Quarterly, 32*, 78-89.

Shu, H. & Anderson, R. C. (1999). Learning to read Chinese: The development of metalinguistic awareness. In J. Wang, A. W. Inhoff & H. -C. Chen (Eds.), *Reading Chinese script* (pp. 1-18). New Jersey: Lawrence Erlbaum Associates, Inc.

E1 Phonological Awareness and Learning to Read: A Cross-Linguistic Perspective

SYLVIA DEFIOR[1]

ABSTRACT

The notion that the ability to segment speech into its phonological units in an explicit conscious manner, commonly termed phonological awareness, is related with learning to read, is one of the most important contributions to cognitive research on reading of the last three decades. This chapter centers on studies designed to determine whether this relationship is universal across language systems, or whether peculiarities of a given system influence the appearance, development and degree of phonological awareness. Three issues are examined. The first is whether the differences in the type of orthography learned, i.e., in the graphic units used to transcribe oral language (basically phonemes in alphabetic systems, syllables in syllabic systems, and morphemes in logographic systems) influence the development of conscious phonological representations. The second is whether the course of development of phonological awareness in alphabetic systems is affected by differences in the degree of orthographic transparency with respect to phonology. The third question this chapter tries to answer is whether characteristics of oral language, specifically phonology, introduce variations in the developmental course of phonological awareness. The concept of phonological awareness is briefly introduced, and the findings of studies that compared phonological skills in native-speaking children of languages with non-alphabetic (Japanese and Chinese) and alphabetic orthographies are discussed. This is followed by a look at studies that compared children growing up in a context characterized by alphabetic languages with a transparent or opaque orthography. In the concluding section I note that although phonological skills are important in learning to read in any language system and a common substrate of phonological awareness exists in all languages, conscious phonological representations are strongly dependent on the type of orthographic and phonologic input that children process. The degree of phonological awareness attained varies between languages,

[1] Acknowledgements: I thank the Ministerio de Ciencia y Tecnología of Spain for support through project BSO 2000-1251, without which this chapter could not have been written, and Karen Shashok for producing the English-language text.

T. Nunes, P. Bryant (eds.), Handbook of Children's Literacy, 631–649.

with the highest levels, in which the subject is aware of each phoneme that the words are formed of, being reached only in alphabetic languages. Within this group of languages, the degree of orthographic transparency further influences the sequence of development of phonological awareness, in terms of both the time of appearance (earlier in transparent orthographies) and the predominance of specific levels at given times (intrasyllabic units in opaque; phonemes in transparent orthographies). The development of phonological awareness is also shaped by the characteristics of oral language.

INTRODUCTION

Each human community has developed its own linguistic system which, with rare exceptions, comprises two closely related subsystems: oral language and written language. Aside from the morphosyntactic differences, these systems differ in phonology, particularly with regard to the number and type of consonant and vowel phonemes and complexity of syllabic combinations. They also differ in the unit each represents in written language: basically, the morpheme in logographic orthographies, the syllables in syllabic orthographies and the phoneme in alphabetic orthographies. In addition, alphabetic scripts, while sharing the alphabetic principle (i.e. the application of grapheme-phoneme correspondence rules [GPCR]), differ in the code they use, and more importantly, in the degree of consistency and completeness of orthographic representations with respect to phonology. Thus, alphabetic orthographies are classified as transparent or opaque depending on the degree of consistency in the GPCR (see Katz & Frost, 1992, for an explanation of the diversity of writing systems).

The demonstration of a close relationship between literacy acquisition and speech processing skills constitutes one of the most relevant contributions of cognitive research on reading of the last three decades. For alphabetic writing systems – the most widely investigated orthography to date – it is generally agreed that phonological and metaphonological processes are critical components for the successful acquisition of reading (Liberman, 1995), although precisely how these processes come into play, and the factors that influence phonological development, continue to be studied and debated. However, given the differences between language systems, the link between reading and phonological awareness would not be expected to be a universal phenomenon; rather, we would expect the development of conscious phonological representations to display characteristics peculiar to each language. This issue obviously requires investigation from a cross-linguistic perspective.

From this perspective, which analyses and compares the development of phonological awareness in speakers of different languages and readers of different orthographies, three basic issues have been examined. The first is whether there is a universal connection between phonological awareness and reading, i.e., whether phonological awareness, particularly phonemic awareness, plays a role in all languages, and whether the sequence of development is the same in all languages. Experience to date suggests that the units used to transcribe a given language (orthographic input) exert a strong influence on conscious representations of phonological units for readers of that language, and hence on the development of phonological awareness. In principle, this contrasts with the idea that the same representations are developed regardless of whether one learns an alphabet, a syllabary or a logographic orthography. The question is therefore to determine whether phonological skills develop in all these linguistic contexts, to what degree, and what factors influence this development.

Secondly, given that phonological awareness is an important factor in learning alphabetic orthographies, its development may differ depending on the degree of consistency and completeness of the GPCR. In languages that use a transparent orthography, the more precise relationship between orthography and phonology would be expected to facilitate attainment of the highest possible levels of conscious phonological representations, and users of such languages would be expected to acquire them earlier and more efficiently than users of languages with a more opaque orthography.

Thirdly, because languages also differ in phonology (phonological input), the characteristics of spoken language may also affect the development of phonological awareness. It would therefore be desirable to test the following hypothesis: If the development of phonological skills depended only on experience with written language, we would not expect to see differences in phonological skills between subjects who have not yet learned to read.

In this chapter I will use the perspective outlined above to analyse the development of phonological awareness in different languages, and its relationship with learning to read. I will first introduce the concept of phonological awareness, then look at studies that have compared the development of phonological skills in languages that use alphabetic and non-alphabetic orthographies (termed, for the sake of convenience, alphabetic and non-alphabetic languages). The following section will describe studies that compared the development of phonological awareness in transparent and opaque alphabetic languages. It should be noted that from a cross-linguistic perspective, these issues have been investigated in both independent and simultaneous studies; in this chapter I will focus more on the latter. Whenever possible I will emphasize the findings that bear on the influence of orthographic and phonologic input on the development of phonological awareness. I shall end the chapter with a general overview of the research results that shed light on the issues defined above.

Phonological Awareness

Children learn to speak and listen naturally, and use the phonological elements of language unconsciously. The development of linguistic awareness involves a gradual shift in the child's attention from the meaning to the structure of language.

One type of awareness is phonological awareness, i.e., explicit knowledge of the internal phonological structure of words and the ability to deliberately manipulate the sublexical units that make them up (Gombert, 1990).

It is generally agreed that words have three levels of phonological structure: syllabic, intrasyllabic, and phonemic units. Awareness of intrasyllabic units is the ability to detect and manipulate the onset of syllables – composed of the phonemes that precede the vowel – and rime, which comprises the vowel and subsequent phonemes. Phonemic awareness is the ability to detect and manipulate the smallest units that make up words and can change their meaning. It is important to note that awareness of the onset involves the development of some degree of phonemic awareness, as many syllables begin with a single phoneme. However, this does not mean that the person is aware of each of the phonemes that make up a word (Goswami, 1997). Tests of phonological awareness have used different types of tasks that vary with regard to the size of the phonological segments and the mental operations involved, which require different degrees of explicit consciousness (Yopp, 1988). Thus, classifying words on the basis of their initial or final sounds requires less awareness and explicit manipulation than counting, deleting, combining, replacing, adding or inverting segments, which are more difficult tasks (for a classification see Defior, 1996).

Metaphonological skill is therefore not a self-contained, homogeneous skill, but rather a heterogeneous set of skills involving different levels of awareness. In general, before children learn to read, they are able to detect and manipulate syllables, and to a lesser degree intrasyllabic units, although awareness of every phoneme in a given word is practically impossible for them to attain. The pioneering work of Liberman, Shankweiler, Fischer & Carter (1974) showed that certain forms of phonological awareness could arise before reading acquisition, and that the ability to segment phonemes increased markedly at about 6 years of age, when the children are first taught to read; this indicates the influence of learning to read on the development of phonological awareness.

Since the publication of this study, much empirical evidence, both correlational and experimental, has supported the existence of a link between phonological skills and success in learning to read an alphabetic language (see Defior, 1994, for a review.) Fewer studies have looked at this relationship in other linguistic contexts; I will discuss primarily those studies that compared phonological skills in children and adults who had different experiences with oral and written language.

THE DEVELOPMENT OF PHONOLOGICAL AWARENESS: NON-ALPHABETIC VERSUS ALPHABETIC LANGUAGES

This section reviews comparative studies that investigated whether phonological awareness develops similarly in children who use non-alphabetic (i.e., Chinese and Japanese) and alphabetic languages (among which English has received the most attention). Because of the differences between Japanese and Chinese, these languages are considered separately below.

Syllabic versus Alphabetic Orthographies

The Japanese writing system is a syllabary. It is composed of two types of characters: kana (Hiragana and Katakana), which represent mora (rhythmic units corresponding approximately to syllables), and Kanji characters, which are logographs.

The first study to compare the development of phonological awareness in Japanese (first to sixth grade) and American children was carried out by Mann (1986), and consisted of a series of four experiments that used segment counting and deletion tasks. In Experiment I, the author used the same test for counting syllables and phonemes (tapping) as did Liberman et al. (1974) in their study of American children. Mann found that Japanese first-graders were better than their American counterparts in syllable-based tasks (100% correct responses *versus* 90%), but not in phoneme-based tasks (10% *versus* 70%). In the deletion experiment (Experiment III), Japanese first-graders were better at syllable deletion but not at deleting the initial consonant sound. The findings in first-graders clearly showed that there were differences in phonological skill between Japanese (little awareness of phonemes, but high awareness of syllables) and American children (awareness of both segments). The first conclusion suggested by this study was that the type of orthographic input influences the development of conscious phonological representations, such that learning a syllabary does not lead to the development of phonemic awareness. Experiments II and IV confirmed these findings in older children. However, in the phoneme-counting task, Japanese children in third, fourth, fifth and sixth grade scored 56%, 73%, 81% and 75% correct responses respectively; although these performances were as low as those seen in American first-graders, they nonetheless indicated the existence of phonemic awareness in the absence of contact with an alphabetic orthography. This result contrasted with the lack of phonemic awareness found in studies of phonological skill in illiterate adults as compared with ex-illiterate adults (Morais, Cary, Alegria & Bertelson, 1979), and in readers literate only in a logographic orthography as opposed to readers who also knew (alphabetic) pinyin (Read, Zhang, Nie & Ding, 1986). Mann suggested that these unexpected findings might be explained by the fact that increasing experience with a phonographic orthography (kanas represent phonological units) may elicit phonemic awareness regardless of whether the subject has had contact with an alphabetic orthography. As a possible complementary explanation, she added repeated experiences with word games (which are common in Japan) as a factor that might contribute to awareness of the phonological structure of words. The effect of the units represented in the orthographic system on the development of conscious phonological representations was clearly evident in young children, whereas the results in older children, despite the fact that they scored lower than Western children, raise doubts about the generalisability of this effect.

A study by Spagnoletti, Morais, Alegria and Dominici (1989) replicated the results reported by Mann (1986) and shed light on the strategies used by children to perform the tasks. These authors evaluated the metaphonological skills of Japanese first-graders with a set of tasks similar to those used by Mann (1986). Their results confirmed that Japanese children showed excellent syllabic awareness (100% correct responses in the counting task, 60% correct responses in the syllable deletion task), whereas phonemic awareness was poor (no subject reached the criterion of six consecutive correct responses in the phoneme-counting task, and performance on the phoneme deletion task was 40% correct responses). However, their performance in the phoneme deletion task was better than expected, and even more surprisingly, it was apparently easier for them to delete than to count phonemes, in contrast to the findings in children living in Western countries (Content, 1984). Error analysis showed that to count phonemes, the children used a spelling-based strategy (number of kanas), so that they solved the phoneme task without actually being aware of these segments. (This may also have accounted for part of Mann's 1986 findings.) Moreover, the results in a segment inversion task revealed that Japanese adults highly instructed in both syllabic and alphabetic scripts used the matrix of kanas rather than an alphabetic strategy to perform the metaphonological tasks (Nakamura, Kolinsky, Spagnoletti & Morais, 1998). Greater reliance on how the word is written than on how it sounds is, in fact, a behavior characteristic of subjects with difficulties in detecting and manipulating phonemes (Campbell & Butterworth, 1985; Ehri, 1984)

Like the adult subjects described above, some Japanese children in the studies by Mann (1986) and Spagnoletti et al. (1989) were learning an alphabetic language (English and French respectively) at the same time as their first language. However, this knowledge did not transfer to a greater ability to solve phoneme-based tasks. In both studies, the children's responses were apparently based only on their knowledge of Japanese; one issue that these studies failed to resolve is whether the use of Japanese language stimuli might have led the subjects to use a kana-based strategy, which in turn might have affected the transfer of knowledge from one language to the other. This illustrates the need for studies that use stimuli in both languages

In overall terms, the studies described above showed that Japanese children and adults had excellent syllabic awareness but poor phonemic awareness in comparison with Western children, and used a syllable-based strategy to segment speech. Therefore, the findings support the idea that conscious representation of the units that make up speech is influenced by the type of unit represented in the writing system.

Logographic versus Alphabetic Orthographies

In the Chinese writing system each character simultaneously represents a morpheme and a syllable. Of the thousands of different characters, 10% to 20% consist of representations of meaning, whereas the remaining 80% to 90% are ideophonetic compounds which comprise a semantic element (radical) and a phonological element (phonetic). It is therefore important to note that Chinese spelling is not strictly logographic, and orthographic-phonologic correspondence rules (OPCR) exist, although the phonetic component provides an adequate cue to the pronunciation in only 48% of the cases (Ho & Bryant, 1997a, c; Huang & Hanley, 1997; Tzeng, Lin, Hung & Lee, 1995).

It should also be noted that since the 1950s, Chinese first-graders in China (at the age of 6 years) learn to read an alphabetic (pinyin) or phonetic writing system (Zhu-Yin-Fu-Hao) during 10 weeks, in order to learn how the traditional characters are pronounced. In contrast, in Hong Kong, traditional teaching is used, and the children have no contact with either of the alternative methods used in mainland China. This makes it interesting to look at studies that compared Chinese subjects who had different learning experiences, as well as studies that compared Chinese and Western subjects.

Read et al. (1986) were the first to document differences in phonological awareness between readers of Chinese literate only in the logographic system and readers also literate in the alphabetic pinyin system. As in the comparison of illiterate and ex-illiterate Portuguese subjects (Morais et al., 1979), phonemic skills were weaker in the former (20% correct responses) than in subjects who had been instructed in both systems (80% correct responses). These results were confirmed by de Gelder, Vroomen & Bertelson (1996) in their comparison of readers who knew an alphabetic script (pinyin, Vietnamese or Australian English) and readers who were familiar only with the logographic script.

It is only recently that phonological skills of Chinese and Western children have been compared. Huang & Hanley (1995) analysed phonological and visual skills in three groups of 8-year-olds: children instructed in Chinese characters only (Hong Kong), in both Chinese characters and Zhu-Yin-Fu-Hao (Taiwan), and children who learned an alphabetic writing system (United Kingdom). Phonological awareness was tested in two ways: with three versions of the Odd Man Out test (with English, Chinese, and nonsense words), and tests of deletion of the initial and final phoneme with consonant-vowel-consonant-consonant (CVCC) and CCVC words. Items with consonant clusters used only English words, as this type of syllable is nonexistent in Chinese. The use of two types of syllable structures also made it possible to investigate the influence of differences in phonological input, which has been posited for alphabetic languages by other authors (Caravolas & Bruck, 1992; Cossu, Shankweiler, Liberman, Katz & Tola, 1988), as the Chinese language lacks consonant clusters. The subjects also took the Raven test, the British Picture Vocabulary Scale and reading tests.

Huang & Hanley (1995) found a significant relationship between visual skills and reading in Chinese but not in British children. On the other hand, British children showed better phonological skills than Hong Kong or Taiwanese children; in general, there were few differences between these last two groups. Although there was a significant correlation between phonological skills and reading Chinese, the differences in phonological awareness became nonsignificant when the effects of vocabulary and nonverbal intelligence were controlled for. In contrast, this association remained significant in British children. Surprisingly, the performance of Chinese and British children in the initial phoneme deletion task showed unexpected, opposite patterns. British children were better at deleting the initial phoneme of CVCC words, whereas Chinese children were better at CCVC words. The most likely explanation for these results lies in the differences between the two languages in phonological input. Chinese children, who lack experience with consonant clusters in their spoken language, tend to introduce an "implicit" vowel after the initial consonant, so that they were actually performing a syllable deletion task rather than a phoneme deletion task. This is similar to the situation in Japanese children in the study of Spagnoletti et al. (1989), who used a nonphonemic strategy to solve a phonemic task. Huang & Hanley illustrate this strategy with the example of "Clinton" in Chinese, this name is written with three characters which represent the three syllables *kuh-lin-ton*.

The lack of difference between children in Taiwan who had experience with a phonetic system, and children in Hong Kong, led to another study designed to examine the evolution of visual and phonological skills in Taiwanese children before they learned the Zhu-Yin-Fu-Hao system, after 10 weeks of instruction in this system, and at the end of first grade (Huang & Hanley, 1997). These authors found a relationship between reading and phonological awareness before the children learned Zhu-Yin-Fu-Hao, although the scores were low. Learning Zhu-Yin-Fu-Hao greatly increased the scores on phonological tests. After experience with this system, both skills were related with reading, and in contrast with the 1995 findings, the greatest correlation was found between reading and phoneme deletion, even when IQ and vocabulary were controlled for. These results therefore pointed to a clearer connection between phonological awareness and logographic reading when children had had more recent experience with a phonetic system. However, when early reading skill was controlled for, phonological measures were not a good predictor of reading skill.

Recent studies by Ho & Bryant (1997a, b, c) have helped to clarify the role of phonological and visual skills in the initial acquisition of literacy in Chinese. These authors worked with children from Hong Kong who had no previous experience with pinyin or Zhu-Yin-Fu-Hao. In a longitudinal 4-year study of children from the age of 3 years 4 months to 8 years (Ho & Bryant, 1997a) they found that visual skills were important for reading Chinese characters, especially in the initial stages of learning to read. With experience in reading, as the number of characters they knew increased, the influence of phonological skills (detection of rhymes-tones and partial homophones) became stronger, probably because the children attended to the phonetic component of the characters. The authors noted that it was as if reading in Chinese children went from a visual-logographic phase to a phonological phase, as occurs in learning alphabetic languages. However, it would be more appropriate to draw comparisons with English, as the existence of a logographic phase has been questioned in more transparent languages such as German (Wimmer & Hummer, 1990) or French (Sprenger-Charolles & Bonnet, 1996). In a certain sense, Chinese, a non-alphabetic language, can be considered an extreme case of opaqueness with regard to the relationship between orthography and phonology; English, an alphabetic language, is considered a morphophonologic orthography (Liberman, 1995). This may account for the similarities between Chinese and English in certain phases of reading development.

In an indirect comparison of the development of phonological skills in Chinese and English children, Ho & Bryant (1997b) found that the latter acquired awareness of rhyme before the former did, when tested with the Odd Man Out task (based on data from Mclean, Bryant & Bradley, 1987) or with the word similarity task (data of Lenel & Cantor, 1984). Because these studies compared preschool children, the differences can be attributed to the phonological characteristics of the languages (rhyme is an important distinguishing feature in English syllables, but not in Chinese syllables), which once again appeared to be a key factor in the development of phonological awareness. Similarly, English 6- and 7-year-olds acquired awareness of the initial consonant of words earlier than Chinese 7- and 8-year-olds (according to data from Stanovich, Cunningham & Cramer, 1984). In this case the differences were attributable to differences in orthography: English children must attend to initial consonants to read and write, whereas this is not necessary in order to be able to read and write Chinese characters. The authors also found that the sequence of development of phonological awareness reflected the same general trend as in Western children, who appeared to progress from global judgements on the similarity of sounds toward awareness of smaller elements, in this case the rhymes and tones contained in syllables.

In summary, these studies show that, in contrast with the widespread belief that only visual skills are important for logographic reading (Perfetti & Zhang, 1991), phonological skills also come into play, although their relationship with reading is apparently shaped by other skills that will require further study to clarify. Assuming that Chinese also has a phonological component, albeit a limited one, the connection between phonological awareness and reading should not be surprising. Children with good phonological skills can be assumed to learn compound phonetic characters more quickly and easily than children with weaker phonological skills. Additional proof that Chinese primary school children take advantage of phonetic cues and use GPCR to read characters can be found in studies by Ho & Bryant (1997c) and Tzeng et al. (1995).

These results notwithstanding, the development of phonological awareness is affected by the characteristics of oral and written language: Chinese and Japanese children and adults who can read appear to develop conscious phonological representations that do not go beyond the syllable and intrasyllabic unit level; nonetheless they perform worse that children who learn an alphabetic orthography. Moreover, Chinese and Japanese subjects used a strategy of transforming phonemic tasks into syllabic tasks, even though they had experience with a phonetic system. Thus, learning to read characters does not develop phonemic awareness. However, it is too soon to say which types of phonological representations Chinese children develop, as interest in elucidating the role of phonological awareness in learning to read a logographic language has arisen only recently. Longer longitudinal and experimental studies that test different levels of phonological awareness will be necessary before we can clearly establish the characteristics of this representation and the changes that occur as reading experience increases.

Considering the findings in non-alphabetic languages as a whole, it is clear that there exists a connection between phonological awareness and reading. However, phonological awareness develops more slowly than in alphabetic languages, and the level of phonological awareness attained is influenced by the type of unit represented in the orthographic system. Chinese and Japanese children and adults who are able to solve phonemic tasks do so by using non-phonemic strategies. Therefore, it appears clear that complete phonemic awareness is not attained in non-alphabetic languages, whereas learning an alphabetic orthography implies access to smaller elements of speech. Moreover, although there are no specific studies on the influence of phonologic input, some isolated research results suggest that the characteristics of oral language also exert an influence on the development of phonological awareness.

THE DEVELOPMENT OF PHONOLOGICAL AWARENESS: TRANSPARENT VERSUS OPAQUE ALPHABETIC LANGUAGES

The relationship between phonological awareness and reading is well established in different languages that use an alphabetic orthography; examples include highly transparent languages such as German, Spanish, Italian, Greek and Serbo-Croatian and opaque languages such as English and French (Bradley & Bryant, 1985; Caravolas & Bruck, 1993; Cossu et al., 1988; Defior & Tudela, 1994; Frith, Wimmer & Landerl, 1998; Goswami, Gombert & Barrera, 1996; Lukatela, Carello, Shankweiler & Liberman, 1995; Porpodas, 1993; Thorstad, 1991; Wimmer & Goswami, 1994; Wimmer, Landerl, Linortner & Hummer, 1991). Some studies have evaluated the impact of orthographic consistency on learning to read and learning difficulties with reading. However, few of them have been long-term longitudinal studies that have used different phonological awareness tasks to carefully compare the development of phonological representations in children who grow up with a transparent or an opaque alphabetic orthography.

Two studies simultaneously analysed the influence of orthographic input (consistency of GPCR) and the characteristics of oral language. Cossu et al.

(1988) indirectly compared (using data from a previous study by Liberman et al., 1974) the development of syllabic and phonemic awareness (tapping task) in Italian and (English-speaking) American preschoolers (aged 4 and 5 years) and first-graders. Although syllabic segmentation (67%, 80% and 100% correct responses in Italian subjects; 46%, 48% and 90% in American subjects) was easier than phonemic segmentation (13%, 27% and 97% in Italian subjects; 0%, 17% and 70% in American subjects) in both languages, Italian children were better than American children at all ages and in all segmentation tasks. In the preliterate stage, the better performance of Italian children was interpreted as a result of the influence of experience with oral language; the greater presence of open syllables and lower number of vowels in Italian may have favored the development of syllabic awareness earlier in preschool children. Nonetheless, the difference between Italian and American children was accentuated when formal education started, implying that the influence of the greater simplicity of phonological input was enhanced by the greater transparency of Italian GPCR. However, the typical pattern of results was inverted in Italian first- and second-graders, for whom syllable-based tasks were more difficult than phoneme-based tasks. One plausible explanation, which supports the hypothetical influence of the orthography, is that because of the regularity and greater graphemic simplicity of Italian, learning the script also implies direct training in phonemic awareness, thus phonemic skills improve more quickly than syllabic skills as children learn to read. A similar inversion was found by Lukatela et al. (1995) in their study of semiliterate Serbo-Croatian adults who readily recognized letters; this finding supports the notion that a greater degree of orthographic transparency facilitates the acquisition of phonemic awareness, and hence the acquisition of literacy. Similar findings were reported by Lindgren, De Renzi & Richman (1985) in a study of the prevalence of dyslexia. These authors found that dyslexia was more prevalent in the USA than in Italy, and that Italian primary school children were better readers and had better phonological skills than American children matched for age and IQ.

Caravolas & Bruck (1993), in a cross-linguistic study with a carefully matched sample (100 Czech children and 101 English-speaking Canadian children aged 4, 5 and 6 years), and pseudoword and monosyllable tasks designed to be equivalent in the two languages, were able to directly study the effects of the characteristics of oral and written language on the development of phonological awareness (Spoken Czech has a greater variety of consonant clusters than English, and these combinations occur more frequently; moreover, the GPCR are more consistent in Czech). The tasks were judging the similarity of the initial phoneme in pairs of CVCC and CCVC items, isolating the initial phoneme, deleting the initial phoneme in CVC and CCV words, and writing pseudowords. The results showed that before they learned to write, Czech children were more aware of consonant clusters than Canadian children. Thus, the difference was a result of the presence, in oral language, of a larger repertory of initial consonant groups in Czech than in English. As in the study by Cossu et al. (1988), the better performance of

Czech children was even more evident in first-graders, due to the additional influence of the transparency of Czech orthography. All Czech and Canadian first-graders easily solved the first two phonological tasks, leading to the appearance of a ceiling effect; however, in the deletion task Czech children performed better than Canadian subjects in CCV items, and also showed better writing skills. Similar results regarding the influence of the characteristics of oral language were found by Zaretsky (1995) in a study of Russian preschoolers.

With respect to the differences between transparent and opaque languages, an issue that remains unresolved concerns the development of awareness of intrasyllabic units, and their role in learning to reading. A study published by Bradley & Bryant (1985) showed that awareness of the intrasyllabic units onset and rime in the preliterate stage is an important predictor of the acquisition of English literacy, although it is not clear whether this relationship exists in other, more transparent languages. Studies by Goswami and colleagues (Goswami, 1991; Goswami et al., 1998) have shown that English children, and to a lesser degree French children, rely for reading more on information provided by the rhyme because this information is more consistent than that provided by the GPCR. This contrasts with the behavior of children who are learning to read a more transparent language, who depend more on the GPCR. These findings raise the possibility that the development of levels of phonological awareness in alphabetic languages occurs at a different rate, and that the relationship between phonological awareness and reading is different-at least during the initial stages of learning-in transparent and opaque languages. One possible working hypothesis is that the differences in the development of phonological awareness lie in the time needed for such awareness to become fully developed, and in the predominance of different levels of phonological awareness during different stages of development. It should nevertheless be noted that "full development" of phonological awareness means the same degree of awareness regardless of the language's orthographic depth. Longitudinal studies designed to compare several languages simultaneously, and that include measures of different levels of phonological awareness and reading, will be needed to test this hypothesis.

In alphabetic languages, unlike non-alphabetic languages, there is a clear increase in phonological awareness when children learn the script and become able to solve phonemic tasks. However, research has found once again that the development of conscious representations of speech is influenced by character- istics of oral language (type of sounds and syllabic combinations) and orthography. Phonological skills are better, and appear earlier (especially phonemic skills) in transparent languages, which beginning readers also find easier to learn. Moreover, development through different levels of phonological awareness may progress differently in transparent and opaque languages; learners of opaque orthographies spend more time at intermediate levels of phonological awareness, which are the levels that these orthographies represent most consistently.

CONCLUSIONS

Returning to the three issues posed in the Introduction, this section will present some conclusions that can be drawn from the research described above, and will note perspectives for future work and consideration.

Phonological Awareness in Alphabetic and Non-alphabetic Languages

The first question is whether the findings that relate phonological awareness and learning to read in one linguistic context can be generalized to other linguistic contexts, and whether common features of this relationship are shared across languages. There does in fact appear to be a common substrate to phonological awareness, which develops before the acquisition of literacy. In addition, the influence of phonological awareness on reading appears to be a universal phenomenon in non-alphabetic as well as in transparent and opaque alphabetic languages. Thus, phonological awareness plays a role in any language in which reading involves a phonetic component (as is the case in all writing systems analysed to date).

The studies discussed in this chapter confirm the general tendency for phonological awareness to develop from more global elements of greater salience toward smaller elements that are inaccessible to the children's consciousness. Awareness of syllables and intrasyllabic units develops first (generally in the preliterate stage), before awareness of phonemes.

In all languages, learning to read is accompanied by an improvement in phonological skills; apparently, when written language is manipulated during reading or writing, the subject becomes aware simultaneously of two entities: the world and the language (Olson, 1995).

However, specific aspects peculiar to each language are also important, and introduce differences in the development of phonological awareness. Some orthographies appear to make spoken language more visible than others (de Gelder & Morais, 1995). In phonological languages (i.e., those which use syllabaries and alphabets) the size of the phonological unit that a subject is aware of is influenced by the size of the segment of speech represented by the orthography; that is, conscious phonological representations depend on how the orthographic system represents the language. In logographic languages where orthography provides cues to how the characters are pronounced although they do not systematically represent any sublexical unit, phonological awareness plays a role, but its predictive power and the precise nature of its role remain to be elucidated, as the findings of some studies have been explained by intermediate factors. In any case, only acquisition of an alphabetic script promotes the highest level of phonemic awareness, and children who learn non-alphabetic languages do not display the change in phonemic awareness that occurs around the age of 6 years in Western children. Therefore, it is not the acquisition of literacy that develops metalinguistic phonemic skills, but rather, these skills develop mainly when the child learns the graphic symbols that represent phonemes (Morais & Kolinsky, 1995). It is as if the development of phonological awareness were "proportional" to the phonological component of the written language. Moreover, lack awareness of the phonemic elements of speech is a lasting phenomenon observed not only in the initial stages of learning, but also in expert adult readers. This phenomenon has also been observed in studies of bilinguism that analysed the influence of characteristics of the first acquired language on the way subjects approached learning to read and to solve metaphonological tasks in their second language. Although this topic has only recently been investigated, and few studies have been published, it appears that for alphabetic languages, learning the first language accelerates the development of phonological awareness in the second (Campbell & Sais, 1995; Durgunoglu et al., 1993), whereas learning a non-alphabetic language, in contrast, interferes with learning an alphabetic language as a second language (Ben-Dror, Frost & Bentin, 1995; de Gelder et al., 1993; Holm & Dodd, 1996; Nakamura et al., 1998). With respect to the latter case, there are no studies of the effect of learning an alphabetic language first on the acquisition of a non-alphabetic language. This area of research deserves greater attention because it could shed light on theoretical and practical aspects of language acquisition in a world in which increasing numbers of persons of different cultural and linguistic backgrounds relocate to a different setting, and global intercommunication is becoming more and more widespread.

Another specific question is that of visual skills, which play a role in logographic but not alphabetic reading. Visual skills are related with logographic reading both in early stages and in more advanced grades of school. These skills, with the repeated recognition of ever-increasing numbers of characters, may become less important, but longer longitudinal studies will be needed to confirm the possible shift in the relative importance of visual and phonological skills.

Phonological Awareness in Transparent and Opaque Alphabetic Languages

A second issue is the possible influence on the development of phonological awareness of the characteristics of orthography with regard to the degree of consistency of alphabetic GPCR. We have seen that phonological skills develop more rapidly in transparent languages, in which performance is better: tasks are solved with greater precision, the number of errors decreases faster, and the performance ceiling is reached sooner. In contrast, children who learn opaque languages develop phonemic awareness later, and their awareness of intrasyllabic units plays an important role in the initial phases of learning to read. In transparent languages the more rapid development of phonological awareness can be explained by the continuous, direct contact with a consistent set of graphic symbols for phonemes, which present few exceptions. In opaque languages, on the other hand, the correspondence between orthography and phonology is more predictable for intrasyllabic units than for phonemes. This leads us to the idea that alphabetical languages might be classifiable on the basis of their degree of transparency, measured as the time beginning readers need to attain full phonemic awareness (ceiling). This would require comparative studies of several languages simultaneously. In this connection, it has been found that in highly transparent languages, phonological skills soon become irrelevant, and appear to be important only during the initial moments of the process of learning to read, after which they make no further contribution to word recognition (Öney & Durgunoglu, 1997; Wimmer, 1993).

Influence of Oral Language on Phonological Awareness

A third level of analysis considers the effect of characteristics of oral language on the early development of certain phonological skills essentially those that appear before the subject learns to read. Clearly, the nature of oral language (phonological input) is a factor that contributes to the differential development of phonological awareness, which commences in the preliterate phase. This question has been little studied, possibly because of difficulties in establishing precise differences between languages. Nonetheless, it deserves further research: in a certain sense, this influence constitutes proof that the development of phonological awareness, regardless of the specific effect of learning a given orthography, also depends on experiential factors and the degree to which language segments are made explicit in developmental contexts. Studies by Bryant, Bradley, McLean & Crossland (1989) and McLean et al. (1987) indicate that the child's family context has a very early effect on their sensitivity to rhyme. Similarly, certain findings of the earliest studies on the development of phonological awareness indicated that a linguistically rich environment that gave children multiple experiences with segments of oral language could develop their capacity for phonemic analysis without their needing to become familiar with the alphabetic principle. In a study by Read et al. (1986), some non-alphabetic literates (11%) performed phonemic tasks at the same level or at a higher level than 25% of the subjects in the alphabetic group. Likewise, Mann (1986) found that Japanese children at the fourth grade level and above were able to perform phonemic tasks, and Morais et al. (1979) reported that 20% of a sample of illiterate subjects scored as well as or better than 23% of their literate subjects. Moreover, several studies have noted that there is no critical period for improving phonological skills; instead, these skills can be developed with explicit instruction and corrective feedback (Content, 1984, in preliterate children; Morais, Content, Bertelson, Cary & Kolinsky, 1988, in illiterate subjects). In other words, a variety of linguistic and instructional experiences can also influence the development of conscious phonological representations.

Therefore, children's conscious phonological representations arise, against a background of biological predisposition, as a product of the interaction between the characteristics of oral language, and the characteristics of the writing system; these interactions, in turn, are modulated by the children's own experiences.

To conclude, I will pose two final considerations. One is the scarcity of cross-linguistic studies that have analysed how difficulties in learning to read are manifested in non-alphabetic languages as opposed to alphabetic languages. In the latter, regardless of the degree of consistency of the GPCR, poor readers are distinguishable from normal readers by their difficulties with phonological (mainly phonemic) tasks. Because phonology is present in all orthographies – albeit to very different degrees – the problems of poor readers may be similar, and a phonological deficit may be shared by children who have difficulties in learning to read, regardless of whether their language is non-alphabetic or alphabetic. By way of example, Tzeng et al. (1995) found that among Chinese third- and sixth-graders, good readers showed a better knowledge of the GPCR than poor readers.

It is also worth observing that despite the relative abundance of research on phonological awareness, many issues remain open, and research from a cross-linguistic perspective may well help to shed light on some questions that await an answer. However, methodological issues will require particular attention, as problems with matching subjects and tasks make it difficult to ensure that the findings are comparable across languages, and to draw clear conclusions. In addition, because most comparisons to date have centred on the English language – which presents the particular difficulties of a complex phonological input and inconsistent orthographic input – future studies should attempt to look simultaneously at other languages with different degrees of transparency. Moreover, the cross-linguistic perspective should be extended to comparative studies of the development of other forms of linguistic awareness; this would provide a more integrated view of how people attain literacy.

Cross-linguistic studies, by considering the differences between language systems, are a powerful tool that can bring us closer to a more realistic description of the processes involved in reading, and can help define strategies to enhance how reading is taught and learned, in ways more in accord with the characteristics of each language system.

REFERENCES

Ben-Dror, I., Frost, R., & Bentin, S. (1995). Orthographic representation and phonemic segmentation in skilled readers: A cross-language comparison. *Psychological Science, 6(3)*, 176-181.

Bradley, L., & Bryant, P. (1985). *Rhyme and reason in reading and spelling*. Ann Arbor: University of Michigan Press.

Bryant, P., Bradley, L., McLean, M., & Crossland, J. (1989). Nursery rhymes, phonological skills and reading. *Journal of Child Language, 16*, 407-428.

Campbell, R., & Butterworth, B. (1985). Phonological dyslexia and dysgraphia in a high literate subject: A developmental case with associated deficits of phonemic processing and awareness. *Quarterly Journal of Experimental Psychology, 35A*, 435-475.

Campbell, R., & Sais, E. (1995). Accelerated metalinguistic (phonological) awareness in bilingual children. *British Journal of Developmental Psychology, 13*, 61-68.

Caravolas, M., & Bruck, M. (1993). The effect of oral and written language input on children's phonological awareness: A cross-linguistic study. *Journal of Experimental Child Psychology*, 55, 1-30.

Content, A. (1984). L'analyse phonétique explicite de la parole et l'acquisition de la lecture [Explicite phonetical analysis of speech and reading acquisition]. *L'Année Psychologique, 84*, 555-572.

Cossu, G., Shankweiler, D., Liberman, I. Y., Katz, L., & Tola, G. (1988). Awareness of phonological segments and reading ability in Italian children. *Applied Psycholinguistics*, 9, 1-16.

Defior, S. (1994). La consciencia fonológica y el aprendizaje de la lectoescritura. [Phonological awareness and learning to read and write] *Infancia y Aprendizaje, 67-68*, 90-113.

Defior, S. (1996). Una clasificación de las tareas utilizadas en la evaluación de las habilidades fonológicas y algunas ideas para su mejora. [A classification of phonological skill assessment tasks and some ideas to improve them] *Infancia y Aprendizaje, 73*, 49-63.

Defior, S., & Tudela, P. (1994). Effect of phonological training on reading and writing acquisition. *Reading & Writing. An Interdisciplinary Journal, 6*, 299-320. de Gelder, B., & Morais, J. (1995). Introduction Speech and Reading:One Side to Two Coins. In B. de Gelder, & J. Morais (Eds.), *Speech and Reading: A Comparative Approach*, 1-13. Hove: Erlbaum (UK) Taylor & Francis.

de Gelder, B., Vroomen, J., & Bertelson, P. (1993). The effects of alphabetic-reading competence on language representation in bilingual Chinese subjects. *Psychological Research, 55*, 315-321.

Durgunoglu, A. Y., Nagy, W. E., & Hancin-Bhatt, B. J. (1993). Cross-language transfer of phonological awareness. *Journal of Educational Psychology, 85(3)*, 453-465.

Ehri, L. (1984). How orthography alters spoken language competencies in children learning to read and spell. In J. Downing, & R. Valtin (Eds.), *Language awareness and learning to read*, 119-147. New York: Springer-Verlag.

Frith, U., Wimmer, H., & Landerl, K. (1998). Differences in phonological recoding in German- and English-speaking children. *Scientific Studies of Reading, 2(1)*, 31-54.

Gombert, J. E. (1992). *Le dévelopment métalinguistique*. [Metalinguistic development] Paris: PUF.

Goswami, U. (1991). Learning about spelling sequences: The role of onsets and rimes in analogies in reading. *Child Development, 62*, 1110-1123.

Goswami, U. (1997). Learning to read in different orthographies: phonological awareness, orthographic representations and dyslexia. In C. Hulme, & M. Snowling (Eds.), *Dyslexia: Biology, Cognition and Intervention*, 131-152. London:Whurr.

Goswami, U.; Gombert, J. E., & Barrera, L. F. (1998). Children's orthographic representations and linguistic transparency: Nonsense word reading in English, French and Spanish. *Applied Psycholinguistics*, 19, 19-52.

Ho, C. S.-H., & Bryant, P. E. (1997a). Phonological skills are important in learning to read Chinese. *Developmental Psychology*, 33(6), 946-951.

Ho, C. S.-H., & Bryant, P. E. *(1997b)*. Phonological awareness and visual skills can predict success in learning to read Chinese and English: A cross-cultural research with two longitudinal studies. *Journal of Psycholinguistic Research, 26(1)*, 109-127.

Ho, C. S.-H., & Bryant, P. E. (1997c). Learning to read Chinese beyond the logographic phase. *Reading Research Quarterly, 32(3)*, 276-289.

Holm, A., & Dodd, B. (1996). The effect of first written language on the acquisition of English literacy. *Cognition, 59*, 119-147

Huang, H. S., & Hanley, J. R. (1995). Phonological awareness and visual skills in learning to read Chinese and English. *Cognition, 54*, 73-98.

Huang, H. S., & Hanley, R. (1997). A longitudinal study of phonological awareness, visual skills, and Chinese reading acquisition among first-graders in Taiwan. *International Journal of Behavioral Development, 20(2)*, 249-268.

Katz, L., & Frost, R. (1992). The reading process is different for different orthographies: The orthographic depth hypothesis. In R. Frost, & L. Katz (Eds.), *Orthography, Phonology, Morphology and Meaning*, 67-85. Amsterdam: Elsevier Science Publishers.

Lenel J. C., & Cantor, J. H. (1981). Rhyme recognition and phonemic perception in young children. *Journal of Psycholinguistic Research, 10*, 57-67.

Liberman, A. M. (1995). The relation of speech to reading and writing. In B. de Gelder, & J. Morais (Eds.), *Speech and Reading: A Comparative Approach*, 17-31.Hove: Erlbaum (UK) Taylor & Francis.

Liberman, I. Y., Shankweiler, D., Fischer, F. W., & Carter, B. (1974). Explicit syllable and phoneme segmentation in the young child. *Journal of Experimental Child Psychology, 18,* 201-212.

Lindgren, S. D., Renzi, E., & Richman L.C. (1985). Cross-national comparisons of developmental dyslexia in Italy and the United States. *Child Development, 56,* 1404-1417.

Lukatela, K., Carello, C., Shankweiler, D., & Liberman, I. Y. (1995). Phonological awareness in illiterates: Observations from Serbo-Croatian. *Applied Psycholinguistics, 16,* 463-487.

MacLean, M., Bryant, P., & Bradley, L. (1987). Rhymes, nursery rhymes, and reading in early childhood. *Merrill-Palmer Quarterly, 33,* 255-281.

Mann, V. A. (1986). Phonological awareness: The role of reading experience. *Cognition, 24,* 65-92.

Morais, J., Cary, L., Alegria, J., & Bertelson P. (1979). Does awareness of speech as a sequence of phones arise spontaneously? *Cognition, 7,* 323-331.

Morais, J., Content, A., Bertelson, P., Cary, L., & Kolinsky, R. (1988). Is there a critical period for the acquisition of segmental analysis? *Cognitive Neuropsychology, 5,* 347-352.

Morais, J., & Kolinsky, R. (1995). The consequences of phoneme awareness. In B. de Gelder, & J. Morais (Eds.), *Speech and Reading: A Comparative Approach*, 317-337. Hove: Erlbaum (UK) Taylor & Francis.

Nakamura, M., Kolinsky, R., Spagnoletti, C., & Morais, J. (1998). Phonemic awareness in alphabetically literate Japanese adults: The influence of the first acquired writing system. *Cahiers de Psychologie Cognitive, 17(2),* 417-450.

Olson, D. R. (1995). La cultura escrita como actividad metalingüística. [Literacy as metalinguistic activity] In D. R. Olson & N. Torrace (Comps.), *Cultura escrita y oralidad* [Literacy and orality] , 333-356. Barcelona: Gedisa.

Öney, B., & Durgunoglu, A. Y. (1997). Beginning to read in Turkish: A phonologically transparent ortography. *Applied Psycholinguistics, 18,* 1-15.

Perfetti, C. A., & Zhang, S. (1991). Phonological processes in reading Chinese characters. *Journal of Experimental Psychology, 17(4),* 633-643.

Porpodas, C. D. (1989). The relation between phonemic awareness and reading and spelling of Greek words in the first school years. In M. Carretero, M. Pope, R. Simons, & J. Pozo (Eds.), *Learning and Instruction. European Research in an International Context.* Vol.3, 203-217. Oxford: Pergamon Press.

Read, C. A., Zhang, Y., Nie, H., & Ding, B. (1986). The ability to manipulate speech sounds depends on knowing alphabetic writing. *Cognition, 24,* 31-44.

Spagnoletti, C., Morais, J., Alegria, J., & Dominicy, M. (1989). Metaphonological abilities of Japanese children. *Reading and Writing. An interdisciplinary Journal, 2,* 221-244.

Sprenger-Charolles, L., & Bonnet, P. (1996). New doubts on the importance of the logographic stage: A longitudinal study of French children. *Cahiers de Psychologie Cognitive, 15(2),* 173-208.

Stanovich, K. E., Cunningham, A. E., & Cramer, B. B. (1984). Assessing phonological awareness in kindergarten children: Issues of task comparability. *Journal of Experimental Child Psychology, 38,* 175-190.

Thorstad, G. (1991). The effect of orthography on the acquisition of literacy skills. *British Journal of Psychology, 82,* 527-537.

Tzeng, O. J. L., Lin, Z.H., Hung, D., & Lee, W.L. (1995). Learning to be a conspirator: A tale of becoming a good Chinese reader. In B. de Gelder, & J. Morais (Eds.), *Speech and Reading: A Comparative Approach*, 227-246. Hove: Erlbaum (UK) Taylor & Francis.

Wimmer, H. (1993). Characteristics of developmental dyslexia in a regular writing system. *Applied Psycholonguistics, 14,* 1-33.

Wimmer, H., & Goswami, U. (1994). The influence of orthographic consistency on reading development: Word recognition in English and German children. *Cognition, 51,* 91-103.

Wimmer, H., & Hummer, P. (1990). How German-speaking first graders read and spell: Doubts on the importance of the logographic stage. *Applied Psycholinguistics, 11,* 349-368

Wimmer, H., Landerl, K., Linortner, R., & Hummer, P. (1991). The relationship of phonemic awareness to reading acquisition: More consequence than precondition but still important. *Cognition, 40,* 219-249.

Yopp, H.K. (1988). The validity and reliability of phonemic awareness tests. *Reading Research Quarterly, 23,* 159-177.

Zaretsky, E. (1995). The influence of spoken language structure on phonological awareness in Russian and English-speaking prereaders. Paper presented at the Meetings of the Society for the Scientific Study of Reading, San Francisco.

SUGGESTED FURTHER READING

de Gelder, B., & Morais, J. (1995). *Speech and Reading: A Comparative Approach.* Hove: Erlbaum (UK) Taylor & Francis.

Gombert, J. E. (1992). *Le développment métalinguistique.* [Metalinguistic development] Paris: Presses Universitaires de France.

Hatano, G., & Harris, M. (1998). *A cross-linguistic perspective on learning to read.* Cambridge University Press.

Frost, R., & Katz, L. (1992). *Orthography, Phonology, Morphology and Meaning.* Amsterdam: Elsevier Science Publishers.

Goswami, U., & Bryant, P. (1990). *Phonological skills and learning to read.* Hillsdale, NJ: Lawrence Erlbaum Assoc.

Taylor, I., & Olson, D. (1995). *Scripts and literacy.* Dordrecht: Kluwer.

E2 Morphology, Reading and Spelling: Looking Across Languages

TEREZINHA NUNES & GIYOO HATANO

ABSTRACT

This chapter considers the significance of morphology and morphological awareness for reading and spelling in different languages. Research on children's language acquisition shows that morphology and grammar play an important role in the acquisition of vocabulary in oral language. This suggests that children have at least some implicit knowledge of morphology, which can be used in the process of reading acquisition. It is possible, however, that this implicit knowledge will have to become at least to some extent explicit in order to contribute to the use of morphological information in reading and spelling. This chapter examines the hypotheses that (i) morphological awareness plays a role in children's literacy learning in different types of language, and that (ii) awareness of morphology in one language can be transferred to another language.

Languages differ in how morphemes are used in word formation. In English, for example, grammatical morphemes (such as inflexional and derivational suffixes) are used in concatenation with a stem to form a word: for example, the word "disheartened" contains a stem, "heart", which is a word by itself and to which the prefix "dis" and two suffixes, "en" (a derivational morpheme) and "ed" (an inflexional morpheme) were added. In Hebrew, the root is composed of (generally) three consonants, which by themselves do not form a pronounceable word; word patterns, which contain vowels, must be intermingled with the root in order to form a word. In spite of these differences in how morphology works across the two languages, children's awareness of morphology and their progress in spelling shows a similar pattern in these two languages: children's awareness of morphology is a predictor of children's progress in spelling and also their progress in spelling seems to strengthen their awareness of morphology.

Languages also differ in how words are represented through script. Thus evidence about morphological awareness in alphabetic scripts must be contrasted with evidence about morphological awareness in non-alphabetic scripts. Evidence from Japanese students reading and spelling with Hiragana – a syllabary – and Kanji – Chinese characters used in Japanese – suggests remarkable similarities in the connection between morphological awareness and literacy across alphabetic

651

T. Nunes, P. Bryant (eds.), Handbook of Children's Literacy, 651–672.

and non-alphabetic scripts. Japanese primary school children seem to face difficulties in learning to read and spell letters that have a morphological function and a different pronunciation determined by this function and master this through a series of steps similar to those described for the mastery of the use of "ed" endings for past tense in English. Furthermore, the facilitative effect between morphological awareness and spelling also goes both ways in Japanese, as it does in English and Hebrew: morphological awareness is predictive of correct spellings of conventional morphemes and progress in the use of morphological components in writing facilitates the acquisition of morphologically complex words. In spite of similarities across such different scripts, it should be pointed out that learning to read and write Chinese characters also requires morphological awareness that is specific to these scripts, such as the awareness of general categories of meaning encapsulated in semantic radicals.

Finally, research is reviewed that shows transfer of morphological awareness in literacy across languages. This transfer is not restricted to cases where there is surface similarity between morphology (such as the use of "s" to mark the plural of nouns in English and French would be an example) but is actually documented in languages where the morphological principle is marked differently in the surface of the languages. Two types of research paradigm, predictive studies and the comparison of monolingual with bilingual children, provide evidence to support transfer of knowledge of morphology across languages.

It is concluded that learning to use morphological principles in writing may be quite similar to learning to use the alphabetic principle. The principle of representing morphology in writing is only acquired once; when we acquire a second language, we only need to learn the particular examples that occur in this second language.

INTRODUCTION

Bryant & Nunes argued in an earlier chapter that children's awareness of morphology plays as important role in learning to read and spell in English. In this chapter, we will expand on this theme by looking across languages, to investigate whether the connection between morphological awareness and reading is language specific. In the first section, we will consider briefly why children's knowledge of syntax and morphology in oral language has the potential to become a source of support for literacy learning. We argue that, if the process of learning an oral language involves syntax and morphology, the knowledge gained in oral language can become integrated into literacy learning in any language. The second section considers the ways in which morphology is represented in different languages and analyses whether different types of morphology are connected with literacy in similar ways. The third section considers some research on non-alphabetic scripts and their representation of morphology. In the forth section we examine the possibility of transfer of morphological awareness across languages in bilingual children. We argue that the possibility of transfer indicates that the connection between morphology and reading is not language specific. In the last section we draw general conclusions from the evidence reviewed in the chapter.

YOUNG CHILDREN'S KNOWLEDGE OF MORPHOLOGY

The interest in young children's knowledge of morphology was first sparkled in the context of studies of how children learn vocabulary. To anyone who is learning a foreign language, it may seem that vocabulary learning is only a matter of learning the sounds of a word and its meaning. When attempting to learn, for example, the word for "vocabulary" in German, we may simply repeat "Wortshatz-vocabulary" to ourselves several times, and hope that we will later remember this German word when we need to use it. In this section, we will try to show that it is unlikely that vocabulary learning only works in this way, by simply repeating a phonological sequence and establishing an association between the sequence of sounds as a whole and its meaning.

Writing about the difficulty of vocabulary learning, researchers often refer to a dilemma posed by the philosopher Quine (1960), which we paraphrase here. Imagine that you are in a foreign country and you hear a native friend say "Gavagai", while looking at a rabbit scurrying past. You may be perfectly able to repeat this sequence of sounds to yourself, and try to start to learn the vocabulary of that language in this way. But how will you know what it means? It could mean "Look!" or "A rabbit!" or "There!" or even "What was that?", if your friend did not actually see the rabbit but only caught the vision of an animal moving. You will be in a difficult position to figure out what "Gavagai" means. Quine's dilemma is, our view, an artificial one. Learning an isolated word is an atypical situation because vocabulary learning usually does not happen in a linguistic vacuum. We learn words and sentences at the same time. The sentences provide learners with input for learning the grammar of the language – and grammar supports vocabulary learning.

Psychologists have for a long time investigated whether children use grammatical cues in the process of learning vocabulary. The pioneer investigations in this domain were carried out by Roger Brown (1957), who used a technique often employed by psychologists when they want to find out about how children deal with novel items. Roger Brown presented the children with a made-up word in the context of a sentence. While the children heard the sentence, they were shown a picture depicting an action on a substance in a container not easily identified as something they would know from everyday life. For example, the child saw a pair of hands kneading a substance in a container and was told: "In this picture you can see some sib". The child was then shown three pictures, one repeating the action with a different material in a different container, one where there was an identical container with an identical substance but the action was different, and a third where the action and the container were different but the substance was the same. The child was asked to select the picture showing "some sib". In this case, the grammatical cues in the sentence indicate that "sib" must refer to the substance. Other examples were used, where the sentence indicated that the word must be a verb (e.g., "In this picture you can see sibbing') or an object ('In this picture you can see a sib').

The children were able to select the correct picture more often than expected by chance. These examples allow us to conclude that children have some knowledge of the implications of these grammatical features of the sentences, even if implicit, and use the grammatical features as cues when they are learning new vocabulary.

What sort of grammatical cues are present in these sentences? In the first example, the main cue is "some"; in the second, the ending of the verb – or the morpheme – "ing"; in the third sentence, the function word "a". These linguistic elements (and others such as the final "s" as a mark for plural, the "ed" ending to mark the past of verbs etc.) are known as "grammatical morphemes". Grammatical morphemes signal characteristics of words such as tense, aspect, plurality, or express relationships between content words in a sentence. Grammatical morphemes are known as bound morphemes because they cannot occur on their own and must be attached to a word. Those morphemes that can appear on their own are termed free morphemes.

Young children do not use knowledge of grammar and morphemes only to learn vocabulary: they also deploy this knowledge when, after learning a new word, they wish to use it in a different grammatical context. Jean Berko (1958) designed a study using the same idea of made-up words used by Brown. In her study, however, instead to asking the children to show that they understood the meaning of a novel word, she asked the children to use novel words in a new grammatical context. To do so appropriately, the children would have to either add or delete morphemes from the model that they had heard. For example, the children were shown a picture of an unfamiliar character and were told: "This is a wug." Then a second picture was shown, with a second identical character, and the children were told: "Now there is another one. Now there are two of them." The child was then encouraged to complete the sentence "There are two...?" In this case, the child would need to add the grammatical morpheme for plurality, "s".

Berko's task is known as a productive morphology task, because the children have to use their knowledge of morphemes in order to produce the correct word, which they never heard before in that particular form. Children's performance in Berko's productive morphology task improved with age. Differences were also observed across grammatical morphemes within the same age level. The inflectional morphemes were easier than the derivational morphemes. For example, the majority of the kindergarten children (aged between 4 and 5.5 years) mastered the plural (wug-wugs). However, both kindergarten and first grade (6 to 7 years) children had much difficulty with inflecting pseudo-words where the plural morpheme appeared in a modified form (known as allomorphs) because of the phonological context (niz-nizzes). In contrast, the use of derivational morphemes was significantly more difficult. For example, whereas adults unanimously said that a man who "zibs" is a "zibber", only 11% of the children provided this answer. In conclusion, Berko's work provides evidence indicating that pre-school children can inflect novel words, although they may not use allomorphs when necessary, but they have considerable difficulty with one kind of grammatical morpheme, namely derivational morphemes, used to form new words.

Since the early work of Brown and Berko, many other researchers have shown that processes in vocabulary learning include the use of syntactic information. Gleitman and colleagues (see, for example, Gleitman, 1990; Gleitman & Gleitman, 1992; Naigles, 1990; Naigles, Gleitman, & Gleitman, 1992) analysed how children use syntax to learn verb meaning. They proposed a Syntactic Bootstrapping hypothesis, according to which children exploit the correlations between syntax and meaning to learn new verbs and narrow down the particular action to which a verb refers. For example, if the child observes a scene where a parent pushes a truck and the trucks skids across the floor, the child will use the syntactic frame to interpret a novel verb used in this situation. If the child is told that "Mum is blicking the truck", the child will interpret this as a causative verb, because it is a transitive verb. If the child is told that "the truck is blicking," the child will interpret the novel verb to refer to a non-causative meaning, the mode of movement of the truck. Even toddlers and pre-school children vary their conjectures about the meaning of verbs according to whether the verb is transitive or intransitive. These results show that quite sophisticated grammatical distinctions are involved in vocabulary learning from an early age.

Another way in which the connection between knowledge of word structure – that is, of morphemes – and vocabulary learning can be demonstrated is by analysing what types of word children are learning at any particular time. Anglin (1993) analysed vocabulary learning in primary school children and showed that a major aspect of vocabulary learning at this age level is learning morphologically complex words. He thus suggested that a major mechanism in vocabulary learning in primary school is the use of morphology to deduce word meaning. We emphasise here the connection between the results on Berko's productive morphology task and this increase in the number of morphologically complex words. The pre-schoolers and first graders had great difficulty in producing derived pseudo-words (zib-zibber). If this difficulty is surmounted in primary school, the children will then be in the position to make use of the recently acquired morphological knowledge and expand their vocabulary.

To summarise, the studies reviewed in this section show that children use their knowledge of grammatical relations and of the morphological structure of words to understand the meaning of novel stimuli, to generate new forms (e.g., plurals, past tense) for novel words which they have not heard, and to actively increase their vocabulary by deduction and without instruction.

We conclude that children have some knowledge of morphology that can be used as a basis for learning in oral language development. It is thus quite reasonable to expect them to use their knowledge of morphology in mastering written language.

The studies that we reviewed in this section include what is known as "implicit knowledge" of grammar. In all of these studies the children used language in its usual function – that is, in communication. We assume that implicit syntactic knowledge is likely to be a stepping stone for the emergence of more explicit forms of syntactic knowledge, which are likely to be implicated in word reading and spelling. We know that children use implicit knowledge of phonology in oral language but that this implicit knowledge is not sufficient for literacy acquisition: children must develop some level of phonological awareness in order to understand how the alphabet represents language (see chapters in Section I for further details). Similarly, children's implicit knowledge of morphology and grammar, detected in the studies reviewed here, may have to become more explicit in order for them to use this knowledge in reading and spelling.

In the section that follows, we consider the fact that there are different types of morphology and different ways in which units of meaning are represented in writing. We will consider some examples of different word structures in oral and written language and also research that analyses the connection between children's understanding of word structure and learning.

DIFFERENT TYPES OF MORPHOLOGY AND THE CONNECTION BETWEEN MORPHOLOGY AND SPELLING ACROSS DIFFERENT LANGUAGES

Morphology in the English language is agglutinative: that is, morphemes are strung together, one after the other. Consider, for example, the word "disheartened". This is a four-morpheme word: each morpheme is placed after the other. The base form – that is, the free morpheme that can be used on its own – is "heart". The prefix "dis" indicates negation; the suffix "en" transforms a noun into a verb; the final suffix, "ed", indicates the tense of the verb, past participle. If we were to encounter this word for the first time – for example in the sentence "I felt disheartened" – we would guess that the speaker was in a negative emotional state, as "heart" is taken here figuratively to signify "emotion".

Morphology does not always follow this pattern, as there are languages in which it is non-concatenative. Hebrew can be used here as an example. Hebrew is a Semitic language and what is said of Hebrew may also apply to other Semitic languages. Bentin and Frost (1995) described concisely and clearly how words are structured in Hebrew:

"As a rule, word formation in Hebrew is based on mounting a "word-pattern" of vowels and consonants onto a "root" which is (usually) a skeleton of consonants.

In contrast to the base-morpheme or stem in English, the Hebrew root is never a word by itself. In fact, the root is not even a phonological unit. Rather, it is an abstract linguistic entity represented by a sequence of usually three (but sometimes four) phonemes (viz., consonants). Roots convey general semantic information which is, in many cases, transparent to the reader. A specific meaning, however, cannot be accessed unless a word is formed by mounting a particular word-pattern on a root. Nevertheless, a speaker of Hebrew can form new words by mounting other word-patterns on the same root and can usually deduce the meaning of new words by extracting the root." (Bentin & Frost, 1995, p. 273).

An example may be useful here. In English, we often add the suffix "er" to verbs in order to form the noun for the agent: clean-cleaner; swim-swimmer; sing-singer. In Hebrew, a frequently used word pattern to form agents is [a – - an]; mounting this word pattern on the root **R**eish **K**uf **D**alet, which means "dancing", forms the word **r**ak**d**an, which means "dancer" (Benting & Frost, 1995, p. 275).

Is it possible that, in spite of such different ways of forming words, English and Hebrew will show similarities in the way that morphology affects the processes of reading and spelling?

Research with adults has shown that there are many similarities between the psychological processes involving morphology used in word recognition in these two languages. We describe here only one example of research with adults in order to illustrate this convergence in results.

Research on adult word recognition often uses an experimental paradigm that is known as "priming". In this paradigm, the participants are asked to name written words presented to them as fast as they can. The "target" word – that is, the word that the experimenter is interested in – is preceded by another word, termed a "prime". The experimenter measures the amount of time that it takes the participant to name the target word. Priming experiments are most often carried out with the support of computers, as the time between the words presented to the participants must be well controlled. Also, the time that it takes the participants to identify the target word – known as recognition time – is measured in milliseconds and thus can only be measured reliably by machines.

Different researchers have investigated what happens to the reaction time when the target word is preceded either by a morphologically related prime (for example, "harmless" is the target word and "harm" is the prime) or by a word that is similar in sound but not related to the target word morphologically (for example, "harmony" is the target and "harm" is the prime). The control condition in these experiments is an unrelated prime, that is, a word that is not similar to the target word either phonologically or morphologically. These experiments consistently show that a morphologically related prime reduces the time that it takes adults to recognise the target word and a prime that is similar in sound but morphologically unrelated increases the recognition time. These results are observed in English (Stolz & Feldman, 1995) and in Italian (Laudana, Badecker & Caramazza, 1989) as well as in Hebrew (Bentin & Frost, 1995).

Research with adults is important for analyses of reading acquisition because it poses a question about the end point of development: If skilled readers use morphology in word recognition, how does this process develop in children?

Bryant and Nunes argued in an earlier chapter in this handbook that awareness of morphology is the basis for children's learning to use morphological strategies in spelling. When spelling, young children represent first and foremost the sounds of words. It is only as their awareness of morphology develops that they become able to represent morphemes in spelling systematically. They also argued that awareness of morphology and spelling with morphemes are two linguistic abilities that influence each other: children need some awareness of morphology in order to spell correctly with morphemes and, as they do so, they become more aware of morphology. Is there similar evidence for the role of morphological awareness in learning to spell Hebrew?

A significant contribution in the domain of morphological strategies in spelling in Hebrew comes from the work by Levin, Ravid and Rapaport (1999). Their study was longitudinal, and included assessing the children in kindergarten and then seven months later, when the children were in first grade. The children were assessed in three oral measures of morphological knowledge and in one writing task. Their measures of morphological knowledge involved a sentence completion task, where the children were asked to provide the adjective that was related to a word included earlier on in the sentence. For example: "A baby who looks like an angel (mal'ax) is an _____ (angel-ic: mal'axi) baby". Levin et al. indicate that this is the last type of adjective to emerge in Hebrew child language and is therefore a good measure of the morphological knowledge of kindergarten children. A second measure of the children's knowledge of morphology used in their study was a transformation of an expanded form – such as ha-gil shel-o (literally, the "age of him') – to the compacted form gil-o ('his age'). The expanded form is acquired early and is characteristic of spoken, less formal discourse. The compacted form involves the use of a suffix marker for gender, number and person and thus involves three simultaneous choices with respect to morphology. Their third task required the children to provide a compound noun from a descriptive sentence. For example, the answer to "what do you call a *room* (xéder) where *children* (yeladim) live?" would be "xadar^yeladim".

Their writing task consisted of 32 words, including some where there is more than one acceptable way of representing one sound: the correct form in these cases was determined by morphology. The spelling received a higher score if the child used the correct spelling than if a phonetically acceptable but orthographically incorrect spelling was used.

Levin et al. observed that the children's knowledge of oral morphology in kindergarten was a good predictor of how well they used the correct spelling in first grade, even after they controlled for how well the children were already writing in kindergarten. Conversely, the children's level of writing in kindergarten was also a good predictor of their knowledge of oral morphology assessed in the first year of school, even after controlling for their knowledge of oral morphology in kindergarten. Similarly to Nunes, Bryant and Bindman (1997), Levin and colleagues concluded that learning about morphology and spelling are two related skills that influence each other. The more you know about morphology, the easier it is to learn the conventional spelling of morphologically related words; this, in turn, makes you more aware of morphology.

In conclusion, the evidence available from languages with distinct word structures – such as agglutinative morphology in English and non-concatenative morphology in Hebrew – indicates that these differences in the characteristics of oral morphology do not imply different processes in the connection between awareness of morphology and literacy. In both languages, skilled readers use morphological information in word identification and children use their knowledge of morphology in order to master conventional spelling that does not conform in a simple way to phonological representation.

In the next section we examine the evidence related to literacy learning in languages with different written word structure.

THE ROLE OF MORPHOLOGY IN DIFFERENT TYPES OF SCRIPT

English and Hebrew represent diverse types of morphology but written English and Hebrew are both alphabetic scripts. In this section we consider different types of script – a syllabic script, the Japanese Hiragana – and a very different script, Chinese characters. We will argue that morphological knowledge plays a significant role in learning to read and write letters and characters representing a larger phonological unit than a phoneme: that is, learning of Hiragana (syllabaries) in the Japanese writing system and learning Chinese characters in Chinese and Japanese depends on children's morphological knowledge. We will consider each script in turn.

Morphological influences on syllabic scripts

Hiragana, one of the two kinds of kana syllabaries used in Japan, are 71 letters. Although they are called syllabaries, each of them in fact represents a mora – a subsyllabic rhythmic unit, more specifically, a vocalic nucleus, a nucleus preceded by a syllable onset, the postvocalic portion of a syllable, or an extended portion of the vowel. Thus, for example, the word "nintendou' has six letters when written in Hiragana that correspond to six morae, though it has only three syllables.

Most kana letters, when used as individual units, have one and the same pronunciation, but there are two exceptions, "ha' and "he'. These letters are pronounced differently when they indicate particles representing cases in a broad sense: "ha' indicates that the preceding noun is the subject or another focus of the sentence ("Tokyo-ha shiranai" meaning "Tokyo, I do not know" with Tokyo as the focus), and "he', the destination or another goal state ("Tokyo-he iku" meaning "I go to Tokyo"). More specifically, "ha' and "he' are usually pronounced /ha/ and /he/, respectively, but when they are case particles they are pronounced /wa/ and /e/. Thus, the letters "ha' and "he' have two distinct pronunciations, one when they have a phonological function only, as an element in a word, and the second when they are grammatical morphemes.

The bi-univocal correspondence between letters and sounds in Japanese Hiragana is violated not only in reading "ha' and "he' as /wa/ and /e/ but also when writing these sounds. There are letters that are pronounced /wa/ and /e/, respectively, which could be used for writing these sounds. However, they are only used for writing these sounds when the sounds are phonological elements in words, not when they are grammatical morphemes. So when writing a word or a sentence, one has to choose the correct letter for these sounds according to whether they correspond to a grammatical morpheme or not.

There are three further pronunciations that can be represented by either of the pairs of kana letters. Which letter is to be used for writing is affected by a morphological rule and a more specific piece of morphological information, in other words, knowledge about substantive morphemes as well as syntactic morphemes – the choice of kana letters for a compound (multi-morphemic) word is often determined by what morphemes it consists of. For example, a variety of pickles are called "xx-zuke', and "zuke' comes from "tsukeru' (pickling). Thus "zu' in this case must be "tsu with a special mark for voicing', not the more common alternative of "su with the voicing mark'. Children have to learn and apply morphological knowledge, if they do not want to learn many different instances just by rote.

Most children learn to read perfectly a sentence written in kana letters (including "ha' and "he') by the end of the first grade, that is, after they have been taught systematically for a year. But some children can infer the special morphological rules by themselves before they start their formal education. How can they acquire the rules? How do they learn that, for example, the letters mentioned above have two pronunciations and thus become able to choose one of them? Is it by judging whether each letter is used as a case particle or not?

Akita and Hatano (1998) tested five-years-old children twice, with an interval of four months between the testing sessions, using three types of short sentence involving the letters "ha' or "he'. In the first type of sentence, "ha' or "he' were embedded in a word and had their usual pronunciation. For example, "Taroukun, hanashitene" ("Taro, please tell me"). The second type of sentence included "ha' or "he' as a case particle, with its other pronunciation /wa/ or /e/: "Taroukunha otonashii" ("Taro is obedient"). The third type also included "ha' or "he' as a case particle, but here they were followed by another particle, a sentence-final one, like "Taroukunhane, yasashiiyo' ("Taro is kind"). "Ha" and "he" as a case particles usually come at the end of a sentence segment consisting of a noun and post-positional particle(s). Correctly pronouncing the letters as /wa/ or /e/ is likely to be harder for the third type of sentence because it violates this positional expectation. In other words, if children use a strategy to identify the morphemic status of "ha" or "he" just based on the letter's position, they will read correctly the second type of sentence but fail to read the third type.

The results of the study suggest three developmental stages for reading "ha" or "he". At the first stage children don't know its pronunciation as a case particle. They read "ha" always /ha/, without any doubt. In the interview, a child at this stage said, "I can read all sentences. They are very easy for me", though his reading was not all correct.

Children at the second stage know that "ha" or "he" may be pronounced /wa/ or /e/, and overextend this pronunciation to the letter when it is a phonological element embedded in words. For example, they pronounce the word "Yokohama" (the name of a city near Tokyo) as Yokowama. These errors occurred especially often in unfamiliar words. They do not overextend it to highly familiar words such as "hana" (flower) and "ohayou" (good morning). At this stage, however, the special pronunciation as case particle tends to have priority over the usual pronunciations.

Through an intermediate stage, children reach the third, final stage, in which they can discriminate the morphemic status of these letters and pronounce them correctly. During the intermediate stage children seem to gradually increase the amount of information that they consider when reading the letters and take different steps in approaching the complete correct solution. One of these steps is to consider the position of these letters in a sentence segment. So, they can read the letter correctly in the last position of the segment, "Tarouha" (as in the above second type of the experimental sentences), but they fail to do so if the letter is not the last segment, "Tarouhane" (as in the third type). This suggests that they are still not sensitive enough to the morphemic status of the letters.

The number of children who reach the third stage of complete differentiation before the first grade is very small. This small number of children may induce an implicit rule for discrimination, apply it to various situations, and receive feedback from adults.

This pattern of acquisition is remarkably similar to the pattern described by Nunes, Bryant and Bindman (1997) for the acquisition of the spelling of "-ed" endings for regular verbs. English children initially spell past verbs phonetically; then they realise that the "ed" ending is a correct form and start using it but don't know yet where it belongs and thus overgeneralise it; finally they restrict it to the correct morphological function. The transition between overgeneralising and correct use in English, like in Japanese, involves progressive steps, because the English children continue to generalise the "-ed" to irregular verbs even after they have stopped using it in non-verbs. In their earlier chapter, Bryant and Nunes provided evidence suggesting that children's progress in these stages is connected to their awareness of morphology and grammar. Akita and Hatano (1999) investigated whether a similar process could be identified in the learning of "ha" and "he".

The measure of awareness of the grammatical morpheme that Akita and Hatano (1999) used was based on the children's ability to recognise the difference in the use of the particle in two short sentences. This task was analogous to judging whether "He carried the box into the house" and "He carried the box to the house" are identical or not, and if not, telling what the difference is. The children's performance in this task was correlated with their developmental stage in reading these letters. In contrast, the reading stage was not correlated with a similar task for a content word (a noun or a verb) – comparable to judging the same/difference between "Birds sing" and "Birds swing". Knowledge about bound morphemes, but not that about free morphemes, seems to be correlated with the proper reading of "ha" and "he".

Akita (1999) has been able to replicate these results in a later study which showed that the ability to recognise and to manipulate a grammatical particle, but not a content word, significantly contributes to reading performance on these letters, even when the effect of the general reading level is partialled out. Her task was similar to the sentence analogy task used by Nunes et al. (1997): it required children to change a particle, or a noun as the control, in the same way as in the given example. For instance, the model sentences for particles were "She put a ball in the box" was changed into "She put a ball on the box"; the children were then asked to make an analogous transformation on "He stored oranges in the container". In the control sentences using content words, the model sentences were "Haruko pinched Akiko" changed to "Akiko pinched Haruko"; the children were then asked to transform "Taro hit Jiro". The results suggest that proper reading of these letters presupposes attention to grammatical particles in sentence processing. Akita also found that children's writing of these letters was based on their pronunciation, even when they could discriminate the letters' morphemic status and read them correctly. More specifically, they often wrote the "wa" or "e" letter for "ha" or "he" as a particle. Thus in Japanese kana orthography, as in English, morphological knowledge plays a role in learning to read and write, at least for these two and a few other letters.

Morphological knowledge in learning to read and write Chinese characters

Chinese characters are similar to Japanese Hiragana because each Chinese character represents a syllable. However, differently from the Japanese Hiragana, Chinese characters have an internal structure. Taft and Zhu (1995) provide a concise description of the structure of Chinese characters:

> "In Chinese [Mandarin] there is no doubt about the internal orthographic and phonological structure of a word. Every word is made up of one or more (usually two) characters, where each character is pronounced as a monosyllable. A character typically provides semantic information about the word, and for this reason, Chinese characters are said to be equivalent to single morphemes. Most characters are composed of two components: a 'semantic radical' which is typically on the left side and provides a guide to the meaning of the word, and a 'phonetic radical' which typically occurs on the right side and provides a guide to pronunciation" (Taft & Zhu, 1995, pp. 301-302).

Nagy and Anderson (1998) concur in asserting that morphological knowledge plays a critical role in learning to read and write Chinese characters, because they represent morphemes. The authors also point out that the internal structure of Chinese words and characters provides readers with a clue for meanings.

Chinese characters are used not only in China but also in a few neighbouring countries. For example, about 2,000 Chinese characters (called *kanji*, literally meaning Chinese characters) are designated as kanji for daily use in Japan. Educated Japanese adults are able to read at least a few times this number. About half of the 2,000 are taught in elementary school.

Because the number of kinds of syllables is much smaller than the number of morphemes (or characters), single-morphemic words that have distinct meanings often have the same pronunciation. This is especially notable in Japanese, a language with a highly limited phonological inventory. For example, more than 70 of the 2,000 kanji for daily use have the Chinese reading of /kou/. Technical terms and other infrequently used words can often be distinguished from their homonyms only by being written in kanji.

Then, how can Chinese and Japanese readers choose the correct component characters in writing? They must rely on the characters' specific morphological information (the meaning and syntactic property). It is like English readers writing "coleslaw" for salad and "coalfish" for a black fish, choosing either COLE or COAL depending on whether its meaning is suitable to the given context. In other words, here readers use specific morphological information in writing.

This is not always straightforward because, though each character has its core meaning, it can be extended metaphorically. For example, a character possessing the core, prototypical meaning of "water" may be used for such expanded meanings as sea, flood, or moisture when combined with other characters. Learning to choose the proper Chinese character for writing is thus based on the accumulation of specific morphological information, probably enhanced most by extensive reading.

Using a Chinese character as a phonetic symbol rather than for its meaning is often considered a sign of being uneducated. Students may fail to choose the correct character, but even when they do so, the characters they choose are close to the correct one in meaning (Hatano, 1986).

Two aspects of morphological awareness, in addition to specific morphological knowledge about each character, seem to facilitate the learning of reading and writing Chinese characters. They are radical awareness and word composition awareness. The former concerns the awareness of the internal structure of Chinese characters, and the latter, the composition of multisyllabic-multicharacter words.

Awareness of internal structure

Many semantic radicals and phonetic components are themselves simple characters, which students are likely to learn before they learn ideo-phonetic compounds. Because of this, learning to read and write Chinese characters is far from rote learning. If students have acquired radical and phonetic awareness – that is, if they are aware that most compound characters have a phonetic component and a semantic radical – they can use this knowledge to interpret new characters. When presented with a new character, students should be able to make an educated guess about its pronunciation and meaning, based on their radical and phonetic component.

There are already some studies in Chinese, using the techniques of unfamiliar and pseudo-word interpretation, production, and learning, that indicate that Chinese children are sensitive to the intra-character structure of ideo-phonetic compounds. For example, Shu and Anderson (1997) showed that the third grade children could choose characters containing the correct radicals for known words in oral language even when the characters as a whole were unfamiliar to them, and use known radicals to infer the meaning of new characters.

Chan and Nunes (1998) used two ingenious tasks to investigate children's knowledge of the written structure of the Chinese ideo-phonetic compound. In one task, the children were presented with pictures of strange but recognisable objects which, they were told, had been found by a boy in his adventurous trips to other planets. The children, all Chinese and living in Hong Kong, were asked to invent a character to name those objects and a pronunciation for the character. As support, they were given stroke patterns (that is, graphic units used to compose characters) written on transparent cards, which they could manipulate to create the novel name for the objects. Chan and Nunes argued that, if the children correctly selected appropriate semantic radicals and combined them with phonetic components, this would demonstrate that they have at least implicit knowledge of the structure of Chinese characters (i.e., written morphemes).

The performance of the 4 year-olds was not above chance level in producing pseudo-words with an ideo-phonetic compound structure but 5-year-olds already performed above chance level, producing more than 70% pseudo-words with this structure. The percentages of pseudo-characters with an ideo-phonetic compound structure was above 80 for the 6- and 7-year-olds and above 90 for the 8-year-olds; all pseudo-words created by 9-year-olds were ideo-phonetic compounds.

Chan and Nunes also examined whether the children had made adequate choices of semantic radicals for their pseudo-characters: the only age group who failed to do so above chance was the group of 4 year-olds. Thus, this task of productive written morphology provides evidence to suggest that even 5 year-olds already display some knowledge of the structure of Chinese characters.

Tsai and Nunes (2000) further explored children's knowledge of the structure of ideo-phonetic compounds by asking children in Taiwan to learn how to write or read pseudo-characters. The children were presented with a series of pictures of strange but identifiable objects (as in the Chan & Nunes' study) and a character, which was said to be the name of the object. A pronunciation for the character was also provided. Half of the pseudo-characters had an appropriate ideo-phonetic compound structure for the meaning they had been assigned: their semantic radical was consistent with the category of the object it represented and their pronunciation was related to the phonetic component. The other half of the characters, although composed of a semantic radical and a phonetic element, were incongruent with the meaning and pronunciation they were assigned in the learning task. Tsai and Nunes suggested that, if the children are sensitive to the structure of characters, they will find the congruent pseudo-words easier to learn than the incongruous ones. The children in their study were in the age range 6 to 11 years. All age groups showed a significant difference between the number of congruous and incongruous pseudo-characters leaned. Although the older children learned more characters, the proportion of congruous characters that they learned was similar to the proportion of congruous characters learned by the younger children. These results were independent of response mode – that is, they were the same irrespective of whether the children were asked to write down the pseudo-words when presented with the picture (the writing task) or asked to identify and pronounce the pseudo-character that went with a picture (the reading task).

In conclusion, there is robust evidence indicating that young Chinese readers are sensitive to the intra-character structure of written Chinese. Because characters are written morphemes, it is possible to conclude that the children use knowledge of morphology in learning novel characters. To our regret, there are no predictive studies to date, similar to those described earlier on in the chapter by Bryant and Nunes, where knowledge of syntax and morphology in oral language was shown both to predict and to be strengthened by literacy learning.

Awareness of the composition of multisyllabic-multicharacter words

Many Chinese words consist of two or more morphemes, syllables, or characters. In other words, component characters can be combined to make new words with more extended or precise meanings. This composition of multimorphemic words is fairly systematic and regulated by what might be called compounding schemata (Hatano, 1986). For example, when two nouns are compounded, the new word belongs to the family of the last noun. Thus, "milk-cow" means a cow for milking and "cow-milk" means milk from a cow. Word composition awareness means the recognition that the meaning of a compound word can be inferred from the prototypical meaning of component characters and a compounding schema.

It has been shown that Japanese college students are good at inferring the meaning of unfamiliar technical terms consisting of two or more Chinese characters (Hatano, Kuhara & Akiyama, 1981). When required to match the terms (e.g., limnology or piscivorous) with their definitions ("the scientific study of physical, chemical, and biological conditions in lakes and ponds" or "eating fish as a regular diet") in Japanese, they performed much better than the American counterparts who were tested in English. Their superiority was not surprising when the word list was presented in kanji, because the kanji expression for the terms clearly indicated constituent morphemes (e.g., for limnology "lake(s)", "pond(s)", and "study (studies)" and for piscivorous "fish", "eat" and "nature". However, the Japanese students showed respectable performances even when the word list was given in Hiragana. Their success should thus be attributed in part to their word composition awareness or ability to infer the meaning of multi-morphemic words.

In conclusion, studies of languages that use non-alphabetic scripts indicate that morphological knowledge is an important part of reading and writing in these scripts. This is surprisingly so even in the case of Japanese Hiragana, which show a high level of consistency at the phonological level and where the examples that involve morphological processes are reduced in number. The initial studies available about the learning of Chinese characters seem to indicate an active involvement of knowledge of written-word structure in young children's literacy learning although very little is known about the nature of this knowledge, whether it is implicit or explicit. Experimental studies would be of great value in clarifying whether systematic teaching of the structure of characters can facilitate literacy learning in Chinese.

TRANSFER OF AWARENESS OF MORPHO-SYNTAX ACROSS LANGUAGES

In this last section we examine the level of representation of children's syntactic and morphological knowledge. There are two distinct possibilities here (for a more extensive discussion, see Bindman, 1997).

First, it is possible that children learn surface-level facts about their language, without developing any representation of the deep structure of the grammar manifested in the morphology. If we consider children's learning of the past tense, for example, it is possible that what they learn is that you can say "I open" and "I opened". If you are speaking about something you already did, then you use "opened". Many verbs work in the same way and have a form ending in "ed" and another form without the "ed". Another example: children may know that if you are speaking about people who carry out certain actions (e.g., swim), you can call them by a name made up by the verb plus an "er" ending (swimmer). If this hypothesis about the children's knowledge is correct, because all they know is the specific "facts" about their language, their knowledge is not useful in another language, unless the same facts hold true in the other language. An example of a fact that holds true across languages is the use of "s" as a marker of plural. If you refer to more than one object in English, you use an "s" at the end of the word; because this is also true of Portuguese, Spanish and French nouns, when you are learning these languages, you can transfer your knowledge of plural from English to these languages.

The second hypothesis is that children learn not only surface-level facts about their language but also the deep-structure principles manifested in the surface level. Their knowledge of past tense, then, would be better described as an understanding that verbs can be inflected to show tense, and that in English the marker of the past is the "ed". If children's knowledge is represented also at this deep-structure level, then their knowledge should be transferable across languages even if the specific facts of surface level grammar are very different across the languages. In this case, the fact that the past is marked by "ed" in English (adding a suffix) and by "ta" in Japanese (adding a particle) should not interfere significantly with learning past forms of verbs in Japanese: all that changes is the surface, the deep-structure principles remain the same.

These two alternative hypotheses are distinct only in the predictions they make regarding transfer across languages that mark the same grammatical distinctions but do so in different ways. When the surface level is distinct (that is, the specific morphemes are different), the first hypotheses predicts no transfer across languages and the second hypotheses predicts positive transfer across languages.

It is important to distinguish between these alternatives both for theoretical and practical reasons. Theoretically, an adequate description of how linguistic knowledge is represented by learners is central to any theory of literacy learning. In the context of learning about the representation of sounds by letters in alphabetic scripts, it has been argued that children's initial and most important task is to acquire an "alphabetic conception" of writing (Read, 1971; Ferrero & Teberosky, 1983) or to understand the alphabetic principle (Byrne & Fielding-Barnsley, 1990). Only then can the specific letter-sound correspondences be utilised for writing and reading words. The practical corollary of this theory is that we only learn to read once. If we learn to read in a second language, the only new acquisition is of letter-sound correspondences: we already knew how to read.

Similarly, it must be investigated whether children develop an understanding that writing represents morphology and transfer this understanding across languages. When children learn a second language, do they need to acquire a "morphological principle" again or do they have to learn only the new facts about how morphology is recorded in writing?

Unfortunately, few studies so far have examined this question. We review here three studies that considered the transfer of grammatical and morphological knowledge across languages. These studies provide an overview of the methods used in the investigation of transfer of the morphological principle across languages.

Geva and Siegel (1994) and Geva (1995) investigated the transfer of grammatical knowledge in oral language. If bilingual children have a deep-structure representation of grammar, their performance in a test of grammatical knowledge in the two languages should show a significant correlation. In order to test this prediction, Geva and her colleagues used a sentence completion task to assess the children's grammatical ability. In this task, known as Oral Cloze Task, the children hear a sentence where one word is missing; the children are asked to produce a word that would fit in that particular place in the sentence. The position of the missing word is signalled by the experimenter tapping on the table. For example, in the sentence "*tap* knocked on the door?", the child would have to provide a word that can be used in the first slot in this sentence frame. Geva administered the Cloze Task twice, once in English and once in Hebrew, to Canadian children attending an English-Hebrew bilingual school. She observed a correlation of .46 between the children's performance in the two languages. Because this correlation might result from the children's level of general intelligence, she ran a regression analysis where she controlled for the children's performance in a test of general intelligence, the Raven's Colored Progressive Matrix. Even after controlling for intelligence, the correlation between the children's performance in the two languages continued to be significant (r = .44). Geva's results suggest that there must be a level at which children represent deep-structure grammatical principles and use their knowledge of these principles across languages, even if the surface grammar of the languages is very different.

An alternative methodological approach to investigate this question was used by Galambos and Goldin-Meadow (1990), whose work involved a comparison between bilingual Spanish-English and monolingual Spanish speaking children. The paradigm of comparing monolingual and bilingual children is based on another feature of the transfer hypothesis. In a typical transfer paradigm, children are given experience in a task that is not identical to the target task, but is hypothesised to share a critical feature with the target task. A control group of children has experience in a third task, which is not hypothesised to share the same feature. When the two groups are tested in the target task, if there is positive transfer across tasks, the transfer group should perform better in the target task than the control group. This reasoning can be easily applied to the analysis of transfer of grammatical and morphological knowledge across languages. Bilingual children have experience with one language, which is not the same as the other language they know but shares with it grammatical and morphological principles at a deep-structure level. Monolingual children lack this extra linguistic experience. Thus the comparison between bilingual and monolingual children offers the opportunity for a natural experiment in the investigation of transfer across languages.

Galambos and Goldin-Meadow investigated whether bilingual children (in the age range 5 to 7 years) were better than monolingual children in making judgements of grammaticality. They were given grammatically correct sentences and incorrect sentences. They were also asked to explain what was wrong with the sentences they thought were incorrect. The bilingual children were better at detecting errors and offering grammatical corrections than the monolingual children, who seemed to be more content-oriented than grammar-oriented in their corrections. Once the error had been detected, children in the two groups were equally competent at explaining what was wrong with the sentence. Thus this natural experiment indicates that there is transfer in grammatical knowledge of oral language between English and Spanish.

Findings indicating that there is transfer of grammatical knowledge of oral language support the hypothesis that the representation of grammatical knowledge involves not only surface features but also deep-level principles. Bindman (1997) investigated whether this transfer can also be observed in the representation of grammatical morphemes in written language. She used in her studies both paradigms described above: a correlational one, where transfer leads to the prediction that there is a significant correlation between grammatical and morphological knowledge across languages, and a bilingual-monolingual comparison, where transfer leads to the prediction that bilingual children will perform better in the target tasks.

Bindman's bilingual group was composed of English children attending English-Hebrew bilingual schools in London. Bindman used both oral and written tasks. Her oral tasks were similar to the Cloze Task used by Geva. To test the use of morphological knowledge in written language, Bindman asked the children to spell words which could have different spellings if only phonology were taken into account, but whose correct spelling is determined by morphology. For example, the word "magician" would be spelled as "magishian" if the children were simply representing the sounds they hear. The use of the letter "c" in "magician" is determined morphologically: the base form, "magic", from which "magician" is derived, ends in "c". Bindman chose a few pairs of words that share the same base form and asked the children to spell one of the words in the pair on one testing occasion and the other word on a second occasion. She scored the children's consistency in spelling the base form across the words in the pair. Because Hebrew was the children's second language, Bindman devised an easier task for assessing the children's knowledge of morphology in written Hebrew. As explained earlier on in this chapter, Hebrew words contain a root formed by three consonants. Bindman presented the children with a target word and three choices, asking the children to identify amongst the three choices which one shared the root with the target word. All three choice words shared three letters with the target one, but only one shared the three consonants that form the root in the correct order. Assuming that morpho-syntactic knowledge is represented at the deep-structure level, Bindman predicted that there would be transfer across the two languages and that the children's performance across languages would be correlated both in the oral and the written mode. Results supported this prediction: the correlations across languages were significant even after controlling for vocabulary knowledge as an abbreviated measure of verbal intelligence.

The second part of Bindman's study used the paradigm of bilingual-monolingual comparison. The same English tasks were given to English monolingual children attending English schools in London. The two groups of children were matched for their verbal ability in English (using the WISC vocabulary task) so that differences between the bilingual and monolingual groups in morpho-syntactic tasks in English could not be attributed to differences in general verbal ability. Bindman's results showed an interaction between the bilingual children's knowledge of Hebrew and their performance in the English tasks of grammatical and morphological knowledge in oral and written language. Bilingual children with high levels of Hebrew knowledge performed significantly better than monolingual English children in both oral and written English tasks of morpho-syntactic knowledge. In contrast, the bilingual children whose knowledge of Hebrew was weak sometimes performed better than the monolingual group but sometimes showed the same level of performance. Bindman concluded that her studies provide strong support to the idea that morpho-syntactic knowledge can be transferred across languages. Thus this knowledge must be represented at the deep-structure level.

In summary, children do not have to learn the concept of representing morphology in writing twice when they learn to read and write in two languages. It is likely that, similarly to the acquisition of the alphabetic principle, the morphological principle is learned only once. When we learn to read and spell in a second language, all we need to learn is which morphemes are represented in writing and how they are represented.

SUMMARY AND CONCLUSIONS

This chapter investigated whether the connection between morpho-syntactic knowledge and literacy is language specific. We reviewed evidence supporting the hypothesis that children's knowledge of morphology in oral language participates in the processes of vocabulary learning. This makes the hypothesis that morphological knowledge participates in literacy learning more plausible and that the connection between morphological awareness and literacy might not be language specific. We then reviewed evidence showing that there is a connection between morphology and literacy in languages with different types of morphology and also in different types of script. The evidence on the stages of acquisition of morphological strategies in reading and spelling in English and Japanese show striking similarity. At first, children seem to concentrate on phonology; later, they seem to notice exceptions in the letter-sound correspondences but do not seem to understand that there is a morphological basis for these exceptions, and thus overgeneralise the use of the newly acquired forms; finally, they are able (often through successive approximations) to implement the adequate morphological strategy and succeed in all instances. In the last section, we discussed the way in which morphological knowledge is represented by children. The evidence we reviewed on transfer of morpho-syntactic knowledge across languages supports the hypothesis of a deep-structure level of representation rather than only a surface level. Thus we conclude that it is most likely that the connection between morphology and literacy is not language specific.

REFERENCES

Akita, K. (1999) *Learning to read and write "ha" or "he" and particle awareness (2)*. Paper presented at the Annual Convention of the Japanese Association of Developmental Psychology, Osaka. [in Japanese]

Akita, K. & Hatano, G. (1998) *Learning to read and write "ha" or "he" and particle awareness*. Paper presented at the Annual Convention of the Japanese Association of Educational Psychology, Tokyo. [in Japanese]

Anglin, J. M. (1993). Vocabulary development: A morphological analysis. *Monographs of the Society for Research in Child Development, 238*, 1-165.

Bentin, S. & Frost, R. (1995). Morphological factors in visual word identification in Hebrew. In L. B. Feldman (Ed.), *Morphological aspects of language processing* (pp. 271-292). Hillsdale (NJ): Lawrence Erlbaum.

Berko, J. B. (1958). The child's learning of English morphology. *Word, 14*, 150-177.

Bindman, M. (1997). Relationships between metalinguistic and spelling development across languages: Evidence from English and Hebrew. Unpublished Ph D Thesis, Child Development and Learning, Institute of Education, University of London.

Brown, R. (1957). Linguistic determinism and parts of speech. *Journal of Abnormal and Social Psychology, 55*, 1-5.

Byrne, B. & Fielding-Barnsley, R. (1990). Acquiring the alphabetic principle: A case for teaching recognition of phoneme identify. *Journal of Educational Psychology, 82*, 805-812.

Chan, L. & Nunes, T. (1998). Children's understanding of formal and functional characteristics of written Chinese. *Applied Psycholinguistics, 19*, 115-131.

Ferreiro, E. & Teberosky, A. (1983) *Literacy before schooling*. London: Heineman Educational.

Galambos, S. J. & Goldin-Meadow, S. (1990). The effects of learning two languages on levels of metalinguistic awareness. *Cognition, 34*, 1-56.

Geva, E. (1995). Orthographic and cognitive processing in learning to read English and Hebrew. In I. Taylor & D. R. Olson (Eds.), *Scripts and literacy* (pp. 81-114). Dordrecth (The Netherlands): Kluwer.

Geva, E. & Siegel, L. (1994). The role of orthography and cognitive factors in the concurrent development of basic reading skills in bilingual children. Unpublished manuscript. Toronto (Canada): OISE.

Gleitman, L. R. (1990). The structural sources of verb meaning. *Language acquisiton, 1*, 3-55.

Gleitman, L. R. & Gleitman, H. (1992). A picture is worth a thousand words, but that's the problem: The role of syntax in vocabulary acquisition. *Current Directions in Psychological Science, 1*, 31-35.

Hatano, G. (1986) How do Japanese children learn to read: Orthographic and eco-cultural variables. In B. Foorman & A. Siegel (Eds.), *Acquisition of reading skills: Cultural constraints and cognitive universals* (pp. 81-114). Hillsdale, NJ: Erlbaum.

Hatano, G., Kuhara, K. and Akiyama, M. (1981) Kanji help readers of Japanese infer the meaning of unfamiliar words. *The Quarterly Newsletter of the Laboratory of Comparative Human Cognition, 3*, 30-33.

Levin, I., Ravid, D., & Rapaport, S. (1999). Developing morphological awareness and learning to write: A two-way street. In T. Nunes (Ed.), *Learning to read: An intergrated view from research and practice* (pp. 77-104). Dordrecht (The Netherlands): Kluwer Academic.

Nagy, W. E. and Anderson, R. C. (1999) Metalinguistic awareness and the acquisition of literacy in different languages. In D. Wagner, R. Venezky, & B. Street (Eds.), *Literacy: An International Handbook* (pp. 155-160). Westminster, CO: West View Press.

Naigles, L. (1990). Children use syntax to learn verb meanings. *Journal of Child Language, 17*, 357-374.

Naigles, L, Gleitman, L. R., & Gleitman, H. (1992). Children acquire word meaning components from syntactic evidence. In E. Dromi (Eds.), *Language and cognition: A developmental perspective* (pp. 104-140). Norwood, NJ: Ablex.

Quine, W. V. O. (1960). *Word and object*. Cambridge (MA): MIT Press.

Read, C. (1971). Pre-school children's knowledge of English phonology. *Harvard Educational Review, 41*, 1-34.

Shu, H. & Anderson, R.C. (1997) Role of radical awareness in the character and word acquisition of Chinese children. *Reading Research Quarterly, 32*, 78-89.

Taft, M. & Zhu, X. (1995). The representation of bound morphemes in the lexicon: A Chinese study. In L. B. Feldman (Ed.), *Morphological Aspects of Language Processing* (pp. 293-216). Hillsdale, (NJ): Lawrence Erlbaum.

Tsai, K. & Nunes, T. (2000). Chinese children's use of character structure in learning new characters. Paper presented at the Annual Meeting of the Developmental Section of the British Psychological Society, Bristol, September.

SUGGESTED FURTHER READING

Foorman, B. & Siegel, A. (1986.), *Acquisition of reading skills: Cultural constraints and cognitive universals.* Hillsdale, NJ: Erlbaum.

Taylor & D. R. Olson (1995), *Scripts and literacy.* Dordrecht (The Netherlands): Kluwer

Wagner, D., Venezky, R. & Street, B. (1998), *Literacy: An International Handbook.* Westminster, CO: West View Press.

E3 Bilingualism and Reading

LINDA SIEGEL

ABSTRACT

This chapter examines the connection between learning bilingualism and learning to read with a special focus on the processes of word identification and spelling. The learners who participated in the different studies considered were bilingual as defined by a certain fluency in the two of more languages they were exposed to. The social and cultural context of the studies varied in that some of the children were immigrants or children of immigrants and spoke one language at home and a second at school whereas others lived in bilingual environments. Although it is recognised that the socio-political context in which the second language is learned is important for the learners' motivation, socio-economic status and the value placed on bilingualism, these were considered less critical for the analysis of processes in word identification and spelling that linguistic differences such as the type and regularity of the scripts being learned. Thus the effects of the linguistic variables were examined more systematically in this review than the effects of the socio-political context.

The research reviewed here analyses individual and group differences in phonological processing, phonological awareness, syntactic awareness, working memory, reading and spelling, and orthographic awareness. These issues are examined in an attempt to provide an answer to two basic questions: (i) whether immigrant children learning to read English as a second language (ESL) are at a disadvantage in comparison to native speakers; and (ii) whether it is possible that transfer of reading and spelling skills can occur between two languages.

The research reveals that immigrant children with little knowledge of English at the start of school may be at a disadvantage in some but not all aspects in learning to read, and may quickly catch up with native speakers in some cases. For example, their restricted exposure to English may result in smaller vocabulary and lower levels of performance in syntactic awareness tasks but they seem to quickly develop phonological awareness and phonological processing skills as they participate in school instruction. Their initial disadvantage in phonological skills is not similar to those of poor readers, whose difficulties remain after instruction. However, bilingual children may remain slower in reading even if their accuracy levels are comparable to those of native speakers.

The possibility of transfer of skills across languages is supported by research

T. Nunes, P. Bryant (eds.), Handbook of Children's Literacy, 673–689.
© 2004 *Kluwer Academic Publishers. Printed in Great Britain.*

that shows significant correlations in phonological awareness across languages. Thus some support is found for a model assuming a common underlying proficiency between languages and also for the possibility of some advantages to learning to read in two languages over learning to read in one language only. In particular, positive transfer from one language to the other was observed when the children learned to read a more regular orthography (such as Portuguese or Spanish) and transfer was analysed in a less regular orthography (such as English). Nevertheless, this transfer is moderated by the level of congruence between the languages. Japanese students, whose orthography is not alphabetic and is visually complex, showed positive transfer is tasks that could be performed at the visual level but no transfer in tasks that required the use of grapheme-phoneme conversion rules. In the latter case, Spanish and Arabic students, who use a second alphabetic language, showed more positive transfer than Japanese students.

It is concluded that bilingualism does not interfere with the development of reading skills and that it may be an advantage to learn two languages in that there is some evidence of positive transfer from one language to another, particularly in the case of transfer from more regular orthographies to English.

INTRODUCTION

There are many types of bilingualism and various contexts in which bilingualism occurs. The term bilingualism implies a certain fluency with two (or more) languages. The discussion of bilingualism and reading in this chapter will be limited to a consideration of the research with children and adults who are acquiring reading skills in a language that is not their first language. Most often, learning to read in a bilingual context occurs because individuals are learning to read in the language of the place in which they live but not the language that they speak at home.

THE CONTEXT OF BILINGUALISM

In major cities in many parts of the world, children grow up speaking two or more languages because of political factors or immigration. In terms of political factors, the area in which children are educated may be bilingual, for example, Quebec, Canada (English and French), Catalan region of Spain (Catalan and Spanish), Hong Kong (Chinese and English). In terms of immigration, their parents may immigrate to a new country but continue to speak the language of the "old country" at home. These children of immigrants speak one language at home and go to school and become educated in a second or sometimes even a third or fourth language. The children themselves may be immigrants. The purpose of this chapter is to discuss reading skills in the context of this type of bilingualism.

The designation ESL (English as a second language) refers to a variety of conditions and indicates varying degrees of bilingualism. LI refers to the language that they speak at home, that is, their first or native language; L2 refers to the language that they are acquiring. In most of the cases discussed in this chapter that language is English. In the case of our research in Canada, much of the bilingualism is children who speak English as a second language and come to school and are instructed in English, so they are learning English from the very beginning of their school experience. This is quite a different matter for children who enter into English language instruction having spoken another language for a longer degree of time and having been schooled in another language until the point that they enter into a school in which English is the language of instruction. Obviously, these are some of the many variables that are relevant to the consideration of bilingualism and reading.

There are many other variables that are relevant to bilingualism and reading. The social setting in which students learn to read English, the instructional method, the congruence between the learners' native language and culture and the target language and culture, and whether or not the school is an elementary or secondary one are all relevant.

In terms of the congruence between the languages, languages vary on at least two important dimensions One of these dimensions is from the alphabetic to the non alphabetic: for example, the character system used in Chinese and a part of Japanese and Korean writing differs from the alphabetic languages in which sounds are represented by letters or groups of letters in English, French, Spanish, German etc. The second important dimension is the predictability of grapheme-phoneme correspondences, that is, how well can one read the language knowing the relationship between letters and their sounds. This dimension is conceptualized by a concept called orthographic depth. Orthographic depth refers to the differences between alphabetic orthographies in terms of how the graphemes of the writing system and the pronunciation of words can be mapped onto each other. In a shallow orthography, there is a one to one correspondence between letters and sounds; a deep orthography uses a more complex set of relationships between letters and sounds. Even in a shallow orthography for decoding, the relationship between the language may be deep or non transparent for spelling in that there may be several ways to represent a sound.

The sociopolitical context in which the second language is learned is important. For example, there are bilingual students in their home cultures who are learning a foreign language and bilingual immigrants to a new country who must learn a new language. These groups may be different in motivation, socioeconomic status and the value placed on bilingualism.

The critical variables in the evaluation of reading skills in a bilingual situation are, among others the point in the acquisition of L2 when reading occurs, whether or not there has been literacy instruction in LI, the differences and similarities between the syntactic structure, the alphabetic nature of the script, the regularity of grapheme-phoneme correspondences, and the overlap of vocabulary.

In this chapter, the relationship between bilingualism and reading will be examined in the context of some of the processes that are significant in the development of reading skills in the English language. These processes are phonological, syntactic awareness, working memory, semantics (or the understanding of meaning), and orthographic awareness.

PHONOLOGICAL PROCESSING

Phonological processing involves a variety of skills, but in the context of the development of reading skills, one of the most significant is the association of sounds with letters, that is, the understanding of grapheme-phoneme conversion rules and the exceptions to these rules. This skill is the basis of decoding print, and although other routes can be used to obtain meaning from print, the phonological route is clearly an important one and critical in the early development of reading skills (e.g., Jorm, 1979; Stanovich, 1988a, 1988b).

English has an irregular spelling system. It is sometimes called orthographically deep in that the mapping of graphemes to phonemes that they represent is, at best, unreliable and erratic. Vowels and consonant clusters are difficult and vowels are especially unpredictable. In English, no one-to-one correspondence exists between a letter (or letters) and a sound. The same letter represents different sounds and the same sound may be represented by different letters.

Current theories of the development of reading skills in English stress that phonological processing is the most significant underlying cognitive process. Arguments for this position were outlined by Stanovich (1988a, 1988b). This function is referred to as the understanding of grapheme-phoneme conversion rules and because of the irregular nature of the correspondences in English, the learning of these rules is a very complex process. The child who is learning to read must map oral language onto written language by decomposing the word into phonemes and associating each letter (or combination of letters) with these phonemes.

The task of the beginning reader is to extract these grapheme-phoneme conversion rules. The alternative is simply to memorise each word as a visual configuration and to associate a meaning with it. This kind of learning may occur, but it is inefficient and makes tremendous demands on visual memory. In an alphabetic language such as English, one of the best measure of phonological processing skills is the reading of pseudowords, that is, pronounceable combinations of letters that can be read by the application of grapheme-phoneme conversion rules, but that are, of course, not real words in English. Examples include pseudowords, such as *shum, laip*, and *cigbet*. Pseudowords can be read by anyone who is familiar with the grapheme-phoneme conversion rules of English even though they are not real words and have not been encountered in print or in spoken language before.

The development of the ability to read pseudowords has been studied extensively and there is ample evidence that this ability develops during childhood. The evidence also indicates that children with dyslexia have a great deal of difficulty reading pseudowords (e.g., Bruck, 1988; Ehri and Wilce, 1983; Snowling, 1980; Siegel and Ryan, 1988; and Waters, Bruck and Seidenberg, 1985). A number of studies have shown that disabled readers have more difficulty reading pseudowords than normal readers matched on either chronological age or reading level (For a review see Rack, Snowling & Olson, 1992).

For children learning to read English, the learning of grapheme-phoneme conversion rules is a result of systematic instruction and the extraction of the rules is a result of repeated encounters with print. No evidence is available to provide information about how much of the development of decoding skills is a result of specific instruction in the grapheme-phoneme conversion rules and how much is a result of experience with print. In any case, the understanding of the grapheme-phoneme conversion rules develops rapidly in the first years of experience with print under normal conditions.

The relationship between reading pseudowords in the individual's first language and the second language is quite strong. In our studies of the correlation between pseudoword reading in two different languages, we have found a high correlation between reading of pseudowords in English and Portuguese (da Fontoura & Siegel, 1995) between pseudowords in Arabic and pseudowords in English, and Hebrew (Abu Rabia & Siegel, 2002) and between pseudowords in Italian and English (D'Anguilli, Serra & Siegel, 2002).

Bilingual children who have difficulty learning to read Portuguese have difficulty reading pseudowords (DaFontoura & Siegel, 1995) and children with reading difficulties learning Hebrew as a second language also have difficulty with pseudowords (Geva & Siegel, 2000).

BILINGUALISM AND PHONOLOGICAL AWARENESS

Another important aspect of learning to read is phonological awareness. Phonological awareness is the ability to segment speech into smaller units called phonemes. Phonological awareness transfers from the first to second language (Chiappe & Siegel, 1999; Cicero & Royer, 1995; Durgonoglu, Nagy, & Hancin-Bhatt, 1993; Verhoeven, 1994). Chiappe and Siegel found that Punjabi speaking children in the first grade had comparable decoding and phonological skills in English to their native speaking peers. However, their syntactic skills lagged behind the native English speakers.

There was some evidence that children who are learning English as a second language showed poorer performance on phonological measures than native English speakers (Wade-Woolley, Chiappe & Siegel, 1998). Wade-Woolley et al found that ESL children performed more poorly than native English speakers on measures of phonological awareness in kindergarten but not the following year in grade 1. Therefore, the age at which ESL children are assessed may influence whether or not their performance on phonological awareness and other linguistic measures show impairments relative to native English speakers. Chiappe, Siegel & Gottardo (1999) found that native speaking and ESL children had similar scores on letter identification, spelling and reading tasks in kindergarten but ESL children had lower scores on rhyme detection, phoneme deletion and a rapid naming task. On the rapid naming task, the ESL children named pictures more slowly than the native speakers in November but by May had caught up to their native speaking peers. These studies show that for young bilingual children, their initial difficulties in the phonological areas are resolved after 12–18 months of instruction in their second language.

Phonological awareness transfers from one language to another (e.g., Cisero & Royer, 1995; Durgonaglou, Nagy & Hassenbat, 1993; Geva, Wade-Woolley & Shaney, 1993; Verhoeven, 1994). For example, Verhoeven (1994) found that phonological skills transferred from LI to L2 while lexical and syntactic processing did not. Durgonaglou et al (1993) showed that phonological awareness in LI was a significant predictor of word recognition and pseudoword decoding in L2 and also phonological awareness in English was a significant predictor of English word reading ability but oral proficiency in English was not. Chiappe & Siegel (1999) found that L2 children may have comparable skills to LI children in both phonological awareness and reading in English, despite poor oral language proficiency.

Cicero and Royer (1995) compared monolingual English-speaking and bilingual Spanish-speaking children with limited English proficiency. First grade students were also administered tasks in the opposite language, Spanish for English speakers and English for Spanish speakers. They used for measures of phonological awareness, rhyme detection, initial phoneme detection and final phoneme detection. For the initial phoneme task, children heard *rat* and *rib* and were asked if they had the same initial phoneme; for Spanish the stimuli were *ven* and *vid*. All students were faster and more accurate on the rhyme task than on the initial phoneme task and slowest and least accurate on the final phoneme task. Each group performed more accurately in their own language. Native-English students were slower than the bilingual students on English rhyme, initial phoneme and final phoneme tasks on both languages but had higher levels of accuracy. Both native and second language performance at time I contributed significantly to the prediction of second language performance at time 2.

Wade-Woolley, Chiappe & Siegel (1998) compared native speakers of English with children who spoke Punjabi at home entered the schools speaking little or no English. In kindergarten there were no differences between ESL and native speakers in their ability to read letters and simple words. There were, however, differences in syntax and vocabulary, sentence repetition, receptive vocabulary and phonological skills especially rhyme detection, phoneme deletion, rhyme production. In grade one, however, the differences between the two groups were significantly smaller. The groups did not differ on measures of reading, pseudoword reading and letter identification. They did not differ on phonological tasks including rhyme detection, phoneme deletion and rhyme production. They did not differ on naming speed of simple pictures. There were significant differences in tasks with a significant linguistic component, that is, a working memory and a task requiring the identification of syntactic errors. There were no differences in basic reading skills, that is, word and pseudoword reading. Therefore, the acquisition of the alphabetic principle and early literacy skills may have more to do with instruction and individual differences than with language status because the ESL children as a group were functioning at a level equivalent to chronological age matched mature speakers on tasks involving phonological awareness.

Phoneme deletion and phoneme deletion substitution were most strongly associated with word reading for both Punjabi and native English speakers. These results show the strong transfer of phonological skills between languages as a function of bilingualism.

In a study of kindergarten ESL and native speakers, Chiappe, Siegel and Gottardo (1999) found that the ESL and native speakers did not differ on measures of early literacy but the ESL children performed more poorly on measures of phonological processing, syntactic awareness and verbal working memory. Therefore, in young children beginning to learn English, initially there is very little transfer for phonological skills from one language to another.

READING AND SPELLING

There is a large body of evidence that indicates that phonological skills are important in successful reading and spelling acquisition in an individual's first language (see Vandervelden & Siegel, 1995 for a review). If L2 learners have phonological deficits in their L2 relative to native speakers of that language, these deficits should be manifested in reading and spelling difficulties. If, however, despite these phonological deficits, L2 learners' reading and spelling abilities equal that of native speakers, then the phonological deficit model should be refined.

Children in grade two learning English as a second language, who are developing primary literacy skills in their second language were compared to native speakers (NS) on their ability to achieve accurate English spellings (Wade-Woolley & Siegel, 1997). The children in the study were grade two students who did not speak English at home. The languages that they spoke at home included Cantonese, Mandarin, Gujarati, Urdu and Punjabi. Most were born in Canada and had attended school since the age of 4. Junior and senior kindergarten in Ontario, Canada, are half-days so they had two half-day years and two full-day years as the study was conducted toward the end of grade two. The children were grouped into good and poor readers on the basis of their word recognition skills as measured by the Wide Range Achievement Test (WRAT-3). ESL students had lower scores than the native speakers on pseudoword repetition, phoneme deletion (for example, if you take away /p/ from pink, what word is left?), on two measures of syntax. The poor readers had lower scores than the good readers on all these tasks. The two measures of syntax were the Oral Cloze task, in which the children were required to insert the missing word in a sentence, e.g., "Fred put the turkey _____ the oven", that they heard orally and a syntactic judgment task where they heard well-formed sentences, e.g., "The boy was chased by the dog", and ill-formed sentences, e.g., "The tall thin man playing was basketball" and had to say whether it was a good sentence.

There were no differences in the spelling scores of the native-speaking and the ESL group although the poor readers had significantly lower scores than the good readers. The native-speakers could represent tense vowels equally well through spelling. Tense vowels need some alteration of the traditional spelling to indicate their pronunciation. For example, the vowel *ea* represents the sound /ii/ so tense vowels were not more difficult for the ESL group although they were more difficult for the poor reading group. Poor readers spelled words with consonant clusters more poorly than those without clusters, but average readers, whether they were ESL or native-speakers, did not show a difference between these two types of words. The accuracy of real word spelling was predicted by pseudoword decoding and phoneme deletion in similar proportions for ESL and native-speaking groups. Pseudoword decoding was the sole predictor for pseudoword spelling for both language groups.

On the basis of these results it appears that spelling does not reflect differences in oral language competence, but does reflect individual differences unrelated to whether children are learning to read and spell in their first or second language, although the ESL speakers were somewhat less sensitive to the syntactic and semantic features of English. The ESL group was poorer than the native-speaking group on two different phonological tasks. The pseudoword repetition task requires the accurate perception and production of non-native -language speech sounds while the phoneme deletion task demanded that the children show the ability to sequence and segment phonemes from their second language and perform complex operations. The results suggest that ESL children have not yet fully acquired the sound system of the second language and yet, their reading and spelling was at a level equivalent to their native speaking peers.

Language status was not a dominant factor in spelling performance. Reading skills were more significantly correlated with spelling than first language was. Average readers were more accurate than poor readers but the process of acquiring a second language does not appear to influence the spelling ability of ESL children. The implication of different patterns of poor readers and ESL speakers on phonological tasks presents an interesting challenge to the phonological core deficit model of reading. One possibility is that the phonological deficit applies to reading disability in native speakers only and the failure of non-native speakers of English who have a reading failure must be attributed to some other cause. Another possibility is that the concept of phonemic awareness must be refined and that there may be more isolated phonological processes. It also may be that orthographic or visual memory processes may be useful in English in terms of understanding how print is translated into sound and meaning.

Geva, Wade-Woolley and Shaney (1993) examined whether individual difference factors or factors related to the orthographic complexity of the language were the determinant of reading and spelling. Hebrew orthography is shallow, that is the sounds of the letters are predictable. The hypothesis that differences between first language (LI) and second language (L2) reading and spelling profiles could be accounted for by lack of proficiency in the L2 or differences in orthographic complexity of the two languages was explored in a longitudinal study of 45 children acquiring reading and spelling skills concurrently in English (LI) and Hebrew (L2). The children were tested in Grades I and 2 on literacy measures in both languages. The less complex Hebrew orthography facilitated subjects' decoding performance, but failed to maintain that facilitation in spelling. The findings showed that, despite LI-L2 differences in orthographic complexity and language proficiency, the profiles of emergent spelling in both languages are strikingly similar. The rate of acquisition of conventional spelling, however, differentiates LI from L2 performance.

Geva et al (1993) note that word frequency in one language, which is a determinant of word reading in that language) does not necessarily mean that the same word frequency applies to another language. For the less proficient L2 learner, there may be no difference between decoding an unfamiliar word and decoding a pseudoword because there are many words that are not known. There were strong within language correlations, that is, correlations between pseudo-word and word reading within each language. A phoneme deletion task predicted reading and spelling skills in English.

Chiappe, Siegel and Gottardo (1999) found that the ESL children showed comparable performance to native English speakers on measures of letter identification, word recognition and spelling. However, there were differences in phonological processing and on measures which required interpretation and manipulation of the language. These differences were still evident at the end of kindergarten. These differences might be expected since they require a new phonology with a new phonemic contrast. Similar results have been found in other studies (Gholamein & Geva, in press; Wade-Woolley & Siegel, 1997). However, in spite of slower word retrieval in November, ESL children named pictures as rapidly as native speakers in May. There were, however, differences in syntactic awareness and verbal working memory throughout kindergarten.

However, the groups did differ in ability to understand and manipulate language (WadeWoolley, Chiappe & Siegel, 1998). The children who spoke Indian languages showed a disadvantage relative to native speakers on phonological tasks in kindergarten. This might be expected since they were acquiring a new phonology with new phonemic contrasts. Similar results have been found in other studies Gholamein & Geva, in press; Wade-Woolley & Siegel, 1997). These findings are consistent with a different sample of English and Punjabi speaking children in grade 1 (Chiappe & Siegel, 1999).

The Special Case of Vowels

Bilingualism provides an interesting context to study vowels. English vowels tend to have more complex and irregular pronunciations than English consonants. English vowels have the property that their pronunciation can change depending on the context. An example is the rule that an e at the end of a word usually makes the vowel long. The grapheme-phoneme correspondences of English vowels are very unpredictable. Consequently, misreadings of vowels occur more frequently than misreadings of consonants (e.g., Fowler, Shankweiler, & Liberman, 1979; Weber, 1970).

In languages other than English, vowels have more regular patterns with fewer representations of each vowel sound. One such language is Hebrew, in which the orthography is transparent, that is, the grapheme-phoneme conversion rules are predictable. Although vowels are omitted from text for older children and adults, in the beginning stages of reading vowels are included. Children learning to read both English and Hebrew can be tested to compare these two very different orthographies. In a comparison of English speaking children learning to read Hebrew as a second language, Geva and Siegel (in press) found that the incidence of errors in reading vowels was significantly higher in English than in Hebrew. Other children who had reading disabilities (in both languages) made many vowel errors in English but very few in Hebrew. Younger children with reading disabilities made vowel errors in both languages. It should be noted that Francophone children learning French, a more transparent language than English, rarely experience difficulties with vowels.

However, other types of errors were more common in Hebrew. Hebrew has many visually similar letters and more errors were made involving visually confusable letters in Hebrew than in English. In addition, because Hebrew has a transparent orthography one can decode it syllable by syllable and pronounce it properly and read the word without the proper stress. Failure to read the word with the stress on the correct syllable was more common in Hebrew than English. In English, a syllable by syllable decoding would usually result in vowel errors (e.g., pronouncing the vowel as a short vowel when the word ends in e and perhaps even pronouncing the final silent e.) Order errors, in which a consonant was omitted or the order of the consonants was confused[1] were more common in English than Hebrew, possibly because Hebrew words can be decoded in a linear manner from right to left and the linear strategy does not always work successfully in English. In general, these results indicate that the structure of the language and its alphabetic system as well as individual difference variables are significantly related to the acquisition of literacy skills in a bilingual context.

SYNTACTIC AWARENESS AND BILINGUALISM

Syntactic awareness, also called grammatical sensitivity, refers to the ability to understand the syntax of the language. Syntactic awareness is the ability to understand the basic grammatical structure of the language in question. Siegel and Ryan (1988) have investigated the development of these skills in an Oral Cloze task. In the Oral Cloze task, a sentence is read aloud to the child and the child is required to fill in the missing word. Examples of are: "Jane _____ her sister ran up the hill"; "Betty _____ dug a hole with her shovel"; "The girl_____ is tall plays basketball." This ability appears to be critical for fluent and efficient reading of text, and it requires making predictions about the words that come next in the sequence. Syntactic factors may influence the difficulty of reading single words, such as function words, prepositions, and auxiliary verbs, which are difficult to integrate in a semantic network. Ehri and Wilce (1980) have shown that beginning readers acquire information about the syntactic properties of function words when they have been trained to read these words in the context of a sentence. Therefore, the ability to process syntax may be an important aspect of word learning.

Syntactic awareness appears to have a relationship to good reading skills in a variety of languages that have been studied. It has been reported that children with ESL have deficits in syntactic awareness, e.g., (Bentin, Deutsch & Liberman, 1990; da Fontoura & Siegel, 1995; So & Siegel, 1997). The ESL children had lower scores than the normal speaking children on the oral doze and memory sentence tasks (Chiappe, Siegel & Gottardo, 1999). For example, da Fontura and Siegel studied Canadian children who spoke Portuguese as a first language, received instruction in reading in English, and attended a Heritage Language Program in Portuguese. The children who had low scores on Portuguese word and pseudoword reading tests had significantly lower scores on both Portuguese and English oral doze tasks than children who were good readers of Portuguese. In both English and Portuguese, syntactic skills are significantly correlated with word and pseudoword reading skills.

WORKING MEMORY AND BILINGUALISM

Working memory refers to the retention of information in short-term storage while processing incoming information and retrieving information from long-term storage. Working memory is relevant to reading because the reader must decode and/or recognize words while remembering what has been read and retrieving information such as grapheme-phoneme conversion rules. Working memory may also be critical to the reading of individual words particularly in the beginning of the acquisition of word reading skills because the grapheme-phoneme conversion rules for each segment of the word must be held in memory while the remaining segments of the word are processed. Longer words, in terms of the number of syllables, place increasing demands on working memory. In addition, the complexity of a particular rule will influence the difficulty of word recognition because the number of possible alternative grapheme-phoneme pronunciations may have an influence on ease or difficulty of reading a particular word. Given more alternative pronunciations, reading will be slower and less accurate until the individual items are mastered. More rules must be searched and applied to the word being read. For example, c and g have multiple pronunciations at the beginning of. English words, and, therefore, words or pseudowords starting with these letters may be more difficult than words or pseudowords beginning with other letters, especially for beginning readers.

Siegel and Ryan (1989a) studied working memory in normal and disabled readers and dyslexics, using a task based on one developed by Daneman and Carpenter (1980). In the modified version of this task, the child is read aloud 2, 3, 4, or 5 sentences and is asked to fill in a missing word at the end of each sentence. The child is then required to remember the missing words. Examples are: "In the summer it is very _____. People go to see monkeys in a _____ With dinner we sometimes eat bread and _____." The child was then required to repeat the three words that he or she selected in the order of presentation of the sentences. The disabled readers performed significantly more poorly than the normal readers on this task, indicating significant difficulties with working memory in the disabled readers. Similar difficulties with working memory have been noted in Chinese (So & Siegel, 1997), Hebrew (Geva & Siegel, 1991), and Portuguese (DaFontoura & Siegel, 1995). da Fontura and Siegel (1995) found that verbal working memory and the syntactic skills of Portuguese-English bilingual children who had been born in Canada still lagged behind in skills of English monolingual children in grades 4, 5, and 6.

ORTHOGRAPHIC AWARENESS

Another aspect of reading is orthographic processing. Orthographic processing refers to the understanding of the writing conventions of the language in question and knowledge of the correct and incorrect spellings of words. All alphabetic systems include legal and illegal and more and less probable sequences of letters, and a fluent reader uses knowledge of these sequences to some extent. Positional constraints and probabilities that letters will occur in certain positions are additional aspects of orthographic knowledge used by the skilled reader.

Siegel, Share, and Geva (1995) developed a task to assess the awareness of orthographic structure. Children were shown 17 pairs of pronounceable pseudo-words, one containing a bigram that never occurs in an English word in a particular position and the other containing a bigram that occurs in English. Examples are filv-filk, moke-moje, vism-visn, and powl-lowp. This task was administered to disabled and normal readers, aged 7-16 years. The disabled readers were significantly poorer in this task than the age-matched normal readers. However, when matched on reading level, the disabled readers performed at a significantly higher level than the normal readers. The orthographic processing of the reading disabled is quite good for their reading level. These data indicate that orthographic processing is not as impaired in dyslexics as is phonological processing. Abu Rabia and Siegel (1999) found that orthographic process did not show any transfer *between* Arabic and English in bilingual speakers and that orthographic skills did not correlate significantly with reading skills.

Orthography influences reading skills. An interesting case is Hebrew-English bilinguals. Hebrew is read for right to left, English from left to right. Pollatsek (1988) studied Hebrew-English bilinguals and found that they perceived more letters to the left of the fixation point when reading Hebrew and more to the right of the fixation point when reading English. Henderson (1983) studied the reading of English by bilingual speakers and found that the native Spanish speakers read more slowly than native English speakers but Arabic speakers who use a different orthography read much more slowly than the Spanish bilinguals. Brown and Haynes (1985) presented bilinguals with tasks involving matching pairs of English words. Spanish speakers were faster than Arabic but Japanese were the fastest, probably because of the visual processing required in Japanese. However, when the determination of whether words (or nonwords) were the same or different the Japanese were the slowest of all of the groups.

TRANSFER BETWEEN LANGUAGES

Transfer between the two languages can be either positive, that is one language enhancing another, negative, one language interfering with the other, or neutral in that the two languages have no influence on each other.

There are two contrasting theories which address the issues of the transfer of reading between two languages; the interdependence hypothesis and the script dependent hypothesis. The Interdependence hypothesis predicts that similar difficulties will appear in both languages owing to a central processing deficit. In regard to the acquisition of reading in a second language, the model of Cummins (1981) assumes a "common underlying proficiency". That is, there is a transfer of knowledge of skills from native language orality or literacy to ESL literacy. A common set of proficiencies underlies both languages. In contrast, the script dependent hypothesis predicts that grapheme phoneme irregularities in English will result in greater difficulties for individuals who speak languages with more predictable grapheme-phoneme correspondences than English. Literacy skills do seem to transfer from one language to another. In a study of relationships among languages, the reading skills of bilingual Hebrew-English speaking children in Israel (Abu Rabia, 1995) were investigated. There was a significant correlation between Hebrew and English skills except for phonological and orthographic tasks. A transfer of linguistic skills is likely to occur but there are some language dependent variables. Abu Rabia administered tests of working memory, oral cloze, a visual task, which involved recognizing which of two words was spelled correctly, a homophone and a pseudohomophone task (for example brane-brain), a phonological test in which the participants had to decide which of two pseudowords sounded like a real word, (for example joak or joap), an orthographic test in which one member of a pair contained an orthographically illegal but pronounceable pseudoword and the other word contained an orthographically legal pseudoword (for example filv and filk), and Word Attack and Word Recognition tests. There were significant correlations between all the tests in Hebrew and English except for the phonological and orthographic tests. Children who were less skilled in Hebrew were also less skilled in English. The correlations between reading skills in English and Hebrew were similar to those found between French and Arabic (Wagner, Spratt & Ezzaki, 1989). The lack of correlation between orthographic skills in English and Hebrew suggest that they do not transfer knowledge of orthographic patterns, which are language specific, from one language to another.

Barry (1992) studied English-Welsh bilinguals. Welsh is a very regular language with a predictable correspondence between grapheme and phonemes. There are some slight deviations and some context sensitive rules, for example, the letter *y* can be pronounced differently depending on its position in the word. In some parts of Wales, the letters *i u* and *y* are pronounced in the same way in the final syllable of the word. Bilingual Welsh-English speakers were presented with words that primed the particular spelling of the particular spelling using the *i*, *u*, or *y* so they were sensitive to these priming effects. They were then presented with English words, priming a certain spelling. There were some priming effects in English. They were also required to spell nonwords. The Welsh speakers were very similar to monolingual English speakers in a task that involved the spelling of nonwords. There is additional evidence to support the interdependence hypothesis. SkutnabbKangas and Toukomaa (1976) found that Finnish immigrant children in Sweden learned their second language, Swedish, in relationship to their proficiency in Finnish at the time that they started learning Swedish. Durgunoglu (1993) found that for Spanish speaking grade one students learning English, performance on English word and pseudoword recognition tests was predicted by levels of Spanish phonological awareness and Spanish word recognition. Verhoeven (1990) studied Turkish children going to school in the Netherlands and found that there was no transfer of lexicon and syntax from one language to another. In phonological skills, there-were some moderate transfers and pragmatic skills showed strong positive transfer.

Verhoeven (1994) studied Turkish children in the Netherlands and found that the type of transfer (positive or negative) from one language to the other depends on the type of skill in question. For vocabulary and syntax, transfer was quite limited but for pragmatic, phonological and reading skills there was significant positive transfer. Verhoeven used language samples, and sentence completion tasks to measure grammatical abilities. The phonological task was the discrimination between same and different phonemes. Vocabulary was larger in Turkish than in Dutch. There was a positive transfer in phonological skills between languages. Verhoeven speculates that this may be due to the high level of metalinguistic awareness required by the phonological awareness task. The transfer of reading skills in the two languages indicates that there may be non-specific language processes related to phonological and higher level reading skills. Vocabulary and syntax appear to be more language specific with little transfer between languages, especially when they are quite different in structure as are Turkish and Dutch. Pragmatic skills were similar in the two languages and there was a positive transfer from reading skills between the two languages.

Brown and Haynes (1985) compared Japanese, Arabic and Spanish speaking students learning reading in English. The Spanish and English share a common alphabet and a similar orthographic system. Arabic writing system is alphabetic but it uses a different set of letters and is read from right to left. Japanese is syllabic and logographic and differs from English in the relationship between writing and speech. They had a task involving matching whether words or pseudowords were the same or different using Roman alphabetic patterns. The Spanish speaking students, not surprisingly, were slower than the Arabic students, the Japanese were the fastest and the most accurate indicating that visual processes are important. When abstract, complex figures were used, the Japanese also performed better than the Spanish and Arabic-speaking student whose scores were essentially the same. The Japanese students did show efficiency in visual processing. In a comparison of reading of pseudowords, the Japanese students were not as fast or accurate in reading pseudowords as the Spanish or Arabic-speaking. Therefore, the visual discrimination superiority of the Japanese was not related to understanding or use of grapheme-phoneme correspondence; the Japanese students tended to rely more on sight word knowledge and less on rule governed letter to sound correspondence than the Arabic and Spanish-speaking students. Word length was a critical factor for the Japanese. For the Spanish and Arabic students, listening and reading were highly correlated, but this was not true for the Japanese. These may represent separate skill domains. The Japanese students showed smaller differences between words and pseudowords and between pseudowords and nonsense strings than the other groups. This was observed in a same-different matching task, again suggesting that they are relying more on visual or orthographic visual strategies than phonological ones. Accuracy in reading was related in the Japanese groups as in the other groups to sensitivity to grapheme-phoneme correspondences.

CONCLUSIONS

Bilingualism, especially if the two languages are acquired at an early age, clearly does not impede the development of reading skills. It may be an advantage to learn two languages in that there is some evidence of positive transfer from one language to another, particularly in the case of transfer from more regular orthographies to English.

REFERENCES

Abu Rabia, S. (1995). Attitudes and cultural background and their relationship to English in a multicultural social context: the case of male and female Arab immigrants in Canada. *Journal of Educational Psychology 15*, 323-335.

Abu-Rabia, S., & Siegel, L. S. (1995). Different orthographies, different context effects: The effects of Arabic sentence context in skilled and poor readers. *Reading Psychology, 16*, 1-19.

Abu Rabia, S. & Siegel, L. S. (2002). Reaching, syntactic, orthographic and working memory skills of bilingual Arabic-English speaking children. *Journal of Psycholinguistic Research, 31*, 661-678.

Barry, C. (1992). Interactions between lexical and assembled spelling (in English, Italian, and Welsh). In C. Sterling & C. Robinson (Eds.), *Psychology, Spelling and Education* (pp.71-86). Clevedon, England: Multilingual Malteus Ltd.

Bentin, S., Deutsch, A., & Liberman, I. Y. (1990). The development of cross language transfer of phonological awareness. *Contemporary Educational Psychology, 20*, 275-303.

Brown, T. L. & Haynes, M. (1985). Literacy background and reading development in a second language (pp.19-34). In T. H. Carr (Ed.) *The Development of Reading Skills: New Directions for Child Development, (27)*. San Francisco: Jossey-Bass.

Bruck, M. (1988). The word recognition and spelling of dyslexia children. *Reading Research Quarterly, 23*, 51-68.

Chiappe, P. & Siegel, L. S. (1 999). Phonological awareness and reading acquisition in English and Punjabi-speaking Canadian children. *Journal of Educational Psychology*, 20-28.

Chiappe, P., Siegel, L. S. & Gottardo, A. (1999). Linguistic diversity and the identification of children at-risk for reading disability.

Cisero, C. A. & Royer, J. M. (1995). The development of cross language transfer of phonological awareness. *Journal of Contemporary Educational Psychology 20*, 275-303.

Cummins, J. (1981). The role of primary language development in promoting educational success for language minority students. In California State Department of Education, *Schooling and language minority students: A theoretical framework*. Evaluating, Dissemination and Assessment Center, California State University, Los Angeles.

D'Anguilli, A., Siegel, L. S. & Serra, E. (2002). The development of reading in English and Italian in bilingual children. *Applied Psycholinguistics, 22*, 479–507.

da Fontoura, H. A. & Siegel, L. 5. (1995). Reading, syntactic and memory skills of bilingual Portuguese-English Canadian children. *Reading and Writing: An Interdisciplinary Journal, 7*,139-153.

Daneman, M., & Carpenter, P. A. (1 980). Individual differences in working memory and reading. *Journal of Verbal Learning and Verbal Behavior 19*, 450-466.

Durgonoglu, A. Y., Nagy, W. E., Hancin-Bhatt, B. J. (1 993). Cross-language transfer of phonological awareness. *Journal of Educational Psychology, 85*, 453-465.

Ehri, L.C., & Wilce, L. 5. (1980). The influence of orthography on readers' conceptualization of the phonemic of words. *Applied Psycholinguistics, 1* 371-385.

Ehri, L.C., & Wilce, L. S. (1983). Development of word identification speed in skilled and less-skilled beginning readers. *Journal of Educational Psychology, 75*, 3-18.

Fowler,C., Shankweiler, D., & Liberman, I. (1979). Apprehending spelling patterns for vowels: A developmental study. *Language and Speech, 22*, 243-251.

Geva, E., & Siegel, L. S. (2000). Orthographic and cognitive factors in the concurrent development of basic reading skills in two languages. *Reading and Writing: An Interdisciplinary Journal, 12*, 1-30.

Geva, E., Wade-Woolley, L. & Shaney, M. (1993). The concurrent development of spelling and decoding in different orthographies. *Journal of Reading Behavior, 25*, 383-406.

Gholamein, M. & Geva, E. (1999) Orthographic and cognitive factors in the concurrent development of basic reading skills in English and Persian. *Language Learning, 2*, 183-217

Haynes, M. & Carr, T. H. (1990). Writing system background and second language reading: A component skills analysis of English reading by native-speaking readers of Chinese. *Reading and its Development*, 375-421.

Jorm, A. F. (1979). The cognitive and neurological basis of developmental dyslexia: A theoretical framework and review. *Cognition, 7,* 19-33.

Murphy, L.A., Pollatsek, A. & Well, A. D. 1988. Developmental dyslexia and word retrieval deficits. *Brain and Language, 35,* 1-23.

Rack, J. P., Snowling, M. & Olson, R. (1 992). The nonword reading deficit in developmental dyslexia: A review. *Reading Research Quarterly, 27,* 28-53.

Shimron, J., Savan, T. (1994). Reading proficiency and orthography: Evidence from Hebrew and English. *Language Learning, 44,* 5-27.

Siegel, L. S. & Ryan, E. B. (1989). The development of working memory in normally achieving and subtypes of learning disabled children. *Child Development, 60,* 973-980.

Siegel, L.S. (1989). Why we do not need IQ test scores in the definition and analyses of learning disability. *Journal of Learning Disabilities, 22,* 514-518.

Siegel, L. S., & Ryan, E. B. (1988). Development of grammatical sensitivity, phonological, and short-term memory in normally achieving and learning disabled children. *Developmental Psychology, 24,* 28-37.

Siegel, L. S., Share, D., & Geva, E. (1995). Evidence for superior orthographic skills in dyslexics. *Psychological Science, 6,* 250-254.

Skutnabb-Kangas, T., Toukomaa, P. (1976). Teaching migrant children their mother tongue and learning the language of the host county in the context of the socio-cultural situation of the migrant family. Helsinki: The Finnish National Commission for UNESCO.

Snowling, M.J. (1 980). The development of grapheme-phoneme correspondence in normal and dyslexic readers. *Journal of Experimental Child Psychology, 29,* 294-305.

So, D., & Siegel, L. 5. (1997). Learning to read Chinese: Semantic, syntactic, phonological and working memory skills in normally achieving and poor Chinese readers. *Reading and Writing: An Interdisciplinary Journal, 9,*1-21.

Stanovich, K. E. (I 988a). Explaining the differences between the dyslexic and garden variety poor reader: The phonological-core variance-difference model. *Journal of Learning Disabilities, 21,* 590-604.

Stanovich, K. E. (I 988b). The right and wrong places to look for the cognitive locus of reading disability. *Annals of Dyslexia, 38,* 154-177

Vandervelden, M. C. & Siegel, L. S. (1995). Phonological recoding and phonemic awareness in early literacy: A developmental approach. *Reading Research Quarterly, 30,* 854-875.

Verhoeven, L. (1994). Transfer in bilingual development: The linguistic interdependence hypothesis revisited. *Language Learning, 44,* 381-415.

Verhoeven, L.T. (1990). Acquisition of reading in a second language. *Reading Research Quarterly, 25,* 90-114.

Wade-Woolley, L., Chiappe, P., & Siegel, L. S. (1998, April). Learning to read in a second language: Does phonological awareness really matter? Paper presented at the annual meeting of the Society for the Scientific Studies of Reading, San Diego, California.

Wade-Woolley, L. & Siegel, L. S. (1997). The spelling performance of ESL & Native speakers of English as a function of reading skill. *Reading and Writing: An interdisciplinary Journal, 9,* 387-406.

Wagner, D., Spratt, J. E., Ezzaki, A. (1989). Does learning to read in a second language always put the child at a disadvantage? Counter evidence from Morocco. *Applied Psycholinguistics, 10,* 31-48.

Weber, R. (1970). A linguistic analysis of first-grade reading errors. *Reading Research Quarterly, 5,* 427-451.

SUGGESTED FURTHER READING

Bindman, M. (2003). Grammatical awareness across languages and the role of social context: Evidence from English and Hebrew. This volume.

Bryant, P., Nunes, T. & Aidinis, A. (1999). Different morphemes, same spelling problems: cross-linguistic developmental studies. In Harris, M. & Hatano, G. (Eds), *Learning to read and write A cross linguistic perspective* (pp. 112-133). Cambridge Studies in Cognitive and Perceptual Development. Cambridge: Cambridge University Press.

E4 Grammatical Awareness Across Languages and the Role of Social Context: Evidence from English and Hebrew

MIRIAM BINDMAN

ABSTRACT

This chapter describes a study investigating cross-language transfer of morpho-syntactic awareness in children with experience of two languages. The hypotheses were (i) that morpho-syntactic awareness gained in one language and orthography can be used for the other, even where the languages are dissimilar and use different scripts, and (ii) that the type of knowledge children transfer across their oral and written languages depends partly on the social practices of those languages. 116 children (6-10 years) with English as a first language (L1) and learning Hebrew as a second language (L2) in two Jewish schools in the UK were given vocabulary and oral and written morpho-syntactic awareness tasks in both languages. The children learn classical written Hebrew for religious purposes and modern spoken Hebrew for communication; however, exposure to the spoken form is emphasised in one school and minimal in the other. Multiple regression analyses revealed cross-language relationships between oral morpho-syntactic tasks, suggesting transfer of knowledge between L1 and L2. L2 morphological knowledge (e.g. of the written three-consonant Hebrew root) was related to L1 morphological spelling (e.g. consistency in spelling semantically related word stems), providing evidence that knowledge of morphological principles (e.g. that words from the same root are spelled similarly) gained in one language can be used for spelling in another. A different pattern of relationships across some L1 and L2 tasks was observed in the two schools. These results are discussed in relation to the different literacy and language practices involved in learning an ancient language for biblical study and prayer, and a modern spoken language for communication. The study highlights the importance of taking language and literacy practices into account when drawing conclusions about cross-language transfer in bilingual learning contexts.

INTRODUCTION

This chapter describes a study conducted in two Jewish primary schools in the UK.

T. Nunes, P. Bryant (eds.), Handbook of Children's Literacy, 691–709.
© 2004 *Kluwer Academic Publishers. Printed in Great Britain.*

The children speak English as their first language (L1) and are taught Hebrew as a second language (L2) at school. Hebrew has a modern, spoken form, and a classical form which is used for religious purposes but which is not used for spoken communication. In their Hebrew teaching programmes, the two schools differ in their emphasis on modern and classical forms. The study examines the possibility that morpho-syntactic awareness gained in one language and orthography can be used for learning in another language. It also considers the effect of different social language and literacy practices on the types of knowledge that may be transferred across the child's two languages.

Transfer of metalinguistic knowledge across languages

In an earlier chapter, Nunes and Hatano raised the hypothesis that children learning a second language can use metalinguistic awareness of morphology gained in one language and orthography, for their other language and orthography, even if these languages are unrelated and have dissimilar structures at a surface level. What transfers at this deep, metalinguistic level is an understanding of the underlying principles or concepts shared by the two languages. For example, an understanding that verbs can be inflected to show tense can be applied to both languages, even if at a surface level they mark tense differently. Transfer at this deep level need not necessarily occur only from L1 to L2. Children who are still developing grammatical awareness in L1 may gain insights about grammatical principles in L2 before they do so in L1. This is particularly likely if an aspect of grammar is more obviously marked in L2 than in L1, or if L2 teaching includes explicit instruction on that aspect (Bindman, 1997).

Research on cross-language transfer of children's metalinguistic and literacy knowledge has so far focussed mainly on phonological awareness and alphabetic literacy knowledge. Relationships between children's ability to reflect on phonology in L1 and L2 have been demonstrated in children exposed to Turkish and Dutch (Verhoeven, 1994), English and Spanish (Durgonoglu, Nagy & Hancin-Bhatt, 1993), and English and Chinese (Gottardo, Yan, Siegel & Wade-Woolley, 2001). Relationships have also been shown between phonological awareness in one language and performance on reading and spelling tasks requiring phonological analysis skills in the other language (Durgonoglu et al., 1993; Gottardo et al., 2001; Geva, Wade-Woolley & Shany, 1993), and between reading and spelling performance across orthographies (Wagner, Spratt & Ezzaki, 1989; da Fontoura & Siegel, 1995; Geva et al., 1993), even in languages using different scripts. Bilingual and biliterate children have been shown to outperform monolingual children on phonological, reading and spelling tasks (Rubin & Turner, 1989; Rubin, Reichman, Crabtree & Kantor, 1991; Mumtaz & Humphreys, 2001).

Although the connection between morpho-syntactic awareness and progress with reading and spelling has now been established in monolingual children (e.g.

Tunmer, Nesdale & Wright, 1987; Rego & Bryant, 1993; Nunes, Bryant & Bindman, 1997; Bryant, Nunes & Bindman, 2000; Muter & Snowling, 1997; Levin, Ravid & Rapaport, 1999; Carlisle, 2000), few studies to date have examined relationships in bilingual children between the L1 and L2 morpho-syntactic skills that are known to relate to morphological spelling, or between morpho-syntactic awareness in one language and morphological spelling another. In one study, da Fontoura & Siegel (1995) examined L1-L2 morpho-syntactic awareness in 37 nine- to twelve-year old children bilingual in English and Portuguese, using an oral cloze task. This consisted of 20 orally presented sentences, each with a word missing, and the child had to fill in the missing word. They found a correlation of .63 between performance on English and Portuguese versions of the task, but did not control for age, or other aspects of language ability. Performance on the morpho-syntactic task was correlated with word and pseudoword reading within but not across languages; however, their reading tasks were designed primarily to tap phonological rather than morpho-syntactic analysis skills. Geva (1995) and Geva & Siegel (2000) also found a cross-language correlation on oral cloze tasks, in children who had English as L1 and Hebrew as L2, even though they were less proficient in Hebrew, and despite surface-level dissimilarities between the grammatical structures of the two languages. This cross-language relationship was not explained by underlying differences in non-verbal intelligence. However, verbal intelligence was not controlled.

The present study examines relationships between performance on morpho-syntactic awareness tasks in English (L1) and Hebrew (L2), and between L2 morpho-syntactic awareness and L1 morphological spelling, in two groups of children aged six to eleven years. One group attends a Jewish day school in which gaining proficiency in the modern, spoken form of Hebrew is emphasised, alongside religious study of texts written in the classical, biblical form. The other group attends a school in which there is minimal exposure to the modern, spoken form, and Hebrew is learned mainly via the study of religious classical Hebrew texts. The aims of the study were to explore whether children are able to use grammatical awareness gained in one language for their other language, even where these languages are dissimilar at a surface-level, whether grammatical awareness gained in L2 can be applied to morphological spelling in L1, and whether the kind of knowledge children are able to transfer across languages depends on the purposes for which L2 is studied, and the language and literacy practices associated with these purposes.

Bilingual education and second language learning contexts

Studies of cross-language transfer in children have been generally been conducted in school-based second language programmes. Broadly speaking, these can be divided into three main types: submersion, immersion, and heritage language (or developmental maintenance) programmes (Baker, 2001).

In submersion, children who speak a minority language at home receive their schooling in the majority language of the country and must therefore make a home-school language switch (Cummins & Swain, 1986). The child is taught entirely through L2, L1 is not fostered or maintained by the school, teachers are unlikely to be bilingual, and bilingualism is not a defined outcome of schooling, although it may result (Baker, 2001). Submersion is probably the most common L2 learning experience of children from ethnic minorities in the UK, who speak languages other than English at home.

Immersion refers to programmes aiming to teach proficiency in L2 while maintaining and developing L1. Immersion originated in Montreal, Canada. Its goal was to teach English-speaking students to become competent to speak, read and write in French, without detriment to their English or other academic competences. Similar programmes now exist in several countries and language contexts (e.g. Wales, Ireland, Spain). In immersion, the school curriculum is taught through L2 for part or the whole of the day, so that L2 learning occurs in an uncontrived and meaningful way. L1 is valued by the school, children start school with similar (minimal) levels of L2, and teachers are likely to be bilingual. Immersion programmes vary in the proportion of the day spent learning through L2 and the age at which L2 exposure begins (Baker, 2001).

In heritage language or developmental maintenance education, language minority children are educated through the minority language, or a mixture of the minority and the majority language. The minority language is usually one spoken at home with parents. Heritage language classes are commonly supported by the ethnic or linguistic community or religious organisation, where the community language is in danger of being lost. They vary in the amount of time spent on the minority language, and whether minority language classes are part of the school timetable or occur outside school hours.

The relevance of social language and literacy practices

The bilingual education programmes outlined above on the whole aim to teach oral proficiency in L2. However, for children in some cultures and minority language contexts, L2 is learned primarily for religious purposes, and oral proficiency may not be a priority, or in the case of a classical language, may not indeed be possible. The case of Jewish children learning classical Hebrew in the diaspora, and of Muslim children learning Qur'anic Arabic are examples. In such cases, L2 is a written language which is rarely or never used for spoken communication. The purpose of instruction is to impart knowledge of the child's heritage and to enable them to participate in cultural and religious community practices, rather than to speak the language. Very few studies have investigated the effects of second language learning for religious purposes, on metalinguistic awareness and L1 literacy development.

Studies of literacy practices in different cultural contexts have shown that the effects of literacy depend on the specific ways in which that literacy is embedded in the culture and the purposes for which it is used. In a classic study of the effects of literacy or nonliteracy on thinking amongst the Vai people in Liberia, Scribner and Cole (1981) gave metalinguistic tasks to 255 Vai men, who fell into the following groups: nonliterates, Vai script monoliterates, Arabic literates, and Vai-Arabic biliterates. They found an effect of Vai but not Arabic script literacy on the ability to judge, correct and explain grammatical errors in Vai sentences. The reason for the effect of Vai script literacy apparently lay in the social practices of Vai script literates. When writing or reading in Vai script, it was a common practice to "maintain a running commentary on whether a particular piece of language was good or correct Vai'. Qur'anic Arabic literacy practices on the other hand involved memorising portions of the Qur'an for religious purposes. This had a different effect on cognitive skills: it was associated with greater recall in an incremental memory task. Scribner and Cole concluded that it was not being literate per se that affected metalinguistic awareness or thinking, but rather that the social practices associated with a specific literacy had specific effects.

In a similar way, the effects of learning a second language on metalinguistic awareness may also depend on the specific cultural uses and practices of the second language and literacy. Different L2 practices may provide different opportunities for acquiring specific aspects of metalinguistic knowledge and place different constraints on the kinds of knowledge children exposed to a second language and literacy are able to transfer across languages. Different models of literacy instruction in a bilingual context may result in different skills on the part of the learner (Hornberger, 1989; Verhoeven & Durgonoglu, 1998). If so, generalisations about cross-language transfer drawn from findings in a specific social context may not apply in all other L2 learning contexts (see Baynham, 1995). Although there is increasing recognition amongst literacy researchers working from a psychological perspective that research needs to take social and cultural practices into account, the effects of different practices are rarely explored systematically. The present study attempts to analyse the effects of L2 learning in two educational contexts which are culturally similar, but which differ in the purpose for which L2 is learned, and in some of the L2 practices emphasised in their teaching programmes. It is proposed that learning L2 as a modern, spoken language for the purposes of communication provides different opportunities for learning about morphology and syntax than learning a written, classical language for religious purposes, and that cross-language relationships will differ according-ly. The development of Hebrew, its uses by Orthodox British Jews, the script and language characteristics will now be outlined.

THE HEBREW LANGUAGE

Historical development

Hebrew is a Semitic language with both classical and modern forms. The most important Jewish holy texts, including the Torah (the Jewish bible), are written in the ancient classical form. Modern Hebrew is the principal official language of modern Israel.

Ancient Hebrew probably ceased to spoken in the second century A.D. (Weinberg, 1981). However, it continued to develop as a written language, and was used by rabbis from different Jewish communities across the world, to communicate about religious, legal and academic matters (Keiner, 1991). It has continued to be used for religious study and prayer to this day.

Hebrew was revived as a spoken language during the half-century before the establishment of the state of Israel in 1948. The revival of the ancient language of the Jewish religion as an everyday, secular language was seen both as a means of linguistically uniting Jews from diverse linguistic backgrounds who were settling in the new state, and as a rejection of the diaspora and the historical oppression associated with it. The sources of the revived language were Biblical and Mishnaic Hebrew (the language of the ancient rabbis), and Medieval and early Modern 19th and 20th century writings (Berman, 1985). Modernising Hebrew required a great deal of inventiveness in semantics and lexicon (Ben-Rafael, 1994). Old meanings were adapted to express modern concepts, and new words were invented, where possible applying Hebrew word-patterns and existing consonantal roots. International words were incorporated either without Hebraicisation, or with the addition of Hebrew morphemes or superimposition of Hebrew word patterns. Modern Hebrew vocabulary therefore differs from but also overlaps with that of classical Hebrew. The two forms also differ to a degree in the grammatical structures commonly used, although the distinction is often one of formal versus more colloquial usage.

The use of Hebrew in British Jewish life

Glinert (1993) has described the Hebrew used by British Jews (and non-Israeli Jews in other countries) as a "quasilect", that is, a historical language which is used for cultural purposes, but not for open-ended active or receptive communication. Hebrew usage varies slightly according to membership of ethnoreligious subgroupings. In the Orthodox tradition, to which the schools in this study adhere, Hebrew is the main language of Jewish worship. In addition to prayer in the synagogue and recitation of the Torah, Hebrew prayers are recited in the home, for example before and after eating, at bedtime and in the morning, on religious acts, and to bless the beginning and end of the Sabbath. There are also festival recitations and songs, notably the communal reading of the *haggadah* (a traditional book) at Passover. Although a basic ability to read and recite Hebrew is necessary for religious practice, a high level of comprehension is not necessary (although viewed as desirable). Reading without comprehension is possible due to the phonological regularity of the vowelised script used in religious texts, and is acceptable because Hebrew is seen as a holy tongue, utterance of which has intrinsic value. The Jewish schools described here, however, attempt to impart a deeper knowledge of Hebrew than the ability to read by rote.

Modern Hebrew is on the whole spoken in Britain only by Israelis living in Britain, children who have Israeli parents, or British Jews who have learned it as a second language, commonly by living and studying in Israel for a period of time.

Hebrew script

Hebrew uses an alphabetic script which is read from right to left. Consonants and vowels are written separately. Consonants (and a few vowels) are represented by letters, and vowels are mostly represented by tiny diacritic marks (dots and lines). Religious texts, and texts produced for young children and second language learners are usually printed with diacritic marks, to aid pronunciation, and with these marks, Hebrew is a shallow orthography for reading (but somewhat less so for spelling). Texts for experienced readers of Modern Hebrew are printed without diacritics, but the children in the present study are generally exposed only to text with diacritics.

Hebrew word formation

Hebrew is a highly inflected, morphologically rich language. Most words are at least bi-morphemic. The derivational and inflectional morphology of Hebrew are very briefly sketched below (for more detail, see Ravid, 2001).

All verbs, and most nouns and adjectives, are made up of a root (usually three consonants) combined with a word-pattern, which may be made up of prefixes, suffixes and infixes (see the chapter by Nunes and Hatano). There are seven types of verbal word-pattern, three of which are active, three passive, and one reflexive. Nominal word patterns are more numerous (about three dozen) and are less systematic than verbal patterns. Some nominal word-patterns consist of vowels only, and since most vowels are represented in writing by diacritic marks and not letters, the orthographic integrity of the root is preserved in these words. Other patterns, on the other hand, contain vowel letters which are infixed between the root consonants, thus interrupting the root (Bentin & Frost, 1995).

The Hebrew inflectional system is much richer and more complicated than in English. Verbs must be inflected for person, gender, number and tense. Nouns and adjectives are inflected for gender and number. Nouns can also be inflected for possessive, locative, and a construct which applies to compound words (Bentin & Frost, 1995).

THE STUDY

Jewish children learning Hebrew as a second language: two educational contexts

The two participating schools both have a strictly orthodox code of behaviour and religious practice, but differ in the emphasis they place upon children becoming proficient in the modern, oral form of Hebrew. Both schools are state-funded, and follow the English language National Curriculum in addition to the Hebrew and religious studies curriculum. Secular subjects are taught in English, which is the main language of communication outside the classroom. Both English and Hebrew are highly valued by school staff, parents, and the wider Orthodox Jewish community. The majority of children come from middle-class backgrounds and speak English as their first language. A small number of children in both schools have Israeli parents and speak Hebrew at home; however, only children speaking English at home were selected for the study. The schools are also Zionist in outlook and the teaching of Modern Hebrew is an expression of solidarity with Israel, as well as a practical advantage for those children who visit Israel or may in future settle there. In both schools, children begin formal literacy instruction in Hebrew and English at the same time, in the pre-school year at four and a half years old. It is considered important for children to be able to read the prayerbook as soon as they are able.

In the first school, which I shall call the Oral school, the children are taught a combination of Modern Hebrew and religious studies, which includes study of classical Hebrew texts, for approximately 2 hours daily. The school day is slightly extended to accommodate this. Oral Hebrew is first introduced in the pre-school year. Once a week, children attend an additional religious studies lesson after school. Most Hebrew teachers are Israeli and bilingual in Modern Hebrew and English. Modern Hebrew is used as the medium of instruction during Hebrew lessons, religious studies lessons, and all other non-secular activities (such as assemblies); however, the teacher may use some English if the children do not understand. The educational programme is therefore similar to a partial immersion programme.

In the second school, which I shall call the Classical school, children are taught Modern Hebrew for less than one hour a week, and religious studies for approximately 3 hours per week. The language of instruction during these lessons is English, and most Hebrew teachers do not speak Modern Hebrew as their first language, or at all. The weekly Modern Hebrew lesson is taught by a British teacher who has learnt to speak Hebrew as L2. The children have little exposure to the spoken language outside this lesson and are not expected to attain a high level of oral proficiency. It is probably closest to a heritage language type of programme, although it differs from many heritage programmes in that the heritage language is L2, is not used for everyday communication in the home, and is used for a specific purpose, namely religious practice.

In religious studies lessons at the Classical school, traditional methods are used to teach biblical Hebrew text. This includes but does not exclusively involve memorising verses and their English translations. Children are not expected to produce Hebrew constructions of their own. Hebrew study involves detailed analysis and discussion of different possible interpretations of biblical text and religious rulings, the subtleties of which may be lost in studying the translation alone. To this aim, the children are taught some aspects of Hebrew morphology and morpho-syntax, and are encouraged to attempt translation of unfamiliar text. They are taught the principle of the three-consonant root, to guess or work out the meaning of an unfamiliar word which shares the root of a word they already know, to recognise the meanings of particular common morphemes, such as those indicating possession, person, gender, and grammatical status of a word (for example, infinitive of a verb), and to break down morphologically complex words into their constituent morphemes. Because of the morphological complexity of many Hebrew words (e.g. one word may contain morphemes indicating the semantic root, word class, gender, possession and plural), a whole lesson may be spent on the analysis and translation of a very small portion of text.

Children in the Oral school also experience this type of biblical text analysis in their religious studies lessons, and are expected to achieve a similar level of knowledge of classical Hebrew. The main distinction between the schools, then, is that the Oral school allocates considerably more time to, and aims to teach proficiency in the modern spoken language for communication, additional to religious study.

Participants

56 children from the Oral school, and 60 from the Classical school took part in the study. In the Oral school, children were selected from school years 2 to 5 (aged 6 to 9 years), and in the Classical school, from years 3 to 6 inclusive (aged 7 to 10 years). An older group was selected from the Classical school to ensure that they would have enough Hebrew knowledge to perform the L2 tasks. The effects of age were then controlled statistically in analyses of cross-language relationships.

Tasks

The children were given the following oral tasks in English (L1):

Vocabulary The Vocabulary subtest of the Wechsler Intelligence Scale for Children-Third Edition (Wechsler, 1992) was given. This is a word-definition task and was used as an abbreviated measure of verbal intelligence in statistical analyses.

Oral-cloze (Siegel and Ryan, 1988). This task requires the use of syntactic, morphological and semantic information to complete sentences. After two practice trials, 15 sentences, each with one word missing, are spoken, and the child is asked to say the missing word, marked by a tap on the table, (for example "*The boy ——— down and hurt his knees"*). Missing words included nouns, adjectives, prepositions, conjunctions, interrogatives and verbs. Answers were scored as grammatically correct or incorrect.

Word Analogy (adapted from Nunes, Bryant & Bindman, 1997). This morpho-syntactic task aimed to measure awareness of parts of speech and tense in spoken language. The analogy method was used in order to avoid the confounding of morpho-syntactic and semantic abilities which occurs in cloze tasks. One example and eight test trials were given. The task was presented to the child orally with the support of two puppets. In the first pair of words in each trial, the first puppet "said" a word (e.g. *happy*) and the second puppet "repeated" it but with a change to the part of speech or tense (e.g. *happiness*). Then the first puppet said a second word (e.g. *high*) and the child was asked to play the role of the second puppet and transform this word in the same way as the puppet had to the first (e.g. *height*).

Sentence Analogy (adapted from Nunes, Bryant & Bindman, 1997). This had a similar design to Word Analogy, except that this time the first puppet spoke a sentence containing a verb in one tense (e.g. *David helps Sarah*) and the second puppet changed the tense of the verb (e.g. *David helped Sarah*). The child then had to play the role of the second puppet and make an analogous transformation to a second sentence spoken by the first puppet (e.g. *David sees Sarah* to *David saw Sarah*).

The children also completed two English morphological spelling tasks:

Past tense "-ed" ending on regular verbs (Nunes, Bryant & Bindman, 1997). This was to test whether the child understood that the "ed" ending belonged only on past tense regular verbs, and not on past tense irregular verbs or nonverbs which end in the same sound (in the original study, /t/ or /d/ sounds; here I gave a shortened version, only using words ending in a /t/ sound). Using the "-ed" spelling correctly requires the child to distinguish past tense and different parts of speech. 3 categories of words ending with a /t/ sound were chosen: regular past-tense verbs such as "kissed" (5 words), irregular past-tense verbs such as "sent" (5 words), and nonverbs such as "except" (4 words).

Consistency in spelling root morphemes (Nunes, Bryant & Bindman, 1997). This was designed to test children's awareness that word pairs related in meaning are likely to share spelling in one morpheme (the stem), even if they do not sound exactly alike (e.g. *know* and *knowledge*). In order to check that the children were actually making the connection between the meaning and spelling rather than spelling by rote, pseudowords as well as real words were used. In each of the 10 word pairs, the shared morpheme's spelling was unpredictable from phonology, so it could not be spelled correctly by sound. There were six pseudoword pairs, in which one of the pair was a real word, and the other was a pseudoword. Five of these were fictional dinosaur names, whose stems were real words (e.g. *knot* and *knotosaurus*). A cartoon picture of the dinosaur was shown to make the semantic link clear (e.g. a dinosaur with a knotted neck). The other pseudoword pair was *specialness, special*. Although *specialness* is a plausible word with the regular *-ness* ending, it does not appear in the dictionary. The other 4 word pairs consisted of real words only, for example *magic, magician*; *strong, strength*. The first word of each pair was given on one occasion, and the second one at a later occasion.

The following tasks were given in Hebrew (L2):

Vocabulary This receptive test was designed by the author as part of a larger study (Bindman, 1997). For each item, the child was shown four pictures and asked to point to the picture that went best with a word spoken by the tester. Items were selected from a list of high-frequency Hebrew words relevant to Jewish diaspora children learning Hebrew, compiled by Rivlin (1994). Words were ordered by Rivlin according to difficulty, based on ratings by diaspora Hebrew teachers, and included words from modern and biblical Hebrew, Jewish festivals and culture. In order to reflect the Hebrew curriculum in the two schools, three modern words and 3 biblical/religious words were chosen from each of seven levels of difficulty in Rivlin's wordlist, by an experienced Hebrew teacher. In reality there is an overlap between these categories; therefore modern words were chosen which children would not or were unlikely to encounter in classical Hebrew (e.g. *car, icecream, to ring*), and biblical/religious words were chosen which were unlikely to put children who learn mainly religious Hebrew at a disadvantage (e.g. *saying, to light, wicked*). There were 42 items in total. Responses were scored as correct or incorrect.

Oral Cloze This was adapted from a test devised by Geva and Siegel (2000) for children attending Canadian Jewish day schools, and parallels the English version described earlier in its design. The missing words covered various word classes, inflected for person, plurality, tense, and/or gender. Because the children were doing this test in their second language and had to understand the sentence in order to be able to use their grammatical knowledge, performance also depended on Hebrew vocabulary level. In the Canadian schools studied by Geva and Siegel, children spend more time learning Modern Hebrew than in the British schools studied here, particularly the Classical school, and test items required higher levels of oral proficiency than the Classical school children were likely to have. Therefore 10 Modern Hebrew items were taken from the original test, and 10 new classical Hebrew sentences were added. These were taken or adapted from the Bible, prayers, or commandments, or were invented by the researcher using vocabulary which appears frequently in religious study. To avoid testing rote memory for biblical text, the original word order of familiar sentences was changed. Answers were scored as grammatically correct (inflected for gender, plurality, person and tense, as appropriate), or incorrect.

Root morphemes This task was designed to assess children's understanding of the three-consonant Hebrew root. The child's task was to extract the root from written Hebrew words, by judging which of four words shared a root with ("means something like") a stimulus word. As in English, two words which share root meaning are likely to share part of their spelling, and therefore the semantic relation between the words can be detected from the shared spelling. Hebrew root letters can be at the beginning of the word as in English stems, but can appear in other positions. They must be in the same order in both words. Homophones which are spelled differently in the root (this is possible because for some phonemes, two different letters can represent the sound) cannot be highly related in meaning. In order to extract a shared root from two written words, the child must understand the principles above, know that roots normally have three letters, that vowel diacritics and word pattern are irrelevant, and must be able to distinguish the root letters from letters or morphemes that indicate aspects of the word's meaning other than the root meaning (e.g. the final morphemes -*im* and -*ot*, which mark plurality and gender, the final letter *hay*, which marks the feminine, and the initial morpheme *le-*, which indicates the infinitive of a verb). Three practice trials were given in which the shared root letters and meaning were pointed out, and eight test trials. Each of the three incorrect words in each trial had one or two of the following non-root features in common with the stimulus word: it rhymed, was a homophone, shared vowels, shared root letters but in mixed-up order, had less than three letters altogether, had two but not three shared root letters, shared prefixes or suffixes, or began with the same three letters but these were not the root. The root letters could appear at the beginning of the word (three trials) or in other positions.

Findings

Is morpho-syntactic awareness transferable across languages?

My hypothesis was that morpho-syntactic awareness would be transferable across the two languages, despite their surface-level dissimilarities. I therefore expected a correlation between performance on Hebrew and English morpho-syntactic awareness tasks, and that Hebrew morpho-syntactic awareness would significantly predict English morpho-syntactic awareness even when age and verbal ability were controlled. No correlation was expected between Hebrew and English vocabulary, as Hebrew and English are unrelated, dissimilar languages, so lexical knowledge was not expected to transfer across languages.

As expected, performance on the Hebrew Oral Cloze task was correlated with all three English morpho-syntactic awareness tasks, although these correlations were weak (between .3 and .39; n = 116; p < .001). Performance on the Hebrew

Roots task correlated with the three English grammatical measures, and most strongly with Sentence Analogy (.51, p < .001) and Word Analogy (.53, p < .001).

Fixed-order hierarchical regression analyses were carried out to test the relationship between performance on Hebrew and English tasks after controls for age and verbal ability. Age was entered as the first step and English vocabulary at the second step. Each analysis shared these first two steps. At the third step, either Hebrew Oral Cloze or Hebrew Roots was entered. The response variable in each analysis was the English morpho-syntactic task.

Neither Hebrew task predicted English Oral Cloze after these controls (perhaps due to a ceiling effect on the English task), but both predicted performance on Sentence Analogy and Word Analogy. Hebrew Oral Cloze explained 5% and 3% of the variance in Sentence Analogy and Word Analogy respectively. Hebrew Roots explained 3% and 4% respectively.

Hebrew and English vocabulary were not correlated, and Hebrew vocabulary did not correlate with any of the English grammatical tasks either.

Is morpho-syntactic awareness in L2 related to morphological spelling in L1?

If transfer of morpho-syntactic awareness can occur across languages, and if children's awareness of L1 morphology in oral language is related to L1 morphological spelling knowledge, then L2 morpho-syntactic awareness should also relate to L1 morphological spelling. I therefore predicted that performance on Hebrew morpho-syntactic tasks would be related to performance on the English morphological spelling tasks. Of the two Hebrew measures, I expected Hebrew Roots to correlate more strongly with consistency in spelling English stems, as performance on both tasks depends on understanding the principle that words sharing meaning also share spelling of the root morpheme.

The correlation between Hebrew Oral Cloze and spelling of the past tense morpheme did not quite reach significance. Hebrew Oral Cloze did, however, correlate significantly, though weakly (.21; p = .04), with the number of consistently spelled stems. Hebrew Roots correlated significantly but weakly with use of the "ed' ending (.23; p = .02). As expected, the strongest cross-language correlation was between Hebrew Roots and consistency in spelling stems (.44; p < .001). Fixed order regression analyses with age, English vocabulary and Hebrew morpho-syntactic task as the first, second and third steps, and English spelling as the response variable, showed that both Hebrew tasks significantly predicted consistency in spelling stems (each explained 4% of the variance), but neither task predicted use of "ed" on regular verbs. The weaker relationships with the "ed" spelling may be partly explained by a near ceiling effect on this task.

Does transfer across languages depend on the type of L2 learning experienced?

My hypothesis was that the relationship between L1 and L2 metalinguistic awareness would depend on the purpose for which L2 was taught and the way in which it was learned, and that different patterns of L1-L2 relationships would therefore be seen when the data from each school were examined separately. Specifically, I expected performance on the Hebrew Oral Cloze task, which demands a high level of spoken Hebrew, to predict performance on the English morpho-syntactic tasks for children in the Oral school. I did not expect this task to be as good a predictor of performance on the English tasks for children in the Classical school. For Classical school children, I expected performance on the Hebrew Roots task to predict performance on the English tasks, as children learn about the Hebrew root in their study of classical texts. The Hebrew Roots task should also predict performance on the English tasks for children from the Oral school, as they too learn about the root in their study of both Modern and Classical Hebrew.

In order to investigate whether the relationships between Hebrew and English morpho-syntactic knowledge were different in the two schools, a series of multiple regressions were carried out in which the predictor variables were age, English vocabulary, Hebrew morpho-syntactic knowledge (Oral Cloze or Roots), a dummy variable for school, and a term representing the interaction between school and Hebrew morpho-syntactic knowledge (the product of school and the Hebrew variable). These predictor variables were entered simultaneously. The response variable in each analysis was the English morpho-syntactic task. If the relationship between Hebrew and English morpho-syntactic awareness were different in the two schools, then a significant interaction was expected between Hebrew morpho-syntactic awareness and school, when the main effects of age, vocabulary, school and Hebrew morpho-syntactic awareness were controlled.

There were significant interactions between Hebrew Oral Cloze score and school for the analysis in which English Oral Cloze was the response variable, and for the analysis in which the English Word Analogy was the response. There were no significant effects of the interaction term for Hebrew Oral Cloze and school on Sentence Analogy, or of the interaction term for Hebrew Roots and school on any of the English tasks.

To clarify the nature of the interactions, correlations between Hebrew Oral Cloze and English Oral Cloze, and between Hebrew Oral Cloze and English Word Analogy, were examined in separately for each school, and, as in previous analyses, fixed-order hierarchical multiple regression analyses were carried out to see if the correlations were still significant when age and verbal ability (English vocabulary) were controlled.

In the Oral school, the correlation between the Hebrew Oral Cloze and the English Oral Cloze tasks was strong ($r = .68$; $n = 56$; $p < .001$). After age and vocabulary had been controlled in the regression analysis, Hebrew Oral Cloze significantly predicted English Oral Cloze, explaining 6% of the variance ($p = . < .001$).

In the Classical school, the correlation between Hebrew Oral Cloze and English Oral Cloze was not significant (r = .17; n = 60; p = .19).

Turning now to the Hebrew Oral Cloze – English Word Analogy relationship, in the Oral school, there was a significant correlation between the two tasks, but this was not strong (r = .32; n = 56; p = .015), and when age and English vocabulary were controlled, did not reach significance.

In the Classical school, on the other hand, the correlation between Hebrew Oral Cloze and English Word Analogy was strong (r = .67; n = 60; p < .001), and in the multiple regression analysis, Hebrew Oral Cloze significantly predicted English Word Analogy even when age and vocabulary were controlled, explaining 16% of the variance (p = .0001).

Discussion

The results of the study showed evidence that English-speaking children learning Hebrew as a second language could transfer metalinguistic knowledge of grammar between their languages, despite surface-level dissimilarities between them. The significant cross-language relationships between most of the morpho-syntactic tasks suggest that explicit awareness of morphology and syntax is not language-specific: children who are aware of these aspects of grammar in one language tend to be aware of them in their other language. These findings are consistent with the results of da Fontoura and Siegel (1995), Geva and Siegel (2000), and Geva (1995). These studies did not partial out the effects of age and verbal ability. The fact that the cross-language relationships were still observed when these factors were controlled statistically suggests that it is not just a question of children learning more about about grammar in each language as they get older, or of children who are good at language in general being good at it in both languages, but rather that there is genuine transfer of grammatical knowledge.

Turning to the relationship between L2 morpho-syntactic awareness and L1 morphological spelling knowledge, there was evidence from the relatively strong correlation between the Hebrew Roots and English spelling consistency tasks, that even where two languages form roots in different ways (here, the three-consonant root in Hebrew in contrast with word stems in English), children can transfer their knowledge of the principle of roots between their languages. The idea that the integrity of the root is preserved in the spelling of semantically related words is similar in the two languages, so understanding of this principle can be applied to both. However, cross-language relationships were not only seen between those aspects of morphological understanding which were conceptually similar. Significant but weaker relationships were also observed between Hebrew Oral Cloze and English spelling consistency, and between Hebrew Roots and "ed" spelling (despite the near ceiling effect on the "ed" task), even after controlling for age and vocabulary. So it seems that what is transferable is an ability to reflect in a more general way about morphology, although the relationships between specific aspects of morphology which are similar in the two languages may be stronger.

The main issue raised in this study was whether the kind of knowledge transferred across languages depends on the purposes for which the second language is learned, the ways in which it is embedded in social and cultural context, and the social language and literacy practices of that language. To answer this question, cross language relationships were examined separately for children in each of the two participating schools, one of which taught Hebrew as both a classical, religious language and a modern, spoken language, and the other of which emphasised mainly the classical form of the language in its Hebrew curriculum.

A different pattern of results emerged in the two schools for two of the three English morpho-syntactic tasks. In the Oral school, there was a strong correlation between the English and Hebrew Oral Cloze tasks (.68). This was stronger than that reported by either da Fontoura and Siegel (1995) or Geva and Siegel (2000), who reported correlations of .63 and .46 respectively, and the relationship remained significant after controls for age and verbal ability. In the Classical school on the other hand, the English and Hebrew Oral Cloze tasks were not related. This could be because for Classical school children, the Hebrew Oral Cloze task was difficult, even though an attempt had been made to include religious Hebrew sentences with which they would have some familiarity. The distribution of scores was skewed towards the lower end. The heavy semantic demands of an oral cloze task may have prevented the children from revealing the kind of grammatical knowledge they actually had, or, they may simply not have had a high enough level of morpho-syntactic knowledge in Hebrew oral language for there to be any relation to similar tasks in English.

However, despite the difficulty of the task, the Hebrew Oral Cloze still correlated significantly with the Word Analogy task for these Classical school children. In fact, the correlation with Word Analogy was higher than for Oral school children, and remained highly significant even after age and verbal ability were controlled, while in the Oral school Hebrew Oral Cloze did not predict Word Analogy at all after these controls.

What is being observed here is a school effect and it is not possible to fully explain the reasons for the school difference in the Hebrew-English relationships. It may be explained, however, by the children's different experiences of Hebrew. For children learning primarily religious Hebrew, Hebrew morpho-syntactic awareness predicted ability to analyse and manipulate in English the relationships between single words presented without any context (Word Analogy), whereas for children learning to speak the oral language as well, Hebrew knowledge was related to the ability to solve English grammatical tasks which made demands on semantic and syntactic knowledge (oral cloze). These observations do seem to relate to differences in the Hebrew experiences of the two groups.

In the Classical school, children experience Hebrew mainly as a formal, written language presenting conceptually difficult material. The children explicitly analyse this text word for word when translating, in order to obtain the meaning. Oral school children, on the other hand, experience Hebrew also as a colloquial spoken language which they can understand without explicitly analysing word for word. Furthermore, Oral school children have a larger vocabulary than Classical school children. It is possible that the Oral school children's experience of Hebrew as a meaningful, comprehensible spoken language leads them to become aware of syntax and morphology as they feature in meaningful contexts, while Classical school children, on the other hand, with their more restricted access to meaning, are caused to analyse morphology in single words, in their attempts to translate difficult religious text. Because of their restricted vocabulary and also the difficulty of the text, these children are probably less able to use syntactic or semantic context to help them understand, so they have to look to the information available in individual words. The demands of the English Word Analogy task, in which they have to analyse the relationships between pairs of single words, may be more similar to the kind of analysis they do in their study of literary Hebrew than metalinguistic tasks demanding sentence level analysis are. In the Oral school, on the other hand, the children are more likely to understand a sentence and to be able to use the grammatical context. Thus their experience may be more similar to the kinds of English tasks which provide sentence level context (i.e. oral cloze tasks).

The school effect was not seen for the Hebrew Roots task: performance was similar in both schools, as were the cross-language relationships between this task and the English tasks. This showed that even children who are learning Hebrew mainly via religious text learn about Hebrew morphology, even if they have little oral proficiency.

CONCLUSIONS

This chapter investigated transfer of morpho-syntactic awareness across two unrelated languages and scripts, in English-speaking Jewish children learning Hebrew as a second language. Evidence for cross-language transfer of morphological knowledge at a metalinguistic level was found, despite differences in the specific processes of word-formation in the two languages, and how they are represented in the orthography. Learning to speak, read and write a modern L2 and learning a classical, written L2 for religious purposes had different effects on some aspects of L1 morpho-syntactic awareness. This preliminary finding highlights the importance of systematically examining not only the relationships across children's languages and orthographies, but also of the specific social and cultural practices of those languages, which may vary in the opportunities they provide for learning (e.g. about morphology). Such an examination needs to include analysis of the purposes for which the languages are learned, how they are used within the school and in the child's community, and the specific teaching practices. Otherwise, conclusions drawn from studies of cross-language transfer in some social contexts may not be generalisable to other contexts.

708   *Miriam Bindman*

REFERENCES

Baker, C. (2001). Foundations of Bilingual Education and Bilingualism, 3rd Edition. Clevedon: Multilingual Matters.

Baynham, M. (1995). Literacy practices: Investigating literacy in social contexts. Harlow: Longman.

Ben-Rafael, E. (1994). *Language, identity and social division: The case of Israel.* Oxford: Clarendon Press.

Bentin, S., & Frost, R. (1995). Morphological factors in visual word identification in Hebrew. In L. B. Feldman (Eds.), *Morphological Aspects of Language Processing.* Hillsdale, N.J.: Erlbaum.

Berman, R. A. (1985). The acquisition of Hebrew. In D. I. Slobin (Eds.), *Crosslinguistic study of language acquisition.* London: Lawrence Erlbaum.

Bindman, M. (1997). Relationships between metalinguistic and spelling development across languages: Evidence from English and Hebrew. PhD thesis, Institute of Education, University of London.

Bryant, P., Nunes, T. & Bindman, M. (2000). The relations between children's linguistic awareness and spelling: The case of the apostrophe. *Reading and Writing. An Interdisciplinary Journal, 12,* (3-4), 253-276.

Carlisle, J. F. (2000). Awareness of the structure and meaning of morphologically complex words: Impact on reading. *Reading and Writing, 12* (3-4), 169-190.

Cummins, J. & Swain, M. (1986). *Bilingualism in Education.* Longman.

da Fontoura, H. A., & Siegel, L. S. (1995). Reading, syntactic and working memory skills of bilingual Portuguese-Canadian children. *Reading and Writing. An Interdisciplinary Journal, 7,* (1), 139-153.

Durgunoglu, A., Nagy, W., & Hancin-Bhatt, B. (1993). Cross-language transfer of phonological awareness. *Journal of Educational Psychology, 85,* (3), 453-465.

Geva, E. (1995). Orthographic and cognitive processing in learning to read English and Hebrew. In I. Taylor & D. R. Olson (Eds.), *Scripts and Literacy.* The Netherlands: Kluwer Academic Publishers.

Geva, E., Wade-Woolley, L., & Shany, M. (1993). The concurrent development of spelling and decoding in two different orthographies. *Journal of Reading Behavior, 25,* (4), 383-406.

Geva, E., & Siegel, L. (2000). The role of orthography and cognitive factors in the concurrent development of basic reading skills in bilingual children. *Reading and Writing. An Interdisciplinary Journal, 12,* (1-2), 1-30.

Geva, E. & Wade-Woolley, L.(1998). Component processes in becoming English-Hebrew biliterate. In Durgonoglu, A.Y. & Verhoeven, L. *Literacy development in a multilingual context: Cross-cultural perspectives.* Mahwah: Lawrence Erlbaum Associates.

Gottardo, A., Yan, B., Siegel, L. S. & Wade-Woolley, L. (2001). Factors related to English reading performance in children with Chinese as a first language: More evidence of cross-language transfer of phonological processing. *Journal of Educational Psychology, 93,* (3), 530-542.

Hornberger, N. H. (1989). Continua of biliteracy. *Review of Educational Research, 59,* 271-296.

Keiner, J. (1991). The Hebrew Speech Community. In S. Alladina & V. Edwards (Eds.), *Multilingualism in the British Isles.* London: Longman.

Levin, I., Ravid, D., & Rapaport, S. (1999). Developing morphological awareness and learning to write: A two-way street. In T. Nunes (Ed.), *Learning to read: An integrated view from research and practice* (pp. 77-104). Dordrecht (The Netherlands): Kluwer Academic.

Mumtaz, S. & Humphreys, G. (2001). The effects of bilingualism on learning to read English: Evidence from the contrast between Urdu-English bilingual and English monolingual children. *Journal of Research in Reading, 24,* (2), 113-134.

Muter, V. & Snowling, M. (1997). Grammar and phonology predict spelling in middle childhood. *Reading and Writing. An Interdisciplinary Journal, 9,* 407-420.

Nunes, T., Bryant, P. & Bindman, M. (1997). Morphological spelling strategies: Developmental stages and processes. *Developmental Psychology, 33,* (4), 637-649.

Ravid, D. (2001). Learning to spell in Hebrew: Phonological and morphological factors. *Reading and Writing. An Interdisciplinary Journal, 14,* 459-485.

Rego, L. L. B., & Bryant, P. E. (1993). The connection between phonological, syntactic and semantic skills and children's reading and spelling. *European Journal of Psychology of Education, 8,* (3), 235-246.

Rivlin, A. E. (1994). *Madregot (Steps): Curriculum for the study of Hebrew as an additional language in Jewish schools in the Diaspora*. Jerusalem: Department of Education and Culture in the Diaspora, World Zionist Organization.

Rubin, H., Reichman, S., Crabtree, S. H., & Kantor, M. (1991). Linguistic analysis and reading skills of first graders in partial French and Hebrew immersion programs. *Reading and Writing. An Interdisciplinary Journal, 3,* 101-114.

Rubin, H., & Turner, A. (1989). Linguistic awareness skills in grade one children in a French immersion setting. *Reading and Writing. An Interdisciplinary Journal, 1,* 73-86.

Scribner, S. & Cole, M. (1981). *The psychology of literacy*. Cambridge, Mass: Harvard University Press.

Tunmer, W. E., Nesdale, A. R., & Wright, A. D. (1987). Syntactic awareness and reading acquisition. *British Journal of Developmental Psychology, 5,* 25-34.

Verhoeven, L. T. (1994). Transfer in bilingual development: The linguistic interdependence hypothesis revisited. *Language Learning, 44,* (3), 381-415.

Verhoeven, L. & Durgonoglu, A.Y. (1998). Perspectives on literacy development in multilingual contexts. *Literacy development in a multilingual context: Cross-cultural perspectives.* Mahwah: Lawrence Erlbaum Associates.

Wagner, D. A., Spratt, J. E., & Ezzaki, A. (1989). Does learning to read in a second language always put the child at a disadvantage? *Applied Psycholinguistics, 10,* 31-48.

Wechsler, D. (1992). *Wechsler Intelligence Scale for Children – 3rd UK Edition.* London: The Psychological Corporation.

Weinberg, W. (1981). A Concise History of the Hebrew Language. In M. Nahir (Eds.), *Hebrew Teaching and Applied Linguistics.* Washington, DC: University Press of America.

SUGGESTIONS FOR FURTHER READING

Baynham, M. (1995). Literacy practices: Investigating literacy in social contexts. Harlow: Longman.

Durgonoglu, A. Y. & Verhoeven, L. (1998). Literacy development in a multilingual context: Cross-cultural perspectives. Mahwah: Lawrence Erlbaum Associates.

Harris, M. & Hatano, G. (1999). Learning to read and write: A cross-linguistic perspective. Cambridge studies in perceptual development.

Share, D. & Levin, I. (1999). Learning to read and write in Hebrew. In Harris, M. & Hatano, G. (Eds). *Learning to read and write: A cross-linguistic perspective.* Cambridge studies in perceptual development.

E5 Literacy, Socialisation and the Social Order

KRISHNA KUMAR

ABSTRACT

In this chapter, the breadth of the concept of literacy is brought out by the analysis of school instruction in India, where the official use of the term "literacy" is actually quite restricted in meaning. If we agree to view literacy in the context of what is there to read in school and outside, rather than simply the acquisition of the ability to read and write, it becomes necessary to talk about "literacies" in India (as elsewhere), given the disparity of school experiences and the class differences reflected in the written materials available to youngsters.

Although all schools in India ostensibly subscribe to multilingual education through the daily teaching of three languages, many private schools use English as the medium of instruction whereas state-supported schools use Hindi and offer Indian languages as the medium of instruction. This choice appears to have far reaching implications for the socialisation of youngsters for the reading materials available to youngsters educated in English medium schools and the reading materials available to those educated in Hindi medium schools is quite different.

The reading materials used in the schools are themselves distinct. English medium schools promote the development of youngsters' fluency in English, thereby increasing the variety of what the youngsters are able to understand as written text. Because English medium schools are private, they are not restricted to the use of government produced textbooks; youngsters can read a vast amount of literary texts produced in the UK and the US and available in bookshops. The youngsters in these schools are not hindered in the development of their potential for reading Hindi texts, as they use Hindi outside school. In contrast, Hindi medium schools cannot promote fluency in English and the understanding of texts in the same way and the materials in English available to their students are basically the government produced textbooks, which focus on grammar and use a limited vocabulary.

English and Hindi readers also have access to reading materials of different nature outside school. The children's sections of English and Hindi newspapers and magazines for teen-agers include different uses of literacy and reflect different messages about the position of youngsters in the Indian context.

It is concluded that the analysis of bilingual education should consider not only the consequences for youngsters with respect to the development of their

T. Nunes, P. Bryant (eds.), Handbook of Children's Literacy, 711–720.
© 2004 *Kluwer Academic Publishers. Printed in Great Britain.*

reading potential but also those that are related to socialisation through literacy, a subtle and almost invisible aspect of education, which nevertheless is of great significance to the youngsters themselves and the society in which they live.

INTRODUCTION

In India, as in many other countries of the so-called "developing" world, the term "literacy" has a restricted, rather enfeebled meaning. It denotes an absolutely minimum capacity to decode writing or print, and to carry out rudimentary functions that require writing, such as signing on an application form. The restriction of "literacy" to this minimal sense has as much to do with the clientele which is said to be in need of literacy, as with the distinction between "education" and "literacy". The remarkably limited reach of institutionalised education is at the heart of this distinction. The system of education permits no more than a third of the child population to complete eight years of formal education. Enrolment and retention figures are subject to controversy, but it is hardly in doubt that schooling does not constitute a common experience. Those who stay outside the school gates unenrolled or forced out by factors ranging from poverty and hunger to the inability to cope with the school await inclusion in an adult literacy programme[2]. For them acquisition of "literacy" symbolises a shaky first step towards the outskirts of the civil society served by modern institutions. The outskirts are heavily populated, and the modes in which literacy nominally qualifies someone to participate in the functioning of modern institutions are highly competitive. Yet, literacy is said to be extremely important, as it constitutes the first operational step towards such participation. This is the basis of the axiom: literacy eradicates illiteracy. Policy documents of Third World governments and global organisations like the World Bank and UNESCO routinely use this axiom, including the verb "eradicate", which connotes that illiteracy is a kind of disease. The individual who goes through the remediation indicated in this axiom is inevitably adult, poor and rural, or else a migrant who now inhabits an urban slum.

The term "literacy" is simply never used in India in the context of children or their education. Its use in policy documents, research journals and the media does not refer to the teaching of reading and writing in schools and the ability to use these skills with ease. Although schools spend a considerable effort in the child's initial year following enrolment – usually at the age of five – to impart acquaintance with the basic tasks involved in reading, remarkably little attention is given to the development of reading abilities in the later years. Like writing, reading is assumed to develop on its own once its rudiments have been learned. The curriculum does not recognize it as an ability requiring continued special encouragement. The absence of specialised scholarship on the pedagogy of reading may be one explanation for this. A reading unit existed in India's apex body of educational research and training, the NCERT, during its initial years; it was soon wound up. Research and policy documents now seldom refer to "reading" with any seriousness of concern or differentiated awareness regarding its acquisition and application by different groups of children. The other explanation for the lack of attention shown to reading may be found in the cultural context of schooling. As Sarangapani (forthcoming) has noted in her ethnographic study of the meaning children associate with school-related tasks, "parhana" – the Hindi word for reading – connotes the general process of attending a school rather than merely a component of literacy. In this culturally rooted parlance, the ability to read fluently or the habit of reading are not necessarily associated with being a student or a literate young person.

The complete appropriation of "literacy" by adult education and the absence of "reading" from among the matters of concern in children's life at school are jointly responsible for a conceptual vacuum. On account of this vacuum, we remain incapable of noticing the manner in which literacy plays a key role in children's socialisation and, thereby, in shaping the social order. As a skill, reading is applied by children and adolescents to the material presented to them at school in the shape of prescribed textbooks and on whatever they can find in the marketplace. If we agree to view literacy in the context of what is there to read in school and outside, we will need to talk about "literacies", given the disparity of school experiences and the class differences reflected in the linguistic environment at home. Once the term is pluralised with reference to the characteristics of children's social backgrounds and the ethos of schools, literacy ceases to connote the effects or outcomes associated with adult education. These effects are routinely discussed in terms of a benign, psycho-social process which supposedly expands the adult learner's awareness, freeing it first from the shackles of traditional modes of thought and a superstitious mindset, and then equipping, even empowering, the learner to participate without hindrance in the worlds of knowledge, business and the state. In contrast to this kind of familiar discussion, we will look at literacy as a socialising force, which functions in association with other sources of children's socialisation, strengthening the orbits these other forces draw, and thereby consolidating the social order. Literacy acquires its specific function in this larger context from the historically rooted legacy of particular languages used for schooling.

All over India one sees the term "English-medium" in the sign-boards propped up outside school buildings or attached to their gates. In the landscape of metropolitan and provincial cities, and now district towns as well, the sign conveys the well-understood message that the institution located behind or under it is a private school, as distinguished from schools run either directly by the government or with the help of its grants. It is a generic sign, denoting a wide range of schools, from well-established, old institutions to the thousands that have mushroomed in the recent years. The two kinds of schools differ in terms of the efficiency with which the daily routine is conducted and the physical infrastructure is maintained. English-medium schools make an explicit effort to uphold the institution's name as a sign of standards in these matters as well as in the more crucial matter of examination results. The Hindi-medium government school, in contrast, literally lacks a name, i.e. it is known by the general title, "Government Boys/Girls Senior Secondary School"; the only indicator of a school's specific identity is the name of the area in which it is located. It has little autonomy as it functions strictly under the framework of the state department of education. Unlike its English-medium counterpart, a government school has little control on enrolment and staffing, and therefore it has no means of ensuring a high pass percentage or distinction in examination results.

Above all else, government schools have no institutional history, whereas English-medium private schools assiduously attempt to construct a history by means of alumni networks, signboards announcing the names of past principals and high achievers, and regular publication of a school magazine. In short, while English-medium schools attempt to impart a sense of institutional identity as a means of building self-esteem and commanding loyalty, schools run by the government merely provide a facility to attend classes in order to earn a certificate of education (Kumar, 1996). The total number of such schools cannot be reported with any accuracy, mainly because official statistics do not recognize the category "English medium". The growth of such schools over the recent years has been both rapid and diffuse: the rapidity indicating both the demand for private schooling and the erosion of the state-system's credibility, and the diffuseness indicating the vast range one may find within the world of English-medium schools in terms of the quality of instruction, the amount of fees charged, and the motive of the entrepreneurs who set up and run private schools. The "English-medium" sign separates the world of the upwardly mobile strata of society from that of the masses who have no choice. While the former are busy finding every means they can to alienate their children from the rest, the majority of the latter are first generation parents of school-going children. They have no choice in the matter of enrolling their children in the nearby government school. Across the north Indian Hindi belt (which includes the states of Haryana, Uttar Pradesh, Himachal Pradesh, Uttaranchal, Madhya Pradesh, Rajasthan and Bihar), the schools run by the government or financially aided by it use Hindi as the medium of instruction in all subjects.

The literacies produced by the two kinds of schools outlined above are markedly distinct though the official curriculum policy claims to favour bilingual or multilingual skills. Hindi is compulsory as a subject in all English-medium schools, and all Hindi-medium schools teach English as a subject. However, the teaching of Hindi and English as subjects in the curriculum, constituting a period of thirty-five minutes in a typical school day, does not disturb the patterns of behaviour and competence associated with the two kinds of school. The English-medium children are usually conversant with spoken Hindi, which is the language used all around them in out-of-school life. At school, they learn Hindi in one period every day. Children studying in government schools hardly ever acquire a comparable familiarity with spoken English. Indeed, the single period devoted to the teaching of English in a normal school day does not aim at imparting the ability to speak fluently: its main purpose is to familiarise children with grammar and writing. Their fluency in Hindi does not give them the kind of self-esteem that the English-medium school children exude as a privileged class on account of their enrolment in a private school. The government school children's difficulty with English acts as an additional factor contributing to the sense of general deficiency they already feel as people who do not belong to the exclusive world of private schools. Competence in English in their case and the lack of such competence in the case of the government school children strengthen the larger patterns of socialisation that find expression in public events, such as the sports day or annual function and in examination results. The textbooks they study at school and the popular literature they have access to outside school demarcate the discrete symbolic orbits their respective schools prepare them to inhabit.

HINDI AND ENGLISH: CONTEST OVER STATUS

To make sense of the reading that the children studying in the two kinds of schools do, we need first to take an overview of the nature and logic of the status-differential we see between English and Hindi. It is a not a simple differential, for while the status of English as a global language introduced in India during the prolonged period of history when India was a part of the British empire, is well recognised, Hindi too is not without formally assigned status. It is a language associated with India's identity as an independent nation-state, and it is mentioned in the Constitution as the official language of the union or federal government. The difference of social status between the two languages has to do with the hegemony of the classes formed during colonial rule. It is also related to the politics of language in India's federal structure, especially with the cost that Hindi has had to pay for appearing to be part of the populous north's dominance over other parts of the country. Hindi's political challenge to English has not succeeded in mitigating the symbolic value of the latter as a means of social advantage and mobility. The status of the socio-economic groups which monopolised educational opportunities during colonial rule has faced all-round contestation but mastery over English has become the prime instrument of that contestation. That is why English-medium schools have continued to proliferate.

As languages of school instruction English and Hindi coexist in cities and provincial towns, but the relationship between the two is highly complex and hard to define. In certain cities like Delhi we can map the geography of English and Hindi literacies by locating the stores where books and magazines of either language can be purchased. Commentaries made in one language on the politics associated with the other suggest a more complex picture. Every week one sees articles and letters to the editor in the Hindi press, protesting against the dominance of English. The writers inevitably berate politicians for their hypocritical patronage of Hindi, and the westernised upper classes for their slavish mentality. The proliferation of English-medium schools is cited as evidence of the deceptive role that the state has played. In the English press on the other hand, suspicion towards Hindi surfaces when a minister in the centre or in one of the Hindi states proclaims his resolve to promote Hindi in office use, education, or the state-owned media. The commentary made on such moves typically reminds the reader that English is an international language, and that India cannot get very far if it ignores or shuns English. The focus of such commentary is on "exposing" the politics of Hindi. The writers remind their English readers that politicians cheat the ordinary public by using language and education for their own narrow political ends. The role played by the English-medium "public"[1] schools in maintaining high educational standards is also emphasised. In the rival discourse of opposition to English, these schools are cited as citadels of elitism and divisiveness.

These are two parallel discourses. Implicit in their arguments and content is the awareness that Hindi and English readers form two discrete audiences. It is quite evident that the two discourses do not constitute a relationship of mutual response. Rather, they can be seen as frozen sets of arguments, which validate and enliven the chronic affective stances that have evolved in the course of a diffuse and prolonged socio-political struggle. In the pre-independence phase of modern India's history, the cause of Hindi was espoused by a regional literati (Kumar, 1989). Today, that association has become obsolete though the discourse of Hindi and some aspects of its linguistic character still carry the imprint of that earlier phase. The moral overtone we see in the arguments put forward for the cause of Hindi arises from the memory of the anti-colonial struggle in which Hindi served as a means to reify national identity. The discourse of English, on the other hand, upholds the promise of modernity, and evokes an imagery of material prosperity. Fluency in English acts as a sign which indicates that the speaker is a part of the national elite, capable of representing a linguistically diverse nation in a cohesive fashion as it did during the struggle for independence. In the present-day context, individual mobility, across the nation and the world, ranks high among the dreams that English-medium schooling signifies, while the government school, which uses Hindi as the medium of instruction, stands for the didactic dream of national freedom and resurgence.

Teaching in both English-medium schools and Hindi-medium schools is centred around textbooks, but the textbooks used in the two kinds of schools are strikingly different in their content and character. To begin with, English-medium schools have a range of textbooks to choose from as they feel free to use textbooks published by private publishers. Hindi-medium government schools, on the other hand, have no choice. From grade one onwards they are obliged to use textbooks published by state agencies. These texts are meant to be low-priced and usually display a poorer quality of production and design. The difference between privately published and state-published textbooks is particularly pronounced in the case of the texts used for the teaching of language. Privately published textbooks for the teaching of English feature a broad range of themes and topics,

---

[1] The term "public" school in British English denotes "private" schools in US usage (editors' note).

including adventure, science fiction, suspense and humour. Since these textbooks are designed for children who study all the subjects in English from the beginning of their school life and therefore have considerable fluency in reading, the editors feel free to select readings from a wide range of literary and other writings. By contrast, the textbooks used for the teaching of English in Hindi-medium schools offer a set of lessons especially written for children with a strict control over vocabulary and syntactical choice. And when this text is published by a state agency, the state's discourse and perspective shape the themes reflected in the lessons. Idealised images of the nation, and popular political themes like national integration, inter-religious brotherhood and rural development comprise the deep structure of most of the content. In a study of state textbooks of English, Advani (1996) found a frequent occurrence of stereotypical references to India's rural population. She says that these bucolic images of rural life "legitimise the partial modernisation of India" in an attempt to construct the national imagination.

This tendency of state-published textbooks is reflected far more strongly in the books prepared for the teaching of Hindi. These textbooks consist of writings selected or composed afresh mainly on the basis of their didactic content. National goals and personal ethics are the two key areas which nearly all the lessons included in a Hindi text cover, irrespective of the genre in which they may be written. Thus, a poem may be included to cover loyalty to the nation, love for nature, or the value of self-discipline. Some of the lessons use biography as a means of highlighting a set of values and attributes of personality; others use a myth, a legend or an episode from history designed as drama or narrative. In every case, the content explicitly emphasises the moral advantage that the child may gain. It is not surprising that themes like suspense and adventure are rare in a Hindi textbook, and humour is altogether absent. Moreover, the lessons reflect an ethos which is quite different from the ethos one notices in a privately published English textbook. The imagery and the metaphors used in poems, the plots and characters used in narratives, and the illustrations depict a conservative Hindu ethos which echoes the ideology of cultural revivalism. Some of the stories are taken directly from epics like the Ramayana and the Mahabharata; some others use medieval history as a resource to dramatise a Hindu-Muslim encounter. A handful of references to India's multi-religious society attempts to pay lip-service to the state policy of secularism, but the underlying allegory of the textbook as a whole suggests a construction of Indianness in terms of north-Indian, upper caste Hindu symbols (e.g. Krishnan, 1997).

At this allegorical level, the state-published Hindi textbook continues to carry the imprint of an old domestic conflict which shaped the politics of identity in the north-Indian Hindi heartland during the second quarter of the twentieth century. The conflict between Hindi and Urdu, which had its roots in the nineteenth century, reached its peak during this period and found its most pronounced expression in school pedagogy, especially the pedagogy of language. During the late thirties, the conflict made a significant contribution to the empowerment of separatist elements recognised in the discourse of modern Indian history as "communal" (Kumar, 1989, Rai, 2000). The complex battle fought mainly over language but extending to national sovereignty continued after independence, imparting to the officially-favoured Hindi a Sanskritised flavour. The textbooks used for the teaching of Hindi reflect this legacy of the political battles fought over the question of Hindi's official status and linguistic character.

Sanskritisation is also evident in the textbooks used in Hindi-medium schools for the teaching of science, mathematics and social studies. The textbooks produced by the National Council for Educational Research and Training (NCERT) for these subjects in Hindi are, without exception, translations from the English original. For translation, a highly Sanskritised technical vocabulary, devised by state committees, is used. This vocabulary is quite unrelated to the everyday Hindi that children use, and it poses a major block for comprehension. Teachers of government schools, where textbooks of this kind are used, often take recourse to the English variant of a technical term in order to explain it in the classroom. By the time Hindi-medium school children enter the higher secondary classes, they realise that textbooks available in Hindi are not as good as the ones available in English. This realisation is consistent with their broader socialisation into a mindset which recognizes the subservient socio-economic status of Hindi.

Just as the study of textbooks at school has a socialising component for the two kinds of clientele, popular reading material available outside the school has a socialising component too, which reinforces the pattern established by the school. The reading that Sunday papers offers to children and the magazines published for the young are an important resource for us to probe the larger spheres of socialisation available to the Hindi-medium and the English-medium school children. One striking difference between the Hindi and English Sunday papers' page for children is in the range of topics and themes dealt with. The range is substantially wider in the English papers. The child whose parents subscribe to an English newspaper can find on the page for young readers, short articles on topics like monsoon, terrorism and black holes, a travelogue on a journey by ship to Maldives or an interview with an architect. The space for stories is limited, sometimes non-existent, and the same is true of poetry, except for the poems children have themselves written. In the Sunday section of the Hindi papers, on the other hand, stories and poems take up most of the available space; the rest is filled up by puzzles, jokes and pictures, including the photographs of children whose birthday falls during the following week. The stories include fables and folk tales, mythological fiction, including myths associated with the Hindu religious traditions, and biographical accounts of national leaders. The poetry is typically *about* something, rather than a reconstruction of experience; for instance, it can be about the rainy season, India's victory in a battle with Pakistan, or a festival. These poems are written for children by adult contributors, but the ones written by children have a similar thematic character to them.

If we compare the popular magazines published for teenagers in English and Hindi, we come across a similar contrast. An issue of *Teens Today* usually has no fiction or poetry; in contrast, the Hindi monthly *Suman Saurabh* is full of stories and poems. The former has features on technology, health, fashion, careers, cinema and music; the latter has hardly any space for such a range; but occasionally, it may have a write-up on a new discovery in science or medicine, or a biographical account of an eminent person. Most of the available space is devoted to short stories. Both magazines have a regular feature where young people can seek advice on personal or emotional problems. The problems on which advice is sought are at times similar, but the advice given is strikingly different. To take an example, a question like how one should deal with one's injured feelings after a friend of the opposite sex has moved on to be friendly with someone else would be answered in *Teens Today* with a consoling thought like there is no point in brooding on what has already happened: one must try again. The advice offered in *Suman Saurabh,* on the other hand, usually asks the questioner to assess whether it was a good idea to spend the valuable time of one's student life on romance.

The key to this divergence is evident enough. The English-medium school child's world is synonymous with the upwardly mobile urban middle class, whereas the Hindi-medium school child's world is that of the lower rungs of the same middle class. Confidence and a sense of freedom to move on are as characteristic of the former's world as uncertainty and the urge to hold back are of the latter's. It would be too simplistic to place these characteristics in the general frame of the well-established concept of westernisation (Srinivas, 1966). It is true that westernisation constitutes an important component of modernisation in post-colonial societies like India, but it is too general a process to be useful for making sense of the variety we notice in the stances towards social change across the urban middle class. Processes like negotiation with the market economy and the state – which have been going through a rapid change of character since the seventies – may be more relevant for the moods or psycho-social characteristics we have noted above. The message that children and adolescents of the lower rungs of the middle class receive from the popular writing addressed to them is about the importance of "watching out" in the face of risks embedded in a volatile cultural ethos. By contrast, those occupying the higher rungs of the middle class and reading the English press receive the message: "work it out".

Fiction – in the shape of short stories – appears to be the favoured medium for conveying the theme of "risk" and the attendant message – watch out – to the young Hindi reader. The stories one sees in magazines like *Suman Saurabh* are about the consequences of reckless living and the gains of caution. The opportunity for learning by vicariously experiencing a character's dilemma that short fiction presents, along with the convenient benefit of seeing a problem resolved within a short space, makes it a suitable genre for conveying a message. Why fiction has so limited a place in the magazines and newspaper spaces addressed to English-medium-school children may be partly because they have access to book-length fiction imported in large quantities from the United Kingdom and the United States. This popular, imported literature, ranging from Enid Blyton's novels to the Harry Potter series, introduces Indian youngsters to a globally hegemonic culture.

CONCLUSION

This paper has made an attempt to show that what literacy does to shape the social landscape can be understood by asking what is there to read. In the case of India's urban youngsters, textbooks studied at school and the magazines read at home have a mutually consistent socialising role. Both kinds of readings habituate the English-medium school children to perceive the world as a place to be explored for the exciting choices it offers. On the other hand, the textbooks and magazines that the Hindi-medium school children read train them to inhabit a world full of uncertainty and demanding loyalty to idealised visions of personal morality and the nation. Going by this analysis, we can say that literacy cannot be seen merely as an enabling skill or a set of skills. The ability and the desire to read which are basic to any worthwhile definition of literacy have very different consequences for young readers in urban India, depending on what they can find to read in the favoured language of their school. The English-medium school, itself a symbol of aspiration and status, imparts entry into the mobile world of market relations and tempting opportunities for the individual. The Hindi-medium school, run by the state for those who cannot afford to pay for their education, socialises its clientele to live in a world which has limited spaces to manoeuvre one's way out of a plethora of perceived risks, both moral and material. These very different kinds of socialisation and facets of the social landscape remain quite invisible under the official and common use of the term "literacy" to refer to the rudimentary skills of reading and writing that rural, typically poor adults are supposed to pick up from nationally sponsored and globally propagated literacy programmes.

REFERENCES

Advani, S. (1996) "Educating the National Imagination", *Economic & Political Weekly*. (31 31, Aug. 3). pp. 2077-2088.
Krishnan, K. (1997) "Educating a Nation" : NCERT Hindi textbooks and the construction of Indianness", unpublished. M.Phil. dissertation, Jawaharlal Nehru University, New Delhi.
Kumar, K. (1989). *Political Agenda of Education*. New Delhi: Sage.
Kumar, K. (1996). *Learning from Conflict*. New Delhi: Orient Longman.
Rai, A. (2000) *Hindi Nationalism*. New Delhi: Orient Longman.
Sarangapani, Padma M. *Constructing School knowledge*. (New Delhi: Sage, 2002)
Srinivas, M. N., *Social Change in Modern India* (Berkeley: University of California Press, 1966)

SUGGESTED FURTHER READING

Baynham, M. (1995). Literacy practices: Investigating literacy in social contexts. Harlow: Longman.
Durgonoglu, A. Y. & Verhoeven, L. (1998). Literacy development in a multilingual context: Cross-cultural perspectives. Mahwah: Lawrence Erlbaum Associates.

E6 Segmentation in the Writing of Mayan Language Statements by Indigenous Children with Primary Schooling

ALEJANDRA PELLICER

ABSTRACT

This chapter investigates children's approach to writing their mother tongue – in this case, Maya – when they were instructed in a second language – here, Spanish. The question examined is whether the children can use principles acquired in Spanish instruction for determining how Maya should be written. The focus of the investigation was how children create blank spaces between units that will be termed here "words': what sort of criteria do they use? Previous research has shown that counting words in oral sentences is not an easy task for illiterate people (Scribner & Cole, 1981). Can the principles for word identification learned in literacy in one language be used in a second language that do not have consolidated written tradition?

The children were asked to work in small groups in order to facilitate discussion amongst them and the researcher. They listened to tape-recorded sentences in Mayan, which they then wrote using the Latin alphabet, learned in Spanish instruction. The analysis of their use of blanks within the different sentences suggests that the children used some principles learned in Spanish but also considered the specificity of their own mother tongue. For example, the children often joined verbs and pronouns in writing, as it is often the case in Spanish with clitic pronouns, and consistently separated with blanks lexical items even if these were written with only a few letters. These principles may have been learned in the acquisition of Spanish literacy. However, they did not restrict their criteria to principles that can be identified in Spanish. Principles that are related to the structure of the syllable in Maya could also be observed. Specifically, Mayan syllables are simple, and can have the form CV or CVC. At the beginning of a word, Mayan syllables always have a consonant, although in the middle of a word there may be syllables that start with a vowel. The children respected this principle and tended to consistently join pronouns with verbs when the pronouns were written with only one letter, a vowel. Furthermore, Mayan syllables do not have dipthongs, and the children recognised this in their consistent segmentation of pronouns from verbs when the verbs ended in a vowel and the pronoun started

T. Nunes, P. Bryant (eds.), Handbook of Children's Literacy, 721–739.

with a vowel. These results lead to the conclusion that the children learned principles about the segmentation of sentences into words from their experience with written Spanish and used these principles in writing Maya, but they did not do so without consideration of the particularities of their mother tongue. The principles were adapted and used in conjunction with others, specific to Maya, revealing the children's metalinguistic knowledge and their potential as informants about their own mother tongue.

INTRODUCTION
A STUDY OF HOW MAYAN CHILDREN SEGMENT WORDS THEIR MOTHER TONGUE IN WRITTEN LANGUAGE

The present chapter intends to describe and explain the segmentation criteria used by Mayan children when writing a list of sentences spoken in their mother tongue – Maya. The children in our sample attended a regular indigenous primary school and were literate in Spanish.

Context and Justification

The purpose of the study was to investigate the conceptualisations that Mayan children, receiving their primary schooling in a bilingual education programme, have about written language. Over the last two decades the understanding of children's ideas about writing have been a recurrent theme in psychological, psycholinguistic and didactic research (Ferreiro, 1997). The present investigation contributes to the analysis of children's conceptualisation of written language. The original contribution of this study is that the children's conceptions and notations are being explored in the context of a written language that is practically non-existent in the children's socio-cultural environment, the Mayan language. Children who speak Maya at home and in their village environment were asked to write in Maya and reflect upon their mother tongue, although they were in the process of becoming literate in Spanish, not in their mother tongue. This situation is a consequence of the present conditions of bilingual education in Mexico, which cannot be described in a simple manner. In this case, the dominant oral language is neither that which the school intends the children to master in the written format – Spanish- nor a language in widespread social use. Nevertheless, as will be demonstrated, this paradoxical situation does not hinder the process of investigating how Mayan children think how their language should be written.

   The task of asking the children to write their mother tongue without explicit knowledge of how to do so is not a novel task in the history of written Maya. The Spanish missionaries of the sixteenth century were the first, of a long chain of people, who undertook the task of using the Latin alphabet as a model for writing Maya. Although others (Mayan chiefs and other adults, foreign linguists) have also attempted this task, it is still to be completed. These different attempts have led to alternatives in the representation of Maya with the Latin alphabet. Asking the children to try to write Maya represents a similar challenge, keeping the differences between the children and their predecessors in mind.

The principal objective in this work is to explore how the Mayan children construct particular strategies to systematise the representation of their language using an alphabetic script given the regularities of written Spanish as a starting point. The hypothesis guiding the study was that writing, as a representational system, possesses general principles that can be applied to any language. Similarly to the first Spanish Evangelists, children are sensitive to these principles and can use them in a novel situation. At the same time, as a result of the sensitivity to these principles, the children adapt the graphical properties – the alphabet, spelling and segmentation – to meet their needs in the differentiation of the two languages.

Using a methodology previously developed in Spanish by Ferreiro and Teberosky (1979), the study attempts to infer children's conceptualisation from their written productions. The recognition and understanding of the phenomena of conceptualisation of writing in bilingual situations will, undoubtedly, in the long or medium term, have direct repercussions in the design of literacy studies and instruction.

About the sample

Before discussing the central issues of the present investigation, the rationale for making two particular choices in the study will be described: why the choice was to work with children, and in particular with speakers of the Mayan language.

Children were chosen as the principal actors in the study because they have been absent in the diverse studies concerning indigenous cultures, more from inexcusable neglect rather than through injustice. The Mayan language has been studied often and from a variety of different disciplinary fields; anthropologists, linguists, historians, sociologists and pedagogues have all studied the Mayan language and culture from various conceptions and perspectives. However, in all the work derived from these disciplines, adult people has been the privileged informant. This is likely to result from the common assumption that children are unable of proposing and solving problems intelligently. Children's reasoning is often pre-judged as puerile and lacking logic. From the behaviouristic perspective of learning psychology, the child is considered predominantly as a passive receptor of external stimuli.

So, why have children been chosen as the principal actors in a study that intends to address an issue that has occupied generations of adults, namely the construction of spelling and segmentation of Mayan writing? On the one hand, because there is now evidence from Piaget's psychogenetic theory (Piaget, 1977, 1978; Piaget & García, 1989), and in particular from studies carried out in the field of psycholinguistics, that the child is intellectually able of tackling a variety of domains of knowledge. The child is an active and creative being who transforms data and constructs original ideas from which understanding is organised. "The child's thinking works like ours and possesses the same special functions of coherence, classification, explanation and relation etc. However, the particular logical structures that recreate the functions are susceptible to development and variation." (Piaget, 1969: 191).

Using Piagetian theory as a base, it can be shown that what is commonly referred to as "errors" in children's reasoning is actually evidence for a logic in children that differs considerably from the logic of adults (Casávola, Castorina *et al.*, 1988). One of the greatest contributions of Piagetian theory is to have recovered the child's point of view as an epistemological condition necessary for explaining the mechanisms of the construction of understanding. For example, Ferreiro believes that a cognitive process exists, that is not just perceptual, in the acquisition of an alphabet. Merely presenting the graphical information neither guarantees its faithful incorporation nor the comprehension of the function of the writing system. In many of her works (e.g., Ferreiro, 1986*a* and *b*; Ferreiro & Teberosky, 1979), Ferreiro has clearly indicated and provided evidence about how the process of acquisition of the written language occurs in school children. "We cannot hope that children will know how to do something that they are just learning to do. Above all, it is inappropriate to apply to material obtained from children, judgements derived from a normal adult conceived as universal, accomplished, which would lead to analysing the children's productions with the aim of categorising and counting errors. What interests us is to understand what these deviations mean, what could be their evolutionary importance and to what extent it gives us an indirect access to a specific representation of the text and its elements (Ferreiro, et al. 1996, p. 33).

The interest in studying children arises from here: to understand how the child's thinking modifies, transforms and constructs understanding. Our specific concern is to understand how the Mayan child deals with written language, but starting from the child's own understanding, which is supported by a logic that guarantees coherence and a systematic approach to his/her intellectual work.

Furthermore, children were elected as the participants for this investigation because they are not involved in adults" discussions about the use of orthographies to represent oral language. Thus they are not influenced by the adult view of linguistic norms. It should be made clear that the Mayan children, when encountering an intellectual task such as writing a list of sentences or sentences spoken in their language, centre their attention and efforts on the various linguistic aspects that the activity requires, without considering whether the choices made are socially appropriate. The children will write their own language according to what they have assimilated and the way they have organised information about the graphic system of Spanish and according to their mastery of the structure of their language. In doing so, they transform and adapt these sources of information with ingenuity and creativity according to their vision, as many adults would. If the children do transform knowledge in this way, if their written productions reflect previous characteristics and conditions, why not introduce into the discussion the different psycho-linguistic elements that the children consider when writing their language, and which are not necessarily evident to the adult eye? These could include the written elaboration and solutions for Mayan graphemes and spelling generated by various specialists in Maya as elements for consideration and discussion. In addition, what the children are capable of doing offers a starting point for educators to understand their thinking and for the design of activities that can promote the progress of the children's understanding. In this sense, even though the objective of the study is not essentially didactic, it can offer valuable information for bilingual education.

The Mayan language was chosen because its investigation presents a series of advantages with respect to other indigenous languages. It is a language with the fewest differences in dialect in the region where Yucatan Maya is spoken and the variations are basically lexical.[1] At present Yucatan Maya is spoken in the Mexican states of Yucatán, Campeche and Quintana Roo. It is also spoken in Guatemala and Belize. Maya is the third most spoken language in various sectors of the Yucatan population and possesses such a positive status that Güemez (1994) reports that in some regions, for example the maize growing region of Cantamayec, Yucatan Maya practically functions as the official language. Some official documents such as IOUs, receipts and contracts are written in Maya. It should be mentioned, however, that although written confirmation of official documents in the Mayan language is not necessary in the regions where the present research was carried out, Maya does enjoy a prestigious social status. People feel proud to speak Maya, even in the presence of people from outside the community.

Thus, the central aim of the study is to understand how the Mayan child acquires written language (Spanish and Maya) under the precarious conditions that the bilingual school offers. The study is necessarily anchored in the psycholinguistic perspective. Although historically some independent Mayan groups have demanded that the Mayan language be the language of instruction and literacy, there are still a great number of teachers and parents that make very

---

[1] According to data from the National Census Population (INEGI, 1995) Yucatán, has a population of 1,555,576 inhabitants, of whom 545,902 (considering only those of 5 years of age or above) are speakers of the Mayan language. This means that 39.8% of the state population is considered as indigenous. Of this last percentage, only 3.4% are considered as monolingual in the Mayan language. This gradual decrease of numbers of Yucactán people that only speak Maya is striking (Güemez, 1995; Pfeiler, 1993). To give an example, it should be mentioned that in the decade of the sixties in the city of Valladolid, 30.2% of the population was monolingual. In contrast, in the nineties, in the same city, only 9.9% of the population was monolingual. This does not mean that the Mayan language is disappearing. The converse is true, and the percentage of Mayan speakers has been increasing in the last decades. What is emphasised is the absolute growth of bilingualism that rests on a descending monolingualism. The explanation of the causes for this increase of bilingualism in this Mayan zone exceeds the limits of the present work.

different demands. They believe that teaching of Spanish should be the fundamental aim of schools, given that fluency in Spanish provides important work opportunities.

These demands from outside school contrast with the present national policy for bilingual education of promoting literacy instruction in the mother tongue and with the efforts of the General Directorate of Indigenous Education (DGEI-SEP), particularly in the last decade, to consolidate this policy through the publication of textbooks in indigenous languages. In spite of these efforts, it has not been possible to develop and consolidate the mechanisms that could make the policy of literacy instruction in the mother tongue a reality. The facts clearly show that the tendency to teach in Spanish persists. In a great number of indigenous schools in the state of Yucatán, the teachers not only continue to rely on traditional pedagogic practices but also consider teaching Spanish as the primary objective of schooling.

Thus, the present investigation fits well with this reality: children in the sample attended indigenous primary schools but they became literate in Spanish. What implications and consequences does this literacy instruction in Spanish have? How does the child assimilate written language?

When entering school, Mayan children have much greater oral competency in their own language than in Spanish. Nevertheless, they learn to read and write in Spanish. For all practical purposes, a child entering first grade is monolingual in Mayan, and after continuing in school for three or four years learns to communicate in Spanish. So, without underestimating the importance of other possible contexts where Spanish can be heard outside school, especially the radio and television, the assumption is made that the main contact the Mayan child has with the Spanish language is inside school and in particular through writing, because the first grade teacher rarely speaks in Spanish to the children. In this sense, Spanish has the status of a written language before that of an oral language. It can be assumed that the children manage to focus their attention on the graphic form of Spanish and that reflection about writing is an important route to access oral Spanish. In contrast, the situation is different with the Mayan language: the child and the teacher talk in Maya, the Mayan language is used as the language for instruction and, as opposed to Spanish, written Maya rarely enters the school. Spanish is introduced progressively from the start to the end of primary school, when it comes to dominate all the uses of oral and written language. The Mayan language, in contrast, is no longer used in the upper grades and remains reserved as the mode of communication between the children. Finding themselves immersed in a supposed bilingual school environment, the children are in fact exposed to a diglosia[2] situation which is certainly interesting:

---

[2] Diglosia normally refers to the existence of two forms of the same language, one of which has a higher level of prestige. The term is extended here to describe the use of Spanish as a language of higher prestige and associated with writing, whereas Maya is used orally and is associated with a lower level of prestige (editors' note).

the Mayan language is used exclusively in an oral form and constitutes the bases for school learning, whereas Spanish is associated with writing.

The teachers of the schools where this investigation was carried out were not convinced that there may be advantages in developing writing in Maya; consequently, the children not only do not write in Maya but also have internalised the idea that writing is associated with Spanish. In this way written Spanish has become the privileged reference "model" for the acquisition of the written language. Of course, this model is not developed by school because the socio-cultural environment of the child is invaded with writing in Spanish. It should be recognised that not everything that surrounds the child is written in Spanish, as many place-names, surnames and some religious texts written in Maya and children have access to them to a certain extent. However, the scarcity of written Maya and the abundance of Spanish does create such a disparity that written Maya has not become an overt model for writing.

Segmentation in writing and information about the Mayan language

Many specialists in written language have had difficulties in defining the term "word". For the purpose of the study, this term will be considered as a string of letters bordered by two blank spaces. In this way, it is proposed that the blank spaces themselves constitute objects for research.

This definition of "word" allows us to achieve two aims. Firstly, to describe the criteria and graphic strategies that the children apply to identify the different parts of a sentence, to segment the sentence in these parts and to write a list of sentences in their mother tongue. Secondly, to help identify, indirectly, what conception of written word guides and guarantees the creation of "blank spaces" in children's writing (Ferreiro, Pontecorvo *et al.*, 1996).

It is widely recognised that the segmentation in writing among children learning literacy in Spanish is an unresolved problem throughout basic schooling (see Ferreiro, 1999). Segmentation in writing involves judgements that are grammatical, semantical and morphological and vary across languages.[3] Thus it seemed worthwhile to investigate how Mayan children would use their knowledge from Spanish instruction to determine segmentation in Mayan language.

A large number of studies that investigate children's analysis of sentences and texts into words do so from a normative focus. Such studies aim to identify how children deviate from the norm in terms of spelling, conventional segmentation and appropriate punctuation. It is not the aim of this study to categorise children's productions into correct or incorrect segmentations. The aim was to

---

[3] Languages differ in the segmentation of words and the use of blank spaces in writing. In English, "Give this to me" contains four words separated by blanks; in Spanish, the same sentence "Damelo" has no blank spaces as the grammatical elements, the pronouns, are joined with the verb (editors' note).

treat the Mayan children's productions as sources of information about their thinking and their linguistic conceptions. If the study limited itself to looking at children's productions from a correct-incorrect dichotomy, it would not be possible to identify the reasons that motivate them to produce a written text. Despite the fact that the Mayan language has an agreed proposed alphabet since 1984, it has not been possible to achieve a consensus for this supposed norm. At present, a great number of possible spellings exist. Some are in general use particularly in the circle of indigenous writers, but no particular system has been able to predominate over the others. In this sense, it is not possible to study Spanish and the Mayan language through the same lens because the second does not enjoy the same tradition as a literate culture nor the consensus about spelling as does Spanish. For these reasons, the study does not propose to explain why the children create "conventional" segmentations; from many perspectives, this goes beyond the present state of affairs.

The study of the acquisition process of written language, in particular words and sentences, allows for the examination of the mechanisms that the indigenous children put into play to represent their language graphically, in spite of the fact that they can rarely see written Maya in their closest socio-cultural environment. These results can be compared to others derived from studies carried out in a diversity of languages, and amply justifies the choice of studying the process of acquisition of written language by children who are speakers of indigenous languages, in particular, children who speak Maya.

For the purpose of this work, suffice it to indicate two fundamental aspects of the Mayan language. The first relates to its syllabic pattern, that coincides with the simple syllable present in many languages: CV – CVC. The other, and perhaps the more revealing, indicates that the syllabic unit often coincides with morphemes; in other words, the smallest unit of meaning in the Mayan language corresponds to the syllable. It is necessary to point out two more considerations about syllables in Maya. (1) In the initial position of the word, all syllables in Maya start with a consonant. All syllables that initiate with a vowel are found in the middle or last positions of the word (Romero, 1964, p. 182). (2) Maya is a language that generally avoids vowel groups; in its syllabic structure there is only one vowel position.

The sentence presented below illustrates the syllabic and morphological analysis of the language. These descriptions correspond to a linguistic analysis that is independent of the choice of spelling. The written format used here is that which coincides with the majority consensus and follows the 1984 agreement as a reference.

Yaan u k'u" p'eex tu k'ab le che'a" (*)
"There is a nest (of) squirrels in the branch (of) this tree"

Mayan word	Syllabic composition	Grammatical category	English meaning
yaan	cvc	Verb	to have
U	v	Article	one
K'u'	cvc	Noun	nest
p'eex	cvc	Noun	squirrels
Tu	cv	Pronoun	its
k'ab	cvc	Noun	hand
Le	cv	Demonstrative	this
Che'a'	cv-cvc	Noun	wood

(*) Note: The long vowels represented with the duplication of the same vowel are considered as a single vowel. The apostrophe placed after the consonant (k') does not represent a consonant. It only represents the gutturalisation of (/k/). Any gutturalarised consonat (such as /k'/) is considered as a single consonant. In the case of the apostrophe situated next to the vowel, this represents a guttural consonant (/'/).

Participants

For this research, two different samples were studied. The first sample comprised a total of 75 children, 25 in 6th grade, 25 in 4th and 25 in 2nd grade attending primary school in the town of Yalcobá, situated in the east of the state of Yucatán, Mexico. The other sample consisted of 60 children, 30 from 3rd grade and 30 5th graders from the Peto region, in the South of the state of Yucatán.

Children's writings were obtained in group sessions. Each session was approximately one hour long. In each case, a small groups of 2 or 3 boys and girls was asked to write a list a sentences. A native speaker of Maya recorded all the sentences previously. In this way, it was guaranteed that all the children heard exactly the same list of sentences, in the same order and with the same intonation that corresponds to that of the native speaker.

In the Yalcobá school the sessions were held in the library. In the other schools, sessions took place in offices or classrooms that were empty during physical education or playtime. In all the interviews the groups were of three, or four, children because that facilitated communication during the interviews. Because many of the children preferred to speak Maya amongst themselves, it was difficult for the researcher to ask questions during the sessions. For this reason, the assistance of an interpreter was required, especially for the work carried out with 2nd grade children, who had the least command of Spanish. In Yalcobá, the interpreter was a colleague who was a native speaker of Maya; in the schools of

Peto, a teacher, also a native speaker of Maya, acted as interpreter.[4] The fact that some of the children in the higher grades were more fluent than others in Spanish, meant that they often took the initiative to act as interpreters when the adult interpreter was absent.

Nearly all the sessions were carried out with groups of children of the same gender. This matching of gender within the groups was introduced when it became clear that it generated better communication between the children because the girls tended to be more silent when working in the same session with boys. Nevertheless, when it was feasible, heterogeneous groups were formed.

It should also be pointed out that, contrary to what may be thought, the children were excellently disposed to the paradoxical and strange task of writing their mother tongue. The task is paradoxical and strange considering that it can be assumed, with a high degree of certainty, that for a majority of the children this was the first time that an adult had asked them, in a more or less scholarly context, not only to write Maya, but also to do so in their own way. In other words, they were asked to write the words and sentences in the way they thought they should be written, they were not asked to reproduce something that they had been previously taught.

The situation had its own attraction for the children. The elicitation of Mayan words and writing sentences turned out to be a fun activity because the children treated it as a puzzle. Additionally, they also showed an interest and willingness to teach the Mayan language to the researchers, who confessed from the outset that they were not fluent in Maya. The researchers' position of lack of knowledge of Maya had positive effects on the children because it immediately placed them in the role of experts. This resulted in the children putting in maximum efforts in the task as informants.

A last clarification about the spelling convention adopted here for the writing of Mayan words and sentences is required. The authors were aware of the consequences of deciding to adopt one and not another of the proposed alphabets for writing Maya. The disputes between the followers of one or the other alphabet have become a chain of unending agreements, counter-agreements, clarifications and complaints. It is not the intention to favour one side in particular. The requirements are simply practical and this should be emphasised. The principal interest was to analyse and understand how the children make graphic decisions to represent their language when asked to write it. For this purpose, in the following examples, Maya is written using the Dictionary of the Mayan Language (1990) published by the INEA (National Institute for Adult Literacy) as a reference, which uses the alphabet in accordance to the 1984 meeting.

---

[4] We are grateful for the collaboration of the teacher Fidencio Briceño (linguist and teacher at the National School of Anthropology and History – ENAH) and of the teacher Zoila Cabrera (teacher and researcher of the subdirectory of Indigenous Education of the Yucatán state).

List of sentences administered to the Yalcobá sample

Conventional segmentation according to the 1984 agreement

Maya	English
1. P'ukukbal chan t'u'ul	"The little rabbit is bent over"
2. Nuuktak u p'u'uk le k'éek'eno'	"The pig has big cheeks"
3. Yaan in kíinsik le kaana'	"I am going to kill the snake"
4. Jach yaj u pool in píix	"My kneecap hurts a lot"
5. Tin manaj óoxp'éel p'uru'us	"I am going to buy three balloons"
6. Tin manaj óoxp'éel p'uru'us	"The baby's bellybutton is sticking out"
7. P'iitil u tuuch le chan paalo'	"The dog has fleas"
8. Le miisa' jach ku chukik ch'o'	"The cat caught spiders"
9. Jach ts'u'uy le che'a'	"The wood is hard"
10. Le máako' ts'o'ok u p'áatal jack ts'oya'an	"The man ended up thin"
11. Tin tsíiktaj u najil in chiich	"I roofed my grandmother's house with palm leaves"
12. Ku chi'ibal in pool wa kin chintal	"My head hurts when I lean over"
13. Ts'o'ok u p'oltal u ja'il in k'ab	"A blister has already formed on my hand"
14. T'ub le ch'óoy ichil le ja'o'	Submerge the bucket in the water"
15. Jach p'eex tu ch'iijil le chan xi'ipala	"The boy grows up very ill"
16. Yaan u k'u' p'eex tu k'ab le che'a	"There is a nest of squirrels in the branch of the tree"

The list of sentences administered to the Peto sample

Conventional segmentation according to the 1984 agreement

Maya	English
1. In kiike' tu xotajuba o'neak	"My sister cut himself yesterday night"
2. Jach istikyaj in wóok'ot	"I dance with a lot of difficulty"
3. Yaan u taal a kiik wa a wíits'in	"Your brother or sister has to come"
4. Le ko' paalo' tu yéensaj ya'ax abal	"The naughty boy got down the green plum"
5. In suku'une' tu yuk'aj in wo'och chokoj áak sa'	"My brother took my hot atole*"
6. Ts'o'ok u lúubul ich luuk'	"It has already fallen in the mud"
7. Le úululmo' ts'o'ok u chukik am	"The turkey caught spiders"
8. Sen áakamnaj ich áak'ab in nool	"My grandfather grumbled in the night"
9. Sen nojoch le 'oopa'	"This anona is very big"
10. Le máako' kulukbal tu k'áanche	"The man is sitting on his bench"

11. Sen k'a'am le cháak tin koolo'   "It rains hard on the cornfield"
12. Ku síit' ajch ka'anal in walak   "My horse jumps very high"
    tsíimin
13. Yaan k píibtik le kéejo'   "We have to oven-cook the venison"
14. T áantajba oxo'on   "We are going to de-grain the corn-cob"
15. Áak' iib tu konik le   "That woman is selling green bean"
    x-ch'úupalo'

* Atole is a Mexican drink made of maize flour.
† Anona is a fruit similar to the custard apple.

Results

The presentation of the results concentrates on the description of the criteria that children use for segmentation in order to answer the following questions: What is separated? What is joined? Where are the separations?

It is possible to segment oral speech in several different ways. Despite recognising many forms of segmentation, literate people prefer to use the same type of segments that they represent when writing in the segmentation of speech. Much research shows how writing affects segmentation possibilities (Ehri, 1984; Scholes & Willis, 1995). But, what are the preferences for a person whose mother tongue is not written in the surrounding environment? What can guide segmentation in this case? Is the syllabic analysis of the Mayan tongue the guiding criterion for making decisions about the production of blank spaces?

We will try to show that the units that are joined correspond to segments that we will tentatively call "words", and that these are not the result of a simple sequence or chain of letters chosen at random.

Qualitative analysis

The first step consists in identifying the elements or sequences that are delimited by blank spaces. In all the sentences we asked the children to write, there were lexical and grammatical elements which could be written together or be separated by blank spaces. After analysing the data it was found that the segmentation was carried out in agreement with the three following variables: (a) the grammatical elements tend to be grouped under certain conditions; (b) the lexical grammatical elements tend to be definitely separated; and (c) a grammatical element tends to be joined with a lexical element under certain conditions.

In the subsequent analyses each of these variables is considered in turn.

a) Between one blank space and another appears a single graphic chain formed of two elements of highly grammatical significance. The following is an example by Irving (5th grade, Peto):

[Le uúlmo **tsocú** chukik am][5]

Note that Irving's written sentence contains five segments separated by blanks. According to our chosen model we have:

Le	úulumo'	ts'o'ok	u	chukik	am	"The turkey caught spiders"
(1)	(2)	(3)	(4)	(5)	(6)	

In this sentence there are six segments that, according to a linguistic description, can be described in the following way: (G-L-**G-G**-L-L)

(1) *Le:*	Grammatical element	Demonstrative	(G)[6]
(2) *úulumo':*	Lexical element	Noun	(L)
(3) ts'o'ok:	Grammatical element	Aspect (Verbal form)	(G)
(4) *u:*	Grammatical element	Pronoun	(G)
(5) chukik:	Lexical element	Verb	(L)
(6) *am:*	Lexical element	Noun	(L)

It is possible to see why Irving constructed his phrase with five segments. The third segment, [tsocú], is formed of two grammatical elements. In the majority of the children's responses the two types of grammatical segments that were joined were of the type: verb (3) and pronoun (4).

This particular way of separating the elements was not universal because the children seemed to consider a variety of criteria in placing blanks between words. Another way of segmenting two grammatical elements was found, which considered the form of the Mayan syllable along with the grammatical and lexical elements. Instead of joining two adjacent grammatical elements, these were separated, but not in an expected manner if only the grammatical elements were considered: the blank spaces were not placed at the limits of the grammatical element but instead respected the boundaries of the simple syllable. In other words, it seems that the children use and apply a syllabic model (CV) as a ruler, which guides them in the placement of blank spaces. The following is an example by Jesús (6th grade, Yalcobá):

[**ya nu** k'u b'ex tu **k'abe** che'a]

According to the model chosen, we have:

'**Yaan u** k'u" p'eex tu k'ab le che'a (**G-G**-L-L-G-L-**G-L**)
"There is a nest of squirrels in the branch of the tree"

It is striking that Jesús, as indeed many other children, placed a blank space in the sequence *Yaan u*, thereby creating a non-conventional cut between two

---

[5] The children's writing will always be placed within square brackets, the Maya written according to model chosen will be in italics and its meaning within quotation marks.

[6] From this point onwards these letters between brackets only will be used to refer to grammatical or lexical elements.

grammatical elements, producing the following sequence: [**ya nu**]. This type of solution is interesting because it shows that, when children carry out the task of identifying elements in a sentence (that is, separating and joining grammatical elements in order to obtain segmentation), they achieve the simultaneous co-ordination of different types of criteria: graphic criteria, syllabic patterns and stress. The pronouns that have few letters (such as "u") lend themselves to joining with or separation from other grammatical elements to create sequences such as (CVCV): [tsocú] or (CV # CV): [ya nu]. The following example shows what Felipe J. (5th grade, Peto) did when writing the same sentence as Irving:

[lee uúlmoo **Dzo kúu** chukik aam]

Felipe J. constructed the same type of sequence as Jesús (CV # CV).

b) A second significant result was the very clear use of blank spaces to separate two adjacent lexical elements. On no occasion was it found that two or more lexical elements were joined. Despite the fact that some of the lexical elements had few letters, they were never joined. The following shows the example of Alejandro (5th grade, Peto):

[**ak iip** ku konike chupalo]

According to the model chosen we have:

' **Áak" iib** tu konik le x-ch'úupalo" (**L-L-G-L-G-L**)
"That woman is selling green bean"

The first element (Áak') is an adjective that means "green" and the second (iib), a noun that means "bean". In the data from the sample there were no examples of writing where these appeared together. However, a union between the verb (konik) and the demonstrative (le) was found. This example also shows a method of segmenting grammatical elements as was indicated in the previous section. Later we shall return to examples concerning the demonstrative (le).

c) Finally, between one blank space and another appears a single graphic chain formed of two elements, one grammatical and the other lexical. Let us see the example of Maria Carmen (6th grade, Yalcobá):

[**pitilu** tuch le chen palo]

According to the model chosen we have:

' **P'iitil u** tuuch le chan paalo" (**L-G-L-G-L-L**)
"The baby's bellybutton is sticking out"

As can be appreciated, Maria Carmen produces a single sequence formed of a lexical element (P'iitil) and another grammatical (u). It seems that, where there are short elements with are usually represented by only a few letters, Children either join these short, grammatical elements to another, lexical element (like Mari Carmen, in the example above), or introduce some other kind of graphic segmentation that respects the usual syllabic boundaries (leaving, for example, two segments whose syllabic structure is CVCV # CV), but does not respect the morphological boundaries. The following is an example by Maria Concepción (6th grade, Yalcobá):

[**piti lu** tuché chan palo]

Thus far, the conditions or places where different forms of segmentations were found have been presented. Now we will present the criteria that the Mayan children use to carry out these segmentations.

According to the results, the following hypotheses are proposed.

There is a tendency to join two non-stressed elements. That is, those words with grammatical meaning; or a stressed and a non-stressed element, with lexical and grammatical meaning respectively. This is done with the intention of respecting the patterns of stress within a sentence.

There is a tendency to respect the general syllabic principles, that is to say, the children were guided and restrained by the principle of the simple syllable: CV or CVC to create blank spaces.

Given that the quantitative criterion is one of the criteria that is known to have a place in the initial stages of learning a written language before the consolidation of the alphabetic written system (Ferreiro, 1986b), it is proposed that the children could be considering the quantity of letters of the elements to be written and this could influence decisions about segmentation.

If it is correct that children join two grammatical segments or one lexical elements with a grammatical element, as was seen in the examples provided by Irving and Maria Carmen, that they create segmentations following a syllabic model, as was seen in the examples provided by Jesús and Felipe and Maria Concepción, and that in each of these cases the grammatical and lexical elements consisted of few letters, how does one distinguish which criteria are operating as the guiding principles in children's writing, especially when the three considerations appear simultaneously? In what order and hierarchy are these considerations presented? These questions are meaningful because it is interesting to know to what extent the children decide to segment, join or separate two elements, guided by criteria that are based on the syllabic pattern, the stress in the sentence and the quantity of letters necessary to write a word.

Before answering these questions a few more examples are reviewed to show how these criteria are present in the children's segmentations.

The data show clearly that the two elements most frequently joined together are:

(a) adjacent verb and pronoun (two grammatical elements) that will be referred to as follows: (G-G)

(b) one lexical and one grammatical element, that will be referred to as follows: (G-L) or (L-G), depending on the order they appear in the sentence.

Illustrations of how the children proceed according to the following hypotheses are presented using the following phrase:

'**Yaan u** k'u" p'eex tu **k'ab le** che'a'
"There is a nest of squirrels in the branch of the tree"

With respect to the type of elements present in the above sentence the first two elements in bold letters correspond to a (G-G) and the last two to a (L-G).

If a syllabic analysis is carried out for each element (all of them monosyllabic words), it forms the following syllabic sequence:

(CVC # (V) # (CVC) # (CVC) # (CV) # (CVC) # (CV) # (CVC-VC)

In the above sentence, the second grammatical element (**u**), which corresponds to the personal pronoun of the second personal singular, is only one letter (a vowel). It must be considered that the seventh grammatical element (**le**) corresponds to a demonstrative of great complexity (Briceño, 1996). It is a discontinuous morpheme that, together with the vowel (a') from the last element in the sentence, marks the position with regards to the speaker (le ... a'/le che'a'), conveying the meaning "this or that", and in speech is converted to a single letter element. Despite being represented with two letters (le), when spoken quickly it is pronounced as a single vowel (e). It is common to observe the phenomenon of elision of the consonant (l) when it is preceded by another consonant and followed by a vowel; because in Maya there are no consonant groups. This results in a sentence that has, for practical purposes, two elements formed with a single vowel.

The types of changes and adjustments that the children carry out when faced with this sentence can now be examined. What many children do is to construct a sequence of six segments instead of eight. The following is the example of Felipe (Fourth grade, Yalcobá):

[*llanu* cú bech to *cabe* cea]

In this case, Felipe joined two elements (G-G) (**Yaan u**) forming a sequence: [llanu],[7] and elsewhere he joined the lexical element (**k'ab**) and another grammatical element (**le** = "that'); because of the elision described above, (le) becomes converted to (e), leaving the sequence: [cabe]. Therefore, the segmentation carried out by Felipe presents the following syllabic sequence that, as can be observed, does not coincide with the standard model:

CV-CV # CV # CVC # CV # CV-CV # CVV

Felipe clearly shows how his production is governed by general syllabic principles. The data show that the children have a tendency not to respect boundaries between words exactly because they adjust to external models based on the syllabic regularisation. That is to say, they join two elements that have a vowel and consonant under the following conditions: a consonant at the end of the word and a vowel at the beginning of the following word (C # V).

---

[7] pronunciation of the "ll" in Spanish is the same as the "y".

Once more it can be seen that the two joined elements always start with a consonant. Felipe could have also joined the pronoun (u) to the noun (k'u') in the following manner: (ucú). However, no child in the sample constructed sequences such as this one. What was found was that blank space were placed between elements of a single vowel or, alternatively, between two elements thus ignoring the boundaries between words. As the example shows, children like Maria Concepción (6th grade, Yalcobá) segment in the following manner:

[**ya nu** kuú peex tu gabe chea]

It is interesting to see that no child constructed blank spaces between the noun (k'ab) and the demonstrative (le) in the following way: (ka be), despite the fact that both segments conserve the syllabic structure (CV # CV). An explanation for this cannot be offered at the moment and for this reason the article is limited to reporting that the demonstratives of few letters (le) have a tendency to be joined with the preceding element (lexical or grammatical) constructing a single chain of the type (CVCV). Actually, written chains of two or more elements beginning with a vowel did not appear in the children's productions. Although this may appear contradictory, this does not mean that a grammatical element formed by a single vowel is not delimited by blank spaces when written. This does not mean, however, that children cannot write longer words that start with a vowel.

Finally, the following shows a sentence where elements of few letters appear:

Yaan **u** taal **a** kiik **wa a** wíits'in
"Your brother or sister has to come"

Antonia (5th grade, Peto) wrote:

[Yanu tala tik wa a witsin]

If the quantity of letters was the determining factor for Antonia in her segmentation, why did she not join the grammatical element of two letters (wa) with the following grammatical element of one letter (a)? Given the progress that has been made in research, it is difficult to offer, at this moment, an explanation for the "conventional" segmentation used here, but it can be speculated that the criteria of most weight in the construction of blank spaces is related to the process of "syllable-making". This conjecture is based on the fact that the majority of the children never joined the conditional conjunctions (wa) with the possessive (a), or any two other elements whose final or initial contexts were vowels; V # V is not permissible in the syllabic pattern in Maya and children did not produce this kind of response, despite the fact that both elements in the example were grammatical elements with few letters.

After analysing the data that are, as can be appreciated, of great complexity, we are in the position to propose that:

The process of "syllable-making" or the regularisation of the maya syllable tends to predominate as a criterion for segmentation.

The three criteria described are simultaneously used by the children: type of element (lexical or grammatical), "syllable-making" and quantity of letters. Even though the three criteria are used, "syllable-making" dominates over the other two when there is conflict in their application.

Finally, it should be indicated that, although the data show that elements are certainly joined or separated guided by syllabic principles, it is not possible to discard other considerations such as the identification of stress patterns that might be playing an important role in segmentation. Consider the following sentence:

'Le úulumo ts'o'ok u chukik am'
"The turkey caught spiders"

Here there is a tendency to join the verb in the past tense with the pronoun (u), thus creating a sequence of two grammatical elements such as those already highlighted: [tsoku] or [tso ku]. However, the verbal element (chukik) and the following lexical element – the noun (am) – were never joined or separated to create sequences such as (chukikam) or (chuki kam), despite presenting similar consonantal and vocalic contexts to the previous two elements (a verb ending in -k, and an initial vowel in the following element).

Indicators such as these will probably have to be tackled, analysed and explained in future investigations.

CONCLUSION

To conclude this chapter, one point will be emphasised. Mayan children do not write without separating words, neither do they fill their writing with blank spaces placed at random: they delimit units creating blank spaces with certain rationality. Writing requires these cuts and they know this. However, it is one thing to know about the necessity of blank spaces when writing sentences, but it is quite a different matter to know where to put these blank paces so as to conform to how native linguists would do.

Once more, we sustained that Mayan children know that written language possesses general principles, common characteristics and criteria that unify and direct the representation they provide for oral language. In this sense, the children use their understanding of principles to write in Spanish and Maya. Furthermore, they know that their language, the Mayan language, has peculiarities and that writing their language should present specific graphical characteristics that simultaneously conform to general principles but distinguish it from Spanish.

The data presented offer an opportunity to penetrate a territory that is little explored. They also point to the possibility of placing the child in the position of a reliable informant who can offer a metalinguistic reflection and suggest to us viable hypotheses for the consolidation and elaboration of the proposals for the writing of an indigenous language.

REFERENCES

Briceño, Fidencio (1996) *La frase nominal en el maya yucatecto* (The nominal phrase in Yucatan Maya) Departamento de Lenguas. Escuela Nacional de Antropologia e Historia (Unpublished research paper).

Casávola, H. M. Castorina, J. A. *et al.* (1988) *El rol constructivo de los errores en la adquisición de los conocimientos. Aportes para una teoría de los aprendizajes.* (The constructive role of errors in the acquisition of understanding). En J. A. Castorina, S. L. Fernández et al. *Psicología Genética, Aspectos metodológicos e implicancias pedagógicas (*43-61). (Genetic Psychology: Methodological aspects and pedagogic implications) Buenos Aires: Miño y Dávila.

Dicconario de la lengua maya (Dictionary of the Mayan language) (1990). México: SEP-OEA (INEA).

Ehri, L. (1984) How orthography alters spoken language competencies in children to read and spell. In J. Downing & R. Valtin (eds.) *Language awareness and Learning to Read.* Berlin: Springer-Verlag.

Ferreiro, E. (1986a) La complejidad conceptual de la escritura. (The conceptual complexities of writing.) In L. F. Lara & F. Garrido (Eds.) *Escritura y Alfabetización* (pp. 60-81). (Writing and literacy.) México: Ediciones del Ermitaño.

Ferreiro, E. (1986b) *Proceso de alfabetización. La alfabetización.* (The process of literacy: Literacy) Buenos Aires: Centro Edito de América Latina.

Ferreiro, E. (1997) *Alfabetización. Teoría y práctica.* (Literacy: Theory and Practice.) México: Siglo XXI.

Ferreiro, E. (1999). Oral and written words. Are they the same units? In T. Nunes (Ed.). *Learning to Read: An Integrated View from Research and Practice* (pp. 65-76). Dordrecht (Netherlands), Kluwer.

Ferreiro, E. and Teberosky, A. (1979) *Los sistemas de escritura en el desarrollo del ñino.* (Systems of writing in the development of the child) México: Siglo XXI.

Ferreiro, E., Pontecorvo, C. *et al.* (1996) *Caperucita Roja aprende a escribir.* (Little Red Riding Hood learns to write.) Barcelona: Gedisa Colección LEA, Núm. 10.

Güemez, P. Ángel, M. (1994) Situación actual de la lengua maya en Yucactán. Un enfoque demográfico. (The present situation of the Mayan language in Yucatán: A demographic focus.) En *INAH*. Mérida: INAH-Cultura. pp. 3-17.

Güemez, P. Ángel, M. (1995) Bilingües y monolingües en la población yucateca. Un perfil sociolingüistico. (Bilinguals and monolinguals in the Yucatan population: A sociolinguistic profile.) In *Working papers* series 17. Duke University, University of North Carolina, Program in Latin American Studies.

Pfeiler, B. (1993) La lealtad lingüistica del indígena Maya Yucateco. Validación de la prueba de *matched-guise*. (The linguistic loyalty of the indigenous Yucatan Maya. Validation of the matched-guise test.) *Estudios de Lingüística Aplicada, 17*, 82-93. (Studies of Applied Linguistics.) México: CELE'UNAM.

Piaget, J. (1969) *Psicología y Pedagogía.* (Psychology and Pedagogy.) Barcelona: Ariel.

Piaget, J. (1977) *Psicología de la intelligencia.* (Psychology of intelligence.) Buenos Aires: Psique.

Piaget, J. (1978) *La equilibración de las estructuras cognitivas. Problema central del desarollo.* (The equilibrium of cognitive structures. The central problem of development.) Madrid: Siglo XXI.

Piaget, J. & García, R. (1989) *Hacia una lógica de significaciones.* (Towards a logic of meaning.) México: Gedisa.

Romero, M. (1964) Los fenomenos del maya-yutateco. (The phenomena of the Yucatan Maya.) En *Anales del Instituto Nacional de Antropología e Historia. Tomo XVI.* (Annuals of the National Institute of Anthropology and History. Volume 16.) México: SEP: pp. 179-192.

Scholes, R. J. & Willis B. J. (1995) Los lingüistas, la cultura escrita y la intencionalidad del hombre occidental (The linguists, the written culture and the intentions of the Western man.) de Marshall McLuhan. En D. Olson & N. Torrance (comps.) *Cultura Escrita y Oralidad* (pp. 285-311). (Oral and written culture.) Barcelona: Gedisa.

Suggested further reading

Ferreiro, E. (1999). Oral and written words. Are they the same units? In T. Nunes (Ed.). *Learning to Read: An Integrated View from Research and Practice* (pp.65-76). Dordrecht (Netherlands), Kluwer.

Ferreiro, E. and Teberosky, A. (1979) *Los sistemas de escritura en el desarrollo del ñino.* (Systems of writing in the development of the child) México: Siglo XXI.

E7 Paths to Literacy for Deaf British Sign Language (BSL) Users

DIANA BURMAN & URSULA PRETZLIK

ABSTRACT

Congenitally Deaf children, whose speech is largely unintelligible due to pre-lingual and profound deafness and whose first language is British Sign Language (BSL), need to be literate in order to communicate effectively in a hearing society. Literacy facilitates the communication between Deaf and hearing in a variety of ways, particularly today when email and other technology for communicating (e.g., minicom, fax machines, text messages) at a distance can use writing instead of voice. Congenitally Deaf children have to learn the orthography of a spoken language without the auditory clues that hearing children use. Those children, who were not educated in oral environments for a variety of reasons, will have learned a language, BSL that differs from English in many ways. This makes literacy learning for them a difficult task. This chapter examines some of these difficulties, and describes how learning to use morphology and grammar can prove beneficial to Deaf children learning literacy in a special school.

INTRODUCTION

During one year we have had the privilege of closely working with the children in this study. Diana Burman – the bilingual teacher who carried out the fieldwork – and the children communicated through British Sign Language (BSL). The children in the study are profoundly deaf. Profoundly deaf children are faced with major challenges in acquiring English literacy, for not only are they learning a second language that is produced and perceived differently from their first language, but also they are confronted with learning a language that they have never heard.

Profound deafness, which precludes the ability to hear speech, occurs in approximately one in a thousand babies born in the U.K. each year. Only one in ten of babies born deaf are born to deaf parents. Those children born to Deaf parents, whose primary language is BSL, consequently use sign as their first language. Those born to hearing parents may develop signed communication

T. Nunes, P. Bryant (eds.), Handbook of Children's Literacy, 741–766.

learned from their hearing parents (as their parents learn BSL), learned in school – if they are educated in a signing school for the deaf – or learned both at home and at school (Ballantyne, Martin & Martin, 1993; Gregory, Knight, McCracken, Powers & Watson, 1998). Many profoundly deaf children grow to adulthood with speech that is unintelligible to strangers, even if they were educated in oral environments; the task of learning to speak without hearing is extremely hard. Gregory (Gregory, Bishop & Sheldon, 1995) reports that about 50% of the deaf young adults she interviewed, although educated in oral environments as children, did prefer BSL as young people. Sadly, almost 20% of the young people in her sample did not learn either BSL or English sufficiently well to be able to communicate satisfactorily with strangers.

This chapter considers the difficulties faced by a group of Deaf children in learning literacy and by their teacher – we analyse a teaching experiment that took place in two classrooms with 18 profoundly deaf children over one academic year. In the first section, an attempt is made to provide a description of the level of deafness of the children initially through an explanation of an audiogram and then through examples of their own experience – or, more specifically, lack of experience – with sounds. In the second section, a brief description of BSL is provided in order to make salient some of the differences between BSL and English. We believe that these differences are related to obstacles faced by deaf children in the mastery of English literacy. The third section considers relevant work of how these children become literate in English. The review is selective, as its function was to support the design of a study that aimed to improve Deaf children's spelling. The final sections report the method and findings from the study.

In this narrative the word "Deaf" has been used to denote those who share the Deaf culture, and does not refer to partially hearing people or to those who have lost their hearing but remain in the hearing culture.

Deafness, communication and the lack of experience of sound

The communication methods used by deaf children are heavily influenced by a number of factors – for example the type and degree of hearing loss, the age of onset of deafness and the amount of use a child is able to make of residual hearing. Level of deafness is measured through an audiometer, an instrument which utilises a technique in which sounds are presented separately to each ear – the child is then asked to indicate whether s/he heard these sounds. The child's responses are plotted on a graph, as in Figure 1, to indicate at what level s/he was able to respond to sound.

The *decibels* (dB) describe the volume: for example, when a person whispers the level reaches approximately 20dB and when that person speaks the level is between 30dB and 60dB. Noise levels in excess of speech include for example a dog barking nearby (85dB), a chain saw (95dB) or a helicopter in close proximity (110dB).

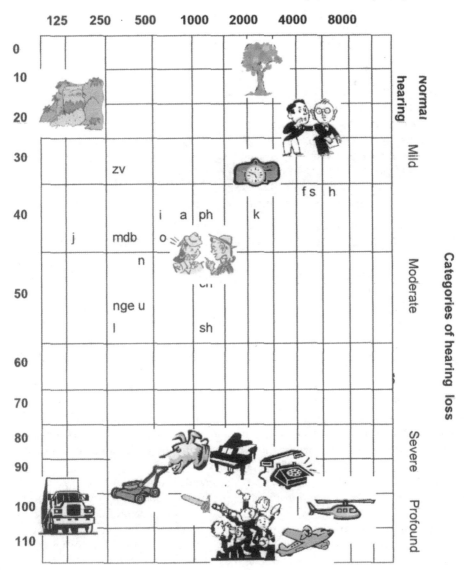

Figure 1. An Audiogram

Other approximate dB noise levels are as follows:

0 Threshold of hearing / the faintest sound audible to humans
10 Leaves rustling in the wind
20 The background noise of a quiet country lane
30 The tick of a watch/rustle of paper
40 A quiet office; a quiet conversation
50 A quiet street; inside an average home
60 A normal conversation
70 A busy street; a large shop
80 A noisy office; an alarm clock; a dog barking; a telephone ringing
90 An underground train; a large truck
100 A food mixer at 2 feet; a helicopter
110 A power mower at 4 feet; a power saw
120 A jet engine at 100 feet; an pneumatic drill; a full orchestra

The *frequencies* are described in cycles per second and denote the pitch, with "middle C" at 256cps, lower pitch 125cps, at the high pitch of a whistle 6000cps. Speech sounds are emitted at various frequencies, as illustrated – approximately – in Figure 1.

Hearing is described in decibels (dB) by plotting an audiogram – that is to say a graph displaying of the number of decibels required for a child to respond to sound at different frequencies, or pitch. The terms used to describe the bands of hearing loss are printed on the right hand side of the audiogram, and denote the volume required when the listener indicated hearing a pure tone (one single frequency). Each of the frequencies on the audiogram are emitted separately and so form a graph of hearing ability.

The children in this study were *born* with a profound loss – in excess of 100dB in the better ear (see Figure 1 for an interpretation of this level of loss). Such children, who are unable to hear a passing bus or underground train, require substantial amplification through hearing aids in order to hear any speech. Many of the children who took part in this study, are unable to respond to sound, even at 120dB to frequencies of 2000 cps and above.

Children, who are born hearing, but become deaf after about the age of three, are considered to differ from profoundly, pre-lingually deaf children. They possess the advantage of having experienced sound and an oral/aural communication system. They have absorbed, without being taught simple experiences that are taken for granted by the hearing community, unlike those who have never been able to hear. The following two true stories illustrate the reality of children living in a silent world. The first concerns Tom when he was nine years old.

Animals that can hear

"What's the dog saying?" asked Tom as he watched his teacher talking to her dog. Tom used BSL to communicate his question.

"Dogs don't talk," she answered.

"Yes. You talk to your dog. Dogs talk."

"Yes, I talk to my dog because my dog can hear."

"What's hear?" asked Tom.

"You know what hear is. When you touch the piano or the tape recorder at school, they vibrate, remember?"

"Yes."

"Well, my dog can hear, but he can't speak. He says "woof, woof," but that's not talking."

"No! Dogs talk," he argued.

On returning to school, Tom went to the bookcase and produces copies of "Little Red Riding Hood" and "The Three Little Pigs".

"Wolf can talk! Pig can talk!" he said.

"Oh no," she answered, "That's just pretend. They don't really talk."

It took a further two months to convince Tom that spoken language is a communication system that has only been mastered by humans.

Six months later Tom attended a talk promoting "Hearing Dogs for the Deaf". The teacher of the deaf translated the talk into BSL, and told Tom that the dogs are trained to make their owners aware of the minicom (a telephone system used by deaf people for communicating text messages). Tom asked if the dogs were *taught to speak* on the telephone. Tom is taught speech, so why are the dogs not taught if they are like him – unable to speak?

The second illustration concerns Robert, aged eight, whose parents are hearing.

Sound diminishes with distance

Robert asked his mother, in BSL, "What time will Daddy be at the station?"

Mum	"I don't know. Daddy didn't tell me."
Robert	"Ask Daddy now, what time he's arriving."
Mum	"I can't. Daddy's on the train."
Robert	"Well *talk* to Daddy."
Mum	"No. Daddy can't hear me."
Robert	"Yes, Daddy can hear you. Daddy's not deaf."
Mum	"No, Daddy's not deaf, but Daddy can't hear me because he's too far away."

Robert did not understand and thought his mother was being difficult. He ran out of the room slamming the door behind him. He had no concept of the distance limitation applicable to hearing people.

These are two examples of how lack of hearing prevents certain concepts from being acquired implicitly and without teaching. People, who are born hearing, but become deaf, possess knowledge of sound and, most importantly, they will have heard the language that is represented by English orthography. When being taught to read, they are able to decode the written symbols and relate them to speech sounds already in their auditory memory.

It is this lack of hearing of speech that makes learning written English so difficult for those born profoundly deaf. Profoundly and pre-lingually deaf children lack the phonological information that we use when we learn letter-sound correspondences, which allow us to produce written words, even those that we never saw before or heard before. Yet when deafness and unintelligible speech preclude communication between Deaf and hearing people, who have not learned to sign, literacy provides an important access to communication and to another world.

BRITISH SIGN LANGUAGE (BSL)

BSL is a language that has evolved in the Deaf community independently of English and has its own lexicon, morphology and syntax; it is not the English language transcribed in sign. The only part of BSL, which directly represents English words is the finger spelling system or manual alphabet. This is generally used to communicate names, places and specific words for which there is no appropriate sign. Finger spelling has arisen as hearing educators attempted to bridge English orthography with sign; it is not a communication system devised by Deaf people. Deaf children who learn through BSL are taught English finger spelling and the corresponding written letter as a precursor to literacy. They need to memorise variations in letter order without the aid of the auditory clues available to hearing children: a difficult task that often results in spelling errors – errors that lead to communication difficulties.

In the same way that spoken language differs across countries, different nations have developed their own systems of sign communication; hence there is no universal sign language. British Sign Language and American Sign Language are also distinct though they are both used in countries where the oral language is the same.

BSL is a multi-channel language where a range of information is communicated simultaneously. Signed languages are described (Dufour, 1997) as involving at least four major features that differentiate between the signs: hand-shape (which may involve one or both hands), movement (which differs in shape and speed), location of the sign, and non-manual features such as facial expression and body language. For example, the same hand-shape with different movements has different meanings; the same movements in the same place with different hand-shapes also have different meanings; the same hand-shape, with the same movement and location but different speeds of movements has different meanings – and so on. Location plays an important role in BSL. Users of BSL can place people, buildings, objects and ideas in different positions around them, and refer back to them by pointing at their location.

Features of objects are often apparent in the sign – be it large or small, fragile or robust, or light or heavy, and both placement and description would be present in the signing of the following sentences:

"Open the door; on the right is the T.V. and on the left is the table. The book is on the floor to the left of the T.V."

Information in the signing for "door" would convey whether it is hinged on the left or right, the height and type of the door handle, the ease, or otherwise, with which the door is opened, and so on. The signing of the "table" would give information regarding its shape and height and so on because those are inherent visual features that are a part of British Sign Language.

This brief description of BSL illustrates why BSL has no orthography in common usage: the multi-channel features of the language make transcription difficult. There are transcriptions of sign languages for scientific purposes, which have attempted to represent signed features, but these do not provide a communication system utilised by Deaf people within their community, nor one that is accessible to the hearing community without special training.

The drawing in Figure 2 helps to illustrate difficulties encountered in the transcription of BSL. It depicts the signs for "interested" and "excited" – the two words share the same hand-shapes and are produced with the same part of the body. It is only the intensity of movement of the hands that denotes the difference in the meaning – excited having greater intensity than interesting. This difference is hard to represent in written form, as are signs that rely on facial expression. Drawings and photographs are at risk of ambiguity because they are two-dimensional and therefore unable to convey the necessary information for the reader to be able to tell them apart. It is only video records of BSL that provide a more accurate medium for imparting information.

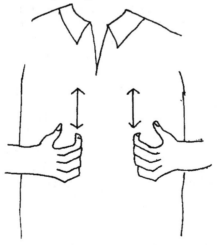

Figure 2. BSL for "excited"/"interested//

BSL is not yet an official language, which means, for example that video recordings of BSL announcements are not available to substitute for spoken or written English for notices of train delays, benefit claim forms, instruction leaflets, ATMs, emails and so on. Hence native BSL users have a need to be literate in a second language – in the UK, English.

Differences and links between BSL and English

It is not possible to present an exhaustive comparison of BSL and English. We presented some aspects that we found to be particularly relevant to the teaching of English literacy to children whose preferred or first language is BSL. There are differences at the word level – grammatical differences – and also morphological differences.

At the word level, three differences can be pointed out. First, there is not always a one to one correspondence between a sign and a word. For example, "up until now" uses three English words, but only one sign. For some signs it is impossible to write an exact English equivalent, and vice versa. Thus the length of sentences varies between the two languages. If a teacher is reading a sentence in English and the child is thinking in BSL, the child may not know what a particular word means. Conversely, if a child wants to write in English a particular sign, s/he may need to use more than one word. In a sense, the concept of "word" is different in BSL and English (see chapter by Pellicer, this volume, for the significance of the concept of "word" in literacy acquisition).

Second, BSL does not contain many of the English function words such as "to" and "at" or content words such as "is" and "was". It does not use the definite or indefinite article ('the", "a"), hence these words are often absent in examples of deaf children's early attempts at writing in English. Consequently, if a child is asked to read for the class or the teacher the *English* in books, as opposed to reading for him/herself for *meaning*, the signer fingerspells these small words, as there is no sign equivalent, constructing sentences that are not a part of his/her language.

Third, colloquialisms in English cannot be literally translated into BSL without misconstruing the meaning e.g. "in the run up to Christmas", "top dog", "he fell for it" etc. In English we use the same word in a variety of contexts, e.g. "run out of sugar", "run a meeting, "run a mile". In BSL it is the meaning that is translated – not the individual words. So reading English holds different goals – to read the words but to sign in BSL, to convey comprehension or to read every word in order to learn literacy. In the latter case, many words will be finger spelled and some "made up" signs might be introduced when there is no equivalent sign.

There are so many differences at the grammatical level that only those that are significant for this study will be considered here. Firstly, BSL has a different sentence structure to English. For example, the sentence "I have a cat at home" would be signed in BSL as "Cat home have I". But note that the word order in BSL is not fixed grammatically; a sentence generally starts with *the topic* in order to cue the viewer into the subject of the communication – in this instance, "cat". Differences in word order exacerbate the difficulty of moving between BSL and written English that will be encountered by a Deaf child learning English literacy.

Secondly, English has different word order for affirmative and interrogative sentences and negation is explicitly represented by "not'/'do not". BSL expresses the interrogative and negative through non-manual features – that is, through facial expression. Thus a Deaf child thinking in BSL and trying to write interrogative and negative sentences in English has to learn a different method for doing so.

Thirdly, unlike English, BSL does not use tenses to denote time; time is communicated by reference to imagined, visual time lines within the three dimensional space; the verb remains the same. The placement of the time lines vary, for instance, "tomorrow"/"yesterday" are signed from the cheek, "in two weeks time"/ "two weeks ago" on the forearm, and "years" with both hands held in front of the chest. The direction of the signed movement denotes past or future, and the use of the fingers denotes the number of weeks or years. The learning of verb tenses in English therefore, introduces an altogether new concept to the BSL user.

Fourth, plurality in English and BSL are marked differently. In the case of English nouns, either a morpheme is added to mark the plural form of a noun – "s"/"es", as in dogs or glasses to the noun – or the noun changes, as in child/ children. In BSL nouns do not carry a plural mark. Plurality can be indicated through a sign that denotes quantity; for example "one dog"; "four dog"; "lots of dog". In the case of verbs, English uses the mark "s" for the third person singular; other contrasts between singular and plural are not marked (e.g., I/we). BSL does not mark verbs for plurality.

The last grammatical differences may also imply differences in the way we think about language. Speakers of English are used to the idea that affixes and suffixes can be added to words as inflexions to form the plural or the past, for example. Although BSL does have composite nouns where two signs are joined to form a new meaning (for example, "psychology" and "experience" are composite nouns that share the same initial sign), the idea of inflectional suffixes may be foreign to BSL users, and may have to be learned. This does not mean that BSL users are deficient in any way, but it may mean that the idea of inflexions should be taught to signers learning English literacy.

In spite of these differences, there are also links between English and BSL. Three main links will be pointed out here. Firstly, finger-spelling for names, places and words, which do not have an appropriate sign – where the finger spelling is an exact transliteration of English letters – is an important link. Secondly, in cases where BSL is communicated simultaneously with lip-patterns, the lip-pattern mirrors speech as used by hearing people. The third link occurs where some BSL signs use the English initial letter in the sign. For example, "chocolate" is signed by the finger-spelt "c" rubbing the chin, "mummy" is signed by the finger-spelt "m" touching the head, and so on. Possibly these signs adopted by the BSL user from English – like finger spelling – are the result of hearing educators" attempts to assist the learning processes of literacy.

These links do provide some connections between English and BSL, but have little impact on the scale of the task facing Deaf children wanting to learn to read and write in English.

A selected review of the literature

Research into the development of literacy in hearing children has frequently focused on the phonological route, a path that uses hearing to establish links with orthography. Deaf children use phonological information, which is learned through "speech" sessions, in reading and spelling (Alegria, Charlier & Hage, 1992; Leybaert & Alegria, 1993; Leybaert, 1993; Hanson, Liberman & Shankweiler, 1984) but much of this information, which relates to the sound system, may be difficult for the Deaf pupil to access.

It is now recognised (Nunes, Bryant & Bindman, 1997; Bryant, Nunes & Bindman, 1999; Nunes, Bryant, Pretzlik & Hurry, 2002) that in order to read and spell English words correctly, the child must use the morphological route as well as the phonological. Morphemes are the smallest units of meaning that can be identified in the language and have a fixed form. When morphemes are combined into words it is termed *morphology*, for example, the morpheme "teach" can be combined with "ing", "er" and "es" (morphology); how words are combined in sentences is termed "syntax".

There are words whose spelling would be unpredictable from phonology but are regular if their morphological composition is considered. The word "magician", for example, cannot be spelled correctly on the basis of its constituent sounds. The letter "c", which is maintained in the word because it is part of the stem in "magic", stands in "magician" for a sound normally represented by the digraph "sh". The final vowel sound is known as a schwa vowel, that is, a vowel whose pronunciation is not distinct; many hearing children would spell "magician" as "magishen" in their attempts to represent the sound in the word. Another example of spellings that are unpredictable if only phonology is considered, which become predictable when morphology is considered is the spelling of end sounds /ks/. These end sounds can be spelled with "x", as in box, or "cks", as in socks. Singular nouns ending in the sounds /ks/ are spelled with "x" whereas plural nouns ending in these sounds are spelled with "cks". This is a rule based on morphology – the "s" at the end of "socks" marks the plural – rather than phonology.

It has been demonstrated (Bryant et al, 1999) that there is a developmental sequence in the acquisition of spelling strategies from phonology to morphology. The morphological route, which focuses on spelling rules based on morphology and grammar, might be deemed the more suitable route to literacy for a pre-lingually, profoundly Deaf child.

Morphology follows rules and rules can be learned and are predictable. The English language has exceptions to the rules and students do not always remember the exceptions. Yet through the use of the rules the *meaning* of verbs or nouns can usually be construed; for example, if we hear a young child say "buyed" for "bought" or "mouses" for "mice", we know what the child means. However, exceptions are less common and mistakes of this kind would not render the writing of deaf children uninterpretable to an English reader.

The findings by Bryant et al (1999) suggest that hearing children can usefully employ their awareness of morphology and grammar to enhance their spelling. In their study, the children were not taught about grammar in school but still showed awareness of grammar as measured through analogy tasks (see Bryant & Nunes, this volume).

There is a paucity of work on deaf children's awareness of morphology and grammar in English. Yet it is important to establish whether deaf children show awareness of English morphology and can use it to spell correctly. Cooper (1967) carried out one of the few studies reported in the literature. He assessed the ability of deaf and hearing students' application of morphological rules.

One hundred and seventy six hearing students aged 7 to 18 and 140 deaf students aged 7 to 19 completed a 48-item morphology test. The deaf students in this study were either congenitally deaf or had become deaf by the age of three. It may therefor be that some students had a period in earlier years when they were exposed to sound and experienced the oral communication system. The average hearing loss of the participants in was 88dB in the better ear (average of the three main speech frequencies are 250, 500 and 1000cps see Figure 1) – a loss that, though severe, still indicates a useful hearing level for communication purposes.

Pseudo words were used to test the students' knowledge of the inflection rule where the students selected pictures, which were identified or cued, by nonsense words. Multiple-choice tasks were set; for example, a picture of an animal was labelled a mogg. Below the pictures were four more pictures: one of *two moggs*, one of one mogg and another animal and one of the second animal. The right choice of picture suggested comprehension of the –s plural rule. And asking the students to modify nonsense words under a drawing of a man performing an acrobatic activity assessed their productive knowledge of inflection rules. For example, "This is a man who knows how to hibb. He did it yesterday. What did he do yesterday? Yesterday he h. ..." If the students completed the statement by writing hibb*ed*, evidence existed that they had production knowledge of the past tense form –ed. Irregular inflectional patterns were also tested (e.g. tife, tives; zife, zives).

The same method was used to test the comprehension of derivative rules. For example, "Mary knows how to zugg. She zuggs every day. She knows a lot about (zuggy, zugged, zuggness, zugg*ing*).'and the productive understanding of derivative rules required the students to complete the statement "John's dog

has wabbs on it. Wabbs are all over the dog. What kind of dog is it? It is a w. ...
dog." The students who wrote down wabby or wabbed displayed evidence that
they had productive knowledge of the rule.

The three scores were obtained from the test: first a receptive score (reading)
based on 26 items; second a productive score (writing) based on 22 items; and
finally a total score was obtained based on all 48 items.

However, it is difficult to form general conclusions about deaf children's
morphological knowledge from a single study as the level of hearing loss and
teaching methods are likely to affect results. It could also be argued that using
nonsense words only to test deaf children's knowledge of written English is very
hard in the first place. Cooper's study focused on one school for the deaf, and
much of deaf children's language ability is directly related to the level of
instruction they receive. The fact that the deaf students in Cooper's research
revealed that they had less knowledge of morphology than their hearing peers is
therefore not necessarily surprising.

The Deaf are not unique in learning to read and write symbols for which there
is no audible correspondence. The French have written markers that have no
corresponding pronunciation. For example, the oral rendering of "le merle siffle"
(the blackbird sings" and "les merles sifflent" (the blackbirds sing) is exactly the
same: oral French does not mark the plural of nouns, adjectives and verbs in the
third person. However, written French does distinguish between singular and
plural in all three grammatical categories. Research by Fayol, Thevenin, Jarousse
and Totereau (1999) shows the essential role that morphological knowledge plays
in the learning of French orthography. They observed that French children in the
first three years of school cannot spell words in the plural correctly; in the first
two years, they cannot distinguish between singular and plural sentences of this
type only from reading. Nevertheless, they found that it was possible to rapidly
improve pupils" performance through explicit training in nominal, adjectival and
verbal plurals, with the introduction of the grammatical concepts of noun,
adjective and verb together with rules of agreement. Fayol et al.'s results are
encouraging as they suggest that, even in the absence of phonological cues, the
explicit teaching of grammar and morphology can improve pupils" representations of morphology in written language.

Considering the importance of morphological awareness for hearing children
learning English literacy and the positive results of explicit instruction on
grammar and morphology obtained by Fayol et al., two studies were designed to
investigate the use of morphological information by Deaf pupils in spelling. The
first study was descriptive, and aimed at analysing the use of morphology in Deaf
children's spelling which can be observed when they have not received explicit
instruction on the target spellings. The second study was an intervention study
and aimed at observing the effects of instruction on the use of morphological
information in written English by Deaf children. The programme of investigation
aimed to increase accuracy in spelling English by Deaf children whose first
language is sign.

THE DESCRIPTIVE STUDY

Permission was obtained for the Deaf children to participate in this study from the school head-teacher, the parents and the children at a special school for Deaf children. A spelling and a morphological awareness task were given to seven 10-year-olds who were congenitally deaf and BSL users. The children belonged to one class, and all the work was based in their classroom.

The words used in the spelling task were chosen to investigate morphological and phonological difficulties in spelling that are obstacles for younger hearing pupils. Because the intervention study concentrated on the morphological difficulties, the phonological aspects will not be discussed in this chapter.

The dictation task involved saying and signing the word in the context of a sentence and then saying and signing the word again in isolation; the children's task was to fill in the gap in the sentence. Further cues were used to ensure that the children spelled the target word – showing pictures or actual articles or miming actions.

In order to investigate the use of morphology, we selected for analysis the use of "s" to mark the plural and third person singular of verbs. The children had failed to use an "s" at the end of words. This error could have been due to their difficulties with phonology – that is, they may have been unable to hear the final / s/ sound – or it could have been due to their lack of awareness of morphology – that is, the children may not have known that there is a need to mark plurals and third person singular verbs in English. Therefore it was necessary to include several different words in the list which ended with an /s/ sound, but where the /s/ sound was part of the word, not a marker of plural. We decided to include words ending in /ks/, which have been investigated earlier by Da Mota (1996). Da Mota asked hearing children aged 7 and 8 to spell words such as "fox" and "mix", which are singular, and "socks" and sticks", which are plural and end in the same sounds. She observed that hearing children represented the /s/ sound in all these words, but that their spelling does not distinguish the cases when the /s/ was part of the word (fox, mix) from its use as a morpheme (socks, sticks). Young children are just as likely to spell fox with "ks" or "cs" as they are to spell socks with "x". In other words, they do not identify the "s" as a morpheme used to mark the plural.

A second morphological marker investigated was the use of "ed" to signify the past in regular verbs. Nunes, Bryant, and Bindman (1997) show that hearing children go through a long process before they achieve mastery of this morpheme. Younger children spell past verbs phonetically, often spelling "kissed" as "kist" and "opened" as "opend" for example (see Bryant & Nunes, this volume). They are significantly more successful in spelling irregular past verbs, which do not have the "ed", and are spelled phonetically, than regular past verbs because they do not realise that the "ed" has this morphological function. It seemed important therefore to investigate whether Deaf children would spell the past tense of regular verbs phonetically or whether they would use the "ed". Whereas phonetic spelling may be difficult for them, the use of "ed" may be even more difficult because BSL does not use inflexional suffixes.

The results are briefly summarised here.

- Not one of the seven children confused the spellings of the identical final sounds /ks/, which hearing children are apt to confuse (Da Mota, 1996). Instead, the Deaf children tended to spell all the singular nouns correctly with "x", but failed to use the "s" as a marker of plural in a systematic fashion. The final "s" appeared occasionally and none of the children marked the plural systematically. This suggests that the deaf children were not failing to use the final "s" for plurals simply due to their phonological difficulties because they did use a representation for the /s/ sound in the singular nouns. Interestingly, their omission of the final /s/ sound in the plural words makes them less prone to a spelling mistake common in hearing children.
- Not one of the seven children spelled the third person singular with "s" at the end of the word. ("She walk*s* to school" was spelled as "walk").
- Six of the seven children made a number of transposition errors. (e.g. "worte" for "wrote; "parnets" for "parents".) This could be attributed to a visual knowledge of the letters that appear in a word, and a lack of phonological information to give a cue as to the order of the letters.
- The children were tested on six regular past tense verbs ending with –ed (e.g. "cooked"; "washed"); 60% of the verbs were spelled correctly (BSL does not use tenses; see above.)
- 50% of the six irregular past tense verbs (drank, bought) were spelled correctly – showing that the regular verbs were easier for the children than the irregular verbs.

The pilot study highlights some areas of concern with regard to deaf children's use of morphology in spelling; the results suggested that regular intervention sessions might prove beneficial. It is clear that teaching the children to use morphological markers would be a starting point – these can be learned in a logical way and are independent of the children's difficulties with phonology. Teaching deaf children to mark plurals, the third person singular, and the past tense in their writing is a modest aim when considered in isolation, but it is a test of whether this approach to improving deaf children's literacy can succeed. A successful outcome suggests that the approach, if employed systematically over time, could have significant implications for the teaching of literacy to deaf children in the longer term.

THE MAIN STUDY

The aims of the study were to determine (a) if the teaching of grammatical and morphological rules enhances the development of Deaf children's spelling as far as the use of morphological markers is concerned and (b) if this teaching also has beneficial effects on text writing.

The design

This was an intervention study based on a two-group design – the *intervention* group and the *control* group. Eighteen children, who were attending the same signing school for the deaf, formed the intervention group. The control group was formed by 19 Deaf children, who had the same level of hearing loss, in the same age range and who were all users of sign as a primary language and had no further special needs. All the children were attending special schools for the deaf. They completed identical pre- and post-tests in reading, writing and spelling at the beginning, and at the end of the academic year. The *intervention group* received the teaching programme in the form of a half hour teaching session each week, in addition to classroom teaching, while the *control group* received the usual classroom teaching only.

Recruiting participants

The control group was recruited by contacting signing schools for the deaf to request their collaboration. They were asked to allow their Years 5 and 6 children, age range 9 to 11 years, who were pre-lingually, profoundly Deaf (with hearing losses between 100-130dB in the better ear) to take part in reading, writing and spelling tests on two occasions (at the beginning of the academic year in September and again the following June, at the end of the academic year). Children in these age groups were chosen because they had been in the education system long enough to have acquired a basic word knowledge of English, and were ready to learn morphological strategies to help them progress in English literacy. Three schools agreed to participate in the study. Nineteen children fitted the criteria, 14 boys and 5 girls. Permission was then obtained for their participation in the study.

Pupils attending Years 5 and 6 in one signing school for the deaf, whose head teacher, teachers and parents had given their consent, made up the intervention group. This group included five pupils for whom BSL was their second language – their first language being the sign language from their country of origin – from Norway, France, Somalia and two from India. Their experience of BSL ranged from three weeks to two years.

The pre- and post-test

The pre- and post-test consisted of reading (not reported here) and spelling tests and a text-writing assessment.

The spelling test included words that contained morphological markers (plural of nouns, third person singular and past tense of verbs). In the case of the plural and third person singular marks, where the mark is "s", two categories of words were used – those where the stem ended in a /k/ sound and those which ended in a different sound. This distinction was considered important because of the possibility of confusion between "ks" and "x" as an ending if the children learned that there was an extra /s/ sound at the end of the words and did not realise its morphological significance.

For the writing task, an enlarged, coloured version of a four-picture sequence was displayed to the intervention and control groups. The children were invited to suggest answers to, "Who are the people?" "What are they doing?" "Where are they going?" and so on. The children were then requested to write their own story about the pictures within 30 minutes.

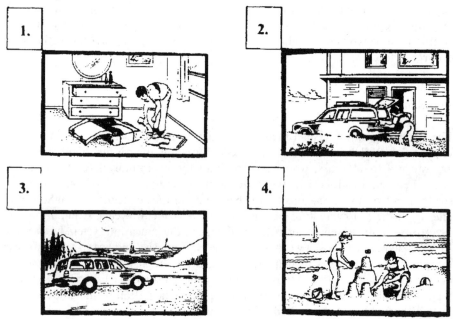

Figure 3. The writing task

Due to the difficulties of marking deaf children's literacy with scores designed for hearing children's attainments, six independent, experienced teachers of the deaf individually assessed the children's writing papers without having known to which group the children belonged. The teachers were asked first to order the writing papers into five bands – from the least to the most proficient samples of English literacy. Band E = 1 represents the weakest and Band A = 5 the strongest knowledge of English literacy. After this initial classification, the teachers ranked the work in each group from weakest to strongest. This provided a rank for each child by each teacher. For analytical purposes, the ranks assigned for each child by the teachers were averaged to offer a single score. An example of children's production in Bands E to A with comments is given in Table 1. The children's real names have not been used.

Table 1. A sample of each of the writing bands

Band "E" – the weakest group, included 9 boys and 2 girls.

The author, Wilf, arrived in England from India 18 months ago. He is able to form letters correctly. He asked for the spelling (in BSL) of "clothes"; the letters were fingerspelt and he was able to write the correct symbol for the fingerspelt letter. Not all children in Band "E" were able to do this. He has a level of literacy commensurate with a person learning an unfamiliar script – perhaps Arabic / Chinese for instance, and being asked to describe pictures in that orthography.

The difference is that he has no auditory clues. He is struggling to recreate a visual "pattern".

Band "D" 5 boys; 2 girls.

The author, Estelle, has committed some appropriate words to memory. She is the only Deaf member of her English family; her mother and sister know a few signs only.

Band "C" 5 boys; 1 girl.

We Mum and Dad and Boy and gril. we went to Sea Holiday and big dipperlane. Get you in

This author, Max, has committed an English phrase to memory. He lives with his English Mother who is learning BSL.

Band "B" 4 boys; 3 girls.

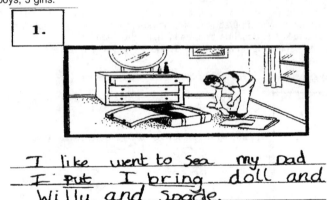

I like went to Sea my Dad I put I bring doll and Willy and Spade.

('Willy" refers to Lucy's buoyancy aid).

Lucy's entire family are pre-lingually, profoundly Deaf and her writing, if signed, makes some sense. She has learned to write some English words that correspond to her first language.

Band "A" 1 boy; 3 girls.

The author, Liz, has tried to begin her story in an "English" fashion, but it is unclear if she intended "One morning", or whether she thought "On morning" was correct, as it is for "On Saturday", for instance. English poses stumbling blocks for Deaf students who have never heard, e.g. *"At the* weekend" / *"In the* morning" / *"On* Tuesday".

She has remembered both the indefinite "a" and definite article, "the"; BSL uses neither. Maybe she inserted both knowing one would be correct.

The word "suitcase" is not known to her; she has described it as "big bag for clothes inside", which would be understood if translated into BSL.

Likewise, the sign for "have", denoting possession, is used in BSL in conjunction with lip-pattern. The word "has" is not part of BSL vocabulary, nor are future, present or past tenses. She probably terms "the sea-side holiday" as "the new house" – her only experience of visiting the sea-side having been with her parents who are buying "a new house" beside the sea.

The intervention

The intervention consisted of eighteen sessions designed to build on the children's knowledge of phonology and to teach morphological spellings and grammar. The 18 children in the intervention group were divided into two English ability groups according to their writing and reading skills. The children in the intervention group were in Bands A – E at pre-test and they were assigned to one of two ability groups of nine children.

There was a carefully considered sequence to the teaching. It was necessary to start the children in the process of understanding grammatical categories before they could learn about morphological markers that apply to nouns and verbs.

The conceptual organisation of the sessions is described briefly below and an example of how the tasks were implemented then follows. The order of description here is according to the order of presentation of the groups of sessions.

a)   Nouns and verbs and the third person singular. This task targeted the third person singular for the Bands A – C children (*Mum* cooks dinner; *Dad* shaves in the bathroom) and gave Bands C – E children practice in writing the names of their peers together with an action (*Mark* cooks; *Emma* walks).

b)   Past and present tenses of regular and irregular verbs: this continued work on verbs, gave revision practice for reading and spelling, and added the concept that English verbs change to denote tense, unlike BSL. (cook/cook*ed*; walk/walk*ed*; shave/shav*ed*; and swim/sw*a*m; drink/dr*a*nk)

c)   Singular and plurals (table/table*s*): As BSL has a different way of communicating plurals, the English rules need to be learned. This not only taught the pupils grammar, but also gave access to the reading and spellings of nouns. Thus the children's writing would expand to "Mark clean*s* cups"; or "Emma drank coke".

Repetition was a key feature of the sessions, particularly for those whose writing tests fell into the C, D and E Bands. Whereas hearing children are exposed to repetition of work learned in the classroom through the medium of song, or a conversation overheard on the radio or television, Deaf children are less likely to encounter the same words before they return to the classroom. Therefore, contrived repetition became an essential ingredient in the weekly intervention sessions. The following sessions illustrate the implementation of repetition. The topic of irregular verbs succeeded the learning of regular present and regular past tense verbs.

   The Teddy Story (see Figure 4) was designed to teach five irregular past tense verbs, all containing "a": swam; sat; drank; ate and ran.

   In the first of three sessions, the words "drinks", "eats", "sits", "swims" and "runs" were displayed on flashcards. The children were asked to sign and mime the meanings of the words. This they were able to do, as it was revision from previous sessions. They were then asked if they could remember how to change verbs to the past tense in English. The "ed" morpheme at the end of the verb was revised.

   It was explained that the five "flashcard" words were different, and the words *swam*, *sat*, *drank*, *ate* and *ran* were shown to them. A teddy bear was then put through these five actions, and the children were asked which of the past tense verbs they thought corresponded to each action. The five words were discussed, and the children were made aware of the "a" spelling in each word. A phonological change in the vowel stem from present to past is a mark of the irregularity of verbs in English; in this case, the children worked with a change in the spelling, which also represents a phonological change. The flashcards were placed randomly on the table, and the children took turns at finding the correct spelling to match teddy's action and to place the word either in the present tense or the past tense board provided.

   The plenary time – the time at the end of the session to reinforce the verbs learned – involved a game for two friends. Each child took a turn at finger spelling one of the verbs, their friend then performed the corresponding action and had to denote whether it was happening now, present tense, or before, past tense.

In the next session, one week later, a child was asked to demonstrate the actions the teddy performed the previous week. The rest of the group were given a set of the five present and five past tense verbs written on flashcards. Their job was to hold up the correct verb as the child placed teddy in a bowl, sat him on a chair, gave him a can of coke and a packet of crisps, and then made him run home.

After practising the present and past tense verbs in this activity, a further set of flashcards and a sequence of five pictures were given to each child. Their task was to watch the teacher use signed English (for many English words there is no BSL equivalent, so these words have been given a sign to correspond with English orthography) and to match their flashcards to create the following sentences:

My Story About Teddy by *name of child*
Teddy swam in the swimming pool.
Then he sat on a chair.
Then he drank coke.
Then he ate crisps.
Then he ran home.

A final production by one child is presented in Figure 4.

2.

Teddy swam in the swimming Pool.

Then he sat on a chair.

4.

Then he drank coke.

Then he ate crisps.

5.

Then he ran home.

Figure 4. The five-part story using irregular past tense verbs, all containing an "a".

Once these phrases had been placed under the corresponding picture, the less literate children glued the phrases into their book and copied the sentences underneath. The more literate children wrote the sentences from memory.

In the last lesson the children were video-recorded signing their story – not an easy task for some. They practiced diligently, seeking confirmation of signed English signs in order to perform their story correctly. Whilst waiting for their turn to be filmed they found past tense words in a Word Search. They subsequently viewed their recordings, which gave them an opportunity for further repetition. As the sessions progressed to singular and plural rules, regular and irregular past tense verbs were revised in games of Bingo.

Results

The children's use of morphological markers in spelling was scored by ignoring the correctness of the spelling of the stem and concentrating on the presence or absence of the morphological mark for plural of nouns, for the third person singular or past tense of verbs. The mean number correct and the standard deviation for the control and intervention groups in the pre- and post-tests are reported in Table 2. Separate means are reported for the plural and third person singular of words with stems ending in a /k/ sound in order to identify whether these would present significantly greater difficulty.

Figure 1 and Table 2 describe the results form the spelling test (maximum score 6).

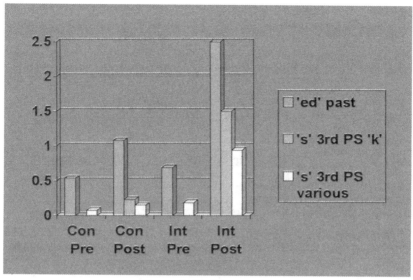

Figure 5. Spelling results

Table 2. Pre- and post-spelling test results of the control and intervention groups (Maximum score 6)

	Use of "ed" in regular verbs			
	Control	Intervention		
Pre-test	0.54	0.69	F = 5.85	P = 0.02
Post-test	1.08	2.5		
	Use of "s" for 3rd person singular in verbs ending in various sounds			
	Control	Intervention		
Pre-test	0.08	0.19	F = 4.27	P = 0.05
Post-test	0.15	0.94		

Analysis of covariance controlling for pre-test scores

As the results for the use of "s" for 3rd person singular in verbs ending in "k" of the Control group and the Intervention group were both "0" in the pre-test, an analysis of covariance was unnecessary. These results (in Table 3) were therefore submitted to analysis of a T-Test.

Table 3 Pre- and post spelling test results of the control and intervention groups t-test (Maximum score 6)

	Use of "s" for 3rd person singular in verbs ending in "k"			
	Control	Intervention		
Pre-test	0.0	0.0	F = 17.27	P = 0.01
Post-test	0.23	1.5	t = -2.541	

Table 2 shows a better performance by the intervention group in the post-test in all cases. In order to test whether these differences could have been observed by chance or whether they are the product of initial differences between the groups, the scores were submitted to analyses of covariance, which allowed us to control for the children's performance in the pre-test. The children's score in the post-test was the dependent variable. In all the analysis, a significant difference was found in the post-test, and in all the cases this difference was in favour of the intervention group.

These results permit the conclusion that the activities used to increase the children's awareness of grammar and morphology and their association with the specific spelling patterns had a positive and significant effect on the children's performance.

The analysis of children's text writing

- Only 16 of the 18 children in the intervention group were able to participate in the June test of the writing assessment. Taking as a yardstick the September samples of Bands, 7 children moved up a Band and 9 children stayed the same. In the control group 10 children moved up a Band, 3 stayed in the same Band and 3 regressed to the Band below. The result may infer that Deaf Children expressive skills in English syntax are harder to acquire than expressive skills in morphology.

The encouraging result of the intervention should be interpreted with caution. It may just be that children, who start from an impoverished level of English, can rapidly improve their performance given appropriate teaching.

Summary of the results

The phonological information acquired by Deaf children, often through the teaching of lip patterns, was used as a basis for teaching morphological rules to the intervention group. Bryant et al (1999) also observed this developmental sequence in hearing children, and this progression, delivered through "explicit training" as advocated by Fayol et al (1999), proved beneficial to the children who took part in this study.

This study made use of learning to read and spell by incorporating lip-pattern and finger spelling (see Hirsh-Pasek, 1983), as well as orthography. These two methods in combination dramatically increased the spelling knowledge of the children in the intervention group. However, it must be remembered the children were all attending the same school for the deaf; further research is necessary to find if the same strategies will be of equal benefit to other groups of Deaf children.

"We identify children who are deficient in linguistic behaviour and then, as if to punish them for this, we focus our educational curriculum on their weakest point." Hans Furth, (1966)

Lack of literacy is a major disadvantage in contemporary society, especially in cases of pre-lingual, profound deafness where verbal communication is not an option. The extensive use of text messages on mobile telephones and emails, ATMs, operating manuals, "delay" messages in railway station and airports, and so on, render the Deaf illiterate adult only limited access to a predominantly hearing society. Therefore attempts to improve the paths to literacy for the Deaf child should not be overlooked.

REFERENCES

Alegria, J., Charlier, B. & Hage, C. (1992). On the origin of phonological representations in the deaf; Listening to the Lips and Hands. Dordrecht, Holland, Elsevier.

Ballantyne, J., Martin, M. & Martin, A. (eds.) (1993). *Deafness*. Whurr Publisher Ltd London.

Bryant, T., T. Nunes, et al. (1999). Morphemes and spelling. *Learning to Read: An Integrated View from Research and Practice*. T. Nunes. Dordrecht, Kluwer: 15-42.

Cooper, R. (1967). The ability of deaf and hearing children to apply morphological rules. *Journal of Speech and Hearing*. Yeshiva University, New York.

Da Mota, M. (1996). The role of grammatical knowledge in spelling. Doctoral Thesis. Department of Experimental Psychology, University of Oxford, UK.

Dufour, R. (1997). Sign language and bilingualism: Modality implications for bilingual language representation. In A. de Groot & J. Kroll (Eds.). *Tutorials in Biligualism*. Lawrence Erlbaum Associates: Mahwah, New Jersey.

Fayol, M., Thevenin, M.G., Jarousse, J. P. & Totereau, C. (1999). From Learning to Teaching to Learning French Written Morphology. *Learning To Read: An Integrated View From Research To Practice*. Kluwer Academic Publishers, Netherlands.

Furth, H. G. *Thinking without Language* (1966). The Free Press, New York.

Gregory, S., Bishop, J. & Sheldon, L. (1995). *Deaf Young People and their Families*. Cambridge University Press.

Gregory, S., Knight, P., McCracken, W., Powers, S. & Watson, L. (1998). *Issues in Deaf Education*. David Fulton Publishers London.

Hanson, V. L., Liberman, I. Y. & Shankweiler, D. (1984). Linguistic coding by deaf children in relation to beginning reading success. Journal of Experimental Psychology, 37, 378-393.

Hirsh-Pasek, K. & Freyd, P. (1983). What Deaf Individuals Bring To The Reading Task: A Focus On Word Identification Strategies. International Reading Association Conference, Pennsylvania, U.S.

Leybaert, J. (1993). Determinants of Reading Ability In Deaf Individuals: The roles of phonological codes. In M. Marschark & D. Clark (Eds), Psychological Perspectives on Deafness. Hillsdale, NJ.: LEA, 269-310.

Leybaert, J. & Alegria J., (1993). The development of written word processing: the case of deaf children. *British Journal of Experimental Psychology*, 11, 1-29.

Nunes, T., Bryant P. & Bindman, M. (1997). Morphological Spelling Strategies: Developmental Stages and Processes. *Developmental Psychology*, *33*, 637-649.

Nunes, T. Bryant, P., Pretzlik, U., & Hurry, J. (2002). Teaching to the strengths or overcoming weaknesses: what is best for dyslexic children? *Literacy Today*, 30, 20-21.

SUGGESTED FURTHER READING

Nunes, T., Bryant P. & Bindman, M. (1997). Morphological Spelling Strategies: Developmental Stages and Processes. *Developmental Psychology*, *33*, 637-649.

Nunes, T. Bryant, P., Pretzlik, U., & Hurry, J. (2002). Teaching to the strengths or overcoming weaknesses: what is best for dyslexic children? *Literacy Today*, 30, 20-21.

Sutton-Spence, R. and Woll, B. (1999), *The Linguistics of British Sign Language – An Introduction*. Cambridge: Cambridge University Press.

Taylor, G. and Bishop, J. (1991), *Being Deaf: The experiences of deafness*, London: The Open University.

Index